Corporations and Other Business Associations

Selected Statutes, Rules, and Forms

Corporations and Other Business Associations

Selected Statutes, Rules, and Forms
2023 Edition

Charles R.T. O'Kelley
Professor and Director
Adolf A. Berle, Jr. Center on Corporations,
Law and Society
Seattle University School of Law

Robert B. Thompson
Peter P. Weidenbruch Jr. Professor of Business Law
Georgetown University Law Center

Dorothy S. Lund
Associate Professor of Law
USC Gould School of Law, University of Southern
California

ASPEN
PUBLISHING

To contact Customer Service, e-mail customer.service@aspenpublishing.com, call 1-800-950-5259, or mail correspondence to:

Aspen Publishing
Attn: Order Department
1 Wall Street
Burlington, MA 01803

Printed in the United States of America.

1 2 3 4 5 6 7 8 9 0

ISBN 979-8-8890-6230-1

About Aspen Publishing

Aspen Publishing is a leading provider of educational content and digital learning solutions to law schools in the U.S. and around the world. Aspen provides best-in-class solutions for legal education through authoritative textbooks, written by renowned authors, and breakthrough products such as Connected eBooks, Connected Quizzing, and PracticePerfect.

The Aspen Casebook Series (famously known among law faculty and students as the "red and black" casebooks) encompasses hundreds of highly regarded textbooks in more than eighty disciplines, from large enrollment courses, such as Torts and Contracts, to emerging electives, such as Sustainability and the Law of Policing. Study aids such as the *Examples & Explanations* and the *Emanuel Law Outlines* series, both highly popular collections, help law students master complex subject matter.

Major products, programs, and initiatives include:

- **Connected eBooks** are enhanced digital textbooks and study aids that come with a suite of online content and learning tools designed to maximize student success. Designed in collaboration with hundreds of faculty and students, the Connected eBook is a significant leap forward in the legal education learning tools available to students.
- **Connected Quizzing** is an easy-to-use formative assessment tool that tests law students' understanding and provides timely feedback to improve learning outcomes. Delivered through CasebookConnect.com, the learning platform already used by students to access their Aspen casebooks, Connected Quizzing is simple to implement and integrates seamlessly with law school course curricula.
- **Practice Perfect** is a visually engaging, interactive study aid to explain commonly encountered legal doctrines through easy-to-understand animated videos, illustrative examples, and numerous practice questions. Developed by a team of experts, PracticePerfect is the ideal study companion for today's law students.
- The **Aspen Learning Library** enables law schools to provide their students with access to the most popular study aids on the market across all of their courses. Available through an annual subscription, the online library consists of study aids in e-book, audio, and video formats with full text search, note-taking, and highlighting capabilities.
- Aspen's **Digital Bookshelf** is an institutional-level online education bookshelf, consolidating everything students and professors need to ensure success. This program ensures that every student has access to affordable course materials from day one.
- **Leading Edge** is a community centered on thinking differently about legal education and putting those thoughts into actionable strategies. At the core of the program is the Leading Edge Conference, an annual gathering of legal education thought leaders looking to pool ideas and identify promising directions of exploration.

Contents

Other Federal Regulations *1189*

Acknowledgments

We would like to thank the following authors and copyright holders for permission to use their works.

American Bar Association, Selections from the Model Business Corporation Act. Copyright © 2023 American Bar Association. Reprinted with permission. All rights reserved. This information or any portion thereof may not be copied or disseminated in any form or by any means or stored in an electronic database or retrieval system without the express written consent of the American Bar Association.

The American Law Institute, Selections from the Restatement of the Law, Third, Agency. Copyright © 2006 by The American Law Institute. Reproduced with permission. All rights reserved.

National Conference of Commissioners on Uniform State Laws. Uniform Partnership Act (1914), reprinted through permission of the Uniform Law Commission.

National Conference of Commissioners on Uniform State Laws, Uniform Partnership Act (1997). Copyright © 1994, 1996, and 1997 by National Conference of Commissioners on Uniform State Laws. Reprinted through permission of the Uniform Law Commission.

National Conference of Commissioners on Uniform State Laws, Uniform Limited Liability Company Act (2006). Copyright © 2006 by National Conference of Commissioners on Uniform State Laws. Reprinted through permission of the Uniform Law Commission.

New York Stock Exchange Listed Company Manual, as available on NYSE's website at the time of publication. Copyright © 2023 NYSE Group, Inc. Used with permission of NYSE Group, Inc.

O'Neal, F.H. and Robert B. Thompson, *O'Neal & Thompson's Close Corporations and LLCs: Law and Practice* (Rev. 3rd ed. 2004). Reprinted with permission from the publisher, Thomson Reuters.

Preface

With the 2023 edition, we continue to provide a comprehensive but carefully edited selection of statutes, rules, and forms for use in the typical business association class. Materials are current through May 2023.

Corporation Statutes

Model Business Corporation Act

§§1.01-17.06

CHAPTER 1. GENERAL PROVISIONS

CHAPTER 8. DIRECTORS AND OFFICERS

Subchapter A. Board of Directors

Subchapter B. Meetings and Action of the Board

Subchapter C. Directors

Subchapter D. Officers

Subchapter E. Indemnification and Advance for Expenses

Chapter 1. General Provisions

SUBCHAPTER A. SHORT TITLE AND RESERVATION OF POWER

§1.01. Short Title

This Act shall be known and may be cited as the "[name of state] Business Corporation Act."

§1.02. Reservation of Power to Amend or Repeal

The [name of state legislature] has power to amend or repeal all or part of this Act at any time and all domestic and foreign corporations subject to this Act are governed by the amendment or repeal.

OFFICIAL COMMENT

The purpose of section 1.02 is to avoid any possible argument that a corporation has contractual or vested rights in any specific statutory provision and to ensure that the state may in the future modify its corporation statutes as it deems appropriate and require existing corporations to comply with the statutes as modified.

All articles of incorporation and foreign registration statements are subject to the reservation of power set forth in section 1.02. Further, corporations "governed" by this Act—which includes all corporations formed or qualified or registered under earlier general incorporation statutes that contain such a reservation of power—are also subject to the reservation of power of section 1.02 and bound by subsequent amendments to the Act.

SUBCHAPTER B. FILING DOCUMENTS

§1.20. Requirements for Documents; Extrinsic Facts

(a) A document must satisfy the requirements of this section, and of any other section that adds to or varies these requirements, to be entitled to filing by the secretary of state.

(b) This Act must require or permit filing the document in the office of the secretary of state.

(c) The document must contain the information required by this Act and may contain other information.

(d) The document must be typewritten or printed or, if electronically transmitted, it must be in a format that can be retrieved or reproduced in typewritten or printed form.

(e) The document must be in the English language. A corporate name need not be in English if written in English letters or Arabic or Roman numerals.

(f) The document must be signed:

(1) by the chairman of the board of directors of a domestic or foreign corporation, by its president, or by another of its officers;

(2) if directors have not been selected or the corporation has not been formed, by an incorporator; or

(3) if the corporation is in the hands of a receiver, trustee, or other court-appointed fiduciary, by that fiduciary.

(g) The person executing the document shall sign it and state beneath or opposite the person's signature the person's name and the capacity in which the document is signed. The document may but need not contain a corporate seal, attestation, acknowledgment, or verification.

(h) If the secretary of state has prescribed a mandatory form for the document under section 1.21(a), the document must be in or on the prescribed form.

(i) The document must be delivered to the office of the secretary of state for filing. Delivery may be made by electronic transmission if and to the extent permitted by the secretary of state. If it is filed in typewritten or printed form and not transmitted electronically, the secretary of state may require one exact or conformed copy to be delivered with the document.

(j) When the document is delivered to the office of the secretary of state for filing, the correct filing fee, and any franchise tax, license fee, or penalty required by this Act or other law to be paid at the time of delivery for filing must be paid or provision for payment made in a manner permitted by the secretary of state.

(k) Whenever a provision of this Act permits any of the terms of a plan or a filed document to be dependent on facts objectively ascertainable outside the plan or filed document, the following provisions apply:

(1) The manner in which the facts will operate upon the terms of the plan or filed document must be set forth in the plan or filed document.

(2) The facts may include:

(i) any of the following that is available in a nationally recognized news or information medium either in print or electronically: statistical or market indices, market prices of any security or group of securities, interest rates, currency exchange rates, or similar economic or financial data;

(ii) a determination or action by any person or body, including the corporation or any other party to a plan or filed document; or

(iii) the terms of, or actions taken under, an agreement to which the corporation is a party, or any other agreement or document.

(3) As used in this subsection (k):

(i) "filed document" means a document filed by the secretary of state under any provision of this Act except chapter 15 or section 16.21; and

(ii) "plan" means a plan of domestication, conversion, merger, or share exchange.

(4) The following provisions of a plan or filed document may not be made dependent on facts outside the plan or filed document:

(i) the name and address of any person required in a filed document;

(ii) the registered office of any entity required in a filed document;

(iii) the registered agent of any entity required in a filed document;

(iv) the number of authorized shares and designation of each class or series of shares;

(v) the effective date of a filed document; and

(vi) any required statement in a filed document of the date on which the underlying transaction was approved or the manner in which that approval was given.

(5) If a provision of a filed document is made dependent on a fact ascertainable outside of the filed document, and that fact is neither ascertainable by reference to a source described in subsection (k)(2)(i) or a document that is a matter of public record, nor have the affected shareholders received notice of the fact from the corporation, then the corporation shall file with the secretary of state articles of amendment to the filed document setting forth the fact promptly after the time when the fact referred to is first ascertainable or thereafter changes. Articles of amendment under this subsection (k)(5) are deemed to be authorized by the authorization of the original filed document to which they relate and may be filed by the corporation without further action by the board of directors or the shareholders.

§1.23. Effective Date of Filed Document

(a) Except to the extent otherwise provided in section 1.24(c) and subchapter E of this chapter, a document accepted for filing is effective:

(1) on the date and at the time of filing, as provided in section 1.25(b);

(2) on the date of filing and at the time specified in the document as its effective time if later than the time under subsection (a)(1);

(3) at a specified delayed effective date and time which may not be more than 90 days after filing; or

(4) if a delayed effective date is specified, but no time is specified, at 12:01 a.m. on the date specified, which may not be more than 90 days after the date of filing.

(b) If a filed document does not specify the time zone or place at which a date or time or both is to be determined, the date or time or both at which it becomes effective shall be those prevailing at the place of filing in this state.

§1.25. Filing Duty of Secretary of State

(a) If a document delivered to the office of the secretary of state for filing satisfies the requirements of section 1.20, the secretary of state shall file it.

(b) The secretary of state files a document by recording it as filed on the date and time of receipt. After filing a document, the secretary of state shall return to the person who delivered the document for filing a copy of the document with an acknowledgement of the date and time of filing.

(c) If the secretary of state refuses to file a document, it shall be returned to the person who delivered the document for filing within five days after the document was delivered, together with a brief, written explanation of the reason for the refusal.

(d) The secretary of state's duty to file documents under this section is ministerial. The secretary of state's filing or refusing to file a document does not create a presumption that: (i) the document does or does not conform to the requirements of the Act; or (ii) the information contained in the document is correct or incorrect.

SUBCHAPTER D. DEFINITIONS

§1.40. Act Definitions

In this Act, unless otherwise specified:

- "Articles of incorporation" means the articles of incorporation described in section 2.02, all amendments to the articles of incorporation, and any other documents permitted or required to be delivered for filing by a domestic business corporation with the secretary of state under any provision of this Act that modify, amend, supplement, restate or replace the articles of incorporation. After an amendment of the articles of incorporation or any other document filed under this Act that restates the articles of incorporation in their entirety, the articles of incorporation shall not include any prior documents. When used with respect to a foreign corporation or a domestic or foreign nonprofit corporation, the "articles of incorporation" of such an entity means the document of such entity that is equivalent to the articles of incorporation of a domestic business corporation.
- "Authorized shares" means the shares of all classes a domestic or foreign corporation is authorized to issue.
- "Beneficial shareholder" means a person who owns the beneficial interest in shares, which may be a record shareholder or a person on whose behalf shares are registered in the name of an intermediary or nominee.
- "Conspicuous" means so written, displayed, or presented that a reasonable person against whom the writing is to operate should have noticed it.
- "Corporation," "domestic corporation," "business corporation" or "domestic business corporation" means a corporation for profit, which is not a foreign corporation, incorporated under this Act.
- "Deliver" or "delivery" means any method of delivery used in conventional commercial practice, including delivery by hand, mail, commercial delivery, and, if authorized in accordance with section 1.41, by electronic transmission.
- "Distribution" means a direct or indirect transfer of cash or other property (except a corporation's own shares) or incurrence of indebtedness by a corporation to or for the benefit of its shareholders in respect of any of its shares. A distribution may be in the form of a payment of a dividend; a purchase, redemption, or other acquisition of shares; a distribution of indebtedness; a distribution in liquidation; or otherwise.
- "Document" means (i) any tangible medium on which information is inscribed, and includes handwritten, typed, printed or similar instruments, and copies of such instruments, or (ii) an electronic record.
- "Domestic," with respect to an entity, means an entity governed as to its internal affairs by the law of this state.
- "Effective date," when referring to a document accepted for filing by the secretary of state, means the time and date determined in accordance with section 1.23.

– "Electronic" means relating to technology having electrical, digital, magnetic, wireless, optical, electromagnetic, or similar capabilities.

– "Electronic mail" means an electronic transmission directed to a unique electronic mail address.

– "Electronic mail address" means a destination, commonly expressed as a string of characters, consisting of a unique user name or mailbox (commonly referred to as the "local part" of the address) and a reference to an internet domain (commonly referred to as the "domain part" of the address), whether or not displayed, to which an electronic mail may be sent or delivered.

– "Electronic record" means information that is stored in an electronic or other nontangible medium and is retrievable in paper form through an automated process used in conventional commercial practice, unless otherwise authorized in accordance with section 1.41(j).

– "Electronic transmission" or "electronically transmitted" means any form or process of communication not directly involving the physical transfer of paper or another tangible medium, which (i) is suitable for the retention, retrieval, and reproduction of information by the recipient, and (ii) is retrievable in paper form by the recipient through an automated process used in conventional commercial practice, unless otherwise authorized in accordance with section 1.41(j).

– "Eligible entity" means a domestic or foreign unincorporated entity or a domestic or foreign nonprofit corporation.

– "Eligible interests" means interests or memberships.

– "Employee" includes an officer but not a director. A director may accept duties that make the director also an employee.

– "Entity" includes domestic and foreign business corporation; domestic and foreign nonprofit corporation; estate; trust; domestic and foreign unincorporated entity; and state, United States, and foreign government.

– "Expenses" means reasonable expenses of any kind that are incurred in connection with a matter.

– "Filing entity" means an unincorporated entity, other than a limited liability partnership, that is of a type that is created by filing a public organic record or is required to file a public organic record that evidences its creation.

– "Foreign," with respect to an entity, means an entity governed as to its internal affairs by the organic law of a jurisdiction other than this state.

– "Foreign corporation" or "foreign business corporation" means a corporation incorporated under a law other than the law of this state which would be a business corporation if incorporated under the law of this state.

– "Foreign nonprofit corporation" means a corporation incorporated under a law other than the law of this state which would be a nonprofit corporation if incorporated under the law of this state.

- "Foreign registration statement" means the foreign registration statement described in section 15.03.
- "Governmental subdivision" includes authority, county, district, and municipality.
- "Governor" means any person under whose authority the powers of an entity are exercised and under whose direction the activities and affairs of the entity are managed pursuant to the organic law governing the entity and its organic rules.
- "Includes" and "including" denote a partial definition or a nonexclusive list.
- "Individual" means a natural person.
- "Interest" means either or both of the following rights under the organic law governing an unincorporated entity:

  (i) the right to receive distributions from the entity either in the ordinary course or upon liquidation; or

  (ii) the right to receive notice or vote on issues involving its internal affairs, other than as an agent, assignee, proxy or person responsible for managing its business and affairs.
- "Interest holder" means a person who holds of record an interest.
- "Interest holder liability" means:

  (i) personal liability for a debt, obligation, or other liability of a domestic or foreign corporation or eligible entity that is imposed on a person:

  (A) solely by reason of the person's status as a shareholder, member or interest holder; or

  (B) by the articles of incorporation of the domestic corporation or the organic rules of the eligible entity or foreign corporation that make one or more specified shareholders, members, or interest holders, or categories of shareholders, members, or interest holders, liable in their capacity as shareholders, members, or interest holders for all or specified liabilities of the corporation or eligible entity; or

  (ii) an obligation of a shareholder, member, or interest holder under the articles of incorporation of a domestic corporation or the organic rules of an eligible entity or foreign corporation to contribute to the entity.

  For purposes of the foregoing, except as otherwise provided in the articles of incorporation of a domestic corporation or the organic law or organic rules of an eligible entity or a foreign corporation, interest holder liability arises under clause (i) when the corporation or eligible entity incurs the liability.
- "Jurisdiction of formation" means the state or country the law of which includes the organic law governing a domestic or foreign corporation or eligible entity.
- "Means" denotes an exhaustive definition.
- "Membership" means the rights of a member in a domestic or foreign nonprofit corporation.
- "Merger" means a transaction pursuant to section 11.02.

- "Nonfiling entity" means an unincorporated entity that is of a type that is not created by filing a public organic record.
- "Nonprofit corporation" or "domestic nonprofit corporation" means a corporation incorporated under the laws of this state and subject to the provisions of the [name of state] Nonprofit Corporation Act.
- "Organic law" means the statute governing the internal affairs of a domestic or foreign business or nonprofit corporation or unincorporated entity.
- "Organic rules" means the public organic record and private organic rules of a domestic or foreign corporation or eligible entity.
- "Person" includes an individual and an entity.
- "Principal office" means the office (in or out of this state) so designated in the annual report or foreign registration statement where the principal executive offices of a domestic or foreign corporation are located.
- "Private organic rules" means (i) the bylaws of a domestic or foreign business or nonprofit corporation or (ii) the rules, regardless of whether in writing, that govern the internal affairs of an unincorporated entity, are binding on all its interest holders, and are not part of its public organic record, if any. Where private organic rules have been amended or restated, the term means the private organic rules as last amended or restated.
- "Proceeding" includes civil suit and criminal, administrative, and investigatory action.
- "Public organic record" means (i) the articles of incorporation of a domestic or foreign business or nonprofit corporation or (ii) the document, if any, the filing of which is required to create an unincorporated entity, or which creates the unincorporated entity and is required to be filed. Where a public organic record has been amended or restated, the term means the public organic record as last amended or restated.
- "Record date" means the date fixed for determining the identity of the corporation's shareholders and their shareholdings for purposes of this Act. Unless another time is specified when the record date is fixed, the determination shall be made as of the close of business at the principal office of the corporation on the date so fixed.
- "Record shareholder" means (i) the person in whose name shares are registered in the records of the corporation or (ii) the person identified as the beneficial owner of shares in a beneficial ownership certificate pursuant to section 7.23 on file with the corporation to the extent of the rights granted by such certificate.
- "Registered foreign corporation" means a foreign corporation registered to do business in the state pursuant to chapter 15.
- "Secretary" means the corporate officer to whom the board of directors has delegated responsibility under section 8.40(c) to maintain the minutes of the

meetings of the board of directors and of the shareholders and for authenticating records of the corporation.

- "Share exchange" means a transaction pursuant to section 11.03.
- "Shareholder" means a record shareholder.
- "Shares" means the units into which the proprietary interests in a domestic or foreign corporation are divided.
- "Sign" or "signature" means, with present intent to authenticate or adopt a document:

(i) to execute or adopt a tangible symbol to a document, and includes any manual, facsimile, or conformed signature; or

(ii) to attach to or logically associate with an electronic transmission an electronic sound, symbol, or process, and includes an electronic signature in an electronic transmission.

- "State," when referring to a part of the United States, includes a state and commonwealth (and their agencies and governmental subdivisions) and a territory and insular possession (and their agencies and governmental subdivisions) of the United States.
- "Subscriber" means a person who subscribes for shares in a corporation, whether before or after incorporation.

"Type of entity" means a generic form of entity:

(i) recognized at common law; or

(ii) formed under an organic law, regardless of whether some entities formed under that law are subject to provisions of that law that create different categories of the form of entity.

- "Unincorporated entity" means an organization or artificial legal person that either has a separate legal existence or has the power to acquire an estate in real property in its own name and that is not any of the following: a domestic or foreign business or nonprofit corporation, a series of a limited liability company or of another type of entity, an estate, a trust, a state, United States, or foreign government. The term includes a general partnership, limited liability company, limited partnership, business trust, joint stock association and unincorporated nonprofit association.
- "United States" includes district, authority, bureau, commission, department, and any other agency of the United States.
- "Unrestricted voting trust beneficial owner" means, with respect to any shareholder rights, a voting trust beneficial owner whose entitlement to exercise the shareholder right in question is not inconsistent with the voting trust agreement.
- "Voting group" means all shares of one or more classes or series that under the articles of incorporation or this Act are entitled to vote and be counted together collectively on a matter at a meeting of shareholders. All shares entitled by the

articles of incorporation or this Act to vote generally on the matter are for that purpose a single voting group.

- "Voting power" means the current power to vote in the election of directors.
- "Voting trust beneficial owner" means an owner of a beneficial interest in shares of the corporation held in a voting trust established pursuant to section 7.30(a).

"Writing" or "written" means any information in the form of a document.

Notices and Other Communications

(a) A notice under this Act must be in writing unless oral notice is reasonable in the circumstances. Unless otherwise agreed between the sender and the recipient, words in a notice or other communication under this Act must be in English.

(b) A notice or other communication may be given by any method of delivery, except that notice or other communication by electronic transmission must be in accordance with this section. If the methods of delivery are impracticable, a notice or other communication from the corporation may be given by means of a broad non-exclusionary distribution to the public (which may include a newspaper of general circulation in the area where published; radio, television, or other form of public broadcast communication; or other methods of distribution that the corporation has previously identified to its shareholders).

(c) A notice or other communication to a domestic corporation or to a registered foreign corporation may be delivered to the corporation's registered agent at its registered office or to the secretary at the corporation's principal office shown in its most recent annual report or, in the case of a foreign corporation that has not yet delivered an annual report, in its foreign registration statement.

(d) A notice or other communication from the corporation to a shareholder may be delivered by electronic mail to the electronic mail address for the shareholder required to be included in the record of shareholders maintained pursuant to section 16.01(d) unless the shareholder has previously notified the corporation in writing that it objects to receiving notices and other communications by electronic mail. Any notice or other communication may be delivered to a shareholder by another form of electronic transmission if consented to by the shareholder or if authorized by subsection (j). Any notice or other communication from the corporation to any other person may be delivered by electronic transmission if consented to by the recipient or if authorized by subsection (j). Any consent under this subsection or subsection (j) may be revoked with respect to future notices or communications by the person who consented by giving written notice to the person to whom the consent was delivered.

(e) A notice or other communication may no longer be delivered to an electronic mail address or other electronic transmission address pursuant to subsection (d) if (i) the corporation receives notice from the information processing system into which such notice or other communication was entered that two consecutive notices or other communications given by electronic transmission have not been delivered to the electronic mail address or other electronic transmission address to which such notice or other communication was directed, and (ii) such notice of non-delivery becomes known to the secretary, the transfer agent, or another person responsible for the giving of notices or other communications for the corporation; provided, however, that the inadvertent failure to recognize such notice of non-delivery as a cessation of authority to provide a shareholder with notice by electronic mail or other electronic transmission shall not invalidate any meeting or other action.

(f) Unless otherwise agreed between the sender and the recipient, a notice or other communication by electronic transmission is received when:

(1) it enters an information processing system directed to (i) in the case of a shareholder, the electronic mail address for the shareholder required to be included in the record of shareholders maintained pursuant to section 16.01(d) or other electronic transmission address at which the shareholder has consented to receive notice or other communications by electronic transmission, or (ii) in the case of any other recipient, the electronic transmission address at which the recipient has consented to receive notice or other communications by electronic transmission; and

(2) it is in a form capable of being processed by that system.

(g) Receipt of an electronic acknowledgement from an information processing system described in subsection (f)(1) establishes that an electronic transmission was received but, by itself, does not establish that the content sent corresponds to the content received.

(h) An electronic transmission is received under this section even if no person is aware of its receipt.

(i) A notice or other communication, if in a comprehensible form or manner, is effective at the earliest of the following:

(1) if in a physical form, the earliest of when it is actually received, or when it is left at:

(i) a shareholder's address included on on the record of shareholders maintained pursuant to section 16.01(d);

(ii) a director's residence or usual place of business; or

(iii) the domestic or registered foreign corporation's principal office;

(2) if mailed postage prepaid and addressed to a shareholder at the shareholder's address included in the record of shareholders pursuant to section 16.01(d), upon deposit in the mail;

(3) if mailed by United States mail postage prepaid and addressed to a recipient other than a shareholder at the address included in the corporation's records, the earliest of when it is actually received, or:

(i) if sent by registered or certified mail, return receipt requested, the date shown on the return receipt signed by or on behalf of the addressee; or

(ii) five days after it is deposited in the United States mail;

(4) if an electronic transmission, when it is received as provided in subsection (f); and

(5) if oral, when communicated.

(j) A notice or other communication may be in the form of an electronic transmission that cannot be directly reproduced in paper form by the recipient through an automated process used in conventional commercial practice only if (i) the electronic transmission is otherwise retrievable in perceivable form, and (ii) the sender and the recipient have consented in writing to the use of such form of electronic transmission.

(k) If this Act prescribes requirements for notices or other communications in particular circumstances, those requirements govern. If articles of incorporation or bylaws prescribe requirements for notices or other communications, not inconsistent with this section or other provisions of this Act, those requirements govern. The articles of incorporation or bylaws may authorize or require delivery of notices of meetings of directors by electronic transmission.

(l) In the event that any provisions of this Act are deemed to modify, limit, or supersede the federal Electronic Signatures in Global and National Commerce Act, 15 U.S.C. §§7001 *et seq.*, the provisions of this Act shall control to the maximum extent permitted by section 102(a)(2) of that federal act.

(m) Whenever notice would otherwise be required to be given under any provision of this Act to a shareholder, the notice need not be given if the corporation is not permitted to deliver notice by electronic transmission pursuant to subsections (d) and (e) and:

(1) notices to shareholders of two consecutive annual meetings, and all notices of meetings during the period between such two consecutive annual meetings, have been sent, to such shareholder at such shareholder's address included in the record of shareholders maintained pursuant to section 16.01(d) and have been returned undeliverable or could not be delivered; or

(2) all, but not less than two, distributions to shareholders during a 12-month period, or two consecutive distributions to shareholders during a period of more than 12 months, have been sent to such shareholder at such shareholder's address included in the record of shareholders maintained pursuant to section 16.01(d) and have been returned undeliverable or could not be delivered; or

(3) no address has been provided to the corporation by or on behalf of a shareholder and the corporation has not otherwise obtained an address for the shareholder it believes is reliable.

In addition, if any shareholder to which this subsection (m) applies delivers to the corporation a written notice setting forth such shareholder's then-current address, the requirement that notice be given to such shareholder shall be reinstated.

§1.42. Number of Shareholders

(a) For purposes of this Act, the following identified as a shareholder in a corporation's current record of shareholders constitutes one shareholder:

(1) three or fewer co-owners;

(2) a corporation, partnership, trust, estate, or other entity; and

(3) the trustees, guardians, custodians, or other fiduciaries of a single trust, estate, or account.

(b) For purposes of this Act, shareholdings registered in substantially similar names constitute one shareholder if it is reasonable to believe that the names represent the same person.

§1.43. Qualified Director

(a) A "qualified director" is a director who, at the time action is to be taken under:

(1) section 2.02(b)(6), is not a director (i) to whom the limitation or elimination of the duty of an officer to offer potential business opportunities to the corporation would apply, or (ii) who has a material relationship with any other person to whom the limitation or elimination would apply;

(2) section 7.44, does not have (i) a material interest in the outcome of the proceeding, or (ii) a material relationship with a person who has such an interest;

(3) section 8.53 or 8.55, (i) is not a party to the proceeding, (ii) is not a director as to whom a transaction is a director's conflicting interest transaction or who sought a disclaimer of the corporation's interest in a business opportunity under section 8.70, which transaction or disclaimer is challenged in the proceeding, and (iii) does not have a material relationship with a director described in either clause (i) or clause (ii) of this subsection (a)(3);

(4) section 8.62, is not a director (i) as to whom the transaction is a director's conflicting interest transaction, or (ii) who has a material relationship with another director as to whom the transaction is a director's conflicting interest transaction; or

(5) section 8.70, is not a director who (i) pursues or takes advantage of the business opportunity, directly, or indirectly through or on behalf of another person, or (ii) has a material relationship with a director or officer who pursues or takes advantage of the business opportunity, directly, or indirectly through or on behalf of another person.

(b) For purposes of this section:

(1) "material relationship" means a familial, financial, professional, employment or other relationship that would reasonably be expected to impair the objectivity of the director's judgment when participating in the action to be taken; and

(2) "material interest" means an actual or potential benefit or detriment (other than one which would devolve on the corporation or the shareholders generally) that would reasonably be expected to impair the objectivity of the director's judgment when participating in the action to be taken.

(c) The presence of one or more of the following circumstances shall not automatically prevent a director from being a qualified director:

(1) nomination or election of the director to the current board by any director who is not a qualified director with respect to the matter (or by any person that has a material relationship with that director), acting alone or participating with others;

(2) service as a director of another corporation of which a director who is not a qualified director with respect to the matter (or any individual who has a material relationship with that director), is or was also a director; or

(3) with respect to action to be taken under section 7.44, status as a named defendant, as a director against whom action is demanded, or as a director who approved the conduct being challenged.

OFFICIAL COMMENT

The definition of the term "qualified director" identifies those directors: (i) who may take action on the dismissal of a derivative proceeding (section 7.44); (ii) who are eligible to make, in the first instance, the authorization and determination required in connection with the decision on a request for advance for expenses (section 8.53(c)) or for indemnification (sections 8.55(b) and (c)); (iii) who may authorize a director's conflicting interest transaction (section 8.62); (iv) who may disclaim the corporation's interest in a business opportunity (section 8.70(a)); and (v) who may make applicable the limitation or elimination of a duty of an officer to offer the corporation business opportunities before the officer or a related person of the officer pursues or takes the opportunity (section 2.02(b)(6)).

Although the term "qualified director" embraces the concept of independence, it does so only in relation to the director's interest or involvement in the specific situations to which the definition applies. The judicial decisions that have examined the qualifications of directors for such purposes have generally required that directors be both *disinterested,* in the sense of not having exposure to an actual or potential benefit or detriment arising out of the action being taken (as opposed to an actual or potential benefit or detriment to the corporation or all shareholders generally), and *independent,* in the sense of having no personal or other relationship with an interested director (*e.g.,* a director who is a party to a transaction with the corporation) that presents a reasonable likelihood that the director's objectivity will be impaired. The "qualified director" concept embraces both of those requirements, and its application is situation-specific; that is, "qualified director" determinations will depend upon the directly relevant facts and circumstances, and the disqualification of a director to act arises from factors that would reasonably be expected to impair the objectivity of the director's judgment. On the other hand, the concept does not suggest that a "qualified director" has or should have special expertise to act on the matter in question.

1. Disqualification Due to Conflicting Interest

The "qualified director" concept prescribes significant disqualifications, depending upon the purpose for which a director might be considered eligible to participate in the action to be taken. These disqualifications include the following:

- In the case of action under a provision adopted under the authority of section 2.02(b)(6) to limit or eliminate any duty of an officer to offer the corporation business opportunities, the definition excludes any director who is also an officer and to whom the provision would apply.
- In the case of action on dismissal of a derivative proceeding under section 7.44, the definition excludes any director who has a material interest in the outcome of the proceeding, such as where the proceeding involves a challenge to the validity of a transaction in which the director has a material financial interest.
- In the case of action to approve indemnification or advance of funds for expenses, the definition excludes any director who is a party to the proceeding (see section 8.50 for the definition of "party" and for the definition of "proceeding").
- In the case of action to approve a director's conflicting interest transaction, the definition excludes any director whose interest, knowledge or status results in the transaction being treated as a "director's conflicting interest transaction." See section 8.60 for the definition of "director's conflicting interest transaction."
- In the case of action under section 8.70(a) to disclaim corporate interest in a business opportunity, the definition excludes any director who directly or

indirectly pursues or takes advantage of the business opportunity, or who has a material relationship with another director or officer who does so.

Whether a director has a material interest in the outcome of a proceeding in which the director does not have a conflicting personal interest is heavily fact-dependent. At one end of the spectrum, if a claim against a director is clearly frivolous or is not supported by particularized and well-pleaded facts, the director should not be deemed to have a "material interest in the outcome of the proceeding" within the meaning of section 1.43(a)(2), even though the director is named as a defendant. At the other end of the spectrum, a director normally should be deemed to have a "material interest in the outcome of the proceeding" within the meaning of section 1.43(a)(2) if a claim against the director is supported by particularized and well-pleaded facts which, if true, would be likely to give rise to a significant adverse outcome against the director.

2. Disqualification Due to Relationships with Interested Persons

In each context in which the "qualified director" definition applies, it also excludes any director who has a "material relationship" with another director (or, with respect to a provision applying to an officer under section 2.02(b)(6) or section 8.70, a "material relationship" with that officer) who is not disinterested for one or more of the reasons outlined in the preceding paragraph. Any relationship with such a person, whether the relationship is familial, financial, professional, employment or otherwise, is a "material relationship," as that term is defined in section 1.43(b)(1), if it would reasonably be expected to impair the objectivity of the director's judgment when voting or otherwise participating in action to be taken on a matter referred to in section 1.43(a). The determination of whether there is a "material relationship" should be based on the practicalities of the situation rather than on formalistic considerations. For example, a director employed by a corporation controlled by another director should be regarded as having an employment relationship with that director. On the other hand, a casual social acquaintance with another director should not be regarded as a disqualifying relationship.

The term "qualified director" is distinct from the generic term "independent director," which is not used in the Act. As a result, a director who might typically be viewed as an "independent director" may in some circumstances not be a "qualified director," and vice versa. See also the Official Comment to section 8.01.

3. Elimination of Automatic Disqualification in Certain Circumstances

Section 1.43(c) addresses three categories of circumstances that, if present alone or together, do not automatically prevent a director from being a qualified director:

- Subsection (c)(1) makes it clear that the participation of nonqualified directors (or interested shareholders or other interested persons) in the nomination or election of a director does not automatically prevent the director so nominated or elected from being qualified. Special litigation committees acting with regard to derivative litigation often consist of directors nominated or elected (after the alleged wrongful acts) by directors named as defendants in the action. In other settings, directors who are seeking indemnification, or who are interested in a director's conflicting interest transaction, may have participated in the nomination or election of an individual director who is otherwise a "qualified director."

- Subsection (c)(2) provides, in a similar fashion, that the mere fact that an individual director is or was a director of another corporation—on the board of which a director who is not a "qualified director" also serves or has served—does not automatically prevent qualification to act.
- Subsection (c)(3) confirms a number of decisions, involving dismissal of derivative proceedings, in which the court rejected a disqualification claim predicated on the mere fact that a director had been named as a defendant, was an individual against whom action has been demanded, or had approved the action being challenged. These cases have held that, where a director's approval of the challenged action is at issue, approval does not automatically make the director ineligible to act. On the other hand, for example, director approval of a challenged transaction, in combination with other particularized facts showing that the director's ability to act objectively on a proposal to dismiss a derivative proceeding is impaired by a material conflicting personal interest in the transaction, disqualifies a director from acting on the proposal to dismiss the proceeding.

The effect of section 1.43(c), while significant, is limited. It merely precludes an automatic inference of director disqualification from the circumstances specified in that subsection.

SUBCHAPTER E. RATIFICATION OF DEFECTIVE CORPORATE ACTIONS

§1.45. Definitions

In this subchapter:

- "Corporate action" means any action taken by or on behalf of the corporation, including any action taken by the incorporator, the board of directors, a committee of the board of directors, an officer or agent of the corporation or the shareholders.
- "Date of the defective corporate action" means the date (or the approximate date, if the exact date is unknown) the defective corporate action was purported to have been taken.
- "Defective corporate action" means (i) any corporate action purportedly taken that is, and at the time such corporate action was purportedly taken would have been, within the power of the corporation, but is void or voidable due to a failure of authorization, and (ii) an overissue.

- "Failure of authorization" means the failure to authorize, approve or otherwise effect a corporate action in compliance with the provisions of this Act, the articles of incorporation or bylaws, a corporate resolution or any plan or agreement to which the corporation is a party, if and to the extent such failure would render such corporate action void or voidable.

- "Overissue" means the purported issuance of:

  (i) shares of a class or series in excess of the number of shares of a class or series the corporation has the power to issue under section 6.01 at the time of such issuance; or

  (ii) shares of any class or series that is not then authorized for issuance by the articles of incorporation.

- "Putative shares" means the shares of any class or series (including shares issued upon exercise of rights, options, warrants or other securities convertible into shares of the corporation, or interests with respect to such shares) that were created or issued as a result of a defective corporate action, that (i) but for any failure of authorization would constitute valid shares, or (ii) cannot be determined by the board of directors to be valid shares.

- "Valid shares" means the shares of any class or series that have been duly authorized and validly issued in accordance with this Act, including as a result of ratification or validation under this subchapter.

- "Validation effective time" with respect to any defective corporate action ratified under this subchapter means the later of:

  (i) the time at which the ratification of the defective corporate action is approved by the shareholders, or if approval of shareholders is not required, the time at which the notice required by section 1.49 becomes effective in accordance with section 1.41; and

  (ii) the time at which any articles of validation filed in accordance with section 1.51 become effective.

The validation effective time shall not be affected by the filing or pendency of a judicial proceeding under section 1.52 or otherwise, unless otherwise ordered by the court.

§1.46. Defective Corporate Actions

(a) A defective corporate action shall not be void or voidable if ratified in accordance with section 1.47 or validated in accordance with section 1.52.

(b) Ratification under section 1.47 or validation under section 1.52 shall not be deemed to be the exclusive means of ratifying or validating any defective corporate action, and the absence or failure of ratification in accordance with this subchapter shall not, of itself, affect the validity or effectiveness of any corporate action properly ratified under common law or otherwise, nor shall it create a presumption that any such corporate action is or was a defective corporate action or void or voidable.

(c) In the case of an overissue, putative shares shall be valid shares effective as of the date originally issued or purportedly issued upon:

(1) the effectiveness under this subchapter and under chapter 10 of an amendment to the articles of incorporation authorizing, designating or creating such shares; or

(2) the effectiveness of any other corporate action under this subchapter ratifying the authorization, designation or creation of such shares.

§1.47. Ratification of Defective Corporate Actions

(a) To ratify a defective corporate action under this section (other than the ratification of an election of the initial board of directors under subsection (b)), the board of directors shall take action ratifying the action in accordance with section 1.48, stating:

(1) the defective corporate action to be ratified and, if the defective corporate action involved the issuance of putative shares, the number and type of putative shares purportedly issued;

(2) the date of the defective corporate action;

(3) the nature of the failure of authorization with respect to the defective corporate action to be ratified; and

(4) that the board of directors approves the ratification of the defective corporate action.

(b) In the event that a defective corporate action to be ratified relates to the election of the initial board of directors of the corporation under section 2.05(a)(2), a majority of the persons who, at the time of the ratification, are exercising the powers of directors may take an action stating:

(1) the name of the person or persons who first took action in the name of the corporation as the initial board of directors of the corporation;

(2) the earlier of the date on which such persons first took such action or were purported to have been elected as the initial board of directors; and

(3) that the ratification of the election of such person or persons as the initial board of directors is approved.

(c) If any provision of this Act, the articles of incorporation or bylaws, any corporate resolution or any plan or agreement to which the corporation is a party in effect at the time action under subsection (a) is taken requires shareholder approval or would have required shareholder approval at the date of the occurrence of the defective corporate action, the ratification of the defective corporate action approved in the action taken by the directors under subsection (a) shall be submitted to the shareholders for approval in accordance with section 1.48.

(d) Unless otherwise provided in the action taken by the board of directors under subsection (a), after the action by the board of directors has been taken and, if required, approved by the shareholders, the board of directors may abandon the ratification at any time before the validation effective time without further action of the shareholders.

§1.50. Effect of Ratification

From and after the validation effective time, and without regard to the 120-day period during which a claim may be brought under section 1.52:

(a) Each defective corporate action ratified in accordance with section 1.47 shall not be void or voidable as a result of the failure of authorization identified in the action taken under section 1.47(a) or (b) and shall be deemed a valid corporate action effective as of the date of the defective corporate action;

(b) The issuance of each putative share or fraction of a putative share purportedly issued pursuant to a defective corporate action identified in the action taken under section 1.47 shall not be void or voidable, and each such putative share or fraction of a putative share shall be deemed to be an identical share or fraction of a valid share as of the time it was purportedly issued; and

(c) Any corporate action taken subsequent to the defective corporate action ratified in accordance with this subchapter in reliance on such defective corporate action having been validly effected and any subsequent defective corporate action resulting directly or indirectly from such original defective corporate action shall be valid as of the time taken.

§1.51. Filings

(a) If the defective corporate action ratified under this subchapter would have required under any other section of this Act a filing in accordance with this Act, then, regardless of whether a filing was previously made in respect of such defective corporate action and in lieu of a filing otherwise required by this Act, the corporation shall file articles of validation in accordance with this section, and such articles of validation shall serve to amend or substitute for any other filing with respect to such defective corporate action required by this Act.

(b) The articles of validation must set forth:

(1) the defective corporate action that is the subject of the articles of validation (including, in the case of any defective corporate action involving the issuance of putative shares, the number and type of putative shares issued and the date or dates upon which such putative shares were purported to have been issued);

(2) the date of the defective corporate action;

(3) the nature of the failure of authorization in respect of the defective corporate action;

(4) a statement that the defective corporate action was ratified in accordance with section 1.47, including the date on which the board of directors ratified such defective corporate action and the date, if any, on which the shareholders approved the ratification of such defective corporate action; and

(5) the information required by subsection (c).

(c) The articles of validation must also contain the following information:

(1) if a filing was previously made in respect of the defective corporate action and no changes to such filing are required to give effect to the ratification of such defective corporate action in accordance with section 1.47, the articles of validation must set forth (i) the name, title and filing date of the filing previously made and any articles of correction to that filing and (ii) a statement that a copy of the filing previously made, together with any articles of correction to that filing, is attached as an exhibit to the articles of validation;

(2) if a filing was previously made in respect of the defective corporate action and such filing requires any change to give effect to the ratification of such defective corporate action in accordance with section 1.47, the articles of validation must set forth (i) the name, title and filing date of the filing previously made and any articles of correction to that filing and (ii) a statement that a filing containing all of the information required to be included under the applicable section or sections of the Act to give effect to such defective corporate action is attached as an exhibit to the articles of validation, and (iii) the date and time that such filing is deemed to have become effective; or

(3) if a filing was not previously made in respect of the defective corporate action and the defective corporate action ratified under section 1.47 would have required a filing under any other section of the Act, the articles of validation must set forth (i) a statement that a filing containing all of the information required to be included under the applicable section or sections of the Act to give effect to such defective corporate action is attached as an exhibit to the articles of validation, and (ii) the date and time that such filing is deemed to have become effective.

§1.52. Judicial Proceedings Regarding Validity of Corporate Actions

(a) Upon application by the corporation, any successor entity to the corporation, a director of the corporation, any shareholder, beneficial shareholder or unrestricted voting trust beneficial owner of the corporation, including any such shareholder, beneficial shareholder or unrestricted voting trust beneficial owner as of the date of the defective corporate action ratified under section 1.47, or any other person claiming to be substantially and adversely affected by a ratification under section 1.47, the [name or describe court] may:

(1) determine the validity and effectiveness of any corporate action or defective corporate action;

(2) determine the validity and effectiveness of any ratification under section 1.47;

(3) determine the validity of any putative shares; and

(4) modify or waive any of the procedures specified in section 1.47 or 1.48 to ratify a defective corporate action.

(b) In connection with an action under this section, the court may make such findings or orders, and take into account any factors or considerations, regarding such matters as it deems proper under the circumstances.

(c) Service of process of the application under subsection (a) on the corporation may be made in any manner provided by statute of this state or by rule of the applicable court for service on the corporation, and no other party need be joined in order for the court to adjudicate the matter. In an action filed by the corporation, the court may require notice of the action be provided to other persons specified by the court and permit such other persons to intervene in the action.

(d) Notwithstanding any other provision of this section or otherwise under applicable law, any action asserting that the ratification of any defective corporate action and any putative shares issued as a result of such defective corporate action should not be effective, or should be effective only on certain conditions, shall be brought within 120 days of the validation effective time.

Chapter 2. Incorporation

§2.01. Incorporators

One or more persons may act as the incorporator or incorporators of a corporation by delivering articles of incorporation to the secretary of state for filing.

§2.02. Articles of Incorporation

(a) The articles of incorporation must set forth:

(1) a corporate name for the corporation that satisfies the requirements of section 4.01;

(2) the number of shares the corporation is authorized to issue;

(3) the street and mailing addresses of the corporation's initial registered office and the name of its initial registered agent at that office; and

(4) the name and address of each incorporator.

(b) The articles of incorporation may set forth:

(1) the names and addresses of the individuals who are to serve as the initial directors;

(2) provisions not inconsistent with law regarding:

(i) the purpose or purposes for which the corporation is organized;

(ii) managing the business and regulating the affairs of the corporation;

(iii) defining, limiting, and regulating the powers of the corporation, its board of directors, and shareholders;

(iv) a par value for authorized shares or classes of shares; or

(v) the imposition of interest holder liability on shareholders;

(3) any provision that under this Act is required or permitted to be set forth in the bylaws;

(4) a provision eliminating or limiting the liability of a director to the corporation or its shareholders for money damages for any action taken, or any failure to take any action, as a director, except liability for (i) the amount of a financial benefit received by a director to which the director is not entitled; (ii) an intentional infliction of harm on the corporation or the shareholders; (iii) a violation of section 8.32; or (iv) an intentional violation of criminal law;

(5) a provision permitting or making obligatory indemnification of a director for liability as defined in section 8.50 to any person for any action taken, or any failure to take any action, as a director, except liability for (i) receipt of a financial benefit to which the director is not entitled, (ii) an intentional infliction of harm on the corporation or its shareholders, (iii) a violation of section 8.32, or (iv) an intentional violation of criminal law; and

(6) a provision limiting or eliminating any duty of a director or any other person to offer the corporation the right to have or participate in any, or one or more classes or categories of, business opportunities, before the pursuit or taking of the opportunity by the director or other person; provided that any application of such a provision to an officer or a related person of that officer (i) also requires approval of that application by the board of directors, subsequent to the effective date of the provision, by action of qualified directors taken in compliance with

the same procedures as are set forth in section 8.62, and (ii) may be limited by the authorizing action of the board.

(c) The articles of incorporation need not set forth any of the corporate powers enumerated in this Act.

(d) Provisions of the articles of incorporation may be made dependent upon facts objectively ascertainable outside the articles of incorporation in accordance with section 1.20(k).

(e) As used in this section, "related person" has the meaning specified in section 8.60.

§2.03. Incorporation

(a) Unless a delayed effective date is specified, the corporate existence begins when the articles of incorporation are filed.

(b) The secretary of state's filing of the articles of incorporation is conclusive proof that the incorporators satisfied all conditions precedent to incorporation except in a proceeding by the state to cancel or revoke the incorporation or involuntarily dissolve the corporation.

§2.04. Liability for Preincorporation Transactions

All persons purporting to act as or on behalf of a corporation, knowing there was no incorporation under this Act, are jointly and severally liable for all liabilities created while so acting.

OFFICIAL COMMENT

Ordinarily, only the filing of articles of incorporation should create the privilege of limited liability. Situations may arise, however, in which the protection of limited liability arguably should be recognized even though the simple incorporation process established by the Act has not been completed.

As a result, the Act imposes liability only on persons who act as or on behalf of corporations "knowing" that no corporation exists. In addition, section 2.04 does not foreclose the possibility that persons who urge defendants to execute contracts in the corporate name knowing that no steps to incorporate have been taken may be estopped to impose personal liability on individual defendants. This estoppel may be based on the inequity perceived when persons, unwilling or reluctant to enter into a commitment under their own name, are persuaded to use the name of a nonexistent corporation, and then are sought to be held personally liable under section 2.04 by the party advocating execution in the name of the corporation.

§2.05. Organization of Corporation

(a) After incorporation:

(1) if initial directors are named in the articles of incorporation, the initial directors shall hold an organizational meeting, at the call of a majority of the directors, to complete the organization of the corporation by appointing officers, adopting bylaws, and carrying on any other business brought before the meeting; or

(2) if initial directors are not named in the articles of incorporation, the incorporator or incorporators shall hold an organizational meeting at the call of a majority of the incorporators:

(i) to elect initial directors and complete the organization of the corporation; or

(ii) to elect a board of directors who shall complete the organization of the corporation.

(b) Action required or permitted by this Act to be taken by incorporators at an organizational meeting may be taken without a meeting if the action taken is evidenced by one or more written consents describing the action taken and signed by each incorporator.

(c) An organizational meeting may be held in or out of this state.

§2.06. Bylaws

(a) The incorporators or board of directors of a corporation shall adopt initial bylaws for the corporation.

(b) The bylaws of a corporation may contain any provision that is not inconsistent with law or the articles of incorporation.

(c) The bylaws may contain one or both of the following provisions:

(1) a requirement that if the corporation solicits proxies or consents with respect to an election of directors, the corporation include in its proxy statement and any form of its proxy or consent, to the extent and subject to such procedures or conditions as are provided in the bylaws, one or more individuals nominated by a shareholder in addition to individuals nominated by the board of directors; and

(2) a requirement that the corporation reimburse the expenses incurred by a shareholder in soliciting proxies or consents in connection with an election of directors, to the extent and subject to such procedures and conditions as are provided in the bylaws, provided that no bylaw so adopted shall apply to elections for which any record date precedes its adoption.

(d) Notwithstanding section 10.20(b)(2), the shareholders in amending, repealing, or adopting a bylaw described in subsection (c) may not limit the authority of the board of directors to amend or repeal any condition or procedure set forth in or to add any procedure or condition to such a bylaw to provide for a reasonable, practical, and orderly process.

OFFICIAL COMMENT

The responsibility for adopting the original bylaws is placed on the person or persons completing the organization of the corporation. Section 2.06(b) permits any bylaw provision that is not inconsistent with law or the articles of incorporation. This limitation precludes bylaw provisions that limit the managerial authority of directors established by section 8.01(b). For a list of provisions that may be included in the bylaws, see the Official Comment to section 2.02.

The power to amend or repeal bylaws, or adopt new bylaws after the organization of the corporation is completed, is addressed in sections 10.20, 10.21 and 10.22.

Section 2.06(c) expressly authorizes bylaws that require the corporation to include individuals nominated by shareholders for election as directors in its proxy statement and proxy cards (or consents) and that require the reimbursement by the corporation of expenses incurred by a shareholder in soliciting proxies (or consents) in an election of directors, in each case subject to such procedures or conditions as may be provided in the bylaws. Expenses reimbursed under section 2.06(c)(2) must be reasonable as contemplated in the definition of expenses set forth in section 1.40.

Examples of the procedures and conditions that may be included in bylaws contemplated by section 2.06(c) include provisions that relate to the ownership of shares (including requirements as to the duration of ownership); informational requirements; restrictions on the number of directors to be nominated or on the use of the provisions by shareholders seeking to acquire control; provisions requiring the nominating shareholder to indemnify the corporation; limitations on reimbursement based on the amount spent by the corporation or the proportion of votes cast for the nominee; and limitations concerning the election of directors by cumulative voting.

Section 2.06(c) clarifies that proxy access and expense reimbursement provisions do not infringe upon the scope of authority granted to the board of directors of a corporation under section 8.01(b). Section 2.06(c) underscores the model of corporate governance embodied by the Act and reflected in section 8.01, but recognizes that different corporations may wish to grant shareholders varying rights in selecting directors through the election process.

Section 2.06(d) limits the rule set forth in section 10.20(b)(2) that shareholder adopted bylaws may limit the authority of directors to amend bylaws, by specifying that such a limit will not apply absolutely to conditions and procedures set forth in access or reimbursement bylaws authorized by section 2.06(c). Section 2.06(d) allows directors to ensure that such bylaws adequately provide for a reasonable, practical, and orderly process, but is not intended to allow the board of directors to frustrate the purpose of a shareholder-adopted proxy access or expense reimbursement provision.

§2.07. *Emergency Bylaws*

(a) Unless the articles of incorporation provide otherwise, the board of directors may adopt bylaws to be effective only in an emergency defined in subsection (d). The emergency bylaws, which are subject to amendment or repeal by the shareholders, may make all provisions necessary for managing the corporation during the emergency, including:

(1) procedures for calling a meeting of the board of directors;

(2) quorum requirements for the meeting; and

(3) designation of additional or substitute directors.

(b) All provisions of the regular bylaws not inconsistent with the emergency bylaws remain effective during the emergency. The emergency bylaws are not effective after the emergency ends.

(c) Corporate action taken in good faith in accordance with the emergency bylaws:

(1) binds the corporation; and

(2) may not be used to impose liability on a director, officer, employee, or agent of the corporation.

(d) An emergency exists for purposes of this section if a quorum of the board of directors cannot readily be assembled because of some catastrophic event.

§2.08. Forum Selection Provisions

(a) The articles of incorporation or the bylaws may require that any or all internal corporate claims shall be brought exclusively in any specified court or courts of this state and, if so specified, in any additional courts in this state or in any other jurisdictions with which the corporation has a reasonable relationship.

(b) A provision of the articles of incorporation or bylaws adopted under subsection (a) shall not have the effect of conferring jurisdiction on any court or over any person or claim, and shall not apply if none of the courts specified by such provision has the requisite personal and subject matter jurisdiction. If the court or courts of this state specified in a provision adopted under subsection (a) do not have the requisite personal and subject matter jurisdiction and another court of this state does have such jurisdiction, then the internal corporate claim may be brought in such other court of this state, notwithstanding that such other court of this state is not specified in such provision, and in any other court specified in such provision that has the requisite jurisdiction.

(c) No provision of the articles of incorporation or the bylaws may prohibit bringing an internal corporate claim in the courts of this state or require such claims to be determined by arbitration.

(d) "Internal corporate claim" means, for the purposes of this section, (i) any claim that is based upon a violation of a duty under the laws of this state by a current or former director, officer, or shareholder in such capacity, (ii) any derivative action or proceeding brought on behalf of the corporation, (iii) any action asserting a claim arising pursuant to any provision of this Act or the articles of incorporation or bylaws, or (iv) any action asserting a claim governed by the internal affairs doctrine that is not included in (i) through (iii) above.

Chapter 3. Purposes and Powers

§3.01. Purposes

(a) Every corporation incorporated under this Act has the purpose of engaging in any lawful business unless a more limited purpose is set forth in the articles of incorporation.

(b) A corporation engaging in a business that is subject to regulation under another statute of this state may incorporate under this Act only if permitted by, and subject to all limitations of, the other statute.

§3.02. General Powers

Unless its articles of incorporation provide otherwise, every corporation has perpetual duration and succession in its corporate name and has the same powers as an individual to do all things necessary or convenient to carry out its business and affairs, including power:

(a) to sue and be sued, complain and defend in its corporate name;

(b) to have a corporate seal, which may be altered at will, and to use it, or a facsimile of it, by impressing or affixing it or in any other manner reproducing it;

(c) to make and amend bylaws, not inconsistent with its articles of incorporation or with the laws of this state, for managing the business and regulating the affairs of the corporation;

(d) to purchase, receive, lease, or otherwise acquire, and own, hold, improve, use, and otherwise deal with, real or personal property, or any legal or equitable interest in property, wherever located;

(e) to sell, convey, mortgage, pledge, lease, exchange, and otherwise dispose of all or any part of its property;

(f) to purchase, receive, subscribe for, or otherwise acquire, own, hold, vote, use, sell, mortgage, lend, pledge, or otherwise dispose of, and deal in and with shares or other interests in, or obligations of, any other entity;

(g) to make contracts and guarantees, incur liabilities, borrow money, issue its notes, bonds, and other securities and obligations (which may be convertible into or include the option to purchase other securities of the corporation), and secure any of its obligations by mortgage or pledge of any of its property, franchises, or income;

(h) to lend money, invest and reinvest its funds, and receive and hold real and personal property as security for repayment;

(i) to be a promoter, partner, member, associate, or manager of any partnership, joint venture, trust, or other entity;

(j) to conduct its business, locate offices, and exercise the powers granted by this Act within or without this state;

(k) to elect directors and appoint officers, employees, and agents of the corporation, define their duties, fix their compensation, and lend them money and credit;

(*l*) to pay pensions and establish pension plans, pension trusts, profit sharing plans, share bonus plans, share option plans, and benefit or incentive plans for any or all of its current or former directors, officers, employees, and agents;

(m) to make donations for the public welfare or for charitable, scientific, or educational purposes;

(n) to transact any lawful business that will aid governmental policy; and

(o) to make payments or donations, or do any other act, not inconsistent with law, that furthers the business and affairs of the corporation.

§3.03. Emergency Powers

(a) In anticipation of or during an emergency defined in subsection (d), the board of directors of a corporation may:

(1) modify lines of succession to accommodate the incapacity of any director, officer, employee, or agent; and

(2) relocate the principal office, designate alternative principal offices or regional offices, or authorize the officers to do so.

(b) During an emergency defined in subsection (d), unless emergency bylaws provide otherwise:

(1) notice of a meeting of the board of directors need be given only to those directors whom it is practicable to reach and may be given in any practicable manner; and

(2) one or more officers of the corporation present at a meeting of the board of directors may be deemed to be directors for the meeting, in order of rank and within the same rank in order of seniority, as necessary to achieve a quorum.

(c) Corporate action taken in good faith during an emergency under this section to further the ordinary business affairs of the corporation:

(1) binds the corporation; and

(2) may not be used to impose liability on a director, officer, employee, or agent.

(d) An emergency exists for purposes of this section if a quorum of the board of directors cannot readily be assembled because of some catastrophic event.

§3.04. Lack of Power to Act

(a) Except as provided in subsection (b), the validity of corporate action may not be challenged on the ground that the corporation lacks or lacked power to act.

(b) A corporation's power to act may be challenged:

(1) in a proceeding by a shareholder against the corporation to enjoin the act;

(2) in a proceeding by the corporation, directly, derivatively, or through a receiver, trustee, or other legal representative, against an incumbent or former director, officer, employee, or agent of the corporation; or

(3) in a proceeding by the attorney general under section 14.30.

(c) In a shareholder's proceeding under subsection (b)(1) to enjoin an unauthorized corporate act, the court may enjoin or set aside the act, if equitable and if all affected persons are parties to the proceeding, and may award damages for loss (other than anticipated profits) suffered by the corporation or another party because of enjoining the unauthorized act.

CHAPTER 4. NAME

§4.01. Corporate Name

(a) A corporate name:

(1) must contain the word "corporation," "incorporated," "company," or "limited," or the abbreviation "corp.," "inc.," "co.," or "ltd.," or words or abbreviations of like import in another language; and

(2) may not contain language stating or implying that the corporation is organized for a purpose other than that permitted by section 3.01 and its articles of incorporation.

(b) Except as authorized by subsections (c) and (d), a corporate name must be distinguishable upon the records of the secretary of state from:

(1) the corporate name of a corporation incorporated in this state which is not administratively dissolved;

(2) a corporate name reserved or registered under section 4.02 or 4.03 or any similar provision of the law of this state;

(3) the name of a foreign corporation registered to do business in this state or an alternate name adopted by a foreign corporation registered to do business in this state because its corporate name is unavailable;

(4) the corporate name of a nonprofit corporation incorporated in this state which is not administratively dissolved;

(5) the name of a foreign nonprofit corporation registered to do business in this state or an alternate name adopted by a foreign nonprofit corporation registered to conduct activities in this state because its real name is unavailable;

(6) the name of a domestic filing entity or limited liability partnership which is not administratively dissolved;

(7) the name of a foreign unincorporated entity registered to do business in this state or an alternate name adopted by such an entity registered to conduct activities in this state because its real name is unavailable; and

(8) an assumed name registered under [state's assumed name statute].

(c) A corporation may apply to the secretary of state for authorization to use a name that is not distinguishable upon the secretary of state's records from one or more of the names described in subsection (b). The secretary of state shall authorize use of the name applied for if:

(1) the other corporation or unincorporated entity consents to the use in writing and submits an undertaking in form satisfactory to the secretary of state to change its name to a name that is distinguishable upon the records of the secretary of state from the name of the applying corporation; or

(2) the applicant delivers to the secretary of state a certified copy of the final judgment of a court of competent jurisdiction establishing the applicant's right to use the name applied for in this state.

(d) This Act does not control the use of fictitious names.

Chapter 5. Office and Agent

§5.01. Registered Office and Agent of Domestic and Registered Foreign Corporations

(a) Each corporation shall continuously maintain in this state:

(1) a registered office that may be the same as any of its places of business; and

(2) a registered agent, which may be:

(i) an individual who resides in this state and whose business office is identical with the registered office; or

(ii) a domestic or foreign corporation or eligible entity whose business office is identical with the registered office and, in the case of a foreign corporation or foreign eligible entity, is registered to do business in this state.

(b) As used in this chapter, "corporation" means both a domestic corporation and a registered foreign corporation.

§5.04. Service on Corporation

(a) A corporation's registered agent is the corporation's agent for service of process, notice, or demand required or permitted by law to be served on the corporation.

(b) If a corporation has no registered agent, or the agent cannot with reasonable diligence be served, the corporation may be served by registered or certified mail, return receipt requested, addressed to the secretary at the corporation's principal office. Service is perfected under this subsection at the earliest of:

(1) the date the corporation receives the mail;

(2) the date shown on the return receipt, if signed on behalf of the corporation; or

(3) five days after its deposit in the United States mail, as evidenced by the postmark, if mailed postpaid and correctly addressed.

(c) If process, notice, or demand (i) cannot be served on a corporation pursuant to subsection (a) or (b), or (ii) is to be served on a registered foreign corporation that has withdrawn its registration pursuant to section 15.07 or 15.09, or the registration of which has been terminated pursuant to section 15.11, then the secretary of state shall be an agent of the corporation upon whom process, notice, or demand may be served. Service of any process, notice, or demand on the secretary of state as agent for a corporation may be made by delivering to the secretary of state duplicate copies of the process, notice, or demand. If process, notice, or demand is served on the secretary of state, the secretary of state shall forward one of the copies by registered or certified mail, return receipt requested, to the corporation at the last address shown in the records of the secretary of state. Service is effected under this subsection (c) at the earliest of:

(1) the date the corporation receives the process, notice, or demand;

(2) the date shown on the return receipt, if signed on behalf of the corporation; or

(3) five days after the process, notice, or demand is deposited with the United States mail by the secretary of state.

(d) This section does not prescribe the only means, or necessarily the required means, of serving a corporation.

Chapter 6. Shares and Distributions

SUBCHAPTER A. SHARES

§6.01. Authorized Shares

(a) The articles of incorporation must set forth any classes of shares and series of shares within a class, and the number of shares of each class and series, that the corporation is authorized to issue. If more than one class or series of shares is authorized, the articles of incorporation must prescribe a distinguishing designation for each class or series and, before the issuance of shares of a class or series, describe the terms, including the preferences, rights, and limitations, of that class or series. Except to the extent varied as permitted by this section, all shares of a class or series must have terms, including preferences, rights, and limitations, that are identical with those of other shares of the same class or series.

(b) The articles of incorporation must authorize:

(1) one or more classes or series of shares that together have full voting rights, and

(2) one or more classes or series of shares (which may be the same class, classes or series as those with voting rights) that together are entitled to receive the net assets of the corporation upon dissolution.

(c) The articles of incorporation may authorize one or more classes or series of shares that:

(1) have special, conditional, or limited voting rights, or no right to vote, except to the extent otherwise provided by this Act;

(2) are redeemable or convertible as specified in the articles of incorporation:

(i) at the option of the corporation, the shareholder, or another person or upon the occurrence of a specified event;

(ii) for cash, indebtedness, securities, or other property; and

(iii) at prices and in amounts specified or determined in accordance with a formula;

(3) entitle the holders to distributions calculated in any manner, including dividends that may be cumulative, noncumulative, or partially cumulative; or

(4) have preference over any other class or series of shares with respect to distributions, including distributions upon the dissolution of the corporation.

(d) Terms of shares may be made dependent upon facts objectively ascertainable outside the articles of incorporation in accordance with section 1.20(k).

(e) Any of the terms of shares may vary among holders of the same class or series so long as such variations are expressly set forth in the articles of incorporation.

(f) The description of the preferences, rights, and limitations of classes or series of shares in subsection (c) is not exhaustive.

OFFICIAL COMMENT

1. *Section 6.01(a)*

Section 6.01(a) requires that the articles of incorporation prescribe the classes and series of shares and the number of shares of each class and series that the corporation is authorized to issue. If the articles of incorporation authorize the issue of only one class of shares, no designation or description of the shares is required, it being understood that these shares have both the power to vote and the power to receive the net assets of the corporation upon dissolution. See section 6.01(b). Shares with both of these characteristics are usually referred to as "common shares" but no specific designation is required by the Act. The articles of incorporation may set forth the number of shares authorized and permit the board of directors under section 6.02 to allocate the authorized shares among designated classes or series of shares.

The preferences, rights and limitations of each class or series of shares constitute the "contract" of the holders of those classes and series of shares with respect to the holders' interest in the corporation and must be set forth in sufficient detail reasonably to define their interest. The terms, including the preferences, rights and limitations, of shares with one or more special or preferential rights which may be authorized are further described in section 6.01(c).

If more than one class or series is authorized (or if only one class or series is originally authorized but at some future time one or more other classes or series of shares are added by amendment), the terms, including the preferences, rights and limitations of each class, classes or series of shares, including the class, classes or series that possess the fundamental characteristics of voting and residual equity financial interests, must be described before shares of those classes or series are issued. If both fundamental characteristics are placed exclusively in a single class of shares, that class may be described simply as "common shares" or by statements such as the "shares have the general distribution and voting rights," the "shares have all the rights of common shares," or the "shares have all rights not granted to the class A shares."

If the articles of incorporation create classes or series of shares that divide these fundamental rights among two or more classes or series of shares, it is necessary that the rights be clearly allocated among the classes and series. Specificity is required only to the extent necessary to differentiate the relative rights of the respective classes and series. For example, where one class or series has a liquidation preference over another, it is necessary to specify only the preferential liquidation right of that class or series; in the absence of a contrary provision in the articles of incorporation, the remaining class or series would be entitled to receive the net assets remaining after the liquidation preference has been satisfied. More than one class or series of shares may be designated as "common shares;" however, each must have a "distinguishing designation" under section 6.01(a), *e.g.*, "nonvoting common shares" or "class A common shares," and the rights of the classes and series must be described. For example, if a corporation authorizes two classes of shares with equal rights to share in all distributions and with identical voting rights except that one class is entitled exclusively to elect one director and the second class is entitled exclusively to elect a second director, the two classes may be designated, *e.g.*, as "Class A common" and "Class B common." What is required is language that makes the allocation of these rights clear.

Rather than describing the terms of each class or series of shares in the articles of incorporation, the corporation may delegate to the board of directors under section 6.02 the power to establish the terms of a class of shares or a series within a class if no shares of that class or series have previously been issued. Those terms, however, must be set forth in an amendment to the articles of incorporation that is effective before the shares are issued.

2. *Section 6.01(b)*

Section 6.01(b) requires that every corporation authorize one or more classes or series of shares that in the aggregate have the two fundamental characteristics of full voting rights and the right to receive the net assets of the corporation upon its dissolution. The phrase "full voting rights" refers to the right to vote on all matters for which voting is required by either the Act or the articles of incorporation.

The two fundamental characteristics need not be placed in a single class or series of shares but may be divided as desired. It is nevertheless essential that the corporation always have authorized shares having in the aggregate these two characteristics, and section 6.03 requires that shares having in the aggregate these characteristics always be outstanding.

3. *Section 6.01(c)*

Section 6.01(c) provides a non-exhaustive list of the principal features that are customarily incorporated into classes or series of shares.

a. In general

Section 6.01(c) authorizes creation of classes or series of shares with a range of preferences, rights and limitations as further described below. The Act permits the creation of shares convertible into, or redeemable in exchange for, cash, other property, or shares or debt securities of the corporation ranking senior to the shares, at the option of either the holder or the corporation. Such a conversion or redemption is subject to the restrictions on distributions under section 6.40.

b. Voting of shares

Any class or series of shares may be granted multiple or fractional votes per share without limitation. See section 7.21. Shares of any class or series may also be made nonvoting "except to the extent otherwise provided by this Act." This "except" clause refers to the provisions in the Act that permit shares which are designated to be nonvoting to vote as separate voting groups on amendments to articles of incorporation and other organic changes in the corporation that directly affect that class or series (see sections 7.26 and 10.04). In addition, shares may be given voting rights that are limited or conditional (*e.g.*, voting rights triggered by the failure to pay specified dividends).

c. Redemption and conversion of shares

Section 6.01(c)(2) permits redemption for any class or series of shares and thereby permits the creation of redeemable or callable shares without limitation (subject only to the provisions that the class, classes or series of shares described in section 6.01(b) must always be authorized and that at least one or more shares which together have those rights must be outstanding under section 6.03).

The prices to be paid upon the redemption of shares under section 6.01(c)(2) and the amounts to be redeemed may be fixed in the articles of incorporation or "determined in accordance with a formula." The formula could be self contained or, pursuant to the provisions of section 6.01(d), could be determined by reference to extrinsic data or events. This permits the redemption price and the amounts to be redeemed to be established on the basis of matters external to the corporation, such as the purchase price of other shares, the level of market reference rates, the effective interest rate at which the corporation may obtain short or long-term financing, the consumer price index or a designated currency ratio.

All redemptions of shares are subject to the restrictions on distributions set forth in section 6.40. See section 6.03(b).

Section 6.01(c)(2) also permits shares of any class or series to be made convertible into shares of any other class or series or into cash, indebtedness, securities, or other property of the corporation or another person.

D. Extrinsic facts

Section 6.01(d) permits the creation of classes or series of shares with terms that are dependent upon facts objectively ascertainable outside the articles of incorporation. See section 1.20(k) and the related Official Comment for an explanation of the meaning of the phrase "facts objectively ascertainable" and the requirement for the filing of articles of amendment under the circumstances set forth in that section. Terms that depend upon reference to extrinsic facts may include dividend rates that vary according to some external index or event. Because such a "variable rate" class or series of shares would be intended to respond to current market conditions, it would most often be used with "blank check" provisions in the articles of incorporation with the terms of shares set by the board of directors immediately before issuance. See the Official Comment to section 6.02. Note that section 6.21 requires the board to determine the adequacy of consideration received or to be received by the corporation before issuing shares. If shares with terms to be determined by reference to extrinsic facts are to be authorized for issuance, the board should take care to establish appropriately defined parameters for such terms.

E. Variation among holders

Section 6.01(e) permits the creation of classes or series of shares with terms that may vary among holders of the same class or series of shares. An example of such variation would be a provision that shares held by a bank or bank holding company in excess of a certain percentage would not have voting rights. In addition, section 6.24(b) expressly permits the issuance of rights, options or warrants for the purchase of shares or other securities of the corporation that contain terms and conditions which vary the rights of the holders of such rights, warrants or options based on a holder's ownership of, or offer to acquire, a specified number or percentage of the outstanding shares or other securities of the corporation.

4. *Examples of Classes or Series of Shares Permitted by Section 6.01*

Section 6.01 is enabling rather than restrictive given that corporations often find it necessary to create new classes or series of shares for a variety of reasons, for instance in connection with raising debt or equity capital. Classes or series of shares may also be used in connection with desired control relationships among the participants in a venture. Under section 7.21, only securities classified as "shares" in the articles of incorporation can have the power to vote.

Examples of such classes and series of shares include:

- Shares of one class or series may be authorized to elect a specified number of directors while shares of a second class or series may be authorized to elect the same or a different number of directors.
- Shares of one class or series may be entitled to vote as a separate voting group on certain transactions, but shares of two or more classes or series may be only entitled to vote together as a single voting group on the election of directors and other matters.
- Shares of one class or series may be nonvoting or may be given multiple or fractional votes per share.
- Shares of one class or series may be entitled to different dividend rights or rights on dissolution than shares of another class or series.
- Shares of one class or series may be created to include some characteristics of debt securities.

A corporation has power to issue debt securities under section 3.02. Although 6.01 authorizes the creation of interests that usually will be classed as "equity" rather than "debt," it is permissible to create classes or series of securities under section 6.01 that have some of the characteristics of debt securities. These securities are often referred to as "hybrid securities." Section 6.01 does not limit the development of hybrid securities, and equity securities may be created under the Act that embody any characteristics of debt. As noted above, however, the Act restricts the power to vote to securities classified as "shares" in the articles of incorporation.

§6.02. *Terms of Class or Series Determined by Board of Directors*

(a) If the articles of incorporation so provide, the board of directors is authorized, without shareholder approval, to:

(1) classify any unissued shares into one or more classes or into one or more series within a class;

(2) reclassify any unissued shares of any class into one or more classes or into one or more series within one or more classes; or

(3) reclassify any unissued shares of any series of any class into one or more classes or into one or more series within a class.

(b) If the board of directors acts pursuant to subsection (a), it shall determine the terms, including the preferences, rights, and limitations, to the same extent permitted under section 6.01, of:

(1) any class of shares before the issuance of any shares of that class, or

(2) any series within a class before the issuance of any shares of that series.

(c) Before issuing any shares of a class or series created under this section, the corporation shall deliver to the secretary of state for filing articles of amendment setting forth the terms determined under subsection (a).

OFFICIAL COMMENT

Section 6.02 permits the board of directors, if authority to do so is contained in the articles of incorporation, to determine the terms of a class of shares or of a series of shares within a class to meet corporate needs, including current requirements of the securities markets or the flexibility needed for acquisitions, without the necessity of holding a shareholders' meeting to amend the articles of incorporation. If given that authority, the board of directors may create new series within a class and may also determine the terms of a class or series if there are no outstanding shares of that class or series.

A provision in the articles of incorporation authorizing shares to be issued in different classes or series with terms to be set by the board of directors is sometimes referred to as a "blank check" provision. The power to make the terms of shares so created dependent on facts objectively ascertainable outside the articles of incorporation and to vary their terms among holders of the same class or series extends to all the permitted provisions set forth in section 6.01(c).

Sections 6.02(a) and (b) make it clear that the board of directors has the same broad flexibility with regard to setting the terms of a class or series under this section as is permitted under section 6.01(c). Section 6.02(c) requires a filing to amend the articles of incorporation so there will be a public record of the class or series which the corporation intends to issue. The amendment does not require shareholder action. See section 10.05(h).

§6.03. *Issued and Outstanding Shares*

(a) A corporation may issue the number of shares of each class or series authorized by the articles of incorporation. Shares that are issued are outstanding shares until they are reacquired, redeemed, converted, or cancelled.

(b) The reacquisition, redemption, or conversion of outstanding shares is subject to the limitations of subsection (c) and to section 6.40.

(c) At all times that shares of the corporation are outstanding, one or more shares that together have full voting rights and one or more shares that together are entitled to receive the net assets of the corporation upon dissolution must be outstanding.

§6.04. Fractional Shares

(a) A corporation may issue fractions of a share or in lieu of doing so may:

(1) pay in cash the value of fractions of a share;

(2) issue scrip in certificated or uncertificated form entitling the holder to receive a full share upon surrendering enough scrip to equal a full share; or

(3) dispose of the fractional shares and pay the proceeds to the holders of those shares.

(b) Each certificate representing scrip must be conspicuously labeled "scrip" and must contain the information required by section 6.25(b). A corporation may not issue scrip certificates in bearer form. Within a reasonable time after the issuance or transfer of scrip without certificates, the corporation shall deliver to the scripholder a written statement of the information required on certificates by section 6.25(b) and the terms of the scrip.

(c) The holder of a fractional share is entitled to exercise the rights of a shareholder, including the rights to vote, to receive dividends, and to receive distributions upon dissolution. The holder of scrip is not entitled to any of these rights unless the scrip provides for them.

(d) The board of directors may authorize the issuance of scrip subject to any condition, including that:

(1) the scrip will become void if not exchanged for full shares before a specified date; and

(2) the shares for which the scrip is exchangeable may be sold and the proceeds paid to the scripholders.

SUBCHAPTER B. ISSUANCE OF SHARES

§6.20. Subscription for Shares Before Incorporation

(a) A subscription for shares entered into before incorporation is irrevocable for six months unless the subscription agreement provides a longer or shorter period or all the subscribers agree to revocation.

(b) The board of directors may determine the payment terms of subscriptions for shares that were entered into before incorporation, unless the subscription agreement specifies them. A call for payment by the board of directors must be uniform so far as practicable as to all shares of the same class or series, unless the subscription agreement specifies otherwise.

(c) Shares issued pursuant to subscriptions entered into before incorporation are fully paid and nonassessable when the corporation receives the consideration specified in the subscription agreement.

(d) If a subscriber defaults in payment of cash or property under a subscription agreement entered into before incorporation, the corporation may collect the amount owed as any other debt. Alternatively, unless the subscription agreement provides otherwise, the corporation may rescind the agreement and may sell the shares if the debt remains unpaid for more than 20 days after the corporation delivers a written demand for payment to the subscriber.

§6.21. *Issuance of Shares*

(a) The powers granted in this section to the board of directors may be reserved to the shareholders by the articles of incorporation.

(b) The board of directors may authorize shares to be issued for consideration consisting of any tangible or intangible property or benefit to the corporation, including cash, promissory notes, services performed, contracts for services to be performed, or other securities of the corporation.

(c) Before the corporation issues shares, the board of directors shall determine that the consideration received or to be received for shares to be issued is adequate. That determination by the board of directors is conclusive insofar as the adequacy of consideration for the issuance of shares relates to whether the shares are validly issued, fully paid, and nonassessable.

(d) When the corporation receives the consideration for which the board of directors authorized the issuance of shares, the shares issued therefor are fully paid and nonassessable.

(e) The corporation may place in escrow shares issued for a contract for future services or benefits or a promissory note, or make other arrangements to restrict the transfer of the shares, and may credit distributions in respect of the shares against their purchase price, until the services are performed, the benefits are received, or the note is paid. If the services are not performed, the benefits are not received, or the note is not paid, the shares escrowed or restricted and the distributions credited may be cancelled in whole or part.

(f) (1) An issuance of shares or other securities convertible into or rights exercisable for shares in a transaction or a series of integrated transactions requires approval of the shareholders, at a meeting at which a quorum consisting of a majority (or such greater number as the articles of incorporation may prescribe) of the votes entitled to be cast on the matter exists, if:

(i) the shares, other securities, or rights are to be issued for consideration other than cash or cash equivalents, and

(ii) the voting power of shares that are issued and issuable as a result of the transaction or series of integrated transactions will comprise more than 20% of the voting power of the shares of the corporation that were outstanding immediately before the transaction.

(2) In this subsection:

(i) For purposes of determining the voting power of shares issued and issuable as a result of a transaction or series of integrated transactions, the voting power of shares or other securities convertible into or rights exercisable for shares shall be the greater of (A) the voting power of the shares to be issued, or (B) the voting power of the shares that would be outstanding after giving effect to the conversion of convertible shares and other securities and the exercise of rights to be issued.

(ii) A series of transactions is integrated only if consummation of one transaction is made contingent on consummation of one or more of the other transactions.

OFFICIAL COMMENT

Because a statutory structure embodying "par value" and "stated capital" concepts does not protect creditors and senior security holders from payments to junior security holders, section 6.21 does not use these concepts.

1. Consideration

Because shares need not have a par value under section 6.21, there is no minimum price at which shares must be issued. . . .

2. Shareholder Approval Requirement for Certain Issuances

The shareholder approval requirement of section 6.21(f) is generally patterned after the listing standards of national securities exchanges. The calculation of the 20% compares the maximum number of votes entitled to be cast by the shares to be issued or that could be outstanding after giving effect to the conversion of convertible securities and the exercise of rights being issued, with the actual number of votes entitled to be cast by outstanding shares before the transaction.

In making the 20% determination under section 6.21(f), shares that are issuable in a transaction of any kind, including a merger, share exchange, or acquisition of assets, on a contingent basis are counted as shares or securities to be issued as a result of the transaction. On the other hand, shares that are issuable under antidilution clauses, such as those designed to take account of future share splits or share dividends, are not counted as shares or securities to be issued as a result of the transaction, because they are issuable only as a result of a later corporate action authorizing the split or dividend. If a transaction involves an earn-out provision, under which the total amount of shares or securities to be issued will depend on future earnings or other performance measures, the maximum amount of shares or securities that can be issued under the earn-out must be included in the determination.

If the number of shares to be issued or issuable is not fixed, but is subject to a formula, the application of the test in section 6.21(f)(2)(i) requires a calculation of the maximum amount that could be issued under the formula, whether stated as a range or otherwise, in the governing agreement. Even if ultimate issuance of the maximum amount is unlikely, a vote will be required if the maximum amount would result in an issuance of more than 20% of the voting power of shares outstanding immediately before the transaction.

Shares that have or would have only contingent voting rights when issued or issuable are not shares that carry voting power for purposes of the calculation under section 6.21(f).

The vote required to approve issuances that fall within section 6.21(f) is the basic voting rule under the Act, set forth in section 7.25, that more shares must be voted in favor of the issuance than are voted against. This is the same voting rule that applies under chapter 9 for domestications and conversions, chapter 10 for amendments of the articles of incorporation, chapter 11 for mergers and share exchanges, chapter 12 for dispositions of assets that require shareholder approval, and chapter 14 for voluntary dissolutions. The quorum rule under section 6.21(f) is also the same as the quorum rule under chapters 9, 10, 11, 12, and 14.

Section 6.21(f) does not apply to an issuance for cash or cash equivalents, regardless of whether in connection with a public offering. "Cash equivalents" are generally short-term investments that are both readily convertible to known amounts of cash and present insignificant risk of changes in interest rates. Shares that are issued partly for cash or cash equivalents and partly for other consideration are "issued for consideration other than cash or cash equivalents" within the meaning of section 6.21(f).

The term "rights" in section 6.21(f) includes warrants, options, and rights of exchange, whether at the option of the holder, the corporation, or another person. The term "voting power" is defined in section 1.40 as the current power to vote in the election of directors. See also the Official Comment to that section. Because transactions are integrated within the meaning of section 6.21(f) only where consummation of one transaction is made contingent on consummation of one or more of the other transactions, transactions are not integrated for purposes of section 6.21(f) merely because they are proximate in time or because the kind of consideration for which the corporation issues shares is similar in each transaction.

Section 6.21(f) only applies to issuances for consideration. Accordingly, section 6.21(f) does not require shareholder approval for share dividends or for shareholder rights plans. See section 6.23 and its Official Comment.

Illustrations of the application of section 6.21(f) follow:

1. C corporation, which has 2,000,000 shares of Class A voting common stock outstanding (carrying one vote per share), proposes to issue 600,000 shares of authorized but unissued Class B nonvoting common stock in exchange for a business owned by D Corporation. The proposed issuance does not require shareholder approval under section 6.21(f) because the Class B shares do not carry voting power.

2. The facts being otherwise as stated in Illustration 1, C proposes to issue 600,000 additional shares of its Class A voting common stock. The proposed issuance requires shareholder approval under section 6.21(f) because the voting power carried by the shares to be issued will comprise more than 20% of the voting power of C's shares outstanding immediately before the issuance.

3. The facts being otherwise as stated in Illustration 1, C proposes to issue 400,000 shares of authorized but unissued voting preferred stock, each share of which carries one vote and is convertible into 1.5 shares of Class A voting common stock. The proposed issuance requires shareholder approval under section 6.21(f). Although the voting power of the preferred shares to be issued will not comprise more than 20% of the voting power of C's shares outstanding immediately before the issuance, the voting power of the shares issuable upon conversion of the preferred shares will carry more than 20% of such voting power.

4. The facts being otherwise as stated in Illustration 1, C proposes to issue 200,000 shares of its Class A voting common stock, and 100,000 shares of authorized but unissued nonvoting preferred stock, each share of which is convertible into 2.5 shares of C's Class A voting common stock. The proposed issuance requires shareholder approval under section 6.21(f) because the voting power of the Class A shares to be issued, after giving effect to the common stock that is issuable upon conversion of the preferred shares, would comprise more than 20% of the voting power of C's outstanding shares immediately before the issuance.

5. The facts being otherwise as stated in Illustration 4, each share of the preferred stock is convertible into 1.2 shares of the Class A voting common stock. The proposed issuance does not require shareholder approval under section 6.21(f) because neither the voting power of the shares to be issued at the outset (200,000) nor the voting power of the shares that would be outstanding after giving effect to the common stock issuable upon conversion of the preferred shares (a total of 320,000) constitutes more than 20% of the voting power of C's outstanding shares immediately before the issuance.

6. The facts being otherwise as stated in Illustration 1, C proposes to acquire businesses from Corporations G, H, and I for 200,000, 300,000, and 400,000 shares of Class

A voting common stock, respectively, within a short period of time. None of the transactions is conditioned on the negotiation or completion of the other transactions. The proposed issuance of voting shares does not require shareholder approval, because the three transactions are not integrated within the meaning of section 6.21(f), and none of the transactions individually involves the issuance of more than 20% of the voting power of C's outstanding shares immediately before each issuance.

§6.22. *Liability of Shareholders*

(a) A purchaser from a corporation of the corporation's own shares is not liable to the corporation or its creditors with respect to the shares except to pay the consideration for which the shares were authorized to be issued or specified in the subscription agreement.

(b) A shareholder of a corporation is not personally liable for any liabilities of the corporation (including liabilities arising from acts of the corporation) except (i) to the extent provided in a provision of the articles of incorporation permitted by section 2.02(b)(2)(v), and (ii) that a shareholder may become personally liable by reason of the shareholder's own acts or conduct.

§6.23. *Share Dividends*

(a) Unless the articles of incorporation provide otherwise, shares may be issued pro rata and without consideration to the corporation's shareholders or to the shareholders of one or more classes or series of shares. An issuance of shares under this subsection is a share dividend.

(b) Shares of one class or series may not be issued as a share dividend in respect of shares of another class or series unless (i) the articles of incorporation so authorize, (ii) a majority of the votes entitled to be cast by the class or series to be issued approve the issue, or (iii) there are no outstanding shares of the class or series to be issued.

(c) The board of directors may fix the record date for determining shareholders entitled to a share dividend, which date may not be retroactive. If the board of directors does not fix the record date for determining shareholders entitled to a share dividend, the record date is the date the board of directors authorizes the share dividend.

OFFICIAL COMMENT

A share dividend is solely a paper transaction: no assets are received by the corporation for the shares and any "dividend" paid in shares does not involve the distribution of property by the corporation to its shareholders. Section 6.23 therefore recognizes that such a transaction involves the issuance of shares "without consideration," and section 1.40 excludes it from the definition of a "distribution."

§6.24. *Share Rights, Options, Warrants and Awards*

(a) A corporation may issue rights, options, or warrants for the purchase of shares or other securities of the corporation. The board of directors shall determine

(i) the terms and conditions upon which the rights, options, or warrants are issued and (ii) the terms, including the consideration for which the shares or other securities are to be issued. The authorization by the board of directors for the corporation to issue such rights, options, or warrants constitutes authorization of the issuance of the shares or other securities for which the rights, options or warrants are exercisable.

(b) The terms and conditions of such rights, options or warrants may include restrictions or conditions that:

(1) preclude or limit the exercise, transfer or receipt of such rights, options or warrants by any person or persons owning or offering to acquire a specified number or percentage of the outstanding shares or other securities of the corporation or by any transferee or transferees of any such person or persons, or

(2) invalidate or void such rights, options, or warrants held by any such person or persons or any such transferee or transferees.

(c) The board of directors may authorize one or more officers to (i) designate the recipients of rights, options, warrants, or other equity compensation awards that involve the issuance of shares and (ii) determine, within an amount and subject to any other limitations established by the board of directors and, if applicable, the shareholders, the number of such rights, options, warrants, or other equity compensation awards and the terms of such rights, options, warrants or awards to be received by the recipients, provided that an officer may not use such authority to designate himself or herself or any other persons as the board of directors may specify as a recipient of such rights, options, warrants, or other equity compensation awards.

OFFICIAL COMMENT

Section 6.24 specifically authorizes the creation of rights, options and warrants and confirms the broad discretion of the board of directors in determining the consideration to be received by the corporation for their issuance, including the creation of compensation plans for directors, officers, agents, and employees.

Section 6.24(a) does not require shareholder approval of rights, options, warrants or compensation plans. Of course, prior shareholder approval may be sought as a discretionary matter, or required to comply with the rules of national securities exchanges or to acquire federal income tax benefits that may be conditioned upon shareholder approval of such plans.

Section 6.24(b) confirms that the issuance of rights, options or warrants as part of a shareholder rights plan is permitted. The permissible scope of shareholder rights plans may, however, be limited by the courts.

Section 6.24(c) provides express authority for the delegation to officers of the designation of recipients of compensatory awards involving the issuance of shares, either directly or upon exercise of rights to acquire shares, and the determination of the amount and other terms of the awards, subject to any applicable limitations established by the board of directors or the shareholders. A board of directors (or a board committee with authority delegated to it under section 8.25, typically a compensation committee) may decide whether to exercise the authority under section 6.24(c) and, to the extent it does so, the board must specify the total amount that may be awarded and may impose any other limits it desires as part of the board's oversight of the award process. A board or committee delegating authority under section 6.24(c) would typically include appropriate limits. These limits might include, for example, the amount or range of shares to be awarded to different classes of employees, the timing and pricing of awards, and the vesting terms or other variable provisions of awards.

§6.25. Form and Content of Certificates

(a) Shares may, but need not, be represented by certificates. Share certificates may not be issued in bearer form. Unless this Act or another statute expressly provides otherwise, the rights and obligations of shareholders are identical regardless of whether their shares are represented by certificates.

(b) At a minimum each share certificate must state on its face:

(1) the name of the corporation and that it is organized under the law of this state;

(2) the name of the person to whom issued; and

(3) the number and class of shares and the designation of the series, if any, the certificate represents.

(c) If the corporation is authorized to issue different classes of shares or series of shares within a class, the front or back of each certificate must summarize (i) the preferences, rights, and limitations applicable to each class and series, (ii) any variations in preferences, rights, and limitations among the holders of the same class or series, and (iii) the authority of the board of directors to determine the terms of future classes or series. Alternatively, each certificate may state conspicuously on its front or back that the corporation will furnish the shareholder this information on request in writing and without charge.

(d) Each share certificate must be signed by two officers designated in the bylaws.

(e) If the person who signed a share certificate no longer holds office when the certificate is issued, the certificate is nevertheless valid.

§6.26. Shares Without Certificates

(a) Unless the articles of incorporation or bylaws provide otherwise, the board of directors of a corporation may authorize the issuance of some or all of the shares of any or all of its classes or series without certificates. The authorization does not affect shares already represented by certificates until they are surrendered to the corporation.

(b) Within a reasonable time after the issuance or transfer of shares without certificates, the corporation shall deliver to the shareholder a written statement of the information required on certificates by sections 6.25(b) and (c), and, if applicable, section 6.27.

§6.27. Restriction on Transfer of Shares

(a) The articles of incorporation, the bylaws, an agreement among shareholders, or an agreement between shareholders and the corporation may impose restrictions on the transfer or registration of transfer of shares of the corporation. A restriction does not affect shares issued before the restriction was adopted unless the holders of the shares are parties to the restriction agreement or voted in favor of the restriction.

(b) A restriction on the transfer or registration of transfer of shares is valid and enforceable against the holder or a transferee of the holder if the restriction is authorized by this section and its existence is noted conspicuously on the front or back of the certificate or is contained in the information statement required by section 6.26(b). Unless so noted or contained, a restriction is not enforceable against a person without knowledge of the restriction.

(c) A restriction on the transfer or registration of transfer of shares is authorized:

(1) to maintain the corporation's status when it is dependent on the number or identity of its shareholders;

(2) to preserve exemptions under federal or state securities law; or

(3) for any other reasonable purpose.

(d) A restriction on the transfer or registration of transfer of shares may:

(1) obligate the shareholder first to offer the corporation or other persons (separately, consecutively, or simultaneously) an opportunity to acquire the restricted shares;

(2) obligate the corporation or other persons (separately, consecutively, or simultaneously) to acquire the restricted shares;

(3) require the corporation, the holders of any class or series of its shares, or other persons to approve the transfer of the restricted shares, if the requirement is not manifestly unreasonable; or

(4) prohibit the transfer of the restricted shares to designated persons or classes of persons, if the prohibition is not manifestly unreasonable.

(e) For purposes of this section, "shares" includes a security convertible into or carrying a right to subscribe for or acquire shares.

OFFICIAL COMMENT

Share transfer restrictions are used by corporations for a variety of purposes. Section 6.27(c) enumerates certain purposes for which share transfer restrictions may be imposed, but does not limit the purposes given that section 6.27(c)(3) permits restrictions "for any other reasonable purpose." Examples of the "status" referred to in section 6.27(c)(1) include the subchapter S election under the Internal Revenue Code, and entitlement to a program or eligibility for a privilege administered by governmental agencies or national securities exchanges.

Examples of the uses of share transfer restrictions include:

- a corporation with few shareholders may impose share transfer restrictions to ensure that shareholders do not transfer their shares to a person not acceptable to the corporation or other shareholders;
- a corporation with few shareholders may impose share transfer restrictions to establish the value of the shares of deceased shareholders;
- a professional corporation may impose share transfer restrictions to ensure that its treatment of departing, retiring or deceased shareholders is consistent with rules applicable to the profession in question;
- a corporation may impose share transfer restrictions to ensure that its election of subchapter S treatment under the Internal Revenue Code will not be unexpectedly terminated; and

- a corporation issuing securities pursuant to an exemption from federal or state securities registration may impose share transfer restrictions to ensure that subsequent transfers of shares will not result in the loss of the exemption being relied upon.

Section 6.27(d) describes the types of restrictions that may be imposed. The types of restrictions referred to in sections 6.27(d)(1) (rights of first offer) and (d)(2) (buy-sell agreements) are imposed as a matter of contractual negotiation and do not prohibit the outright transfer of shares. Rather, they designate to whom shares or other securities must be offered at a price established in the agreement or by a formula or method agreed to in advance. By contrast, the restrictions described in clauses sections 6.27(d)(3) and (d)(4) may permanently limit the market for shares by disqualifying all or some potential purchasers. The restrictions imposed by these two provisions must not be "manifestly unreasonable."

SUBCHAPTER C. SUBSEQUENT ACQUISITION OF SHARES BY SHAREHOLDERS AND CORPORATION

§6.30. Shareholders' Preemptive Rights

(a) The shareholders of a corporation do not have a preemptive right to acquire the corporation's unissued shares except to the extent the articles of incorporation so provide.

(b) A statement included in the articles of incorporation that "the corporation elects to have preemptive rights" (or words of similar effect) means that the following principles apply except to the extent the articles of incorporation expressly provide otherwise:

(1) The shareholders of the corporation have a preemptive right, granted on uniform terms and conditions prescribed by the board of directors to provide a fair and reasonable opportunity to exercise the right, to acquire proportional amounts of the corporation's unisssued shares upon the decision of the board of directors to issue them.

(2) A preemptive right may be waived by a shareholder. A waiver evidenced by a writing is irrevocable even though it is not supported by consideration.

(3) There is no preemptive right with respect to:

(i) shares issued as compensation to directors, officers, employees or agents of the corporation, its subsidiaries or affiliates;

(ii) shares issued to satisfy conversion or option rights created to provide compensation to directors, officers, employees or agents of the corporation, its subsidiaries or affiliates;

(iii) shares authorized in the articles of incorporation that are issued within six months from the effective date of incorporation; or

(iv) shares sold otherwise than for cash.

(4) Holders of shares of any class or series without voting power but with preferential rights to distributions have no preemptive rights with respect to shares of any class or series.

(5) Holders of shares of any class or series with voting power but without preferential rights to distributions have no preemptive rights with respect to

shares of any class or series with preferential rights to distributions unless the shares with preferential rights are convertible into or carry a right to subscribe for or acquire the shares without preferential rights.

(6) Shares subject to preemptive rights that are not acquired by shareholders may be issued to any person for a period of one year after being offered to shareholders at a consideration set by the board of directors that is not lower than the consideration set for the exercise of preemptive rights. An offer at a lower consideration or after the expiration of one year is subject to the shareholders' preemptive rights.

(c) For purposes of this section, "shares" includes a security convertible into or carrying a right to subscribe for or acquire shares.

§6.31. *Corporation's Acquisition of Its Own Shares*

(a) A corporation may acquire its own shares, and shares so acquired constitute authorized but unissued shares.

(b) If the articles of incorporation prohibit the reissue of the acquired shares, the number of authorized shares is reduced by the number of shares acquired.

SUBCHAPTER D. DISTRIBUTIONS

§6.40. *Distributions to Shareholders*

(a) A board of directors may authorize and the corporation may make distributions to its shareholders subject to restriction by the articles of incorporation and the limitation in subsection (c).

(b) The board of directors may fix the record date for determining shareholders entitled to a distribution, which date may not be retroactive. If the board of directors does not fix a record date for determining shareholders entitled to a distribution (other than one involving a purchase, redemption, or other acquisition of the corporation's shares), the record date is the date the board of directors authorizes the distribution.

(c) No distribution may be made if, after giving it effect:

(1) the corporation would not be able to pay its debts as they become due in the usual course of business; or

(2) the corporation's total assets would be less than the sum of its total liabilities plus (unless the articles of incorporation permit otherwise) the amount that would be needed, if the corporation were to be dissolved at the time of the distribution, to satisfy the preferential rights upon dissolution of shareholders whose preferential rights are superior to those receiving the distribution.

(d) The board of directors may base a determination that a distribution is not prohibited under subsection (c) either on financial statements prepared on the basis of accounting practices and principles that are reasonable in the circumstances or on a fair valuation or other method that is reasonable in the circumstances.

(e) Except as provided in subsection (g), the effect of a distribution under subsection (c) is measured:

(1) in the case of distribution by purchase, redemption, or other acquisition of the corporation's shares, as of the earlier of (i) the date cash or other property is transferred or debt to a shareholder is incurred by the corporation or (ii) the date the shareholder ceases to be a shareholder with respect to the acquired shares;

(2) in the case of any other distribution of indebtedness, as of the date the indebtedness is distributed; and

(3) in all other cases, as of (i) the date the distribution is authorized if the payment occurs within 120 days after the date of authorization or (ii) the date the payment is made if it occurs more than 120 days after the date of authorization.

(f) A corporation's indebtedness to a shareholder incurred by reason of a distribution made in accordance with this section is at parity with the corporation's indebtedness to its general, unsecured creditors except to the extent subordinated by agreement.

(g) Indebtedness of a corporation, including indebtedness issued as a distribution, is not considered a liability for purposes of determinations under subsection (c) if its terms provide that payment of principal and interest are made only if and to the extent that payment of a distribution to shareholders could then be made under this section. If such indebtedness is issued as a distribution, each payment of principal or interest is treated as a distribution, the effect of which is measured on the date the payment is actually made.

(h) This section shall not apply to distributions in liquidation under chapter 14.

OFFICIAL COMMENT

1. *The Scope of Section 6.40*

Section 6.40 imposes a single, uniform test on all distributions other than distributions in liquidation under chapter 14. Section 1.40 defines "distribution" broadly to include transfers of cash and other property (excluding a corporation's own shares) to a shareholder in respect of the corporation's shares. Examples of such transfers are cash or property dividends, payments by a corporation to purchase its own shares, and distributions of promissory notes or indebtedness. The financial provisions of the Act do not use the concept of surplus but do have restrictions on distributions built around both equity insolvency and balance sheet tests.

2. *Equity Insolvency Test*

In most cases involving a corporation operating as a going concern in the normal course, it will be apparent from information generally available that no particular inquiry concerning the equity insolvency test in section 6.40(c)(1) is needed. Although neither a balance sheet nor an income statement can be conclusive as to this test, the existence of significant shareholders' equity and normal operating conditions are of themselves a strong indication that no issue should arise under that test. In the case of a corporation having regularly audited financial statements, the absence of any qualification in the most recent auditor's opinion as to the corporation's status as a "going concern," coupled with a lack of subsequent adverse events, would normally be decisive.

It is only when circumstances indicate that the corporation is encountering difficulties or is in an uncertain position concerning its liquidity and operations that the board of directors or, more commonly, the officers or others upon whom they may place reliance under section 8.30(d), may need to address the issue. Because of the overall judgment required in evaluating the equity insolvency test, no "bright line" test is provided. . . .

In exercising their judgment, the directors are entitled to rely, as provided in section 8.30(e), on information, opinions, reports, and statements prepared by others. Ordinarily, they should not be expected to become involved in the details of the various analyses or market or economic projections that may be relevant.

3. *Balance Sheet Test*

The determination of a corporation's assets and liabilities for purposes of the balance sheet test of section 6.40(c)(2) and the choice of the permissible basis on which to do so are left to the judgment of its board of directors. In making a judgment under section 6.40(d), the board may rely as provided in section 8.30(e) upon information, opinions, reports, and statements, including financial statements and other financial data, prepared or presented by public accountants or others.

Section 6.40 does not utilize particular accounting terminology of a technical nature or specify particular accounting concepts. In making determinations under this section, the board of directors may make judgments about accounting matters. . . .

Section 6.40(d) specifically permits determinations to be made under section 6.40(c)(2) on the basis of a fair valuation or other method that is reasonable in the circumstances. The statute authorizes departures from historical cost accounting and permits the use of appraisal and current value methods to determine the amount available for distribution. No particular method of valuation is prescribed in the statute, as different methods may have validity depending upon the circumstances, including the type of enterprise and the purpose for which the determination is made. In most cases, a fair valuation method or a going concern basis would be appropriate if it is believed that the enterprise will continue as a going concern.

Ordinarily a corporation should not selectively revalue assets. It should consider the value of all of its material assets, regardless of whether they are reflected in the financial statements (*e.g.*, a valuable executory contract). Likewise, all of a corporation's material obligations should be considered and revalued to the extent appropriate and possible. In any event, section 6.40(d) calls for the application under section 6.40(c)(2) of a method of determining the aggregate amount of assets and liabilities that is reasonable in the circumstances.

The phrase "other method that is reasonable in the circumstances means that under section 6.40(c)(2) a wide variety of methods may be considered reasonable in a particular case even if any such method might not be a "fair valuation" or "current value" method.

4. *Relationship to the Federal Bankruptcy Code and Other Fraudulent Conveyance Statutes*

The Act establishes the validity of distributions from the corporate law standpoint under section 6.40 and determines the potential liability of directors for improper distributions under sections 8.30 and 8.32. The federal bankruptcy laws and state fraudulent conveyance statutes, on the other hand, are designed to enable the trustee or other representative to recapture for the benefit of creditors funds distributed to others in some circumstances. Accordingly, the tests of section 6.40 are different from the tests for insolvency under those statutes.

5. Preferential Dissolution Rights and the Balance Sheet Test

Section 6.40(c)(2) treats preferential dissolution rights of shares for distribution purposes as if they were liabilities for the sole purpose of determining the amount available for distributions. In making the calculation of the amount that must be added to the liabilities of the corporation to reflect the preferential dissolution rights, the assumption should be made that the preferential dissolution rights are to be established pursuant to the articles of incorporation as of the date of the distribution or proposed distribution. The amount so determined must include arrearages in preferential dividends if the articles of incorporation require that they be paid upon the dissolution of the corporation. In the case of shares having both preferential rights upon dissolution and other non-preferential rights, only the preferential rights should be taken into account. The treatment of preferential dissolution rights of classes or series of shares set forth in section 6.40(c)(2) is applicable only to the balance sheet test and is not applicable to the equity insolvency test of section 6.40(c)(1). The treatment of preferential rights mandated by section 6.40(c)(2) may always be eliminated by an appropriate provision in the articles of incorporation. . . .

Chapter 7. Shareholders

Subchapter A. Meetings

§7.01. Annual Meeting

(a) Unless directors are elected by written consent in lieu of an annual meeting as permitted by section 7.04, a corporation shall hold a meeting of shareholders annually at a time stated in or fixed in accordance with the bylaws at which directors shall be elected.

(b) Unless the board of directors determines to hold the meeting solely by means of remote communication in accordance with section 7.09(c), annual meetings may be held (i) in or out of this state at the place stated in or fixed in accordance with the bylaws, or (ii) if no place is stated in or fixed in accordance with the bylaws, at the corporation's principal office.

(c) The failure to hold an annual meeting at the time stated in or fixed in accordance with a corporation's bylaws does not affect the validity of any corporate action.

§7.02. Special Meeting

(a) A corporation shall hold a special meeting of shareholders:

(1) on call of its board of directors or the person or persons authorized to do so by the articles of incorporation or bylaws; or

(2) if shareholders holding at least 10% of all the votes entitled to be cast on an issue proposed to be considered at the proposed special meeting sign, date, and deliver to the corporation one or more written demands for the meeting describing the purpose or purposes for which it is to be held, provided that the articles of incorporation may fix a lower percentage or a

higher percentage not exceeding 25% of all the votes entitled to be cast on any issue proposed to be considered. Unless otherwise provided in the articles of incorporation, a written demand for a special meeting may be revoked by a writing to that effect received by the corporation before the receipt by the corporation of demands sufficient in number to require the holding of a special meeting.

(b) If not otherwise fixed under section 7.03 or 7.07, the record date for determining shareholders entitled to demand a special meeting shall be the first date on which a signed shareholder demand is delivered to the corporation. No written demand for a special meeting shall be effective unless, within 60 days of the earliest date on which such a demand delivered to the corporation as required by this section was signed, written demands signed by shareholders holding at least the percentage of votes specified in or fixed in accordance with subsection (a)(2) have been delivered to the corporation.

(c) Unless the board of directors determines to hold the meeting solely by remote participation in accordance with section 7.09(c), special meetings of shareholders may be held (i) in or out of this state at the place stated in or fixed in accordance with the bylaws, or (ii) if no place is stated in or fixed in accordance with the bylaws, at the corporation's principal office.

(d) Only business within the purpose or purposes described in the meeting notice required by section 7.05(c) may be conducted at a special meeting of shareholders.

§7.03. Court-Ordered Meeting

(a) The [name or describe court] may summarily order a meeting to be held:

(1) on application of any shareholder of the corporation if an annual meeting was not held or action by written consent in lieu of an annual meeting did not become effective within the earlier of six months after the end of the corporation's fiscal year or 15 months after its last annual meeting; or

(2) on application of one or more shareholders who signed a demand for a special meeting valid under section 7.02, if:

(i) notice of the special meeting was not given within 30 days after the first day on which the requisite number of such demands have been delivered to the corporation; or

(ii) the special meeting was not held in accordance with the notice.

(b) The court may fix the time and place of the meeting, determine the shares entitled to participate in the meeting, specify a record date or dates for determining shareholders entitled to notice of and to vote at the meeting, prescribe the form and content of the meeting notice, fix the quorum required for specific matters to be considered at the meeting (or direct that the shares represented at the meeting constitute a quorum for action on those matters), and enter other orders necessary to accomplish the purpose or purposes of the meeting.

(c) For purposes of subsection (a)(1), "shareholder" means a record shareholder, a beneficial shareholder, and an unrestricted voting trust beneficial owner.

§7.04. Action Without Meeting

(a) Action required or permitted by this Act to be taken at a shareholders' meeting may be taken without a meeting if the action is taken by all the shareholders entitled to vote on the action. The action must be evidenced by one or more written consents bearing the date of signature and describing the action taken, signed by all the shareholders entitled to vote on the action and delivered to the corporation for filing by the corporation with the minutes or corporate records.

(b) The articles of incorporation may provide that any action required or permitted by this Act to be taken at a shareholders' meeting may be taken without a meeting, and without prior notice, if consents in writing setting forth the action so taken are signed by the holders of outstanding shares having not less than the minimum number of votes that would be required to authorize or take the action at a meeting at which all shares entitled to vote on the action were present and voted; provided, however, that if a corporation's articles of incorporation authorize shareholders to cumulate their votes when electing directors pursuant to section 7.28, directors may not be elected by less than unanimous written consent. A written consent must bear the date of signature of the shareholder who signs the consent and be delivered to the corporation for filing by the corporation with the minutes or corporate records.

(c) If not otherwise fixed under section 7.07 and if prior action by the board of directors is not required respecting the action to be taken without a meeting, the record date for determining the shareholders entitled to take action without a meeting shall be the first date on which a signed written consent is delivered to the corporation. If not otherwise fixed under section 7.07 and if prior action by the board of directors is required respecting the action to be taken without a meeting, the record date shall be the close of business on the day the resolution of the board of directors taking such prior action is adopted. No written consent shall be effective to take the corporate action referred to therein unless, within 60 days of the earliest date on which a consent delivered to the corporation as required by this section was signed, written consents signed by sufficient shareholders to take the action have been delivered to the corporation. A written consent may be revoked by a writing to that effect delivered to the corporation before unrevoked written consents sufficient in number to take the corporate action have been delivered to the corporation.

(d) A consent signed pursuant to the provisions of this section has the effect of a vote taken at a meeting and may be described as such in any document. Unless the articles of incorporation, bylaws or a resolution of the board of directors provides for a reasonable delay to permit tabulation of written consents, the action taken by written consent shall be effective when written consents signed by sufficient shareholders to take the action have been delivered to the corporation.

(e) If this Act requires that notice of a proposed action be given to nonvoting shareholders and the action is to be taken by written consent of the voting shareholders, the corporation shall give its nonvoting shareholders written notice of the action not more than 10 days after (i) written consents sufficient to take the action have been delivered to the corporation, or (ii) such later date that tabulation of consents is completed pursuant to an authorization under subsection (d). The notice must reasonably describe the action taken and contain or be accompanied by the same material that, under any provision of this Act, would have been required to be sent to nonvoting shareholders in a notice of a meeting at which the proposed action would have been submitted to the shareholders for action.

(f) If action is taken by less than unanimous written consent of the voting shareholders, the corporation shall give its nonconsenting voting shareholders written notice of the action not more than 10 days after (i) written consents sufficient to take the action have been delivered to the corporation, or (ii) such later date that tabulation of consents is completed pursuant to an authorization under subsection (d). The notice must reasonably describe the action taken and contain or be accompanied by the same material that, under any provision of this Act, would have been required to be sent to voting shareholders in a notice of a meeting at which the action would have been submitted to the shareholders for action.

(g) The notice requirements in subsections (e) and (f) shall not delay the effectiveness of actions taken by written consent, and a failure to comply with such notice requirements shall not invalidate actions taken by written consent, provided that this subsection shall not be deemed to limit judicial power to fashion any appropriate remedy in favor of a shareholder adversely affected by a failure to give such notice within the required time period.

§7.05. *Notice of Meeting*

(a) A corporation shall notify shareholders of the date, time, and place, if any, of each annual and special shareholders' meeting no fewer than 10 nor more than 60 days before the meeting date. If the board of directors has authorized participation by means of remote communication pursuant to section 7.09 for holders of any class or series of shares, the notice to the holders of such class or series of shares must describe the means of remote communication to be used. The notice must include the record date for determining the shareholders entitled to vote at the meeting, if such date is different from the record date for determining shareholders entitled to notice of the meeting. Unless this Act or the articles of incorporation require otherwise, the corporation is required to give notice only to shareholders entitled to vote at the meeting as of the record date for determining the shareholders entitled to notice of the meeting.

(b) Unless this Act or the articles of incorporation require otherwise, the notice of an annual meeting of shareholders need not include a description of the purpose or purposes for which the meeting is called.

(c) Notice of a special meeting of shareholders must include a description of the purpose or purposes for which the meeting is called.

(d) If not otherwise fixed under section 7.03 or 7.07, the record date for determining shareholders entitled to notice of and to vote at an annual or special shareholders' meeting is the day before the first notice is delivered to shareholders.

(e) Unless the bylaws require otherwise, if an annual or special shareholders' meeting is adjourned to a different date, time, or place, if any, notice need not be given of the new date, time, or place, if any, if the new date, time, or place, if any, is announced at the meeting before adjournment. If a new record date for the adjourned meeting is or must be fixed under section 7.07, however, notice of the adjourned meeting shall be given under this section to shareholders entitled to vote at such adjourned meeting as of the record date fixed for notice of such adjourned meeting.

§7.06. *Waiver of Notice*

(a) A shareholder may waive any notice required by this Act or the articles of incorporation or bylaws, before or after the date and time stated in the notice. The waiver must be in writing, be signed by the shareholder entitled to the notice, and be delivered to the corporation for filing by the corporation with the minutes or corporate records.

(b) A shareholder's attendance at a meeting:

(1) waives objection to lack of notice or defective notice of the meeting, unless the shareholder at the beginning of the meeting objects to holding the meeting or transacting business at the meeting; and

(2) waives objection to consideration of a particular matter at the meeting that is not within the purpose or purposes described in the meeting notice, unless the shareholder objects to considering the matter when it is presented.

§7.07. *Record Date for Meeting*

(a) The bylaws may fix or provide the manner of fixing the record date or dates for one or more voting groups to determine the shareholders entitled to notice of a shareholders' meeting, to demand a special meeting, to vote, or to take any other action. If the bylaws do not fix or provide for fixing a record date, the board of directors may fix the record date.

(b) A record date fixed under this section may not be more than 70 days before the meeting or action requiring a determination of shareholders and may not be retroactive.

(c) A determination of shareholders entitled to notice of or to vote at a shareholders' meeting is effective for any adjournment of the meeting unless the board of directors fixes a new record date or dates, which it shall do if the meeting is adjourned to a date more than 120 days after the date fixed for the original meeting.

(d) If a court orders a meeting adjourned to a date more than 120 days after the date fixed for the original meeting, it may provide that the original record date or dates continues in effect or it may fix a new record date or dates.

(e) The record dates for a shareholders' meeting fixed by or in the manner provided in the bylaws or by the board of directors shall be the record date for determining shareholders entitled both to notice of and to vote at the shareholders' meeting, unless in the case of a record date fixed by the board of directors and to the extent not prohibited by the bylaws, the board, at the time it fixes the record date for shareholders entitled to notice of the meeting, fixes a later record date on or before the date of the meeting to determine the shareholders entitled to vote at the meeting.

§7.08. *Conduct of Meeting*

(a) At each meeting of shareholders, a chair shall preside. The chair shall be appointed as provided in the bylaws or, in the absence of such provision, by the board of directors.

(b) The chair, unless the articles of incorporation or bylaws provide otherwise, shall determine the order of business and shall have the authority to establish rules for the conduct of the meeting.

(c) Any rules adopted for, and the conduct of, the meeting shall be fair to shareholders.

(d) The chair of the meeting shall announce at the meeting when the polls close for each matter voted upon. If no announcement is made, the polls shall be deemed to have closed upon the final adjournment of the meeting. After the polls close, no ballots, proxies or votes nor any revocations or changes to such ballots, proxies or votes may be accepted.

§7.09. *Remote Participation in Shareholders' Meetings; Meetings Held Solely by Remote Participation*

(a) Shareholders of any class or series of shares may participate in any meeting of shareholders by means of remote communication to the extent the board of directors authorizes such participation for such class or series. Participation as a shareholder by means of remote communication shall be subject to such guidelines and procedures as the board of directors adopts, and shall be in conformity with subsection (b).

(b) Shareholders participating in a shareholders' meeting by means of remote communication shall be deemed present and may vote at such a meeting if the corporation has implemented reasonable measures:

(1) to verify that each person participating remotely as a shareholder is a shareholder; and

(2) to provide such shareholders a reasonable opportunity to participate in the meeting and to vote on matters submitted to the shareholders, including an opportunity to communicate, and to read or hear the proceedings of the meeting, substantially concurrently with such proceedings.

(c) Unless the bylaws require the meeting of shareholders to be held at a place, the board of directors may determine that any meeting of shareholders shall not be held at any place and shall instead be held solely by means of remote communication, but only if the corporation implements the measures specified in subsection (b).

SUBCHAPTER B. VOTING

§7.20. *Shareholders' List for Meeting*

(a) After fixing a record date for a meeting, a corporation shall prepare an alphabetical list of the names of all its shareholders who are entitled to notice of the shareholders' meeting. If the board of directors fixes a different record date under section 7.07(e) to determine the shareholders entitled to vote at the meeting, a corporation also shall prepare an alphabetical list of the names of all its shareholders who are entitled to vote at the meeting. The list must be arranged by voting group (and within each voting group by class or series of shares) and contain the address of, and number and class or series of shares held by, each shareholder and, if the notice or other communications regarding the meeting have been or will be sent by the corporation to a shareholder by electronic mail or other electronic transmission, the electronic mail or other electronic transmission address of that shareholder.

(b) The list of shareholders entitled to notice shall be available for inspection by any shareholder, beginning two business days after notice of the meeting is given for which the list was prepared and continuing through the meeting, (i) at the corporation's principal office or at a place identified in the meeting notice in the city where the meeting will be held, or (ii) on a reasonably accessible electronic network, provided that the information required to gain access to such list is provided with the notice of the meeting. The list of shareholders entitled to vote shall be similarly available for inspection promptly after the record date for voting. In the event that the corporation determines to make the list available on an electronic network, the corporation may take reasonable steps to ensure that such information is available only to shareholders of the corporation. A shareholder, or the shareholder's agent or attorney, is entitled on written demand to inspect and, subject to the requirements of section 16.02(c), to copy a list of shareholders, during regular business hours and at the shareholder's expense, during the period it is available for inspection. A corporation may satisfy the shareholder's right to copy a list of shareholders by furnishing a copy in the manner described in section 16.03 (b). A shareholder and the shareholder's agent or attorney who inspects or is furnished a copy of a list of shareholders under this subsection (b) or under subsection (c) or who copies the list under this subsection (b) may use the information on that list only for purposes related to the meeting and its subject matter and must keep the information on that list confidential.

(c) If the meeting is to be held at a place, the corporation shall make the list of shareholders entitled to vote available at the meeting and any adjournment, and any shareholder, or the shareholder's agent or attorney, is entitled to inspect the list at any time during the meeting and any adjournment. If the meeting is to be held solely by means of remote communication, then such list shall also be available for such inspection during the meeting and any adjournment on a reasonably accessible electronic network, and the information required to access such list shall be provided with the notice of the meeting. The corporation may satisfy its obligation to make such list available for inspection during a meeting by furnishing a copy of the list in the manner described in section 16.03(b) to the shareholders prior to the meeting.

(d) If the corporation refuses to allow a shareholder, or the shareholder's agent or attorney, to inspect a list of shareholders before or at the meeting or any adjournment (or copy a list as permitted by subsection (b)), the [name or describe court], on application of the shareholder, may summarily order the inspection or copying at the corporation's expense and may postpone the meeting for which the list was prepared until the inspection or copying is complete.

(e) Refusal or failure to prepare or make available the list of shareholders does not affect the validity of action taken at the meeting.

§7.21. *Voting Entitlement of Shares*

(a) Except as provided in subsections (b) and (d) or unless the articles of incorporation provide otherwise, each outstanding share, regardless of class or series, is entitled to one vote on each matter voted on at a shareholders' meeting. Only shares are entitled to vote.

(b) Shares of a corporation are not entitled to vote if they are owned by or otherwise belong to the corporation directly, or indirectly through an entity of which a majority of the voting power is held directly or indirectly by the corporation or which is otherwise controlled by the corporation.

(c) Shares held by the corporation in a fiduciary capacity for the benefit of any person are entitled to vote unless they are held for the benefit of, or otherwise belong to, the corporation directly, or indirectly through an entity of which a majority of the voting power is held directly or indirectly by the corporation or which is otherwise controlled by the corporation.

(d) Redeemable shares are not entitled to vote after delivery of written notice of redemption is effective and a sum sufficient to redeem the shares has been deposited with a bank, trust company, or other financial institution under an irrevocable obligation to pay the holders the redemption price on surrender of the shares.

(e) For purposes of this section, "voting power" means the current power to vote in the election of directors of a corporation or to elect, select or appoint governors of another entity.

§7.22. *Proxies*

(a) A shareholder may vote the shareholder's shares in person or by proxy.

(b) A shareholder, or the shareholder's agent or attorney-in-fact, may appoint a proxy to vote or otherwise act for the shareholder by signing an appointment form, or by an electronic transmission. An electronic transmission must contain or be accompanied by information from which the recipient can determine the date of the transmission and that the transmission was authorized by the sender or the sender's agent or attorney-in-fact.

(c) An appointment of a proxy is effective when a signed appointment form or an electronic transmission of the appointment is received by the inspector of election or the officer or agent of the corporation authorized to count votes. An appointment is valid for the term provided in the appointment form, and, if no term is provided, is valid for 11 months unless the appointment is irrevocable under subsection (d).

(d) An appointment of a proxy is revocable unless the appointment form or electronic transmission states that it is irrevocable and the appointment is coupled with an interest. Appointments coupled with an interest include the appointment of:

(1) a pledgee;

(2) a person who purchased or agreed to purchase the shares;

(3) a creditor of the corporation who extended it credit under terms requiring the appointment;

(4) an employee of the corporation whose employment contract requires the appointment; or

(5) a party to a voting agreement created under section 7.31.

(e) The death or incapacity of the shareholder appointing a proxy does not affect the right of the corporation to accept the proxy's authority unless notice of the death or incapacity is received by the secretary or other officer or agent authorized to tabulate votes before the proxy exercises authority under the appointment.

(f) An appointment made irrevocable under subsection (d) is revoked when the interest with which it is coupled is extinguished.

(g) Unless it otherwise provides, an appointment made irrevocable under subsection (d) continues in effect after a transfer of the shares and a transferee takes subject to the appointment, except that a transferee for value of shares subject to an irrevocable appointment may revoke the appointment if the transferee did not know of its existence when acquiring the shares and the existence of the irrevocable appointment was not noted conspicuously on the certificate representing the shares or on the information statement for shares without certificates.

(h) Subject to section 7.24 and to any express limitation on the proxy's authority stated in the appointment form or electronic transmission, a corporation is entitled to accept the proxy's vote or other action as that of the shareholder making the appointment.

§7.23. Shares Held by Intermediaries and Nominees

(a) A corporation's board of directors may establish a procedure under which a person on whose behalf shares are registered in the name of an intermediary or nominee may elect to be treated by the corporation as the record shareholder by filing with the corporation a beneficial ownership certificate. The terms, conditions, and limitations of this treatment shall be specified in the procedure. To the extent such person is treated under such procedure as having rights or privileges that the record shareholder otherwise would have, the record shareholder shall not have those rights or privileges.

(b) The procedure must specify:

(1) the types of intermediaries or nominees to which it applies;

(2) the rights or privileges that the corporation recognizes in a person with respect to whom a beneficial ownership certificate is filed;

(3) the manner in which the procedure is selected which must include that the beneficial ownership certificate be signed or assented to by or on behalf of the record shareholder and the person on whose behalf the shares are held;

(4) the information that must be provided when the procedure is selected;

(5) the period for which selection of the procedure is effective;

(6) requirements for notice to the corporation with respect to the arrangement; and

(7) the form and contents of the beneficial ownership certificate.

(c) The procedure may specify any other aspects of the rights and duties created by the filing of a beneficial ownership certificate.

§7.24. Acceptance of Votes and Other Instruments

(a) If the name signed on a vote, ballot, consent, waiver, shareholder demand, or proxy appointment corresponds to the name of a shareholder, the corporation, if acting in good faith, is entitled to accept the vote, ballot, consent, waiver, shareholder demand, or proxy appointment and give it effect as the act of the shareholder.

(b) If the name signed on a vote, ballot, consent, waiver, shareholder demand, or proxy appointment does not correspond to the name of its shareholder, the corporation, if acting in good faith, is nevertheless entitled to accept the vote, ballot, consent, waiver, shareholder demand, or proxy appointment and give it effect as the act of the shareholder if:

(1) the shareholder is an entity and the name signed purports to be that of an officer or agent of the entity;

(2) the name signed purports to be that of an administrator, executor, guardian, or conservator representing the shareholder and, if the corporation requests, evidence of fiduciary status acceptable to the corporation has been presented with respect to the vote, ballot, consent, waiver, shareholder demand, or proxy appointment;

(3) the name signed purports to be that of a receiver or trustee in bankruptcy of the shareholder and, if the corporation requests, evidence of this status acceptable to the corporation has been presented with respect to the vote, ballot, consent, waiver, shareholder demand, or proxy appointment;

(4) the name signed purports to be that of a pledgee, beneficial owner, or attorney-in-fact of the shareholder and, if the corporation requests, evidence acceptable to the corporation of the signatory's authority to sign for the shareholder has been presented with respect to the vote, ballot, consent, waiver, shareholder demand, or proxy appointment; or

(5) two or more persons are the shareholder as co-tenants or fiduciaries and the name signed purports to be the name of at least one of the co-owners and the person signing appears to be acting on behalf of all the co-owners.

(c) The corporation is entitled to reject a vote, ballot, consent, waiver, shareholder demand, or proxy appointment if the person authorized to accept or reject such instrument, acting in good faith, has reasonable basis for doubt about the validity of the signature on it or about the signatory's authority to sign for the shareholder.

(d) Neither the corporation or any person authorized by it, nor an inspector of election appointed under section 7.29, that accepts or rejects a vote, ballot,, consent, waiver, shareholder demand, or proxy appointment in good faith and in accordance with the standards of this section 7.24 or section 7.22(b) is liable in damages to the shareholder for the consequences of the acceptance or rejection.

(e) Corporate action based on the acceptance or rejection of a vote, ballot, consent, waiver, shareholder demand, or proxy appointment under this section is valid unless a court of competent jurisdiction determines otherwise.

(f) If an inspector of election has been appointed under section 7.29, the inspector of election also has the authority to request information and make determinations under subsections (a), (b), and (c). Any determination made by the inspector of election under those subsections is controlling.

§7.25. *Quorum and Voting Requirements for Voting Groups*

(a) Shares entitled to vote as a separate voting group may take action on a matter at a meeting only if a quorum of those shares exists with respect to that matter. Unless the articles of incorporation provide otherwise, shares representing a majority of the votes entitled to be cast on the matter by the voting group constitutes a quorum of that voting group for action on that matter. Whenever this Act requires a particular quorum for a specified action, the articles of incorporation may not provide for a lower quorum.

(b) Once a share is represented for any purpose at a meeting, it is deemed present for quorum purposes for the remainder of the meeting and for any adjournment of that meeting unless a new record date is or must be fixed for that adjourned meeting.

(c) If a quorum exists, action on a matter (other than the election of directors) by a voting group is approved if the votes cast within the voting group favoring the action exceed the votes cast opposing the action, unless the articles of incorporation require a greater number of affirmative votes.

(d) An amendment of the articles of incorporation adding, changing, or deleting a quorum or voting requirement for a voting group greater than specified in subsection (a) or (c) is governed by section 7.27.

(e) The election of directors is governed by section 7.28.

(f) Whenever a provision of this Act provides for voting of classes or series as separate voting groups, the rules provided in section 10.04(c) for amendments of the articles of incorporation apply to that provision.

§7.26. *Action by Single and Multiple Voting Groups*

(a) If the articles of incorporation or this Act provide for voting by a single voting group on a matter, action on that matter is taken when voted upon by that voting group as provided in section 7.25.

(b) If the articles of incorporation or this Act provide for voting by two or more voting groups on a matter, action on that matter is taken only when voted upon by each of those voting groups counted separately as provided in section 7.25. Action may be taken by different voting groups on a matter at different times.

§7.27. *Modifying Quorum or Voting Requirements*

An amendment to the articles of incorporation that adds, changes, or deletes a quorum or voting requirement shall meet the same quorum requirement and be adopted by the same vote and voting groups required to take action under the quorum and voting requirements then in effect or proposed to be adopted, whichever is greater.

§7.28. *Voting for Directors; Cumulative Voting*

(a) Unless otherwise provided in the articles of incorporation, directors are elected by a plurality of the votes cast by the shares entitled to vote in the election at a meeting at which a quorum is present.

(b) Shareholders do not have a right to cumulate their votes for directors unless the articles of incorporation so provide.

(c) A statement included in the articles of incorporation that "[all] [a designated voting group of] shareholders are entitled to cumulate their votes for directors" (or words of similar import) means that the shareholders designated are entitled to multiply the number of votes they are entitled to cast by the number of directors for whom they are entitled to vote and cast the product for a single candidate or distribute the product among two or more candidates.

(d) Shares otherwise entitled to vote cumulatively may not be voted cumulatively at a particular meeting unless:

(1) the meeting notice or proxy statement accompanying the notice states conspicuously that cumulative voting is authorized; or

(2) a shareholder who has the right to cumulate the shareholder's votes gives notice to the corporation not less than 48 hours before the time set for the meeting of the shareholder's intent to cumulate votes during the meeting, and if one shareholder gives this notice all other shareholders in the same voting group participating in the election are entitled to cumulate their votes without giving further notice.

§7.29. Inspectors of Election

(a) A corporation that has a class of equity securities registered pursuant to section 12 of the Securities Exchange Act of 1934 shall, and any other corporation may, appoint one or more inspectors to act at a meeting of shareholders in connection with determining voting results. Each inspector shall verify in writing that the inspector will faithfully execute the duties of inspector with strict impartiality and according to the best of the inspector's ability. An inspector may be an officer or employee of the corporation. The inspectors may appoint or retain other persons to assist the inspectors in the performance of the duties of inspector under subsection (b), and may rely on information provided by such persons and other persons, including those appointed to tabulate votes, unless the inspectors believe reliance is unwarranted.

(b) The inspectors shall:

(1) ascertain the number of shares outstanding and the voting power of each;

(2) determine the shares represented at a meeting;

(3) determine the validity of proxy appointments and ballots;

(4) count the votes; and

(5) make a written report of the results.

(c) In performing their duties, the inspectors may examine (i) the proxy appointment forms and any other information provided in accordance with section 7.22(b), (ii) any envelope or related writing submitted with those appointment forms, (iii) any ballots, (iv) any evidence or other information specified in section 7.24 and (v) the relevant books and records of the corporation relating to its shareholders and their entitlement to vote, including any securities position list provided by a depository clearing agency.

(d) The inspectors also may consider other information that they believe is relevant and reliable for the purpose of performing any of the duties assigned to them pursuant to subsection (b), including for the purpose of evaluating inconsistent, incomplete or erroneous information and reconciling information submitted on behalf of banks, brokers, their nominees or similar persons that indicates more votes being cast than a proxy authorized by the record shareholder is entitled to cast. If the inspectors consider other information allowed by this subsection, they shall in their report under subsection (b) specify the information considered by them, including the purpose or purposes for which the information was considered, the person or persons from whom they obtained the information, when the information was obtained, the means by which the information was obtained, and the basis for the inspectors' belief that such information is relevant and reliable.

(e) Determinations of law by the inspectors of election are subject to de novo review by a court in a proceeding under section 7.49 or other judicial proceeding.

SUBCHAPTER C. VOTING TRUSTS AND AGREEMENTS

§7.30. *Voting Trusts*

(a) One or more shareholders may create a voting trust, conferring on a trustee the right to vote or otherwise act for them, by signing an agreement setting out the provisions of the trust (which may include anything consistent with its purpose) and transferring their shares to the trustee. When a voting trust agreement is signed, the trustee shall prepare a list of the names and addresses of all voting trust beneficial owners, together with the number and class of shares each transferred to the trust, and deliver copies of the list and agreement to the corporation at its principal office.

(b) A voting trust becomes effective on the date the first shares subject to the trust are registered in the trustee's name.

(c) Limits, if any, on the duration of a voting trust shall be as set forth in the voting trust. A voting trust that became effective when this Act provided a 10-year limit on its duration remains governed by the provisions of this section concerning duration then in effect, unless the voting trust is amended to provide otherwise by unanimous agreement of the parties to the voting trust.

§7.31. *Voting Agreements*

(a) Two or more shareholders may provide for the manner in which they will vote their shares by signing an agreement for that purpose. A voting agreement created under this section is not subject to the provisions of section 7.30.

(b) A voting agreement created under this section is specifically enforceable.

§7.32. *Shareholder Agreements*

(a) An agreement among the shareholders of a corporation that complies with this section is effective among the shareholders and the corporation even though it is inconsistent with one or more other provisions of this Act in that it:

(1) eliminates the board of directors or restricts the discretion or powers of the board of directors;

(2) governs the authorization or making of distributions, regardless of whether they are in proportion to ownership of shares, subject to the limitations in section 6.40;

(3) establishes who shall be directors or officers of the corporation, or their terms of office or manner of selection or removal;

(4) governs, in general or in regard to specific matters, the exercise or division of voting power by or between the shareholders and directors or by or among any of them, including use of weighted voting rights or director proxies;

(5) establishes the terms and conditions of any agreement for the transfer or use of property or the provision of services between the corporation and any shareholder, director, officer or employee of the corporation or among any of them;

(6) transfers to one or more shareholders or other persons all or part of the authority to exercise the corporate powers or to manage the business and affairs of the corporation, including the resolution of any issue about which there exists a deadlock among directors or shareholders;

(7) requires dissolution of the corporation at the request of one or more of the shareholders or upon the occurrence of a specified event or contingency; or

(8) otherwise governs the exercise of the corporate powers or the management of the business and affairs of the corporation or the relationship among the shareholders, the directors and the corporation, or among any of them, and is not contrary to public policy.

(b) An agreement authorized by this section shall be:

(1) as set forth (i) in the articles of incorporation or bylaws and approved by all persons who are shareholders at the time of the agreement, or (ii) in a written agreement that is signed by all persons who are shareholders at the time of the agreement and is made known to the corporation; and

(2) subject to amendment only by all persons who are shareholders at the time of the amendment, unless the agreement provides otherwise.

(c) The existence of an agreement authorized by this section shall be noted conspicuously on the front or back of each certificate for outstanding shares or on the information statement required by section 6.26(b). If at the time of the agreement the corporation has shares outstanding represented by certificates, the corporation shall recall the outstanding certificates and issue substitute certificates that comply with this subsection. The failure to note the existence of the agreement on the certificate or information statement shall not affect the validity of the agreement or any action taken pursuant to it. Any purchaser of shares who, at the time of purchase, did not have knowledge of the existence of the agreement shall be entitled to rescission of the purchase. A purchaser shall be deemed to have knowledge of the existence of the agreement if its existence is noted on the certificate or information statement for the shares in compliance with this subsection and, if the shares are not represented by a certificate, the information statement is delivered to the purchaser at or before the time of purchase of the shares. An action to enforce the right of rescission authorized by this subsection shall be commenced within the earlier of 90 days after discovery of the existence of the agreement or two years after the time of purchase of the shares.

(d) If the agreement ceases to be effective for any reason, the board of directors may, if the agreement is contained or referred to in the corporation's articles of incorporation or bylaws, adopt an amendment to the articles of incorporation or bylaws, without shareholder action, to delete the agreement and any references to it.

(e) An agreement authorized by this section that limits the discretion or powers of the board of directors shall relieve the directors of, and impose upon the person or persons in whom such discretion or powers are vested, liability for acts or omissions imposed by law on directors to the extent that the discretion or powers of the directors are limited by the agreement.

(f) The existence or performance of an agreement authorized by this section shall not be a ground for imposing personal liability on any shareholder for the acts or debts of the corporation even if the agreement or its performance treats the corporation as if it were a partnership or results in failure to observe the corporate formalities otherwise applicable to the matters governed by the agreement.

(g) Incorporators or subscribers for shares may act as shareholders with respect to an agreement authorized by this section if no shares have been issued when the agreement is made.

(h) Limits, if any, on the duration of an agreement authorized by this section must be set forth in the agreement. An agreement that became effective when this Act provided for a 10-year limit on duration of shareholder agreements, unless the agreement provided otherwise, remains governed by the provisions of this section concerning duration then in effect.

OFFICIAL COMMENT

Shareholders of some corporations, especially those that are closely held, frequently enter into agreements that govern the operation of the enterprise.

Section 7.32 provides, within the context of the traditional corporate structure, legal certainty to such agreements that embody various aspects of the business arrangement established by the shareholders to meet their business and personal needs. The subject matter of these arrangements includes governance of the entity, allocation of the economic return from the business, and other aspects of the relationships among shareholders, directors, and the corporation which are part of the business arrangement. Section 7.32 also recognizes that many of the corporate norms contained in the Act were designed with an eye towards corporations whose management and share ownership are distinct. These functions are often conjoined in some corporations, such as the close corporation. Thus, section 7.32 validates agreements among shareholders even when the agreements are inconsistent with the statutory norms contained in the Act.

Importantly, section 7.32 only addresses the parties to the shareholder agreement, their transferees, and the corporation, and does not have any binding legal effect on the state, creditors, or other third persons.

Section 7.32 supplements the other provisions of the Act. If an agreement is not in conflict with another section of the Act, no resort need be made to section 7.32 with its requirement of unanimity. For example, special provisions may be included in the articles of incorporation or bylaws with less than unanimous shareholder agreement so long as such provisions are not in conflict with other provisions of the Act. Similarly, section 7.32 would not have to be relied upon to validate typical buy-sell agreements among two or more shareholders or the covenants and other terms of a stock purchase agreement entered into in connection with the issuance of shares by a corporation. . . .

SUBCHAPTER D. DERIVATIVE PROCEEDINGS

§7.40. *Subchapter Definitions*

In this subchapter:

– "Derivative proceeding" means a civil suit in the right of a domestic corporation or, to the extent provided in section 7.47, in the right of a foreign corporation.

– "Shareholder" means a record shareholder, a beneficial shareholder, and an unrestricted voting trust beneficial owner.

§7.41. *Standing*

A shareholder may not commence or maintain a derivative proceeding unless the shareholder (i) was a shareholder of the corporation at the time of the act or omission complained of or became a shareholder through transfer by operation of law from one who was a shareholder at that time and (ii) fairly and adequately represents the interests of the corporation in enforcing the right of the corporation.

OFFICIAL COMMENT

Section 7.41 requires (i) the plaintiff to be a shareholder and therefore does not permit, for example, creditors or holders of options, warrants, or conversion rights to commence a derivative proceeding, and (ii) that the plaintiff fairly and adequately represent the interests of *the corporation,* rather than *shareholders similarly situated* as provided in some rules of procedure, because the reference to the corporation more clearly reflects the nature of the derivative suit.

The introductory language of section 7.41 refers both to the commencement and maintenance of the proceeding to make it clear that the proceeding should be dismissed if, after commencement, the plaintiff ceases to be a shareholder or a fair and adequate representative. The latter would occur, for example, if the plaintiff were using the proceeding for personal advantage. If a plaintiff no longer has standing, courts have in a number of instances provided an opportunity for one or more other shareholders to intervene.

§7.42. *Demand*

No shareholder may commence a derivative proceeding until (i) a written demand has been made upon the corporation to take suitable action and (ii) 90 days have expired from the date delivery of the demand was made unless the shareholder has earlier been notified that the demand has been rejected by the corporation or unless irreparable injury to the corporation would result by waiting for the expiration of the 90-day period.

OFFICIAL COMMENT

Section 7.42 requires a written demand for two reasons. First, even though no director may be "qualified" (see section 1.43), the demand will give the corporation the opportunity to re-examine the act complained of in the light of a potential lawsuit and take corrective action. Second, the provision eliminates the time and expense of litigating whether demand is required. Requiring a demand in all cases does not impose an onerous burden given the relatively short waiting period and that this period may be shortened if irreparable injury to the corporation would result by waiting for the expiration of the 90-day period.

1. *Form of Demand*

Section 7.42 specifies only that the demand shall be in writing. Detailed pleading is not required given that the corporation can contact the shareholder for clarification if there are any questions, and cases have noted that a demand which sets forth the facts concerning share ownership and is sufficiently specific should apprise the corporation of the action sought to be taken and the grounds for that action so that the demand can be evaluated.

2. *Upon Whom Demand Should Be Made*

To ensure that the demand reaches the appropriate person for review, it should be addressed to the board of directors, chief executive officer, or secretary at the corporation's principal office. In most cases the board of directors will be the appropriate body to review the demand but there may be instances, such as a decision to sue a third party for an injury to the corporation, in which the taking of, or refusal to take, action would fall within the authority of an officer of the corporation.

3. *The 90-Day Period*

The 90-day period in section 7.42 was chosen as a reasonable time within which the board of directors can meet, conduct the necessary inquiry into the charges, receive the results of the inquiry and make its decision. A fixed time period also eliminates litigation over what is or is not a reasonable time. If additional time is needed, the corporation may request counsel for the shareholder to delay filing suit until the inquiry has been completed or, if suit is commenced, the corporation can apply to the court for a stay under section 7.43.

Two exceptions are provided to the 90-day waiting period. The first exception is the situation where the shareholder has been notified of the rejection of the demand before the end of the 90 days. The standard under the second exception for irreparable injury to the corporation is intended to be the same as that governing the entry of a preliminary injunction. Other factors may also be considered, such as the possible expiration of the statute of limitations, although this would depend on the period of time during which the shareholder was aware of the grounds for the proceeding.

The shareholder bringing suit does not necessarily have to be the person making the demand. Only one demand need be made in order for the corporation to consider whether to take corrective action.

4. *Response by the Corporation*

There is no obligation on the part of the corporation to respond to the demand. However, if the corporation, after receiving the demand, decides to institute litigation or, after a derivative proceeding has commenced, decides to assume control of the litigation, the shareholder's right to commence or control the proceeding normally ends unless it can be shown that the corporation will not adequately pursue the matter.

§7.43. *Stay of Proceedings*

If the corporation commences an inquiry into the allegations made in the demand or complaint, the court may stay any derivative proceeding for such period as the court deems appropriate.

OFFICIAL COMMENT

A stay may be appropriate where, for example, the complaint is filed 90 days after demand but the inquiry into matters raised by the demand has not been completed or where a demand has not been investigated but the corporation commences the inquiry after the complaint has been filed. In any case, the court will likely monitor the course of the inquiry to ensure that the corporation is proceeding expeditiously and in good faith.

§7.44. *Dismissal*

(a) A derivative proceeding shall be dismissed by the court on motion by the corporation if one of the groups specified in subsection (b) or subsection (e) has determined in good faith, after conducting a reasonable inquiry upon which its conclusions are based, that the maintenance of the derivative proceeding is not in the best interests of the corporation.

(b) Unless a panel is appointed pursuant to subsection (e), the determination in subsection (a) shall be made by:

(1) a majority vote of qualified directors present at a meeting of the board of directors if the qualified directors constitute a quorum; or

(2) a majority vote of a committee consisting of two or more qualified directors appointed by majority vote of qualified directors present at a meeting of the board of directors, regardless of whether such qualified directors constitute a quorum.

(c) If a derivative proceeding is commenced after a determination has been made rejecting a demand by a shareholder, the complaint shall allege with particularity facts establishing either (1) that a majority of the board of directors did not consist of qualified directors at the time the determination was made or (2) that the requirements of subsection (a) have not been met.

(d) If a majority of the board of directors consisted of qualified directors at the time the determination was made, the plaintiff shall have the burden of proving that the requirements of subsection (a) have not been met; if not, the corporation shall have the burden of proving that the requirements of subsection (a) have been met.

(e) Upon motion by the corporation, the court may appoint a panel of one or more individuals to make a determination whether the maintenance of the derivative proceeding is in the best interests of the corporation. In such case, the plaintiff shall have the burden of proving that the requirements of subsection (a) have not been met.

OFFICIAL COMMENT

The procedures set forth in section 7.44 are not intended to be exclusive. Discretion is left with the courts to determine when a derivative action should be dismissed under circumstances other than those set forth in section 7.44. For example, as noted in the comment to section 7.42, there may be instances where a decision to commence an action falls within the authority of an officer of the corporation, depending upon the amount of the claim and the identity of the potential defendants.

1. *The Persons Making the Determination and Timing*

The determination under section 7.44(b) that the maintenance of the proceeding is not in the best interests of the corporation can be made before commencement of the derivative action in response to a demand or after commencement of the action upon examination of the allegations of the complaint. Section 7.44(b) allows the determination to be made by "qualified directors" as defined in section 1.43. These provisions parallel the mechanics for authorizing an officer's pursuit of a business opportunity pursuant to a provision in the articles of incorporation (section 2.02(b)(6)), for determining entitlement to indemnification (section 8.55), for authorizing directors' conflicting interest transactions (section 8.62), and for renunciation of the corporation's interests in a business opportunity (section 8.70). Section 7.44(e) provides for the appointment of a panel only upon motion by the corporation. This would not, however, prevent the court on its own initiative from appointing a special master if permitted under applicable state rules of procedure.

This panel procedure may be desirable in a number of circumstances, particularly if there are no qualified directors available. In addition, even if there are qualified directors, they may not be in a position to conduct the inquiry.

2. *Standards to be Applied*

Section 7.44(a) contemplates that the court will examine the "good faith" of the persons making the determination. Both the determination and the inquiry in section 7.44(a) must be made in "good faith." Section 7.44(a) does not authorize the court to review the reasonableness of the determination to reject a demand or seek a dismissal. The "good faith" standard, which is also found in section 8.30 (general standards of conduct for directors) and 8.51 (authority to indemnify), is a subjective one, meaning "honestly or in an honest manner."

The word "inquiry"—rather than "investigation"—has been used to make it clear that the scope of the inquiry will depend upon the issues raised and the knowledge of the group making the determination with respect to those issues. In some cases, the issues may be within the knowledge of the group so that extensive additional investigation is not necessary. In other cases, the group may need to engage counsel and possibly other professionals to conduct an investigation and assist the group in its evaluation of the issues.

The phrase "upon which its conclusions are based" requires that the conclusions follow logically from the inquiry. The burden of convincing the court about this issue lies with whichever party has the burden under section 7.44(d). This phrase does not require the persons making the determination to prepare a written report that sets forth their determination and its bases, as circumstances will vary as to the need for such a report.

Section 7.44 is not intended to modify the general standards of conduct for directors set forth in section 8.30 but rather to make those standards more explicit in the derivative proceeding context. In this regard, the qualified directors making the determination would be entitled to rely on information and reports from other persons in accordance with section 8.30.

§7.45. Discontinuance or Settlement

A derivative proceeding may not be discontinued or settled without the court's approval. If the court determines that a proposed discontinuance or settlement will substantially affect the interests of the corporation's shareholders or a class or series of shareholders, the court shall direct that notice be given to the shareholders affected.

OFFICIAL COMMENT

Section 7.45's requirement that all proposed settlements and discontinuances receive judicial approval supports the proposition that a derivative suit is brought for the benefit of all shareholders and thus should not be settled privately.

By requiring that notice be given to all affected shareholders if the court determines that the proposed settlement may substantially affect their interests, section 7.45 permits the court to decide whether notice to shareholders (or holders of a class or series of shares) need be given. For example, the court may decide not to require notice of dismissal if, in the court's judgment, the proceeding is frivolous or has become moot. Section 7.45 also makes a distinction between classes or series of shareholders, an approach that could be used, for example, to eliminate the costs of notice to preferred shareholders where the settlement does not have an effect on their rights, such as their rights to dividends or a liquidation preference.

Section 7.45 does not address the issue of which party should bear the cost of giving this notice, which is left to the discretion of the court reviewing the proposed settlement.

§7.46. Payment of Expenses

On termination of the derivative proceeding the court may:

(1) order the corporation to pay the plaintiff's expenses incurred in the proceeding if it finds that the proceeding has resulted in a substantial benefit to the corporation;

(2) order the plaintiff to pay any defendant's expenses incurred in defending the proceeding if it finds that the proceeding was commenced or maintained without reasonable cause or for an improper purpose; or

(3) order a party to pay an opposing party's expenses incurred because of the filing of a pleading, motion or other paper, if it finds that the pleading, motion or other paper (i) was not well grounded in fact, after reasonable inquiry, or warranted by existing law or a good faith argument for the extension, modification or reversal of existing law or (ii) was interposed for an improper purpose, such as to harass or cause unnecessary delay or needless increase in the cost of litigation.

OFFICIAL COMMENT

The requirement in section 7.46(a) that the court may order the corporation to pay the plaintiff's expenses if it finds that the proceeding has resulted in a "substantial" benefit to the corporation, should discourage a plaintiff from proposing inconsequential matters to justify the payment of counsel fees. The provision does not specify the method for calculating attorneys' fees given that there is a substantial body of case law that delineates this issue, which usually includes taking into account the amount or character of the benefit to the corporation.

The standard under section 7.46(b) for the court to require the plaintiff to pay the defendants' expenses if the action was commenced without reasonable cause or for an improper purpose is intended to discourage proceedings brought for the sole purpose of obtaining early settlement payments by defendants to avoid significant defense costs, while also protecting plaintiffs whose suits have a reasonable foundation. This test is similar to but not identical to the test utilized in section 13.31, relating to dissenters' rights, where the standard for award of expenses is that dissenters "acted arbitrarily, vexatiously or not in good faith" in demanding a judicial appraisal of their shares. The derivative action situation is sufficiently different from the dissenters' rights situation to justify a different and less onerous test for imposing costs on the plaintiff.

Section 7.46(c) addresses other abuses in the conduct of derivative litigation which may occur on the part of the defendants and their counsel as well as by the plaintiffs and their counsel. This provision may be unnecessary if these abuses are already addressed under applicable rules of civil procedure.

§7.47. *Applicability to Foreign Corporations*

In any derivative proceeding in the right of a foreign corporation, the matters covered by this subchapter shall be governed by the laws of the jurisdiction of incorporation of the foreign corporation except for sections 7.43, 7.45, and 7.46.

SUBCHAPTER E. JUDICIAL PROCEEDINGS

§7.48. *Shareholder Action to Appoint a Custodian or Receiver*

(a) The [name or describe court] may appoint one or more persons to be custodians, or, if the corporation is insolvent, to be receivers, of and for a corporation in a proceeding by a shareholder where it is established that:

(1) the directors are deadlocked in the management of the corporate affairs, the shareholders are unable to break the deadlock, and irreparable injury to the corporation is threatened or being suffered; or

(2) the directors or those in control of the corporation are acting fraudulently and irreparable injury to the corporation is threatened or being suffered.

(b) The court:

(1) may issue injunctions, appoint a temporary custodian or temporary receiver with all the powers and duties the court directs, take other action to preserve the corporate assets wherever located, and carry on the business of the corporation until a full hearing is held;

(2) shall hold a full hearing, after notifying all parties to the proceeding and any interested persons designated by the court, before appointing a custodian or receiver; and

(3) has jurisdiction over the corporation and all of its property, wherever located.

(c) The court may appoint an individual or domestic or foreign corporation (registered to do business in this state) as a custodian or receiver and may require the custodian or receiver to post bond, with or without sureties, in an amount the court directs.

(d) The court shall describe the powers and duties of the custodian or receiver in its appointing order, which may be amended from time to time. Among other powers:

(1) a custodian may exercise all of the powers of the corporation, through or in place of its board of directors, to the extent necessary to manage the business and affairs of the corporation; and

(2) a receiver (i) may dispose of all or any part of the assets of the corporation wherever located, at a public or private sale, if authorized by the court; and (ii) may sue and defend in the receiver's own name as receiver in all courts of this state.

(e) The court during a custodianship may redesignate the custodian a receiver, and during a receivership may redesignate the receiver a custodian, if doing so is in the best interests of the corporation.

(f) The court from time to time during the custodianship or receivership may order compensation paid and expense disbursements or reimbursements made to the custodian or receiver from the assets of the corporation or proceeds from the sale of its assets.

(g) In this section, "shareholder" means a record shareholder, a beneficial shareholder, and an unrestricted voting trust beneficial owner.

§7.49. *Judicial Determination of Corporate Offices and Review of Elections and Shareholder Votes*

(a) Upon application of or in a proceeding commenced by a person specified in subsection (b), the [name or describe court] may determine:

(1) the result or validity of the election, appointment, removal or resignation of a director or officer of the corporation;

(2) the right of an individual to hold the office of director or officer of the corporation;

(3) the result or validity of any vote by the shareholders of the corporation;

(4) the right of a director to membership on a committee of the board of directors; and

(5) the right of a person to nominate or an individual to be nominated as a candidate for election or appointment as a director of the corporation, and any right under a bylaw adopted pursuant to section 2.06(c) or any comparable right under any provision of the articles of incorporation, contract, or applicable law.

(b) An application or proceeding pursuant to subsection (a) of this section may be filed or commenced by any of the following persons:

(1) the corporation;

(2) any record shareholder, beneficial shareholder or unrestricted voting trust beneficial owner of the corporation;

(3) a director of the corporation, an individual claiming the office of director, or a director whose membership on a committee of the board of directors is

contested, in each case who is seeking a determination of his or her right to such office or membership;

(4) an officer of the corporation or an individual claiming to be an officer of the corporation, in each case who is seeking a determination of his or her right to such office; and

(5) a person claiming a right covered by subsection (a)(5) and who is seeking a determination of such right.

(c) In connection with any application or proceeding under subsection (a), the following shall be named as defendants, unless such person made the application or commenced the proceeding:

(1) the corporation;

(2) any individual whose right to office or membership on a committee of the board of directors is contested;

(3) any individual claiming the office or membership at issue; and

(4) any person claiming a right covered by subsection (a)(5) that is at issue.

(d) In connection with any application or proceeding under subsection (a), service of process may be made upon each of the persons specified in subsection (c) either by:

(1) service of process on the corporation addressed to such person in any manner provided by statute of this state or by rule of the applicable court for service on the corporation; or

(2) service of process on the person in any manner provided by statute of this state or by rule of the applicable court.

(e) When service of process is made upon a person other than the corporation by service upon the corporation pursuant to subsection (d)(1), the plaintiff and the corporation or its registered agent shall promptly provide written notice of such service, together with copies of all process and the application or complaint, to the person at the person's last known residence or business address, or as permitted by statute of this state or by rule of the applicable court.

(f) In connection with any application or proceeding under subsection (a), the court shall dispose of the application or proceeding on an expedited basis and also may:

(1) order such additional or further notice as the court deems proper under the circumstances;

(2) order that additional persons be joined as parties to the proceeding if the court determines that such joinder is necessary for a just adjudication of matters before the court;

(3) order an election or meeting be held in accordance with the provisions of section 7.03(b) or otherwise;

(4) appoint a master to conduct an election or meeting;

(5) enter temporary, preliminary or permanent injunctive relief;

(6) resolve solely for the purpose of this proceeding any legal or factual issues necessary for the resolution of any of the matters specified in subsection (a), including the right and power of persons claiming to own shares to vote at any meeting of the shareholders; and

(7) order such other relief as the court determines is equitable, just and proper.

(g) It is not necessary to make shareholders a party to a proceeding or application pursuant to this section unless the shareholder is a required defendant under subsection (c)(4), relief is sought against the shareholder individually, or the court orders joinder pursuant to subsection (f)(2).

(h) Nothing in this section limits, restricts, or abolishes the subject matter jurisdiction or powers of the court as existed before the enactment of this section, and an application or proceeding pursuant to this section is not the exclusive remedy or proceeding available with respect to the matters specified in subsection (a).

CHAPTER 8. DIRECTORS AND OFFICERS

SUBCHAPTER A. BOARD OF DIRECTORS

§8.01. Requirement for and Functions of Board of Directors

(a) Except as may be provided in an agreement authorized under section 7.32, each corporation shall have a board of directors.

(b) Except as may be provided in an agreement authorized under section 7.32, and subject to any limitation in the articles of incorporation permitted by section 2.02(b), all corporate powers shall be exercised by or under the authority of the board of directors, and the business and affairs of the corporation shall be managed by or under the direction, and subject to the oversight, of the board of directors.

OFFICIAL COMMENT

As provided in Section 8.01(a), the board of directors is the traditional form of governance, but the shareholders of a corporation may, in an agreement that satisfies the requirements of section 7.32, dispense with a board of directors and structure the corporation's management and governance to address specific needs of the enterprise.

In section 8.01(b), the phrase "by or under the direction, and subject to the oversight, of" encompasses the varying functions of boards of directors of different corporations. In some corporations, particularly closely held corporations, the board of directors may be involved in the day-to-day business and affairs and it may be reasonable to describe management as being "by" the board of directors. In many other corporations, including most public corporations, the business and affairs are managed "under the direction, and subject to the oversight, of" the board of directors, and operational management is delegated to executive officers and other professional managers.

Section 8.01(b) often is considered to constitute the heart of the governance provisions of the Act. Giving the board of directors the power, and the responsibility, to oversee and direct the business of the corporation permits separation of ownership of the corporation from control of its oversight and direction. The Act's broad grant of authority and responsibility to the board of directors constitutes the rejection of the concept that the directors, having been elected by the shareholders, merely serve as agents to implement the will of the shareholders. See section 8.30.

Section 8.01(b), in providing for corporate powers to be exercised under the direction of the board of directors, allows the board of directors to delegate to appropriate officers, employees or agents of the corporation authority to exercise powers and perform functions not required by law to be exercised or performed by the board of directors itself. Although such delegation does not relieve the board of directors from its responsibility to oversee the business and affairs of the corporation, directors are not personally responsible for actions or omissions of officers, employees, or agents of the corporation so long as the directors have relied reasonably and in good faith upon these officers, employees, or agents. See sections 8.30 and 8.31 and their Official Comments.

The scope of the board's oversight responsibility will vary depending on the nature of the corporation and its business. At least for public corporations, the board's responsibilities generally include oversight of the following:

- business performance, plans and strategy;
- management's assessment of major risks to which the corporation is or may be exposed;
- the performance and compensation of executive officers;
- policies and practices to foster the corporation's compliance with law and ethical conduct;
- management's preparation of the corporation's financial statements;
- management's design and assessment of effectiveness of the corporation's internal controls;
- plans for the succession of the chief executive officer and other executive officers;
- the composition of the board and of board committees; and
- whether the corporation has information and reporting systems in place to provide directors with appropriate information in a timely manner.

In giving attention to the composition of the board, directors of public corporations should consider the corporation's processes for obtaining and evaluating the views of shareholders, including processes for considering individuals proposed by shareholders as nominees for election as directors. Directors of public corporations also should take into account the important role of independent directors. When ownership is separated from responsibility for oversight and direction, as is the case with public corporations, having nonmanagement independent directors who participate actively in the board's oversight functions increases the likelihood that actions taken by the board, if challenged, will be given deference by the courts. The listing standards of most public securities markets have requirements for independent directors to serve on boards; in many cases, they must constitute a majority of the board, and certain board committees must be composed entirely of independent directors. The listing standards have differing rules as to what constitutes an independent director. The Act does not attempt to define "independent director." Ordinarily, an independent director may not be a present or recent member of senior management and must be free of significant professional, financial or similar relationships with the corporation, and the director and members of the director's immediate family must be free of similar relationships with the corporation's senior management. Judgment is required to determine independence in light of the particular circumstances, subject to any specific requirements of a listing standard. The qualifications for disinterestedness required of directors for specific purposes under the Act are similar, but not necessarily identical, to those that are prerequisites to independence. For the requirements for a director to be considered disinterested and qualified to act in those specified situations, see section 1.43. An individual who is an independent director may not be eligible to act in a particular case under those other provisions of the Act. Conversely, a director who is not independent (for example, a member of management) may be disinterested and qualified to act in a particular case.

Section 8.01(b) recognizes that the powers of the board of directors may be limited by express provisions in the articles of incorporation and in an agreement among all shareholders under section 7.32. In an agreement under section 7.32, board powers also may be assigned to others. Because all of the shareholders must approve a section 7.32 agreement, the only restriction on limiting or assigning board powers is that any limitation or assignment must be provided for in sections 7.32(a)(1) through (a)(7) or must not be contrary to public policy under section 7.32(a)(8). In contrast, as is provided in section 2.02(b)(2), any limitation on board powers in the articles of incorporation cannot be "inconsistent with law." As a result of this difference in standards, any such limitation under section 2.02 should not, for example, be inconsistent with requirements of section 8.30 regarding standards of conduct for directors or otherwise preclude the directors from fulfilling their duties to the corporation.

§8.02. *Qualifications of Directors*

(a) The articles of incorporation or bylaws may prescribe qualifications for directors or for nominees for directors. Qualifications must be reasonable as applied to the corporation and be lawful.

(b) A requirement that is based on a past, prospective, or current action, or expression of opinion, by a nominee or director that could limit the ability of a nominee or director to discharge his or her duties as a director is not a permissible qualification under this section. Notwithstanding the foregoing, qualifications may include not being or having been subject to specified criminal, civil, or regulatory sanctions or not having been removed as a director by judicial action or for cause.

(c) A director need not be a resident of this state or a shareholder unless the articles of incorporation or bylaws so prescribe.

(d) A qualification for nomination for director prescribed before a person's nomination shall apply to such person at the time of nomination. A qualification for nomination for director prescribed after a person's nomination shall not apply to such person with respect to such nomination.

(e) A qualification for director prescribed before a director has been elected or appointed may apply only at the time an individual becomes a director or may apply during a director's term. A qualification prescribed after a director has been elected or appointed shall not apply to that director before the end of that director's term.

OFFICIAL COMMENT

Some corporations have adopted qualifications for individuals to be directors or to be nominated as directors. One use of qualifications may be by closely held corporations, to ensure representation and voting power on the board of directors. Other provisions of the Act also are designed to accomplish these purposes. See, for example, section 7.32 providing for shareholder agreements. See also section 2.02(b).

Qualifications may apply to all board members or to a specified percentage or number of directors. An example of a qualification applying to fewer than all directors would be a requirement that at least two directors must have specified business or professional experience or a particular educational degree or background. Careful consideration should be given to the intended effect of the application of any qualification that applies to fewer than all directors in the context of an election contest in which only some of the nominees satisfy this qualification. In the event that specified qualifications for some or all directors are not satisfied, remedial steps could be addressed in the articles of incorporation or bylaws, or can be left to other mechanisms available to a corporation and its board and shareholders, such as the provisions permitting changes in the number of directors and providing for the filling of vacancies on the board. See sections 8.03 and 8.10.

The purpose of section 8.02(a) is to permit qualifications that may benefit the corporation by enhancing the board's ability to perform its role effectively. However, this needs to be balanced against the risk that qualifications could be misused for entrenchment purposes by incumbents or for other improper purposes. To address these concerns, section 8.02(a) requires that qualifications must be reasonable as applied to the corporation and must be lawful. For example, a qualification that seeks to favor incumbent directors or distinguish between a director elected from the slate nominated by a corporation's board and a director elected as the result of being nominated by one or more shareholders, including under a bylaw adopted pursuant to section 2.06(c), would not ordinarily be reasonable and thus not ordinarily authorized by section 8.02(a). An example of a qualification that would not be lawful would be a requirement that is impermissibly discriminatory under the Civil Rights Act of 1964.

1. *Scope of Permitted Qualifications*

Examples of qualifications that may be permissible under section 8.02 are eligibility requirements based on residence, shareholdings, age, length of service, experience, expertise, and professional licenses or certifications.

Under section 8.02(b) a qualification that is based on a past, current, or prospective action, or expression of opinion, by a nominee or director that could limit the ability of a nominee or director to discharge his or her duties as a director is not a permissible qualification. The discharge of duties of a director is referenced in section 8.30. A requirement based on a director's having voted for or against, or expressed an intent to vote for or against, a particular type of resolution, such as a resolution in favor of or against a bylaw pursuant to section 2.06(c) or a resolution in favor of or against a shareholder rights plan, would be impermissible.

A shareholder agreement that meets the requirements of section 7.32 could override the terms of section 8.02, including with respect to the requirement of reasonableness in section 8.02(a) and the limitation on permitted qualifications in section 8.02(b).

2. *Timing and Applicability of Qualifications*

Sections 8.02(d) and (e) prohibit "springing" qualifications. A qualification for a director that is prescribed during the term of that director shall, assuming it remains in effect, apply to that director upon the start of any additional term of that director.

To avoid ambiguity as to whether a qualification for director only applies at the start of a term or applies during the term, a qualification provision should provide clearly when it applies. In the event that a qualification provision does not so specify, customary principles of interpretation and construction will apply. Examples of qualifications the nature of which would generally indicate an intent that they apply throughout a term would be a citizenship or residence qualification or a qualification that a director have a particular license or government clearance.

A director who ceases to meet a qualification that applies during a term will not satisfy that qualification at that time. For example, if a bylaw provision that is in effect at the start of a director's term requires that all directors be residents of state X during their terms, and that director at the start of his or her term is a resident of state X but during the term becomes a resident of state Y, then that director would cease to satisfy the qualification and, therefore, cease to be a director at the time the director becomes a resident of state Y.

§8.03. Number and Election of Directors

(a) A board of directors shall consist of one or more individuals, with the number specified in or fixed in accordance with the articles of incorporation or bylaws.

(b) The number of directors may be increased or decreased from time to time by amendment to, or in the manner provided in, the articles of incorporation or bylaws.

(c) Directors are elected at the first annual shareholders' meeting and at each annual shareholders' meeting thereafter unless elected by written consent in lieu of an annual meeting as permitted by section 7.04 or unless their terms are staggered under section 8.06.

OFFICIAL COMMENT

Section 8.03 prescribes rules for (i) the determination of the size of the board of directors of corporations, and (ii) changes in the number of directors once the board's size has been established.

1. Number of Directors

Under section 8.03(a), the size of the board of directors may be fixed initially in one or more of the fundamental corporate documents, or the decision as to the size of the initial board of directors may be made thereafter in the manner authorized in those documents.

2. Changes in the Size of the Board of Directors

Section 8.03(b) provides a corporation with the freedom to design its articles of incorporation and bylaw provisions relating to the size of its board with a view to achieving the combination of flexibility for the board of directors and protection for shareholders that it deems appropriate. The articles of incorporation could provide for a specified number of directors or a board size within a range from a minimum to a maximum, or an unlimited size not fewer than one as determined by the board or the shareholders. If the shareholders or the board of directors want to change the specified size of the board, to change the range established for the size of the board or to change from a board size within a range or of unlimited size to a specified board size or vice versa, board of directors and shareholder action would be required to make those changes by amending the articles of incorporation. Alternatively, the bylaws could provide for a specified number of directors or a size within a stated range or unlimited size, with the number to be fixed by the board of directors. Any change would be made in the manner provided by the bylaws. The bylaws could permit amendment by the board of directors or the bylaws could require that any amendment, in whole or in part, be made only by the shareholders in accordance with section 10.20(a). Typically, the board of directors would be permitted to change the board size within the established range. If a corporation wishes to ensure that any change in the number of directors be approved by shareholders, then an appropriate restriction would have to be included in the articles of incorporation or bylaws.

The board's power to change the number of directors, like all other board powers, is subject to compliance with applicable standards governing director conduct. In particular, it may be inappropriate to change the size of the board for the primary purpose of maintaining control or defeating particular candidates for the board.

In many closely held corporations, shareholder approval for a change in the size of the board of directors may be readily accomplished if that is desired. In many closely held corporations a board of directors of a fixed size may be an essential part of a control arrangement. In these situations, an increase or decrease in the size of the board of directors by even a single member may significantly affect control. To maintain control arrangements dependent on a board of directors of a fixed size, the power of the board of directors to change its own size must be negated. This may be accomplished by fixing the size of the board of directors in the articles of incorporation or by expressly negating the power of the board of directors to change the size of the board, whether by amendment of the bylaws or otherwise. See section 10.20(a).

§8.04. Election of Directors by Certain Classes or Series of Shares

If the articles of incorporation or action by the board of directors pursuant to section 6.02 authorize dividing the shares into classes or series, the articles of incorporation may also authorize the election of all or a specified number of directors by the holders of one or more authorized classes or series of shares. A class or series (or multiple classes or series) of shares entitled to elect one or more directors is a separate voting group for purposes of the election of directors.

OFFICIAL COMMENT

Provisions allowing separate classes or series of shares each to elect a specified number of directors are often used in corporations to effect an agreed upon allocation of control, for example, to ensure representation on the board of directors by particular shareholders by issuing to those shareholders a class or series of shares entitled to elect one or more directors. Each class or series (or multiple classes or series) entitled to elect separately one or more directors constitutes a separate voting group for this purpose, and the quorum and voting requirements must be separately met by each voting group as provided in sections 7.25, 7.26 and 7.28.

§8.05. Terms of Directors Generally

(a) The terms of the initial directors of a corporation expire at the first shareholders' meeting at which directors are elected.

(b) The terms of all other directors expire at the next, or if their terms are staggered in accordance with section 8.06, at the applicable second or third, annual shareholders' meeting following their election, except to the extent (i) provided in section 10.22 if a bylaw electing to be governed by that section is in effect, or (ii) a shorter term is specified in the articles of incorporation in the event of a director nominee failing to receive a specified vote for election.

(c) A decrease in the number of directors does not shorten an incumbent director's term.

(d) The term of a director elected to fill a vacancy expires at the next shareholders' meeting at which directors are elected.

(e) Except to the extent otherwise provided in the articles of incorporation or under section 10.22 if a bylaw electing to be governed by that section is in effect, despite the expiration of a director's term, the director continues to serve until the director's successor is elected and qualifies or there is a decrease in the number of directors.

OFFICIAL COMMENT

Section 8.05 provides for the annual election of directors at the annual shareholders' meeting with the single exception that terms may be staggered as permitted in section 8.06.

Under section 8.05(d), if terms are staggered, the term of a director elected to fill a vacant term with more than a year to run is shorter than the term of the director's predecessor. The board of directors may take appropriate steps, by designation of short terms or otherwise, to return the rotation of election of directors to the original staggered terms established or fixed by the articles of incorporation or bylaws.

Section 8.05(e), with two exceptions, provides for "holdover" directors so that directorships do not automatically become vacant at the expiration of their terms. This means that the power of the board of directors to act continues uninterrupted even if an annual shareholders' meeting is not held or the shareholders are deadlocked or otherwise do not elect directors at the meeting. The articles of incorporation may modify or eliminate this holdover concept. Also, if a bylaw is adopted invoking section 10.22, the effect will be that directors who are elected by a plurality vote but receive more votes against than for their election will not hold over past the abbreviated 90-day term of office specified in section 10.22.

§8.06. Staggered Terms for Directors

The articles of incorporation may provide for staggering the terms of directors by dividing the total number of directors into two or three groups, with each group containing half or one-third of the total, as near as may be practicable. In that event, the terms of directors in the first group expire at the first annual shareholders' meeting after their election, the terms of the second group expire at the second annual shareholders' meeting after their election, and the terms of the third group, if any, expire at the third annual shareholders' meeting after their election. At each annual shareholders' meeting held thereafter, directors shall be elected for a term of two years or three years, as the case may be, to succeed those whose terms expire.

OFFICIAL COMMENT

Section 8.06 permits the practice of "classifying" the board or "staggering" the terms of directors. The requirement that these provisions be in the articles of incorporation ensures that, unless included in the corporation's original articles, a staggered board may only be implemented with shareholder approval.

§8.07. *Resignation of Directors*

(a) A director may resign at any time by delivering a written notice of resignation to the board of directors or its chair, or to the secretary.

(b) A resignation is effective as provided in section 1.41(i) unless the resignation provides for a delayed effectiveness, including effectiveness determined upon a future event or events. A resignation that is conditioned upon failing to receive a specified vote for election as a director may provide that it is irrevocable.

OFFICIAL COMMENT

In addition to permitting resignations effective at a date later than the date of delivery of the resignation, section 8.07(b) permits a director resignation to be conditioned upon "future events," which might include the director failing to achieve a specified vote for reelection, *e.g.*, more votes "for" than "against" coupled with board acceptance of the resignation. Corporations and individual directors may thus give effect, in a manner subsequently enforceable by the corporation, to voting standards for the election of directors that exceed the plurality default standard in section 7.28. Section 8.07(b) also makes it clear that such arrangements do not contravene public policy. The express reference to the failure to receive a specified vote is not to be construed to address or negate the possible validity of other appropriate conditions for an irrevocable resignation.

Under section 8.10, a vacancy that will occur at a specific later date by reason of a resignation effective at a later date may be filled before the vacancy occurs, but the new director may not take office until the vacancy occurs. Because the individual tendering that resignation is still a member of the board, he or she may participate in all decisions until the specified date, including the choice of his or her successor under section 8.10.

§8.08. *Removal of Directors by Shareholders*

(a) The shareholders may remove one or more directors with or without cause unless the articles of incorporation provide that directors may be removed only for cause.

(b) If a director is elected by a voting group of shareholders, only the shareholders of that voting group may participate in the vote to remove that director.

(c) A director may be removed if the number of votes cast to remove exceeds the number of votes cast not to remove the director, except to the extent the articles of incorporation or bylaws require a greater number; provided that if cumulative voting is authorized, a director may not be removed if, in the case of a meeting, the number of votes sufficient to elect the director under cumulative voting is voted against removal and, if action is taken by less than unanimous written consent, voting shareholders entitled to the number of votes sufficient to elect the director under cumulative voting do not consent to the removal.

(d) A director may be removed by the shareholders only at a meeting called for the purpose of removing the director and the meeting notice must state that removal of the director is a purpose of the meeting.

OFFICIAL COMMENT

Section 8.08(a) provides a default rule that shareholders have the power to change the directors at will. However, that section permits the power to remove directors without cause to be eliminated by a provision in the articles of incorporation. Section 8.08(c) assures that a minority faction with sufficient votes to guarantee the election of a director under cumulative voting will be able to protect that director from removal by the remaining shareholders. In computing whether a director elected by cumulative voting is protected from removal under that section, the votes should be counted as though (i) the vote to remove the director occurred in an election to elect the number of directors normally elected by the relevant voting group along with the director whose removal is sought, (ii) the number of votes cast cumulatively against removal had been cast for election of the director, and (iii) all votes cast for removal of the director had been cast cumulatively in an efficient pattern for the election of a sufficient number of candidates so as to deprive the director whose removal is being sought of the director's office.

Although sections 8.08(b) and (c) have specific requirements with respect to removal of directors elected by particular voting groups or by cumulative voting, such directors nevertheless may be removed by court proceeding under section 8.09. Section 8.08(d) acknowledges the seriousness of director removal by requiring the meeting notice to state that removal of specific directors will be proposed. Section 8.08(d) governs removal of directors at a meeting of shareholders, but does not preclude removal by means of shareholder action by written consent under section 7.04. Unless cumulative voting is authorized, and in the absence of a greater vote requirement in the articles of incorporation or bylaws, removal of a director by less than unanimous written consent would require that a majority of the outstanding shares of the relevant voting group consent to the removal.

§8.09. *Removal of Directors by Judicial Proceeding*

(a) The [name or describe court] may remove a director from office or may order other relief, including barring the director from reelection for a period prescribed by the court, in a proceeding commenced by or in the right of the corporation if the court finds that (i) the director engaged in fraudulent conduct with respect to the corporation or its shareholders, grossly abused the position of director, or intentionally inflicted harm on the corporation; and (ii) considering the director's course of conduct and the inadequacy of other available remedies, removal or such other relief would be in the best interest of the corporation.

(b) A shareholder proceeding on behalf of the corporation under subsection (a) shall comply with all of the requirements of subchapter 7D, except clause (i) of section 7.41.

OFFICIAL COMMENT

Section 8.09 is designed to operate in the limited circumstance where other remedies are inadequate to address serious misconduct by a director and it is impracticable for shareholders to invoke removal under section 8.08. A proceeding under section 8.09 may be brought by the corporation or by a shareholder suing derivatively. If an action is brought derivatively, all of the provisions of chapter 7D, including dismissal under section 7.44, are applicable to the action with the exception of the contemporaneous ownership requirement of clause (i) of section 7.41. This extraordinary remedy of judicial removal is only for the kind of misconduct described in clause (i) of section 8.09(a) and does not reach matters falling within an individual director's lawful exercise of business judgment.

The court may determine that the director's continuation in office is inimical to the best interest of the corporation. Judicial removal might be the most appropriate remedy if shareholder removal under section 8.08 is impracticable because of situations such as the following:

- The director charged with serious misconduct personally owns or controls sufficient shares to block removal.
- The director was elected by voting group or cumulative voting, and the shareholders with voting power to prevent removal will exercise that power despite the director's serious misconduct and without regard to what the court deems to be the best interest of the corporation.
- A shareholders' meeting to consider removal under section 8.08 will entail considerable expense and a period of delay that will be contrary to the corporation's best interest.

§8.10. Vacancy on Board of Directors

(a) Unless the articles of incorporation provide otherwise, if a vacancy occurs on a board of directors, including a vacancy resulting from an increase in the number of directors:

(1) the shareholders may fill the vacancy;

(2) the board of directors may fill the vacancy; or

(3) if the directors remaining in office are less than a quorum, they may fill the vacancy by the affirmative vote of a majority of all the directors remaining in office.

(b) If the vacant office was held by a director elected by a voting group of shareholders, only the holders of shares of that voting group are entitled to vote to fill the vacancy if it is filled by the shareholders, and only the remaining directors elected by that voting group, even if less than a quorum, are entitled to fill the vacancy if it is filled by the directors.

(c) A vacancy that will occur at a specific later date (by reason of a resignation effective at a later date under section 8.07(b) or otherwise) may be filled before the vacancy occurs but the new director may not take office until the vacancy occurs.

§8.11. Compensation of Directors

Unless the articles of incorporation or bylaws provide otherwise, the board of directors may fix the compensation of directors.

OFFICIAL COMMENT

Section 8.11 reflects the view that director compensation is an appropriate function of the board of directors. Board action on directors' compensation and benefits is a director's conflicting interest transaction subject to chapter 8F. See Official Comment to section 8.61, Note on Directors' Compensation.

SUBCHAPTER B. MEETINGS AND ACTION OF THE BOARD

§8.20. Meetings

(a) The board of directors may hold regular or special meetings in or out of this state.

(b) Unless restricted by the articles of incorporation or bylaws, any or all directors may participate in any meeting of the board of directors through the use of any means of communication by which all directors participating may simultaneously hear each other during the meeting. A director participating in a meeting by this means is deemed to be present in person at the meeting.

§8.21. Action Without Meeting

(a) Except to the extent that the articles of incorporation or bylaws require that action by the board of directors be taken at a meeting, action required or permitted by this Act to be taken by the board of directors may be taken without a meeting if each director signs a consent describing the action to be taken and delivers it to the corporation.

(b) Action taken under this section is the act of the board of directors when one or more consents signed by all the directors are delivered to the corporation. The consent may specify a later time as the time at which the action taken is to be effective. A director's consent may be withdrawn by a revocation signed by the director and delivered to the corporation before delivery to the corporation of unrevoked written consents signed by all the directors.

(c) A consent signed under this section has the effect of action taken at a meeting of the board of directors and may be described as such in any document.

§8.22. Notice of Meeting

(a) Unless the articles of incorporation or bylaws provide otherwise, regular meetings of the board of directors may be held without notice of the date, time, place, or purpose of the meeting.

(b) Unless the articles of incorporation or bylaws provide for a longer or shorter period, special meetings of the board of directors shall be preceded by at least two days' notice of the date, time, and place of the meeting. The notice need not describe the purpose of the special meeting unless required by the articles of incorporation or bylaws.

§8.23. Waiver of Notice

(a) A director may waive any notice required by this Act, the articles of incorporation or the bylaws before or after the date and time stated in the notice. Except as provided by subsection (b), the waiver must be in writing, signed by the director entitled to the notice and delivered to the corporation for filing by the corporation with the minutes or corporate records.

(b) A director's attendance at or participation in a meeting waives any required notice to the director of the meeting unless the director at the beginning of the meeting (or promptly upon arrival) objects to holding the meeting or transacting business at the meeting and does not after objecting vote for or assent to action taken at the meeting.

§8.24. Quorum and Voting

(a) Unless the articles of incorporation or bylaws provide for a greater or lesser number or unless otherwise expressly provided in this Act, a quorum of a board of directors consists of a majority of the number of directors specified in or fixed in accordance with the articles of incorporation or bylaws.

(b) The quorum of the board of directors specified in or fixed in accordance with the articles of incorporation or bylaws may not consist of less than one-third of the specified or fixed number of directors.

(c) If a quorum is present when a vote is taken, the affirmative vote of a majority of directors present is the act of the board of directors unless the articles of incorporation or bylaws require the vote of a greater number of directors or unless otherwise expressly provided in this Act.

(d) A director who is present at a meeting of the board of directors or a committee when corporate action is taken is deemed to have assented to the action taken unless: (i) the director objects at the beginning of the meeting (or promptly upon arrival) to holding it or transacting business at the meeting; (ii) the dissent or abstention from the action taken is entered in the minutes of the meeting; or (iii) the director delivers written notice of the director's dissent or abstention to the presiding officer of the meeting before its adjournment or to the corporation immediately after adjournment of the meeting. The right of dissent or abstention is not available to a director who votes in favor of the action taken.

§8.25. Committees of the Board

(a) Unless this Act, the articles of incorporation or the bylaws provide otherwise, a board of directors may establish one or more board committees composed exclusively of one or more directors to perform functions of the board of directors.

(b) The establishment of a board committee and appointment of members to it shall be approved by the greater of (i) a majority of all the directors in office when the action is taken or (ii) the number of directors required by the articles of incorporation or bylaws to take action under section 8.24, unless, in either case, this Act or the articles of incorporation provide otherwise.

(c) Sections 8.20 through 8.24 apply to board committees and their members.

(d) A board committee may exercise the powers of the board of directors under section 8.01, to the extent specified by the board of directors or in the articles of incorporation or bylaws, except that a board committee may not:

(1) authorize or approve distributions, except according to a formula or method, or within limits, prescribed by the board of directors;

(2) approve or propose to shareholders action that this Act requires be approved by shareholders;

(3) fill vacancies on the board of directors or, subject to subsection (e), on any board committees; or

(4) adopt, amend, or repeal bylaws.

(e) The board of directors may appoint one or more directors as alternate members of any board committee to replace any absent or disqualified member during the member's absence or disqualification. If the articles of incorporation, the bylaws, or the resolution creating the board committee so provide, the member or members present at any board committee meeting and not disqualified from voting may, by unanimous action, appoint another director to act in place of an absent or disqualified member during that member's absence or disqualification.

§8.26. Submission of Matters for Shareholder Vote

A corporation may agree to submit a matter to a vote of its shareholders even if, after approving the matter, the board of directors determines it no longer recommends the matter.

OFFICIAL COMMENT

Section 8.26 authorizes a corporation to enter into an agreement, such as a merger agreement, containing a provision that requires a shareholder vote on the matter despite a subsequent change in the recommendation of the board of directors. Otherwise, a board is not required to submit a matter to the shareholders, even if it has been approved by the board. Section 8.26 also applies to the provisions of the Act that require the board of directors to approve a matter before recommending that the shareholders vote to approve it. Section 8.26 does not change the standards of conduct or liability applicable when considering whether to authorize such agreement by the corporation.

SUBCHAPTER C. DIRECTORS

§8.30. Standards of Conduct for Directors

(a) Each member of the board of directors, when discharging the duties of a director, shall act: (i) in good faith, and (ii) in a manner the director reasonably believes to be in the best interests of the corporation.

(b) The members of the board of directors or a board committee, when becoming informed in connection with their decision-making function or devoting attention to their oversight function, shall discharge their duties with the care that a person in a like position would reasonably believe appropriate under similar circumstances.

(c) In discharging board or board committee duties, a director shall disclose, or cause to be disclosed, to the other board or committee members information not already known by them but known by the director to be material to the discharge of their decision-making or oversight functions, except that disclosure is not required to the extent that the director reasonably believes that doing so would violate a duty imposed under law, a legally enforceable obligation of confidentiality, or a professional ethics rule.

(d) In discharging board or board committee duties, a director who does not have knowledge that makes reliance unwarranted is entitled to rely on the performance by any of the persons specified in subsection (f)(1) or subsection (f)(3) to whom the board may have delegated, formally or informally by course of conduct, the authority or duty to perform one or more of the board's functions that are delegable under applicable law.

(e) In discharging board or board committee duties, a director who does not have knowledge that makes reliance unwarranted is entitled to rely on information, opinions, reports, or statements, including financial statements and other financial data, prepared or presented by any of the persons specified in subsection (f).

(f) A director is entitled to rely, in accordance with subsection (d) or (e), on:

(1) one or more officers or employees of the corporation whom the director reasonably believes to be reliable and competent in the functions performed or the information, opinions, reports or statements provided;

(2) legal counsel, public accountants, or other persons retained by the corporation as to matters involving skills or expertise the director reasonably believes are matters (i) within the particular person's professional or expert competence, or (ii) as to which the particular person merits confidence; or

(3) a board committee of which the director is not a member if the director reasonably believes the committee merits confidence.

OFFICIAL COMMENT

Section 8.30 sets standards of conduct for directors that focus on the manner in which directors make their decisions, not the correctness of the decisions made. Section 8.30 should be read in light of the basic role of directors set forth in section 8.01(b), which provides that the "business and affairs of a corporation shall be managed by or under the direction and subject to the oversight of the board of directors," as supplemented by various provisions of the Act assigning specific powers or responsibilities to the board. The standards of conduct for directors established by section 8.30 are analogous to those generally articulated by courts in evaluating director conduct, often referred to as the duties of care and loyalty.

Section 8.30 addresses standards of conduct—the level of performance expected of directors undertaking the role and responsibilities of the office of director. The section does not address the liability of a director, although exposure to liability may result from a failure to honor the standards of conduct required to be observed. The issue of director liability is addressed in sections 8.31 and 8.32. Section 8.30 does, however, play an important role in evaluating a director's conduct and the effectiveness of board action. It has relevance in assessing, under section 8.31, the reasonableness of a director's belief. Similarly, it has relevance in assessing a director's timely attention to appropriate inquiry when particular facts and circumstances of significant concern materialize. It also serves as a frame of reference for determining, under section 8.32(a), liability for an unlawful distribution. Finally, section 8.30 compliance may influence a court's analysis where injunctive relief against a transaction is being sought. Directors act both individually and collectively as a board in performing their functions and discharging their duties. Section 8.30 addresses actions in both capacities.

Under the standards of section 8.30, the board may delegate or assign to appropriate officers or employees of the corporation the authority or duty to exercise powers that the law does not require the board to retain. Because the directors are entitled to rely on these persons absent knowledge making reliance unwarranted, the directors will not be in breach of the standards under section 8.30 as a result of their delegatees' actions or omissions so long as the board acted in good faith and complied with the other standards of conduct set forth in section 8.30 in delegating responsibility and, where appropriate, monitoring performance of the duties delegated. In addition, subsections (d), (e) and (f) permit a director to rely on enumerated third parties for specified purposes, although reliance is prohibited when a director has knowledge that makes reliance unwarranted. Section 8.30(a)'s standards of good faith and reasonable belief in the best interests of the corporation also apply to a director's reliance under subsections (d), (e) and (f).

1. Section 8.30(a)

Section 8.30(a) establishes the basic standards of conduct for all directors and its mandate governs all aspects of directors' conduct, including the requirements in other subsections. It includes concepts courts have used in defining the duty of loyalty. Two of the phrases used in section 8.30(a) deserve further comment:

- The phrase "reasonably believes" is both subjective and objective in character. Its first level of analysis is geared to what the particular director, acting in good faith, actually believes—not what objective analysis would lead another director (in a like position and acting in similar circumstances) to conclude. The second level of analysis is focused specifically on "reasonably." Although a director has wide discretion in gathering information and reaching conclusions, whether a director's belief is reasonable (*i.e.*, could—not would—a reasonable person in a like position and acting in similar circumstances, taking into account that director's knowledge and experience, have arrived at that belief) ultimately involves an overview that is objective in character.
- The phrase "best interests of the corporation" is key to an understanding of a director's duties. The term "corporation" is a surrogate for the business enterprise as well as a frame of reference encompassing the shareholder body. In determining the corporation's "best interests," the director has wide discretion in deciding how to weigh near-term opportunities versus long-term benefits as well as in making judgments where the interests of various groups of shareholders or other corporate constituencies may differ.

Section 8.30 operates as a "baseline" principle governing director conduct in circumstances uncomplicated by self-interest. The Act recognizes, however, that directors' personal interests may not always align with the corporation's best interests and provides procedures by which situations and transactions involving conflicts of interest can be processed. See subchapter D (derivative proceedings) of chapter 7 and subchapters E (indemnification and advance for expenses), F (directors' conflicting interest transactions), and G (business opportunities) of this chapter 8. Those procedures generally contemplate that the interested director will provide appropriate disclosure and will not be involved in taking action on the matter giving rise to the conflict of interest.

2. Section 8.30(b)

Section 8.30(b) establishes a general standard of care for directors in the context of their dealing with the board's decision-making and oversight functions. Although certain aspects will involve individual conduct (*e.g.*, preparation for meetings), these functions are generally performed by the board of directors through collective action, as recognized by the reference in subsection (b) to board and committee "members" and "their duties." In contrast with section 8.30(a)'s individual conduct mandate, section 8.30(b) has a two-fold thrust: it provides a standard of conduct for individual action and, more broadly, it states a conduct obligation—"shall discharge their duties"—concerning the degree of care to be used collectively by the directors when performing those functions. The standard is not what care a particular director might believe appropriate in the circumstances but what a person—in a like position and acting under similar circumstances—would reasonably believe to be appropriate. Thus, the degree of care that directors should employ under section 8.30(b) involves an objective standard.

The process by which a director becomes informed, in carrying out the decision-making and oversight functions, will vary. The directors' decision-making function is reflected in various sections of the Act, including: the issuance of shares (section 6.21); distributions (section 6.40); dismissal of derivative proceedings (section 7.44); indemnification (section 8.55); conflict of interest transaction authorization (section 8.62); articles of incorporation amendments (sections 10.02 and 10.03); bylaw amendments (section 10.20); mergers and share exchanges (section 11.04); asset dispositions (section 12.02); and dissolution (section 14.02). The directors' oversight function is established under section 8.01. In discharging the section 8.01 duties associated with the board's oversight function, the standard of care entails primarily a requirement of attention. In contrast with the board's decision-making function, which generally involves informed action at a point in time, the oversight function is concerned with a continuum and the attention of the directors accordingly involves participatory performance over a period of time.

Several of the phrases chosen to define the standard of conduct in section 8.30(b) deserve specific mention:

- The phrase "becoming informed," in the context of the decision–making function, refers to the process of gaining sufficient familiarity with the background facts and circumstances to make an informed judgment. Unless the circumstances would permit a reasonable director to conclude that he or she is already sufficiently informed, the standard of care requires every director to take steps to become informed about the background facts and circumstances before taking action on the matter at hand. The process typically involves review of written materials provided before or at the meeting and attention to or participation in the deliberations leading up to a vote. In addition to considering information and data on which a director is expressly entitled to rely under section 8.30(e), "becoming informed" can also involve consideration of information and data generated by other persons, for example, review of industry studies or research articles prepared by third parties. It can also involve direct communications, outside of the boardroom, with members of management or other directors. There is no one way for "becoming informed," and both the method and measure—"how to" and "how much"—are matters of reasonable judgment for the director to exercise.
- The phrase "devoting attention," in the context of the oversight function, refers to considering such matters as the corporation's information and reporting systems generally and not to an independent investigation into particular system inadequacies or noncompliance. Although directors typically give attention to future plans and trends as well as current activities, they should not be expected to anticipate any particular problems which the corporation may face except in those circumstances where something has occurred to make it obvious to the

board that the corporation should be addressing a particular problem. The standard of care associated with the oversight function involves gaining assurances from management and advisers that appropriate systems have been established, such as those concerned with legal compliance, risk assessment or internal controls. Such assurances also should cover establishment of ongoing monitoring of the systems in place, with appropriate follow-up responses when alerted to the issues requiring attention.

- The reference to "person," without embellishment, is intended to avoid implying any qualifications, such as specialized expertise or experience requirements, beyond the basic attributes of common sense, practical wisdom, and informed judgment (however, see the last bullet below).
- The phrase "reasonably believe appropriate" refers to the array of possible options that a person possessing the basic attributes of common sense, practical wisdom and informed judgment would recognize to be available, in terms of the degree of care that might be appropriate, and from which a choice by such person would be made. The measure of care that such person might determine to be appropriate, in a given instance, would normally involve a selection from the range of options and any choice within the realm of reason would be an appropriate decision under the standard of care called for under section 8.30(b). However, a decision that is so removed from the realm of reason, or is so unreasonable, that it falls outside the permissible bounds of sound discretion, and thus is an abuse of discretion, will not satisfy the standard.
- The phrase "in a like position" recognizes that the "care" under consideration is that which would be used by the "person" if he or she were a director of the particular corporation.
- The combined phrase "in a like position ... under similar circumstances" is intended to recognize that (i) the nature and extent of responsibilities will vary, depending upon such factors as the size, complexity, urgency, and location of activities carried on by the particular corporation, (ii) decisions must be made on the basis of the information known to the directors without the benefit of hindsight, and (iii) the special background, qualifications, and oversight responsibilities of a particular director may be relevant in evaluating that director's compliance with the standard of care.

3. *Section 8.30(c)*

A requirement to disclose to other directors information that a director knows to be material to the decision-making or oversight functions of the board of directors or a board committee is implicit in the standards of conduct set forth in sections 8.30(a) and (b), but section 8.30(c) makes this explicit. Thus, for example, when a member of the board of directors knows information that the director recognizes is material to a decision by the board but is not known to the other directors, the director is obligated to disclose that information to the other members of the board. Such disclosure can occur through direct statements in meetings of the board, or by any other timely means, including, for example, communicating the information to the chairman of the board or the chairman of a committee, or to the corporation's general counsel, and requesting that the recipient inform the other board or committee members of the information.

Section 8.30(c) recognizes that a duty of confidentiality to a third party can override a director's obligation to share with other directors information pertaining to a current corporate matter. In some circumstances, a duty of confidentiality to a third party may even prohibit disclosure of the nature or the existence of the duty itself. Ordinarily, however, a director who withholds material information based on a reasonable belief that a duty of confidentiality to a third party prohibits disclosure should advise the other directors of the existence and nature of that duty. Under the standards of conduct set forth in section 8.30(a), the withholding of material information may, depending on the nature of the material information and of the matter before the board of directors or a board committee, require that a director abstain or recuse himself or herself from all or a portion of the other directors' deliberation or vote on the matter to which the undisclosed information is material, or even resign as a director. See Official Comment to section 8.62. . . .

In connection with a director's conflicting interest transaction, the required disclosure (as defined in section 8.60) that must be made under section 8.62(a) and the exceptions to the required disclosure in that context under section 8.62(b) have elements that parallel the disclosure obligation of directors under section 8.30(c). The demands of section 8.62, however, are more detailed and specific. They apply to just one situation—a director's conflicting interest transaction—while the requirements of section 8.30(c) apply generally to all other decision-making and oversight functions. For example, the specific requirements of section 8.62(a)(1) for deliberation and a vote outside the presence of the conflicted director are not imposed universally for all decision-making matters or for oversight matters that do not involve decisions. Although they may be different from the generally applicable provisions of section 8.30(c), the specific provisions of subchapter 8F control and are exclusive with respect to director conflicting interest transactions.

The requirement that a director disclose information to other directors as set forth in section 8.30(c) is different from any common law duty the board may have to cause the corporation to make disclosures to shareholders under certain circumstances. The Act does not seek to codify such a duty of disclosure, but leaves its existence and scope, the circumstances for its application, and the consequences of any failure to satisfy it, to be developed by courts on a case-by-case basis. . . .

4. Section 8.30(d) . . .

Although the board of directors may delegate the authority or duty to perform one or more of its functions, delegation and reliance under section 8.30(d) may not alone constitute compliance with sections 8.30(a) and (b) and the action taken by the delegatee may not alone satisfy the directors or a noncommittee board member's section 8.01 responsibilities. On the other hand, failure of the board committee or the corporate officer or employee performing the function delegated to meet section 8.30(b)'s standard of care will not automatically result in violation by the board of section 8.01. Factors to be considered in determining whether a violation of section 8.01 has occurred will include the care used in the delegation to and supervision over the delegatee, and the amount of knowledge regarding the particular matter which is reasonably available to the particular director. Care in delegation and supervision includes appraisal of the capabilities and diligence of the delegatee in light of the subject and its relative importance and may be satisfied, in the usual case, by receipt of reports concerning the delegatee's activities. The enumeration of these factors is intended to emphasize that directors may not abdicate their responsibilities and avoid accountability simply by delegating authority to others. Rather, a director who is accountable for the acts of delegatees will fulfill the director's duties if the standards contained in section 8.30 are met.

5. Section 8.30(e)

Reliance under section 8.30(e) on a report, statement, opinion, or other information is permitted only if the director has read or heard orally presented the information, opinion, report or statement in question, or took other steps to become generally familiar with it. A director must comply with the general standard of care of section 8.30(b) in making a judgment as to the reliability and competence of the source of information upon which the director proposes to rely or, as appropriate, that it otherwise merits confidence.

6. Section 8.30(f)

In determining whether a corporate officer or employee is "reliable," for purposes of section 8.30(f)(1), the director would typically consider (i) the individual's background experience and scope of responsibility within the corporation in gauging the individual's familiarity and knowledge respecting the subject matter and (ii) the individual's record and reputation for honesty, care and ability in discharging responsibilities which he or she undertakes. In determining whether a person is "competent," the director would normally take into account the same considerations and, if expertise should be relevant, the director would consider the individual's technical skills as well. Recognition of the right of one director to rely on the expertise and experience of another director, in the context of board or committee deliberations, is unnecessary, for reliance on shared experience and wisdom of other board members is an implicit underpinning of collective board conduct. In relying on another member of the board, a director would quite properly take advantage of the colleague's knowledge and experience in becoming informed about the matter at hand before taking action; however, the director would be expected to exercise independent judgment when it comes time to vote. . . .

7. Application to Officers

Section 8.30 generally deals only with directors. Section 8.42 and its Official Comment explain the extent to which the principles set forth in section 8.30 apply to officers.

§8.31. Standards of Liability for Directors

(a) A director shall not be liable to the corporation or its shareholders for any decision to take or not to take action, or any failure to take any action, as a director, unless the party asserting liability in a proceeding establishes that:

(1) no defense interposed by the director based on (i) any provision in the articles of incorporation authorized by section 2.02(b)(4) or by section 2.02(b)(6), (ii) the protection afforded by section 8.61 (for action taken in compliance with section 8.62 or section 8.63), or (iii) the protection afforded by section 8.70, precludes liability; and

(2) the challenged conduct consisted or was the result of:

(i) action not in good faith; or

(ii) a decision

(A) which the director did not reasonably believe to be in the best interests of the corporation, or

(B) as to which the director was not informed to an extent the director reasonably believed appropriate in the circumstances; or

(iii) a lack of objectivity due to the director's familial, financial or business relationship with, or a lack of independence due to the director's domination or control by, another person having a material interest in the challenged conduct,

(A) which relationship or which domination or control could reasonably be expected to have affected the director's judgment respecting the challenged conduct in a manner adverse to the corporation, and

(B) after a reasonable expectation to such effect has been established, the director shall not have established that the challenged conduct was reasonably believed by the director to be in the best interests of the corporation; or

(iv) a sustained failure of the director to devote attention to ongoing oversight of the business and affairs of the corporation, or a failure to devote timely attention, by making (or causing to be made) appropriate inquiry, when particular facts and circumstances of significant concern materialize that would alert a reasonably attentive director to the need for such inquiry; or

(v) receipt of a financial benefit to which the director was not entitled or any other breach of the director's duties to deal fairly with the corporation and its shareholders that is actionable under applicable law.

(b) The party seeking to hold the director liable:

(1) for money damages, shall also have the burden of establishing that:

(i) harm to the corporation or its shareholders has been suffered, and

(ii) the harm suffered was proximately caused by the director's challenged conduct; or

(2) for other money payment under a legal remedy, such as compensation for the unauthorized use of corporate assets, shall also have whatever persuasion burden may be called for to establish that the payment sought is appropriate in the circumstances; or

(3) for other money payment under an equitable remedy, such as profit recovery by or disgorgement to the corporation, shall also have whatever persuasion burden may be called for to establish that the equitable remedy sought is appropriate in the circumstances.

(c) Nothing contained in this section shall (i) in any instance where fairness is at issue, such as consideration of the fairness of a transaction to the corporation under section 8.61(b)(3), alter the burden of proving the fact or lack of fairness otherwise applicable, (ii) alter the fact or lack of liability of a director under another section of this Act, such as the provisions governing the consequences of an unlawful distribution under section 8.32 or a transactional interest under section 8.61, or (iii) affect any rights to which the corporation or a shareholder may be entitled under another statute of this state or the United States.

OFFICIAL COMMENT

Boards of directors and corporate managers make numerous decisions that involve the balancing of risks and benefits for the enterprise. Although some decisions turn out to have been unwise or the result of a mistake of judgment, it is not reasonable to impose liability for an informed decision made in good faith which with the benefit of hindsight turns out to be wrong or unwise. Therefore, as a general rule, a director is not exposed to personal liability for injury or damage caused by an unwise decision and conduct conforming with the standards of section 8.30 will almost always be protected regardless of the end result. Moreover, the fact that a director's performance fails to meet the standards of section 8.30 does not in itself establish personal liability for damages that the corporation or its shareholders may have suffered as a consequence. Nevertheless, a director can be held liable for misfeasance or nonfeasance in performing his or her duties. Section 8.31

sets forth the standards of liability of directors as distinct from the standards of conduct set forth in section 8.30.

Courts have developed the broad common law concept of the business judgment rule. Although formulations vary, in basic principle, a board of directors generally enjoys a presumption of sound business judgment and its decisions will not be disturbed by a court substituting its own notions of what is or is not sound business judgment if the board's decisions can be attributed to any rational business purpose. It is also presumed that, in making a business decision, directors act in good faith, on an informed basis, and in the honest belief that the action taken is in the best interests of the corporation. The elements of the business judgment rule and the circumstances for its application continue to be developed and refined by courts. Accordingly, it would not be desirable to freeze the concept in a statute. Thus, section 8.31 does not codify the business judgment rule as a whole, although certain of its principal elements, relating to personal liability issues, are reflected in section 8.31(a)(2). . . .

§8.32. Directors' Liability for Unlawful Distributions

(a) A director who votes for or assents to a distribution in excess of what may be authorized and made pursuant to section 6.40(a) or 14.09(a) is personally liable to the corporation for the amount of the distribution that exceeds what could have been distributed without violating section 6.40(a) or 14.09(a) if the party asserting liability establishes that when taking the action the director did not comply with section 8.30.

(b) A director held liable under subsection (a) for an unlawful distribution is entitled to:

(1) contribution from every other director who could be held liable under subsection (a) for the unlawful distribution; and

(2) recoupment from each shareholder of the pro-rata portion of the amount of the unlawful distribution the shareholder accepted, knowing the distribution was made in violation of section 6.40(a) or 14.09(a).

(c) A proceeding to enforce:

(1) the liability of a director under subsection (a) is barred unless it is commenced within two years after the date (i) on which the effect of the distribution was measured under section 6.40(e) or (g), (ii) as of which the violation of section 6.40(a) occurred as the consequence of disregard of a restriction in the articles of incorporation, or (iii) on which the distribution of assets to shareholders under section 14.09(a) was made; or

(2) contribution or recoupment under subsection (b) is barred unless it is commenced within one year after the liability of the claimant has been finally adjudicated under subsection (a).

SUBCHAPTER D. OFFICERS

§8.40. Officers

(a) A corporation has the officers described in its bylaws or appointed by the board of directors in accordance with the bylaws.

(b) The board of directors may elect individuals to fill one or more offices of the corporation. An officer may appoint one or more officers if authorized by the bylaws or the board of directors.

(c) The bylaws or the board of directors shall assign to an officer responsibility for maintaining and authenticating the records of the corporation required to be kept under section 16.01(a).

(d) The same individual may simultaneously hold more than one office in a corporation.

OFFICIAL COMMENT

Section 8.40 permits every corporation to designate the officers it will have. No particular officers are required.

The board of directors, as well as duly authorized officers, employees or agents, may also appoint other agents for the corporation. In addition, a board of directors has the intrinsic power to organize its own internal affairs, including designating officers of the board.

The officer who has the responsibility to maintain the minutes and authenticate the corporate records referred to in section 16.01(a) is referred to as the "secretary" of the corporation throughout the Act. See section 1.40. The person so designated has authority to bind the corporation by that officer's authentication under this section. This assignment of authority, traditionally vested in the corporate "secretary," allows third persons to rely on authenticated records without inquiry as to their truth or accuracy.

§8.41. Functions of Officers

Each officer has the authority and shall perform the functions set forth in the bylaws or, to the extent consistent with the bylaws, the functions prescribed by the board of directors or by direction of an officer authorized by the board of directors to prescribe the functions of other officers.

OFFICIAL COMMENT

The methods of investing officers with formal authority in section 8.41 do not exhaust the sources of an officer's actual or apparent authority. Specific officers, particularly the chief executive officer, may have implied authority to take certain actions on behalf of a corporation merely by virtue of their positions. Officers may also be vested with apparent authority by reason of corporate conduct on which third persons reasonably rely.

In addition to express, implied, or apparent authority, a corporation is bound by unauthorized acts of officers if they are ratified by the board of directors. Generally, ratification may extend only to acts that could have been authorized as an original matter. Ratification may itself be express or implied and may in some cases serve as the basis of apparent authority.

§8.42. Standards of Conduct for Officers

(a) An officer, when performing in such capacity, has the duty to act:

(1) in good faith;

(2) with the care that a person in a like position would reasonably exercise under similar circumstances; and

(3) in a manner the officer reasonably believes to be in the best interests of the corporation.

(b) The duty of an officer includes the obligation:

(1) to inform the superior officer to whom, or the board of directors or the board committee to which, the officer reports of information about the affairs of the corporation known to the officer, within the scope of the officer's functions, and known to the officer to be material to such superior officer, board or committee; and

(2) to inform his or her superior officer, or another appropriate person within the corporation, or the board of directors, or a board committee, of any actual or probable material violation of law involving the corporation or material breach of duty to the corporation by an officer, employee, or agent of the corporation, that the officer believes has occurred or is likely to occur.

(c) In discharging his or her duties, an officer who does not have knowledge that makes reliance unwarranted is entitled to rely on:

(1) the performance of properly delegated responsibilities by one or more employees of the corporation whom the officer reasonably believes to be reliable and competent in performing the responsibilities delegated; or

(2) information, opinions, reports or statements, including financial statements and other financial data, prepared or presented by one or more employees of the corporation whom the officer reasonably believes to be reliable and competent in the matters presented or by legal counsel, public accountants, or other persons retained by the corporation as to matters involving skills or expertise the officer reasonably believes are matters (i) within the particular person's professional or expert competence or (ii) as to which the particular person merits confidence.

(d) An officer shall not be liable to the corporation or its shareholders for any decision to take or not to take action, or any failure to take any action, as an officer, if the duties of the office are performed in compliance with this section. Whether an officer who does not comply with this section shall have liability will depend in such instance on applicable law, including those principles of section 8.31 that have relevance.

OFFICIAL COMMENT

Under section 8.42(a), an officer, when performing in such officer's official capacity, has to meet standards of conduct generally specified for directors under section 8.30. This section is not intended to modify, diminish or qualify the duties or standards of conduct that may be imposed upon specific officers by other law or regulation.

Common law has generally recognized a duty on the part of officers and key employees to disclose to their superiors material information relevant to the affairs of the corporation. This duty is implicit in, and embraced under, the broader standard of section 8.42(a), but section 8.42(b) sets forth this disclosure obligation explicitly. Section 8.42(b)(1) specifies that business information shall be transmitted through the officer's regular reporting channels. Section 8.42(b)(2) specifies the reporting responsibility differently with respect to actual or probable material violations of law or material breaches of duty. The use of the term "appropriate" in subsection (b)(2) accommodates any normative standard that the corporation may have prescribed for reporting potential violations of law or duty to a specified person, such as an ombudsperson, ethics officer, internal auditor, general counsel or the like, as well as situations where there is no designated person but the officer's immediate superior is not appropriate (for example, because the officer believes that individual is complicit in the unlawful activity or breach of duty).

Section 8.42(b)(1) should not be interpreted so broadly as to discourage efficient delegation of functions. It addresses the flow of information to the board of directors and to superior officers necessary to enable them to perform their decision-making and oversight functions. See the Official Comment to section 8.31. The officer's duties under subsection (b) may not be negated by agreement; however, their scope under section 8.42(b)(1) may be shaped by prescribing the scope of an officer's functional responsibilities.

With respect to the duties under section 8.42(b)(2), codes of conduct or codes of ethics may prescribe the circumstances in which and mechanisms by which officers and employees may discharge their duty to report material information to superior officers or the board of directors, or to other designated persons.

The term "material" modifying violations of law or breaches of duty in section 8.42(b)(2) denotes a qualitative as well as quantitative standard. It relates not only to the potential direct financial impact on the corporation, but also to the nature of the violation or breach. For example, an embezzlement of $10,000, or even less, would be material because of the seriousness of the offense, even though the amount involved would ordinarily not be material to the financial position or results of operations of the corporation.

The duty under section 8.42(b)(2) is triggered by an officer's subjective belief that a material violation of law or breach of duty actually or probably has occurred or is likely to occur. This duty is not triggered by objective knowledge concepts, such as whether the officer should have concluded that such misconduct was occurring. The subjectivity of the trigger under subsection (b)(2), however, does not excuse officers from their obligations under subsection (a) to act in good faith and with due care in the performance of the functions assigned to them, including oversight duties within their respective areas of responsibility. There may be occasions when the principles applicable under section 8.30(c) limiting the duty of disclosure by directors where a duty of confidentiality is overriding may also apply to officers. See the Official Comment to section 8.30(c).

An officer's ability to rely on others in meeting the standards prescribed in section 8.42 may be more limited, depending upon the circumstances of the particular case, than the measure and scope of reliance permitted a director under section 8.30, in view of the greater obligation the officer may have to be familiar with the affairs of the corporation. The proper delegation of responsibilities by an officer, separate and apart from the exercise of judgment as to the delegatee's reliability and competence, is concerned with the procedure employed. This will involve, in the usual case, sufficient communication such that the delegatee understands the scope of the assignment and, in turn, manifests to the officer a willingness and commitment to undertake its performance. The entitlement to rely upon employees assumes that a delegating officer will maintain a sufficient level of communication with the officer's subordinates to fulfill his or her supervisory responsibilities. The definition of "employee" in section 1.40 includes an officer; accordingly, section 8.42 contemplates the delegation of responsibilities to other officers as well as to non-officer employees.

Although under section 8.42(d), performance meeting that section's standards of conduct will eliminate an officer's exposure to any liability to the corporation or its shareholders, failure by an officer to meet that section's standards will not automatically result in liability. Deficient performance of duties by an officer, depending upon the facts and circumstances, will normally be dealt with through intracorporate disciplinary procedures, such as reprimand, compensation adjustment, delayed promotion, demotion or discharge. These procedures may be subject to (and limited by) the terms of an officer's employment agreement. See section 8.44.

In some cases, failure to observe relevant standards of conduct can give rise to an officer's liability to the corporation or its shareholders. A court review of challenged conduct will involve an evaluation of the particular facts and circumstances in light of applicable law. In this connection, section 8.42(d) recognizes that relevant principles of section 8.31, such as duties to deal fairly with the corporation and its shareholders and the challenger's burden of establishing proximately caused harm, should be taken into account. In addition, the business judgment rule will normally apply to decisions within an officer's discretionary authority. Liability to others can also arise from an officer's own acts or omissions (*e.g.*, violations of law or tort claims) and, in some cases, an officer with supervisory responsibilities can have risk exposure in connection with the acts or omissions of others.

The Official Comment to section 8.30 supplements this Official Comment to the extent that it can be appropriately viewed as generally applicable to officers as well as directors.

§8.43. Resignation and Removal of Officers

(a) An officer may resign at any time by delivering a written notice to the board of directors, or its chair, or to the appointing officer or the secretary. A resignation is effective as provided in section 1.41(i) unless the notice provides for a delayed effectiveness, including effectiveness determined upon a future event or events. If effectiveness of a resignation is stated to be delayed and the board of directors or the appointing officer accepts the delay, the board of directors or the appointing officer may fill the pending vacancy before the delayed effectiveness but the new officer may not take office until the vacancy occurs.

(b) An officer may be removed at any time with or without cause by (i) the board of directors; (ii) the appointing officer, unless the bylaws or the board of directors provide otherwise; or (iii) any other officer if authorized by the bylaws or the board of directors.

(c) In this section, "appointing officer" means the officer (including any successor to that officer) who appointed the officer resigning or being removed.

OFFICIAL COMMENT

In part because of the unlimited power of removal under section 8.43(b), a corporation may enter into an employment agreement with the holder of an office that gives the officer rights in the event of removal or failure to be reelected or reappointed to office. This type of contract is binding on the corporation even if the articles of incorporation or bylaws provide that officers are elected for a term shorter than the period of the employment contract. Such an employment agreement does not override the removal power set forth in section 8.43(b) and may give the officer the right to damages, but not specific performance, if employment is terminated before the end of the contract term.

Section 8.43(b) provides the corporation with the flexibility to determine when, if ever, an officer will be permitted to remove another officer. To the extent that the corporation wishes to permit an officer, other than the appointing officer, to remove another officer, the bylaws or a board resolution should set forth clearly the persons having removal authority.

A person may be removed from office irrespective of contract rights or the presence or absence of "cause" in a legal sense.

§8.44. Contract Rights of Officers

(a) The election or appointment of an officer does not itself create contract rights.

(b) An officer's removal does not affect the officer's contract rights, if any, with the corporation. An officer's resignation does not affect the corporation's contract rights, if any, with the officer.

OFFICIAL COMMENT

The removal of an officer with contract rights is without prejudice to the officer's rights in a proceeding seeking damages for breach of contract. See the Official Comment to section 8.43. Similarly, an officer with an employment contract who prematurely resigns may be in breach of his or her employment contract. The mere election or appointment of an officer for a term does not create a contractual obligation on the officer's part to complete the term.

SUBCHAPTER E. INDEMNIFICATION AND ADVANCE FOR EXPENSES

INTRODUCTORY COMMENT

1. Policy Issues Raised by Indemnification and Advance for Expenses

Indemnification (including advance for expenses) provides financial protection by the corporation for its directors against exposure to expenses and liabilities that may be incurred by them in connection with legal proceedings based on an alleged breach of duty in their service to or on behalf of the corporation.

The concept of indemnification recognizes that there will be situations in which even though the director does not satisfy all of the elements of the standard of conduct set forth in section 8.30(a) or the requirements of some other applicable law, the corporation should nevertheless be permitted (or required) to absorb the economic costs incurred by the director in any ensuing litigation.

Subchapter 8E is an integrated treatment of indemnification and advance for expenses and strikes a balance among important public policies. It would be difficult to persuade responsible persons to serve as directors if they were compelled to bear personally the cost of vindicating the propriety of their conduct in every instance in which it might be challenged. If permitted too broadly, however, indemnification may violate equally basic tenets of public policy. For example, a director who intentionally inflicts harm on the corporation should not expect to receive assistance from the corporation for legal or other expenses and should be required to satisfy from his or her personal assets not only any adverse judgment but also expenses incurred in connection with the proceeding. A similar policy issue is raised in connection with indemnification against liabilities or sanctions imposed under state or federal civil or criminal statutes. A shift of the economic cost of these liabilities from the individual director to the corporation by way of indemnification may in some instances frustrate the public policy of those statutes.

Some of the same policy considerations apply to the indemnification of officers and, in many cases, employees and agents. The indemnification of officers, whose duties are specified in section 8.42, is dealt with separately in section 8.56. The indemnification of employees and agents, whose duties are prescribed by sources of law other than corporation law (*e.g.*, contract and agency law), is beyond the scope of this subchapter. Section 8.58(d), however, makes clear that subchapter E does not limit a corporation's power to indemnify or advance expenses to employees and agents in accordance with applicable law.

2. *Relationship of Indemnification to Other Policies Established in the Act*

Indemnification is closely related to the standards of conduct for directors and officers established elsewhere in chapter 8. The structure of the Act is based on the assumption that if a director acts consistently with the standards of conduct described in section 8.30 or with the standards of a liability-limitation provision in the articles of incorporation (as authorized by section 2.02(b)(4)), the director will not have exposure to liability to the corporation or to shareholders and any expenses necessary to establish a defense will be borne by the corporation (under section 8.52). The converse, however, is not necessarily true. The basic standards for indemnification set forth in section 8.51 for a civil action, in the absence of an indemnification provision in the articles of incorporation (as authorized by section 2.02(b)(5)), are good faith and reasonable belief that the conduct was in or not opposed to the best interests of the corporation. In some circumstances, a director or officer may be found to have violated a statutory or common law duty and yet be able to establish eligibility for indemnification under these standards of conduct. In addition, subchapter E permits a director or officer who is held liable for violating a statutory or common law duty, but who does not meet the relevant standard of conduct, to petition a court to order indemnification under section 8.54 if the court determines that it would be fair and reasonable to do so.

§8.50. Subchapter Definitions

In this subchapter:

- "Corporation" includes any domestic or foreign predecessor entity of a corporation in a merger.
- "Director" or "officer" means an individual who is or was a director or officer, respectively, of a corporation or who, while a director or officer of the corporation, is or was serving at the corporation's request as a director, officer, manager, partner, trustee, employee, or agent of another entity or employee benefit plan. A director or officer is considered to be serving an employee benefit plan at the corporation's request if the individual's duties to the corporation also impose duties on, or otherwise involve services by, the individual to the plan or to participants in or beneficiaries of the plan. "Director" or "officer" includes, unless the context requires otherwise, the estate or personal representative of a director or officer.
- "Liability" means the obligation to pay a judgment, settlement, penalty, fine (including an excise tax assessed with respect to an employee benefit plan), or expenses incurred with respect to a proceeding.
- "Official capacity" means: (i) when used with respect to a director, the office of director in a corporation; and (ii) when used with respect to an officer, as contemplated in section 8.56, the office in a corporation held by the officer. "Official capacity" does not include service for any other domestic or foreign corporation or any joint venture, trust, employee benefit plan, or other entity.

– "Party" means an individual who was, is, or is threatened to be made, a defendant or respondent in a proceeding.

"Proceeding" means any threatened, pending, or completed action, suit, or proceeding, whether civil, criminal, administrative, arbitrative, or investigative and whether formal or informal.

OFFICIAL COMMENT

The definitions set forth in section 8.50 apply only to subchapter E and have no application elsewhere in the Act, except for the use of "liability" in section 2.02(b)(5). The term "qualified director," which is used in sections 8.53 and 8.55, is defined in section 1.43.

1. Corporation

Subchapter E's definition of "corporation" includes predecessor entities that have been absorbed in mergers to negate any argument that a different result might be reached under section 11.07(a), which provides for the assumption of liabilities by operation of law upon a merger. The express responsibility of successor entities for the liabilities of their predecessors under this subchapter is broader than under section 11.07(a) and may impose liability on a successor although section 11.07(a) does not. The definition of "corporation" in section 8.50 is thus an essential aspect of the protection provided by this subchapter for persons eligible for indemnification.

2. Director and Officer

A special definition of "director" and "officer" is included in subchapter E to cover individuals who are made parties to proceedings because they are or were directors or officers or, while serving as directors or officers, also serve or served at the corporation's request in another capacity for another entity. The purpose of the latter part of this definition is to give directors and officers the benefits of the protection of this subchapter while serving at the corporation's request in a responsible position for employee benefit plans, trade associations, nonprofit or charitable entities, domestic or foreign entities, or other kinds of profit or nonprofit ventures. To avoid misunderstanding, it is good practice from both the corporation's and director's or officer's viewpoint for this type of request to be evidenced by resolution, memorandum or other writing.

Even without such a formal action, the second sentence of the definition of "director" or "officer" in section 8.50 addresses the question of liabilities arising under the Employee Retirement Income Security Act of 1974 (ERISA). It makes clear that a director or officer who is serving as a fiduciary of an employee benefit plan is automatically viewed for purposes of this subchapter as having been requested by the corporation to act in that capacity. Special treatment is believed necessary because of ERISA's broad definition of "fiduciary" and the requirement that a "fiduciary" must discharge his or her duties "solely in the interest" of the participants and beneficiaries of the employee benefit plan. Decisions by a director or officer, who is serving as a fiduciary under the plan on questions regarding, for example, (i) eligibility for benefits, (ii) investment decisions, or (iii) interpretation of plan provisions respecting (a) qualifying service, (b) years of service, or (c) retroactivity, are all subject to the protections of this subchapter. See also the definition of "official capacity" in section 8.50.

In the last sentence of the definition of "director" or "officer" in section 8.50, the phrase "unless the context requires otherwise" is intended to clarify that the estate or personal representative does not have the right to participate in decisions by directors authorized in this subchapter. . . .

§8.51. Permissible Indemnification

(a) Except as otherwise provided in this section, a corporation may indemnify an individual who is a party to a proceeding because the individual is a director against liability incurred in the proceeding if:

(1) (i) the director conducted himself or herself in good faith; and

(ii) the director reasonably believed:

(A) in the case of conduct in an official capacity, that his or her conduct was in the best interests of the corporation; and

(B) in all other cases, that his or her conduct was at least not opposed to the best interests of the corporation; and

(iii) in the case of any criminal proceeding, the director had no reasonable cause to believe his or her conduct was unlawful; or

(2) the director engaged in conduct for which broader indemnification has been made permissible or obligatory under a provision of the articles of incorporation (as authorized by section 2.02(b)(5)).

(b) A director's conduct with respect to an employee benefit plan for a purpose the director reasonably believed to be in the interests of the participants in, and the beneficiaries of, the plan is conduct that satisfies the requirement of subsection (a)(1)(ii)(B).

(c) The termination of a proceeding by judgment, order, settlement, or conviction, or upon a plea of nolo contendere or its equivalent, is not, of itself, determinative that the director did not meet the relevant standard of conduct described in this section.

(d) Unless ordered by a court under section 8.54(a)(3), a corporation may not indemnify a director:

(1) in connection with a proceeding by or in the right of the corporation, except for expenses incurred in connection with the proceeding if it is determined that the director has met the relevant standard of conduct under subsection (a); or

(2) in connection with any proceeding with respect to conduct for which the director was adjudged liable on the basis of receiving a financial benefit to which he or she was not entitled, regardless of whether it involved action in the director's official capacity.

OFFICIAL COMMENT

1. Section 8.51(a) . . .

In section 8.51(a)(1)(ii)(B), the words "at least" qualify "not opposed to" and make clear that this standard is for conduct other than in an official capacity. Although this provision deals with indemnification by the corporation, a director serving another entity at the request of the corporation remains subject to the provisions of the law governing service to that other entity, including provisions dealing with conflicts of interest. Compare sections 8.60 through 8.63. Should indemnification from the requesting corporation be sought by a director for acts done while serving another entity, which acts involved breach of a duty owed to that other entity, nothing in section 8.51(a)(1)(ii)(B) would preclude the requesting corporation from considering, in assessing its own best interests, whether the fact that its director had engaged in a violation of the duty owed to the other entity was in fact "opposed to" the interests of the indemnifying corporation.

If the relevant standards are met, section 8.51 also permits indemnification in connection with a proceeding involving an alleged failure to satisfy legal standards other than the standards of conduct in section 8.30, *e.g.*, violations of antitrust, environmental or securities laws. . . .

2. *Section 8.51(b)*

As discussed in the Official Comment to the definition of "director" or "officer" in section 8.50, ERISA requires that a "fiduciary" (as defined in ERISA) discharge the fiduciary's duties "solely in the interest" of the participants in and beneficiaries of an employee benefit plan. The standard in section 8.51(b) for indemnification of a director who is serving as a trustee or fiduciary for an employee benefit plan under ERISA is arguably an exception to the more general standard that conduct not in an official corporate capacity is indemnifiable if it is "at least not opposed to" the best interests of the corporation. However, a corporation that causes a director to undertake fiduciary duties in connection with an employee benefit plan should expect the director to act in the best interests of the plan's beneficiaries or participants. Thus, subsection (b) establishes and provides a standard for indemnification that is consistent with the statutory policies embodied in ERISA. See Official Comment to section 8.50(2).

3. *Section 8.51(c)*

Section 8.51(c) rejects the argument that indemnification is automatically improper whenever a proceeding has been concluded on a basis that does not exonerate the director claiming indemnification. However, any judicial determination of substantive liability should be taken into account in determining whether the standards of section 8.51(a) were met. By the same token, it is clear that the termination of a proceeding by settlement or plea of no contest should not of itself create a presumption either that conduct met or did not meet the relevant standard of subsection (a) since a settlement or nolo plea may be agreed to for many reasons unrelated to the merits of the claim. On the other hand, a final determination of non-liability (including one based on a liability-limitation provision adopted under section 2.02(b)(4)) or an acquittal in a criminal case automatically entitles the director to indemnification of expenses under section 8.52.

4. *Section 8.51(d)*

Section 8.51(d) does not permit indemnification of settlements and judgments in derivative proceedings which would give rise to a circularity in which the corporation receiving payment of damages by the director in the settlement or judgment (less attorneys' fees) would then immediately return the same amount to the director (including attorneys' fees) as indemnification. Thus, the corporation would be in a poorer economic position than if there had been no proceeding. . . .

§8.52. Mandatory Indemnification

A corporation shall indemnify a director who was wholly successful, on the merits or otherwise, in the defense of any proceeding to which the director was a party because he or she was a director of the corporation against expenses incurred by the director in connection with the proceeding.

§8.53. Advance for Expenses

(a) A corporation may, before final disposition of a proceeding, advance funds to pay for or reimburse expenses incurred in connection with the proceeding by an individual who is a party to the proceeding because that individual is a director if the director delivers to the corporation a signed written undertaking of the director to repay any funds advanced if (i) the director is not entitled to mandatory indemnification under section 8.52 and (ii) it is ultimately determined under section 8.54 or section 8.55 that the director is not entitled to indemnification.

(b) The undertaking required by subsection (a) must be an unlimited general obligation of the director but need not be secured and may be accepted without reference to the financial ability of the director to make repayment.

(c) Authorizations under this section shall be made:

(1) by the board of directors:

(i) if there are two or more qualified directors, by a majority vote of all the qualified directors (a majority of whom shall for such purpose constitute a quorum) or by a majority of the members of a committee consisting solely of two or more qualified directors appointed by such a vote; or

(ii) if there are fewer than two qualified directors, by the vote necessary for action by the board of directors in accordance with section 8.24(c), in which authorization directors who are not qualified directors may participate; or

(2) by the shareholders, but shares owned by or voted under the control of a director who at the time is not a qualified director may not be voted on the authorization.

OFFICIAL COMMENT

Section 8.53 authorizes, but does not require, a corporation to advance or reimburse a director's reasonable expenses, subject to the delivery of the repayment undertaking required by subsection (a) and any limitations set forth in the articles of incorporation pursuant to section 8.58(d). The repayment undertaking required by section 8.53 is also required in connection with obligatory advancement pursuant to section 8.58(a).

Section 8.53 recognizes an important difference between indemnification and an advance for expenses: indemnification is retrospective and, therefore, enables the persons determining whether to indemnify to do so on the basis of known facts, including the outcome of the proceeding. Indemnification may include reimbursement for non-advanced expenses. Advance for expenses is necessarily prospective and, in situations where advancement is not obligatory, the individuals making the decision whether to authorize expense advancement generally have fewer known facts on which to base their decision.

Section 8.53 reflects a determination that it is sound public policy to permit the corporation to advance (by direct payment or by reimbursement) the defense expenses of a director so long as the director agrees to repay any amounts advanced if it is ultimately determined that the director is not entitled to indemnification. This policy is based upon the view that a person who serves an entity in a representative capacity should not be required to finance his or her own defense of actions taken in that capacity. Moreover, adequate legal representation often involves substantial expenses during the course of the proceeding and many individuals are willing to serve as directors only if they have the assurance that the corporation will advance these expenses. Accordingly, many corporations enter into contractual obligations (*e.g.*, by a provision in the articles of incorporation or bylaws or by individual agreements) to advance expenses for directors. See section 8.58(a). . . .

A corporation may obligate itself pursuant to section 8.58(a) to advance for expenses under section 8.53 by means of a provision set forth in the articles of incorporation or bylaws, by a resolution of its board of directors or shareholders, or by an agreement. Unless provided otherwise, section 8.58(a) deems a general obligatory provision requiring indemnification to the fullest extent permitted by law to include advance for expenses to the fullest extent permitted by law, even if not specifically mentioned, subject to providing the required repayment undertaking. . . .

§8.54. Court-Ordered Indemnification and Advance for Expenses

(a) A director who is a party to a proceeding because he or she is a director may apply for indemnification or an advance for expenses to the court conducting the proceeding or to another court of competent jurisdiction. After receipt of an application and after giving any notice it considers necessary, the court shall:

(1) order indemnification if the court determines that the director is entitled to mandatory indemnification under section 8.52;

(2) order indemnification or advance for expenses if the court determines that the director is entitled to indemnification or advance for expenses pursuant to a provision authorized by section 8.58(a); or

(3) order indemnification or advance for expenses if the court determines, in view of all the relevant circumstances, that it is fair and reasonable (i) to indemnify the director, or (ii) to advance expenses to the director, even if, in the case of (i) or (ii), he or she has not met the relevant standard of conduct set forth in section 8.51(a), failed to comply with section 8.53 or was adjudged liable in a proceeding referred to in section 8.51(d)(1) or (d)(2), but if the director was adjudged so liable indemnification shall be limited to expenses incurred in connection with the proceeding.

(b) If the court determines that the director is entitled to indemnification under subsection (a)(1) or to indemnification or advance for expenses under subsection (a)(2), it shall also order the corporation to pay the director's expenses incurred in connection with obtaining court-ordered indemnification or advance for expenses. If the court determines that the director is entitled to indemnification or advance for expenses under subsection (a)(3), it may also order the corporation to pay the director's expenses to obtain court-ordered indemnification or advance for expenses.

§8.55. Determination and Authorization of Indemnification

(a) A corporation may not indemnify a director under section 8.51 unless authorized for a specific proceeding after a determination has been made that indemnification is permissible because the director has met the relevant standard of conduct set forth in section 8.51.

(b) The determination shall be made:

(1) if there are two or more qualified directors, by the board of directors by a majority vote of all the qualified directors (a majority of whom shall for such purpose constitute a quorum), or by a majority of the members of a committee of two or more qualified directors appointed by such a vote;

(2) by special legal counsel:

(i) selected in the manner prescribed in subsection (b)(1); or

(ii) if there are fewer than two qualified directors, selected by the board of directors (in which selection directors who are not qualified directors may participate); or

(3) by the shareholders, but shares owned by or voted under the control of a director who at the time is not a qualified director may not be voted on the determination.

(c) Authorization of indemnification shall be made in the same manner as the determination that indemnification is permissible except that if there are fewer than two qualified directors, or if the determination is made by special legal counsel, authorization of indemnification shall be made by those entitled to select special legal counsel under subsection (b)(2)(ii).

§8.56. Indemnification of Officers

(a) A corporation may indemnify and advance expenses under this subchapter to an officer who is a party to a proceeding because he or she is an officer

(1) to the same extent as a director; and

(2) if he or she is an officer but not a director, to such further extent as may be provided by the articles of incorporation or the bylaws, or by a resolution adopted or a contract approved by the board of directors or shareholders, except for

(i) liability in connection with a proceeding by or in the right of the corporation other than for expenses incurred in connection with the proceeding, or

(ii) liability arising out of conduct that constitutes

(A) receipt by the officer of a financial benefit to which he or she is not entitled,

(B) an intentional infliction of harm on the corporation or the shareholders, or

(C) an intentional violation of criminal law.

(b) Subsection (a)(2) shall apply to an officer who is also a director if he or she is made a party to the proceeding based on an act or omission solely as an officer.

(c) An officer who is not a director is entitled to mandatory indemnification under section 8.52, and may apply to a court under section 8.54 for indemnification or an advance for expenses, in each case to the same extent to which a director may be entitled to indemnification or advance for expenses under those sections.

§8.57. Insurance

A corporation may purchase and maintain insurance on behalf of an individual who is a director or officer of the corporation, or who, while a director or officer of the corporation, serves at the corporation's request as a director, officer, partner, trustee, employee, or agent of another domestic or foreign corporation or a joint venture, trust, employee benefit plan, or other entity, against liability asserted against or incurred by the individual in that capacity or arising from the individual's status as a director or officer, regardless of whether the corporation would have power to indemnify or advance expenses to the individual against the same liability under this subchapter.

§8.58. Variation by Corporate Action; Application of Subchapter

(a) A corporation may, by a provision in its articles of incorporation or bylaws or in a resolution adopted or a contract approved by the board of directors or shareholders, obligate itself in advance of the act or omission giving rise to a proceeding to provide indemnification in accordance with section 8.51 or advance funds to pay for or reimburse expenses in accordance with section 8.53. Any such obligatory provision shall be deemed to satisfy the requirements for authorization referred to in section 8.53(c) and in section 8.55(c). Any such provision that obligates the corporation to provide indemnification to the fullest extent permitted by law shall be deemed to obligate the corporation to advance funds to pay for or reimburse expenses in accordance with section 8.53 to the fullest extent permitted by law, unless the provision expressly provides otherwise.

(b) A right of indemnification or to advances for expenses created by this subchapter or under subsection (a) and in effect at the time of an act or omission shall not be eliminated or impaired with respect to such act or omission by an amendment of the articles of incorporation or bylaws or a resolution of the board of directors or shareholders, adopted after the occurrence of such act or omission, unless, in the case of a right created under subsection (a), the provision creating such right and in effect at the time of such act or omission explicitly authorizes such elimination or impairment after such act or omission has occurred.

(c) Any provision pursuant to subsection (a) shall not obligate the corporation to indemnify or advance expenses to a director of a predecessor of the corporation, pertaining to conduct with respect to the predecessor, unless otherwise expressly provided. Any provision for indemnification or advance for expenses in the articles of incorporation or bylaws, or a resolution of the board of directors or shareholders of a predecessor of the corporation in a merger or in a contract to which the predecessor is a party, existing at the time the merger takes effect, shall be governed by section 11.07(a)(4).

(d) Subject to subsection (b), a corporation may, by a provision in its articles of incorporation, limit any of the rights to indemnification or advance for expenses created by or pursuant to this subchapter.

(e) This subchapter does not limit a corporation's power to pay or reimburse expenses incurred by a director or an officer in connection with appearing as a witness in a proceeding at a time when he or she is not a party.

(f) This subchapter does not limit a corporation's power to indemnify, advance expenses to or provide or maintain insurance on behalf of an employee or agent.

§8.59. Exclusivity of Subchapter

A corporation may provide indemnification or advance expenses to a director or an officer only as permitted by this subchapter.

OFFICIAL COMMENT

Subchapter E is the exclusive source for the power of a corporation to indemnify or advance expenses to a director or an officer.

Section 8.59 does not preclude provisions in the articles of incorporation, the bylaws, resolutions, or contracts designed to provide procedural machinery in addition to (but not inconsistent with) that provided by subchapter E. For example, a corporation may properly obligate the board of directors to consider and act expeditiously on an application for indemnification or advance for expenses or to cooperate in the procedural steps required to obtain a judicial determination under section 8.54.

SUBCHAPTER F. DIRECTOR'S CONFLICTING INTEREST TRANSACTIONS

INTRODUCTORY COMMENT

1. *Overview*

There are four basic elements in subchapter F.

First, subchapter F defines, with bright-line rules, the transactions that are to be treated as director's conflicting interest transactions.

Second, subchapter F provides that a director's transaction that is not within the statutory definition of a director's conflicting interest transaction is not subject to judicial review for fairness on the ground that it involved a conflict of interest (although circumstances that fall outside the statutory definition may afford the basis for a legal attack on the transaction on some other ground), even if the transaction involves some sort of conflict lying outside the statutory definition, such as a remote familial relationship.

Third, subchapter F provides that if a director's conflicting interest transaction is properly approved by disinterested (or "qualified") directors or shareholders, the transaction is insulated from judicial review for fairness (although, again, it might be open to attack on some basis other than the conflict).

Fourth, subchapter F also provides that if a director's conflicting interest transaction is properly approved by disinterested (or "qualified") directors or shareholders, the conflicted director may not be subject to an award of damages or other sanctions (although the director could be subject to claims on some basis other than the conflict).

Bright-line provisions of any kind represent a trade-off between the benefits of certainty and the danger that some transactions or conduct that fall outside the area circumscribed by the bright-lines may be so similar to the transactions and conduct that fall within the area that different treatment may seem anomalous. Subchapter F reflects the judgment that in corporate matters, where planning is critical, the clear and important efficiency gains that result from certainty through defining director's conflicting interest transactions exceed any potential and uncertain efficiency losses that might follow from excluding other director's transactions from judicial review for fairness on conflict-of-interest grounds.

2. *Scope of Subchapter F*

Subchapter F addresses legal challenges based on director conflicts of interest only. Subchapter F does not undertake to define, regulate, or provide any form of procedure regarding other possible claims. For example, subchapter F does not address a claim that a controlling shareholder has violated a duty owed to the corporation or minority shareholders. So, although transactions between a corporation and a parent corporation or other controlling shareholder who owns less than all of its shares may give rise to the possibility of abuse of power by the controlling shareholder, subchapter F does not address proceedings brought on that basis because section 8.61 concerns only proceedings that are brought on the ground that a "director has an interest respecting the transaction."

Subchapter F applies only when there is a "transaction" by or with the corporation. For purposes of subchapter F, "transaction" generally connotes negotiations or consensual arrangements between the corporation and another party or parties that concern their respective and differing economic rights or interests—not a unilateral action by the corporation or a director. Whether safe harbor procedures of some kind might be available to the director and the corporation with respect to non-transactional matters is discussed in numbered part 3 of this Introductory Comment.

Subchapter F does not preclude the assertion of defenses, such as statute of limitations or failure of a condition precedent, that are based on grounds other than the defenses set forth in this subchapter.

The voting procedures and conduct standards prescribed in subchapter F deal solely with the complicating element presented by the director's conflicting interest in a transaction. A transaction that receives favorable directors' or shareholders' action complying with subchapter F may still fail to satisfy a different quorum requirement or to achieve a different vote than may be needed for substantive approval of the transaction under other applicable statutory provisions or under the articles of incorporation, and vice versa. (Under the Act, a corporation may set higher voting requirements and different quorum requirements in the articles of incorporation. See sections 2.02(b)(2) and 7.27). In addition, subchapter F does not shield misbehavior by a director or other person that is actionable under other provisions of the Act, such as section 8.31, or under other legal rules, regardless of whether the misbehavior is incident to a transaction with the corporation and regardless of whether the rule is one of corporate law.

Finally, certain corporate transactions or arrangements in which directors inherently have a special personal interest are of a unique character and are regulated by special procedural provisions of the Act. See sections 8.51 and 8.52 dealing with indemnification arrangements, and section 7.44 dealing with termination of derivative proceedings by board action. Any corporate transactions or arrangements affecting directors that are governed by such regulatory sections of the Act are not governed by subchapter F.

3. *Nontransactional Situations Involving Interest Conflicts*

A. Corporate or Business Opportunity

Subchapter F does not apply by its terms to corporate or business opportunities because no transaction between the corporation and the director is involved in the taking of an opportunity. However, subchapter 8G provides, in effect, that the safe harbor procedures of section 8.62 or 8.63 may be employed, at the interested director's election, to protect the taking of a business opportunity that might be challenged under the corporate opportunity doctrine. Also, section 2.02(b)(6) permits a corporation to include in its articles of incorporation a provision that limits or eliminates the duty to present a business opportunity to the corporation.

B. Other Situations

Many other kinds of situations can give rise to divergent economic interests between a director and the corporation. For example, a director's personal financial interests can be affected by a nontransactional policy decision of the board of directors, such as where it decides to establish a divisional headquarters in the director's small hometown. In other situations, simple inaction by a board might work to a director's personal advantage, or a flow of ongoing business relationships between a director and the corporation may, without centering upon any discrete "transaction," raise questions of possible favoritism, unfair dealing, or undue influence. If a director decides to engage in business activity that directly competes with the corporation's own business, the economic interest in that competing activity ordinarily will conflict with the best interests of the corporation and put in issue the breach of the director's duties to the corporation. Basic conflicts and improprieties can also arise out of a director's personal appropriation of corporate assets or improper use of corporate proprietary or inside information.

The circumstances in which such nontransactional conflict situations should be brought to the board of directors or shareholders for clearance, and the legal effect, if any, of such clearance, are matters for development under the common law and lie outside the ambit of subchapter F. Although these nontransactional situations are not covered by the provisions of subchapter F, a court may well recognize that the subchapter F procedures provide a useful analogy for dealing with such situations.

* * * * *

Note on Terms in Official Comments

In the Official Comments to subchapter F, the director who has a conflicting interest is for convenience referred to as "the director" or "D," and the corporation of which he or she is a director is referred to as "the corporation" or "X Co." A subsidiary of the corporation is referred to as "S Co." Another corporation dealing with X Co. is referred to as "Y Co."

§8.60. *Subchapter Definitions*

In this subchapter:

– "Control" (including the term "controlled by") means (i) having the power, directly or indirectly, to elect or remove a majority of the members of the board of directors or other governing body of an entity, whether through the ownership of voting shares or interests, by contract, or otherwise, or (ii) being subject to a majority of the risk of loss from the entity's activities or entitled to receive a majority of the entity's residual returns.

- "Director's conflicting interest transaction" means a transaction effected or proposed to be effected by the corporation (or by an entity controlled by the corporation)

    (i) to which, at the relevant time, the director is a party;

    (ii) respecting which, at the relevant time, the director had knowledge and a material financial interest known to the director; or

    (iii) respecting which, at the relevant time, the director knew that a related person was a party or had a material financial interest.

- "Fair to the corporation" means, for purposes of section 8.61(b)(3), that the transaction as a whole was beneficial to the corporation, taking into appropriate account whether it was (i) fair in terms of the director's dealings with the corporation, and (ii) comparable to what might have been obtainable in an arm's length transaction, given the consideration paid or received by the corporation.

- "Material financial interest" means a financial interest in a transaction that would reasonably be expected to impair the objectivity of the director's judgment when participating in action on the authorization of the transaction.

- "Related person" means:

    (i) the individual's spouse;

    (ii) a child, stepchild, grandchild, parent, step parent, grandparent, sibling, step sibling, half sibling, aunt, uncle, niece or nephew (or spouse of any such person) of the individual or of the individual's spouse;

    (iii) a natural person living in the same home as the individual;

    (iv) an entity (other than the corporation or an entity controlled by the corporation) controlled by the individual or any person specified above in this definition;

    (v) a domestic or foreign (A) business or nonprofit corporation (other than the corporation or an entity controlled by the corporation) of which the individual is a director, (B) unincorporated entity of which the individual is a general partner or a member of the governing body, or (C) individual, trust or estate for whom or of which the individual is a trustee, guardian, personal representative or like fiduciary; or

    (vi) a person that is, or an entity that is controlled by, an employer of the individual.

- "Relevant time" means (i) the time at which directors' action respecting the transaction is taken in compliance with section 8.62, or (ii) if the transaction is not brought before the board of directors (or a committee) for action under section 8.62, at the time the corporation (or an entity controlled by the corporation) becomes legally obligated to consummate the transaction.

- "Required disclosure" means disclosure of (i) the existence and nature of the director's conflicting interest, and (ii) all facts known to the director respecting the subject matter of the transaction that a director free of such conflicting interest would reasonably believe to be material in deciding whether to proceed with the transaction.

OFFICIAL COMMENT

The definitions set forth in section 8.60 apply only to subchapter F and section 2.02(b)(6) and, where relevant to subchapter G. They have no application elsewhere in the Act. (For the meaning and use of certain terms used below, such as "D," "X Co." and "Y Co.," see the Note on Terms at the end of the Introductory Comment of subchapter F.)

1. *Director's Conflicting Interest Transaction*

The definition of "director's conflicting interest transaction" in section 8.60 is the core concept underlying subchapter F. The definition operates preclusively in that, as used in section 8.61, it denies the power of a court to invalidate transactions or otherwise to remedy conduct on the ground that the director has a conflict of interest if it falls outside the statutory definition of "director's conflicting interest transaction."

a. Transaction

For purposes of subchapter F, "transaction" requires a bilateral (or multilateral) arrangement to which the corporation or an entity controlled by the corporation is a party. Subchapter F does not apply to transactions to which no such entity is a party. For example, a purchase or sale by the director of the corporation's shares on the open market or from or to a third party is not a "director's conflicting interest transaction" within the meaning of subchapter F.

b. Party to the transaction—the corporation or a controlled entity

In the usual case, the transaction would be effected by X Co. Assume, however, that X Co. controls the vote for directors of S Co. D wishes to sell a building D owns to X Co. and X Co. is willing to buy it. As a business matter, it makes no difference to X Co. whether it takes the title directly or indirectly through its subsidiary S Co. or some other entity that X Co. controls. The applicability of subchapter F does not depend upon that formal distinction, because the subchapter includes within its operative framework transactions by entities controlled by X Co. Thus, subchapter F would apply to a sale of the building by D to S Co.

c. Party to the transaction—the director or a related person

D can have a conflicting interest in only two ways.

First, a conflicting interest can arise under either clause (i) or (ii) of the definition of "director's conflicting interest transaction." This will be the case if, under clause (i), the transaction is between D and X Co. A conflicting interest also will arise under clause (ii) if D is not a party to the transaction, but knows about it and knows that he or she has a material financial interest in it. The personal economic stake of the director must be in the transaction itself—that is, the director's gain must flow directly from the transaction. A remote gain (for example, a future reduction in tax rates in the local community) is not enough to give rise to a conflicting interest under clause (ii) of the definition.

Second, a conflicting interest for D can arise under clause (iii) of the definition from the involvement in the transaction of a "related person" of D that is either a party to the transaction or has a "material financial interest" in it. "Related person" is defined in section 8.60.

Circumstances may arise where a director could have a conflicting interest under more than one clause of the definition. For example, if Y Co. is a party to or interested in the transaction with X Co. and Y Co. is a related person of D, the matter would fall under clause (iii), but D also may have a conflicting interest under clause (ii) if D's economic interest in Y Co. is sufficiently material and if the importance of the transaction to Y Co. is sufficiently material.

A director may have relationships and connections to persons and institutions that are not specified in clause (iii) of the definition. Such relationships and connections fall outside subchapter F because the categories of persons described in clause (iii) constitute the exclusive universe for purposes of subchapter F. For example, in a challenged transaction between X Co. and Y Co., suppose the court confronts the argument that D also is a major creditor of Y Co. and that creditor status in Y Co. gives D a conflicting interest. The court should rule that D's creditor status in Y Co. does not fit any category of the definition; and therefore, the conflict of interest claim must be rejected by reason of section 8.61(a). The result would be different if Y Co.'s debt to D were of such economic significance to D that it would either fall under clause (ii) of the definition or, if it placed D in control of Y Co., it would fall under clause (iii) (because Y Co. is a related person of D under clause (iv) of the definition). To explore the example further, if D is also a shareholder of Y Co., but D does not have a material financial interest in the transaction and does not control Y Co., no director's conflicting interest transaction arises and the transaction cannot be challenged on conflict of interest grounds. To avoid any appearance of impropriety, D, nonetheless, could consider recusal from the other directors' deliberations and voting on the transaction between X Co. and Y Co.

Any director's interest in a transaction that meets the criteria of the definition renders the transaction a "director's conflicting interest transaction." If the director's interest satisfies those criteria, subchapter F draws no distinction between a director's interest that clashes with the interests of the corporation and a director's interest that coincides with, or is parallel to, or even furthers the interests of the corporation.

Routine business transactions frequently occur between companies with overlapping directors. If X Co. and Y Co. have routine, frequent business dealings with terms dictated by competitive market forces, then even if a director of X Co. has a relevant relationship with Y Co., the transactions would almost always be defensible, regardless of approval by disinterested directors or shareholders, on the ground that they are "fair." For example, a common transaction involves a purchase of the corporation's products or services by Y Co., or perhaps by D or a related person, at prices normally charged by the corporation. In such circumstances, it usually will not be difficult for D to show that the transaction was on arms-length terms and was fair. Even a purchase by D of a product of X Co. at a usual "employee's discount," although technically assailable as a conflicting interest transaction, would customarily be viewed as a routine incident of the office of director and, thus, "fair" to the corporation.

2. *Control*

The definition of "control" in section 8.60 contains two independent clauses. The first clause addresses the ability to elect or remove a majority of the members of an entity's governing body. That power can arise, for example, from articles of incorporation or a shareholders' agreement. The second clause addresses economic interest in the entity and may include, among other circumstances, financial structures that do not have voting interests or a governing body in the traditional sense, such as special purpose entities.

3. Relevant Time

The definition of director's conflicting interest transaction requires that, except where he or she is a party, the director know of the transaction at the "relevant time" as defined in section 8.60. Where the director lacks such knowledge, the risk to the corporation that the director's judgment might be improperly influenced, or the risk of unfair dealing by the director, is not present. In a corporation of significant size, routine transactions in the ordinary course of business, which typically involve decision making at lower management levels, normally will not be known to the director and, if that is the case, will not meet the "knowledge" requirement of clauses (ii) or (iii) of the definition of director's conflicting interest transaction.

4. Material Financial Interest

The "interest" of a director or a related person in a transaction can be direct or indirect (*e.g.*, as an owner of an entity or a beneficiary of a trust or estate), but it must be financial for there to exist a "director's conflicting interest transaction." Thus, for example, an interest in a transaction between X Co. and a director's alma mater, or any other transaction involving X Co. and a party with which D might have emotional involvement but no financial interest, would not give rise to a director's conflicting interest transaction. Moreover, whether a financial interest is material does not turn on any assertion by the possibly conflicted director that the interest in question would not impair his or her objectivity if called upon to vote on the authorization of the transaction. Instead, assuming a court challenge asserting the materiality of the financial interest, the standard calls upon the trier of fact to determine whether the objectivity of the director would reasonably be expected to have been impaired by the financial interest when voting on the matter. Thus, the standard is objective, not subjective.

Under clause (ii) of the definition of "director's conflicting interest transaction," at the relevant time a director must have knowledge of his or her financial interest in the transaction in addition to knowing about the transaction itself. As a practical matter, a director could not be influenced by a financial interest about which that director had no knowledge. For example, the possibly conflicted director might know about X Co.'s transaction with Y Co., but might not know that his or her money manager recently established a significant position in Y Co. stock for the director's portfolio. In such circumstances, the transaction with Y Co. would not fall within clause (ii), notwithstanding the portfolio investment's significance. If the director did not know about the Y Co. portfolio investment, it could not reasonably be expected to impair the objectivity of that director's judgment.

Similarly, under clause (iii) of that definition, a director must know about his or her related person's financial interest in the transaction for the matter to give rise to a "material financial interest" as defined in section 8.60. If there is such knowledge and "interest" (*i.e.*, the financial interest could reasonably be expected to influence the director's judgment), then the matter involves a director's conflicting interest transaction.

5. Related Person

Six categories of "related person" of the director are set out in the definition of that term. These categories are specific, exclusive and preemptive.

The first three categories involve closely related family, or near-family, individuals as specified in clauses (i) through (iii). These clauses are exclusive insofar as family relationships are concerned and include adoptive relationships. The references to a "spouse" include a common law spouse. Clause (iii) covers personal, as opposed to business, relationships; for example, clause (iii) does not cover a lessee.

Regarding the subcategories of persons described in clause (v) from the perspective of X Co., certain of D's relationships with other entities and D's fiduciary relationships are always a sensitive concern, separate and apart from whether D has a financial interest in the transaction. Clause (v) reflects the policy judgment that D cannot escape D's legal obligation to act in the best interests of another person for whom D has such a relationship and, accordingly, that such a relationship (without regard to any financial interest on D's part) should cause the relevant entity to have "related person" status.

The term "employer" as used in clause (vi) is not separately defined but should be interpreted in light of the purpose of subchapter F. The relevant inquiry is whether D, because of an employment relationship with an employer who has a significant stake in the outcome of the transaction, is likely to be influenced to act in the interest of that employer rather than in the interest of X Co.

References in the foregoing to "director" or "D" include the term "officer" where relevant in section 2.02(b)(6) and section 8.70.

6. *Fair to the Corporation*

The term "fair" to the corporation in subchapter F has a special meaning. The transaction, viewed as a whole, must have been beneficial to the corporation.

In considering the "fairness" of the transaction, the court will be required to consider not only the market fairness of the terms of the deal—whether it is comparable to what might have been obtainable in an arm's length transaction—but also (as the board of directors would have been required to do) whether the transaction was one that was reasonably likely to yield favorable results (or reduce detrimental results). Thus, if a manufacturing company that lacks sufficient working capital allocates some of its scarce funds to purchase at a market price a sailing yacht owned by one of its directors, it will not be easy to persuade the court that the transaction was "fair" in the sense that it was reasonably made to further the business interests of the corporation. The fact that the price paid for the yacht was a "fair" market price, and that the full measure of disclosures made by the director is beyond challenge, may still not be enough to defend and uphold the transaction.

a. Consideration and other terms of the transaction

The fairness of the consideration and other transaction terms are to be judged at the relevant time. See section 8.61(b)(3). The relevant inquiry is whether the consideration paid or received by the corporation or the benefit expected to be realized by the corporation was adequate in relation to the obligations assumed or received or other consideration provided by or to the corporation. If the issue in a transaction is the "fairness" of a price, "fair" is not to be taken to imply that there is one single "fair" price, all others being "unfair." Generally a "fair" price is any price within a range that an unrelated party might have been willing to pay or willing to accept, as the case may be, for the relevant property, asset, service or commitment, following a normal arm's-length business negotiation. The same approach applies not only to gauging the fairness of price, but also to the fairness evaluation of any other key term of the deal.

Although the "fair" criterion used to assess the consideration under section 8.61(b)(3) is also a range rather than a point, the width of that range may be narrower than would be the case in an arm's-length transaction. For example, the quality and completeness of disclosures, if any, made by the conflicted director that bear upon the consideration in question are relevant in determining whether the consideration paid or received by the corporation, although otherwise commercially reasonable, was "fair" for purposes of section 8.61(b)(3).

b. Process of decision and the director's conduct

In some circumstances, the behavior of the director having the conflicting interest may affect the finding and content of "fairness." Fair dealing requires that the director make "required disclosure" at the "relevant time" (both as defined) even if the director plays no role in arranging or negotiating the terms of the transaction. One illustration of unfair dealing is the director's failure to disclose fully the director's interest or hidden defects known to the director regarding the transaction. Another illustration would be the exertion by the director of improper pressure upon the other directors or other parties that might be involved with the transaction. Whether a transaction can be successfully challenged by reason of deficient or improper conduct, notwithstanding the fairness of the economic terms, will turn on the court's evaluation of the conduct and its impact on the transaction.

7. *Required Disclosure*

An important element of subchapter F's safe harbor procedures is that those acting for the corporation be able to make an informed judgment. As an example of "required disclosure" (as defined), if D knows that the land the corporation is proposing to buy from D is sinking into an abandoned coal mine, D must disclose not only D's interest in the transaction but also that the land is subsiding. As a director of X Co., D may not invoke the "buyer beware" doctrine. On the other hand, D does not have any obligation to reveal the price that D paid for the property 10 years ago, or the fact that D inherited the property, because that information is not material to the board's evaluation of the property and its business decision whether to proceed with the transaction. Further, although material facts respecting the subject of the transaction must be disclosed, D is not required to reveal personal or subjective information that bears upon D's negotiating position (such as, for example, D's urgent need for cash, or the lowest price D would be willing to accept). This is true even though such information would be highly relevant to the corporation's decision-making in that, if the information were known to the corporation, it could enable the corporation to hold out for more favorable terms.

§8.61. Judicial Action

(a) A transaction effected or proposed to be effected by the corporation (or by an entity controlled by the corporation) may not be the subject of equitable relief, or give rise to an award of damages or other sanctions against a director of the corporation, in a proceeding by a shareholder or by or in the right of the corporation, on the ground that the director has an interest respecting the transaction, if it is not a director's conflicting interest transaction.

(b) A director's conflicting interest transaction may not be the subject of equitable relief, or give rise to an award of damages or other sanctions against a director of the corporation, in a proceeding by a shareholder or by or in the right of the corporation, on the ground that the director has an interest respecting the transaction, if:

(1) directors' action respecting the transaction was taken in compliance with section 8.62 at any time; or

(2) shareholders' action respecting the transaction was taken in compliance with section 8.63 at any time; or

(3) the transaction, judged according to the circumstances at the relevant time, is established to have been fair to the corporation.

Shareholders' action, see §8.63.
Standards of conduct for directors, see §8.30.

OFFICIAL COMMENT

Section 8.61 is the operational section of subchapter F, as it prescribes the judicial consequences of the other sections. In general terms:

- If the section 8.62 or 8.63 procedures are complied with, or if it is established that at the relevant time a director's conflicting interest transaction was fair to the corporation, then a director's conflicting interest transaction is immune from attack by a shareholder or the corporation on the ground of an interest of the director. However, if the transaction is vulnerable to attack on some other ground, observance of subchapter F's procedures does not make it less so.
- If a transaction is *not* a director's conflicting interest transaction as defined in section 8.60, then the transaction may *not* be enjoined, rescinded, or made the basis of other sanction on the ground of a conflict of interest of a director, regardless of whether it went through the procedures of subchapter F. In that sense, subchapter F is specifically intended to be both comprehensive and exclusive.
- If a director's conflicting interest transaction that was not at any time the subject of action taken in compliance with section 8.62 or 8.63 is challenged on grounds of the director's conflicting interest, and is not shown to be fair to the corporation, then the court may take such remedial action as it considers appropriate under the applicable law of the jurisdiction.

1. Section 8.61(a)

Section 8.61(a) makes clear that the bright-line definition of "director's conflicting interest transaction" is exclusive with respect to a court's review of a director's interest in a transaction. So, for example, a transaction will not constitute a director's conflicting interest transaction and, therefore, will not be subject to judicial review on the ground that a director had an interest in the transaction, where the transaction is made with a relative of a director who is not one of the relatives specified in the definition of "related person," or on the ground of an alleged interest other than a material financial interest, such as a financial interest of the director that is not material, as defined in section 8.60, or a nonfinancial interest. If, however, there is reason to believe that the fairness of a transaction involving D could be questioned, D should subject the transaction to the safe harbor procedures of subchapter F. The procedures of section 8.62 (and, to a lesser extent, section 8.63) may be used for many transactions that lie outside the definitions of section 8.60.

2. *Section 8.61(b)*

Section 8.61(b)(1) provides a defense in a proceeding challenging a director's conflicting interest transaction if the procedures of section 8.62 have been properly followed.

The plaintiff may challenge the availability of that defense based on a failure to meet the specific requirements of section 8.62 or to conform with general standards of director conduct. For example, a challenge addressed to section 8.62 compliance might question whether the acting directors were "qualified directors" or might dispute the quality and completeness of the disclosures made by D to the qualified directors. If such a challenge is successful, the board action is ineffective for purposes of section 8.61(b)(1) and both D and the transaction may be subject to the full range of remedies that might apply, absent the safe harbor, unless the fairness of the transaction can be established under section 8.61(b)(3). The fact that a transaction has been nominally passed through safe harbor procedures does not preclude a subsequent challenge based on any failure to meet the requirements of section 8.62. A challenge to the effectiveness of board action for purposes of section 8.61(b)(1) might also assert that, although the conflicted director's conduct in connection with the process of approval by qualified directors may have been consistent with the statute's expectations, the qualified directors dealing with the matter did not act in good faith or on reasonable inquiry. The kind of relief that may be appropriate when qualified directors have approved a transaction but have not acted in good faith or have failed to become reasonably informed—and, again, where the fairness of the transaction has not been established under section 8.61(b)(3)—will depend heavily on the facts of the individual case.

Section 8.61(b)(2) regarding shareholders' approval of the transaction is the matching piece to section 8.61(b)(1) regarding directors' approval.

The language "at any time" in these provisions permits the directors or the shareholders to ratify a director's conflicting interest transaction after the fact for purposes of subchapter F.

Section 8.61(b)(3) permits a showing that a director's conflicting interest transaction was fair to the corporation even if there was no compliance with section 8.62 or 8.63. Under section 8.61(b)(3) the interested director has the burden of establishing that the transaction was fair.

* * * * *

Note on Directors' Compensation

Although directors' fees and other forms of director compensation are typically set by the board of directors and are specifically authorized by section 8.11 of the Act, they do involve a director's conflicting interest transaction in which most if not all of the directors may not be qualified directors. Therefore, board action on directors' compensation and benefits would be subject to judicial sanction if they are not favorably acted upon by shareholders pursuant to section 8.63 or if they are not in the circumstances fair to the corporation pursuant to section 8.61(b)(3).

§8.62. Directors' Action

(a) Directors' action respecting a director's conflicting interest transaction is effective for purposes of section 8.61(b)(1) if the transaction has been authorized by the affirmative vote of a majority (but no fewer than two) of the qualified directors who voted on the transaction, after required disclosure by the conflicted director of information not already known by such qualified directors, or after modified disclosure in compliance with subsection (b), provided that:

(1) the qualified directors have deliberated and voted outside the presence of and without the participation by any other director; and

(2) where the action has been taken by a board committee, all members of the committee were qualified directors, and either (i) the committee was composed of all the qualified directors on the board of directors or (ii) the members of the committee were appointed by the affirmative vote of a majority of the qualified directors on the board of directors.

(b) Notwithstanding subsection (a), when a transaction is a director's conflicting interest transaction only because a related person described in clause (v) or (vi) of the definition of "related person" in section 8.60 is a party to or has a material financial interest in the transaction, the conflicted director is not obligated to make required disclosure to the extent that the director reasonably believes that doing so would violate a duty imposed under law, a legally enforceable obligation of confidentiality, or a professional ethics rule, provided that the conflicted director discloses to the qualified directors voting on the transaction:

(1) all information required to be disclosed that is not so violative,

(2) the existence and nature of the director's conflicting interest, and

(3) the nature of the conflicted director's duty not to disclose the confidential information.

(c) A majority (but no fewer than two) of all the qualified directors on the board of directors, or on the board committee, constitutes a quorum for purposes of action that complies with this section.

(d) Where directors' action under this section does not satisfy a quorum or voting requirement applicable to the authorization of the transaction by reason of the articles of incorporation or bylaws or a provision of law, independent action to satisfy those authorization requirements shall be taken by the board of directors or a board committee, in which action directors who are not qualified directors may participate.

OFFICIAL COMMENT

Section 8.62 provides the procedure for action by the board of directors or by a board committee under subchapter F. In the normal course this section, together with section 8.61(b), will be the key method for addressing directors' conflicting interest transactions. Any discussion of section 8.62 must have in mind the requirements that directors act in good faith and on reasonable inquiry. See section 8.30. Director action that does not comply with those requirements, even if otherwise in compliance with section 8.62, will be subject to challenge and not be given effect under section 8.62. See the Official Comment to section 8.61(b).

1. Section 8.62(a)

The definition of "qualified director" in section 1.43(a)(4) excludes not only a director who is conflicted directly or because of a person specified in the categories of the "related person" definition in section 8.60, but also any director with a familial, financial, employment, professional or other relationship with *another director for whom the transaction is a director's conflicting interest transaction* that would be likely to impair the objectivity of the first director's judgment when participating in a vote on the transaction.

Action under section 8.62 may take the form of committee action meeting the requirements of subsection (a)(2). The requirements for effective committee action are intended to preclude the appointment as committee members of a favorably inclined minority from among all the qualified directors. With respect to required disclosure under subsection (a), if there is more than one conflicted director interested in the transaction, the need for required disclosure would apply to each.

2. *Section 8.62(b)*

Section 8.62(b) accommodates situations where a director who has a conflicting interest is not able to comply fully with the disclosure requirement of subsection (a) because of an extrinsic duty of confidentiality that such director reasonably believes to exist. The director may, for example, be prohibited from making full disclosure because of legal restrictions that happen to apply to the transaction (*e.g.*, grand jury seal or national security statute) or professional ethics rule (*e.g.*, attorney-client confidentiality). The most frequent use of subsection (b), however, will likely involve directors who have conflicting fiduciary obligations. If D is also a director of Y Co., D may have acquired confidential information from one or both directorships relevant to a transaction between X Co. and Y Co., that D cannot reveal to one without violating a fiduciary duty owed to the other. In such circumstances, subsection (b) enables the conflicting interest complication to be presented for consideration under subsection (a), and thereby enables X Co. (and Y Co.) and D to secure for the transaction the protection afforded by subchapter F even though D cannot, by reason of applicable law, confidentiality strictures or a professional ethics rule, make the full disclosure otherwise required.

To comply with section 8.62(b), D must meet all three requirements set forth in clauses (1), (2) and (3). D must then play no personal role in the board's (or committee's) ultimate deliberations or action. The purpose of subsection (b) is to make it clear that the provisions of subchapter F may be employed to "safe harbor" a transaction in circumstances where a conflicted director cannot, because of enforced fiduciary silence, disclose all the known facts. A director could, of course, encounter the same problem of mandated silence with regard to any matter that comes before the board; that is, the problem of forced silence is not linked at all to the problems of transactions involving a conflicting interest of a director. It could happen that at the same board meeting of X Co. at which D invokes subsection (b), another director who has no financial interest in the transaction might conclude that under applicable law he or she is bound to silence (because of attorney-client confidentiality, for example) and would under general principles of sound director conduct withdraw from participation in the board's deliberations and action. Of course, if D invokes subsection (b) and does not make disclosures that would otherwise be required under subsection (a) before leaving the meeting, the qualified directors may decline to act on the transaction out of concern that D knows (or may know) something they do not. On the other hand, if D is subject to an extrinsic duty of confidentiality but has no knowledge of material facts that should otherwise be disclosed, D would normally state just that and subsection (b) would be irrelevant. Having disclosed the existence and nature of the conflicting interest, D would thereby comply with the "required disclosure" as defined under section 8.60.

Although section 8.62(b) will apply to the recurring situation where transacting corporations have common directors (or where a director of one party is an officer of the other), it should not otherwise be read as attempting to address the scope, or mandate the consequences, of various silence-privileges.

Section 8.62(b) is available to D if a transaction is a director's conflicting interest transaction only because a related person described in clauses (v) or (vi) of the definition of that term in section 8.60 is a party to or has a material financial interest in the transaction. Its availability is so limited because in those instances a director owes a fiduciary duty to such a related person. If D or a related person of D other than a related person described in clauses (v) or (vi) of the definition of is a party to or has a material financial interest in the transaction, D's only options are satisfying the required disclosure obligation on an unrestricted basis, abandoning the transaction, or accepting the risk of establishing fairness under section 8.61(b)(3), if the transaction is challenged in a court proceeding.

Whenever a conflicted director proceeds in the manner provided in subsection (b), the other directors should recognize that the conflicted director may have information that, but for the narrow exception set forth in subsection (b), D would be required to reveal to the qualified directors who are acting on the transaction—information that could well indicate that the transaction would be either favorable or unfavorable for *X* Co.

3. Section 8.62(d).

Subsection 8.62(d) underscores the fact that the directors' voting procedures and requirements set forth in subsections (a) through (c) address only the director's conflicting interest. Thus, in any case where the quorum or voting requirements for substantive approval of a transaction differ from the quorum or voting requirements for "safe harbor" protection under section 8.62, the directors may find it necessary to conduct (and record in the minutes of the proceedings) two separate votes—one for section 8.62 purposes and the other for substantive approval purposes.

§8.63. Shareholders' Action

(a) Shareholders' action respecting a director's conflicting interest transaction is effective for purposes of section 8.61(b)(2) if a majority of the votes cast by the holders of all qualified shares are in favor of the transaction after (i) notice to shareholders describing the action to be taken respecting the transaction, (ii) provision to the corporation of the information referred to in subsection (b), and (iii) communication to the shareholders entitled to vote on the transaction of the information that is the subject of required disclosure, to the extent the information is not known by them. In the case of shareholders' action at a meeting, the shareholders entitled to vote shall be determined as of the record date for notice of the meeting.

(b) A director who has a conflicting interest respecting the transaction shall, before the shareholders' vote, inform the secretary or other officer or agent of the corporation authorized to tabulate votes, in writing, of the number of shares that the director knows are not qualified shares under subsection (c), and the identity of the holders of those shares.

(c) For purposes of this section: (i) "holder" means and "held by" refers to shares held by a record shareholder, a beneficial shareholder, and an unrestricted voting trust beneficial owner; and (ii) "qualified shares" means all shares entitled to be voted with respect to the transaction except for shares that the secretary or other officer or agent of the corporation authorized to tabulate votes either knows, or under subsection (b) is notified, are held by (A) a director who has a conflicting interest respecting the transaction or (B) a related person of the director (excluding a person described in clause (vi) of the definition of "related person" in section 8.60).

(d) A majority of the votes entitled to be cast by the holders of all qualified shares constitutes a quorum for purposes of compliance with this section. Subject to the provisions of subsection (e), shareholders' action that otherwise complies with this section is not affected by the presence of holders, or by the voting, of shares that are not qualified shares.

(e) If a shareholders' vote does not comply with subsection (a) solely because of a director's failure to comply with subsection (b), and if the director establishes that the failure was not intended to influence and did not in fact determine the outcome of the vote, the court may take such action respecting the transaction and the director, and may give such effect, if any, to the shareholders' vote, as the court considers appropriate in the circumstances.

(f) Where shareholders' action under this section does not satisfy a quorum or voting requirement applicable to the authorization of the transaction by reason of the articles of incorporation or the bylaws or a provision of law, independent action to satisfy those authorization requirements shall be taken by the shareholders, in which action shares that are not qualified shares may participate.

OFFICIAL COMMENT

Section 8.63 provides the machinery for shareholders' action that confers safe harbor protection for a director's conflicting interest transaction, just as section 8.62 provides the machinery for directors' action that confers subchapter F safe harbor protection for such a transaction.

1. *Section 8.63(a)*

Section 8.63(a) specifies the procedure required to confer effective safe harbor protection for a director's conflicting interest transaction through a vote of shareholders. In advance of the vote, three steps must be taken: (i) shareholders must be given timely and adequate notice describing the transaction; (ii) D must disclose the information called for in subsection (b); and (iii) required disclosure (as defined in section 8.60) must be made to the shareholders entitled to vote. Shareholder action that complies with subsection (a) may be taken at any time, before or after the corporation becomes legally obligated to complete the transaction.

Section 8.63 does not contain a "limited disclosure" provision that is comparable to section 8.62(b). Thus, the safe harbor protection of subchapter F is not available through shareholder action under section 8.63 in a case where D either remains silent or makes less than required disclosure because of an extrinsic duty of confidentiality.

2. *Section 8.63(b)*

In many circumstances, the secretary or other person charged with counting votes on behalf of X Co. will have no way to know which of X Co.'s outstanding shares should be excluded from the vote. Section 8.63(b) (together with subsection (c)) therefore obligates a director who has a conflicting interest respecting the transaction, as a prerequisite to safe harbor protection by shareholder action, to provide information known to the director with respect to the shares that are not qualified.

If the person counting the votes knows, or is notified under subsection (b), that particular shares should be excluded but for some reason fails to exclude them from the count and their inclusion in the vote does not affect its outcome, the shareholders' vote will stand. If the improper inclusion determines the outcome, the shareholders' vote fails because it does not comply with subsection (a). Subsection (e) permits the court to take the appropriate action in cases where the notification under subsection (b) is defective but not determinative of the outcome of the vote.

3. Section 8.63(c)

The definition of "qualified shares" in section 8.63(c) does not exclude shares held by entities or persons described in clause (vi) of the definition of "related person" in section 8.60, *i.e.*, a person that is, or is an entity that is controlled by, an employer of D. If D is an employee of Y Co., that fact does not prevent Y Co. from exercising its usual rights to vote any shares it may hold in X Co. D may be unaware of, and would not necessarily monitor, whether his or her employer holds X Co. shares. Moreover, D will typically have no control over his or her employer and how it may vote its X Co. shares.

4. Section 8.63(e)

If D did not provide the information required under section 8.63(b), on its face the shareholders' action is not in compliance with subsection (a) and D has no safe harbor under subsection (a). In the absence of that safe harbor, D can be put to the burden of establishing the fairness of the transaction under section 8.61(b)(3).

That result is proper where D's failure to inform was determinative of the vote results or, worse, was part of a deliberate effort on D's part to influence the outcome. If, however, D's omission was not motivated by D's effort to influence the integrity of the voting process (for example, it was the result of D's negligence), and the voting of the unreported shares was not determinative of the outcome of the vote, then the court should be free to fashion an appropriate response to the situation in light of all the considerations at the time of its decision.

Despite the presumption of regularity customarily accorded the secretary's record, a plaintiff may go behind the secretary's record for purposes of subsection (e).

5. Section 8.63(f)

Section 8.63(f) underscores that the shareholders' voting procedures and requirements set forth in subsections (a) through (e) treat only the director's conflicting interest. A transaction that receives a shareholders' vote that complies with subchapter F may well fail to achieve a different vote or quorum that may be required for substantive approval of the transaction under other applicable statutory provisions or provisions contained in X Co.'s articles of incorporation or bylaws, and vice versa. Thus, in any case where the quorum or voting requirements for substantive approval of a transaction differ from the quorum or voting requirements for "safe harbor" protection under section 8.63, the corporation may find it necessary to conduct (and record in the minutes of the proceedings) two separate shareholder votes—one for section 8.63 purposes and the other for substantive approval purposes (or, if appropriate, conduct two separate tabulations of one vote).

SUBCHAPTER G. BUSINESS OPPORTUNITIES

§8.70. Business Opportunities

(a) If a director or officer pursues or takes advantage of a business opportunity directly, or indirectly through or on behalf of another person, that action may not be the subject of equitable relief, or give rise to an award of damages or other sanctions against the director, officer or other person, in a proceeding by or in the right of the corporation on the ground that the opportunity should have first been offered to the corporation, if

(1) before the director, officer or other person becomes legally obligated respecting the opportunity the director or officer brings it to the attention of the corporation and either:

(i) action by qualified directors disclaiming the corporation's interest in the opportunity is taken in compliance with the same procedures as are set forth in section 8.62, or

(ii) shareholders' action disclaiming the corporation's interest in the opportunity is taken in compliance with the procedures set forth in section 8.63, in either case as if the decision being made concerned a director's conflicting interest transaction, except that, rather than making "required disclosure" as defined in section 8.60, the director or officer shall have made prior disclosure to those acting on behalf of the corporation of all material facts concerning the business opportunity known to the director or officer; or

(2) the duty to offer the corporation the business opportunity has been limited or eliminated pursuant to a provision of the articles of incorporation adopted (and where required, made effective by action of qualified directors) in accordance with section 2.02(b)(6).

(b) In any proceeding seeking equitable relief or other remedies based upon an alleged improper pursuit or taking advantage of a business opportunity by a director or officer, directly, or indirectly through or on behalf of another person, the fact that the director or officer did not employ the procedure described in subsection (a)(1)(i) or (ii) before pursuing or taking advantage of the opportunity shall not create an implication that the opportunity should have been first presented to the corporation or alter the burden of proof otherwise applicable to establish that the director or officer breached a duty to the corporation in the circumstances.

OFFICIAL COMMENT

Section 8.70(a)(1) provides a safe harbor for a director or officer weighing possible involvement with a prospective business opportunity that might constitute a "corporate opportunity." The phrase "directly, or indirectly through or on behalf of another person" recognizes the need to cover transactions pursued or effected either directly by the director or officer or indirectly through or on behalf of another person, which might be a related person as defined in section 8.60 or a person which is not a related person. By action of the board of directors or shareholders of the corporation under section 8.70(a)(1), the director or officer can obtain a disclaimer of the corporation's interest in the matter before proceeding with such involvement. In the alternative, the corporation may, among other things, (i) decline to disclaim its interest, (ii) delay a decision respecting granting a disclaimer pending receipt from the director or officer of additional information (or for any other reason), or (iii) attach conditions to the disclaimer it grants under section 8.70(a)(1).

The safe harbor provided under section 8.70(a)(1) may be utilized only for a specific business opportunity. A broader advance safe harbor for any, or one or more classes or categories of, business opportunities must meet the requirements of section 2.02(b)(6). Section 8.70(a)(2) confirms that if the duty of an officer or director to present an opportunity has been limited or eliminated by a provision in the articles of incorporation under section 2.02(b)(6) (and, in the case of officers, appropriate action by qualified directors as required by that section), a safe harbor exists in connection with the pursuit or taking of the opportunity. The common law doctrine of "corporate opportunity" has long been recognized as a part of the director's duty of loyalty and, under court decisions, extends to officers. See section 8.30(a) and its Official Comment. The doctrine recognizes that the corporation has a right prior to that of its directors or officers to act on certain business opportunities that come to the attention of the directors or officers. In such situations, a director or officer who acts on the opportunity for the benefit of the director or officer or another person without having first presented it to the corporation can be held to have "usurped" or "intercepted" a right of the corporation. A defendant director or officer who is found by a court to have violated the duty of loyalty in this regard, as well as related or other persons involved in the transaction, may be subject to damages or possible equitable remedies, including injunction, disgorgement or the imposition of a constructive trust in favor of the corporation. Although the doctrine's concept is easily described, whether it will be found to apply in a given case depends on the facts and circumstances of the particular situation and is thus frequently unpredictable.

In recognition that the corporation need not pursue every business opportunity of which it becomes aware, an opportunity coming within the doctrine's criteria that has been properly presented to and declined by the corporation may then be pursued or taken by the presenting director or officer without breach of the duty of loyalty.

The fact-intensive nature of the corporate opportunity doctrine resists statutory definition. Instead, subchapter G employs the broader notion of "business opportunity" that encompasses any opportunity, without regard to whether it would come within the judicial definition of a "corporate opportunity," as it may have been developed by courts in a jurisdiction. When properly employed, subchapter G provides a safe-harbor mechanism enabling a director or officer to pursue an opportunity directly, or indirectly through or on behalf of another person, free of possible challenge claiming conflict with the director's or officer's duty on the ground that the opportunity should first have been offered to the corporation. Section 8.70 is modeled on the safe-harbor and approval procedures of subchapter F pertaining to directors' conflicting interest transactions with, however, some modifications necessary to accommodate differences in the two matters addressed.

1. Section 8.70(a)(1)

Section 8.70(a)(1) describes the safe harbor available to a director or officer who elects to subject a business opportunity, regardless of whether the opportunity would be classified as a "corporate opportunity," to the disclosure and approval procedures set forth in that section. The safe harbor provided is as broad as that provided for a director's conflicting interest transaction in section 8.61. If the director or officer makes the prescribed disclosure of the facts specified and the corporation's interest in the opportunity is disclaimed by director action under subsection (a)(1)(i) or shareholder action under subsection (a)(1)(ii), the director or officer has foreclosed any claimed breach of the duty of loyalty and may not be subject to equitable relief, damages or other sanctions if the director or officer thereafter pursues or takes the opportunity for his or her own account or through or for the benefit of another person. As a general proposition, disclaimer by director action under subsection (a)(1)(i) must meet all of the requirements provided in section 8.62 with respect to a director's conflicting interest transaction and disclaimer by shareholder action under subsection (a)(1)(ii) must likewise meet all of the requirements for shareholder action under section 8.63. Note, however, several important differences.

First, in contrast to director or shareholder action under sections 8.62 and 8.63, which may be taken at any time, section 8.70(a)(1) requires that the director or officer present the opportunity and secure director or shareholder action disclaiming it *before* the director of officer or other person involved through or on behalf of the director or officer becomes legally obligated respecting the opportunity. The safe harbor concept contemplates that the corporation's decision maker will have full freedom of action in deciding whether the corporation should take over a proffered opportunity or disclaim the corporation's interest in it. If the director or officer could seek ratification after the legal obligation respecting the opportunity arises, the option of taking over the opportunity would, in most cases, be foreclosed to the corporation. The safe harbor's benefit is available only when the corporation can entertain the opportunity in a fully objective way.

The second difference relates to the necessary disclosure. Instead of employing section 8.60's definition of "required disclosure" which is incorporated in sections 8.62 and 8.63 and includes "the existence and nature of the director's conflicting interest," the disclosure obligation of section 8.70(a)(1) requires only that the director or officer reveal all material facts concerning the business opportunity known to the director or officer. The safe harbor procedure shields the director or officer even if a material fact regarding the business opportunity is not disclosed, so long as the proffering director or officer had no knowledge of that fact.

2. *Section 8.70(b)*

Section 8.70(b) reflects a fundamental difference between the coverage of subchapters F and G. Because subchapter F provides an exclusive definition of "director's conflicting interest transaction," any transaction meeting the definition that is not approved in accordance with the provisions of subchapter F is not entitled to its safe harbor. Unless the interested director can, upon challenge, establish the transaction's fairness, the director's conduct is presumptively actionable and subject to the full range of remedies that might otherwise be awarded by a court. In contrast, the concept of "business opportunity" under section 8.70 is not defined but is intended to be broader than what might be regarded as an actionable "corporate opportunity." This approach reflects the fact-intensive nature of the corporate opportunity doctrine, with the result that a director or officer may be inclined to seek safe harbor protection under section 8.70 before pursuing an opportunity that may or may not be a "corporate opportunity." Likewise, a director or officer may conclude that a business opportunity is not a "corporate opportunity" under applicable law and choose to pursue it without seeking a disclaimer by the corporation under subsection (a)(1). Accordingly, subsection (b) provides that a decision not to seek the safe harbor offered by subsection (a)(1) neither creates a negative implication nor alters the burden of proof in any subsequent proceeding seeking damages or equitable relief based upon an alleged improper taking of a "corporate opportunity."

Chapter 10. Amendment of Articles of Incorporation and Bylaws

SUBCHAPTER A. AMENDMENT OF ARTICLES OF INCORPORATION

§10.01. Authority to Amend

(a) A corporation may amend its articles of incorporation at any time to add or change a provision that is required or permitted in the articles of incorporation as of the effective date of the amendment or to delete a provision that is not required to be contained in the articles of incorporation.

(b) A shareholder of the corporation does not have a vested property right resulting from any provision in the articles of incorporation, including provisions relating to management, control, capital structure, dividend entitlement, or purpose or duration of the corporation.

§10.02. Amendment Before Issuance of Shares

If a corporation has not yet issued shares, its board of directors, or its incorporators if it has no board of directors, may adopt one or more amendments to the corporation's articles of incorporation.

§10.03. Amendment by Board of Directors and Shareholders

If a corporation has issued shares, an amendment to the articles of incorporation shall be adopted in the following manner:

(a) The proposed amendment shall first be adopted by the board of directors.

(b) Except as provided in sections 10.05, 10.07, and 10.08, the amendment shall then be approved by the shareholders. In submitting the proposed amendment to the shareholders for approval, the board of directors shall recommend that the shareholders approve the amendment, unless (i) the board of directors makes a determination that because of conflicts of interest or other special circumstances it should not make such a recommendation, or (ii) section 8.26 applies. If either (i) or (ii) applies, the board must inform the shareholders of the basis for its so proceeding.

(c) The board of directors may set conditions for the approval of the amendment by the shareholders or the effectiveness of the amendment.

(d) If the amendment is required to be approved by the shareholders, and the approval is to be given at a meeting, the corporation shall notify each shareholder, regardless of whether entitled to vote, of the meeting of shareholders at which the amendment is to be submitted for approval. The notice must state that the purpose, or one of the purposes, of the meeting is to consider the amendment. The notice must contain or be accompanied by a copy of the amendment.

(e) Unless the articles of incorporation, or the board of directors acting pursuant to subsection (c), require a greater vote or a greater quorum, approval of the amendment requires the approval of the shareholders at a meeting at which a quorum consisting of a majority of the votes entitled to be cast on the amendment exists, and, if any class or series of shares is entitled to vote as a separate group on the amendment, except as provided in section 10.04(c), the approval of each such separate voting group at a meeting at which a quorum of the voting group exists consisting of a majority of the votes entitled to be cast on the amendment by that voting group.

(f) If as a result of an amendment of the articles of incorporation one or more shareholders of a domestic corporation would become subject to new interest holder liability, approval of the amendment requires the signing in connection with the amendment, by each such shareholder, of a separate written consent to become subject to such new interest holder liability, unless in the case of a shareholder that already has interest holder liability the terms and conditions of the new interest holder liability (i) are substantially identical to those of the existing interest holder liability, or (ii) are substantially identical to those of the existing interest holder liability (other than changes that eliminate or reduce such interest holder liability).

(g) For purposes of subsection (f) and section 10.09, "new interest holder liability" means interest holder liability of a person resulting from an amendment of the articles of incorporation if (i) the person did not have interest holder liability before the amendment becomes effective, or (ii) the person had interest holder liability before the amendment becomes effective, the terms and conditions of which are changed when the amendment becomes effective.

OFFICIAL COMMENT

Section 10.03 governs amendments to the articles of incorporation after shares have been issued. Most such amendments will require a shareholder vote. When submitting an amendment to the articles of incorporation to shareholders, the board of directors must recommend the amendment, subject to two exceptions in section 10.03(b). The board might exercise the exception under clause (i) where the number of directors having a conflicting interest makes it inadvisable for the board to recommend the amendment or where the board is evenly divided as to the merits of the amendment but is able to agree that shareholders should be permitted to consider it. Alternatively, the board of directors might exercise the exception under clause (ii), which recognizes that, under section 8.26, a board of directors may agree to submit an amendment to a vote of shareholders even if, after approving the amendment, the board of directors determines that it no longer recommends the amendment.

Section 10.03(c) permits the board of directors to set conditions for its submission of an amendment to the shareholders or effectiveness of an amendment. Examples of conditions that a board might impose are that the amendment will not be deemed approved (i) unless it is approved by a specified vote of the shareholders, or by one or more specified classes or series of shares, voting as a separate voting group, or by a specified percentage of votes of disinterested shareholders, or (ii) if shareholders holding more than a specified number or percentage of outstanding shares assert appraisal rights. . . .

§10.04. Voting on Amendments by Voting Groups

(a) The holders of the outstanding shares of a class are entitled to vote as a separate voting group (if shareholder voting is otherwise required by this Act) on a proposed amendment to the articles of incorporation if the amendment would:

(1) effect an exchange or reclassification of all or part of the shares of the class into shares of another class;

(2) effect an exchange or reclassification, or create the right of exchange, of all or part of the shares of another class into shares of the class;

(3) change the rights, preferences, or limitations of all or part of the shares of the class;

(4) change the shares of all or part of the class into a different number of shares of the same class;

(5) create a new class of shares having rights or preferences with respect to distributions that are prior or superior to the shares of the class;

(6) increase the rights, preferences, or number of authorized shares of any class that, after giving effect to the amendment, have rights or preferences with respect to distributions that are prior or superior to the shares of the class;

(7) limit or deny an existing preemptive right of all or part of the shares of the class; or

(8) cancel or otherwise affect rights to distributions that have accumulated but not yet been authorized on all or part of the shares of the class.

(b) If a proposed amendment would affect a series of a class of shares in one or more of the ways described in subsection (a), the holders of shares of that series are entitled to vote as a separate voting group on the proposed amendment.

(c) If a proposed amendment that entitles the holders of two or more classes or series of shares to vote as separate voting groups under this section would affect those two or more classes or series in the same or a substantially similar way, the holders of shares of all the classes or series so affected shall vote together as a single voting group on the proposed amendment, unless otherwise provided in the articles of incorporation or added as a condition by the board of directors pursuant to section 10.03(c).

(d) A class or series of shares is entitled to the voting rights granted by this section even if the articles of incorporation provide that the shares are nonvoting shares.

OFFICIAL COMMENT

Section 10.04(a) requires separate approval by voting groups for certain types of amendments to the articles of incorporation where the corporation has more than one class or series of shares outstanding. Even if a class or series of shares is described as "nonvoting" or the articles purport to make that class or series nonvoting "for all purposes," that class or series nonetheless has the voting rights provided by this section. Likewise, shares are entitled to vote as separate voting groups under this section even though the articles of incorporation purport to allow other classes or series of shares to vote as part of the same voting group. However, an amendment that does not require shareholder approval does not trigger the right to vote by voting groups under this section. This would include a determination by the board, pursuant to authority granted in the articles of incorporation, of the rights, preferences and limitations of any class before the issuance of any shares of that class, or of one or more series within a class before the issuance of any shares of that series. See sections 6.02(a) and (b).

The right to vote as a separate voting group provides a major protection for classes or series of shares with preferential rights, or classes or series of limited or nonvoting shares, against amendments that affect that class or series. This section, however, does not make the right to vote by a separate voting group dependent on an evaluation of whether the amendment is detrimental to that class or series; if the amendment is one of those described in section 10.04(a), the class or series is automatically entitled to vote as a separate voting group on the amendment.

An amendment that changes the number of shares owned by one or more shareholders of a class into a fraction of a share, through a "reverse split," falls within subsection (a)(4) and therefore requires approval by the class, voting as a separate voting group, whether the fractional share is to be issued or otherwise paid in cash under section 6.04. Sections 10.04(a)(5) and (6) refer to preferences with respect to distributions, including distributions in liquidation or dissolution. See section 1.40 and the Official Comment to section 1.40 under "Distributions."

Sections 7.25 and 7.26 set forth the mechanics of voting by multiple voting groups. Section 10.04(b) extends the privilege of voting as a separate voting group to a series of a class of shares if the series is affected in one or more of the ways described in subsection (a). Any distinguishing feature of a series, which an amendment affects or alters, should trigger the right of voting as a separate voting group for that series. However, if a proposed amendment that affects two or more classes or series of shares in the same or a substantially similar way, under subsection (c), the shares of all the class or series so affected must vote together, as a single voting group, unless otherwise provided in the articles of incorporation or a condition set by the board of directors pursuant to section 10.03(c).

The application of sections 10.04(b) and (c) may best be illustrated by the following examples, all of which assume there is no provision in the articles of incorporation providing otherwise and that the board has not set an additional voting condition.

First, assume there is a class of shares comprised of three series, each with different preferential dividend rights. A proposed amendment would reduce the rate of dividend applicable to the "Series A" shares and would change the dividend right of the "Series B" shares from a cumulative to a noncumulative right. The amendment would not affect the preferential dividend right of the "Series C" shares. Both Series A and B would be entitled to vote as separate voting groups on the proposed amendment; the holders of the Series C shares, not directly affected by the amendment, would not be entitled to vote unless the Series C shares are voting shares under the articles of incorporation, in which case the Series C shares would not vote as a separate voting group but would vote in the voting group consisting of all shares in the class, as well as in the voting group consisting of all shares with general voting rights under the articles of incorporation.

Second, if the proposed amendment would reduce the dividend right of Series A and change the dividend right of both Series B and C from a cumulative to a noncumulative right, the holders of Series A would be entitled to vote as a single voting group, and the holders of Series B and C would be required to vote together as a single, separate voting group.

Third, assume that a corporation has common stock and two classes of preferred stock. A proposed amendment would create a new class of senior preferred that would have priority in distribution rights over both the common stock and the existing classes of preferred stock. Because the creation of the new senior preferred would affect all three classes of stock in the same or a substantially similar way, all three classes would vote together as a single voting group on the proposed amendment.

§10.05. Amendment by Board of Directors

Unless the articles of incorporation provide otherwise, a corporation's board of directors may adopt amendments to the corporation's articles of incorporation without shareholder approval:

(a) to extend the duration of the corporation if it was incorporated at a time when limited duration was required by law;

(b) to delete the names and addresses of the initial directors;

(c) to delete the name and address of the initial registered agent or registered office, if a statement of change is on file with the secretary of state;

(d) if the corporation has only one class of shares outstanding:

(1) to change each issued and unissued authorized share of the class into a greater number of whole shares of that class; or

(2) to increase the number of authorized shares of the class to the extent necessary to permit the issuance of shares as a share dividend;

(e) to change the corporate name by substituting the word "corporation," "incorporated," "company," "limited," or the abbreviation "corp.," "inc.," "co.," or "ltd.," for a similar word or abbreviation in the name, or by adding, deleting, or changing a geographical attribution for the name;

(f) to reflect a reduction in authorized shares, as a result of the operation of section 6.31(b), when the corporation has acquired its own shares and the articles of incorporation prohibit the reissue of the acquired shares;

(g) to delete a class of shares from the articles of incorporation, as a result of the operation of section 6.31(b), when there are no remaining shares of the class because the corporation has acquired all shares of the class and the articles of incorporation prohibit the reissue of the acquired shares; or

(h) to make any change expressly permitted by section 6.02(a) or (b) to be made without shareholder approval.

OFFICIAL COMMENT

The amendments described in subsections (a) through (h) are so routine and ministerial in nature as not to require approval by shareholders. None affects the substantive rights of shareholders in any meaningful way. Although the board of directors' designation of the preferences, rights and limitations of a new class or series of shares under section 6.02 may have substantive effects, amendments of the articles of incorporation to set forth the terms of a new class or series are already permitted by section 6.02(c). Amendments provided for in this section may be included in restated articles of incorporation under section 10.07 or in articles of merger under chapter 11.

§10.06. *Articles of Amendment*

(a) After an amendment to the articles of incorporation has been adopted and approved in the manner required by this Act and by the articles of incorporation, the corporation shall deliver to the secretary of state for filing articles of amendment, which must set forth:

(1) the name of the corporation;

(2) the text of each amendment adopted, or the information required by section 1.20(k)(5);

(3) if an amendment provides for an exchange, reclassification, or cancellation of issued shares, provisions for implementing the amendment if not contained in the amendment itself, (which may be made dependent upon facts objectively ascertainable outside the articles of amendment in accordance with section 1.20(k)(5);

(4) the date of each amendment's adoption; and

(5) if an amendment:

(i) was adopted by the incorporators or board of directors without shareholder approval, a statement that the amendment was duly adopted by the incorporators or by the board of directors, as the case may be, and that shareholder approval was not required;

(ii) required approval by the shareholders, a statement that the amendment was duly approved by the shareholders in the manner required by this Act and by the articles of incorporation; or

(iii) is being filed pursuant to section 1.20(k)(5), a statement to that effect.

(b) Articles of amendment shall take effect at the effective date determined in accordance with section 1.23.

§10.07. *Restated Articles of Incorporation*

(a) A corporation's board of directors may restate its articles of incorporation at any time, without shareholder approval, to consolidate all amendments into a single document.

(b) If the restated articles include one or more new amendments that require shareholder approval, the amendments shall be adopted and approved as provided in section 10.03.

(c) A corporation that restates its articles of incorporation shall deliver to the secretary of state for filing articles of restatement setting forth:

(1) the name of the corporation;

(2) the text of the restated articles of incorporation;

(3) a statement that the restated articles consolidate all amendments into a single document; and

(4) if a new amendment is included in the restated articles, the statements required under section 10.06 with respect to the new amendment.

(d) Duly adopted restated articles of incorporation supersede the original articles of incorporation and all amendments to the articles of incorporation.

(e) The secretary of state may certify restated articles of incorporation as the articles of incorporation currently in effect, without including the statements required by subsection (c)(4).

§10.08. Amendment Pursuant to Reorganization

(a) A corporation's articles of incorporation may be amended without action by the board of directors or shareholders to carry out a plan of reorganization ordered or decreed by a court of competent jurisdiction under the authority of a law of the United States.

(b) The individual or individuals designated by the court shall deliver to the secretary of state for filing articles of amendment setting forth:

(1) the name of the corporation;

(2) the text of each amendment approved by the court;

(3) the date of the court's order or decree approving the articles of amendment;

(4) the title of the reorganization proceeding in which the order or decree was entered; and

(5) a statement that the court had jurisdiction of the proceeding under federal statute.

(c) This section does not apply after entry of a final decree in the reorganization proceeding even though the court retains jurisdiction of the proceeding for limited purposes unrelated to consummation of the reorganization plan.

§10.09. Effect of Amendment

(a) An amendment to the articles of incorporation does not affect a cause of action existing against or in favor of the corporation, a proceeding to which the corporation is a party, or the existing rights of persons other than the shareholders. An amendment changing a corporation's name does not affect a proceeding brought by or against the corporation in its former name.

(b) A shareholder who becomes subject to new interest holder liability in respect of the corporation as a result of an amendment to the articles of incorporation shall have that new interest holder liability only in respect of interest holder liabilities that arise after the amendment becomes effective.

(c) Except as otherwise provided in the articles of incorporation of the corporation, the interest holder liability of a shareholder who had interest holder liability in respect of the corporation before the amendment becomes effective and has new interest holder liability after the amendment becomes effective shall be as follows:

(1) The amendment does not discharge that prior interest holder liability with respect to any interest holder liabilities that arose before the amendment becomes effective.

(2) The provisions of the articles of incorporation of the corporation relating to interest holder liability as in effect immediately prior to the amendment shall continue to apply to the collection or discharge of any interest holder liabilities preserved by subsection (c)(1), as if the amendment had not occurred.

(3) The shareholder shall have such rights of contribution from other persons as are provided by the articles of incorporation relating to interest holder liability as in effect immediately prior to the amendment with respect to any interest holder liabilities preserved by subsection (c)(1), as if the amendment had not occurred.

(4) The shareholder shall not, by reason of such prior interest holder liability, have interest holder liability with respect to any interest holder liabilities that arise after the amendment becomes effective.

SUBCHAPTER B. AMENDMENT OF BYLAWS

§10.20. Authority to Amend

(a) A corporation's shareholders may amend or repeal the corporation's bylaws.

(b) A corporation's board of directors may amend or repeal the corporation's bylaws, unless:

(1) the articles of incorporation, section 10.21 or, if applicable, section 10.22 reserve that power exclusively to the shareholders in whole or part; or

(2) except as provided in section 2.06(d), the shareholders in amending, repealing, or adopting a bylaw expressly provide that the board of directors may not amend, repeal, or adopt that bylaw.

(c) A shareholder of the corporation does not have a vested property right resulting from any provision in the bylaws.

OFFICIAL COMMENT

The power to amend or repeal bylaws is shared by the board of directors and the shareholders, unless that power is reserved exclusively to the shareholders by an appropriate provision in the articles of incorporation. Section 10.20(b)(1) permits the reservation of amendment power to the shareholders to be limited to specific articles or sections of the bylaws or to specific subjects or topics addressed in the bylaws.

The authority granted to the shareholders in section 10.20(b)(2) to prevent the board of directors from further changing a bylaw which the shareholders have amended, repealed, or adopted is expressly subject to section 2.06(d), which limits the authority of shareholders to restrict board action on bylaws with regard to procedures or conditions set forth in certain bylaws regulating the election of directors. See the Official Comment to section 2.06. . . .

§10.21. Bylaw Increasing Quorum or Voting Requirement for Directors or Requiring a Meeting Place

(a) A bylaw that increases a quorum or voting requirement for the board of directors or that requires a meeting of shareholders to be held at a place may be amended or repealed:

(1) if originally adopted by the shareholders, only by the shareholders, unless the bylaw otherwise provides; or

(2) if adopted by the board of directors, either by the shareholders or by the board of directors.

(b) A bylaw adopted or amended by the shareholders that increases a quorum or voting requirement for the board of directors may provide that it can be amended or repealed only by a specified vote of either the shareholders or the board of directors.

(c) Action by the board of directors under subsection (a) to amend or repeal a bylaw that changes a quorum or voting requirement for the board of directors shall meet the same quorum requirement and be adopted by the same vote required to take action under the quorum and voting requirement then in effect or proposed to be adopted, whichever is greater.

§10.22. Bylaw Provisions Relating to the Election of Directors

(a) Unless the articles of incorporation (i) specifically prohibit the adoption of a bylaw pursuant to this section, (ii) alter the vote specified in section 7.28(a), or (iii) provide for cumulative voting, a corporation may elect in its bylaws to be governed in the election of directors as follows:

(1) each vote entitled to be cast may be voted for or against up to that number of candidates that is equal to the number of directors to be elected, or a shareholder may indicate an abstention, but without cumulating the votes;

(2) to be elected, a nominee shall have received a plurality of the votes cast by holders of shares entitled to vote in the election at a meeting at which a quorum is present, provided that a nominee who is elected but receives more votes against than for election shall serve as a director for a term that shall terminate on the date that is the earlier of (i) 90 days from the date on which the voting results are determined pursuant to section 7.29(b)(5) or (ii) the date on which an individual is selected by the board of directors to fill the office held by such director, which selection shall be deemed to constitute the filling of a vacancy by the board to which section 8.10 applies. Subject to subsection (a)(3), a nominee who is elected but receives more votes against than for election shall not serve as a director beyond the 90-day period referenced above; and

(3) the board of directors may select any qualified individual to fill the office held by a director who received more votes against than for election.

(b) Subsection (a) does not apply to an election of directors by a voting group if (i) at the expiration of the time fixed under a provision requiring advance notification of director candidates, or (ii) absent such a provision, at a time fixed by the board of directors which is not more than 14 days before notice is given of the meeting at which the election is to occur, there are more candidates for election by the voting group than the number of directors to be elected, one or more of whom are properly proposed by shareholders. An individual shall not be considered a candidate for purposes of this subsection if the board of directors determines before the notice of meeting is given that such individual's candidacy does not create a bona fide election contest.

(c) A bylaw electing to be governed by this section may be repealed:

(1) if originally adopted by the shareholders, only by the shareholders, unless the bylaw otherwise provides;

(2) if adopted by the board of directors, by the board of directors or the shareholders.

OFFICIAL COMMENT

Section 10.22 is effective only if a corporation elects in a bylaw to be governed by its terms. The provisions of section 10.22 effectively modify the term and holdover provisions of section 8.05 pursuant to a limited exception for section 10.22 that is recognized in section 8.05. Accordingly, a bylaw provision that would seek to alter the term and holdover provision of section 8.05 that varied in any manner from section 10.22 would not be effective.

1. *Section 10.22(a)*

The rule in subsection (a) is straightforward if the nominees for director equal the number of directorships up for election. In that case, and by way of example, the holder of a single share could vote either for or against each director. In the unusual case that section 10.22(a) were applicable to a contested election notwithstanding the provisions of section 10.22(b) (*e.g.*, in the absence of an advance notice bylaw, a contest arises as a result of candidates for director being proposed subsequent to the determination date under section 10.22(b)), the holder of a share would have to choose whether to indicate opposition to a slate by voting in favor of a candidate on the preferred slate or by voting against a candidate on the disfavored slate, or to abstain. Because it would be in the interests of all contestants to explain in their proxy materials that against votes would not be counted in favor of any candidate in a contested election, the rational voter in a contested election might be expected to vote in favor of all candidates on the preferred slate to promote a simple plurality victory rather than voting against candidates on the disfavored slate. Nothing in section 10.22 would prevent the holder of more than one share from voting differently with respect to each share held.

Section 10.22(a) specifically contemplates that a corporate ballot for the election of directors would provide for "against" votes. Although there is no prohibition in the Act against a corporation offering shareholders the opportunity to vote "against" candidates at any time, unless the corporation elects to be governed by section 10.22 or the articles of incorporation are amended to make such a vote meaningful, an "against" vote is given no effect under the Act.

Section 10.22(a)(2) does not conflict with or alter the plurality voting default standard. However, because section 10.22 shortens the term of a director who is elected but receives more votes against election than in favor of election, a vacancy will exist if no action is taken to fill the vacancy before the expiration of the shortened term. As contemplated by section 8.10, that vacancy may be filled by shareholders or by the board of directors, unless the articles of incorporation provide otherwise. In the alternative, action could be taken by amendment to, or in the manner provided in, the articles of incorporation or bylaws to reduce the size of the board of directors. See section 8.03.

Under section 8.05(d), the director appointed to fill the vacancy would be up for reelection at the next annual meeting, even if the term for that directorship would otherwise have been for more than one year, as in the case of a staggered board.

There is also no limitation in section 10.22 or elsewhere in the Act on the power of either the board of directors or shareholders to fill a vacancy with the person who held such directorship before the vacancy arose.

2. *Section 10.22(b)*

Under section 10.22(b), when there are more candidates for election as directors by a voting group (as defined in section 1.40) than director positions to be filled, the resulting election contest would not be subject to the voting regime under section 10.22(a). Instead, it would be conducted by means of a plurality vote under section 7.28(a). Such plurality voting is appropriate in that circumstance because shareholders will have a choice between competing candidates.

The timing provided in clauses (i) and (ii) of subsection (b) for determining when section 10.22(a) does not apply to an election assures that the voting regime that will apply will be known in advance of the giving of notice, and that the disclosure of the voting rules and the proxy appointment form will be clear and reflect the applicable voting regime. The determination of how many candidates there are to fill the number of director positions up for election may be made by the board of directors. The board's determination of whether an individual shall not be considered a candidate for purposes of section 10.22(b) because the candidacy does not create a bona fide election contest must be made before notice of the meeting is given. The board of directors might choose, for example, to exercise this authority to preserve the voting regime under section 10.22(a) when it is clear that an individual has designated himself or herself as a candidate without intending to solicit votes or for the purpose of frustrating the availability of the section 10.22(a) voting regime.

The contested or uncontested nature of the election can change following the date for determining the voting regime that will apply. For example, an election that is contested at that date could become uncontested if a candidate withdraws. Conversely, unless the bylaws require advance notice of director nomination, an uncontested election could become contested before the vote is taken but after notice of the meeting has been given because there is no limitation on the ability of shareholders to nominate candidates for directorships up until the time nominations are closed at the meeting. Section 10.22(b) does not authorize changing the voting regime in those circumstances.

Chapter 11. Mergers and Share Exchanges

§11.01. Definitions

As used in this chapter:

- "Acquired entity" means the domestic or foreign corporation or eligible entity that will have all of one or more classes or series of its shares or eligible interests acquired in a share exchange.
- "Acquiring entity" means the domestic or foreign corporation or eligible entity that will acquire all of one or more classes or series of shares or eligible interests of the acquired entity in a share exchange.
- "New interest holder liability" means interest holder liability of a person, resulting from a merger or share exchange, that is (i) in respect of an entity which is different from the entity in which the person held shares or eligible interests immediately before the merger or share exchange became effective; or (ii) in respect of the same entity as the one in which the person held shares or eligible interests immediately before the merger or share exchange became effective if (A) the person did not have interest holder liability immediately before

the merger or share exchange became effective, or (B) the person had interest holder liability immediately before the merger or share exchange became effective, the terms and conditions of which were changed when the merger or share exchange became effective.

- "Party to a merger" means any domestic or foreign corporation or eligible entity that will merge under a plan of merger but does not include a survivor created by the merger.
- "Survivor" in a merger means the domestic or foreign corporation or eligible entity into which one or more other corporations or eligible entities are merged.

§11.02. Merger

(a) By complying with this chapter:

(1) one or more domestic business corporations may merge with one or more domestic or foreign business corporations or eligible entities pursuant to a plan of merger, resulting in a survivor; and

(2) two or more foreign business corporations or domestic or foreign eligible entities may merge, resulting in a survivor that is a domestic business corporation created in the merger.

(b) By complying with the provisions of this chapter applicable to foreign entities, a foreign business corporation or a foreign eligible entity may be a party to a merger with a domestic business corporation, or may be created as the survivor in a merger in which a domestic business corporation is a party, but only if the merger is permitted by the organic law of the foreign business corporation or eligible entity.

(c) If the organic law or organic rules of a domestic eligible entity do not provide procedures for the approval of a merger, a plan of merger may nonetheless be adopted and approved by the unanimous consent of all of the interest holders of such eligible entity, and the merger may thereafter by effected as provided in the other provisions of this chapter; and for the purposes of applying this chapter in such a case:

(1) the eligible entity, its members or interest holders, eligible interests and articles of incorporation or other organic rules taken together shall be deemed to be a domestic business corporation, shareholders, shares and articles of incorporation, respectively and vice versa as the context may require; and

(2) if the business and affairs of the eligible entity are managed by a person or persons that are not identical to the members or interest holders, that group shall be deemed to be the board of directors.

(d) The plan of merger must include:

(1) as to each party to the merger, its name, jurisdiction of formation, and type of entity;

(2) the survivor's name, jurisdiction of formation, and type of entity, and, if the survivor is to be created in the merger, a statement to that effect;

(3) the terms and conditions of the merger;

(4) the manner and basis of converting the shares of each merging domestic or foreign business corporation and eligible interests of each merging domestic

or foreign eligible entity into shares or other securities, eligible interests, obligations, rights to acquire shares, other securities or eligible interests, cash, other property, or any combination of the foregoing;

(5) the articles of incorporation of any domestic or foreign business or nonprofit corporation, or the public organic record of any domestic or foreign unincorporated entity, to be created by the merger, or if a new domestic or foreign business or nonprofit corporation or unincorporated entity is not to be created by the merger, any amendments to the survivor's articles of incorporation or other public organic record; and

(6) any other provisions required by the laws under which any party to the merger is organized or by which it is governed, or by the articles of incorporation or organic rules of any such party.

(e) In addition to the requirements of subsection (d), a plan of merger may contain any other provision not prohibited by law.

(f) Terms of a plan of merger may be made dependent on facts objectively ascertainable outside the plan in accordance with section 1.20(k).

(g) A plan of merger may be amended only with the consent of each party to the merger, except as provided in the plan. A domestic party to a merger may approve an amendment to a plan:

(1) in the same manner as the plan was approved, if the plan does not provide for the manner in which it may be amended; or

(2) in the manner provided in the plan, except that shareholders, members, or interest holders that were entitled to vote on or consent to approval of the plan are entitled to vote on or consent to any amendment of the plan that will change:

(i) the amount or kind of shares or other securities, eligible interests, obligations, rights to acquire shares, other securities or eligible interests, cash, or other property to be received under the plan by the shareholders, members, or interest holders of any party to the merger;

(ii) the articles of incorporation of any domestic or foreign business or nonprofit corporation, or the organic rules of any unincorporated entity, that will be the survivor of the merger, except for changes permitted by section 10.05 or by comparable provisions of the organic law of any such foreign corporation or domestic or foreign nonprofit corporation or unincorporated entity; or

(iii) any of the other terms or conditions of the plan if the change would adversely affect such shareholders, members, or interest holders in any material respect.

OFFICIAL COMMENT

1. *In General*

Section 11.02 authorizes domestic corporations to merge with each other. It also authorizes one or more domestic corporations to merge with one or more foreign corporations or domestic or foreign eligible entities (such as limited liability companies or partnerships). In addition, it provides for the merger of two or more foreign corporations or foreign or domestic eligible entities, even if no domestic business corporation is a party to the merger, but only if the survivor is a domestic business corporation created by the merger.

2. Applicability to Foreign Corporations and Eligible Entities and to Domestic Eligible Entities

A foreign corporation or a foreign eligible entity may be a party to or be the survivor in a merger authorized by chapter 11 only if the merger is permitted by the laws under which the foreign corporation or eligible entity is organized. Whether and on what terms a foreign corporation or a foreign eligible entity is authorized to merge is governed by those laws. If a foreign corporation or eligible entity is so authorized, it must comply with the applicable provisions of chapter 11 in addition to the requirements of its own governing laws. For example, section 11.02(d) sets forth certain requirements for the contents of a plan of merger with a domestic corporation, and section 11.07(d) provides that upon a merger becoming effective, a foreign corporation or foreign eligible entity that is the survivor is deemed to appoint the secretary of state as its agent for service of process in a proceeding to enforce appraisal rights of shareholders of each domestic corporation that is a party to the merger.

With respect to a domestic eligible entity, if the law under which it is organized does not expressly authorize it to be a party to or survive a merger under chapter 11, section 11.02(c) provides procedures for such an entity to adopt and effect a plan of merger.

3. Terms and Conditions of Merger

Chapter 11 imposes no restrictions or limitations on the terms or conditions of a merger, except for those set forth in section 11.02(g). The list in section 11.02(d) of provisions in a plan of merger is not exhaustive.

4. Amendments of Articles of Incorporation

Under section 11.02, a corporation's articles of incorporation may be amended by a merger, and section 11.02(d)(5) provides that a plan of merger must include any such amendments. If the plan of merger is approved and the survivor is a domestic entity, section 11.07 provides that the amendments will become effective with the merger. If the plan includes amendments to the articles of incorporation of a surviving domestic corporation, section 11.04(f)(1)(ii), by reference to the voting requirements of section 10.04 relating to amendments of the articles of incorporation, may impose voting requirements by separate voting groups that would not otherwise apply.

Although the plan of merger must include any amendments to the articles of incorporation or public organic record of the survivor, the survivor's articles of incorporation or public organic record are not required to be included in the plan unless the survivor is created by the merger. However, if approval of the plan of merger by the shareholders of a domestic corporation is required under section 11.04, section 11.04(d) requires that its shareholders be furnished with a copy or summary of the articles of incorporation or public organic record of the survivor in connection with voting on approval.

§11.03. Share Exchange

(a) By complying with this chapter:

(1) a domestic corporation may acquire all of the shares of one or more classes or series of shares of another domestic or foreign corporation, or all of the eligible interests of one or more classes or series of interests of a domestic or foreign eligible entity, in exchange for shares or other securities, eligible interests, obligations, rights to acquire shares or other securities or eligible interests, cash, other property, or any combination of the foregoing, pursuant to a plan of share exchange; or

(2) all of the shares of one or more classes or series of shares of a domestic corporation may be acquired by another domestic or foreign corporation or eligible entity, in exchange for shares or other securities, eligible interests, obligations, rights to acquire shares or other securities or eligible interests, cash, other property, or any combination of the foregoing, pursuant to a plan of share exchange.

(b) A foreign corporation or eligible entity may be the acquired entity in a share exchange only if the share exchange is permitted by the organic law of that corporation or other entity.

(c) If the organic law or organic rules of a domestic eligible entity do not provide procedures for the approval of a share exchange, a plan of share exchange may be adopted and approved, and the share exchange effected, in accordance with the procedures, if any, for a merger. If the organic law or organic rules of a domestic eligible entity do not provide procedures for the approval of either a share exchange or a merger, a plan of share exchange may nonetheless be adopted and approved by the unanimous consent of all of the interest holders of such eligible entity whose interests will be exchanged under the plan of share exchange, and the share exchange may thereafter be effected as provided in the other provisions of this chapter; and for purposes of applying this chapter in such a case:

(1) the eligible entity, its interest holders, interests and articles of incorporation or other organic rules taken together shall be deemed to be a domestic business corporation, shareholders, shares and articles of incorporation, respectively and vice versa as the context may require; and

(2) if the business and affairs of the eligible entity are managed by a person or persons that are not identical to the members or interest holders, that person or those persons shall be deemed to be the board of directors.

(d) The plan of share exchange must include:

(1) the name of each domestic or foreign corporation or other eligible entity the shares or eligible interests of which will be acquired and the name of the domestic or foreign corporation or eligible entity that will acquire those shares or eligible interests;

(2) the terms and conditions of the share exchange;

(3) the manner and basis of exchanging shares of a domestic or foreign corporation or eligible interests in a domestic or foreign eligible entity the shares or eligible interests of which will be acquired under the share exchange for shares or other securities, eligible interests, obligations, rights to acquire shares, other

securities, or eligible interests, cash, other property, or any combination of the foregoing; and

(4) any other provisions required by the organic law governing the acquired entity or its articles of incorporation or organic rules.

(e) Terms of a plan of share exchange may be made dependent on facts objectively ascertainable outside the plan in accordance with section 1.20(k).

(f) A plan of share exchange may be amended only with the consent of each party to the share exchange, except as provided in the plan. A domestic entity may approve an amendment to a plan:

(1) in the same manner as the plan was approved, if the plan does not provide for the manner in which it may be amended; or

(2) in the manner provided in the plan, except that shareholders, members, or interest holders that were entitled to vote on or consent to approval of the plan are entitled to vote on or consent to any amendment of the plan that will change:

(i) the amount or kind of shares or other securities, eligible interests, obligations, rights to acquire shares, other securities or eligible interests, cash, or other property to be received under the plan by the shareholders, members or interest holders of the acquired entity; or

(ii) any of the other terms or conditions of the plan if the change would adversely affect such shareholders, members or interest holders in any material respect.

OFFICIAL COMMENT

1. *In General*

It is often desirable to structure a corporate combination so that the separate existence of one or more parties to the combination does not cease although another corporation or other entity obtains ownership of the shares or interests of those parties. This objective is often particularly important in the formation of insurance and bank holding companies, but is not limited to those contexts. In the absence of the procedure authorized in section 11.03, this kind of result often can be accomplished only by a reverse triangular merger, which involves the formation by a corporation, A, of a new subsidiary, followed by a merger of that subsidiary into another party to the merger, B, effected through the exchange of A's securities for securities of B. Section 11.03 authorizes a more straightforward procedure to accomplish the same result.

Section 11.03 authorizes a share exchange—a transaction in which the acquiring entity acquires all of the shares or eligible interests of one or more classes or series of shares or eligible interests of the acquired entity. The shares or eligible interests of one or more other classes or series of the acquired entity may be excluded from the share exchange or may be included on different bases. Shares or eligible interests of the affected class or series of the acquired entity owned at the effective time of the share exchange by the acquiring entity (or any parent of the acquiring entity or by any wholly owned subsidiary of the acquiring entity or of any such parent, each as defined in section 11.04(k)), may also be excluded from the share exchange.

After the plan of share exchange is adopted and approved as required by section 11.04, it is binding on all holders of the shares or eligible interests of the class or series to be acquired. Section 11.03 does not limit the power of a domestic corporation to acquire shares of another corporation or interests in another entity in a transaction other than a share exchange. In contrast to mergers, the articles of incorporation or public organic record of a party to a share exchange may not be amended by a plan of share exchange. Such an amendment to the articles of incorporation may, however, be effected under chapter 10 as a separate element of a corporate combination that involves a share exchange.

2. *Applicability to Foreign Corporations and Foreign and Domestic Eligible Entities*

A foreign corporation or a foreign eligible entity may be an acquired entity in a share exchange authorized by chapter 11 only if the share exchange is permitted by the organic law of the foreign corporation or eligible entity. Whether and on what terms a foreign corporation or a foreign eligible entity is authorized to be a party to a share exchange is governed by its organic law. If a foreign corporation or eligible entity is so authorized, it must also comply with the applicable terms of chapter 11 in addition to the requirements of its organic law. For example, section 11.03(d) sets forth certain requirements for the content of a plan of share exchange.

With respect to a domestic eligible entity, if the law under which it is organized does not expressly authorize it to be a party to a share exchange under chapter 11, section 11.03(a) is intended to provide the necessary authority. In that case, section 11.03(c) provides procedures for adopting, approving and effecting a plan of share exchange.

3. *Terms and Conditions of Share Exchange*

Chapter 11 imposes no restrictions or limitations on the terms or conditions of a share exchange, except for those contained in section 11.03(f), and the requirement in section 11.03(a) that the acquiring entity must acquire all the shares or eligible interests of the acquired class or series of shares or eligible interests. However, shares or interests of the acquired class or series owned at the effective time of the share exchange by the acquiring entity or any of its parents or their wholly owned subsidiaries may be excluded from the exchange. The list in section 11.03(d) of provisions in a plan of share exchange is not exhaustive.

§11.04. Action on a Plan of Merger or Share Exchange

In the case of a domestic corporation that is a party to a merger or the acquired entity in a share exchange, the plan of merger or share exchange shall be adopted in the following manner:

(a) The plan of merger or share exchange shall first be adopted by the board of directors.

(b) Except as provided in subsections (h), (j) and (l) and in section 11.05, the plan of merger or share exchange shall then be approved by the shareholders. In submitting the plan of merger or share exchange to the shareholders for approval, the board of directors shall recommend that the shareholders approve the plan or, in the case of an offer referred to in subsection (j)(2), that the shareholders tender their shares to the offeror in response to the offer, unless (i) the board of directors makes a determination that because of conflicts of interest or other special circumstances it should not make such a recommendation or (ii) section 8.26 applies. If either (i) or (ii) applies, the board shall inform the shareholders of the basis for its so proceeding.

(c) The board of directors may set conditions for the approval of the plan of merger or share exchange by the shareholders or the effectiveness of the plan of merger or share exchange.

(d) If the plan of merger or share exchange is required to be approved by the shareholders, and if the approval is to be given at a meeting, the corporation shall notify each shareholder, regardless of whether entitled to vote, of the meeting of shareholders at which the plan is to be submitted for approval. The notice must state that the purpose, or one of the purposes, of the meeting is to consider the plan and must contain or be accompanied by a copy or summary of the plan. If the corporation is to be merged into an existing foreign or domestic corporation or eligible entity, the notice must also include or be accompanied by a copy or summary of the articles of incorporation and bylaws or the organic rules of that corporation or eligible entity. If the corporation is to be merged with a domestic or foreign corporation or eligible entity and a new domestic or foreign corporation or eligible entity is to be created pursuant to the merger, the notice must include or be accompanied by a copy or a summary of the articles of incorporation and bylaws or the organic rules of the new corporation or eligible entity.

(e) Unless the articles of incorporation, or the board of directors acting pursuant to subsection (c), require a greater vote or a greater quorum, approval of the plan of merger or share exchange requires the approval of the shareholders at a meeting at which a quorum exists consisting of a majority of the votes entitled to be cast on the plan, and, if any class or series of shares is entitled to vote as a separate group on the plan of merger or share exchange, the approval of each such separate voting group at a meeting at which a quorum of the voting group is present consisting of a majority of the votes entitled to be cast on the merger or share exchange by that voting group.

(f) Subject to subsection (g), separate voting by voting groups is required:

(1) on a plan of merger, by each class or series of shares that:

(i) are to be converted under the plan of merger into shares, other securities, eligible interests, obligations, rights to acquire shares, other securities or eligible interests, cash, other property, or any combination of the foregoing; or

(ii) are entitled to vote as a separate group on a provision in the plan that constitutes a proposed amendment to the articles of incorporation of a surviving corporation that requires action by separate voting groups under section 10.04;

(2) on a plan of share exchange, by each class or series of shares included in the exchange, with each class or series constituting a separate voting group; and

(3) on a plan of merger or share exchange, if the voting group is entitled under the articles of incorporation to vote as a voting group to approve a plan of merger or share exchange, respectively.

(g) The articles of incorporation may expressly limit or eliminate the separate voting rights provided in subsections (f)(1)(i) and (f)(2) as to any class or series of shares, except when the plan of merger or share exchange (i) includes what is or would be in effect an amendment subject to subsection (f)(1)(ii), and (ii) will not effect a substantive business combination.

(h) Unless the articles of incorporation otherwise provide, approval by the corporation's shareholders of a plan of merger is not required if:

(1) the corporation will survive the merger;

(2) except for amendments permitted by section 10.05, its articles of incorporation will not be changed;

(3) each shareholder of the corporation whose shares were outstanding immediately before the effective date of the merger or share exchange will hold the same number of shares, with identical preferences, rights and limitations, immediately after the effective date of the merger; and

(4) the issuance in the merger of shares or other securities convertible into or rights exercisable for shares does not require a vote under section 6.21(f).

(i) If as a result of a merger or share exchange one or more shareholders of a domestic corporation would become subject to new interest holder liability, approval of the plan of merger or share exchange requires the signing in connection with the transaction, by each such shareholder, of a separate written consent to become subject to such new interest holder liability, unless in the case of a shareholder that already has interest holder liability with respect to such domestic corporation, (i) the new interest holder liability is with respect to a domestic or foreign corporation (which may be a different or the same domestic corporation in which the person is a shareholder), and (ii) the terms and conditions of the new interest holder liability are substantially identical to those of the existing interest holder liability (other than for changes that eliminate or reduce such interest holder liability).

(j) Unless the articles of incorporation otherwise provide, approval by the shareholders of a plan of merger or share exchange is not required if:

(1) the plan of merger or share exchange expressly (i) permits or requires the merger or share exchange to be effected under this subsection and (ii) provides that, if the merger or share exchange is to be effected under this subsection, the merger or share exchange will be effected as soon as practicable following the satisfaction of the requirement set forth in subsection (j)(6);

(2) another party to the merger, the acquiring entity in the share exchange, or a parent of another party to the merger or the acquiring entity in the share exchange, makes an offer to purchase, on the terms provided in the plan of merger or share exchange, any and all of the outstanding shares of the corporation that, absent this subsection, would be entitled to vote on the plan of merger or share exchange, except that the offer may exclude shares of the corporation that are owned at the commencement of the offer by the corporation, the offeror, or any parent of the offeror, or by any wholly owned subsidiary of any of the foregoing;

(3) the offer discloses that the plan of merger or share exchange provides that the merger or share exchange will be effected as soon as practicable following the satisfaction of the requirement set forth in subsection (j)(6) and that the shares of the corporation that are not tendered in response to the offer will be treated as set forth in subsection (j)(8);

(4) the offer remains open for at least 10 days;

(5) the offeror purchases all shares properly tendered in response to the offer and not properly withdrawn;

(6) the shares listed below are collectively entitled to cast at least the minimum number of votes on the merger or share exchange that, absent this subsection, would be required by this chapter and by the articles of incorporation for the approval of the merger or share exchange by the shareholders and by any other voting group entitled to vote on the merger or share exchange at a meeting at which all shares entitled to vote on the approval were present and voted:

(i) shares purchased by the offeror in accordance with the offer;

(ii) shares otherwise owned by the offeror or by any parent of the offeror or any wholly owned subsidiary of any of the foregoing; and

(iii) shares subject to an agreement that they are to be transferred, contributed or delivered to the offeror, any parent of the offeror, or any wholly owned subsidiary of any of the foregoing in exchange for shares or eligible interests in such offeror, parent or subsidiary;

(7) the offeror or a wholly owned subsidiary of the offeror merges with or into, or effects a share exchange in which it acquires shares of, the corporation; and

(8) each outstanding share of each class or series of shares of the corporation that the offeror is offering to purchase in accordance with the offer, and that is not purchased in accordance with the offer, is to be converted in the merger into, or into the right to receive, or is to be exchanged in the share exchange for, or for the right to receive, the same amount and kind of securities, eligible interests, obligations, rights, cash, or other property to be paid or exchanged in accordance with the offer for each share of that class or series of shares that is tendered in response to the offer, except that shares of the corporation that are owned by the corporation or that are described in clause (ii) or (iii) of subsection (j)(6) need not be converted into or exchanged for the consideration described in this subsection (j)(8).

(k) As used in subsection (j):

(1) "offer" means the offer referred to in subsection (j)(2);

(2) "offeror" means the person making the offer;

(3) "parent" of an entity means a person that owns, directly or indirectly (through one or more wholly owned subsidiaries), all of the outstanding shares of or eligible interests in that entity;

(4) shares tendered in response to the offer shall be deemed to have been "purchased" in accordance with the offer at the earliest time as of which (i) the offeror has irrevocably accepted those shares for payment and (ii) either (A) in the case of shares represented by certificates, the offeror, or the offeror's designated depository or other agent, has physically received the certificates representing those shares or (B) in the case of shares without certificates, those shares have been transferred into the account of the offeror or its designated depository or other agent, or an agent's message relating to those shares has been received by the offeror or its designated depository or other agent; and

(5) "wholly owned subsidiary" of a person means an entity of or in which that person owns, directly or indirectly (through one or more wholly owned subsidiaries), all of the outstanding shares or eligible interests.

(*l*) Unless the articles of incorporation otherwise provide,

(1) approval of a plan of share exchange by the shareholders of a domestic corporation is not required if the corporation is the acquiring entity in the share exchange; and

(2) shares not to be exchanged under the plan of share exchange are not entitled to vote on the plan.

OFFICIAL COMMENT

1. *In General*

Subject to the exceptions set forth in section 11.04(b), a plan of merger must always be approved by the shareholders of a corporation that is a party to a merger and a plan of share exchange must always be approved by shareholders of the class or series that is being acquired in a share exchange. Under section 11.04(h) approval of a plan of merger by the shareholders of a surviving corporation is not required if the conditions stated in that section are satisfied. Under section 11.04(j), shareholder action by selling shares in a tender offer or exchange offer is accepted as an alternative to the traditional consent by voting if the conditions specified in section 11.04(j) are met.

Section 11.04(g), together with the appraisal rights provisions of chapter 13, is designed to assure that in transactions or actions that may occur under chapters 9, 10, 11 and 12, a shareholder has either a group voting right or an appraisal right.

Under section 10.04(c), and therefore under section 11.04(f)(1)(ii), if a change that requires voting by separate voting groups affects two or more classes or two or more series in the same or a substantially similar way, the relevant classes or series vote together, rather than separately, on the change, unless otherwise provided in the articles of incorporation or required by the board of directors. If separate voting by voting groups is required for a merger or a share exchange under section 11.04(f), it will not fall within the exception to shareholder approval provided by section 11.04(h). For the mechanics of voting where voting by voting groups is required under section 11.04(f), see sections 7.25 and 7.26 and the Official Comments to those sections.

If a merger would amend the articles of incorporation of a survivor that is a domestic corporation in such a way as to affect the voting requirements on future amendments, the transaction must also be approved by the vote required by section 7.27.

2. *Submission to the Shareholders*

When submitting a plan of merger or share exchange to shareholders, the board of directors must recommend the transaction, subject to two exceptions in section 11.04(b). The board might exercise the exception under clause (i) where the number of directors having a conflicting interest makes it inadvisable for them to recommend the transaction or where the board is evenly divided as to the merits of the transaction but is able to agree that shareholders should be permitted to consider the transaction. Alternatively, the board of directors might exercise the exception in clause (ii), which recognizes that, under section 8.26, a board of directors may include a "force the vote" clause in a plan of merger or share exchange, agreeing to submit the plan to shareholders even if, after approving the plan, the board of directors determines that it no longer recommends the plan. Section 11.04(c) permits the board of directors to condition its submission of a plan of merger or share exchange to the shareholders or the effectiveness of a plan of merger or share exchange. Among the conditions that a board of directors might impose are that the plan will not be deemed approved (i) unless it is approved by a specified vote of the shareholders, or by one or more specified classes or series of shares, voting as a separate voting group, or by a specified percentage of disinterested shareholders or (ii) if shareholders holding more than a specified fraction of the outstanding shares assert appraisal rights.

Section 11.04(d) sets forth the notice requirements if a plan of merger or share exchange is to be considered by the shareholders at a meeting. Requirements concerning the timing and content of a notice of meeting are set out in section 7.05. Section 11.04(d) does not address the notice to be given to nonvoting or nonconsenting shareholders where the merger or share exchange is approved, without a meeting, by written consent. However, that requirement is imposed by section 7.04. . . .

4. *Two-Step Transactions*

Section 11.04(j) authorizes a two-step transaction meeting the requirements of that section to proceed without the shareholder vote that would otherwise be required by section 11.04(b). The first step is an offer to the shareholders to tender their shares in response to which enough shareholders tender so that, upon consummation of the offer, the offering party (and any parent or wholly owned subsidiary) owns or has the right to acquire shares with sufficient voting power to satisfy the shareholder approval that would otherwise be required to approve the plan of merger or share exchange pursuant to section 11.04. The second step is a merger or share exchange providing the remaining shareholders the same consideration as was offered to their class or series in the first step offer. The shareholder action in selling in response to the offer provides the necessary consent for the transaction, in lieu of a shareholder vote, if the other conditions set forth in section 11.04(j) are met. The requirements of section 11.04(j), together with sections 11.04(b), 13.20, 13.21 and 13.22, are intended to ensure that shareholders are not disadvantaged by the absence of a vote, and that they receive the same protection in terms of timing, director duties and appraisal rights that they would in a transaction approved by a shareholder vote. For example, section 11.04(b) requires, subject to limited exceptions, that the board of directors make a recommendation with respect to the offer that shareholders tender their shares. This ensures that there is a corporate action implicated by the offer, and that the same director duties will apply to the recommendation to tender into the offer as to conversion or exchange pursuant to a plan of merger or share exchange.

5. *Personal Liability of Shareholders*

The approval provisions of section 11.04(i) apply only in situations where a shareholder is becoming subject to "new interest holder liability" as defined in section 11.01, for example, where a corporation is merging into a general partnership or a cap on the shareholder's interest holder liability is increased. The effect of a merger or share exchange on interest holder liability will be determined as provided in section 11.07(e).

§11.05. Merger Between Parent and Subsidiary or Between Subsidiaries

(a) A domestic or foreign parent entity that owns shares of a domestic corporation which carry at least 90% of the voting power of each class and series of the outstanding shares of the subsidiary that has voting power may (i) merge the subsidiary into itself (if it is a domestic or foreign corporation or eligible entity) or into another domestic or foreign corporation or eligible entity in which the parent entity owns at least 90% of the voting power of each class and series of the outstanding shares or eligible interests which have voting power, or (ii) merge itself (if it is a domestic or foreign corporation or eligible entity) into such subsidiary, in either case without the approval of the board of directors or shareholders of the subsidiary, unless the articles of incorporation or organic rules of the parent entity or the articles of incorporation of the subsidiary corporation otherwise provide. Section 11.04(i) applies to a merger under this section. The articles of merger relating to a merger under this section do not need to be signed by the subsidiary.

(b) A parent entity shall, within 10 days after the effective date of a merger approved under subsection (a), notify each of the subsidiary's shareholders that the merger has become effective.

(c) Except as provided in subsections (a) and (b), a merger between a parent entity and a domestic subsidiary corporation shall be governed by the provisions of chapter 11 applicable to mergers generally.

OFFICIAL COMMENT

If the conditions of section 11.05 are met, no approval is required by the board of directors and the shareholders of a subsidiary that is merged into the parent or another subsidiary. In other respects, mergers between parents and 90%-owned subsidiaries are governed by the other provisions of chapter 11, including section 11.04(i).

§11.06. Articles of Merger or Share Exchange

(a) After (i) a plan of merger has been adopted and approved as required by this Act, or (ii) if the merger is being effected under section 11.02(a)(2), the merger has been approved as required by the organic law governing the parties to the merger, then articles of merger shall be signed by each party to the merger except as provided in section 11.05(a). The articles must set forth:

(1) the name, jurisdiction of formation, and type of entity of each party to the merger;

(2) the name, jurisdiction of formation, and type of entity of the survivor;

(3) if the survivor of the merger is a domestic corporation and its articles of incorporation are amended, or if a new domestic corporation is created as a result of the merger:

(i) the amendments to the survivor's articles of incorporation; or

(ii) the articles of incorporation of the new corporation;

(4) if the survivor of the merger is a domestic eligible entity and its public organic record is amended, or if a new domestic eligible entity is created as a result of the merger:

(i) the amendments to the public organic record of the survivor; or

(ii) the public organic record of the new eligible entity;

(5) if the plan of merger required approval by the shareholders of a domestic corporation that is a party to the merger, a statement that the plan was duly approved by the shareholders and, if voting by any separate voting group was required, by each such separate voting group, in the manner required by this Act and the articles of incorporation;

(6) if the plan of merger or share exchange did not require approval by the shareholders of a domestic corporation that is a party to the merger, a statement to that effect;

(7) as to each foreign corporation that is a party to the merger, a statement that the participation of the foreign corporation was duly authorized as required by its organic law;

(8) as to each domestic or foreign eligible entity that is a party to the merger, a statement that the merger was approved in accordance with its organic law or section 11.02(c); and

(9) if the survivor is created by the merger and is a domestic limited liability partnership, the filing required to become a limited liability partnership, as an attachment.

(b) After a plan of share exchange in which the acquired entity is a domestic corporation or eligible entity has been adopted and approved as required by this Act, articles of share exchange shall be signed by the acquired entity and the acquiring entity. The articles shall set forth:

(1) the name of the acquired entity;

(2) the name, jurisdiction of formation, and type of entity of the domestic or foreign corporation or eligible entity that is the acquiring entity; and

(3) a statement that the plan of share exchange was duly approved by the acquired entity by:

(i) the required vote or consent of each class or series of shares or eligible interests included in the exchange; and

(ii) the required vote or consent of each other class or series of shares or eligible interests entitled to vote on approval of the exchange by the articles of incorporation or organic rules of the acquired entity or section 11.03(c).

(c) In addition to the requirements of subsection (a) or (b), articles of merger or share exchange may contain any other provision not prohibited by law.

(d) The articles of merger or share exchange shall be delivered to the secretary of state for filing and, subject to subsection (e), the merger or share exchange shall take effect at the effective date determined in accordance with section 1.23.

(e) With respect to a merger in which one or more foreign entities is a party or a foreign entity created by the merger is the survivor, the merger itself shall become effective at the later of:

(1) when all documents required to be filed in foreign jurisdictions to effect the merger have become effective, or

(2) when the articles of merger take effect.

(f) Articles of merger filed under this section may be combined with any filing required under the organic law governing any domestic eligible entity involved in the transaction if the combined filing satisfies the requirements of both this section and the other organic law.

§11.07. *Effect of Merger or Share Exchange*

(a) When a merger becomes effective:

(1) the domestic or foreign corporation or eligible entity that is designated in the plan of merger as the survivor continues or comes into existence, as the case may be;

(2) the separate existence of every domestic or foreign corporation or eligible entity that is a party to the merger, other than the survivor, ceases;

(3) all property owned by, and every contract right possessed by, each domestic or foreign corporation or eligible entity that is a party to the merger, other than the survivor, are the property and contract rights of the survivor without transfer, reversion or impairment;

(4) all debts, obligations and other liabilities of each domestic or foreign corporation or eligible entity that is a party to the merger, other than the survivor, are debts, obligations or liabilities of the survivor;

(5) the name of the survivor may, but need not be, substituted in any pending proceeding for the name of any party to the merger whose separate existence ceased in the merger;

(6) if the survivor is a domestic entity, the articles of incorporation and bylaws or the organic rules of the survivor are amended to the extent provided in the plan of merger;

(7) the articles of incorporation and bylaws or the organic rules of a survivor that is a domestic entity and is created by the merger become effective;

(8) the shares of each domestic or foreign corporation that is a party to the merger, and the eligible interests in an eligible entity that is a party to a merger, that are to be converted in accordance with the terms of the merger into shares or other securities, eligible interests, obligations, rights to acquire shares, other securities, or eligible interests, cash, other property, or any combination of the foregoing, are converted, and the former holders of such shares or eligible interests are entitled only to the rights provided to them by those terms or to any rights they may have under chapter 13 or the organic law governing the eligible entity or foreign corporation;

(9) except as provided by law or the terms of the merger, all the rights, privileges, franchises, and immunities of each entity that is a party to the merger, other than the survivor, are the rights, privileges, franchises, and immunities of the survivor; and

(10) if the survivor exists before the merger:

(i) all the property and contract rights of the survivor remain its property and contract rights without transfer, reversion, or impairment;

(ii) the survivor remains subject to all its debts, obligations, and other liabilities; and

(iii) except as provided by law or the plan of merger, the survivor continues to hold all of its rights, privileges, franchises, and immunities.

(b) When a share exchange becomes effective, the shares or eligible interests in the acquired entity that are to be exchanged for shares or other securities, eligible interests, obligations, rights to acquire shares, other securities or eligible interests, cash, other property, or any combination of the foregoing, are entitled only to the rights provided to them in the plan of share exchange or to any rights they may have under chapter 13 or under the organic law governing the acquired entity.

(c) Except as otherwise provided in the articles of incorporation of a domestic corporation or the organic law governing or organic rules of a foreign corporation or a domestic or foreign eligible entity, the effect of a merger or share exchange on interest holder liability is as follows:

(1) A person who becomes subject to new interest holder liability in respect of an entity as a result of a merger or share exchange shall have that new interest holder liability only in respect of interest holder liabilities that arise after the merger or share exchange becomes effective.

(2) If a person had interest holder liability with respect to a party to the merger or the acquired entity before the merger or share exchange becomes effective with respect to shares or eligible interests of such party or acquired entity which were (i) exchanged in the merger or share exchange, (ii) were cancelled in the merger or (iii) the terms and conditions of which relating to interest holder liability were amended pursuant to the merger:

(i) The merger or share exchange does not discharge that prior interest holder liability with respect to any interest holder liabilities that arose before the merger or share exchange becomes effective.

(ii) The provisions of the organic law governing any entity for which the person had that prior interest holder liability shall continue to apply to the collection or discharge of any interest holder liabilities preserved by subsection (c)(2)(i), as if the merger or share exchange had not occurred.

(iii) The person shall have such rights of contribution from other persons as are provided by the organic law governing the entity for which the person had that prior interest holder liability with respect to any interest holder liabilities preserved by subsection (c)(2)(i), as if the merger or share exchange had not occurred.

(iv) The person shall not, by reason of such prior interest holder liability, have interest holder liability with respect to any interest holder liabilities that arise after the merger or share exchange becomes effective.

(3) If a person has interest holder liability both before and after a merger becomes effective with unchanged terms and conditions with respect to the entity that is the survivor by reason of owning the same shares or eligible interests before and after the merger becomes effective, the merger has no effect on such interest holder liability.

(4) A share exchange has no effect on interest holder liability related to shares or eligible interests of the acquired entity that were not exchanged in the share exchange.

(d) Upon a merger becoming effective, a foreign corporation, or a foreign eligible entity, that is the survivor of the merger is deemed to:

(1) appoint the secretary of state as its agent for service of process in a proceeding to enforce the rights of shareholders of each domestic corporation that is a party to the merger who exercise appraisal rights; and

(2) agree that it will promptly pay the amount, if any, to which such shareholders are entitled under chapter 13.

(e) Except as provided in the organic law governing a party to a merger or in its articles of incorporation or organic rules, the merger does not give rise to any rights that an interest holder, governor, or third party would have upon a dissolution, liquidation, or winding up of that party. The merger does not require a party to the merger to wind up its affairs and does not constitute or cause its dissolution or termination.

(f) Property held for a charitable purpose under the law of this state by a domestic or foreign corporation or eligible entity immediately before a merger becomes effective may not, as a result of the transaction, be diverted from the objects for which it was donated, granted, devised, or otherwise transferred except and to the extent permitted by or pursuant to the laws of this state addressing cy près or dealing with nondiversion of charitable assets.

(g) A bequest, devise, gift, grant, or promise contained in a will or other instrument of donation, subscription, or conveyance which is made to an entity that is a party to a merger that is not the survivor and which takes effect or remains payable after the merger inures to the survivor.

(h) A trust obligation that would govern property if transferred to a nonsurviving entity applies to property that is transferred to the survivor after a merger becomes effective.

OFFICIAL COMMENT

Under section 11.07(a), in a merger the parties that merge become one. The survivor automatically becomes the owner of all real and personal property and becomes subject to all the liabilities, actual or contingent, of each other party to the merger. A merger is not a conveyance, transfer, or assignment. It does not give rise to claims of reverter or impairment of title based on a prohibited conveyance, transfer, or assignment. It does not give rise to a claim that a contract with a party to the merger is no longer in effect on the ground of nonassignability, unless the contract specifically addresses that issue. All pending proceedings involving either the survivor or a party whose separate existence ceased as a result of the merger are continued.

In contrast to a merger, a share exchange does not vest in the acquiring entity the assets of the acquired entity, or render the acquiring entity liable for the liabilities of the acquired entity. The statements in sections 11.07(a)(8) and 11.07(b) regarding the rights of former holders of shares or eligible interests are not intended to preclude an otherwise proper question concerning the validity of the merger or share exchange, or to override or otherwise affect any provisions of chapter 13 concerning the exclusiveness of rights under that chapter.

The deemed appointment and agreement in section 11.07(d) by a foreign survivor is based on the implied consent of such a foreign corporation, or foreign eligible entity, to the terms of chapter 11 by reason of entering into an agreement that is governed by this chapter.

Section 11.07(e) sets forth the impact of mergers and share exchanges on interest holder liability. Section 11.04(i) sets forth when approval of a merger or share exchange requires the consent of shareholders who would otherwise become subject to new interest holder liability.

§11.08. Abandonment of a Merger or Share Exchange

(a) After a plan of merger or share exchange has been adopted and approved as required by this chapter, and before articles of merger or share exchange have become effective, the plan may be abandoned by a domestic business corporation that is a party to the plan without action by its shareholders in accordance with any procedures set forth in the plan of merger or share exchange or, if no such procedures are set forth in the plan, in the manner determined by the board of directors.

(b) If a merger or share exchange is abandoned under subsection (a) after articles of merger or share exchange have been delivered to the secretary of state for filing but before the merger or share exchange has become effective, a statement of abandonment signed by all the parties that signed the articles of merger or share exchange shall be delivered to the secretary of state for filing before the articles of merger or share exchange become effective. The statement shall take effect on filing and the merger or share exchange shall be deemed abandoned and shall not become effective. The statement of abandonment must contain:

(1) the name of each party to the merger or the names of the acquiring and acquired entities in a share exchange;

(2) the date on which the articles of merger or share exchange were filed by the secretary of state; and

(3) a statement that the merger or share exchange has been abandoned in accordance with this section.

Chapter 12. Disposition of Assets

§12.01. Disposition of Assets not Requiring Shareholder Approval

No approval of the shareholders is required, unless the articles of incorporation otherwise provide:

(a) to sell, lease, exchange, or otherwise dispose of any or all of the corporation's assets in the usual and regular course of business;

(b) to mortgage, pledge, dedicate to the repayment of indebtedness (whether with or without recourse), or otherwise encumber any or all of the corporation's assets, regardless of whether in the usual and regular course of business;

(c) to transfer any or all of the corporation's assets to one or more domestic or foreign corporations or other entities all of the shares or interests of which are owned by the corporation; or

(d) to distribute assets pro rata to the holders of one or more classes or series of the corporation's shares.

OFFICIAL COMMENT

Section 12.01 specifies dispositions for which shareholder approval is not required, and section 12.02 specifies dispositions requiring shareholder approval.

Examples of dispositions in the usual and regular course of business under section 12.01(a) include the sale of a building that was the corporation's only major asset where the corporation was formed for the purpose of constructing and selling that building, the sale by a corporation of its only major business where the corporation was formed to buy and sell businesses and the proceeds of the sale are to be reinvested in the purchase of a new business, or sales of assets by an open- or closed-end investment company the portfolio of which turns over many times in short periods.

No shareholder approval is required for a transaction involving a pro rata distribution because it comes within section 12.01(d). An example is a spin-off in which shares of a subsidiary are distributed pro rata to the holders of one or more classes or series of shares. On the other hand, a non pro rata distribution—for example, a split-off in which shares of a subsidiary are distributed only to some shareholders in exchange for some or all of their shares—would require shareholder approval under section 12.02(a) if the disposition would leave the corporation without a significant continuing business activity. When the transaction involves a distribution in liquidation—for example, when two or more subsidiaries (whether they have existed previously or are newly formed) representing all of a dissolved corporation's business activities are distributed to shareholders (sometimes referred to as a split-up)—the transaction will be governed by chapter 14 (dissolution), not by chapter 12.

§12.02. Shareholder Approval of Certain Dispositions

(a) A sale, lease, exchange, or other disposition of assets, other than a disposition described in section 12.01, requires approval of the corporation's shareholders if the disposition would leave the corporation without a significant continuing business activity. A corporation will conclusively be deemed to have retained a significant continuing business activity if it retains a business activity that represented, for the corporation and its subsidiaries on a consolidated basis, at least (i) 25% of total assets at the end of the most recently completed fiscal year, and (ii) either 25% of either income from continuing operations before taxes or 25% of revenues from continuing operations, in each case for the most recently completed fiscal year.

(b) To obtain the approval of the shareholders under subsection (a) the board of directors shall first adopt a resolution authorizing the disposition. The disposition shall then be approved by the shareholders. In submitting the disposition to the shareholders for approval, the board of directors shall recommend that the shareholders approve the disposition, unless (i) the board of directors makes a determination that because of conflicts of interest or other special circumstances it should not make such a recommendation, or (ii) section 8.26 applies. If either (i) or (ii) applies, the board shall inform the shareholders of the basis for its so proceeding.

(c) The board of directors may set conditions for the approval by the shareholders of a disposition or the effectiveness of the disposition.

(d) If a disposition is required to be approved by the shareholders under subsection (a), and if the approval is to be given at a meeting, the corporation shall notify each shareholder, regardless of whether entitled to vote, of the meeting of shareholders at which the disposition is to be submitted for approval. The notice must state that the purpose, or one of the purposes, of the meeting is to consider the disposition and must contain a description of the disposition, including the terms and conditions of the disposition and the consideration to be received by the corporation.

(e) Unless the articles of incorporation or the board of directors acting pursuant to subsection (c) require a greater vote or a greater quorum, the approval of a disposition by the shareholders shall require the approval of the shareholders at a meeting at which a quorum exists consisting of a majority of the votes entitled to be cast on the disposition.

(f) After a disposition has been approved by the shareholders under this chapter, and at any time before the disposition has been consummated, it may be abandoned by the corporation without action by the shareholders, subject to any contractual rights of other parties to the disposition.

(g) A disposition of assets in the course of dissolution under chapter 14 is not governed by this section.

(h) The assets of a direct or indirect consolidated subsidiary shall be deemed to be the assets of the parent corporation for the purposes of this section.

OFFICIAL COMMENT

1. *In General*

Section 12.02(a) requires shareholder approval for a sale, lease, exchange or other disposition of assets by a corporation that would leave the corporation without a significant continuing business activity, other than as provided in section 12.01. Whether a disposition leaves a corporation with a significant continuing business activity, within the meaning of section 12.02(a), depends on whether the corporation's remaining business activity is significant when compared to the corporation's business before the disposition. The 25% safe harbor provides a measure of certainty in making this determination. The safe-harbor test is applied to assets and to revenue or income for the fiscal year ended immediately before the decision by the board of directors to make the disposition in question.

If a corporation disposes of assets for the purpose of reinvesting the proceeds of the disposition in substantially the same business in a somewhat different form (for example, by selling the corporation's only plant for the purpose of buying or building a replacement plant), the disposition and reinvestment should be treated together, so that the transaction should not be deemed to leave the corporation without a significant continuing business activity.

In determining whether a disposition would leave a corporation without a significant continuing business activity, the test combines a parent corporation with subsidiaries that are or should be consolidated with it under applicable accounting principles. For example, if a corporation's only significant business is owned by a consolidated subsidiary, a sale of that business requires approval of the parent's shareholders under section 12.02. Correspondingly, if a corporation owns one significant business directly, and several other significant businesses through one or more wholly or almost wholly owned subsidiaries, a sale by the corporation of the single business it owns directly does not require shareholder approval under section 12.02 (for example, the 25% retention tests of section 12.02(a) are met).

If all or a large part of a corporation's assets are held for investment, the corporation actively manages those assets, and it has no other significant business, for purposes of chapter 12 the corporation should be considered to be in the business of investing in assets, so that a sale of most of those assets without a reinvestment should be considered a sale that would leave the corporation without a significant continuing business activity. In applying the 25% tests of section 12.02(a), an issue could arise if a corporation had more than one business activity, one or more of which might be traditional operating activities, such as manufacturing or distribution, and another of which might be considered managing investments in other securities or enterprises. If the activity constituting the management of investments is to be a continuing business activity as a result of the active engagement of the management of the corporation in that process and the 25% retention tests were met upon the disposition of the other businesses, shareholder approval would not be required.

A board of directors may determine that a retained continuing business falls within the 25% bright-line tests of the safe harbor in section 12.02(a) based either on accounting principles and practices that are reasonable in the circumstances or (in applying the asset test) on a fair valuation or other method that is reasonable in the circumstances in a manner similar to that described in section 6.40(d) and the Official Comment 4 to that section.

The use of the term "significant" and the specific 25% safe harbor test for purposes of this section do not imply a standard for the test of significance or materiality for any other purposes under the Act or otherwise.

2. *Submission to Shareholders*

When submitting a proposal to shareholders for a disposition of assets, the board of directors must recommend the disposition, subject to two exceptions in section 12.02(b). The board might exercise the exception under clause (i) where the number of directors having a conflicting interest makes it inadvisable for the board to recommend the disposition or where the board is evenly divided as to the merits of the proposal but is able to agree that shareholders should be permitted to consider it. Alternatively, the board of directors might exercise the exception under clause (ii), which recognizes that, under section 8.26, a board of directors may agree to submit a proposal for a disposition to a vote of shareholders even if, after approving the proposal, the board of directors determines that it no longer recommends the proposal.

Section 12.02(c) permits the board of directors to condition its submission to the shareholders of a proposal for a disposition of assets or the effectiveness of the disposition. Among the conditions that a board of directors might impose are that the proposal will not be deemed approved: (i) unless it is approved by a specified percentage of the shareholders, or by one or more specified classes or series of shares, voting as a separate voting group, or by a specified percentage of disinterested shareholders; or (ii) if shareholders holding more than a specified fraction of the outstanding shares exercise appraisal rights. . . .

CHAPTER 13. APPRAISAL RIGHTS

SUBCHAPTER A. RIGHT TO APPRAISAL AND PAYMENT FOR SHARES

§13.01. Definitions

In this chapter:

- "Affiliate" means a person that directly or indirectly through one or more intermediaries controls, is controlled by, or is under common control with another person or is a senior executive of such person. For purposes of section 13.02(b)(4), a person is deemed to be an affiliate of its senior executives.
- "Corporation" means the domestic corporation that is the issuer of the shares held by a shareholder demanding appraisal and, for matters covered in sections 13.22 through 13.31, includes the survivor of a merger.
- "Fair value" means the value of the corporation's shares determined:

(i) immediately before the effectiveness of the corporate action to which the shareholder objects;

(ii) using customary and current valuation concepts and techniques generally employed for similar businesses in the context of the transaction requiring appraisal; and

(iii) without discounting for lack of marketability or minority status except, if appropriate, for amendments to the articles of incorporation pursuant to section 13.02(a)(4).

- "Interest" means interest from the date the corporate action becomes effective until the date of payment, at the rate of interest on judgments in this state on the effective date of the corporate action.
- "Interested transaction" means a corporate action described in section 13.02(a), other than a merger pursuant to section 11.05, involving an interested person in which any of the shares or assets of the corporation are being acquired or converted. As used in this definition:

(i) "Interested person" means a person, or an affiliate of a person, who at any time during the one-year period immediately preceding approval by the board of directors of the corporate action:

(A) was the beneficial owner of 20% or more of the voting power of the corporation, other than as owner of excluded shares;

(B) had the power, contractually or otherwise, other than as owner of excluded shares, to cause the appointment or election of 25% or more of the directors to the board of directors of the corporation; or

(C) was a senior executive or director of the corporation or a senior executive of any affiliate of the corporation, and that senior executive or director will receive, as a result of the corporate action, a financial benefit not generally available to other shareholders as such, other than:

(I) employment, consulting, retirement, or similar benefits established separately and not as part of or in contemplation of the corporate action;

(II) employment, consulting, retirement, or similar benefits established in contemplation of, or as part of, the corporate action that are not more favorable than those existing before the corporate action or, if more favorable, that have been approved on behalf of the corporation in the same manner as is provided in section 8.62; or

(III) in the case of a director of the corporation who will, in the corporate action, become a director or governor of the acquiror or any of its affiliates, rights and benefits as a director or governor that are provided on the same basis as those afforded by the acquiror generally to other directors or governors of such entity or such affiliate.

(ii) "Beneficial owner" means any person who, directly or indirectly, through any contract, arrangement, or understanding, other than a revocable proxy, has or shares the power to vote, or to direct the voting of, shares; except that a member of a national securities exchange is not deemed to be a beneficial owner of securities held directly or indirectly by it on behalf of another person if the member is precluded by the rules of the exchange from voting without instruction on contested matters or matters that may affect substantially the rights or privileges of the holders of the securities to be voted. When two or more persons agree to act together for the purpose of voting their shares of the corporation, each member of the group formed thereby is deemed to have acquired beneficial ownership, as of the date of the agreement, of all shares having voting power of the corporation beneficially owned by any member of the group.

(iii) "Excluded shares" means shares acquired pursuant to an offer for all shares having voting power if the offer was made within one year before the corporate action for consideration of the same kind and of a value equal to or less than that paid in connection with the corporate action.

- "Preferred shares" means a class or series of shares whose holders have preference over any other class or series of shares with respect to distributions.
- "Senior executive" means the chief executive officer, chief operating officer, chief financial officer, and any individual in charge of a principal business unit or function.
- "Shareholder" means a record shareholder, a beneficial shareholder, and a voting trust beneficial owner.

OFFICIAL COMMENT

1. *Overview*

Chapter 13 proceeds from the premise that judicial appraisal should be provided by statute only when two conditions co-exist. First, a proposed corporate action as approved by a majority will result in a fundamental change in the shares to be affected by the action. Second, uncertainty concerning the fair value of the affected shares may cause reasonable persons to differ about the fairness of the terms of the corporate action. Uncertainty is reduced, however, in the case of publicly traded shares. This explains both the market exception described below and the limits provided to that exception.

When these two conditions exist in connection with domestications and conversions under chapter 9, mergers and share exchanges under chapter 11, and dispositions of assets requiring shareholder approval under chapter 12, chapter 13 provides for appraisal rights. Each of these actions will result in a fundamental change in the shares that a disapproving shareholder may believe was not adequately compensated by the terms approved by the majority. Shareholders are not entitled to appraisal, however, if the change will not alter the terms of the class or series of securities that they hold. For example, statutory appraisal rights are not available for shares of any class or series of the surviving corporation in a merger that are not being changed in the merger or for shares of any class or series that is not included in a share exchange. Appraisal is also not triggered by a voluntary dissolution under chapter 14 because the dissolution does not affect liquidation rights of the shares of any class or series.

With the exception of reverse stock splits that result in cashing out some of the shares of a class or series, chapter 13 does not grant appraisal rights in connection with amendments to the articles of incorporation. This does not reflect a judgment that an amendment changing the terms of a particular class or series may not have significant economic effects. Rather, it reflects a judgment that distinguishing among different types of amendments for the purposes of statutory appraisal is necessarily arbitrary. Chapter 13 delineates in section 13.02(a)(5) a list of actions for which the corporation may voluntarily choose to provide appraisal. It also allows, under section 13.02(c), a provision in the articles of incorporation that eliminates, in whole or in part, statutory appraisal rights for preferred shares, subject to certain conditions.

Chapter 13 provides an exception to appraisal rights for publicly traded shares, referred to as the "market exception." This exception is available in those situations when shareholders are likely to receive fair value if they sell their shares in the market after the announcement of an appraisal-triggering transaction. For the market exception to apply under chapter 13, there must be a liquid market for the shares. The market exception does not apply where the appraisal-triggering action is a conflict transaction.

2. *Definitions*

Section 13.01 contains specialized definitions applicable only to chapter 13.

A. Corporation

The definition of "corporation" in section 13.01 includes, for purposes of the post-transaction matters covered in sections 13.22 through 13.31, a successor entity in a merger where the corporation is not the surviving entity. The definition does not include an acquiring entity in a share exchange or disposition of assets because the corporation whose shares or assets were acquired continues in existence in both of these instances and remains responsible for the appraisal obligations. Whether a foreign corporation or other form of domestic or foreign entity is subject to appraisal rights in connection with any of these transactions depends upon the applicable law of the relevant jurisdiction.

B. Fair value

Clause (i) of the definition of "fair value" in section 13.01 specifies that fair value is to be determined immediately before the effectiveness of the corporate action, which will be after the shareholder vote. Accordingly, section 13.01 permits consideration of changes in the value of the corporation's shares after the shareholder vote but before the effectiveness of the transaction, to the extent such changes are relevant. Similarly, in a two-step transaction culminating in a merger, fair value is determined immediately before the second step merger, taking into account any interim changes in value.

Clause (ii) of the definition of "fair value" in section 13.01 adopts the view that different transactions and different contexts may warrant different valuation methodologies. Customary valuation concepts and techniques will typically take into account numerous relevant factors, and will normally result in a range of values, not a particular single value. A court determining fair value under chapter 13 should give great deference to the aggregate consideration accepted or approved by a disinterested board of directors for an appraisal-triggering transaction.

Valuation discounts for lack of marketability or minority status are inappropriate in most appraisal actions, both because most transactions that trigger appraisal rights affect the corporation as a whole and because such discounts may give the majority the opportunity to take advantage of minority shareholders who have been forced against their will to accept the appraisal-triggering transaction. Clause (iii) of the definition of "fair value" adopts the view that appraisal should generally award a shareholder his or her proportional interest in the corporation after valuing the corporation as a whole, rather than the value of the shareholder's shares when valued alone.

C. Interest

The specification of the rate of interest on judgments, rather than a more subjective rate, eliminates a possible issue of contention and should facilitate voluntary settlements. Other state law determines whether interest is compound or simple.

D. Interested Transaction

The term "interested transaction" addresses two groups of conflict transactions: those in subsections (i)(A) and (B) of the definition, which involve large shareholders; and those in subsection (i)(C), which involve senior executives and directors. The phrase "involving an interested person" as applied to subsections (i)(A) and (B) denotes participation beyond merely voting or participating on the same basis as other holders of securities of the same or a similar class or series. When a transaction fits within the definition of an interested transaction there are two consequences: the market exception will not be applicable, and the exclusion of other remedies under section 13.40 will not be applicable unless certain disinterested approvals have been obtained.

The definition of "beneficial owner" in subsection (ii) of the definition of "interested transaction" is used to identify possible conflict situations by deeming each member of a group that agrees to vote in concert to be a beneficial owner of all the voting shares owned by the members of the group. (In contrast, the term "beneficial shareholder," as defined in section 1.40, is used to identify those persons entitled to appraisal rights.) When an acquisition is effected in two steps (a tender offer followed by a merger) within one year, and the consideration in the merger is of the same kind and of at least the same value as that in the tender offer, the two-step acquisition is properly considered a single transaction for purposes of identifying conflict transactions, regardless of whether the second-step merger is governed by section 11.04 or 11.05. Therefore the shares acquired in such an offer (defined as "excluded shares" in subsection (iii)) are excluded in subsections (i)(A) and (B) from the determination of whether a person is an "interested person" for purposes of the second-step merger.

A reverse split in which small shareholders are cashed out will constitute an interested transaction if there is an affiliate of the corporation who satisfies the test in subsections (i)(A) or (B). In that case, the corporation itself will be considered an affiliate of the large shareholder and fall within the definition of "interested person," such that when the corporation acquires and cashes out the shares of the small shareholders the acquisition will be an interested transaction.

Subsection (i)(C) applies to management buyouts because management's participation in the buyout group is itself "a financial benefit not generally available to other shareholders." It also applies to transactions involving other types of economic benefits (excluding benefits afforded to shareholders generally) afforded to senior executives (as defined in section 13.01) and directors in specified conflict situations, unless specific objective or procedural standards are met. It would also apply to less common situations, such as where the vote of a director is manipulated by providing the director with special consideration to secure his or her vote in favor of the transaction. Section 13.01 specifically defines the term "affiliate" to include an entity of which a person is a senior executive. As a result of this definition, if a senior executive of the corporation is to continue and is to receive enumerated employment and other financial benefits after the transaction, exempting the transaction from the category of "interested transactions" will depend on meeting one of the three conditions specified in subsection (i)(C), for example:

- If an individual has an arrangement under which benefits will be triggered on a "change of control," such as accelerated vesting of options, retirement benefits, deferred compensation and similar items, or is afforded the opportunity to retire or leave the employ of the enterprise with more favorable economic results than would be the case absent a change of control, the existence of these arrangements would not mean that the transaction is an interested transaction if the arrangements had been established as a general condition of the individual's employment or continued employment, rather than in contemplation of the particular transaction.
- If such arrangements are established as part of, or as a condition of, the transaction, the transaction will still not be considered an interested transaction if the arrangements are either not more favorable to the officer or director than those already in existence or, if they treat the director or officer more favorably, are approved by "qualified" directors (*i.e.*, meeting the standard specified in section 1.43), in the same manner as provided for conflicting interest transactions generally with the corporation under section 8.62. This category would include arrangements with the corporation that have been negotiated as part of, or as a condition to, the transaction or arrangements with the acquiring company or one or more of its other subsidiaries.
- If a person who is a director of the corporation and, in connection with the transaction, is to become a director of the acquiror or its parent, or to continue as a director of the corporation when it becomes a subsidiary of the acquiror, the transaction will not be considered an interested transaction as long as that person will not be treated more favorably as a director than are other persons who are serving in the same director positions.

F. Senior executive

The definition of "senior executive" in section 13.01 encompasses the group of individuals in control of corporate information and the corporation's day-to-day operations. An employee of a subsidiary organization is a "senior executive" of the parent if the employee is "in charge of a principal business unit or function" of the parent and its subsidiaries on a combined or consolidated basis.

F. Shareholder

The definition of "shareholder" in section 13.01 encompasses beneficial shareholders and voting trust beneficial owners. This recognizes that these persons have or hold on behalf of others an economic interest in the shares. Use of the term "beneficial shareholder" for this purpose is to be contrasted with the use of the term "beneficial owner" in subsection (ii) of the definition of "interested transaction" to identify possible conflict situations. The distinction between "record shareholder" and "beneficial shareholder" appears primarily in section 13.03, which establishes the manner in which beneficial shareholders, and record shareholders who are acting on behalf of beneficial shareholders, perfect appraisal rights.

§13.02. Right to Appraisal

(a) A shareholder is entitled to appraisal rights, and to obtain payment of the fair value of that shareholder's shares, in the event of any of the following corporate actions:

(1) consummation of a merger to which the corporation is a party (i) if shareholder approval is required for the merger by section 11.04, or would be required but for the provisions of section 11.04(j), except that appraisal rights shall not be available to any shareholder of the corporation with respect to shares of any class or series that remain outstanding after consummation of the merger, or (ii) if the corporation is a subsidiary and the merger is governed by section 11.05;

(2) consummation of a share exchange to which the corporation is a party the shares of which will be acquired, except that appraisal rights shall not be available to any shareholder of the corporation with respect to any class or series of shares of the corporation that is not acquired in the share exchange;

(3) consummation of a disposition of assets pursuant to section 12.02 if the shareholder is entitled to vote on the disposition, except that appraisal rights shall not be available to any shareholder of the corporation with respect to shares of any class or series if (i) under the terms of the corporate action approved by the shareholders there is to be distributed to shareholders in cash the corporation's net assets, in excess of a reasonable amount reserved to meet claims of the type described in sections 14.06 and 14.07, (A) within one year after the shareholders' approval of the action and (B) in accordance with their respective interests determined at the time of distribution, and (ii) the disposition of assets is not an interested transaction;

(4) an amendment of the articles of incorporation with respect to a class or series of shares that reduces the number of shares of a class or series owned by the shareholder to a fraction of a share if the corporation has the obligation or right to repurchase the fractional share so created;

(5) any other merger, share exchange, disposition of assets or amendment to the articles of incorporation, in each case to the extent provided by the articles of incorporation, bylaws or a resolution of the board of directors;

(6) consummation of a domestication pursuant to section 9.20 if the shareholder does not receive shares in the foreign corporation resulting from the domestication that have terms as favorable to the shareholder in all material respects, and represent at least the same percentage interest of the total voting rights of the outstanding shares of the foreign corporation, as the shares held by the shareholder before the domestication;

(7) consummation of a conversion of the corporation to a nonprofit corporation pursuant to section 9.30; or

(8) consummation of a conversion of the corporation to an unincorporated entity pursuant to section 9.30.

(b) Notwithstanding subsection (a), the availability of appraisal rights under subsections (a)(1), (2), (3), (4), (6) and (8) shall be limited in accordance with the following provisions:

(1) Appraisal rights shall not be available for the holders of shares of any class or series of shares which is:

(i) a covered security under section 18(b)(1)(A) or (B) of the Securities Act of 1933;

(ii) traded in an organized market and has at least 2,000 shareholders and a market value of at least $20 million (exclusive of the value of such shares held by the corporation's subsidiaries, senior executives and directors and by any beneficial shareholder and any voting trust beneficial owner owning more than 10% of such shares); or

(iii) issued by an open end management investment company registered with the Securities and Exchange Commission under the Investment Company Act of 1940 and which may be redeemed at the option of the holder at net asset value.

(2) The applicability of subsection (b)(1) shall be determined as of:

(i) the record date fixed to determine the shareholders entitled to receive notice of the meeting of shareholders to act upon the corporate action requiring appraisal rights or, in the case of an offer made pursuant to section 11.04(j), the date of such offer; or

(ii) if there is no meeting of shareholders and no offer made pursuant to section 11.04(j), the day before the consummation of the corporate action or effective date of the amendment of the articles of incorporation, as applicable.

(3) Subsection (b)(1) shall not be applicable and appraisal rights shall be available pursuant to subsection (a) for the holders of any class or series of shares (i) who are required by the terms of the corporate action requiring appraisal rights to accept for such shares anything other than cash or shares of any class or any series of shares of any corporation, or any other proprietary interest of any other entity, that satisfies the standards set forth in subsection (b)(1) at the time the corporate action becomes effective, or (ii) in the case of the consummation of a disposition of assets pursuant to section 12.02, unless the cash, shares, or proprietary interests received in the disposition are, under the terms of the corporate action approved by the shareholders, to be distributed to the shareholders, as part of a distribution to shareholders of the net assets of the corporation

in excess of a reasonable amount to meet claims of the type described in sections 14.06 and 14.07, (A) within one year after the shareholders' approval of the action, and (B) in accordance with their respective interests determined at the time of the distribution.

(4) Subsection (b)(1) shall not be applicable and appraisal rights shall be available pursuant to subsection (a) for the holders of any class or series of shares where the corporate action is an interested transaction.

(c) Notwithstanding any other provision of section 13.02, the articles of incorporation as originally filed or any amendment to the articles of incorporation may limit or eliminate appraisal rights for any class or series of preferred shares, except that (i) no such limitation or elimination shall be effective if the class or series does not have the right to vote separately as a voting group (alone or as part of a group) on the action or if the action is a conversion under section 9.30, or a merger having a similar effect as a conversion in which the converted entity is an eligible entity, and (ii) any such limitation or elimination contained in an amendment to the articles of incorporation that limits or eliminates appraisal rights for any of such shares that are outstanding immediately before the effective date of such amendment or that the corporation is or may be required to issue or sell thereafter pursuant to any conversion, exchange or other right existing immediately before the effective date of such amendment shall not apply to any corporate action that becomes effective within one year after the effective date of such amendment if such action would otherwise afford appraisal rights.

OFFICIAL COMMENT

1. *Transactions Requiring Appraisal Rights*

Section 13.02(a) establishes the scope of appraisal rights by identifying those transactions that afford this right. Statutory appraisal is made available only for corporate actions that will result in a fundamental change in the shares to be affected by the action and then only when uncertainty concerning the fair value of the affected shares may cause reasonable differences about the fairness of the terms of the corporate action. The transactions that satisfy both of these criteria are set forth in section 13.02(a), subject to the exceptions set forth in section 13.02(b). In a two-step transaction authorized by section 11.04(j), shareholders at the time of the second step merger could have appraisal rights even though there is no shareholder vote. Shareholders who tender in response to the offer in the first step of such a transaction would not have appraisal rights; their tendering in response to the offer has the same effect on appraisal rights as if they had voted for the transaction.

Under section 13.02(b)(4), the reasons for granting appraisal rights in a reverse stock split in which shares are cashed out are similar to those for granting such rights in cases of cash-out mergers, as both transactions could compel affected shareholders to accept cash for their investment in an amount established by the corporation. Appraisal is afforded only for those shareholders of a class or series whose interest is so affected by the amendment. As provided in section 12.02(g), a disposition of assets by a corporation in the course of dissolution under chapter 14 is governed by that chapter, not chapter 12, and thus does not implicate appraisal rights.

An express grant of voluntary appraisal rights under section 13.02(a)(5) overrides any of the exceptions to the availability of appraisal rights in section 13.02(a). Any voluntary grant of appraisal rights by the corporation to the holders of one or more of its classes or series of shares in connection with a corporate action will automatically make all of the provisions of chapter 13 applicable to the corporation and such holders regarding that corporate action.

2. *Market Exception to Appraisal Rights*

.Because section 13.02(b)(3)(i) excludes from the market exception those transactions that require shareholders to accept anything other than cash or securities that also meet the liquidity tests of section 13.02(b)(1), shareholders are assured of receiving either appraisal rights, cash from the transaction, or shares or other proprietary interests in the survivor entity that are liquid. Section 13.02(b)(2) specifies the date on which the corporation must satisfy the requirements of section 13.02(b)(1) for the market exception to be applicable. Section 13.02(b)(4) recognizes that the market price of, or consideration for, shares of a corporation that proposes to engage in an interested transaction of the type listed in section 13.02(a) may be subject to influences where a corporation's management, controlling shareholders or directors have conflicting interests that could, if not dealt with appropriately, adversely affect the consideration that otherwise could have been expected. Section 13.02(b)(4) thus provides that the market exception will not apply in those instances where the transaction constitutes an interested transaction (as defined in section 13.01).

3. *Elimination of Appraisal Rights for Preferred Shares*

Section 13.02(c) permits the corporation to eliminate or limit appraisal rights that would otherwise be available for the holders of one or more series or classes of preferred shares provided that the standards in that section are met. Chapter 13 does not permit the corporation to eliminate or limit the appraisal rights of common shares.

§13.03. Assertion of Rights by Nominees and Beneficial Shareholders

(a) A record shareholder may assert appraisal rights as to fewer than all the shares registered in the record shareholder's name but owned by a beneficial shareholder or a voting trust beneficial owner only if the record shareholder objects with respect to all shares of a class or series owned by the beneficial shareholder or the voting trust beneficial owner and notifies the corporation in writing of the name and address of each beneficial shareholder or voting trust beneficial owner on whose behalf appraisal rights are being asserted. The rights of a record shareholder who asserts appraisal rights for only part of the shares held of record in the record shareholder's name under this subsection shall be determined as if the shares as to which the record shareholder objects and the record shareholder's other shares were registered in the names of different record shareholders.

(b) A beneficial shareholder and a voting trust beneficial owner may assert appraisal rights as to shares of any class or series held on behalf of the shareholder only if such shareholder:

(1) submits to the corporation the record shareholder's written consent to the assertion of such rights no later than the date referred to in section 13.22(b)(2)(ii); and

(2) does so with respect to all shares of the class or series that are beneficially owned by the beneficial shareholder or the voting trust beneficial owner.

SUBCHAPTER B. PROCEDURE FOR EXERCISE OF APPRAISAL RIGHTS

§13.20. Notice of Appraisal Rights

(a) Where any corporate action specified in section 13.02(a) is to be submitted to a vote at a shareholders' meeting, the meeting notice (or where no approval of such action is required pursuant to section 11.04(j), the offer made pursuant to section 11.04(j)), must state that the corporation has concluded that appraisal rights are, are not or may be available under this chapter. If the corporation concludes that appraisal rights are or may be available, a copy of this chapter must accompany the meeting notice or offer sent to those record shareholders entitled to exercise appraisal rights.

(b) In a merger pursuant to section 11.05, the parent entity shall notify in writing all record shareholders of the subsidiary who are entitled to assert appraisal rights that the corporate action became effective. Such notice shall be sent within 10 days after the corporate action became effective and include the materials described in section 13.22.

(c) Where any corporate action specified in section 13.02(a) is to be approved by written consent of the shareholders pursuant to section 7.04:

(1) written notice that appraisal rights are, are not or may be available shall be sent to each record shareholder from whom a consent is solicited at the time consent of such shareholder is first solicited and, if the corporation has concluded that appraisal rights are or may be available, the notice must be accompanied by a copy of this chapter; and

(2) written notice that appraisal rights are, are not or may be available must be delivered together with the notice to nonconsenting and nonvoting shareholders required by sections 7.04(e) and (f), may include the materials described in section 13.22 and, if the corporation has concluded that appraisal rights are or may be available, must be accompanied by a copy of this chapter.

(d) Where corporate action described in section 13.02(a) is proposed, or a merger pursuant to section 11.05 is effected, the notice referred to in subsection (a) or (c), if the corporation concludes that appraisal rights are or may be available, and in subsection (b) must be accompanied by:

(1) financial statements of the corporation that issued the shares that may be subject to appraisal, consisting of a balance sheet as of the end of a fiscal year ending not more than 16 months before the date of the notice, an income statement for that year, and a cash flow statement for that year; provided that, if such financial statements are not reasonably available, the corporation shall provide reasonably equivalent financial information; and

(2) the latest interim financial statements of such corporation, if any.

(e) The right to receive the information described in subsection (d) may be waived in writing by a shareholder before or after the corporate action.

§13.21. Notice of Intent to Demand Payment and Consequences of Voting or Consenting

(a) If a corporate action specified in section 13.02(a) is submitted to a vote at a shareholders' meeting, a shareholder who wishes to assert appraisal rights with respect to any class or series of shares:

(1) shall deliver to the corporation, before the vote is taken, written notice of the shareholder's intent to demand payment if the proposed action is effectuated; and

(2) shall not vote, or cause or permit to be voted, any shares of such class or series in favor of the proposed action.

(b) If a corporate action specified in section 13.02(a) is to be approved by written consent, a shareholder who wishes to assert appraisal rights with respect to any class or series of shares shall not sign a consent in favor of the proposed action with respect to that class or series of shares.

(c) If a corporate action specified in section 13.02(a) does not require shareholder approval pursuant to section 11.04(j), a shareholder who wishes to assert appraisal rights with respect to any class or series of shares (i) shall deliver to the corporation before the shares are purchased pursuant to the offer written notice of the shareholder's intent to demand payment if the proposed action is effected; and (ii) shall not tender, or cause or permit to be tendered, any shares of such class or series in response to such offer.

(d) A shareholder who fails to satisfy the requirements of subsection (a), (b) or (c) is not entitled to payment under this chapter.

§13.22. Appraisal Notice and Form

(a) If a corporate action requiring appraisal rights under section 13.02(a) becomes effective, the corporation shall deliver a written appraisal notice and form required by subsection (b) to all shareholders who satisfy the requirements of sections 13.21(a), (b) or (c). In the case of a merger under section 11.05, the parent shall deliver an appraisal notice and form to all record shareholders who may be entitled to assert appraisal rights.

(b) The appraisal notice shall be delivered no earlier than the date the corporate action specified in section 13.02(a) became effective, and no later than 10 days after such date, and must:

(1) supply a form that (i) specifies the first date of any announcement to shareholders made before the date the corporate action became effective of the principal terms of the proposed corporate action, and (ii) if such announcement was made, requires the shareholder asserting appraisal rights to certify whether beneficial ownership of those shares for which appraisal rights are asserted was acquired before that date, and (iii) requires the shareholder asserting appraisal rights to certify that such shareholder did not vote for or consent to the transaction as to the class or series of shares for which appraisal is sought;

(2) state:

(i) where the form shall be sent and where certificates for certificated shares shall be deposited and the date by which those certificates must be deposited, which date may not be earlier than the date by which the corporation must receive the required form under subsection (b)(2)(ii);

(ii) a date by which the corporation shall receive the form, which date may not be fewer than 40 nor more than 60 days after the date the subsection (a) appraisal notice is sent, and state that the shareholder shall have waived the right to demand appraisal with respect to the shares unless the form is received by the corporation by such specified date;

(iii) the corporation's estimate of the fair value of the shares;

(iv) that, if requested in writing, the corporation will provide, to the shareholder so requesting, within 10 days after the date specified in subsection (b)(2)(ii) the number of shareholders who return the forms by the specified date and the total number of shares owned by them; and

(v) the date by which the notice to withdraw under section 13.23 shall be received, which date shall be within 20 days after the date specified in subsection (b)(2)(ii); and

(3) be accompanied by a copy of this chapter.

§13.23. Perfection of Rights; Right to Withdraw

(a) A shareholder who receives notice pursuant to section 13.22 and who wishes to exercise appraisal rights shall sign and return the form sent by the corporation and, in the case of certificated shares, deposit the shareholder's certificates in accordance with the terms of the notice by the date referred to in the notice pursuant to section 13.22(b)(2)(ii). In addition, if applicable, the shareholder shall certify on the form whether the beneficial owner of such shares acquired beneficial ownership of the shares before the date required to be set forth in the notice pursuant to section 13.22(b)(1)(i). If a shareholder fails to make this certification, the corporation may elect to treat the shareholder's shares as after-acquired shares under section 13.25. Once a shareholder deposits that shareholder's certificates or, in the case of uncertificated shares, returns the signed forms, that shareholder loses all rights as a shareholder, unless the shareholder withdraws pursuant to subsection (b).

(b) A shareholder who has complied with subsection (a) may nevertheless decline to exercise appraisal rights and withdraw from the appraisal process by so notifying the corporation in writing by the date set forth in the appraisal notice pursuant to section 13.22(b)(2)(v). A shareholder who fails to so withdraw from the appraisal process may not thereafter withdraw without the corporation's written consent.

(c) A shareholder who does not sign and return the form and, in the case of certificated shares, deposit that shareholder's share certificates where required, each by the date set forth in the notice described in section 13.22(b), shall not be entitled to payment under this chapter.

§13.24. Payment

(a) Except as provided in section 13.25, within 30 days after the form required by section 13.22(b)(2)(ii) is due, the corporation shall pay in cash to those shareholders who complied with section 13.23(a) the amount the corporation estimates to be the fair value of their shares, plus interest.

(b) The payment to each shareholder pursuant to subsection (a) must be accompanied by:

(1) (i) financial statements of the corporation that issued the shares to be appraised, consisting of a balance sheet as of the end of a fiscal year ending not more than 16 months before the date of payment, an income statement for that year, and a cash flow statement for that year; provided that, if such annual financial statements are not reasonably available, the corporation shall provide reasonably equivalent financial information, and (ii) the latest interim financial statements of such corporation, if any;

(2) a statement of the corporation's estimate of the fair value of the shares, which estimate shall equal or exceed the corporation's estimate given pursuant to section 13.22(b)(2)(iii); and

(3) a statement that shareholders described in subsection (a) have the right to demand further payment under section 13.26 and that if any such shareholder does not do so within the time period specified in section 13.26(b), such shareholder shall be deemed to have accepted the payment under subsection (a) in full satisfaction of the corporation's obligations under this chapter.

§13.25. After-Acquired Shares

(a) A corporation may elect to withhold payment required by section 13.24 from any shareholder who was required to, but did not certify that beneficial ownership of all of the shareholder's shares for which appraisal rights are asserted was acquired before the date set forth in the appraisal notice sent pursuant to section 13.22(b)(1).

(b) If the corporation elected to withhold payment under subsection (a), it shall, within 30 days after the form required by section 13.22(b)(2)(ii) is due, notify all shareholders who are described in subsection (a):

(1) of the information required by section 13.24(b)(1);

(2) of the corporation's estimate of fair value pursuant to section 13.24(b)(2);

(3) that they may accept the corporation's estimate of fair value, plus interest, in full satisfaction of their demands or demand appraisal under section 13.26;

(4) that those shareholders who wish to accept such offer shall so notify the corporation of their acceptance of the corporation's offer within 30 days after receiving the offer; and

(5) that those shareholders who do not satisfy the requirements for demanding appraisal under section 13.26 shall be deemed to have accepted the corporation's offer.

(c) Within 10 days after receiving the shareholder's acceptance pursuant to subsection (b)(4), the corporation shall pay in cash the amount it offered under subsection (b)(2) plus interest to each shareholder who agreed to accept the corporation's offer in full satisfaction of the shareholder's demand.

(d) Within 40 days after delivering the notice described in subsection (b), the corporation shall pay in cash the amount it offered to pay under subsection (b)(2) plus interest to each shareholder described in subsection (b)(5).

§13.26. Procedure if Shareholder Dissatisfied with Payment or Offer

(a) A shareholder paid pursuant to section 13.24 who is dissatisfied with the amount of the payment shall notify the corporation in writing of that shareholder's estimate of the fair value of the shares and demand payment of that estimate (less any payment under section 13.24) plus interest. A shareholder offered payment under section 13.25 who is dissatisfied with that offer shall reject the offer and demand payment of the shareholder's stated estimate of the fair value of the shares plus interest.

(b) A shareholder who fails to notify the corporation in writing of that shareholder's demand to be paid the shareholder's stated estimate of the fair value plus interest under subsection (a) within 30 days after receiving the corporation's payment or offer of payment under section 13.24 or section 13.25, respectively, waives the right to demand payment under this section and shall be entitled only to the payment made or offered pursuant to those respective sections.

SUBCHAPTER C. JUDICIAL APPRAISAL OF SHARES

§13.30. Court Action

(a) If a shareholder makes demand for payment under section 13.26 which remains unsettled, the corporation shall commence a proceeding within 60 days after receiving the payment demand and petition the court to determine the fair value of the shares and accrued interest. If the corporation does not commence the proceeding within the 60-day period, it shall pay in cash to each shareholder the amount the shareholder demanded pursuant to section 13.26 plus interest.

(b) The corporation shall commence the proceeding in the [name or describe court].

(c) The corporation shall make all shareholders (regardless of whether they are residents of this state) whose demands remain unsettled parties to the proceeding as in an action against their shares, and all parties shall be served with a copy of the petition. Nonresidents may be served by registered or certified mail or by publication as provided by law.

(d) The jurisdiction of the court in which the proceeding is commenced under subsection (b) is plenary and exclusive. The court may appoint one or more persons as appraisers to receive evidence and recommend a decision on the question of fair value. The appraisers shall have the powers described in the order appointing them, or in any amendment to it. The shareholders demanding appraisal rights are entitled to the same discovery rights as parties in other civil proceedings. There shall be no right to a jury trial.

(e) Each shareholder made a party to the proceeding is entitled to judgment (i) for the amount, if any, by which the court finds the fair value of the shareholder's shares exceeds the amount paid by the corporation to the shareholder for such shares, plus interest, or (ii) for the fair value, plus interest, of the shareholder's shares for which the corporation elected to withhold payment under section 13.25.

§13.31. Court Costs and Expenses

(a) The court in an appraisal proceeding commenced under section 13.30 shall determine all court costs of the proceeding, including the reasonable compensation and expenses of appraisers appointed by the court. The court shall assess the court costs against the corporation, except that the court may assess court costs against all or some of the shareholders demanding appraisal, in amounts which the court finds equitable, to the extent the court finds such shareholders acted arbitrarily, vexatiously, or not in good faith with respect to the rights provided by this chapter.

(b) The court in an appraisal proceeding may also assess the expenses of the respective parties in amounts the court finds equitable:

(1) against the corporation and in favor of any or all shareholders demanding appraisal if the court finds the corporation did not substantially comply with the requirements of sections 13.20, 13.22, 13.24, or 13.25; or

(2) against either the corporation or a shareholder demanding appraisal, in favor of any other party, if the court finds the party against whom expenses are assessed acted arbitrarily, vexatiously, or not in good faith with respect to the rights provided by this chapter.

(c) If the court in an appraisal proceeding finds that the expenses incurred by any shareholder were of substantial benefit to other shareholders similarly situated and that such expenses should not be assessed against the corporation, the court may direct that such expenses be paid out of the amounts awarded the shareholders who were benefited.

(d) To the extent the corporation fails to make a required payment pursuant to sections 13.24, 13.25, or 13.26, the shareholder may sue directly for the amount owed, and to the extent successful, shall be entitled to recover from the corporation all expenses of the suit.

SUBCHAPTER D. OTHER REMEDIES

§13.40. Other Remedies Limited

(a) The legality of a proposed or completed corporate action described in section 13.02(a) may not be contested, nor may the corporate action be enjoined, set aside or rescinded, in a legal or equitable proceeding by a shareholder after the shareholders have approved the corporate action.

(b) Subsection (a) does not apply to a corporate action that:

(1) was not authorized and approved in accordance with the applicable provisions of:

(i) chapter 9, 10, 11, or 12;

(ii) the articles of incorporation or bylaws; or

(iii) the resolution of the board of directors authorizing the corporate action;

(2) was procured as a result of fraud, a material misrepresentation, or an omission of a material fact necessary to make statements made, in light of the circumstances in which they were made, not misleading;

(3) is an interested transaction, unless it has been recommended by the board of directors in the same manner as is provided in section 8.62 and has been approved by the shareholders in the same manner as is provided in section 8.63 as if the interested transaction were a director's conflicting interest transaction; or

(4) is approved by less than unanimous consent of the voting shareholders pursuant to section 7.04 if:

(i) the challenge to the corporate action is brought by a shareholder who did not consent and as to whom notice of the approval of the corporate action was not effective at least 10 days before the corporate action was effected; and

(ii) the proceeding challenging the corporate action is commenced within 10 days after notice of the approval of the corporate action is effective as to the shareholder bringing the proceeding.

OFFICIAL COMMENT

The principle underlying section 13.40 generally is that when the holders of a majority of the shares have approved a corporate change, the corporation should be permitted to proceed even if a minority considers the change unwise or disadvantageous. The existence of an appraisal remedy recognizes that shareholders may disagree about the financial consequences that a corporate action may have and that some may hold such strong views that they will want to vindicate them in a judicial proceeding. Accordingly, if an appraisal proceeding results in an award of additional consideration to the shareholders who pursued appraisal, no inference should be drawn that the judgment of the majority was wrong or that compensation is now owed to shareholders who did not seek appraisal. The limitations are not confined to cases where appraisal is available. The liquidity and reliability considerations that justify the market exception also justify imposing the same limitation on post-shareholder approval remedies that apply when appraisal is available.

Section 13.40 permits proceedings contesting the legality of a transaction, or seeking to enjoin, rescind or set aside the corporate action after the action has been approved by shareholders under the four circumstances described in section 13.40(b)(1). In the case of a corporate action that is an interested transaction, the same reasoning that supports the provision of appraisal rights in situations where the market exception would otherwise apply under section 13.02(b) also supports the approach in section 13.40(b)(3) not to preclude judicial review or relief in connection with such transactions, unless other strong safeguards are present. Those safeguards are drawn from the treatment of director conflicting interest transactions in sections 8.60 through 8.63. In those sections, a conflict of interest transaction may be protected if either qualified director or disinterested shareholder approval is obtained after required disclosure. Here, the protection is made available only if both those requirements are met. Absent compliance with those safeguards, the standard of review to be applied, and the extent of the relief that may be available is not addressed by this section.

The scope of section 13.40(b) is limited and does not otherwise affect applicable state law. Section 13.40(b) does not create any cause of action; it merely removes the bar to the types of post-transaction claims provided in section 13.40(a). Even then, whether the specific facts of a transaction subject to section 13.40(b) warrant invalidation or rescission is left to the discretion of the court. Similarly, section 13.40 leaves to applicable state law the question of remedies, such as injunctive relief, that may be available before the corporate action is approved by shareholders in light of other remedies that may be available after the transaction is approved or completed. Where post-shareholder approval claims outside the scope of section 13.40 are asserted, the availability of judicial review, the remedies (such as damages) that shareholders may have, and questions relating to election of remedies, will be determined by applicable state law. Section 13.40 addresses challenges only to the corporate action and does not address remedies, if any, that shareholders may have against directors or other persons as a result of the corporate action, even where subsection (b)(4) applies. See section 8.31 and the related Official Comment and the introductory Official Comment to chapter 8F under the heading "Scope of Subchapter F."

CHAPTER 14. DISSOLUTION

SUBCHAPTER A. VOLUNTARY DISSOLUTION

§14.01. *Dissolution by Incorporators or Initial Directors*

A majority of the incorporators or initial directors of a corporation that has not issued shares or has not commenced business may dissolve the corporation by delivering to the secretary of state for filing articles of dissolution that set forth:

(a) the name of the corporation;

(b) the date of its incorporation;

(c) either (i) that none of the corporation's shares has been issued or (ii) that the corporation has not commenced business;

(d) that no debt of the corporation remains unpaid;

(e) that the net assets of the corporation remaining after winding up have been distributed to the shareholders, if shares were issued; and

(f) that a majority of the incorporators or initial directors authorized the dissolution.

§14.02. *Dissolution by Board of Directors and Shareholders*

(a) The board of directors may propose dissolution for submission to the shareholders by first adopting a resolution authorizing the dissolution.

(b) For a proposal to dissolve to be adopted, it shall then be approved by the shareholders. In submitting the proposal to dissolve to the shareholders for approval, the board of directors shall recommend that the shareholders approve the dissolution, unless (i) the board of directors determines that because of conflict of interest or other special circumstances it should make no recommendation or (ii) section 8.26 applies. If either (i) or (ii) applies, the board shall inform the shareholders of the basis for its so proceeding.

(c) The board of directors may set conditions for the approval of the proposal for dissolution by shareholders or the effectiveness of the dissolution.

(d) If the approval of the shareholders is to be given at a meeting, the corporation shall notify each shareholder, regardless of whether entitled to vote, of the meeting of shareholders at which the dissolution is to be submitted for approval. The notice must state that the purpose, or one of the purposes, of the meeting is to consider dissolving the corporation.

(e) Unless the articles of incorporation or the board of directors acting pursuant to subsection (c) require a greater vote, a greater quorum, or a vote by voting groups, adoption of the proposal to dissolve shall require the approval of the shareholders at a meeting at which a quorum exists consisting of a majority of the votes entitled to be cast on the proposal to dissolve.

§14.03. Articles of Dissolution

(a) At any time after dissolution is authorized, the corporation may dissolve by delivering to the secretary of state for filing articles of dissolution setting forth:

(1) the name of the corporation;

(2) the date that dissolution was authorized; and

(3) if dissolution was approved by the shareholders, a statement that the proposal to dissolve was duly approved by the shareholders in the manner required by this Act and by the articles of incorporation.

(b) The articles of dissolution shall take effect at the effective date determined in accordance with section 1.23. A corporation is dissolved upon the effective date of its articles of dissolution.

(c) For purposes of this subchapter, "dissolved corporation" means a corporation whose articles of dissolution have become effective and includes a successor entity to which the remaining assets of the corporation are transferred subject to its liabilities for purposes of liquidation.

§14.04. Revocation of Dissolution

(a) A corporation may revoke its dissolution within 120 days after its effective date.

(b) Revocation of dissolution shall be authorized in the same manner as the dissolution was authorized unless that authorization permitted revocation by action of the board of directors alone, in which event the board of directors may revoke the dissolution without shareholder action.

(c) After the revocation of dissolution is authorized, the corporation may revoke the dissolution by delivering to the secretary of state for filing articles of revocation of dissolution, together with a copy of its articles of dissolution, that set forth:

(1) the name of the corporation;

(2) the effective date of the dissolution that was revoked;

(3) the date that the revocation of dissolution was authorized;

(4) if the corporation's board of directors (or incorporators) revoked the dissolution, a statement to that effect;

(5) if the corporation's board of directors revoked a dissolution as authorized by the shareholders, a statement that revocation was permitted by action by the board of directors alone pursuant to that authorization; and

(6) if shareholder action was required to revoke the dissolution, a statement that the revocation was duly approved by the shareholders in the manner required by this Act and by the articles of incorporation.

(d) The articles of revocation of dissolution shall take effect at the effective date determined in accordance with section 1.23. Revocation of dissolution is effective upon the effective date of the articles of revocation of dissolution.

(e) When the revocation of dissolution is effective, it relates back to and takes effect as of the effective date of the dissolution and the corporation resumes carrying on its business as if dissolution had never occurred.

§14.05. Effect of Dissolution

(a) A corporation that has dissolved continues its corporate existence but the dissolved corporation may not carry on any business except that appropriate to wind up and liquidate its business and affairs, including:

(1) collecting its assets;

(2) disposing of its properties that will not be distributed in kind to its shareholders;

(3) discharging or making provision for discharging its liabilities;

(4) making distributions of its remaining assets among its shareholders according to their interests; and

(5) doing every other act necessary to wind up and liquidate its business and affairs.

(b) Dissolution of a corporation does not:

(1) transfer title to the corporation's property;

(2) prevent transfer of its shares or securities;

(3) subject its directors or officers to standards of conduct different from those prescribed in chapter 8;

(4) change (i) quorum or voting requirements for its board of directors or shareholders; (ii) provisions for selection, resignation, or removal of its directors or officers or both; or (iii) provisions for amending its bylaws;

(5) prevent commencement of a proceeding by or against the corporation in its corporate name;

(6) abate or suspend a proceeding pending by or against the corporation on the effective date of dissolution; or

(7) terminate the authority of the registered agent of the corporation.

(c) A distribution in liquidation under this section may only be made by a dissolved corporation. For purposes of determining the shareholders entitled to receive a distribution in liquidation, the board of directors may fix a record date for determining shareholders entitled to a distribution in liquidation, which date may not be retroactive. If the board of directors does not fix a record date for determining shareholders entitled to a distribution in liquidation, the record date is the date the board of directors authorizes the distribution in liquidation.

§14.06. Known Claims Against Dissolved Corporation

(a) A dissolved corporation may dispose of the known claims against it by notifying its known claimants in writing of the dissolution at any time after its effective date.

(b) The written notice must:

(1) describe information that must be included in a claim;

(2) provide a mailing address where a claim may be sent;

(3) state the deadline, which may not be fewer than 120 days after the written notice is effective, by which the dissolved corporation shall receive the claim; and

(4) state that the claim will be barred if not received by the deadline.

(c) A claim against the dissolved corporation is barred:

(1) if a claimant who was given written notice under subsection (b) does not deliver the claim to the dissolved corporation by the deadline; or

(2) if a claimant whose claim was rejected by the dissolved corporation does not commence a proceeding to enforce the claim within 90 days after the rejection notice is effective.

(d) For purposes of this section, "claim" does not include a contingent liability or a claim based on an event occurring after the effective date of dissolution.

§14.07. Other Claims Against Dissolved Corporation

(a) A dissolved corporation may publish notice of its dissolution and request that persons with claims against the dissolved corporation present them in accordance with the notice.

(b) The notice must:

(1) be published (i) one time in a newspaper of general circulation in the county where the dissolved corporation's principal office (or, if none in this state, its registered office) is or was last located or (ii) be posted conspicuously for at least 30 days on the dissolved corporation's website;

(2) describe the information that must be included in a claim and provide a mailing address where the claim may be sent; and

(3) state that a claim against the dissolved corporation will be barred unless a proceeding to enforce the claim is commenced within three years after the publication of the notice.

(c) If the dissolved corporation publishes a notice in accordance with subsection (b), the claim of each of the following claimants is barred unless the claimant commences a proceeding to enforce the claim against the dissolved corporation within three years after the publication date of the notice:

(1) a claimant who was not given written notice under section 14.06;

(2) a claimant whose claim was timely sent to the dissolved corporation but not acted on by the corporation;

(3) a claimant whose claim is contingent or based on an event occurring after the effective date of dissolution.

(d) A claim that is not barred by section 14.06(c) or section 14.07(c) may be enforced:

(1) against the dissolved corporation, to the extent of its undistributed assets; or

(2) except as provided in section 14.08(d), if the assets have been distributed in liquidation, against a shareholder of the dissolved corporation to the

extent of the shareholder's pro rata share of the claim or the corporate assets distributed to the shareholder in liquidation, whichever is less, but a shareholder's total liability for all claims under this section may not exceed the total amount of assets distributed to the shareholder.

§14.08. Court Proceedings

(a) A dissolved corporation that has published a notice under section 14.07 may file an application with the [name or describe court] for a determination of the amount and form of security to be provided for payment of claims that are contingent or have not been made known to the dissolved corporation or that are based on an event occurring after the effective date of dissolution but that, based on the facts known to the dissolved corporation, are reasonably estimated to arise after the effective date of dissolution. Provision need not be made for any claim that is or is reasonably anticipated to be barred under section 14.07(c).

(b) Within 10 days after the filing of the application, notice of the proceeding shall be given by the dissolved corporation to each claimant holding a contingent claim whose contingent claim is shown on the records of the dissolved corporation.

(c) The court may appoint a guardian ad litem to represent all claimants whose identities are unknown in any proceeding brought under this section. The reasonable fees and expenses of such guardian, including all reasonable expert witness fees, shall be paid by the dissolved corporation.

(d) Provision by the dissolved corporation for security in the amount and the form ordered by the court under section 14.08(a) shall satisfy the dissolved corporation's obligations with respect to claims that are contingent, have not been made known to the dissolved corporation or are based on an event occurring after the effective date of dissolution, and such claims may not be enforced against a shareholder who received assets in liquidation.

§14.09. Director Duties

(a) Directors shall cause the dissolved corporation to discharge or make reasonable provision for the payment of claims and make distributions in liquidation of assets to shareholders after payment or provision for claims.

(b) Directors of a dissolved corporation which has disposed of claims under section 14.06, 14.07, or 14.08 shall not be liable for breach of section 14.09(a) with respect to claims against the dissolved corporation that are barred or satisfied under section 14.06, 14.07 or 14.08.

SUBCHAPTER B. ADMINISTRATIVE DISSOLUTION

§14.20. Grounds for Administrative Dissolution

The secretary of state may commence a proceeding under section 14.21 to dissolve a corporation administratively if:

(a) the corporation does not pay within 60 days after they are due any fees, taxes, interest or penalties imposed by this Act or other laws of this state;

(b) the corporation does not deliver its annual report to the secretary of state within 60 days after it is due;

(c) the corporation is without a registered agent or registered office in this state for 60 days or more;

(d) the secretary of state has not been notified within 60 days that the corporation's registered agent or registered office has been changed, that its registered agent has resigned, or that its registered office has been discontinued; or

(e) the corporation's period of duration stated in its articles of incorporation expires.

§14.21. Procedure for and Effect of Administrative Dissolution

(a) If the secretary of state determines that one or more grounds exist under section 14.20 for dissolving a corporation, the secretary of state shall serve the corporation with written notice of such determination under section 5.04.

(b) If the corporation does not correct each ground for dissolution or demonstrate to the reasonable satisfaction of the secretary of state that each ground determined by the secretary of state does not exist within 60 days after service of the notice under section 5.04, the secretary of state shall administratively dissolve the corporation by signing a certificate of dissolution that recites the ground or grounds for dissolution and its effective date. The secretary of state shall file the original of the certificate and serve a copy on the corporation under section 5.04.

(c) A corporation administratively dissolved continues its corporate existence but may not carry on any business except that necessary to wind up and liquidate its business and affairs under section 14.05 and notify claimants under sections 14.06 and 14.07.

(d) The administrative dissolution of a corporation does not terminate the authority of its registered agent.

§14.22. Reinstatement Following Administrative Dissolution

(a) A corporation administratively dissolved under section 14.21 may apply to the secretary of state for reinstatement within two years after the effective date of dissolution. The application must:

(1) state the name of the corporation and the effective date of its administrative dissolution;

(2) state that the ground or grounds for dissolution either did not exist or have been eliminated;

(3) state that the corporation's name satisfies the requirements of section 4.01; and

(4) contain a certificate from the [taxing authority] reciting that all taxes owed by the corporation have been paid.

(b) If the secretary of state determines that the application contains the information required by subsection (a) and that the information is correct, the secretary of state shall cancel the certificate of dissolution and prepare a certificate of reinstatement that recites such determination and the effective date of reinstatement, file the original of the certificate, and serve a copy on the corporation under section 5.04.

(c) When the reinstatement is effective, it relates back to and takes effect as of the effective date of the administrative dissolution and the corporation resumes carrying on its business as if the administrative dissolution had never occurred.

§14.23. Appeal from Denial of Reinstatement

(a) If the secretary of state denies a corporation's application for reinstatement following administrative dissolution, the secretary of state shall serve the corporation under section 5.04 with a written notice that explains the reason or reasons for denial.

(b) The corporation may appeal the denial of reinstatement to the [name or describe court] within 30 days after service of the notice of denial is effected. The corporation appeals by petitioning the court to set aside the dissolution and attaching to the petition copies of the secretary of state's certificate of dissolution, the corporation's application for reinstatement, and the secretary of state's notice of denial.

(c) The court may summarily order the secretary of state to reinstate the dissolved corporation or may take other action the court considers appropriate.

(d) The court's final decision may be appealed as in other civil proceedings.

SUBCHAPTER C. JUDICIAL DISSOLUTION

§14.30. Grounds for Judicial Dissolution

(a) The [name or describe court or courts] may dissolve a corporation:

(1) in a proceeding by the attorney general if it is established that:

(i) the corporation obtained its articles of incorporation through fraud; or

(ii) the corporation has continued to exceed or abuse the authority conferred upon it by law;

(2) in a proceeding by a shareholder if it is established that:

(i) the directors are deadlocked in the management of the corporate affairs, the shareholders are unable to break the deadlock, and irreparable injury to the corporation is threatened or being suffered, or the business and affairs of the corporation can no longer be conducted to the advantage of the shareholders generally, because of the deadlock;

(ii) the directors or those in control of the corporation have acted, are acting, or will act in a manner that is illegal, oppressive, or fraudulent;

(iii) the shareholders are deadlocked in voting power and have failed, for a period that includes at least two consecutive annual meeting dates, to elect successors to directors whose terms have expired; or

(iv) the corporate assets are being misapplied or wasted;

(3) in a proceeding by a creditor if it is established that:

(i) the creditor's claim has been reduced to judgment, the execution on the judgment returned unsatisfied, and the corporation is insolvent; or

(ii) the corporation has admitted in writing that the creditor's claim is due and owing and the corporation is insolvent;

(4) in a proceeding by the corporation to have its voluntary dissolution continued under court supervision; or

(5) in a proceeding by a shareholder if the corporation has abandoned its business and has failed within a reasonable time to liquidate and distribute its assets and dissolve.

(b) Subsection (a)(2) shall not apply in the case of a corporation that, on the date of the filing of the proceeding, has a class or series of shares which is:

(1) a covered security under section 18(b)(1)(A) or (B) of the Securities Act of 1933; or

(2) not a covered security, but is held by at least 300 shareholders and the shares outstanding have a market value of at least $20 million (exclusive of the value of such shares held by the corporation's subsidiaries, senior executives, directors and beneficial shareholders and voting trust beneficial owners owning more than 10% of such shares).

(c) In subsection (a), "shareholder" means a record shareholder, a beneficial shareholder, and an unrestricted voting trust beneficial owner, and in subsection (b), "shareholder" means a record shareholder, a beneficial shareholder, and a voting trust beneficial owner.

OFFICIAL COMMENT

Section 14.30 provides grounds for the judicial dissolution of a corporation at the request of the state, a shareholder, a creditor, or when a corporation that has commenced voluntary dissolution seeks judicial oversight. Judicial oversight may be useful to protect the corporation from suits by creditors or shareholders. Under this section, the court has discretion as to whether dissolution is appropriate even though the specified grounds for judicial dissolution exist. . . .

2. *Involuntary Dissolution by Shareholders*

Section 14.30(a)(2) provides for involuntary dissolution at the request of a shareholder under circumstances involving deadlock or significant abuse of power by controlling shareholders or directors. Section 14.30(c) extends the ability to seek judicial dissolution under section 14.30(a)(2) to beneficial shareholders and unrestricted voting trust beneficial owners, as these persons have, or hold on behalf of others, an economic interest in the shares. The remedy of judicial dissolution is available only for shareholders of corporations that do not meet the tests in section 14.30(b). Even for those corporations to which section 14.30(a)(2) applies, however, the court can take into account the number of shareholders and the nature of the trading market for the shares in deciding whether to exercise its discretion to order dissolution. Shareholders of corporations that meet the tests of section 14.30(b) may often have the ability to sell their shares if they are dissatisfied with current management or may seek other remedies under the Act. See, for example, sections 7.48(a) and 8.09. The grounds for dissolution under section 14.30(a)(2) are broader than those required to be shown for the appointment of a custodian or receiver under section 7.48(a). The difference is attributable to the different focus of the two proceedings. Although some of the circumstances listed in 14.30(a)(2), such as deadlock, may implicate the welfare of the corporation as a whole, the primary focus is on the effect of actions by those in control on the value of the complaining shareholder's individual investment. For example, "oppressive" behavior in section 14.30(a)(2)(ii) generally describes action directed against a particular shareholder. In contrast, the focus of protection in an action to appoint a custodian or receiver under section 7.48(a) is the corporate entity, and the remedy is intended to protect the interests of all shareholders, creditors and others who may have an interest therein. In other instances, action that is "illegal" or "fraudulent" under section 14.30(a)(2)(ii) may be severely prejudicial to the interests of an individual shareholder, whereas conduct that is illegal with respect to the entire corporation may be remedied by other causes of action under the Act.

Section 14.30(a)(5) provides a basis for a shareholder to obtain involuntary dissolution in the event the corporation has abandoned its business, but those in control of the corporation have delayed unreasonably in either liquidating and distributing its assets or completing the necessary procedures to dissolve the corporation. . . .

§14.31. Procedure for Judicial Dissolution

(a) Venue for a proceeding by the attorney general to dissolve a corporation lies in [name or describe court]. Venue for a proceeding brought by any other party named in section 14.30(a) lies in [name or describe court].

(b) It is not necessary to make shareholders parties to a proceeding to dissolve a corporation unless relief is sought against them individually.

(c) A court in a proceeding brought to dissolve a corporation may issue injunctions, appoint a receiver or custodian during the proceeding with all powers and duties the court directs, take other action required to preserve the corporate assets wherever located, and carry on the business of the corporation until a full hearing can be held.

(d) Within 10 days of the commencement of a proceeding to dissolve a corporation under section 14.30(a)(2), the corporation shall deliver to all shareholders, other than the petitioner, a notice stating that the shareholders are entitled to avoid the dissolution of the corporation by electing to purchase the petitioner's shares under section 14.34 and accompanied by a copy of section 14.34.

§14.32. Receivership or Custodianship

(a) Unless an election to purchase has been filed under section 14.34, a court in a judicial proceeding brought to dissolve a corporation may appoint one or more receivers to wind up and liquidate, or one or more custodians to manage, the business and affairs of the corporation. The court shall hold a hearing, after notifying all parties to the proceeding and any interested persons designated by the court, before appointing a receiver or custodian. The court appointing a receiver or custodian has jurisdiction over the corporation and all of its property wherever located.

(b) The court may appoint an individual or a domestic or foreign corporation or eligible entity as a receiver or custodian, which, if a foreign corporation or foreign eligible entity, must be registered to do business in this state. The court may require the receiver or custodian to post bond, with or without sureties, in an amount the court directs.

(c) The court shall describe the powers and duties of the receiver or custodian in its appointing order, which may be amended from time to time. Among other powers:

(1) the receiver (i) may dispose of all or any part of the assets of the corporation wherever located, at a public or private sale; and (ii) may sue and defend in the receiver's own name as receiver of the corporation in all courts of this state;

(2) the custodian may exercise all of the powers of the corporation, through or in place of its board of directors, to the extent necessary to manage the affairs of the corporation in the best interests of its shareholders and creditors.

The receiver or custodian shall have such other powers and duties as the court may provide in the appointing order, which may be amended from time to time.

(d) The court during a receivership may redesignate the receiver a custodian and during a custodianship may redesignate the custodian a receiver.

(e) The court from time to time during the receivership or custodianship may order compensation paid and expenses paid or reimbursed to the receiver or custodian from the assets of the corporation or proceeds from the sale of the assets.

§14.33. Decree of Dissolution

(a) If after a hearing the court determines that one or more grounds for judicial dissolution described in section 14.30 exist, it may enter a decree dissolving the corporation and specifying the effective date of the dissolution, and the clerk of the court shall deliver a certified copy of the decree to the secretary of state for filing.

(b) After entering the decree of dissolution, the court shall direct the winding-up and liquidation of the corporation's business and affairs in accordance with section 14.05 and the notification of claimants in accordance with sections 14.06 and 14.07.

§14.34. Election to Purchase in Lieu of Dissolution

(a) In a proceeding under section 14.30(a)(2) to dissolve a corporation, the corporation may elect or, if it fails to elect, one or more shareholders may elect to purchase all shares owned by the petitioning shareholder at the fair value of the shares. An election pursuant to this section shall be irrevocable unless the court determines that it is equitable to set aside or modify the election.

(b) An election to purchase pursuant to this section may be filed with the court at any time within 90 days after the filing of the petition under section 14.30(a)(2) or at such later time as the court in its discretion may allow. If the election to purchase is filed by one or more shareholders, the corporation shall, within 10 days thereafter, give written notice to all shareholders, other than the petitioner. The notice must state the name and number of shares owned by the petitioner and the name and number of shares owned by each electing shareholder and must advise the recipients of their right to join in the election to purchase shares in accordance with this section. Shareholders who wish to participate shall file notice of their intention to join in the purchase no later than 30 days after the effectiveness of the notice to them. All shareholders who have filed an election or notice of their intention to participate in the election to purchase thereby become parties to the proceeding and shall participate in the purchase in proportion to their ownership of shares as of the date the first election was filed, unless they otherwise agree or the court otherwise directs. After an election has been filed by the corporation or one or more shareholders, the proceeding under section 14.30(a)(2) may not be discontinued or settled, nor may the petitioning shareholder sell or otherwise dispose of his or her shares, unless the court determines that it would be equitable to the corporation and the shareholders, other than the petitioner, to permit such discontinuance, settlement, sale, or other disposition.

(c) If, within 60 days of the filing of the first election, the parties reach agreement as to the fair value and terms of purchase of the petitioner's shares, the court shall enter an order directing the purchase of the petitioner's shares upon the terms and conditions agreed to by the parties.

(d) If the parties are unable to reach an agreement as provided for in subsection (c), the court, upon application of any party, shall stay the proceedings under section 14.30(a)(2) and determine the fair value of the petitioner's shares as of the day before the date on which the petition under section 14.30(a)(2) was filed or as of such other date as the court deems appropriate under the circumstances.

(e) Upon determining the fair value of the shares, the court shall enter an order directing the purchase upon such terms and conditions as the court deems appropriate, which may include payment of the purchase price in installments, where necessary in the interests of equity, provision for security to assure payment of the purchase price and any additional expenses as may have been awarded, and, if the shares are to be purchased by shareholders, the allocation of shares among them. In allocating the petitioner's shares among holders of different classes or series of shares, the court should attempt to preserve the existing distribution of voting rights among holders of different classes or series insofar as practicable and may direct that holders of a specific class or classes or series shall not participate in the purchase. Interest may be allowed at the rate and from the date determined by the court to be equitable, but if the court finds that the refusal of the petitioning shareholder to accept an offer of payment was arbitrary or otherwise not in good faith, no interest shall be allowed. If the court finds that the petitioning shareholder had probable grounds for relief under sections 14.30(a)(2)(ii) or (iv), it may award expenses to the petitioning shareholder.

(f) Upon entry of an order under subsections (c) or (e), the court shall dismiss the petition to dissolve the corporation under section 14.30(a)(2), and the petitioning shareholder shall no longer have any rights or status as a shareholder of the corporation, except the right to receive the amounts awarded by the order of the court which shall be enforceable in the same manner as any other judgment.

(g) The purchase ordered pursuant to subsection (e) shall be made within 10 days after the date the order becomes final.

(h) Any payment by the corporation pursuant to an order under subsections (c) or (e), other than an award of expenses pursuant to subsection (e), is subject to the provisions of section 6.40.

OFFICIAL COMMENT

It is not always necessary to dissolve a corporation and liquidate its assets to provide relief for the situations covered in section 14.30(a)(2). Section 14.34 provides an alternative by means of which a dissolution proceeding under section 14.30(a)(2) can be terminated upon payment of the fair value of the petitioner's shares, allowing the corporation to continue in existence for the benefit of the remaining shareholders.

1. *Availability*

There are two prerequisites to filing an election to purchase under section 14.34. First, a proceeding to dissolve the corporation under section 14.30(a)(2) must have been commenced. Second, the election may be made only by the corporation or by shareholders other than the shareholder who is seeking to dissolve the corporation under section 14.30(a)(2).

2. *Effect of Filing*

The election to purchase is wholly voluntary, but it may only be made as a matter of right within 90 days after the filing of the petition under section 14.30(a)(2). After 90 days, leave of court is required to make an election to purchase.

Sections 14.34(a) and (b) include provisions with respect to the irrevocability of an election and the inability to discontinue a dissolution proceeding or dispose of shares following the filing of an election. These provisions are intended to reduce the risk that either the dissolution proceeding or the buyout election will be used other than in good faith, because under section 14.34 a petitioner using section 14.30(a)(2) becomes irrevocably committed to sell these shares pursuant to section 14.34 once an election is filed. The petitioning shareholder may not thereafter discontinue the dissolution proceeding or dispose of the petitioner's shares without permission of the court, which is specifically directed to consider whether such action would be equitable from the standpoint of the corporation and the other shareholders.

If the corporation or the other shareholders fail to elect to purchase the petitioner's shares within the first 90 days, they run the risk that the court will decline to accept a subsequent election and will, instead, allow the dissolution proceeding to go forward. The dissolution proceeding is not affected by the filing of an election; it will be stayed only upon an application to the court to determine the fair value of the petitioner's shares filed after the expiration of the 60-day negotiating period provided for in section 14.34(c).

Once an election is filed, it may be set aside or modified only for reasons that the court finds equitable. If the court sets aside the election, the corporation or the electing shareholders are released from their obligation to purchase the petitioner's shares. Under section 14.34(a), the court also has discretion to "modify" the election by releasing one or more electing shareholders without releasing the others.

3. *Election by Corporation or Shareholders*

Because any change in the allocation of shareholdings may upset control or other arrangements that have been previously negotiated by the parties, the corporation's election to purchase is given preference during the 90-day period provided for in section 14.34(b). This preference does not affect the order of filing, and any shareholder may file an election (thus triggering the provisions of subsection (b)) as soon as the dissolution proceeding is commenced. If the corporation thereafter files an election within the 90-day period, its election takes precedence over any previously filed election by shareholders. An election by the corporation after 90 days may be filed only with the court's approval. Section 14.34 does not affect an agreement between the corporation and the other shareholders to participate jointly in the purchase of the petitioner's shares.

Section 14.34(b) requires the corporation to notify all other shareholders of their right to join in the purchase "in proportion to their ownership of shares as of the date the first election was filed." This may raise the question of whether shareholders of a class different from the class of shares owned by the petitioner may participate in the purchase. Given the wide variety of capital structures adopted by corporations, it is not possible to state a general rule that would be appropriate in all cases. Any allocation that is agreed to by the electing shareholders controls regardless of whether the other terms and conditions of the purchase are set by the parties' agreement pursuant to subsection (c) or are determined by the court pursuant to subsection (e). If electing shareholders cannot agree, the court, under subsection (e), must determine an allocation.

4. *Court Order*

If the parties come to terms within the 60-day negotiating period provided for in section 14.34(c), their agreement will be incorporated in an order of the court and will thereafter be enforceable as such. If the parties are unable to reach agreement, any party may apply to the court to determine the fair value of the shares. After the court makes that determination, section 14.34(e) requires it to enter an order directing the sale on such terms as the court finds appropriate. Section 14.34(e) does place some limitations on when the court may provide for installment payments or award interest or expenses and does state that the court should attempt to preserve the distribution of certain voting rights. Otherwise, the contents of the order under subsection (e) are subject to the court's discretion.

The entry of an order under section 14.34(c) or (e) requires the court to dismiss the dissolution proceeding under section 14.30(a)(2) and terminates all rights of the petitioner as a shareholder. Thus, the order also terminates all claims that the petitioner may have had in his or her capacity as a shareholder, and the value of such claims must either be asserted as part of the "fair value" of the petitioner's shares or forever lost. Under subsection (f), claims asserted by the petitioner in any nonshareholder capacity, such as claims for back wages or indemnification, are not affected by the entry of an order nor does the order affect any rights the petitioner may have as a creditor with respect to shares pledged as security for the purchase price. Otherwise, the order is enforceable only in the same manner as any other judgment, and the petitioner may not seek to reopen the proceedings in the event of a default.

After the entry of an order under section 14.34(c) or (e), the petitioner is a creditor with respect to the electing shareholders who participate in the purchase, but any payments to be made by the corporation, other than expenses awarded under section 14.34(e), fall within the definition of "distribution" and are subject to section 6.40.

CHAPTER 15. FOREIGN CORPORATIONS

§15.01. *Governing Law*

(a) The law of the jurisdiction of formation of a foreign corporation governs:

(1) the internal affairs of the foreign corporation; and

(2) the interest holder liability of its shareholders.

(b) A foreign corporation is not precluded from registering to do business in this state because of any difference between the law of the foreign corporation's jurisdiction of formation and the law of this state.

(c) Registration of a foreign corporation to do business in this state does not permit the foreign corporation to engage in any business or affairs or exercise any power that a domestic corporation may not engage in or exercise in this state.

§15.02. Registration to do Business in this State

(a) A foreign corporation may not do business in this state until it registers with the secretary of state under this chapter.

(b) A foreign corporation doing business in this state may not maintain a proceeding in any court of this state until it is registered to do business in this state.

(c) The failure of a foreign corporation to register to do business in this state does not impair the validity of a contract or act of the foreign corporation or preclude it from defending a proceeding in this state.

(d) A limitation on the liability of a shareholder or director of a foreign corporation is not waived solely because the foreign corporation does business in this state without registering.

(e) Section 15.01(a) applies even if a foreign corporation fails to register under this chapter.

§15.05. Activities not Constituting Doing Business

(a) Activities of a foreign corporation that do not constitute doing business in this state for purposes of this chapter include:

(1) maintaining, defending, mediating, arbitrating, or settling a proceeding;

(2) carrying on any activity concerning the internal affairs of the foreign corporation, including holding meetings of its shareholders or board of directors;

(3) maintaining accounts in financial institutions;

(4) maintaining offices or agencies for the transfer, exchange, and registration of securities of the foreign corporation or maintaining trustees or depositories with respect to those securities;

(5) selling through independent contractors;

(6) soliciting or obtaining orders by any means if the orders require acceptance outside this state before they become contracts;

(7) creating or acquiring indebtedness, mortgages, or security interests in property;

(8) securing or collecting debts or enforcing mortgages or security interests in property securing the debts, and holding, protecting, or maintaining property so acquired;

(9) conducting an isolated transaction that is not in the course of similar transactions;

(10) owning, protecting and maintaining property; and

(11) doing business in interstate commerce.

(b) This section does not apply in determining the contacts or activities that may subject a foreign corporation to service of process, taxation, or regulation under the laws of this state other than this Act.

Chapter 16. Records and Reports

SUBCHAPTER A. RECORDS

§16.01. Corporate Records

(a) A corporation shall maintain the following records:

(1) its articles of incorporation as currently in effect;

(2) any notices to shareholders referred to in section 1.20(k)(5) specifying facts on which a filed document is dependent if those facts are not included in the articles of incorporation or otherwise available as specified in section 1.20(k)(5);

(3) its bylaws as currently in effect;

(4) all written communications within the past three years to shareholders generally;

(5) minutes of all meetings of, and records of all actions taken without a meeting by, its shareholders, its board of directors, and board committees established under section 8.25;

(6) a list of the names and business addresses of its current directors and officers; and

(7) its most recent annual report delivered to the secretary of state under section 16.21.

(b) A corporation shall maintain all annual financial statements prepared for the corporation for its last three fiscal years (or such shorter period of existence) and any audit or other reports with respect to such financial statements.

(c) A corporation shall maintain accounting records in a form that permits preparation of its financial statements.

(d) A corporation shall maintain a record of its current shareholders in alphabetical order by class or series of shares showing the address of, each shareholder to which notices and other communications from the corporation are to be sent, and which shall include the number and class or series of shares held by each such shareholder. In addition, if a shareholder has provided an electronic mail address to the corporation or has consented to receive notices or other communications by electronic mail or other electronic transmission, the record of shareholders shall include the electronic mail or other electronic transmission address of the shareholder if notices or other communications are being delivered by the corporation to the shareholder at such electronic mail or other electronic transmission address pursuant to section 1.41(d). An electronic mail address of a shareholder shall be deemed to be provided by a shareholder if it is contained in a communication to the corporation by or on behalf of the shareholder unless the communication expressly indicates that the electronic mail address may not be used to deliver notices or other communications.

(e) A corporation shall maintain the records specified in this section in a manner so that they may be made available for inspection within a reasonable time.

§16.02. *Inspection Rights of Shareholders*

(a) A shareholder of a corporation is entitled to inspect and copy, during regular business hours at the corporation's principal office, any of the records of the corporation described in section 16.01(a), excluding minutes of meetings of, and records of actions taken without a meeting by, the corporation's board of directors and board committees established under section 8.25, if the shareholder gives the corporation a signed written notice of the shareholder's demand at least five business days before the date on which the shareholder wishes to inspect and copy.

(b) A shareholder of a corporation is entitled to inspect and copy, during regular business hours at a reasonable location specified by the corporation, any of the following records of the corporation if the shareholder meets the requirements of subsection (c) and gives the corporation a signed written notice of the shareholder's demand at least five business days before the date on which the shareholder wishes to inspect and copy:

(1) the financial statements of the corporation maintained in accordance with section 16.01(b);

(2) accounting records of the corporation;

(3) excerpts from minutes of any meeting of, or records of any actions taken without a meeting by, the corporation's board of directors and board committees maintained in accordance with section 16.01(a); and

(4) the record of shareholders maintained in accordance with section 16.01(d).

(c) A shareholder may inspect and copy the records described in subsection (b) only if:

(1) the shareholder's demand is made in good faith and for a proper purpose;

(2) the shareholder's demand describes with reasonable particularity the shareholder's purpose and the records the shareholder desires to inspect; and

(3) the records are directly connected with the shareholder's purpose.

(d) The corporation may impose reasonable restrictions on the confidentiality, use or distribution of records described in subsection (b).

(e) For any meeting of shareholders for which the record date for determining shareholders entitled to vote at the meeting is different than the record date for notice of the meeting, any person who becomes a shareholder subsequent to the record date for notice of the meeting and is entitled to vote at the meeting is entitled to obtain from the corporation upon request the notice and any other information provided by the corporation to shareholders in connection with the meeting, unless the corporation has made such information generally available to shareholders by posting it on its website or by other generally recognized means. Failure of a corporation to provide such information does not affect the validity of action taken at the meeting.

(f) The right of inspection granted by this section may not be abolished or limited by a corporation's articles of incorporation or bylaws.

(g) This section does not affect:

(1) the right of a shareholder to inspect records under section 7.20 or, if the shareholder is in litigation with the corporation, to the same extent as any other litigant; or

(2) the power of a court, independently of this Act, to compel the production of corporate records for examination and to impose reasonable restrictions as provided in section 16.04(c), provided that, in the case of production of records described in subsection (b) of this section at the request of a shareholder, the shareholder has met the requirements of subsection (c).

(h) For purposes of this section, "shareholder" means a record shareholder, a beneficial shareholder, and an unrestricted voting trust beneficial owner.

§16.03. Scope of Inspection Right

(a) A shareholder may appoint an agent or attorney to exercise the shareholder's inspection and copying rights under section 16.02.

(b) The corporation may, if reasonable, satisfy the right of a shareholder to copy records under section 16.02 by furnishing to the shareholder copies by photocopy or other means chosen by the corporation, including furnishing copies through an electronic transmission.

(c) The corporation may comply at its expense with a shareholder's demand to inspect the record of shareholders under section 16.02(b)(4) by providing the shareholder with a list of shareholders that was compiled no earlier than the date of the shareholder's demand.

(d) The corporation may impose a reasonable charge to cover the costs of providing copies of documents to the shareholder, which may be based on an estimate of such costs.

§16.04. Court-Ordered Inspection

(a) If a corporation does not allow a shareholder who complies with section 16.02(a) to inspect and copy any records required by that section to be available for inspection, the [name or describe court] may summarily order inspection and copying of the records demanded at the corporation's expense upon application of the shareholder.

(b) If a corporation does not within a reasonable time allow a shareholder who complies with section 16.02(b) to inspect and copy the records required by that section, the shareholder who complies with section 16.02(c) may apply to the [name or describe court] for an order to permit inspection and copying of the records demanded. The court shall dispose of an application under this subsection on an expedited basis.

(c) If the court orders inspection and copying of the records demanded under section 16.02(b), it may impose reasonable restrictions on their confidentiality, use or distribution by the demanding shareholder and it shall also order the corporation to pay the shareholder's expenses incurred to obtain the order unless the corporation establishes that it refused inspection in good faith because the corporation had:

(1) a reasonable basis for doubt about the right of the shareholder to inspect the records demanded; or

(2) required reasonable restrictions on the confidentiality, use or distribution of the records demanded to which the demanding shareholder had been unwilling to agree.

§16.05. Inspection Rights of Directors

(a) A director of a corporation is entitled to inspect and copy the books, records and documents of the corporation at any reasonable time to the extent reasonably related to the performance of the director's duties as a director, including duties as a member of a board committee, but not for any other purpose or in any manner that would violate any duty to the corporation.

(b) The [name or describe court] may order inspection and copying of the books, records and documents at the corporation's expense, upon application of a director who has been refused such inspection rights, unless the corporation establishes that the director is not entitled to such inspection rights. The court shall dispose of an application under this subsection on an expedited basis.

(c) If an order is issued, the court may include provisions protecting the corporation from undue burden or expense, and prohibiting the director from using information obtained upon exercise of the inspection rights in a manner that would violate a duty to the corporation, and may also order the corporation to reimburse the director for the director's expenses incurred in connection with the application.

OFFICIAL COMMENT

The purpose of section 16.05(a) is to confirm the principle that a director always is entitled to inspect books, records and documents to the extent reasonably related to the performance of the director's duties, provided that the requested inspection is not for an improper purpose and the director's use of the information obtained would not violate any duty to the corporation. In addition, section 16.05 sets forth a remedy for the director in circumstances where the corporation improperly denies the right of inspection.

Section 16.05(b) provides for a court order on an expedited basis because there is a presumption that significant latitude and discretion should be granted to the director, and the corporation has the burden of establishing that the director is not entitled to inspection of the documents requested. There may be circumstances where the director's inspection right might be denied, for example, when it would be contrary to the interest of the corporation because of adversity with the director, and the courts have broad discretion to address these circumstances. Section 16.05 does not directly deal with the ability of a director to inspect records of a subsidiary of which he or she is not also a director. A director's ability to inspect records of a subsidiary generally should be exercised through the parent's rights or power and section 16.05(a) does not independently provide that right or power to a director of the parent. In the case of wholly-owned subsidiaries, a director's ability to inspect should approximate his or her rights with respect to the parent.

SUBCHAPTER B. REPORTS

§16.20. Financial Statements for Shareholders

(a) Upon the written request of a shareholder, a corporation shall deliver or make available to such requesting shareholder by posting on its website or by other generally recognized means annual financial statements for the most recent fiscal year of the corporation for which annual financial statements have been prepared for the corporation. If financial statements have been prepared for the corporation on the basis of generally accepted accounting principles for such specified period, the corporation shall deliver or make available such financial statements to the requesting shareholder. If the annual financial statements to be delivered or made available to the requesting shareholder are audited or otherwise reported upon by a public accountant, the report shall also be delivered or made available to the requesting shareholder.

(b) A corporation shall deliver, or make available and provide written notice of availability of, the financial statements required under subsection (a) to the requesting shareholder within five business days of delivery of such written request to the corporation.

(c) A corporation may fulfill its responsibilities under this section by delivering the specified financial statements, or otherwise making them available, in any manner permitted by the applicable rules and regulations of the United States Securities and Exchange Commission.

(d) Notwithstanding the provisions of subsections (a), (b) and (c) of this section:

(1) as a condition to delivering or making available financial statements to a requesting shareholder, the corporation may require the requesting shareholder to agree to reasonable restrictions on the confidentiality, use and distribution of such financial statements; and

(2) the corporation may, if it reasonably determines that the shareholder's request is not made in good faith or for a proper purpose, decline to deliver or make available such financial statements to that shareholder.

(e) If a corporation does not respond to a shareholder's request for annual financial statements pursuant to this section in accordance with subsection (b) within five business days of delivery of such request to the corporation:

(1) The requesting shareholder may apply to the [name or describe court] for an order requiring delivery of or access to the requested financial statements. The court shall dispose of an application under this subsection on an expedited basis.

(2) If the court orders delivery or access to the requested financial statements, it may impose reasonable restrictions on their confidentiality, use or distribution.

(3) In such proceeding, if the corporation has declined to deliver or make available such financial statements because the shareholder had been unwilling to agree to restrictions proposed by the corporation on the confidentiality, use and distribution of such financials statements, the corporation shall have the burden of demonstrating that the restrictions proposed by the corporation were reasonable.

(4) In such proceeding, if the corporation has declined to deliver or make available such financial statements pursuant to section 16.20(d)(2), the corporation shall have the burden of demonstrating that it had reasonably determined that the shareholder's request was not made in good faith or for a proper purpose.

(5) If the court orders delivery or access to the requested financial statements it shall order the corporation to pay the shareholder's expenses incurred to obtain such order unless the corporation establishes that it had refused delivery or access to the requested financial statements because the shareholder had refused to agree to reasonable restrictions on the confidentiality, use or distribution of the financial statements or that the corporation had reasonably determined that the shareholder's request was not made in good faith or for a proper purpose.

§16.21. Annual Report for Secretary of State

(a) Each domestic corporation shall deliver to the secretary of state for filing an annual report that sets forth:

(1) the name of the corporation;

(2) the street and mailing address of its registered office and the name of its registered agent at that office in this state;

(3) the street and mailing address of its principal office;

(4) the names and business addresses of its directors and principal officers;

(5) a brief description of the nature of its business;

(6) the total number of authorized shares, itemized by class and series, if any, within each class; and

(7) the total number of issued and outstanding shares, itemized by class and series, if any, within each class.

(b) Each foreign corporation registered to do business in this state shall deliver to the secretary of state for filing an annual report that sets forth:

(1) the name of the foreign corporation and, if the name does not comply with section 4.01, an alternate name as required by section 15.06;

(2) the foreign corporation's jurisdiction of formation;

(3) the street and mailing addresses of the foreign corporation's principal office and, if the law of the foreign corporation's jurisdiction of formation requires the foreign corporation to maintain an office in that jurisdiction, the street and mailing addresses of that office;

(4) the street and mailing addresses of the foreign corporation's registered office in this state and the name of its registered agent at that office;

(5) the names and business addresses of its directors and principal officers; and

(6) a brief description of the nature of its business conducted in this state.

(c) Information in the annual report must be current as of the date the annual report is signed on behalf of the corporation.

(d) The first annual report shall be delivered to the secretary of state between January 1 and April 1 of the year following the calendar year in which a domestic corporation was incorporated or a foreign corporation was registered to do business. Subsequent annual reports shall be delivered to the secretary of state between January 1 and April 1 of the following calendar years.

(e) If an annual report does not contain the information required by this section, the secretary of state shall promptly notify the reporting domestic or foreign corporation in writing and return the report to it for correction. If the report is corrected to contain the information required by this section and delivered to the secretary of state within 30 days after the notice from the secretary of state becomes effective as determined in accordance with section 1.41, it is deemed to be timely filed.

CHAPTER 17. BENEFIT CORPORATIONS

§17.01. Application of Chapter; Definitions

(a) A corporation electing to become a benefit corporation under this chapter in the manner prescribed in this chapter is subject in all respects to the provisions of this Act, except to the extent this chapter imposes additional or different requirements, in which case such requirements apply. The inclusion of a provision in this chapter does not imply that a contrary or different rule of law applies to a corporation that is not a benefit corporation. This chapter does not affect a statute or rule of law that applies to a corporation that is not a benefit corporation.

(b) As used in this chapter:

"Benefit corporation" means a corporation that includes in its articles of incorporation a statement that the corporation is subject to this chapter.

"Public benefit" means a positive effect, or reduction of negative effects, on one or more communities or categories of persons (other than shareholders solely in their capacity as shareholders) or on the environment, including effects of an artistic, charitable, economic, educational, cultural, literary, medical, religious, social, ecological, or scientific nature.

"Public benefit provision" means a provision in the articles of incorporation which states that the corporation shall pursue one or more identified public benefits.

"Responsible and sustainable manner" means a manner that:

(i) pursues through the business of the corporation the creation of a positive effect on society and the environment, taken as a whole, that is material taking into consideration the corporation's size and the nature of its business; and

(ii) considers, in addition to the interests of shareholders generally, the separate interests of stakeholders known to be affected by the conduct of the business of the corporation.

§17.02. Name; Share Certificates

(a) The name of a benefit corporation may contain the words "benefit corporation," the abbreviation "B.C.," or the designation "BC," any of which shall be deemed to satisfy the requirements of section 4.01(a)(1).

(b) Any share certificate issued by a benefit corporation, and any information statement delivered by a benefit corporation pursuant to section 6.26(b), must note conspicuously that the corporation is a benefit corporation subject to this chapter.

§17.03. *Certain Amendments and Transactions; Votes Required*

(a) Unless the articles of incorporation require a greater vote, in addition to any other approval of shareholders required under this Act, the approval of at least two-thirds of the votes entitled to be cast thereon, and, if any class or series of shares is entitled to vote as a separate group thereon, the approval of at least two-thirds of the votes entitled to be cast by that voting group, shall be required for a corporation that is not a benefit corporation to:

(1) amend its articles of incorporation to include a statement that it is subject to this chapter; or

(2) merge with or into, or enter into a share exchange with, another entity, or effect a domestication or conversion, if, as a result of the merger, share exchange, domestication, or conversion, the shares of any voting group would become, or be converted into or exchanged for the right to receive, shares of a benefit corporation or shares or interests in an entity subject to provisions of organic law analogous to those in this chapter; provided, however, that in the case of this subsection (a)(2), if the shares of one or more, but not all, voting groups are so affected, then only the shares in the voting groups so affected shall be entitled to cast votes under this subsection (a).

(b) Unless the articles of incorporation require a greater vote, in addition to any other approval of shareholders required under this Act, the approval of at least two-thirds of the votes entitled to be cast thereon, and, if any class or series of shares is entitled to vote as a separate group thereon, the approval of at least two-thirds of the votes entitled to be cast by that voting group, shall be required for a benefit corporation to:

(1) amend its articles of incorporation to eliminate a statement that the corporation is subject to this chapter; or

(2) merge with or into, or enter into a share exchange with, another entity, or effect a domestication or conversion if, as a result of the merger, share exchange, domestication, or conversion, the shares of any voting group would become, or be converted into or exchanged for the right to receive, shares or interests in an entity that is neither a benefit corporation nor an entity subject to provisions of organic law analogous to those in this chapter; provided, however, that in the case of this subsection (b)(2), if the shares of one or more, but not all, voting groups are so affected, then only the shares in the voting groups so affected shall be entitled to cast votes under this subsection (b).

§17.04. *Duties of Directors*

(a) Each member of the board of directors of a benefit corporation, when discharging the duties of a director, shall act: (i) in a responsible and sustainable manner, and (ii) in a manner that pursues the public benefit or benefits identified in any public benefit provision.

(b) In fulfilling the duties under subsection (a), a director shall consider, to the extent affected, in addition to the interests of shareholders generally, the separate interests of stakeholders known to be affected by the business of the corporation including:

(1) the employees and work forces of the corporation, its subsidiaries, and its suppliers;

(2) customers;

(3) communities or society, including those of each community in which offices or facilities of the corporation, its subsidiaries, or its suppliers are located; and

(4) the local and global environment.

(c) A director of a benefit corporation shall not, by virtue of the duties imposed by subsections (a) and (b), owe any duty to a person other than the benefit corporation due to any interest of the person in the status of the corporation as a benefit corporation or in any public benefit provision.

(d) Unless otherwise provided in the articles of incorporation, the violation by a director of the duties imposed by subsections (a) and (b) shall not constitute an intentional infliction of harm on the corporation or the shareholders for purposes of sections 2.02(b)(4) and (5).

§17.05. Annual Benefit Report

(a) No less than annually, a benefit corporation shall prepare a benefit report addressing the efforts of the corporation during the preceding year to operate in a responsible and sustainable manner, to pursue any public benefit or benefits identified in any public benefit provision, and to consider the interests described in section 17.04(b). The annual benefit report must include:

(1) the objectives that the board of directors has established for the corporation to operate in a responsible and sustainable manner, to pursue the public benefit or benefits identified in any public benefit provision, and to consider the interests described in section 17.04(b);

(2) the standards the board of directors has adopted to measure the corporation's progress in operating in a responsible and sustainable manner, in pursuing the public benefit or benefits identified in any public benefit provision, and in considering the interests described in section 17.04(b);

(3) if the articles of incorporation or bylaws require that the corporation use an independent third-party standard in reporting on the corporation's progress in operating in a responsible and sustainable manner, in pursuing the public benefit or benefits identified in any public benefit provision, or in considering the interests described in section 17.04(b), or if the board of directors has chosen to use such a standard, the applicable standard so required or chosen; and

(4) an assessment of the corporation's success in meeting the objectives and standards identified in subsections (a)(1) and (a)(2) and, if applicable, subsection (a)(3), and the basis for that assessment.

(b) The benefit corporation shall deliver to each shareholder, or make available and provide written notice to each shareholder of the availability of, the annual benefit report required by subsection (a) on or before the earlier of:

(1) 120 days following the end of the fiscal year of the benefit corporation; or

(2) The time that the benefit corporation delivers any other annual reports or annual financial statements to its shareholders.

(c) Any shareholder that has not received or been given access to an annual benefit report within the time required by subsection (b) may make a written request that the corporation deliver or make available the annual benefit report to the shareholder. If a benefit corporation does not deliver or make available an annual benefit report to the shareholder within five business days of receiving such request, the requesting shareholder may apply to the [name or describe court] for an order requiring delivery of or access to the annual benefit report. The court shall dispose of an action under this subsection (c) on an expedited basis

(d) A benefit corporation shall post all of its annual benefit reports on the public portion of its website, if any. If a benefit corporation does not have a website, the benefit corporation shall provide a copy of its most recent annual benefit report, without charge, to any person that requests a copy in writing.

§17.06. *Rights of Action*

(a) Except in a proceeding authorized under section 17.05(c) or this section, no person other than the corporation, or a shareholder in the right of the corporation pursuant to subsection (b), may bring an action or assert a claim with respect to the violation of any duty applicable to a benefit corporation or any of its directors under this chapter.

(b) Except for a proceeding brought under section 17.05(c), a proceeding by a shareholder of a benefit corporation claiming violation of any duty applicable to a benefit corporation or any of its directors under this chapter:

(1) must be brought in a derivative proceeding pursuant to subchapter 7D; and

(2) may be brought only by a shareholder of the benefit corporation that at the time of the act or omission complained of either individually, or together with other shareholders bringing such action collectively, owned directly or indirectly at least five percent of a class of the corporation's outstanding shares or, in the case of a corporation with shares traded on an organized market as described in section 13.02(b)(1)(ii), either that percentage of shares or shares with a market value of at least $5 million at the time the proceeding is commenced.

(c) A suit under subsection (b) may not be maintained if, during the pendency of the suit, the shareholder individually fails, or the shareholders collectively fail, to continue to own directly or indirectly the lesser of (i) the number of shares owned at the time the proceeding is commenced, (ii) a number of shares representing five percent of a class of the corporation's shares, or (iii) a number of shares with a market value of at least $5 million.

Delaware General Corporation Law

SUBCHAPTER I. FORMATION

§101. Incorporators; How Corporation Formed; Purposes

(a) Any person, partnership, association or corporation, singly or jointly with others, and without regard to such person's or entity's residence, domicile or state of incorporation, may incorporate or organize a corporation under this chapter by filing with the Division of Corporations in the Department of State a certificate of incorporation which shall be executed, acknowledged and filed in accordance with §103 of this title.

(b) A corporation may be incorporated or organized under this chapter to conduct or promote any lawful business or purposes, except as may otherwise be provided by the Constitution or other law of this State.

(c) Corporations for constructing, maintaining and operating public utilities, whether in or outside of this State, may be organized under this chapter, but corporations for constructing, maintaining and operating public utilities within this State shall be subject to, in addition to this chapter, the special provisions and requirements of Title 26 applicable to such corporations.

§102. Contents of Certificate of Incorporation

(a) The certificate of incorporation shall set forth:

(1) The name of the corporation, which (i) shall contain 1 of the words "association," "company," "corporation," "club," "foundation," "fund," "incorporated," "institute," "society," "union," "syndicate," or "limited," (or abbreviations

thereof, with or without punctuation), or words (or abbreviations thereof, with or without punctuation) of like import of foreign countries or jurisdictions (provided they are written in roman characters or letters); provided, however, that the Division of Corporations in the Department of State may waive such requirement (unless it determines that such name is, or might otherwise appear to be, that of a natural person) if such corporation executes, acknowledges and files with the Secretary of State in accordance with §103 of this title a certificate stating that its total assets, as defined in §503(i) of this title, are not less than $10,000,000, or, in the sole discretion of the Division of Corporations in the Department of State, if the corporation is both a nonprofit nonstock corporation and an association of professionals, (ii) shall be such as to distinguish it upon the records in the office of the Division of Corporations in the Department of State from the names that are reserved on such records and from the names on such records of each other corporation, partnership, limited partnership, limited liability company, registered series of a limited liability company, registered series of a limited partnership or statutory trust organized or registered as a domestic or foreign corporation, partnership, limited partnership, limited liability company, registered series of a limited liability company, registered series of a limited partnership or statutory trust under the laws of this State, except with the written consent of the person who has reserved such name or such other foreign corporation or domestic or foreign partnership, limited partnership, limited liability company, registered series of a limited liability company, registered series of a limited partnership or statutory trust, executed, acknowledged and filed with the Secretary of State in accordance with §103 of this title, or except that, without prejudicing any rights of the person who has reserved such name or such other foreign corporation or domestic or foreign partnership, limited partnership, limited liability company, registered series of a limited liability company, registered series of a limited partnership or statutory trust, the Division of Corporations in the Department of State may waive such requirement if the corporation demonstrates to the satisfaction of the Secretary of State that the corporation or a predecessor entity previously has made substantial use of such name or a substantially similar name, that the corporation has made reasonable efforts to secure such written consent, and that such waiver is in the interest of the State, (iii) except as permitted by §395 of this title, shall not contain the word "trust," and (iv) shall not contain the word "bank," or any variation thereof, except for the name of a bank reporting to and under the supervision of the State Bank Commissioner of this State or a subsidiary of a bank or savings association (as those terms are defined in the Federal Deposit Insurance Act, as amended, at 12 U.S.C. §1813), or a corporation regulated under the Bank Holding Company Act of 1956, as amended, 12 U.S.C. §1841 et seq., or the Home Owners' Loan Act, as amended, 12 U.S.C. §1461 et seq.; provided, however, that this section shall not be construed to prevent the use of the word "bank," or any variation thereof, in a context clearly not purporting to refer to a banking business or otherwise likely to mislead the public about the nature of the business of the corporation or to lead to a pattern and practice of abuse that might cause harm to the interests of the public or the State as determined by the Division of Corporations in the Department of State;

(2) The address (which shall be stated in accordance with §131(c) of this title) of the corporation's registered office in this State, and the name of its registered agent at such address;

(3) The nature of the business or purposes to be conducted or promoted. It shall be sufficient to state, either alone or with other businesses or purposes, that the purpose of the corporation is to engage in any lawful act or activity for which corporations may be organized under the General Corporation Law of Delaware, and by such statement all lawful acts and activities shall be within the purposes of the corporation, except for express limitations, if any;

(4) If the corporation is to be authorized to issue only 1 class of stock, the total number of shares of stock which the corporation shall have authority to issue and the par value of each of such shares, or a statement that all such shares are to be without par value. If the corporation is to be authorized to issue more than 1 class of stock, the certificate of incorporation shall set forth the total number of shares of all classes of stock which the corporation shall have authority to issue and the number of shares of each class and shall specify each class the shares of which are to be without par value and each class the shares of which are to have par value and the par value of the shares of each such class. The certificate of incorporation shall also set forth a statement of the designations and the powers, preferences and rights, and the qualifications, limitations or restrictions thereof, which are permitted by §151 of this title in respect of any class or classes of stock or any series of any class of stock of the corporation and the fixing of which by the certificate of incorporation is desired, and an express grant of such authority as it may then be desired to grant to the board of directors to fix by resolution or resolutions any thereof that may be desired but which shall not be fixed by the certificate of incorporation. The foregoing provisions of this paragraph shall not apply to nonstock corporations. In the case of nonstock corporations, the fact that they are not authorized to issue capital stock shall be stated in the certificate of incorporation. The conditions of membership, or other criteria for identifying members, of nonstock corporations shall likewise be stated in the certificate of incorporation or the bylaws. Nonstock corporations shall have members, but failure to have members shall not affect otherwise valid corporate acts or work a forfeiture or dissolution of the corporation. Nonstock corporations may provide for classes or groups of members having relative rights, powers and duties, and may make provision for the future creation of additional classes or groups of members having such relative rights, powers and duties as may from time to time be established, including rights, powers and duties senior to existing classes and groups of members. Except as otherwise provided in this chapter, nonstock corporations may also provide that any member or class or group of members shall have full, limited, or no voting rights or powers, including that any member or class or group of members shall have the right to vote on a specified transaction even if that member or class or group of members does not have the right to vote for the election of the members of the governing body of the corporation. Voting by members of a nonstock corporation may be on a per capita, number, financial interest, class, group, or any other basis set forth. The provisions referred to in the 3 preceding sentences may be set forth in the certificate of incorporation or

the bylaws. If neither the certificate of incorporation nor the bylaws of a nonstock corporation state the conditions of membership, or other criteria for identifying members, the members of the corporation shall be deemed to be those entitled to vote for the election of the members of the governing body pursuant to the certificate of incorporation or bylaws of such corporation or otherwise until thereafter otherwise provided by the certificate of incorporation or the bylaws;

(5) The name and mailing address of the incorporator or incorporators;

(6) If the powers of the incorporator or incorporators are to terminate upon the filing of the certificate of incorporation, the names and mailing addresses of the persons who are to serve as directors until the first annual meeting of stockholders or until their successors are elected and qualify.

(b) In addition to the matters required to be set forth in the certificate of incorporation by subsection (a) of this section, the certificate of incorporation may also contain any or all of the following matters:

(1) Any provision for the management of the business and for the conduct of the affairs of the corporation, and any provision creating, defining, limiting and regulating the powers of the corporation, the directors, and the stockholders, or any class of the stockholders, or the governing body, members, or any class or group of members of a nonstock corporation; if such provisions are not contrary to the laws of this State. Any provision which is required or permitted by any section of this chapter to be stated in the bylaws may instead be stated in the certificate of incorporation;

(2) The following provisions, in haec verba,

(i), for a corporation other than a nonstock corporation, viz:

Whenever a compromise or arrangement is proposed between this corporation and its creditors or any class of them and/or between this corporation and its stockholders or any class of them, any court of equitable jurisdiction within the State of Delaware may, on the application in a summary way of this corporation or of any creditor or stockholder thereof or on the application of any receiver or receivers appointed for this corporation under §291 of Title 8 of the Delaware Code or on the application of trustees in dissolution or of any receiver or receivers appointed for this corporation under §279 of Title 8 of the Delaware Code order a meeting of the creditors or class of creditors, and/or of the stockholders or class of stockholders of this corporation, as the case may be, to be summoned in such manner as the said court directs. If a majority in number representing three fourths in value of the creditors or class of creditors, and/or of the stockholders or class of stockholders of this corporation, as the case may be, agree to any compromise or arrangement and to any reorganization of this corporation as consequence of such compromise or arrangement, the said compromise or arrangement and the said reorganization shall, if sanctioned by the court to which the said application has been made, be binding on all the creditors or class of creditors, and/or on all the stockholders or class of stockholders, of this corporation, as the case may be, and also on this corporation; or

(ii), for a nonstock corporation, viz:

Whenever a compromise or arrangement is proposed between this corporation and its creditors or any class of them and/or between this corporation and its members or any class of them, any court of equitable jurisdiction within the State of Delaware may, on the application in a summary way of this corporation or of any creditor or member thereof or on the application of any receiver or receivers appointed for this corporation under §291 of Title 8 of the Delaware Code or on the application of trustees in dissolution or of any receiver or receivers appointed for this corporation under §279 of Title 8 of the Delaware Code order a meeting of the creditors or class of creditors, and/or of the members or class of members of this corporation, as the case may be, to be summoned in such manner as the said court directs. If a majority in number representing three fourths in value of the creditors or class of creditors, and/or of the members or class of members of this corporation, as the case may be, agree to any compromise or arrangement and to any reorganization of this corporation as consequence of such compromise or arrangement, the said compromise or arrangement and the said reorganization shall, if sanctioned by the court to which the said application has been made, be binding on all the creditors or class of creditors, and/or on all the members or class of members, of this corporation, as the case may be, and also on this corporation;

(3) Such provisions as may be desired granting to the holders of the stock of the corporation, or the holders of any class or series of a class thereof, the preemptive right to subscribe to any or all additional issues of stock of the corporation of any or all classes or series thereof, or to any securities of the corporation convertible into such stock. No stockholder shall have any preemptive right to subscribe to an additional issue of stock or to any security convertible into such stock unless, and except to the extent that, such right is expressly granted to such stockholder in the certificate of incorporation. All such rights in existence on July 3, 1967, shall remain in existence unaffected by this paragraph unless and until changed or terminated by appropriate action which expressly provides for the change or termination;

(4) Provisions requiring for any corporate action, the vote of a larger portion of the stock or of any class or series thereof, or of any other securities having voting power, or a larger number of the directors, than is required by this chapter;

(5) A provision limiting the duration of the corporation's existence to a specified date; otherwise, the corporation shall have perpetual existence;

(6) A provision imposing personal liability for the debts of the corporation on its stockholders to a specified extent and upon specified conditions; otherwise, the stockholders of a corporation shall not be personally liable for the payment of the corporation's debts except as they may be liable by reason of their own conduct or acts;

(7) A provision eliminating or limiting the personal liability of a director or officer to the corporation or its stockholders for monetary damages for breach of fiduciary duty as a director or officer, provided that such provision shall not eliminate or limit the liability of: (i) a director or officer for any breach of the director's

duty of loyalty to the corporation or its stockholders; (ii) a director or officer for acts or omissions not in good faith or which involve intentional misconduct or a knowing violation of law; (iii) a director under §174 of this title; (iv) a director or officer for any transaction from which the director derived an improper personal benefit; or (v) an officer in any action by or in the right of the corporation. No such provision shall eliminate or limit the liability of a director for any act or omission occurring prior to the date when such provision becomes effective. An amendment, repeal or elimination of such a provision shall not affect its application with respect to an act or omission by a director occurring before such amendment, repeal or elimination unless the provision provides otherwise at the time of such act or omission. All references in this paragraph to a director shall also be deemed to refer to such other person or persons, if any, who, pursuant to a provision of the certificate of incorporation in accordance with §141(a) of this title, exercise or perform any of the powers or duties otherwise conferred or imposed upon the board of directors by this title. All references in this paragraph to an officer shall mean only a person who at the time of an act or omission as to which liability is asserted is deemed to have consented to service by the delivery of process to the registered agent of the corporation pursuant to §3114(b) of Title 10 (for purposes of this sentence only, treating residents of this State as they were nonresidents to apply §3114(b) of Title 10 to this sentence.[1]

(c) It shall not be necessary to set forth in the certificate of incorporation any of the powers conferred on corporations by this chapter.

(d) Except for provisions included pursuant to paragraphs (a)(1), (a)(2), (a)(5), (a)(6), (b)(2), (b)(5), (b)(7) of this section, and provisions included pursuant to paragraph (a)(4) of this section specifying the classes, number of shares, and par value of shares a corporation other than a nonstock corporation is authorized to issue, any provision of the certificate of incorporation may be made dependent upon facts ascertainable outside such instrument, provided that the manner in which such facts shall operate upon the provision is clearly and explicitly set forth therein. The term "facts," as used in this subsection, includes, but is not limited to, the occurrence

---

1. §3114 [of Title 10]. Service of process on nonresident directors, trustees, members of the governing body or officers of Delaware corporations . . .

(b) Every nonresident of this State who after January 1, 2004, accepts election or appointment as an officer of a corporation organized under the laws of this State, or who after such date serves in such capacity . . . shall, by such acceptance or by such service, be deemed thereby to have consented to the [service by the delivery of process to the registered agent of the corporation.] As used in this section, the word "officer" means an officer of the corporation who:

(1) Is or was the president, chief executive officer, chief operating officer, chief financial officer, chief legal officer, controller, treasurer or chief accounting officer of the corporation at any time during the course of conduct alleged in the action or proceeding to be wrongful;

(2) Is or was identified in the corporation's public filings with the United States Securities and Exchange Commission because such person is or was 1 of the most highly compensated executive officers of the corporation at any time during the course of conduct alleged in the action or proceeding to be wrongful; or

(3) Has, by written agreement with the corporation, consented to be identified as an officer for purposes of this section.

of any event, including a determination or action by any person or body, including the corporation.

(e) The exclusive right to the use of a name that is available for use by a domestic or foreign corporation may be reserved by or on behalf of:

(1) Any person intending to incorporate or organize a corporation with that name under this chapter or contemplating such incorporation or organization;

(2) Any domestic corporation or any foreign corporation qualified to do business in the State of Delaware, in either case, intending to change its name or contemplating such a change;

(3) Any foreign corporation intending to qualify to do business in the State of Delaware and adopt that name or contemplating such qualification and adoption; and

(4) Any person intending to organize a foreign corporation and have it qualify to do business in the State of Delaware and adopt that name or contemplating such organization, qualification and adoption.

The reservation of a specified name may be made by filing with the Secretary of State an application, executed by the applicant, certifying that the reservation is made by or on behalf of a domestic corporation, foreign corporation or other person described in paragraphs (e)(1)-(4) of this section above, and specifying the name to be reserved and the name and address of the applicant. If the Secretary of State finds that the name is available for use by a domestic or foreign corporation, the Secretary shall reserve the name for the use of the applicant for a period of 120 days. The same applicant may renew for successive 120-day periods a reservation of a specified name by filing with the Secretary of State, prior to the expiration of such reservation (or renewal thereof), an application for renewal of such reservation, executed by the applicant, certifying that the reservation is renewed by or on behalf of a domestic corporation, foreign corporation or other person described in paragraphs (e)(1)-(4) of this section above and specifying the name reservation to be renewed and the name and address of the applicant. The right to the exclusive use of a reserved name may be transferred to any other person by filing in the office of the Secretary of State a notice of the transfer, executed by the applicant for whom the name was reserved, specifying the name reservation to be transferred and the name and address of the transferee. The reservation of a specified name may be cancelled by filing with the Secretary of State a notice of cancellation, executed by the applicant or transferee, specifying the name reservation to be cancelled and the name and address of the applicant or transferee. Unless the Secretary of State finds that any application, application for renewal, notice of transfer, or notice of cancellation filed with the Secretary of State as required by this subsection does not conform to law, upon receipt of all filing fees required by law the Secretary of State shall prepare and return to the person who filed such instrument a copy of the filed instrument with a notation thereon of the action taken by the Secretary of State. A fee as set forth in §391 of this title shall be paid at the time of the reservation of any name, at the time of the renewal of any such reservation and at the time of the filing of a notice of the transfer or cancellation of any such reservation.

(f) The certificate of incorporation may not contain any provision that would impose liability on a stockholder for the attorneys' fees or expenses of the corporation or any other party in connection with an internal corporate claim, as defined in §115 of this title.

§106. Commencement of Corporate Existence

Upon the filing with the Secretary of State of the certificate of incorporation, executed and acknowledged in accordance with §103 of this title, the incorporator or incorporators who signed the certificate, and such incorporator's or incorporators' successors and assigns, shall, from the date of such filing, be and constitute a body corporate, by the name set forth in the certificate, subject to §103(d) of this title and subject to dissolution or other termination of its existence as provided in this chapter.

§107. Powers of Incorporators

If the persons who are to serve as directors until the first annual meeting of stockholders have not been named in the certificate of incorporation, the incorporator or incorporators, until the directors are elected, shall manage the affairs of the corporation and may do whatever is necessary and proper to perfect the organization of the corporation, including the adoption of the original bylaws of the corporation and the election of directors.

§108. Organization Meeting of Incorporators or Directors Named in Certificate of Incorporation

(a) After the filing of the certificate of incorporation an organization meeting of the incorporator or incorporators, or of the board of directors if the initial directors were named in the certificate of incorporation, shall be held, either within or without this State, at the call of a majority of the incorporators or directors, as the case may be, for the purposes of adopting bylaws, electing directors (if the meeting is of the incorporators) to serve or hold office until the first annual meeting of stockholders or until their successors are elected and qualify, electing officers if the meeting is of the directors, doing any other or further acts to perfect the organization of the corporation, and transacting such other business as may come before the meeting.

(b) The persons calling the meeting shall give to each other incorporator or director, as the case may be, at least 2 days' notice thereof in writing or by electronic transmission by any usual means of communication, which notice shall state the time, place and purposes of the meeting as fixed by the persons calling it. Notice of the meeting need not be given to anyone who attends the meeting or who waives notice either before or after the meeting.

(c) Unless otherwise restricted by the certificate of incorporation, (1) any action permitted to be taken at the organization meeting of the incorporators or directors, as the case may be, may be taken without a meeting if each incorporator or director, where there is more than 1, or the sole incorporator or director where there is only 1, consents thereto in writing or by electronic transmission and (2) a consent may be documented, signed and delivered in any manner permitted by §116 of this title. Any person (whether or not then an incorporator or director) may provide, whether through instruction to an agent or otherwise, that a consent to action will be effective at a future time (including a time determined upon the happening of an event), no later than 60 days after such instruction is given or such provision is made and such consent shall be deemed to have been given for purposes of this subsection at such effective time so long as such person is then an incorporator or director, as the case may be, and did not revoke the consent prior to such time. Any such consent shall be revocable prior to its becoming effective.

(d) If any incorporator is not available to act, then any person for whom or on whose behalf the incorporator was acting directly or indirectly as employee or agent, may take any action that such incorporator would have been authorized to take under this section or §107 of this title; provided that any instrument signed by such other person, or any record of the proceedings of a meeting in which such person participated, shall state that such incorporator is not available and the reason therefor, that such incorporator was acting directly or indirectly as employee or agent for or on behalf of such person, and that such person's signature on such instrument or participation in such meeting is otherwise authorized and not wrongful.

§109. Bylaws

(a) The original or other bylaws of a corporation may be adopted, amended or repealed by the incorporators, by the initial directors of a corporation other than a nonstock corporation or initial members of the governing body of a nonstock corporation if they were named in the certificate of incorporation, or, before a corporation other than a nonstock corporation has received any payment for any of its stock, by its board of directors. After a corporation other than a nonstock corporation has received any payment for any of its stock, the power to adopt, amend or repeal bylaws shall be in the stockholders entitled to vote. In the case of a nonstock corporation, the power to adopt, amend or repeal bylaws shall be in its members entitled to vote. Notwithstanding the foregoing, any corporation may, in its certificate of incorporation, confer the power to adopt, amend or repeal bylaws upon the directors or, in the case of a nonstock corporation, upon its governing body. The fact that such power has been so conferred upon the directors or governing body, as the case may be, shall not divest the stockholders or members of the power, nor limit their power to adopt, amend or repeal bylaws.

(b) The bylaws may contain any provision, not inconsistent with law or with the certificate of incorporation, relating to the business of the corporation, the conduct of its affairs, and its rights or powers or the rights or powers of its stockholders, directors, officers or employees. The bylaws may not contain any provision that would impose liability on a stockholder for the attorneys' fees or expenses of the corporation or any other party in connection with an internal corporate claim, as defined in §115 of this title.

§110. Emergency Bylaws and Other Powers in Emergency

(a) The board of directors of any corporation may adopt emergency bylaws, subject to repeal or change by action of the stockholders, which, notwithstanding any different provision elsewhere in this chapter or in Chapters 3 [repealed] and 5 [repealed] of Title 26, or in Chapter 7 of Title 5, or in the certificate of incorporation or bylaws, shall be operative during any emergency resulting from an attack on the United States or on a locality in which the corporation conducts its business or customarily holds meetings of its board of directors or its stockholders, or during any nuclear or atomic disaster, or during the existence of any catastrophe, including, but not limited to, an epidemic or pandemic, and a declaration of a national emergency by the United States government, or other similar emergency condition, irrespective of whether a quorum of the board of directors or a standing committee thereof can readily be convened for action. The emergency bylaws contemplated by this section may be adopted by the board of directors or, if a quorum cannot be readily convened for a meeting, by a majority of the directors present. The emergency bylaws may make any provision that may be practical and necessary for the circumstances of the emergency, including provisions that:

(1) A meeting of the board of directors or a committee thereof may be called by any officer or director in such manner and under such conditions as shall be prescribed in the emergency bylaws;

(2) The director or directors in attendance at the meeting, or any greater number fixed by the emergency bylaws, shall constitute a quorum; and

(3) The officers or other persons designated on a list approved by the board of directors before the emergency, all in such order of priority and subject to such conditions and for such period of time (not longer than reasonably necessary after the termination of the emergency) as may be provided in the emergency bylaws or in the resolution approving the list, shall, to the extent required to provide a quorum at any meeting of the board of directors, be deemed directors for such meeting.

(b) The board of directors, either before or during any such emergency, may provide, and from time to time modify, lines of succession in the event that during such emergency any or all officers or agents of the corporation shall for any reason be rendered incapable of discharging their duties.

(c) The board of directors, either before or during any such emergency, may, effective in the emergency, change the head office or designate several alternative head offices or regional offices, or authorize the officers so to do.

(d) No officer, director or employee acting in accordance with any emergency bylaws shall be liable except for wilful misconduct.

(e) To the extent not inconsistent with any emergency bylaws so adopted, the bylaws of the corporation shall remain in effect during any emergency and upon its termination the emergency bylaws shall cease to be operative.

(f) Unless otherwise provided in emergency bylaws, notice of any meeting of the board of directors during such an emergency may be given only to such of the directors as it may be feasible to reach at the time and by such means as may be feasible at the time, including publication or radio.

(g) To the extent required to constitute a quorum at any meeting of the board of directors during such an emergency, the officers of the corporation who are present shall, unless otherwise provided in emergency bylaws, be deemed, in order of rank and within the same rank in order of seniority, directors for such meeting.

(h) Nothing contained in this section shall be deemed exclusive of any other provisions for emergency powers consistent with other sections of this title which have been or may be adopted by corporations created under this chapter.

(i) During any emergency condition of a type described in subsection (a) of this section, the board of directors (or, if a quorum cannot be readily convened for a meeting, a majority of the directors present) may (i) take any action that it determines to be practical and necessary to address the circumstances of such emergency condition with respect to a meeting of stockholders of the corporation notwithstanding anything to the contrary in this chapter or in Chapter 7 of Title 5 or in the certificate of incorporation or bylaws, including, but not limited to, (1) to postpone any such meeting to a later time or date (with the record date for determining the stockholders entitled to notice of, and to vote at, such meeting applying to the postponed meeting irrespective of §213 of this title), and (2) with respect to a corporation subject to the reporting requirements of §13(a) or §15(d) of the Securities Exchange Act of 1934 [15 U.S.C. §78m(a) or 78o(d)], as amended, and the rules and regulations promulgated thereunder, to notify stockholders of any postponement or a change of the place of the meeting (or a change to hold the meeting solely by means of remote communication) solely by a document publicly filed by the corporation with the Securities and Exchange Commission pursuant to §13, §14 or §15(d) of such Act [15 U.S.C. §78m, §78n or 78o(d)] and such rules and regulations; and (ii) with respect to any dividend that has been declared as to which the record date has not occurred, change each of the record date and payment date to a later date or dates (provided the payment date as so changed is not more than 60 days after the record date as so changed); provided that, in either case, the corporation gives notice of such change to stockholders as promptly as practicable thereafter (and in any event before the record date theretofore in effect), which notice, in the case of a corporation subject to the reporting requirements of §13(a) or §15(d) of the Securities Exchange Act of 1934 [15 U.S.C. §78m(a) or 78o(d)], as amended, and the rules and regulations promulgated thereunder, may be given solely by a document publicly filed with the Securities and Exchange Commission pursuant to §13, §14 or §15(d) of such Act [15 U.S.C. §78m, §78n or 78o(d)] and such rules and regulations. No person shall be liable, and no meeting of stockholders shall be postponed or voided, for the failure to make a stocklist available pursuant to §219 of this title if it was not practicable to allow inspection during any such emergency condition.

§111. Jurisdiction to Interpret, Apply, Enforce or Determine the Validity of Corporate Instruments and Provisions of This Title

(a) Any civil action to interpret, apply, enforce or determine the validity of the provisions of:

(1) The certificate of incorporation or the bylaws of a corporation;

(2) Any instrument, document or agreement (i) by which a corporation creates or sells, or offers to create or sell, any of its stock, or any rights or options respecting its stock, or (ii) to which a corporation and 1 or more holders of its stock are parties, and pursuant to which any such holder or holders sell or offer to sell any of such stock, or (iii) by which a corporation agrees to sell, lease or exchange any of its property or assets, and which by its terms provides that 1 or more holders of its stock approve of or consent to such sale, lease or exchange;

(3) Any written restrictions on the transfer, registration of transfer or ownership of securities under §202 of this title;

(4) Any proxy under §212 or §215 of this title;

(5) Any voting trust or other voting agreement under §218 of this title;

(6) Any agreement, certificate of merger or consolidation, or certificate of ownership and merger governed by §§251-253, §§255-258, §§263-264, or §267 of this title;

(7) Any certificate of conversion under §265 or §266 of this title;

(8) Any certificate of domestication, transfer or continuance under §388, §389 or §390 of this title; or

(9) Any other instrument, document, agreement, or certificate required by any provision of this title; may be brought in the Court of Chancery, except to the extent that a statute confers exclusive jurisdiction on a court, agency or tribunal other than the Court of Chancery.

(b) Any civil action to interpret, apply or enforce any provision of this title may be brought in the Court of Chancery.

§112. Access to Proxy Solicitation Materials

The bylaws may provide that if the corporation solicits proxies with respect to an election of directors, it may be required, to the extent and subject to such procedures or conditions as may be provided in the bylaws, to include in its proxy solicitation materials (including any form of proxy it distributes), in addition to individuals nominated by the board of directors, 1 or more individuals nominated by a stockholder. Such procedures or conditions may include any of the following:

(1) A provision requiring a minimum record or beneficial ownership, or duration of ownership, of shares of the corporation's capital stock, by the nominating stockholder, and defining beneficial ownership to take into account options or other rights in respect of or related to such stock;

(2) A provision requiring the nominating stockholder to submit specified information concerning the stockholder and the stockholder's nominees, including information concerning ownership by such persons of shares of the corporation's capital stock, or options or other rights in respect of or related to such stock;

(3) A provision conditioning eligibility to require inclusion in the corporation's proxy solicitation materials upon the number or proportion of directors nominated by stockholders or whether the stockholder previously sought to require such inclusion;

(4) A provision precluding nominations by any person if such person, any nominee of such person, or any affiliate or associate of such person or nominee, has acquired or publicly proposed to acquire shares constituting a specified percentage of the voting power of the corporation's outstanding voting stock within a specified period before the election of directors;

(5) A provision requiring that the nominating stockholder undertake to indemnify the corporation in respect of any loss arising as a result of any false or misleading information or statement submitted by the nominating stockholder in connection with a nomination; and

(6) Any other lawful condition.

§113. *Proxy Expense Reimbursement*

(a) The bylaws may provide for the reimbursement by the corporation of expenses incurred by a stockholder in soliciting proxies in connection with an election of directors, subject to such procedures or conditions as the bylaws may prescribe, including:

(1) Conditioning eligibility for reimbursement upon the number or proportion of persons nominated by the stockholder seeking reimbursement or whether such stockholder previously sought reimbursement for similar expenses;

(2) Limitations on the amount of reimbursement based upon the proportion of votes cast in favor of 1 or more of the persons nominated by the stockholder seeking reimbursement, or upon the amount spent by the corporation in soliciting proxies in connection with the election;

(3) Limitations concerning elections of directors by cumulative voting pursuant to §214 of this title; or

(4) Any other lawful condition.

(b) No bylaw so adopted shall apply to elections for which any record date precedes its adoption.

§114. *Application of Chapter to Nonstock Corporations*

(a) Except as otherwise provided in subsections (b) and (c) of this section, the provisions of this chapter and of chapter 5 of this title shall apply to nonstock corporations in the manner specified in the following paragraphs (a)(1)-(4) of this section:

(1) All references to stockholders of the corporation shall be deemed to refer to members of the corporation;

(2) All references to the board of directors of the corporation shall be deemed to refer to the governing body of the corporation;

(3) All references to directors or to members of the board of directors of the corporation shall be deemed to refer to members of the governing body of the corporation; and

(4) All references to stock, capital stock, or shares thereof of a corporation authorized to issue capital stock shall be deemed to refer to memberships of a nonprofit nonstock corporation and to membership interests of any other nonstock corporation.

(b) Subsection (a) of this section shall not apply to:

(1) Sections 102(a)(4), (b)(1) and (2), 109(a), 114, 141, 154, 215, 228, 230(b), 241, 242, 253, 254, 255, 256, 257, 258, 271, 276, 311, 312, 313, 390, and 503 of this title, which apply to nonstock corporations by their terms;

(2) Sections 102(f), 109(b) (last sentence), 151, 152, 153, 155, 156, 157(d), 158, 161, 162, 163, 164, 165, 166, 167, 168, 203, 211, 212, 213, 214, 216, 219, 222, 231, 243, 244, 251, 252, 267, 274, 275, 324, 364, 366(a), 391 and 502(a)(5) of this title; and

(3) Subchapter XIV and Subchapter XVI of this chapter.

(c) In the case of a non-profit nonstock corporation, subsection (a) of this section shall not apply to:

(1) The sections and subchapters listed in subsection (b) of this section;

(2) Sections 102(b)(3), 111(a)(2) and (3), 144(a)(2), 217, 218(a) and (b), and 262 of this title; and

(3) Subchapter V, subchapter VI (other than §§204 and 205 of this title) and subchapter XV of this chapter.

(d) For purposes of this chapter:

(1) A 'charitable nonstock corporation' is any nonprofit nonstock corporation that is exempt from taxation under §501(c)(3) of the United States Internal Revenue Code, or any successor provisions;

(2) a 'membership interest' is, unless otherwise provided in a nonstock corporation's certificate of incorporation, a member's share of the profits and losses of a nonstock corporation, or a member's right to receive distributions of the nonstock corporation's assets, or both;

(3) a 'nonprofit nonstock corporation' is a nonstock corporation that does not have membership interests; and

(4) A 'nonstock corporation' is any corporation organized under this chapter that is not authorized to issue capital stock.

§115. *Forum Selection Provisions*

The certificate of incorporation or the bylaws may require, consistent with applicable jurisdictional requirements, that any or all internal corporate claims shall be brought solely and exclusively in any or all of the courts in this State, and no provision of the certificate of incorporation or the bylaws may prohibit bringing such claims in the courts of this State. "Internal corporate claims" means claims, including claims in the right of the corporation, (i) that are based upon a violation of a duty by a current or former director or officer or stockholder in such capacity, or (ii) as to which this title confers jurisdiction upon the Court of Chancery.

§116. *Document Form, Signature and Delivery*

(a) Except as provided in subsection (b) of this section, without limiting the manner in which any act or transaction may be documented, or the manner in which a document may be signed or delivered:

(1) Any act or transaction contemplated or governed by this chapter or the certificate of incorporation or bylaws may be provided for in a document, and an electronic transmission shall be deemed the equivalent of a written document. "Document" means:

a. Any tangible medium on which information is inscribed, and includes handwritten, typed, printed or similar instruments, and copies of such instruments; and

b. An electronic transmission.

(2) Whenever this chapter or the certificate of incorporation or bylaws requires or permits a signature, the signature may be a manual, facsimile, conformed or electronic signature. "Electronic signature" means an electronic symbol or process that is attached to, or logically associated with, a document and executed or adopted by a person with an intent to execute, authenticate or adopt the document. A person may execute a document with such person's signature.

(3) Unless otherwise agreed between the sender and recipient (and in the case of proxies or consents given by or on behalf of a stockholder, subject to the additional requirements set forth in §212(c)(2) and (3) and §228(d)(1) of this title, respectively), an electronic transmission shall be deemed delivered to a person for purposes of this chapter and the certificate of incorporation and bylaws when it enters an information processing system that the person has designated for the purpose of receiving electronic transmissions of the type delivered, so long as the electronic transmission is in a form capable of being processed by that system and such person is able to retrieve the electronic transmission. Whether a person has so designated an information processing system is determined by the certificate of incorporation, the bylaws or from the context and surrounding circumstances, including the parties' conduct. An electronic transmission is delivered under this section even if no person is aware of its receipt. Receipt of an electronic acknowledgement from an information processing system establishes that an electronic transmission was received but, by itself, does not establish that the content sent corresponds to the content received.

This chapter shall not prohibit 1 or more persons from conducting a transaction in accordance with Chapter 12A of Title 6 so long as the part or parts of the transaction that are governed by this chapter are documented, signed and delivered in accordance with this subsection or otherwise in accordance with this chapter. This subsection shall apply solely for purposes of determining whether an act or transaction has been documented, and the document has been signed and delivered, in accordance with this chapter, the certificate of incorporation and the bylaws.

(b) Subsection (a) of this section shall not apply to:

(1) a document filed with or submitted to the Secretary of State, the Register in Chancery, or a court or other judicial or governmental body of this State;

(2) A document comprising part of the stock ledger;

(3) A certificate representing a security;

(4) Any document expressly referenced as a notice (or waiver of notice) by this chapter, the certificate of incorporation or bylaws;

(5) [Repealed.]

(6) A ballot to vote on actions at a meeting of stockholders; and

(7) An act or transaction effected pursuant to §280 of this title or subchapters III, XIII or XVI of this chapter.

The foregoing shall not create any presumption about the lawful means to document a matter addressed by this subsection, or the lawful means to sign or deliver a document addressed by this subsection. No provision of the certificate of incorporation or bylaws shall limit the application of subsection (a) of this section except for a provision that expressly restricts or prohibits the use of an electronic transmission or electronic signature (or any form thereof) or expressly restricts or prohibits the delivery of an electronic transmission to an information processing system.

(c) In the event that any provision of this chapter is deemed to modify, limit or supersede the Electronic Signatures in Global and National Commerce Act, [15 U.S.C. [§§]7001 et. seq.], the provisions of this chapter shall control to the fullest extent permitted by §7002(a)(2) of such act.

SUBCHAPTER II. POWERS

§121. General Powers

(a) In addition to the powers enumerated in §122 of this title, every corporation, its officers, directors and stockholders shall possess and may exercise all the powers and privileges granted by this chapter or by any other law or by its certificate of incorporation, together with any powers incidental thereto, so far as such powers and privileges are necessary or convenient to the conduct, promotion or attainment of the business or purposes set forth in its certificate of incorporation.

(b) Every corporation shall be governed by the provisions and be subject to the restrictions and liabilities contained in this chapter.

§122. Specific Powers

Every corporation created under this chapter shall have power to:

(1) Have perpetual succession by its corporate name, unless a limited period of duration is stated in its certificate of incorporation;

(2) Sue and be sued in all courts and participate, as a party or otherwise, in any judicial, administrative, arbitrative or other proceeding, in its corporate name;

(3) Have a corporate seal, which may be altered at pleasure, and use the same by causing it or a facsimile thereof, to be impressed or affixed or in any other manner reproduced;

(4) Purchase, receive, take by grant, gift, devise, bequest or otherwise, lease, or otherwise acquire, own, hold, improve, employ, use and otherwise deal in and with real or personal property, or any interest therein, wherever situated, and to sell, convey, lease, exchange, transfer or otherwise dispose of, or mortgage or pledge, all or any of its property and assets, or any interest therein, wherever situated;

(5) Appoint such officers and agents as the business of the corporation requires and to pay or otherwise provide for them suitable compensation;

(6) Adopt, amend and repeal bylaws;

(7) Wind up and dissolve itself in the manner provided in this chapter;

(8) Conduct its business, carry on its operations and have offices and exercise its powers within or without this State;

(9) Make donations for the public welfare or for charitable, scientific or educational purposes, and in time of war or other national emergency in aid thereof;

(10) Be an incorporator, promoter or manager of other corporations of any type or kind;

(11) Participate with others in any corporation, partnership, limited partnership, joint venture or other association of any kind, or in any transaction, undertaking or arrangement which the participating corporation would have power to conduct by itself, whether or not such participation involves sharing or delegation of control with or to others;

(12) Transact any lawful business which the corporation's board of directors shall find to be in aid of governmental authority;

(13) Make contracts, including contracts of guaranty and suretyship, incur liabilities, borrow money at such rates of interest as the corporation may

determine, issue its notes, bonds and other obligations, and secure any of its obligations by mortgage, pledge or other encumbrance of all or any of its property, franchises and income, and make contracts of guaranty and suretyship which are necessary or convenient to the conduct, promotion or attainment of the business of (a) a corporation all of the outstanding stock of which is owned, directly or indirectly, by the contracting corporation, or (b) a corporation which owns, directly or indirectly, all of the outstanding stock of the contracting corporation, or (c) a corporation all of the outstanding stock of which is owned, directly or indirectly, by a corporation which owns, directly or indirectly, all of the outstanding stock of the contracting corporation, which contracts of guaranty and suretyship shall be deemed to be necessary or convenient to the conduct, promotion or attainment of the business of the contracting corporation, and make other contracts of guaranty and suretyship which are necessary or convenient to the conduct, promotion or attainment of the business of the contracting corporation;

(14) Lend money for its corporate purposes, invest and reinvest its funds, and take, hold and deal with real and personal property as security for the payment of funds so loaned or invested;

(15) Pay pensions and establish and carry out pension, profit sharing, stock option, stock purchase, stock bonus, retirement, benefit, incentive and compensation plans, trusts and provisions for any or all of its directors, officers and employees, and for any or all of the directors, officers and employees of its subsidiaries;

(16) Provide insurance for its benefit on the life of any of its directors, officers or employees, or on the life of any stockholder for the purpose of acquiring at such stockholder's death shares of its stock owned by such stockholder.

(17) Renounce, in its certificate of incorporation or by action of its board of directors, any interest or expectancy of the corporation in, or in being offered an opportunity to participate in, specified business opportunities or specified classes or categories of business opportunities that are presented to the corporation or 1 or more of its officers, directors or stockholders.

§124. Effect of Lack of Corporate Capacity or Power; Ultra Vires

No act of a corporation and no conveyance or transfer of real or personal property to or by a corporation shall be invalid by reason of the fact that the corporation was without capacity or power to do such act or to make or receive such conveyance or transfer, but such lack of capacity or power may be asserted:

(1) In a proceeding by a stockholder against the corporation to enjoin the doing of any act or acts or the transfer of real or personal property by or to the corporation. If the unauthorized acts or transfer sought to be enjoined are being, or are to be, performed or made pursuant to any contract to which the corporation is a party, the court may, if all of the parties to the contract are parties to the proceeding and if it deems the same to be equitable, set aside and enjoin the performance of such contract, and in so doing may allow to the corporation or to the other parties to the contract, as the case may be, such compensation as may be equitable for the loss or damage sustained by any of them which may result from the action of the court in setting aside and enjoining the performance of

such contract, but anticipated profits to be derived from the performance of the contract shall not be awarded by the court as a loss or damage sustained;

(2) In a proceeding by the corporation, whether acting directly or through a receiver, trustee or other legal representative, or through stockholders in a representative suit, against an incumbent or former officer or director of the corporation, for loss or damage due to such incumbent or former officer's or director's unauthorized act;

(3) In a proceeding by the Attorney General to dissolve the corporation, or to enjoin the corporation from the transaction of unauthorized business.

SUBCHAPTER III. REGISTERED OFFICE AND REGISTERED AGENT

§131. Registered Office in State; Principal Office or Place of Business in State

(a) Every corporation shall have and maintain in this State a registered office which may, but need not be, the same as its place of business.

(b) Whenever the term "corporation's principal office or place of business in this State" or "principal office or place of business of the corporation in this State," or other term of like import, is or has been used in a corporation's certificate of incorporation, or in any other document, or in any statute, it shall be deemed to mean and refer to, unless the context indicates otherwise, the corporation's registered office required by this section; and it shall not be necessary for any corporation to amend its certificate of incorporation or any other document to comply with this section. . . .

§132. Registered Agent in State; Resident Agent

(a) Every corporation shall have and maintain in this State a registered agent, which agent may be any of:

(1) The corporation itself;

(2) An individual resident in this State;

(3) A domestic corporation (other than the corporation itself), a domestic partnership (whether general (including a limited liability partnership) or limited (including a limited liability limited partnership)), a domestic limited liability company or a domestic statutory trust; or

(4) A foreign corporation, a foreign limited liability partnership, a foreign limited partnership, a foreign limited liability limited partnership, a foreign limited liability company or a foreign statutory trust.

(b) Every registered agent for a domestic corporation or a foreign corporation shall:

(1) If an entity, maintain a business office in this State which is generally open, or if an individual, be generally present at a designated location in this State, at sufficiently frequent times to accept service of process and otherwise perform the functions of a registered agent;

(2) If a foreign entity, be authorized to transact business in this State;

(3) Accept service of process and other communications directed to the corporations for which it serves as registered agent and forward same to the corporation to which the service or communication is directed; and

(4) Forward to the corporations for which it serves as registered agent the annual report required by §502 of this title or an electronic notification of same in a form satisfactory to the Secretary of State ("Secretary"). . . .

SUBCHAPTER IV. DIRECTORS AND OFFICERS

§141. Board of Directors; Powers; Number, Qualifications, Terms and Quorum; Committees; Classes of Directors; Nonstock Corporations; Reliance upon Books; Action Without Meeting; Removal

(a) The business and affairs of every corporation organized under this chapter shall be managed by or under the direction of a board of directors, except as may be otherwise provided in this chapter or in its certificate of incorporation. If any such provision is made in the certificate of incorporation, the powers and duties conferred or imposed upon the board of directors by this chapter shall be exercised or performed to such extent and by such person or persons as shall be provided in the certificate of incorporation.

(b) The board of directors of a corporation shall consist of 1 or more members, each of whom shall be a natural person. The number of directors shall be fixed by, or in the manner provided in, the bylaws, unless the certificate of incorporation fixes the number of directors, in which case a change in the number of directors shall be made only by amendment of the certificate. Directors need not be stockholders unless so required by the certificate of incorporation or the bylaws. The certificate of incorporation or bylaws may prescribe other qualifications for directors. Each director shall hold office until such director's successor is elected and qualified or until such director's earlier resignation or removal. Any director may resign at any time upon notice given in writing or by electronic transmission to the corporation. A resignation is effective when the resignation is delivered unless the resignation specifies a later effective date or an effective date determined upon the happening of an event or events. A resignation which is conditioned upon the director failing to receive a specified vote for reelection as a director may provide that it is irrevocable. A majority of the total number of directors shall constitute a quorum for the transaction of business unless the certificate of incorporation or the bylaws require a greater number. Unless the certificate of incorporation provides otherwise, the bylaws may provide that a number less than a majority shall constitute a quorum which in no case shall be less 1/3 than of the total number of directors. The vote of the majority of the directors present at a meeting at which a quorum is present shall be the act of the board of directors unless the certificate of incorporation or the bylaws shall require a vote of a greater number.

(c) (1) All corporations incorporated prior to July 1, 1996, shall be governed by this paragraph (c)(1) of this section, provided that any such corporation may by a resolution adopted by a majority of the whole board elect to be governed by paragraph (c)(2) of this section, in which case this paragraph (c)(1) of this section shall not apply to such corporation. All corporations incorporated on or after July 1, 1996, shall be governed by paragraph (c)(2) of this section. The board of directors may, by resolution passed by a majority of the whole board, designate 1 or more committees, each committee to consist of 1 or more of the directors of the corporation. The board may designate 1 or more directors as alternate members of any committee, who may replace any absent or disqualified member at any meeting of the committee. The bylaws may provide that in the absence or disqualification of a member of a committee, the member or members present at any meeting and not disqualified from voting, whether or not the member or members present constitute a quorum, may unanimously appoint another member of the board of directors to act at the meeting in the place of any such absent or disqualified member. Any such committee, to the extent provided in the resolution of the board of directors, or in the bylaws of the corporation, shall have and may exercise all the powers and authority of the board of directors in the management of the business and affairs of the corporation, and may authorize the seal of the corporation to be affixed to all papers which may require it; but no such committee shall have the power or authority in reference to amending the certificate of incorporation (except that a committee may, to the extent authorized in the resolution or resolutions providing for the issuance of shares of stock adopted by the board of directors as provided in §151(a) of this title, fix the designations and any of the preferences or rights of such shares relating to dividends, redemption, dissolution, any distribution of assets of the corporation or the conversion into, or the exchange of such shares for, shares of any other class or classes or any other series of the same or any other class or classes of stock of the corporation or fix the number of shares of any series of stock or authorize the increase or decrease of the shares of any series), adopting an agreement of merger or consolidation under §251, §252, §254, §255, §256, §257, §258, §263 or §264 of this title, recommending to the stockholders the sale, lease or exchange of all or substantially all of the corporation's property and assets, recommending to the stockholders a dissolution of the corporation or a revocation of a dissolution, or amending the bylaws of the corporation; and, unless the resolution, bylaws or certificate of incorporation expressly so provides, no such committee shall have the power or authority to declare a dividend, to authorize the issuance of stock or to adopt a certificate of ownership and merger pursuant to §253 of this title.

(2) The board of directors may designate 1 or more committees, each committee to consist of 1 or more of the directors of the corporation. The board may designate 1 or more directors as alternate members of any committee, who may replace any absent or disqualified member at any meeting of the committee. The bylaws may provide that in the absence or disqualification of a member of a committee, the member or members present at any meeting and not disqualified from voting, whether or not such member or members constitute a quorum, may unanimously appoint another member of the board of directors to act at the meeting in the place of any such absent or disqualified member. Any such committee, to the extent provided in the resolution of the board of directors, or in the bylaws of the corporation, shall have and may exercise all the powers and authority of the board of directors in the management of the business and affairs of the corporation, and may authorize the seal of the corporation to be affixed to all papers which may require it; but no such committee shall have the power or authority in reference to the following matter: (i) approving or adopting, or recommending to the stockholders, any action or matter (other than the election or removal of

directors) expressly required by this chapter to be submitted to stockholders for approval or (ii) adopting, amending or repealing any bylaw of the corporation.

(3) Unless otherwise provided in the certificate of incorporation, the bylaws or the resolution of the board of directors designating the committee, a committee may create 1 or more subcommittees, each subcommittee to consist of 1 or more members of the committee, and delegate to a subcommittee any or all of the powers and authority of the committee. Except for references to committees and members of committees in subsection (c) of this section, every reference in this chapter to a committee of the board of directors or a member of a committee shall be deemed to include a reference to a subcommittee or member of a subcommittee.

(4) A majority of the directors then serving on a committee of the board of directors or on a subcommittee of a committee shall constitute a quorum for the transaction of business by the committee or subcommittee, unless the certificate of incorporation, the bylaws, a resolution of the board of directors or a resolution of a committee that created the subcommittee requires a greater or lesser number, provided that in no case shall a quorum be less than 1/3 of the directors then serving on the committee or subcommittee. The vote of the majority of the members of a committee or subcommittee present at a meeting at which a quorum is present shall be the act of the committee or subcommittee, unless the certificate of incorporation, the bylaws, a resolution of the board of directors or a resolution of a committee that created the subcommittee requires a greater number.

(d) The directors of any corporation organized under this chapter may, by the certificate of incorporation or by an initial bylaw, or by a bylaw adopted by a vote of the stockholders, be divided into 1, 2 or 3 classes; the term of office of those of the first class to expire at the first annual meeting held after such classification becomes effective; of the second class 1 year thereafter; of the third class 2 years thereafter; and at each annual election held after such classification becomes effective, directors shall be chosen for a full term, as the case may be, to succeed those whose terms expire. The certificate of incorporation or bylaw provision dividing the directors into classes may authorize the board of directors to assign members of the board already in office to such classes at the time such classification becomes effective. The certificate of incorporation may confer upon holders of any class or series of stock the right to elect 1 or more directors who shall serve for such term, and have such voting powers as shall be stated in the certificate of incorporation. The terms of office and voting powers of the directors elected separately by the holders of any class or series of stock may be greater than or less than those of any other director or class of directors. In addition, the certificate of incorporation may confer upon 1 or more directors, whether or not elected separately by the holders of any class or series of stock, voting powers greater than or less than those of other directors. Any such provision conferring greater or lesser voting power shall apply to voting in any committee, unless otherwise provided in the certificate of incorporation or bylaws. If the certificate of incorporation provides that 1 or more directors shall have more or less than 1 vote per director on any matter, every reference in this chapter to a majority or other proportion of the directors shall refer to a majority or other proportion of the votes of the directors.

(e) A member of the board of directors, or a member of any committee designated by the board of directors, shall, in the performance of such member's duties, be fully protected in relying in good faith upon the records of the corporation and upon such information, opinions, reports or statements presented to the corporation by any of the corporation's officers or employees, or committees of the board of directors, or by any other person as to matters the member reasonably believes are within such other person's professional or expert competence and who has been selected with reasonable care by or on behalf of the corporation.

(f) Unless otherwise restricted by the certificate of incorporation or bylaws, (1) any action required or permitted to be taken at any meeting of the board of directors or of any committee thereof may be taken without a meeting if all members of the board or committee, as the case may be, consent thereto in writing, or by electronic transmission, and (2) a consent may be documented, signed and delivered in any manner permitted by §116 of this title. Any person (whether or not then a director) may provide, whether through instruction to an agent or otherwise, that a consent to action will be effective at a future time (including a time determined upon the happening of an event), no later than 60 days after such instruction is given or such provision is made and such consent shall be deemed to have been given for purposes of this subsection at such effective time so long as such person is then a director and did not revoke the consent prior to such time. Any such consent shall be revocable prior to its becoming effective. After an action is taken, the consent or consents relating thereto shall be filed with the minutes of the proceedings of the board of directors, or the committee thereof, in the same paper or electronic form as the minutes are maintained.

(g) Unless otherwise restricted by the certificate of incorporation or bylaws, the board of directors of any corporation organized under this chapter may hold its meetings, and have an office or offices, outside of this State.

(h) Unless otherwise restricted by the certificate of incorporation or bylaws, the board of directors shall have the authority to fix the compensation of directors.

(i) Unless otherwise restricted by the certificate of incorporation or bylaws, members of the board of directors of any corporation, or any committee designated by the board, may participate in a meeting of such board, or committee by means of conference telephone or other communications equipment by means of which all persons participating in the meeting can hear each other, and participation in a meeting pursuant to this subsection shall constitute presence in person at the meeting.

(j) The certificate of incorporation of any nonstock corporation may provide that less than 1/3 of the members of the governing body may constitute a quorum thereof and may otherwise provide that the business and affairs of the corporation shall be managed in a manner different from that provided in this section. Except as may be otherwise provided by the certificate of incorporation, this section shall apply to such a corporation, and when so applied, all references to the board of directors, to members thereof, and to stockholders shall be deemed to refer to the governing body of the corporation, the members thereof and the members of the corporation, respectively; and all references to stock, capital stock, or shares thereof shall be deemed to refer to memberships of a non-profit nonstock corporation and to membership interests of any other nonstock corporation.

(k) Any director or the entire board of directors may be removed, with or without cause, by the holders of a majority of the shares then entitled to vote at an election of directors, except as follows:

(1) Unless the certificate of incorporation otherwise provides, in the case of a corporation whose board is classified as provided in subsection (d) of this section, stockholders may effect such removal only for cause; or

(2) In the case of a corporation having cumulative voting, if less than the entire board is to be removed, no director may be removed without cause if the votes cast against such director's removal would be sufficient to elect such director if then cumulatively voted at an election of the entire board of directors, or, if there be classes of directors, at an election of the class of directors of which such director is a part.

Whenever the holders of any class or series are entitled to elect 1 or more directors by the certificate of incorporation, this subsection shall apply, in respect to the removal without cause of a director or directors so elected, to the vote of the holders of the outstanding shares of that class or series and not to the vote of the outstanding shares as a whole.

§142. Officers; Titles, Duties, Selection, Term; Failure to Elect; Vacancies

(a) Every corporation organized under this chapter shall have such officers with such titles and duties as shall be stated in the bylaws or in a resolution of the board of directors which is not inconsistent with the bylaws and as may be necessary to enable it to sign instruments and stock certificates which comply with §§103(a)(2) and 158 of this title. One of the officers shall have the duty to record the proceedings of the meetings of the stockholders and directors in a book to be kept for that purpose. Any number of offices may be held by the same person unless the certificate of incorporation or bylaws otherwise provide.

(b) Officers shall be chosen in such manner and shall hold their offices for such terms as are prescribed by the bylaws or determined by the board of directors or other governing body. Each officer shall hold office until such officer's successor is elected and qualified or until such officer's earlier resignation or removal. Any officer may resign at any time upon written notice to the corporation.

(c) The corporation may secure the fidelity of any or all of its officers or agents by bond or otherwise.

(d) A failure to elect officers shall not dissolve or otherwise affect the corporation.

(e) Any vacancy occurring in any office of the corporation by death, resignation, removal or otherwise, shall be filled as the bylaws provide. In the absence of such provision, the vacancy shall be filled by the board of directors or other governing body.

§143. Loans to Employees and Officers; Guaranty of Obligations of Employees and Officers

Any corporation may lend money to, or guarantee any obligation of, or otherwise assist any officer or other employee of the corporation or of its subsidiary, including any officer or employee who is a director of the corporation or its subsidiary, whenever, in the judgment of the directors, such loan, guaranty or assistance may reasonably be expected to benefit the corporation. The loan, guaranty or other assistance may be with or without interest, and may be unsecured, or secured in such manner as the board of directors shall approve, including, without limitation, a pledge of shares of stock of the corporation. Nothing in this section contained shall be deemed to deny, limit or restrict the powers of guaranty or warranty of any corporation at common law or under any statute.

§144. Interested Directors; Quorum

(a) No contract or transaction between a corporation and 1 or more of its directors or officers, or between a corporation and any other corporation, partnership, association, or other organization in which 1 or more of its directors or officers, are directors or officers, or have a financial interest, shall be void or voidable solely for this reason, or solely because the director or officer is present at or participates in the meeting of the board or committee which authorizes the contract or transaction, or solely because any such director's or officer's votes are counted for such purpose, if:

(1) The material facts as to the director's or officer's relationship or interest and as to the contract or transaction are disclosed or are known to the board of directors or the committee, and the board or committee in good faith authorizes the contract or transaction by the affirmative votes of a majority of the disinterested directors, even though the disinterested directors be less than a quorum; or

(2) The material facts as to the director's or officer's relationship or interest and as to the contract or transaction are disclosed or are known to the stockholders entitled to vote thereon, and the contract or transaction is specifically approved in good faith by vote of the stockholders; or

(3) The contract or transaction is fair as to the corporation as of the time it is authorized, approved or ratified, by the board of directors, a committee or the stockholders.

(b) Common or interested directors may be counted in determining the presence of a quorum at a meeting of the board of directors or of a committee which authorizes the contract or transaction.

§145. Indemnification of Officers, Directors, Employees and Agents; Insurance

(a) A corporation shall have power to indemnify any person who was or is a party or is threatened to be made a party to any threatened, pending or completed action, suit or proceeding, whether civil, criminal, administrative or investigative (other than an action by or in the right of the corporation) by reason of the fact that the person is or was a director, officer, employee or agent of the corporation, or is or was serving at the request of the corporation as a director, officer, employee or agent of another corporation, partnership, joint venture, trust or other enterprise, against expenses (including attorneys' fees), judgments, fines and amounts paid in settlement actually and reasonably incurred by the person in connection with such action, suit or proceeding if the person acted in good faith and in a manner the person reasonably believed to be in or not opposed to the best interests of the corporation, and, with respect to any criminal action or proceeding, had no reasonable cause to believe the person's conduct was unlawful. The termination of any action, suit or proceeding by judgment, order, settlement, conviction, or upon a plea of nolo contendere or its equivalent, shall not, of itself, create a presumption that the person did not act in good faith and in a manner which the person reasonably believed to be in or not opposed to the best interests of the corporation, and, with respect to any criminal action or proceeding, had reasonable cause to believe that the person's conduct was unlawful.

(b) A corporation shall have power to indemnify any person who was or is a party or is threatened to be made a party to any threatened, pending or completed action or suit by or in the right of the corporation to procure a judgment in its favor by reason of the fact that the person is or was a director, officer, employee or agent of the corporation, or is or was serving at the request of the corporation as a director, officer, employee or agent of another corporation, partnership, joint venture, trust or other enterprise against expenses (including attorneys' fees) actually and reasonably incurred by the person in connection with the defense or settlement of such action or suit if the person acted in good faith and in a manner the person reasonably believed to be in or not opposed to the best interests of the corporation and except that no indemnification shall be made in respect of any claim, issue or matter as to which such person shall have been adjudged to be liable to the corporation unless and only to the extent that the Court of Chancery or the court in which such action or suit was brought shall determine upon application that, despite the adjudication of liability but in view of all the circumstances of the case, such person is fairly and reasonably entitled to indemnity for such expenses which the Court of Chancery or such other court shall deem proper.

(c) (1) To the extent that a present or former director or officer of a corporation has been successful on the merits or otherwise in defense of any action, suit or proceeding referred to in subsections (a) and (b) of this section, or in defense of any claim, issue or matter therein, such person shall be indemnified against expenses (including attorneys' fees) actually and reasonably incurred by such person in connection therewith. For indemnification with respect to any act or omission occurring after December 31, 2020, references to "officer" for purposes of paragraphs (c)(1) and (2) of this section shall mean only a person who at the time of such act or omission is deemed to have consented to service by the delivery of process to the registered agent of the corporation pursuant to §3114(b) of Title 10 (for purposes of this sentence only, treating residents of this State as if they were nonresidents to apply §3114(b) of Title 10 to this sentence).

(2) The corporation may indemnify any other person who is not a present or former director or officer of the corporation against expenses (including attorneys' fees) actually and reasonably incurred by such person to the extent he or she has been successful on the merits or otherwise in defense of any action, suit or proceeding referred to in subsections (a) and (b) of this section, or in defense of any claim, issue or matter therein.

(d) Any indemnification under subsections (a) and (b) of this section (unless ordered by a court) shall be made by the corporation only as authorized in the specific case upon a determination that indemnification of the present or former director, officer, employee or agent is proper in the circumstances because the person has met the applicable standard of conduct set forth in subsections (a) and (b) of this section. Such determination shall be made, with respect to a person who is a director or officer of the corporation at the time of such determination:

(1) by a majority vote of the directors who are not parties to such action, suit or proceeding, even though less than a quorum; or

(2) by a committee of such directors designated by majority vote of such directors, even though less than a quorum; or

(3) if there are no such directors, or if such directors so direct, by independent legal counsel in a written opinion; or

(4) by the stockholders.

(e) Expenses (including attorneys' fees) incurred by an officer or director of the corporation in defending any civil, criminal, administrative or investigative action, suit or proceeding may be paid by the corporation in advance of the final disposition of such action, suit or proceeding upon receipt of an undertaking by or on behalf of such director or officer to repay such amount if it shall ultimately be determined that such person is not entitled to be indemnified by the corporation as authorized in this section. Such expenses (including attorneys' fees) incurred by former directors and officers or other employees and agents of the corporation or by persons serving at the request of the corporation as directors, officers, employees or agents of another corporation, partnership, joint venture, trust or other enterprise may be so paid upon such terms and conditions, if any, as the corporation deems appropriate.

(f) The indemnification and advancement of expenses provided by, or granted pursuant to, the other subsections of this section shall not be deemed exclusive of any other rights to which those seeking indemnification or advancement of expenses may be entitled under any bylaw, agreement, vote of stockholders or disinterested directors or otherwise, both as to action in such person's official capacity and as to action in another capacity while holding such office. A right to indemnification or to advancement of expenses arising under a provision of the certificate of incorporation or a bylaw shall not be eliminated or impaired by an amendment to or repeal or elimination of the certificate of incorporation or the bylaws after the occurrence of the act or omission that is the subject of the civil, criminal, administrative or investigative action, suit or proceeding for which indemnification or advancement of expenses is sought, unless the provision in effect at the time of such act or omission explicitly authorizes such elimination or impairment after such action or omission has occurred.

(g) A corporation shall have power to purchase and maintain insurance on behalf of any person who is or was a director, officer, employee or agent of the corporation, or is or was serving at the request of the corporation as a director, officer, employee or agent of another corporation, partnership, joint venture, trust or other enterprise against any liability asserted against such person and incurred by such person in any such capacity, or arising out of such person's status as such, whether or not the corporation would have the power to indemnify such person against such liability under this section. For purposes of this subsection, insurance shall include any insurance provided directly or indirectly (including pursuant to any fronting or reinsurance arrangement) by or through a captive insurance company organized and licensed in compliance with the laws of any jurisdiction, including any captive insurance company licensed under Chapter 69 of Title 18 of the Delaware Code, provided that the terms of any such captive insurance shall:

(1) exclude from coverage thereunder, and provide that the insurer shall not make any payment for, loss in connection with any claim made against any person arising out of, based upon or attributable to any (i) personal profit or other financial advantage to which such person was not legally entitled or

(ii) deliberate criminal or deliberate fraudulent act of such person, or a knowing violation of law by such person, if (in the case of the foregoing clause (i) or (ii)) established by a final, non-appealable adjudication in the underlying proceeding in respect of such claim (which shall not include an action or proceeding initiated by the insurer or the insured to determine coverage under the policy), unless and only to the extent such person is entitled to be indemnified therefor under this section;

(2) require that any determination to make a payment under such insurance in respect of a claim against a current director or officer (as defined in paragraph (c)(1) of this section) of the corporation shall be made by a independent claims administrator or in accordance with the provisions of paragraphs (d)(1) through (4) of this section; and

(3) require that, prior to any payment under such insurance in connection with any dismissal or compromise of any action, suit or proceeding brought by or in the right of a corporation as to which notice is required to be given to stockholders, such corporation shall include in such notice that a payment is proposed to be made under such insurance in connection with such dismissal or compromise.

For purposes of paragraph (1) of this subsection, the conduct of an insured person shall not be imputed to any other insured person. A corporation that establishes or maintains a captive insurance company that provides insurance pursuant to this section shall not, solely by virtue thereof, be subject to the provisions of Title 18 of the Delaware Code.

(h) For purposes of this section, references to "the corporation" shall include, in addition to the resulting corporation, any constituent corporation (including any constituent of a constituent) absorbed in a consolidation or merger which, if its separate existence had continued, would have had power and authority to indemnify its directors, officers, and employees or agents, so that any person who is or was a director, officer, employee or agent of such constituent corporation, or is or was serving at the request of such constituent corporation as a director, officer, employee or agent of another corporation, partnership, joint venture, trust or other enterprise, shall stand in the same position under this section with respect to the resulting or surviving corporation as such person would have with respect to such constituent corporation if its separate existence had continued.

(i) For purposes of this section, references to "other enterprises" shall include employee benefit plans; references to "fines" shall include any excise taxes assessed on a person with respect to any employee benefit plan; and references to "serving at the request of the corporation" shall include any service as a director, officer, employee or agent of the corporation which imposes duties on, or involves services by, such director, officer, employee or agent with respect to an employee benefit plan, its participants or beneficiaries; and a person who acted in good faith and in a manner such person reasonably believed to be in the interest of the participants and beneficiaries of an employee benefit plan shall be deemed to have acted in a manner "not opposed to the best interests of the corporation" as referred to in this section.

(j) The indemnification and advancement of expenses provided by, or granted pursuant to, this section shall, unless otherwise provided when authorized or ratified, continue as to a person who has ceased to be a director, officer, employee or agent and shall inure to the benefit of the heirs, executors and administrators of such a person.

(k) The Court of Chancery is hereby vested with exclusive jurisdiction to hear and determine all actions for advancement of expenses or indemnification brought under this section or under any bylaw, agreement, vote of stockholders or disinterested directors, or otherwise. The Court of Chancery may summarily determine a corporation's obligation to advance expenses (including attorneys' fees).

§146. *Submission of Matters for Stockholder Vote*

A corporation may agree to submit a matter to a vote of its stockholders whether or not the board of directors determines at any time subsequent to approving such matter that such matter is no longer advisable and recommends that the stockholders reject or vote against the matter.

SUBCHAPTER V. STOCK AND DIVIDENDS

§151. *Classes and Series of Stock; Redemption; Rights*

(a) Every corporation may issue 1 or more classes of stock or 1 or more series of stock within any class thereof, any or all of which classes may be of stock with par value or stock without par value and which classes or series may have such voting powers, full or limited, or no voting powers, and such designations, preferences and relative, participating, optional or other special rights, and qualifications, limitations or restrictions thereof, as shall be stated and expressed in the certificate of incorporation or of any amendment thereto, or in the resolution or resolutions providing for the issue of such stock adopted by the board of directors pursuant to authority expressly vested in it by the provisions of its certificate of incorporation. Any of the voting powers, designations, preferences, rights and qualifications, limitations or restrictions of any such class or series of stock may be made dependent upon facts ascertainable outside the certificate of incorporation or of any amendment thereto, or outside the resolution or resolutions providing for the issue of such stock adopted by the board of directors pursuant to authority expressly vested in it by its certificate of incorporation, provided that the manner in which such facts shall operate upon the voting powers, designations, preferences, rights and qualifications, limitations or restrictions of such class or series of stock is clearly and expressly set forth in the certificate of incorporation or in the resolution or resolutions providing for the issue of such stock adopted by the board of directors. The term "facts," as used in this subsection, includes, but is not limited to, the occurrence of any event, including a determination or action by any person or body, including the corporation. The power to increase or decrease or otherwise adjust the capital stock as provided in this chapter shall apply to all or any such classes of stock.

(b) Any stock of any class or series may be made subject to redemption by the corporation at its option or at the option of the holders of such stock or upon the happening of a specified event; provided however, that immediately following any such redemption the corporation shall have outstanding 1 or more shares of 1 or more classes or series of stock, which share, or shares together, shall have full voting powers. Notwithstanding the limitation stated in the foregoing proviso:

(1) Any stock of a regulated investment company registered under the Investment Company Act of 1940 [15 U.S.C. §80a-1 et seq.], as heretofore or hereafter amended, may be made subject to redemption by the corporation at its option or at the option of the holders of such stock.

(2) Any stock of a corporation which holds (directly or indirectly) a license or franchise from a governmental agency to conduct its business or is a member of a national securities exchange, which license, franchise or membership is conditioned upon some or all of the holders of its stock possessing prescribed qualifications, may be made subject to redemption by the corporation to the extent necessary to prevent the loss of such license, franchise or membership or to reinstate it.

Any stock which may be made redeemable under this section may be redeemed for cash, property or rights, including securities of the same or another corporation, at such time or times, price or prices, or rate or rates, and with such adjustments, as shall be stated in the certificate of incorporation or in the resolution or resolutions providing for the issue of such stock adopted by the board of directors pursuant to subsection (a) of this section.

(c) The holders of preferred or special stock of any class or of any series thereof shall be entitled to receive dividends at such rates, on such conditions and at such times as shall be stated in the certificate of incorporation or in the resolution or resolutions providing for the issue of such stock adopted by the board of directors as hereinabove provided, payable in preference to, or in such relation to, the dividends payable on any other class or classes or of any other series of stock, and cumulative or noncumulative as shall be so stated and expressed. When dividends upon the preferred and special stocks, if any, to the extent of the preference to which such stocks are entitled, shall have been paid or declared and set apart for payment, a dividend on the remaining class or classes or series of stock may then be paid out of the remaining assets of the corporation available for dividends as elsewhere in this chapter provided.

(d) The holders of the preferred or special stock of any class or of any series thereof shall be entitled to such rights upon the dissolution of, or upon any distribution of the assets of, the corporation as shall be stated in the certificate of incorporation or in the resolution or resolutions providing for the issue of such stock adopted by the board of directors as hereinabove provided.

(e) Any stock of any class or of any series thereof may be made convertible into, or exchangeable for, at the option of either the holder or the corporation or upon the happening of a specified event, shares of any other class or classes or any other series of the same or any other class or classes of stock of the corporation, at such price or prices or at such rate or rates of exchange and with such adjustments as shall be stated in the certificate of incorporation or in the resolution or resolutions providing for the issue of such stock adopted by the board of directors as hereinabove provided.

(f) If any corporation shall be authorized to issue more than 1 class of stock or more than 1 series of any class, the powers, designations, preferences and relative, participating, optional, or other special rights of each class of stock or series thereof and the qualifications, limitations or restrictions of such preferences and/or rights shall be set forth in full or summarized on the face or back of the certificate which the corporation shall issue to represent such class or series of stock, provided that, except as otherwise provided in §202 of this title, in lieu of the foregoing requirements, there may be set forth on the face or back of the certificate which the corporation shall issue to represent such class or series of stock, a statement that the corporation will furnish without charge to each stockholder who so requests the powers, designations, preferences and relative, participating, optional, or other special rights of each class of stock or series thereof and the qualifications, limitations or restrictions of such preferences and/or rights. Within a reasonable time after the issuance or transfer of uncertificated stock, the registered owner thereof shall be given a notice, in writing or by electronic transmission, containing the information required to be set forth or stated on certificates pursuant to this section or §156, §202(a), §218(a) or §364 of this title or with respect to this section a statement that the corporation will furnish without charge to each stockholder who so requests the powers, designations, preferences and relative participating, optional or other special rights of each class of stock or series thereof and the qualifications, limitations or restrictions of such preferences and/or rights. Except as otherwise expressly provided by law, the rights and obligations of the holders of uncertificated stock and the rights and obligations of the holders of certificates representing stock of the same class and series shall be identical.

(g) When any corporation desires to issue any shares of stock of any class or of any series of any class of which the powers, designations, preferences and relative, participating, optional or other rights, if any, or the qualifications, limitations or restrictions thereof, if any, shall not have been set forth in the certificate of incorporation or in any amendment thereto but shall be provided for in a resolution or resolutions adopted by the board of directors pursuant to authority expressly vested in it by the certificate of incorporation or any amendment thereto, a certificate of designations setting forth a copy of such resolution or resolutions and the number of shares of stock of such class or series as to which the resolution or resolutions apply shall be executed, acknowledged, filed and shall become effective, in accordance with §103 of this title. Unless otherwise provided in any such resolution or resolutions, the number of shares of stock of any such series to which such resolution or resolutions apply may be increased (but not above the total number of authorized shares of the class) or decreased (but not below the number of shares thereof then outstanding) by a certificate likewise executed, acknowledged, and filed setting forth a statement that a specified increase or decrease therein had been authorized and directed by a resolution or resolutions likewise adopted by the board of directors. In case the number of such shares shall be decreased the number of shares so specified in the certificate shall resume the status which they had prior to the adoption of the first resolution or resolutions. When no shares of any such class or series are outstanding, either because none were issued or because no issued shares of any such class or series remain outstanding, a certificate setting forth a resolution or resolutions adopted by the board of directors that none of the authorized shares of such class or series are outstanding, and that none will be issued subject to the certificate of designations previously filed with respect to such class or series, may be executed, acknowledged and filed in accordance with §103 of this title and, when such certificate becomes effective, it shall have the effect of eliminating from the certificate of incorporation all matters set forth in the certificate of designations with respect to such class or series of stock. Unless otherwise provided in the certificate of incorporation, if no shares of stock have been issued of a class or series of stock established by a resolution of the board of directors, the voting powers, designations, preferences and relative, participating, optional or other rights, if any, or the qualifications, limitations or restrictions thereof, may be amended by a resolution or resolutions adopted by the board of directors. A certificate which:

(1) states that no shares of the class or series have been issued;

(2) sets forth a copy of the resolution or resolutions; and

(3) if the designation of the class or series is being changed, indicates the original designation and the new designation, shall be executed, acknowledged and filed and shall become effective, in accordance with §103 of this title. When any certificate filed under this subsection becomes effective, it shall have the effect of amending the certificate of incorporation; except that neither the filing of such certificate nor the filing of a restated certificate of incorporation pursuant to §245 of this title shall prohibit the board of directors from subsequently adopting such resolutions as authorized by this subsection.

§152. Issuance of Stock; Lawful Consideration; Fully Paid Stock

(a) The consideration, as determined pursuant to §153(a) and (b) of this title, for subscriptions to, or the purchase of, the capital stock to be issued by a corporation shall be paid in the form and in the manner that the board of directors shall determine. The board of directors may authorize capital stock to be issued for consideration consisting of cash, any tangible or intangible property or any benefit to the corporation, or any combination thereof. Stock may be issued in 1 or more transactions, in the numbers, at the times and for the consideration as set forth in a resolution of the board of directors.

(b) A resolution of the board of directors may delegate to a person or body, in addition to the board of directors, the authority to enter into 1 or more transactions to issue stock, and with respect to such transactions, shares of stock may be issued in the numbers, at the times and for the consideration as such person or body may determine; provided the resolution fixes (i) a maximum number of shares that may be issued pursuant to such resolution, (ii) a time period during which such shares may be issued and (iii) a minimum amount of consideration for which such shares may be issued. No such resolution shall permit a person or body to issue stock to such person or body.

(c) Any provision of a resolution contemplated by subsection (a) or (b) of this section may be made dependent on facts ascertainable outside the resolution, provided the manner in which such facts shall operate upon the resolution is clearly and expressly set forth in such resolution. The term "facts," as used in this section, includes, but is not limited to, the occurrence of any event, including a determination or action by any person or body, including the corporation; provided that, if the resolution delegates to a person or body the authority to enter into 1 or more transactions to issue stock pursuant to subsection (b) of this section, the provisions contemplated by subsection (b)(i) through (iii) of this section may not be made dependent on a determination or action by such person or body.

(d) In the absence of actual fraud in the transaction, the judgment of the directors as to the value of the consideration (or minimum amount of consideration) received by the corporation for the issuance of stock shall be conclusive. The capital stock issued in accordance with this section shall be deemed to be fully paid and nonassessable stock upon receipt by the corporation of such consideration; provided, however, nothing contained herein shall prevent the board of directors from issuing partly paid shares under §156 of this title.

§153. Consideration for Stock

(a) Shares of stock with par value may be issued for such consideration, having a value not less than the par value of the shares so issued, as determined from time to time in accordance with §152 of this title, or by the stockholders if the certificate of incorporation so provides.

(b) Shares of stock without par value may be issued for such consideration as is determined from time to time in accordance with §152 of this title, or by the stockholders if the certificate of incorporation so provides.

(c) Treasury shares may be disposed of by the corporation in the same manner that shares of stock are issued pursuant to §152 of this title, or may be disposed of for such consideration as determined by the stockholders if the certificate of incorporation so provides.

(d) If the certificate of incorporation reserves to the stockholders the right to determine the consideration for the issue of any shares, the stockholders shall, unless the certificate requires a greater vote, do so by a vote of a majority of the outstanding stock entitled to vote thereon.

§154. Determination of Amount of Capital; Capital, Surplus and Net Assets Defined

Any corporation may, by resolution of its board of directors, determine that only a part of the consideration which shall be received by the corporation for any of the shares of its capital stock which it shall issue from time to time shall be capital; but, in case any of the shares issued shall be shares having a par value, the amount of the part of such consideration so determined to be capital shall be in excess of the aggregate par value of the shares issued for such consideration having a par value, unless all the shares issued shall be shares having a par value, in which case the amount of the part of such consideration so determined to be capital need be only equal to the aggregate par value of such shares. In each such case the board of directors shall specify in dollars the part of such consideration which shall be capital. If the board of directors shall not have determined (1) at the time of issue of any shares of the capital stock of the corporation issued for cash or (2) within 60 days after the issue of any shares of the capital stock of the corporation issued for consideration other than cash what part of the consideration for such shares shall be capital, the capital of the corporation in respect of such shares shall be an amount equal to the aggregate par value of such shares having a par value, plus the amount of the consideration for such shares without par value. The amount of the consideration so determined to be capital in respect of any shares without par value shall be the stated capital of such shares. The capital of the corporation may be increased from time to time by resolution of the board of directors directing that a portion of the net assets of the corporation in excess of the amount so determined to be capital be transferred to the capital account. The board of directors may direct that the portion of such net assets so transferred shall be treated as capital in respect of any shares of the corporation of any designated class or classes. The excess, if any, at any given time, of the net assets of the corporation over the amount so determined to be capital shall be surplus. Net assets means the amount by which total assets exceed total liabilities. Capital and surplus are not liabilities for this purpose. Notwithstanding anything in this section to the contrary, for purposes of this section and §§160 and 170 of this title, the capital of any nonstock corporation shall be deemed to be zero.

§155. Fractions of Shares

A corporation may, but shall not be required to, issue fractions of a share. If it does not issue fractions of a share, it shall (1) arrange for the disposition of fractional interests by those entitled thereto, (2) pay in cash the fair value of fractions of a share as of the time when those entitled to receive such fractions are determined or (3) issue scrip or warrants in registered form (either represented by a certificate or uncertificated) or in bearer form (represented by a certificate) which shall entitle the holder to receive a full share upon the surrender of such scrip or warrants aggregating a full share. A certificate for a fractional share or an uncertificated fractional share shall, but scrip or warrants shall not unless otherwise provided therein, entitle the holder to exercise voting rights, to receive dividends thereon and to participate in any of the assets of the corporation in the event of liquidation. The board of directors may cause scrip or warrants to be issued subject to the conditions that they shall become void if not exchanged for certificates representing the full shares or uncertificated full shares before a specified date, or subject to the conditions that the shares for which scrip or warrants are exchangeable may be sold by the corporation and the proceeds thereof distributed to the holders of scrip or warrants, or subject to any other conditions which the board of directors may impose.

§156. Partly Paid Shares

Any corporation may issue the whole or any part of its shares as partly paid and subject to call for the remainder of the consideration to be paid therefor. Upon the face or back of each stock certificate issued to represent any such partly paid shares, or upon the books and records of the corporation in the case of uncertificated partly paid shares, the total amount of the consideration to be paid therefor and the amount paid thereon shall be stated. Upon the declaration of any dividend on fully paid shares, the corporation shall declare a dividend upon partly paid shares of the same class, but only upon the basis of the percentage of the consideration actually paid thereon.

§157. Rights and Options Respecting Stock

(a) Subject to any provisions in the certificate of incorporation, every corporation may create and issue, whether or not in connection with the issue and sale of any shares of stock or other securities of the corporation, rights or options entitling the holders thereof to acquire from the corporation any shares of its capital stock of any class or classes of the corporation.

(b) The terms upon which, including the time or times which may be limited or unlimited in duration, at or within which, and the consideration, including a formula by which such consideration may be determined, for which any such shares may be acquired from the corporation upon the exercise of any such right or option, shall be such as shall be stated in the certificate of incorporation, or in a resolution adopted by the board of directors or by another person or body authorized pursuant to this section.

(c) The board of directors may adopt a resolution to delegate to a person or body, in addition to the board of directors, the authority to enter into 1 or more transactions to issue rights or options, and with respect to such transactions, the rights or options may be issued in such numbers, at such times and for such consideration as such person or body may determine; provided that the resolution fixes (i) the maximum number of rights or options, and the maximum number of shares issuable upon exercise thereof, that may be issued pursuant to such resolution, (ii) a time period during which such rights or options, and during which the shares issuable upon exercise thereof, may be issued, and (iii) a minimum amount of consideration (if any) for which such rights or options may be issued and a minimum amount of consideration for the shares issuable upon exercise thereof. No such resolution shall permit a person or body to issue rights or options to such person or body.

(d) Any provision in a resolution contemplated by subsection (b) or (c) of this section may be made dependent on facts ascertainable outside the resolution, provided the manner in which such facts shall operate upon the resolution is clearly and expressly set forth in such resolution. The term "facts," as used in this section, includes, but is not limited to, the occurrence of any event, including a determination or action by any person or body, including the corporation; provided that, if the resolution delegates to a person or body the authority to enter into 1 or more transactions to issue rights or options pursuant to subsection (c) of this section, the provisions contemplated by subsection (c)(i) through (iii) of this section may not be made dependent on a determination or action by such person or body.

(e) The minimum consideration to be received for the shares of stock of the corporation to be issued upon exercise of such rights or options shall be no less than the amount set forth in §153 of this title.

§158. Stock Certificates; Uncertificated Shares

The shares of a corporation shall be represented by certificates, provided that the board of directors of the corporation may provide by resolution or resolutions that some or all of any or all classes or series of its stock shall be uncertificated shares. Any such resolution shall not apply to shares represented by a certificate until such certificate is surrendered to the corporation. Every holder of stock represented by certificates shall be entitled to have a certificate signed by, or in the name of the corporation by any 2 authorized officers of the corporation representing the number of shares registered in certificate form. Any or all the signatures on the certificate may be a facsimile. In case any officer, transfer agent or registrar who has signed or whose facsimile signature has been placed upon a certificate shall have ceased to be such officer, transfer agent or registrar before such certificate is issued, it may be issued by the corporation with the same effect as if such person were such officer, transfer agent or registrar at the date of issue. A corporation shall not have power to issue a certificate in bearer form.

§160. Corporation's Powers Respecting Ownership, Voting, etc., of Its Own Stock; Rights of Stock Called for Redemption

(a) Every corporation may purchase, redeem, receive, take or otherwise acquire, own and hold, sell, lend, exchange, transfer or otherwise dispose of, pledge, use and otherwise deal in and with its own shares; provided, however, that no corporation shall:

(1) Purchase or redeem its own shares of capital stock for cash or other property when the capital of the corporation is impaired or when such purchase or redemption would cause any impairment of the capital of the corporation, except that a corporation other than a nonstock corporation may purchase or redeem out of capital any of its own shares which are entitled upon any distribution of its assets, whether by dividend or in liquidation, to a preference over another class or series of its stock, or, if no shares entitled to such a preference are outstanding, any of its own shares, if such shares will be retired upon their acquisition and the capital of the corporation reduced in accordance with §243 and 244 of this title. Nothing in this subsection shall invalidate or otherwise affect a note, debenture or other obligation of a corporation given by it as consideration for its acquisition by purchase, redemption or exchange of its shares of stock if at the time such note, debenture or obligation was delivered by the corporation its capital was not then impaired or did not thereby become impaired;

(2) Purchase, for more than the price at which they may then be redeemed, any of its shares which are redeemable at the option of the corporation; or

(3) a. In the case of a corporation other than a nonstock corporation, redeem any of its shares, unless their redemption is authorized by §151(b) of this title and then only in accordance with such section and the certificate of incorporation, or

b. in the case of a nonstock corporation, redeem any of its membership interests, unless their redemption is authorized by the certificate of incorporation and then only in accordance with the certificate of incorporation.

(b) Nothing in this section limits or affects a corporation's right to resell any of its shares theretofore purchased or redeemed out of surplus and which have not been retired, for such consideration as shall be fixed by the board of directors.

(c) Shares of a corporation's capital stock shall neither be entitled to vote nor be counted for quorum purposes if such shares belong to:

(1) The corporation;

(2) Another corporation, if a majority of the shares entitled to vote in the election of directors of such other corporation is held, directly or indirectly; or

(3) Any other entity, if a majority of the voting power of such other entity is held, directly or indirectly, by the corporation or if such other entity is otherwise controlled, directly or indirectly, by the corporation.

Nothing in this section shall be construed as limiting the right of any corporation to vote stock, including but not limited to its own stock, held by it in a fiduciary capacity.

(d) Shares which have been called for redemption shall not be deemed to be outstanding shares for the purpose of voting or determining the total number of shares entitled to vote on any matter on and after the date on which notice of redemption has been sent to holders thereof and a sum sufficient to redeem such shares has been irrevocably deposited or set aside to pay the redemption price to the holders of the shares upon surrender of certificates therefor.

§161. Issuance of Additional Stock; When and by Whom

The directors may, at any time and from time to time, if all of the shares of capital stock which the corporation is authorized by its certificate of incorporation to issue have not been issued, subscribed for, or otherwise committed to be issued, issue or take subscriptions for additional shares of its capital stock up to the amount authorized in its certificate of incorporation.

§162. Liability of Stockholder or Subscriber for Stock Not Paid in Full

(a) When the whole of the consideration payable for shares of a corporation has not been paid in, and the assets shall be insufficient to satisfy the claims of its creditors, each holder of or subscriber for such shares shall be bound to pay on each share held or subscribed for by such holder or subscriber the sum necessary to complete the amount of the unpaid balance of the consideration for which such shares were issued or are to be issued by the corporation.

(b) The amounts which shall be payable as provided in subsection (a) of this section may be recovered as provided in §325 of this title, after a writ of execution against the corporation has been returned unsatisfied as provided in said §325.

(c) Any person becoming an assignee or transferee of shares or of a subscription for shares in good faith and without knowledge or notice that the full consideration therefor has not been paid shall not be personally liable for any unpaid portion of such consideration, but the transferor shall remain liable therefor.

(d) No person holding shares in any corporation as collateral security shall be personally liable as a stockholder but the person pledging such shares shall be considered the holder thereof and shall be so liable. No executor, administrator, guardian, trustee or other fiduciary shall be personally liable as a stockholder, but the estate or funds held by such executor, administrator, guardian, trustee or other fiduciary in such fiduciary capacity shall be liable.

(e) No liability under this section or under §325 of this title shall be asserted more than 6 years after the issuance of the stock or the date of the subscription upon which the assessment is sought.

(f) In any action by a receiver or trustee of an insolvent corporation or by a judgment creditor to obtain an assessment under this section, any stockholder or subscriber for stock of the insolvent corporation may appear and contest the claim or claims of such receiver or trustee.

§163. *Payment for Stock Not Paid in Full*

The capital stock of a corporation shall be paid for in such amounts and at such times as the directors may require. The directors may, from time to time, demand payment, in respect of each share of stock not fully paid, of such sum of money as the necessities of the business may, in the judgment of the board of directors, require, not exceeding in the whole the balance remaining unpaid on said stock, and such sum so demanded shall be paid to the corporation at such times and by such installments as the directors shall direct. The directors shall give notice of the time and place of such payments, which notice shall be given at least 30 days before the time for such payment, to each holder of or subscriber for stock which is not fully paid at such holder's or subscriber's last known address.

§164. *Failure to Pay for Stock; Remedies*

When any stockholder fails to pay any installment or call upon such stockholder's stock which may have been properly demanded by the directors, at the time when such payment is due, the directors may collect the amount of any such installment or call or any balance thereof remaining unpaid, from the said stockholder by an action at law, or they shall sell at public sale such part of the shares of such delinquent stockholder as will pay all demands then due from such stockholder with interest and all incidental expenses, and shall transfer the shares so sold to the purchaser, who shall be entitled to a certificate therefor.

Notice of the time and place of such sale and of the sum due on each share shall be given by advertisement at least 1 week before the sale, in a newspaper of the county in this State where such corporation's registered office is located, and such notice shall be mailed by the corporation to such delinquent stockholder at such stockholder's last known post-office address, at least 20 days before such sale.

If no bidder can be had to pay the amount due on the stock, and if the amount is not collected by an action at law, which may be brought within the county where the corporation has its registered office, within 1 year from the date of the bringing of such action at law, the said stock and the amount previously paid in by the delinquent stockholder on the stock shall be forfeited to the corporation.

§165. *Revocability of Preincorporation Subscriptions*

Unless otherwise provided by the terms of the subscription, a subscription for stock of a corporation to be formed shall be irrevocable, except with the consent of all other subscribers or the corporation, for a period of 6 months from its date.

§166. *Formalities Required of Stock Subscriptions*

A subscription for stock of a corporation, whether made before or after the formation of a corporation, shall not be enforceable against a subscriber, unless in writing and signed by the subscriber or by such subscriber's agent.

§169. *Situs of Ownership of Stock*

For all purposes of title, action, attachment, garnishment and jurisdiction of all courts held in this State, but not for the purpose of taxation, the situs of the ownership of the capital stock of all corporations existing under the laws of this State, whether organized under this chapter or otherwise, shall be regarded as in this State.

§170. *Dividends; Payment; Wasting Asset Corporations*

(a) The directors of every corporation, subject to any restrictions contained in its certificate of incorporation, may declare and pay dividends upon the shares of its capital stock either:

(1) out of its surplus, as defined in and computed in accordance with §§154 and 244 of this title; or

(2) in case there shall be no such surplus, out of its net profits for the fiscal year in which the dividend is declared and/or the preceding fiscal year.

If the capital of the corporation, computed in accordance with §§154 and 244 of this title, shall have been diminished by depreciation in the value of its property, or by losses, or otherwise, to an amount less than the aggregate amount of the capital represented by the issued and outstanding stock of all classes having a preference upon the distribution of assets, the directors of such corporation shall not declare and pay out of such net profits any dividends upon any shares of any classes of its capital stock until the deficiency in the amount of capital represented by the issued and outstanding stock of all classes having a preference upon the distribution of assets shall have been repaired. Nothing in this subsection shall invalidate or otherwise affect a note, debenture or other obligation of the corporation paid by it as a dividend on shares of its stock, or any payment made thereon, if at the time such note, debenture or obligation was delivered by the corporation, the corporation had either surplus or net profits as provided in (a)(1) or (2) of this section from which the dividend could lawfully have been paid.

(b) Subject to any restrictions contained in its certificate of incorporation, the directors of any corporation engaged in the exploitation of wasting assets (including but not limited to a corporation engaged in the exploitation of natural resources or other wasting assets, including patents, or engaged primarily in the liquidation of specific assets) may determine the net profits derived from the exploitation of such wasting assets or the net proceeds derived from such liquidation without taking into consideration the depletion of such assets resulting from lapse of time, consumption, liquidation or exploitation of such assets.

§171. *Special Purpose Reserves*

The directors of a corporation may set apart out of any of the funds of the corporation available for dividends a reserve or reserves for any proper purpose and may abolish any such reserve.

§172. *Liability of Directors and Committee Members as to Dividends or Stock Redemption*

A member of the board of directors, or a member of any committee designated by the board of directors, shall be fully protected in relying in good faith upon the records of the corporation and upon such information, opinions, reports or statements presented to the corporation by any of its officers or employees, or committees of the board of directors, or by any other person as to matters the director reasonably believes are within such other person's professional or expert competence and who has been selected with reasonable care by or on behalf of the corporation, as to the value and amount of the assets, liabilities and/or net profits of the corporation or any other facts pertinent to the existence and amount of surplus or other funds from which dividends might properly be declared and paid, or with which the corporation's stock might properly be purchased or redeemed.

§173. *Declaration and Payment of Dividends*

No corporation shall pay dividends except in accordance with this chapter. Dividends may be paid in cash, in property, or in shares of the corporation's capital stock. If the dividend is to be paid in shares of the corporation's theretofore unissued capital stock the board of directors shall, by resolution, direct that there be designated as capital in respect of such shares an amount which is not less than the aggregate par value of par value being declared as a dividend and, in the case of shares without par value shares being declared as a dividend, such amount as shall be determined by the board of directors. No such designation as capital shall be necessary if shares are being distributed by a corporation pursuant to a split-up or division of its stock rather than as payment of a dividend declared payable in stock of the corporation.

§174. *Liability of Directors for Unlawful Payment of Dividend or Unlawful Stock Purchase or Redemption; Exoneration from Liability; Contribution Among Directors; Subrogation*

(a) In case of any wilful or negligent violation of §§160 or 173 of this title, the directors under whose administration the same may happen shall be jointly and severally liable, at any time within 6 years after paying such unlawful dividend or after such unlawful stock purchase or redemption, to the corporation, and to its creditors in the event of its dissolution or insolvency, to the full amount of the dividend unlawfully paid, or to the full amount unlawfully paid for the purchase or redemption of the corporation's stock, with interest from the time such liability accrued. Any director who may have been absent when the same was done, or who may have dissented from the act or resolution by which the same was done, may be exonerated from such liability by causing his or her dissent to be entered on the books containing the minutes of the proceedings of the directors at the time the same was done, or immediately after such director has notice of the same.

(b) Any director against whom a claim is successfully asserted under this section shall be entitled to contribution from the other directors who voted for or concurred in the unlawful dividend, stock purchase or stock redemption.

(c) Any director against whom a claim is successfully asserted under this section shall be entitled, to the extent of the amount paid by such director as a result of such claim, to be subrogated to the rights of the corporation against stockholders who received the dividend on, or assets for the sale or redemption of, their stock with knowledge of facts indicating that such dividend, stock purchase or redemption was unlawful under this chapter, in proportion to the amounts received by such stockholders respectively.

SUBCHAPTER VI. STOCK TRANSFERS

§201. Transfer of Stock, Stock Certificates and Uncertificated Stock

Except as otherwise provided in this chapter, the transfer of stock and the certificates of stock which represent the stock or uncertificated stock shall be governed by [UCC] Article 8. To the extent that any provision of this chapter is inconsistent with any provision of [the UCC], this chapter shall be controlling.

§202. Restrictions on Transfer and Ownership of Securities

(a) A written restriction or restrictions on the transfer or registration of transfer of a security of a corporation, or on the amount of the corporation's securities that may be owned by any person or group of persons, if permitted by this section and noted conspicuously on the certificate or certificates representing the security or securities so restricted or, in the case of uncertificated shares, contained in the notice or notices given pursuant to §151(f) of this title, may be enforced against the holder of the restricted security or securities or any successor or transferee of the holder including an executor, administrator, trustee, guardian or other fiduciary entrusted with like responsibility for the person or estate of the holder. Unless noted conspicuously on the certificate or certificates representing the security or securities so restricted or, in the case of uncertificated shares, contained in the notice or notices given pursuant to §151(f) of this title, a restriction, even though permitted by this section, is ineffective except against a person with actual knowledge of the restriction.

(b) A restriction on the transfer or registration of transfer of securities of a corporation, or on the amount of a corporation's securities that may be owned by any person or group of persons, may be imposed by the certificate of incorporation or by the bylaws or by an agreement among any number of security holders or among such holders and the corporation. No restrictions so imposed shall be binding with respect to securities issued prior to the adoption of the restriction unless the holders of the securities are parties to an agreement or voted in favor of the restriction.

(c) A restriction on the transfer or registration of transfer of securities of a corporation or on the amount of such securities that may be owned by any person or group of persons is permitted by this section if it:

(1) Obligates the holder of the restricted securities to offer to the corporation or to any other holders of securities of the corporation or to any other person or to any combination of the foregoing, a prior opportunity, to be exercised within a reasonable time, to acquire the restricted securities; or

(2) Obligates the corporation or any holder of securities of the corporation or any other person or any combination of the foregoing, to purchase the securities which are the subject of an agreement respecting the purchase and sale of the restricted securities; or

(3) Requires the corporation or the holders of any class or series of securities of the corporation to consent to any proposed transfer of the restricted

securities or to approve the proposed transferee of the restricted securities, or to approve the amount of securities of the corporation that may be owned by any person or group of persons; or

(4) Obligates the holder of the restricted securities to sell or transfer an amount of restricted securities to the corporation or to any other holders of securities of the corporation or to any other person or to any combination of the foregoing, or causes or results in the automatic sale or transfer of an amount of restricted securities to the corporation or to any other holders of securities of the corporation or to any other person or to any combination of the foregoing; or

(5) Prohibits or restricts the transfer of the restricted securities to, or the ownership of restricted securities by, designated persons or classes of persons or groups of persons, and such designation is not manifestly unreasonable.

(d) Any restriction on the transfer or the registration of transfer of the securities of a corporation, or on the amount of securities of a corporation that may be owned by a person or group of persons, for any of the following purposes shall be conclusively presumed to be for a reasonable purpose:

(1) maintaining any local, state, federal or foreign tax advantage to the corporation or its stockholders, including without limitation:

a. maintaining the corporation's status as an electing small business corporation under subchapter S of the United States Internal Revenue Code [26 U.S.C.A. §1371 et seq.], or

b. maintaining or preserving any tax attribute (including without limitation net operating losses), or

c. qualifying or maintaining the qualification of the corporation as a real estate investment trust pursuant to the United States Internal Revenue Code or regulations adopted pursuant to the United States Internal Revenue Code, or

(2) maintaining any statutory or regulatory advantage or complying with any statutory or regulatory requirements under applicable local, state, federal or foreign law.

(e) Any other lawful restriction on transfer or registration of transfer of securities, or on the amount of securities that may be owned by any person or group of persons, is permitted by this section.

§203. Business Combinations with Interested Stockholders

(a) Notwithstanding any other provisions of this chapter, a corporation shall not engage in any business combination with any interested stockholder for a period of 3 years following the time that such stockholder became an interested stockholder, unless:

(1) Prior to such time the board of directors of the corporation approved either the business combination or the transaction which resulted in the stockholder becoming an interested stockholder;

(2) Upon consummation of the transaction which resulted in the stockholder becoming an interested stockholder, the interested stockholder owned at least 85% of the voting stock of the corporation outstanding at the time the transaction commenced, excluding for purposes of determining the voting stock

outstanding (but not the outstanding voting stock owned by the interested stockholder) those shares owned (i) by persons who are directors and also officers and (ii) employee stock plans in which employee participants do not have the right to determine confidentially whether shares held subject to the plan will be tendered in a tender or exchange offer; or

(3) At or subsequent to such time the business combination is approved by the board of directors and authorized at an annual or special meeting of stockholders, and not by written consent, by the affirmative vote of at least 2/3 of the outstanding voting stock which is not owned by the interested stockholder.

(b) The restrictions contained in this section shall not apply if:

(1) The corporation's original certificate of incorporation contains a provision expressly electing not to be governed by this section;

(2) The corporation, by action of its board of directors, adopts an amendment to its bylaws within 90 days of February 2, 1988, expressly electing not to be governed by this section, which amendment shall not be further amended by the board of directors;

(3) The corporation, by action of its stockholders, adopts an amendment to its certificate of incorporation or bylaws expressly electing not to be governed by this section; provided that, in addition to any other vote required by law, such amendment to the certificate of incorporation or bylaws must be adopted by the affirmative vote of a majority of the outstanding stock entitled to vote thereon. In the case of a corporation that both (i) has never had a class of voting stock that falls within any of the 2 categories set out in paragraph (b)(4) of this section, and (ii) has not elected by a provision in its original certificate of incorporation or any amendment thereto to be governed by this section, such amendment shall become effective upon (i) in the case of an amendment to the certificate of incorporation, the date and time at which the certificate filed in accordance with §103 of this title becomes effective thereunder or (ii) in the case of an amendment to the bylaws, the date of the adoption of such amendment. In all other cases, an amendment adopted pursuant to this paragraph shall become effective (i) in the case of an amendment to the certificate of incorporation, 12 months after the date and time at which the certificate filed in accordance with §103 of this title becomes effective thereunder or (ii) in the case of an amendment to the bylaws, 12 months after the date of the adoption of such amendment, and, in either case, the election not to be governed by this section shall not apply to any business combination between such corporation and any person who became an interested stockholder of such corporation on or before (A) in the case of an amendment to the certificate of incorporation, the date and time at which the certificate filed in accordance with §103 of this title becomes effective thereunder or (B) in the case of an amendment to the bylaws, the date of the adoption of such amendment. A bylaw amendment adopted pursuant to this paragraph shall not be further amended by the board of directors;

(4) The corporation does not have a class of voting stock that is: (i) Listed on a national securities exchange; or (ii) held of record by more than 2,000 stockholders, unless any of the foregoing results from action taken, directly or indirectly, by an interested stockholder or from a transaction in which a person becomes an interested stockholder;

(5) A stockholder becomes an interested stockholder inadvertently and (i) as soon as practicable divests itself of ownership of sufficient shares so that the stockholder ceases to be an interested stockholder; and (ii) would not, at any time within the 3-year period immediately prior to a business combination between the corporation and such stockholder, have been an interested stockholder but for the inadvertent acquisition of ownership;

(6) The business combination is proposed prior to the consummation or abandonment of and subsequent to the earlier of the public announcement or the notice required hereunder of a proposed transaction which (i) constitutes 1 of the transactions described in the second sentence of this paragraph; (ii) is with or by a person who either was not an interested stockholder during the previous 3 years or who became an interested stockholder with the approval of the corporation's board of directors or during the period described in paragraph (b)(7) of this section; and (iii) is approved or not opposed by a majority of the members of the board of directors then in office (but not less than 1) who were directors prior to any person becoming an interested stockholder during the previous 3 years or were recommended for election or elected to succeed such directors by a majority of such directors. The proposed transactions referred to in the preceding sentence are limited to (x) a merger or consolidation of the corporation (except for a merger in respect of which, pursuant to §251(f) of this title, no vote of the stockholders of the corporation is required); (y) a sale, lease, exchange, mortgage, pledge, transfer or other disposition (in 1 transaction or a series of transactions), whether as part of a dissolution or otherwise, of assets of the corporation or of any direct or indirect majority-owned subsidiary of the corporation (other than to any direct or indirect wholly-owned subsidiary or to the corporation) having an aggregate market value equal to 50% or more of either [the] aggregate market value of all of the assets of the corporation determined on a consolidated basis or the aggregate market value of all the outstanding stock of the corporation; or (z) a proposed tender or exchange offer for 50% or more of the outstanding voting stock of the corporation. The corporation shall give not less than 20 days' notice to all interested stockholders prior to the consummation of any of the transactions described in clause (x) or (y) of the second sentence of this paragraph; or

(7) The business combination is with an interested stockholder who became an interested stockholder at a time when the restrictions contained in this section did not apply by reason of any of paragraphs (b)(1) through (4) of this section, provided, however, that this paragraph (b)(7) shall not apply if, at the time such interested stockholder became an interested stockholder, the corporation's certificate of incorporation contained a provision authorized by the last sentence of this subsection (b).

Notwithstanding paragraphs (b)(1), (2), (3) and (4) of this section, a corporation may elect by a provision of its original certificate of incorporation or any amendment thereto to be governed by this section; provided that any such amendment to the certificate of incorporation shall not apply to restrict a business combination between the corporation and an interested stockholder of the corporation if the interested stockholder became such before the date and time at which the certificate filed in accordance with §103 of this title becomes effective thereunder.

(c) As used in this section only, the term:

(1) "Affiliate" means a person that directly, or indirectly through 1 or more intermediaries, controls, or is controlled by, or is under common control with, another person.

(2) "Associate," when used to indicate a relationship with any person, means:

(i) Any corporation, partnership, unincorporated association or other entity of which such person is a director, officer or partner or is, directly or indirectly, the owner of 20% or more of any class of voting stock;

(ii) any trust or other estate in which such person has at least a 20% beneficial interest or as to which such person serves as trustee or in a similar fiduciary capacity; and

(iii) any relative or spouse of such person, or any relative of such spouse, who has the same residence as such person.

(3) "Business combination," when used in reference to any corporation and any interested stockholder of such corporation, means:

(i) Any merger or consolidation of the corporation or any direct or indirect majority-owned subsidiary of the corporation with (A) the interested stockholder, or (B) with any other corporation, partnership, unincorporated association or other entity if the merger or consolidation is caused by the interested stockholder and as a result of such merger or consolidation subsection (a) of this section is not applicable to the surviving entity;

(ii) Any sale, lease, exchange, mortgage, pledge, transfer or other disposition (in 1 transaction or a series of transactions), except proportionately as a stockholder of such corporation, to or with the interested stockholder, whether as part of a dissolution or otherwise, of assets of the corporation or of any direct or indirect majority-owned subsidiary of the corporation which assets have an aggregate market value equal to 10% or more of either the aggregate market value of all the assets of the corporation determined on a consolidated basis or the aggregate market value of all the outstanding stock of the corporation;

(iii) Any transaction which results in the issuance or transfer by the corporation or by any direct or indirect majority-owned subsidiary of the corporation of any stock of the corporation or of such subsidiary to the interested stockholder, except: (A) Pursuant to the exercise, exchange or conversion of securities exercisable for, exchangeable for or convertible into stock of such corporation or any such subsidiary which securities were outstanding prior to the time that the interested stockholder became such; (B) pursuant to a merger under §251(g) of this title; (C) pursuant to a dividend or distribution paid or made, or the exercise, exchange or conversion of securities exercisable for, exchangeable for or convertible into stock of such corporation or any such subsidiary which security is distributed, pro rata to all holders of a class or series of stock of such corporation subsequent to the time the interested stockholder became such; (D) pursuant to an exchange offer by the corporation to purchase stock made on the same terms to all holders of said stock; or (E) any issuance or transfer of stock by the corporation; provided however, that in no case under items (C)-(E) of this subparagraph shall there be an increase in the interested stockholder's proportionate share of the stock of any class or series of the corporation or of the voting stock of the corporation;

(iv) Any transaction involving the corporation or any direct or indirect majority-owned subsidiary of the corporation which has the effect, directly or indirectly, of increasing the proportionate share of the stock of any class or series, or securities convertible into the stock of any class or series, of the corporation or of any such subsidiary which is owned by the interested stockholder, except as a result of immaterial changes due to fractional share adjustments or as a result of any purchase or redemption of any shares of stock not caused, directly or indirectly, by the interested stockholder; or

(v) Any receipt by the interested stockholder of the benefit, directly or indirectly (except proportionately as a stockholder of such corporation), of any loans, advances, guarantees, pledges or other financial benefits (other than those expressly permitted in paragraphs (c)(3)(i)-(iv) of this section) provided by or through the corporation or any direct or indirect majority-owned subsidiary.

(4) "Control," including the terms "controlling," "controlled by" and "under common control with," means the possession, directly or indirectly, of the power to direct or cause the direction of the management and policies of a person, whether through the ownership of voting stock, by contract or otherwise. A person who is the owner of 20% or more of the outstanding voting stock of any corporation, partnership, unincorporated association or other entity shall be presumed to have control of such entity, in the absence of proof by a preponderance of the evidence to the contrary; Notwithstanding the foregoing, a presumption of control shall not apply where such person holds voting stock, in good faith and not for the purpose of circumventing this section, as an agent, bank, broker, nominee, custodian or trustee for 1 or more owners who do not individually or as a group have control of such entity.

(5) "Interested stockholder" means any person (other than the corporation and any direct or indirect majority-owned subsidiary of the corporation) that (i) is the owner of 15% or more of the outstanding voting stock of the corporation, or (ii) is an affiliate or associate of the corporation and was the owner of 15% or more of the outstanding voting stock of the corporation at any time within the 3-year period immediately prior to the date on which it is sought to be determined whether such person is an interested stockholder, and the affiliates and associates of such person; provided, however, that the term "interested stockholder" shall not include (x) any person who (A) owned shares in excess of the 15% limitation set forth herein as of, or acquired such shares pursuant to a tender offer commenced prior to, December 23, 1987, or pursuant to an exchange offer announced prior to the aforesaid date and commenced within 90 days thereafter and either (I) continued to own shares in excess of such 15% limitation or would have but for action by the corporation or (II) is an affiliate or associate of the corporation and so continued (or so would have continued but for action by the corporation) to be the owner of 15% or more of the outstanding voting stock of the corporation at any time within the 3-year period immediately prior to the date on which it is sought to be determined whether such a person

is an interested stockholder or (B) acquired said shares from a person described in item (A) of this paragraph by gift, inheritance or in a transaction in which no consideration was exchanged; or (y) any person whose ownership of shares in excess of the 15% limitation set forth herein is the result of action taken solely by the corporation; provided that such person shall be an interested stockholder if thereafter such person acquires additional shares of voting stock of the corporation, except as a result of further corporate action not caused, directly or indirectly, by such person. For the purpose of determining whether a person is an interested stockholder, the voting stock of the corporation deemed to be outstanding shall include stock deemed to be owned by the person through application of paragraph (9) of this subsection but shall not include any other unissued stock of such corporation which may be issuable pursuant to any agreement, arrangement or understanding, or upon exercise of conversion rights, warrants or options, or otherwise.

(6) "Person" means any individual, corporation, partnership, unincorporated association or other entity.

(7) "Stock" means, with respect to any corporation, capital stock and, with respect to any other entity, any equity interest.

(8) "Voting stock" means, with respect to any corporation, stock of any class or series entitled to vote generally in the election of directors and, with respect to any entity that is not a corporation, any equity interest entitled to vote generally in the election of the governing body of such entity. Every reference to a percentage of voting stock shall refer to such percentage of the votes of such voting stock.

(9) "Owner," including the terms "own" and "owned," when used with respect to any stock, means a person that individually or with or through any of its affiliates or associates:

(i) Beneficially owns such stock, directly or indirectly; or

(ii) Has (A) the right to acquire such stock (whether such right is exercisable immediately or only after the passage of time) pursuant to any agreement, arrangement or understanding, or upon the exercise of conversion rights, exchange rights, warrants or options, or otherwise; provided, however, that a person shall not be deemed the owner of stock tendered pursuant to a tender or exchange offer made by such person or any of such person's affiliates or associates until such tendered stock is accepted for purchase or exchange; or (B) the right to vote such stock pursuant to any agreement, arrangement or understanding; provided, however, that a person shall not be deemed the owner of any stock because of such person's right to vote such stock if the agreement, arrangement or understanding to vote such stock arises solely from a revocable proxy or consent given in response to a proxy or consent solicitation made to 10 or more persons; or

(iii) Has any agreement, arrangement or understanding for the purpose of acquiring, holding, voting (except voting pursuant to a revocable proxy or consent as described in item (B) of subparagraph (ii) of this paragraph), or disposing of such stock with any other person that beneficially owns, or whose affiliates or associates beneficially own, directly or indirectly, such stock.

(d) No provision of a certificate of incorporation or bylaw shall require, for any vote of stockholders required by this section, a greater vote of stockholders than that specified in this section.

(e) The Court of Chancery is hereby vested with exclusive jurisdiction to hear and determine all matters with respect to this section.

§204. Ratification of Defective Corporate Acts and Stock

(a) Subject to subsection (f) of this section, no defective corporate act or putative stock shall be void or voidable solely as a result of a failure of authorization if ratified as provided in this section or validated by the Court of Chancery in a proceeding brought under §205 of this title.

(b) (1) In order to ratify 1 or more defective corporate acts pursuant to this section (other than the ratification of an election of the initial board of directors pursuant to paragraph (b)(2) of this section), the board of directors of the corporation shall adopt resolutions stating:

(A) The defective corporate act or acts to be ratified;

(B) The date of each defective corporate act or acts;

(C) If such defective corporate act or acts involved the issuance of shares of putative stock, the number and type of shares of putative stock issued and the date or dates upon which such putative shares were purported to have been issued;

(D) The nature of the failure of authorization in respect of each defective corporate act to be ratified; and

(E) That the board of directors approves the ratification of the defective corporate act or acts.

Such resolutions may also provide that, at any time before the validation effective time in respect of any defective corporate act set forth therein, notwithstanding the approval of the ratification of such defective corporate act by stockholders, the board of directors may abandon the ratification of such defective corporate act without further action of the stockholders. The quorum and voting requirements applicable to the ratification by the board of directors of any defective corporate act shall be the quorum and voting requirements applicable to the type of defective corporate act proposed to be ratified at the time the board adopts the resolutions ratifying the defective corporate act; provided that if the certificate of incorporation or bylaws of the corporation, any plan or agreement to which the corporation was a party or any provision of this title, in each case as in effect as of the time of the defective corporate act, would have required a larger number or portion of directors or of specified directors for a quorum to be present or to approve the defective corporate act, such larger number or portion of such directors or such specified directors shall be required for a quorum to be present or to adopt the resolutions to ratify the defective corporate act, as applicable, except that the presence or approval of any director elected, appointed or nominated by holders of any class or series of which no shares are then outstanding, or by any person that is no longer a stockholder, shall not be required.

(2) In order to ratify a defective corporate act in respect of the election of the initial board of directors of the corporation pursuant to §108 of this title, a majority of the persons who, at the time the resolutions required by

this paragraph (b)(2) of this section are adopted, are exercising the powers of directors under claim and color of an election or appointment as such may adopt resolutions stating:

(A) The name of the person or persons who first took action in the name of the corporation as the initial board of directors of the corporation;

(B) The earlier of the date on which such persons first took such action or were purported to have been elected as the initial board of directors; and

(C) That the ratification of the election of such person or persons as the initial board of directors is approved.

(c) Each defective corporate act ratified pursuant to paragraph (b)(1) of this section shall be submitted to stockholders for approval as provided in subsection (d) of this section, unless:

(1) (A) No other provision of this title, and no provision of the certificate of incorporation or bylaws of the corporation, or of any plan or agreement to which the corporation is a party, would have required stockholder approval of such defective corporate act to be ratified, either at the time of such defective corporate act or at the time the board of directors adopts the resolutions ratifying such defective corporate act pursuant to paragraph (b)(1) of this section; and (B) such defective corporate act did not result from a failure to comply with §203 of this title; or

(2) As of the record date for determining the stockholders entitled to vote on the ratification of such defective corporate act, there are no shares of valid stock outstanding and entitled to vote thereon, regardless of whether there then exist any shares of putative stock.

(d) If the ratification of a defective corporate act is required to be submitted to stockholders for approval pursuant to subsection (c) of this section, due notice of the time, place, if any, and purpose of the meeting shall be given at least 20 days before the date of the meeting to each holder of valid stock and putative stock, whether voting or nonvoting, at the address of such holder as it appears or most recently appeared, as appropriate, on the records of the corporation. The notice shall also be given to the holders of record of valid stock and putative stock, whether voting or nonvoting, as of the time of the defective corporate act (or, in the case of any defective corporate act that involved the establishment of a record date for notice of or voting at any meeting of stockholders, for action by written consent of stockholders in lieu of a meeting, or for any other purpose, the record date for notice of or voting at such meeting, the record date for action by written consent, or the record date for such other action, as the case may be), other than holders whose identities or addresses cannot be determined from the records of the corporation. The notice shall contain a copy of the resolutions adopted by the board of directors pursuant to paragraph (b)(1) of this section or the information required by paragraphs (b)(1)(A) through (E) of this section and a statement that any claim that the defective corporate act or putative stock ratified hereunder is void or voidable due to the failure of authorization, or that the Court of Chancery should declare in its discretion that a ratification in accordance with this section not be effective or be effective only on certain conditions must be brought within 120 days from the applicable validation effective time. At such meeting, the quorum and voting requirements applicable to ratification of such defective corporate act shall be the quorum and voting requirements applicable to the type of defective corporate act proposed to be ratified at the time of the approval of the ratification, except that:

(1) If the certificate of incorporation or bylaws of the corporation, any plan or agreement to which the corporation was a party or any provision of this title in effect as of the time of the defective corporate act would have required a larger number or portion of stock or of any class or series thereof or of specified stockholders for a quorum to be present or to approve the defective corporate act, the presence or approval of such larger number or portion of stock or of such class or series thereof or of such specified stockholders shall be required for a quorum to be present or to approve the ratification of the defective corporate act, as applicable, except that the presence or approval of shares of any class or series of which no shares are then outstanding, or of any person that is no longer a stockholder, shall not be required;

(2) The approval by stockholders of the ratification of the election of a director shall require the affirmative vote of the majority of shares present at the meeting and entitled to vote on the election of such director, except that if the certificate of incorporation or bylaws of the corporation then in effect or in effect at the time of the defective election require or required a larger number or portion of stock or of any class or series thereof or of specified stockholders to elect such director, the affirmative vote of such larger number or portion of stock or of any class or series thereof or of such specified stockholders shall be required to ratify the election of such director, except that the presence or approval of shares of any class or series of which no shares are then outstanding, or of any person that is no longer a stockholder, shall not be required; and

(3) In the event of a failure of authorization resulting from failure to comply with the provisions of §203 of this title, the ratification of the defective corporate act shall require the vote set forth in §203(a)(3) of this title, regardless of whether such vote would have otherwise been required.

Shares of putative stock on the record date for determining stockholders entitled to vote on any matter submitted to stockholders pursuant to subsection (c) of this section (and without giving effect to any ratification that becomes effective after such record date) shall neither be entitled to vote nor counted for quorum purposes in any vote to ratify any defective corporate act.

(e) If a defective corporate act ratified pursuant to this section would have required under any other section of this title the filing of a certificate in accordance with §103 of this title, then, whether or not a certificate was previously filed in respect of such defective corporate act and in lieu of filing the certificate otherwise required by this title, the corporation shall file a certificate of validation with respect to such defective corporate act in accordance with §103 of this title. A separate certificate of validation shall be required for each defective corporate act requiring the filing of a certificate of validation under this section, except that (i) 2 or more defective corporate acts may be included in a single certificate of validation if the corporation filed, or to comply with this title would have filed, a single certificate under another provision of this title to effect such acts, and (ii) 2 or more overissues of shares of any class, classes or series of stock may be included in a single certificate of validation, provided that the increase in the number of authorized shares of each such class or series set forth in the certificate of validation shall be effective as of the date of the first such overissue. The certificate of validation shall set forth:

(1) Each defective corporate act that is the subject of the certificate of validation (including, in the case of any defective corporate act involving the issuance of shares of putative stock, the number and type of shares of putative stock issued and the date or dates upon which such putative shares were purported to have been issued), the date of such defective corporate act, and the nature of the failure of authorization in respect of such defective corporate act;

(2) A statement that such defective corporate act was ratified in accordance with this section, including the date on which the board of directors ratified such defective corporate act and the date, if any, on which the stockholders approved the ratification of such defective corporate act; and

(3) Information required by 1 of the following paragraphs:

a. If a certificate was previously filed under §103 of this title in respect of such defective corporate act and no changes to such certificate are required to give effect to such defective corporate act in accordance with this section, the certificate of validation shall set forth (x) the name, title and filing date of the certificate previously filed and of any certificate of correction thereto and (y) a statement that a copy of the certificate previously filed, together with any certificate of correction thereto, is attached as an exhibit to the certificate of validation;

b. If a certificate was previously filed under §103 of this title in respect of the defective corporate act and such certificate requires any change to give effect to the defective corporate act in accordance with this section (including a change to the date and time of the effectiveness of such certificate), the certificate of validation shall set forth (x) the name, title and filing date of the certificate so previously filed and of any certificate of correction thereto, (y) a statement that a certificate containing all of the information required to be included under the applicable section or sections of this title to give effect to the defective corporate act is attached as an exhibit to the certificate of validation, and (z) the date and time that such certificate shall be deemed to have become effective pursuant to this section; or

c. If a certificate was not previously filed under §103 of this title in respect of the defective corporate act and the defective corporate act ratified pursuant to this section would have required under any other section of this title the filing of a certificate in accordance with §103 of this title, the certificate of validation shall set forth (x) a statement that a certificate containing all of the information required to be included under the applicable section or sections of this title to give effect to the defective corporate act is attached as an exhibit to the certificate of validation, and (y) the date and time that such certificate shall be deemed to have become effective pursuant to this section.

A certificate attached to a certificate of validation pursuant to paragraph (e)(3)b. or c. of this section need not be separately executed and acknowledged and need not include any statement required by any other section of this title that such instrument has been approved and adopted in accordance with the provisions of such other section.

(f) From and after the validation effective time, unless otherwise determined in an action brought pursuant to §205 of this title:

(1) Subject to the last sentence of subsection (d) of this section, each defective corporate act ratified in accordance with this section shall no longer be deemed void or voidable as result of a the failure of authorization described in the resolutions adopted pursuant to subsection (b) of this section and such effect shall be retroactive to the time of the defective corporate act; and

(2) Subject to the last sentence of subsection (d) of this section, each share or fraction of a share of putative stock issued or purportedly issued pursuant to any such defective corporate act shall no longer be deemed void or voidable and shall be deemed to be an identical share or fraction of a share of outstanding stock as of the time it was purportedly issued.

(g) In respect of each defective corporate act ratified by the board of directors pursuant to subsection (b) of this section, prompt notice of the ratification shall be given to all holders of valid stock and putative stock, whether voting or nonvoting, as of the date the board of directors adopts the resolutions approving such defective corporate act, or as of a date within 60 days after such date of adoption, as established by the board of directors, at the address of such holder as it appears or most recently appeared, as appropriate, on the records of the corporation. The notice shall also be given to the holders of record of valid stock and putative stock, whether voting or nonvoting, as of the time of the defective corporate act, other than holders whose identities or addresses cannot be determined from the records of the corporation. The notice shall contain a copy of the resolutions adopted pursuant to subsection (b) of this section or the information specified in paragraphs (b)(1)(A) through (E) or paragraphs (b)(2)(A) through (C) of this section, as applicable, and a statement that any claim that the defective corporate act or putative stock ratified hereunder is void or voidable due to the failure of authorization, or that the Court of Chancery should declare in its discretion that a ratification in accordance with this section not be effective or be effective only on certain conditions must be brought within 120 days from the later of the validation effective time or the time at which the notice required by this subsection is given. Notwithstanding the foregoing, (i) no such notice shall be required if notice of the ratification of the defective corporate act is to be given in accordance with subsection (d) of this section, and (ii) in the case of a corporation that has a class of stock listed on a national securities exchange, the notice required by this subsection and the second sentence of subsection (d) of this section may be deemed given if disclosed in a document publicly filed by the corporation with the Securities and Exchange Commission pursuant to §§13, 14 or 15(d) of the Securities Exchange Act of 1934, as amended, and the rules and regulations promulgated thereunder, or the corresponding provisions of any subsequent United States federal securities laws, rules or regulations. If any defective corporate act has been approved by stockholders acting pursuant to §228 of this title, the notice required by this subsection may be included in any notice required to be given pursuant to §228(e) of this title and, if so given, shall be sent to the stockholders entitled thereto under §228(e) and to all holders of valid and putative stock to whom notice would be required under this subsection if the defective corporate act had been approved at a meeting other than any stockholder who approved the action by consent in lieu of a meeting pursuant to §228 of this title or any holder of putative stock who otherwise consented thereto in writing. Solely for purposes of subsection (d) of this section and this subsection, notice to holders of putative stock, and notice to holders of valid stock and putative stock as of the time of the defective corporate act, shall be treated as notice to holders of valid stock for purposes of §§222 and 228, 229, 230, 232 and 233 of this title.

(h) As used in this section and in §205 of this title only, the term:

(1) "Defective corporate act" means an overissue, an election or appointment of directors that is void or voidable due to a failure of authorization, or any act or transaction purportedly taken by or on behalf of the corporation that is, and at the time such act or transaction was purportedly taken would have been, within the power of a corporation under subchapter II of this chapter (without regard to the failure of authorization identified in §204(b)(1)(D) of this title), but is void or voidable due to a failure of authorization;

(2) "Failure of authorization" means: (i) the failure to authorize or effect an act or transaction in compliance with (A) the provisions of this title, (B) the certificate of incorporation or bylaws of the corporation, or (C) any plan or agreement to which the corporation is a party or the disclosure set forth in any proxy or consent solicitation statement, if and to the extent such failure would render such act or transaction void or voidable; or (ii) the failure of the board of directors or any officer of the corporation to authorize or approve any act or transaction taken by or on behalf of the corporation that would have required for its due authorization the approval of the board of directors or such officer;

(3) "Overissue" means the purported issuance of:

a. Shares of capital stock of a class or series in excess of the number of shares of such class or series the corporation has the power to issue under §161 of this title at the time of such issuance; or

b. Shares of any class or series of capital stock that is not then authorized for issuance by the certificate of incorporation of the corporation;

(4) "Putative stock" means the shares of any class or series of capital stock of the corporation (including shares issued upon exercise of options, rights, warrants or other securities convertible into shares of capital stock of the corporation, or interests with respect thereto that were created or issued pursuant to a defective corporate act) that:

a. But for any failure of authorization, would constitute valid stock; or

b. Cannot be determined by the board of directors to be valid stock;

(5) "Time of the defective corporate act" means the date and time the defective corporate act was purported to have been taken;

(6) "Validation effective time" with respect to any defective corporate act ratified pursuant to this section means the latest of:

a. The time at which the defective corporate act submitted to the stockholders for approval pursuant to subsection (c) of this section is approved by such stockholders or if no such vote of stockholders is required to approve the ratification of the defective corporate act, the time at which the board of directors adopts the resolutions required by paragraph (b)(1) or (b)(2) of this section;

b. Where no certificate of validation is required to be filed pursuant to subsection (e) of this section, the time, if any, specified by the board of directors in the resolutions adopted pursuant to paragraph (b)(1) or (b)(2) of this section, which time shall not precede the time at which such resolutions are adopted; and

c. The time at which any certificate of validation filed pursuant to subsection (e) of this section shall become effective in accordance with §103 of this title.

(7) "Valid stock" means the shares of any class or series of capital stock of the corporation that have been duly authorized and validly issued in accordance with this title.

In the absence of actual fraud in the transaction, the judgment of the board of directors that shares of stock are valid stock or putative stock shall be conclusive, unless otherwise determined by the Court of Chancery in a proceeding brought pursuant to §205 of this title.

(i) Ratification under this section or validation under §205 of this title shall not be deemed to be the exclusive means of ratifying or validating any act or transaction taken by or on behalf of the corporation, including any defective corporate act, or any issuance of stock, including any putative stock, or of adopting or endorsing any act or transaction taken by or in the name of the corporation prior to the commencement of its existence, and the absence or failure of ratification in accordance with either this section or validation under §205 of this title shall not, of itself, affect the validity or effectiveness of any act or transaction or the issuance of any stock properly ratified under common law or otherwise, nor shall it create a presumption that any such act or transaction is or was a defective corporate act or that such stock is void or voidable.

§205. Proceedings Regarding Validity of Defective Corporate Acts and Stock

(a) Subject to subsection (f) of this section, upon application by the corporation, any successor entity to the corporation, any member of the board of directors, any record or beneficial holder of valid stock or putative stock, any record or beneficial holder of valid or putative stock as of the time of a defective corporate act ratified pursuant to §204 of this title, or any other person claiming to be substantially and adversely affected by a ratification pursuant to §204 of this title, the Court of Chancery may:

(1) Determine the validity and effectiveness of any defective corporate act ratified pursuant to §204 of this title;

(2) Determine the validity and effectiveness of the ratification of any defective corporate act pursuant to §204 of this title;

(3) Determine the validity and effectiveness of any defective corporate act not ratified or not ratified effectively pursuant to §204 of this title;

(4) Determine the validity of any corporate act or transaction and any stock, rights or options to acquire stock; and

(5) Modify or waive any of the procedures set forth in §204 of this title to ratify a defective corporate act.

(b) In connection with an action under this section, the Court of Chancery may:

(1) Declare that a ratification in accordance with and pursuant to §204 of this title is not effective or shall only be effective at a time or upon conditions established by the Court;

(2) Validate and declare effective any defective corporate act or putative stock and impose conditions upon such validation by the Court;

(3) Require measures to remedy or avoid harm to any person substantially and adversely affected by a ratification pursuant to §204 of this title or from any order of the Court pursuant to this section, excluding any harm that would have resulted if the defective corporate act had been valid when approved or effectuated;

(4) Order the Secretary of State to accept an instrument for filing with an effective time specified by the Court, which effective time may be prior or subsequent to the time of such order, provided that the filing date of such instrument shall be determined in accordance with §103(c)(3) of this title;

(5) Approve a stock ledger for the corporation that includes any stock ratified or validated in accordance with this section or with §204 of this title;

(6) Declare that shares of putative stock are shares of valid stock or require a corporation to issue and deliver shares of valid stock in place of any shares of putative stock;

(7) Order that a meeting of holders of valid stock or putative stock be held and exercise the powers provided to the Court under §227 of this title with respect to such a meeting;

(8) Declare that a defective corporate act validated by the Court shall be effective as of the time of the defective corporate act or at such other time as the Court shall determine;

(9) Declare that putative stock validated by the Court shall be deemed to be an identical share or fraction of a share of valid stock as of the time originally issued or purportedly issued or at such other time as the Court shall determine; and

(10) Make such other orders regarding such matters as it deems proper under the circumstances.

(c) Service of the application under subsection (a) of this section upon the registered agent of the corporation shall be deemed to be service upon the corporation, and no other party need be joined in order for the Court of Chancery to adjudicate the matter. In an action filed by the corporation, the Court may require notice of the action be provided to other persons specified by the Court and permit such other persons to intervene in the action.

(d) In connection with the resolution of matters pursuant to subsections (a) and (b) of this section, the Court of Chancery may consider the following:

(1) Whether the defective corporate act was originally approved or effectuated with the belief that the approval or effectuation was in compliance with the provisions of this title, the certificate of incorporation or bylaws of the corporation;

(2) Whether the corporation and board of directors has treated the defective corporate act as a valid act or transaction and whether any person has acted in reliance on the public record that such defective corporate act was valid;

(3) Whether any person will be or was harmed by the ratification or validation of the defective corporate act, excluding any harm that would have resulted if the defective corporate act had been valid when approved or effectuated;

(4) Whether any person will be harmed by the failure to ratify or validate the defective corporate act; and

(5) Any other factors or considerations the Court deems just and equitable.

(e) The Court of Chancery is hereby vested with exclusive jurisdiction to hear and determine all actions brought under this section.

(f) Notwithstanding any other provision of this section, no action asserting:

(1) That a defective corporate act or putative stock ratified in accordance with §204 of this title is void or voidable due to a failure of authorization identified in the resolution adopted in accordance with 204(b) of this title; or

(2) That the Court of Chancery should declare in its discretion that a ratification in accordance with §204 of this title not be effective or be effective only on certain conditions,

may be brought after the expiration of 120 days from the later of the validation effective time and the time notice, if any, that is required to be given pursuant to §204(g) of this title is given with respect to such ratification, except that this subsection shall not apply to an action asserting that a ratification was not accomplished in accordance with §204 of this title or to any person to whom notice of the ratification was required to have been given pursuant to §204(d) or (g) of this title, but to whom such notice was not given.

SUBCHAPTER VII. MEETINGS, ELECTIONS, VOTING AND NOTICE

§211. Meetings of Stockholders

(a)(1) Meetings of stockholders may be held at such place, either within or without this State as may be designated by or in the manner provided in the certificate of incorporation or bylaws, or if not so designated, as determined by the board of directors. If, pursuant to this paragraph or the certificate of incorporation or the bylaws of the corporation, the board of directors is authorized to determine the place of a meeting of stockholders, the board of directors may, in its sole discretion, determine that the meeting shall not be held at any place, but may instead be held solely by means of remote communication as authorized by paragraph (a)(2) of this section.

(2) If authorized by the board of directors in its sole discretion, and subject to such guidelines and procedures as the board of directors may adopt, stockholders and proxyholders not physically present at a meeting of stockholders may, by means of remote communication:

a. Participate in a meeting of stockholders; and

b. Be deemed present in person and vote at a meeting of stockholders whether such meeting is to be held at a designated place or solely by means of remote communication, provided that (i) the corporation shall implement reasonable measures to verify that each person deemed present and permitted to vote at the meeting by means of remote communication is a stockholder or proxyholder, (ii) the corporation shall implement reasonable measures to provide such stockholders and proxyholders a reasonable opportunity to participate in the meeting and to vote on matters submitted to the stockholders, including an opportunity to read or hear the proceedings of the meeting substantially concurrently with such proceedings, and (iii) if any stockholder or proxyholder votes or takes other action at the meeting by means of remote communication, a record of such vote or other action shall be maintained by the corporation.

(b) Unless directors are elected by written consent in lieu of an annual meeting as permitted by this subsection, an annual meeting of stockholders shall be held for the election of directors on a date and at a time designated by or in the manner provided in the bylaws. Stockholders may, unless the certificate of incorporation otherwise provides, act by written consent to elect directors; provided, however, that, if such consent is less than unanimous, such action by written consent may be in lieu of holding an annual meeting only if all of the directorships to which directors could be elected at an annual meeting held at the effective time of such action are vacant and are filled by such action. Any other proper business may be transacted at the annual meeting.

(c) A failure to hold the annual meeting at the designated time or to elect a sufficient number of directors to conduct the business of the corporation shall not affect otherwise valid corporate acts or work a forfeiture or dissolution of the corporation except as may be otherwise specifically provided in this chapter. If the annual meeting for election of directors is not held on the date designated therefor or action by written consent to elect directors in lieu of an annual meeting has not been taken, the directors shall cause the meeting to be held as soon as is convenient. If there be a failure to hold the annual meeting or to take action by written consent to elect directors in lieu of an annual meeting for a period of 30 days after the date designated for the annual meeting, or if no date has been designated, for a period of 13 months after the latest to occur of the organization of the corporation, its last annual meeting or the last action by written consent to elect directors in lieu of an annual meeting, the Court of Chancery may summarily order a meeting to be held upon the application of any stockholder or director. The shares of stock represented at such meeting, either in person or by proxy, and entitled to vote thereat, shall constitute a quorum for the purpose of such meeting, notwithstanding any provision of the certificate of incorporation or bylaws to the contrary. The Court of Chancery may issue such orders as may be appropriate, including, without limitation, orders designating the time and place of such meeting, the record date or dates for determination of stockholders entitled to notice of the meeting and to vote thereat, and the form of notice of such meeting.

(d) Special meetings of the stockholders may be called by the board of directors or by such person or persons as may be authorized by the certificate of incorporation or by the bylaws.

(e) All elections of directors shall be by written ballot unless otherwise provided in the certificate of incorporation; if authorized by the board of directors, such requirement of a written ballot shall be satisfied by a ballot submitted by electronic transmission, provided that any such electronic transmission must either set forth or be submitted with information from which it can be determined that the electronic transmission was authorized by the stockholder or proxy holder.

§212. Voting Rights of Stockholders; Proxies; Limitations

(a) Unless otherwise provided in the certificate of incorporation and subject to §213 of this title, each stockholder shall be entitled to 1 vote for each share of capital stock held by such stockholder. If the certificate of incorporation provides for more or less than 1 vote for any share, on any matter, every reference in this chapter to a majority or other proportion of stock, voting stock or shares shall refer to such majority or other proportion of the votes of such stock, voting stock or shares.

(b) Each stockholder entitled to vote at a meeting of stockholders or to express consent or dissent to corporate action in writing without a meeting may authorize another person or persons to act for such stockholder by proxy, but no such proxy shall be voted or acted upon after 3 years from its date, unless the proxy provides for a longer period.

(c) Without limiting the manner in which a stockholder may authorize another person or persons to act for such stockholder as proxy pursuant to subsection (b) of this section, the following shall constitute a valid means by which a stockholder may grant such authority:

(1) A stockholder, or such stockholder's authorized officer, director, employee or agent, may execute a document authorizing another person or persons to act for such stockholder as proxy.

(2) A stockholder may authorize another person or persons to act for such stockholder as proxy by transmitting or authorizing the transmission of an electronic transmission to the person who will be the holder of the proxy or to a proxy solicitation firm, proxy support service organization or like agent duly authorized by the person who will be the holder of the proxy to receive such transmission, provided that any such transmission must either set forth or be submitted with information from which it can be determined that the transmission was authorized by the stockholder. If it is determined that such transmissions are valid, the inspectors or, if there are no inspectors, such other persons making that determination shall specify the information upon which they relied.

(3) The authorization of a person to act as a proxy may be documented, signed and delivered in accordance with §116 of this title, provided that such authorization shall set forth, or be delivered with information enabling the corporation to determine, the identity of the stockholder granting such authorization.

(d) Any copy, facsimile telecommunication or other reliable reproduction of the document (including any electronic transmission) created pursuant to subsection (c) of this section may be substituted or used in lieu of the original document for any and all purposes for which the original document could be used, provided that such copy, facsimile telecommunication or other reproduction shall be a complete reproduction of the entire original document.

(e) A duly executed proxy shall be irrevocable if it states that it is irrevocable and if, and only as long as, it is coupled with an interest sufficient in law to support an irrevocable power. A proxy may be made irrevocable regardless of whether the interest with which it is coupled is an interest in the stock itself or an interest in the corporation generally.

§213. Fixing Date for Determination of Stockholders of Record

(a) In order that the corporation may determine the stockholders entitled to notice of any meeting of stockholders or any adjournment thereof, the board of directors may fix a record date, which record date shall not precede the date upon which the resolution fixing the record date is adopted by the board of directors, and which record date shall not be more than 60 nor less than 10 days before the date of such meeting. If the board of directors so fixes a date, such date shall also be the record date for determining the stockholders entitled to vote at such meeting unless the board of directors determines, at the time it fixes such record date, that a later date on or before the date of the meeting shall be the date for making such determination. If no record date is fixed by the board of directors, the record date for determining stockholders entitled to notice of and to vote at a meeting of stockholders shall be at the close of business on the day next preceding the day on which notice is given, or, if notice is waived, at the close of business on the day next preceding the day on which the meeting is held. A determination of stockholders of record entitled to notice of or to vote at a meeting of stockholders shall apply to any adjournment of the meeting; provided, however, that the board of directors may fix a new record date for determination of stockholders entitled to vote at the adjourned meeting, and in such case shall also fix as the record date for stockholders entitled to notice of such adjourned meeting the same or an earlier date as that fixed for determination of stockholders entitled to vote in accordance with the foregoing provisions of this subsection (a) at the adjourned meeting.

(b) In order that the corporation may determine the stockholders entitled to consent to corporate action without a meeting in accordance with §228 of this title, the board of directors may fix a record date, which record date shall not precede the date upon which the resolution fixing the record date is adopted by the board of directors, and which date shall not be more than 10 days after the date upon which the resolution fixing the record date is adopted by the board of directors. If no record date has been fixed by the board of directors, the record date for determining stockholders entitled to consent to corporate action without a meeting, when no prior action by the board of directors is required by this chapter, shall be the first date on which a signed consent setting forth the action taken or proposed to be taken is delivered to the corporation in accordance with §228 (d) of this title. If no record date has been fixed by the board of directors and prior action by the board of directors is required by this chapter, the record date for determining stockholders entitled to consent to corporate action in writing without a meeting shall be at the close of business on the day on which the board of directors adopts the resolution taking such prior action.

(c) In order that the corporation may determine the stockholders entitled to receive payment of any dividend or other distribution or allotment of any rights or the stockholders entitled to exercise any rights in respect of any change, conversion or exchange of stock, or for the purpose of any other lawful action, the board of directors may fix a record date, which record date shall not precede the date upon which the resolution fixing the record date is adopted, and which record date shall be not more than 60 days prior to such action. If no record date is fixed, the record date for determining stockholders for any such purpose shall be at the close of business on the day on which the board of directors adopts the resolution relating thereto.

§214. Cumulative Voting

The certificate of incorporation of any corporation may provide that at all elections of directors of the corporation, or at elections held under specified circumstances, each holder of stock or of any class or classes or of a series or series thereof shall be entitled to as many votes as shall equal the number of votes which (except for such provision as to cumulative voting) such holder would be entitled to cast for the election of directors with respect to such holder's shares of stock multiplied by the number of directors to be elected by such holder, and that such holder may cast all of such votes for a single director or may distribute them among the number to be voted for, or for any 2 or more of them as such holder may see fit.

§215. Voting Rights of Members of Nonstock Corporations; Quorum; Proxies

(a) Sections 211 through 214 and 216 of this title shall not apply to nonstock corporations, except that §211(a) and (d) of this title and §212(c), (d), and (e) of this title shall apply to such corporations, and, when so applied, all references therein to stockholders and to the board of directors shall be deemed to refer to the members and the governing body of a nonstock corporation, respectively; and all references to stock, capital stock, or shares thereof shall be deemed to refer to memberships of a nonprofit nonstock corporation and to membership interests of any other nonstock corporation.

(b) Unless otherwise provided in the certificate of incorporation or the bylaws of a nonstock corporation, and subject to subsection (f) of this section, each member shall be entitled at every meeting of members to 1 vote on each matter submitted to a vote of members. A member may exercise such voting rights in person or by proxy, but no proxy shall be voted on after 3 years from its date, unless the proxy provides for a longer period.

(c) Unless otherwise provided in this chapter, the certificate of incorporation or bylaws of a nonstock corporation may specify the number of members having voting power who shall be present or represented by proxy at any meeting in order to constitute a quorum for, and the votes that shall be necessary for, the transaction of any business. In the absence of such specification in the certificate of incorporation or bylaws of a nonstock corporation:

(1) One-third of the members of such corporation shall constitute a quorum at a meeting of such members;

(2) In all matters other than the election of the governing body of such corporation, the affirmative vote of a majority of such members present in person or represented by proxy at the meeting and entitled to vote on the subject matter shall be the act of the members, unless the vote of a greater number is required by this chapter;

(3) Members of the governing body shall be elected by a plurality of the votes of the members of the corporation present in person or represented by proxy at the meeting and entitled to vote thereon; and

(4) Where a separate vote by a class or group or classes or groups is required, a majority of the members of such class or group or classes or groups, present in person or represented by proxy, shall constitute a quorum entitled to take action with respect to that vote on that matter and, in all matters other than the election of members of the governing body, the affirmative vote of the majority of the members of such class or group or classes or groups present in person or represented by proxy at the meeting shall be the act of such class or group or classes or groups.

(d) If the election of the governing body of any nonstock corporation shall not be held on the day designated by the bylaws, the governing body shall cause the election to be held as soon thereafter as convenient. The failure to hold such an election at the designated time shall not work any forfeiture or dissolution of the corporation, but the Court of Chancery may summarily order such an election to be held upon the application of any member of the corporation. At any election pursuant to such order the persons entitled to vote in such election who shall be present at such meeting, either in person or by proxy, shall constitute a quorum for such meeting, notwithstanding any provision of the certificate of incorporation or the bylaws of the corporation to the contrary.

(e) If authorized by the governing body, any requirement of a written ballot shall be satisfied by a ballot submitted by electronic transmission, provided that any such electronic transmission must either set forth or be submitted with information from which it can be determined that the electronic transmission was authorized by the member or proxy holder.

(f) Except as otherwise provided in the certificate of incorporation, in the bylaws, or by resolution of the governing body, the record date for any meeting or corporate action shall be deemed to be the date of such meeting or corporate action; provided, however, that no record date may precede any action by the governing body fixing such record date.

§216. Quorum and Required Vote for Stock Corporations

Subject to this chapter in respect of the vote that shall be required for a specified action, the certificate of incorporation or bylaws of any corporation authorized to issue stock may specify the number of shares and/or the amount of other securities having voting power the holders of which shall be present or represented by proxy at any meeting in order to constitute a quorum for, and the votes that shall be necessary for, the transaction of any business, but in no event shall a quorum consist of less than 1/3 of the shares entitled to vote at the meeting, except that, where a separate vote by a class or series or classes or series is required, a quorum shall consist of no less than 1/3 of the shares of such class or series or classes or series. In the absence of such specification in the certificate of incorporation or bylaws of the corporation:

(1) A majority of the shares entitled to vote, present in person or represented by proxy, shall constitute a quorum at a meeting of stockholders;

(2) In all matters other than the election of directors, the affirmative vote of the majority of shares present in person or represented by proxy at the meeting and entitled to vote on the subject matter shall be the act of the stockholders;

(3) Directors shall be elected by a plurality of the votes of the shares present in person or represented by proxy at the meeting and entitled to vote on the election of directors; and

(4) Where a separate vote by a class or series or classes or series is required, a majority of the outstanding shares of such class or series or classes or series, present in person or represented by proxy, shall constitute a quorum entitled to take action with respect to that vote on that matter and, in all matters other than the election of directors, the affirmative vote of the majority of shares of such class or series or classes or series present in person or represented by proxy at the meeting shall be the act of such class or series or classes or series.

A bylaw amendment adopted by stockholders which specifies the votes that shall be necessary for the election of directors shall not be further amended or repealed by the board of directors.

§217. Voting Rights of Fiduciaries, Pledgors and Joint Owners of Stock

(a) Persons holding stock in a fiduciary capacity shall be entitled to vote the shares so held. Persons whose stock is pledged shall be entitled to vote, unless in the transfer by the pledgor on the books of the corporation such person has expressly empowered the pledgee to vote thereon, in which case only the pledgee, or such pledgee's proxy, may represent such stock and vote thereon.

(b) If shares or other securities having voting power stand of record in the names of 2 or more persons, whether fiduciaries, members of a partnership, joint tenants, tenants in common, tenants by the entirety or otherwise, or if 2 or more persons have the same fiduciary relationship respecting the same shares, unless the secretary of the corporation is given written notice to the contrary and is furnished with a copy of the instrument or order appointing them or creating the relationship wherein it is so provided, their acts with respect to voting shall have the following effect:

(1) If only 1 votes, such person's act binds all;

(2) If more than 1 vote, the act of the majority so voting binds all;

(3) If more than 1 vote, but the vote is evenly split on any particular matter, each faction may vote the securities in question proportionally, or any person voting the shares, or a beneficiary, if any, may apply to the Court of Chancery or such other court as may have jurisdiction to appoint an additional person to act with the persons so voting the shares, which shall then be voted as determined by a majority of such persons and the person appointed by the Court. If the instrument so filed shows that any such tenancy is held in unequal interests, a majority or even split for the purpose of this subsection shall be a majority or even split in interest.

§218. Voting Trusts and Other Voting Agreements

(a) One stockholder or 2 or more stockholders may by agreement in writing deposit capital stock of an original issue with or transfer capital stock to any person or persons, or entity or entities authorized to act as trustee, for the purpose of vesting in such person or persons, entity or entities, who may be designated voting trustee, or voting trustees, the right to vote thereon for any period of time determined by such agreement, upon the terms and conditions stated in such agreement. The agreement may contain any other lawful provisions not inconsistent with such purpose. After delivery of a copy of the agreement to the registered office of the corporation in this State or the principal place of business of the corporation, which copy shall be open to the inspection of any stockholder of the corporation or any beneficiary of the trust under the agreement daily during business hours, certificates of stock or uncertificated stock shall be issued to the voting trustee or trustees to represent any stock of an original issue so deposited with such voting trustee or trustees, and any certificates of stock or uncertificated stock so transferred to the voting trustee or trustees shall be surrendered and cancelled and new certificates or uncertificated stock shall be issued therefore to the voting trustee or trustees. In the certificate so issued, if any, it shall be stated that it is issued pursuant to such agreement, and that fact shall also be stated in the stock ledger of the corporation. The voting trustee or trustees may vote the stock so issued or transferred during the period specified in the agreement. Stock standing in the name of the voting trustee or trustees may be voted either in person or by proxy, and in voting the stock, the voting trustee or trustees shall incur no responsibility as stockholder, trustee or otherwise, except for their own individual malfeasance. In any case where 2 or more persons or entities are designated as voting trustees, and the right and method of voting any stock standing in their names at any meeting of the corporation are not fixed by the agreement appointing the trustees, the right to vote the stock and the manner of voting it at the meeting shall be determined by a majority of the trustees, or if they be equally divided as to the right and manner of voting the stock in any particular case, the vote of the stock in such case shall be divided equally among the trustees.

(b) Any amendment to a voting trust agreement shall be made by a written agreement, a copy of which shall be delivered to the registered office of the corporation in this State or principal place of business of the corporation.

(c) An agreement between 2 or more stockholders, if in writing and signed by the parties thereto, may provide that in exercising any voting rights, the shares held by them shall be voted as provided by the agreement, or as the parties may agree, or as determined in accordance with a procedure agreed upon by them.

(d) This section shall not be deemed to invalidate any voting or other agreement among stockholders or any irrevocable proxy which is not otherwise illegal.

§219. List of Stockholders Entitled to Vote; Penalty for Refusal to Produce; Stock Ledger

(a) The corporation shall prepare, no later than the tenth day before each meeting of stockholders, a complete list of the stockholders entitled to vote at the meeting; provided, however, if the record date for determining the stockholders entitled to vote is less than 10 days before the meeting date, the list shall reflect the stockholders entitled to vote as of the tenth day before the meeting date, arranged in alphabetical order, and showing the address of each stockholder and the number of shares registered in the name of each stockholder. Nothing contained in this section shall require the corporation to include electronic mail addresses or other electronic contact information on such list. Such list shall be open to the examination of any stockholder for any purpose germane to the meeting for a period of 10 days ending on the day before the meeting date: (i) on a reasonably accessible electronic network, provided that the information required to gain access to such list is provided with the notice of the meeting, or (ii) during ordinary business hours, at the principal place of business of the corporation. In the event that the corporation determines to make the list available on an electronic network, the corporation may take reasonable steps to ensure that such information is available only to stockholders of the corporation.

(b) If the corporation, or an officer or agent of the corporation, refuses to permit examination of the list by a stockholder, such stockholder may apply to the Court of Chancery for an order to compel the corporation to permit such examination. The burden of proof shall be on the corporation to establish that the examination such stockholder seeks is for a purpose not germane to the meeting. The Court may summarily order the corporation to permit examination of the list upon such conditions as the Court may deem appropriate, and may make such additional orders as may be appropriate, including, without limitation, postponing the meeting or voiding the results of the meeting.

(c) For purposes of this chapter, "stock ledger" means 1 or more records administered by or on behalf of the corporation in which the names of all of the corporation's stockholders of record, the address and number of shares registered in the name of each such stockholder, and all issuances and transfers of stock of the corporation are recorded in accordance with §224 of this title. The stock ledger shall be the only evidence as to who are the stockholders entitled by this section to examine the list required by this section or to vote in person or by proxy at any meeting of stockholders.

§220. Inspection of Books and Records

(a) As used in this section:

(1) "Stockholder" means a holder of record of stock in a stock corporation, or a person who is the beneficial owner of shares of such stock held either in a voting trust or by a nominee on behalf of such person.

(2) "Subsidiary" means any entity directly or indirectly owned, in whole or in part, by the corporation of which the stockholder is a stockholder and over the affairs of which the corporation directly or indirectly exercises control, and includes, without limitation, corporations, partnerships, limited partnerships, limited liability partnerships, limited liability companies, statutory trusts and/or joint ventures.

(3) "Under oath" includes statements the declarant affirms to be true under penalty of perjury under the laws of the United States or any state.

(b) Any stockholder, in person or by attorney or other agent, shall, upon written demand under oath stating the purpose thereof, have the right during the usual hours for business to inspect for any proper purpose, and to make copies and extracts from:

(1) The corporation's stock ledger, a list of its stockholders, and its other books and records; and

(2) A subsidiary's books and records, to the extent that:

a. The corporation has actual possession and control of such records of such subsidiary; or

b. The corporation could obtain such records through the exercise of control over such subsidiary, provided that as of the date of the making of the demand:

1. The stockholder inspection of such books and records of the subsidiary would not constitute a breach of an agreement between the corporation or the subsidiary and a person or persons not affiliated with the corporation; and

2. The subsidiary would not have the right under the law applicable to it to deny the corporation access to such books and records upon demand by the corporation.

In every instance where the stockholder is other than a record holder of stock in a stock corporation, or a member of a nonstock corporation, the demand under oath shall state the person's status as a stockholder, be accompanied by documentary evidence of beneficial ownership of the stock, and state that such documentary evidence is a true and correct copy of what it purports to be. A proper purpose shall mean a purpose reasonably related to such person's interest as a stockholder. In every instance where an attorney or other agent shall be the person who seeks the right to inspection, the demand under oath shall be accompanied by a power of attorney or such other writing which authorizes the attorney or other agent to so act on behalf of the stockholder. The demand under oath shall be directed to the corporation at its registered office in this State or at its principal place of business.

(c) If the corporation, or an officer or agent thereof, refuses to permit an inspection sought by a stockholder or attorney or other agent acting for the stockholder pursuant to subsection (b) of this section or does not reply to the demand within 5 business days after the demand has been made, the stockholder may apply to the Court of Chancery for an order to compel such inspection. The Court of Chancery is hereby vested with exclusive jurisdiction to determine whether or not the person seeking inspection is entitled to the inspection sought. The Court may summarily order the corporation to permit the stockholder to inspect the corporation's stock ledger, an existing list of stockholders, and its other books and records, and to make copies or extracts therefrom; or the Court may order the corporation to furnish to the stockholder a list of its stockholders as of a specific date on condition that the stockholder first pay to the corporation the reasonable cost of obtaining and furnishing such list and on such other conditions as the Court deems appropriate. Where the stockholder seeks to inspect the corporation's books and records, other than its stock ledger or list of stockholders, such stockholder shall first establish that:

(1) Such stockholder is a stockholder;

(2) Such stockholder has complied with this section respecting the form and manner of making demand for inspection of such documents; and

(3) The inspection such stockholder seeks is for a proper purpose.

Where the stockholder seeks to inspect the corporation's stock ledger or list of stockholders and establishes that such stockholder is a stockholder and has complied with this section respecting the form and manner of making demand for inspection of such documents, the burden of proof shall be upon the corporation to establish that the inspection such stockholder seeks is for an improper purpose. The Court may, in its discretion, prescribe any limitations or conditions with reference to the inspection, or award such other or further relief as the Court may deem just and proper. The Court may order books, documents and records, pertinent extracts therefrom, or duly authenticated copies thereof, to be brought within this State and kept in this State upon such terms and conditions as the order may prescribe.

(d) Any director shall have the right to examine the corporation's stock ledger, a list of its stockholders and its other books and records for a purpose reasonably related to the director's position as a director. The Court of Chancery is hereby vested with the exclusive jurisdiction to determine whether a director is entitled to the inspection sought. The Court may summarily order the corporation to permit the director to inspect any and all books and records, the stock ledger and the list of stockholders and to make copies or extracts therefrom. The burden of proof shall be upon the corporation to establish that the inspection such director seeks is for an improper purpose. The Court may, in its discretion, prescribe any limitations or conditions with reference to the inspection, or award such other and further relief as the Court may deem just and proper.

§221. Voting, Inspection and Other Rights of Bondholders and Debenture Holders

Every corporation may in its certificate of incorporation confer upon the holders of any bonds, debentures or other obligations issued or to be issued by the corporation the power to vote in respect to the corporate affairs and management of the corporation to the extent and in the manner provided in the certificate of incorporation and may confer upon such holders of bonds, debentures or other obligations the same right of inspection of its books, accounts and other records, and also any other rights, which the stockholders of the corporation have or may have by reason of this chapter or of its certificate of incorporation. If the certificate of incorporation so provides, such holders of bonds, debentures or other obligations shall be deemed to be stockholders, and their bonds, debentures or other obligations shall be deemed to be shares of stock, for the purpose of any provision of this chapter which requires the vote of stockholders as a prerequisite to any corporate action and the certificate of incorporation may divest the holders of capital stock, in whole or in part, of their right to vote on any corporate matter whatsoever, except as set forth in §242(b)(2) of this title.

§222. Notice of Meetings and Adjourned Meetings

(a) Whenever stockholders are required or permitted to take any action at a meeting, a notice of the meeting shall be given in accordance with §232 of this title, and such notice shall state the place, if any, date and hour of the meeting, the means of remote communications, if any, by which stockholders and proxy holders may be deemed to be present in person and vote at such meeting, the record date for determining the stockholders entitled to vote at the meeting, if such date is different from the record date for determining stockholders entitled to notice of the meeting, and, in the case of a special meeting, the purpose or purposes for which the meeting is called.

(b) Unless otherwise provided in this chapter, the notice of any meeting shall be given not less than 10 nor more than 60 days before the date of the meeting to each stockholder entitled to vote at such meeting as of the record date for determining the stockholders entitled to notice of the meeting.

(c) Unless the bylaws otherwise require, when a meeting is adjourned to another time or place, (including an adjournment taken to address a technical failure to convene or continue a meeting using remote communication), notice need not be given of the adjourned meeting if the time, place, if any, thereof, and the means of remote communications, if any, by which stockholders and proxy holders may be deemed to be present in person and vote at such adjourned meeting are (i) announced at the meeting at which the adjournment is taken, (ii) displayed, during the time scheduled for the meeting, on the same electronic network used to enable stockholders and proxy holders to participate in the meeting by means of remote communication or (iii) set forth in the notice of meeting given in accordance with sub-section (a) of this section . At the adjourned meeting the corporation may transact any business which might have been transacted at the original meeting. If the adjournment is for more than 30 days, a notice of the adjourned meeting shall be given to each stockholder of record entitled to vote at the meeting. If after the adjournment a new record date for stockholders entitled to vote is fixed for the adjourned meeting, the board of directors shall fix a new record date for notice of such adjourned meeting in accordance with §213(a) of this title, and shall give notice of the adjourned meeting to each stockholder of record entitled to vote at such adjourned meeting as of the record date fixed for notice of such adjourned meeting.

§223. Vacancies and Newly Created Directorships

(a) Unless otherwise provided in the certificate of incorporation or bylaws:

(1) Vacancies and newly created directorships resulting from any increase in the authorized number of directors elected by all of the stockholders having the right to vote as a single class may be filled by a majority of the directors then in office, although less than a quorum, or by a sole remaining director;

(2) Whenever the holders of any class or classes of stock or series thereof are entitled to elect 1 or more directors by the certificate of incorporation, vacancies and newly created directorships of such class or classes or series may be filled by a majority of the directors elected by such class or classes or series thereof then in office, or by a sole remaining director so elected.

If at any time, by reason of death or resignation or other cause, a corporation should have no directors in office, then any officer or any stockholder or an executor, administrator, trustee or guardian of a stockholder, or other fiduciary entrusted with like responsibility for the person or estate of a stockholder, may call a special meeting of stockholders in accordance with the certificate of incorporation or the bylaws, or may apply to the Court of Chancery for a decree summarily ordering an election as provided in §211 or §215 of this title.

(b) In the case of a corporation the directors of which are divided into classes, any directors chosen under subsection (a) of this section shall hold office until the next election of the class for which such directors shall have been chosen, and until their successors shall be elected and qualified.

(c) If, at the time of filling any vacancy or any newly created directorship, the directors then in office shall constitute less than a majority of the whole board (as constituted immediately prior to any such increase), the Court of Chancery may, upon application of any stockholder or stockholders holding at least 10 percent of the voting stock at the time outstanding having the right to vote for such directors, summarily order an election to be held to fill any such vacancies or newly created directorships, or to replace the directors chosen by the directors then in office as aforesaid, which election shall be governed by §211 or §215 of this title as far as applicable.

(d) Unless otherwise provided in the certificate of incorporation or bylaws, when 1 or more directors shall resign from the board, effective at a future date, a majority of the directors then in office, including those who have so resigned, shall have power to fill such vacancy or vacancies, the vote thereon to take effect when such resignation or resignations shall become effective, and each director so chosen shall hold office as provided in this section in the filling of other vacancies.

§224. Form of Records

Any records administered by or on behalf of the corporation in the regular course of its business, including its stock ledger, books of account, and minute books, may be kept on, or by means of, or be in the form of, any information storage device, method, or 1 or more electronic networks or databases (including 1 or more distributed electronic networks or databases), provided that the records so kept can be converted into clearly legible paper form within a reasonable time, and, with respect to the stock ledger, that the records so kept (i) can be used to prepare the list of stockholders specified in §§219 and 220 of this title, (ii) record the information specified in §§156, 159, 217(a) and 218 of this title, and (iii) record transfers of stock as governed by Article 8 of subtitle I of Title 6. Any corporation shall convert any records so kept into clearly legible paper form upon the request of any person entitled to inspect such records pursuant to any provision of this chapter. When records are kept in such manner, a clearly legible paper form prepared from or by means of the information storage device, method, or 1 or more electronic networks or databases (including 1 or more distributed electronic networks or databases) shall be valid and admissible in evidence, and accepted for all other purposes, to the same extent as an original paper record of the same information would have been, provided the paper form accurately portrays the record.

§225. Contested Election of Directors; Proceedings to Determine Validity

(a) Upon application of any stockholder or director, or any officer whose title to office is contested, the Court of Chancery may hear and determine the validity of any election, appointment, removal or resignation of any director or officer of any corporation, and the right of any person to hold or continue to hold such office, and, in case any such office is claimed by more than 1 person, may determine the person entitled thereto; and to that end make such order or decree in any such case as may be just and proper, with power to enforce the production of any books, papers and records of the corporation relating to the issue. In case it should be determined that no valid election has been held, the Court of Chancery may order an election to be held in accordance with §211 or §215 of this title. In any such application, service of copies of the application upon the registered agent of the corporation shall be deemed to be service upon the corporation and upon the person whose title to office is contested and upon the person, if any, claiming such office; and the registered agent shall forward immediately a copy of the application to the corporation and to the person whose title to office is contested and to the person, if any, claiming such office, in a postpaid, sealed, registered letter addressed to such corporation and such person at their post-office addresses last known to the registered agent or furnished to the registered agent by the applicant stockholder. The Court may make such order respecting further or other notice of such application as it deems proper under the circumstances.

(b) Upon application of any stockholder or upon application of the corporation itself, the Court of Chancery may hear and determine the result of any vote of stockholders upon matters other than the election of directors or officers. Service of the application upon the registered agent of the corporation shall be deemed to be service upon the corporation, and no other party need be joined in order for the Court to adjudicate the result of the vote. The Court may make such order respecting notice of the application as it deems proper under the circumstances.

(c) If 1 or more directors has been convicted of a felony in connection with the duties of such director or directors to the corporation, or if there has been a prior judgment on the merits by a court of competent jurisdiction that 1 or more directors has committed a breach of the duty of loyalty in connection with the duties of such director or directors to that corporation, then, upon application by the corporation, or derivatively in the right of the corporation by any stockholder, in a subsequent action brought for such purpose, the Court of Chancery may remove from office such director or directors if the Court determines that the director or directors did not act in good faith in performing the acts resulting in the prior conviction or judgment and judicial removal is necessary to avoid irreparable harm to the corporation. In connection with such removal, the Court may make such orders as are necessary to effect such removal. In any such application, service of copies of the application upon the registered agent of the corporation shall be deemed to be service upon the corporation and upon the director or directors whose removal is sought; and the registered agent shall forward immediately a copy of the application to the corporation and to such director or directors, in a postpaid, sealed, registered letter addressed to such corporation and such director or directors at their post office addresses last known to the registered agent or furnished to the registered agent by the applicant. The Court may make such order respecting further or other notice of such application as it deems proper under the circumstances.

§226. *Appointment of Custodian or Receiver of Corporation on Deadlock or for Other Cause*

(a) The Court of Chancery, upon application of any stockholder, may appoint 1 or more persons to be custodians, and, if the corporation is insolvent, to be receivers, of and for any corporation when:

(1) At any meeting held for the election of directors the stockholders are so divided that they have failed to elect successors to directors whose terms have expired or would have expired upon qualification of their successors; or

(2) The business of the corporation is suffering or is threatened with irreparable injury because the directors are so divided respecting the management of the affairs of the corporation that the required vote for action by the board of directors cannot be obtained and the stockholders are unable to terminate this division; or

(3) The corporation has abandoned its business and has failed within a reasonable time to take steps to dissolve, liquidate or distribute its assets.

(b) A custodian appointed under this section shall have all the powers and title of a receiver appointed under §291 of this title, but the authority of the custodian is to continue the business of the corporation and not to liquidate its affairs and distribute its assets, except when the Court shall otherwise order and except in cases arising under (a)(3) of this section or §352(a)(2) of this title.

(c) In the case of a charitable nonstock corporation, the applicant shall provide a copy of any application referred to in subsection (a) of this section to the Attorney General of the State of Delaware within 1 week of its filing with the Court of Chancery.

§227. *Powers of Court in Elections of Directors*

(a) The Court of Chancery, in any proceeding instituted under §211, 215 or 225 of this title may determine the right and power of persons claiming to own stock to vote at any meeting of the stockholders.

(b) The Court of Chancery may appoint a Master to hold any election provided for in §211, 215 or 225 of this title under such orders and powers as it deems proper; and it may punish any officer or director for contempt in case of disobedience of any order made by the Court; and, in case of disobedience by a corporation of any order made by the Court, may enter a decree against such corporation for a penalty of not more than $5,000.

§228. *Consent of Stockholders or Members in Lieu of Meeting*

(a) Unless otherwise provided in the certificate of incorporation, any action required by this chapter to be taken at any annual or special meeting of stockholders of a corporation, or any action which may be taken at any annual or special meeting of such stockholders, may be taken without a meeting, without prior notice and without a vote, if a consent or consents, setting forth the action so taken, shall be signed by the holders of outstanding stock having not less than the minimum number of votes that would be necessary to authorize or take such action at a meeting at which all shares entitled to vote thereon were present and voted and shall be delivered to the corporation in the manner required by this section.

(b) Unless otherwise provided in the certificate of incorporation, any action required by this chapter to be taken at a meeting of the members of a nonstock corporation, or any action which may be taken at any meeting of the members of a nonstock corporation, may be taken without a meeting, without prior notice and without a vote, if a consent or consents, setting forth the action so taken, shall be signed by members having not less than the minimum number of votes that would be necessary to authorize or take such action at a meeting at which all members having a right to vote thereon were present and voted and shall be delivered to the corporation in the manner required by this section.

(c) Unless the bylaws otherwise require, when a meeting is adjourned to another time or place, (including an adjournment taken to address a technical failure to convene or continue a meeting using remote communication), notice need not be given of the adjourned meeting if the time, place, if any, thereof, and the means of remote communications, if any, by which stockholders and proxy holders may be deemed to be present in person and vote at such adjourned meeting are (i) announced at the meeting at which the adjournment is taken, (ii) displayed, during the time scheduled for the meeting, on the same electronic network used to enable stockholders and proxy holders to participate in the meeting by means of remote communication or (iii) set forth in the notice of meeting given in accordance with subsection (a) of this section. At the adjourned meeting the corporation may transact any business which might have been transacted at the original meeting. If the adjournment is for more than 30 days, a notice of the adjourned meeting shall be given to each stockholder of record entitled to vote at the meeting. If after the adjournment a new record date for stockholders entitled to vote is fixed for the adjourned meeting, the board of directors shall fix a new record date for notice of such adjourned meeting in accordance with §213(a) of this title, and shall give notice of the adjourned meeting to each stockholder of record entitled to vote at such adjourned meeting as of the record date fixed for notice of such adjourned meeting.

(d)(1) A consent permitted by this section shall be delivered: (i) to the principal place of business of the corporation; (ii) to an officer or agent of the corporation having custody of the book in which proceedings of meetings of stockholders or members are recorded; (iii) to the registered office of the corporation in this State by hand or by certified or registered mail, return receipt requested; or (iv) subject to the next sentence, in accordance with §116 of this title to an information processing system, if any, designated by the corporation for receiving such consents. In the case of delivery pursuant to the foregoing clause (iv), such consent must set forth or be delivered with information that enables the corporation to determine the date of delivery of such consent and the identity of the person giving such consent, and, if such consent is given by a person authorized to act for a stockholder or member as proxy, such consent must comply with the applicable provisions of §212(c)(2) and (3) of this title.

(2) Any copy, facsimile or other reliable reproduction of a consent in writing may be substituted or used in lieu of the original writing for any and all purposes for which the original writing could be used, provided that such copy, facsimile or other reproduction shall be a complete reproduction of the entire original

writing. A consent may be documented and signed in accordance with §116 of this title, and when so documented or signed shall be deemed to be in writing for purposes of this title; provided that if such consent is delivered pursuant to clause (i), (ii) or (iii) of paragraph (d)(1) of this section, such consent must be reproduced and delivered in paper form.

(e) Prompt notice of the taking of the corporate action without a meeting by less than unanimous consent shall be given to those stockholders or members who have not consented and who, if the action had been taken at a meeting, would have been entitled to notice of the meeting if the record date for notice of such meeting had been the date that consents signed by a sufficient number of holders or members to take the action were delivered to the corporation as provided in this section. In the event that the action which is consented to is such as would have required the filing of a certificate under any other section of this title, if such action had been voted on by stockholders or by members at a meeting thereof, the certificate filed under such other section shall state, in lieu of any statement required by such section concerning any vote of stockholders or members, that consent has been given in accordance with this section.

§229. Waiver of Notice

Whenever notice is required to be given under any provision of this chapter or the certificate of incorporation or bylaws, a written waiver, signed by the person entitled to notice, or a waiver by electronic transmission by the person entitled to notice, whether before or after the time stated therein, shall be deemed equivalent to notice. Attendance of a person at a meeting shall constitute a waiver of notice of such meeting, except when the person attends a meeting for the express purpose of objecting at the beginning of the meeting, to the transaction of any business because the meeting is not lawfully called or convened. Neither the business to be transacted at, nor the purpose of, any regular or special meeting of the stockholders, directors or members of a committee of directors need be specified in any written waiver of notice or any waiver by electronic transmission unless so required by the certificate of incorporation or the bylaws.

§230. Exception to Requirements of Notice

(a) Whenever notice is required to be given, under any provision of this chapter or of the certificate of incorporation or bylaws of any corporation, to any person with whom communication is unlawful, the giving of such notice to such person shall not be required and there shall be no duty to apply to any governmental authority or agency for a license or permit to give such notice to such person. Any action or meeting which shall be taken or held without notice to any such person with whom communication is unlawful shall have the same force and effect as if such notice had been duly given. In the event that the action taken by the corporation is such as to require the filing of a certificate under any of the other sections of this title, the certificate shall state, if such is the fact and if notice is required, that notice was given to all persons entitled to receive notice except such persons with whom communication is unlawful.

(b) Whenever notice is required to be given, under any provision of this title or the certificate of incorporation or bylaws of any corporation, to any stockholder or, if the corporation is a nonstock corporation, to any member, to whom (1) notice of 2 consecutive annual meetings, and all notices of meetings or of the taking of action by written consent without a meeting to such person during the period between such 2 consecutive annual meetings, or (2) all, and at least 2, payments (if sent by first-class mail) of dividends or interest on securities during a 12-month period, have been mailed addressed to such person at such person's address as shown on the records of the corporation and have been returned undeliverable, the giving of such notice to such person shall not be required. Any action or meeting which shall be taken or held without notice to such person shall have the same force and effect as if such notice had been duly given. If any such person shall deliver to the corporation a written notice setting forth such person's then current address, the requirement that notice be given to such person shall be reinstated. In the event that the action taken by the corporation is such as to require the filing of a certificate under any of the other sections of this title, the certificate need not state that notice was not given to persons to whom notice was not required to be given pursuant to this subsection.

(c) The exception in paragraph (b)(1) of this section to the requirement that notice be given shall not be applicable to any notice returned as undeliverable if the notice was given by electronic transmission. The exception in paragraph (b)(1) of this section to the requirement that notice be given shall not be applicable to any stockholder or member whose electronic mail address appears on the records of the corporation and to whom notice by electronic transmission is not prohibited by §232 of this title.

§231. Voting Procedures and Inspectors of Elections

(a) The corporation shall, in advance of any meeting of stockholders, appoint 1 or more inspectors to act at the meeting and make a written report thereof. The corporation may designate 1 or more persons as alternate inspectors to replace any inspector who fails to act. If no inspector or alternate is able to act at a meeting of stockholders, the person presiding at the meeting shall appoint 1 or more inspectors to act at the meeting. Each inspector, before entering upon the discharge of the duties of inspector, shall take and sign an oath faithfully to execute the duties of inspector with strict impartiality and according to the best of such inspector's ability.

(b) The inspectors shall:

(1) Ascertain the number of shares outstanding and the voting power of each;

(2) Determine the shares represented at a meeting and the validity of proxies and ballots;

(3) Count all votes and ballots;

(4) Determine and retain for a reasonable period a record of the disposition of any challenges made to any determination by the inspectors; and

(5) Certify their determination of the number of shares represented at the meeting, and their count of all votes and ballots.

The inspectors may appoint or retain other persons or entities to assist the inspectors in the performance of the duties of the inspectors.

(c) The date and time of the opening and the closing of the polls for each matter upon which the stockholders will vote at a meeting shall be announced at the meeting. No ballot, proxies or votes, nor any revocations thereof or changes thereto, shall be accepted by the inspectors after the closing of the polls unless the Court of Chancery upon application by a stockholder shall determine otherwise.

(d) In determining the validity and counting of proxies and ballots, the inspectors shall be limited to an examination of the proxies, any envelopes submitted with those proxies, any information provided in accordance with §211(e) or §212(c)(2) of this title, or any information provided pursuant to §211(a)(2)b.(i) or (iii) of this title, ballots and the regular books and records of the corporation, except that the inspectors may consider other reliable information for the limited purpose of reconciling proxies and ballots submitted by or on behalf of banks, brokers, their nominees or similar persons which represent more votes than the holder of a proxy is authorized by the record owner to cast or more votes than the stockholder holds of record. If the inspectors consider other reliable information for the limited purpose permitted herein, the inspectors at the time they make their certification pursuant to paragraph (b)(5) of this section shall specify the precise information considered by them including the person or persons from whom they obtained the information, when the information was obtained, the means by which the information was obtained and the basis for the inspectors' belief that such information is accurate and reliable.

(e) Unless otherwise provided in the certificate of incorporation or bylaws, this section shall not apply to a corporation that does not have a class of voting stock that is:

(1) Listed on a national securities exchange;

(2) Authorized for quotation on an interdealer quotation system of a registered national securities association; or

(3) Held of record by more than 2,000 stockholders.

§232. Delivery of notice; notice by electronic transmission

(a) Without limiting the manner by which notice otherwise may be given effectively to stockholders, any notice to stockholders given by the corporation under any provision of this chapter, the certificate of incorporation, or the bylaws may be given in writing directed to the stockholder's mailing address (or by electronic transmission directed to the stockholder's electronic mail address, as applicable) as it appears on the records of the corporation and shall be given:

(1) If mailed, when the notice is deposited in the U.S. mail, postage prepaid;

(2) If delivered by courier service, the earlier of when the notice is received or left at such stockholder's address; or

(3) If given by electronic mail, when directed to such stockholder's electronic mail address unless the stockholder has notified the corporation in writing or by electronic transmission of an objection to receiving notice by electronic mail or such notice is prohibited by subsection (e) of this section.

A notice by electronic mail must include a prominent legend that the communication is an important notice regarding the corporation.

(b) Without limiting the manner by which notice otherwise may be given effectively to stockholders, but subject to subsection (e) of this section, any notice to stockholders given by the corporation under any provision of this chapter, the certificate of incorporation, or the bylaws shall be effective if given by a form of electronic transmission consented to by the stockholder to whom the notice is given. Any such consent shall be revocable by the stockholder by written notice or electronic transmission to the corporation. A corporation may give a notice by electronic mail in accordance with subsection (a) of this section without obtaining the consent required by this subsection.

(c) Notice given pursuant to subsection (b) of this section shall be deemed given:

(1) If by facsimile telecommunication, when directed to a number at which the stockholder has consented to receive notice;

(2) If by a posting on an electronic network together with separate notice to the stockholder of such specific posting, upon the later of:

a. Such posting; and

b. The giving of such separate notice; and

(3) If by any other form of electronic transmission, when directed to the stockholder.

(d) For purposes of this chapter:

(1) "Electronic transmission" means any form of communication, not directly involving the physical transmission of paper, including the use of, or participation in, 1 or more electronic networks or databases (including 1 or more distributed electronic networks or databases), that creates a record that may be retained, retrieved and reviewed by a recipient thereof, and that may be directly reproduced in paper form by such a recipient through an automated process;

(2) "Electronic mail" means an electronic transmission directed to a unique electronic mail address (which electronic mail shall be deemed to include any files attached thereto and any information hyperlinked to a website if such electronic mail includes the contact information of an officer or agent of the corporation who is available to assist with accessing such files and information); and

(3) "Electronic mail address" means a destination, commonly expressed as a string of characters, consisting of a unique user name or mailbox (commonly referred to as the "local part" of the address) and a reference to an internet domain (commonly referred to as the "domain part" of the address), whether or not displayed, to which electronic mail can be sent or delivered.

(e) Notwithstanding the foregoing, a notice may not be given by an electronic transmission from and after the time that:

(1) The corporation is unable to deliver by such electronic transmission 2 consecutive notices given by the corporation; and

(2) Such inability becomes known to the secretary or an assistant secretary of the corporation or to the transfer agent, or other person responsible for the giving of notice, provided, however, the inadvertent failure to discover such inability shall not invalidate any meeting or other action.

(f) An affidavit of the secretary or an assistant secretary or of the transfer agent or other agent of the corporation that notice has been given shall, in the absence of fraud, be prima facie evidence of the facts stated therein.

(g) No provision of this section, except for paragraphs (a)(1), (d)(2) and (d)(3) of this section, shall apply to §164, §296, §311, §312, or §324 of this title.

SUBCHAPTER VIII. AMENDMENT OF CERTIFICATE OF INCORPORATION; CHANGES IN CAPITAL AND CAPITAL STOCK

§241. *Amendment of Certificate of Incorporation before Receipt of Payment for Stock*

(a) Before a corporation has received any payment for any of its stock, it may amend its certificate of incorporation at any time or times, in any and as many respects as may be desired, so long as its certificate of incorporation as amended would contain only such provisions as it would be lawful and proper to insert in an original certificate of incorporation filed at the time of filing the amendment.

(b) The amendment of a certificate of incorporation authorized by this section shall be adopted by a majority of the incorporators, if directors were not named in the original certificate of incorporation or have not yet been elected, or, if directors were named in the original certificate of incorporation or have been elected and have qualified, by a majority of the directors. A certificate setting forth the amendment and certifying that the corporation has not received any payment for any of its stock, or that the corporation has no members, as applicable, and that the amendment has been duly adopted in accordance with this section shall be executed, acknowledged and filed in accordance with §103 of this title. Upon such filing, the corporation's certificate of incorporation shall be deemed to be amended accordingly as of the date on which the original certificate of incorporation became effective, except as to those persons who are substantially and adversely affected by the amendment and as to those persons the amendment shall be effective from the filing date.

(c) This section will apply to a nonstock corporation before such a corporation has any members; provided, however, that all references to directors shall be deemed to be references to members of the governing body of the corporation.

§242. *Amendment of Certificate of Incorporation after Receipt of Payment for Stock; Nonstock Corporations*

(a) After a corporation has received payment for any of its capital stock, or after a nonstock corporation has members, it may amend its certificate of incorporation, from time to time, in any and as many respects as may be desired, so long as its certificate of incorporation as amended would contain only such provisions as it would be lawful and proper to insert in an original certificate of incorporation filed at the time of the filing of the amendment; and, if a change in stock or the rights of stockholders, or an exchange, reclassification, subdivision, combination or cancellation of stock or rights of stockholders is to be made, such provisions as may be necessary to effect such change, exchange, reclassification, subdivision, combination or cancellation. In particular, and without limitation upon such general power of amendment, a corporation may amend its certificate of incorporation, from time to time, so as:

(1) To change its corporate name; or

(2) To change, substitute, enlarge or diminish the nature of its business or its corporate powers and purposes; or

(3) To increase or decrease its authorized capital stock or to reclassify the same, by changing the number, par value, designations, preferences, or relative, participating, optional, or other special rights of the shares, or the qualifications, limitations or restrictions of such rights, or by changing shares with par value into shares without par value, or shares without par value into shares with par value either with or without increasing or decreasing the number of shares, or by subdividing or combining the outstanding shares of any class or series of a class of shares into a greater or lesser number of outstanding shares; or

(4) To cancel or otherwise affect the right of the holders of the shares of any class to receive dividends which have accrued but have not been declared; or

(5) To create new classes of stock having rights and preferences either prior and superior or subordinate and inferior to the stock of any class then authorized, whether issued or unissued; or

(6) To change the period of its duration; or

(7) To delete:

a. Such provisions of the original certificate of incorporation which named the incorporator or incorporators, the initial board of directors and the original subscribers for shares; and

b. Such provisions contained in any amendment to the certificate of incorporation as were necessary to effect a change, exchange, reclassification, subdivision, combination or cancellation of stock, if such change, exchange, reclassification, subdivision, combination or cancellation has become effective.

Any or all such changes or alterations may be effected by 1 certificate of amendment.

(b) Every amendment authorized by subsection (a) of this section shall be made and effected in the following manner:

(1) If the corporation has capital stock, its board of directors shall adopt a resolution setting forth the amendment proposed, declaring its advisability, and either calling a special meeting of the stockholders entitled to vote in respect thereof for the consideration of such amendment or directing that the amendment proposed be considered at the next annual meeting of the stockholders; provided, however, that unless otherwise expressly required by the certificate of incorporation, no meeting or vote of stockholders shall be required to adopt an amendment that effects only changes described in paragraph (a)(1) or (7) of this section. Such special or annual meeting shall be called and held upon notice in accordance with §222 of this title. The notice shall set forth such amendment in full or a brief summary of the changes to be effected thereby unless such notice constitutes a notice of internet availability of proxy materials under the rules promulgated under the Securities Exchange Act of 1934. At the meeting a vote of the stockholders entitled to vote thereon shall be taken for and against any proposed amendment that requires adoption by stockholders. If no vote of stockholders is required to effect such amendment, or if a majority of the outstanding stock entitled to vote thereon, and a majority of the outstanding stock of each class entitled to vote thereon as a class has been voted in favor of the amendment, a certificate setting forth the amendment and certifying that such amendment has been duly adopted in accordance with this section shall be executed,

acknowledged and filed and shall become effective in accordance with §103 of this title.

(2) The holders of the outstanding shares of a class shall be entitled to vote as a class upon a proposed amendment, whether or not entitled to vote thereon by the certificate of incorporation, if the amendment would increase or decrease the aggregate number of authorized shares of such class, increase or decrease the par value of the shares of such class, or alter or change the powers, preferences, or special rights of the shares of such class so as to affect them adversely. If any proposed amendment would alter or change the powers, preferences, or special rights of 1 or more series of any class so as to affect them adversely, but shall not so affect the entire class, then only the shares of the series so affected by the amendment shall be considered a separate class for the purposes of this paragraph. The number of authorized shares of any such class or classes of stock may be increased or decreased (but not below the number of shares thereof then outstanding) by the affirmative vote of the holders of a majority of the stock of the corporation entitled to vote irrespective of this subsection, if so provided in the original certificate of incorporation, in any amendment thereto which created such class or classes of stock or which was adopted prior to the issuance of any shares of such class or classes of stock, or in any amendment thereto which was authorized by a resolution or resolutions adopted by the affirmative vote of the holders of a majority of such class or classes of stock.

(3) If the corporation is a nonstock corporation, then the governing body thereof shall adopt a resolution setting forth the amendment proposed and declaring its advisability. If a majority of all the members of the governing body shall vote in favor of such amendment, a certificate thereof shall be executed, acknowledged and filed and shall become effective in accordance with §103 of this title. The certificate of incorporation of any nonstock corporation may contain a provision requiring any amendment thereto to be approved by a specified number or percentage of the members or of any specified class of members of such corporation in which event such proposed amendment shall be submitted to the members or to any specified class of members of such corporation in the same manner, so far as applicable, as is provided in this section for an amendment to the certificate of incorporation of a stock corporation; and in the event of the adoption thereof by such members, a certificate evidencing such amendment shall be executed, acknowledged and filed and shall become effective in accordance with §103 of this title.

(4) Whenever the certificate of incorporation shall require for action by the board of directors of a corporation other than a nonstock corporation or by the governing body of a nonstock corporation, by the holders of any class or series of shares or by the members, or by the holders of any other securities having voting power the vote of a greater number or proportion than is required by any section of this title, the provision of the certificate of incorporation requiring such greater vote shall not be altered, amended or repealed except by such greater vote.

(c) The resolution authorizing a proposed amendment to the certificate of incorporation may provide that at any time prior to the effectiveness of the filing of the amendment with the Secretary of State, notwithstanding authorization of the proposed amendment by the stockholders of the corporation or by the members of a nonstock corporation, the board of directors or governing body may abandon such proposed amendment without further action by the stockholders or members.

§243. *Retirement of Stock*

(a) A corporation, by resolution of its board of directors, may retire any shares of its capital stock that are issued but are not outstanding.

(b) Whenever any shares of the capital stock of a corporation are retired, they shall resume the status of authorized and unissued shares of the class or series to which they belong unless the certificate of incorporation otherwise provides. If the certificate of incorporation prohibits the reissuance of such shares, or prohibits the reissuance of such shares as a part of a specific series only, a certificate stating that reissuance of the shares (as part of the class or series) is prohibited identifying the shares and reciting their retirement shall be executed, acknowledged and filed and shall become effective in accordance with §103 of this title. When such certificate becomes effective, it shall have the effect of amending the certificate of incorporation so as to reduce accordingly the number of authorized shares of the class or series to which such shares belong or, if such retired shares constitute all of the authorized shares of the class or series to which they belong, of eliminating from the certificate of incorporation all reference to such class or series of stock.

(c) If the capital of the corporation will be reduced by or in connection with the retirement of shares, the reduction of capital shall be effected pursuant to §244 of this title.

§244. *Reduction of Capital*

(a) A corporation, by resolution of its board of directors, may reduce its capital in any of the following ways:

(1) By reducing or eliminating the capital represented by shares of capital stock which have been retired;

(2) By applying to an otherwise authorized purchase or redemption of outstanding shares of its capital stock some or all of the capital represented by the shares being purchased or redeemed, or any capital that has not been allocated to any particular class of its capital stock;

(3) By applying to an otherwise authorized conversion or exchange of outstanding shares of its capital stock some or all of the capital represented by the shares being converted or exchanged, or some or all of any capital that has not been allocated to any particular class of its capital stock, or both, to the extent that such capital in the aggregate exceeds the total aggregate par value or the stated capital of any previously unissued shares issuable upon such conversion or exchange; or

(4) By transferring to surplus (i) some or all of the capital not represented by any particular class of its capital stock; (ii) some or all of the capital represented by issued shares of its par value capital stock, which capital is in excess of

the aggregate par value of such shares; or (iii) some of the capital represented by issued shares of its capital stock without par value.

(b) Notwithstanding the other provisions of this section, no reduction of capital shall be made or effected unless the assets of the corporation remaining after such reduction shall be sufficient to pay any debts of the corporation for which payment has not been otherwise provided. No reduction of capital shall release any liability of any stockholder whose shares have not been fully paid.

(c) [Repealed.]

SUBCHAPTER IX. MERGER, CONSOLIDATION OR CONVERSION

§251. Merger or Consolidation of Domestic Corporations

(a) Any 2 or more corporations of this State may merge into a single surviving corporation, which may be any 1 of the constituent corporations or may consolidate into a new resulting corporation formed by the consolidation, pursuant to an agreement of merger or consolidation, as the case may be, complying and approved in accordance with this section.

(b) The board of directors of each corporation which desires to merge or consolidate shall adopt a resolution approving an agreement of merger or consolidation and declaring its advisability. The agreement shall state:

(1) The terms and conditions of the merger or consolidation;

(2) The mode of carrying the same into effect;

(3) In the case of a merger, such amendments or changes in the certificate of incorporation of the surviving corporation as are desired to be effected by the merger (which amendments or changes may amend and restate the certificate of incorporation of the surviving corporation in its entirety), or, if no such amendments or changes are desired, a statement that the certificate of incorporation of the surviving corporation shall be its certificate of incorporation;

(4) In the case of a consolidation, that the certificate of incorporation of the resulting corporation shall be as is set forth in an attachment to the agreement;

(5) The manner, if any, of converting the shares of each of the constituent corporations into shares or other securities of the corporation surviving or resulting from the merger or consolidation, or of cancelling some or all of such shares, and, if any shares of any of the constituent corporations are not to remain outstanding, to be converted solely into shares or other securities of the surviving or resulting corporation or to be cancelled, the cash, property, rights or securities of any other corporation or entity which the holders of such shares are to receive in exchange for, or upon conversion of such shares and the surrender of any certificates evidencing them, which cash, property, rights or securities of any other corporation or entity may be in addition to or in lieu of shares or other securities of the surviving or resulting corporation; and

(6) Such other details or provisions as are deemed desirable, including, without limiting the generality of the foregoing, a provision for the payment of cash in lieu of the issuance or recognition of fractional shares, rights or other securities of the surviving or resulting corporation or of any other corporation

or entity the shares, rights or other securities of which are to be received in the merger or consolidation, or for any other arrangement with respect thereto, consistent with §155 of this title.

The agreement so adopted shall be executed by an authorized person, provided that if the agreement is filed, it shall be executed and acknowledged in accordance with §103 of this title. Any of the terms of the agreement of merger or consolidation may be made dependent upon facts ascertainable outside of such agreement, provided that the manner in which such facts shall operate upon the terms of the agreement is clearly and expressly set forth in the agreement of merger or consolidation. The term "facts," as used in the preceding sentence, includes, but is not limited to, the occurrence of any event, including a determination or action by any person or body, including the corporation.

(c) The agreement required by subsection (b) of this section shall be submitted to the stockholders of each constituent corporation at an annual or special meeting for the purpose of acting on the agreement. Due notice of the time, place and purpose of the meeting shall be given to each holder of stock, whether voting or nonvoting, of the corporation at the stockholder's address as it appears on the records of the corporation, at least 20 days prior to the date of the meeting. The notice shall contain a copy of the agreement or a brief summary thereof. At the meeting, the agreement shall be considered and a vote taken for its adoption or rejection. If a majority of the outstanding stock of the corporation entitled to vote thereon shall be voted for the adoption of the agreement, that fact shall be certified on the agreement by the secretary or assistant secretary of the corporation, provided that such certification on the agreement shall not be required if a certificate of merger or consolidation is filed in lieu of filing the agreement. If the agreement shall be so adopted and certified by each constituent corporation, it shall then be filed and shall become effective, in accordance with §103 of this title. In lieu of filing the agreement of merger or consolidation required by this section, the surviving or resulting corporation may file a certificate of merger or consolidation, executed in accordance with §103 of this title, which states:

(1) The name and state of incorporation of each of the constituent corporations;

(2) That an agreement of merger or consolidation has been approved, adopted, executed and acknowledged by each of the constituent corporations in accordance with this section;

(3) The name of the surviving or resulting corporation;

(4) In the case of a merger, such amendments or changes in the certificate of incorporation of the surviving corporation as are desired to be effected by the merger (which amendments or changes may amend and restate the certificate of incorporation of the surviving corporation in its entirety), or, if no such amendments or changes are desired, a statement that the certificate of incorporation of the surviving corporation shall be its certificate of incorporation;

(5) In the case of a consolidation, that the certificate of incorporation of the resulting corporation shall be as set forth in an attachment to the certificate;

(6) That the executed agreement of consolidation or merger is on file at an office of the surviving or resulting corporation, stating the address thereof; and

(7) That a copy of the agreement of consolidation or merger will be furnished by the surviving or resulting corporation, on request and without cost, to any stockholder of any constituent corporation.

(d) Any agreement of merger or consolidation may contain a provision that at any time prior to the time that the agreement (or a certificate in lieu thereof) filed with the Secretary of State becomes effective in accordance with §103 of this title, the agreement may be terminated by the board of directors of any constituent corporation notwithstanding approval of the agreement by the stockholders of all or any of the constituent corporations; in the event the agreement of merger or consolidation is terminated after the filing of the agreement (or a certificate in lieu thereof) with the Secretary of State but before the agreement (or a certificate in lieu thereof) has become effective, a certificate of termination or merger or consolidation shall be filed in accordance with §103 of this title. Any agreement of merger or consolidation may contain a provision that the boards of directors of the constituent corporations may amend the agreement at any time prior to the time that the agreement (or a certificate in lieu thereof) filed with the Secretary of State becomes effective in accordance with §103 of this title, provided that an amendment made subsequent to the adoption of the agreement by the stockholders of any constituent corporation shall not (1) alter or change the amount or kind of shares, securities, cash, property and/or rights to be received in exchange for or on conversion of all or any of the shares of any class or series thereof of such constituent corporation, (2) alter or change any term of the certificate of incorporation of the surviving corporation to be effected by the merger or consolidation, or (3) alter or change any of the terms and conditions of the agreement if such alteration or change would adversely affect the holders of any class or series thereof of such constituent corporation; in the event the agreement of merger or consolidation is amended after the filing thereof with the Secretary of State but before the agreement has become effective, a certificate of amendment of merger or consolidation shall be filed in accordance with §103 of this title.

(e) In the case of a merger, the certificate of incorporation of the surviving corporation shall automatically be amended to the extent, if any, that changes in the certificate of incorporation are set forth in the agreement of merger.

(f) Notwithstanding the requirements of subsection (c) of this section, unless required by its certificate of incorporation, no vote of stockholders of a constituent corporation surviving a merger shall be necessary to authorize a merger if (1) the agreement of merger does not amend in any respect the certificate of incorporation of such constituent corporation, (2) each share of stock of such constituent corporation outstanding immediately prior to the effective date of the merger is to be an identical outstanding or treasury share of the surviving corporation after the effective date of the merger, and (3) either no shares of common stock of the surviving corporation and no shares, securities or obligations convertible into such stock are to be issued or delivered under the plan of merger, or the authorized unissued shares or the treasury shares of common stock of the surviving corporation to be issued or delivered under the plan of merger plus those initially issuable upon conversion of any other shares, securities or obligations to be issued or delivered under such plan do not exceed 20% of the shares of common stock of such constituent corporation outstanding immediately prior to the effective date of the merger. No vote of stockholders of a constituent corporation shall be necessary to authorize a merger or consolidation if no shares of the stock of such corporation shall have been issued prior to the adoption by the board of directors of the resolution approving the agreement of merger or consolidation. If an agreement of merger is adopted by the constituent corporation surviving the merger, by action of its board of directors and without any vote of its stockholders pursuant to this subsection, the secretary or assistant secretary of that corporation shall certify on the agreement that the agreement has been adopted pursuant to this subsection and, (1) if it has been adopted pursuant to the first sentence of this subsection, that the conditions specified in that sentence have been satisfied, or (2) if it has been adopted pursuant to the second sentence of this subsection, that no shares of stock of such corporation were issued prior to the adoption by the board of directors of the resolution approving the agreement of merger or consolidation, provided that such certification on the agreement shall not be required if a certificate of merger or consolidation is filed in lieu of filing the agreement. The agreement so adopted and certified shall then be filed and shall become effective, in accordance with §103 of this title. Such filing shall constitute a representation by the person who executes the agreement that the facts stated in the certificate remain true immediately prior to such filing.

(g) Notwithstanding the requirements of subsection (c) of this section, unless expressly required by its certificate of incorporation, no vote of stockholders of a constituent corporation shall be necessary to authorize a merger with or into a single direct or indirect wholly-owned subsidiary of such constituent corporation if:

(1) Such constituent corporation and the direct or indirect wholly-owned subsidiary of such constituent corporation are the only constituent entities to the merger;

(2) Each share or fraction of a share of the capital stock of the constituent corporation outstanding immediately prior to the effective time of the merger is converted in the merger into a share or equal fraction of share of capital stock of a holding company having the same designations, rights, powers and preferences, and the qualifications, limitations and restrictions thereof, as the share of stock of the constituent corporation being converted in the merger;

(3) The holding company and the constituent corporation are corporations of this State and the direct or indirect wholly-owned subsidiary that is the other constituent entity to the merger is a corporation or limited liability company of this State;

(4) The certificate of incorporation and bylaws of the holding company immediately following the effective time of the merger contain provisions identical to the certificate of incorporation and bylaws of the constituent corporation immediately prior to the effective time of the merger (other than provisions, if any, regarding the incorporator or incorporators, the corporate name, the registered office and agent, the initial board of directors and the initial subscribers for shares and such provisions contained in any amendment to the certificate of incorporation as were necessary to effect a change, exchange, reclassification, subdivision, combination or cancellation of stock, if such change, exchange, reclassification, subdivision, combination, or cancellation has become effective);

(5) As a result of the merger, the constituent corporation or its successor becomes or remains a direct or indirect wholly-owned subsidiary of the holding company;

(6) The directors of the constituent corporation become or remain the directors of the holding company upon the effective time of the merger;

(7) The organizational documents of the surviving entity immediately following the effective time of the merger contain provisions requiring that (A) any act or transaction by or involving the surviving entity, other than the election or removal of directors or managers, managing members or other members of the governing body of the surviving entity, that, if taken by the constituent corporation immediately prior to the effective time of the merger, would require, for its adoption under this chapter or under the certificate of incorporation or bylaws of the constituent corporation immediately prior to the effective time of the merger, the approval of the stockholders of the constituent corporation, shall, by specific reference to this subsection, require, in addition to approval of the stockholders or members of the surviving entity, the approval of the stockholders of the holding company (or any successor by merger), by the same vote as is required by this chapter and/or by the certificate of incorporation or bylaws of the constituent corporation immediately prior to the effective time of the merger; provided, however, that for purposes of this paragraph (g)(7)(A), any amendment of the organizational documents of a surviving entity that is not a corporation, which amendment would, if adopted by a corporation subject to this chapter, be required to be included in the certificate of incorporation of such corporation, shall, by specific reference to this subsection, require, in addition, the approval of the stockholders of the holding company (or any successor by merger), by the same vote as is required by this chapter and/or by the certificate of incorporation or bylaws of the constituent corporation immediately prior to the effective time of the merger; and (B) the business and affairs of a surviving entity that is not a corporation shall be managed by or under the direction of a board of directors, board of managers or other governing body consisting of individuals who are subject to the same fiduciary duties applicable to, and who are liable for breach of such duties to the same extent as, directors of a corporation subject to this chapter; and

(8) The stockholders of the constituent corporation do not recognize gain or loss for United States federal income tax purposes as determined by the board of directors of the constituent corporation. Neither paragraph (g)(7)(A) and (B) of this section nor any provision of a surviving entity's organizational documents required by paragraph (g)(7)(A) and (B) of this section shall be deemed or construed to require approval of the stockholders of the holding company to elect or remove directors or managers, managing members or other members of the governing body of the surviving entity. The term "organizational documents", as used in paragraph (g)(7) of this section and in the preceding sentence, shall, when used in reference to a corporation, mean the certificate of incorporation of such corporation, and when used in reference to a limited liability company, mean the limited liability company agreement of such limited liability company.

As used in this subsection only, the term "holding company" means a corporation which, from its incorporation until consummation of a merger governed by this subsection, was at all times a direct or indirect wholly-owned subsidiary of the constituent corporation and whose capital stock is issued in such merger. From and after the effective time of a merger adopted by a constituent corporation by action of its board of directors and without any vote of stockholders pursuant to this subsection: (i) to the extent the restrictions of §203 of this title applied to the constituent corporation and its stockholders at the effective time of the merger, such restrictions shall apply to the holding company and its stockholders immediately after the effective time of the merger as though it were the constituent corporation, and all shares of stock of the holding company acquired in the merger shall for purposes of §203 of this title be deemed to have been acquired at the time that the shares of stock of the constituent corporation converted in the merger were acquired, and provided further that any stockholder who immediately prior to the effective time of the merger was not an interested stockholder within the meaning of §203 of this title shall not solely by reason of the merger become an interested stockholder of the holding company, (ii) if the corporate name of the holding company immediately following the effective time of the merger is the same as the corporate name of the constituent corporation immediately prior to the effective time of the merger, the shares of capital stock of the holding company into which the shares of capital stock of the constituent corporation are converted in the merger shall be represented by the stock certificates that previously represented shares of capital stock of the constituent corporation and (iii) to the extent a stockholder of the constituent corporation immediately prior to the merger had standing to institute or maintain derivative litigation on behalf of the constituent corporation, nothing in this section shall be deemed to limit or extinguish such standing. If an agreement of merger is adopted by a constituent corporation by action of its board of directors and without any vote of stockholders pursuant to this subsection, the secretary or assistant secretary of the constituent corporation shall certify on the agreement that the agreement has been adopted pursuant to this subsection and that the conditions specified in the first sentence of this subsection have been satisfied, provided that such certification on the agreement shall not be required if a certificate of merger or consolidation is filed in lieu of filing the agreement. The agreement so adopted and certified shall then be filed and become effective, in accordance with §103 of this title. Such filing shall constitute a representation by the person who executes the agreement that the facts stated in the certificate remain true immediately prior to such filing.

(h) Notwithstanding the requirements of subsection (c) of this section, unless expressly required by its certificate of incorporation, no vote of stockholders of a constituent corporation that has a class or series of stock that is listed on a national securities exchange or held of record by more than 2,000 holders immediately prior to the execution of the agreement of merger by such constituent corporation shall be necessary to authorize a merger if:

(1) The agreement of merger expressly:

a. Permits or requires such merger to be effected under this sub-section; and

b. Provides that such merger shall be effected as soon as practicable following the consummation of the offer referred to in paragraph (h)(2) of this section if such merger is effected under this subsection;

(2) A corporation consummates an offer for all of the outstanding stock of such constituent corporation on the terms provided in such agreement of merger that, absent this subsection, would be entitled to vote on the adoption or rejection of the agreement of merger; provided, however, that such offer may be conditioned on the tender of a minimum number or percentage of shares of the stock of such constituent corporation, or of any class or series thereof, and such offer may exclude any excluded stock and provided further that the corporation may consummate separate offers for separate classes or series of the stock of such constituent corporation;

a.-d. [Repealed.]

(3) Immediately following the consummation of the offer referred to in paragraph (h)(2) of this section, the stock irrevocably accepted for purchase or exchange pursuant to such offer and received by the depository prior to expiration of such offer, together with the stock otherwise owned by the consummating corporation or its affiliates and any rollover stock, equals at least such percentage of the shares of stock of such constituent corporation, and of each class or series thereof, that, absent this subsection, would be required to adopt the agreement of merger by this chapter and by the certificate of incorporation of such constituent corporation;

(4) The corporation consummating the offer referred to in paragraph (h)(2) of this section merges with or into such constituent corporation pursuant to such agreement; and

(5) Each outstanding share (other than shares of excluded stock) of each class or series of stock of such constituent corporation that is the subject of and is not irrevocably accepted for purchase or exchange in the offer referred to in paragraph (h)(2) of this section is to be converted in such merger into, or into the right to receive, the same amount and kind of cash, property, rights or securities to be paid for shares of such class or series of stock of such constituent corporation irrevocably accepted for purchase or exchange in such offer.

(6) As used in this section only, the term:

a. "Affiliate" means, in respect of the corporation making the offer referred to in paragraph (h)(2) of this section, any person that (i) owns, directly or indirectly, all of the outstanding stock of such corporation or (ii) is a direct or indirect wholly-owned subsidiary of such corporation or of any person referred to in clause (i) of this definition;

b. "Consummates" (and with correlative meaning, "consummation" and "consummating") means irrevocably accepts for purchase or exchange stock tendered pursuant to an offer;

c. "Depository" means an agent, including a depository, appointed to facilitate consummation of the offer referred to in paragraph (h)(2) of this section;

d. "Excluded stock" means (i) stock of such constituent corporation that is owned at the commencement of the offer referred to in paragraph (h)(2) of this section by such constituent corporation, the corporation making the offer referred to in paragraph (h)(2) of this section, any person that owns, directly or indirectly, all of the outstanding stock of the corporation making such offer, or any direct or indirect wholly-owned subsidiary of any of the foregoing and (ii) rollover stock;

e. "Person" means any individual, corporation, partnership, limited liability company, unincorporated association or other entity;

f. "Received" (solely for purposes of paragraph (h)(3) of this section) means (a) with respect to certificated shares, physical receipt of a stock certificate accompanied by an executed letter of transmittal, (b) with respect to uncertificated shares held of record by a clearing corporation as nominee, transfer into the depository's account by means of an agent's message, and (c) with respect to uncertificated shares held of record by a person other than a clearing corporation as nominee, physical receipt of an executed letter of transmittal by the depository; provided, however, that shares shall cease to be "received" (i) with respect to certificated shares, if the certificate representing such shares was canceled prior to consummation of the offer referred to in paragraph (h)(2) of this section, or (ii) with respect to uncertificated shares, to the extent such uncertificated shares have been reduced or eliminated due to any sale of such shares prior to consummation of the offer referred to in paragraph (h)(2) of this section; and

g. "Rollover stock" means any shares of stock of such constituent corporation that are the subject of a written agreement requiring such shares to be transferred, contributed or delivered to the consummating corporation or any of its affiliates in exchange for stock or other equity interests in such consummating corporation or an affiliate thereof; provided, however, that such shares of stock shall cease to be rollover stock for purposes of paragraph (h)(3) of this section if, immediately prior to the time the merger becomes effective under this chapter, such shares have not been transferred, contributed or delivered to the consummating corporation or any of its affiliates pursuant to such written agreement.

If an agreement of merger is adopted without the vote of stockholders of a corporation pursuant to this subsection, the secretary or assistant secretary of the surviving corporation shall certify on the agreement that the agreement has been adopted pursuant to this subsection and that the conditions specified in this subsection (other than the condition listed in paragraph (h)(4) of this section) have been satisfied; provided that such certification on the agreement shall not be required if a certificate of merger is filed in lieu of filing the agreement. The agreement so adopted and certified shall then be filed and shall become effective, in accordance with §103 of this title. Such filing shall constitute a representation by the person who executes the agreement that the facts stated in the certificate remain true immediately prior to such filing.

§252. *Merger or Consolidation of Domestic and Foreign Corporations; Service of Process upon Surviving or Resulting Corporation*

(a) Any 1 or more corporations of this State may merge or consolidate with 1 or more foreign corporations, unless the laws of the jurisdiction or jurisdictions under which such foreign corporation or corporations are organized prohibit such merger or consolidation. The constituent corporations may merge into a single surviving corporation, which may be any 1 of the constituent corporations, or they may consolidate into a new resulting corporation formed by the consolidation, which may be a corporation of the jurisdiction of organization of any 1 of the constituent corporations, pursuant to an agreement of merger or consolidation, as the case may be, complying and approved in accordance with this section.

(b) All the constituent corporations shall enter into an agreement of merger or consolidation. The agreement shall state:

(1) The terms and conditions of the merger or consolidation;

(2) The mode of carrying the same into effect;

(3) In the case of a merger in which the surviving corporation is a corporation of this State, such amendments or changes in the certificate of incorporation of the surviving corporation as are desired to be effected by the merger (which amendments or changes may amend and restate the certificate of incorporation of the surviving corporation in its entirety), or, if no such amendments or changes are desired, a statement that the certificate of incorporation of the surviving corporation shall be its certificate of incorporation;

(4) In the case of a consolidation in which the resulting corporation is a corporation of this State, that the certificate of incorporation of the resulting corporation shall be as is set forth in an attachment to the agreement;

(5) The manner, if any, of converting the shares of each of the constituent corporations into shares or other securities of the corporation surviving or resulting from the merger or consolidation, or of cancelling some or all of such shares, and, if any shares of any of the constituent corporations are not to remain outstanding, to be converted solely into shares or other securities of the surviving or resulting corporation or to be cancelled, the cash, property, rights or securities of any other corporation or entity which the holders of such shares are to receive in exchange for, or upon conversion of, such shares and the surrender of any certificates evidencing them, which cash, property, rights or securities of any other corporation or entity may be in addition to or in lieu of the shares or other securities of the surviving or resulting corporation;

(6) Such other details or provisions as are deemed desirable, including, without limiting the generality of the foregoing, a provision for the payment of cash in lieu of the issuance or recognition of fractional shares, rights or other securities of the surviving or resulting corporation or of any other corporation or entity the shares, rights or other securities of which are to be received in the merger or consolidation, or for some other arrangement with respect thereto, consistent with §155 of this title; and

(7) Such other provisions or facts as shall be required to be set forth in an agreement of merger or consolidation (including any provision for amendment of the certificate of incorporation (or equivalent document) of a surviving or resulting foreign corporation) by the laws of each jurisdiction under which any of the foreign corporations are organized.

Any of the terms of the agreement of merger or consolidation may be made dependent upon facts ascertainable outside of such agreement, provided that the manner in which such facts shall operate upon the terms of the agreement is clearly and expressly set forth in the agreement of merger or consolidation. The term "facts," as used in the preceding sentence, includes, but is not limited to, the occurrence of any event, including a determination or action by any person or body, including the corporation.

(c) The agreement shall be adopted, approved, certified, executed and acknowledged by each of the constituent corporations in accordance with the laws under which it is organized, and, in the case of a corporation of this State, in the same manner as is provided in §251 of this title. The agreement shall be filed and shall become effective for all purposes of the laws of this State when and as provided in §251 of this title with respect to the merger or consolidation of corporations of this State. In lieu of filing the agreement of merger or consolidation, the surviving or resulting corporation may file a certificate of merger or consolidation, executed in accordance with §103 of this title, which states:

(1) The name and jurisdiction of organization of each of the constituent corporations;

(2) That an agreement of merger or consolidation has been approved, adopted, certified, executed and acknowledged by each of the constituent corporations in accordance with this subsection;

(3) The name of the surviving or resulting corporation;

(4) In the case of a merger in which the surviving corporation is a corporation of this State, such amendments or changes in the certificate of incorporation of the surviving corporation as are desired to be effected by the merger (which amendments or changes may amend and restate the certificate of incorporation of the surviving corporation in its entirety), or, if no such amendments or changes are desired, a statement that the certificate of incorporation of the surviving corporation shall be its certificate of incorporation;

(5) In the case of a consolidation in which the resulting corporation is a corporation of this State, that the certificate of incorporation of the resulting corporation shall be as is set forth in an attachment to the certificate;

(6) That the executed agreement of consolidation or merger is on file at an office of the surviving or resulting corporation and the address thereof;

(7) That a copy of the agreement of consolidation or merger will be furnished by the surviving or resulting corporation, on request and without cost, to any stockholder of any constituent corporation;

(8) If the corporation surviving or resulting from the merger or consolidation is a corporation of this State, the authorized capital stock of each constituent corporation which is not a corporation of this State; and

(9) The agreement, if any, required by subsection (d) of this section.

(d) If the corporation surviving or resulting from the merger or consolidation is a foreign corporation, it shall agree that it may be served with process in this State in any proceeding for enforcement of any obligation of any constituent corporation of this State, as well as for enforcement of any obligation of the surviving or resulting corporation arising from the merger or consolidation, including any suit or other proceeding to enforce the right of any stockholders as determined in appraisal proceedings pursuant to §262 of this title, and shall irrevocably appoint the Secretary of State as its agent to accept service of process in any such suit or other proceedings and shall specify the address to which a copy of such process shall be mailed by the

Secretary of State. Process may be served upon the Secretary of State under this subsection by means of electronic transmission but only as prescribed by the Secretary of State. The Secretary of State is authorized to issue such rules and regulations with respect to such service as the Secretary of State deems necessary or appropriate. In the event of such service upon the Secretary of State in accordance with this subsection, the Secretary of State shall forthwith notify such surviving or resulting corporation thereof by letter, directed to such surviving or resulting corporation at its address so specified, unless such surviving or resulting corporation shall have designated in writing to the Secretary of State a different address for such purpose, in which case it shall be mailed to the last address so designated. Such letter shall be sent by a mail or courier service that includes a record of mailing or deposit with the courier and a record of delivery evidenced by the signature of the recipient. Such letter shall enclose a copy of the process and any other papers served on the Secretary of State pursuant to this subsection. It shall be the duty of the plaintiff in the event of such service to serve process and any other papers in duplicate, to notify the Secretary of State that service is being effected pursuant to this subsection and to pay the Secretary of State the sum of $50 for the use of the State, which sum shall be taxed as part of the costs in the proceeding, if the plaintiff shall prevail therein. The Secretary of State shall maintain an alphabetical record of any such service setting forth the name of the plaintiff and the defendant, the title, docket number and nature of the proceeding in which process has been served, the fact that service has been effected pursuant to this subsection, the return date thereof, and the day and hour service was made. The Secretary of State shall not be required to retain such information longer than 5 years from receipt of the service of process.

(e) Section 251(d) of this title shall apply to any merger or consolidation under this section; §251 (e) of this title shall apply to a merger under this section in which the surviving corporation is a corporation of this State; and §251 (f) and (h) of this title shall apply to any merger under this section.

§253. Merger of Parent Corporation and Subsidiary or Subsidiaries

(a) In any case in which: (1) at least 90% of the outstanding shares of each class of the stock of a corporation or corporations (other than a corporation which has in its certificate of incorporation the provision required by §251(g)(7)(A) and (B) of this title), of which class there are outstanding shares that, absent this subsection, would be entitled to vote on such merger, is owned by a corporation of this State or a foreign corporation, and (2) 1 or more of such corporations is a corporation of this State, unless the laws of the jurisdiction or jurisdictions under which the foreign corporation or corporations are organized prohibit such merger, the parent corporation may either merge the subsidiary corporation or corporations into itself and assume all of its or their obligations, or merge itself, or itself and 1 or more of such other subsidiary corporations, into 1 of the subsidiary corporations by executing, acknowledging and filing, in accordance with §103 of this title, a certificate of such ownership and merger setting forth a copy of the resolution of its board of directors to so merge and the date of the adoption; provided, however, that in case the parent corporation shall not own all the outstanding stock of all the subsidiary corporations, parties to a merger as aforesaid, the resolution of the board of directors of the parent corporation shall state the terms and conditions of the merger, including the securities, cash, property, or rights to be issued, paid, delivered or granted by the surviving corporation upon surrender of each share of the subsidiary corporation or corporations not owned by the parent corporation, or the cancellation of some or all of such shares. Any of the terms of the resolution of the board of directors to so merge may be made dependent upon facts ascertainable outside of such resolution, provided that the manner in which such facts shall operate upon the terms of the resolution is clearly and expressly set forth in the resolution. The term "facts," as used in the preceding sentence, includes, but is not limited to, the occurrence of any event, including a determination or action by any person or body, including the corporation. If the parent corporation be not the surviving corporation, the resolution shall include provision for the pro rata issuance of stock of the surviving corporation to the holders of the stock of the parent corporation on surrender of any certificates therefor, and the certificate of ownership and merger shall state that the proposed merger has been approved by a majority of the outstanding stock of the parent corporation entitled to vote thereon at a meeting duly called and held after 20 days' notice of the purpose of the meeting given to each such stockholder at the stockholder's address as it appears on the records of the corporation if the parent corporation is a corporation of this State or state that the proposed merger has been adopted, approved, certified, executed and acknowledged by the parent corporation in accordance with the laws under which it is organized if the parent corporation is a foreign corporation. If the surviving corporation is a foreign corporation:

(1) Section 252(d) of this title or §258(c) of this title, as applicable, shall also apply to a merger under this section; and

(2) The terms and conditions of the merger shall obligate the surviving corporation to provide the agreement, and take the actions, required by §252(d) of this title or §258(c) of this title, as applicable.

(b) If the surviving corporation is a Delaware corporation, it may change its corporate name by the inclusion of a provision to that effect in the resolution of merger adopted by the directors of the parent corporation and set forth in the certificate of ownership and merger, and upon the effective date of the merger, the name of the corporation shall be so changed.

(c) Section §251(d) of this title shall apply to a merger under this section, and §251(e) of this title shall apply to a merger under this section in which the surviving corporation is the subsidiary corporation and is a corporation of this State. References to "agreement of merger" in §251(d) and (e) of this title shall mean for purposes of this subsection the resolution of merger adopted by the board of directors of the parent corporation. Any merger which effects any changes other than those authorized by this section or made applicable by this subsection shall be accomplished under §251, §252, §257, or §258 of this title. Section 262 of this title shall not apply to any merger effected under this section, except as provided in subsection (d) of this section.

(d) In the event all of the stock of a subsidiary Delaware corporation party to a merger effected under this section is not owned by the parent corporation immediately prior to the merger, the stockholders of the subsidiary Delaware corporation party to the merger shall have appraisal rights as set forth in §262 of this title.

(e) This section shall apply to nonstock corporations if the parent corporation is such a corporation and is the surviving corporation of the merger; provided, however, that references to the directors of the parent corporation shall be deemed to be references to members of the governing body of the parent corporation, and references to the board of directors of the parent corporation shall be deemed to be references to the governing body of the parent corporation.

(f) Nothing in this section shall be deemed to authorize the merger of a corporation with a charitable nonstock corporation, if the charitable status of such charitable nonstock corporation would thereby be lost or impaired.

§259. Status, Rights, Liabilities, of Constituent and Surviving or Resulting Corporations Following Merger or Consolidation

(a) When any merger or consolidation shall have become effective under this chapter, for all purposes of the laws of this State the separate existence of all the constituent corporations, or of all such constituent corporations except the one into which the other or others of such constituent corporations have been merged, as the case may be, shall cease and the constituent corporations shall become a new corporation, or be merged into 1 of such corporations, as the case may be, possessing all the rights, privileges, powers and franchises as well of a public as of a private nature, and being subject to all the restrictions, disabilities and duties of each of such corporations so merged or consolidated; and all and singular, the rights, privileges, powers and franchises of each of said corporations, and all property, real, personal and mixed, and all debts due to any of said constituent corporations on whatever account, as well for stock subscriptions as all other things in action or belonging to each of such corporations shall be vested in the corporation surviving or resulting from such merger or consolidation; and all property, rights, privileges, powers and franchises, and all and every other interest shall be thereafter as effectually the property of the surviving or resulting corporation as they were of the several and respective constituent corporations, and the title to any real estate vested by deed or otherwise, under the laws of this State, in any of such constituent corporations, shall not revert or be in any way impaired by reason of this chapter; but all rights of creditors and all liens upon any property of any of said constituent corporations shall be preserved unimpaired, and all debts, liabilities and duties of the respective constituent corporations shall thenceforth attach to said surviving or resulting corporation, and may be enforced against it to the same extent as if said debts, liabilities and duties had been incurred or contracted by it. . . .

§260. Powers of Corporation Surviving or Resulting from Merger or Consolidation; Issuance of Stock, Bonds or Other Indebtedness

When 2 or more corporations are merged or consolidated, the corporation surviving or resulting from the merger may issue bonds or other obligations, negotiable or otherwise, and with or without coupons or interest certificates thereto attached, to an amount sufficient with its capital stock to provide for all the payments it will be required to make, or obligations it will be required to assume, in order to effect the merger or consolidation. For the purpose of securing the payment of any such bonds and obligations, it shall be lawful for the surviving or resulting corporation to mortgage its corporate franchise, rights, privileges and property, real, personal or mixed. The surviving or resulting corporation may issue certificates of its capital stock or uncertificated stock if authorized to do so and other securities to the stockholders of the constituent corporations in exchange or payment for the original shares, in such amount as shall be necessary in accordance with the terms of the agreement of merger or consolidation in order to effect such merger or consolidation in the manner and on the terms specified in the agreement.

§261. *Effect of Merger upon Pending Actions*

Any action or proceeding, whether civil, criminal or administrative, pending by or against any corporation which is a party to a merger or consolidation shall be prosecuted as if such merger or consolidation had not taken place, or the corporation surviving or resulting from such merger or consolidation may be substituted in such action or proceeding.

§262. *Appraisal Rights*

(a) Any stockholder of a corporation of this State who holds shares of stock on the date of the making of a demand pursuant to subsection (d) of this section with respect to such shares, who continuously holds such shares through the effective date of the merger, consolidation, or conversion, who has otherwise complied with subsection (d) of this section and who has neither voted in favor of the merger, consolidation or conversion nor consented thereto in writing pursuant to §228 of this title shall be entitled to an appraisal by the Court of Chancery of the fair value of the stockholder's shares of stock under the circumstances described in subsections (b) and (c) of this section. As used in this section, the word "stockholder" means a holder of record of stock in a corporation; the words "stock" and "share" mean and include what is ordinarily meant by those words; the words "depository receipt" mean a receipt or other instrument issued by a depository representing an interest in 1 or more shares, or fractions thereof, solely of stock of a corporation, which stock is deposited with the depository; the words "beneficial owner" mean a person who is the beneficial owner of shares of stock held either in voting trust or by a nominee on behalf of such person ; and the word "person" means any individual, corporation, partnership, unincorporated association or other entity .

(b) Appraisal rights shall be available for the shares of any class or series of stock of a constituent or converting corporation in a merger, consolidation or conversion to be effected pursuant to §251 (other than a merger effected pursuant to §251(g) of this title), §252, §254, §255, §256, §257, §258, §263 , §264 or §266 of this title (other than, in each case and solely with respect to a domesticated corporation, a merger, consolidation or conversion authorized pursuant to and in accordance with the provisions of §388 of this title):

(1) Provided, however, that no appraisal rights under this section shall be available for the shares of any class or series of stock, which stock, or depository

receipts in respect thereof, at the record date fixed to determine the stockholders entitled to receive notice of the meeting of stockholders, or at the record date fixed to determine the stockholders entitled to consent pursuant to §228, to act upon the agreement of merger or consolidation or the resolution providing for conversion (or, in the case of a merger pursuant to §251(h), as of immediately prior to the execution of the agreement of merger), were either: (i) listed on a national securities exchange or (ii) held of record by more than 2,000 holders; and further provided that no appraisal rights shall be available for any shares of stock of the constituent corporation surviving a merger if the merger did not require for its approval the vote of the stockholders of the surviving corporation as provided in §251(f) of this title.

(2) Notwithstanding paragraph (b)(1) of this section, appraisal rights under this section shall be available for the shares of any class or series of stock of a constituent or converting corporation if the holders thereof are required by the terms of an agreement of merger or consolidation, or by the terms of a resolution providing for conversion, pursuant to §§251, 252, 254, 255, 256, 257, 258, 263 , 264 or 266 of this title to accept for such stock anything except:

a. Shares of stock of the corporation surviving or resulting from such merger or consolidation, or of the converted entity if such entity is a corporation as a result of the conversion, or depository receipts in respect thereof;

b. Shares of stock of any other corporation, or depository receipts in respect thereof, which shares of stock (or depository receipts in respect thereof) or depository receipts at the effective date of the merger or, consolidation or conversion will be either listed on a national securities exchange or held of record by more than 2,000 holders;

c. Cash in lieu of fractional shares or fractional depository receipts described in the foregoing paragraphs (b)(2)a. and b. of this section; or

d. Any combination of the shares of stock, depository receipts and cash in lieu of fractional shares or fractional depository receipts described in the foregoing paragraphs (b)(2)a., b. and c. of this section.

(3) In the event all of the stock of a subsidiary Delaware corporation party to a merger effected under §253 or §267 of this title is not owned by the parent immediately prior to the merger, appraisal rights shall be available for the shares of the subsidiary Delaware corporation.

(4) [Repealed.]

(c) Any corporation may provide in its certificate of incorporation that appraisal rights under this section shall be available for the shares of any class or series of its stock as a result of an amendment to its certificate of incorporation, any merger or consolidation in which the corporation is a constituent corporation, the sale of all or substantially all of the assets of the corporation or a conversion effected pursuant to §266 of this title. If the certificate of incorporation contains such a provision, the provisions of this section, including those set forth in subsections (d), (e), and (g) of this section, shall apply as nearly as is practicable.

(d) Appraisal rights shall be perfected as follows:

(1) If a proposed merger, consolidation or conversion for which appraisal rights are provided under this section is to be submitted for approval at a meeting

of stockholders, the corporation, not less than 20 days prior to the meeting, shall notify each of its stockholders who was such on the record date for notice of such meeting (or such members who received notice in accordance with §255(c) of this title) with respect to shares for which appraisal rights are available pursuant to subsection (b) or (c) of this section that appraisal rights are available for any or all of the shares of the constituent corporations or the converting corporation, and shall include in such notice either a copy of this section (and, if 1 of the constituent corporations or the converting corporation is a nonstock corporation, a copy of §114 of this title) or information directing the stockholders to a publicly available electronic resource at which this section (and, §114 of this title, if applicable) may be accessed without subscription or cost. Each stockholder electing to demand the appraisal of such stockholder's shares shall deliver to the corporation, before the taking of the vote on the merger, consolidation or conversion, a written demand for appraisal of such stockholder's shares; provided that a demand may be delivered to the corporation by electronic transmission if directed to an information processing system (if any) expressly designated for that purpose in such notice. Such demand will be sufficient if it reasonably informs the corporation of the identity of the stockholder and that the stockholder intends thereby to demand the appraisal of such stockholder's shares. A proxy or vote against the merger, consolidation or conversion shall not constitute such a demand. A stockholder electing to take such action must do so by a separate written demand as herein provided. Within 10 days after the effective date of such merger, consolidation or conversion, the surviving, resulting or converted entity shall notify each stockholder of each constituent or converting corporation who has complied with this subsection and has not voted in favor of or consented to the merger, consolidation or conversion, and any beneficial owner who has demanded appraisal under subsection (d)(3) of this section, of the date that the merger, consolidation or conversion has become effective; or

(2) If the merger, consolidation or conversion was approved pursuant to §228, §251(h), §253, or §267 of this title, then either a constituent or converting corporation before the effective date of the merger, consolidation or conversion, or the surviving, resulting or converted entity within 10 days after such effective date, shall notify each stockholder of any class or series of stock of such constituent or converting corporation who is entitled to appraisal rights of the approval of the merger, consolidation or conversion and that appraisal rights are available for any or all shares of such class or series of stock of such constituent or converting corporation, and shall include in such notice either a copy of this section (and, if 1 of the constituent corporations or the converting corporation is a nonstock corporation, a copy of §114 of this title) or information directing the stockholders to a publicly available electronic resource at which this section (and §114 of this title, if applicable) may be accessed without subscription or cost. Such notice may, and, if given on or after the effective date of the merger, consolidation or conversion, shall, also notify such stockholders of the effective date of the merger, consolidation or conversion. Any stockholder entitled to appraisal rights may, within 20 days after the date of giving such notice or, in the case of a merger approved pursuant to §251(h) of this title, within the later of the consummation of the offer contemplated by §251(h) of this title and 20 days after the date of giving such

notice, demand in writing from the surviving or resulting entity the appraisal of such holder's shares; provided that a demand may be delivered to such entity by electronic transmission if directed to an information processing system (if any) expressly designated for that purpose in such notice. Such demand will be sufficient if it reasonably informs such entity of the identity of the stockholder and that the stockholder intends thereby to demand the appraisal of such holder's shares. If such notice did not notify stockholders of the effective date of the merger, consolidation or conversion, either (i) each such constituent corporation or the converting corporation shall send a second notice before the effective date of the merger, consolidation notifying each of the holders of any class or series of stock of such constituent or converting corporation that are entitled to appraisal rights of the effective date of the merger, consolidation or conversion or (ii) the surviving, resulting or converted entity shall send such a second notice to all such holders on or within 10 days after such effective date; provided, however, that if such second notice is sent more than 20 days following the sending of the first notice or, in the case of a merger approved pursuant to §251(h) of this title, later than the later of the consummation of the offer contemplated by §251(h) of this title and 20 days following the sending of the first notice, such second notice need only be sent to each stockholder who is entitled to appraisal rights and who has demanded appraisal of such holder's shares in accordance with this subsection and any beneficial owner who has demanded appraisal under subsection (d)(3) of this section. An affidavit of the secretary or assistant secretary or of the transfer agent of the corporation or entity that is required to give either notice that such notice has been given shall, in the absence of fraud, be prima facie evidence of the facts stated therein. For purposes of determining the stockholders entitled to receive either notice, each constituent corporation or the converting corporation may fix, in advance, a record date that shall be not more than 10 days prior to the date the notice is given, provided, that if the notice is given on or after the effective date of the merger, consolidation or conversion, the record date shall be such effective date. If no record date is fixed and the notice is given prior to the effective date, the record date shall be the close of business on the day next preceding the day on which the notice is given.

(3) Notwithstanding subsection (a) of this section (but subject to this subsection (d)(3)), a beneficial owner may, in such person's name, demand in writing an appraisal of such beneficial owner's shares in accordance with either subsection (d)(1) or (2) of this section, as applicable; provided that (i) such beneficial owner continuously owns such shares through the effective date of the merger, consolidation or conversion and otherwise satisfies the requirements applicable to a stockholder under the first sentence of subsection (a) and (ii) the demand made by such beneficial owner reasonably identifies the holder of record of the shares for which the demand is made, is accompanied by documentary evidence of such beneficial owner's beneficial ownership of stock and a statement that such documentary evidence is a true and correct copy of what it purports to be, and provides an address at which such beneficial owner consents to receive notices given by the surviving, resulting or converted entity hereunder and to be set forth on the verified list required by subsection (f) of this section.

(e) Within 120 days after the effective date of the merger, consolidation or conversion , the surviving, resulting or converted entity, or any person who has complied with subsections (a) and (d) of this section hereof and who is otherwise entitled to appraisal rights, may commence an appraisal proceeding by filing a petition in the Court of Chancery demanding a determination of the value of the stock of all such stockholders. Notwithstanding the foregoing, at any time within 60 days after the effective date of the merger, consolidation or conversion, any person entitled to appraisal rights who has not commenced an appraisal proceeding or joined that proceeding as a named party shall have the right to withdraw such person's demand for appraisal and to accept the terms offered upon the merger, consolidation or conversion. Within 120 days after the effective date of the merger, consolidation or conversion, any person who has complied with the requirements of subsections (a) and (d) of this section hereof, upon request given in writing (or by electronic transmission directed to an information processing system (if any) expressly designated for that purpose in the notice of appraisal), shall be entitled to receive from the surviving, resulting or converted entity a statement setting forth the aggregate number of shares not voted in favor of the merger, consolidation or conversion (or, in the case of a merger approved pursuant to §251(h) of this title, the aggregate number of shares (other than any excluded stock (as defined in §251(h)(6)d. of this title)) that were the subject of, and were not tendered into, and accepted for purchase or exchange in, the offer referred to in §251(h)(2)), and, in either case, with respect to which demands for appraisal have been received and the aggregate number of stockholders or beneficial owners holding or owning such shares (provided that, where a beneficial owner makes a demand pursuant to paragraph (d)(3) of this section, the record holder of such shares shall not be considered a separate stockholder holding such shares for purposes of such aggregate number). Such statement shall be given to the person within 10 days after such person's request for such a statement is received by the surviving, resulting or converted entity or within 10 days after expiration of the period for delivery of demands for appraisal under subsection (d) of this section hereof, whichever is later.

(f) Upon the filing of any such petition by any person other than the surviving, resulting or converted entity, service of a copy thereof shall be made upon such entity, which shall within 20 days after such service file in the office of the Register in Chancery in which the petition was filed a duly verified list containing the names and addresses of all persons who have demanded appraisal for their shares and with whom agreements as to the value of their shares have not been reached by such entity. If the petition shall be filed by the surviving or, resulting or converted entity, the petition shall be accompanied by such a duly verified list. The Register in Chancery, if so ordered by the Court, shall give notice of the time and place fixed for the hearing of such petition by registered or certified mail to the surviving or, resulting or converted entity and to the persons shown on the list at the addresses therein stated. The forms of the notices by mail and by publication shall be approved by the Court, and the costs thereof shall be borne by the surviving, resulting or converted entity.

(g) At the hearing on such petition, the Court shall determine the persons who have complied with this section and who have become entitled to appraisal rights.

The Court may require the persons who have demanded an appraisal for their shares and who hold stock represented by certificates to submit their certificates of stock to the Register in Chancery for notation thereon of the pendency of the appraisal proceedings; and if any person fails to comply with such direction, the Court may dismiss the proceedings as to such person. If immediately before the merger, consolidation or conversion the shares of the class or series of stock of the constituent or converting corporation as to which appraisal rights are available were listed on a national securities exchange, the Court shall dismiss the proceedings as to all holders of such shares who are otherwise entitled to appraisal rights unless (1) the total number of shares entitled to appraisal exceeds 1% of the outstanding shares of the class or series eligible for appraisal, (2) the value of the consideration provided in the merger, consolidation or conversion for such total number of shares exceeds $1 million, or (3) the merger was approved pursuant to §253 or §267 of this title.

(h) After the Court determines the persons entitled to an appraisal, the appraisal proceeding shall be conducted in accordance with the rules of the Court of Chancery, including any rules specifically governing appraisal proceedings. Through such proceeding the Court shall determine the fair value of the shares exclusive of any element of value arising from the accomplishment or expectation of the merger, consolidation or conversion, together with interest, if any, to be paid upon the amount determined to be the fair value. In determining such fair value, the Court shall take into account all relevant factors. Unless the Court in its discretion determines otherwise for good cause shown, and except as provided in this subsection, interest from the effective date of the merger, consolidation or conversion through the date of payment of the judgment shall be compounded quarterly and shall accrue at 5% over the Federal Reserve discount rate (including any surcharge) as established from time to time during the period between the effective date of the merger, consolidation or conversion and the date of payment of the judgment. At any time before the entry of judgment in the proceedings, the surviving, resulting or converted entity may pay to each person entitled to appraisal an amount in cash, in which case interest shall accrue thereafter as provided herein only upon the sum of (1) the difference, if any, between the amount so paid and the fair value of the shares as determined by the Court, and (2) interest theretofore accrued, unless paid at that time. Upon application by the surviving, resulting or converted entity or by any person entitled to participate in the appraisal proceeding, the Court may, in its discretion, proceed to trial upon the appraisal prior to the final determination of the persons entitled to an appraisal. Any person whose name appears on the list filed by the surviving, resulting or converted entity pursuant to subsection (f) of this section may participate fully in all proceedings until it is finally determined that such person is not entitled to appraisal rights under this section.

(i) The Court shall direct the payment of the fair value of the shares, together with interest, if any, by the surviving, resulting or converted entity to the persons entitled thereto. Payment shall be so made to each such person upon such terms and conditions as the Court may order. The Court's decree may be enforced as other decrees in the Court of Chancery may be enforced, whether such surviving, resulting or converted entity be an entity of this State or of any state.

(j) The costs of the proceeding may be determined by the Court and taxed upon the parties as the Court deems equitable in the circumstances. Upon application of a person whose name appears on the list filed by the surviving, resulting or converted entity pursuant to subsection (f) of this section who participated in the proceeding and incurred expenses in connection therewith, the Court may order all or a portion of such expenses, including, without limitation, reasonable attorney's fees and the fees and expenses of experts, to be charged pro rata against the value of all the shares entitled to an appraisal not dismissed pursuant to subsection (k) of this section or subject to such an award pursuant to a reservation of jurisdiction under subsection (k) of this section.

(k) From and after the effective date of the merger, consolidation or conversion, no person who has demanded appraisal rights with respect to some or all of such person's shares as provided in subsection (d) of this section shall be entitled to vote such shares for any purpose or to receive payment of dividends or other distributions on such shares (except dividends or other distributions payable to stockholders of record at a date which is prior to the effective date of the merger, consolidation or conversion); provided, however, that if no petition for an appraisal is filed within the time provided in subsection (e) of this section, or if a person who has made a demand for an appraisal in accordance with this section shall deliver to the surviving, resulting or converted entity a written withdrawal of such person's demand for an appraisal in respect of some or all of such person's shares in accordance with subsection (e) of this section, then the right of such person to an appraisal of the shares subject to the withdrawal shall cease. Notwithstanding the foregoing, no appraisal proceeding in the Court of Chancery shall be dismissed as to any person without the approval of the Court, and such approval may be conditioned upon such terms as the Court deems just, including without limitation, a reservation of jurisdiction for any application to the Court made under subsection (j) of this section; provided, however that this provision shall not affect the right of any person who has not commenced an appraisal proceeding or joined that proceeding as a named party to withdraw such person's demand for appraisal and to accept the terms offered upon the merger, consolidation or conversion within 60 days after the effective date of the merger, consolidation or conversion, as set forth in subsection (e) of this section.

(*l*) The shares or other equity interests of the surviving, resulting or converted entity to which the shares of stock subject to appraisal under this section would have otherwise converted but for an appraisal demand made in accordance with this section shall have the status of authorized but not outstanding shares of stock or other equity interests of the surviving, resulting or converted entity, unless and until the person that has demanded appraisal is no longer entitled to appraisal pursuant to this section.

§265. Conversion of Other Entities to a Domestic Corporation

(a) As used in this section, the term "other entity" means a limited liability company, statutory trust, business trust or association, real estate investment trust, common-law trust or any other unincorporated business including a partnership (whether general (including a limited liability partnership) or limited (including a limited liability limited partnership)), or a foreign corporation.

(b) Any other entity may convert to a corporation of this State by complying with subsection (h) of this section and filing in the office of the Secretary of State:

(1) A certificate of conversion to corporation that has been executed in accordance with subsection (i) of this section and filed in accordance with §103 of this title; and

(2) A certificate of incorporation that has been executed, acknowledged and filed in accordance with §103 of this title.

Each of the certificates required by this subsection (b) shall be filed simultaneously in the office of the Secretary of State and, if such certificates are not to become effective upon their filing as permitted by §103(d) of this title, then each such certificate shall provide for the same effective date or time in accordance with §103(d) of this title.

(c) The certificate of conversion to corporation shall state:

(1) The date on which and jurisdiction where the other entity was first created, incorporated, formed or otherwise came into being and, if it has changed, its jurisdiction immediately prior to its conversion to a domestic corporation;

(2) The name and type of entity of the other entity immediately prior to the filing of the certificate of conversion to corporation; and

(3) The name of the corporation as set forth in its certificate of incorporation filed in accordance with subsection (b) of this section.

(4) [Repealed.]

(d) Upon the effective time of the certificate of conversion to corporation and the certificate of incorporation, the other entity shall be converted to a corporation of this State and the corporation shall thereafter be subject to all of the provisions of this title, except that notwithstanding §106 of this title, the existence of the corporation shall be deemed to have commenced on the date the other entity commenced its existence in the jurisdiction in which the other entity was first created, formed, incorporated or otherwise came into being.

(e) The conversion of any other entity to a corporation of this State shall not be deemed to affect any obligations or liabilities of the other entity incurred prior to its conversion to a corporation of this State or the personal liability of any person incurred prior to such conversion.

(f) When an other entity has been converted to a corporation of this State pursuant to this section, the corporation of this State shall, for all purposes of the laws of the State of Delaware, be deemed to be the same entity as the converting other entity. When any conversion shall have become effective under this section, for all purposes of the laws of the State of Delaware, all of the rights, privileges and powers of the other entity that has converted, and all property, real, personal and mixed, and all debts due to such other entity, as well as all other things and causes of action belonging to such other entity, shall remain vested in the domestic corporation to which such other entity has converted and shall be the property of such domestic corporation and the title to any real property vested by deed or otherwise in such other entity shall not revert or be in any way impaired by reason of this chapter; but all rights of creditors and all liens upon any property of such other entity shall be preserved unimpaired, and all debts, liabilities and duties of the other entity that has converted shall remain attached to the corporation of this State to which such other entity has converted, and may be enforced against it to the same extent as if said debts, liabilities and duties had originally been incurred or contracted by it in its capacity as a corporation of this State. The rights, privileges, powers and interests in property of the other entity, as well as the debts, liabilities and duties of the other entity, shall not be deemed, as a consequence of the conversion, to have been transferred to the domestic corporation to which such other entity has converted for any purpose of the laws of the State of Delaware.

(g) Unless otherwise agreed, for all purposes of the laws of the State of Delaware or as required under applicable non-Delaware law, the converting other entity shall not be required to wind up its affairs or pay its liabilities and distribute its assets, and the conversion shall not be deemed to constitute a dissolution of such other entity and shall constitute a continuation of the existence of the converting other entity in the form of a corporation of this State.

(h) Prior to the time a certificate of conversion to corporation becomes effective in accordance with §103 of this title, the conversion shall be approved in the manner provided for by the document, instrument, agreement or other writing, as the case may be, governing the internal affairs of the other entity and the conduct of its business or by applicable law, as appropriate, and a certificate of incorporation shall be approved by the same authorization required to approve the conversion.

(i) The certificate of conversion to corporation shall be signed by any person who is authorized to sign the certificate of conversion to corporation on behalf of the other entity.

(j) In connection with a conversion hereunder, rights or securities of, or interests in, the other entity which is to be converted to a corporation of this State may be exchanged for or converted into cash, property, or shares of stock, rights or securities of such corporation of this State or, in addition to or in lieu thereof, may be exchanged for or converted into cash, property, or shares of stock, rights or securities of or interests in another domestic corporation or other entity or may be cancelled.

SUBCHAPTER X. SALE OF ASSETS, DISSOLUTION, AND WINDING UP

§271. Sale, Lease or Exchange of Assets; Consideration; Procedure

(a) Every corporation may at any meeting of its board of directors or governing body sell, lease or exchange all or substantially all of its property and assets, including its goodwill and its corporate franchises, upon such terms and conditions and for such consideration, which may consist in whole or in part of money or other property, including shares of stock in, and/or other securities of, any other corporation or corporations, as its board of directors or governing body deems expedient and for the best interests of the corporation, when and as authorized by a resolution adopted by the holders of a majority of the outstanding stock of the corporation entitled to vote thereon or, if the corporation is a nonstock corporation, by a majority of the members having the right to vote for the election of the members of the governing body and any other members entitled to vote thereon under the certificate of incorporation or the bylaws of such corporation, at a meeting duly called upon at least 20 days' notice. The notice of the meeting shall state that such a resolution will be considered.

(b) Notwithstanding authorization or consent to a proposed sale, lease or exchange of a corporation's property and assets by the stockholders or members, the board of directors or governing body may abandon such proposed sale, lease or exchange without further action by the stockholders or members, subject to the rights, if any, of third parties under any contract relating thereto.

(c) For purposes of this section only, the property and assets of the corporation include the property and assets of any subsidiary of the corporation. As used in this subsection, "subsidiary" means any entity wholly-owned and controlled, directly or indirectly, by the corporation and includes, without limitation, corporations, partnerships, limited partnerships, limited liability partnerships, limited liability companies, and/or statutory trusts. Notwithstanding subsection (a) of this section, except to the extent the certificate of incorporation otherwise provides, no resolution by stockholders or members shall be required for a sale, lease or exchange of property and assets of the corporation to a subsidiary.

§272. *Mortgage or Pledge of Assets*

The authorization or consent of stockholders to the mortgage or pledge of a corporation's property and assets shall not be necessary, except to the extent that the certificate of incorporation otherwise provides.

§273. *Dissolution of Joint Venture Corporation Having 2 Stockholders*

(a) If the stockholders of a corporation of this State, having only 2 stockholders each of which own 50% of the stock therein, shall be engaged in the prosecution of a joint venture and if such stockholders shall be unable to agree upon the desirability of discontinuing such joint venture and disposing of the assets used in such venture, either stockholder may, unless otherwise provided in the certificate of incorporation of the corporation or in a written agreement between the stockholders, file with the Court of Chancery a petition stating that it desires to discontinue such joint venture and to dispose of the assets used in such venture in accordance with a plan to be agreed upon by both stockholders or that, if no such plan shall be agreed upon by both stockholders, the corporation be dissolved. Such petition shall have attached thereto a copy of the proposed plan of discontinuance and distribution and a certificate stating that copies of such petition and plan have been transmitted in writing to the other stockholder and to the directors and officers of such corporation. The petition and certificate shall be executed and acknowledged in accordance with §103 of this title.

(b) Unless both stockholders file with the Court of Chancery:

(1) Within 3 months of the date of the filing of such petition, a certificate similarly executed and acknowledged stating that they have agreed on such plan, or a modification thereof, and

(2) Within 1 year from the date of the filing of such petition, a certificate similarly executed and acknowledged stating that the distribution provided by such plan had been completed,

the Court of Chancery may dissolve such corporation and may by appointment of 1 or more trustees or receivers with all the powers and title of a trustee or receiver appointed under §279 of this title, administer and wind up its affairs. Either or both of the above periods may be extended by agreement of the stockholders, evidenced by a certificate similarly executed, acknowledged and filed with the Court of Chancery prior to the expiration of such period.

(c) In the case of a charitable nonstock corporation, the petitioner shall provide a copy of any petition referred to in subsection (a) of this section to the Attorney General of the State of Delaware within 1 week of its filing with the Court of Chancery.

§275. *Dissolution Generally; Procedure*

(a) If it should be deemed advisable in the judgment of the board of directors of any corporation that it should be dissolved, the board, after the adoption of a resolution to that effect by a majority of the whole board at any meeting called for that purpose, shall cause notice of the adoption of the resolution and of a meeting of stockholders to take action upon the resolution to be given to each stockholder entitled to vote thereon as of the record date for determining the stockholders entitled to notice of the meeting.

(b) At the meeting a vote shall be taken upon the proposed dissolution. If a majority of the outstanding stock of the corporation entitled to vote thereon shall vote for the proposed dissolution, a certification of dissolution shall be filed with the Secretary of State pursuant to subsection (d) of this section.

(c) Dissolution of a corporation may also be authorized without action of the directors if all the stockholders entitled to vote thereon shall consent in writing and a certificate of dissolution shall be filed with the Secretary of State pursuant to subsection (d) of this section.

(d) If dissolution is authorized in accordance with this section, a certificate of dissolution shall be executed, acknowledged and filed, and shall become effective, in accordance with §103 of this title. Such certificate of dissolution shall set forth:

(1) The name of the corporation;

(2) The date dissolution was authorized;

(3) That the dissolution has been authorized by the board of directors and stockholders of the corporation, in accordance with subsections (a) and (b) of this section, or that the dissolution has been authorized by all of the stockholders of the corporation entitled to vote on a dissolution, in accordance with subsection (c) of this section;

(4) The names and addresses of the directors and officers of the corporation; and

(5) The date of filing of the corporation's original certificate of incorporation with the Secretary of State.

(e) The resolution authorizing a proposed dissolution may provide that notwithstanding authorization or consent to the proposed dissolution by the stockholders, or the members of a nonstock corporation pursuant to §276 of this title, the board of directors or governing body may abandon such proposed dissolution without further action by the stockholders or members.

(f) If a corporation has included in its certificate of incorporation a provision limiting the duration of its existence to a specified date in accordance with §102(b)(5) of this title, a certificate of dissolution shall be executed, acknowledged and filed in accordance with §103 of this title within 90 days before such specified date and shall become effective on such specified date. Such certificate of dissolution shall set forth:

(1) The name of the corporation;

(2) The date specified in the corporation's certificate of incorporation limiting the duration of its existence;

(3) The names and addresses of the directors and officers of the corporation; and

(4) The date of filing of the corporation's original certificate of incorporation with the Secretary of State.

The failure to timely file a certificate of dissolution pursuant to this subsection with respect to any corporation shall not affect the expiration of such corporation's existence on the date specified in its certificate of incorporation pursuant to §102(b)(5) of this title and shall not eliminate the requirement to file a certificate of dissolution as contemplated by this subsection. If a certificate of good standing is issued by the Secretary of State after the date specified in a corporation's certificate of incorporation pursuant to §102(b)(5) of this title, such certificate of good standing shall be of no force or effect.

(g) A corporation shall be dissolved upon the earlier of (1) the date specified in such corporation's certificate of incorporation pursuant to §102(b)(5) of this title or (2) the effectiveness in accordance with §103 of this title of a certificate of dissolution filed in accordance with this section.

§278. *Continuation of Corporation after Dissolution for Purposes of Suit and Winding Up Affairs*

All corporations, whether they expire by their own limitation or are otherwise dissolved, shall nevertheless be continued, for the term of 3 years from such expiration or dissolution or for such longer period as the Court of Chancery shall in its discretion direct, bodies corporate for the purpose of prosecuting and defending suits, whether civil, criminal or administrative, by or against them, and of enabling them gradually to settle and close their business, to dispose of and convey their property, to discharge their liabilities and to distribute to their stockholders any remaining assets, but not for the purpose of continuing the business for which the corporation was organized. With respect to any action, suit or proceeding begun by or against the corporation either prior to or within 3 years after the date of its expiration or dissolution, the action shall not abate by reason of the dissolution of the corporation; the corporation shall, solely for the purpose of such action, suit or proceeding, be continued as a body corporate beyond the 3-year period and until any judgments, orders or decrees therein shall be fully executed, without the necessity for any special direction to that effect by the Court of Chancery. Sections 279 through 282 of this title shall apply to any corporation that has expired by its own limitation, and when so applied, all references in those sections to a dissolved corporation or dissolution shall include a corporation that has expired by its own limitation and to such expiration, respectively.

§279. *Trustees or Receivers for Dissolved Corporations; Appointment; Powers; Duties*

When any corporation organized under this chapter shall be dissolved in any manner whatever, the Court of Chancery, on application of any creditor, stockholder or director of the corporation, or any other person who shows good cause therefor, at any time, may either appoint 1 or more of the directors of the corporation to be trustees, or appoint 1 or more persons to be receivers, of and for the corporation, to take charge of the corporation's property, and to collect the debts and property due and belonging to the corporation, with power to prosecute and defend, in the name of the corporation, or otherwise, all such suits as may be necessary or proper for the purposes aforesaid, and to appoint an agent or agents under them, and to do all other acts which might be done by the corporation, if in being, that may be necessary for the final settlement of the unfinished business of the corporation. The powers of the trustees or receivers may be continued as long as the Court of Chancery shall think necessary for the purposes aforesaid.

§280. Notice to Claimants; Filing of Claims

(a)(1) After a corporation has been dissolved in accordance with the procedures set forth in this chapter, the corporation or any successor entity may give notice of the dissolution, requiring all persons having a claim against the corporation other than a claim against the corporation in a pending action, suit or proceeding to which the corporation is a party to present their claims against the corporation in accordance with such notice. Such notice shall state:

a. That all such claims must be presented in writing and must contain sufficient information reasonably to inform the corporation or successor entity of the identity of the claimant and the substance of the claim;

b. The mailing address to which such claim must be sent;

c. The date by which such a claim must be received by the corporation or successor entity, which date shall be no earlier than 60 days from the date thereof; and

d. That such claim will be barred if not received by the date referred to in paragraph (a)(1)c. of this section; and

e. That the corporation or a successor entity may make distributions to other claimants and the corporation's stockholders or persons interested as having been such without further notice to the claimant; and

f. The aggregate amount, on an annual basis, of all distributions made by the corporation to its stockholders for each of the 3 years prior to the date the corporation dissolved.

Such notice shall also be published at least once a week for 2 consecutive weeks in a newspaper of general circulation in the county in which the office of the corporation's last registered agent in this State is located and in the corporation's principal place of business and, in the case of a corporation having $10,000,000 or more in total assets at the time of its dissolution, at least once in all editions of a daily newspaper with a national circulation. On or before the date of the first publication of such notice, the corporation or successor entity shall mail a copy of such notice by certified or registered mail, return receipt requested, to each known claimant of the corporation including persons with claims asserted against the corporation in a pending action, suit or proceeding to which the corporation is a party.

(2) Any claim against the corporation required to be presented pursuant to this subsection is barred if a claimant who was given actual notice under this subsection does not present the claim to the dissolved corporation or successor entity by the date referred to in paragraph (a)(1)c. of this section.

(3) A corporation or successor entity may reject, in whole or in part, any claim made by a claimant pursuant to this subsection by mailing notice of such rejection by certified or registered mail, return receipt requested, to the claimant within 90 days after receipt of such claim and, in all events, at least 150 days before the expiration of the period described in §278 of this title; provided however, that in the case of a claim filed pursuant to §295 of this title against a corporation or successor entity for which a receiver or trustee has been appointed by the Court of Chancery the time period shall be as provided in §296 of this title, and the 30-day appeal period provided for in §296 of this title shall be applicable. A notice sent by a corporation or successor entity pursuant to this subsection shall state that any claim rejected therein will be barred if an action, suit or proceeding with respect to the claim is not commenced within 120 days of the date thereof, and shall be accompanied by a copy of §§278-283 of this title and, in the case of a notice sent by a court-appointed receiver or trustee and as to which a claim has been filed pursuant to §295 of this title, copies of §§295 and 296 of this title.

(4) A claim against a corporation is barred if a claimant whose claim is rejected pursuant to paragraph (a)(3) of this section does not commence an action, suit or proceeding with respect to the claim no later than 120 days after the mailing of the rejection notice.

(b)(1) A corporation or successor entity electing to follow the procedures described in subsection (a) of this section shall also give notice of the dissolution of the corporation to persons with contractual claims contingent upon the occurrence or nonoccurrence of future events or otherwise conditional or unmatured, and request that such persons present such claims in accordance with the terms of such notice. Provided however, that as used in this section and in §281 of this title, the term "contractual claims" shall not include any implied warranty as to any product manufactured, sold, distributed or handled by the dissolved corporation. Such notice shall be in substantially the form, and sent and published in the same manner, as described in paragraph (a)(1) of this section.

(2) The corporation or successor entity shall offer any claimant on a contract whose claim is contingent, conditional or unmatured such security as the corporation or successor entity determines is sufficient to provide compensation to the claimant if the claim matures. The corporation or successor entity shall mail such offer to the claimant by certified or registered mail, return receipt requested, within 90 days of receipt of such claim and, in all events, at least 150 days before the expiration of the period described in §278 of this title. If the claimant offered such security does not deliver in writing to the corporation or successor entity a notice rejecting the offer within 120 days after receipt of such offer for security, the claimant shall be deemed to have accepted such security as the sole source from which to satisfy the claim against the corporation.

(c)(1) A corporation or successor entity which has given notice in accordance with subsection (a) of this section shall petition the Court of Chancery to determine the amount and form of security that will be reasonably likely to be sufficient to provide compensation for any claim against the corporation which is the subject of a pending action, suit or proceeding to which the corporation is a party other than a claim barred pursuant to subsection (a) of this section.

(2) A corporation or successor entity which has given notice in accordance with subsections (a) and (b) of this section shall petition the Court of Chancery to determine the amount and form of security that will be sufficient to provide compensation to any claimant who has rejected the offer for security made pursuant to paragraph (b)(2) of this section.

(3) A corporation or successor entity which has given notice in accordance with subsection (a) of this section shall petition the Court of Chancery to determine the amount and form of security which will be reasonably likely to be sufficient to provide compensation for claims that have not been made known to the corporation or that have not arisen but that, based on facts known to the corporation or successor entity, are likely to arise or to become known to the corporation or successor entity within 5 years after the date of dissolution or such longer period of time as the Court of Chancery may determine not to exceed 10 years after the date of dissolution. The Court of Chancery may appoint a guardian ad litem in respect of any such proceeding brought under this subsection. The reasonable fees and expenses of such guardian, including all reasonable expert witness fees, shall be paid by the petitioner in such proceeding.

(d) The giving of any notice or making of any offer pursuant to this section shall not revive any claim then barred or constitute acknowledgment by the corporation or successor entity that any person to whom such notice is sent is a proper claimant and shall not operate as a waiver of any defense or counterclaim in respect of any claim asserted by any person to whom such notice is sent.

(e) As used in this section, the term "successor entity" shall include any trust, receivership or other legal entity governed by the laws of this State to which the remaining assets and liabilities of a dissolved corporation are transferred and which exists solely for the purposes of prosecuting and defending suits, by or against the dissolved corporation, enabling the dissolved corporation to settle and close the business of the dissolved corporation, to dispose of and convey the property of the dissolved corporation to discharge the liabilities of the dissolved corporation, and to distribute to the dissolved corporation's stockholders any remaining assets, but not for the purpose of continuing the business for which the dissolved corporation was organized.

(f) The time periods and notice requirements of this section shall, in the case of a corporation or successor entity for which a receiver or trustee has been appointed by the Court of Chancery, be subject to variation by, or in the manner provided in, the Rules of the Court of Chancery.

(g) In the case of a nonstock corporation, any notice referred to in the last sentence of paragraph (a)(3) of this section shall include a copy of §114 of this title. In the case of a nonprofit nonstock corporation, provisions of this section regarding distributions to members shall not apply to the extent that those provisions conflict with any other applicable law or with that corporation's certificate of incorporation or bylaws.

§281. *Payment and Distribution to Claimants and Stockholders*

(a) A dissolved corporation or successor entity which has followed the procedures described in §280 of this title:

(1) Shall pay the claims made and not rejected in accordance with §280(a) of this title,

(2) Shall post the security offered and not rejected pursuant to §280(b)(2) of this title,

(3) Shall post any security ordered by the Court of Chancery in any proceeding under §280(c) of this title, and

(4) Shall pay or make provision for all other claims that are mature, known and uncontested or that have been finally determined to be owing by the corporation or such successor entity.

Such claims or obligations shall be paid in full and any such provision for payment shall be made in full if there are sufficient assets. If there are insufficient assets, such claims and obligations shall be paid or provided for according to their priority, and, among claims of equal priority, ratably to the extent of assets legally available therefor. Any remaining assets shall be distributed to the stockholders of the dissolved corporation; provided, however, that such distribution shall not be made before the expiration of 150 days from the date of the last notice of rejections given pursuant to §280(a)(3) of this title. In the absence of actual fraud, the judgment of the directors of the dissolved corporation or the governing persons of such successor entity as to the provision made for the payment of all obligations under paragraph (a)(4) of this section shall be conclusive.

(b) A dissolved corporation or successor entity which has not followed the procedures described in §280 of this title shall, prior to the expiration of the period described in §278 of this title, adopt a plan of distribution pursuant to which the dissolved corporation or successor entity (i) shall pay or make reasonable provision to pay all claims and obligations, including all contingent, conditional or unmatured contractual claims known to the corporation or such successor entity, (ii) shall make such provision as will be reasonably likely to be sufficient to provide compensation for any claim against the corporation which is the subject of a pending action, suit or proceeding to which the corporation is a party and (iii) shall make such provision as will be reasonably likely to be sufficient to provide compensation for claims that have not been made known to the corporation that have not arisen but that, based on facts known to the corporation or successor entity, are likely to arise or to become known to the corporation or successor entity within 10 years after the date of dissolution. The plan of distribution shall provide that such claims shall be paid in full and any such provision for payment made shall be made in full if there are sufficient assets. If there are insufficient assets, such plan shall provide that such claims and obligations shall be paid or provided for according to their priority and, among claims of equal priority, ratably to the extent of assets legally available therefor. Any remaining assets shall be distributed to the stockholders of the dissolved corporation.

(c) Directors of a dissolved corporation or governing persons of a successor entity which has complied with subsection (a) or (b) of this section shall not be personally liable to the claimants of the dissolved corporation.

(d) As used in this section, the term "successor entity" has the meaning set forth in §280(e) of this title.

(e) The term "priority," as used in this section, does not refer either to the order of payments set forth in paragraph (a)(1)-(4) of this section or to the relative times at which any claims mature or are reduced to judgment.

(f) In the case of a nonprofit nonstock corporation, provisions of this section regarding distributions to members shall not apply to the extent that those provisions conflict with any other applicable law or with that corporation's certificate of incorporation or bylaws.

§282. Liability of Stockholders of Dissolved Corporations

(a) A stockholder of a dissolved corporation the assets of which were distributed pursuant to §281(a) or (b) of this title shall not be liable for any claim against the corporation in an amount in excess of such stockholder's pro rata share of the claim or the amount so distributed to such stockholder, whichever is less.

(b) A stockholder of a dissolved corporation the assets of which were distributed pursuant to §281(a) of this title shall not be liable for any claim against the corporation on which an action, suit or proceeding is not begun prior to the expiration of the period described in §278 of this title.

(c) The aggregate liability of any stockholder of a dissolved corporation for claims against the dissolved corporation shall not exceed the amount distributed to such stockholder in dissolution.

§284. Revocation or Forfeiture of Charter; Proceedings

(a) Upon motion by the Attorney General, the Court of Chancery shall have jurisdiction to revoke or forfeit the charter of any corporation for abuse, misuse or nonuse of its corporate powers, privileges or franchises. The Attorney General shall proceed for this purpose by complaint in the Court of Chancery.

(b) The Court of Chancery shall have power, by appointment of trustees, receivers or otherwise, to administer and wind up the affairs of any corporation whose charter shall be revoked or forfeited by the Court of Chancery under this section, and to make such orders and decrees with respect thereto as shall be just and equitable respecting its affairs and assets and the rights of its stockholders and creditors.

(c) No proceeding shall be instituted under this section for nonuse of any corporation's powers, privileges or franchises during the first 2 years after its incorporation.

SUBCHAPTER XIII. SUITS AGAINST CORPORATIONS, DIRECTORS, OFFICERS OR STOCKHOLDERS

§325. Actions Against Officers, Directors or Stockholders to Enforce Liability of Corporation; Unsatisfied Judgment Against Corporation

(a) When the officers, directors or stockholders of any corporation shall be liable by the provisions of this chapter to pay the debts of the corporation, or any part thereof, any person to whom they are liable may have an action, at law or in equity, against any 1 or more of them, and the complaint shall state the claim against the corporation, and the ground on which the plaintiff expects to charge the defendants personally.

(b) No suit shall be brought against any officer, director or stockholder for any debt of a corporation of which such person is an officer, director or stockholder, until judgment be obtained therefor against the corporation and execution thereon returned unsatisfied.

§327. Stockholders' Derivative Action; Allegation of Stock Ownership

In any derivative suit instituted by a stockholder of a corporation, it shall be averred in the complaint that the plaintiff was a stockholder of the corporation at the time of the transaction of which such stockholder complains or that such stockholder's stock thereafter devolved upon such stockholder by operation of law.

§329. Defective Organization of Corporation as Defense

(a) No corporation of this State and no person sued by any such corporation shall be permitted to assert the want of legal organization as a defense to any claim.

(b) This section shall not be construed to prevent judicial inquiry into the regularity or validity of the organization of a corporation, or its lawful possession of any corporate power it may assert in any other suit or proceeding where its corporate existence or the power to exercise the corporate rights it asserts is challenged, and evidence tending to sustain the challenge shall be admissible in any such suit or proceeding.

SUBCHAPTER XIV. CLOSE CORPORATIONS; SPECIAL PROVISIONS

§341. Law Applicable to Close Corporation

(a) This subchapter applies to all close corporations, as defined in §342 of this title. Unless a corporation elects to become a close corporation under this subchapter in the manner prescribed in this subchapter, it shall be subject in all respects to this chapter, except this subchapter.

(b) This chapter shall be applicable to all close corporations, as defined in §342 of this title, except insofar as this subchapter otherwise provides.

§342. Close Corporation Defined; Contents of Certificate of Incorporation

(a) A close corporation is a corporation organized under this chapter whose certificate of incorporation contains the provisions required by §102 of this title and, in addition, provides that:

(1) All of the corporation's issued stock of all classes, exclusive of treasury shares, shall be represented by certificates and shall be held of record by not more than a specified number of persons, not exceeding 30; and

(2) All of the issued stock of all classes shall be subject to 1 or more of the restrictions on transfer permitted by §202 of this title; and

(3) The corporation shall make no offering of any of its stock of any class which would constitute a "public offering" within the meaning of the United

States Securities Act of 1933 [15 U.S.C. §77a et seq.] as it may be amended from time to time.

(b) The certificate of incorporation of a close corporation may set forth the qualifications of stockholders, either by specifying classes of persons who shall be entitled to be holders of record of stock of any class, or by specifying classes of persons who shall not be entitled to be holders of stock of any class or both.

(c) For purposes of determining the number of holders of record of the stock of a close corporation, stock which is held in joint or common tenancy or by the entireties shall be treated as held by 1 stockholder.

§343. Formation of a Close Corporation

A close corporation shall be formed in accordance with §§101, 102 and 103 of this title, except that:

(1) Its certificate of incorporation shall contain a heading stating the name of the corporation and that it is a close corporation; and

(2) Its certificate of incorporation shall contain the provisions required by §342 of this title.

§344. Election of Existing Corporation to Become a Close Corporation

Any corporation organized under this chapter may become a close corporation under this subchapter by executing, acknowledging and filing in accordance with §103 of this title, a certificate of amendment of its certificate of incorporation which shall contain a statement that it elects to become a close corporation, the provisions required by §342 of this title to appear in the certificate of incorporation of a close corporation, and a heading stating the name of the corporation and that it is a close corporation. Such amendment shall be adopted in accordance with the requirements of §§241 or 242 of this title, except that it must be approved by a vote of the holders of record of at least 2/3 of the shares of each class of stock of the corporation which are outstanding.

§345. Limitations on Continuation of Close Corporation Status

A close corporation continues to be such and to be subject to this subchapter until:

(1) It files with the Secretary of State a certificate of amendment deleting from its certificate of incorporation the provisions required or permitted by §342 of this title to be stated in the certificate of incorporation to qualify it as a close corporation; or

(2) Any 1 of the provisions or conditions required or permitted by §342 of this title to be stated in a certificate of incorporation to qualify a corporation as a close corporation has in fact been breached and neither the corporation nor any of its stockholders takes the steps required by §348 of this title to prevent such loss of status or to remedy such breach.

§346. *Voluntary Termination of Close Corporation Status by Amendment of Certificate of Incorporation; Vote Required*

(a) A corporation may voluntarily terminate its status as a close corporation and cease to be subject to this subchapter by amending its certificate of incorporation to delete therefrom the additional provisions required or permitted by §342 of this title to be stated in the certificate of incorporation of a close corporation. Any such amendment shall be adopted and shall become effective in accordance with §242 of this title, except that it must be approved by a vote of the holders of record of at least 2/3 of the shares of each class of stock of the corporation which are outstanding.

(b) The certificate of incorporation of a close corporation may provide that on any amendment to terminate its status as a close corporation, a vote greater than 2/3 or a vote of all shares of any class shall be required; and if the certificate of incorporation contains such a provision, that provision shall not be amended, repealed or modified by any vote less than that required to terminate the corporation's status as a close corporation.

§347. *Issuance or Transfer of Stock of a Close Corporation in Breach of Qualifying Conditions*

(a) If stock of a close corporation is issued or transferred to any person who is not entitled under any provision of the certificate of incorporation permitted by §342(b) of this title to be a holder of record of stock of such corporation, and if the certificate for such stock conspicuously notes the qualifications of the persons entitled to be holders of record thereof, such person is conclusively presumed to have notice of the fact of such person's ineligibility to be a stockholder.

(b) If the certificate of incorporation of a close corporation states the number of persons, not in excess of 30, who are entitled to be holders of record of its stock, and if the certificate for such stock conspicuously states such number, and if the issuance or transfer of stock to any person would cause the stock to be held by more than such number of persons, the person to whom such stock is issued or transferred is conclusively presumed to have notice of this fact.

(c) If a stock certificate of any close corporation conspicuously notes the fact of a restriction on transfer of stock of the corporation, and the restriction is one which is permitted by §202 of this title, the transferee of the stock is conclusively presumed to have notice of the fact that such person has acquired stock in violation of the restriction, if such acquisition violates the restriction.

(d) Whenever any person to whom stock of a close corporation has been issued or transferred has, or is conclusively presumed under this section to have, notice either:

(1) That such person is a person not eligible to be a holder of stock of the corporation; or

(2) That transfer of stock to such person would cause the stock of the corporation to be held by more than the number of persons permitted by its certificate of incorporation to hold stock of the corporation; or (3) That the

transfer of stock is in violation of a restriction on transfer of stock, the corporation may, at its option, refuse to register transfer of the stock into the name of the transferee.

(e) Subsection (d) of this section shall not be applicable if the transfer of stock, even though otherwise contrary to subsection (a), (b) or (c), of this section has been consented to by all the stockholders of the close corporation, or if the close corporation has amended its certificate of incorporation in accordance with §346 of this title.

(f) The term "transfer," as used in this section, is not limited to a transfer for value.

(g) The provisions of this section do not in any way impair any rights of a transferee regarding any right to rescind the transaction or to recover under any applicable warranty express or implied.

§348. Involuntary Termination of Close Corporation Status; Proceeding to Prevent Loss of Status

(a) If any event occurs as a result of which 1 or more of the provisions or conditions included in a close corporation's certificate of incorporation pursuant to §342 of this title to qualify it as a close corporation has been breached, the corporation's status as a close corporation under this subchapter shall terminate unless:

(1) Within 30 days after the occurrence of the event, or within 30 days after the event has been discovered, whichever is later, the corporation files with the Secretary of State a certificate, executed and acknowledged in accordance with §103 of this title, stating that a specified provision or condition included in its certificate of incorporation pursuant to §342 of this title to qualify it as a close corporation has ceased to be applicable, and furnishes a copy of such certificate to each stockholder; and

(2) The corporation concurrently with the filing of such certificate takes such steps as are necessary to correct the situation which threatens its status as a close corporation, including, without limitation, the refusal to register the transfer of stock which has been wrongfully transferred as provided by §347 of this title, or a proceeding under subsection (b) of this section.

(b) The Court of Chancery, upon the suit of the corporation or any stockholder, shall have jurisdiction to issue all orders necessary to prevent the corporation from losing its status as a close corporation, or to restore its status as a close corporation by enjoining or setting aside any act or threatened act on the part of the corporation or a stockholder which would be inconsistent with any of the provisions or conditions required or permitted by §342 of this title to be stated in the certificate of incorporation of a close corporation, unless it is an act approved in accordance with §346 of this title. The Court of Chancery may enjoin or set aside any transfer or threatened transfer of stock of a close corporation which is contrary to the terms of its certificate of incorporation or of any transfer restriction permitted by §202 of this title, and may enjoin any public offering, as defined in §342 of this title, or threatened public offering of stock of the close corporation.

§349. Corporate Option Where a Restriction on Transfer of a Security Is Held Invalid

If a restriction on transfer of a security of a close corporation is held not to be authorized by §202 of this title, the corporation shall nevertheless have an option, for a period of 30 days after the judgment setting aside the restriction becomes final, to acquire the restricted security at a price which is agreed upon by the parties, or if no agreement is reached as to price, then at the fair value as determined by the Court of Chancery. In order to determine fair value, the Court may appoint an appraiser to receive evidence and report to the Court such appraiser's findings and recommendation as to fair value.

§350. Agreements Restricting Discretion of Directors

A written agreement among the stockholders of a close corporation holding a majority of the outstanding stock entitled to vote, whether solely among themselves or with a party not a stockholder, is not invalid, as between the parties to the agreement, on the ground that it so relates to the conduct of the business and affairs of the corporation as to restrict or interfere with the discretion or powers of the board of directors. The effect of any such agreement shall be to relieve the directors and impose upon the stockholders who are parties to the agreement the liability for managerial acts or omissions which is imposed on directors to the extent and so long as the discretion or powers of the board in its management of corporate affairs is controlled by such agreement.

§351. Management by Stockholders

The certificate of incorporation of a close corporation may provide that the business of the corporation shall be managed by the stockholders of the corporation rather than by a board of directors. So long as this provision continues in effect:

(1) No meeting of stockholders need be called to elect directors;

(2) Unless the context clearly requires otherwise, the stockholders of the corporation shall be deemed to be directors for purposes of applying provisions of this chapter; and

(3) The stockholders of the corporation shall be subject to all liabilities of directors.

Such a provision may be inserted in the certificate of incorporation by amendment if all incorporators and subscribers or all holders of record of all of the outstanding stock, whether or not having voting power, authorize such a provision. An amendment to the certificate of incorporation to delete such a provision shall be adopted by a vote of the holders of a majority of all outstanding stock of the corporation, whether or not otherwise entitled to vote. If the certificate of incorporation contains a provision authorized by this section, the existence of such provision shall be noted conspicuously on the face or back of every stock certificate issued by such corporation.

§352. Appointment of Custodian for Close Corporation

(a) In addition to §226 of this title respecting the appointment of a custodian for any corporation, the Court of Chancery, upon application of any stockholder, may appoint 1 or more persons to be custodians, and, if the corporation is insolvent, to be receivers, of any close corporation when:

(1) Pursuant to §351 of this title the business and affairs of the corporation are managed by the stockholders and they are so divided that the business of the corporation is suffering or is threatened with irreparable injury and any remedy with respect to such deadlock provided in the certificate of incorporation or bylaws or in any written agreement of the stockholders has failed; or

(2) The petitioning stockholder has the right to the dissolution of the corporation under a provision of the certificate of incorporation permitted by §355 of this title.

(b) In lieu of appointing a custodian for a close corporation under this section or §226 of this title the Court of Chancery may appoint a provisional director, whose powers and status shall be as provided in §353 of this title if the Court determines that it would be in the best interest of the corporation. Such appointment shall not preclude any subsequent order of the Court appointing a custodian for such corporation.

§353. Appointment of a Provisional Director in Certain Cases

(a) Notwithstanding any contrary provision of the certificate of incorporation or the bylaws or agreement of the stockholders, the Court of Chancery may appoint a provisional director for a close corporation if the directors are so divided respecting the management of the corporation's business and affairs that the votes required for action by the board of directors cannot be obtained with the consequence that the business and affairs of the corporation can no longer be conducted to the advantage of the stockholders generally.

(b) An application for relief under this section must be filed (1) by at least one half of the number of directors then in office, (2) by the holders of at least one third of all stock then entitled to elect directors, or, (3) if there be more than 1 class of stock then entitled to elect 1 or more directors, by the holders of two thirds of the stock of any such class; but the certificate of incorporation of a close corporation may provide that a lesser proportion of the directors or of the stockholders or of a class of stockholders may apply for relief under this section.

(c) A provisional director shall be an impartial person who is neither a stockholder nor a creditor of the corporation or of any subsidiary or affiliate of the corporation, and whose further qualifications, if any, may be determined by the Court of Chancery. A provisional director is not a receiver of the corporation and does not have the title and powers of a custodian or receiver appointed under §§226 and 291 of this title. A provisional director shall have all the rights and powers of a duly elected director of the corporation, including the right to notice of and to vote at meetings of directors, until such time as such person shall be removed by order of the Court of Chancery or by the holders of a majority of all shares then entitled to vote to elect directors or by the holders of two thirds of the shares of that class of voting shares which filed the application for appointment of a provisional director. A provisional director's compensation shall be determined by agreement between such person and the corporation subject to approval of the Court of Chancery, which may fix such person's compensation in the absence of agreement or in the event of disagreement between the provisional director and the corporation.

(d) Even though the requirements of subsection (b) of this section relating to the number of directors or stockholders who may petition for appointment of a provisional director are not satisfied, the Court of Chancery may nevertheless appoint a provisional director if permitted by §352(b) of this title.

§354. Operating Corporation as Partnership

No written agreement among stockholders of a close corporation, nor any provision of the certificate of incorporation or of the bylaws of the corporation, which agreement or provision relates to any phase of the affairs of such corporation, including but not limited to the management of its business or declaration and payment of dividends or other division of profits or the election of directors or officers or the employment of stockholders by the corporation or the arbitration of disputes, shall be invalid on the ground that it is an attempt by the parties to the agreement or by the stockholders of the corporation to treat the corporation as if it were a partnership or to arrange relations among the stockholders or between the stockholders and the corporation in a manner that would be appropriate only among partners.

§355. Stockholders' Option to Dissolve Corporation

(a) The certificate of incorporation of any close corporation may include a provision granting to any stockholder, or to the holders of any specified number or percentage of shares of any class of stock, an option to have the corporation dissolved at will or upon the occurrence of any specified event or contingency. Whenever any such option to dissolve is exercised, the stockholders exercising such option shall give written notice thereof to all other stockholders. After the expiration of 30 days following the sending of such notice, the dissolution of the corporation shall proceed as if the required number of stockholders having voting power had consented in writing to dissolution of the corporation as provided by §228 of this title.

(b) If the certificate of incorporation as originally filed does not contain a provision authorized by subsection (a) of this section, the certificate may be amended to include such provision if adopted by the affirmative vote of the holders of all the outstanding stock, whether or not entitled to vote, unless the certificate of incorporation specifically authorizes such an amendment by a vote which shall be not less than 2/3 of all the outstanding stock whether or not entitled to vote.

(c) Each stock certificate in any corporation whose certificate of incorporation authorizes dissolution as permitted by this section shall conspicuously note on the face thereof the existence of the provision. Unless noted conspicuously on the face of the stock certificate, the provision is ineffective.

§356. Effect of This Subchapter on Other Laws

This subchapter shall not be deemed to repeal any statute or rule of law which is or would be applicable to any corporation which is organized under this chapter but is not a close corporation.

SUBCHAPTER XV. PUBLIC BENEFIT CORPORTIONS

§361. Law Applicable to Public Benefit Corporations; How Formed

This subchapter applies to all public benefit corporations, as defined in §362 of this title. If a corporation elects to become a public benefit corporation under this subchapter in the manner prescribed in this subchapter, it shall be subject in all respects to the provisions of this chapter, except to the extent this subchapter imposes additional or different requirements, in which case such requirements shall apply.

§362. Public Benefit Corporation Defined; Contents of Certificate of Incorporation

(a) A "public benefit corporation" is a for-profit corporation organized under and subject to the requirements of this chapter that is intended to produce a public benefit or public benefits and to operate in a responsible and sustainable manner. To that end, a public benefit corporation shall be managed in a manner that balances the stockholders' pecuniary interests, the best interests of those materially affected by the corporation's conduct, and the public benefit or public benefits identified in its certificate of incorporation. In the certificate of incorporation, a public benefit corporation shall:

(1) Identify within its statement of business or purpose pursuant to §102(a)(3) of this title one or more specific public benefits to be promoted by the corporation; and

(2) State within its heading that it is a public benefit corporation.

(b) "Public benefit" means a positive effect (or reduction of negative effects) on 1 or more categories of persons, entities, communities or interests (other than stockholders in their capacities as stockholders) including, but not limited to, effects of an artistic, charitable, cultural, economic, educational, environmental, literary, medical, religious, scientific or technological nature. "Public benefit provisions" means the provisions of a certificate of incorporation contemplated by this subchapter.

(c) The name of the public benefit corporation may contain the words "public benefit corporation," or the abbreviation "P.B.C.," or the designation "PBC," which shall be deemed to satisfy the requirements of §102(a)(1)(i) of this title. If the name does not contain such language, the corporation shall, prior to issuing unissued shares of stock or disposing of treasury shares, provide notice to any person to whom such stock is issued or who acquires such treasury shares that it is a public benefit corporation; provided that such notice need not be provided if the issuance or disposal is pursuant to an offering registered under the Securities Act of 1933 or if, at the time of issuance or disposal, the corporation has a class of securities that is registered under the Securities Exchange Act of 1934.

§363. Nonprofit Nonstock Corporations

A nonprofit nonstock corporation may not be a constituent corporation to any merger or consolidation with a public benefit corporation or in which the certificate of incorporation of the surviving corporation is amended to include a provision authorized by §362 (a)(1) of this title.

§364. *Stock Certificates; Notices Regarding Uncertificated Stock*

Any stock certificate issued by a public benefit corporation shall note conspicuously that the corporation is a public benefit corporation formed pursuant to this subchapter. Any notice given by a public benefit corporation pursuant to §151(f) of this title shall state conspicuously that the corporation is a public benefit corporation formed pursuant to this subchapter.

§365. *Duties of Directors*

(a) The board of directors shall manage or direct the business and affairs of the public benefit corporation in a manner that balances the pecuniary interests of the stockholders, the best interests of those materially affected by the corporation's conduct, and the specific public benefit or public benefits identified in its certificate of incorporation.

(b) A director of a public benefit corporation shall not, by virtue of the public benefit provisions or §362(a) of this title, have any duty to any person on account of any interest of such person in the public benefit or public benefits identified in the certificate of incorporation or on account of any interest materially affected by the corporation's conduct and, with respect to a decision implicating the balance requirement in subsection (a) of this section, will be deemed to satisfy such director's fiduciary duties to stockholders and the corporation if such director's decision is both informed and disinterested and not such that no person of ordinary, sound judgment would approve.

(c) A director's ownership of or other interest in the stock of the public benefit corporation shall not alone, for the purposes of this section, create a conflict of interest on the part of the director with respect to the director's decision implicating the balancing requirement in subsection (a) of this section, except to the extent that such ownership or interest would create a conflict of interest if the corporation were not a public benefit corporation. In the absence of a conflict of interest, no failure to satisfy that balancing requirement shall, for the purposes of §102(b)(7) or §145 of this title, constitute an act or omission not in good faith, or a breach of the duty of loyalty, unless the certificate of incorporation so provides.

§366. *Periodic Statements and Third Party Certification*

(a) A public benefit corporation shall include in every notice of a meeting of stockholders a statement to the effect that it is a public benefit corporation formed pursuant to this subchapter.

(b) A public benefit corporation shall no less than biennially provide its stockholders with a statement as to the corporation's promotion of the public benefit or public benefits identified in the certificate of incorporation and of the best interests of those materially affected by the corporation's conduct. The statement shall include:

(1) The objectives the board of directors has established to promote such public benefit or public benefits and interests;

(2) The standards the board of directors has adopted to measure the corporation's progress in promoting such public benefit or public benefits and interests;

(3) Objective factual information based on those standards regarding the corporation's success in meeting the objectives for promoting such public benefit or public benefits and interests; and

(4) An assessment of the corporation's success in meeting the objectives and promoting such public benefit or public benefits and interests.

(c) The certificate of incorporation or bylaws of a public benefit corporation may require that the corporation:

(1) Provide the statement described in subsection (b) more frequently than biennially;

(2) Make the statement described in subsection (b) available to the public; and/or

(3) Use a third party standard in connection with and/or attain a periodic third party certification addressing the corporation's promotion of the public benefit or public benefits identified in the certificate of incorporation and/or the best interests of those materially affected by the corporation's conduct.

§367. *Suits to Enforce the Requirements of §365(a) of this Title*

Any action to enforce the balancing requirement of §365(a) of this title, including any individual, derivative or any other type of action, may not be brought unless the plaintiffs in such action own individually or collectively, as of the date of instituting such action, at least 2% of the corporation's outstanding shares or, in the case of a corporation with shares listed on a national securities exchange, the lesser of such percentage or shares of the corporation with at least $2,000,000 as of the date the action is instituted. This section shall not relieve the plaintiffs from complying with any other conditions applicable to filing a derivative action including §327 of this title and any rules of the court in which the action is filed.

§368. *No Effect on Other Corporations*

This subchapter shall not affect a statute or rule of law that is applicable to a corporation that is not a public benefit corporation, except as provided in §363 of this title.

SUBCHAPTER XVII. DOMESTICATION AND TRANSFER

§390. *Transfer or Continuance of Domestic Corporations*

(a) Upon compliance with the provisions of this section, any corporation existing under the laws of this State may transfer to or domesticate or continue in any foreign jurisdiction and, in connection therewith, may elect to continue its existence as a corporation of this State. As used in this section, the term:

(1) "Foreign jurisdiction" means any foreign country, or other foreign jurisdiction (other than the United States, any state, the District of Columbia, or any possession or territory of the United States); and

(2) "Resulting entity" means the entity formed, incorporated, created or otherwise coming into being as a consequence of the transfer of the corporation

to, or its domestication or continuance in, a foreign jurisdiction pursuant to this section.

(b) The board of directors of the corporation which desires to transfer to or domesticate or continue in a foreign jurisdiction shall adopt a resolution approving such transfer, domestication or continuance specifying the foreign jurisdiction to which the corporation shall be transferred or in which the corporation shall be domesticated or continued and, if applicable, that in connection with such transfer, domestication or continuance the corporation's existence as a corporation of this State is to continue and recommending the approval of such transfer or domestication or continuance by the stockholders of the corporation. Such resolution shall be submitted to the stockholders of the corporation at an annual or special meeting. Due notice of the time, place and purpose of the meeting shall be given to each holder of stock, whether voting or nonvoting, of the corporation at the address of the stockholder as it appears on the records of the corporation, at least 20 days prior to the date of the meeting. At the meeting, the resolution shall be considered and a vote taken for its adoption or rejection. If all outstanding shares of stock of the corporation, whether voting or nonvoting, shall be voted for the adoption of the resolution, the corporation shall file with the Secretary of State a certificate of transfer if its existence as a corporation of this State is to cease or a certificate of transfer and domestic continuance if its existence as a corporation of this State is to continue, executed in accordance with §103 of this title, which certifies:

(1) The name of the corporation, and if it has been changed, the name under which it was originally incorporated.

(2) The date of filing of its original certificate of incorporation with the Secretary of State.

(3) The foreign jurisdiction to which the corporation shall be transferred or in which it shall be domesticated or continued and the name of the resulting entity.

(4) That the transfer, domestication or continuance of the corporation has been approved in accordance with the provisions of this section.

(5) In the case of a certificate of transfer, (i) that the existence of the corporation as a corporation of this State shall cease when the certificate of transfer becomes effective, and (ii) the agreement of the corporation that it may be served with process in this State in any proceeding for enforcement of any obligation of the corporation arising while it was a corporation of this State which shall also irrevocably appoint the Secretary of State as its agent to accept service of process in any such proceeding and specify the address (which may not be that of the corporation's registered agent without the written consent of the corporation's registered agent, such consent to be filed along with the certificate of transfer) to which a copy of such process shall be mailed by the Secretary of State. Process may be served upon the Secretary of State under this subsection by means of electronic transmission but only as prescribed by the Secretary of State. The Secretary of State is authorized to issue such rules and regulations with respect to such service as the Secretary of State deems necessary or appropriate. In the event of service upon the Secretary of State in accordance with this subsection, the Secretary of State shall forthwith notify such corporation that has transferred out of the State

of Delaware by letter, directed to such corporation that has transferred out of the State of Delaware at the address so specified, unless such corporation shall have designated in writing to the Secretary of State a different address for such purpose, in which case it shall be mailed to the last address designated. Such letter shall be sent by a mail or courier service that includes a record of mailing or deposit with the courier and a record of delivery evidenced by the signature of the recipient. Such letter shall enclose a copy of the process and any other papers served on the Secretary of State pursuant to this subsection. It shall be the duty of the plaintiff in the event of such service to serve process and any other papers in duplicate, to notify the Secretary of State that service is being effected pursuant to this subsection and to pay the Secretary of State the sum of $50 for the use of the State, which sum shall be taxed as part of the costs in the proceeding, if the plaintiff shall prevail therein. The Secretary of State shall maintain an alphabetical record of any such service setting forth the name of the plaintiff and the defendant, the title, docket number and nature of the proceeding in which process has been served, the fact that service has been effected pursuant to this subsection, the return date thereof, and the day and hour service was made. The Secretary of State shall not be required to retain such information longer than 5 years from receipt of the service of process.

(6) In the case of a certificate of transfer and domestic continuance, that the corporation will continue to exist as a corporation of this State after the certificate of transfer and domestic continuance becomes effective.

(c) Upon the filing of a certificate of transfer in accordance with subsection (b) of this section and payment to the Secretary of State of all fees prescribed under this title, the Secretary of State shall certify that the corporation has filed all documents and paid all fees required by this title, and thereupon the corporation shall cease to exist as a corporation of this State at the time the certificate of transfer becomes effective in accordance with §103 of this title. Such certificate of the Secretary of State shall be prima facie evidence of the transfer, domestication or continuance by such corporation out of this State.

(d) The transfer, domestication or continuance of a corporation out of this State in accordance with this section and the resulting cessation of its existence as a corporation of this State pursuant to a certificate of transfer shall not be deemed to affect any obligations or liabilities of the corporation incurred prior to such transfer, domestication or continuance, the personal liability of any person incurred prior to such transfer, domestication or continuance, or the choice of law applicable to the corporation with respect to matters arising prior to such transfer, domestication or continuance. Unless otherwise agreed or otherwise provided in the certificate of incorporation, the transfer, domestication or continuance of a corporation out of the State of Delaware in accordance with this section shall not require such corporation to wind up its affairs or pay its liabilities and distribute its assets under this title and shall not be deemed to constitute a dissolution of such corporation.

(e) If a corporation files a certificate of transfer and domestic continuance, after the time the certificate of transfer and domestic continuance becomes effective, the corporation shall continue to exist as a corporation of this State, and the law of the State of Delaware, including this title, shall apply to the corporation to the same extent as prior to such time. So long as a corporation continues to exist as a corporation of the State of Delaware following the filing of a certificate of transfer and domestic continuance, the continuing corporation and the resulting entity shall, for all purposes of the laws of the State of Delaware, constitute a single entity formed, incorporated, created or otherwise having come into being, as applicable, and existing under the laws of the State of Delaware and the laws of the foreign jurisdiction.

(f) When a corporation has transferred, domesticated or continued pursuant to this section, for all purposes of the laws of the State of Delaware, the resulting entity shall be deemed to be the same entity as the transferring, domesticating or continuing corporation and shall constitute a continuation of the existence of such corporation in the form of the resulting entity. When any transfer, domestication or continuance shall have become effective under this section, for all purposes of the laws of the State of Delaware, all of the rights, privileges and powers of the corporation that has transferred, domesticated or continued, and all property, real, personal and mixed, and all debts due to such corporation, as well as all other things and causes of action belonging to such corporation, shall remain vested in the resulting entity (and also in the corporation that has transferred, domesticated or continued, if and for so long as such corporation continues its existence as a corporation of this State) and shall be the property of such resulting entity (and also of the corporation that has transferred, domesticated or continued, if and for so long as such corporation continues its existence as a corporation of this State), and the title to any real property vested by deed or otherwise in such corporation shall not revert or be in any way impaired by reason of this title; but all rights of creditors and all liens upon any property of such corporation shall be preserved unimpaired, and all debts, liabilities and duties of such corporation shall remain attached to the resulting entity (and also to the corporation that has transferred, domesticated or continued, if and for so long as such corporation continues its existence as a corporation of this State), and may be enforced against it to the same extent as if said debts, liabilities and duties had originally been incurred or contracted by it in its capacity as such resulting entity. The rights, privileges, powers and interests in property of the corporation, as well as the debts, liabilities and duties of the corporation, shall not be deemed, as a consequence of the transfer, domestication or continuance, to have been transferred to the resulting entity for any purpose of the laws of the State of Delaware.

(g) In connection with a transfer, domestication or continuance under this section, shares of stock of the transferring, domesticating or continuing corporation may be exchanged for or converted into cash, property, or shares of stock, rights or securities of, or interests in, the resulting entity or, in addition to or in lieu thereof, may be exchanged for or converted into cash, property, or shares of stock, rights or securities of, or interests in, another corporation or other entity or may be cancelled.

(h) No vote of the stockholders of a corporation shall be necessary to authorize a transfer, domestication or continuance if no shares of the stock of such corporation shall have been issued prior to the adoption by the board of directors of the resolution approving the transfer, domestication or continuance.

(i) Whenever it shall be desired to transfer to or domesticate or continue in any foreign jurisdiction any nonstock corporation, the governing body shall perform all the acts necessary to effect a transfer, domestication or continuance which are required by this section to be performed by the board of directors of a corporation having capital stock. If the members of a nonstock corporation are entitled to vote for the election of members of its governing body or are entitled under the certificate of incorporation or the bylaws of such corporation to vote on such transfer, domestication or continuance or on a merger, consolidation, or dissolution of the corporation, they, and any other holder of any membership interest in the corporation, shall perform all the acts necessary to effect a transfer, domestication or continuance which are required by this section to be performed by the stockholders of a corporation having capital stock. If there is no member entitled to vote thereon, nor any other holder of any membership interest in the corporation, the transfer, domestication or continuance of the corporation shall be authorized at a meeting of the governing body, upon the adoption of a resolution to transfer or domesticate or continue by the vote of a majority of members of its governing body then in office. In all other respects, the method and proceedings for the transfer, domestication or continuance of a nonstock corporation shall conform as nearly as may be to the proceedings prescribed by this section for the transfer, domestication or continuance of corporations having capital stock. In the case of a charitable nonstock corporation, due notice of the corporation's intent to effect a transfer, domestication or continuance shall be mailed to the Attorney General of the State of Delaware 10 days prior to the date of the proposed transfer, domestication or continuance.

SUBCHAPTER XVIII. MISCELLANEOUS PROVISIONS

§391. Taxes and Fees Payable to Secretary of State upon Filing Certificate or Other Paper

(a) The following fees and penalties shall be collected by and paid to the Secretary of State, for the use of the State:

(1) Upon the receipt for filing of an original certificate of incorporation, the fee shall be computed on the basis of $0.02 for each share of authorized capital stock having par value up to and including 20,000 shares, $0.01 for each share in excess of 20,000 shares up to and including 200,000 shares, and 2/5 of a $0.01 for each share in excess of 200,000 shares; $0.01 for each share of authorized capital stock without par value up to and including 20,000 shares, 1/2 of $0.01 for each share in excess of 20,000 shares up to and including 2,000,000 shares, and 2/5 of a $0.01 for each share in excess of 2,000,000 shares. In no case shall the amount paid be less than $15. For the purpose of computing the fee on par value stock each $100 unit of the authorized capital stock shall be counted as 1 assessable share.

(2) Upon the receipt for filing of a certificate of amendment of certificate of incorporation, or a certificate of amendment of certificate of incorporation before payment of capital, or a restated certificate of incorporation, increasing the

authorized capital stock of a corporation, the fee shall be an amount equal to the difference between the fee computed at the foregoing rates upon the total authorized capital stock of the corporation including the proposed increase, and the fee computed at the foregoing rates upon the total authorized capital stock excluding the proposed increase. In no case shall the amount paid be less than $30. . . .

(4) Upon the receipt for filing of a certificate of merger or consolidation of 2 or more corporations, the fee shall be an amount equal to the difference between the fee computed at the foregoing rates upon the total authorized capital stock of the corporation created by the merger or consolidation, and the fee so computed upon the aggregate amount of the total authorized capital stock of the constituent corporations. In no case shall the amount paid be less than $75. The foregoing fee shall be in addition to any tax or fee required under any other law of this State to be paid by any constituent entity that is not a corporation in connection with the filing of the certificate of merger or consolidation. . . .

§394. Reserved Power of State to Amend or Repeal Chapter; Chapter Part of Corporation's Charter or Certificate of Incorporation

This chapter may be amended or repealed, at the pleasure of the General Assembly, but any amendment or repeal shall not take away or impair any remedy under this chapter against any corporation or its officers for any liability which shall have been previously incurred. This chapter and all amendments thereof shall be a part of the charter or certificate of incorporation of every corporation except so far as the same are inapplicable and inappropriate to the objects of the corporation.

California Corporations Code (Selected Sections)

CHAPTER 1. GENERAL PROVISIONS AND DEFINITIONS

CHAPTER 2. ORGANIZATION AND BYLAWS

CHAPTER 3. DIRECTORS AND MANAGEMENT

CHAPTER 1. GENERAL PROVISIONS AND DEFINITIONS

§114. Financial Statements or Comparable Statements or Items

All references in this division to financial statements, balance sheets, income statements, and statements of cashflows, and all references to assets, liabilities, earnings, retained earnings, and similar accounting items of a corporation mean those financial statements or comparable statements or items prepared or determined in conformity with generally accepted accounting principles then applicable, fairly presenting in conformity with generally accepted accounting principles the matters that they purport to present, subject to any specific accounting treatment required by a particular section of this division. Unless otherwise expressly stated, all references in this division to financial statements mean, in the case of a corporation that has subsidiaries, consolidated statements of the corporation and each of its subsidiaries as are required to be included in the consolidated statements under generally accepted accounting principles then applicable and all references to accounting items mean the items determined on a consolidated basis in accordance with the consolidated financial statements. Financial statements other than annual statements may be condensed or otherwise presented as permitted by authoritative accounting pronouncements.

§150. Affiliate; Affiliated

A corporation is an "affiliate" of, or a corporation is "affiliated" with, another specified corporation if it directly, or indirectly through one or more intermediaries, controls, is controlled by or is under common control with the other specified corporation.

§151. Approved by (or Approval of) the Board

"Approved by (or approval of) the board" means approved or ratified by the vote of the board or by the vote of a committee authorized to exercise the powers of the board, except as to matters not within the competence of the committee under Section 311.

§152. Approved by (or Approval of) the Outstanding Shares

"Approved by (or approval of) the outstanding shares" means approved by the affirmative vote of a majority of the outstanding shares entitled to vote. Such approval shall include the affirmative vote of a majority of the outstanding shares of each class or series entitled, by any provision of the articles or of this division, to vote as a class or series on the subject matter being voted upon and shall also include the affirmative vote of such greater proportion (including all) of the outstanding shares of any class or series if such greater proportion is required by the articles or this division.

§153. Approved by (or Approval of) the Shareholders

"Approved by (or approval of) the shareholders" means approved or ratified by the affirmative vote of a majority of the shares represented and voting at a duly held meeting at which a quorum is present (which shares voting affirmatively also constitute at least a majority of the required quorum) or by the written consent of shareholders (Section 603) or by the affirmative vote or written consent of such greater proportion (including all) of the shares of any class or series as may be provided in the articles or in this division for all or any specified shareholder action.

§158. Close Corporation

(a) "Close corporation" means a corporation, including a close social purpose corporation, whose articles contain, in addition to the provisions required by Section 202, a provision that all of the corporation's issued shares of all classes shall be held of record by not more than a specified number of persons, not exceeding 35, and a statement, "This corporation is a close corporation."

(b) The special provisions referred to in subdivision (a) may be included in the articles by amendment, but if such amendment is adopted after the issuance of shares only by the affirmative vote of all of the issued and outstanding shares of all classes.

(c) The special provisions referred to in subdivision (a) may be deleted from the articles by amendment, or the number of shareholders specified may be changed by amendment, but if such amendment is adopted after the issuance of shares, only by the affirmative vote of at least two-thirds of each class of the outstanding shares; provided, however, that the articles may provide for a lesser vote, but not less than a majority of the outstanding shares, or may deny a vote to any class, or both.

(d) In determining the number of shareholders for the purposes of the provision in the articles authorized by this section, spouses and the personal representative of either shall be counted as one regardless of how shares may be held by either or both of them, a trust or personal representative of a decedent holding shares shall be counted as one regardless of the number of trustees or beneficiaries, and a partnership or corporation or business association holding shares shall be counted as one (except that any such trust or entity the primary purpose of which was the acquisition or voting of the shares shall be counted according to the number of beneficial interests therein).

(e) A corporation shall cease to be a close corporation upon the filing of an amendment to its articles pursuant to subdivision (c) or, if it shall have more than the maximum number of holders of record of its shares specified in its articles as a result of an inter vivos transfer of shares which is not void under subdivision (d) of Section 418, the transfer of shares on distribution by will or pursuant to the laws of descent and distribution, the dissolution of a partnership or corporation or business association, or the termination of a trust which holds shares, by court decree upon dissolution of a marriage or otherwise by operation of law. Promptly upon acquiring more than the specified number of holders of record of its shares, a close corporation shall execute and file an amendment to its articles deleting the special provisions referred to in subdivision (a) and deleting any other provisions not permissible for a corporation which is not a close corporation, which amendment shall be promptly approved and filed by the board and need not be approved by the outstanding shares.

(f) Nothing contained in this section shall invalidate any agreement among the shareholders to vote for the deletion from the articles of the special provisions referred to in subdivision (a) upon the lapse of a specified period of time or upon the occurrence of a certain event or condition or otherwise.

(g) The following sections contain specific references to close corporations: Sections 186, 202, 204, 300, 418, 421, 1111, 1201, 1800, and 1904.

§160. Control

(a) Except as provided in subdivision (b), "control" means the possession, direct or indirect, of the power to direct or cause the direction of the management and policies of a corporation.

(b) "Control" in Sections 181, 1001, and 1200 means the ownership directly or indirectly of shares or equity securities possessing more than 50 percent of the voting power of a domestic corporation, a foreign corporation, or an other business entity.

§161. *Constituent Corporation*

"Constituent corporation" means a corporation which is merged with or into one or more other corporations or one or more other business entities and includes a surviving corporation.

§165. *Disappearing Corporation*

"Disappearing corporation" means a constituent corporation which is not the surviving corporation.

§166. *Distribution to Its Shareholders*

"Distribution to its shareholders" means the transfer of cash or property by a corporation to its shareholders without consideration, whether by way of dividend or otherwise, except a dividend in shares of the corporation, or the purchase or redemption of its shares for cash or property, including the transfer, purchase, or redemption by a subsidiary of the corporation. The time of any distribution by way of dividend shall be the date of declaration thereof and the time of any distribution by purchase or redemption of shares shall be the date cash or property is transferred by the corporation, whether or not pursuant to a contract of an earlier date; provided, that where a debt obligation that is a security (as defined in Section 8102 of the Commercial Code) is issued in exchange for shares the time of the distribution is the date when the corporation acquires the shares in the exchange. In the case of a sinking fund payment, cash or property is transferred within the meaning of this section at the time that it is delivered to a trustee for the holders of preferred shares to be used for the redemption of the shares or physically segregated by the corporation in trust for that purpose. "Distribution to its shareholders" shall not include (a) satisfaction of a final judgment of a court or tribunal of appropriate jurisdiction ordering the rescission of the issuance of shares, (b) the rescission by a corporation of the issuance of it [sic] shares, if the board determines (with any director who is, or would be, a party to the transaction not being entitled to vote) that (1) it is reasonably likely that the holder or holders of the shares in question could legally enforce a claim for the rescission, (2) that the rescission is in the best interests of the corporation, and (3) the corporation is likely to be able to meet its liabilities (except those for which payment is otherwise adequately provided) as they mature, or (c) the repurchase by a corporation of its shares issued by it pursuant to Section 408, if the board determines (with any director who is, or would be, a party to the transaction not being entitled to vote) that (1) the repurchase is in the best interests of the corporation and that (2) the corporation is likely to be able to meet its liabilities (except those for which payment is otherwise adequately provided) as they mature.

§168. *Equity Security*

"Equity security" in Sections 181, 1001, 1113, 1200, and 1201 means any share or membership of a domestic or foreign corporation; any partnership interest, membership interest, or equivalent equity interest in an other business entity; and any security convertible with or without consideration into, or any warrant or right to subscribe to or purchase, any of the foregoing.

§172. Liquidation Price; Liquidation Preference

"Liquidation price" or "liquidation preference" means amounts payable on shares of any class upon voluntary or involuntary dissolution, winding up or distribution of the entire assets of the corporation, including any cumulative dividends accrued and unpaid, in priority to shares of another class or classes.

§174.5. Other Business Entity

"Other business entity" means a domestic or foreign limited liability company, limited partnership, general partnership, business trust, real estate investment trust, unincorporated association (other than a nonprofit association), or a domestic reciprocal insurer. . . .

§175. Parent

Except as used in Sections 1001, 1101, and 1113, a "parent" of a specified corporation is an affiliate in control (Section 160(a)) of that corporation directly or indirectly through one or more intermediaries. In Sections 1001, 1101, and 1113, "parent" means a person in control (Section 160(b)) of a domestic corporation, a foreign corporation, or an other business entity.

§181. Reorganization

"Reorganization" means either:

(a) A merger pursuant to Chapter 11 (commencing with Section 1100) other than a short-form merger (a "merger reorganization").

(b) The acquisition by one domestic corporation, foreign corporation, or other business entity in exchange, in whole or in part, for its equity securities (or the equity securities of a domestic corporation, a foreign corporation, or another business entity which is in control of the acquiring entity) of equity securities of another domestic corporation, foreign corporation, or other business entity if, immediately after the acquisition, the acquiring entity has control of the other entity (an "exchange reorganization").

(c) The acquisition by one domestic corporation, foreign corporation, or other business entity in exchange in whole or in part for its equity securities (or the equity securities of a domestic corporation, a foreign corporation, or an other business entity which is in control of the acquiring entity) or for its debt securities (or debt securities of a domestic corporation, foreign corporation, or other business entity which is in control of the acquiring entity) which are not adequately secured and which have a maturity date in excess of five years after the consummation of the reorganization, or both, of all or substantially all of the assets of another domestic corporation, foreign corporation, or other business entity (a "sale-of-assets reorganization").

§183.5. *Share Exchange Tender Offer*

"Share exchange tender offer" means any acquisition by one corporation in exchange in whole or in part for its equity securities (or the equity securities of a corporation which is in control of the acquiring corporation) of shares of another corporation, other than an exchange reorganization (subdivision (b) of Section 181).

§184. *Shares*

"Shares" means the units into which the proprietary interests in a corporation are divided in the articles.

§186. *Shareholders' Agreement*

"Shareholders' agreement" means a written agreement among all of the shareholders of a close corporation, or if a close corporation has only one shareholder between such shareholder and the corporation, as authorized by subdivision (b) of Section 300.

§190. *Surviving Corporation*

"Surviving corporation" means a corporation into which one or more other corporations or one or more other business entities are merged.

§194.7. *Voting Shift*

"Voting shift" means a change, pursuant to or by operation of a provision of the articles, in the relative rights of the holders of one or more classes or series of shares, voting as one or more separate classes or series, to elect one or more directors.

Chapter 2. Organization and Bylaws

§204. *Articles of Incorporation; Optional Provisions*

The articles of incorporation may set forth:

(a) Any or all of the following provisions, which shall not be effective unless expressly provided in the articles: . . .

(10) Provisions eliminating or limiting the personal liability of a director for monetary damages in an action brought by or in the right of the corporation for breach of a director's duties to the corporation and its shareholders, as set forth in Section 309, provided, however, that (A) such a provision may not eliminate or limit the liability of directors (i) for acts or omissions that involve intentional misconduct or a knowing and culpable violation of law, (ii) for acts or omissions that a director believes to be contrary to the best interests of the corporation or

its shareholders or that involve the absence of good faith on the part of the director, (iii) for any transaction from which a director derived an improper personal benefit, (iv) for acts or omissions that show a reckless disregard for the director's duty to the corporation or its shareholders in circumstances in which the director was aware, or should have been aware, in the ordinary course of performing a director's duties, of a risk of serious injury to the corporation or its shareholders, (v) for acts or omissions that constitute an unexcused pattern of inattention that amounts to an abdication of the director's duty to the corporation or its shareholders, (vi) under Section 310, or (vii) under Section 316, (B) no such provision shall eliminate or limit the liability of a director for any act or omission occurring prior to the date when the provision becomes effective, and (C) no such provision shall eliminate or limit the liability of an officer for any act or omission as an officer, notwithstanding that the officer is also a director or that his or her actions, if negligent or improper, have been ratified by the directors.

(11) A provision authorizing, whether by bylaw, agreement, or otherwise, the indemnification of agents (as defined in Section 317) in excess of that expressly permitted by Section 317 for those agents of the corporation for breach of duty to the corporation and its stockholders, provided, however, that the provision may not provide for indemnification of any agent for any acts or omissions or transactions from which a director may not be relieved of liability as set forth in the exception to paragraph (10) or as to circumstances in which indemnity is expressly prohibited by Section 317.

Notwithstanding this subdivision, in the case of a close corporation any of the provisions referred to above may be validly included in a shareholders' agreement. Notwithstanding this subdivision, bylaws may require for all or any actions by the board the affirmative vote of a majority of the authorized number of directors. Nothing contained in this subdivision shall affect the enforceability, as between the parties thereto, of any lawful agreement not otherwise contrary to public policy. . .

§204.5. Director Liability; Limiting Provision in Articles; Wording; Disclosure to Shareholders Regarding Provision

(a) If the articles of a corporation include a provision reading substantially as follows: "The liability of the directors of the corporation for monetary damages shall be eliminated to the fullest extent permissible under California law"; the corporation shall be considered to have adopted a provision as authorized by paragraph (10) of subdivision (a) of Section 204 and more specific wording shall not be required.

(b) This section shall not be construed as setting forth the exclusive method of adopting an article provision as authorized by paragraph (10) of subdivision (a) of Section 204.

(c) This section shall not change the otherwise applicable standards or duties to make full and fair disclosure to shareholders when approval of such a provision is sought.

Chapter 3. Directors and Management

§300. *Powers of Board; Delegation; Close Corporations; Shareholders' Agreements; Validity; Liability; Failure to Observe Formalities*

(a) Subject to the provisions of this division and any limitations in the articles relating to action required to be approved by the shareholders (Section 153) or by the outstanding shares (Section 152), or by a less than majority vote of a class or series of preferred shares (Section 402.5), the business and affairs of the corporation shall be managed and all corporate powers shall be exercised by or under the direction of the board. The board may delegate the management of the day-to-day operation of the business of the corporation to a management company or other person provided that the business and affairs of the corporation shall be managed and all corporate powers shall be exercised under the ultimate direction of the board.

(b) Notwithstanding subdivision (a) or any other provision of this division, but subject to subdivision (c), no shareholders' agreement, which relates to any phase of the affairs of a close corporation, including but not limited to management of its business, division of its profits or distribution of its assets on liquidation, shall be invalid as between the parties thereto on the ground that it so relates to the conduct of the affairs of the corporation as to interfere with the discretion of the board or that it is an attempt to treat the corporation as if it were a partnership or to arrange their relationships in a manner that would be appropriate only between partners. A transferee of shares covered by such an agreement which is filed with the secretary of the corporation for inspection by any prospective purchaser of shares, who has actual knowledge thereof or notice thereof by a notation on the certificate pursuant to Section 418, is bound by its provisions and is a party thereto for the purposes of subdivision (d). Original issuance of shares by the corporation to a new shareholder who does not become a party to the agreement terminates the agreement, except that if the agreement so provides it shall continue to the extent it is enforceable apart from this subdivision. The agreement may not be modified, extended or revoked without the consent of such a transferee, subject to any provision of the agreement permitting modification, extension or revocation by less than unanimous agreement of the parties. A transferor of shares covered by such an agreement ceases to be a party thereto upon ceasing to be a shareholder of the corporation unless the transferor is a party thereto other than as a shareholder. An agreement made pursuant to this subdivision shall terminate when the corporation ceases to be a close corporation, except that if the agreement so provides it shall continue to the extent it is enforceable apart from this subdivision. This subdivision does not apply to an agreement authorized by subdivision (a) of Section 706.

(c) No agreement entered into pursuant to subdivision (b) may alter or waive any of the provisions of Sections 158, 417, 418, 500, 501, and 1111, subdivision (e) of Section 1201, Sections 2009, 2010, and 2011, or of Chapters 15 (commencing with Section 1500), 16 (commencing with Section 1600), 18 (commencing with Section 1800), and 22 (commencing with Section 2200). All other provisions of this division may be altered or waived as between the parties thereto in a shareholders' agreement, except the required filing of any document with the Secretary of State.

(d) An agreement of the type referred to in subdivision (b) shall, to the extent and so long as the discretion or powers of the board in its management of corporate affairs is controlled by such agreement, impose upon each shareholder who is a party thereto liability for managerial acts performed or omitted by such person pursuant thereto that is otherwise imposed by this division upon directors, and the directors shall be relieved to that extent from such liability.

(e) The failure of a close corporation to observe corporate formalities relating to meetings of directors or shareholders in connection with the management of its affairs, pursuant to an agreement authorized by subdivision (b), shall not be considered a factor tending to establish that the shareholders have personal liability for corporate obligations.

§301.4 Minimum of Directors from Underrepresented Community; Reports; Adoption of Regulations; Fines

(a) No later than the close of the 2021 calendar year, a publicly held domestic or foreign corporation whose principal executive offices, according to the corporation's SEC 10-K form, are located in California shall have a minimum of one director from an underrepresented community on its board. A corporation may increase the number of directors on its board to comply with this section.

(b) No later than the close of the 2022 calendar year, a publicly held domestic or foreign corporation whose principal executive offices, according to the corporation's SEC 10-K form, are located in California shall comply with the following:

(1) If its number of directors is nine or more, the corporation shall have a minimum of three directors from underrepresented communities.

(2) If its number of directors is more than four but fewer than nine, the corporation shall have a minimum of two directors from underrepresented communities.

(3) If its number of directors is four or fewer, the corporation shall have a minimum of one director from an underrepresented community.

(c) No later than March 1, 2022, and annually thereafter, the Secretary of State shall include in its report required by subdivision (d) of Section 301.3, at a minimum, all of the following:

(1) The number of corporations subject to this section that were in compliance with the requirements of this section during at least one point during the preceding calendar year.

(2) The number of publicly held corporations that moved their United States headquarters to California from another state or out of California into another state during the preceding calendar year.

(3) The number of publicly held corporations that were subject to this section during the preceding year, but are no longer publicly traded.

(d) (1) The Secretary of State may adopt regulations to implement this section. The Secretary of State may impose fines for violations of this section as follows:

(A) For failure to timely file board member information with the Secretary of State pursuant to a regulation adopted pursuant to this paragraph, the amount of one hundred thousand dollars ($100,000).

(B) For a first violation, as described in paragraph (2), the amount of one hundred thousand dollars ($100,000).

(C) For a second or subsequent violation, as described in paragraph (2), the amount of three hundred thousand dollars ($300,000).

(2) For the purposes of this subdivision, both of the following apply:

(A) Each director seat required by this section to be held by a director from an underrepresented community, which is not held by a director from an underrepresented community during at least a portion of a calendar year, shall count as a violation.

(B) A director from an underrepresented community having held a seat for at least a portion of the year shall not be a violation.

(3) Fines collected pursuant to this section shall be available, upon appropriation by the Legislature, for use by the Secretary of State to offset the cost of administering this section.

(e) For purposes of this section, the following definitions apply:

(1) "Director from an underrepresented community" means an individual who self-identifies as Black, African American, Hispanic, Latino, Asian, Pacific Islander, Native American, Native Hawaiian, or Alaska Native, or who self-identifies as gay, lesbian, bisexual, or transgender.

(2) "Publicly held corporation" means a corporation with outstanding shares listed on a major United States stock exchange.

§301.5. Listed Corporations; Classes of Directors; Cumulative Voting; Election of Directors; Amendment of Articles and Bylaws

(a) A listed corporation may, by amendment of its articles or bylaws, adopt provisions to divide the board of directors into two or three classes to serve for terms of two or three years respectively, or to eliminate cumulative voting, or both. After the issuance of shares, a corporation that is not a listed corporation may, by amendment of its articles or bylaws, adopt provisions to be effective when the corporation becomes a listed corporation to divide the board of directors into two or three classes to serve for terms of two or three years respectively, or to eliminate cumulative voting, or both. An article or bylaw amendment providing for division of the board of directors into classes, or any change in the number of classes, or the elimination of cumulative voting may only be adopted by the approval of the board and the outstanding shares (Section 152) voting as a single class, notwithstanding Section 903.

(b) If the board of directors is divided into two classes pursuant to subdivision (a), the authorized number of directors shall be no less than six and one-half of the directors or as close an approximation as possible shall be elected at each annual meeting of shareholders. If the board of directors is divided into three classes, the authorized number of directors shall be no less than nine and one-third of the directors or as close an approximation as possible shall be elected at each annual meeting of shareholders. Directors of a listed corporation may be elected by classes at a meeting of shareholders at which an amendment to the articles or bylaws described in subdivision (a) is approved, but the extended terms for directors are contingent on that approval, and in the case of an amendment to the articles, the filing of any necessary amendment to the articles pursuant to Section 905 or 910.

(c) If directors for more than one class are to be elected by the shareholders at any one meeting of shareholders and the election is by cumulative voting pursuant to Section 708, votes may be cumulated only for directors to be elected within each class.

(d) For purposes of this section, a "listed corporation" means a corporation with outstanding shares listed on the New York Stock Exchange, the NYSE American, the NASDAQ Global Market, or the NASDAQ Capital Market.

(e) Subject to subdivision (h), if a listed corporation having a board of directors divided into classes pursuant to subdivision (a) ceases to be a listed corporation for any reason, unless the articles of incorporation or bylaws of the corporation provide for the elimination of classes of directors at an earlier date or dates, the board of directors of the corporation shall cease to be divided into classes as to each class of directors on the date of the expiration of the term of the directors in that class and the term of each director serving at the time the corporation ceases to be a listed corporation (and the term of each director elected to fill a vacancy resulting from the death, resignation, or removal of any of those directors) shall continue until its expiration as if the corporation had not ceased to be a listed corporation.

(f) Subject to subdivision (h), if a listed corporation having a provision in its articles or bylaws eliminating cumulative voting pursuant to subdivision (a) or permitting noncumulative voting in the election of directors pursuant to that subdivision, or both, ceases to be a listed corporation for any reason, the shareholders shall be entitled to cumulate their votes pursuant to Section 708 at any election of directors occurring while the corporation is not a listed corporation notwithstanding that provision in its articles of incorporation or bylaws.

(g) Subject to subdivision (i), if a corporation that is not a listed corporation adopts amendments to its articles of incorporation or bylaws to divide its board of directors into classes or to eliminate cumulative voting, or both, pursuant to subdivision (a) and then becomes a listed corporation, unless the articles of incorporation or bylaws provide for those provisions to become effective at some other time and, in cases where classes of directors are provided for, identify the directors who, or the directorships that, are to be in each class or the method by which those directors or directorships are to be identified, the provisions shall become effective for the next election of directors after the corporation becomes a listed corporation at which all directors are to be elected.

(h) If a corporation ceases to be a listed corporation on or after the record date for a meeting of shareholders and before the conclusion of the meeting, including the conclusion of the meeting after an adjournment or postponement that does not require or result in the setting of a new record date, then, solely for purposes of subdivisions (e) and (f), the corporation shall not be deemed to have ceased to be a listed corporation until the conclusion of the meeting of shareholders.

(i) If a corporation becomes a listed corporation on or after the record date for a meeting of shareholders and before the conclusion of the meeting, including the conclusion of the meeting after an adjournment or postponement that does not require or result in the setting of a new record date, then, solely for purposes of subdivision (g), the corporation shall not be deemed to have become a listed corporation until the conclusion of the meeting of shareholders.

(j) If an article amendment referred to in subdivision (a) is adopted by a listed corporation, the certificate of amendment shall include a statement of the facts showing that the corporation is a listed corporation within the meaning of subdivision (d). If an article or bylaw amendment referred to in subdivision (a) is adopted by a corporation which is not a listed corporation, the provision, as adopted, shall include the following statement or the substantial equivalent: "This provision shall become effective only when the corporation becomes a listed corporation within the meaning of Section 301.5 of the Corporations Code."

§303. Directors; Removal Without Cause

(a) Any or all of the directors may be removed without cause if the removal is approved by the outstanding shares (Section 152), subject to the following:

(1) Except for a corporation to which paragraph (3) is applicable, no director may be removed (unless the entire board is removed) when the votes cast against removal, or not consenting in writing to the removal, would be sufficient to elect the director if voted cumulatively at an election at which the same total number of votes were cast (or, if the action is taken by written consent, all shares entitled to vote were voted) and the entire number of directors authorized at the time of the director's most recent election were then being elected.

(2) When by the provisions of the articles the holders of the shares of any class or series, voting as a class or series, are entitled to elect one or more directors, any director so elected may be removed only by the applicable vote of the holders of the shares of that class or series.

(3) A director of a corporation whose board of directors is classified pursuant to Section 301.5 may not be removed if the votes cast against removal of the director, or not consenting in writing to the removal, would be sufficient to elect the director if voted cumulatively (without regard to whether shares may otherwise be voted cumulatively) at an election at which the same total number of votes were cast (or, if the action is taken by written consent, all shares entitled to vote were voted) and either the number of directors elected at the most recent annual meeting of shareholders, or if greater, the number of directors for whom removal is being sought, were then being elected.

(b) Any reduction of the authorized number of directors or amendment reducing the number of classes of directors does not remove any director prior to the expiration of the director's term of office.

(c) Except as provided in this section and Sections 302 and 304, a director may not be removed prior to the expiration of the director's term of office.

§304. Removal for Cause; Shareholders Suit

The superior court of the proper county may, at the suit of shareholders holding at least 10 percent of the number of outstanding shares of any class, remove from office any director in case of fraudulent or dishonest acts or gross abuse of authority or discretion with reference to the corporation and may bar from reelection any director so removed for a period prescribed by the court. The corporation shall be made a party to such action.

§305. Filling of Vacancies; Resignation

(a) Unless otherwise provided in the articles or bylaws and except for a vacancy created by the removal of a director, vacancies on the board may be filled by approval of the board (Section 151) or, if the number of directors then in office is less than a quorum, by (1) the unanimous written consent of the directors then in office, (2) the affirmative vote of a majority of the directors then in office at a meeting held pursuant to notice or waivers of notice complying with Section 307 or (3) a sole remaining director. Unless the articles or a bylaw adopted by the shareholders provide that the board may fill vacancies occurring in the board by reason of the removal of directors, such vacancies may be filled only by approval of the shareholders (Section 153).

(b) The shareholders may elect a director at any time to fill any vacancy not filled by the directors. Any such election by written consent other than to fill a vacancy created by removal, which requires the unanimous consent of all shares entitled to vote for the election of directors, requires the consent of a majority of the outstanding shares entitled to vote.

(c) If, after the filling of any vacancy by the directors, the directors then in office who have been elected by the shareholders shall constitute less than a majority of the directors then in office, then both of the following shall be applicable:

(1) Any holder or holders of an aggregate of 5 percent or more of the total number of shares at the time outstanding having the right to vote for those directors may call a special meeting of shareholders, or

(2) The superior court of the proper county shall, upon application of such shareholder or shareholders, summarily order a special meeting of shareholders, to be held to elect the entire board. The term of office of any director shall terminate upon that election of a successor.

The hearing on any application filed pursuant to this subdivision shall be held on not less than 10 business days notice to the corporation. If the corporation intends to oppose the application, it shall file with the court a notice of opposition not later than five business days prior to the date set for the hearing. The application and any notice of opposition shall be supported by appropriate affidavits and the court's determination shall be made on the basis of the papers in the record; but, for good cause shown, the court may receive and consider at the hearing additional evidence, oral or documentary, and additional points and authorities. The hearing shall take precedence over all other matters not of a similar nature pending on the date set for the hearing.

(d) Any director may resign effective upon giving written notice to the chairperson of the board, the president, the secretary or the board of directors of the corporation, unless the notice specifies a later time for the effectiveness of such resignation. If the resignation is effective at a future time, a successor may be elected to take office when the resignation becomes effective.

§309. Performance of Duties by Director; Liability

(a) A director shall perform the duties of a director, including duties as a member of any committee of the board upon which the director may serve, in good faith, in a manner such director believes to be in the best interests of the corporation and its shareholders and with such care, including reasonable inquiry, as an ordinarily prudent person in a like position would use under similar circumstances.

(b) In performing the duties of a director, a director shall be entitled to rely on information, opinions, reports or statements, including financial statements and other financial data, in each case prepared or presented by any of the following:

(1) One or more officers or employees of the corporation whom the director believes to be reliable and competent in the matters presented.

(2) Counsel, independent accountants or other persons as to matters which the director believes to be within such person's professional or expert competence.

(3) A committee of the board upon which the director does not serve, as to matters within its designated authority, which committee the director believes to merit confidence,

so long as, in any such case, the director acts in good faith, after reasonable inquiry when the need therefor is indicated by the circumstances and without knowledge that would cause such reliance to be unwarranted.

(c) A person who performs the duties of a director in accordance with subdivisions (a) and (b) shall have no liability based upon any alleged failure to discharge the person's obligations as a director. In addition, the liability of a director for monetary damages may be eliminated or limited in a corporation's articles to the extent provided in paragraph (10) of subdivision (a) of Section 204.

§310. *Contracts in Which Director Has Material Financial Interest; Validity*

(a) No contract or other transaction between a corporation and one or more of its directors, or between a corporation and any corporation, firm or association in which one or more of its directors has a material financial interest, is either void or voidable because such director or directors or such other corporation, firm or association are parties or because such director or directors are present at the meeting of the board or a committee thereof which authorizes, approves or ratifies the contract or transaction, if

(1) The material facts as to the transaction and as to such director's interest are fully disclosed or known to the shareholders and such contract or transaction is approved by the shareholders (Section 153) in good faith, with the shares owned by the interested director or directors not being entitled to vote thereon, or

(2) The material facts as to the transaction and as to such director's interest are fully disclosed or known to the board or committee, and the board or committee authorizes, approves or ratifies the contract or transaction in good faith by a vote sufficient without counting the vote of the interested director or directors and the contract or transaction is just and reasonable as to the corporation at the time it is authorized, approved or ratified, or

(3) As to contracts or transactions not approved as provided in paragraph (1) or (2) of this subdivision, the person asserting the validity of the contract or transaction sustains the burden of proving that the contract or transaction was just and reasonable as to the corporation at the time it was authorized, approved or ratified.

A mere common directorship does not constitute a material financial interest within the meaning of this subdivision. A director is not interested within the meaning of this subdivision in a resolution fixing the compensation of another director as a director, officer or employee of the corporation, notwithstanding the fact that the first director is also receiving compensation from the corporation.

(b) No contract or other transaction between a corporation and any corporation or association of which one or more of its directors are directors is either void or voidable because such director or directors are present at the meeting of the board or a committee thereof which authorizes, approves or ratifies the contract or transaction, if

(1) The material facts as to the transaction and as to such director's other directorship are fully disclosed or known to the board or committee, and the board or committee authorizes, approves or ratifies the contract or transaction in good faith by a vote sufficient without counting the vote of the common director or directors or the contract or transaction is approved by the shareholders (Section 153) in good faith, or

(2) As to contracts or transactions not approved as provided in paragraph (1) of this subdivision, the contract or transaction is just and reasonable as to the corporation at the time it is authorized, approved or ratified.

This subdivision does not apply to contracts or transactions covered by subdivision (a).

(c) Interested or common directors may be counted in determining the presence of a quorum at a meeting of the board or a committee thereof which authorizes, approves or ratifies a contract or transaction.

§315. Loans or Guarantees of Obligations of Directors, Officers or Other Persons

(a) A corporation shall not make any loan of money or property to, or guarantee the obligation of, any director or officer of the corporation or of its parent, unless the transaction, or an employee benefit plan authorizing the loans or guaranties after disclosure of the right under such a plan to include officers or directors, is approved by a majority of the shareholders entitled to act thereon.

(b) Notwithstanding subdivision (a), if the corporation has outstanding shares held of record by 100 or more persons . . . on the date of approval by the board, and has a bylaw approved by the outstanding shares (Section 152) authorizing the board alone to approve such a loan or guaranty to an officer, whether or not a director, or an employee benefit plan authorizing such a loan or guaranty to an officer, such a loan or guaranty or employee benefit plan may be approved by the board alone by a vote sufficient without counting the vote of any interested director or directors if the board determines that such a loan or guaranty or plan may reasonably be expected to benefit the corporation. . . .

§316. Corporate Actions Subjecting Directors to Joint and Several Liability; Actions; Damages

(a) Subject to the provisions of Section 309, directors of a corporation who approve any of the following corporate actions shall be jointly and severally liable to the corporation for the benefit of all of the creditors or shareholders entitled to institute an action under subdivision (c):

(1) The making of any distribution to its shareholders to the extent that it is contrary to the provisions of Sections 500 to 503, inclusive.

(2) The distribution of assets to shareholders after institution of dissolution proceedings of the corporation, without paying or adequately providing for all known liabilities of the corporation. . . .

(3) The making of any loan or guaranty contrary to Section 315. . . .

§317. Indemnification of Agent of Corporation in Proceedings or Actions

(a) For the purposes of this section, "agent" means any person who is or was a director, officer, employee or other agent of the corporation, or is or was serving at the request of the corporation as a director, officer, employee or agent of another foreign or domestic corporation, partnership, joint venture, trust or other enterprise, or was a director, officer, employee or agent of a foreign or domestic corporation which was a predecessor corporation of the corporation or of another enterprise at the request of the predecessor corporation; "proceeding" means any threatened, pending or completed action or proceeding, whether civil, criminal, administrative or investigative; and "expenses" includes without limitation attorneys' fees and any expenses of establishing a right to indemnification under subdivision (d) or paragraph (4) of subdivision (e).

(b) A corporation shall have power to indemnify any person who was or is a party or is threatened to be made a party to any proceeding (other than an action by or in the right of the corporation to procure a judgment in its favor) by reason of the fact that the person is or was an agent of the corporation, against expenses, judgments, fines, settlements, and other amounts actually and reasonably incurred in connection with the proceeding if that person acted in good faith and in a manner the person reasonably believed to be in the best interests of the corporation and, in the case of a criminal proceeding, had no reasonable cause to believe the conduct of the person was unlawful. The termination of any proceeding by judgment, order, settlement, conviction, or upon a plea of nolo contendere or its equivalent shall not, of itself, create a presumption that the person did not act in good faith and in a manner which the person reasonably believed to be in the best interests of the corporation or that the person had reasonable cause to believe that the person's conduct was unlawful.

(c) A corporation shall have power to indemnify any person who was or is a party or is threatened to be made a party to any threatened, pending, or completed action by or in the right of the corporation to procure a judgment in its favor by reason of the fact that the person is or was an agent of the corporation, against expenses actually and reasonably incurred by that person in connection with the defense or settlement of the action if the person acted in good faith, in a manner the person believed to be in the best interests of the corporation and its shareholders.

No indemnification shall be made under this subdivision for any of the following:

(1) In respect of any claim, issue or matter as to which the person shall have been adjudged to be liable to the corporation in the performance of that

person's duty to the corporation and its shareholders, unless and only to the extent that the court in which the proceeding is or was pending shall determine upon application that, in view of all the circumstances of the case, the person is fairly and reasonably entitled to indemnity for expenses and then only to the extent that the court shall determine.

(2) Of amounts paid in settling or otherwise disposing of a pending action without court approval.

(3) Of expenses incurred in defending a pending action which is settled or otherwise disposed of without court approval.

(d) To the extent that an agent of a corporation has been successful on the merits in defense of any proceeding referred to in subdivision (b) or (c) or in defense of any claim, issue, or matter therein, the agent shall be indemnified against expenses actually and reasonably incurred by the agent in connection therewith.

(e) Except as provided in subdivision (d), any indemnification under this section shall be made by the corporation only if authorized in the specific case, upon a determination that indemnification of the agent is proper in the circumstances because the agent has met the applicable standard of conduct set forth in subdivision (b) or (c), by any of the following:

(1) A majority vote of a quorum consisting of directors who are not parties to such proceeding.

(2) If such a quorum of directors is not obtainable, by independent legal counsel in a written opinion.

(3) Approval of the shareholders (Section 153), with the shares owned by the person to be indemnified not being entitled to vote thereon.

(4) The court in which the proceeding is or was pending upon application made by the corporation or the agent or the attorney or other person rendering services in connection with the defense, whether or not the application by the agent, attorney or other person is opposed by the corporation.

(f) Expenses incurred in defending any proceeding may be advanced by the corporation prior to the final disposition of the proceeding upon receipt of an undertaking by or on behalf of the agent to repay that amount if it shall be determined ultimately that the agent is not entitled to be indemnified as authorized in this section. The provisions of subdivision (a) of Section 315 do not apply to advances made pursuant to this subdivision.

(g) The indemnification authorized by this section shall not be deemed exclusive of any additional rights to indemnification for breach of duty to the corporation and its shareholders while acting in the capacity of a director or officer of the corporation to the extent the additional rights to indemnification are authorized in an article provision adopted pursuant to paragraph (11) of subdivision (a) of Section 204. The indemnification provided by this section for acts, omissions, or transactions while acting in the capacity of, or while serving as, a director or officer of the corporation but not involving breach of duty to the corporation and its shareholders shall not be deemed exclusive of any other rights to which those seeking indemnification may be entitled under any bylaw, agreement, vote of shareholders or disinterested directors, or otherwise, to the extent the additional rights to indemnification are authorized in the articles of the corporation. An article provision authorizing indemnification "in excess of that otherwise permitted by Section 317" or "to the fullest extent permissible under California law" or the substantial equivalent thereof shall be construed to be both a provision for additional indemnification for breach of duty to the corporation and its shareholders as referred to in, and with the limitations required by, paragraph (11) of subdivision (a) of Section 204 and a provision for additional indemnification as referred to in the second sentence of this subdivision. The rights to indemnity hereunder shall continue as to a person who has ceased to be a director, officer, employee, or agent and shall inure to the benefit of the heirs, executors, and administrators of the person. Nothing contained in this section shall affect any right to indemnification to which persons other than the directors and officers may be entitled by contract or otherwise.

(h) No indemnification or advance shall be made under this section, except as provided in subdivision (d) or paragraph (4) of subdivision (e), in any circumstance where it appears:

(1) That it would be inconsistent with a provision of the articles, bylaws, a resolution of the shareholders, or an agreement in effect at the time of the accrual of the alleged cause of action asserted in the proceeding in which the expenses were incurred or other amounts were paid, which prohibits or otherwise limits indemnification.

(2) That it would be inconsistent with any condition expressly imposed by a court in approving a settlement.

(i) A corporation shall have power to purchase and maintain insurance on behalf of any agent of the corporation against any liability asserted against or incurred by the agent in that capacity or arising out of the agent's status as such whether or not the corporation would have the power to indemnify the agent against that liability under this section. . . .

Chapter 6. Shareholders' Meetings and Consents

§603. Actions Without Meeting; Written Consent of Shareholders; Procedure with Consents from Less Than All Shareholders; Revocation of Consent

(a) Unless otherwise provided in the articles, any action that may be taken at any annual or special meeting of shareholders may be taken without a meeting and without prior notice, if a consent in writing, as specified in Section 195, setting forth the action so taken, shall be provided by the holders of outstanding shares having not less than the minimum number of votes that would be necessary to authorize or take that action at a meeting at which all shares entitled to vote thereon were present and voted.

(b) Unless the consents of all shareholders entitled to vote have been solicited in writing, both of the following shall apply:

(1) Notice of any shareholder approval pursuant to Section 310, 317, 1152, 1201 (except for a reorganization as to which shareholders have the right, pursuant to Chapter 13 (commencing with Section 1300) to demand payment of cash for their shares), or 2007 without a meeting by less than unanimous written consent shall be given at least 10 days before the consummation of the action authorized by that approval. Notice shall be given as provided in subdivision (b) of Section 601.

(2) Prompt notice shall be given of the taking of any other corporate action approved by shareholders without a meeting by less than unanimous written consent, to those shareholders entitled to vote who have not consented in writing. Notice shall be given as provided in subdivision (b) of Section 601.

(c) Any shareholder giving a written consent, or the shareholder's proxyholders, or a transferee of the shares or a personal representative of the shareholder or their respective proxyholders, may revoke the consent personally or by proxy by a writing received by the corporation prior to the time that written consents of the number of shares required to authorize the proposed action have been filed with the secretary of the corporation, but may not do so thereafter. The revocation is effective upon its receipt by the secretary of the corporation.

(d) Notwithstanding subdivision (a), directors may not be elected by written consent except by unanimous written consent of all shares entitled to vote for the election of directors; provided that the shareholders may elect a director to fill a vacancy, other than a vacancy created by removal, by the written consent of a majority of the outstanding shares entitled to vote.

§604. *Proxies or Written Consents; Contents; Form*

(a) Any form of proxy or written consent distributed to 10 or more shareholders of a corporation with outstanding shares held of record by 100 or more persons shall afford an opportunity on the proxy or form of written consent to specify a choice between approval and disapproval of each matter or group of related matters intended to be acted upon at the meeting for which the proxy is solicited or by such written consent, other than elections to office, and shall provide, subject to reasonable specified conditions, that where the person solicited specifies a choice with respect to any such matter the shares will be voted in accordance therewith.

(b) In any election of directors, any form of proxy in which the directors to be voted upon are named therein as candidates and which is marked by a shareholder "withhold" or otherwise marked in a manner indicating that the authority to vote for the election of directors is withheld shall not be voted for the election of a director.

(c) Failure to comply with this section shall not invalidate any corporate action taken, but may be the basis for challenging any proxy at a meeting and the superior court may compel compliance therewith at the suit of any shareholder.

(d) This section does not apply to any corporation with an outstanding class of securities registered under Section 12 of the Securities Exchange Act of 1934 or whose securities are exempted from such registration by Section 12(g)(2) of that act.

Chapter 7. Voting of Shares

§707. *Inspectors of Election*

(a) In advance of any meeting of shareholders the board may appoint inspectors of election to act at the meeting and any adjournment thereof. If inspectors of election are not so appointed, or if any persons so appointed fail to appear or refuse to act, the chairperson of any meeting of shareholders may, and on the request of any shareholder or a shareholder's proxy shall, appoint inspectors of election (or persons to replace those who so fail or refuse) at the meeting. The number of inspectors shall be either one or three. If appointed at a meeting on the request of one or more shareholders or proxies, the majority of shares represented in person or by proxy shall determine whether one or three inspectors are to be appointed.

(b) The inspectors of election shall determine the number of shares outstanding and the voting power of each, the shares represented at the meeting, the existence of a quorum and the authenticity, validity and effect of proxies, receive votes, ballots or consents, hear and determine all challenges and questions in any way arising in connection with the right to vote, count and tabulate all votes or consents, determine when the polls shall close, determine the result and do such acts as may be proper to conduct the election or vote with fairness to all shareholders.

(c) The inspectors of election shall perform their duties impartially, in good faith, to the best of their ability and as expeditiously as is practical. If there are three inspectors of election, the decision, act or certificate of a majority is effective in all respects as the decision, act or certificate of all. Any report or certificate made by the inspectors of election is prima facie evidence of the facts stated therein.

§708. Directors; Cumulative Voting; Election by Ballot

(a) Except as provided in Sections 301.5 and 708.5, every shareholder complying with subdivision (b) and entitled to vote at any election of directors may cumulate such shareholder's votes and give one candidate a number of votes equal to the number of directors to be elected multiplied by the number of votes to which the shareholder's shares are normally entitled, or distribute the shareholder's votes on the same principle among as many candidates as the shareholder thinks fit.

(b) No shareholder shall be entitled to cumulate votes (i.e., cast for any candidate a number of votes greater than the number of votes that the shareholder normally is entitled to cast) unless the candidate or candidates' names have been placed in nomination prior to the voting and the shareholder has given notice at the meeting prior to the voting of the shareholder's intention to cumulate the shareholder's votes. If any one shareholder has given that notice, all shareholders may cumulate their votes for candidates in nomination.

(c)Except as provided in Section 708.5, in any election of directors, the candidates receiving the highest number of affirmative votes of the shares entitled to be voted for them up to the number of directors to be elected by those shares are elected; votes against the director and votes withheld shall have no legal effect. . . .

§710. Supermajority Vote Requirement; Approval

(a) This section applies to a corporation with outstanding shares held of record by 100 or more persons (determined as provided in Section 605) that files an amendment of articles or certificate of determination containing a "supermajority vote" provision on or after January 1, 1989. This section shall not apply to a corporation that files an amendment of articles or certificate of determination on or after January 1, 1994, if, at the time of filing, the corporation has (1) outstanding shares of more than one class or series of stock, (2) no class of equity securities registered under Section 12(b) or 12(g) of the Securities Exchange Act of 1934, and (3) outstanding shares held of record by fewer than 300 persons determined as provided by Section 605.

(b) A "supermajority vote" is a requirement set forth in the articles or in a certificate of determination authorized under any provision of this division that specified corporate action or actions be approved by a larger proportion of the outstanding shares than a majority, or by a larger proportion of the outstanding shares of a class or series than a majority, but no supermajority vote that is subject to this section shall require a vote in excess of $66\frac{2}{3}$ percent of the outstanding shares or $66\frac{2}{3}$ percent of the outstanding shares of any class or series of those shares.

(c) An amendment of the articles or a certificate of determination that includes a supermajority vote requirement shall be approved by at least as large a proportion of the outstanding shares (Section 152) as is required pursuant to that amendment or certificate of determination for the approval of the specified corporate action or actions. . . .

Chapter 8. Shareholder Derivative Actions

§800. Conditions; Security; Motion for Order; Determination

(a) As used in this section, "corporation" includes an unincorporated association; "board" includes the managing body of an unincorporated association; "shareholder" includes a member of an unincorporated association; and "shares" includes memberships in an unincorporated association.

(b) No action may be instituted or maintained in right of any domestic or foreign corporation by any holder of shares or of voting trust certificates of the corporation unless both of the following conditions exist:

(1) The plaintiff alleges in the complaint that plaintiff was a shareholder, of record or beneficially, or the holder of voting trust certificates at the time of the transaction or any part thereof of which plaintiff complains or that plaintiff's shares or voting trust certificates thereafter devolved upon plaintiff by operation of law from a holder who was a holder at the time of the transaction or any part thereof complained of; provided, that any shareholder who does not meet these requirements may nevertheless be allowed in the discretion of the court to maintain the action on a preliminary showing to and determination by the court, by motion and after a hearing, at which the court shall consider such evidence, by affidavit or testimony, as it deems material, that (i) there is a strong prima facie case in favor of the claim asserted on behalf of the corporation, (ii) no other similar action has been or is likely to be instituted, (iii) the plaintiff acquired the shares before there was disclosure to the public or to the plaintiff of the wrongdoing of which plaintiff complains, (iv) unless the action can be maintained the defendant may retain a gain derived from defendant's willful breach of a fiduciary duty, and (v) the requested relief will not result in unjust enrichment of the corporation or any shareholder of the corporation; and

(2) The plaintiff alleges in the complaint with particularity plaintiff's efforts to secure from the board such action as plaintiff desires, or the reasons for not making such effort, and alleges further that plaintiff has either informed the

corporation or the board in writing of the ultimate facts of each cause of action against each defendant or delivered to the corporation or the board a true copy of the complaint which plaintiff proposes to file.

(c) In any action referred to in subdivision (b), at any time within 30 days after service of summons upon the corporation or upon any defendant who is an officer or director of the corporation, or held such office at the time of the acts complained of, the corporation or the defendant may move the court for an order, upon notice and hearing, requiring the plaintiff to furnish a bond as hereinafter provided. The motion shall be based upon one or both of the following grounds:

(1) That there is no reasonable possibility that the prosecution of the cause of action alleged in the complaint against the moving party will benefit the corporation or its shareholders.

(2) That the moving party, if other than the corporation, did not participate in the transaction complained of in any capacity.

The court on application of the corporation or any defendant may, for good cause shown, extend the 30-day period for an additional period or periods not exceeding 60 days.

(d) At the hearing upon any motion pursuant to subdivision (c), the court shall consider such evidence, written or oral, by witnesses or affidavit, as may be material (1) to the ground or grounds upon which the motion is based, or (2) to a determination of the probable reasonable expenses, including attorneys' fees, of the corporation and the moving party which will be incurred in the defense of the action. If the court determines, after hearing the evidence adduced by the parties, that the moving party has established a probability in support of any of the grounds upon which the motion is based, the court shall fix the amount of the bond, not to exceed fifty thousand dollars ($50,000), to be furnished by the plaintiff for reasonable expenses, including attorneys' fees, which may be incurred by the moving party and the corporation in connection with the action, including expenses for which the corporation may become liable pursuant to Section 317. A ruling by the court on the motion shall not be a determination of any issue in the action or of the merits thereof. If the court, upon the motion, makes a determination that a bond shall be furnished by the plaintiff as to any one or more defendants, the action shall be dismissed as to the defendant or defendants, unless the bond required by the court has been furnished within such reasonable time as may be fixed by the court.

(e) If the plaintiff shall, either before or after a motion is made pursuant to subdivision (c), or any order or determination pursuant to the motion, furnish a bond in the aggregate amount of fifty thousand dollars ($50,000) to secure the reasonable expenses of the parties entitled to make the motion, the plaintiff has complied with the requirements of this section and with any order for a bond theretofore made, and any such motion then pending shall be dismissed and no further or additional bond shall be required.

(f) If a motion is filed pursuant to subdivision (c), no pleadings need be filed by the corporation or any other defendant and the prosecution of the action shall be stayed until 10 days after the motion has been disposed of.

Chapter 9. Amendment of Articles . . .

§902. Adoption After Issuance of Shares

(a) After any shares have been issued, amendments may be adopted if approved by the board and approved by the outstanding shares (Section 152), either before or after the approval by the board. . . .

(e) Whenever the articles require for corporate action the vote of a larger proportion or of all of the shares of any class or series, or of a larger proportion or of all of the directors, than is otherwise required by this division, the provision in the articles requiring such greater vote shall not be altered, amended or repealed except by such greater vote unless otherwise provided in the articles.

(f) Notwithstanding subdivision (a), any amendment reducing the vote required for an amendment pursuant to subdivision (c) of Section 158 may not be adopted unless approved by the affirmative vote of at least two-thirds of each class of outstanding shares or such other vote as may then be specified by the articles of the corporation.

Chapter 10. Sales of Assets

§1001. Disposition of Substantially All Assets; Approval

(a) A corporation may sell, lease, convey, exchange, transfer, or otherwise dispose of all or substantially all of its assets when the principal terms are approved by the board, and, unless the transaction is in the usual and regular course of its business, approved by the outstanding shares (Section 152), either before or after approval by the board and before or after the transaction. A transaction constituting a reorganization (Section 181) is subject to the provisions of Chapter 12 (commencing with Section 1200) and not this section (other than subdivision (d)). A transaction constituting a conversion (Section 161.9) is subject to the provisions of Chapter 11.5 (commencing with Section 1150) and not this section.

(b) Notwithstanding approval of the outstanding shares (Section 152), the board may abandon the proposed transaction without further action by the shareholders, subject to the contractual rights, if any, of third parties.

(c) The sale, lease, conveyance, exchange, transfer, or other disposition may be made upon those terms and conditions and for that consideration as the board may deem in the best interests of the corporation. The consideration may be money, securities, or other property.

(d) If the acquiring party in a transaction pursuant to subdivision (a) of this section or subdivision (g) of Section 2001 is in control of or under common control with the disposing corporation, the principal terms of the sale must be approved by at least 90 percent of the voting power of the disposing corporation unless the disposition is to a domestic or foreign corporation or other business entity in consideration of the nonredeemable common shares or nonredeemable equity securities of the acquiring party or its parent.

(e) Subdivision (d) does not apply to any transaction if the Commissioner of Financial Protection and Innovation, the Insurance Commissioner, or the Public Utilities Commission has approved the terms and conditions of the transaction and the fairness of those terms and conditions pursuant to Section 25142 of this code, or Section 1209, 5750, or 5802 of the Financial Code, Section 838.5 of the Insurance Code, or Section 822 of the Public Utilities Code.

CHAPTER 11. MERGER

§1100. Authorization

Any two or more corporations may be merged into one of those corporations. A corporation may merge with one or more domestic corporations (Section 167), social purpose corporations (Section 171.08), foreign corporations (Section 171), or other business entities (Section 174.5) pursuant to this chapter. Mergers in which a foreign corporation but no other business entity is a constituent party are governed by Section 1108, mergers in which a social purpose corporation but no other business entity is a constituent party are governed by Section 1112.5, and mergers in which an other business entity is a constituent party are governed by Section 1113.

§1101. Agreement of Merger; Approval of Boards; Contents

(a) The board of each corporation that desires to merge shall approve an agreement of merger. The constituent corporations shall be parties to the agreement of merger and other persons, including a parent party (Section 1200), may be parties to the agreement of merger. The agreement shall state all of the following:

(1) The terms and conditions of the merger.

(2) The amendments, subject to Sections 900 and 907, to the articles of the surviving corporation to be effected by the merger, if any. If any amendment changes the name of the surviving corporation the new name may be the same as or similar to the name of a disappearing domestic or foreign corporation, subject to subdivision (b) of Section 201.

(3) The name and place of incorporation of each constituent corporation and which of the constituent corporations is the surviving corporation.

(4) The manner of converting the shares of each of the constituent corporations into shares or other securities of the surviving corporation and, if any shares of any of the constituent corporations are not to be converted solely into shares or other securities of the surviving corporation, the cash, rights, securities, or other property which the holders of those shares are to receive in exchange for the shares, which cash, rights, securities, or other property may be in addition to or in lieu of shares or other securities of the surviving corporation, or that the shares are canceled without consideration.

(5) Other details or provisions as are desired, if any, including, without limitation, a provision for the payment of cash in lieu of fractional shares or for any other arrangement with respect thereto consistent with the provisions of Section 407.

(b) Each share of the same class or series of any constituent corporation (other than the cancellation of shares held by a constituent corporation or its parent or a wholly owned subsidiary of either in another constituent corporation) shall, unless all shareholders of the class or series consent and except as provided in Section 407, be treated equally with respect to any distribution of cash, rights, securities, or other property. Notwithstanding paragraph (4) of subdivision (a), except in a short-form merger, and in the merger of a corporation into its subsidiary in which it owns at least 90 percent of the outstanding shares of each class, the nonredeemable common shares or nonredeemable equity securities of a constituent corporation may be converted only into nonredeemable common shares of the surviving party or a parent party if a constituent corporation or its parent owns, directly or indirectly, before the merger shares of another constituent corporation representing more than 50 percent of the voting power of the other constituent corporation before the merger, unless all of the shareholders of the class consent and except as provided in Section 407.

§1110. Short Form Merger of 90% or More Owned Subsidiary Into Parent or Parent and Any Other Subsidiary Into Subsidiary

(a) If a domestic corporation owns all the outstanding shares, or owns less than all the outstanding shares but at least 90 percent of the outstanding shares of each class, of a corporation or corporations, domestic or foreign, the merger of the subsidiary corporation or corporations into the parent corporation or the merger into the subsidiary corporation of the parent corporation and any other subsidiary corporation or corporations, may be effected by a resolution or plan of merger adopted and approved by the board of the parent corporation and the filing of a certificate of ownership as provided in subdivision (e). The resolution or plan of merger shall provide for the merger and shall provide that the surviving corporation assumes all the liabilities of each disappearing corporation and shall include any other provisions required by this section. . . .

§1111. Close Corporation as Disappearing but Not Surviving Corporation; Approval of Shareholders

If any disappearing corporation in a merger is a close corporation and the surviving corporation is not a close corporation, the merger shall be approved by the affirmative vote of at least two-thirds of each class of the outstanding shares of such disappearing corporation; provided, however, that the articles may provide for a lesser vote, but not less than a majority of the outstanding shares of each class.

Chapter 12. Reorganizations

§1200. Approval by Board

A reorganization (Section 181) or a share exchange tender offer (Section 183.5) shall be approved by the board of:

(a) Each constituent corporation in a merger reorganization;

(b) The acquiring corporation in an exchange reorganization;

(c) The acquiring corporation and the corporation whose property and assets are acquired in a sale-of-assets reorganization;

(d) The acquiring corporation in a share exchange tender offer (Section 183.5); and

(e) The corporation in control of any constituent or acquiring domestic or foreign corporation or other business entity under subdivision (a), (b) or (c) and whose equity securities are issued, transferred, or exchanged in the reorganization (a "parent party").

LEGISLATIVE COMMITTEE COMMENT (1975)—ASSEMBLY

Under the new law, various methods of corporate fusion are treated as different means to the same end for the purpose of codifying the "de facto merger" doctrine.

§1201. Shareholder Approval; Board Abandonment

(a) The principal terms of a reorganization shall be approved by the outstanding shares (Section 152) of each class of each corporation the approval of whose board is required under Section 1200, except as provided in subdivision (b) and except that (unless otherwise provided in the articles) no approval of any class of outstanding preferred shares of the surviving or acquiring corporation or parent party shall be required if the rights, preferences, privileges, and restrictions granted to or imposed upon that class of shares remain unchanged (subject to the provisions of subdivision (c)). For the purpose of this subdivision, two classes of common shares differing only as to voting rights shall be considered as a single class of shares.

(b) No approval of the outstanding shares (Section 152) is required by subdivision (a) in the case of any corporation if that corporation, or its shareholders immediately before the reorganization, or both, shall own (immediately after the reorganization) equity securities, other than any warrant or right to subscribe to or purchase those equity securities, of the surviving or acquiring corporation or a parent party (subdivision (e) of Section 1200) possessing more than five-sixths of the voting power of the surviving or acquiring corporation or parent party. In making the determination of ownership by the shareholders of a corporation, immediately after the reorganization, of equity securities pursuant to the preceding sentence, equity securities which they owned immediately before the reorganization as shareholders of another party to the transaction shall be disregarded. For the purpose of this section only, the voting power of a corporation shall be calculated by assuming the conversion of all equity securities convertible (immediately or at some future time) into shares entitled to vote but not assuming the exercise of any warrant or right to subscribe to or purchase those shares.

(c) Notwithstanding subdivision (b), the principal terms of a reorganization shall be approved by the outstanding shares (Section 152) of the surviving corporation in a merger reorganization if any amendment is made to its articles that would otherwise require that approval.

(d) Notwithstanding subdivision (b), the principal terms of a reorganization shall be approved by the outstanding shares (Section 152) of any class of a corporation that is a party to a merger or sale-of-assets reorganization if holders of shares of that class receive shares of the surviving or acquiring corporation or parent party having different rights, preferences, privileges, or restrictions than those surrendered. Shares in a foreign corporation received in exchange for shares in a domestic corporation have different rights, preferences, privileges, and restrictions within the meaning of the preceding sentence.

(e) Notwithstanding subdivisions (a) and (b), the principal terms of a reorganization shall be approved by the affirmative vote of at least two-thirds of each class, or a greater vote if required in the articles, of the outstanding shares (Section 152) of any close corporation if the reorganization would result in their receiving shares of a corporation that is not a close corporation. However, the articles may provide for a lesser vote, but not less than a majority of the outstanding shares of each class.

(f) Notwithstanding subdivisions (a) and (b), the principal terms of a reorganization shall be approved by at least two-thirds of each class, or a greater vote if required in the articles, of the outstanding shares (Section 152) of a corporation that is a party to a merger reorganization if holders of shares receive shares of a surviving social purpose corporation in the merger.

(g) Notwithstanding subdivisions (a) and (b), the principal terms of a reorganization shall be approved by the outstanding shares (Section 152) of any class of a corporation that is a party to a merger reorganization if holders of shares of that class receive interests of a surviving other business entity in the merger.

(h) Notwithstanding subdivisions (a) and (b), the principal terms of a reorganization shall be approved by all shareholders of any class or series if, as a result of the reorganization, the holders of that class or series become personally liable for any obligations of a party to the reorganization, unless all holders of that class or series have the dissenters' rights provided in Chapter 13 (commencing with Section 1300).

(i) Any approval required by this section may be given before or after the approval by the board. Notwithstanding approval required by this section, the board may abandon the proposed reorganization without further action by the shareholders, subject to the contractual rights, if any, of third parties.

§1201.5. Share Exchange Tender Offer; Approval of Principal Terms

(a) The principal terms of a share exchange tender offer (Section 183.5) shall be approved by the outstanding shares (Section 152) of each class of the corporation making the tender offer or whose shares are to be used in the tender offer, except as provided in subdivision (b) and except that (unless otherwise provided in the articles) no approval of any class of outstanding preferred shares of either corporation shall be required, if the rights, preferences, privileges, and restrictions granted to or imposed upon that class of shares remain unchanged. For the purpose of this subdivision, two classes of common shares differing only as to voting rights shall be considered as a single class of shares.

(b) No approval of the outstanding shares (Section 152) is required by subdivision (a) in the case of any corporation if the corporation, or its shareholders immediately before the tender offer, or both, shall own (immediately after the completion of the share exchange proposed in the tender offer) equity securities, (other than any warrant or right to subscribe to or purchase the equity securities), of the corporation making the tender offer or of the corporation whose shares were used in the tender offer, possessing more than five-sixths of the voting power of either corporation. In making the determination of ownership by the shareholders of a corporation, immediately after the tender offer, of equity securities pursuant to the preceding sentence, equity securities which they owned immediately before the tender offer as shareholders of another party to the transaction shall be disregarded. For the purpose of this section only, the voting power of a corporation shall be calculated by assuming the conversion of all equity securities convertible (immediately or at some future time) into shares entitled to vote but not assuming the exercise of any warrant or right to subscribe to, or purchase, shares.

§1202. Terms of Merger Reorganization or Sale-of-Assets Reorganization; Approval by Shareholders; Foreign Corporations

(a) In addition to the requirements of Section 1201, the principal terms of a merger reorganization shall be approved by all the outstanding shares of a corporation if the agreement of merger provides that all the outstanding shares of that corporation are canceled without consideration in the merger.

(b) In addition to the requirements of Section 1201, if the terms of a merger reorganization or sale-of-assets reorganization provide that a class or series of preferred shares is to have distributed to it a lesser amount than would be required by applicable article provisions, the principal terms of the reorganization shall be approved by the same percentage of outstanding shares of that class or series which would be required to approve an amendment of the article provisions to provide for the distribution of that lesser amount.

(c) If a parent party within the meaning of Section 1200 is a foreign corporation (other than a foreign corporation to which subdivision (a) of Section 2115 is applicable), any requirement or lack of a requirement for approval by the outstanding shares of the foreign corporation shall be based, not on the application of Sections 1200 and 1201, but on the application of the laws of the state or place of incorporation of the foreign corporation.

§1203. Interested Party Proposal or Tender Offer to Shareholders; Affirmative Opinion; Delivery; Approval; Later Proposal or Tender Offer; Withdrawal of Vote, Consent, or Proxy; Procedures

(a) If a tender offer, including a share exchange tender offer (Section 183.5), or a written proposal for approval of a reorganization subject to Section 1200 or for a sale of assets subject to subdivision (a) of Section 1001 is made to some or all of a corporation's shareholders by an interested party (herein referred to as an "Interested Party Proposal"), an affirmative opinion in writing as to the fairness of the consideration to the shareholders of that corporation shall be delivered as follows:

(1) If no shareholder approval or acceptance is required for the consummation of the transaction, the opinion shall be delivered to the corporation's board of directors not later than the time that consummation of the transaction is authorized and approved by the board of directors.

(2) If a tender offer is made to the corporation's shareholders, the opinion shall be delivered to the shareholders at the time that the tender offer is first made in writing to the shareholders. However, if the tender offer is commenced by publication and tender offer materials are subsequently mailed or otherwise distributed to the shareholders, the opinion may be omitted in that publication if the opinion is included in the materials distributed to the shareholders.

(3) If a shareholders' meeting is to be held to vote on approval of the transaction, the opinion shall be delivered to the shareholders with the notice of the meeting (Section 601).

(4) If consents of all shareholders entitled to vote are solicited in writing (Section 603), the opinion shall be delivered at the same time as that solicitation.

(5) If the consents of all shareholders are not solicited in writing, the opinion shall be delivered to each shareholder whose consent is solicited prior to that shareholder's consent being given, and to all other shareholders at the time they are given the notice required by subdivision (b) of Section 603.

For purposes of this section, the term "interested party" means a person who is a party to the transaction and (A) directly or indirectly controls the corporation that is the subject of the tender offer or proposal, (B) is, or is directly or indirectly controlled by, an officer or director of the subject corporation, or (C) is an entity in which a material financial interest (subdivision (a) of Section 310) is held by any director or executive officer of the subject corporation. For purposes of the preceding sentence, "any executive officer" means the president, any vice president in charge of a principal business unit, division, or function such as sales, administration, research, development, or finance, and any other officer or other person who performs a policymaking function or has the same duties as those of a president or vice president. The opinion required by this subdivision shall be provided by a person who is not affiliated with the offeror and who, for compensation, engages in the business of advising others as to the value of properties, businesses, or securities. The fact that the opining person previously has provided services to the offeror or a related entity or is simultaneously engaged in providing advice or assistance with respect to the proposed transaction in a manner which makes its compensation contingent on the success of the proposed transaction shall not, for those reasons, be deemed to affiliate the opining person with the offeror. Nothing in this subdivision shall limit the applicability of the standards of review of the transaction in the event of a challenge thereto under Section 310 or subdivision (c) of Section 1312.

This subdivision shall not apply to an Interested Party Proposal if the corporation that is the subject thereof does not have shares held of record by 100 or more persons. . . .

(b) If a tender of shares or a vote or written consent is being sought pursuant to an Interested Party Proposal and a later tender offer or written proposal for a reorganization subject to Section 1200 or sale of assets subject to subdivision (a) of Section 1001 that would require a vote or written consent of shareholders is made to the corporation or its shareholders (herein referred to as a "Later Proposal") by any other person at least 10 days prior to the date for acceptance of the tendered shares or the vote or notice of shareholder approval on the Interested Party Proposal, then each of the following shall apply:

(1) The shareholders shall be informed of the Later Proposal and any written material provided for this purpose by the later offeror shall be forwarded to the shareholders at that offeror's expense.

(2) The shareholders shall be afforded a reasonable opportunity to withdraw any vote, consent, or proxy previously given before the vote or written consent on the Interested Party Proposal becomes effective, or a reasonable time to withdraw any tendered shares before the purchase of the shares pursuant to the Interested Party Proposal. For purposes of this subdivision, a delay of 10 days from the notice or publication of the Later Proposal shall be deemed to provide a reasonable opportunity or time to effect that withdrawal.

Chapter 13. Dissenters' Rights

§1300. Reorganization or Short-Form Merger; Dissenting Shares; Corporate Purchase at Fair Market Value; Definitions

(a) If the approval of the outstanding shares (Section 152) of a corporation is required for a reorganization under subdivisions (a) and (b) or subdivision (e) or (f) of Section 1201, each shareholder of the corporation entitled to vote on the transaction and each shareholder of a subsidiary corporation in a short-form merger may, by complying with this chapter, require the corporation in which the shareholder holds shares to purchase for cash at their fair market value the shares owned by the shareholder which are dissenting shares as defined in subdivision (b). The fair market value shall be determined as of the day of, and immediately prior to, the first announcement of the terms of the proposed reorganization or short-form merger, excluding any appreciation or depreciation in consequence of the proposed reorganization or short-form merger, as adjusted for any stock split, reverse stock split, or share dividend that becomes effective thereafter.

(b) As used in this chapter, "dissenting shares" means shares to which all of the following apply:

(1) That were not, immediately prior to the reorganization or short-form merger, listed on any national securities exchange certified by the Commissioner of Business Oversight under subdivision (o) of Section 25100, and the notice of meeting of shareholders to act upon the reorganization summarizes this section and Sections 1301, 1302, 1303, and 1304; provided, however, that this provision does not apply to any shares with respect to which there exists any restriction on transfer imposed by the corporation or by any law or regulation; and provided, further, that this provision does not apply to any shares where the holder of those shares is required, by the terms of the reorganization or short-form merger, to accept for the shares anything except: (A) shares of any other corporation, which shares, at the time the reorganization or short-form merger is effective, are listed on any national securities exchange certified by the Commissioner of Business Oversight under subdivision (o) of Section 25100; (B) cash in lieu of fractional shares described in the foregoing subparagraph (A); or (C) any combination of

the shares and cash in lieu of fractional shares described in the foregoing subparagraphs (A) and (B).

(2) That were outstanding on the date for the determination of shareholders entitled to vote on the reorganization and (A) were not voted in favor of the reorganization or, (B) if described in paragraph (1), were voted against the reorganization, or were held of record on the effective date of a short-form merger; provided, however, that subparagraph (A) rather than subparagraph (B) of this paragraph applies in any case where the approval required by Section 1201 is sought by written consent rather than at a meeting.

(3) That the dissenting shareholder has demanded that the corporation purchase at their fair market value, in accordance with Section 1301.

(4) That the dissenting shareholder has submitted for endorsement, in accordance with Section 1302.

(c) As used in this chapter, "dissenting shareholder" means the recordholder of dissenting shares and includes a transferee of record.

§1311. Exempt Shares

This chapter, except Section 1312, does not apply to classes of shares whose terms and provisions specifically set forth the amount to be paid in respect to such shares in the event of a reorganization or merger.

§1312. Right of Dissenting Shareholder to Attack, Set Aside or Rescind Merger or Reorganization; Restraining Order or Injunction; Conditions

(a) No shareholder of a corporation who has a right under this chapter to demand payment of cash for the shares held by the shareholder shall have any right at law or in equity to attack the validity of the reorganization or short-form merger, or to have the reorganization or short-form merger set aside or rescinded, except in an action to test whether the number of shares required to authorize or approve the reorganization have been legally voted in favor thereof; but any holder of shares of a class whose terms and provisions specifically set forth the amount to be paid in respect to them in the event of a reorganization or short-form merger is entitled to payment in accordance with those terms and provisions or, if the principal terms of the reorganization are approved pursuant to subdivision (b) of Section 1202, is entitled to payment in accordance with the terms and provisions of the approved reorganization.

(b) If one of the parties to a reorganization or short-form merger is directly or indirectly controlled by, or under common control with, another party to the reorganization or short-form merger, subdivision (a) shall not apply to any shareholder of such party who has not demanded payment of cash for such shareholder's shares pursuant to this chapter; but if the shareholder institutes any action to attack the validity of the reorganization or short-form merger or to have the reorganization or short-form merger set aside or rescinded, the shareholder shall not thereafter have any right to demand payment of cash for the shareholder's shares pursuant to this chapter. The court in any action attacking the validity of the reorganization or short-form merger or to have the reorganization or short-form merger set aside or rescinded shall not restrain or enjoin the consummation of the transaction except upon 10 days' prior notice to the corporation and upon a determination by the court that clearly no other remedy will adequately protect the complaining shareholder or the class of shareholders of which such shareholder is a member.

(c) If one of the parties to a reorganization or short-form merger is directly or indirectly controlled by, or under common control with, another party to the reorganization or short-form merger, in any action to attack the validity of the reorganization or short-form merger or to have the reorganization or short-form merger set aside or rescinded, (1) a party to a reorganization or short-form merger which controls another party to the reorganization or short-form merger shall have the burden of proving that the transaction is just and reasonable as to the shareholders of the controlled party, and (2) a person who controls two or more parties to a reorganization shall have the burden of proving that the transaction is just and reasonable as to the shareholders of any party so controlled.

Chapter 18. Involuntary Dissolution

§1800. Verified Complaint; Plaintiffs; Grounds; Intervention by Shareholder or Creditor; Exempt Corporations

(a) A verified complaint for involuntary dissolution of a corporation on any one or more of the grounds specified in subdivision (b) may be filed in the superior court of the proper county by any of the following persons:

(1) One-half or more of the directors in office.

(2) A shareholder or shareholders who hold shares representing not less than $33\frac{1}{3}$ percent of (i) the total number of outstanding shares (assuming conversion of any preferred shares convertible into common shares) or (ii) the outstanding common shares or (iii) the equity of the corporation, exclusive in each case of shares owned by persons who have personally participated in any of the transactions enumerated in paragraph (4) of subdivision (b), or any shareholder or shareholders of a close corporation.

(3) Any shareholder if the ground for dissolution is that the period for which the corporation was formed has terminated without extension thereof.

(4) Any other person expressly authorized to do so in the articles.

(b) The grounds for involuntary dissolution are that:

(1) The corporation has abandoned its business for more than one year.

(2) The corporation has an even number of directors who are equally divided and cannot agree as to the management of its affairs, so that its business can no longer be conducted to advantage or so that there is danger that its property and business will be impaired or lost, and the holders of the voting shares of the corporation are so divided into factions that they cannot elect a board consisting of an uneven number.

(3) There is internal dissension and two or more factions of shareholders in the corporation are so deadlocked that its business can no longer be conducted with advantage to its shareholders or the shareholders have failed at two consecutive annual meetings at which all voting power was exercised, to elect successors to directors whose terms have expired or would have expired upon election of their successors.

(4) Those in control of the corporation have been guilty of or have knowingly countenanced persistent and pervasive fraud, mismanagement or abuse of authority or persistent unfairness toward any shareholders or its property is being misapplied or wasted by its directors or officers.

(5) In the case of any corporation with 35 or fewer shareholders (determined as provided in Section 605), liquidation is reasonably necessary for the protection of the rights or interests of the complaining shareholder or shareholders.

(6) The period for which the corporation was formed has terminated without extension of such period.

(c) At any time prior to the trial of the action any shareholder or creditor may intervene therein. . . .

Chapter 19. Voluntary Dissolution

§1900. *Election by Shareholders; Required Vote; Election by Board; Grounds*

(a) Any corporation may elect voluntarily to wind up and dissolve by the vote of shareholders holding shares representing 50 percent or more of the voting power. . . .

Chapter 20. General Provisions Relating to Dissolution

§2000. *Avoidance of Dissolution by Purchase of Plaintiffs' Shares; Valuation; Vote Required; Stay of Dissolution Proceedings; Appraisal under Court Order; Confirmation by Court; Appeal*

(a) Subject to any contrary provision in the articles, which may include a reference to a separate written agreement between two or more shareholders pertaining to the purchase of shares:

In any suit for involuntary dissolution, or in any proceeding for voluntary dissolution initiated by the vote of shareholders representing only 50 percent of the voting power, the corporation or, if it does not elect to purchase, the holders of 50 percent or more of the voting power of the corporation (the "purchasing parties") may avoid the dissolution of the corporation and the appointment of any receiver by purchasing for cash the shares owned by the plaintiffs or by the shareholders so initiating the proceeding (the "moving parties") at their fair value. The fair value shall be determined on the basis of the liquidation value as of the valuation date but taking into account the possibility, if any, of sale of the entire business as a going concern in a liquidation. In fixing the value, the amount of any damages resulting if the initiation of the dissolution is a breach by any moving party or parties of an agreement with the purchasing party or parties may be deducted from the amount payable to the moving party or parties, unless the ground for dissolution is that specified in paragraph (4) of subdivision (b) of Section 1800. The election of the corporation to purchase may be made by the approval of the outstanding shares (Section 152) excluding shares held by the moving parties.

(b) If the purchasing parties (1) elect to purchase the shares owned by the moving parties, and (2) are unable to agree with the moving parties upon the fair value of the shares, and (3) give bond with sufficient security to pay the estimated reasonable expenses (including attorneys' fees) of the moving parties if those expenses are recoverable under subdivision (c), the court upon application of the purchasing parties, either in the pending action or in a proceeding initiated in the superior court of the proper county by the purchasing parties in the case of a voluntary election to wind up and dissolve, shall stay the winding up and dissolution proceeding and shall proceed to ascertain and fix the fair value of the shares owned by the moving parties.

(c) The court shall appoint three disinterested appraisers to appraise the fair value of the shares owned by the moving parties, and shall make an order referring the matter to the appraisers so appointed for the purpose of ascertaining the value. The order shall prescribe the time and manner of producing evidence, if evidence is required. The award of the appraisers or of a majority of them, when confirmed by the court, shall be final and conclusive upon all parties. The court shall enter a decree which shall provide in the alternative for winding up and dissolution of the corporation unless payment is made for the shares within the time specified by the decree. If the purchasing parties do not make payment for the shares within the time specified, judgment shall be entered against them and the surety or sureties on the bond for the amount of the expenses (including attorneys' fees) of the moving parties. Any shareholder aggrieved by the action of the court may appeal therefrom. . . .

(f) For the purposes of this section, the valuation date shall be (1) in the case of a suit for involuntary dissolution under Section 1800, the date upon which that action was commenced, or (2) in the case of a proceeding for voluntary dissolution initiated by the vote of shareholders representing only 50 percent of the voting power, the date upon which that proceeding was initiated. However, in either case the court may, upon the hearing of a motion by any party, and for good cause shown, designate some other date as the valuation date.

Chapter 21. Foreign Corporations

§2115. Foreign Corporations Subject to Corporate Laws of State; Tests to Determine Subject Corporations; Laws Applicable; Time of Application

(a) A foreign corporation (other than a foreign association or foreign nonprofit corporation but including a foreign parent corporation even though it does not itself transact intrastate business) is subject to the requirements of subdivision (b) commencing on the date specified in subdivision (d) and continuing until the date specified in subdivision (e) if:

(1) The average of the property factor, the payroll factor, and the sales factor (as defined in Sections 25129, 25132, and 25134 of the Revenue and Taxation Code) with respect to it is more than 50 percent during its latest full income year and

(2) more than one-half of its outstanding voting securities are held of record by persons having addresses in this state appearing on the books of the corporation on the record date for the latest meeting of shareholders held during its latest full income year or, if no meeting was held during that year, on the last day of the latest full income year. The property factor, payroll factor, and sales factor shall be those used in computing the portion of its income allocable to this state in its franchise tax return or, with respect to corporations the allocation of whose income is governed by special formulas or that are not required to file separate or any tax returns, which would have been so used if they were governed by this three-factor formula. The determination of these factors with respect to any parent corporation shall be made on a consolidated basis, including in a unitary computation (after elimination of intercompany transactions) the property, payroll, and sales of the parent and all of its subsidiaries in which it owns directly or indirectly more than 50 percent of the outstanding shares entitled to vote for the election of directors, but deducting a percentage of the property, payroll, and sales of any subsidiary equal to the percentage minority ownership, if any, in the subsidiary. For the purpose of this subdivision, any securities held to the knowledge of the issuer in the names of broker-dealers, nominees for broker-dealers (including clearing corporations), or banks, associations, or other entities holding securities in a nominee name or otherwise on behalf of a beneficial owner (collectively "nominee holders"), shall not be considered outstanding. However, if the foreign corporation requests all nominee holders to certify, with respect to all beneficial owners for whom securities are held, the number of shares held for those beneficial owners having addresses (as shown on the records of the nominee holder) in this state and outside of this state, then all shares so certified shall be considered outstanding and held of record by persons having addresses either in this state or outside of this state as so certified, provided that the certification so provided shall be retained with the record of shareholders and made available for inspection and copying in the same manner as is provided in Section 1600 with respect to that record. A current list of beneficial owners of a foreign corporation's securities provided to the corporation by one or more nominee holders or their agent pursuant to the requirements of Rule 14b-1(b)(3) or 14b-2(b)(3) as adopted on January 6, 1992, promulgated under the Securities Exchange Act of 1934, shall constitute an acceptable certification with respect to beneficial owners for the purposes of this subdivision.

(b) Except as provided in subdivision (c), the following chapters and sections of this division shall apply to a foreign corporation as defined in subdivision (a) (to the exclusion of the law of the jurisdiction in which it is incorporated):

Chapter 1 (general provisions and definitions), to the extent applicable to the following provisions;

Section 301 (annual election of directors);

Section 303 (removal of directors without cause);

Section 304 (removal of directors by court proceedings);

Section 305, subdivision (c) (filling of director vacancies where less than a majority in office elected by shareholders);

Section 309 (directors' standard of care);

Section 316 (excluding paragraph (3) of subdivision (a) and paragraph (3) of subdivision (f)) (liability of directors for unlawful distributions);

Section 317 (indemnification of directors, officers, and others);

Sections 500 to 505, inclusive (limitations on corporate distributions in cash or property);

Section 506 (liability of shareholder who receives unlawful distribution);

Section 600, subdivisions (b) and (c) (requirement for annual shareholders' meeting and remedy if same not timely held);

Section 708, subdivisions (a), (b), and (c) (shareholder's right to cumulate votes at any election of directors);

Section 710 (supermajority vote requirement);

Section 1001, subdivision (d) (limitations on sale of assets);

Section 1101, subdivision (b) (limitations on mergers);

Section 1151 (first sentence only) (limitations on conversions);

Section 1152 (requirements of conversions);

Chapter 12 (commencing with Section 1200) (reorganizations);

Chapter 13 (commencing with Section 1300) (dissenters' rights);

Sections 1500 and 1501 (records and reports);

Section 1508 (action by Attorney General);

Chapter 16 (commencing with Section 1600) (rights of inspection).

(c) This section does not apply to any corporation (1) with outstanding securities listed on the New York Stock Exchange, the NYSE American, the NASDAQ Global Market, or the NASDAQ Capital Market, or (2) if all of its voting shares (other than directors' qualifying shares) are owned directly or indirectly by a corporation or corporations not subject to this section.

(d) For purp0oses of subdivision (a), the requirements of subdivision (b) shall become applicable to a foreign corporation only upon the first day of the first income year of the corporation (1) commencing on or after the 135th day of the income year immediately following the latest income year with respect to which the tests referred to in subdivision (a) have been met or (2) commencing on or after the entry of a final order by a court of competent jurisdiction declaring that those tests have been met.

(e) For purposes of subdivision (a), the requirements of subdivision (b) shall cease to be applicable to a foreign corporation (1) at the end of the first income year of the corporation immediately following the latest income year with respect to which at least one of the tests referred to in subdivision (a) is not met or (2) at the end of the income year of the corporation during which a final order has been entered by a court of competent jurisdiction declaring that one of those tests is not met, provided that a contrary order has not been entered before the end of the income year.

(f) Any foreign corporation that is subject to the requirements of subdivision (b) shall advise any shareholder of record, any officer, director, employee, or other agent (within the meaning of Section 317) and any creditor of the corporation in writing, within 30 days of receipt of written request for that information, whether or not it is subject to subdivision (b) at the time the request is received. Any party who obtains a final determination by a court of competent jurisdiction that the corporation failed to provide to the party information required to be provided by this subdivision or provided the party information of the kind required to be provided by this subdivision that was incorrect, then the court, in its discretion, shall have the power to include in its judgment recovery by the party from the corporation of all court costs and reasonable attorneys' fees incurred in that legal proceeding to the extent they relate to obtaining that final determination.

New York Business Corporation Law (Selected Sections)

Article 4 — Formation of Corporations

§402. Certificate of Incorporation; Contents

. . . (b) The certificate of incorporation may set forth a provision eliminating or limiting the personal liability of directors to the corporation or its shareholders for damages for any breach of duty in such capacity, provided that no such provision shall eliminate or limit:

(1) the liability of any director if a judgment or other final adjudication adverse to him establishes that his acts or omissions were in bad faith or involved intentional misconduct or a knowing violation of law or that he personally gained in fact a financial profit or other advantage to which he was not legally entitled or that his acts violated section 719, or

(2) the liability of any director for any act or omission prior to the adoption of a provision authorized by this paragraph.

(c) The certificate of incorporation may set forth any provision, not inconsistent with this chapter or any other statute of this state, relating to the business of the corporation, its affairs, its rights or powers, or the rights or powers of its shareholders, directors or officers including any provision relating to matters which under this chapter are required or permitted to be set forth in the by-laws. It is not necessary to set forth in the certificate of incorporation any of the powers enumerated in this chapter.

ARTICLE 6 — SHAREHOLDERS

§601. *By-Laws*

(a) The initial by-laws of a corporation shall be adopted by its incorporator or incorporators at the organization meeting. Thereafter, subject to section 613 (Limitations on right to vote), by-laws may be adopted, amended or repealed by a majority of the votes cast by the shares at the time entitled to vote in the election of any directors. When so provided in the certificate of incorporation or a by-law adopted by the shareholders, by-laws may also be adopted, amended or repealed by the board by such vote as may be therein specified, which may be greater than the vote otherwise prescribed by this chapter, but any by-law adopted by the board may be amended or repealed by the shareholders entitled to vote thereon as herein provided. Any reference in this chapter to a "by-law adopted by the shareholders" shall include a by-law adopted by the incorporator or incorporators.

(b) The by-laws may contain any provision relating to the business of the corporation, the conduct of its affairs, its rights or powers or the rights or powers of its shareholders, directors or officers, not inconsistent with this chapter or any other statute of this state or the certificate of incorporation.

§602. *Meetings of Shareholders*

(a) Meetings of shareholders may be held at such place, within or without this state, as may be fixed by or under the by-laws, or if not so fixed, as determined by the board of directors. If, pursuant to this paragraph or the by-laws of the corporation, the board of directors is authorized to determine the place of a meeting of shareholders, the board of directors may, in its sole discretion, determine that the meeting be held solely by means of electronic communication, the platform/service of which shall be the place of the meeting for purpose of this article.

(b)

(i) A corporation may, if authorized by the board of directors: (1) implement reasonable measures to provide shareholders not physically present at a shareholders' meeting a reasonable opportunity to participate in the proceedings of the meeting substantially concurrently with such proceedings; and/or (2) provide reasonable measures to enable shareholders to vote or grant proxies with respect to matters submitted to the shareholders at a shareholders' meeting by means of electronic communication; provided that the corporation shall, if applicable, (A) implement reasonable measures to verify that each person deemed present and permitted to vote at the meeting by means of electronic communication is a shareholder of record and (B) keep a record of any vote or other action taken by a shareholder participating and voting by means of electronic communications at a shareholders' meeting. A shareholder participating in a shareholders' meeting by this means is deemed to be present in person at the meeting.

(ii) Nothing required in subparagraph (i) of this paragraph shall limit, restrict or supersede other forms of voting and participation.

(iii) For purposes of this paragraph, "reasonable measures" with respect to participating in proceedings shall include, but not be limited to, audio webcast or other broadcast of the meeting and for voting shall include but not be limited to telephonic and internet voting.

(c) A meeting of shareholders shall be held annually for the election of directors and the transaction of other business on a date fixed by or under the by-laws. A failure to hold the annual meeting on the date so fixed or to elect a sufficient number of directors to conduct the business of the corporation shall not work a forfeiture or give cause for dissolution of the corporation, except as provided in paragraph (c) of section 1104 (Petition in case of deadlock among directors or shareholders).

(d) Special meetings of the shareholders may be called by the board and by such person or persons as may be so authorized by the certificate of incorporation or the by-laws. At any such special meeting only such business may be transacted which is related to the purpose or purposes set forth in the notice required by section 605 (Notice of meetings of shareholders).

(e) Except as otherwise required by this chapter, the by-laws may designate reasonable procedures for the calling and conduct of a meeting of shareholders, including but not limited to specifying: (i) who may call and who may conduct the meeting, (ii) the means by which the order of business to be conducted shall be established, (iii) the procedures and requirements for the nomination of directors, (iv) the procedures with respect to the making of shareholder proposals, and (v) the procedures to be established for the adjournment of any meeting of shareholders. No amendment of the by-laws pertaining to the election of directors or the procedures for the calling and conduct of a meeting of shareholders shall affect the election of directors or the procedures for the calling or conduct in respect of any meeting of shareholders unless adequate notice thereof is given to the shareholders in a manner reasonably calculated to provide shareholders with sufficient time to respond thereto prior to such meeting.

§614. *Vote of Shareholders*

(a) Directors shall, except as otherwise required by this chapter or by the by-laws or certificate of incorporation as permitted by this chapter, be elected by a plurality of the votes cast at a meeting of shareholders by the holders of shares entitled to vote in the election.

(b) Whenever any corporate action, other than the election of directors, is to be taken under this chapter by vote of the shareholders, it shall, except as otherwise required by this chapter or by the certificate of incorporation as permitted by this chapter or by the specific provisions of a by-law adopted by the shareholders, be authorized by a majority of the votes cast in favor of or against such action at a meeting of shareholders by the holders of shares entitled to vote thereon. Except as otherwise provided in the certificate of incorporation or the specific provision of a by-law adopted by the shareholders, an abstention shall not constitute a vote cast.

§615. Written Consent of Shareholders, Subscribers or Incorporators Without a Meeting

(a) Whenever under this chapter shareholders are required or permitted to take any action by vote, such action may be taken without a meeting on written consent, setting forth the action so taken, signed by the holders of all outstanding shares entitled to vote thereon or, if the certificate of incorporation so permits, signed by the holders of outstanding shares having not less than the minimum number of votes that would be necessary to authorize or take such action at a meeting at which all shares entitled to vote thereon were present and voted. In addition, this paragraph shall not be construed to alter or modify the provisions of any section or any provision in a certificate of incorporation not inconsistent with this chapter under which the written consent of the holders of less than all outstanding shares is sufficient for corporate action. . . .

§616. Greater Requirement as to Quorum and Vote of Shareholders

(a) The certificate of incorporation may contain provisions specifying either or both of the following:

(1) That the proportion of votes of shares, or the proportion of votes of shares of any class or series thereof, the holders of which shall be present in person or by proxy at any meeting of shareholders, including a special meeting for election of directors under section 603 (Special meeting for election of directors), in order to constitute a quorum for the transaction of any business or of any specified item of business, including amendments to the certificate of incorporation, shall be greater than the proportion prescribed by this chapter in the absence of such provision.

(2) That the proportion of votes of shares, or votes of shares of a particular class or series of shares, that shall be necessary at any meeting of shareholders for the transaction of any business or of any specified item of business, including amendments to the certificate of incorporation, shall be greater than the proportion prescribed by this chapter in the absence of such provision.

(b) An amendment of the certificate of incorporation which changes or strikes out a provision permitted by this section, shall be authorized at a meeting of shareholders by two-thirds of the votes of the shares entitled to vote thereon, or of such greater proportion of votes of shares, or votes of shares of a particular class or series of shares, as may be provided specifically in the certificate of incorporation for changing or striking out a provision permitted by this section.

(c) If the certificate of incorporation of any corporation contains a provision authorized by this section, the existence of such provision shall be noted conspicuously on the face or back of every certificate for shares issued by such corporation, except that this requirement shall not apply to any corporation having any class of any equity security registered pursuant to Section twelve of the Securities Exchange Act of 1934, as amended.

§618. Cumulative voting

The certificate of incorporation of any corporation may provide that in all elections of directors of such corporation each shareholder shall be entitled to as many votes as shall equal the number of votes which, except for such provisions as to cumulative voting, he would be entitled to cast for the election of directors with respect to his shares multiplied by the number of directors to be elected, and that he may cast all of such votes for a single director or may distribute them among the number to be voted for, or any two or more of them, as he may see fit, which right, when exercised, shall be termed cumulative voting.

§620. Agreements as to Voting; Provision in Certificate of Incorporation as to Control of Directors

(a) An agreement between two or more shareholders, if in writing and signed by the parties thereto, may provide that in exercising any voting rights, the shares held by them shall be voted as therein provided, or as they may agree, or as determined in accordance with a procedure agreed upon by them.

(b) A provision in the certificate of incorporation otherwise prohibited by law because it improperly restricts the board in its management of the business of the corporation, or improperly transfers to one or more shareholders or to one or more persons or corporations to be selected by him or them, all or any part of such management otherwise within the authority of the board under this chapter, shall nevertheless be valid:

(1) If all the incorporators or holders of record of all outstanding shares, whether or not having voting power, have authorized such provision in the certificate of incorporation or an amendment thereof; and

(2) If, subsequent to the adoption of such provision, shares are transferred or issued only to persons who had knowledge or notice thereof or consented in writing to such provision.

(c) A provision authorized by paragraph (b) shall be valid only so long as no shares of the corporation are listed on a national securities exchange or regularly quoted in an over-the-counter market by one or more members of a national or affiliated securities association.

(d)(1) Except as provided in paragraph (e), an amendment to strike out a provision authorized by paragraph (b) shall be authorized at a meeting of shareholders by

(A) (i) for any corporation in existence on the effective date of subparagraph (2) of this paragraph, two-thirds of the votes of the shares entitled to vote thereon and

(ii) for any corporation in existence on the effective date of this clause the certificate of incorporation of which expressly provides such and for any corporation incorporated after the effective date of subparagraph (2) of this paragraph, a majority of the votes of the shares entitled to vote thereon or

(B) in either case, by such greater proportion of votes of shares as may be required by the certificate of incorporation for that purpose.

(2) Any corporation may adopt an amendment of the certificate of incorporation in accordance with the applicable clause or subclause of subparagraph (1) of this paragraph to provide that any further amendment of the certificate of incorporation that strikes out a provision authorized by paragraph (b) of this section shall be authorized at a meeting of the shareholders by a specified proportion of votes of outstanding shares, or votes of a particular class or series of shares, entitled to vote thereon, provided that such proportion may not be less than a majority.

(e) Alternatively, if a provision authorized by paragraph (b) shall have ceased to be valid under this section, the board may authorize a certificate of amendment under section 805 (Certificate of amendment; contents) striking out such provision. Such certificate shall set forth the event by reason of which the provision ceased to be valid.

(f) The effect of any such provision authorized by paragraph (b) shall be to relieve the directors and impose upon the shareholders authorizing the same or consenting thereto the liability for managerial acts or omissions that is imposed on directors by this chapter to the extent that and so long as the discretion or powers of the board in its management of corporate affairs is controlled by any such provision.

(g) If the certificate of incorporation of any corporation contains a provision authorized by paragraph (b), the existence of such provision shall be noted conspicuously on the face or back of every certificate for shares issued by such corporation.

§622. *Preemptive Rights*

(a) As used in this section, the term:

(1) "Unlimited dividend rights" means the right without limitation as to amount either to all or to a share of the balance of current or liquidating dividends after the payment of dividends on any shares entitled to a preference.

(2) "Equity shares" means shares of any class, whether or not preferred as to dividends or assets, which have unlimited dividend rights.

(3) "Voting rights" means the right to vote for the election of one or more directors, excluding a right so to vote which is dependent on the happening of an event specified in the certificate of incorporation which would change the voting rights of any class of shares.

(4) "Voting shares" means shares of any class which have voting rights, but does not include bonds on which voting rights are conferred under section 518 (Corporate bonds).

(5) "Preemptive right" means the right to purchase shares or other securities to be issued or subject to rights or options to purchase, as such right is defined in this section.

(b) (1) With respect to any corporation incorporated prior to the effective date of subparagraph (2) of this paragraph, except as otherwise provided in the certificate of incorporation, and except as provided in this section, the holders of equity shares of any class, in case of the proposed issuance by the corporation of, or the proposed granting by the corporation of rights or options to purchase, its equity shares of any class or any shares or other securities convertible into or carrying rights or options to purchase its equity shares of any class, shall, if the issuance of the equity shares proposed to be issued or issuable upon exercise of such rights or options or upon conversion of such other securities would adversely affect the unlimited dividend rights of such holders, have the right during a reasonable time and on reasonable conditions, both to be fixed by the board, to purchase such shares or other securities in such proportions as shall be determined as provided in this section.

(2) With respect to any corporation incorporated on or after the effective date of this subparagraph, the holders of such shares shall not have any preemptive right, except as otherwise expressly provided in the certificate of incorporation.

(c) Except as otherwise provided in the certificate of incorporation, and except as provided in this section, the holders of voting shares of any class having any preemptive right under this paragraph on the date immediately prior to the effective date of subparagraph (2) of paragraph (b) of this section, in case of the proposed issuance by the corporation of, or the proposed granting by the corporation of rights or options to purchase, its voting shares of any class or any shares or other securities convertible into or carrying rights or options to purchase its voting shares of any class, shall, if the issuance of the voting shares proposed to be issued or issuable upon exercise of such rights or options or upon conversion of such other securities would adversely affect the voting rights of such holders, have the right during a reasonable time and on reasonable conditions, both to be fixed by the board, to purchase such shares or other securities in such proportions as shall be determined as provided in this section.

(d) The preemptive right provided for in paragraphs (b) and (c) shall entitle shareholders having such rights to purchase the shares or other securities to be offered or optioned for sale as nearly as practicable in such proportions as would, if such preemptive right were exercised, preserve the relative unlimited dividend rights and voting rights of such holders and at a price or prices not less favorable than the price or prices at which such shares or other securities are proposed to be offered for sale to others, without deduction of such reasonable expenses of and compensation for the sale, underwriting or purchase of such shares or other securities by underwriters or dealers as may lawfully be paid by the corporation. In case each of the shares entitling the holders thereof to preemptive rights does not confer the same unlimited dividend right or voting right, the board shall apportion the shares or other securities to be offered or optioned for sale among the shareholders having preemptive rights to purchase them in such proportions as in the opinion of the board shall preserve as far as practicable the relative unlimited dividend rights and voting rights of the holders at the time of such offering. The apportionment made by the board shall, in the absence of fraud or bad faith, be binding upon all shareholders.

(e) Unless otherwise provided in the certificate of incorporation, shares or other securities offered for sale or subjected to rights or options to purchase shall not be subject to preemptive rights under paragraph (b) or (c) of this section if they:

(1) Are to be issued by the board to effect a merger or consolidation or offered or subjected to rights or options for consideration other than cash;

(2) Are to be issued or subjected to rights or options under paragraph (d) of section 505 (Rights and options to purchase shares; issue of rights and options to directors, officers and employees);

(3) Are to be issued to satisfy conversion or option rights theretofore granted by the corporation;

(4) Are treasury shares;

(5) Are part of the shares or other securities of the corporation authorized in its original certificate of incorporation and are issued, sold or optioned within two years from the date of filing such certificate; or

(6) Are to be issued under a plan of reorganization approved in a proceeding under any applicable act of congress relating to reorganization of corporations.

(f) Shareholders of record entitled to preemptive rights on the record date fixed by the board under section 604 (Fixing record date), or, if no record date is fixed, then on the record date determined under section 604, and no others shall be entitled to the right defined in this section.

(g) The board shall cause to be given to each shareholder entitled to purchase shares or other securities in accordance with this section, a notice directed to him in the manner provided in section 605 (Notice of meetings of shareholders) setting forth the time within which and the terms and conditions upon which the shareholder may purchase such shares or other securities and also the apportionment made of the right to purchase among the shareholders entitled to preemptive rights. Such notice shall be given personally or by mail at least fifteen days prior to the expiration of the period during which the shareholder shall have the right to purchase. All shareholders entitled to preemptive rights to whom notice shall have been given as aforesaid shall be deemed conclusively to have had a reasonable time in which to exercise their preemptive rights.

(h) Shares or other securities which have been offered to shareholders having preemptive rights to purchase and which have not been purchased by them within the time fixed by the board may thereafter, for a period of not exceeding one year following the expiration of the time during which shareholders might have exercised such preemptive rights, be issued, sold or subjected to rights or options to any other person or persons at a price, without deduction of such reasonable expenses of and compensation for the sale, underwriting or purchase of such shares by underwriters or dealers as may lawfully be paid by the corporation, not less than that at which they were offered to such shareholders. Any such shares or other securities not so issued, sold or subjected to rights or options to others during such one year period shall thereafter again be subject to the preemptive rights of shareholders.

(i) Except as otherwise provided in the certificate of incorporation and except as provided in this section, no holder of any shares of any class shall as such holder have any preemptive right to purchase any other shares or securities of any class which at any time may be sold or offered for sale by the corporation. Unless otherwise provided in the certificate of incorporation, holders of bonds on which voting rights are conferred under section 518 shall have no preemptive rights.

§623. *Procedure to Enforce Shareholder's Right to Receive Payment for Shares*

(a) A shareholder intending to enforce his right under a section of this chapter to receive payment for his shares if the proposed corporate action referred to therein is taken shall file with the corporation, before the meeting of shareholders at which the action is submitted to a vote, or at such meeting but before the vote, written objection to the action. The objection shall include a notice of his election to dissent, his name and residence address, the number and classes of shares as to which he dissents and a demand for payment of the fair value of his shares if the action is taken. Such objection is not required from any shareholder to whom the corporation did not give notice of such meeting in accordance with this chapter or where the proposed action is authorized by written consent of shareholders without a meeting.

(b) Within ten days after the shareholders' authorization date, which term as used in this section means the date on which the shareholders' vote authorizing such action was taken, or the date on which such consent without a meeting was obtained from the requisite shareholders, the corporation shall give written notice of such authorization or consent by registered mail to each shareholder who filed written objection or from whom written objection was not required, excepting any shareholder who voted for or consented in writing to the proposed action and who thereby is deemed to have elected not to enforce his right to receive payment for his shares.

(c) Within twenty days after the giving of notice to him, any shareholder from whom written objection was not required and who elects to dissent shall file with the corporation a written notice of such election, stating his name and residence address, the number and classes of shares as to which he dissents and a demand for payment of the fair value of his shares. Any shareholder who elects to dissent from a merger under section 905 (Merger of subsidiary corporation) or paragraph (c) of section 907 (Merger or consolidation of domestic and foreign corporations) or from a share exchange under paragraph (g) of section 913 (Share exchanges) shall file a written notice of such election to dissent within twenty days after the giving to him of a copy of the plan of merger or exchange or an outline of the material features thereof under section 905 or 913.

(d) A shareholder may not dissent as to less than all of the shares, as to which he has a right to dissent, held by him of record, that he owns beneficially. A nominee or fiduciary may not dissent on behalf of any beneficial owner as to less than all of the shares of such owner, as to which such nominee or fiduciary has a right to dissent, held of record by such nominee or fiduciary.

(e) Upon consummation of the corporate action, the shareholder shall cease to have any of the rights of a shareholder except the right to be paid the fair value of his shares and any other rights under this section. A notice of election may be withdrawn by the shareholder at any time prior to his acceptance in writing of an offer made by the corporation, as provided in paragraph (g), but in no case later than sixty days from the date of consummation of the corporate action except that if the corporation fails to make a timely offer, as provided in paragraph (g), the time for withdrawing a notice of election shall be extended until sixty days from the date an offer is made. Upon expiration of such time, withdrawal of a notice of election shall require the written consent of the corporation. In order to be effective, withdrawal of a notice of election must be accompanied by the return to the corporation of any advance payment made to the shareholder as provided in paragraph (g). If a notice of election is withdrawn, or the corporate action is rescinded, or a court shall determine that the shareholder is not entitled to receive payment for his shares, or the shareholder shall otherwise lose his dissenter's rights, he shall not have the right to receive payment for his shares and he shall be reinstated to all his rights as a shareholder as of the consummation of the corporate action, including any intervening preemptive rights and the right to payment of any intervening dividend or other distribution or, if any such rights have expired or any such dividend or distribution other than in cash has been completed, in lieu thereof, at the election of the corporation, the fair value thereof in cash as determined by the board as of the time of such expiration or completion, but without prejudice otherwise to any corporate proceedings that may have been taken in the interim.

(f) At the time of filing the notice of election to dissent or within one month thereafter the shareholder of shares represented by certificates shall submit the certificates representing his shares to the corporation, or to its transfer agent, which shall forthwith note conspicuously thereon that a notice of election has been filed and shall return the certificates to the shareholder or other person who submitted them on his behalf. Any shareholder of shares represented by certificates who fails to submit his certificates for such notation as herein specified shall, at the option of the corporation exercised by written notice to him within forty-five days from the date of filing of such notice of election to dissent, lose his dissenter's rights unless a court, for good cause shown, shall otherwise direct. Upon transfer of a certificate bearing such notation, each new certificate issued therefor shall bear a similar notation together with the name of the original dissenting holder of the shares and a transferee shall acquire no rights in the corporation except those which the original dissenting shareholder had at the time of transfer.

(g) Within fifteen days after the expiration of the period within which shareholders may file their notices of election to dissent, or within fifteen days after the proposed corporate action is consummated, whichever is later (but in no case later than ninety days from the shareholders' authorization date), the corporation or, in the case of a merger or consolidation, the surviving or new corporation, shall make a written offer by registered mail to each shareholder who has filed such notice of election to pay for his shares at a specified price which the corporation considers to be their fair value. Such offer shall be accompanied by a statement setting forth the aggregate number of shares with respect to which notices of election to dissent have been received and the aggregate number of holders of such shares. If the corporate action has been consummated, such offer shall also be accompanied by (1) advance payment to each such shareholder who has submitted the certificates representing his shares to the corporation, as provided in paragraph (f), of an amount equal to eighty percent of the amount of such offer, or (2) as to each shareholder who has not yet submitted his certificates a statement that advance payment to him of an amount equal to eighty percent of the amount of such offer will be made by the corporation promptly upon submission of his certificates. If the corporate action has not been consummated at the time of the making of the offer, such advance payment or statement as to advance payment shall be sent to each shareholder entitled thereto forthwith upon consummation of the corporate action. Every advance payment or statement as to advance payment shall include advice to the shareholder to the effect that acceptance of such payment does not constitute a waiver of any dissenters' rights. If the corporate action has not been consummated upon the expiration of the ninety day period after the shareholders' authorization date, the offer may be conditioned upon the consummation of such action. Such offer shall be made at the same price per share to all dissenting shareholders of the same class, or if divided into series, of the same series and shall be accompanied by a balance sheet of the corporation whose shares the dissenting shareholder holds as of the latest available date, which shall not be earlier than twelve months before the making of such offer, and a profit and loss statement or statements for not less than a twelve month period ended on the date of such balance sheet or, if the corporation was not in existence throughout such twelve month period, for the portion thereof during which it was in existence. Notwithstanding the foregoing, the corporation shall not be required to furnish a balance sheet or profit and loss statement or statements to any shareholder to whom such balance sheet or profit and loss statement or statements were previously furnished, nor if in connection with obtaining the shareholders' authorization for or consent to the proposed corporate action the shareholders were furnished with a proxy or information statement, which included financial statements, pursuant to Regulation 14A or Regulation 14C of the United States Securities and Exchange Commission. If within thirty days after the making of such offer, the corporation making the offer and any shareholder agree upon the price to be paid for his shares, payment therefor shall be made within sixty days after the making of such offer or the consummation of the proposed corporate action, whichever is later, upon the surrender of the certificates for any such shares represented by certificates.

(h) The following procedure shall apply if the corporation fails to make such offer within such period of fifteen days, or if it makes the offer and any dissenting shareholder or shareholders fail to agree with it within the period of thirty days thereafter upon the price to be paid for their shares:

(1) The corporation shall, within twenty days after the expiration of whichever is applicable of the two periods last mentioned, institute a special proceeding in the supreme court in the judicial district in which the office of the corporation is located to determine the rights of dissenting shareholders and to fix the fair value of their shares. If, in the case of merger or consolidation, the surviving or new corporation is a foreign corporation without an office in this state, such

proceeding shall be brought in the county where the office of the domestic corporation, whose shares are to be valued, was located.

(2) If the corporation fails to institute such proceeding within such period of twenty days, any dissenting shareholder may institute such proceeding for the same purpose not later than thirty days after the expiration of such twenty day period. If such proceeding is not instituted within such thirty day period, all dissenter's rights shall be lost unless the supreme court, for good cause shown, shall otherwise direct.

(3) All dissenting shareholders, excepting those who, as provided in paragraph (g), have agreed with the corporation upon the price to be paid for their shares, shall be made parties to such proceeding, which shall have the effect of an action quasi in rem against their shares. The corporation shall serve a copy of the petition in such proceeding upon each dissenting shareholder who is a resident of this state in the manner provided by law for the service of a summons, and upon each nonresident dissenting shareholder either by registered mail and publication, or in such other manner as is permitted by law. The jurisdiction of the court shall be plenary and exclusive.

(4) The court shall determine whether each dissenting shareholder, as to whom the corporation requests the court to make such determination, is entitled to receive payment for his shares. If the corporation does not request any such determination or if the court finds that any dissenting shareholder is so entitled, it shall proceed to fix the value of the shares, which, for the purposes of this section, shall be the fair value as of the close of business on the day prior to the shareholders' authorization date. In fixing the fair value of the shares, the court shall consider the nature of the transaction giving rise to the shareholder's right to receive payment for shares and its effects on the corporation and its shareholders, the concepts and methods then customary in the relevant securities and financial markets for determining fair value of shares of a corporation engaging in a similar transaction under comparable circumstances and all other relevant factors. The court shall determine the fair value of the shares without a jury and without referral to an appraiser or referee. Upon application by the corporation or by any shareholder who is a party to the proceeding, the court may, in its discretion, permit pretrial disclosure, including, but not limited to, disclosure of any expert's reports relating to the fair value of the shares whether or not intended for use at the trial in the proceeding and notwithstanding subdivision (d) of section 3101 of the civil practice law and rules.

(5) The final order in the proceeding shall be entered against the corporation in favor of each dissenting shareholder who is a party to the proceeding and is entitled thereto for the value of his shares so determined.

(6) The final order shall include an allowance for interest at such rate as the court finds to be equitable, from the date the corporate action was consummated to the date of payment. In determining the rate of interest, the court shall consider all relevant factors, including the rate of interest which the corporation would have had to pay to borrow money during the pendency of the proceeding. If the court finds that the refusal of any shareholder to accept the corporate offer

of payment for his shares was arbitrary, vexatious or otherwise not in good faith, no interest shall be allowed to him.

(7) Each party to such proceeding shall bear its own costs and expenses, including the fees and expenses of its counsel and of any experts employed by it. Notwithstanding the foregoing, the court may, in its discretion, apportion and assess all or any part of the costs, expenses and fees incurred by the corporation against any or all of the dissenting shareholders who are parties to the proceeding, including any who have withdrawn their notices of election as provided in paragraph (e), if the court finds that their refusal to accept the corporate offer was arbitrary, vexatious or otherwise not in good faith. The court may, in its discretion, apportion and assess all or any part of the costs, expenses and fees incurred by any or all of the dissenting shareholders who are parties to the proceeding against the corporation if the court finds any of the following: (A) that the fair value of the shares as determined materially exceeds the amount which the corporation offered to pay; (B) that no offer or required advance payment was made by the corporation; (C) that the corporation failed to institute the special proceeding within the period specified therefor; or (D) that the action of the corporation in complying with its obligations as provided in this section was arbitrary, vexatious or otherwise not in good faith. In making any determination as provided in clause (A), the court may consider the dollar amount or the percentage, or both, by which the fair value of the shares as determined exceeds the corporate offer.

(8) Within sixty days after final determination of the proceeding, the corporation shall pay to each dissenting shareholder the amount found to be due him, upon surrender of the certificates for any such shares represented by certificates.

(i) Shares acquired by the corporation upon the payment of the agreed value therefor or of the amount due under the final order, as provided in this section, shall become treasury shares or be cancelled as provided in section 515 (Reacquired shares), except that, in the case of a merger or consolidation, they may be held and disposed of as the plan of merger or consolidation may otherwise provide.

(j) No payment shall be made to a dissenting shareholder under this section at a time when the corporation is insolvent or when such payment would make it insolvent. In such event, the dissenting shareholder shall, at his option:

(1) Withdraw his notice of election, which shall in such event be deemed withdrawn with the written consent of the corporation; or

(2) Retain his status as a claimant against the corporation and, if it is liquidated, be subordinated to the rights of creditors of the corporation, but have rights superior to the non-dissenting shareholders, and if it is not liquidated, retain his right to be paid for his shares, which right the corporation shall be obliged to satisfy when the restrictions of this paragraph do not apply.

(3) The dissenting shareholder shall exercise such option under subparagraph (1) or (2) by written notice filed with the corporation within thirty days after the corporation has given him written notice that payment for his shares cannot be made because of the restrictions of this paragraph. If the dissenting shareholder fails to exercise such option as provided, the corporation shall exercise the option by written notice given to him within twenty days after the expiration of such period of thirty days.

(k) The enforcement by a shareholder of his right to receive payment for his shares in the manner provided herein shall exclude the enforcement by such shareholder of any other right to which he might otherwise be entitled by virtue of share ownership, except as provided in paragraph (e), and except that this section shall not exclude the right of such shareholder to bring or maintain an appropriate action to obtain relief on the ground that such corporate action will be or is unlawful or fraudulent as to him.

(l) Except as otherwise expressly provided in this section, any notice to be given by a corporation to a shareholder under this section shall be given in the manner provided in section 605 (Notice of meetings of shareholders).

(m) This section shall not apply to foreign corporations except as provided in subparagraph (e)(2) of section 907 (Merger or consolidation of domestic and foreign corporations).

§626. *Shareholders' Derivative Action Brought in the Right of the Corporation to Procure a Judgment in Its Favor*

(a) An action may be brought in the right of a domestic or foreign corporation to procure a judgment in its favor, by a holder of shares or of voting trust certificates of the corporation or of a beneficial interest in such shares or certificates.

(b) In any such action, it shall be made to appear that the plaintiff is such a holder at the time of bringing the action and that he was such a holder at the time of the transaction of which he complains, or that his shares or his interest therein devolved upon him by operation of law.

(c) In any such action, the complaint shall set forth with particularity the efforts of the plaintiff to secure the initiation of such action by the board or the reasons for not making such effort.

(d) Such action shall not be discontinued, compromised or settled, without the approval of the court having jurisdiction of the action. If the court shall determine that the interests of the shareholders or any class or classes thereof will be substantially affected by such discontinuance, compromise, or settlement, the court, in its discretion, may direct that notice, by publication or otherwise, shall be given to the shareholders or class or classes thereof whose interest it determines will be so affected; if notice is so directed to be given, the court may determine which one or more of the parties to the action shall bear the expense of giving the same, in such amount as the court shall determine and find to be reasonable in the circumstances, and the amount of such expense shall be awarded as special costs of the action and recoverable in the same manner as statutory taxable costs.

(e) If the action on behalf of the corporation was successful, in whole or in part, or if anything was received by the plaintiff or plaintiffs or a claimant or claimants as the result of a judgment, compromise or settlement of an action or claim, the court may award the plaintiff or plaintiffs, claimant or claimants, reasonable expenses, including reasonable attorney's fees, and shall direct him or them to account to the corporation for the remainder of the proceeds so received by him or them. This paragraph shall not apply to any judgment rendered for the benefit of injured shareholders only and limited to a recovery of the loss or damage sustained by them.

§627. *Security for Expenses in Shareholders' Derivative Action Brought in the Right of the Corporation to Procure a Judgment in Its Favor*

In any action specified in section 626 (Shareholders' derivative action brought in the right of the corporation to procure a judgment in its favor), unless the plaintiff or plaintiffs hold five percent or more of any class of the outstanding shares or hold voting trust certificates or a beneficial interest in shares representing five percent or more of any class of such shares, or the shares, voting trust certificates and beneficial interest of such plaintiff or plaintiffs have a fair value in excess of fifty thousand dollars, the corporation in whose right such action is brought shall be entitled at any stage of the proceedings before final judgment to require the plaintiff or plaintiffs to give security for the reasonable expenses, including attorney's fees, which may be incurred by it in connection with such action and by the other parties defendant in connection therewith for which the corporation may become liable under this chapter, under any contract or otherwise under law, to which the corporation shall have recourse in such amount as the court having jurisdiction of such action shall determine upon the termination of such action. The amount of such security may thereafter from time to time be increased or decreased in the discretion of the court having jurisdiction of such action upon showing that the security provided has or may become inadequate or excessive.

§630. *Liability of Shareholders for Wages Due to Laborers, Servants or Employees*

(a) The ten largest shareholders, as determined by the fair value of their beneficial interest as of the beginning of the period during which the unpaid services referred to in this section are performed, of every domestic corporation or of any foreign corporation, when the unpaid services were performed in the state, no shares of which are listed on a national securities exchange or regularly quoted in an over-the-counter market by one or more members of a national or an affiliated securities association, shall jointly and severally be personally liable for all debts, wages or salaries due and owing to any of its laborers, servants or employees other than contractors, for services performed by them for such corporation. Before such laborer, servant or employee shall charge such shareholder for such services, he shall give notice in writing to such shareholder that he intends to hold him liable under this section. Such notice shall be given within one hundred and eighty days after termination of such services, except that if, within such period, the laborer, servant or employee demands an examination of the record of shareholders under paragraph (b) of section 624 (Books and records; right of inspection, prima facie evidence) of this article, such notice may be given within sixty days after he has been given the opportunity to examine the record of shareholders. An action to enforce such liability shall be commenced within ninety days after the return of an execution unsatisfied against the corporation upon a judgment recovered against it for such services. The provisions of this paragraph shall not apply to an investment company registered as such under an act of congress entitled "Investment Company Act of 1940."

(b) For the purposes of this section, wages or salaries shall mean all compensation and benefits payable by an employer to or for the account of the employee for personal services rendered by such employee. These shall specifically include but not be limited to salaries, overtime, vacation, holiday and severance pay; employer contributions to or payments of insurance or welfare benefits; employer contributions to pension or annuity funds; and any other moneys properly due or payable for services rendered by such employee.

(c) A shareholder who has paid more than his pro rata share under this section shall be entitled to contribution pro rata from the other shareholders liable under this section with respect to the excess so paid, over and above his pro rata share, and may sue them jointly or severally or any number of them to recover the amount due from them. Such recovery may be had in a separate action. As used in this paragraph, "pro rata" means in proportion to beneficial share interest. Before a shareholder may claim contribution from other shareholders under this paragraph, he shall, unless they have been given notice by a laborer, servant or employee under paragraph (a), give them notice in writing that he intends to hold them so liable to him. Such notice shall be given by him within twenty days after the date that notice was given to him by a laborer, servant or employee under paragraph (a).

Article 7 — Directors and Officers

§701. Board of Directors

Subject to any provision in the certificate of incorporation authorized by paragraph (b) of section 620 (Agreements as to voting; provision in certificate of incorporation as to control of directors) or by paragraph (b) of section 715 (Officers), the business of a corporation shall be managed under the direction of its board of directors, each of whom shall be at least eighteen years of age. The certificate of incorporation or the by-laws may prescribe other qualifications for directors.

§706. Removal of Directors

(a) Any or all of the directors may be removed for cause by vote of the shareholders. The certificate of incorporation or the specific provisions of a by-law adopted by the shareholders may provide for such removal by action of the board, except in the case of any director elected by cumulative voting, or by the holders of the shares of any class or series, or holders of bonds, voting as a class, when so entitled by the provisions of the certificate of incorporation.

(b) If the certificate of incorporation or the by-laws so provide, any or all of the directors may be removed without cause by vote of the shareholders.

(c) The removal of directors, with or without cause, as provided in paragraphs (a) and (b) is subject to the following:

(1) In the case of a corporation having cumulative voting, no director may be removed when the votes cast against his removal would be sufficient to elect him if voted cumulatively at an election at which the same total number of votes were cast and the entire board, or the entire class of directors of which he is a member, were then being elected; and

(2) When by the provisions of the certificate of incorporation the holders of the shares of any class or series, or holders of bonds, voting as a class, are entitled to elect one or more directors, any director so elected may be removed only by

the applicable vote of the holders of the shares of that class or series, or the holders of such bonds, voting as a class.

(d) An action to procure a judgment removing a director for cause may be brought by the attorney-general or by the holders of ten percent of the outstanding shares, whether or not entitled to vote. The court may bar from reelection any director so removed for a period fixed by the court.

§709. Greater Requirement as to Quorum and Vote of Directors

(a) The certificate of incorporation may contain provisions specifying either or both of the following:

(1) That the proportion of directors that shall constitute a quorum for the transaction of business or of any specified item of business shall be greater than the proportion prescribed by this chapter in the absence of such provision.

(2) That the proportion of votes of directors that shall be necessary for the transaction of business or of any specified item of business shall be greater than the proportion prescribed by this chapter in the absence of such provision.

(b)(1) An amendment of the certificate of incorporation which changes or strikes out a provision permitted by this section shall be authorized at a meeting of shareholders by

(A)(i) for any corporation in existence on the effective date of subparagraph (2) of this paragraph, two-thirds of the votes of all outstanding shares entitled to vote thereon, and

(ii) for any corporation in existence on the effective date of this clause the certificate of incorporation of which expressly provides such and for any corporation incorporated after the effective date of subparagraph (2) of this paragraph, a majority of the votes of all outstanding shares entitled to vote thereon or

(B) in either case, such greater proportion of votes of shares, or votes of a class or series of shares, as may be provided specifically in the certificate of incorporation for changing or striking out a provision permitted by this section.

(2) Any corporation may adopt an amendment of the certificate of incorporation in accordance with any applicable clause or subclause of subparagraph (1) of this paragraph to provide that any further amendment of the certificate of incorporation that changes or strikes out a provision permitted by this section shall be authorized at a meeting of the shareholders by a specified proportion of the votes of the shares, or particular class or series of shares, entitled to vote thereon, provided that such proportion may not be less than a majority.

(c) [Repealed.]

§713. Interested Directors

(a) No contract or other transaction between a corporation and one or more of its directors, or between a corporation and any other corporation, firm, association or other entity in which one or more of its directors are directors or officers, or have a substantial financial interest, shall be either void or voidable for this reason alone or by reason alone that such director or directors are present at the meeting of the board, or of a committee thereof, which approves such contract or transaction, or that his or their votes are counted for such purpose:

(1) If the material facts as to such director's interest in such contract or transaction and as to any such common directorship, officership or financial interest are disclosed in good faith or known to the board or committee, and the board or committee approves such contract or transaction by a vote sufficient for such purpose without counting the vote of such interested director or, if the votes of the disinterested directors are insufficient to constitute an act of the board as defined in section 708 (Action by the board), by unanimous vote of the disinterested directors; or

(2) If the material facts as to such director's interest in such contract or transaction and as to any such common directorship, officership or financial interest are disclosed in good faith or known to the shareholders entitled to vote thereon, and such contract or transaction is approved by vote of such shareholders.

(b) If a contract or other transaction between a corporation and one or more of its directors, or between a corporation and any other corporation, firm, association or other entity in which one or more of its directors are directors or officers, or have a substantial financial interest, is not approved in accordance with paragraph (a), the corporation may avoid the contract or transaction unless the party or parties thereto shall establish affirmatively that the contract or transaction was fair and reasonable as to the corporation at the time it was approved by the board, a committee or the shareholders.

(c) Common or interested directors may be counted in determining the presence of a quorum at a meeting of the board or of a committee which approves such contract or transaction.

(d) The certificate of incorporation may contain additional restrictions on contracts or transactions between a corporation and its directors and may provide that contracts or transactions in violation of such restrictions shall be void or voidable by the corporation.

(e) Unless otherwise provided in the certificate of incorporation or the by-laws, the board shall have authority to fix the compensation of directors for services in any capacity.

§714. Loans to Directors

(a) A corporation may not lend money to or guarantee the obligation of a director of the corporation unless:

(1) the particular loan or guarantee is approved by the shareholders, with the holders of a majority of the votes of the shares entitled to vote thereon constituting a quorum, but shares held of record or beneficially by directors who are benefitted by such loan or guarantee shall not be entitled to vote or to be included in the determination of a quorum; or

(2) with respect to any corporation in existence on the effective date of this subparagraph (2) the certificate of incorporation of which expressly provides such and with respect to any corporation incorporated after the effective date of

this subparagraph (2), the board determines that the loan or guarantee benefits the corporation and either approves the specific loan or guarantee or a general plan authorizing loans and guarantees.

(b) The fact that a loan or guarantee is made in violation of this section does not affect the borrower's liability on the loan.

§715. Officers

(a) The board may elect or appoint a president, one or more vice-presidents, a secretary and a treasurer, and such other officers as it may determine, or as may be provided in the by-laws.

(b) The certificate of incorporation may provide that all officers or that specified officers shall be elected by the shareholders instead of by the board. . . .

(g) All officers as between themselves and the corporation shall have such authority and perform such duties in the management of the corporation as may be provided in the by-laws or, to the extent not so provided, by the board. . . .

§716. Removal of Officers

(a) Any officer elected or appointed by the board may be removed by the board with or without cause. An officer elected by the shareholders may be removed, with or without cause, only by vote of the shareholders, but his authority to act as an officer may be suspended by the board for cause.

(b) The removal of an officer without cause shall be without prejudice to his contract rights, if any. The election or appointment of an officer shall not of itself create contract rights.

(c) An action to procure a judgment removing an officer for cause may be brought by the attorney-general or by ten percent of the votes of the outstanding shares, whether or not entitled to vote. The court may bar from re-election or reappointment any officer so removed for a period fixed by the court.

§717. Duty of Directors

(a) A director shall perform his duties as a director, including his duties as a member of any committee of the board upon which he may serve, in good faith and with that degree of care which an ordinarily prudent person in a like position would use under similar circumstances. In performing his duties, a director shall be entitled to rely on information, opinions, reports or statements including financial statements and other financial data, in each case prepared or presented by:

(1) one or more officers or employees of the corporation or of any other corporation of which at least fifty percentum of the outstanding shares of stock entitling the holders thereof to vote for the election of directors is owned directly or indirectly by the corporation, whom the director believes to be reliable and competent in the matters presented,

(2) counsel, public accountants or other persons as to matters which the director believes to be within such person's professional or expert competence, or

(3) a committee of the board upon which he does not serve, duly designated in accordance with a provision of the certificate of incorporation or the by-laws, as to matters within its designated authority, which committee the director believes to merit confidence, so long as in so relying he shall be acting in good faith and with such degree of care, but he shall not be considered to be acting in good faith if he has knowledge concerning the matter in question that would cause such reliance to be unwarranted. A person who so performs his duties shall have no liability by reason of being or having been a director of the corporation.

(b) In taking action, including, without limitation, action which may involve or relate to a change or potential change in the control of the corporation, a director shall be entitled to consider, without limitation, (1) both the long-term and the short-term interests of the corporation and its shareholders and (2) the effects that the corporation's actions may have in the short-term or in the long-term upon any of the following:

(i) the prospects for potential growth, development, productivity and profitability of the corporation;

(ii) the corporation's current employees;

(iii) the corporation's retired employees and other beneficiaries receiving or entitled to receive retirement, welfare or similar benefits from or pursuant to any plan sponsored, or agreement entered into, by the corporation;

(iv) the corporation's customers and creditors; and

(v) the ability of the corporation to provide, as a going concern, goods, services, employment opportunities and employment benefits and otherwise to contribute to the communities in which it does business.

Nothing in this paragraph shall create any duties owed by any director to any person or entity to consider or afford any particular weight to any of the foregoing or abrogate any duty of the directors, either statutory or recognized by common law or court decisions.

For purposes of this paragraph, "control" shall mean the possession, directly or indirectly, of the power to direct or cause the direction of the management and policies of the corporation, whether through the ownership of voting stock, by contract, or otherwise.

§719. Liability of Directors in Certain Cases

(a) Directors of a corporation who vote for or concur in any of the following corporate actions shall be jointly and severally liable to the corporation for the benefit of its creditors or shareholders, to the extent of any injury suffered by such persons, respectively, as a result of such action:

(1) The declaration of any dividend or other distribution to the extent that it is contrary to the provisions of paragraphs (a) and (b) of section 510 (Dividends or other distributions in cash or property).

(2) The purchase of the shares of the corporation to the extent that it is contrary to the provisions of section 513 (Purchase or redemption by a corporation of its own shares).

(3) The distribution of assets to shareholders after dissolution of the corporation without paying or adequately providing for all known liabilities of the

corporation, excluding any claims not filed by creditors within the time limit set in a notice given to creditors under articles 10 (Non-judicial dissolution) or 11 (Judicial dissolution).

(4) The making of any loan contrary to section 714 (Loans to directors).

(b) A director who is present at a meeting of the board, or any committee thereof, when action specified in paragraph (a) is taken shall be presumed to have concurred in the action unless his dissent thereto shall be entered in the minutes of the meeting, or unless he shall submit his written dissent to the person acting as the secretary of the meeting before the adjournment thereof, or shall deliver or send by registered mail such dissent to the secretary of the corporation promptly after the adjournment of the meeting. Such right to dissent shall not apply to a director who voted in favor of such action. A director who is absent from a meeting of the board, or any committee thereof, when such action is taken shall be presumed to have concurred in the action unless he shall deliver or send by registered mail his dissent thereto to the secretary of the corporation or shall cause such dissent to be filed with the minutes of the proceedings of the board or committee within a reasonable time after learning of such action.

(c) Any director against whom a claim is successfully asserted under this section shall be entitled to contribution from the other directors who voted for or concurred in the action upon which the claim is asserted.

(d) Directors against whom a claim is successfully asserted under this section shall be entitled, to the extent of the amounts paid by them to the corporation as a result of such claims:

(1) Upon payment to the corporation of any amount of an improper dividend or distribution, to be subrogated to the rights of the corporation against shareholders who received such dividend or distribution with knowledge of facts indicating that it was not authorized by section 510, in proportion to the amounts received by them respectively.

(2) Upon payment to the corporation of any amount of the purchase price of an improper purchase of shares, to have the corporation rescind such purchase of shares and recover for their benefit, but at their expense, the amount of such purchase price from any seller who sold such shares with knowledge of facts indicating that such purchase of shares by the corporation was not authorized by section 513.

(3) Upon payment to the corporation of the claim of any creditor by reason of a violation of subparagraph (a)(3), to be subrogated to the rights of the corporation against shareholders who received an improper distribution of assets.

(4) Upon payment to the corporation of the amount of any loan made contrary to section 714, to be subrogated to the rights of the corporation against a director who received the improper loan.

(e) A director shall not be liable under this section if, in the circumstances, he performed his duty to the corporation under paragraph (a) of section 717.

(f) This section shall not affect any liability otherwise imposed by law upon any director.

§720. Action against Directors and Officers for Misconduct

(a) An action may be brought against one or more directors or officers of a corporation to procure a judgment for the following relief:

(1) Subject to any provision of the certificate of incorporation authorized pursuant to paragraph (b) of section 402, to compel the defendant to account for his official conduct in the following cases:

(A) The neglect of, or failure to perform, or other violation of his duties in the management and disposition of corporate assets committed to his charge.

(B) The acquisition by himself, transfer to others, loss or waste of corporate assets due to any neglect of, or failure to perform, or other violation of his duties.

(C) In the case of directors or officers of a benefit corporation organized under article seventeen of this chapter: (i) the failure to pursue the general public benefit purpose of a benefit corporation or any specific public benefit set forth in its certificate of incorporation; (ii) the failure by a benefit corporation to deliver or post an annual report as required by section seventeen hundred eight of article seventeen of this chapter; or (iii) the neglect of, or failure to perform, or other violation of his or her duties or standard of conduct under article seventeen of this chapter.

(2) To set aside an unlawful conveyance, assignment or transfer of corporate assets, where the transferee knew of its unlawfulness.

(3) To enjoin a proposed unlawful conveyance, assignment or transfer of corporate assets, where there is sufficient evidence that it will be made.

(b) An action may be brought for the relief provided in this section, and in paragraph (a) of section 719 (Liability of directors in certain cases) by a corporation, or a receiver, trustee in bankruptcy, officer, director or judgment creditor thereof, or, under section 626 (Shareholders' derivative action brought in the right of the corporation to procure a judgment in its favor), by a shareholder, voting trust certificate holder, or the owner of a beneficial interest in shares thereof.

(c) This section shall not affect any liability otherwise imposed by law upon any director or officer.

§721. Nonexclusivity of Statutory Provisions for Indemnification of Directors and Officers

The indemnification and advancement of expenses granted pursuant to, or provided by, this article shall not be deemed exclusive of any other rights to which a director or officer seeking indemnification or advancement of expenses may be entitled, whether contained in the certificate of incorporation or the by-laws or, when authorized by such certificate of incorporation or by-laws, (i) a resolution of shareholders, (ii) a resolution of directors, or (iii) an agreement providing for such indemnification, provided that no indemnification may be made to or on behalf of any director or officer if a judgment or other final adjudication adverse to the director or officer establishes that his acts were committed in bad faith or were the result of active and deliberate dishonesty and were material to the cause of action so adjudicated, or that he personally gained in fact a financial profit or other advantage to which he was not legally entitled. Nothing contained in this article shall affect any rights to indemnification to which corporate personnel other than directors and officers may be entitled by contract or otherwise under law.

§722. *Authorization for Indemnification of Directors and Officers*

(a) A corporation may indemnify any person made, or threatened to be made, a party to an action or proceeding (other than one by or in the right of the corporation to procure a judgment in its favor), whether civil or criminal, including an action by or in the right of any other corporation of any type or kind, domestic or foreign, or any partnership, joint venture, trust, employee benefit plan or other enterprise, which any director or officer of the corporation served in any capacity at the request of the corporation, by reason of the fact that he, his testator or intestate, was a director or officer of the corporation, or served such other corporation, partnership, joint venture, trust, employee benefit plan or other enterprise in any capacity, against judgments, fines, amounts paid in settlement and reasonable expenses, including attorneys' fees actually and necessarily incurred as a result of such action or proceeding, or any appeal therein, if such director or officer acted, in good faith, for a purpose which he reasonably believed to be in, or, in the case of service for any other corporation or any partnership, joint venture, trust, employee benefit plan or other enterprise, not opposed to, the best interests of the corporation and, in criminal actions or proceedings, in addition, had no reasonable cause to believe that his conduct was unlawful.

(b) The termination of any such civil or criminal action or proceeding by judgment, settlement, conviction or upon a plea of nolo contendere, or its equivalent, shall not in itself create a presumption that any such director or officer did not act, in good faith, for a purpose which he reasonably believed to be in, or, in the case of service for any other corporation or any partnership, joint venture, trust, employee benefit plan or other enterprise, not opposed to, the best interests of the corporation or that he had reasonable cause to believe that his conduct was unlawful.

(c) A corporation may indemnify any person made, or threatened to be made, a party to an action by or in the right of the corporation to procure a judgment in its favor by reason of the fact that he, his testator or intestate, is or was a director or officer of the corporation, or is or was serving at the request of the corporation as a director or officer of any other corporation of any type or kind, domestic or foreign, of any partnership, joint venture, trust, employee benefit plan or other enterprise, against amounts paid in settlement and reasonable expenses, including attorneys' fees, actually and necessarily incurred by him in connection with the defense or settlement of such action, or in connection with an appeal therein, if such director or officer acted, in good faith, for a purpose which he reasonably believed to be in, or, in the case of service for any other corporation or any partnership, joint venture, trust, employee benefit plan or other enterprise, not opposed to, the best interests of the corporation, except that no indemnification under this paragraph shall be made in respect of (1) a threatened action, or a pending action which is settled or otherwise disposed of, or (2) any claim, issue or matter as to which such person shall have been adjudged to be liable to the corporation, unless and only to the extent that the court in which the action was brought, or, if no action was brought, any court of competent jurisdiction, determines upon application that, in view of all the circumstances of the case, the person is fairly and reasonably entitled to indemnity for such portion of the settlement amount and expenses as the court deems proper. . . .

§723. Payment of Indemnification Other Than by Court Award

(a) A person who has been successful, on the merits or otherwise, in the defense of a civil or criminal action or proceeding of the character described in section 722 shall be entitled to indemnification as authorized in such section.

(b) Except as provided in paragraph (a), any indemnification under section 722 or otherwise permitted by section 721, unless ordered by a court under section 724 (Indemnification of directors and officers by a court), shall be made by the corporation, only if authorized in the specific case:

(1) By the board acting by a quorum consisting of directors who are not parties to such action or proceeding upon a finding that the director or officer has met the standard of conduct set forth in section 722 or established pursuant to section 721, as the case may be, or,

(2) If a quorum under subparagraph (1) is not obtainable or, even if obtainable, a quorum of disinterested directors so directs;

(A) By the board upon the opinion in writing of independent legal counsel that indemnification is proper in the circumstances because the applicable standard of conduct set forth in such sections has been met by such director or officer, or

(B) By the shareholders upon a finding that the director or officer has met the applicable standard of conduct set forth in such sections.

(c) Expenses incurred in defending a civil or criminal action or proceeding may be paid by the corporation in advance of the final disposition of such action or proceeding upon receipt of an undertaking by or on behalf of such director or officer to repay such amount as, and to the extent, required by paragraph (a) of section 725.

§724. Indemnification of Directors and Officers by a Court

(a) Notwithstanding the failure of a corporation to provide indemnification, and despite any contrary resolution of the board or of the shareholders in the specific case under section 723 (Payment of indemnification other than by court award), indemnification shall be awarded by a court to the extent authorized under section 722 (Authorization for indemnification of directors and officers), and paragraph (a) of section 723. Application therefor may be made, in every case, either:

(1) In the civil action or proceeding in which the expenses were incurred or other amounts were paid, or

(2) To the supreme court in a separate proceeding, in which case the application shall set forth the disposition of any previous application made to any court for the same or similar relief and also reasonable cause for the failure to make application for such relief in the action or proceeding in which the expenses were incurred or other amounts were paid.

(b) The application shall be made in such manner and form as may be required by the applicable rules of court or, in the absence thereof, by direction of a court to which it is made. Such application shall be upon notice to the corporation. The court may also direct that notice be given at the expense of the corporation to the shareholders and such other persons as it may designate in such manner as it may require.

(c) Where indemnification is sought by judicial action, the court may allow a person such reasonable expenses, including attorneys' fees, during the pendency of the litigation as are necessary in connection with his defense therein, if the court shall find that the defendant has by his pleadings or during the course of the litigation raised genuine issues of fact or law.

§725. Other Provisions Affecting Indemnification of Directors and Officers

(a) All expenses incurred in defending a civil or criminal action or proceeding which are advanced by the corporation under paragraph (c) of section 723 (Payment of indemnification other than by court award) or allowed by a court under paragraph (c) of section 724 (Indemnification of directors and officers by a court) shall be repaid in case the person receiving such advancement or allowance is ultimately found, under the procedure set forth in this article, not to be entitled to indemnification or, where indemnification is granted, to the extent the expenses so advanced by the corporation or allowed by the court exceed the indemnification to which he is entitled.

(b) No indemnification, advancement or allowance shall be made under this article in any circumstance where it appears:

(1) That the indemnification would be inconsistent with the law of the jurisdiction of incorporation of a foreign corporation which prohibits or otherwise limits such indemnification;

(2) That the indemnification would be inconsistent with a provision of the certificate of incorporation, a by-law, a resolution of the board or of the shareholders, an agreement or other proper corporate action, in effect at the time of the accrual of the alleged cause of action asserted in the threatened or pending action or proceeding in which the expenses were incurred or other amounts were paid, which prohibits or otherwise limits indemnification; or

(3) If there has been a settlement approved by the court, that the indemnification would be inconsistent with any condition with respect to indemnification expressly imposed by the court in approving the settlement.

(c) If any expenses or other amounts are paid by way of indemnification, otherwise than by court order or action by the shareholders, the corporation shall, not later than the next annual meeting of shareholders unless such meeting is held within three months from the date of such payment, mail to its shareholders of record at the time entitled to vote for the election of directors a statement specifying the persons paid, the amounts paid, and the nature and status at the time of such payment of the litigation or threatened litigation.

(d) If any action with respect to indemnification of directors and officers is taken by way of amendment of the by-laws, resolution of directors, or by agreement, then the corporation shall, not later than the next annual meeting of shareholders, unless such meeting is held within three months from the date of such action, mail to its shareholders of record at the time entitled to vote for the election of directors a statement specifying the action taken. . . .

§726. *Insurance for Indemnification of Directors and Officers*

(a) Subject to paragraph (b), a corporation shall have power to purchase and maintain insurance:

(1) To indemnify the corporation for any obligation which it incurs as a result of the indemnification of directors and officers under the provisions of this article, and

(2) To indemnify directors and officers in instances in which they may be indemnified by the corporation under the provisions of this article, and

(3) To indemnify directors and officers in instances in which they may not otherwise be indemnified by the corporation under the provisions of this article provided the contract of insurance covering such directors and officers provides, in a manner acceptable to the superintendent of financial services, for a retention amount and for co-insurance.

(b) No insurance under paragraph (a) may provide for any payment, other than cost of defense, to or on behalf of any director or officer:

(1) if a judgment or other final adjudication adverse to the insured director or officer establishes that his acts of active and deliberate dishonesty were material to the cause of action so adjudicated, or that he personally gained in fact a financial profit or other advantage to which he was not legally entitled, or

(2) in relation to any risk the insurance of which is prohibited under the insurance law of this state.

(c) Insurance under any or all subparagraphs of paragraph (a) may be included in a single contract or supplement thereto. Retrospective rated contracts are prohibited.

(d) The corporation shall, within the time and to the persons provided in paragraph (c) of section 725 (Other provisions affecting indemnification of directors or officers), mail a statement in respect of any insurance it has purchased or renewed under this section, specifying the insurance carrier, date of the contract, cost of the insurance, corporate positions insured, and a statement explaining all sums, not previously reported in a statement to shareholders, paid under any indemnification insurance contract.

(e) This section is the public policy of this state to spread the risk of corporate management, notwithstanding any other general or special law of this state or of any other jurisdiction including the federal government.

ARTICLE 9 — MERGER OR CONSOLIDATION; GUARANTEE; DISPOSITION OF ASSETS

§908. Guarantee Authorized by Shareholders

A guarantee may be given by a corporation, although not in furtherance of its corporate purposes, when authorized at a meeting of shareholders by two-thirds of the votes of all outstanding shares entitled to vote thereon. If authorized by a like vote, such guarantee may be secured by a mortgage or pledge of, or the creation of a security interest in, all or any part of the corporate property, or any interest therein, wherever situated.

§910. Right of Shareholder to Receive Payment for Shares Upon Merger or Consolidation, or Sale, Lease, Exchange or Other Disposition of Assets, or Share Exchange

(a) A shareholder of a domestic corporation shall, subject to and by complying with section 623 (Procedure to enforce shareholder's right to receive payment for shares), have the right to receive payment of the fair value of his shares and the other rights and benefits provided by such section, in the following cases:

(1) Any shareholder entitled to vote who does not assent to the taking of an action specified in clauses (A), (B) and (C).

(A) Any plan of merger or consolidation to which the corporation is a party; except that the right to receive payment of the fair value of his shares shall not be available:

. . . (iii) . . . [T]o a shareholder for the shares of any class or series of stock, which shares or depository receipts in respect thereof, at the record date fixed to determine the shareholders entitled to receive notice of the meeting of shareholders to vote upon the plan of merger or consolidation, were listed on a national securities exchange or designated as a national market system security on an interdealer quotation system by the National Association of Securities Dealers, Inc.

(B) Any sale, lease, exchange or other disposition of all or substantially all of the assets of a corporation which requires shareholder approval under section 909 (Sale, lease, exchange or other disposition of assets) other than a transaction wholly for cash where the shareholders' approval thereof is conditioned upon the dissolution of the corporation and the distribution of substantially all of its net assets to the shareholders in accordance with their respective interests within one year after the date of such transaction. . . .

ARTICLE 10 — NON-JUDICIAL DISSOLUTION

§1001. Authorization of Dissolution

(a) A corporation may be dissolved under this article. Such dissolution shall be authorized at a meeting of shareholders by

(i) for corporations the certificate of incorporation of which expressly provides such or corporations incorporated after the effective date of paragraph (b) of this section, a majority of the votes of all outstanding shares entitled to vote thereon or

(ii) for other corporations, two-thirds of the votes of all outstanding shares entitled to vote thereon, except, in either case, as otherwise provided under section 1002 (Dissolution under provision in certificate of incorporation).

(b) Any corporation may adopt an amendment of the certificate of incorporation providing that such dissolution shall be authorized at a meeting of shareholders by a specified proportion of votes of all outstanding shares entitled to vote thereon, provided that such proportion may not be less than a majority.

Article 11 — Judicial Dissolution

§1102. Directors' Petition for Judicial Dissolution

If a majority of the board adopts a resolution that finds that the assets of a corporation are not sufficient to discharge its liabilities or that a dissolution will be beneficial to the shareholders, it may present a petition for its dissolution.

§1103. Shareholders' Petition for Judicial Dissolution

(a) If the shareholders of a corporation adopt a resolution stating that they find that its assets are not sufficient to discharge its liabilities, or that they deem a dissolution to be beneficial to the shareholders, the shareholders or such of them as are designated for that purpose in such resolution may present a petition for its dissolution.

(b) A shareholders' meeting to consider such a resolution may be called, notwithstanding any provision in the certificate of incorporation, by the holders of shares representing ten percent of the votes of all outstanding shares entitled to vote thereon, or if the certificate of incorporation authorizes a lesser proportion of votes of shares to call the meeting, by such lesser proportion. A meeting under this paragraph may not be called more often than once in any period of twelve consecutive months.

(c) Such a resolution may be adopted at a meeting of shareholders by vote of a majority of the votes of all outstanding shares entitled to vote thereon or if the certificate of incorporation requires a greater proportion of votes to adopt such a resolution, by such greater proportion.

§1104. Petition in Case of Deadlock among Directors or Shareholders

(a) Except as otherwise provided in the certificate of incorporation under section 613 (Limitations on right to vote), the holders of shares representing one-half of the votes of all outstanding shares of a corporation entitled to vote in an election of directors may present a petition for dissolution on one or more of the following grounds:

(1) That the directors are so divided respecting the management of the corporation's affairs that the votes required for action by the board cannot be obtained.

(2) That the shareholders are so divided that the votes required for the election of directors cannot be obtained.

(3) That there is internal dissension and two or more factions of shareholders are so divided that dissolution would be beneficial to the shareholders.

(b) If the certificate of incorporation provides that the proportion of votes required for action by the board, or the proportion of votes of shareholders required for election of directors, shall be greater than that otherwise required by this chapter, such a petition may be presented by the holders of shares representing more than one-third of the votes of all outstanding shares entitled to vote on non-judicial dissolution under section 1001 (Authorization of dissolution).

(c) Notwithstanding any provision in the certificate of incorporation, any holder of shares entitled to vote at an election of directors of a corporation, may present a petition for its dissolution on the ground that the shareholders are so divided that they have failed, for a period which includes at least two consecutive annual meeting dates, to elect successors to directors whose terms have expired or would have expired upon the election and qualification of their successors.

§1104-a. Petition for Judicial Dissolution under Special Circumstances

(a) The holders of shares representing twenty percent or more of the votes of all outstanding shares of a corporation, other than a corporation registered as an investment company under an act of congress entitled "Investment Company Act of 1940", no shares of which are listed on a national securities exchange or regularly quoted in an over-the-counter market by one or more members of a national or an affiliated securities association, entitled to vote in an election of directors may present a petition of dissolution on one or more of the following grounds:

(1) The directors or those in control of the corporation have been guilty of illegal, fraudulent or oppressive actions toward the complaining shareholders;

(2) The property or assets of the corporation are being looted, wasted, or diverted for non-corporate purposes by its directors, officers or those in control of the corporation.

(b) The court, in determining whether to proceed with involuntary dissolution pursuant to this section, shall take into account:

(1) Whether liquidation of the corporation is the only feasible means whereby the petitioners may reasonably expect to obtain a fair return on their investment; and

(2) Whether liquidation of the corporation is reasonably necessary for the protection of the rights and interests of any substantial number of shareholders or of the petitioners.

(c) In addition to all other disclosure requirements, the directors or those in control of the corporation, no later than thirty days after the filing of a petition hereunder, shall make available for inspection and copying to the petitioners under reasonable working conditions the corporate financial books and records for the three preceding years.

(d) The court may order stock valuations be adjusted and may provide for a surcharge upon the directors or those in control of the corporation upon a finding of wilful or reckless dissipation or transfer of assets or corporate property without just or adequate compensation therefor.

§1111. Judgment or Final Order of Dissolution

(a) In an action or special proceeding under this article if, in the court's discretion, it shall appear that the corporation should be dissolved, it shall make a judgment or final order dissolving the corporation.

(b) In making its decision, the court shall take into consideration the following criteria:

(1) In an action brought by the attorney-general, the interest of the public is of paramount importance.

(2) In a special proceeding brought by directors or shareholders, the benefit to the shareholders of a dissolution is of paramount importance.

(3) In a special proceeding brought under section 1104 (Petition in case of deadlock among directors or shareholders) or section 1104-a (Petition for judicial dissolution under special circumstances) dissolution is not to be denied merely because it is found that the corporate business has been or could be conducted at a profit.

(c) If the judgment or final order shall provide for a dissolution of the corporation, the court may, in its discretion, provide therein for the distribution of the property of the corporation to those entitled thereto according to their respective rights.

(d) The clerk of the court or such other person as the court may direct shall transmit certified copies of the judgment or final order of dissolution to the department of state and to the clerk of the county in which the office of the corporation was located at the date of the judgment or order. Upon filing by the department of state, the corporation shall be dissolved.

(e) The corporation shall promptly thereafter transmit a certified copy of the judgment or final order to the clerk of each other county in which its certificate of incorporation was filed.

§1118. Purchase of Petitioner's Shares; Valuation

(a) In any proceeding brought pursuant to section eleven hundred four-a of this chapter, any other shareholder or shareholders or the corporation may, at any time within ninety days after the filing of such petition or at such later time as the court in its discretion may allow, elect to purchase the shares owned by the petitioners at their fair value and upon such terms and conditions as may be approved by the court, including the conditions of paragraph (c) herein. An election pursuant to this section shall be irrevocable unless the court, in its discretion, for just and equitable considerations, determines that such election be revocable.

(b) If one or more shareholders or the corporation elect to purchase the shares owned by the petitioner but are unable to agree with the petitioner upon the fair value of such shares, the court, upon the application of such prospective purchaser or purchasers or the petitioner, may stay the proceedings brought pursuant to section 1104-a of this chapter and determine the fair value of the petitioner's shares as of the day prior to the date on which such petition was filed, exclusive of any element of value arising from such filing but giving effect to any adjustment or surcharge found to be appropriate in the proceeding under section 1104-a of this chapter. In determining the fair value of the petitioner's shares, the court, in its discretion, may award interest from the date the petition is filed to the date of payment for the petitioner's shares at an equitable rate upon [the] judicially determined fair value of his shares.

(c) In connection with any election to purchase pursuant to this section:

(1) If such election is made beyond ninety days after the filing of the petition, and the court allows such petition, the court, in its discretion, may award the petitioner his reasonable expenses incurred in the proceeding prior to such election, including reasonable attorneys' fees;

(2) The court, in its discretion, may require, at any time prior to the actual purchase of petitioner's shares, the posting of a bond or other acceptable security in an amount sufficient to secure petitioner for the fair value of his shares.

ARTICLE 17 — BENEFIT CORPORATIONS

§1701. Application and Effect of Article

(a) This article shall be applicable to all benefit corporations.

(b) The existence of a provision of this article shall not of itself create any implication that a contrary or different rule of law is or would be applicable to a business corporation that is not a benefit corporation. This article shall not affect any statute or rule of law that is or would be applicable to a business corporation that is not a benefit corporation.

(c) Except as otherwise provided in this article, this chapter shall be applicable to all benefit corporations. The specific provisions of this article shall control over the general provisions of this chapter.

§1702. Definitions

As used in this article, unless the context otherwise requires, the term:

(a) "Benefit corporation" means a business corporation incorporated under this article and whose status as a benefit corporation has not been terminated as provided in this article.

(b) "General public benefit" means a material positive impact on society and the environment, taken as a whole, assessed against a third-party standard, from the business and operations of a benefit corporation.

(c) "Independent" means that a person has no material relationship with a benefit corporation or any of its subsidiaries. A material relationship between a person and a benefit corporation or any of its subsidiaries will be conclusively presumed to exist if:

(1) the person is, or has been within the last three years, an employee of the benefit corporation or any of its subsidiaries;

(2) an immediate family member of the person is, or has been within the last three years, an executive officer of the benefit corporation or any of its subsidiaries; or

(3) the person, or an entity of which the person is a director, officer or other manager or in which the person owns beneficially or of record five percent or more of the equity interests, owns beneficially or of record five percent or more of the shares of the benefit corporation. A percentage of ownership in an entity shall be calculated as if all outstanding rights to acquire equity interests in the entity had been exercised.

(d) "Minimum status vote" means that, in addition to any other approval or vote required by this chapter, the certificate of incorporation or a bylaw adopted by the shareholders:

(1) The holders of shares of every class or series that are entitled to vote on the corporate action shall be entitled to vote as a class on the corporate action; and

(2) The corporate action must be approved by vote of the shareholders of each class or series entitled to cast at least three-quarters of the votes that all shareholders of the class or series are entitled to cast thereon.

(e) "Specific public benefit," includes:

(1) providing low-income or underserved individuals or communities with beneficial products or services;

(2) promoting economic opportunity for individuals or communities beyond the creation of jobs in the normal course of business;

(3) preserving the environment;

(4) improving human health;

(5) promoting the arts, sciences or advancement of knowledge;

(6) increasing the flow of capital to entities with a public benefit purpose; and

(7) the accomplishment of any other particular benefit for society or the environment.

(f) "Subsidiary" means an entity in which a person owns beneficially or of record fifty percent or more of the equity interests. A percentage of ownership in an entity shall be calculated as if all outstanding rights to acquire equity interests in the entity had been exercised.

(g) "Third-party standard" means a recognized standard for defining, reporting and assessing general public benefit that is:

(1) developed by a person that is independent of the benefit corporation; and

(2) transparent because the following information about the standard is publicly available:

(A) the factors considered when measuring the performance of a business;

(B) the relative weightings of those factors; and

(C) the identity of the persons who developed and control changes to the standard and the process by which those changes are made.

§1703. Formation of Benefit Corporations

A benefit corporation shall be formed in accordance with this chapter except that its certificate of incorporation shall also state that it is a benefit corporation.

§1704. Election of an Existing Business Corporation to Become a Benefit Corporation

(a) A business corporation may become a benefit corporation under this article by amending its certificate of incorporation so that it contains a statement that the corporation is a benefit corporation. The amendment shall not be effective unless it is adopted by at least the minimum status vote.

(b) Any corporation that is not a benefit corporation that is a party to a merger or consolidation in which the surviving or consolidated corporation will be a benefit corporation must approve the plan of merger or consolidation by at least the minimum status vote in addition to any other vote required by this chapter, the certificate of incorporation or the bylaws.

(c) Any corporation that is not a benefit corporation that is party to a merger or consolidation in which shares of stock of such corporation will be converted into a right to receive shares of stock of a benefit corporation must approve the plan of merger or consolidation by at least the minimum status vote in addition to any other vote required by this chapter, the certificate of incorporation or the bylaws.

§1705. Termination of Benefit Corporation Status

(a) A benefit corporation may terminate its status as such and cease to be subject to this article by amending its certificate of incorporation to delete the statement that the corporation is a benefit corporation. The amendment shall not be effective unless it is adopted by at least the minimum status vote.

(b) If a benefit corporation is a party to a merger or consolidation in which the surviving or new corporation will not be a benefit corporation, the plan of merger or consolidation shall not be effective unless it is adopted by at least the minimum status vote in addition to any other vote required by this chapter, the certificate of incorporation or the bylaws.

(c) Any benefit corporation that is party to a merger or consolidation in which shares of stock of such benefit corporation will be converted into a right to receive shares of stock of a corporation that is not a benefit corporation must approve the plan of merger or consolidation by at least the minimum status vote in addition to any other vote required by this chapter, the certificate of incorporation or the bylaws.

(d) A sale, lease, conveyance, exchange, transfer, or other disposition of all or substantially all of the assets of a benefit corporation, unless the transaction is in the usual and regular course of business of the benefit corporation, shall not be effective unless the transaction is approved by at least the minimum status vote in addition to any other vote required by this chapter, the certificate of incorporation or the bylaws.

§1706. Corporate Purposes

(a) Every benefit corporation shall have a purpose of creating general public benefit. This purpose is in addition to its purposes under section two hundred one of this chapter and any specific purpose set forth in its certificate of incorporation under paragraph (b) of this section. The purpose to create general public benefit shall be a limitation on the other purposes of the benefit corporation, and shall control over any inconsistent purpose of the benefit corporation.

(b) The certificate of incorporation of a benefit corporation may identify one or more specific public benefits that it is the purpose of the benefit corporation to create in addition to its purposes under section two hundred one of this chapter and paragraph (a) of this section. The identification of a specific public benefit under this paragraph does not limit the obligation of a benefit corporation to create general public benefit.

(c) The creation of general and specific public benefits as provided in paragraphs (a) and (b) of this section is in the best interests of the benefit corporation.

(d) A benefit corporation may amend its certificate of incorporation to add, amend or delete the identification of a specific public benefit that it is the purpose of the benefit corporation to create. The amendment shall not be effective unless it is adopted by at least the minimum status vote.

§1707. *Standard of Conduct for Directors and Officers*

(a) In discharging the duties of their respective positions, the board of directors, committees of the board and individual directors and officers of a benefit corporation:

(1) shall consider the effects of any action upon:

(A) the ability for the benefit corporation to accomplish its general and any specific public benefit purpose;

(B) the shareholders of the benefit corporation;

(C) the employees and workforce of the benefit corporation and its subsidiaries and suppliers;

(D) the interests of customers as beneficiaries of the general or specific public benefit purposes of the benefit corporation;

(E) community and societal considerations, including those of any community in which offices or facilities of the benefit corporation or its subsidiaries or suppliers are located;

(F) the local and global environment; and

(G) the short-term and long-term interests of the benefit corporation, including benefits that may accrue to the benefit corporation from its long-term plans and the possibility that these interests may be best served by the continued independence of the benefit corporation;

(2) may consider:

(A) the resources, intent and conduct (past, stated and potential) of any person seeking to acquire control of the corporation; and

(B) any other pertinent factors or the interests of any other group that they deem appropriate; and

(3) shall not be required to give priority to the interests of any particular person or group referred to in subparagraphs one and two of this paragraph over the interests of any other person or group unless the benefit corporation has stated its intention to give priority to interests related to a specific public benefit purpose identified in its certificate of incorporation.

(b) The consideration of interests and factors in the manner required by paragraph (a) of this section:

(1) shall not constitute a violation of the provisions of sections seven hundred fifteen or seven hundred seventeen of this chapter; and

(2) is in addition to the ability of directors to consider interests and factors as provided in section seven hundred seventeen of this chapter.

(c) A director does not have a fiduciary duty to a person that is a beneficiary of the general or specific public benefit purposes of a benefit corporation arising from the status of the person as a beneficiary, unless otherwise stated in the certificate of incorporation or the bylaws of the benefit corporation.

§1708. Annual Benefit Report

(a) A benefit corporation must deliver to each shareholder an annual benefit report including:

(1) a narrative description of:

(A) the process and rationale for selecting the third party standard used to prepare the benefit report;

(B) the ways in which the benefit corporation pursued general public benefit during the year and the extent to which general public benefit was created;

(C) the ways in which the benefit corporation pursued any specific public benefit that the certificate of incorporation states it is the purpose of the benefit corporation to create and the extent to which that specific public benefit was created; and

(D) any circumstances that have hindered the creation by the benefit corporation of general or specific public benefit;

(2) an assessment of the performance of the benefit corporation, relative to its general public benefit purpose assessed against a third-party standard applied consistently with any application of that standard in prior benefit reports or accompanied by an explanation of the reasons for any inconsistent application and, if applicable, assessment of the performance of the benefit corporation, relative to its specific public benefit purpose or purposes;

(3) the compensation paid by the benefit corporation during the year to each director in that capacity; and

(4) the name of each person that owns beneficially or of record five percent or more of the outstanding shares of the benefit corporation.

(b) The benefit report must be sent annually to each shareholder within one hundred twenty days following the end of the fiscal year of the benefit corporation. Delivery of a benefit report to shareholders is in addition to any other requirement to deliver an annual report to shareholders.

(c) A benefit corporation must post its most recent benefit report on the public portion of its website, if any, except that the compensation paid to directors and any financial or proprietary information included in the benefit report may be omitted from the benefit report as posted.

(d) Concurrently with the delivery of the benefit report to shareholders pursuant to paragraph (b) of this section, the benefit corporation must deliver a copy of the benefit report to the department for filing, except that the compensation paid to directors and any financial or proprietary information included in the benefit report may be omitted from the benefit report as filed under this section.

(e) The annual benefit report shall be in addition to all other reporting requirements under this chapter.

§1709. Conspicuous Language on the Face of Certificates

All certificates representing shares of a benefit corporation shall contain, in addition to any other statements required by the business corporation law, the following conspicuous language on the face of the certificate:

"This entity is a benefit corporation organized under article seventeen of the New York business corporation law."

Selected Other Constituencies Statutes

Connecticut Business Corporation Act

§33-756. General Standards for Directors . . .

(d) For purposes of [mergers, consolidations, sales of assets and business combinations with interested shareholders], a director of a corporation which has a class of voting stock registered pursuant to Section 12 of the Securities Exchange Act of 1934 . . . in addition to complying with the provisions of [MBCA §8.30(a)-(c)] shall consider, in determining what he reasonably believes to be in the best interests of the corporation, (1) the long-term as well as the short-term interests of the corporation, (2) the interests of the shareholders, long-term as well as short-term, including the possibility that those interests may be best served by the continued independence of the corporation, (3) the interests of the corporation's employees, customers, creditors and suppliers, and (4) community and societal considerations including those of any community in which any office or other facility of the corporation is located. A director may also in his discretion consider any other factors he reasonably considers appropriate in determining what he reasonably believes to be in the best interests of the corporation. . . .

Georgia Business Corporation Code

§14-2-202. Articles of Incorporation . . .

(b) The articles of incorporation may set forth: . . .

(5) A provision that, in discharging the duties of their respective positions and in determining what is believed to be in the best interests of the corporation, the board of directors, committees of the board of directors, and individual directors, in addition to considering the effects of any action on the corporation or its shareholders, may consider the interests of the employees, customers, suppliers, and creditors of the corporation and its subsidiaries, the communities in which offices or other establishments of the corporation and its subsidiaries are located, and all other factors such directors consider pertinent; provided, however, that any such provision shall be deemed solely to grant discretionary

authority to the directors and shall not be deemed to provide to any constituency any right to be considered.

Maine Business Corporation Act

§831. Standard of Conduct for Directors . . .

6. Interests of Other Constituencies

In discharging their duties, the directors and officers may, in considering the best interests of the corporation and of its shareholders, consider the effects of any action upon employees, suppliers and customers of the corporation, communities in which offices or other establishments of the corporation are located and all other pertinent factors.

Pennsylvania Business Corporation Code

§1715. Exercise of Powers Generally

(a) General rule.—In discharging the duties of their respective positions, the board of directors, committees of the board and individual directors of a business corporation may, in considering the best interests of the corporation, consider to the extent they deem appropriate:

(1) The effects of any action upon any or all groups affected by such action, including shareholders, employees, suppliers, customers and creditors of the corporation, and upon communities in which offices or other establishments of the corporation are located.

(2) The short-term and long-term interests of the corporation, including benefits that may accrue to the corporation from its long-term plans and the possibility that these interests may be best served by the continued independence of the corporation.

(3) The resources, intent and conduct (past, stated and potential) of any person seeking to acquire control of the corporation.

(4) All other pertinent factors.

(b) Consideration of interests and factors.—The board of directors, committees of the board and individual directors shall not be required, in considering the best interests of the corporation or the effects of any action, to regard any corporate interest or the interests of any particular group affected by such action as a dominant or controlling interest or factor. The consideration of interests and factors in the manner described in this subsection and in subsection (a) shall not constitute a violation of section 1712 (relating to standard of care and justifiable reliance).

(c) Specific applications.—In exercising the powers vested in the corporation, including, without limitation, those powers pursuant to section 1502 (relating to general powers), and in no way limiting the discretion of the board of directors, committees of the board and individual directors pursuant to subsections (a) and (b), the fiduciary duty of directors shall not be deemed to require them:

(1) to redeem any rights under, or to modify or render inapplicable, any shareholder rights plan, including, but not limited to, a plan adopted pursuant or made subject to section 2513 (relating to disparate treatment of certain persons);

(2) to render inapplicable, or make determinations under, the provisions of Subchapter E (relating to control transactions), F (relating to business combinations), G (relating to control-share acquisitions) or H (relating to disgorgement by certain controlling shareholders following attempts to acquire control) of Chapter 25 or under any other provision of this title relating to or affecting acquisitions or potential or proposed acquisitions of control; or

(3) to act as the board of directors, a committee of the board or an individual director solely because of the effect such action might have on an acquisition or potential or proposed acquisition of control of the corporation or the consideration that might be offered or paid to shareholders in such an acquisition. . . .

New York Stock Exchange Listed Company Manual

LISTED COMPANY MANUAL . . .

303A.00 *Corporate Governance Standards*

312.00 *Shareholder Approved Policy*

303A.00 Introduction

Equity Listings

Section 303A applies in full to all companies listing common equity securities, with the following exceptions:

Controlled Companies

A company of which more than 50 percent of the voting power for the election of directors is held by an individual, a group, or another company is not required to comply with the requirements of sections 303A.01, .04, or .05. Controlled companies must comply with the remaining provisions of section 303A. . . .

303A.01 Independent Directors.

Listed companies must have a majority of independent directors.

Commentary: Effective boards of directors exercise independent judgment in carrying out their responsibilities. Requiring a majority of independent directors will increase the quality of board oversight and lessen the possibility of damaging conflicts of interest.

303A.02 Independence Tests. In order to tighten the definition of "independent director" for purposes of these standards:

(a)(i) No director qualifies as "independent" unless the board of directors affirmatively determines that the director has no material relationship with the listed company (either directly or as a partner, shareholder or officer of an organization that has a relationship with the company)

(ii) In addition, in affirmatively determining the independence of any director who will serve on the compensation committee of the listed company's board of directors, the board of directors must consider all factors specifically relevant to determining whether a director has a relationship to the listed company which is material to that director's ability to be independent from management in connection with the duties of a compensation committee member, including, but not limited to:

(A) the source of compensation of such director, including any consulting, advisory or other compensatory fee paid by the listed company to such director; and

(B) whether such director is affiliated with the listed company, a subsidiary of the listed company or an affiliate of a subsidiary of the listed company.

Commentary: It is not possible to anticipate, or explicitly to provide for, all circumstances that might signal potential conflicts of interest, or that might bear on the materiality of a director's relationship to a listed company. (references to "listed company" would include any parent or subsidiary in a consolidated group with the listed company). Accordingly, it is best that boards making "independence" determinations broadly consider all relevant facts and circumstances. In particular, when assessing the materiality of a director's relationship with the listed company, the board should consider the issue not merely from the standpoint of the director, but also from that of persons or organizations with which the director has an affiliation. Material relationships can include commercial, industrial, banking, consulting, legal, accounting, charitable, and familial relationships among others. However, as the concern is independence from management, the Exchange does not view ownership of even a significant amount of stock, by itself, as a bar to an independence finding.

When considering the sources of a director's compensation in determining his independence for purposes of compensation committee service, the board should consider whether the director receives compensation from any person or entity that would impair his ability to make independent judgments about the listed company's executive compensation. Similarly, when considering any affiliate relationship a director has with the company, a subsidiary of the company, or an affiliate of a subsidiary of the company, in determining his independence for purposes of compensation committee service, the board should consider whether the affiliate relationship places the director under the direct or indirect control of the listed company or its senior management, or creates a direct relationship between the director and members of senior management, in each case of a nature that would impair his ability to make independent judgments about the listed company's executive compensation.

Disclosure Requirement: The listed company must comply with the disclosure requirements, set forth in Item 407(a) of Regulation S-K.

(b) In addition a director is not independent if:

(i) The director is, or has been within the last three years, an employee of the listed company, or an immediate family member is, or has been within the last three years, an executive officer of the listed company.[1]

Commentary: Employment as an interim Chairman or CEO or other executive officer shall not disqualify a director from being considered independent following that employment.

(ii) The director has received, or has an immediate family member who has received, during any twelve-month period within the last three years, more than $120,000 in direct compensation from the listed company, other than director and committee fees and pension or other forms of deferred compensation for prior service (provided such compensation is not contingent in any way on continued service).

Commentary: Compensation received by a director for former service as an interim Chairman or CEO or other executive officer need not be considered in determining independence under this test. Compensation received by an immediate family member for service as an employee of the listed company (other than executive officer) need not be considered in determining independence under this test.

(iii) (A) The director is a current partner or employee of a firm that is the listed company's internal or external auditor; (B) the director has an immediate family member who is a current partner of such a firm; (C) the director has an immediate family member who is a current employee of such a firm and personally works on the listed company's audit; or (D) the director or an immediate family member was within the last three years a partner or employee of such a firm and personally worked on the listed company's audit within that time.

(iv) The director or an immediate family member is, or has been within the last three years, employed as an executive officer of another company where any of the listed company's present executive officers at the same time serves or served on that company's compensation committee.

1. For purposes of section 303A, the term "executive officer" has the same meaning specified for the term "officer" in Rule 16a-1(f) under the Securities Exchange Act of 1934.

(v) The director is a current employee, or an immediate family member is a current executive officer, of a company that has made payments to, or received payments from, the listed company for property or services in an amount which, in any of the last three fiscal years, exceeds the greater of $1 million, or 2% of such other company's consolidated gross revenues.

Commentary: In applying the test in Section 303A.02(b)(v), both the payments and the consolidated gross revenues to be measured shall be those reported in the last completed fiscal year of such other company. The look-back provision for this test applies solely to the financial relationship between the listed company and the director or immediate family member's current employer; a listed company need not consider former employment of the director or immediate family member.

Disclosure Requirement: Contributions to tax-exempt organizations shall not be considered "payments" for purposes of section 303A.02(b)(v), provided, however, that a listed company shall disclose either on or through its website or in its annual proxy statement, or if the listed company does not file an annual proxy statement, in the listed company's annual report on Form 10-K filed with the SEC, any such contributions made by the listed company to any tax-exempt organization in which any independent director serves as an executive officer if, within the preceding three years, contributions in any single fiscal year from the listed company to the organization exceeded the greater of $1 million, or 2% of such tax-exempt organization's consolidated gross revenues. If this disclosure is made on or through the listed Company's website, the listed company must disclose that fact in its annual proxy statement or annual report, as applicable, and provide the website address. Listed company boards are reminded of their obligations to consider the materiality of any such relationship in accordance with Section 303A.02(a) above.

General Commentary to Section 303A.02(b): An "immediate family member" includes a person's spouse, parents, children, siblings, mothers and fathers-in-law, sons and daughters-in-law, brothers and sisters-in-law, and anyone (other than domestic employees) who shares such person's home. When applying the look-back provisions in Section 303A.02(b), listed companies need not consider individuals who are no longer immediate family members as a result of legal separation or divorce, or those who have died or become incapacitated.

In addition, references to the "listed company" or "company" include any parent or subsidiary in a consolidated group with the listed company. . . .

303A.03 Executive Sessions. To empower non-management directors to serve as a more effective check on management, the non-management directors of each listed company must meet at regularly scheduled executive sessions without management.

Commentary: To promote open discussion among the non-management directors, companies must schedule regular executive sessions in which those directors meet without management participation. "Non-management" directors are all those who are not executive officers, and includes such directors who are not independent by virtue of a material relationship, former status or family membership, or for any other reason.

Regular scheduling of such meetings is important not only to foster better communication among non-management directors, but also to prevent any negative inference from attaching to the calling of executive sessions. A non-management director must preside over each executive session, although the same director is not required to preside at all executive sessions.

While this Section 303A.03 refers to meetings of non-management directors, listed companies may instead choose to hold regular executive sessions of independent directors only.

An independent director must preside over each executive session of the independent directors, although the same director is not required to preside at all executive sessions of the independent directors.

If a listed company chooses to hold regular meetings of all non-management directors, such listed company should hold an executive session including only independent directors at least once a year.

Disclosure Requirements: If one director is chosen to preside at all of these executive sessions, his or her name must be disclosed either on or through the listed company's website or in its annual proxy statement or, if the listed company does not file an annual proxy statement, in its annual report on Form 10-K filed with the SEC. If this disclosure is made on or through the listed company's website, the listed company must disclose that fact in its annual proxy statement or annual report, as applicable, and provide the website address. Alternatively, if the same individual is not the presiding director at every meeting, a listed company must disclose the procedure by which a presiding director is selected for each executive session. For example, a listed company may wish to rotate the presiding position among the chairs of board committees.

In order that all interested parties (not just shareholders) may be able to make their concerns known to the non-management or independent directors, a listed company must also disclose a method for such parties to communicate directly with the presiding director or with those directors as a group either on or through the listed company's website or in its annual proxy statement or, if the listed company does not file an annual proxy statement, in its annual report on Form 10-K filed with the SEC. If this disclosure is made on or through the listed company's website, the listed company must disclose that fact in its annual proxy statement or annual report, as applicable, and provide the website address. Companies may, if they wish, utilize for this purpose the same procedures they have established to comply with the requirement of Rule 10A-3 (b)(3) under the Exchange Act regarding complaints to the audit committee, as applied to listed companies through Section 303A.06.

303A.04 Nominating/Corporate Governance Committee. (a) Listed companies must have a nominating/corporate governance committee composed entirely of independent directors.

(b) The nominating/corporate governance committee must have a written charter that addresses:

(i) the committee's purpose and responsibilities—which, at minimum, must be to: identify individuals qualified to become board members, consistent with criteria approved by the board, and to select, or to recommend that the board select, the director nominees for the next annual meeting of shareholders; develop and recommend to the board a set of corporate governance guidelines applicable to the corporation and oversee the evaluation of the board and management; and

(ii) an annual performance evaluation of the committee.

Commentary: A nominating/corporate governance committee is central to the effective functioning of the board. New director and board committee nominations are among a board's most important functions. Placing this responsibility in the hands of an independent nominating/corporate governance committee can enhance the independence and quality of nominees. The committee is also responsible for taking a leadership role in shaping the corporate governance of a corporation. . . .

Website Posting Requirement: A listed company must make its nominating/corporate governance committee charter available on or through its website. If any function of the nominating/corporate governance committee has been delegated to another committee, the charter of that committee must also be made available on or through the listed company's website.

Disclosure Requirements: A listed company must disclose in its annual proxy statement or, if it does not file an annual proxy statement, in its annual report on Form 10-K filed with the SEC that its nominating/corporate governance committee charter is available on or through its website and provide the website address.

303A.05 Compensation Committee. (a) Listed companies must have a compensation committee composed entirely of independent directors. Compensation committee members must satisfy the additional independence requirements specific to compensation committee membership set forth in Section 303A.02(a)(ii).

(b) The compensation committee must have a written charter that addresses:

(i) the committee's purpose and responsibilities—which, at minimum, must be to have direct responsibility to:

(A) review and approve corporate goals and objectives relevant to CEO compensation, evaluate the CEO's performance in light of those goals and objectives, and either as a committee or together with the other independent directors (as directed by the board), determine and approve the CEO's compensation level based on this evaluation;

(B) make recommendations to the board with respect to non-CEO executive compensation, and incentive-compensation and equity-based plans that are subject to board approval; and

(C) prepare the disclosure required by Item 407(e)(5) of Regulation S-K.

(ii) An annual performance evaluation of the compensation committee.

(iii) The rights and responsibilities of the compensation committee set forth in Section 303A.05(c).

Commentary: In determining the long-term incentive component of CEO compensation, the committee should consider the listed company's performance and relative shareholder return, the value of similar incentive awards to CEOs at comparable companies, and the awards given to the listed company's CEO in past years. To avoid confusion, note that the compensation committee is not precluded from approving awards (with or without ratification of the board) as may be required to comply with applicable tax laws (i.e., Rule 162(m)). Note also that nothing in section 303A.05(b)(i)(B) is intended to preclude the board from delegating its authority over such matters to the compensation committee.

The compensation committee charter should also address the following items: committee member qualifications; committee member appointment and removal; committee structure and operations (including authority to delegate to subcommittees); and committee reporting to the board.

Boards may allocate the responsibilities of the compensation committee to committees of their own denomination, provided that the committees are composed entirely of independent directors. Any such committee must have a committee charter.

Nothing in this provision should be construed as precluding discussion of CEO compensation with the board generally, as it is not the intent of this standard to impair communication among members of the board.

Website Posting Requirement: A listed company must make its compensation committee charter available on or through its website. If any function of the compensation committee has been delegated to another committee, the charter of that committee must also be made available on or through the listed company's website.

Disclosure Requirements: A listed company must disclose in its annual proxy statement or, if it does not file an annual proxy statement, in its annual report on Form 10-K filed with the SEC that its compensation committee charter is available on or through its website and provide the website address.

(c)(i) The compensation committee may, in its sole discretion, retain or obtain the advice of a compensation consultant, independent legal counsel or other adviser.

(ii) The compensation committee shall be directly responsible for the appointment, compensation and oversight of the work of any compensation consultant, independent legal counsel or other adviser retained by the compensation committee.

(iii) The listed company must provide for appropriate funding, as determined by the compensation committee, for payment of reasonable compensation to a compensation consultant, independent legal counsel or any other adviser retained by the compensation committee.

(iv) The compensation committee may select a compensation consultant, legal counsel or other adviser to the compensation committee only after taking into consideration, all factors relevant to that person's independence from management, including the following:

(A) The provision of other services to the listed company by the person that employs the compensation consultant, legal counsel or other adviser;

(B) The amount of fees received from the listed company by the person that employs the compensation consultant, legal counsel or other adviser, as a percentage of the total revenue of the person that employs the compensation consultant, legal counsel or other adviser;

(C) The policies and procedures of the person that employs the compensation consultant, legal counsel or other adviser that are designed to prevent conflicts of interest;

(D) Any business or personal relationship of the compensation consultant, legal counsel or other adviser with a member of the compensation committee;

(E) Any stock of the listed company owned by the compensation consultant, legal counsel or other adviser; and

(F) Any business or personal relationship of the compensation consultant, legal counsel, other adviser or the person employing the adviser with an executive officer of the listed company.

Commentary: Nothing in this Section 303A.05(c) shall be construed: (A) to require the compensation committee to implement or act consistently with the advice or recommendations of the compensation consultant, independent legal counsel or other adviser to the compensation committee; or (B) to affect the ability or obligation of the compensation committee to exercise its own judgment in fulfillment of the duties of the compensation committee.

The compensation committee is required to conduct the independence assessment outlined in Section 303A.05(c)(iv) with respect to any compensation consultant, legal counsel or other adviser that provides advice to the compensation committee, other than (i) in-house legal counsel; and (ii) any compensation consultant, legal counsel or other adviser whose role is limited to the following activities for which no disclosure would be required under Item 407(e)(3)(iii) of Regulation S-K: consulting on any broad-based plan that does not discriminate in scope, terms, or operation, in favor of executive officers or directors of the listed company, and that is available generally to all salaried employees; or providing information that either is not customized for a particular company or that is customized based on parameters that are not developed by the compensation consultant, and about which the compensation consultant does not provide advice.

Nothing in this Section 303A.05(c) requires a compensation consultant, legal counsel or other compensation adviser to be independent, only that the compensation committee consider the enumerated independence factors before selecting or receiving advice from a compensation adviser. The compensation committee may select or receive advice from any compensation adviser they prefer including ones that are not independent, after considering the six independence factors outlined in Section 303A.05(c)(iv)(A)–(F).

303A.06 Audit Committee. Listed companies must have an audit committee that satisfies the requirements of Rule 10A-3 under the Exchange Act.

Commentary: The Exchange will apply the requirements of Rule 10A-3 in a manner consistent with the guidance provided by the Securities and Exchange Commission in SEC Release No. 34-47654 (April 1, 2003). Without limiting the generality of the foregoing, the Exchange will provide companies the opportunity to cure defects provided in Rule 10A-3(a)(3) under the Exchange Act . . .

303A.07 Audit Committee. Additional Requirements. (a) The audit committee must have a minimum of three members. All audit committee members must satisfy the requirements for independence set out in section 303A.02 and, in the absence of an applicable exemption, Rule 10A-3(b)(1).

Commentary: Each member of the audit committee must be financially literate, as such qualification is interpreted by the listed company's board in its business judgment, or must become financially literate within a reasonable period of time after his or her appointment to the audit committee. In addition, at least one member of the audit committee must have accounting or related financial management expertise, as the listed company's board interprets such qualification in its business judgment. While the Exchange does not require that a listed company's audit committee include a person who satisfies the definition of audit committee financial expert set out in Item 407(d)(5)(ii) of Regulation S-K, a board may presume that such a person has accounting or related financial management expertise.

Because of the audit committee's demanding role and responsibilities, and the time commitment attendant to committee membership, each prospective audit committee member should evaluate carefully the existing demands on his or her time before accepting this important assignment.

Disclosure Requirement: If an audit committee member simultaneously serves on the audit committees of more than three public companies, the board must determine that such simultaneous service would not impair the ability of such member to effectively serve on the listed company's audit committee and must disclose such determination either on or through the listed company's website or in its annual proxy statement or, if the listed company does not file an annual proxy statement, in its annual report on Form 10-K filed with the SEC. If this disclosure is made on or through the listed company's website, the listed company must disclose that fact in its annual proxy statement or annual report as applicable, and provide the website address.

(b) The audit committee must have a written charter that addresses:

(i) the committee's purpose—which, at minimum, must be to:

(A) assist board oversight of (1) the integrity of the listed company's financial statements, (2) the listed company's compliance with legal and regulatory requirements, (3) the independent auditor's qualifications and independence, and (4) the performance of the listed company's internal audit function and independent auditors (if the listed company does not yet have an internal audit function because it is availing itself of a transition period pursuant to Section 303A.00, the charter must provide that the committee will assist board oversight of the design and implementation of the internal audit function); and

(B) prepare the disclosure required by Item 407(d)(3)(i) of Regulation S-K;

(ii) an annual performance evaluation of the audit committee; and

(iii) the duties and responsibilities of the audit committee—which, at a minimum, must include those set out in Rule 10A-3(b)(2), (3), (4), and (5) of the Exchange Act, as well as to:

(A) at least annually, obtain and review a report by the independent auditor describing: the firm's internal quality-control procedures; any material issues raised by the most recent internal quality-control review, or peer review, of the firm, or by any inquiry or investigation by governmental or professional authorities, within the preceding five years, respecting one or more independent audits carried out by the firm, and any steps taken to deal with any such issues; and (to assess the auditor's independence) all relationships between the independent auditor and the listed company.

Commentary: After reviewing the foregoing report and the independent auditor's work throughout the year, the audit committee will be in a position to evaluate the auditor's qualifications, performance, and independence. This evaluation should include the review and evaluation of the lead partner of the independent auditor. In making its evaluation, the audit committee should take into account the opinions of management and the listed company's internal auditors (or other personnel responsible for the internal audit function). In addition to assuring the regular rotation of the lead audit partner as required by law, the audit committee should further consider whether, in order to assure continuing auditor independence, there should be regular rotation of the audit firm itself. The audit committee should present its conclusions with respect to the independent auditor to the full board.

(B) meet to review and discuss the listed company's annual audited financial statements and quarterly financial statements with management and the independent auditor, including reviewing the listed company's specific disclosures under "Management's Discussion and Analysis of Financial Condition and Results of Operations";

Commentary: Meetings may be telephonic if permitted under applicable corporate law; polling of audit committee members, however, is not permitted in lieu of meetings . . .

(C) discuss the listed company's earnings press releases, as well as financial information and earnings guidance provided to analysts and rating agencies.

Commentary: The audit committee's responsibility to discuss earnings releases, as well as financial information and earnings guidance, may be done generally (i.e., discussion of the types of information to be disclosed and the type of presentation to be made). The audit committee need not discuss in advance each earnings release or each instance in which a listed company may provide earnings guidance.

(D) discuss policies with respect to risk assessment and risk management.

Commentary: While it is the job of the CEO and senior management to assess and manage the listed company's exposure to risk, the audit committee must discuss guidelines and policies to govern the process by which this is handled. The audit committee should discuss the listed company's major financial risk exposures and the steps management has taken to monitor and control such exposures. The audit committee is not required to be the sole body responsible for risk assessment and management, but as stated above, the committee must discuss guidelines and policies to govern the process by which risk assessment and management is undertaken. Many companies, particularly financial companies, manage and assess their risk through mechanisms other than the audit committee. The processes these companies have in place should be reviewed in a general manner by the audit committee, but they need not be replaced by the audit committee.

(E) meet separately, periodically, with management, with internal auditors (or other personnel responsible for the internal audit function) and with independent auditors.

Commentary: To perform its oversight functions most effectively, the audit committee must have the benefit of separate sessions with management, the independent auditors and those responsible for the internal audit function. As noted herein, all listed companies must have an internal audit function. These separate sessions may be more productive than joint sessions in surfacing issues warranting committee attention. If the listed company does not yet have an internal audit function because it is availing itself of a transition period pursuant to Section 303A.00, the committee must meet periodically with the company personnel primarily responsible for the design and implementation of the internal audit function.

(F) review with the independent auditor any audit problems or difficulties and management's response.

Commentary: The audit committee must regularly review with the independent auditor any difficulties the auditor encountered in the course of the audit work, including any restrictions on the scope of the independent auditor's activities or on access to requested information, and any significant disagreements with management. Among the items the audit committee may want to review with the auditor are: any accounting adjustments that were noted or proposed by the auditor but were "passed" (as immaterial or otherwise); any communications between the audit team and the audit firm's national office respecting auditing or accounting issues presented by the engagement; and any "management" or "internal control" letter issued, or proposed to be issued, by the audit firm to the listed company. The review should also include discussion of the responsibilities, budget and staffing of the listed company's internal audit function. If the listed company does not yet have an internal audit function because it is availing itself of a transition period pursuant to Section 303A.00, the review should include discussion of management's plans with respect to the responsibilities, budget and staffing of the internal audit function and its plans for the implementation of the internal audit function.

(G) set clear hiring policies for employees or former employees of the independent auditors; and

Commentary: Employees or former employees of the independent auditor are often valuable additions to corporate management. Such individuals' familiarity with the business, and personal rapport with the employees, may be attractive qualities when filling a key opening. However, the audit committee should set hiring policies taking into account the pressures that may exist for auditors consciously or subconsciously seeking a job with the listed company they audit.

(H) report regularly to the board of directors.

Commentary: The audit committee should review with the full board any issues that arise with respect to the quality or integrity of the listed company's financial statements, the listed company's compliance with legal or regulatory requirements, the performance and independence of the listed company's independent auditors, or the performance of the internal audit function. If the listed company does not yet have an internal audit function because it is availing itself of a transition period pursuant to Section 303A.00, the committee should review with the board management's activities with respect to the design and implementation of the internal audit function.

General Commentary to Section 303A.07(b): While the fundamental responsibility for the listed company's financial statements and disclosures rests with management and the independent auditor, the audit committee must review: (A) major issues regarding accounting principles and financial statement presentations, including any significant changes in the listed company's selection or application of accounting principles, and major issues as to the adequacy of the listed company's internal controls and any special audit steps adopted in light of material control deficiencies; (B) analyses prepared by management and/or the independent auditor setting forth significant financial reporting issues and judgments made in connection with the preparation of the financial statements, including analyses of the effects of alternative GAAP methods on the financial statements; (C) the effect of regulatory and accounting initiatives, as well as off-balance sheet structures, on the financial statements of the listed company; and (D) the type and presentation of information to be included in earnings press releases (paying particular attention to any use of "pro forma," or "adjusted" non-GAAP, information), as well as review any financial information and earnings guidance provided to analysts and rating agencies.

Website Posting Requirement: A listed company must make its audit committee charter available on or through its website. A closed-end fund is not required to comply with this website posting requirement.

Disclosure Requirements: A listed company must disclose in its annual proxy statement or, if it does not file an annual proxy statement, in its annual report on Form 10-K filed with the SEC that its audit committee charter is available on or through its website and provide the website address.

(c) Each listed company must have an internal audit function.

Commentary: Listed companies must maintain an internal audit function to provide management and the audit committee with ongoing assessments of the listed company's risk management processes and system of internal control. A listed company may choose to outsource this function to a third-party service provider other than its independent auditor. While Section 303A.00 permits certain categories of newly-listed companies to avail themselves of a transition period to comply with the internal audit function requirement, all listed companies must have an internal audit function in place no later than the first anniversary of the company's listing date.

General Commentary to Section 303A.07: To avoid any confusion, note that the audit committee functions specified in Section 303A.07 are the sole responsibility of the audit committee and may not be allocated to a different committee.

303A.08 Shareholder Approval of Equity Compensation Plans. Shareholders must be given the opportunity to vote on all equity-compensation plans and material revisions thereto, with limited exemptions explained below.

Commentary: Equity-compensation plans can help align shareholder and management interests, and equity-based awards are often very important components of employee compensation. To provide checks and balances on the potential dilution resulting from the process of earmarking shares to be used for equity-based awards, the Exchange requires that all equity-compensation plans, and any material revisions to the terms of such plans, be subject to shareholder approval, with the limited exemptions explained below.

Definition of Equity-Compensation Plan

An "equity-compensation plan" is a plan or other arrangement that provides for the delivery of equity securities (either newly issued or treasury shares) of the listed company to any employee, director or other service provider as compensation for services. Even a compensatory grant of options or other equity securities that is not made under a plan is, nonetheless, an "equity-compensation plan" for these purposes.

However, the following are not "equity-compensation plans" even if the brokerage and other costs of the plan are paid for by the listed company:

- Plans that are made available to shareholders generally, such as a typical dividend reinvestment plan.
- Plans that merely allow employees, directors or other service providers to elect to buy shares on the open market or from the listed company for their current fair market value, regardless of whether:
  - the shares are delivered immediately or on a deferred basis; or
  - the payments for the shares are made directly or by giving up compensation that is otherwise due (for example, through payroll deductions).

Material Revisions

A "material revision" of an equity-compensation plan includes (but is not limited to), the following:

- A material increase in the number of shares available under the plan (other than an increase solely to reflect a reorganization, stock split, merger, spinoff or similar transaction).
  - If a plan contains a formula for automatic increases in the shares available (sometimes called an "evergreen formula") or for automatic grants pursuant to a formula, each such increase or grant will be considered a revision requiring shareholder approval *unless* the plan has a term of not more than ten years.

This type of plan (regardless of its term) is referred to below as a "formula plan." Examples of automatic grants pursuant to a formula are (1) annual grants to directors of restricted stock having a certain dollar value, and (2) "matching contributions," whereby stock is credited to a participant's account based upon the amount of compensation the participant elects to defer.

- If a plan contains no limit on the number of shares available and is not a formula plan, then each grant under the plan will require separate shareholder approval *regardless* of whether the plan has a term of not more than ten years.

  This type of plan is referred to below as a "discretionary plan." A requirement that grants be made out of treasury shares or repurchased shares will not, in itself, be considered a limit or pre-established formula so as to prevent a plan from being considered a discretionary plan.

- An expansion of the types of awards available under the plan.
- A material expansion of the class of employees, directors or other service providers eligible to participate in the plan.
- A material extension of the term of the plan.
- A material change to the method of determining the strike price of options under the plan.
  - A change in the method of determining "fair market value" from the closing price on the date of grant to the average of the high and low price on the date of grant is an example of a change that the Exchange would not view as material.
- The deletion or limitation of any provision prohibiting repricing of options. See the next section for details.

Note that an amendment will not be considered a "material revision' if it curtails rather than expands the scope of the plan in question.

Repricings

A plan that does not contain a provision that specifically *permits* repricing of options will be considered for purposes of this listing standard as *prohibiting* repricing. Accordingly, any actual repricing of options will be considered a material revision of a plan even if the plan itself is not revised. This consideration will not apply to a repricing through an exchange offer that commenced before the date this listing standard became effective.

"Repricing" means any of the following or any other action that has the same effect:

- Lowering the strike price of an option after it is granted.
- Any other action that is treated as a repricing under generally accepted accounting principles.
- Canceling an option at a time when its strike price exceeds the fair market value of the underlying stock, in exchange for another option, restricted stock, or other equity, unless the cancellation and exchange occurs in connection with a merger, acquisition, spinoff or other similar corporate transaction.

Exemptions

This listing standard does not require shareholder approval of employment inducement awards, certain grants, plans and amendments in the context of mergers and acquisitions, and certain specific types of plans, all as described below. However, these exempt grants, plans and amendments may be made only with the approval of the listed company's independent compensation committee or the approval of a majority of the listed company's independent directors. Companies must also notify the Exchange in writing when they use one of these exemptions.

Employment Inducement Awards

An employment inducement award is a grant of options or other equity-based compensation as a material inducement to a person or persons being hired by the listed company or any of its subsidiaries, or being rehired following a bona fide period of interruption of employment. Inducement awards include grants to new employees in connection with a merger or acquisition. Promptly following a grant of any inducement award in reliance on this exemption, the listed company must disclose in a press release the material terms of the award, including the recipient(s) of the award and the number of shares involved. . . .

303A.09 Corporate Governance Guidelines. Listed companies must adopt and disclose corporate governance guidelines.

Commentary: No single set of guidelines would be appropriate for every listed company, but certain key areas of universal importance include director qualifications and responsibilities, responsibilities of key board committees, and director compensation.

The following subjects must be addressed in the corporate governance guideline:

- **Director qualification standards.** These standards should, at minimum, reflect the independence requirements set forth in sections 303A.01 and 303A.02. Companies may also address other substantive qualification requirements, including policies limiting the number of boards on which a director may sit, and director tenure, retirement and succession.
- **Director responsibilities.** These responsibilities should clearly articulate what is expected from a director, including basic duties and responsibilities with respect to attendance at board meetings and advance review of meeting materials.
- **Director access to management and, as necessary and appropriate, independent advisors.**
- **Director compensation.** Director compensation guidelines should include general principles for determining the form and amount of director compensation (and for reviewing those principles, as appropriate). The board should be aware that questions as to directors' independence may be raised when directors' fee and emoluments exceed what is customary. Similar concerns may be raised when the listed company makes substantial charitable contributions to organizations in which a director is affiliated, or enters into consulting contracts with (or provides other indirect forms of compensation to) a director. The board should critically evaluate each of these matters when determining the form and amount of director compensation, and the independence of a director.
- **Director orientation and continuing education.**
- **Management succession.** Succession planning should include policies and principles for CEO selection and performance review, as well as policies regarding succession in the event of an emergency or the retirement of the CEO.

- **Annual performance evaluation of the board.** The board should conduct a self-evaluation at least annually to determine whether it and its committees are functioning effectively.

Website Posting Requirement: A listed company must make its corporate governance guidelines available on or through its website.

Disclosure Requirements: A listed company must disclose in its annual proxy statement or, if it does not file an annual proxy statement, in its annual report on Form 10-K filed with the SEC that its corporate governance guidelines are available on or through its website and provide the website address.

303A.10 Code of Business Conduct and Ethics. Listed companies must adopt and disclose a code of business conduct and ethics for directors, officers and employees, and promptly disclose any waivers of the code for directors or executive officers.

Commentary: No code of business conduct and ethics can replace the thoughtful behavior of an ethical director, officer or employee. However, such a code can focus the board and management on areas of ethical risk, provide guidance to personnel to help them recognize and deal with ethical issues, provide mechanisms to report unethical conduct, and help to foster a culture of honesty and accountability.

Each code of business conduct and ethics must require that any waiver of the code for executive officers or directors may be made only by the board or a board committee.

Each code of business conduct and ethics must also contain compliance standards and procedures that will facilitate the effective operation of the code. These standards should ensure the prompt and consistent action against violations of the code.

Each listed company may determine its own policies, but all listed companies should address the most important topics, including the following:

- **Conflicts of interest.** A "conflict of interest" occurs when an individual's private interest interferes in any way—or even appears to interfere—with the interests of the corporation as a whole. A conflict situation can arise when an employee, officer or director takes actions or has interests that may make it difficult to perform his or her company work objectively and effectively. Conflicts of interest also arise when an employee, officer or director, or a member of his or her family, receives improper personal benefits as a result of his or her position in the company. Loans to, or guarantees of obligations of, such persons are of special concern. The listed company should have a policy prohibiting such conflicts of interest, and providing a means for employees, officers and directors to communicate potential conflicts to the listed company.
- **Corporate opportunities.** Employees, officers and directors should be prohibited from (a) taking for themselves personally opportunities that are discovered through the use of corporate property, information or position; (b) using corporate property, information, or position for personal gain; and (c) competing with the company. Employees, officers, and directors owe a duty to the company to advance its legitimate interests when the opportunity to do so arises.
- **Confidentiality.** Employees, officers and directors should maintain the confidentiality of information entrusted to them by the listed company or its customers, except when disclosure is authorized or legally mandated. Confidential information includes all non-public information that might be of use to competitors, or harmful to the company or its customers, if disclosed.
- **Fair dealing.** Each employee, officer and director should endeavor to deal fairly with the listed company's customers, suppliers, competitors and employees. None

should take unfair advantage of anyone through manipulation, concealment, abuse of privileged information, misrepresentation of material facts, or any other unfair-dealing practice. Listed companies may write their codes in a manner that does not alter existing legal rights and obligations of companies and their employees such as "at will" employment arrangements.

- **Protection and proper use of listed company assets.** All employees, officers and directors should protect the listed company's assets and ensure their efficient use. Theft, carelessness and waste have a direct impact on the listed company's profitability. All listed company assets should be used for legitimate business purposes.
- **Compliance with laws, rules and regulations (including insider trading laws).** The listed company should proactively promote compliance with laws, rules and regulations, including insider trading laws. Insider trading is both unethical and illegal, and should be dealt with decisively.
- **Encouraging the reporting of any illegal or unethical behavior.** The listed company should proactively promote ethical behavior. The listed company should encourage employees to talk to supervisors, managers or other appropriate personnel when in doubt about the best course of action in a particular situation. Additionally, employees should report violations of laws, rules, regulations or the code of business conduct to appropriate personnel. To encourage employees to report such violations, the listed company must ensure that employees know that the company will not allow retaliation for reports made in good faith.

Website Posting Requirement: A listed company must make its code of business conduct and ethics available on or through its website.

Disclosure Requirements: A listed company must disclose in its annual proxy statement or, if it does not file an annual proxy statement, in its annual report on Form 10-K filled with the SEC that its code of business conduct and ethics is available on or through its website and provide the website address.

To the extent that a listed company's board or a board committee determines to grant any waiver of the code of business conduct and ethics for an executive officer or director, the waiver must be disclosed to shareholders within four business days of such determination. Disclosure must be made by distributing a press release, providing website disclosure, or by filing a current report on Form 8-K with the SEC.

303A.11 Foreign Private Issuer Disclosure. Listed foreign private issuers must disclose any significant ways in which their corporate governance practices differ from those followed by domestic companies under NYSE listing standards.

Commentary: Foreign private issuers must make their U.S. investors aware of the significant ways in which their corporate governance practices differ from those required of domestic companies under NYSE listing standards. However, foreign private issuers are not required to present a detailed, item-by-item analysis of these differences. Such a disclosure would be long and unnecessarily complicated. Moreover, this requirement is not intended to suggest that one country's corporate governance practices are better or more effective than another. The Exchange believes that U.S. shareholders should be aware of the significant ways that the governance of a listed foreign private issuer differs from that of a U.S. listed company. The Exchange underscores that what is required is a brief, general summary of the significant differences, not a cumbersome analysis.

Disclosure Requirement: A foreign private issuer that is required to file an annual report on Form 20-F with the SEC must include the statement of significant differences in that annual report. All other foreign private issuers may either (i) include the statement of significant differences in an annual report filed with the SEC or (ii) make the statement of significant differences available on or through the listed company's website. If the statement of significant differences is made available on or through the listed company's website, the listed company must disclose that fact in its annual report filed with the SEC and provide the website address.

303A.12 Certification Requirements. (a) Each listed company CEO must certify to the NYSE each year that he or she is not aware of any violation by the listed company of NYSE corporate governance listing standards qualifying the certification to the extent necessary.

Commentary: The CEO's annual certification regarding the NYSE's corporate governance listing standards will focus the CEO and senior management on the listed company's compliance with the listing standards.

(b) Each listed company CEO must promptly notify the NYSE in writing after any executive officer of the listed company becomes aware of any non-compliance with any applicable provisions of this section 303A.

(c) Each listed company must submit an executed Written Affirmation annually to the NYSE. In addition, each listed company must submit an interim Written Affirmation as and when required by the interim Written Affirmation Form specified by the NYSE.

303A.13 Public Reprimand Letter. The NYSE may issue a public reprimand letter to any listed company that violates a NYSE standard.

Commentary: Suspending trading in or delisting a listed company can be harmful to the very shareholders that the NYSE listing standards seek to protect; the NYSE must therefore use these measures sparingly and judiciously. For this reason it is appropriate for the NYSE to have the ability to apply a lesser sanction to deter companies from violating its corporate governance (or other) listing standards. Accordingly, the NYSE may issue a public reprimand letter to any listed company regardless of type of security listed or country of incorporation, that it determines has violated a NYSE listing standard. For companies that repeatedly or flagrantly violate NYSE listing standards, suspension and delisting remain the ultimate penalties. For clarification, this lesser sanction is not intended for use in the case of companies that fall below the financial and other continued listing standards provided in Chapter 8 of the Listed Company Manual or that fail to comply with the audit committee standards set out in section 303A.06. The processes and procedures provided for in Chapter 8 govern the treatment of companies falling below those standards.

312.00 Shareholder Approval Policy

312.03 Shareholder Approval. Shareholder approval is a prerequisite to issuing securities in the following situations:

(a) Shareholder approval is required for equity compensation plans. See section 303A.08.

(b)(i) Shareholder approval is required prior to the issuance of common stock, or of securities convertible into or exercisable for common stock, in any transaction or series of related transactions, to a director, officer or substantial security holder of the company (each a "Related Party") if the number of shares of common stock to be issued, or if the number of shares of common stock into which the securities may be convertible or exercisable, exceeds either one percent of the number of shares of common stock or one percent of the voting power outstanding before the issuance. However, shareholder approval will not be required if such transaction is a cash sale for a price that is at least the Minimum Price.

(ii) Shareholder approval is also required prior to the issuance of common stock, or of securities convertible into or exercisable for common stock, where such securities are issued as consideration in a transaction or series of related transactions in which a Related Party has a five percent or greater interest (or such persons collectively have a ten percent or greater interest), directly or indirectly, in the company or assets to be acquired or in the consideration to be paid in the transaction or series of related transactions and the present or potential issuance of common stock, or securities convertible into common stock, could result in an issuance that exceeds either five percent of the number of shares of common stock or five percent of the voting power outstanding before the issuance.

(iii) Any sale of stock to an employee, director or service provider is also subject to the equity compensation rules in Section 303A.08 of the Manual. For example, a sale of stock to any of such parties at a discount to the then market price would be treated as equity compensation under Section 303A.08 notwithstanding that shareholder approval may not be required under Sections 312.03(b) or 312.03(c). Consequently, the company would be required to either: (i) obtain shareholder approval of such sale, or (ii) issue such shares under an equity compensation plan that had previously been approved by shareholders and for which shareholder approval under Section 303A.08 is not otherwise required. Moreover, shareholder approval is required if any of the subparagraphs of Section 312.03 require such approval, notwithstanding the fact that the transaction does not require approval under this subparagraph or one or more of the other subparagraphs. (See Section 312.04(a).)

(c) Shareholder approval is required prior to the issuance of common stock, or of securities convertible into or exercisable for common stock, in any transaction or series of related transactions if:

(1) the common stock has, or will have upon issuance, voting power equal to or in excess of 20 percent of the voting power outstanding before the issuance of such stock or of securities convertible into or exercisable for common stock; or

(2) the number of shares of common stock to be issued is, or will be upon issuance, equal to or in excess of 20 percent of the number of shares of common stock outstanding before the issuance of the common stock or of securities convertible into or exercisable for common stock.

However, shareholder approval will not be required for any such issuance involving:

- any public offering for cash; or
- any other financing (that is not a public offering for cash) in which the company is selling securities for cash, if such financing involves a sale of common stock, or securities convertible into or exercisable for common stock, at a price at least as great as the Minimum Price, provided that if the securities in such financing are issued in connection with an acquisition of the stock or assets of another company, shareholder approval will be required if the issuance of such securities alone or when combined with any other present or potential issuance of common stock, or securities convertible into common stock in connection with such acquisition, is equal to or exceeds either 20 percent of the number of shares of common stock or 20 percent of the voting power outstanding before the issuance.

(d) Shareholder approval is required prior to an issuance that will result in a change of control of the issuer.

(e) Sections 312.03 (b), (c) and (d) shall not apply to issuances by limited partnerships.

312.04 For the Purpose of Section 312.03

For the purpose of Section 312.03:

(a) Shareholder approval is required if any of the subparagraphs of Section 312.03 require such approval, notwithstanding the fact that the transaction does not require approval under one or more of the other subparagraphs.

(b) Pursuant to Sections 312.03 (b) and (c), shareholder approval is required for the issuance of securities convertible into or exercisable for common stock if the stock that can be issued upon conversion or exercise exceeds the applicable percentages. This is the case even if such convertible or exchangeable securities are not to be listed on the Exchange.

(c) The Exchange's policy regarding the need to apply to list common stock reserved for issuance on the conversion or the exercise of other securities is described in Section 703.07.

(d) Only shares actually issued and outstanding (excluding treasury shares or shares held by a subsidiary) are to be used in making any calculation provided for in Sections 312.03 (b) and (c). Shares reserved for issuance upon conversion of securities or upon exercise of options or warrants will not be regarded as outstanding.

(e) An interest consisting of less than either five percent of the number of shares of common stock or five percent of the voting power outstanding of a company or entity shall not be considered a substantial interest or cause the holder of such an interest to be regarded as a substantial security holder.

(f) "Voting power outstanding" refers to the aggregate number of votes that may be cast by holders of those securities outstanding that entitle the holders thereof to vote generally on all matters submitted to the company's security holders for a vote.

(g) "Officer" has the same meaning as defined by the Securities and Exchange Commission in Rule 16a-1(f) under the Securities Exchange Act of 1934, or any successor rule.

(h) "Minimum Price" means a price that is the lower of: (i) the Official Closing Price immediately preceding the signing of the binding agreement; or (ii) the average Official Closing Price for the five trading days immediately preceding the signing of the binding agreement.

(i) "Official Closing Price" of the issuer's common stock means the official closing price on the Exchange as reported to the Consolidated Tape immediately preceding the signing of a binding agreement to issue the securities. For example, if the transaction is signed after the close of the regular session at 4:00 pm Eastern Standard Time on a Tuesday, then Tuesday's official closing price is used. If the transaction is signed at any time between the close of the regular session on Monday and the close if the regular session on Tuesday, then Monday's official closing price is used.

(j) The issuance of shares from treasury is considered an issuance of shares for purposes of Section 312.03. (See Section 703.01, Part 1, of the Listed Company Manual regarding required notice to the Exchange of issuance of shares from treasury.)

Derivative Complaint

The Walt Disney Company Litigation

IN THE COURT OF CHANCERY OF THE STATE OF DELAWARE
IN AND FOR NEW CASTLE COUNTY

IN RE THE WALT DISNEY COMPANY DERIVATIVE LITIGATION	CONSOLIDATED C.A. No. 15452

SECOND AMENDED CONSOLIDATED DERIVATIVE COMPLAINT

1. For their Second Amended Consolidated Derivative Complaint (the "Complaint"), plaintiffs allege the following upon personal knowledge as to themselves and their own acts and upon information and belief as to all other allegations, based upon inspection and review by plaintiffs' lead counsel of books and records produced by The Walt Disney Company ("Disney" or the "Company") pursuant to 8 Del. C. §220 and upon the investigation by plaintiffs' counsel of other materials pertinent to the claims herein alleged:

NATURE AND SUMMARY OF THE ACTION

2. Plaintiffs bring this action derivatively on behalf of the nominal corporate defendant, Disney, to redress the Director Defendants breaches of their fiduciary duties in (1) causing or permitting adoption of the Ovitz Employment Agreement (the "OEA") (a copy of which is attached hereto as Exhibit A) by which defendant Michael S. Ovitz ("Ovitz") was hired as Disney's President and (2) causing or permitting Ovitz's receipt of a "Non-Fault Termination" of his employment at Disney, only 14 months after the start of his employment, as a result of which Ovitz received severance benefits exceeding $140 million.

3. Defendant Michael D. Eisner ("Eisner"), Disney's Chief Executive Officer, recruited Ovitz, his long-time personal friend, to join Disney. The hiring of Ovitz was also facilitated by defendant Irwin Russell ("Russell"), the Chairman of the Compensation Committee of the Old Board, who was another long-time friend of Eisner as well as Eisner's personal attorney. Russell was paid by Disney $250,000, as additional compensation for his work in securing Ovitz's services for the Company.

4. The Disney Compensation Committee, chaired by Russell, approved a set of general terms that were supposed to provide the basis for the OEA in a meeting in September 1995. Russell and the other members of the Compensation Committee, however, inadequately investigated the proposed terms of the OEA and thus violated their fiduciary duties owed to Disney. The members of the Committee, who did not receive any materials regarding the OEA prior to the meeting, spent an extremely minimal and negligible amount of time, probably as little as ten minutes, considering the terms of the OEA. The Old Board subsequently decided to appoint Ovitz President, paying scant attention to the terms of the OEA. Indeed, both the Old Board and the Compensation Committee devoted more attention to the subject of Russell's additional compensation for working out Ovitz's package than to the terms of the OEA.

5. The members of the Compensation Committee and the Old Board, indifferently and recklessly, failed to obtain and consider all material information reasonably available to them to evaluate whether the OEA was desirable from a corporate standpoint and whether it contained adequate safeguards. They did not obtain the draft of the OEA which was available at the time. They did not obtain any calculations, assessments, or even a general picture of the compensation that Ovitz would receive in the event of Non-Fault Termination at various points in time and of how such compensation would compare with the compensation Ovitz would obtain in the event of serving the full contract term. Moreover, the Compensation Committee and the Old Board never approved more than a set of general terms and conditions that were proposed as a framework whose fine details would be subsequently negotiated and could be approved by defendant Eisner. By doing so, the members of the Old Board knowingly left Eisner, whose very close relations with Ovitz were familiar to all of them, the task of finalizing the agreement without any further scrutiny on their part.

6. The OEA that was produced by this highly flawed and ill-informed process was one that no reasonable person would have accepted had that person been adequately informed, failed to contain adequate safeguards to secure Ovitz's future services, and was wasteful. The OEA provided Ovitz with severance compensation in the event of a Non-Fault Termination that was at least as valuable, if not more so, than if he remained in Disney's employment throughout the entire term of his employment agreement. As a result, rather than provide incentives to Ovitz to continue working for Disney and serve it well, the terms of the OEA perversely made obtaining a Non-Fault Termination far more financially attractive for Ovitz than his serving the full term of the contract. The stock option and severance provisions in the OEA, therefore, failed to secure Ovitz's services for the full contract term and even provided a disincentive for him to perform as President for the full five years. The seriously perverse and counter-productive incentives produced by these terms of the OEA could have been detected and prevented by the directors had they properly studied them and had they obtained a comparative assessment of the benefits provided to Ovitz in the event of a Non-Fault Termination and the benefits of full contract performance by Ovitz.

7. Moreover, the Compensation Committee and the Old Board failed to secure any expert advice regarding the terms of the OEA. Although Graef Crystal ("Crystal")

assisted Russell in certain aspects of the negotiations relating to the OEA, he was never retained to perform such work and merely offered such services as ancillary to advisory work that he was doing for Russell with regard to the restructuring of Eisner's employment agreement. Not surprisingly, Crystal did not render any opinion or other recommendation with regard to the terms of the OEA and never attended any meeting of the Compensation Committee of the Old Board that touched on these matters. Similarly, Crystal neither provided to the Compensation Committee or the Old Board, nor prepared for consideration by either one of them, any analysis of the terms of the OEA.

8. Although Ovitz started serving as President of Disney on October 1, 1995, and the OEA was dated as of October 1, 1995, the OEA was not finalized and executed on that date. Rather, negotiations over the OEA continued beyond this date for at least 10 weeks, and the OEA was executed on or about December 12, 1995 and backdated to October 1, 1995. The final version of the OEA that was worked out by Eisner and Ovitz deviated substantially from the general terms approved earlier by the Disney Compensation Committee. Eisner agreed to generous and unwarranted expansion of the circumstances under which Ovitz would be entitled to a Non-Fault Termination. Furthermore, whereas the Compensation Committee had contemplated the granting of stock options with an exercise price no greater than the market price on the date of the grant, as had typically been the practice at Disney, Eisner agreed to stock option grants that were known at the time of OEA's actual execution to be substantially in-the-money. But for Eisner's close relationship with his "best friend" Ovitz and the other directors' gross and reckless inattention, such lucrative, unearned benefits would never have been provided to Ovitz.

9. Notwithstanding the fact that Ovitz was neither an officer nor a director of Disney prior to the (backdated) effective date of the OEA (October 1, 1995), he was an officer and a director and thus a fiduciary of Disney at the time the OEA was actually executed. As a fiduciary, Ovitz violated his duties of loyalty and good faith owed to Disney in obtaining for himself an arrangement that was adverse to the interests of the Company.

10. During his tenure at Disney, Ovitz performed poorly and acted in disregard of his contractual duties to Disney. His poor performance was recognized as such by Disney's senior management, outside observers, and eventually Ovitz himself. This caused Ovitz to look actively for alternative employment and to start negotiations with Sony Corp. over his joining Sony as a senior executive. To implement this, Ovitz wrote to Eisner on or about October 8, 1996, stating that he wished to leave his position at Disney and that he was seeking approval for his conducting employment negotiations with other companies before actually departing.

11. Confronted with Ovitz's failure as President of Disney, and with Ovitz's express desire to leave Disney, defendant Eisner agreed that he would do everything that he could to ease his friend out of Disney without his suffering any financial cost or recriminations. In a note that Eisner wrote to Ovitz on October 9, 1995, Eisner stated in part that he was "committed to make this a win-win situation, to keep our friendship intact," adding: "Nobody ever needs to know anything other than positive things from either of us . . . you are still the only one who came to my hospital bed [when Eisner underwent heart surgery]—and I do remember." Eisner added:

that "Nobody ever needs to know anything other than positive things from either of us." In a subsequent note, Eisner also stated reassuringly to Ovitz, "I am sure we are now both protected 'every way to and from Sunday'." In that same letter, Eisner conveyed to Ovitz his wish to arrange Ovitz's departure on terms which would avoid any "embarrassment" to Eisner.

12. When Ovitz's efforts to secure another position foundered, Eisner capitulated to his friend's desire to leave, but without sacrificing any of the financial benefits of the OEA. Thus, Eisner put his personal friendship with Ovitz, and his desire to keep this friendship intact, and to avoid his embarrassment, above his fiduciary duties owed to Disney and Disney's interest in avoiding or minimizing any unnecessary payments to the departing Ovitz. He did so by unilaterally agreeing that Ovitz's depârture would be treated as a Non-Fault Termination, triggering Ovitz's lucrative pay-out under the OEA. Eisner never explored any other alternatives that may have been more beneficial to Disney.

13. Consistent with his promises to his friend Ovitz, Eisner never reported to or informed the New Board about his interactions with Ovitz concerning Ovitz's departure, nor brought to the New Board any recommendation or proposal concerning the termination of Ovitz. Rather, he unilaterally caused Disney to pay Ovitz the full benefits of a Non-Fault Termination with the inexcusable acquiescence of the New Board. Although, pursuant to Disney's Bylaws, the President could only be removed by the Board, Disney's records show that, in fact, the New Board abdicated its responsibilities, leaving the decision to Eisner, who was patently conflicted in his dealings with Ovitz. By obtaining and accepting these benefits, Ovitz, acted in concert with defendant Eisner, violated his fiduciary duties to Disney.

PARTIES

14. Plaintiffs were and are holders of shares of Disney common stock who have held such shares from the time of the wrongs complained of through the present.

15. Disney is a Delaware corporation with its principal place of business located at 500 South Buena Vista Street, Burbank, California. Disney identifies itself in its filings with the Securities and Exchange Commission ("SEC") as a "diversified international entertainment company with operations in three business segments: Creative Content; Broadcasting; and Theme Parks and Resorts." Disney is named in this action as a nominal defendant.

16. At all relevant times, defendant Eisner has served as Disney's Chairman of the Board and Chief Executive Officer.

17. (a) Defendant Ovitz served as Disney's President from approximately September 26, 1995 until December 27, 1996. Ovitz also served as a Disney director from January 1996 until his departure from the Company. Ovitz and Disney announced on December 12, 1996, that Ovitz would leave Disney effective January 31, 1997. Ovitz's departure was subsequently accelerated to December 27, 1996.

(b) Prior to his employment at Disney, Ovitz founded and served as Chairman of Creative Artists Agency ("CAA"), a firm of talent agents. Before joining Disney, Ovitz had neither served as an entertainment industry executive nor as an officer of a publicly-traded company.

18. Defendant Stephen F. Bollenbach is the former Senior Executive Vice President and Chief Financial Officer of Disney. Bollenbach served in those positions, and as a Disney director, from approximately April of 1995 until February of 1996.

19. Defendant Sanford M. Litvack, was, at all relevant times, Disney's General Counsel as well as a Disney director.

20. Defendant Russell was, at all relevant times, a Disney director and Chairman of the Disney Board's Compensation Committee, as well as Eisner's personal attorney.

21. Defendants Eisner, Bollenbach, Litvack, Russell, Roy E. Disney, Stanley P. Gold, Richard A. Nunis, Sidney Poitier, Robert A.M. Stern, E. Cardon Walker, Raymond L. Watson, Gary L. Wilson, Reveta F. Bowers, Ignacio E. Lozano Jr., and George J. Mitchell were the members of the "Old Board."

22. Defendants Eisner, Disney, Gold, Litvack, Nunis, Poitier, Russell, Stern, Walker, Watson, Wilson, Bowers, Lozano, Mitchell, Leo J. O'Donovan and Thomas S. Murphy, excluding defendant Ovitz, are sometimes referred to as the "New Board."

23. The members of the Old Board and the New Board (excluding defendant Ovitz) are collectively referred to as the "Director Defendants."

24. Throughout the course of their service with Disney, the Director Defendants and Ovitz owed Disney fiduciary obligations, including those of due care, loyalty and good faith.

SUBSTANTIVE ALLEGATIONS

A. General Background to Ovitz's Hiring by Disney

25. Prior to joining Disney, Ovitz was Chairman of CAA. He had no experience in working as an officer of a public corporation, much less one the size and scope of Disney. Moreover, Ovitz had no experience in many of Disney's principal businesses, including its vast theme parks operations.

26. Further, Ovitz had previously functioned as a virtual kingpin in his limited domain as a talent agent. Thus, Ovitz had no track record of following orders, much less acting as a second-in-command to a powerful executive such as Eisner.

27. In 1994, Eisner lost his highly respected second-in-command, Frank Wells, in a fatal helicopter crash. Within months of Wells' death, Disney also lost the services of Jeffrey Katzenberg, a leading figure in the motion picture and animation fields in which Disney had recently recorded great successes. Eisner had demonstrated a tendency to cause significant turnover of Disney top executives reporting to him. For example, Eisner forced Katzenberg to leave Disney because Eisner was unwilling to name Katzenberg, who was widely regarded as a highly creative and forceful executive, as Disney's President, because this would place a potential rival in the second-most powerful position in the Company—unacceptable to Eisner. In March of 1995, Richard Frank, the Chairman of Disney's television and telecommunications divisions, resigned. Public reports indicated that Frank's departure was caused by Eisner's aggressive and intrusive management style.

28. The departure of Katzenberg and Frank, coupled with Ovitz's lack of experience as an executive, made it especially important for the Old Board to examine the arrangements governing termination of the OEA and to satisfy itself that the OEA contained adequate safeguards to ensure that the Company would receive the benefit of its bargain and was not wasteful.

29. Before Ovitz joined Disney, Ovitz and his wife had been close friends of Eisner and his wife for over 25 years. This bond of friendship was so strong that even the disappointments and troubles caused to Eisner by Ovitz's subsequent failure as the Company's President did not undermine it. As set forth below, in a letter written in October 1996, in the period in which Ovitz and Eisner were already arranging for Ovitz's departure, and despite Ovitz's performance having generated vexing tension and disappointment within the Disney organization, Eisner stressed that it was very important for him to keep his friendship with Ovitz intact, and Ovitz referred to Eisner in a letter to him written in that period as "my best friend."

B. <u>The Hiring of Ovitz</u>

30. The decision to bring Ovitz in as President of Disney was made unilaterally by Eisner, who considered Ovitz his "best friend." At a meeting held at Eisner's Bel Air Home on or about August 13, 1995, Eisner announced to Old Board members Bollenbach, Litvack and Russell that he had hired Ovitz. At that meeting, Bollenbach, Litvack and even Russell (Eisner's personal attorney) protested the decision.

31. On or about August 14, 1995, Eisner send Ovitz a letter memorializing the principal terms of Ovitz's prospective employment by Disney. Prior to Eisner's sending Ovitz this letter, the hiring of Ovitz as President was never considered or discussed by the Old Board or any of its committees.

32. In his letter, Eisner stated that the hiring of Ovitz was subject to the formal approval of the Company's Board and its Compensation Committee. The employment of Ovitz, however, was not brought to the Board until weeks later—September 26, 1995—after much of the OEA had already been formulated. At that meeting, as described herein, the Old Board spent very little time considering Ovitz's employment—only one-half of one page of the fifteen page minutes of that meeting is devoted to this important matter—and acquiesced in Eisner's unilateral choice. Importantly, no written agreement between Ovitz and the Company was presented for consideration at that meeting. Instead, Eisner was authorized to bring such negotiations to closure—negotiations which would and did continue for months after Ovitz began working at Disney.

C. <u>Defendants Breach their Fiduciary Duties in Connection With Entering Into The OEA</u>

33.An internal Disney document created on or about July 7, 1995 raised concerns about the extraordinary number of options that were being negotiated and would apparently be granted to Ovitz:

> *[n]umber of stock options is far beyond standards applied in Company [sic] and in corporate America and will raise very strong criticism.* We should collect survey information to be prepared to answer if it becomes necessary. [Emphasis added.]

34. Neither this document nor any other document providing survey information or otherwise analyzing the benefits provided to Ovitz was submitted to the Compensation Committee or the Old Board when they agreed to Ovitz's hiring.

35. Also, before Ovitz was hired, a letter from Crystal to Russell dated August 12, 1995, noted, with reference to a "large signing bonus," that the "deficiencies of this approach are that the cost is borne immediately, and it is borne in full even though the executive, for one reason or another, fails to serve his full employment term." Neither this document nor any other document discussing, highlighting, criticizing or analyzing the similar problems created by the Non-Fault Termination provision in the OEA was submitted to the Compensation Committee or to the Old Board prior to the hiring of Ovitz.

1. <u>The September 26, 1995 Compensation Committee Meeting</u>

36. The Disney Compensation Committee briefly considered Ovitz's prospective employment in a meeting that was held on or about September 26, 1995. The members of the Compensation Committee were defendants Lozano, Poitier, Russell and Watson. Defendant Russell was the Chairman of the Committee. Defendant Litvack also attended that meeting. The Committee approved in this meeting a set of general terms and conditions that were proposed as a framework whose fine details would be subsequently negotiated and could be approved by defendant Eisner. By doing so, the members of the Old Board knowingly left to Eisner, whose very close relations with Ovitz were familiar to all of them, the task of finalizing the agreement without any further scrutiny on their part.

37. The whole meeting of the Compensation Committee lasted no more than an hour, as the Old Board, including all the members of the Compensation Committee, started a meeting—at which Ovitz was scheduled to be appointed President—one hour after the beginning of the Compensation Committee meeting. Furthermore, the subject of Ovitz's agreement was second among three subjects discussed at the Compensation Committee meeting, and the minutes indicate that the other two subjects attracted substantially more attention and discussion from the Compensation Committee.

38. The minutes of the September 26, 1995, Compensation Committee meeting cover five pages, with the first page largely devoted to preliminary matters such as the list of participants. The next two pages were devoted to a subject unrelated to Ovitz. (A copy of this document which was provided to plaintiffs' counsel pursuant to 8 Del. C. §220 labels those pages as "REDACTED" and "IRRELEVANT.") The last two (less than full) pages include a brief account of the Compensation Committee's consideration of Ovitz's employment (eleven lines) and a slightly longer account (fourteen lines) of the Compensation Committee's consideration of a $250,000 fee to be paid to defendant Russell for his role in "securing" Ovitz's services. Assuming that the fraction of total text in the minutes devoted to a topic is roughly proportional to the amount of time spent on it, less than 10 minutes were spent on Ovitz's employment.

39. The minutes not only illustrate the extreme brevity of the time spent on Ovitz's agreement, but also indicate the absence of any focused attention to the subject by members of the Compensation Committee. In fact, materially more discussion and

attention was devoted to the matter of approving defendant Russell's $250,000 fee (a matter which, needless to say, was far less important to Disney's shareholders). In this regard, the minutes highlight several distinct issues that were raised with respect to Russell's fee by specific directors who are named in the minutes. In contrast, the brief account in the minutes of the consideration of Ovitz's agreement contains no reference to specific issues that were discussed, if any. The minutes only blandly note that Russell reviewed the terms of the OEA and answered questions and that a resolution of approval was then passed.

40. The Compensation Committee failed to obtain several types of information on the terms and conditions of the OEA that were reasonably available to it and were material to assessing the terms of such agreement. For example, even though a draft of the OEA was prepared by Disney and sent to Ovitz's lawyers on September 23, 1995, and even though this draft contained a more complete account of the terms and conditions of the OEA as contemplated at the time, this draft was not distributed to the members of the Compensation Committee before the meeting so that they could read and reflect on the OEA beforehand. Nor was this draft distributed to the members of the Compensation Committee during the meeting.

41. Instead, what the directors received at the meeting was merely a rough summary and substantially incomplete account of the terms and conditions of the OEA as they then stood. For example, the summary of the terms and conditions of the OEA attached to the minutes indicated that Ovitz was to receive options to purchase five million shares. It did not indicate, even though the draft was more specific, what was the contemplated exercise price of the options, which is a critical component to any consideration of a grant of options.

42. Importantly, the Compensation Committee did not receive any materials—whether in the form of a spreadsheet, tables, a list of estimates, or any other form—that could provide its members with some sense of the magnitude of possible pay-outs that Ovitz would receive in the event of a Non-Fault Termination at various points in time. As a result, the Compensation Committee did not possess even a general sense or notion of the amount of compensation that Ovitz would receive in the event of a Non-Fault Termination—much less any precise quantification of the value of the severance package that Ovitz would receive under a variety of scenarios that could reasonable come into play.

43. In a December 23, 1996, article that appeared in the Worldwide Web magazine *Slate,* Crystal expressed his regret that—even though he was not retained to serve as an expert or to provide an expert report—he did not at the time intervene to cause the simple and easy steps needed to remedy the utter failure to inform the decision-making process of the magnitude of compensation involved. He stated in the article as follows: "Of course, the overall costs of the package would go up sharply in the event of Ovitz's termination *and I wish now that I'd made a spreadsheet showing just what the deal would total if Ovitz had been fired at any time*" (emphasis added).

44. Finally, even though the benefits provided to Ovitz were clearly of exceptional magnitude and structure, the Compensation Committee did not receive nor request any materials as to how these striking benefits compared with standard arrangements or even as to whether there had been any precedents for the granting, or proposed structuring, of such benefits.

45. Moreover, in considering the OEA, the Compensation Committee did not receive, and hence did not and could not rely on, any expert advice regarding the terms of the OEA. Although Graef Crystal, who in that period was retained to provide advice with regard to defendant Eisner's new employment contract, had communications with Russell relating to the negotiations and development of the OEA, Crystal was never retained, nor acted, as an expert to render any formal opinion or recommendation concerning the terms of the OEA. In that regard, Crystal did not prepare any written analysis or opinion regarding the OEA that was submitted to the Compensation Committee or the Old Board. Crystal also did not make any oral presentation to the Compensation Committee or the Old Board, and he did not participate in any of the meetings in which the hiring or contract with Ovitz was discussed. The Compensation Committee also did not get any advice or opinion from any other person.

46. Although woefully uninformed, the members of the Compensation Committee nonetheless approved the general terms and conditions of the OEA as they then stood. Although the committee was informed that further negotiations would take place and that Ovitz's "stock option grant would be delayed until final contract details were worked out between Mr. Ovitz and the Corporation," the Compensation Committee did not condition its approval of the summary of terms and conditions of Ovitz's employment on being able to review subsequently the complete text of the OEA. Instead, the Committee approved a resolution under which "the terms and the conditions are hereby approved subject to such reasonable further negotiations within the framework of the terms and conditions described in Exhibit C as may be approved by the Chief Executive Officer of the Walt Disney Company."

2. <u>The September 26, 1995, Old Board Meeting</u>

47. A meeting of the Old Board took place on September 26, 1995, immediately following the meeting of the Compensation Committee. Crystal was not present at that Board meeting and the minutes reflect no mention of his name. Ovitz was designated at the meeting to be President of the Company effective October 1, 1995. However, the Old Board did not obtain any information nor spend any time whatsoever on the matter of Ovitz's compensation.

48. In fact, the only discussion in the minutes of that meeting that was related to the OEA (which amounted to 1½ pages out of the 15 pages of minutes for that meeting) was (1) that Russell should and would receive a payment of $250,000 for his work in connection with retaining Ovitz (one page in the minutes) and (2) that "the Chairman resigned the position of President of the Corporation and then recommended that Michael Ovitz be elected to the office of President of the Corporation and reviewed Mr. Ovitz's professional and education credentials (half a page of the minutes)."

49. The minutes do not reflect that the Old Board received, let alone considered, any recommendation and/or report of the Compensation Committee and/or of defendant Russell with respect to the OEA. Nor did the Old Board receive, let alone consider, any report or advice from any expert with respect to the OEA. Needless to say, the Old Board did not consider the consequences of a Non-Fault Termination and the resultant pay-out to Ovitz that could have been expected under various

scenarios, nor was a spreadsheet presented or reviewed evaluating possible pay-outs (or ranges of pay-outs) at various times if Ovitz obtained a Non-Fault Termination.

3. The October 16, 1995 Compensation Committee Meeting

50. The Compensation Committee received a brief oral report of the still-continuing negotiations over Ovitz's agreement in a meeting which took place on October 16, 1995 (more than two weeks after Ovitz had already commenced his duties as Disney President). The members of the Compensation Committee did not take advantage of this opportunity to obtain any of the information that they failed to obtain earlier and that was reasonably available to them. Again, even though a draft of the OEA was available at this time, it was not distributed to the members of the Committee either before or during the meeting; rather, the members of the Compensation Committee satisfied themselves with a similar summary and incomplete account of the main terms and conditions of the OEA that they received in their meeting of September 26, 1995. Furthermore, the Committee did not obtain any sense of the magnitude of the benefits that Ovitz would obtain in the event of a Non-Fault Termination at various points in time and of how these benefits would compare with those of full-term service. As before, the Compensation Committee did not receive any report, advice or recommendation from any expert with regard to the OEA.

D. The Finalization, Backdating and Execution of the OEA

51. Although Ovitz began serving as Disney's President on October 1, 1995, and the OEA was dated as of October 1, 1995, the OEA was not finalized, approved by Eisner, or executed by Ovitz and Disney on October 1, 1995. Rather, negotiations over the OEA continued beyond that date, and the OEA was finalized and executed only much later, and was then backdated.

52. In the weeks and months after the September 26, 1995, Old Board meeting, Ovitz and Eisner continued to negotiate the language of the OEA. Drafts of the OEA were circulated between and among the parties' lawyers on October 3, 1995, October 10, 1995, October 16, 1995, October 20, 1995, October 23, 1995, and December 12, 1995. The OEA was physically executed only on or about December 12, 1995, and it was then backdated to October 1, 1995—a date more than 10 weeks before the date on which it was actually executed. The OEA was expressly between Michael S. Ovitz, "Executive" and "The Walt Disney Company, a Delaware corporation."

53. The final version of the OEA negotiated by Eisner, Ovitz and their representatives was substantially more favorable toward Ovitz than the general terms and conditions approved by the Compensation Committee at its September 26, 1995 meeting (and again at its October 16, 1995 meeting). In addition, the Stock Option Agreement in connection with the OEA was executed by defendant Eisner on behalf of Disney on April 2, 1996, and Ovitz did not countersign the agreement until November 15, 1996, at which time he was already in discussion with Eisner about leaving the Company.

54. One significant way in which Eisner exceeded the terms and conditions reviewed by the Compensation Committee concerned the circumstances under which Ovitz would receive the benefits of a Non-Fault Termination. According to the summary of the terms and conditions of the OEA, as reported to the Compensation

Committee on September 26, 1995, the Non-Fault Termination benefits would be provided to Ovitz only in the event that Disney "wrongfully" terminated Ovitz's employment (or that Ovitz died or became disabled). A similarly tight definition of the circumstances under which Ovitz would be entitled to the benefits of a Non-Fault Termination was included among the terms and conditions presented to the Compensation Committee on October 16, 1995. However, the OEA finally executed in December 1995 (and backdated to October 1, 1995) provided a much broader definition of the circumstances in which such a generous package would be paid to Ovitz. Instead of protecting Ovitz from "wrongful" behavior by Disney, the provisions concerning Non-Fault Termination now contemplated that Ovitz would have access to these massive benefits as long as he did not engage in detrimental behavior defined as "gross negligence" or "malfeasance."

55. Another way in which Eisner favored Ovitz was taking the extraordinary step of causing Disney to grant Ovitz options that were materially more in-the-money than they were supposed to be. In this regard, Eisner's granting to Ovitz Disney stock options on or about December 12, 1995, which had an exercise price equal not to the market price prevailing at that time (the date as of December 12, 1995) but, to the market price on October 16, 1995, provided Ovitz with materially more stock option value. As a result of this decision, the exercise price of each of the three million options granted to Ovitz was reduced by $5.125 and put in-the-money to that extent.

56. In contrast, the draft OEA as of September 23, 1995, set the exercise price of Ovitz's options at Disney's stock price as of October 2, 1995, i.e., the first trading day after the anticipated effective date of the OEA. Thereafter, at its meeting on October 16, 1995, the Compensation Committee agreed to set the exercise price of Ovitz's options at Disney's stock price as of October 16, 1995 (which was roughly the same as that of October 2, 1995).

57. However, by the time that the OEA was physically executed in December 1995 (which officially granted Ovitz his stock options), the stock market had risen dramatically and so had Disney's stock price. The Dow Jones Industrial Average increased from 4784 on October 16, 1995, to 5175 on December 12, 1995—a gain of approximately 8%. Disney's stock price rose from $56.875 per share on October 16, 1995 to $61.50 per share on December 12, 1995—a similar increase of 8%.

58. Given that the price of Disney's stock went up significantly before the actual execution of the OEA, granting Ovitz Disney stock options in December 1995, with an exercise price equal to the October 16, 1995, price of Disney's stock, as was done, when Disney's stock price had risen approximately 8% from its October price, gave Ovitz a substantial unearned benefit. Whereas granting Ovitz Disney options on October 16, 1995 with an exercise price equal to the market price of that day would have faced Ovitz both with an upside and a downside as far as general market movements are concerned, waiting until December 1995, and granting Ovitz options at that time with an exercise price equal to the October 16, 1995, price, when it was known that the market price went up significantly since then, was equivalent to granting Ovitz a winning lottery ticket not before, but after, the results are known. Eisner, however, agreed to have the OEA grant Ovitz options which he knew at the time of this agreement to be already heavily "in-the-money."

E. The Counter-Productive and Injurious Terms of the OEA

59. The OEA that Ovitz signed with Disney had a term of five years from October 1, 1995, through September 30, 2000. The agreement called for Ovitz to devote his full time and best efforts exclusively to Disney, with exceptions for volunteer work, service on the board of another company and management of his passive interests. In return for his full-time service throughout the contract term, Ovitz was to receive generous compensation consisting of three elements: (a) an annual salary set at $1 million, (b) a discretionary bonus at the end of each full year of service as Disney's President up to $10 million, and (c) most importantly, a series of "A" options that collectively enabled Ovitz to purchase 3 million shares of Disney common stock at an exercise price equal to their market price on October 16, 1995.

60. The terms of the OEA provided that, in the event of a "Non-Fault Termination" before the OEA expired on September 30, 2000, Ovitz would enjoy a package that would be worth at least as much, if not more, than if he stayed with Disney for the full term of the OEA. This was the case for each of the three elements of the compensation package. Hence, the stock option and severance provisions in the OEA actually afforded him an incentive to leave.

61. To start with the salary element, the OEA provided that, in the event of a Non-Fault Termination, Ovitz would immediately receive the full value of the total salary payments expected during the full contract period. Not only would all of Ovitz's remaining salary be accelerated, but it would be discounted to the present value at a risk-free rate that would not reflect the actual risk that Ovitz might be terminated or leave before the end of the contract. As a result, the accelerated salary payment was greater than it would have been on an expected value basis had a more appropriate discount rate been applied.

62. The advantage in favor of a Non-Fault Termination was even more pronounced in the treatment of potential bonuses. As a full-time employee, Ovitz could receive as much as $10 million per year in bonus compensation, but he could also receive nothing. Given Ovitz's unfamiliarity with Disney's operations and need to move up on a learning curve, as well as all the risks and uncertainties that ordinarily go into an award of bonus compensation, Ovitz could never be assured of what his annual bonus compensation would be. By contrast, in the event of a Non-Fault Termination, Ovitz would receive $7.5 million per remaining year on his contract (75% of the maximum), again discounted to present value at a risk-free interest rate keyed to Disney's borrowing costs. Thus, the base amount of bonus compensation for purposes of the severance pay-out was very high, while the discount rate applied to converting that amount to present value was unrealistically low. As a result, Ovitz was markedly better off with regard to the bonus compensation component by leaving Disney early that by staying throughout the full contract term.

63. As to the "A" options, in the event of a Non-Fault Termination, Ovitz would receive the same number of options as he would if he served a full term and, furthermore, the options would vest immediately. If Ovitz were to serve a full term, the options would vest in increments of one million shares on September 30 of each year commencing September 30, 1998 through September 30, 2000. In addition, the exercise period for Ovitz's options was extended until the later of 24 months after the date of a Non-Fault Termination, or September 30, 2002.

64. With respect to the A Options, Ovitz not only would receive as many of those options in the event of a Non-Fault Termination as he would by remaining for the full contract term, he would also receive the full allotment of those options in one block and sooner than if he stayed with Disney for the full five-year term. Thus, instead of providing Ovitz with the incentive to constructively contribute to Disney's success and growth by conditioning the options on certain performance milestones or even just Ovitz's continued tenure at the Company, the options provided incentives for Ovitz to secure a Non-Fault Termination.

65. As yet another benefit from having the OEA terminated prematurely, the OEA also called for Ovitz to receive a "termination payment" of $10,000,000 in the event that he was terminated other than for good cause prior to the September 30, 2000, conclusion of the contract.

66. The OEA also provided that if Ovitz completed the entire five-year term and then entered into a new contract with Disney, he would receive a second set of stock options, the so-called "B" options, for two million additional shares. The Company, however, was completely free to refrain from entering into a new employment contract with Ovitz. Thus, the parties could and should have expected that, in the event that they would later enter into negotiations over a new contract, the presence of this provision would in no way impede the Company from offering less B options or no such options at all, as it would not impede Ovitz from demanding more B options or other types of options.

67. As a result, the OEA provided Ovitz with at least as much by way of option compensation for a Non-Fault Termination as he would receive by working full-time for Disney for the five-year contractual term of his employment. Also, all such options would be received immediately, allowing Ovitz to exercise them without delay, and relieving him of the risk that the options would subsequently go "out of the money" or that Ovitz might be terminated for fault, thus eliminating his entitlement to any such options, risks he would face if he stayed a Disney employee. It was thus in Ovitz's pecuniary interest at all times to have a Non-Fault Termination rather than continue his service as President, particularly since the OEA contained no non-compete restrictions on his ability to earn income outside of Disney if he left its employ. Accordingly, the OEA did not contain adequate safeguards to ensure that Disney would get the bargained-for-benefit and, in fact, should Ovitz at any time develop a preference to leave the Company, the OEA would perversely encourage him to quit rather than hold him to the full-term of his employment.

68. An article published in the January 13, 1997, edition of *California Law Business* reported the assessment of Crystal, who was a contemporaneous observer, with respect to the preparations, and the arrangement of, the OEA. The *California Law Business* article described the perverse nature of the structure of the contract as follows:

> [Ovitz] was given a lucrative exit package that guaranteed him his salary and bonuses over the life of the contract, as well as a $10 million termination payment and options on 3 million shares of Disney stock. *Thus, the contract was most valuable to Ovitz the sooner he left Disney, Crystal says.* [Emphasis added.]

F. Ovitz's Failures As President of Disney

69. From the outset, Ovitz's performance as Disney's President was undistinguished and counter-productive—as judged not only by the outside world but also by other executives and directors at the Company.

70. For example, *The Wall Street Journal* reported in its February 24, 1997, edition that, only months after Ovitz was hired by Disney, Eisner wrote in a memorandum to defendant Watson that he "had made an error in judgment in who I brought into the company." According to Eisner:

> I made it clear to [Watson] and a few other people that if I should get hit by this truck, he should not expand my error and continue it . . . I made it very clear that I had made a mistake, way before it became clear to the public and way before I acted. I knew that it was not going to work and I did not want to leave a legacy of my mistake.

71. *The New York Times* reported in its December 14, 1996, edition a similar account of how Ovitz's tenure at Disney was viewed by the Company's executives:

> Even Disney executives acknowledge that Mr. Eisner's management style was, perhaps, anathema to Mr. Ovitz. But studio executives said Mr. Ovitz bore the brunt of the blame with some highly publicized missteps, including clashes with top Disney officials, an imperious management style that included a huge office and staff, even by Hollywood standards, and a feud with NBC that was set off when he lured a top programmer, Jamie Tarses, from that network to Disney's ABC network.

72. Ovitz's failure as President was in part caused by his deliberate refusal to learn certain important aspects of Disney's business as he was expected to do. An October 7, 1996, article in *The New York Times* reported that Ovitz was instructed by Eisner to meet weekly with defendant Bollenbach during Bollenbach's tenure as Disney's Chief Financial Officer. Those meetings were scheduled to be held on Mondays at 2:00 p.m. As *The New York Times* reported, however, "each Monday . . . Mr. Ovitz canceled the meeting at the last minute, reportedly angering Mr. Bollenbach," who had already noted Ovitz's refusal to meet with him simply for the purpose of becoming better oriented with Disney's affairs. In part because of his conflicts with Ovitz and dissatisfaction with Eisner's choice of Ovitz as Disney's second-in-command, defendant Bollenbach left Disney on February 5, 1996.

73. A harsh account of how Ovitz failed to carry out his duties was delivered by defendant Bollenbach in the December 1996 issue of *Vanity Fair.* The article states:

> [Bollenbach] suggested that his new colleague sit down with briefing books and familiarize himself with the details of company operations. "Let's you and I take a day, a day and a half, and I'll go through all this with you, go through a budget, and you'll understand this business," Bollenbach remember telling Ovitz. "His response was 'Great. I can't thank you enough, let's set up a meeting.' That conversation occurred 25 times. And we never had the meeting. *The point was, Michael Ovitz didn't understand the duties of an executive at a public company and didn't want to learn.*" [Emphasis added.]

74. Even prior to his resignation from Disney, Ovitz had admitted publicly that he was performing poorly in his role as Disney's President and had not learned important aspects of his job. In a September 30, 1996, interview of Eisner and Ovitz on "Larry King Live," held a year after Ovitz had joined Disney, Ovitz stated that "I probably know about 1% of what I need to know."

75. In disregard of his contract with Disney, which required Ovitz to "devote his full time and best efforts exclusively to the Company," Ovitz looked actively for alternative employment while President of Disney. As early as September 12, 1996, *The Wall Street Journal* reported that Ovitz was interviewing for a top position at Sony with Nobuyuki Idei, the Chairman of Sony Corp. of Japan, the parent company of Sony Corporation of America's ("SCA").

76. The fact that Ovitz was actively searching for alternative job prospects could not be kept secret. For example, in its December 12, 1996, edition, *The New York Times* reported that "Michael Ovitz, the president of the Walt Disney Company and one of the most formidable power brokers in Hollywood, has held conversations with Sony in recent weeks about taking a top job there, a high-level entertainment executive said tonight."

G. <u>Eisner and Ovitz Engineer a Lucrative Departure for Ovitz</u>

77. Sometime in or about August or September of 1996, Ovitz determined that he wished to leave Disney provided he could get Eisner's agreement to work together towards an orderly departure that would be placed in the best possible light. He had several reasons for this. First, according to Section 12 of the OEA, Ovitz had the right to terminate his employment only if one of three events occurred (none of which occurred in this case). Moreover, resigning outright would have been a violation of the OEA and would have made Ovitz liable for damages to Disney, and at the very least, would have prevented Ovitz from receiving the benefits of a Non-Fault Termination. A handwritten letter from Ovitz written to Eisner on October 8, 1996, expressed Ovitz's concern that his unilaterally resigning from Disney to pursue other opportunities would be injurious to him:

> If I get an offer I assume that you, Sandy [Litvack] and/or the company will not raise any claims against me or the other company under my employment contract or, if I make a deal that the same applies. . . . I will try to do this in the next few weeks. If I cannot, then I guess you are stuck with me until I can find something to do that works for the both of us . . . Since Sandy relayed his P.O.V. on the company and me I think I need you to acknowledge this note by signing it so that I do not end up in a problem which I do not want with the company or my best friend.

78. Another reason why Ovitz wanted to leave was that he was hoping to use the time that would be freed for him to take advantage of other lucrative opportunities whose realization required Ovitz to free himself of Disney. As set forth herein, Ovitz had a tempting opportunity at Sony and he was also attracted to the idea of setting up a business for himself.

79. Finally, it was important for Ovitz to exit Disney in a way that would tarnish Ovitz's reputation as little as possible. This, again, was something for which he needed Eisner's cooperation and participation, which was readily given.

80. On October 9, 1996, Eisner wrote to Ovitz and stated cooperatively:

> I read your note, and I really appreciate the spirit in which it is written—in light of all our conversations, I am sure you realize that I do not object to your trying to work out a deal for yourself with Sony. And if Sony replaces Disney's financial obligations to you so you come out the same or better, and if Sony handles the "Disney and MDE [Michael D. Eisner] embarrassment equation" by making some strategic deal with us, then we certainly would not stand in the way of closing your deal. I agree with you that we must work together to assure a smooth transition and deal with the public relations brilliantly. I am committed to make this a *win-win situation, to keep our friendship intact,* to be positive to say and write only glowing things. . . . *Nobody ever needs to know anything other than positive things from either of us.* This all can work out! *You are still the only one who came to my hospital bed*—and I do remember. [Emphasis added]

81. As this letter indicates, Eisner attached great importance to his friendship with Ovitz and was willing to elevate his friendship with Ovitz over Disney's interests by cooperating in a sacrifice of the Company's interests to advance their collective public interest concerns and their avoidance of "embarrassment."

82. On or about October 16, 1996, Eisner sought to allay Ovitz's concern about one source of potential liability toward Disney. He wrote to Ovitz enclosing a letter that Eisner had written to Mr. Idei of Sony in which Eisner stated that Ovitz could negotiate with Sony for an employment position there and not fear any repercussion. In his letter, Eisner stated reassuringly to his friend: I am sure *we are now both protected 'every way to and from Sunday'.*" [Emphasis added.]

83. With the green light by Eisner, Sony turned on October 17, 1996, to its outside counsel, the New York law firm of Rosenman & Colin, LLP, to assist Sony in negotiating an employment agreement with Ovitz. The negotiations by Sony were conducted by five of the highest-ranking officials of SCA and Sony Japan, including: Idei, Sony Japan's Chairman; Tsunao Hashimoto, Sony Japan's Vice Chairman; Teruo Masaki, SCA's General Counsel; Marinus Henny, SCA's Executive Vice President and CFO; and Tamotsu Iba, the Executive Deputy President and CFO of Sony Japan and the representative of Sony Japan on the SCA Board.

84. Sony and Rosenman & Colin documents indicate that Ovitz and Sony were contemplating a five-year, $100 million contract. Ovitz was to lead Sony's entertainment business, but the negotiations failed.

85. When Ovitz's efforts to secure another position foundered, Eisner, who had originally sought to arrange Ovitz's exit on terms whereby Sony would effectively absorb the cost, capitulated to his friend's desire to leave, but without sacrificing any of the financial benefits of the OEA—the ideal solution from Ovitz's standpoint. On December 11, 1996, defendants Eisner, Litvack and Ovitz met at Eisner's apartment to finalize Ovitz's Non-Fault Termination from Disney. The next day, December 12, 1996, defendant Litvack sent a letter to Ovitz in which Litvack stated that, by "mutual agreement," (1) the term of Ovitz' employment under the OEA would end on January 31, 1997 and (2) "this letter will for all purposes of the Employment Agreement be given the same effect as though there had been a 'Non-Fault Termination,' and the Company will pay you, on or before February 5, 1997, all amounts due you under the Employment Agreement, including those under Section 11(c) thereof. In addition,

the stock options granted pursuant to Option A, will vest as of January 31, 1997 and will expire in accordance with their terms on September 30, 2002." Ovitz's receipt of a Non-Fault Termination would provide him with severance benefits worth $140 million. Ovitz's departure from Disney was publicly reported on December 12, 1996.

86. The parties apparently perceived a defect in the letter sent to Ovitz on December 12, 1996, as that letter was superseded by a December 27, 1996, letter from defendant Litvack to Ovitz. One apparent defect was the letter's choice of language—providing Ovitz with the benefits of a Non-Fault Termination "as though" there had been a Non-Fault Termination.

87. The December 27, 1996, letter said that (1) the term of Ovitz's employment with Disney would "end at the close of business today. Consequently, your signature confirms the end of your service as an officer, and your resignation as a director, of the Company and its affiliates;" (2) this letter will . . . be treated as a 'Non-Fault Termination' [and,] by mutual agreement, the total amount payable to you . . . is $38,888,230.77, net of withholding; [and] (3) ". . . the option to purchase 3,000,000 shares of [Disney] Common Stock granted to you pursuant to Option A . . . will vest as of today and will expire in accordance with its terms on September 30, 2002." Both Litvack and Ovitz signed the December 27, 1996, letter.

88. Consistent with Eisner's promise to his friend Ovitz that "no one needs to know," Disney has no record that at any point in time during the process described above, or afterwards, Eisner reported to the New Board or to any of its committees, either in writing or orally in a Board meeting, the process leading to Ovitz's departure and his receipt of a Non-Fault Termination. However, between December 12, 1996, when Ovitz's departure was publicly announced, and December 27, 1996, when he left, the Disney Board had ample opportunity to intervene and control this process, but did not. Instead, they left a conflicted Eisner with the task of ushering his friend out the door.

H. The Absence of An Affirmative Board Decision With Regard to Ovitz's Termination

89. According to Disney's Bylaws, the President of the Company may be removed only by the Board. The Bylaws state that in pertinent part that: "[a]ll officers of the corporation shall hold office until their successors are chosen and qualified, or until their earlier resignation or removal. Any officer elected by the Board of Directors may be removed at any time by the Board of Directors with or without cause." A Non-Fault Termination of Ovitz was the functional equivalent of his removal and needed Disney Board action and approval. Eisner had no authority to cause that result himself.

90. As represented by defendants herein to the Delaware Supreme Court in this case:

> the board retained the ability to determine whether or not Mr. Ovitz would leave under a fault or no-fault termination. There is no way, short of Mr. Ovitz's death, that Mr. Ovitz could part with all of the termination benefits unless the board of directors of Disney acted affirmatively. There had to be an affirmative action by the board of directors to enable Mr. Ovitz to depart with all of the benefits.

* * *

> number two; the company received assurance that he (Ovitz) would work for the company unless the board—unless the board determined otherwise during the five-year term of that agreement.

Transcript of Oral Argument, dated June 15, 1999, pages 24-29.

91. However, Ovitz did depart, with all of the termination benefits, without the new Board of Directors of Disney having acted affirmatively. A review of the documents produced by Disney in response to 8 Del. C. § 220 evidences no documents or decisions made by the New Board or any of its committee relating to Ovitz's receipt of a Non-Fault Termination.

92. The New Board, with knowledge that Eisner and Ovitz were working out arrangements for Ovitz's separation, made a tacit, knowing decision to stand aside and permit Eisner to make the decisions that the New Board was charged to make.

93. Each and every member of the New Board was aware that Eisner was negotiating Ovitz's separation from Disney and that, at least as of December 12, 1996, Disney had given Ovitz a Non-Fault Termination effective some time thereafter. The members of the New Board, however, adopted a supine attitude in acquiescing to the lopsided severance that the conflicted Eisner had negotiated with his friend.

94. The New Board, in gross dereliction of its duties and in bad faith, failed to obtain any information or investigate the options that Disney had at that juncture of its relationship with Ovitz. For example, despite Ovitz's failures as President, his refusal to learn his job and his efforts to seek other employment, the Board never examined into whether Ovitz could have been terminated for cause. Similarly, the New Board failed to inquire whether there were any grounds to let Ovitz depart under terms that included none or only some of the benefits provided by a Non-Fault Termination. Throughout the relevant period, the New Board did not seek nor did it receive any advice or recommendation from an expert on these issues.

95. Ovitz's separation from Disney was publicly reported and confirmed on December 12, 1996. There was, therefore, ample time and opportunity for the Disney Board to convene and consider the terms and conditions of Ovitz's separation from Disney even assuming that it was not informed of this matter by Eisner until December 12, 1996, at the latest. However, despite the huge costs to Disney of a Non-Fault Termination, and the plain requirement that the Board be involved, the New Board simply acquiesced in Eisner's willingness to accommodate Ovitz—without investigation, deliberation or even discussion about the respective rights and liabilities of Disney and Ovitz or the relative pros and cons of the course set by Eisner.

96. In fact, there was a second opportunity for the New Board to take affirmative steps when Litvack, acting at Eisner's behest, accelerated Ovitz's departure from January 31, 1997 to December 27, 1996, and accelerated the receipt of all of Ovitz's severance benefits to December 27, 1996. Yet, at this juncture as well, there is no evidence that the New Board took any action other than to abdicate to Eisner the decision to benefit his friend.

97. Moreover, notwithstanding the New Board's apparently passive and supine performance, the legal documentation relating to Ovitz's Non-Fault Termination signed on or about December 27, 1996, included a general release from all claims (the "Release") executed by Ovitz running to Disney and, inter alia, all of its officers

and directors, including all claims relating to or arising from the OEA, the Non-Fault Termination and his tenure with Disney. The Release conferred a tangible benefit on each of the members of the New Board.

I. Ovitz's Breaches of Fiduciary Duties In Connection With His Non-Fault Termination

98. Because Ovitz was an officer and a director of Disney until December 27, 1996, he was an officer and director when he joined forces with Eisner, who Ovitz knew had his own personal agenda, to arrange the payment to himself of the full benefits of a Non-Fault Termination. Accordingly, Ovitz was subject to all the fiduciary duties of an officer and director of Disney at all relevant times and breached those duties.

99. In addition, because Ovitz was a director during this latter period, he was fully aware that the New Board did not make any decisions or take any affirmative steps with respect to his receipt of a Non-Fault Termination. Furthermore, due to the circumstances of his departure and his relationship with Eisner, Ovitz was fully aware that Eisner's unilateral decision to grant him the benefits of a Non-Fault Termination was not based on business reasons. Rather, Eisner's decision was solely or primarily motivated by his desire to keep his friendship intact with Ovitz, appreciation of past acts of kindness (which Ovitz exploited) and by Eisner's motive to neutralize the "MDE embarrassment equation," as he put it in his October 9, 1996 letter to Ovitz.

100. As an officer and director of Disney, Ovitz was duty-bound to pursue departure from Disney only on terms that would be entirely fair to Disney and were consonant with the fiduciary duties of all Board members. By arranging, together with Eisner, the payment of full Non-Fault Termination benefits, Ovitz wrongfully and self-servingly failed in the performance of his duties to the Company.

J. The Magnitude of Ovitz's Severance Benefits at Disney's Expense

101. Because Ovitz's departure from his post as Disney's President was treated as a "Non-Fault Termination," the options to purchase three million shares of Disney common stock became immediately exercisable upon termination of his employment at Disney. Those options were priced at the market price of Disney common stock as of October 16, 1995 (approximately $57 per share). Based on Disney's closing stock price of $71.25 on December 27, 1996 (the date of Ovitz's official departure), the cash value of the options on that date exceeded $42 million. About $16 million of this amount was a product of the setting of the exercise price at the level of the market price two months preceding the date on which the OEA was actually executed, and then backdated.

102. The true value of Ovitz's severance package, however, cannot be calculated solely by determining the cash value of the stock options as if they were exercised on the date of Ovitz's departure. A more accurate approach to calculating the value of Ovitz's Disney stock options is to formulate a present value for those options pursuant to commonly-accepted valuation techniques, such as the Black-Scholes option pricing model. Employing reasonable assumptions, namely, a volatility of Disney stock of 22.5%, a risk-free rate of return of 6.8%, and quarterly dividends of $0.1325 per share, the value of Ovitz's stock options at the end of November 1996 was $101.5 million.

103. In addition to the enormous value of the stock options granted to Ovitz at the time of his departure from Disney, the Company paid him (a) a "Contract Termination Payment" of $10,000,000; and (b) a "Non-Fault Payment" equal to the present value of all base salary due to Ovitz through the end of the OEA on September 30, 2000, plus the present value of an assumed annual bonus of $7,500,000 for all fiscal years not completed at the time Ovitz left Disney.

104. As set forth above, Eisner and Litvack agreed with Ovitz that the then present value of the Non-Fault Payment was $38,869,000, net of withholdings. Accordingly, the total value of Ovitz's severance benefits was approximately $140 million, or about $10 million for each month of his employment at Disney.

105. At $140 million, the payments granted Ovitz upon departure amounted to approximately $0.20 per share of Disney common stock, as compared to Disney's first fiscal quarter 1997 EPS of $1.09. Moreover, the cash severance payment made to Ovitz alone amounted to approximately $0.03 per outstanding Disney share. That expense negatively impacted Disney's earnings for the first fiscal quarter of 1997.

PRE-SUIT DEMAND ON DISNEY'S BOARD OF DIRECTORS IS EXCUSED

106. Plaintiffs did not make pre-suit demand on the Disney Board to seek the relief sought in this complaint because such demand is excused for the following reasons:

A. A majority of the Board, at the time this action was commenced, consisted of members of both the Old Board and New Board. The members of the Old Board and New Board were grossly derelict in discharging their fiduciary obligations to Disney in connection with Ovitz's hiring and Ovitz's receipt of a Non-Fault Termination. The particularized allegations of this Complaint create the requisite reasonable doubt that the members of the Old Board and the New Board fulfilled their duty of care in hiring Ovitz and allowing him to depart from Disney with a Non-Fault Termination.

B. The members of the Compensation Committee and the Old Board were grossly negligent—to the point of recklessness and/or bad faith—in not taking readily available steps to ascertain the rough value of the payout to Ovitz if he were terminated without "fault." As set forth above, the members of the Old Board failed to heed "red flags" posted by Disney's staff about the magnitude and counter-productive nature of the stock option package which accompanied the OEA. Furthermore, Eisner was conflicted because of Ovitz's status as Eisner's "best friend" and Russell was conflicted because he was Eisner's personal lawyer and was paid $250,000 for "securing" Ovitz's services for the Company.

C. In addition, the members of the Compensation Committee and the Old Board abdicated their responsibilities by simply granting to Eisner a general authorization to proceed with and complete the agreement with Ovitz, without reserving to themselves the power to scrutinize and approve its final terms. As one of the results thereof, the OEA substantially deviated in Ovitz's favor from the general guidelines that the directors had approved. The directors knew that Eisner was not independent of Ovitz but failed to insulate him from the process or oversee his activities.

D. Eisner, Ovitz and Russell also had conflicts of interest in connection with the execution of the OEA.

E. Because the members of the Old Board violated their duties of care, good faith and loyalty in connection with the OEA, the execution of the OEA was not the product of properly informed business judgement, nor can defendants invoke the Business Judgement Rule to avoid judicial scrutiny of their actions for fairness. Pre-suit demand on defendants is, therefore, excused.

F. Similarly, the members of the New Board were grossly negligent—to the point of recklessness and/or bad faith—in connection with the termination of Ovitz's employment by Disney. As set forth in the preceding sections of this Complaint, the New Board abdicated its duties to decide whether Disney's President should be removed and whether he should be given the benefits of a Non-Fault Termination. They allowed Eisner, who they knew lacked independence from Ovitz, to arrange all aspects of Ovitz's removal. The New Board also made no effort whatsoever to inform itself about this important termination and about the severance payments, notwithstanding the tens of millions of dollars—aggregating $140 million in value—that Ovitz garnered for a brief and unproductive 14 months as an employee of Disney, despite ample opportunity to do so. The New Board's failure to convene and consider the terms of Ovitz's separation under circumstances where all Board members were aware of the negotiations between Eisner and Ovitz was reckless and unconscionable.

G. The OEA constituted a waste of Disney's assets. While the OEA may have induced Ovitz to join Disney, the terms of the OEA, with the accompanying stock option package, deprived Disney of any reasonable expectation that it would receive the benefit of its bargain—five years of productive service by Ovitz. No reasonable person, if fully informed and acting in his or her interest, would enter into such an agreement. Thus, demand is excused on this basis as well.

H. Furthermore, the Release executed by Ovitz running to the Director Defendants conferred a tangible benefit on each of the members of the New Board in connection with Ovitz's receipt of a Non-Fault Termination and provided each of them with a conflicting interest in responding to a demand.

FIRST CLAIM FOR RELIEF

107. Plaintiffs repeat and reallege each of the foregoing allegations as if fully set forth herein.

108. In allowing the OEA to be entered into without adequate investigation and consideration of all material information reasonable available to the Old Board, and without consulting any expert, the members of the Old Board breached their fiduciary duties of good faith and due care which they owed to Disney.

109. In working out and arranging the terms of the OEA, defendants Eisner and Russell, who lacked the requisite independence, violated their fiduciary duties of good faith and loyalty which they owed to Disney. The other members of the Old Board similarly violated their fiduciary duties by allowing the conflicted Eisner and Russell to arrange with Ovitz the terms on which he would be hired.

110. In negotiating, arranging and finalizing the terms of the OEA, defendant Ovitz violated his fiduciary duties of good faith and loyalty which he owed to Disney.

111. Ovitz and Eisner colluded with each other in causing the OEA to be signed and, as fiduciaries, acted unfairly and in bad faith in doing so. The other directors, by their knowing and wrongful inaction, failed to take such steps as would be necessary to afford this transaction the protection of the Business Judgment Rule and it is, therefore, subject to scrutiny for fairness. The OEA does not pass muster under that standard.

SECOND CLAIM FOR RELIEF

112. Plaintiffs repeat and reallege each of the foregoing allegations as if fully set forth herein.

113. The Old Board approved the OEA and thereby wasted Disney's assets in violation of its members' fiduciary duties of loyalty, good faith and due care. Among other things, the stock option and severance provisions in the OEA failed to secure Ovitz's full and undivided services for the entire contract term and even provided him with a disincentive to stay.

114. Defendant Ovitz wrongfully caused Disney to engage in Waste.

THIRD CLAIM FOR RELIEF

115. Plaintiffs repeat and reallege each of the foregoing allegations as if fully set forth herein.

116. In connection with the Non-Fault Termination received by Ovitz, the members of the New Board wrongfully acquiesced in Eisner's unilateral negotiations, entirely abdicating their duties and failing to inform themselves of all material information reasonably available to them, thereby violating their fiduciary duties of good faith and due care which they owed to Disney.

117. In pursuing and benefitting from the Non-Fault Termination, defendant Ovitz violated his fiduciary duties of loyalty and good faith which he owed to Disney.

118. In accommodating Ovitz's wish for a Non-Fault Termination, defendant Eisner was motivated by friendship and the desire to avoid personal embarrassment rather than undivided loyalty to Disney. Defendant Eisner also violated his fiduciary responsibilities in failing to take any steps to bring the matter of Ovitz's Non-Fault Termination to the New Board for its review, including consideration of the impact of Ovitz's failures in the performance of his duties. Eisner also, due to his conflicting motives, allowed Ovitz to exit the Company without attempting to rework Ovitz's departure in a manner which better served the Company's financial interests. Instead, the characterization of Ovitz's departure as a Non-Fault Termination, proceeding from Eisner's conflicted motives, represented a complete capitulation to Ovitz's position and utter sacrifice of corporate well-being. Defendant Eisner is therefore liable for breaching his duties of loyalty and good faith which he owed to Disney.

119. Ovitz and Eisner, with the active participation of Litvack, colluded with each other in causing the Non-Fault Termination to be granted and, as fiduciaries, acted unfairly and in bad faith in doing so. The other directors, by their knowing and wrongful inaction, failed to take such steps as would be necessary to afford this transaction the protection of the Business Judgment Rule and it is, therefore, subject to scrutiny for fairness. The granting of the Non-Fault Termination does not pass muster under that standard.

120. Furthermore, the actions and inaction of the New Board, ridden by due care violations and bad faith, are subject to scrutiny for fairness and defendants must bear the burden of demonstrating that Ovitz's departure was on terms that were fair to the Company. Such knowing cannot be made because the grant of the Non-Fault Termination represented a complete capitulation to Ovitz and total sacrifice of Disney's rights and best interests.

AS TO ALL CLAIMS

121. As a result of the foregoing, Disney has sustained damages and injuries and defendant Ovitz has justly profited.

122. Plaintiffs have no adequate remedy at law.

WHEREFORE, Plaintiffs demand judgment in their favor and in favor of Disney against all of the Director Defendants and Ovitz as follows:

A. Declaring that the Director Defendants and defendant Ovitz, individually and collectively, breached their fiduciary duties owed to Disney;

B. Directing the Director Defendants and Ovitz to account to Disney for all damages sustained by Disney as a result of the wrongs complained of herein;

C. Directing defendant Ovitz to account to Disney for all profits unlawfully obtained by him as a result of the wrongs complained of herein;

D. Rescinding all stock options granted to defendant Ovitz and not yet exercised;

E. Awarding pre-judgment and post-judgment interest to Disney at the maximum rate allowable by law;

F. Awarding plaintiffs the costs and disbursements of this action, including reasonable allowances for plaintiffs' attorneys' and experts' fees and expenses; and

G. Granting such other or further relief as may be just and proper under the circumstances.

ROSENTHAL, MONHAIT, GROSS & GODDESS, P.A.

By: Joseph A. Rosenthal by Carmella P. Keener
Suite 1401
919 North Market Street
Wilmington, DE 19801
(302) 656-4433

MILBERG WEISS BERSHAD
HYNES & LERACH LLP
Steven G. Schulman
U. Seth Ottensoser
One Pennsylvania Plaza
New York, NY 10119
(212) 594-5300

Plaintiffs' Lead Counsel

EMPLOYMENT AGREEMENT DATED AS OF OCTOBER 1, 1995 BETWEEN THE WALT DISNEY COMPANY AND MICHAEL S. OVITZ

Michael S. Ovitz ("Executive") and The Walt Disney Company, A Delaware corporation ("Company"), hereby agree as follows:

1. Term

The term of Executive's employment by Company under this Agreement shall commence on and as of October 1, 1995 and shall expire on September 30, 2000 (the "**Term**"), unless earlier terminated as hereinafter provided.

2. Title and Duties

During the Term, Executive shall be employed by Company as its President. As President, Executive shall report to Company's Chairman and Chief Executive Officer. Executive shall devote his full time and best efforts exclusively to the Company; *provided, however,* that the foregoing shall not preclude Executive from engaging in charitable and community affairs, managing his personal passive investments and continuing his current board membership with Ziff-Davis Holdings, Inc., provided that none of such activities or managing shall interfere with, or be inconsistent with, the performance of his duties hereunder. Executive shall perform such duties, which shall not be inconsistent with his position as President of Company, as are assigned to him from time to time by the Chairman, and Chief Executive Officer of Company, and any other duties undertaken or accepted by Executive. Company agrees to use its best efforts to cause Executive to be elected to the Board of Directors of Company (or its successor in interest), when a seat on the Board becomes available, and to nominate Executive as a member of the management slate at each annual meeting of stockholders during his employment hereunder at which Executive's director class comes up for election. Executive agrees to serve on the Board if elected.

3. Salary

Executive shall receive a salary of $1,000,000 per annum during the term hereof. Salary payments shall be made in equal installments in accordance with Company's then prevailing payroll policy.

4. Bonus

For each full year of the Term completed by Executive, Executive will be eligible for an annual discretionary bonus which will be determined by the Compensation Committee of the Board of Directors. Pursuant to Company's applicable bonus plan as in effect from time to time, such bonus may be determined according to criteria intended to qualify under Section 162(m) of the Internal Revenue Code, as amended (the "Code").

5. Stock Options

Executive shall be granted two stock options (individually, "Option A" and "Option B") to purchase an aggregate of 5,000,000 shares of common stock of Company pursuant to Company's 1990 Stock Incentive Plan and related rules or pursuant to a stock option plan hereinafter adopted by Company having terms no less favorable to Executive than the 1990 Stock Incentive Plan and related rules (the applicable plan and rules pursuant to which such option shall be granted being hereinafter referred to as the ("Plan") in accordance with, and subject to, the following:

Option A:

(a) The exercise price of Option A shall be equal to the fair market value (determined in accordance with the applicable provisions of the Plan) of Company's common stock on the date of grant, which date shall be October 16, 1995.

(b) Pursuant to Option A Executive shall have the right to purchase 3,000,000 shares, subject to the terms and conditions hereof and of the Plan, and such right shall vest in increments of 1,000,000 shares on September 30 of each year commencing September 30, 1998; *provided, however,* that, notwithstanding the foregoing, any portion of Option A scheduled to vest on a scheduled vesting date shall not vest on such scheduled vesting date (or at any time thereafter) if Executive's employment by Company pursuant to this Agreement shall have terminated for any reason whatsoever more than three months prior to such scheduled vesting date.

(c) In the event that Executive's employment shall be terminated and such termination shall constitute a Non-Fault Termination (as defined in subparagraph (d) below, then the vesting schedule of Option A shall be accelerated and Option A shall become immediately exercisable in its entirety upon such termination.

(d) Option A shall expire on the earlier of ten years from the date of grant or 24 months after termination of Executive's employment with Company; *provided, however,* that notwithstanding the foregoing, in the event that Executive's employment with Company shall be terminated without cause (i.e., in a manner which shall constitute a breach of this Agreement by Company), by reason of default or total and permanent disability pursuant to Section 11(a)(i) or (ii) hereof, or Executive shall validly terminate his employment pursuant to Section 12 hereof (any of the foregoing being herein referred to as a "Non-Fault Termination"), Option A shall expire on the later of September 30, 2002, or 24 months after the date of the Non-Fault Termination (but in no event later than ten years from the date of grant.)

(e) Except as expressly provided herein, Option A shall be subject to all of the standard terms and provisions of the Plan (i.e., those terms and provisions which are automatically applicable to any stock option granted under the Plan in the absence of special action or specification to the contrary with respect to such stock option by the Compensation Committee of the Board of Directors of the Company (which Committee currently administers the Plan)), including without limitation, such modifications and/or substitutions of the Plan and the options granted thereunder as are effected in connection with the acquisition by Company of Cap Cities/ABC, Inc.

Option B:

The terms and provisions of Option B shall be identical to the terms and provisions of Option A in all respects except as follows:

(f) Pursuant to Option B Executive shall have the right to purchase 2,000,000 shares of Company's common stock, subject to the terms and conditions hereof and of the Plan, and such right shall vest in increments of 1,000,000 shares on each of September 30, 2001 and September 30, 2002; *provided, however,* that notwithstanding the foregoing, any portion of Option B scheduled to vest on a scheduled vesting date shall not vest on such vesting date (or at any time thereafter) if Executive's employment with Company shall have terminated for any reason whatsoever more than three months prior to such scheduled vesting date.

(g) Notwithstanding any other term or provision of the Plan or this Agreement, under no circumstances shall Option B vest or become exercisable prior to October 1, 2000, and in the event that Executive's employment with the Company shall terminate prior to such date for any reason whatsoever, Option B and all rights and claims of any nature related thereto shall thereupon irrevocable terminate in their entirety without further action by any party; after such date Option B shall vest in accordance with its terms, if and only if, Executive shall have entered into, prior to the earlier of the first scheduled vesting date of Option B or the date of any event occurring on or after October 1, 2000 which would give rise to accelerated vesting if the conditions of this subparagraph were met, an agreement with Company (which shall be acceptable to Company in its sole and unfettered discretion or which shall have been entered into pursuant to a Qualifying Offer (as herein defined in Section 10 hereof) to continue his employment with Company until at least September 30, 2002; *provided, however,* that notwithstanding the foregoing, if Executive is actually employed by Company on a scheduled vesting date of Option B, the increment of Option B scheduled to vest on such date shall vest in accordance with its terms. . . .

10. Contract Termination Payment

In the event that Company shall not have made a Qualifying Offer (as hereinafter defined) to Executive by July 1, 2000, and no other agreement between Executive and Company relating to the extension of Executive's employment shall have been entered into by September 30, 2000, Executive shall be entitled to receive, after Executive's:

(a) having given Company written notice of its failure to deliver a Qualifying Offer; and

(b) not having received such Qualifying Offer from Company within five business days from the delivery of such notice to Company,

a contract termination payment of $10,000,000 (the "Termination Payment") from Company. Such Termination Payment shall be due by the earlier of 30 days after the date that such payment shall not be subject to Section 162(m) of the Code or four months after the end of the last fiscal year of the Company during which Executive was employed by the Company, but in no event shall such Termination Payment be due earlier than October 1, 2000, except as provided in Section 11(c) hereof. The term "Qualifying Offer" shall mean a written offer of employment to Executive which (i) shall be for a period of not less than five years from October 1, 2000, (ii) shall include the types of compensation contained in this Agreement, (iii) shall constitute a reasonable offer taking into account the compensation to Executive provided for in this Agreement, the Company's financial and operating performance during the term of this Agreement and any other then-current circumstances relevant to the determination of Executive's compensation by Company for the period specified in clause (i) above, (iv) shall not contain any terms or provisions which reduce Executive's title or duties as stated herein, and (vii) shall state that it is irrevocable for 30 days from the date of delivery thereof. Notwithstanding any other term or provision hereof, Executive shall be entitled to receive the Termination Payment in accordance with Section 11(c) hereof in the event of a Non-Fault Termination of Executive's employment for any reason other than death (it being understood that in the event of Executive's death prior to payment of the Termination Payment, Company shall have no obligation under any circumstances to make a Termination Payment to Executive's estate or any other person or entity).

In the event that the parties shall disagree as to whether or not an offer timely made by Company in accordance with the foregoing constitutes a Qualifying Offer, the parties shall submit such disagreement to arbitration by a qualified individual executive compensation expert of national reputation who shall not have had dealings with either party during the preceding five years. Upon failure to agree upon the selection of the arbitrator, each party shall submit a panel of three qualified arbitrators, the other party may strike two from the other's list, and the arbitrator shall be selected by lot from the remaining two names. The arbitrator shall have the authority only to determine (i) whether the matter is arbitrable under the conditions of this Agreement and (ii) whether or not the offer made by the Company is a Qualifying Offer.

11. Termination

(a) Company shall have the right to terminate Executive's employment with Company under the following circumstances:

(i) Upon death of Executive.

(ii) Upon notice from Company to Executive in the event of an illness or other disability which has totally and permanently incapacitated him from performing his duties for six consecutive months as determined in good faith by the Board of Directors.

(iii) For good cause (A) immediately upon notice from Company if Company shall reasonable determine that the conduct or cause specified in such notice is not curable; or (B) upon thirty days' notice from Company, if Company shall determine that the conduct or cause specified in such notice is curable, unless Executive has, within ten days after the date such notice has been given by Company, commenced in good faith to cure the conduct or cause specified in such notice and has completed such cure within 30 days following the date of such notice. Termination by Company of Executive's employment for "good cause" as used in this Agreement shall be limited to gross negligence or malfeasance by Executive in the performance of his duties under this Agreement or the voluntary resignation by Executive prior to expiration of the Term (other than pursuant to a valid termination of employment by Executive in accordance with Section 12 hereof) as an employee of Company without the prior written consent of Company.

(b) If Executive's employment is terminated pursuant to Section 11(a)(iii) above, Executive's rights and Company's obligations hereunder and under all stock options granted in accordance with this Agreement shall forthwith terminate in their entirety, except that, notwithstanding the foregoing, (i) the expiration date of any stock options granted in accordance with this Agreement shall be 30 days after the date of termination pursuant to Section 11 (a)(iii), and (ii) to the extent that any term or provision of this Agreement shall expressly state that any such right or obligation shall survive termination of the Agreement pursuant to Section 11(a)(iii) hereof, it shall so survive.

(c) If a Non-Fault Termination of Executive's employment with the Company shall occur, Executive or his estate shall be entitled to receive a lump sum payment equal to the sum of (x) the present value (based on Company's then current cost of borrowing for the remainder of the scheduled Term) of 100% of Executive's base salary for the balance of the term of this Agreement (the percentage of Executive's salary to be paid in such lump sum after such present value calculation being referred to herein as the "Present Value Percentage") and (y) of an amount equal to $7,500,000 multiplied by the product of (A) the Present Value Percentage (expressed as a decimal) and (B) the number of fiscal years of Company in the Term not yet completed at the time of termination. The sum of clauses (x) and (y) above is hereinafter referred to as the "Non-Fault Payment". In addition, in the event of a Non-Fault Termination for any reason other than death, Executive shall be entitled to receive the Termination Payment. Company may purchase insurance to cover all or any part of its obligations set forth in the preceding sentence, and Executive agrees to take a physical examination to facilitate the obtaining of such insurance. The Non-Fault Payment and Termination Payment (if applicable) shall be made to Executive (or to his estate, if applicable) not later than the earlier of (i) 30 days after the date that such payment shall not be subject to Section 162(m) of the Code, or (ii) four months after the end of the last fiscal year of Company during white Executive was employed by Company.

(d) Whenever compensation is payable to Executive hereunder during a time when he is partially or totally disabled and such disability would entitle him to disability income or to salary continuation payments from Company according to the terms of any plan now or hereafter provided by Company or according to any Company policy in effect at the time of such disability, the compensation payable to him hereunder shall be inclusive of any such disability income or salary continuation and shall not be in addition thereto. If disability income is payable directly to Executive by any insurance company under an insurance policy paid for by Company, the amounts paid to him by said insurance company shall be considered to be part of the payments to be made by Company to him pursuant to this Section 11(d) and shall not be in addition thereto.

12. Termination by Executive

Prior to the expiration of the Term, Executive shall have the right to terminate his employment under this Agreement upon 30 days' notice to Company given within 60 days following the occurrence of any of the following events, provided that Company shall have 20 days after the date such notice has been given to Company in which to cure the conduct or cause specified in such notice;

(a) Executive is not elected or retained in accordance with Section 2 hereof as President (reporting to Company's Chairman and Chief Executive Officer) and a director of the Company.

(b) Company shall assign duties to Executive hereunder which are materially inconsistent with his position as President.

(c) Company shall fail to grant Executive's stock options provided for herein (other than to the extent provided in the last paragraph of Section 5 hereof) or shall reduce his salary or shall deny Executive eligibility for annual discretionary bonuses, or Company shall fail to make any compensation payment required hereunder. . . .

IN WITNESS WHEREOF, the parties have executed this Agreement as of the date first above written.

THE WALT DISNEY COMPANY

Michael S. Ovitz
Michael S. Ovitz

By: *Michael D. Eisner*
Title: Chairman and Chief Executive Officer

Sample Charters, Bylaws, and Merger Agreement

Sample Charters

AMENDED AND RESTATED CERTIFICATE OF INCORPORATION OF ALPHABET INC.
a Delaware Corporation

Alphabet Inc., a corporation organized and existing under the laws of the State of Delaware (the "Corporation"), hereby certifies as follows:

A. The name of the Corporation is Alphabet Inc. The Corporation's original Certificate of Incorporation was filed with the Secretary of State of the State of Delaware on July 23, 2015.

B. This Amended and Restated Certificate of Incorporation was duly adopted in accordance with Sections 242, 245 and 228 (by written consent of the sole stockholder of the Corporation) of the General Corporation Law of the State of Delaware, and restates, integrates and further amends the provisions of the Corporation's Certificate of Incorporation.

C. The text of the Certificate of Incorporation of this Corporation is hereby amended and restated in its entirety, effective October 2, 2015, at 4:01 p.m., EDT, as set forth in Exhibit A attached hereto.

IN WITNESS WHEREOF, the Corporation has caused this Amended and Restated Certificate of Incorporation to be executed by the undersigned officer, thereunto duly authorized, this second day of October 2015.

ALPHABET INC.
a Delaware corporation

By:/s/ LARRY PAGE
Name: Larry Page
Title: Chief Executive Officer

EXHIBIT A

ARTICLE I

The name of this corporation is Alphabet Inc. (hereinafter, the "Corporation").

ARTICLE II

The address of the Corporation's registered office in the State of Delaware is 2711 Centerville Road, Suite 400, City of Wilmington, County of New Castle, Delaware 19808. The name of its registered agent at such address is Corporation Service Company.

ARTICLE III

The nature of the business or purposes to be conducted or promoted by the Corporation is to engage in any lawful act or activity for which corporations may be organized under the General Corporation Law of the State of Delaware.

ARTICLE IV

Section 1. Authorized Shares. This Corporation is authorized to issue nine billion (9,000,000,000) shares of Class A Common Stock, par value $0.001 per share (the "Class A Common Stock"), three billion (3,000,000,000) shares of Class B Common Stock, par value $0.001 per share (the "Class B Common Stock", and together with the Class A Common Stock, the "Common Stock"), three billion (3,000,000,000) shares of Class C Capital Stock, par value $0.001 per share (the "Class C Capital Stock"), and one hundred million (100,000,000) shares of Preferred Stock, par value $0.001 per share. The number of authorized shares of any class or classes of stock may be increased or decreased (but not below the number of shares thereof then outstanding) by the affirmative vote of the holders of at least a majority of the voting power of the issued and outstanding shares of Common Stock of the Corporation, voting together as a single class.

Section 2. Common Stock. A statement of the designations of each class of Common Stock and the powers, preferences and rights and qualifications, limitations or restrictions thereof is as follows:

(a) Voting Rights.

(i) Except as otherwise provided herein or by applicable law, the holders of shares of Class A Common Stock and Class B Common Stock shall at all times vote together as one class on all matters (including the election of directors) submitted to a vote or for the consent of the stockholders of the Corporation.

(ii) Each holder of shares of Class A Common Stock shall be entitled to one (1) vote for each share of Class A Common Stock held as of the applicable date on any matter that is submitted to a vote or for the consent of the stockholders of the Corporation.

(iii) Each holder of shares of Class B Common Stock shall be entitled to ten (10) votes for each share of Class B Common Stock held as of the applicable date on any matter that is submitted to a vote or for the consent of the stockholders of the Corporation.

(b) Dividends. Subject to the preferences applicable to any series of Preferred Stock, if any, outstanding at any time, the holders of Class A Common Stock and the holders of Class B Common Stock shall be entitled to share equally, on a per share basis, in such dividends and other distributions of cash, property or shares of stock of the Corporation as may be declared by the Board of Directors from time to time with respect to the Common Stock out of assets or funds of the Corporation legally available therefor; provided, however, that in the event that such dividend is paid in the form of shares of Common Stock or rights to acquire Common Stock, the holders of Class A Common Stock shall receive Class A Common Stock or rights to acquire Class A Common Stock, as the case may be, and the holders of Class B Common Stock shall receive Class B Common Stock or rights to acquire Class B Common Stock, as the case may be.

(c) Liquidation. Subject to the preferences applicable to any series of Preferred Stock, if any outstanding at any time, in the event of the voluntary or involuntary liquidation, dissolution, distribution of assets or winding up of the Corporation, the holders of Class A Common Stock and the holders of Class B Common Stock shall be entitled to share equally, on a per share basis, all assets of the Corporation of whatever kind available for distribution to the holders of Common Stock.

(d) Subdivision or Combinations. If the Corporation in any manner subdivides or combines the outstanding shares of one class of Common Stock, the outstanding shares of the other class of Common Stock will be subdivided or combined in the same manner.

(e) Equal Status. Except as expressly provided in this Article IV, Class A Common Stock and Class B Common Stock shall have the same rights and privileges and rank equally, share ratably and be identical in all respects as to all matters. Without limiting the generality of the foregoing, (i) in the event of a merger, consolidation or other business combination requiring the approval of the holders of the Corporation's capital stock entitled to vote thereon (whether or not the Corporation is the surviving entity), the holders of the Class A Common Stock shall have the right to receive, or the right to elect to receive, the same form of consideration, if any, as the holders of the Class B Common Stock and the holders of the Class A Common Stock shall have the right to receive, or the right to elect to receive, at least the same amount of consideration, if any, on a per share basis as the holders of the Class B Common Stock, and (ii) in the event of (x) any tender or exchange offer to acquire any shares of Common Stock by any third party pursuant to an agreement to which the Corporation is a party or (y) any tender or exchange offer by the Corporation to acquire any shares of Common Stock, pursuant to the terms of the applicable tender or exchange offer, the holders of the Class A Common Stock shall have the right to receive, or the right to elect to receive, the same form of consideration as the holders of the Class B Common Stock and the holders of the Class A Common Stock shall have the right to receive, or the right to elect to receive, at least the same amount of consideration on a per share basis as the holders of the Class B Common Stock.

(f) Conversion.

(i) As used in this Section 2(f), the following terms shall have the following meanings:

(1) "Founder" shall mean either Larry Page or Sergey Brin, each as a natural living person, and "Founders" shall mean both of them.

(2) "Class B Stockholder" shall mean (a) the Founders, (b) the registered holder of a share of Class B Common Stock of Google Inc. on July 6, 2004 (the "Effective Time"), (c) each natural person who Transferred shares of Class B Common Stock of Google Inc. (or securities convertible into or exchangeable for shares of Class B Common Stock of Google Inc.) prior to the Effective Time to a Permitted Entity that, as of the Effective Time, complies with the applicable exception for such Permitted Entity specified in Section 2(f)(iii)(2), and (d) the initial registered holder of any shares of Class B Common Stock of Google Inc. that were originally issued by the Corporation after the Effective Time.

(3) "Permitted Entity" shall mean, with respect to any individual Class B Stockholder, any trust, account, plan, corporation, partnership, or limited liability company specified in Section 2(f)(iii)(2) established by or for such individual Class B Stockholder, so long as such entity meets the requirements of the exception set forth in Section 2(f)(iii)(2) applicable to such entity.

(4) "Transfer" of a share of Class B Common Stock shall mean any sale, assignment, transfer, conveyance, hypothecation or other transfer or disposition of such share or any legal or beneficial interest in such share, whether or not for value and whether voluntary or involuntary or by operation of law. A "Transfer" shall also include, without limitation, a transfer of a share of Class B Common Stock to a broker or other nominee (regardless of whether or not there is a corresponding change in beneficial ownership), or the transfer of, or entering into a binding agreement with respect to, Voting Control over a share of Class B Common Stock by proxy

or otherwise; provided, however, that the following shall not be considered a "Transfer" within the meaning of this Section 2(f)(i)(4):

a) the granting of a proxy to officers or directors of the Corporation at the request of the Board of Directors of the Corporation in connection with actions to be taken at an annual or special meeting of stockholders;

b) entering into a voting trust, agreement or arrangement (with or without granting a proxy) solely with stockholders who are Class B Stockholders, that (A) is disclosed either in a Schedule 13D filed with the Securities and Exchange Commission or in writing to the Secretary of the Corporation, (B) either has a term not exceeding one (1) year or is terminable by the Class B Stockholder at any time and (C) does not involve any payment of cash, securities, property or other consideration to the Class B Stockholder other than the mutual promise to vote shares in a designated manner; or

c) the pledge of shares of Class B Common Stock by a Class B Stockholder that creates a mere security interest in such shares pursuant to a bona fide loan or indebtedness transaction so long as the Class B Stockholder continues to exercise Voting 5 Control over such pledged shares; provided, however, that a foreclosure on such shares of Class B Common Stock or other similar action by the pledgee shall constitute a "Transfer."

(5) "Voting Control" with respect to a share of Class B Common Stock shall mean the power (whether exclusive or shared) to vote or direct the voting of such share of Class B Common Stock by proxy, voting agreement or otherwise.

(ii) Each share of Class B Common Stock shall be convertible into one (1) fully paid and nonassessable share of Class A Common Stock at the option of the holder thereof at any time upon written notice to the transfer agent of the Corporation.

(iii) Each share of Class B Common Stock shall automatically, without any further action, convert into one (1) fully paid and nonassessable share of Class A Common Stock upon a Transfer of such share, other than a Transfer:

(1) from a Founder, or such Founder's Permitted Entities, to the other Founder, or such Founder's Permitted Entities.

(2) by a Class B Stockholder who is a natural person to any of the following Permitted Entities, and from any of the following Permitted Entities back to such Class B Stockholder and/or any other Permitted Entity established by or for such Class B Stockholder:

a) a trust for the benefit of such Class B Stockholder and for the benefit of no other person, provided such Transfer does not involve any payment of cash, securities, property or other consideration (other than an interest in such trust) to the Class B Stockholder and, provided, further, that in the event such Class B Stockholder is no longer the exclusive beneficiary of such trust, each share of Class B Common Stock then held by such trust shall automatically convert into one (1) fully paid and nonassessable share of Class A Common Stock;

b) a trust for the benefit of persons other than the Class B Stockholder so long as the Class B Stockholder has sole dispositive power and exclusive Voting Control with respect to the shares of Class B Common Stock held by such trust, provided such Transfer does not involve any payment of cash, securities, property or other consideration (other than an interest in such trust) to the Class B Stockholder, and, provided, further, that in the event the Class B Stockholder no longer has sole dispositive power and exclusive Voting Control with respect to the shares of Class B Common Stock held by such trust, each share of Class B Common Stock then held by such trust shall automatically convert into one (1) fully paid and nonassessable share of Class A Common Stock;

c) a trust under the terms of which such Class B Stockholder has retained a "qualified interest" within the meaning of §2702(b)(1) of the Code and/or a reversionary interest so long as the Class B Stockholder has sole dispositive power and exclusive Voting Control with respect to the shares of Class B Common Stock held by such trust; provided, however, that in the event the Class B Stockholder no longer has sole dispositive power and exclusive Voting Control with respect to the shares of Class B Common Stock held 6 by such trust, each share of Class B Common Stock then held by such trust shall automatically convert into one (1) fully paid and nonassessable share of Class A Common Stock;

d) an Individual Retirement Account, as defined in Section 408(a) of the Internal Revenue Code, or a pension, profit sharing, stock bonus or other type of plan or trust of which such Class B Stockholder is a participant or beneficiary and which satisfies the requirements for qualification under Section 401 of the Internal Revenue Code; provided that in each case such Class B Stockholder has sole dispositive power and exclusive Voting Control with respect to the shares of Class B Common Stock held in such account, plan or trust, and provided, further, that in the event the Class B Stockholder no longer has sole dispositive power and exclusive Voting Control with respect to the shares of Class B Common Stock held by such account, plan or trust, each share of Class B Common Stock then held by such trust shall automatically convert into one (1) fully paid and nonassessable share of Class A Common Stock;

e) a corporation in which such Class B Stockholder directly, or indirectly through one or more Permitted Entities, owns shares with sufficient Voting Control in the corporation, or otherwise has legally enforceable rights, such that the Class B Stockholder retains sole dispositive power and exclusive Voting Control with respect to the shares of Class B Common Stock held by such corporation; provided that in the event the Class B Stockholder no longer owns sufficient shares or has sufficient legally enforceable rights to enable the Class B Stockholder to retain sole dispositive power and exclusive Voting Control with respect to the shares of Class B Common Stock held by such corporation, each share of Class B Common Stock then held by such corporation shall automatically convert into one (1) fully paid and nonassessable share of Class A Common Stock;

f) a partnership in which such Class B Stockholder directly, or indirectly through one or more Permitted Entities, owns partnership interests with sufficient Voting Control in the partnership, or otherwise has legally enforceable rights, such that the Class B Stockholder retains sole dispositive power and exclusive Voting Control with respect to the shares of Class B Common Stock held by such partnership; provided that in the event the Class B Stockholder no longer owns sufficient partnership interests or has sufficient legally enforceable rights to enable the Class B Stockholder to retain sole dispositive power and exclusive Voting Control with respect to the shares of Class B Common Stock held by such partnership, each share of Class B Common Stock then held by such partnership shall automatically convert into one (1) fully paid and nonassessable share of Class A Common Stock; or

g) a limited liability company in which such Class B Stockholder directly, or indirectly through one or more Permitted Entities, owns membership interests with sufficient Voting Control in the limited liability company, or otherwise has legally enforceable rights, such that the Class B Stockholder retains sole dispositive power and exclusive Voting Control with respect to the shares of Class B Common Stock held by such limited liability company; provided that in the event the Class B Stockholder no longer owns sufficient membership interests or has sufficient legally enforceable rights to enable the Class B Stockholder to retain sole dispositive power and exclusive Voting Control with respect to the shares of Class B Common Stock held by such limited liability company, each share of Class B 7 Common Stock then held by such limited liability company shall automatically convert into one (1) fully paid and nonassessable share of Class A Common Stock.

Notwithstanding the foregoing, if the shares of Class B Common Stock held by the Permitted Entity of a Class B Stockholder would constitute stock of a "controlled corporation" (as defined in Section 2036(b)(2) of the Code) upon the death of such Class B Stockholder, and the Transfer of shares Class B Common Stock by such Class B Stockholder to the Permitted Entity did not involve a bona fide sale for an adequate and full consideration in money or money's worth (as contemplated by Section 2036(a) of the Code), then such shares will not automatically convert to Class A Common Stock if the Class B Stockholder does not directly or indirectly retain Voting Control over such shares until such time as the shares of Class B Common Stock would no longer constitute stock of a "controlled corporation" pursuant to the Code upon the death of such Class B Stockholder (such time is referred to as the "Voting Shift"). If the Class B Stockholder does not, within five (5) business days following the mailing of the Corporation's proxy statement for the first annual or special meeting of stockholders following the Voting Shift, directly or indirectly through one or more Permitted Entities assume sole dispositive power and exclusive Voting Control with respect to such shares of Class B Common Stock, each such share of Class B Common Stock shall automatically convert into one (1) fully paid and nonassessable share of Class A Common Stock.

(3) by a Class B Stockholder that is a partnership, or a nominee for a partnership, which partnership beneficially held more than five percent (5%) of the total outstanding shares of Class B Common Stock as of the Effective Time, to any person or entity that, at the Effective Time, was a partner of such partnership pro rata in accordance with their ownership interests in the partnership and the terms of any applicable partnership or similar agreement binding the partnership at the Effective Time, and any further Transfer(s) by any such partner that is a partnership or limited liability company to any person or entity that was at such time a partner or member of such partnership or limited liability company pro rata in accordance with their ownership interests in the partnership or limited liability company and the terms of any applicable partnership or similar agreement binding the partnership or limited liability company at the Effective Time. All shares of Class B Common Stock held by affiliated entities shall be aggregated together for the purposes of determining the satisfaction of such five percent (5%) threshold.

(4) by a Class B Stockholder that is a limited liability company, or a nominee for a limited liability company, which limited liability company beneficially held more than five percent (5%) of the total outstanding shares of Class B Common Stock as of the Effective Time, to any person or entity that, at the Effective Time, was a member of such limited liability company pro rata in accordance with their ownership interests in the company and the terms of any applicable agreement binding the company and its members at the Effective Time, and any further Transfer(s) by any such member that is a partnership or limited liability company to any person or entity that was at such time a partner or member of such partnership or limited liability company pro rata in accordance with their ownership interests in the partnership or limited liability company and the terms of any applicable partnership or similar agreement binding the partnership or limited liability company. All shares of Class B Common Stock held by affiliated entities shall be aggregated together for the purposes of determining the satisfaction of such five percent (5%) threshold.

(iv) Each share of Class B Common Stock held of record by a Class B Stockholder who is a natural person, or by such Class B Stockholder's Permitted Entities, shall automatically, without any further action, convert into one (1) fully paid and nonassessable share of Class A Common Stock upon the death of such Class B Stockholder; provided, however, that:

(1) If a Founder, or such Founder's Permitted Entity (in either case, the "Transferring Founder") Transfers exclusive Voting Control (but not ownership) of shares of Class B Common Stock to the other Founder (the "Transferee Founder") which Transfer of Voting Control is contingent or effective upon the death of the Transferring Founder, then each share of Class B Common Stock that is the subject of such Transfer shall automatically convert into one (1) fully paid and nonassessable share of Class A Common Stock upon that date which is the earlier of: (a) nine (9) months after the date upon which the Transferring Founder died, or (b) the date upon which the Transferee Founder ceases to hold exclusive Voting Control over such shares of Class B Common Stock; provided, further, that if the Transferee Founder shall die within nine (9) months following the death of the Transferring Founder, then a trustee designated by the Transferee Founder and approved by the Board of Directors may exercise Voting Control over: (x) the Transferring Founders' shares of Class B Common Stock and, in such instance, each such share of Class B Common Stock shall automatically convert into one (1) fully paid and nonassessable share of Class A Common Stock upon that date which is the earlier of: (A) nine (9) months after the date upon which the Transferring Founder died, or (B) the date upon which such trustee ceases to hold exclusive Voting Control over such shares of Class B Common Stock; and (y) the Transferee Founders' shares of Class B Common Stock (or shares held by an entity of the type referred to in paragraph (2) below established by or for the Transferee Founder) and, in such instance, each such share of Class B Common Stock shall automatically convert into one (1) fully paid and nonassessable share of Class A Common Stock upon that date which is the earlier of: (A) nine (9) months after the date upon which the Transferee Founder died, or (B) the date upon which such trustee ceases to hold exclusive Voting Control over such shares of Class B Common Stock; and

(2) If both Founders die simultaneously, a trustee designated by the Founders and approved by the Board of Directors may exercise Voting Control over the Founders' shares of Class B Common Stock and, in such instance, each such share of Class B Common Stock shall automatically convert into one (1) fully paid and nonassessable share of Class A Common Stock upon that date which is the earlier of: (a) nine (9) months after the date upon which both Founders died, or (b) the date upon which such trustee ceases to hold exclusive Voting Control over such shares of Class B Common Stock.

(v) The Corporation may, from time to time, establish such policies and procedures relating to the conversion of the Class B Common Stock to Class A Common Stock and the general administration of this dual class common stock structure, including the issuance of stock certificates with respect thereto, as it may deem necessary or advisable, and may request that holders of shares of Class B Common Stock furnish affidavits or other proof to the Corporation as it deems necessary to verify the ownership of Class B Common Stock and to confirm that a conversion to Class A Common Stock has not occurred. A determination by the Secretary of the Corporation that a Transfer results in a conversion to Class A Common Stock shall be conclusive.

(vi) In the event of a conversion of shares of Class B Common Stock to shares of Class A Common Stock pursuant to this Section 2, such conversion shall be deemed to have been made at the time that the Transfer of such shares occurred. Upon any conversion of Class B Common Stock to Class A Common Stock, all rights of the holder of shares of Class B Common Stock shall cease and the person or persons in whose names or names the certificate or certificates representing the shares of Class A Common Stock are to be issued shall be treated for all purposes as having become the record holder or holders of such shares of Class A Common Stock. Shares of Class B Common Stock that are converted into shares of Class A Common Stock as provided in this Section 2 shall be retired and may not be reissued.

(g) Reservation of Stock. The Corporation shall at all times reserve and keep available out of its authorized but unissued shares of Class A Common Stock, solely for the purpose of effecting the conversion of the shares of Class B Common Stock, such number of its shares of Class A Common Stock as shall from time to time be sufficient to effect the conversion of all outstanding shares of Class B Common Stock into shares of Class A Common Stock.

Section 3. Change in Control Transaction. The Corporation shall not consummate a Change in Control Transaction without first obtaining the affirmative vote, at a duly called annual or special meeting of the stockholders of the Corporation, of the holders of the greater of: (A) a majority of the voting power of the issued and outstanding shares of capital stock of the Corporation then entitled to vote thereon, voting together as a single class, and (B) sixty percent (60%) of the voting power of the shares of capital stock present in person or represented by proxy at the stockholder meeting called to consider the Change in Control Transaction and entitled to vote thereon, voting together as a single class. For the purposes of this section, a "Change in Control Transaction" means the occurrence of any of the following events:

(a) the sale, encumbrance or disposition (other than non-exclusive licenses in the ordinary course of business and the grant of security interests in the ordinary course of business) by the Corporation of all or substantially all of the Corporation's assets;

(b) the merger or consolidation of the Corporation with or into any other corporation or entity, other than a merger or consolidation which would result in the voting securities of the Corporation outstanding immediately prior thereto continuing to represent (either by remaining outstanding or by being converted into voting securities of the surviving entity or its parent) more than fifty percent (50%) of the total voting power represented by the voting securities of the Corporation or such surviving entity or its parent outstanding immediately after such merger or consolidation; or

(c) the issuance by the Corporation, in a transaction or series of related transactions, of voting securities representing more than two percent (2%) of the total voting power of the Corporation before such issuance, to any person or persons acting as a group as contemplated in Rule 13d-5(b) under the Securities Exchange Act of 1934 (or any successor provision) such that, following such transaction or related transactions, such person or group of persons would hold more than fifty percent (50%) of the total voting power of the Corporation, after giving effect to such issuance.

Section 4. Preferred Stock. The Board of Directors is authorized, subject to any limitations prescribed by law, to provide for the issuance of shares of Preferred Stock in series, and to establish from time to time the number of shares to be included in each such series, and to fix the designation, power, preferences, and rights of the shares of each such series and any qualifications, limitations or restrictions thereof. Except as otherwise required by law, holders of Common Stock shall not be entitled to vote on any amendment to this Certificate of Incorporation (including any certificate of designation filed with respect to any series of Preferred Stock) that relates solely to the terms of one or more outstanding series of Preferred Stock if the holders of such affected series are entitled, either separately or together as a class with the holders of one or more other such series, to vote thereon by law or pursuant to this Certificate of Incorporation (including any certificate of designation filed with respect to any series of Preferred Stock).

Section 5. Class C Capital Stock. A statement of the designation of the Class C Capital Stock and the powers, preferences and rights and qualifications, limitations or restrictions thereof is as follows:

(a) Voting. Except as otherwise required by applicable law, shares of Class C Capital Stock shall have no voting power and the holders thereof, as such, shall not be entitled to vote on any matter that is submitted to a vote or for the consent of the stockholders of the Corporation.

(b) Dividends. Subject to the preferences applicable to any series of Preferred Stock, if any, outstanding at any time, the holders of Class C Capital Stock shall be entitled to receive, on a per share basis, the same form and amount of dividends and other distributions of cash, property or shares of stock of the Corporation as may be declared by the Board of Directors from time to time with respect to shares of the Common Stock out of assets or funds of the Corporation legally available therefor; provided, however, that in the event that such dividend is paid in the form of shares of Common Stock or rights to acquire Common Stock, the holders of Class C Capital Stock shall receive Class C Capital Stock or rights to acquire Class C Capital Stock, as the case may be.

(c) Conversion upon Liquidation. Immediately prior to the earlier of (i) any distribution of assets of the Corporation to the holders of the Common Stock in connection with a voluntary or involuntary liquidation, dissolution, distribution of assets or winding up of the Corporation pursuant to Section 2(c) or (ii) any record date established to determine the holders of capital stock of the Corporation entitled to receive such distribution of assets, each outstanding share of the Class C Capital Stock shall automatically, without any further action, convert into and become one (1) fully paid and nonassessable share of Class A Common Stock. The Corporation shall at all times reserve and keep available out of its authorized but unissued shares of Class A Common Stock, solely for the purpose of effecting the conversion of the shares of Class C Capital Stock pursuant to this Section 5(c), such number of its shares of Class A Common Stock as shall from time to time be sufficient to effect the conversion of all outstanding shares of Class C Capital Stock into shares of Class A Common Stock.

(d) Subdivision or Combinations. If the Corporation in any manner subdivides or combines the outstanding shares of any class of Common Stock, the outstanding 11 shares of the Class C Capital Stock will be subdivided or combined in the same manner. The Corporation shall not subdivide or combine the outstanding shares of the Class C Capital Stock unless a subdivision or combination is made in the same manner with respect to each class of Common Stock.

(e) Equal Status. Except as expressly provided in this Article IV, Class C Capital Stock shall have the same rights and privileges and rank equally, share ratably and be identical in all respects to the Common Stock as to all matters. Without limiting the generality of the foregoing, (i) in the event of a merger, consolidation or other business combination of the Corporation requiring the approval of the holders of the Corporation's capital stock entitled to vote thereon (whether or not the Corporation is the surviving entity), the holders of the Class C Capital Stock shall receive the same amount and form of consideration, if any, on a per share basis as the consideration, if any, received by holders of the Class A Common Stock in connection with such merger, consolidation or combination (provided that if holders of Class A Common Stock are entitled to make an election as to the amount or form of consideration such holders shall receive in any such merger, consolidation or combination with respect to their shares of Class A Common Stock, the holders of Class C Capital Stock shall be entitled to make the same election as to their shares of Class C Capital Stock), and (ii) in the event of (x) any tender or exchange offer to acquire any shares of Common Stock by any third party pursuant to an agreement to which the Corporation is a party or (y) any tender or exchange offer by the Corporation to acquire any shares of Common Stock, pursuant to the terms of the applicable tender or exchange offer, the holders of the Class C Capital Stock shall receive the same amount and form of consideration on a per share basis as the holders of the Class A Common Stock (provided that if holders of Class A Common Stock are entitled to make an election as to the amount or form of consideration such holders shall receive in any such tender or exchange offer with respect to their shares of Class A Common Stock, the holders of Class C Capital Stock shall be entitled to make the same election as to their shares of Class C Capital Stock).

ARTICLE V

The Corporation is to have perpetual existence.

ARTICLE VI

Section 1. The business and affairs of the Corporation shall be managed by or under the direction of the Board of Directors. In addition to the powers and authority expressly conferred upon them by statute or by this Certificate of Incorporation or the Bylaws of the Corporation, the directors are hereby empowered to exercise all such powers and do all such acts and things as may be exercised or done by the Corporation.

Section 2. In furtherance and not in limitation of the powers conferred by statute, the Board of Directors is expressly authorized to adopt, alter, amend or repeal the Bylaws of the Corporation. The affirmative vote of at least a majority of the Board of Directors then in office shall be required in order for the Board of Directors to adopt, amend, alter or repeal the Corporation's Bylaws. The Corporation's Bylaws may also be adopted, amended, altered or repealed by the stockholders of the Corporation. Notwithstanding the above or any other provision of this Certificate of Incorporation, the Bylaws of the Corporation may not be 12 amended, altered or repealed except in accordance with Article X of the Bylaws. No Bylaw hereafter legally adopted, amended, altered or repealed shall invalidate any prior act of the directors or officers of the Corporation that would have been valid if such Bylaw had not been adopted, amended, altered or repealed.

Section 3.

(a) If, at any time during which shares of capital stock of the Corporation are listed for trading on either The Nasdaq National Market ("Nasdaq") or the New York Stock Exchange ("NYSE"), holders of the requisite voting power under the then-applicable Nasdaq or NYSE listing standards notify the Corporation in writing of their election to cause the Corporation to rely upon the applicable "controlled company" exemptions (the "Controlled Company Exemption") to the corporate governance rules and requirements of the Nasdaq or the NYSE (the "Exchange Governance Rules"), the Corporation shall call a special meeting of the stockholders to consider whether to approve the election to be held within ninety (90) days of written notice of such election (or, if the next succeeding annual meeting of stockholders will be held within ninety (90) days of written notice of such election, the Corporation shall include a proposal to the same effect to be considered at such annual meeting). The Corporation shall not elect to rely upon the Controlled Company Exemption until such time as the Corporation shall have received the approval from holders of at least sixty-six and two thirds percent (66 2/3%) of the voting power of the issued and outstanding shares of capital stock of the Corporation at such annual or special meeting.

(b) In the event such approval is obtained, for so long as shares of the capital stock of the Corporation are listed on either the Nasdaq or the NYSE and the Corporation remains eligible for the Controlled Company Exemption under the requirements of the applicable Exchange Governance Rules, then the

Board of Directors shall be constituted such that (i) a majority of the directors on the Board of Directors shall be Outside Directors (as defined below), and (ii) the Corporation's compensation committee and the governance and nominating committee (or such committees serving similar functions as the Board of Directors of the Corporation shall constitute from time to time) shall consist of at least two (2) members of the Board of Directors and shall be composed entirely of Outside Directors. In the event the number of Outside Directors serving on the Board of Directors constitutes less than a majority of the directors on the Board of Directors as a result of the death, resignation or removal of an Outside Director, then the Board of Directors may continue to properly exercise its powers and no action of the Board of Directors shall be so invalidated, provided, that the Board of Directors shall promptly take such action as is necessary to appoint new Outside Director(s) to the Board of Directors.

(c) An "Outside Director" shall mean a director who, currently and for any of the past three years, is and was not an officer of the Corporation (other than service as the chairman of the Board of Directors) or a parent or subsidiary of the Corporation and is not and was not otherwise employed by the corporation or a parent or subsidiary of the Corporation.

Section 4. The chairman of the Board of Directors shall be an Outside Director (as defined above) and shall not hold any other office of the Corporation unless the appointment of the chairman is approved by two-thirds of the members of the Board of Directors then in office, 13 provided, however, that if there is no chief executive officer or president of the Corporation as a result of the death, resignation or removal of such officer, then the chairman of the Board of Directors may also serve in an interim capacity as the chief executive officer of the Corporation until the Board shall appoint a new chief executive officer.

Section 5. The Board of Directors of the Corporation shall establish an audit committee whose principal purpose will be to oversee the Corporation's and its subsidiaries' accounting and financial reporting processes, internal systems of control, independent auditor relationships and audits of consolidated financial statements of the Corporation and its subsidiaries. The audit committee will also determine the appointment of the independent auditors of the Corporation and any change in such appointment and ensure the independence of the Corporation's auditors. In addition, the audit committee will assume such other duties and responsibilities delegated to it by the Board of Directors and specified for it under applicable law and Exchange Governance Rules.

Section 6. The Board of Directors of the Corporation shall establish a corporate governance and nominating committee whose principal duties will be to assist the Board of Directors by identifying individuals qualified to become members of the Board of Directors consistent with criteria approved by the Board of Directors, to recommend to the Board of Directors for its approval the slate of nominees to be proposed by the Board of Directors to the stockholders for election to the Board of Directors, to develop and recommend to the Board of

Directors the governance principles applicable to the Corporation, as well as such other duties and responsibilities delegated to it by the Board of Directors and specified for it under applicable law and Exchange Governance Rules. In the event the corporate governance and nominating committee will not be recommending a then incumbent director for inclusion in the slate of nominees to be proposed by the Board of Directors to the stockholders for election to the Board of Directors, and provided such incumbent director has not notified the committee that he or she will be resigning or that he or she does not intend to stand for re-election to the Board of Directors, then, in the case of an election to be held at an annual meeting of stockholders, the corporate governance and nominating committee will recommend the slate of nominees to the Board of Directors at least thirty (30) days prior to the latest date required by the provisions of Sections 2.14 (advance notice of stockholder business) and 2.15 (advance notice of director nominations) of the Bylaws of the Corporation (as such provisions may be amended from time to time) for stockholders to submit nominations for directors at such annual meeting, or in the case of an election to be held at a special meeting of stockholders, at least ten (10) days prior to the latest date required by the provisions of Sections 2.14 and 2.15 of the Bylaws for stockholders to submit nominations for directors at such special meeting.

Section 7. The Board of Directors of the Corporation shall establish a compensation committee whose principal duties will be to review employee compensation policies and programs as well as the compensation of the chief executive officer and other executive officers of the Corporation, to recommend to the Board of Directors a compensation program for outside members of the Board of Directors, as well as such other duties and responsibilities delegated to it by the Board of Directors and specified for it under applicable law and Exchange Governance Rules.

Section 8. Elections of directors need not be by written ballot unless the Bylaws of the Corporation shall so provide.

Section 9. No stockholder will be permitted to cumulate votes at any election of directors.

Section 10. The number of directors that constitute the whole Board of Directors shall be fixed exclusively in the manner designated in the Bylaws of the Corporation.

ARTICLE VII

Section 1. To the fullest extent permitted by the General Corporation Law of Delaware as the same exists or as may hereafter be amended, a director of the Corporation shall not be personally liable to the Corporation or its stockholders for monetary damages for breach of fiduciary duty as a director. If the General Corporation Law of Delaware is amended to authorize corporate action further eliminating or limiting the personal liability of directors, then the liability of a director of the Corporation shall be eliminated to the fullest extent permitted by the General Corporation Law of Delaware, as so amended.

Section 2. The Corporation may indemnify to the fullest extent permitted by law any person made or threatened to be made a party to an action or proceeding, whether criminal, civil, administrative or investigative, by reason of the fact that he, she, his or her testator or intestate is or was a director, officer, employee or agent at the request of the Corporation or any predecessor to the Corporation or serves or served at any other enterprise as a director, officer, employee or agent at the request of the Corporation or any predecessor to the Corporation.

Section 3. Neither any amendment or repeal of any Section of this Article VII, nor the adoption of any provision of this Certificate of Incorporation inconsistent with this Article VII, shall eliminate or reduce the effect of this Article VII, in respect of any matter occurring, or any action or proceeding accruing or arising or that, but for this Article VII, would accrue or arise, prior to such amendment, repeal or adoption of an inconsistent provision.

ARTICLE VIII

Meetings of stockholders may be held within or without the State of Delaware, as the Bylaws may provide. The books of the Corporation may be kept (subject to any provision contained in the statutes) outside of the State of Delaware at such place or places as may be designated from time to time by the Board of Directors or in the Bylaws of the Corporation.

ARTICLE IX

Section 1. Except as otherwise provided for or fixed by or pursuant to the provisions of Article IV hereof in relation to the rights of the holders of Preferred Stock to elect directors under specified circumstances, newly created directorships resulting from any increase in the number of directors, created in accordance with the Bylaws of the Corporation, and any vacancies on the Board of Directors resulting from death, resignation, disqualification, removal or other cause shall be filled only by the affirmative vote of a majority of the remaining directors then in office, even though less than a quorum of the Board of Directors, or by a sole remaining director. Any director elected in accordance with the preceding sentence shall hold office until the next annual meeting of stockholders and until such director's successor shall have been elected and qualified, or until such director's earlier death, resignation or removal. No decrease in the number of directors constituting the Board of Directors shall shorten the term of any incumbent director.

Section 2. Any director or the entire Board of Directors may be removed from office at any time, with or without cause, by the affirmative vote of the holders of at least a majority of the voting power of the issued and outstanding shares of capital stock of the Corporation then entitled to vote in the election of directors.

ARTICLE X

Advance notice of new business and stockholder nominations for the election of directors shall be given in the manner and to the extent provided in the Bylaws of the Corporation.

ARTICLE XI

Section 1. Unless otherwise required by law, special meetings of the stockholders of the Corporation, for any purpose or purposes, may be called only by (i) the Board of Directors of the Corporation, (ii) the Chairman of the Board of Directors of the Corporation, (iii) the Chief Executive Officer (or, in the absence of a Chief Executive Officer, the President) of the Corporation, or (iv) a holder, or group of holders, of Common Stock holding more than twenty percent (20%) of the total voting power of the outstanding shares of capital stock of the Corporation then entitled to vote.

Section 2. Any action required or permitted to be taken by the stockholders of the Corporation must be effected at a duly called annual or special meeting of stockholders of the Corporation and may not be effected by any consent in writing by such stockholders.

ARTICLE XII

The Corporation reserves the right to amend or repeal any provision contained in this Certificate of Incorporation in the manner prescribed by the laws of the State of Delaware and all rights conferred upon stockholders are granted subject to this reservation; <u>provided</u>, <u>however</u>, that notwithstanding any other provision of this Certificate of Incorporation, or any provision of law that might otherwise permit a lesser vote or no vote, but in addition to any vote of the holders of any class or series of the stock of the Corporation, and, as applicable, such other approvals of the Board of Directors of the Corporation, as are required by law or by this Certificate of Incorporation: (i) the unanimous consent of Board of Directors then in office, and the affirmative vote of the holders at least a majority of the voting power of the issued and outstanding shares of capital stock of the Corporation then entitled to vote, shall be required to amend or repeal Article IV, Section 2, Article IV, Section 5 or this clause (i) of Article XII; (ii) the affirmative vote of the holders of the greater of: (A) a majority of the voting power of the issued and outstanding shares of capital stock of the Corporation then entitled to vote thereon, or (B) sixty percent (60%) of the voting power of the shares of capital stock present in person or represented by proxy at the stockholder meeting and entitled to vote thereon, shall be required to amend or repeal Article IV, Section 3 or this clause (ii) of Article XII; (iii) the consent of a 16 majority of the members of the Board then in office, and the affirmative vote of the holders at least sixty-six and two-thirds percent (66 2/3%) of the voting power of the issued and outstanding shares of capital stock of the Corporation then entitled to vote shall be required to amend or repeal Article IV, Section 4 and Article XI or this clause (iii) of Article XII; (iv) the unanimous consent of the Board of Directors then in office and the consent of at least sixty-six and two-thirds percent (66 2/3%) of the voting power of the issued and outstanding shares of capital stock of the Corporation shall be required to amend or repeal Article VI, Section 3, 5, 6 or 7 or this clause (iv) of Article XII; and (v) the consent of at least two-thirds of the members of the Board of Directors then in office and the affirmative vote of the holders of at least a majority of the voting power of the issued and outstanding shares of capital stock of the Corporation then entitled to vote shall be required to amend or repeal Article VI, Section 4 or this clause (v) of Article XII.

Articles of Incorporation* of The Plasti-Sheen Corporation

The undersigned, acting as an incorporator under the provisions of the Utopia Business Corporation Act (hereafter referred to as the "Act") adopts the following articles of incorporation:

Article I. Name

The name of this corporation is the Plasti-Sheen Corporation.

Article II. Period of Duration

The duration of this corporation is to be perpetual.

Article III. Purposes and Powers

Section 1. Purposes

The purposes for which this corporation is organized are as follows: to engage in the business of manufacturing and selling plastic and other merchandise of whatever kind; to engage in activities which are necessary, suitable or convenient for the accomplishment of that purpose or which are incidental thereto or connected therewith; and to conduct its business and carry out that purpose in any state, territory, district or possession of the United States or in any foreign country, to the extent not forbidden by law.

---

* Reprinted with permission from F.H. O'Neal and Robert B. Thompson, O'Neal & Thompson's Close Corporations and LLCs: Law and Practice (Rev. 3rd ed. 2004), published by Thomson/West. Toll-free 1-800-328-4880. —Eds.

Section 2. Powers

This corporation shall have all the powers specified in sections ________ of the Act.

Article IV. Stock Clauses

The aggregate number of shares which this corporation shall have authority to issue is 5,000 shares with a par value of $10 per share. The corporation shall not have the authority to issue shares in series.

Article V. Minimum Capital for Commencing Business

This corporation will not commence business until at least $1,000 has been received as consideration for the issuance of shares.

Article VI. Preemptive Rights and Related Matter

Section 1. Statement of Preemptive Rights

After the first 2,500 shares of this corporation's authorized shares have once been issued, each holder of shares in this corporation shall have the first right to purchase shares (and securities convertible into shares) of this corporation that may from time to time be issued (whether or not presently authorized), including shares from the treasury of this corporation, in the ratio that the number of shares he holds at the time of issue bears to the total number of shares outstanding exclusive of treasury shares. This right shall be deemed waived by any shareholder who does not exercise it and pay for the shares preempted within thirty days of receipt of a notice in writing from the corporation stating the prices, terms and conditions of the issue of shares and inviting him to exercise his preemptive rights.

Section 2. Prohibition of Issue of Shares for Other Than Money

Shares in this corporation shall not be issued for consideration other than money or in payment of a debt of the corporation, without the unanimous consent of all the shareholders.

Article VII. Provisions for Regulation of the Corporation's Internal Affairs

Section 1. Meetings of Shareholders and Directors

Meetings of the shareholders and directors of this corporation may be held either within or without the state of Utopia at such place or places as may from time to time be designated in the code of bylaws or by resolution of the board of directors.

Section 2. Code of Bylaws

The initial code of bylaws of this corporation shall be adopted by its board of directors. The power to amend or repeal the bylaws or to adopt a new code of bylaws shall be in the shareholders, but the affirmative vote of the holders of three-fourths of the shares outstanding shall be necessary to exercise that power. The code of bylaws may contain any provisions for the regulation and management of this corporation which are consistent with the Act and these articles of incorporation.

Section 3. Contracts in Which Directors Have an Interest

No contract or other transaction of this corporation with any person, firm or corporation or no contract or other transaction in which this corporation is interested shall be invalidated or affected by (a) the fact that one or more of the directors of this corporation is interested in or is a director or officer of another corporation, or (b) the fact that any director, individually or jointly with others, may be a party to or may be interested in the contract or transaction; and each person who may become a director of this corporation is hereby relieved from any liability that might otherwise arise by reason of his contracting with this corporation for the benefit of himself or any firm, or corporation in which he may be interested.

Section 4. Compensation of Directors

The board of directors shall have the authority to make provision for reasonable compensation to its members for their services as directors and to fix the basis and conditions upon which this compensation shall be paid. Any director may also serve the corporation in any other capacity and receive compensation therefrom in any form.

Article VIII. Registered Office and Registered Agent

The address of the initial registered office of this corporation is 491 First National Bank Building, Middletown, Utopia 01234. The name of the initial registered agent of this corporation at that address is J. Harvey Moore.

Article IX. Information on Directors

The initial board of directors shall consist of four members. The names and addresses of the persons who are to serve as directors until the first annual meeting of shareholders or until their successors be elected and qualify are as follows: J. Harvey Moore, 491 First National Bank Building, Middletown, Utopia 01234; Susan Edgar, 491 First National Bank Building, Middletown, Utopia 01234;

Kathleen M. Dodge, 491 First National Bank Building, Middletown, Utopia 01234; and Roger W. Oppenheim, 333 Second National Bank Building, Middletown, Utopia 01234.

Article X. Information on Incorporators

The name and address of the incorporator of this corporation is: James R. Beane, 491 First National Bank Building, Middletown, Utopia 01234.

In witness whereof, the undersigned, being the incorporator of this corporation, executes these articles of incorporation and certifies to the truth of the facts herein stated, this _______ day of _______, 20___.

____

James R. Beane

State of Utopia
County of Sighs

I, the undersigned, a notary public duly commissioned to take acknowledgments and administer oaths in the State of Utopia, certify that James R. Beane, being the incorporator referred to in the foregoing articles of incorporation, personally appeared before me and swore to the truth of the facts therein stated.

Witness my hand and notarial seal this _______ day of _______, 20___.

My commission expires _______________.

____

Lola Barco

Bylaws

Bylaws of the Plasti-Sheen Corporation*

Article I. Name, Registered Office, and Registered Agent

Section 1. Name

The name of this corporation is The Plasti-Sheen Corporation.

Section 2. Registered Office and Registered Agent

The address of the registered office of this corporation is 491 First National Bank Building, Middletown, Utopia 01234. The name of the initial registered agent of this corporation at that address is J. Harvey Moore.

Article II. Seal and Fiscal Year

Section 1. Seal

The seal of this corporation shall have inscribed on it the name of this corporation, the date of its organization, and the words "Corporate Seal, State of Utopia."

Section 2. Fiscal Year

The fiscal year of this corporation shall begin on January 1 and end on December 31.

---

* Reprinted with permission from F.H. O'Neal and Robert B. Thompson, O'Neal & Thompson's Close Corporations and LLCs: Law and Practice (Rev. 3rd ed. 2004), published by Thomson/West. Toll-free 1-800-328-4880. —Eds.

Article III. Shareholders' Meetings

Section 1. Place of Meetings

Meetings of the shareholders shall be held at the registered office of the corporation or at any other place (within or without the State of Utopia) the Board of Directors or shareholders may from time to time select.

Section 2. Annual Meeting

An annual meeting of the shareholders shall be held on the second Tuesday in March of each year, if not a legal holiday, and if a legal holiday, then on the next secular day following that is not a legal holiday, at ten o'clock a.m., and the shareholders shall elect a Board of Directors and transact other business. If an annual meeting has not been called and held within six months after the time designated for it, any shareholder may call it.

Section 3. Special Meetings

Special meetings of the shareholders may be called by the President, by a majority of the Board of Directors, or by the holders of one-tenth or more of the shares outstanding and entitled to vote.

Section 4. Notice of Meeting

A written or printed notice of each shareholders' meeting, stating the place, day and hour of the meeting, and in case of a special meeting the purpose or purposes of the meeting shall be given by the Secretary of the corporation or by the person authorized to call the meeting, to each shareholder of record entitled to vote at the meeting. This notice shall be sent at least ten days before the date named for the meeting (unless a greater period of notice is required by law in a particular case) to each shareholder by United States mail or by telegram, charges prepaid, to his address appearing on the books of the corporation.

Section 5. Waiver of Notice

A shareholder, either before or after a shareholders' meeting, may waive notice of the meeting; and his waiver shall be deemed the equivalent of giving notice. Attendance at a shareholders' meeting, either in person or by proxy, of a person entitled to notice shall constitute a waiver of notice of the meeting unless he attends for the express purpose of objecting to the transaction of business on the ground that the meeting was not lawfully called or convened.

Section 6. Voting Rights

Subject to the provisions of the law of the State of Utopia, each holder of capital stock in this corporation shall be entitled at each shareholders' meeting to one vote for every share of stock standing in his name on the books of the corporation, but, transferees of shares that are transferred on the books of the corporation within ten days next preceding the date set for a meeting shall not be entitled to notice of, or to vote at, the meeting.

Section 7. Proxies

A shareholder entitled to vote may vote in person or by proxy executed in writing by the shareholder or by his attorney-in-fact. A proxy shall not be valid after eleven months from the date of its execution unless a longer period is expressly stated in it.

Section 8. Quorum

The presence, in person or by proxy, of the holders of one-half or more of the shares outstanding and entitled to vote shall constitute a quorum at meetings of shareholders. At a duly organized meeting stockholders present can continue to do business until adjournment even though enough stockholders withdraw to leave less than a quorum.

Section 9. Adjournments

Any meeting of shareholders may be adjourned. Notice of the adjourned meeting or of the business to be transacted there, other than by announcement at the meeting at which the adjournment is taken, shall not be necessary. At an adjourned meeting at which a quorum is present or represented, any business may be transacted which could have been transacted at the meeting originally called.

Section 10. Informal Action by Shareholders

Any action that may be taken at a meeting of shareholders may be taken without a meeting if a consent in writing setting forth the action shall be signed by all of the shareholders entitled to vote on the action and shall be filed with the Secretary of the corporation. This consent shall have the same effect as a unanimous vote at a shareholders' meeting.

Article IV. The Board of Directors

Section 1. Number, Qualifications and Term of Office

The business and affairs of the corporation shall be managed by a board of four directors, none of whom need be resident in the State of Utopia or hold shares in this corporation. Each director, except one appointed to fill a vacancy, shall be elected to serve for the term of one year and until his successor shall be elected and shall qualify.

Section 2. Vacancies

Vacancies on the Board of Directors shall be filled by a majority of the remaining members of the board, though less than a quorum. Each director so selected shall serve until his successor is elected by the shareholders at the next annual meeting or at a special meeting earlier called for that purpose. The other members of the Board of Directors may declare vacant the office of a director who is convicted of a felony or who is declared of unsound mind by an order of court.

Section 3. Compensation

Directors shall not receive a salary for their services as directors; but, by resolution of the board, a fixed sum and expenses of attendance may be allowed for attendance at each meeting of the board. A director may serve the corporation in a capacity other than that of director and receive compensation for the services rendered in that other capacity.

Section 4. Removal

At a meeting of shareholders called for that purpose the entire Board of Directors or any individual director may be removed from office without assignment of cause by the vote of a majority of the shares entitled to vote at an election of directors.

Article V. Meetings of the Board

Section 1. Place of Meetings

The meetings of the Board of Directors may be held at the registered office of the corporation or (subject to Section 2 of Article V of these bylaws) at any place within or without the State of Utopia that a majority of the Board of Directors may from time to time by resolution appoint.

Section 2. Annual Meeting

The Board of Directors shall meet each year immediately after the annual meeting of the shareholders at the place that meeting has been held, to elect officers and consider other business.

Section 3. Special Meetings

Special meetings of the Board of Directors may be called at any time by the President or by any two members of the board.

Section 4. Notice of Meetings

Notice of the annual meeting of the Board of Directors need not be given. Written notice of each special meeting, setting forth the time and place of the meeting shall be given to each director at least twenty-four hours before the meeting. This notice may be given either personally, or by sending a copy of the notice through the United States mail or by telegram, charges prepaid, to the address of each director appearing on the books of the corporation.

Section 5. Waiver of Notice

A director may waive in writing notice of a special meeting of the board either before or after the meeting; and his waiver shall be deemed the equivalent of giving notice. Attendance of a director at a meeting shall constitute waiver of notice of that meeting unless he attends for the express purpose of objecting to the transaction of business because the meeting has not been lawfully called or convened.

Section 6. Quorum

At meetings of the Board of Directors a majority of the directors in office shall be necessary to constitute a quorum for the transaction of business. If a quorum is present, the acts of a majority of the directors in attendance shall be the acts of the board.

Section 7. Adjournment

A meeting of the Board of Directors may be adjourned. Notice of the adjourned meeting or of the business to be transacted there, other than by announcement at the meeting at which the adjournment is taken, shall not be necessary. At an adjourned meeting at which a quorum is present, any business may be transacted which could have been transacted at the meeting originally called.

Section 8. Informal Action

If all the directors severally or collectively consent in writing to any action taken or to be taken by the corporation and the writing or writings evidencing their consent are filed with the Secretary of the corporation, the action shall be as valid as though it had been authorized at a meeting of the board.

Article VI. Officers, Agents, and Employees

Section 1. Officers

The executive officers of the corporation shall be chosen by the Board of Directors and shall consist of a President, Vice-President, Secretary, and Treasurer. Other officers, assistant officers, agents and employees that the Board of Directors from time to time may deem necessary may be elected by the board or be appointed in a manner prescribed by the board.

Two or more offices may be held by the same person except that one person shall not at the same time hold the offices of President and Vice-President or the offices of President and Secretary. Officers shall hold office until their successors are chosen and have qualified, unless they are sooner removed from office as provided in these bylaws.

Section 2. Vacancies

When a vacancy occurs in one of the executive offices by death, resignation or otherwise, it shall be filled by the Board of Directors. The officer so selected shall hold office until his successor is chosen and qualified.

Section 3. Salaries

The Board of Directors shall fix the salaries of the officers of the corporation. The salaries of other agents and employees of the corporation may be fixed by the Board of Directors or by an officer to whom that function has been delegated by the board.

Section 4. Removal of Officers and Agents

An officer or agent of the corporation may be removed by a majority vote of the Board of Directors whenever in their judgment the best interests of the corporation will be served by the removal. The removal shall be without prejudice to the contract rights, if any, of the person so removed.

Section 5. President: Powers and Duties

The President shall be the chief executive officer of the corporation and shall have general supervision of the business of the corporation. He shall preside at all meetings of stockholders and directors and discharge the duties of a presiding officer, shall present at each annual meeting of the shareholders a report of the business of the corporation for the preceding fiscal year, and shall perform whatever other duties the Board of Directors may from time to time prescribe.

Section 6. Vice-President: Powers and Duties

The Vice-President shall, in the absence or disability of the President, perform the duties and exercise the powers of the President. He also shall perform whatever duties and have whatever powers the Board of Directors may from time to time assign him.

Section 7. Secretary: Powers and Duties

The Secretary shall attend all meetings of the directors and of the shareholders and shall keep or cause to be kept a true and complete record of the proceedings of those meetings. He shall keep the corporate seal of the corporation, and when directed by the Board of Directors, shall affix it to any instrument requiring it. He shall give, or cause to be given, notice of all meetings of the directors or of the shareholders and shall perform whatever additional duties the Board of Directors and the President may from time to time prescribe.

Section 8. Treasurer: Powers and Duties

The Treasurer shall have custody of corporate funds and securities. He shall keep full and accurate accounts of receipts and disbursements and shall deposit all corporate monies and other valuable effects in the name and to the credit of the corporation in a depositary or depositaries designated by the Board of Directors. He shall disburse the funds of the corporation and shall render to the President or the Board of Directors, whenever they may require it, an account of his transactions as Treasurer and of the financial condition of the corporation.

The Treasurer shall furnish a bond satisfactory to the Board of Directors.

Section 9. Delegation of Duties

Whenever an officer is absent or whenever for any reason the Board of Directors may deem it desirable, the board may delegate the powers and duties of an officer to any other officer or officers or to any director or directors.

Article VII. Share Certificates and the Transfer of Shares

Section 1. Share Certificates

The share certificates shall be in a form approved by the Board of Directors. Each certificate shall be signed by the President or the Vice-President and the Treasurer, and shall be stamped with the corporate seal.

Section 2. Registered Shareholders

The corporation shall be entitled to treat the holder of record of shares as the holder in fact and, except as otherwise provided by the laws of Utopia, shall not be bound to recognize any equitable or other claim to or interest in the shares.

Section 3. Transfers of Shares

Shares of the corporation shall only be transferred on its books upon the surrender to the corporation of the share certificates duly endorsed or accompanied by proper evidence of succession, assignment or authority to transfer. In that event, the surrendered certificates shall be canceled, new certificates issued to the person entitled to them, and the transaction recorded on the books of the corporation.

Section 4. Lost Certificates

The Board of Directors may direct a new certificate to be issued in place of a certificate alleged to have been destroyed or lost if the owner makes an affidavit that it is destroyed or lost. The board, in its discretion, may as a condition precedent to issuing the new certificate, require the owner to give the corporation a bond as indemnity against any claim that may be made against the corporation on the certificate allegedly destroyed or lost.

Article VIII. Special Corporate Acts

Section 1. Execution of Written Instruments

Contracts, deeds, documents, and instruments shall be executed by the President or the Vice-President under the seal of the corporation affixed and attested by the Secretary unless the Board of Directors shall in a particular situation designate another procedure for their execution.

Section 2. Signing of Checks and Notes

Checks, notes, drafts, and demands for money shall be signed by the officer or officers from time to time designated by the Board of Directors.

Section 3. Voting Shares Held in Other Corporations

In the absence of other arrangements by the Board of Directors, shares of stock issued by any other corporation and owned or controlled by this corporation may be voted at any shareholders' meeting of the other corporation by the President of this corporation or, if he is not present at the meeting, by the Vice-President of this corporation; and in the event neither the President or the Vice-President is to be present at a meeting, the shares may be voted by such person as the President and Secretary of the corporation shall by duly executed proxy designate to represent the corporation at the meeting.

Article IX. Amendments

The power to amend or repeal the bylaws or to adopt a new code of bylaws is reserved to the shareholders, the affirmative vote of holders of not less than three-fourths in number of the total number of shares issued and outstanding being necessary to exercise that power.

Merger Agreement

AGREEMENT AND PLAN OF MERGER

by and among

TIFFANY & CO.,

LVMH MOËT HENNESSY-LOUIS VUITTON SE,

BREAKFAST HOLDINGS ACQUISITION CORP.

and

BREAKFAST ACQUISITION CORP.

Dated as of November 24, 2019

TABLE OF CONTENTS

AGREEMENT AND PLAN OF MERGER

This AGREEMENT AND PLAN OF MERGER (this "Agreement"), dated as of November 24, 2019, is entered into by and among Tiffany & Co., a Delaware corporation (the "Company"), LVMH Moët Hennessy-Louis Vuitton SE, a *societas Europaea* (European company) organized under the laws of France ("Parent"), Breakfast Holdings Acquisition Corp., a Delaware corporation and a Wholly Owned Subsidiary of Parent ("Holding"), and Breakfast Acquisition Corp., a Delaware corporation and a Wholly Owned Subsidiary of Holding ("Merger Sub" and, together with the Company, Holding and Parent, the "Parties" and each, a "Party").

RECITALS

WHEREAS, the Parties intend to effect the acquisition of the Company by Parent through the merger of Merger Sub with and into the Company (the "Merger"), with the Company surviving the Merger as the surviving corporation, in accordance with the General Corporation Law of the State of Delaware (the "DGCL"), pursuant to which each share of the Company's common stock, par value $0.01 per share ("Share"), shall be converted into the right to receive $135.00 in cash, without interest and less any required withholding Taxes (such amount, the "Per Share Merger Consideration"), upon the terms and subject to the conditions set forth herein;

WHEREAS, the Company Board has (a) determined that it is in the best interests of the Company and its stockholders, and declared it advisable, to enter into this Agreement, (b) approved the execution, delivery and performance of this Agreement by the Company and the consummation of the transactions contemplated hereby, including the Merger, (c) directed that the adoption of this Agreement be submitted to a vote at the Company Stockholders Meeting and (d) resolved to recommend that this Agreement be adopted by the holders of Shares;

WHEREAS, the Parent Board has unanimously (a) determined that it is in the best corporate interests (i.e., "*intérêt social*," as defined under the laws of France applicable to Parent) of Parent (including the best interests of its stakeholders), and declared it advisable to enter into this Agreement and consummate the transactions contemplated hereby, including the Merger, and (b) approved the execution, delivery and performance of this Agreement by Parent and the consummation of the transactions contemplated hereby, including the Merger;

WHEREAS, the board of directors of Merger Sub has unanimously (a) determined that it is in the best interests of Merger Sub and its sole stockholder, and declared it advisable, to enter into this Agreement, (b) approved the execution, delivery and performance of this Agreement by Merger Sub and the consummation of the transactions contemplated by this Agreement, including the Merger and (c) resolved to recommend that this Agreement be adopted by Holding as the sole stockholder of Merger Sub;

WHEREAS, Holding, as the sole stockholder of Merger Sub, shall (a) approve the execution, delivery and performance by Merger Sub of this Agreement and the consummation of the transactions contemplated hereby, including the Merger, and (b) adopt this Agreement, in each case, substantially concurrently with (but deemed to occur a moment thereafter) the execution and delivery of this Agreement by each of the Parties; and

WHEREAS, the Parties desire to make certain representations, warranties, covenants and agreements in connection with this Agreement and the transactions contemplated by this Agreement.

NOW, THEREFORE, in consideration of the foregoing premises and the representations, warranties, covenants and agreements set forth in this Agreement, the Parties, intending to be legally bound, agree as follows:

ARTICLE I

DEFINITIONS; INTERPRETATION AND CONSTRUCTION

1.1 Definitions. For the purposes of this Agreement, except as otherwise specifically provided herein, the following terms have meanings set forth in this Section 1.1:

"Acquisition Proposal" means any (a) proposal, offer, inquiry or indication of interest (whether in writing or otherwise) relating to a merger, joint venture, partnership, consolidation, dissolution, liquidation, tender offer, recapitalization, reorganization, spin-off, share exchange, asset purchase, extraordinary dividend, business combination or similar transaction involving the Company or any of its Subsidiaries or (b) direct or indirect acquisition (whether by tender offer, share purchase, share exchange or other manner) in a single transaction or a series of related transactions by any Person or group (as defined under Section 13 of the Exchange Act), or any proposal, offer, inquiry or indication of interest with respect to any such direct or indirect acquisition, which, in each case of (a) or (b), if consummated would result in any Person or group (as defined under Section 13 of the Exchange Act) becoming the beneficial owner of, directly or indirectly, in one or a series of related transactions, fifteen percent (15%) or more (i) measured by either voting power or value, of the Shares and other equity and voting interests in the Company (or any class thereof) or (ii) of the revenue, net income, EBITDA or assets of the Company and its Subsidiaries (taken as a whole), in each case, other than the transactions contemplated by this Agreement.

[. . .] "Alternative Acquisition Agreement" means any Contract, letter of intent, memorandum of understanding, agreement in principle, term sheet, acquisition agreement, merger agreement, arrangement agreement, option agreement, joint venture agreement, partnership agreement, share purchase agreement, asset purchase agreement, share exchange agreement, lease agreement or other similar document, agreement or instrument (other than a Permitted Confidentiality Agreement) from any person (other than Parent and its Subsidiaries) relating to, providing for or contemplating, whether in a single transaction or series of related transactions, any Acquisition Proposal or requiring the Company (or that would require the Company) to abandon, terminate or fail to consummate the Merger or any of the other transactions contemplated by this Agreement.

[. . .] "Material Adverse Effect" means any Effect that, individually or in the aggregate with all other Effects, (a) has had or would be reasonably expected to have a material adverse effect on the business, condition (financial or otherwise), properties, assets, liabilities (contingent or otherwise), business operations or results of operations of the Company and its Subsidiaries, taken as a whole or (b) would or would reasonably be expected to prevent, materially delay or materially impair the ability of the Company to consummate the Merger or to perform any of its obligations under this Agreement by the Outside Date; provided, however, in the case of clause (a) no Effect arising out of or resulting from any of the following shall be deemed either alone or in combination to constitute a Material Adverse Effect: (i) changes or conditions generally affecting the industries in which the Company and any of its Subsidiaries operate, (ii) general economic or political conditions (including U.S.-China relations), commodity pricing or securities, credit, financial or other capital markets conditions, in each case in the United States or any foreign jurisdiction in which the Company or any of its Subsidiaries operate, (iii) any failure, in and of itself, by the Company to meet any internal or published projections, forecasts, estimates or predictions in respect of revenues, earnings or other financial or operating metrics for any period (it being understood that the facts or occurrences giving rise to or contributing to such failure may be deemed to constitute, or be taken into account in determining whether there has been, or is reasonably expected to be, a Material Adverse Effect, to the extent permitted by this definition), (iv) consequences resulting from the execution and delivery of this Agreement or the public announcement or pendency of the transactions contemplated hereby, including the impact thereof on the relationships, contractual or otherwise, of the Company or any of its Subsidiaries with employees, labor unions, customers, suppliers, designers, landlords or partners, (v) any change, in and of itself, in the market price or trading volume of the Company's securities or in its credit ratings (it being understood that the facts or occurrences giving rise to or contributing to such change may be deemed to constitute, or be taken into account in determining whether there has been, or is reasonably expected to be, a Material Adverse Effect, to the extent permitted by this definition), (vi) any change in Law applicable to the Company's business or GAAP (or authoritative interpretation thereof), (vii) geopolitical conditions, the outbreak or escalation of hostilities (including the Hong Kong protests and the "Yellow Vest" movement), any acts of war (whether or not declared), sabotage (including cyberattacks) or terrorism, or any escalation or worsening of any such acts of hostilities, war, sabotage or terrorism threatened or underway as of the date of this Agreement, (viii) any hurricane, tornado, flood, earthquake or other natural disaster or (ix) any actions required to be taken or not taken by the Company or any of its Subsidiaries (other than the Company's obligations under the first sentence of Section 7.1(a)) pursuant to this Agreement or, with Parent's prior written consent, except, in the case of clauses (i), (ii), (vi), (vii) and (viii) to the extent such Effect has a materially disproportionate adverse effect on the Company and its Subsidiaries, taken as a whole, relative to others in the industries and geographical regions in which affected businesses of the Company and its Subsidiaries operate in respect of the business conducted in such industries and applicable geographical regions.

[. . .] "Requisite Company Vote" means the adoption of this Agreement by the holders of a majority of the outstanding Shares entitled to vote on such matter at the Company Stockholders Meeting.

[. . .] "Superior Proposal" means an unsolicited, bona fide written Acquisition Proposal (with all references to fifteen percent (15%) in the definition of Acquisition Proposal deemed to reference eighty and 1/10th percent (80.1%)) that the Company Board has determined in good faith (after consultation with a financial advisor (of nationally recognized reputation) and outside legal counsel), taking into account all financial, legal, regulatory and other aspects of such Acquisition Proposal and this Agreement, (a) to be reasonably likely to be consummated in accordance with its terms and (b) would result in a transaction more favorable to the stockholders of the Company (solely in their capacities as such) from a financial point of view than the transactions contemplated by this Agreement (after taking into account any revisions to the terms of this Agreement proposed by Parent pursuant to Section 7.2(d)(ii)); provided that such Acquisition Proposal was not obtained or made as a direct or indirect result of a breach of Section 7.2.

[. . .]

ARTICLE II

THE MERGER; CLOSING; EFFECTIVE TIME

2.1 The Merger. Upon the terms and subject to conditions set forth in this Agreement, and in accordance with the applicable provisions of the DGCL, at the Effective Time, Merger Sub shall be merged with and into the Company, whereupon the separate corporate existence of Merger Sub shall cease and the Company shall continue as the surviving corporation in the Merger (the "Surviving Corporation") and a Wholly Owned Subsidiary of Parent.

2.2 Closing. Subject to the provisions of this Agreement, the closing of the Merger (the "Closing") shall be effected by the electronic exchange of signatures by electronic transmission or, if such exchange is not practicable, at a Closing to be held at the offices of Skadden, Arps, Slate, Meagher & Flom LLP, 4 Times Square, New York, New York 10036 at 12:00 PM (Eastern Time) on the day no later than the fifth (5th) Business Day following the satisfaction or (to the extent permitted by applicable Law) waiver of the conditions set forth in Article VIII (other than those conditions that by their nature can only be satisfied by action taken at or immediately prior to the Closing, but subject to the satisfaction or (to the extent permitted by applicable Law) waiver of those conditions) or at such other date, time and place (or by means of remote communication) as the Company and Parent may agree in writing. The date on which the Closing occurs is referred to in this Agreement as the "Closing Date."

2.3 Effective Time. Upon the terms and subject to the conditions set forth in this Agreement, as soon as practicable on the Closing Date, the Parties shall (i) cause the Certificate of Merger to be duly executed and properly filed with the Secretary of State of the State of Delaware as provided under the DGCL and (ii) make any and all other filings, recordings or publications required to be made by the Parties under the DGCL in connection with the Merger. The Merger shall become effective at the Effective Time.

2.4 Effects of the Merger. The effects of the Merger shall be as provided in this Agreement and the applicable provisions of the DGCL. Without limiting the generality of the foregoing, and subject thereto, at the Effective Time all of the property, rights, privileges, powers and franchises of each of the Company.

2.5 Capitalization Certificate. Five (5) Business Days prior to the Closing, the Company shall deliver a certificate in the form set forth in Section 2.5 of the Company Disclosure Letter, signed on behalf of the Company by an executive officer of the Company certifying as true, as of such date, the number of (i) outstanding Shares, (ii) Shares underlying Company Options, (iii) Shares with respect to Company PSUs and (iv) Shares with respect to Company RSUs.

ARTICLE III

CERTIFICATE OF INCORPORATION AND BYLAWS; DIRECTORS AND OFFICERS OF THE SURVIVING CORPORATION

3.1 The Certificate of Incorporation of the Surviving Corporation. At the Effective Time, by virtue of the Merger, the Company Charter shall be amended and restated in its entirety to read as the certificate of incorporation of Merger Sub in effect immediately prior to the Effective Time (except (i) the Company's name shall not be amended, (ii) the provisions of the certificate of incorporation of Merger Sub relating to the incorporator of Merger Sub shall be omitted, and (iii) any provisions required to be included in the certificate of incorporation of the Surviving Corporation pursuant to Section 7.9 shall not be amended, altered or repealed), and as so amended shall be the certificate of incorporation of the Surviving Corporation until thereafter duly amended, restated or amended and restated as provided therein or by applicable Law.

3.2 The Bylaws of the Surviving Corporation. At the Effective Time, the Company Bylaws shall be amended and restated in their entirety to read as the bylaws of Merger Sub in effect immediately prior to the Effective Time (except (i) the name of the Company shall remain "Tiffany & Co.", and (ii) any provisions required to be included in the Bylaws of the Surviving Corporation pursuant to Section 7.9 shall not be amended, altered or repealed) and as so amended shall be the Bylaws of the Surviving Corporation until thereafter amended, restated or amended and restated as provided therein, the Company Charter or by applicable Law.

3.3 Directors of the Surviving Corporation. Subject to applicable Law, the Parties shall take all actions necessary so that the board of directors of Merger Sub immediately prior to the Effective Time shall, from and after the Effective Time, be the initial directors of the Surviving Corporation, each to hold office until his or her successor has been duly elected or appointed and qualified or until his or her earlier death, resignation, incapacity or removal, as the case may be.

3.4 Officers of the Surviving Corporation. Except as otherwise determined by Parent prior to the Effective Time, the officers of the Company immediately prior to the Effective Time shall, from and after the Effective Time, be the initial officers of the Surviving Corporation, each to hold office until his or her successor has been duly elected or appointed and qualified or until his or her earlier death, resignation, incapacity or removal, as the case may be.

ARTICLE IV

EFFECT OF THE MERGER ON CAPITAL STOCK; EXCHANGE OF CERTIFICATES

4.1 Effect of the Merger on Capital Stock. At the Effective Time, by virtue of the Merger and without any action on the part of any of the Parties or holders of any capital stock of the Company or on the part of the sole stockholder of Merger Sub:

(a) Merger Consideration. Subject to Section 4.2(g), each Eligible Share shall be automatically converted into the right to receive the Per Share Merger Consideration, shall be automatically cancelled and shall cease to exist, and each holder of Eligible Shares represented by a Certificate or Book-Entry Share shall cease to have any rights with respect thereto, except the right to receive the Per Share Merger Consideration in accordance with the terms of this Agreement.

(b) Treatment of Cancelled Shares. Each Share that is owned or held in treasury immediately prior to the Effective Time by the Company or any Wholly Owned Subsidiary of the Company and each Share that is owned immediately prior to the Effective Time by Parent or any Wholly Owned Subsidiary of Parent (including Holding and Merger Sub) shall be automatically cancelled without payment of any consideration therefor and shall cease to exist (collectively, the "Cancelled Shares").

(c) Merger Sub. Each share of common stock, par value $0.01 per share, of Merger Sub, issued and outstanding immediately prior to the Effective Time shall be converted into and become one validly issued, fully paid and nonassessable share of common stock, par value $0.01 per share, of the Surviving Corporation and, collectively, shall constitute the only outstanding shares of capital stock of the Surviving Corporation.

(d) Dissenting Shares. Notwithstanding anything in this Agreement to the contrary, Shares issued and outstanding immediately prior to the Effective Time (other than Cancelled Shares) and held by a holder of record who did not vote in favor of the adoption of this Agreement and is entitled to demand and validly demands appraisal of such Shares pursuant to, and complies in all respects with, Section 262 of the DGCL (any such shares meeting the requirements of this sentence, the "Dissenting Shares") shall not be converted into the right to receive Per Share Merger Consideration, but instead, at the Effective Time, shall be converted into the right to receive payment of such amounts that are payable in accordance with Section 262 of the DGCL (it being understood and acknowledged that at the Effective Time, such Dissenting Shares shall no longer be outstanding, shall automatically be cancelled and shall cease to exist, and such holder shall cease to have any rights with respect thereto, except the right to receive the fair value of such Dissenting Shares to the extent afforded by Section 262 of the DGCL); provided that if any such holder shall fail to perfect or otherwise shall waive, withdraw or lose the right to payment of the fair value of such Dissenting Shares under Section 262 of the DGCL, then the right of such holder to be paid the fair value of such holder's Dissenting Shares shall cease and such Dissenting Shares shall be deemed to have been converted as of the Effective Time into, and to have become exchangeable solely for the right to receive, without interest or duplication, the Per Share Merger Consideration in accordance with the terms of this Agreement. The Company shall give prompt written notice to Parent of any demands received by the Company for the appraisal of any Shares (or written threats thereof), of any withdrawals (purported or otherwise) of such demands and of any other documents or instruments served pursuant to the DGCL and received by the Company relating to Section 262 of the DGCL and any alleged dissenters' rights. Parent shall have the right to participate in and direct all negotiations and Proceedings with respect to such demands. Prior to the Effective Time, the Company shall not, without the prior written consent of Parent, and Parent shall not direct the Company to, without the written consent of the Company, make any payment or demand with respect to, or settle or compromise or offer to settle or compromise, any such payment or demand, or agree to do any of the foregoing.

[. . .]

ARTICLE V

REPRESENTATIONS AND WARRANTIES OF THE COMPANY

Except as set forth (i) in the Company Reports publicly filed at least two (2) Business Days prior to the date of this Agreement and made available to Parent (to the extent that the relevance of any such disclosure with respect to any section of this Agreement is reasonably apparent on its face), but excluding, in each case, any exhibits or schedules to the Company Reports or disclosures set forth or referenced under the captions "Risk Factors," "Forward-Looking Statements," "Quantitative and Qualitative Disclosures About Market Risk" or any similar section (it being understood that this clause (i) shall not apply to Section 5.1, Section 5.2, Section 5.3 or Section 5.4) or (ii) in the corresponding sections of the Company Disclosure Letter (it being agreed that disclosure of any item in any section or subsection of the Company Disclosure Letter shall be deemed disclosure with respect to any other section or subsection to which the relevance of such item is reasonably apparent from the face of such disclosure), the Company hereby represents and warrants to Parent, Holding and Merger Sub that:

[. . .]

5.10 Absence of Certain Changes.

(a) Since July 31, 2019, and through the date of this Agreement, except in connection with the execution and delivery of this Agreement and the consummation of the transactions contemplated by this Agreement, the Company and its Subsidiaries have conducted their respective businesses in all material respects in the Ordinary Course of Business.

(b) Since July 31, 2019, and through the date of this Agreement, there has not been any event, change, development, circumstance, fact or effect materially adverse to the financial condition, assets, liabilities (contingent or otherwise), business operations or results of operations of the Company and its Subsidiaries (taken as a whole) that, individually or in the aggregate, has had, or would reasonably be expected to have, a Material Adverse Effect.

(c) Since January 1, 2019, and through the date of this Agreement, the Company has not made, declared or paid any dividend or any other distribution, except for (i) $0.55 per Share in cash (declared on February 21, 2019), (ii) $0.58 per Share in cash (declared on June 4, 2019), (iii) $0.58 per Share in cash (declared on August 15, 2019) and (iv) $0.58 per Share in cash (declared on November 21, 2019).

[. . .]

ARTICLE VII
COVENANTS

7.1 Conduct of the Company.

(a) From and after the execution and delivery of this Agreement until the earlier to occur of the Effective Time or the termination of this Agreement in accordance with Article IX, the Company shall, and shall cause each of its Subsidiaries to, except as set forth in Section 7.1(a)(i)-(xxiv) of the Company Disclosure Letter, consented to in writing by Parent (such consent not to be unreasonably conditioned, withheld or delayed) or in compliance with a Company Material Contract, and except as otherwise specifically contemplated by this Agreement or as is required by a Governmental Entity or applicable Law, comply in all material respects with all applicable Laws and the material requirements of all Company Material Contracts, conduct its business in all material respects in the Ordinary Course of Business and, in connection therewith and to the extent consistent with the Ordinary Course of Business, shall use and cause each of its Subsidiaries to use their respective commercially reasonable efforts to preserve its and its Subsidiaries' business organizations substantially intact, maintain its and its Subsidiaries' existing relations and goodwill with Governmental Entities, suppliers, distributors, consultants, licensors, licensees, creditors, lessors, employees and others having significant business dealings with them, keep available the services of its and its Subsidiaries' officers and key employees, preserve and maintain the assets utilized in connection with the business of the Company and its Subsidiaries, maintain in effect all Governmental Authorizations and maintain all material Insurance Policies with reputable insurers; [. . .]

7.2 Acquisition Proposals; Change of Recommendation.

(a) No Solicitation. At all times during the period commencing with the execution and delivery of this Agreement and continuing until the earlier to occur of the termination of this Agreement pursuant to Article IX and the Effective Time, except as expressly permitted by this Section 7.2, the Company shall, and shall cause its Subsidiaries and the Company's directors, executive officers, or controlled Affiliates, and shall instruct its other Representatives to, immediately cease any discussions or negotiations with any Person conducted heretofore with respect to an Acquisition Proposal or proposal that would reasonably be expected to lead to an Acquisition Proposal, terminate access to any physical or electronic dataroom relating to the Company for any such Acquisition Proposal and request the prompt return or destruction of any confidential information provided to any third party in connection with an Acquisition Proposal made in the twelve (12) months prior to the date of this Agreement. From and after the date of this Agreement, the Company and its Subsidiaries and the Company's executive officers and directors shall use their reasonable best efforts to enforce any confidentiality provisions or provisions of similar effect to which the Company or any of its Subsidiaries is a party in connection with an Acquisition Proposal or of which the Company or any of its Subsidiaries is a beneficiary in connection with an Acquisition Proposal. Without prejudice to the foregoing sentences, at all times during the period commencing with the execution and delivery of this Agreement and continuing until the earlier to occur of the termination of this Agreement pursuant to Article IX and the Effective Time, except as expressly permitted by this Section 7.2, the Company shall not, and shall cause its Subsidiaries and its and their respective directors, executive officers or controlled Affiliates, and shall instruct any other Representatives and other employees not to, directly or indirectly:

(i) initiate, solicit, cause, propose or knowingly encourage, assist or facilitate any inquiry, proposal or offer with respect to, or the making, submission or announcement of any Acquisition Proposal or any inquiry, proposal or request for information that would reasonably be expected to lead to, or result in, an Acquisition Proposal;

(ii) engage in, conduct, continue, respond to or otherwise participate in any discussions or negotiations with respect to any Acquisition Proposal or any inquiry, proposal, offer or request for information that would reasonably be expected to lead to, or result in, an Acquisition Proposal;

(iii) disclose or furnish any non-public information or data concerning the Company or its Subsidiaries to any Person in connection with any Acquisition Proposal or any inquiry, proposal, offer or request for information that would reasonably be expected to lead to, or result in, an Acquisition Proposal;

(iv) afford access (other than customer access to retail locations in the Ordinary Course of Business and except pursuant to Section 220 of the DGCL) to the business, properties, assets, books or records of the Company or any of its Subsidiaries to any Person in connection with any Acquisition Proposal or any inquiry, proposal, offer or request for information that would reasonably be expected to lead to, or result in, an Acquisition Proposal;

(v) recommend, authorize, approve, adopt, endorse, declare advisable (or make any public statement recommending, authorizing, approving, adopting, endorsing, declaring advisable) or enter into any Alternative Acquisition Agreement;

(vi) approve any transaction, or any Person becoming an "interested stockholder", under Section 203 of the DGCL or approve any transaction, or any person becoming a "Substantial Stockholder", under Article IX of the Company Charter (in each case, other than with respect to this Agreement, the transactions contemplated hereby or Parent or its Affiliates);

(vii) otherwise knowingly facilitate any effort or attempt to make an Acquisition Proposal; or

(viii) resolve, agree, authorize or commit to do any of the foregoing.

(b) Exceptions. Notwithstanding anything to the contrary set forth in this Agreement, but, for the avoidance of doubt, subject to the provisions of Section 7.2(c), prior to the time, but not after, the Requisite Company Vote is obtained, in response to an unsolicited, bona fide written Acquisition Proposal that is made after the date of this Agreement (and in any event only if the Company did not violate this Section 7.2 with respect to such Person), the Company may (acting upon the recommendation of the Company Board), subject to compliance with this Section 7.2(b) and Section 7.2(c):

(i) provide information and data .concerning the Company and its Subsidiaries and access to the Company and its Subsidiaries' properties, books and records in response to a request to the Person who made such Acquisition Proposal; provided that substantially concurrently (but in any event within twenty-four (24) hours after the provision of such information or data), the Company shall make available to Parent any such information or data concerning the Company or its Subsidiaries that the Company provides to any such Person that was not previously made available to Parent and that, prior to furnishing any such information, the Company receives from the Person making such Acquisition Proposal an executed confidentiality agreement with terms that are at least as restrictive to the other party as the terms in the Confidentiality Agreement are on Parent (it being understood that such confidentiality agreement need not contain a standstill provision or otherwise prohibit the making or amending of an Acquisition Proposal, but shall not include any restrictions that would reasonably be expected to restrain the Company from satisfying its obligations contemplated by Section 7.2(c) or that would otherwise call for an exclusive right to negotiate with the Company prior to the termination of this Agreement) (any confidentiality agreement satisfying such criteria, a "Permitted Confidentiality Agreement"); and

(ii) engage or otherwise participate in any discussions or negotiations with any such Person regarding such unsolicited, bona fide written Acquisition Proposal, in each case of clause (i) and this clause (ii) of this Section 7.2(b), if, and only if, prior to taking any action described in clause (i) or this clause (ii) of this Section 7.2(b), the Company Board determines in good faith (after consultation with its legal advisor) that (A) based on the information then available and after consultation with a financial advisor of nationally recognized reputation that such Acquisition Proposal either constitutes a Superior Proposal or could reasonably be expected to result in a Superior Proposal and (B) based on the information then available, including the terms and conditions of such Acquisition Proposal and those of this Agreement, failure to take such action would be inconsistent with the directors' fiduciary duties under applicable Law; provided that prior to engaging or otherwise participating in any such discussions or negotiations with or furnishing any information to such Person, the Company gives Parent written notice in accordance with Section 7.2(c). The Company acknowledges and agrees that any action, that if taken by the Company would be a breach of this Section 7.2, is taken by a Representative of the Company, such action shall be deemed to constitute a breach of this Section 7.2 by the Company.

(c) Notice of Acquisition Proposals. The Company shall promptly (but, in any event, within twenty-four (24) hours) give notice to Parent if (i) any inquiries, proposals or offers with respect to an Acquisition Proposal or which could reasonably be expected to lead to an Acquisition Proposal are received by, (ii) any non-public information or data concerning the Company or its Subsidiaries is requested in connection with any Acquisition Proposal from, or (iii) any discussions or negotiations relating to an Acquisition Proposal are sought to be engaged in or continued with, it, its Subsidiaries or any of its or any of the Company's officers, directors and financial advisors, setting forth in such notice a summary of the material terms and conditions with respect to any such proposal or offer and a summary of the material content of any such inquiry, as applicable, and thereafter shall (1) keep Parent reasonably informed, on a prompt basis of the status and material terms and conditions of any such Acquisition Proposals or requests (including any amendments, modifications or supplements thereto, within twenty-four (24) hours following receipt thereof) and the status of any such discussions or negotiations and (2) provide Parent (or its outside legal counsel) with unredacted copies of all writings or media containing any terms or conditions of any proposals or proposed transaction agreements relating to any Acquisition Proposal as promptly as practicable (and in any event, within twenty-four (24) hours following the receipt or delivery thereof). The Company agrees that it shall not, and shall cause its Subsidiaries not to, enter into any confidentiality agreement subsequent to the date hereof that prohibits the Company from providing to Parent such material terms and conditions and other information.

(d) No Change of Recommendation.

(i) Except as permitted by Section 7.2(d)(ii) and Section 7.2(e), the Company Board, including any committee thereof, shall not:

(A) withhold, withdraw, qualify, amend or modify (or publicly propose or resolve to withhold, withdraw, qualify, amend or modify) the Company Recommendation with respect to the Merger in any manner adverse to Parent, Holding or Merger Sub;

(B) following the date any Acquisition Proposal or any material modification thereto is first made public or sent or given to stockholders of the Company, fail to issue a press release publicly reaffirming the Company Recommendation within five (5) Business Days (or, if earlier, prior to the Company Stockholders Meeting) following Parent's written request to do so (which request may only be made once with respect to any such Acquisition Proposal, except that Parent may make an additional request after any material change in the terms of such Acquisition Proposal);

(C) following the commencement of any tender or exchange offer relating to the securities of the Company, fail to issue a press release publicly announcing within ten (10) Business Days of such commencement that the Company recommends rejection of such tender or exchange offer and reaffirming the Company Recommendation;

(D) fail to include the Company Recommendation in the Proxy Statement or make or authorize the making of any public statement (oral or written) that has the substantive effect of a withdrawal, qualification or modification of the Company Recommendation;

(E) approve or recommend, or propose publicly to approve or recommend any Acquisition Proposal or proposal reasonably expected to lead to an Acquisition Proposal or approve or recommend, or publicly declare advisable or publicly propose to enter into, or enter into, any Alternative Acquisition Agreement;

(F) except as expressly permitted by, and after compliance with, Section 7.2(d)(ii) and Section 9.3(b), cause or permit the Company to enter into an Alternative Acquisition Agreement; or

(G) agree, authorize or commit to do any of the foregoing.

(ii) Notwithstanding anything to the contrary set forth in this Section 7.2, prior to the time the Requisite Company Vote is obtained, the Company Board may (A) effect a Change of Recommendation if (x)(1) a written Acquisition Proposal that the Company Board determines in good faith (after consultation with outside legal counsel) is bona fide and that did not arise from or in connection with a breach of the obligations set forth in this Section 7.2 is received by the Company after the date of this Agreement and is not withdrawn prior to the Change of Recommendation, and the Company Board determines in good faith, after consultation with outside legal counsel and a financial advisor of nationally recognized reputation, that such Acquisition Proposal constitutes a Superior Proposal or (2) an Intervening Event has occurred, and (y) the Company Board determines in good faith, after consultation with outside legal counsel and a financial advisor of nationally recognized reputation, that failure to effect a Change of Recommendation would reasonably be likely to be inconsistent with the directors' fiduciary duties under applicable Law or (B) take action to terminate this Agreement pursuant to, and in accordance with, Section 9.3(b) to enter into an Alternative Acquisition Agreement with respect to a written Acquisition Proposal that the Company Board determines in good faith (after consultation with outside legal counsel) is bona fide and that did not arise from or in connection with a breach of the obligations set forth in this Section 7.2 and that the Company Board determines in good faith, after consultation with outside legal counsel and a financial advisor of nationally recognized reputation, that (1) such Acquisition Proposal constitutes a Superior Proposal and (2) failure to effect a Change of Recommendation would reasonably be likely to be inconsistent with the directors' fiduciary duties under applicable Law; provided, however, that a Change of Recommendation or action to terminate this Agreement pursuant to Section 9.3(b) may not be made (i) unless the Company shall have complied in all material respects with its obligations under this Section 7.2 and (ii) unless and until the Company has given Parent written notice of such action four (4) Business Days in advance (an "Initial Notice"), setting forth in writing that the Company Board intends to consider whether to take such action, the reasons with respect thereto and (I) in the case of a Superior Proposal, the material terms and conditions of such Superior Proposal and (II) in the case of an Intervening Event, a reasonable description of such Intervening Event (it being agreed that, in each case, the delivery of such notice by the Company shall not constitute a Change of Recommendation). After giving such Initial Notice and prior to effecting such Change of Recommendation or taking such action to terminate the Agreement pursuant to Section 9.3(b), the Company shall, and shall instruct its legal and financial advisors to, negotiate in good faith with Parent and its Representatives throughout such four (4) Business Day period (to the extent Parent wishes to negotiate) to make such revisions to the terms of this Agreement such that the failure of the Company Board to effect a Change of Recommendation or to take such action to terminate this Agreement pursuant to Section 9.3(b) would no longer be reasonably be likely to be inconsistent with its fiduciary duties. At the end of the four (4) Business Day period, prior to taking action to effect a Change of Recommendation or taking action to terminate the Agreement pursuant to Section 9.3(b), the Company Board shall take into account any changes to the terms of this Agreement proposed by Parent in writing and any other information offered by Parent in writing in response to the Initial Notice, and shall have determined in good faith (after consultation with outside legal counsel) that (A) in the case of a Superior Proposal, the Superior Proposal continues to constitute a Superior Proposal, and (B) in the case of an Intervening Event, the failure to effect a Change of Recommendation in response to such Intervening Event would be inconsistent with the directors' fiduciary duties under applicable Law, in each case, if such changes offered in writing were to be given effect. Any material amendment to any Acquisition Proposal will be deemed to be a new Acquisition Proposal for purposes of this Section 7.2(d) except that the obligation to give advance written notice with respect thereto as set forth in this Section 7.2(d) shall be reduced to three (3) Business Days. [. . .]

(f) Standstill Provisions. Notwithstanding anything to the contrary set forth in this Agreement, the Company shall be permitted to terminate, amend or otherwise modify, waive or fail to enforce any provision of any such confidentiality, "standstill" or similar agreement if the Company Board determines in good faith, after consultation with its outside legal counsel, that failure to take such action would be inconsistent with the directors' fiduciary duties under applicable Law.

7.3 Proxy Statement; Other Regulatory Matters.

(a) Proxy Statement.

(i) As promptly as practicable after the date of this Agreement, but in any event within fifteen (15th) Business Days after the date of this Agreement, the Company shall prepare and file with the SEC, a proxy statement (as amended or supplemented, the "Proxy Statement"). Except under the circumstances expressly otherwise permitted by Section 7.2, the Proxy Statement shall include the Company Recommendation. Parent shall cooperate with the Company in the preparation of the Proxy Statement upon reasonable request of the Company and furnish all information concerning Parent as reasonably requested by the Company. [. . .]

7.4 Company Stockholders Meeting.

(a) The Company shall take all action necessary, in accordance with applicable Law and its Organizational Documents, to duly call, give notice of, convene and hold the Company Stockholders Meeting as promptly as practicable (but in no event later than thirty-five (35) days) after the Proxy Statement Clearance Date, to secure the Requisite Company Vote in respect of the approval of the Merger and the adoption of this Agreement, and to cause such vote to be taken. . . . .

(b) Subject to the Company Board's fiduciary obligations under applicable Law, the Company shall use its reasonable best efforts to obtain the Requisite Company Vote, including the solicitation of proxies therefor. [. . .]

ARTICLE VIII

CONDITIONS

8.1 Conditions to Each Party's Obligation to Effect the Merger. The respective obligation of each Party to effect the Merger is subject to the satisfaction or waiver (to the extent permitted by applicable Law) at or prior to the Effective Time of each of the following conditions:

(a) Company Stockholder Approval. The Requisite Company Vote shall have been obtained.

(b) Requisite Regulatory Approvals. (i) The waiting period (and any extension thereof) applicable to the Merger under the HSR Act shall have expired or been earlier terminated, (ii) CFIUS Approval shall have been obtained and (iii) the authorizations, consents, orders and approvals listed in Section 8.1(b) of the Company Disclosure Letter, shall have been obtained or terminated (all such authorizations, consents, orders and approvals and the lapse of all such waiting periods, including under the HSR Act, being the "Requisite Regulatory Approvals").

(c) No Legal Prohibition. (i) No Governmental Entity shall have enacted, issued, promulgated, enforced or entered any Law (whether temporary, preliminary or permanent) or temporary restraining order, preliminary or permanent injunction or other Order, in each case, that is in effect and enjoins, prevents or otherwise prohibits, materially restrains or materially impairs or makes unlawful consummation of the transactions contemplated by this Agreement (a "Legal Restraint") and (ii) no Governmental Entity shall have instituted any Proceeding (which remains pending at what would otherwise be the Closing Date) before any court or other Governmental Entity of competent jurisdiction seeking to temporarily or permanently impose a Legal Restraint.

8.2 Conditions to Obligations of Parent, Holding and Merger Sub. The obligations of Parent, Holding and Merger Sub to consummate the Merger are further subject to the satisfaction, at or prior to the Effective Time, of the following conditions (which may be waived, in whole or in part, to the extent permitted by Law, by Parent):

(a) Representations and Warranties. Each of the representations and warranties set forth in: (i) Section 5.1(a) (Organization, Good Standing and Qualification), Section 5.2(a) and Section 5.2(b)(iv) (Capital Structure) (except for *de minimis* inaccuracies; provided, however, that no inaccuracies in excess of an aggregate 6,000 Shares shall be deemed to be *de minimis*), Section 5.3 (Corporate Authority and Approval), Section 5.10(b) (Absence of Certain Changes), Section 5.20 (Takeover Statutes; No Rights Plan), Section 5.21 (Brokers and Finders) and Section 5.22 (Opinion of Financial Advisor) shall be true and correct in all respects as of the Closing Date as though made on and as of such date and time (except to the extent that any such representation and warranty expressly speaks as of a particular date or period of time, in which case such representation and warranty shall be so true and correct as of such particular date or period of time) and (ii) any other section of Article V shall be true and correct as of the Closing Date as though made on and as of such date and time (except to the extent that any such representation and warranty expressly speaks as of a particular date or period of time, in which case such representation and warranty shall be so true and correct as of such particular date or period of time) (without giving effect to any qualification by "materiality" or "Material Adverse Effect" and words of similar import set forth therein in the case of (ii)), except, in the case of this clause (ii), where the failure of any such representation or warranty to be so true and correct has not had and would not, individually or in the aggregate, reasonably be expected to have, a Material Adverse Effect.

(b) Performance of Obligations of the Company. The Company shall have performed in all material respects all obligations required to be performed by it under this Agreement at or prior to the Closing Date.

(c) Company Closing Certificate. Parent, Holding and Merger Sub shall have received (i) a certificate signed on behalf of the Company by an executive officer of the Company certifying that the conditions set forth in Section 8.2(a) and Section 8.2(b) above have been satisfied.

(d) No Material Adverse Effect. Since the date of this Agreement there shall not have occurred any Material Adverse Effect.

ARTICLE IX

TERMINATION

9.1 Termination by Mutual Written Consent. This Agreement may be terminated and the transactions contemplated by this Agreement may be abandoned at any time prior to the Effective Time, whether before or after the Requisite Company Vote has been obtained, by mutual written consent of the Company and Parent.

9.2 Termination by Either Parent or the Company. This Agreement may be terminated and the transactions contemplated by this Agreement may be abandoned at any time prior to the Effective Time, by either the Company or Parent if:

(a) the Merger shall not have been consummated on or before August 24, 2020 (the "Outside Date"); provided, however, that if the conditions to Closing set forth in Section 8.1(b) or Section 8.1(c) have not been satisfied or waived on or prior to such date but all other conditions to Closing set forth in Article VIII have been satisfied or waived (except for those conditions that by their nature are to be satisfied at the Closing), the Outside Date may be extended by either party to a date not beyond November 24, 2020 and such date, as so extended, shall be the "Outside Date"; provided, further, that the right to terminate this Agreement or extend the Outside Date pursuant to this Section 9.2(a) shall not be available to any Party that has breached in any material respect its obligations set forth in this Agreement in any manner that shall have been the principal cause of, or directly resulted in, the failure of the Closing to occur by the Outside Date

(b) the Requisite Company Vote shall not have been obtained at the Company Stockholders Meeting (or at any adjournment or postponement thereof, subject to Section 7.4) held in accordance with this Agreement; or

(c) any Legal Restraint having the effect set forth in Section 8.1(c) shall be in effect and shall have permanently restrained, enjoined or otherwise prohibited the consummation of the Merger and such Legal Restraint shall have become final and non-appealable; provided that the right to terminate this Agreement pursuant to this Section 9.2(c) shall not be available to any Party that has breached, or whose controlled Affiliate has breached, in any material respect its obligations set forth in this Agreement in any manner that shall have been the principal cause of, or directly resulted in the issuance of such final, non-appealable Legal Restraint.

9.3 Termination by the Company. This Agreement may be terminated and the transactions contemplated by this Agreement may be abandoned by the Company:

(a) if there has been a breach of any representation, warranty, covenant or agreement made by Parent, Holding or Merger Sub set forth in this Agreement, or if any representation or warranty of Parent, Holding or Merger Sub shall have become untrue following the date of this Agreement, in either case such that the conditions in Section 8.3(a) or Section 8.3(b) would not be satisfied (and such breach or failure to be true and correct is not curable prior to the Outside Date, or if curable prior to the Outside Date, has not been cured within the earlier of (i) twenty (20) days after the giving of notice thereof by the Company to Parent describing such breach or failure in reasonable detail and (ii) three (3) Business Days prior to the Outside Date); provided, however, that the right to terminate this Agreement pursuant to this Section 9.3(a) shall not be available to the Company if the Company is then in material breach of this Agreement or if any representation or warranty of the Company shall have become untrue, in either case, so as to result in the failure of any of the conditions set forth in Section 8.2(a) or Section 8.2(b); or

(b) prior to the time the Requisite Company Vote is obtained, to enter into an Alternative Acquisition Agreement in compliance with the terms of this Agreement, including Section 7.2(d)(ii); provided that the Company pays the Company Termination Fee to Parent prior to or concurrently with such termination in accordance with Section 9.5(b).

9.4 Termination by Parent. This Agreement may be terminated and the transactions contemplated by this Agreement may be abandoned by the Parent:

(a) if there has been a breach of any representation, warranty, covenant or agreement made by the Company set forth in this Agreement, or if any representation or warranty of the Company shall have become untrue following the date of this Agreement, in either case such that the conditions in Section 8.2(a) or Section 8.2(b) would not be satisfied (and such breach or failure to be true and correct is not curable prior to the Outside Date, or if curable prior to the Outside Date, has not been cured within the earlier of (i) twenty (20) days after the giving of notice thereof by Parent to the Company describing such breach or failure in reasonable detail and stating Parent's intention to terminate this Agreement and (ii) three (3) Business Days prior to the Outside Date); provided, however, that the right to terminate this Agreement pursuant to this Section 9.4(a) shall not be available to Parent if Parent, Holding or Merger Sub is then in material breach of this Agreement or any representation or warranty of Parent, Holding or Merger Sub shall have become untrue, in either case, so as to result in the failure of any of the conditions set forth in Section 8.3(a) or Section 8.3(b); or

(b) prior to the time the Requisite Company Vote is obtained, there shall have been a Change of Recommendation or if the Company or any of its Representatives shall have materially breached any of its obligations under Section 7.2.

9.5 Effect of Termination and Abandonment.

(a) In the event of the termination of this Agreement by either Parent or the Company as provided in Article IX, written notice thereof shall forthwith be given by the terminating Party to the other Party specifying the provision hereof pursuant to which such termination is made. Except to the extent provided in Section 9.5(b), in the event of termination of this Agreement in compliance with Article IX, this Agreement shall be terminated and this Agreement shall forthwith become void and have no effect, without any liability or obligation on the part of any Party (or any of its Representatives or Affiliates); provided, however, and notwithstanding anything to the contrary set forth in this Agreement, (i) no such termination shall relieve any Party from any liability or damages for Willful Breach of this Agreement prior to such termination or the requirement to make the payments set forth in Section 9.5(b) and (ii) the provisions set forth in this Section 9.5 and Article X shall survive the termination of this Agreement.

(b) The Company shall pay to Parent, by wire transfer of immediately available funds, a termination fee in the amount of $575,000,000 (the "Company Termination Fee") in the event that this Agreement is terminated:

(i) by either the Company or Parent pursuant to Section 9.2(a), or Section 9.2(b) or by Parent pursuant to Section 9.4(a) and, in each case;

(A) any Person shall have made an Acquisition Proposal to the Company or its stockholders (whether or not conditional or not withdrawn) or publicly announced an intention (whether or not conditional and whether or not withdrawn) to make an Acquisition Proposal with respect to the Company or any of its Subsidiaries, and

(B) within twelve (12) months after such termination, the Company enters into any Alternative Acquisition Agreement with respect to any Acquisition Proposal (with "fifty percent (50%)" being substituted in lieu of "fifteen percent (15%)" in each instance thereof in the definition of "Acquisition Proposal" for purposes of this Section 9.5(b)(i)(B)), then immediately prior to or concurrently with the occurrence of such entry into an Alternative Acquisition Agreement, or

(ii) by Parent pursuant to Section 9.4(b), then promptly, but in no event later than two (2) Business Days after the date of such termination; or

(iii) by the Company pursuant to Section 9.3(b), then simultaneously with, and as a condition to, the effectiveness of any such termination.

In no event shall the Company be required to pay the Company Termination Fee on more than one occasion.

(c) The Parties acknowledge that (i) the agreements set forth in this Section 9.5 are an integral part of the transactions contemplated by this Agreement, (ii) the Company Termination Fee is not a penalty, but is liquidated damages, in a reasonable amount that will compensate Parent, in the circumstances in which such fee is payable for the efforts and resources expended and opportunities foregone while negotiating this Agreement and in reliance on this Agreement and on the expectation of the consummation of the transactions contemplated hereby, which amount would otherwise be impossible to calculate with precision, and (iii) without this agreement, the Parties would not enter into this Agreement. Accordingly, if the Company fails to promptly pay the amount due pursuant to this Section 9.5, and, in order to obtain such payment, Parent commences a suit that results in a judgment against the Company for the fees set forth in this Section 9.5 or any portion of such fees, the Company shall pay to Parent its costs and expenses (including attorneys' fees) in connection with such suit, together with interest on the amount due pursuant to this Section 9.5 from the date such payment was required to be made until the date of payment at the annual rate of two percent (2%) *plus* the prime lending rate as published in The Wall Street Journal in effect on the date such payment was required to be made through the date of payment (or such lesser rate as is the maximum permitted by applicable Law). Notwithstanding any other provision of this Agreement, other than in the case of actual or intentional fraud or Willful Breach of this Agreement by the Company and subject to Section 10.6, the Parties agree that in the event this Agreement is terminated under circumstances where the Company Termination Fee is payable pursuant to this Section 9.5, the payment of the Company Termination Fee shall be the sole and exclusive monetary remedy of Parent, Holding and Merger Sub, with respect to this Agreement and the transactions contemplated by this Agreement, against the Company and its Subsidiaries and any of their respective directors, officers, employees and stockholders and Affiliates (the "Company Related Parties") for all losses and damages suffered as a result of the failure of the transactions contemplated by this Agreement to be consummated or for a breach or failure to perform hereunder or otherwise, and upon payment of the Company Termination Fee, other than in the case of actual or intentional fraud or any Willful Breach of this Agreement by the Company, none of the Company Related Parties shall have any further liability or obligation to or arising out of this Agreement or the transactions contemplated hereby.

Agency Law

Restatement (Third) of Agency (Selected Sections)

Chapter 1. Introductory Matters

TOPIC 1. DEFINITIONS AND TERMINOLOGY

§1.01. Agency Defined

Agency is the fiduciary relationship that arises when one person (a "principal") manifests assent to another person (an "agent") that the agent shall act on the principal's behalf and subject to the principal's control, and the agent manifests assent or otherwise consents so to act.

§1.02. Parties' Labeling and Popular Usage Not Controlling

An agency relationship arises only when the elements stated in §1.01 are present. Whether a relationship is characterized as agency in an agreement between parties or in the context of industry or popular usage is not controlling.

§1.03. Manifestation

A person manifests assent or intention through written or spoken words or other conduct.

§1.04. Terminology

(1) *Coagents.* Coagents have agency relationships with the same principal. A coagent may be appointed by the principal or by another agent actually or apparently authorized by the principal to do so.

(2) *Disclosed, undisclosed,* and *unidentified principals.*

(a) *Disclosed principal.* A principal is disclosed if, when an agent and a third party interact, the third party has notice that the agent is acting for a principal and has notice of the principal's identity.

(b) *Undisclosed principal.* A principal is undisclosed if, when an agent and a third party interact, the third party has no notice that the agent is acting for a principal.

(c) *Unidentified principal.* A principal is unidentified if, when an agent and a third party interact, the third party has notice that the agent is acting for a principal but does not have notice of the principal's identity.

(3) *Gratuitous agent.* A gratuitous agent acts without a right to compensation.

(4) *Notice.* A person has notice of a fact if the person knows the fact, has reason to know the fact, has received an effective notification of the fact, or should know

the fact to fulfill a duty owed to another person. Notice of a fact that an agent knows or has reason to know is imputed to the principal as stated in §§5.03 and 5.04. A notification given to or by an agent is effective as notice to or by the principal as stated in §5.02.

(5) *Person.* A person is (a) an individual; (b) an organization or association that has legal capacity to possess rights and incur obligations; (c) a government, political subdivision, or instrumentality or entity created by government; or (d) any other entity that has legal capacity to possess rights and incur obligations.

(6) *Power given as security.* A power given as security is a power to affect the legal relations of its creator that is created in the form of a manifestation of actual authority and held for the benefit of the holder or a third person. It is given to protect a legal or equitable title or to secure the performance of a duty apart from any duties owed the holder of the power by its creator that are incident to a relationship of agency under §1.01.

(7) *Power of attorney.* A power of attorney is an instrument that states an agent's authority.

(8) *Subagent.* A subagent is a person appointed by an agent to perform functions that the agent has consented to perform on behalf of the agent's principal and for whose conduct the appointing agent is responsible to the principal. The relationship between an appointing agent and a subagent is one of agency, created as stated in §1.01.

(9) *Superior* and *subordinate coagents.* A superior coagent has the right, conferred by the principal, to direct a subordinate coagent.

(10) *Trustee* and *agenttrustee.* A trustee is a holder of property who is subject to fiduciary duties to deal with the property for the benefit of charity or for one or more persons, at least one of whom is not the sole trustee. An agenttrustee is a trustee subject to the control of the settlor or of one or more beneficiaries.

Chapter 2. Principles of Attribution

INTRODUCTORY NOTE

This Chapter states, in general form, the three distinct bases on which the common law of agency attributes the legal consequences of one person's action to another person. . . . The three distinct bases for attribution are actual authority, apparent authority, and respondeat superior. These doctrines attribute legal consequences but do not create freestanding or independent causes of action that a third person may assert against a principal. The legal consequences that these doctrines attribute to a principal are not consequences of agency doctrine itself but of other bodies of law.

Descriptions of agency doctrine often mention, as additional distinct principles of attribution, implied authority and inherent authority or agency power. This Restatement treats implied authority as an aspect of the scope of an agent's actual authority and not as a separate type of authority. See §2.02. Moreover, this Chapter, like the remainder of this Restatement, does not use the concept of inherent agency power stated in Restatement Second, Agency §8 A. Situations that inherent agency power is said to govern are covered by other doctrines, as explained specifically where relevant. . . .

TOPIC 1. ACTUAL AUTHORITY

ctual Authority

An agent acts with actual authority when, at the time of taking action that has legal consequences for the principal, the agent reasonably believes, in accordance with the principal's manifestations to the agent, that the principal wishes the agent so to act.

§2.02. *Scope of Actual Authority*

(1) An agent has actual authority to take action designated or implied in the principal's manifestations to the agent and acts necessary or incidental to achieving the principal's objectives, as the agent reasonably understands the principal's manifestations and objectives when the agent determines how to act.

(2) An agent's interpretation of the principal's manifestations is reasonable if it reflects any meaning known by the agent to be ascribed by the principal and, in the absence of any meaning known to the agent, as a reasonable person in the agent's position would interpret the manifestations in light of the context, including circumstances of which the agent has notice and the agent's fiduciary duty to the principal.

(3) An agent's understanding of the principal's objectives is reasonable if it accords with the principal's manifestations and the inferences that a reasonable person in the agent's position would draw from the circumstances creating the agency.

TOPIC 2. APPARENT AUTHORITY

§2.03. *Apparent Authority*

Apparent authority is the power held by an agent or other actor to affect a principal's legal relations with third parties when a third party reasonably believes the actor has authority to act on behalf of the principal and that belief is traceable to the principal's manifestations.

TOPIC 3. RESPONDEAT SUPERIOR

§2.04. *Respondeat Superior*

An employer is subject to liability for torts committed by employees while acting within the scope of their employment.

TOPIC 4. RELATED DOCTRINES

§2.05. *Estoppel to Deny Existence of Agency Relationship*

A person who has not made a manifestation that an actor has authority as an agent and who is not otherwise liable as a party to a transaction purportedly done by the actor on that person's account is subject to liability to a third party who justifiably is induced to make a detrimental change in position because the transaction is believed to be on the person's account, if

(1) the person intentionally or carelessly caused such belief, or

(2) having notice of such belief and that it might induce others to change their positions, the person did not take reasonable steps to notify them of the facts.

§2.06. Liability of Undisclosed Principal

(1) An undisclosed principal is subject to liability to a third party who is justifiably induced to make a detrimental change in position by an agent acting on the principal's behalf and without actual authority if the principal, having notice of the agent's conduct and that it might induce others to change their positions, did not take reasonable steps to notify them of the facts.

(2) An undisclosed principal may not rely on instructions given an agent that qualify or reduce the agent's authority to less than the authority a third party would reasonably believe the agent to have under the same circumstances if the principal had been disclosed.

§2.07. Restitution of Benefit

If a principal is unjustly enriched at the expense of another person by the action of an agent or a person who appears to be an agent, the principal is subject to a claim for restitution by that person.

Chapter 3. Creation and Termination of Authority and Agency Relationships

Topic 1. Creating and Evidencing Actual Authority

§3.01. Creation of Actual Authority

Actual authority, as defined in §2.01, is created by a principal's manifestation to an agent that, as reasonably understood by the agent, expresses the principal's assent that the agent take action on the principal's behalf.

§3.02. Formal Requirements

If the law requires a writing or record signed by the principal to evidence an agent's authority to bind a principal to a contract or other transaction, the principal is not bound in the absence of such a writing or record. A principal may be estopped to assert the lack of such a writing or record when a third party has been induced to make a detrimental change in position by the reasonable belief that an agent has authority to bind the principal that is traceable to a manifestation made by the principal.

TOPIC 2. CREATING APPARENT AUTHORITY

§3.03. Creation of Apparent Authority

Apparent authority, as defined in §2.03, is created by a person's manifestation that another has authority to act with legal consequences for the person who makes the manifestation, when a third party reasonably believes the actor to be authorized and the belief is traceable to the manifestation.

§3.04. Capacity to Act as Principal

(1) An individual has capacity to act as principal in a relationship of agency as defined in §1.01 if, at the time the agent takes action, the individual would have capacity if acting in person.

(2) The law applicable to a person that is not an individual governs whether the person has capacity to be a principal in a relationship of agency as defined in §1.01, as well as the effect of the person's lack or loss of capacity on those who interact with it.

(3) If performance of an act is not delegable, its performance by an agent does not constitute performance by the principal.

§3.05. Capacity to Act as Agent

Any person may ordinarily be empowered to act so as to affect the legal relations of another. The actor's capacity governs the extent to which, by so acting, the actor becomes subject to duties and liabilities to the person whose legal relations are affected or to third parties.

TOPIC 3. TERMINATION OF AGENT'S POWER

§3.06. Termination of Actual Authority—In General

An agent's actual authority may be terminated by:

(1) the agent's death, cessation of existence, or suspension of powers as stated in §3.07(1) and (3); or

(2) the principal's death, cessation of existence, or suspension of powers as stated in §3.07(2) and (4); or

(3) the principal's loss of capacity, as stated in §3.08(1) and (3); or

(4) an agreement between the agent and the principal or the occurrence of circumstances on the basis of which the agent should reasonably conclude that the principal no longer would assent to the agent's taking action on the principal's behalf, as stated in §3.09; or

(5) a manifestation of revocation by the principal to the agent, or of renunciation by the agent to the principal, as stated in §3.10(1); or

(6) the occurrence of circumstances specified by statute.

§3.07. Death, Cessation of Existence, and Suspension of Powers

(1) The death of an individual agent terminates the agent's actual authority.

(2) The death of an individual principal terminates the agent's actual authority. The termination is effective only when the agent has notice of the principal's

death. The termination is also effective as against a third party with whom the agent deals when the third party has notice of the principal's death.

(3) When an agent that is not an individual ceases to exist or commences a process that will lead to cessation of existence or when its powers are suspended, the agent's actual authority terminates except as provided by law.

(4) When a principal that is not an individual ceases to exist or commences a process that will lead to cessation of its existence or when its powers are suspended, the agent's actual authority terminates except as provided by law.

§3.08. *Loss of Capacity*

(1) An individual principal's loss of capacity to do an act terminates the agent's actual authority to do the act. The termination is effective only when the agent has notice that the principal's loss of capacity is permanent or that the principal has been adjudicated to lack capacity. The termination is also effective as against a third party with whom the agent deals when the third party has notice that the principal's loss of capacity is permanent or that the principal has been adjudicated to lack capacity.

(2) A written instrument may make an agent's actual authority effective upon a principal's loss of capacity, or confer it irrevocably regardless of such loss.

(3) If a principal that is not an individual loses capacity to do an act, its agent's actual authority to do the act is terminated.

§3.09. *Termination by Agreement or by Occurrence of Changed Circumstances*

An agent's actual authority terminates (1) as agreed by the agent and the principal, subject to the provisions of §3.10; or (2) upon the occurrence of circumstances on the basis of which the agent should reasonably conclude that the principal no longer would assent to the agent's taking action on the principal's behalf.

TOPIC 4. TERMINATION OF AGENT'S POWER

TITLE A. TERMINATION OF ACTUAL AUTHORITY

§3.10. *Manifestation Terminating Actual Authority*

(1) Notwithstanding any agreement between principal and agent, an agent's actual authority terminates if the agent renounces it by a manifestation to the principal or if the principal revokes the agent's actual authority by a manifestation to the agent. A revocation or a renunciation is effective when the other party has notice of it.

(2) A principal's manifestation of revocation is, unless otherwise agreed, ineffective to terminate a power given as security or to terminate a proxy to vote securities or other membership or ownership interests that is made irrevocable in compliance with applicable legislation. See §§3.12-3.13.

TITLE B. TERMINATION OF APPARENT AUTHORITY

§3.11. Termination of Apparent Authority

(1) The termination of actual authority does not by itself end any apparent authority held by an agent.

(2) Apparent authority ends when it is no longer reasonable for the third party with whom an agent deals to believe that the agent continues to act with actual authority.

CHAPTER 4. RATIFICATION

§4.01. Ratification Defined

(1) Ratification is the affirmance of a prior act done by another, whereby the act is given effect as if done by an agent acting with actual authority.

(2) A person ratifies an act by

(a) manifesting assent that the act shall affect the person's legal relations, or

(b) conduct that justifies a reasonable assumption that the person so consents.

(3) Ratification does not occur unless

(a) the act is ratifiable as stated in §4.03,

(b) the person ratifying has capacity as stated in §4.04,

(c) the ratification is timely as stated in §4.05, and

(d) the ratification encompasses the act in its entirety as stated in §4.07.

§4.02. Effect of Ratification

(1) Subject to the exceptions stated in subsection (2), ratification retroactively creates the effects of actual authority.

(2) Ratification is not effective:

(a) in favor of a person who causes it by misrepresentation or other conduct that would make a contract voidable;

(b) in favor of an agent against a principal when the principal ratifies to avoid a loss; or

(c) to diminish the rights or other interests of persons, not parties to the transaction, that were acquired in the subject matter prior to the ratification.

§4.03. Acts That May Be Ratified

A person may ratify an act if the actor acted or purported to act as an agent on the person's behalf.

§4.04. Capacity to Ratify

(1) A person may ratify an act if

(a) the person existed at the time of the act, and

(b) the person had capacity as defined in §3.04 at the time of ratifying the act.

(2) At a later time, a principal may avoid a ratification made earlier when the principal lacked capacity as defined in §3.04.

§4.05. *Timing of Ratification*

A ratification of a transaction is not effective unless it precedes the occurrence of circumstances that would cause the ratification to have adverse and inequitable effects on the rights of third parties. These circumstances include:

(1) any manifestation of intention to withdraw from the transaction made by the third party;

(2) any material change in circumstances that would make it inequitable to bind the third party, unless the third party chooses to be bound; and

(3) a specific time that determines whether a third party is deprived of a right or subjected to a liability.

§4.06. *Knowledge Requisite to Ratification*

A person is not bound by a ratification made without knowledge of material facts involved in the original act when the person was unaware of such lack of knowledge.

§4.07. *No Partial Ratification*

A ratification is not effective unless it encompasses the entirety of an act, contract, or other single transaction.

§4.08. *Estoppel to Deny Ratification*

If a person makes a manifestation that the person has ratified another's act and the manifestation, as reasonably understood by a third party, induces the third party to make a detrimental change in position, the person may be estopped to deny the ratification.

Chapter 5. Notifications and Notice

§5.01. *Notifications and Notice—In General*

(1) A notification is a manifestation that is made in the form required by agreement among parties or by applicable law, or in a reasonable manner in the absence of an agreement or an applicable law, with the intention of affecting the legal rights and duties of the notifier in relation to rights and duties of persons to whom the notification is given.

(2) A notification given to or by an agent is effective as notification to or by the principal as stated in §5.02.

(3) A person has notice of a fact if the person knows the fact, has reason to know the fact, has received an effective notification of the fact, or should know the fact to fulfill a duty owed to another person.

(4) Notice of a fact that an agent knows or has reason to know is imputed to the principal as stated in §§5.03 and 5.04.

§5.02. *Notification Given by or to an Agent*

(1) A notification given to an agent is effective as notice to the principal if the agent has actual or apparent authority to receive the notification, unless the person

who gives the notification knows or has reason to know that the agent is acting adversely to the principal as stated in §5.04.

(2) A notification given by an agent is effective as notification given by the principal if the agent has actual or apparent authority to give the notification, unless the person who receives the notification knows or has reason to know that the agent is acting adversely to the principal as stated in §5.04.

§5.03. Imputation of Notice of Fact to Principal

For purposes of determining a principal's legal relations with a third party, notice of a fact that an agent knows or has reason to know is imputed to the principal if knowledge of the fact is material to the agent's duties to the principal, unless the agent

(a) acts adversely to the principal as stated in §5.04, or

(b) is subject to a duty to another not to disclose the fact to the principal.

§5.04. An Agent Who Acts Adversely to a Principal

For purposes of determining a principal's legal relations with a third party, notice of a fact that an agent knows or has reason to know is not imputed to the principal if the agent acts adversely to the principal in a transaction or matter, intending to act solely for the agent's own purposes or those of another person. Nevertheless, notice is imputed

(a) when necessary to protect the rights of a third party who dealt with the principal in good faith; or

(b) when the principal has ratified or knowingly retained a benefit from the agent's action.

A third party who deals with a principal through an agent, knowing or having reason to know that the agent acts adversely to the principal, does not deal in good faith for this purpose.

Chapter 6. Contracts and Other Transactions with Third Parties

Topic 1. Parties to Contracts

§6.01. Agent for Disclosed Principal

When an agent acting with actual or apparent authority makes a contract on behalf of a disclosed principal,

(1) the principal and the third party are parties to the contract; and

(2) the agent is not a party to the contract unless the agent and third party agree otherwise.

§6.02. Agent for Unidentified Principal

When an agent acting with actual or apparent authority makes a contract on behalf of an unidentified principal,

(1) the principal and the third party are parties to the contract; and

(2) the agent is a party to the contract unless the agent and the third party agree otherwise.

§6.03. *Agent for Undisclosed Principal*

When an agent acting with actual authority makes a contract on behalf of an undisclosed principal,

(1) unless excluded by the contract, the principal is a party to the contract;

(2) the agent and the third party are parties to the contract; and

(3) the principal, if a party to the contract, and the third party have the same rights, liabilities, and defenses against each other as if the principal made the contract personally, subject to §§6.05-6.09.

§6.04. *Principal Does Not Exist or Lacks Capacity*

Unless the third party agrees otherwise, a person who makes a contract with a third party purportedly as an agent on behalf of a principal becomes a party to the contract if the purported agent knows or has reason to know that the purported principal does not exist or lacks capacity to be a party to a contract.

TOPIC 2. RIGHTS, LIABILITIES, AND DEFENSES . . .

Title C. Agent's Warranties and Representations

§6.10. *Agent's Implied Warranty of Authority*

A person who purports to make a contract, representation, or conveyance to or with a third party on behalf of another person, lacking power to bind that person, gives an implied warranty of authority to the third party and is subject to liability to the third party for damages for loss caused by breach of that warranty, including loss of the benefit expected from performance by the principal, unless

(1) the principal or purported principal ratifies the act as stated in §4.01; or

(2) the person who purports to make the contract, representation, or conveyance gives notice to the third party that no warranty of authority is given; or

(3) the third party knows that the person who purports to make the contract, representation, or conveyance acts without actual authority.

CHAPTER 7. TORTS — LIABILITY OF AGENT AND PRINCIPAL

TOPIC 1. AGENT'S LIABILITY

§7.01. *Agent's Liability to Third Party*

An agent is subject to liability to a third party harmed by the agent's tortious conduct. Unless an applicable statute provides otherwise, an actor remains subject to liability although the actor acts as an agent or an employee, with actual or apparent authority, or within the scope of employment.

§7.02. *Duty to Principal; Duty to Third Party*

An agent's breach of a duty owed to the principal is not an independent basis for the agent's tort liability to a third party. An agent is subject to tort liability to a third party harmed by the agent's conduct only when the agent's conduct breaches a duty that the agent owes to the third party.

TOPIC 2. PRINCIPAL'S LIABILITY

§7.03. Principal's Liability—In General

(1) A principal is subject to direct liability to a third party harmed by an agent's conduct when

(a) as stated in §7.04, the agent acts with actual authority or the principal ratifies the agent's conduct and

(i) the agent's conduct is tortious, or

(ii) the agent's conduct, if that of the principal, would subject the principal to tort liability; or

(b) as stated in §7.05, the principal is negligent in selecting, supervising, or otherwise controlling the agent; or

(c) as stated in §7.06, the principal delegates performance of a duty to use care to protect other persons or their property to an agent who fails to perform the duty.

(2) A principal is subject to vicarious liability to a third party harmed by an agent's conduct when

(a) as stated in §7.07, the agent is an employee who commits a tort while acting within the scope of employment; or

(b) as stated in §7.08, the agent commits a tort when acting with apparent authority in dealing with a third party on or purportedly on behalf of the principal.

CHAPTER 8. DUTIES OF AGENT AND PRINCIPAL TO EACH OTHER

TOPIC 1. AGENT'S DUTIES TO PRINCIPAL

Title A. General Fiduciary Principle

§8.01. General Fiduciary Principle

An agent has a fiduciary duty to act loyally for the principal's benefit in all matters connected with the agency relationship.

Title B. Duties of Loyalty

§8.02. Material Benefit Arising out of Position

An agent has a duty not to acquire a material benefit from a third party in connection with transactions conducted or other actions taken on behalf of the principal or otherwise through the agent's use of the agent's position.

§8.03. Acting as or on Behalf of an Adverse Party

An agent has a duty not to deal with the principal as or on behalf of an adverse party in a transaction connected with the agency relationship.

§8.04. Competition

Throughout the duration of an agency relationship, an agent has a duty to refrain from competing with the principal and from taking action on behalf of or otherwise assisting the principal's competitors. During that time, an agent may take action, not otherwise wrongful, to prepare for competition following termination of the agency relationship.

§8.05. Use of Principal's Property; Use of Confidential Information

An agent has a duty

(1) not to use property of the principal for the agent's own purposes or those of a third party; and

(2) not to use or communicate confidential information of the principal for the agent's own purposes or those of a third party.

§8.06. Principal's Consent

(1) Conduct by an agent that would otherwise constitute a breach of duty as stated in §§8.01, 8.02, 8.03, 8.04, and 8.05 does not constitute a breach of duty if the principal consents to the conduct, provided that

(a) in obtaining the principal's consent, the agent

(i) acts in good faith,

(ii) discloses all material facts that the agent knows, has reason to know, or should know would reasonably affect the principal's judgment unless the principal has manifested that such facts are already known by the principal or that the principal does not wish to know them, and

(iii) otherwise deals fairly with the principal; and

(b) the principal's consent concerns either a specific act or transaction, or acts or transactions of a specified type that could reasonably be expected to occur in the ordinary course of the agency relationship.

(2) An agent who acts for more than one principal in a transaction between or among them has a duty

(a) to deal in good faith with each principal,

(b) to disclose to each principal

(i) the fact that the agent acts for the other principal or principals, and

(ii) all other facts that the agent knows, has reason to know, or should know would reasonably affect the principal's judgment unless the principal has manifested that such facts are already known by the principal or that the principal does not wish to know them, and

(c) otherwise to deal fairly with each principal.

Title C. Duties of Performance

§8.07. Duty Created by Contract

An agent has a duty to act in accordance with the express and implied terms of any contract between the agent and the principal.

§8.08. Duties of Care, Competence, and Diligence

Subject to any agreement with the principal, an agent has a duty to the principal to act with the care, competence, and diligence normally exercised by agents in similar circumstances. Special skills or knowledge possessed by an agent are circumstances to be taken into account in determining whether the agent acted with due care and diligence. If an agent claims to possess special skills or knowledge, the agent has a duty to the principal to act with the care, competence, and diligence normally exercised by agents with such skills or knowledge.

§8.09. Duty to Act Only Within Scope of Actual Authority and to Comply with Principal's Lawful Instructions

(1) An agent has a duty to take action only within the scope of the agent's actual authority.

(2) An agent has a duty to comply with all lawful instructions received from the principal and persons designated by the principal concerning the agent's actions on behalf of the principal.

§8.10. Duty of Good Conduct

An agent has a duty, within the scope of the agency relationship, to act reasonably and to refrain from conduct that is likely to damage the principal's enterprise.

§8.11. Duty to Provide Information

An agent has a duty to use reasonable effort to provide the principal with facts that the agent knows, has reason to know, or should know when

(1) subject to any manifestation by the principal, the agent knows or has reason to know that the principal would wish to have the facts or the facts are material to the agent's duties to the principal; and

(2) the facts can be provided to the principal without violating a superior duty owed by the agent to another person.

§8.12. Duties Regarding Principal's Property—Segregation, Record-Keeping, and Accounting

An agent has a duty, subject to any agreement with the principal,

(1) not to deal with the principal's property so that it appears to be the agent's property;

(2) not to mingle the principal's property with anyone else's; and

(3) to keep and render accounts to the principal of money or other property received or paid out on the principal's account.

TOPIC 2. PRINCIPAL'S DUTIES TO AGENT

§8.13. Duty Created by Contract

A principal has a duty to act in accordance with the express and implied terms of any contract between the principal and the agent.

§8.14. Duty to Indemnify

A principal has a duty to indemnify an agent

(1) in accordance with the terms of any contract between them; and

(2) unless otherwise agreed,

(a) when the agent makes a payment

(i) within the scope of the agent's actual authority, or

(ii) that is beneficial to the principal, unless the agent acts officiously in making the payment; or

(b) when the agent suffers a loss that fairly should be borne by the principal in light of their relationship.

§8.15. Principal's Duty to Deal Fairly and in Good Faith

A principal has a duty to deal with the agent fairly and in good faith, including a duty to provide the agent with information about risks of physical harm or pecuniary loss that the principal knows, has reason to know, or should know are present in the agent's work but unknown to the agent.

Unincorporated Business Association Statutes

Uniform Partnership Act (1914)

Part I. Preliminary Provisions

§1. Name of Act

This act may be cited as Uniform Partnership Act.

§2. Definition of Terms

In this act, "Court" includes every court and judge having jurisdiction in the case.

"Business" includes every trade, occupation, or profession.

"Person" includes individuals, partnerships, corporations, and other associations.

"Bankrupt" includes bankrupt under the Federal Bankruptcy Act or insolvent under any state insolvent act.

"Conveyance" includes every assignment, lease, mortgage, or encumbrance.
"Real property" includes land and any interest or estate in land.

§3. *Interpretation of Knowledge and Notice*

(1) A person has "knowledge" of a fact within the meaning of this act not only when he has actual knowledge thereof, but also when he has knowledge of such other facts as in the circumstances shows bad faith.

(2) A person has "notice" of a fact within the meaning of this act when the person who claims the benefit of the notice:

(a) States the fact to such person, or

(b) Delivers through the mail, or by other means of communication, a written statement of the fact to such person or to a proper person at his place of business or residence.

§4. *Rules of Construction*

(1) The rule that statutes in derogation of the common law are to be strictly construed shall have no application to this act.

(2) The law of estoppel shall apply under this act.

(3) The law of agency shall apply under this act.

(4) This act shall be so interpreted and construed as to effect its general purpose to make uniform the law of those states which enact it.

(5) This act shall not be construed so as to impair the obligations of any contract existing when the act goes into effect, nor to affect any action or proceedings begun or right accrued before this act takes effect.

§5. *Rules for Cases Not Provided for in this Act*

In any case not provided for in this act the rules of law and equity, including the law merchant, shall govern.

PART II. NATURE OF PARTNERSHIP

§6. *Partnership Defined*

(1) A partnership is an association of two or more persons to carry on as co-owners of a business for profit.

(2) But any association formed under any other statute of this state, or any statute adopted by authority, other than the authority of this state, is not a partnership under this act, unless such association would have been a partnership in this state prior to the adoption of this act; but this act shall apply to limited partnerships except in so far as the statutes relating to such partnerships are inconsistent herewith.

§7. *Rules for Determining the Existence of a Partnership*

In determining whether a partnership exists, these rules shall apply:

(1) Except as provided by section 16 persons who are not partners as to each other are not partners as to third persons.

(2) Joint tenancy, tenancy in common, tenancy by the entireties, joint property, common property, or part ownership does not of itself establish a partnership, whether such co-owners do or do not share any profits made by the use of the property.

(3) The sharing of gross returns does not of itself establish a partnership, whether or not the persons sharing them have a joint or common right or interest in any property from which the returns are derived.

(4) The receipt by a person of a share of the profits of a business is prima facie evidence that he is a partner in the business, but no such inference shall be drawn if such profits were received in payment:

(a) As a debt by installments or otherwise,

(b) As wages of an employee or rent to a landlord,

(c) As an annuity to a widow or representative of a deceased partner,

(d) As interest on a loan, though the amount of payment vary with the profits of the business,

(e) As the consideration for the sale of a good-will of a business or other property by installments or otherwise.

§8. Partnership Property

(1) All property originally brought into the partnership stock or subsequently acquired by purchase or otherwise, on account of the partnership, is partnership property.

(2) Unless the contrary intention appears, property acquired with partnership funds is partnership property.

(3) Any estate in real property may be acquired in the partnership name. Title so acquired can be conveyed only in the partnership name.

(4) A conveyance to a partnership in the partnership name, though without words of inheritance, passes the entire estate of the grantor unless a contrary intent appears.

Part III. Relations of Partners to Persons Dealing with the Partnership

§9. Partner Agent of Partnership as to Partnership Business

(1) Every partner is an agent of the partnership for the purpose of its business, and the act of every partner, including the execution in the partnership name of any instrument, for apparently carrying on in the usual way the business of the partnership of which he is a member binds the partnership, unless the partner so acting has in fact no authority to act for the partnership in the particular matter, and the person with whom he is dealing has knowledge of the fact that he has no such authority.

(2) An act of a partner which is not apparently for the carrying on of the business of the partnership in the usual way does not bind the partnership unless authorized by the other partners.

(3) Unless authorized by the other partners or unless they have abandoned the business, one or more but less than all the partners have no authority to:

(a) Assign the partnership property in trust for creditors or on the assignee's promise to pay the debts of the partnership,

(b) Dispose of the good-will of the business,

(c) Do any other act which would make it impossible to carry on the ordinary business of a partnership,

(d) Confess a judgment,

(e) Submit a partnership claim or liability to arbitration or reference.

(4) No act of a partner in contravention of a restriction on authority shall bind the partnership to persons having knowledge of the restriction.

§10. Conveyance of Real Property of the Partnership

(1) Where title to real property is in the partnership name, any partner may convey title to such property by a conveyance executed in the partnership name; but the partnership may recover such property unless the partner's act binds the partnership under the provisions of paragraph (1) of section 9, or unless such property has been conveyed by the grantee or a person claiming through such grantee to a holder for value without knowledge that the partner, in making the conveyance, has exceeded his authority.

(2) Where title to real property is in the name of the partnership, a conveyance executed by a partner, in his own name, passes the equitable interest of the partnership, provided the act is one within the authority of the partner under the provisions of paragraph (1) of section 9.

(3) Where title to real property is in the name of one or more but not all the partners, and the record does not disclose the right of the partnership, the partners in whose name the title stands may convey title to such property, but the partnership may recover such property if the partners' act does not bind the partnership under the provisions of paragraph (1) of section 9, unless the purchaser or his assignee, is a holder for value, without knowledge.

(4) Where the title to real property is in the name of one or more or all the partners, or in a third person in trust for the partnership, a conveyance executed by a partner in the partnership name, or in his own name, passes the equitable interest of the partnership, provided the act is one within the authority of the partner under the provisions of paragraph (1) of section 9.

(5) Where the title to real property is in the names of all the partners a conveyance executed by all the partners passes all their rights in such property.

§11. Partnership Bound by Admission of Partner

An admission or representation made by any partner concerning partnership affairs within the scope of his authority as conferred by this act is evidence against the partnership.

§12. Partnership Charged with Knowledge of or Notice to Partner

Notice to any partner of any matter relating to partnership affairs, and the knowledge of the partner acting in the particular matter, acquired while a partner or then present to his mind, and the knowledge of any other partner who reasonably could and should have communicated it to the acting partner, operate as notice to or knowledge of the partnership, except in the case of a fraud on the partnership committed by or with the consent of that partner.

§13. *Partnership Bound by Partner's Wrongful Act*

Where, by any wrongful act or omission of any partner acting in the ordinary course of the business of the partnership or with the authority of his co-partners, loss or injury is caused to any person, not being a partner in the partnership, or any penalty is incurred, the partnership is liable therefor to the same extent as the partner so acting or omitting to act.

§14. *Partnership Bound by Partner's Breach of Trust*

The partnership is bound to make good the loss:

(a) Where one partner acting within the scope of his apparent authority receives money or property of a third person and misapplies it; and

(b) Where the partnership in the course of its business receives money or property of a third person and the money or property so received is misapplied by any partner while it is in the custody of the partnership.

§15. *Nature of Partner's Liability*

All partners are liable

(a) Jointly and severally for everything chargeable to the partnership under sections 13 and 14.

(b) Jointly for all other debts and obligations of the partnership; but any partner may enter into a separate obligation to perform a partnership contract.

§16. *Partner by Estoppel*

(1) When a person, by words spoken or written or by conduct, represents himself, or consents to another representing him to any one, as a partner in an existing partnership or with one or more persons not actual partners, he is liable to any such person to whom such representation has been made, who has, on the faith of such representation, given credit to the actual or apparent partnership, and if he has made such representation or consented to its being made in a public manner he is liable to such person, whether the representation has or has not been made or communicated to such person so giving credit by or with the knowledge of the apparent partner making the representation or consenting to its being made.

(a) When a partnership liability results, he is liable as though he were an actual member of the partnership.

(b) When no partnership liability results, he is liable jointly with the other persons, if any, so consenting to the contract or representation as to incur liability, otherwise separately.

(2) When a person has been thus represented to be a partner in an existing partnership, or with one or more persons not actual partners, he is an agent of the persons consenting to such representation to bind them to the same extent and in the same manner as though he were a partner in fact, with respect to persons who rely upon the representation. Where all the members of the existing partnership consent to the representation, a partnership act or obligation results; but in all other cases it is the joint act or obligation of the person acting and the persons consenting to the representation.

§17. *Liability of Incoming Partner*

A person admitted as a partner into an existing partnership is liable for all the obligations of the partnership arising before his admission as though he had been a partner when such obligations were incurred, except that this liability shall be satisfied only out of partnership property.

Part IV. Relations of Partners to One Another

§18. *Rules Determining Rights and Duties of Partners*

The rights and duties of the partners in relation to the partnership shall be determined, subject to any agreement between them, by the following rules:

(a) Each partner shall be repaid his contributions, whether by way of capital or advances to the partnership property and share equally in the profits and surplus remaining after all liabilities, including those to partners, are satisfied; and must contribute towards the losses, whether of capital or otherwise, sustained by the partnership according to his share in the profits.

(b) The partnership must indemnify every partner in respect of payments made and personal liabilities reasonably incurred by him in the ordinary and proper conduct of its business, or for the preservation of its business or property.

(c) A partner, who in aid of the partnership makes any payment or advance beyond the amount of capital which he agreed to contribute, shall be paid interest from the date of the payment or advance.

(d) A partner shall receive interest on the capital contributed by him only from the date when repayment should be made.

(e) All partners have equal rights in the management and conduct of the partnership business.

(f) No partner is entitled to remuneration for acting in the partnership business, except that a surviving partner is entitled to reasonable compensation for his services in winding up the partnership affairs.

(g) No person can become a member of a partnership without the consent of all the partners.

(h) Any difference arising as to ordinary matters connected with the partnership business may be decided by a majority of the partners; but no act in contravention of any agreement between the partners may be done rightfully without the consent of all the partners.

§19. Partnership Books

The partnership books shall be kept, subject to any agreement between the partners, at the principal place of business of the partnership, and every partner shall at all times have access to and may inspect and copy any of them.

§20. Duty of Partners to Render Information

Partners shall render on demand true and full information of all things affecting the partnership to any partner or the legal representative of any deceased partner or partner under legal disability.

§21. Partner Accountable as a Fiduciary

(1) Every partner must account to the partnership for any benefit, and hold as trustee for it any profits derived by him without the consent of the other partners from any transaction connected with the formation, conduct, or liquidation of the partnership or from any use by him of its property.

(2) This section applies also to the representatives of a deceased partner engaged in the liquidation of the affairs of the partnership as the personal representatives of the last surviving partner.

§22. Right to an Account

Any partner shall have the right to a formal account as to partnership affairs:

(a) If he is wrongfully excluded from the partnership business or possession of its property by his co-partners,

(b) If the right exists under the terms of any agreement,

(c) As provided by section 21,

(d) Whenever other circumstances render it just and reasonable.

§23. Continuation of Partnership Beyond Fixed Term

(1) When a partnership for a fixed term or particular undertaking is continued after the termination of such term or particular undertaking without any express agreement, the rights and duties of the partners remain the same as they were at such termination, so far as is consistent with a partnership at will.

(2) A continuation of the business by the partners or such of them as habitually acted therein during the term, without any settlement or liquidation of the partnership affairs, is prima facie evidence of a continuation of the partnership.

PART V. PROPERTY RIGHTS OF A PARTNER

§24. Extent of Property Rights of a Partner

The property rights of a partner are (1) his rights in specific partnership property, (2) his interest in the partnership, and (3) his right to participate in the management.

§25. *Nature of a Partner's Right in Specific Partnership Property*

(1) A partner is co-owner with his partners of specific partnership property holding as a tenant in partnership.

(2) The incidents of this tenancy are such that:

(a) A partner, subject to the provisions of this act and to any agreement between the partners, has an equal right with his partners to possess specific partnership property for partnership purposes; but he has no right to possess such property for any other purpose without the consent of his partners.

(b) A partner's right in specific partnership property is not assignable except in connection with the assignment of rights of all the partners in the same property.

(c) A partner's right in specific partnership property is not subject to attachment or execution, except on a claim against the partnership. When partnership property is attached for a partnership debt the partners, or any of them, or the representatives of a deceased partner, cannot claim any right under the homestead or exemption laws.

(d) On the death of a partner his right in specific partnership property vests in the surviving partner or partners, except where the deceased was the last surviving partner, when his right in such property vests in his legal representative. Such surviving partner or partners, or the legal representative of the last surviving partner, has no right to possess the partnership property for any but a partnership purpose.

(e) A partner's right in specific partnership property is not subject to dower, curtesy, or allowances to widows, heirs, or next of kin.

§26. *Nature of Partner's Interest in the Partnership*

A partner's interest in the partnership is his share of the profits and surplus, and the same is personal property.

§27. *Assignment of Partner's Interest*

(1) A conveyance by a partner of his interest in the partnership does not of itself dissolve the partnership, nor, as against the other partners in the absence of agreement, entitle the assignee, during the continuance of the partnership, to interfere in the management or administration of the partnership business or affairs, or to require any information or account of partnership transactions, or to inspect the partnership books; but it merely entitles the assignee to receive in accordance with his contract the profits to which the assigning partner would otherwise be entitled.

(2) In case of a dissolution of the partnership, the assignee is entitled to receive his assignor's interest and may require an account from the date only of the last account agreed to by all the partners.

§28. *Partner's Interest Subject to Charging Order*

(1) On due application to a competent court by any judgment creditor of a partner, the court which entered the judgment, order, or decree, or any other

court, may charge the interest of the debtor partner with payment of the unsatisfied amount of such judgment debt with interest thereon; and may then or later appoint a receiver of his share of the profits, and of any other money due or to fall due to him in respect of the partnership, and make all other orders, directions, accounts and inquiries which the debtor partner might have made, or which the circumstances of the case may require.

(2) The interest charged may be redeemed at any time before foreclosure, or in case of a sale being directed by the court may be purchased without thereby causing a dissolution:

(a) With separate property, by any one or more of the partners, or

(b) With partnership property, by any one or more of the partners with the consent of all the partners whose interests are not so charged or sold.

(3) Nothing in this act shall be held to deprive a partner of his right, if any, under the exemption laws, as regards his interest in the partnership.

PART VI. DISSOLUTION AND WINDING UP

§29. Dissolution Defined

The dissolution of a partnership is the change in the relation of the partners caused by any partner ceasing to be associated in the carrying on as distinguished from the winding up of the business.

§30. Partnership Not Terminated by Dissolution

On dissolution the partnership is not terminated, but continues until the winding up of partnership affairs is completed.

§31. Causes of Dissolution

Dissolution is caused:

(1) Without violation of the agreement between the partners,

(a) By the termination of the definite term or particular undertaking specified in the agreement,

(b) By the express will of any partner when no definite term or particular undertaking is specified,

(c) By the express will of all the partners who have not assigned their interests or suffered them to be charged for their separate debts, either before or after the termination of any specified term or particular undertaking,

(d) By the expulsion of any partner from the business bona fide in accordance with such a power conferred by the agreement between the partners;

(2) In contravention of the agreement between the partners, where the circumstances do not permit a dissolution under any other provision of this section, by the express will of any partner at any time;

(3) By any event which makes it unlawful for the business of the partnership to be carried on or for the members to carry it on in partnership;

(4) By the death of any partner;
(5) By the bankruptcy of any partner or the partnership;
(6) By decree of court under section 32.

§32. *Dissolution by Decree of Court*

(1) On application by or for a partner the court shall decree a dissolution whenever:

(a) A partner has been declared a lunatic in any judicial proceeding or is shown to be of unsound mind,

(b) A partner becomes in any other way incapable of performing his part of the partnership contract,

(c) A partner has been guilty of such conduct as tends to affect prejudicially the carrying on of the business,

(d) A partner wilfully or persistently commits a breach of the partnership agreement, or otherwise so conducts himself in matters relating to the partnership business that it is not reasonably practicable to carry on the business in partnership with him,

(e) The business of the partnership can only be carried on at a loss,

(f) Other circumstances render a dissolution equitable.

(2) On the application of the purchaser of a partner's interest under sections 28 or 29:[1]

(a) After the termination of the specified term or particular undertaking,

(b) At any time if the partnership was a partnership at will when the interest was assigned or when the charging order was issued.

§33. *General Effect of Dissolution on Authority of Partner*

Except so far as may be necessary to wind up partnership affairs or to complete transactions begun but not then finished, dissolution terminates all authority of any partner to act for the partnership,

(1) With respect to the partners,

(a) When the dissolution is not by the act, bankruptcy or death of a partner; or

(b) When the dissolution is by such act, bankruptcy or death of a partner, in cases where section 34 so requires.

(2) With respect to persons not partners, as declared in section 35.

§34. *Right of Partner to Contribution from Co-partners after Dissolution*

Where the dissolution is caused by the act, death or bankruptcy of a partner, each partner is liable to his co-partners for his share of any liability created by any partner acting for the partnership as if the partnership had not been dissolved unless

(a) The dissolution being by act of any partner, the partner acting for the partnership had knowledge of the dissolution, or

[1] So in original. Probably should read "sections 27 or 28."

(b) The dissolution being by the death or bankruptcy of a partner, the partner acting for the partnership had knowledge or notice of the death or bankruptcy.

§35. *Power of Partner to Bind Partnership to Third Persons after Dissolution*

(1) After dissolution a partner can bind the partnership except as provided in paragraph (3):

(a) By any act appropriate for winding up partnership affairs or completing transactions unfinished at dissolution;

(b) By any transaction which would bind the partnership if dissolution had not taken place, provided the other party to the transaction

(I) Had extended credit to the partnership prior to dissolution and had no knowledge or notice of the dissolution; or

(II) Though he had not so extended credit, had nevertheless known of the partnership prior to dissolution, and, having no knowledge or notice of dissolution, the fact of dissolution had not been advertised in a newspaper of general circulation in the place (or in each place if more than one) at which the partnership business was regularly carried on.

(2) The liability of a partner under paragraph (1b) shall be satisfied out of partnership assets alone when such partner had been prior to dissolution

(a) Unknown as a partner to the person with whom the contract is made; and

(b) So far unknown and inactive in partnership affairs that the business reputation of the partnership could not be said to have been in any degree due to his connection with it.

(3) The partnership is in no case bound by any act of a partner after dissolution

(a) Where the partnership is dissolved because it is unlawful to carry on the business, unless the act is appropriate for winding up partnership affairs; or

(b) Where the partner has become bankrupt; or

(c) Where the partner has no authority to wind up partnership affairs; except by a transaction with one who

(I) Had extended credit to the partnership prior to dissolution and had no knowledge or notice of his want of authority; or

(II) Had not extended credit to the partnership prior to dissolution; and, having no knowledge or notice of his want of authority, the fact of his want of authority has not been advertised in the manner provided for advertising the fact of dissolution in paragraph (1bII).

(4) Nothing in this section shall affect the liability under section 16 of any person who after dissolution represents himself or consents to another representing him as a partner in a partnership engaged in carrying on business.

§36. *Effect of Dissolution on Partner's Existing Liability*

(1) The dissolution of the partnership does not of itself discharge the existing liability of any partner.

(2) A partner is discharged from any existing liability upon dissolution of the partnership by an agreement to that effect between himself, the partnership creditor and the person or partnership continuing the business; and such agreement may be inferred from the course of dealing between the creditor having knowledge of the dissolution and the person or partnership continuing the business.

(3) Where a person agrees to assume the existing obligations of a dissolved partnership, the partners whose obligations have been assumed shall be discharged from any liability to any creditor of the partnership who, knowing of the agreement, consents to a material alteration in the nature or time of payment of such obligations.

(4) The individual property of a deceased partner shall be liable for all obligations of the partnership incurred while he was a partner but subject to the prior payment of his separate debts.

§37. Right to Wind Up

Unless otherwise agreed the partners who have not wrongfully dissolved the partnership or the legal representative of the last surviving partner, not bankrupt, has the right to wind up the partnership affairs; provided, however, that any partner, his legal representative or his assignee, upon cause shown, may obtain winding up by the court.

§38. Rights of Partners to Application of Partnership Property

(1) When dissolution is caused in any way, except in contravention of the partnership agreement, each partner, as against his co-partners and all persons claiming through them in respect of their interests in the partnership, unless otherwise agreed, may have the partnership property applied to discharge its liabilities, and the surplus applied to pay in cash the net amount owing to the respective partners. But if dissolution is caused by expulsion of a partner, bona fide under the partnership agreement and if the expelled partner is discharged from all partnership liabilities, either by payment or agreement under section 36(2), he shall receive in cash only the net amount due him from the partnership.

(2) When dissolution is caused in contravention of the partnership agreement the rights of the partners shall be as follows:

(a) Each partner who has not caused dissolution wrongfully shall have,

(I) All the rights specified in paragraph (1) of this section, and

(II) The right, as against each partner who has caused the dissolution wrongfully, to damages for breach of the agreement.

(b) The partners who have not caused the dissolution wrongfully, if they all desire to continue the business in the same name, either by themselves or jointly with others, may do so, during the agreed term for the partnership and for that purpose may possess the partnership property, provided they secure the payment by bond approved by the court, or pay to any partner who has caused the dissolution wrongfully, the value of his interest in the partnership at the dissolution, less any damages recoverable under clause (2a II) of this section, and in like manner indemnify him against all present or future partnership liabilities.

(c) A partner who has caused the dissolution wrongfully shall have:

(I) If the business is not continued under the provisions of paragraph (2b) all the rights of a partner under paragraph (1), subject to clause (2a II), of this section,

(II) If the business is continued under paragraph (2b) of this section the right as against his co-partners and all claiming through them in respect of their interests in the partnership, to have the value of his interest in the partnership, less any damages caused to his co-partners by the dissolution, ascertained and paid to him in cash, or the payment secured by bond approved by the court, and to be released from all existing liabilities of the partnership; but in ascertaining the value of the partner's interest the value of the good-will of the business shall not be considered.

§39. Rights Where Partnership Is Dissolved for Fraud or Misrepresentation

Where a partnership contract is rescinded on the ground of the fraud or misrepresentation of one of the parties thereto, the party entitled to rescind is, without prejudice to any other right, entitled,

(a) To a lien on, or a right of retention of, the surplus of the partnership property after satisfying the partnership liabilities to third persons for any sum of money paid by him for the purchase of an interest in the partnership and for any capital or advances contributed by him; and

(b) To stand, after all liabilities to third persons have been satisfied, in the place of the creditors of the partnership for any payments made by him in respect of the partnership liabilities; and

(c) To be indemnified by the person guilty of the fraud or making the representation against all debts and liabilities of the partnership.

§40. Rules for Distribution

In settling accounts between the partners after dissolution, the following rules shall be observed, subject to any agreement to the contrary:

(a) The assets of the partnership are:

(I) The partnership property,

(II) The contributions of the partners necessary for the payment of all the liabilities specified in clause (b) of this paragraph.

(b) The liabilities of the partnership shall rank in order of payment, as follows:

(I) Those owing to creditors other than partners,

(II) Those owing to partners other than for capital and profits,

(III) Those owing to partners in respect of capital,

(IV) Those owing to partners in respect of profits.

(c) The assets shall be applied in order of their declaration in clause (a) of this paragraph to the satisfaction of the liabilities.

(d) The partners shall contribute, as provided by section 18 (a) the amount necessary to satisfy the liabilities; but if any, but not all, of the partners are insolvent, or, not being subject to process, refuse to contribute, the other partners shall contribute their share of the liabilities, and, in the relative proportions in which they share the profits, the additional amount necessary to pay the liabilities.

(e) An assignee for the benefit of creditors or any person appointed by the court shall have the right to enforce the contributions specified in clause (d) of this paragraph.

(f) Any partner or his legal representative shall have the right to enforce the contributions specified in clause (d) of this paragraph, to the extent of the amount which he has paid in excess of his share of the liability.

(g) The individual property of a deceased partner shall be liable for the contributions specified in clause (d) of this paragraph.

(h) When partnership property and the individual properties of the partners are in possession of a court for distribution, partnership creditors shall have priority on partnership property and separate creditors on individual property, saving the rights of lien or secured creditors as heretofore.

(i) Where a partner has become bankrupt or his estate is insolvent the claims against his separate property shall rank in the following order:

(I) Those owing to separate creditors,

(II) Those owing to partnership creditors,

(III) Those owing to partners by way of contribution.

§41. *Liability of Persons Continuing the Business in Certain Cases*

(1) When any new partner is admitted into an existing partnership, or when any partner retires and assigns (or the representative of the deceased partner assigns) his rights in partnership property to two or more of the partners, or to one or more of the partners and one or more third persons, if the business is continued without liquidation of the partnership affairs, creditors of the first or dissolved partnership are also creditors of the partnership so continuing the business.

(2) When all but one partner retire and assign (or the representative of a deceased partner assigns) their rights in partnership property to the remaining partner, who continues the business without liquidation of partnership affairs, either alone or with others, creditors of the dissolved partnership are also creditors of the person or partnership so continuing the business.

(3) When any partner retires or dies and the business of the dissolved partnership is continued as set forth in paragraphs (1) and (2) of this section, with the consent of the retired partners or the representative of the deceased partner, but without any assignment of his right in partnership property, rights of creditors of the dissolved partnership and of the creditors of the person or partnership continuing the business shall be as if such assignment had been made.

(4) When all the partners or their representatives assign their rights in partnership property to one or more third persons who promise to pay the debts and who

continue the business of the dissolved partnership, creditors of the dissolved partnership are also creditors of the person or partnership continuing the business.

(5) When any partner wrongfully causes a dissolution and the remaining partners continue the business under the provisions of section 38(2b), either alone or with others, and without liquidation of the partnership affairs, creditors of the dissolved partnership are also creditors of the person or partnership continuing the business.

(6) When a partner is expelled and the remaining partners continue the business either alone or with others, without liquidation of the partnership affairs, creditors of the dissolved partnership are also creditors of the person or partnership continuing the business.

(7) The liability of a third person becoming a partner in the partnership continuing the business, under this section, to the creditors of the dissolved partnership shall be satisfied out of partnership property only.

(8) When the business of a partnership after dissolution is continued under any conditions set forth in this section the creditors of the dissolved partnership, as against the separate creditors of the retiring or deceased partner or the representative of the deceased partner, have a prior right to any claim of the retired partner or the representative of the deceased partner against the person or partnership continuing the business, on account of the retired or deceased partner's interest in the dissolved partnership or on account of any consideration promised for such interest or for his right in partnership property.

(9) Nothing in this section shall be held to modify any right of creditors to set aside any assignment on the ground of fraud.

(10) The use by the person or partnership continuing the business of the partnership name, or the name of a deceased partner as part thereof, shall not of itself make the individual property of the deceased partner liable for any debts contracted by such person or partnership.

§42. Rights of Retiring or Estate of Deceased Partner When the Business Is Continued

When any partner retires or dies, and the business is continued under any of the conditions set forth in section 41(1, 2, 3, 5, 6), or section 38(2b) without any settlement of accounts as between him or his estate and the person or partnership continuing the business, unless otherwise agreed, he or his legal representative as against such persons or partnership may have the value of his interest at the date of dissolution ascertained, and shall receive as an ordinary creditor an amount equal to the value of his interest in the dissolved partnership with interest, or, at his option or at the option of his legal representative, in lieu of interest, the profits attributable to the use of his right in the property of the dissolved partnership; provided that the creditors of the dissolved partnership as against the separate creditors, or the representative of the retired or deceased partner, shall have priority on any claim arising under this section, as provided by section 41(8) of this act.

§43. Accrual of Actions

The right to an account of his interest shall accrue to any partner, or his legal representative, as against the winding up partners or the surviving partners or the person or partnership continuing the business, at the date of dissolution, in the absence of any agreement to the contrary.

*Uniform Partnership Act (1997)**

(The Revised Uniform Partnership Act)

ARTICLE 1. GENERAL PROVISIONS

ARTICLE 2. NATURE OF PARTNERSHIP

ARTICLE 3. RELATIONS OF PARTNERS TO PERSONS DEALING WITH PARTNERSHIP

*Including the Amendments adopted July 1997.

ARTICLE 1. GENERAL PROVISIONS

§101. Definitions

In this [Act]:

(1) "Business" includes every trade, occupation, and profession.

(2) "Debtor in bankruptcy" means a person who is the subject of:

(i) an order for relief under Title 11 of the United States Code or a comparable order under a successor statute of general application; or

(ii) a comparable order under federal, state, or foreign law governing insolvency.

(3) "Distribution" means a transfer of money or other property from a partnership to a partner in the partner's capacity as a partner or to the partner's transferee.

(4) "Foreign limited liability partnership" means a partnership that:

(i) is formed under laws other than the laws of this State; and

(ii) has the status of a limited liability partnership under those laws.

(5) "Limited liability partnership" means a partnership that has filed a statement of qualification under Section 1001 and does not have a similar statement in effect in any other jurisdiction.

(6) "Partnership" means an association of two or more persons to carry on as co-owners a business for profit formed under Section 202, predecessor law, or comparable law of another jurisdiction.

(7) "Partnership agreement" means the agreement, whether written, oral or implied, among the partners concerning the partnership, including amendments to the partnership agreement.

(8) "Partnership at will" means a partnership in which the partners have not agreed to remain partners until the expiration of a definite term or the completion of a particular undertaking.

(9) "Partnership interest" or "partner's interest in the partnership" means all of a partner's interests in the partnership, including the partner's transferable interest and all management and other rights.

(10) "Person" means an individual, corporation, business trust, estate, trust, partnership, association, joint venture, government, governmental subdivision, agency, or instrumentality, or any other legal or commercial entity.

(11) "Property" means all property, real, personal, or mixed, tangible or intangible, or any interest therein.

(12) "State" means a State of the United States, the District of Columbia, the Commonwealth of Puerto Rico, or any territory or insular possession subject to the jurisdiction of the United States.

(13) "Statement" means a statement of partnership authority under Section 303, a statement of denial under Section 304, a statement of dissociation under Section 704, a statement of dissolution under Section 805, a statement of merger under Section 907, a statement of qualification under Section 1001, a statement of foreign qualification under Section 1102, or an amendment or cancellation of the foregoing.

(14) "Transfer" includes an assignment, conveyance, lease, mortgage, deed, and encumbrance.

§102. Knowledge and Notice

(a) A person knows a fact if the person has knowledge of it.

(b) A person has notice of a fact if the person:

(1) knows of it;

(2) has received a notification of it; or

(3) has reason to know it exists from all of the facts known to the person at the time in question.

(c) A person notifies or gives a notification to another by taking steps reasonably required to inform the other person in ordinary course, whether or not the other person learns of it.

(d) A person receives a notification when the notification:

(1) comes to the person's attention; or

(2) is duly delivered at the person's place of business or at any other place held out by the person as a place for receiving communications.

(e) Except as otherwise provided in subsection (f), a person other than an individual knows, has notice, or receives a notification of a fact for purposes of a particular transaction when the individual conducting the transaction knows, has notice, or receives a notification of the fact, or in any event when the fact would have been brought to the individual's attention if the person had exercised reasonable diligence. The person exercises reasonable diligence if it maintains reasonable routines for communicating significant information to the individual conducting the transaction and there is reasonable compliance with the routines. Reasonable diligence does not require an individual acting for the person to communicate information unless the communication is part of the individual's regular duties or the individual has reason to know of the transaction and that the transaction would be materially affected by the information.

(f) A partner's knowledge, notice, or receipt of a notification of a fact relating to the partnership is effective immediately as knowledge by, notice to, or receipt of a notification by the partnership, except in the case of a fraud on the partnership committed by or with the consent of that partner.

§103. *Effect of Partnership Agreement; Nonwaivable Provisions*

(a) Except as otherwise provided in subsection (b), relations among the partners and between the partners and the partnership are governed by the partnership agreement. To the extent the partnership agreement does not otherwise provide, this [Act] governs relations among the partners and between the partners and the partnership.

(b) The partnership agreement may not:

(1) vary the rights and duties under Section 105 except to eliminate the duty to provide copies of statements to all of the partners;

(2) unreasonably restrict the right of access to books and records under Section 403(b);

(3) eliminate the duty of loyalty under Section 404(b) or 603(b)(3), but:

(i) the partnership agreement may identify specific types or categories of activities that do not violate the duty of loyalty, if not manifestly unreasonable; or

(ii) all of the partners or a number or percentage specified in the partnership agreement may authorize or ratify, after full disclosure of all material facts, a specific act or transaction that otherwise would violate the duty of loyalty;

(4) unreasonably reduce the duty of care under Section 404(c) or 603(b)(3);

(5) eliminate the obligation of good faith and fair dealing under Section 404(d), but the partnership agreement may prescribe the standards by which the performance of the obligation is to be measured, if the standards are not manifestly unreasonable;

(6) vary the power to dissociate as a partner under Section 602(a), except to require the notice under Section 601(1) to be in writing;

(7) vary the right of a court to expel a partner in the events specified in Section 601(5);

(8) vary the requirement to wind up the partnership business in cases specified in Section 801(4), (5), or (6);

(9) vary the law applicable to a limited liability partnership under Section 106(b); or

(10) restrict rights of third parties under this [Act].

§104. Supplemental Principles of Law

(a) Unless displaced by particular provisions of this [Act], the principles of law and equity supplement this [Act].

(b) If an obligation to pay interest arises under this [Act] and the rate is not specified, the rate is that specified in [applicable statute].

§105. Execution, Filing, and Recording of Statements

(a) A statement may be filed in the office of [the Secretary of State]. A certified copy of a statement that is filed in an office in another State may be filed in the office of [the Secretary of State]. Either filing has the effect provided in this [Act] with respect to partnership property located in or transactions that occur in this State.

(b) A certified copy of a statement that has been filed in the office of the [Secretary of State] and recorded in the office for recording transfers of real property has the effect provided for recorded statements in this [Act]. A recorded statement that is not a certified copy of a statement filed in the office of the [Secretary of State] does not have the effect provided for recorded statements in this [Act].

(c) A statement filed by a partnership must be executed by at least two partners. Other statements must be executed by a partner or other person authorized by this [Act]. An individual who executes a statement as, or on behalf of, a partner or other person named as a partner in a statement shall personally declare under penalty of perjury that the contents of the statement are accurate.

(d) A person authorized by this [Act] to file a statement may amend or cancel the statement by filing an amendment or cancellation that names the partnership, identifies the statement, and states the substance of the amendment or cancellation.

(e) A person who files a statement pursuant to this section shall promptly send a copy of the statement to every non-filing partner and to any other person named as a partner. Failure to send a copy of a statement to a partner or other person does not limit the effectiveness of the statement as to a person not a partner.

(f) The [Secretary of State] may collect a fee for filing or providing a certified copy of a statement. The [officer responsible for] recording transfers of real property may collect a fee for recording a statement.

§106. *Governing Law*

(a) Except as otherwise provided in subsection (b), the law of the jurisdiction in which a partnership has its chief executive office governs relations among the partners and between the partners and the partnership.

(b) The law of this State governs relations among the partners and between the partners and the partnership and the liability of partners for an obligation of a limited liability partnership.

§107. *Partnership Subject to Amendment or Repeal of [Act]*

(a) A partnership governed by this [Act] is subject to any amendment to or repeal of this [Act].

(b) A limited liability partnership continues to be the same entity that existed before the filing of a statement of qualification under Section 1001.

ARTICLE 2. NATURE OF PARTNERSHIP

§201. *Partnership as Entity*

(a) A partnership is an entity distinct from its partners.

(b) A limited liability partnership continues to be the same entity that existed before the filing of a statement of qualification under Section 1001.

§202. *Formation of Partnership*

(a) Except as otherwise provided in subsection (b), the association of two or more persons to carry on as co-owners a business for profit forms a partnership, whether or not the persons intend to form a partnership.

(b) An association formed under a statute other than this [Act], a predecessor statute, or a comparable statute of another jurisdiction is not a partnership under this act.

(c) In determining whether a partnership is formed, the following rules apply:

(1) Joint tenancy, tenancy in common, tenancy by the entireties, joint property, common property, or part ownership does not by itself establish a partnership, even if the co-owners share profits made by the use of the property.

(2) The sharing of gross returns does not by itself establish a partnership, even if the persons sharing them have a joint or common right or interest in property from which the returns are derived.

(3) A person who receives a share of the profits of a business is presumed to be a partner in the business, unless the profits were received in payment:

(i) of a debt by installments or otherwise;

(ii) for services as an independent contractor or of wages or other compensation to an employee;

(iii) of rent;

(iv) of an annuity or other retirement benefit to a beneficiary, representative, or designee of a deceased or retired partner;

(v) of interest or other charge on a loan, even if the amount of payment varies with the profits of the business, including a direct or indirect present or future ownership of the collateral, or rights to income, proceeds, or increase in value derived from the collateral; or

(vi) for the sale of the goodwill of a business or other property by installments or otherwise.

§203. Partnership Property

Property acquired by a partnership is property of the partnership and not of the partners individually.

§204. When Property Is Partnership Property

(a) Property is partnership property if acquired in the name of:

(1) the partnership; or

(2) one or more partners with an indication in the instrument transferring title to the property of the person's capacity as a partner or of the existence of a partnership but without an indication of the name of the partnership.

(b) Property is acquired in the name of the partnership by a transfer to:

(1) the partnership in its name; or

(2) one or more partners in their capacity as partners in the partnership, if the name of the partnership is indicated in the instrument transferring title to the property.

(c) Property is presumed to be partnership property if purchased with partnership assets, even if not acquired in the name of the partnership or one or more partners with an indication in the instrument transferring title to the property of the person's capacity as a partner or of the existence of a partnership.

(d) Property acquired in the name of one or more of the partners, without an indication in the instrument transferring title to the property of the person's capacity as a partner or of the existence of a partnership and without use of partnership assets, is presumed to be separate property, even if used for partnership purposes.

Article 3. Relations of Partners to Persons Dealing with Partnership

§301. Partner Agent of Partnership

Subject to the effect of a statement of partnership authority under Section 303:

(1) Each partner is an agent of the partnership for the purpose of its business. An act of a partner, including the execution of an instrument in the partnership name, for apparently carrying on in the ordinary course the partnership business or business of the kind carried on by the partnership binds the partnership, unless the partner had no authority to act for the partnership in the particular matter and the person with whom the partner was dealing knew or had received a notification that the partner lacked authority.

(2) An act of a partner which is not apparently for carrying on in the ordinary course the partnership business or business of the kind carried on by the partnership binds the partnership only if the act was authorized by the other partners.

§302. *Transfer of Partnership Property*

(a) Partnership property may be transferred as follows:

(1) Subject to the effect of a statement of partnership authority under Section 303, partnership property held in the name of the partnership may be transferred by an instrument of transfer executed by a partner in the partnership name.

(2) Partnership property held in the name of one or more partners with an indication in the instrument transferring the property to them of their capacity as partners or of the existence of a partnership, but without an indication of the name of the partnership, may be transferred by an instrument of transfer executed by the persons in whose name the property is held.

(3) Partnership property held in the name of one or more persons other than the partnership, without an indication in the instrument transferring the property to them of their capacity as partners or of the existence of a partnership, may be transferred by an instrument of transfer executed by the persons in whose name the property is held.

(b) A partnership may recover partnership property from a transferee only if it proves that execution of the instrument of initial transfer did not bind the partnership under Section 301 and:

(1) as to a subsequent transferee who gave value for property transferred under subsection (a)(1) and (2), proves that the subsequent transferee knew or had received a notification that the person who executed the instrument of initial transfer lacked authority to bind the partnership; or

(2) as to a transferee who gave value for property transferred under subsection (a)(3), proves that the transferee knew or had received a notification that the property was partnership property and that the person who executed the instrument of initial transfer lacked authority to bind the partnership.

(c) A partnership may not recover partnership property from a subsequent transferee if the partnership would not have been entitled to recover the property, under subsection (b), from any earlier transferee of the property.

(d) If a person holds all of the partners' interests in the partnership, all of the partnership property vests in that person. The person may execute a document in the name of the partnership to evidence vesting of the property in that person and may file or record the document.

§303. Statement of Partnership Authority

(a) A partnership may file a statement of partnership authority, which:

(1) must include:

(i) the name of the partnership;

(ii) the street address of its chief executive office and of one office in this State, if there is one;

(iii) the names and mailing addresses of all of the partners or of an agent appointed and maintained by the partnership for the purpose of subsection (b); and

(iv) the names of the partners authorized to execute an instrument transferring real property held in the name of the partnership; and

(2) may state the authority, or limitations on the authority, of some or all of the partners to enter into other transactions on behalf of the partnership and any other matter.

(b) If a statement of partnership authority names an agent, the agent shall maintain a list of the names and mailing addresses of all of the partners and make it available to any person on request for good cause shown.

(c) If a filed statement of partnership authority is executed pursuant to Section 105(c) and states the name of the partnership but does not contain all of the other information required by subsection (a), the statement nevertheless operates with respect to a person not a partner as provided in subsections (d) and (e).

(d) Except as otherwise provided in subsection (g) a filed statement of partnership authority supplements the authority of a partner to enter into transactions on behalf of the partnership as follows:

(1) Except for transfers of real property, a grant of authority contained in a filed statement of partnership authority is conclusive in favor of a person who gives value without knowledge to the contrary, so long as and to the extent that a limitation on that authority is not then contained in another filed statement. A filed cancellation of a limitation on authority revives the previous grant of authority.

(2) A grant of authority to transfer real property held in the name of the partnership contained in a certified copy of a filed statement of partnership authority recorded in the office for recording transfers of that real property is conclusive in favor of a person who gives value without knowledge to the contrary, so long as and to the extent that a certified copy of a filed statement containing a limitation on that authority is not then of record in the office for recording transfers of that real property. The recording in the office for recording transfers of that real property of a certified copy of a filed cancellation of a limitation on authority revives the previous grant of authority.

(e) A person not a partner is deemed to know of a limitation on the authority of a partner to transfer real property held in the name of the partnership if a certified copy of the filed statement containing the limitation on authority is of record in the office for recording transfers of that real property.

(f) Except as otherwise provided in subsections (d) and (e) and Sections 704 and 805, a person not a partner is not deemed to know of a limitation on the authority of a partner merely because the limitation is contained in a filed statement.

(g) Unless earlier canceled, a filed statement of partnership authority is canceled by operation of law five years after the date on which the statement, or the most recent amendment, was filed with the [Secretary of State].

§304. Statement of Denial

A partner or other person named as a partner in a filed statement of partnership authority or in a list maintained by an agent pursuant to Section 303(b) may file a statement of denial stating the name of the partnership and the fact that is being denied, which may include denial of a person's authority or status as a partner. A statement of denial is a limitation on authority as provided in Sections 303(d) and (e).

§305. Partnership Liable for Partner's Actionable Conduct

(a) A partnership is liable for loss or injury caused to a person, or for a penalty incurred, as a result of a wrongful act or omission, or other actionable conduct, of a partner acting in the ordinary course of business of the partnership or with authority of the partnership.

(b) If, in the course of the partnership's business or while acting with authority of the partnership, a partner receives or causes the partnership to receive money or property of a person not a partner, and the money or property is misapplied by a partner, the partnership is liable for the loss.

§306. Partner's Liability

(a) Except as otherwise provided in subsections (b) and (c), all partners are liable jointly and severally for all obligations of the partnership unless otherwise agreed by the claimant or provided by law.

(b) A person admitted as a partner into an existing partnership is not personally liable for any partnership obligation incurred before the person's admission as a partner.

(c) An obligation of a partnership incurred while the partnership is a limited liability partnership, whether arising in contract, tort, or otherwise, is solely the obligation of the partnership. A partner is not personally liable, directly or indirectly, by way of contribution or otherwise, for such an obligation solely by reason of being or so acting as a partner. This subsection applies notwithstanding anything inconsistent in the partnership agreement that existed immediately before the vote required to become a limited liability partnership under Section 1001(b).

§307. Action by and Against Partnership and Partners

(a) A partnership may sue and be sued in the name of the partnership.

(b) An action may be brought against the partnership and, to the extent not inconsistent with Section 306, any or all of the partners in the same action or in separate actions.

(c) A judgment against a partnership is not by itself a judgment against a partner. A judgment against a partnership may not be satisfied from a partner's assets unless there is also a judgment against the partner.

(d) A judgment creditor of a partner may not levy execution against the assets of the partner to satisfy a judgment based on a claim against the partnership unless the partner is personally liable for the claim under Section 306 and:

(1) a judgment based on the same claim has been obtained against the partnership and a writ of execution on the judgment has been returned unsatisfied in whole or in part;

(2) the partnership is a debtor in bankruptcy;

(3) the partner has agreed that the creditor need not exhaust partnership assets;

(4) a court grants permission to the judgment creditor to levy execution against the assets of a partner based on a finding that partnership assets subject to execution are clearly insufficient to satisfy the judgment, that exhaustion of partnership assets is excessively burdensome, or that the grant of permission is an appropriate exercise of the court's equitable powers; or

(5) liability is imposed on the partner by law or contract independent of the existence of the partnership.

(e) This section applies to any partnership liability or obligation resulting from a representation by a partner or purported partner under Section 308.

§308. Liability of Purported Partner

(a) If a person, by words or conduct, purports to be a partner, or consents to being represented by another as a partner, in a partnership or with one or more persons not partners, the purported partner is liable to a person to whom the representation is made, if that person, relying on the representation, enters into a transaction with the actual or purported partnership. If the representation, either by the purported partner or by a person with the purported partner's consent, is made in a public manner, the purported partner is liable to a person who relies upon the purported partnership even if the purported partner is not aware of being held out as a partner to the claimant. If partnership liability results, the purported partner is liable with respect to that liability as if the purported partner were a partner. If no partnership liability results, the purported partner is liable with respect to that liability jointly and severally with any other person consenting to the representation.

(b) If a person is thus represented to be a partner in an existing partnership, or with one or more persons not partners, the purported partner is an agent of persons consenting to the representation to bind them to the same extent and in the same manner as if the purported partner were a partner, with respect to persons who enter into transactions in reliance upon the representation. If all of the partners of the existing partnership consent to the representation, a partnership act or obligation results. If fewer than all of the partners of the existing partnership consent to the representation, the person acting and the partners consenting to the representation are jointly and severally liable.

(c) A person is not liable as a partner merely because the person is named by another in a statement of partnership authority.

(d) A person does not continue to be liable as a partner merely because of a failure to file a statement of dissociation or to amend a statement of partnership authority to indicate the partner's dissociation from the partnership.

(e) Except as otherwise provided in subsections (a) and (b), persons who are not partners as to each other are not liable as partners to other persons.

Article 4. Relations of Partners to Each Other and to Partnership

§401. Partner's Rights and Duties

(a) Each partner is deemed to have an account that is:

(1) credited with an amount equal to the money plus the value of any other property, net of the amount of any liabilities, the partner contributes to the partnership and the partner's share of the partnership profits; and

(2) charged with an amount equal to the money plus the value of any other property, net of the amount of any liabilities, distributed by the partnership to the partner and the partner's share of the partnership losses.

(b) Each partner is entitled to an equal share of the partnership profits and chargeable with a share of the partnership losses in proportion to the partner's share of the profits.

(c) A partnership shall reimburse a partner for payments made and indemnify a partner for liabilities incurred by the partner in the ordinary course of the business of the partnership or for the preservation of its business or property.

(d) A partnership shall reimburse a partner for an advance to the partnership beyond the amount of capital the partner agreed to contribute.

(e) A payment or advance made by a partner which gives rise to a partnership obligation under subsection (c) or (d) constitutes a loan to the partnership which accrues interest from the date of the payment or advance.

(f) Each partner has equal rights in the management and conduct of the partnership business.

(g) A partner may use or possess partnership property only on behalf of the partnership.

(h) A partner is not entitled to remuneration for services performed for the partnership, except for reasonable compensation for services rendered in winding up the business of the partnership.

(i) A person may become a partner only with the consent of all of the partners.

(j) A difference arising as to a matter in the ordinary course of business of a partnership may be decided by a majority of the partners. An act outside the ordinary course of business of a partnership and an amendment to the partnership agreement may be undertaken only with the consent of all of the partners.

(k) This section does not affect the obligations of a partnership to other persons under Section 301.

§402. *Distributions in Kind*

A partner has no right to receive, and may not be required to accept, a distribution in kind.

§403. *Partner's Rights and Duties with Respect to Information*

(a) A partnership shall keep its books and records, if any, at its chief executive office.

(b) A partnership shall provide partners and their agents and attorneys access to its books and records. It shall provide former partners and their agents and attorneys access to books and records pertaining to the period during which they were partners. The right of access provides the opportunity to inspect and copy books and records during ordinary business hours. A partnership may impose a reasonable charge, covering the costs of labor and material, for copies of documents furnished.

(c) Each partner and the partnership shall furnish to a partner, and to the legal representative of a deceased partner or partner under legal disability:

(1) without demand, any information concerning the partnership's business and affairs reasonably required for the proper exercise of the partner's rights and duties under the partnership agreement or this [Act]; and

(2) on demand, any other information concerning the partnership's business and affairs, except to the extent the demand or the information demanded is unreasonable or otherwise improper under the circumstances.

§404. *General Standards of Partner's Conduct*

(a) The only fiduciary duties a partner owes to the partnership and the other partners are the duty of loyalty and the duty of care set forth in subsections (b) and (c).

(b) A partner's duty of loyalty to the partnership and the other partners is limited to the following:

(1) to account to the partnership and hold as trustee for it any property, profit, or benefit derived by the partner in the conduct and winding up of the partnership business or derived from a use by the partner of partnership property, including the appropriation of a partnership opportunity;

(2) to refrain from dealing with the partnership in the conduct or winding up of the partnership business as or on behalf of a party having an interest adverse to the partnership; and

(3) to refrain from competing with the partnership in the conduct of the partnership business before the dissolution of the partnership.

(c) A partner's duty of care to the partnership and the other partners in the conduct and winding up of the partnership business is limited to refraining from engaging in grossly negligent or reckless conduct, intentional misconduct, or a knowing violation of law.

(d) A partner shall discharge the duties to the partnership and the other partners under this [Act] or under the partnership agreement and exercise any rights consistently with the obligation of good faith and fair dealing.

(e) A partner does not violate a duty or obligation under this [Act] or under the partnership agreement merely because the partner's conduct furthers the partner's own interest.

(f) A partner may lend money to and transact other business with the partnership, and as to each loan or transaction, the rights and obligations of the partner are the same as those of a person who is not a partner, subject to other applicable law.

(g) This section applies to a person winding up the partnership business as the personal or legal representative of the last surviving partner as if the person were a partner.

§405. *Actions by Partnership and Partners*

(a) A partnership may maintain an action against a partner for a breach of the partnership agreement, or for the violation of a duty to the partnership, causing harm to the partnership.

(b) A partner may maintain an action against the partnership or another partner for legal or equitable relief, with or without an accounting as to partnership business, to:

(1) enforce the partner's rights under the partnership agreement;

(2) enforce the partner's rights under this [Act], including:

(i) the partner's right under Sections 401, 403, or 404;

(ii) the partner's right on dissociation to have the partner's interest in the partnership purchased pursuant to Section 701 or enforce any other right under Article 6 or 7; or

(iii) the partner's right to compel a dissolution and winding up of the partnership business under Section 801 or enforce any other right under Article 8; or

(3) enforce the rights and otherwise protect the interests of the partner, including rights and interests arising independently of the partnership relationship.

(c) The accrual of, and any time limitation on, a right of action for a remedy under this section is governed by other law. A right to an accounting upon a dissolution and winding up does not revive a claim barred by law.

§406. *Continuation of Partnership Beyond Definite Term or Particular Undertaking*

(a) If a partnership for a definite term or particular undertaking is continued, without an express agreement, after the expiration of the term or completion of the undertaking, the rights and duties of the partners remain the same as they were at the expiration or completion, so far as is consistent with a partnership at will.

(b) If the partners, or those of them who habitually acted in the business during the term or undertaking, continue the business without any settlement or liquidation of the partnership, they are presumed to have agreed that the partnership will continue.

Article 5. Transferees and Creditors of Partner

§501. Partner Not Co-Owner of Partnership Property

A partner is not a co-owner of partnership property and has no interest in partnership property which can be transferred, either voluntarily or involuntarily.

§502. Partner's Transferable Interest in Partnership

The only transferable interest of a partner in the partnership is the partner's share of the profits and losses of the partnership and the partner's right to receive distributions. The interest is personal property.

§503. Transfer of Partner's Transferable Interest

(a) A transfer, in whole or in part, of a partner's transferable interest in the partnership:

(1) is permissible;

(2) does not by itself cause a dissolution and winding up of the partnership business; and

(3) does not, as against the other partners or the partnership, entitle the transferee, during the continuance of the partnership, to participate in the management or conduct of the partnership business, to require access to information concerning partnership transactions, or to inspect or copy the partnership books or records.

(b) A transferee of a partner's transferable interest in the partnership has a right:

(1) to receive, in accordance with the transfer, distributions to which the transferor would otherwise be entitled;

(2) to receive upon the dissolution and winding up of the partnership business, in accordance with the transfer, the net amount otherwise distributable to the transferor; and

(3) to seek under Section 801(6) a judicial determination that it is equitable to wind up the partnership business.

(c) In a dissolution and winding up, a transferee is entitled to an account of partnership transactions only from the date of the lastest account agreed to by all of the partners.

(d) Upon transfer, the transferor retains the rights and duties of a partner other than the interest in distributions transferred.

(e) A partnership need not give effect to a transferee's rights under this section until it has notice of the transfer.

(f) A transfer of a partner's transferable interest in the partnership in violation of a restriction on transfer contained in the partnership agreement is ineffective as to a person having notice of the restriction at the time of transfer.

§504. Partner's Transferable Interest Subject to Charging Order

(a) On application by a judgment creditor of a partner or a partner's transferee, a court having jurisdiction may charge the transferable interest of the debtor partner or transferee to satisfy the judgment. The court may appoint a receiver of the share of the distributions due or to become due to the judgment debtor in respect of the partnership and make all other orders, directions, accounts, and inquiries the judgment debtor might have made or which the circumstances of the case may require.

(b) A charging order constitutes a lien on the judgment debtor's transferable interest in the partnership. The court may order a foreclosure of the interest subject to the charging order at any time. The purchaser at the foreclosure sale has the rights of a transferee.

(c) At any time before foreclosure, an interest charged may be redeemed:

(1) by the judgment debtor;

(2) with property other than partnership property, by one or more of the other partners; or

(3) with partnership property, by one or more of the other partners with the consent of all of the partners whose interests are not so charged.

(d) This [Act] does not deprive a partner of a right under exemption laws with respect to the partner's interest in the partnership.

(e) This Section provides the exclusive remedy by which a judgment creditor of a partner or partner's transferee may satisfy a judgment out of the judgment debtor's transferable interest in the partnership.

ARTICLE 6. PARTNER'S DISSOCIATION

§601. Events Causing Partner's Dissociation

A partner is dissociated from a partnership upon the occurrence of any of the following events:

(1) the partnership's having notice of the partner's express will to withdraw as a partner or on a later date specified by the partner;

(2) an event agreed to in the partnership agreement as causing the partner's dissociation;

(3) the partner's expulsion pursuant to the partnership agreement;

(4) the partner's expulsion by the unanimous vote of the other partners if:

(i) it is unlawful to carry on the partnership business with that partner;

(ii) there has been a transfer of all or substantially all of that partner's transferable interest in the partnership, other than a transfer for security purposes, or a court order charging the partner's interest, which has not been foreclosed;

(iii) within 90 days after the partnership notifies a corporate partner that it will be expelled because it has filed a certificate of dissolution or the equivalent, its charter has been revoked, or its right to conduct business has been suspended by the jurisdiction of its incorporation, there is no revocation of the certificate of dissolution or no reinstatement of its charter or its right to conduct business; or

(iv) a partnership that is a partner has been dissolved and its business is being wound up;

(5) on application by the partnership or another partner, the partner's expulsion by judicial determination because:

(i) the partner engaged in wrongful conduct that adversely and materially affected the partnership business;

(ii) the partner willfully or persistently committed a material breach of the partnership agreement or of a duty owed to the partnership or the other partners under Section 404; or

(iii) the partner engaged in conduct relating to the partnership business which makes it not reasonably practicable to carry on the business in partnership with the partner;

(6) the partner's:

(i) becoming a debtor in bankruptcy;

(ii) executing an assignment for the benefit of creditors;

(iii) seeking, consenting to, or acquiescing in the appointment of a trustee, receiver, or liquidator of that partner or of all or substantially all of that partner's property; or

(iv) failing, within 90 days after the appointment, to have vacated or stayed the appointment of a trustee, receiver, or liquidator of the partner or of all or substantially all of the partner's property obtained without the partner's consent or acquiescence, or failing within 90 days after the expiration of a stay to have the appointment vacated;

(7) in the case of a partner who is an individual;

(i) the partner's death;

(ii) the appointment of a guardian or general conservator for the partner; or

(iii) a judicial determination that the partner has otherwise become incapable of performing the partner's duties under the partnership agreement;

(8) in the case of a partner that is a trust or is acting as a partner by virtue of being a trustee of a trust, distribution of the trust's entire transferable interest in the partnership, but not merely by reason of the substitution of a successor trustee;

(9) in the case of a partner that is an estate or is acting as a partner by virtue of being a personal representative of an estate, distribution of the estate's entire transferable interest in the partnership, but not merely by reason of the substitution of a successor personal representative; or

(10) termination of a partner who is not an individual, partnership, corporation, trust, or estate.

§602. *Partner's Power to Dissociate; Wrongful Dissociation*

(a) A partner has the power to dissociate at any time, rightfully or wrongfully, by express will pursuant to Section 601(1).

(b) A partner's dissociation is wrongful only if:

(1) it is in breach of an express provision of the partnership agreement; or

(2) in the case of a partnership for a definite term or particular undertaking, before the expiration of the term or the completion of the undertaking:

(i) the partner withdraws by express will, unless the withdrawal follows within 90 days after another partner's dissociation by death or otherwise under Section 601(6) through (10) or wrongful dissociation under this subsection;

(ii) the partner is expelled by judicial determination under Section 601(5);

(iii) the partner is dissociated by becoming a debtor in bankruptcy; or

(iv) in the case of a partner who is not an individual, trust other than a business trust, or estate, the partner is expelled or otherwise dissociated because it willfully dissolved or terminated.

(c) A partner who wrongfully dissociates is liable to the partnership and to the other partners for damages caused by the dissociation. The liability is in addition to any other obligation of the partner to the partnership or to the other partners.

§603. *Effect of Partner's Dissociation*

(a) If a partner's dissociation results in a dissolution and winding up of the partnership business, Article 8 applies; otherwise, Article 7 applies.

(b) Upon a partner's dissociation:

(1) the partner's right to participate in the management and conduct of the partnership business terminates, except as otherwise provided in Section 803;

(2) the partner's duty of loyalty under Section 404(b)(3) terminates; and

(3) the partner's duty of loyalty under Section 404(b)(1) and (2) and duty of care under Section 404(c) continue only with regard to matters arising and events occurring before the partner's dissociation, unless the partner participates in winding up the partnership's business pursuant to Section 803.

Article 7. Partner's Dissociation When Business Not Wound Up

§701. *Purchase of Dissociated Partner's Interest*

(a) If a partner is dissociated from a partnership without resulting in a dissolution and winding up of the partnership business under Section 801, the partnership shall cause the dissociated partner's interest in the partnership to be purchased for a buyout price determined pursuant to subsection (b).

(b) The buyout price of a dissociated partner's interest is the amount that would have been distributable to the dissociating partner under Section 807(b) if, on the date of dissociation, the assets of the partnership were sold at a price equal to the greater of the liquidation value or the value based on a sale of the entire business as a going concern without the dissociated partner and the partnership were wound up as of that date. Interest must be paid from the date of dissociation to the date of payment.

(c) Damages for wrongful dissociation under Section 602(b), and all other amounts owing, whether or not presently due, from the dissociated partner to the partnership, must be offset against the buyout price. Interest must be paid from the date the amount owed becomes due to the date of payment.

(d) A partnership shall indemnify a dissociated partner whose interest is being purchased against all partnership liabilities, whether incurred before or after the dissociation, except liabilities incurred by an act of the dissociated partner under Section 702.

(e) If no agreement for the purchase of a dissociated partner's interest is reached within 120 days after a written demand for payment, the partnership shall pay, or cause to be paid, in cash to the dissociated partner the amount the partnership estimates to be the buyout price and accrued interest, reduced by any offsets and accrued interest under subsection (c).

(f) If a deferred payment is authorized under subsection (h), the partnership may tender a written offer to pay the amount it estimates to be the buyout price and accrued interest, reduced by any offsets under subsection (c), stating the time of payment, the amount and type of security for payment, and the other terms and conditions of the obligation.

(g) The payment or tender required by subsection (e) or (f) must be accompanied by the following:

(1) a statement of partnership assets and liabilities as of the date of dissociation;

(2) the latest available partnership balance sheet and income statement, if any;

(3) an explanation of how the estimated amount of the payment was calculated; and

(4) written notice that the payment is in full satisfaction of the obligation to purchase unless, within 120 days after the written notice, the dissociated partner commences an action to determine the buyout price, any offsets under subsection (c), or other terms of the obligation to purchase.

(h) A partner who wrongfully dissociates before the expiration of a definite term or the completion of a particular undertaking is not entitled to payment of any portion of the buyout price until the expiration of the term or completion of the undertaking, unless the partner establishes to the satisfaction of the court that earlier payment will not cause undue hardship to the business of the partnership. A deferred payment must be adequately secured and bear interest.

(i) A dissociated partner may maintain an action against the partnership, pursuant to Section 405(b)(2)(ii), to determine the buyout price of that partner's interest, any offsets under subsection (c), or other terms of the obligation to purchase. The action must be commenced within 120 days after the partnership has tendered payment or an offer to pay or within one year after written demand for payment if no payment or offer to pay is tendered. The court shall determine the buyout price of the dissociated partner's interest, any offset due under subsection (c), and accrued interest, and enter judgment for any additional payment or refund. If deferred payment is authorized under subsection (h), the court shall also determine the security for payment and other terms of the obligation to purchase. The court may assess reasonable attorney's fees and the fees and expenses of appraisers or other experts for a party to the action, in amounts the court finds equitable, against a party that the court finds acted arbitrarily, vexatiously, or not in good faith. The finding may be based on the partnership's failure to tender payment or an offer to pay or to comply with subsection (g).

§702. *Dissociated Partner's Power to Bind Partnership*

(a) For two years after a partner dissociates without resulting in a dissolution and winding up of the partnership business, the partnership, including a surviving partnership under Article 9, is bound by an act of the dissociated partner which would have bound the partnership under Section 301 before dissociation only if at the time of entering into the transaction the other party:

(1) reasonably believed that the dissociated partner was then a partner;

(2) did not have notice of the partner's dissociation; and

(3) is not deemed to have had knowledge under Section 303(e) or notice under Section 704(c).

(b) A dissociated partner is liable to the partnership for any loss caused to the partnership arising from an obligation incurred by the dissociated partner after dissociation for which the partnership is liable under subsection (a).

§703. *Dissociated Partner's Liability to Other Persons*

(a) A partner's dissociation does not of itself discharge the partner's liability for a partnership obligation incurred before dissociation. A dissociated partner is not liable for a partnership obligation incurred after dissociation, except as otherwise provided in subsection (b).

(b) A partner who dissociates without resulting in a dissolution and winding up of the partnership business is liable as a partner to the other party in a transaction entered into by the partnership, or a surviving partnership under Article 9, within two years after the partner's dissociation, only if the partner is liable for the obligation under Section 306 and at the time of entering into the transaction the other party:

(1) reasonably believed that the dissociated partner was then a partner;

(2) did not have notice of the partner's dissociation; and

(3) is not deemed to have had knowledge under Section 303(e) or notice under Section 704(c).

(c) By agreement with the partnership creditor and the partners continuing the business, a dissociated partner may be released from liability for a partnership obligation.

(d) A dissociated partner is released from liability for a partnership obligation if a partnership creditor, with notice of the partner's dissociation but without the partner's consent, agrees to a material alteration in the nature or time of payment of a partnership obligation.

§704. Statement of Dissociation

(a) A dissociated partner or the partnership may file a statement of dissociation stating the name of the partnership and that the partner is dissociated from the partnership.

(b) A statement of dissociation is a limitation on the authority of a dissociated partner for the purpose of Section 303(d) and (e).

(c) For the purposes of Sections 702(a)(3) and 703(b)(3), a person not a partner is deemed to have notice of the dissociation 90 days after the statement of dissociation is filed.

§705. Continued Use of Partnership Name

Continued use of a partnership name, or a dissociated partner's name as part thereof, by partners continuing the business does not of itself make the dissociated partner liable for an obligation of the partners or the partnership continuing the business.

ARTICLE 8. WINDING UP PARTNERSHIP BUSINESS

§801. Events Causing Dissolution and Winding Up of Partnership Business

A partnership is dissolved, and its business must be wound up, only upon the occurrence of any of the following events:

(1) in a partnership at will, the partnership's having notice from a partner, other than a partner who is dissociated under Section 601(2) through (10), of that partner's express will to withdraw as a partner, or on a later date specified by the partner;

(2) in a partnership for a definite term or particular undertaking:

(i) within 90 days after a partner's dissociation by death or otherwise under Section 601(6) through (10) or wrongful dissociation under Section 602(b), the express will of at least half of the remaining partners to wind up the partnership business, for which purpose a partner's rightful dissociation pursuant to Section 602(b)(2)(i) constitutes the expression of that partner's will to wind up the partnership business;

(ii) the express will of all of the partners to wind up the partnership business; or

(iii) the expiration of the term or the completion of the undertaking;

(3) an event agreed to in the partnership agreement resulting in the winding up of the partnership business;

(4) an event that makes it unlawful for all or substantially all of the business of the partnership to be continued, but a cure of illegality within 90 days after

notice to the partnership of the event is effective retroactively to the date of the event for purposes of this section;

(5) on application by a partner, a judicial determination that:

(i) the economic purpose of the partnership is likely to be unreasonably frustrated;

(ii) another partner has engaged in conduct relating to the partnership business which makes it not reasonably practicable to carry on the business in partnership with that partner; or

(iii) it is not otherwise reasonably practicable to carry on the partnership business in conformity with the partnership agreement; or

(6) on application by a transferee of a partner's transferable interest, a judicial determination that it is equitable to wind up the partnership business:

(i) after the expiration of the term or completion of the undertaking, if the partnership was for a definite term or particular undertaking at the time of the transfer or entry of the charging order that gave rise to the transfer; or

(ii) at any time, if the partnership was a partnership at will at the time of the transfer or entry of the charging order that gave rise to the transfer.

§802. Partnership Continues after Dissolution

(a) Subject to subsection (b), a partnership continues after dissolution only for the purpose of winding up its business. The partnership is terminated when the winding up of its business is completed.

(b) At any time after the dissolution of a partnership and before the winding up of its business is completed, all of the partners, including any dissociating partner other than a wrongfully dissociating partner, may waive the right to have the partnership's business wound up and the partnership terminated. In that event:

(1) the partnership resumes carrying on its business as if dissolution had never occurred, and any liability incurred by the partnership or a partner after the dissolution and before the waiver is determined as if dissolution had never occurred; and

(2) the rights of a third party accruing under Section 804(1) or arising out of conduct in reliance on the dissolution before the third party knew or received a notification of the waiver may not be adversely affected.

§803. Right to Wind Up Partnership Business

(a) After dissolution, a partner who has not wrongfully dissociated may participate in winding up a partnership's business, but on application of any partner, partner's legal representative, or transferee, the [designate the appropriate court], for good cause shown, may order judicial supervision of the winding up.

(b) The legal representative of the last surviving partner may wind up a partnership's business.

(c) A person winding up a partnership's business may preserve the partnership business or property as a going concern for a reasonable time, prosecute and defend actions and proceedings, whether civil, criminal, or administrative, settle and close the partnership's business, dispose of and transfer the partnership's property, discharge the partnership's liabilities, distribute the assets of the partnership pursuant to Section 807, settle disputes by mediation or arbitration, and perform other necessary acts.

§804. *Partner's Power to Bind Partnership after Dissolution*

Subject to Section 805, a partnership is bound by a partner's act after dissolution that:

(1) is appropriate for winding up the partnership business; or

(2) would have bound the partnership under Section 301 before dissolution, if the other party to the transaction did not have notice of the dissolution.

§805. *Statement of Dissolution*

(a) After dissolution, a partner who has not wrongfully dissociated may file a statement of dissolution stating the name of the partnership and that the partnership has dissolved and is winding up its business.

(b) A statement of dissolution cancels a filed statement of partnership authority for the purposes of Section 303(d) and is a limitation on authority for the purposes of Section 303(e).

(c) For the purposes of Sections 301 and 804, a person not a partner is deemed to have notice of the dissolution and the limitation on the partners' authority as a result of the statement of dissolution 90 days after it is filed.

(d) After filing and, if appropriate, recording a statement of dissolution, a dissolved partnership may file and, if appropriate, record a statement of partnership authority which will operate with respect to a person not a partner as provided in Sections 303(d) and (e) in any transaction, whether or not the transaction is appropriate for winding up the partnership business.

§806. *Partner's Liability to Other Partners after Dissolution*

(a) Except as otherwise provided in subsection (b) and Section 306, after dissolution a partner is liable to the other partners for the partner's share of any partnership liability incurred under Section 804.

(b) A partner who, with knowledge of the dissolution, incurs a partnership liability under Section 804(2) by an act that is not appropriate for winding up the partnership business is liable to the partnership for any damage caused to the partnership arising from the liability.

§807. *Settlement of Accounts Among Partners*

(a) In winding up a partnership's business, the assets of the partnership, including the contributions of the partners required by this section, must be applied to discharge its obligations to creditors, including, to the extent permitted by law, partners who are creditors. Any surplus must be applied to pay in cash the net amount distributable to partners in accordance with their right to distributions under subsection (b).

(b) Each partner is entitled to a settlement of all partnership accounts upon winding up the partnership business. In settling accounts among the partners, the profits and losses that result from the liquidation of the partnership assets must be credited and charged to the partners' accounts. The partnership shall make a distribution to a partner in an amount equal to any excess of the credits over the charges in the partner's account. A partner shall contribute to the partnership an amount equal to any excess of the charges over the credits in the partner's account but excluding from the calculation charges attributable to an obligation for which the partner is not personally liable under Section 306.

(c) If a partner fails to contribute the full amount required under subsection (b), all of the other partners shall contribute, in the proportions in which those partners share partnership losses, the additional amount necessary to satisfy the partnership obligations for which they are personally liable under Section 306. A partner or partner's legal representative may recover from the other partners any contributions the partner makes to the extent the amount contributed exceeds that partner's share of the partnership obligations for which the partner is personally liable under Section 306.

(d) After the settlement of accounts, each partner shall contribute, in the proportion in which the partner shares partnership losses, the amount necessary to satisfy partnership obligations that were not known at the time of the settlement and for which the partner is personally liable under Section 306.

(e) The estate of a deceased partner is liable for the partner's obligation to contribute to the partnership.

(f) An assignee for the benefit of creditors of a partnership or a partner, or a person appointed by a court to represent creditors of a partnership or a partner, may enforce a partner's obligation to contribute to the partnership.

Article 10. Limited Liability Partnership

§1001. Statement of Qualifications

(a) A partnership may become a limited liability partnership pursuant to this section.

(b) The terms and conditions on which a partnership becomes a limited liability partnership must be approved by the vote necessary to amend the partnership agreement except, in the case of a partnership agreement that expressly considers obligations to contribute to the partnership, the vote necessary to amend those provisions.

(c) After the approval required by subsection (b), a partnership may become a limited liability partnership by filing a statement of qualification. The statement must contain:

(1) the name of the partnership;

(2) the street address of the partnership's chief executive office and, if different, the street address of an office in this State, if any;

(3) if the partnership does not have an office in this State, the name and street address of the partnership's agent for service of process;

(4) a statement that the partnership elects to be a limited liability partnership; and

(5) a deferred effective date, if any.

(d) The agent of a limited liability partnership for service of process must be an individual who is a resident of this State or other person authorized to do business in the State.

(e) The status of a partnership as a limited liability partnership is effective on the later of the filing of the statement or a date specified in the statement. The status remains effective, regardless of changes in the partnership, until it is canceled pursuant to Section 105(d) or revoked pursuant to Section 1003.

(f) The status of a partnership as a limited liability partnership and the liability of its partners is not affected by errors or later changes in the information required to be contained in the statement of qualification under subsection (c).

(g) The filing of a statement of qualification establishes that a partnership has satisfied all conditions precedent to the qualification of the partnership as a limited liability partnership.

(h) An amendment or cancellation of a statement of qualification is effective when it is filed or on a deferred effective date specified in the amendment or cancellation.

§1002. Name

The name of a limited liability partnership must end with "Registered Limited Liability Partnership," "Limited Liability Partnership," "R.L.L.P.," "L.L.P.," "RLLP," or "LLP."

§1003. Annual Report

(a) A limited liability partnership, and a foreign limited liability partnership authorized to transact business in this State, shall file an annual report in the office of the [Secretary of State] which contains:

(1) the name of the limited liability partnership and the State or other jurisdiction under whose laws the foreign limited liability partnership is formed;

(2) the street address of the partnership's chief executive office and, if different, the street address of an office of the partnership in this State, if any; and

(3) if the partnership does not have an office in this State, the name and street address of the partnership's current agent for service of process.

(b) An annual report must be filed between [January 1 and April 1] of each year following the calendar year in which a partnership files a statement of qualification or a foreign partnership becomes authorized to transact business in this State.

(c) The [Secretary of State] may revoke the statement of qualification of a partnership that fails to file an annual report when due or pay the required filing fee. To do so, the [Secretary of State] shall provide the partnership at least 60 days' written notice of intent to revoke the statement. The notice must be mailed to the partnership at its chief executive office set forth in the last filed statement of qualification or annual report. The notice must specify the annual report that has not been filed, the fee that has not been paid, and the effective date of the revocation. The revocation is not effective if the annual report is filed and the fee is paid before the effective date of the revocation.

(d) A revocation under subsection (c) only affects a partnership's status as a limited liability partnership and is not an event of dissolution of the partnership.

(e) A partnership whose statement of qualification has been revoked may apply to the [Secretary of State] for reinstatement within two years after the effective date of the revocation. The application must state:

(1) the name of the partnership and the effective date of the revocation; and

(2) that the ground for revocation either did not exist or has been corrected.

(f) A reinstatement under subsection (e) relates back to and takes effect as of the effective date of the revocation, and the partnership's status as a limited liability partnership continues as if the revocation had never occurred.

ARTICLE 11. FOREIGN LIMITED LIABILITY PARTNERSHIP

§1101. Law Governing Foreign Limited Liability Partnership

(a) The law under which a foreign limited liability partnership is formed governs relations among the partners and between the partners and the partnership and the liability of partners for obligations of the partnership.

(b) A foreign limited liability partnership may not be denied a statement of foreign qualification by reason of any difference between the law under which the partnership was formed and the law of this State.

(c) A statement of foreign qualification does not authorize a foreign limited liability partnership to engage in any business or exercise any power that a partnership may not engage in or exercise in this State as a limited liability partnership.

§1102. Statement of Foreign Qualification

(a) Before transacting business in this State, a foreign limited liability partnership must file a statement of foreign qualification. . . .

§1103. Effect of Failure to Qualify

(a) A foreign limited liability partnership transacting business in this State may not maintain an action or proceeding in this State unless it has in effect a statement of foreign qualification.

(b) The failure of a foreign limited liability partnership to have in effect a statement of foreign qualification does not impair the validity of a contract or act of the foreign limited liability partnership or preclude it from defending an action or proceeding in this State.

(c) A limitation on personal liability of a partner is not waived solely by transacting business in this State without a statement of foreign qualification.

(d) If a foreign limited liability partnership transacts business in this State without a statement of foreign qualification, the [Secretary of State] is its agent for service of process with respect to a right of action arising out of the transaction of business in this State.

Article 12. Miscellaneous Provisions . . .

§1206. Applicability

(a) Before January 1, 199__, this [Act] governs only a partnership formed:

(1) after the effective date of this [Act], unless that partnership is continuing the business of a dissolved partnership under [Section 41 of the prior Uniform Partnership Act]; and

(2) before the effective date of this [Act], that elects, as provided by subsection (c), to be governed by this [Act].

(b) After January 1, 199__, this [Act] governs all partnerships.

(c) Before January 1, 199__, a partnership voluntarily may elect, in the manner provided in its partnership agreement or by law for amending the partnership agreement, to be governed by this [Act]. The provisions of this [Act] relating to the liability of the partnership's partners to third parties apply to limit those partners' liability to a third party who had done business with the partnership within one year preceding the partnership's election to be governed by this [Act], only if the third party knows or has received a notification of the partnership's election to be governed by this [Act].

Delaware Limited Liability Company Act

SUBCHAPTER VII. ASSIGNMENT OF LIMITED LIABILITY COMPANY INTERESTS

SUBCHAPTER VIII. DISSOLUTION

SUBCHAPTER IX. FOREIGN LIMITED LIABILITY COMPANIES

SUBCHAPTER X. DERIVATIVE ACTIONS

SUBCHAPTER XI. MISCELLANEOUS

Subchapter I. General Provisions

§18-101. Definitions

As used in this chapter unless the context otherwise requires:

(1) "Bankruptcy" means an event that causes a person to cease to be a member as provided in §18-304 of this title.

(2) "Certificate of formation" means the certificate referred to in §18-201 of this title, and the certificate as amended.

(3) "Contribution" means any cash, property, services rendered or a promissory note or other obligation to contribute cash or property or to perform services, which a person contributes to a limited liability company in the person's capacity as a member.

(4) "Document" means:

a. Any tangible medium on which information is inscribed, and includes handwritten, typed, printed or similar instruments, and copies of such instruments; and

b. An electronic transmission.

(5) "Electronic transmission" means any form of communication not directly involving the physical transmission of paper, including the use of, or participation in, 1 or more electronic networks or databases (including 1 or more distributed electronic networks or databases), that creates a record that may be retained, retrieved and reviewed by a recipient thereof and that may be directly reproduced in paper form by such a recipient through an automated process.

(6) "Foreign limited liability company" means a limited liability company formed under the laws of any state or under the laws of any foreign country or

other foreign jurisdiction. When used in this title in reference to a foreign limited liability company, the terms "limited liability company agreement," "limited liability company interest," "manager" or "member" shall mean a limited liability company agreement, limited liability company interest, manager or member, respectively, under the laws of the state or foreign country or other foreign jurisdiction under which the foreign limited liability company is formed.

(7) "Knowledge" means a person's actual knowledge of a fact, rather than the person's constructive knowledge of the fact.

(8) "Limited liability company" and "domestic limited liability company" means a limited liability company formed under the laws of the State of Delaware and having 1 or more members.

(9) "Limited liability company agreement" means any agreement (whether referred to as a limited liability company agreement, operating agreement or otherwise), written, oral or implied, of the member or members as to the affairs of a limited liability company and the conduct of its business. A member or manager of a limited liability company or an assignee of a limited liability company interest is bound by the limited liability company agreement whether or not the member or manager or assignee executes the limited liability company agreement. A limited liability company (including any protected series or registered series thereof) is not required to execute its limited liability company agreement. A limited liability company (including any protected series or registered series thereof) is bound by its limited liability company agreement whether or not the limited liability company (or any protected series or registered series thereof) executes the limited liability company agreement. A limited liability company agreement of a limited liability company having only 1 member shall not be unenforceable by reason of there being only 1 person who is a party to the limited liability company agreement. A limited liability company agreement is not subject to any statute of frauds (including §2714 of this title). A limited liability company agreement may provide rights to any person, including a person who is not a party to the limited liability company agreement, to the extent set forth therein. A written limited liability company agreement or another written agreement or writing:

a. May provide that a person shall be admitted as a member of a limited liability company, or shall become an assignee of a limited liability company interest or other rights or powers of a member to the extent assigned:

1. If such person (or a representative authorized by such person orally, in writing or by other action such as payment for a limited liability company interest) executes the limited liability company agreement or any other writing evidencing the intent of such person to become a member or assignee; or

2. Without such execution, if such person (or a representative authorized by such person orally, in writing or by other action such as payment for a limited liability company interest) complies with the conditions for becoming a member or assignee as set forth in the limited liability company agreement or any other writing; and

b. Shall not be unenforceable by reason of its not having been signed by a person being admitted as a member or becoming an assignee as provided in paragraph (9)a, of this section, or by reason of its having been signed by a representative as provided in this chapter.

c. May consist of 1 or more agreements, instruments or other writings and may include or incorporate 1 or more schedules, supplements or other writings containing provisions as to the conduct of the business and affairs of the limited liability company or any series thereof.

(10) "Limited liability company interest" means a member's share of the profits and losses of a limited liability company and a member's right to receive distributions of the limited liability company's assets.

(11) "Liquidating trustee" means a person carrying out the winding up of a limited liability company.

(12) "Manager" means a person who is named as a manager of a limited liability company in, or designated as a manager of a limited liability company pursuant to, a limited liability company agreement or similar instrument under which the limited liability company is formed, and includes a manager of the limited liability company generally and a manager associated with a series of the limited liability company. Unless the context otherwise requires, references in this chapter to a manager (including references in this chapter to a manager of a limited liability company) shall be deemed to be references to a manager of the limited liability company generally and to a manager associated with a series with respect to such series.

(13) "Member" means a person who is admitted to a limited liability company as a member as provided in §18-301 of this title, and includes a member of the limited liability company generally and a member associated with a series of the limited liability company. Unless the context otherwise requires, references in this chapter to a member (including references in this chapter to a member of a limited liability company) shall be deemed to be references to a member of the limited liability company generally and to a member associated with a series with respect to such series.

(14) "Person" means a natural person, partnership (whether general or limited), limited liability company, trust (including a common law trust, business trust, statutory trust, voting trust or any other form of trust), estate, association (including any group, organization, cotenancy, plan, board, council or committee), corporation, government (including a country, state, county or any other governmental subdivision, agency or instrumentality), custodian, nominee or any other individual or entity (or series thereof) in its own or any representative capacity, in each case, whether domestic or foreign.

(15) "Personal representative" means, as to a natural person, the executor, administrator, guardian, conservator or other legal representative thereof and, as to a person other than a natural person, the legal representative or successor thereof.

(16) "Protected series" means a designated series of members, managers, limited liability company interests or 4 assets that is established in accordance with §18-215(b) of this title.

(17) "Registered series" means a designated series of members, managers, limited liability company interests or 6 assets that is formed in accordance with §18-218 of this title.

(18) "Series" means a designated series of members, managers, limited liability company interests or assets that is a protected series or a registered series, or that is neither a protected series nor a registered series.

(19) "State" means the District of Columbia or the Commonwealth of Puerto Rico or any state, territory, possession or other jurisdiction of the United States other than the State of Delaware.

§18-102. Name Set Forth in Certificate

The name of each limited liability company as set forth in its certificate of formation:

(1) Shall contain the words "Limited Liability Company" or the abbreviation "L.L.C." or the designation "LLC";

(2) May contain the name of a member or manager;

(3) Must be such as to distinguish it upon the records in the office of the Secretary of State from the name on such records of any corporation, partnership, limited partnership, statutory trust, limited liability company, registered series of a limited liability company or registered series of a limited partnership reserved, registered, formed or organized under the laws of the State of Delaware or qualified to do business or registered as a foreign corporation, foreign limited partnership, foreign statutory trust, foreign partnership, or foreign limited liability company in the State of Delaware; provided however, that a limited liability company may register under any name which is not such as to distinguish it upon the records in the office of the Secretary of State from the name on such records of any domestic or foreign corporation, partnership, limited partnership, statutory trust, registered series of a limited liability company, registered series of a limited partnership, or foreign limited liability company reserved, registered, formed or organized under the laws of the State of Delaware with the written consent of the other corporation, partnership, limited partnership, statutory trust, registered series of a limited liability company, registered series of a limited partnership, or foreign limited liability company, which written consent shall be filed with the Secretary of State; provided further, that, if on July 31, 2011, a limited liability company is registered (with the consent of another limited liability company) under a name which is not such as to distinguish it upon the records in the office of the Secretary of State from the name on such records of such other domestic limited liability company, it shall not be necessary for any such limited liability company to amend its certificate of formation to comply with this subsection;

(4) May contain the following words: "Company," "Association," "Club," "Foundation," "Fund," "Institute," "Society," "Union," "Syndicate," "Limited," "Public Benefit" or "Trust" (or abbreviations of like import); and

(5) Shall not contain the word "bank," or any variation thereof, except for the name of a bank reporting to and under the supervision of the State Bank Commissioner of this State or a subsidiary of a bank or savings association (as those terms are defined in the Federal Deposit Insurance Act, as amended, at 12 U.S.C. §1813), or a limited liability company regulated under the Bank Holding Company Act of 1956, as amended, at 12 U.S.C. §1841 et seq., or the Home Owners' Loan Act, as amended, 12 U.S.C. §1461 et seq.; provided, however, that this section shall not be construed to prevent the use of the word "bank," or any variation thereof, in a context clearly not purporting to refer to a banking business or otherwise likely to mislead the public about the nature of the business of the limited liability company or to lead to a pattern and practice of abuse that might cause harm to the interests

of the public or this State as determined by the Division of Corporations in the Department of State.

§18-104. Registered Office; Registered Agent

(a) Each limited liability company shall have and maintain in the State of Delaware:

(1) A registered office, which may but need not be a place of its business in the State of Delaware; and

(2) A registered agent for service of process on the limited liability company, having a business office identical with such registered office, which agent may be any of:

a. The limited liability company itself,

b. An individual resident in the State of Delaware,

c. A domestic limited liability company (other than the limited liability company itself), a domestic corporation, a domestic partnership (whether general (including a limited liability partnership) or limited (including a limited liability limited partnership)), or a domestic statutory trust, or

d. A foreign corporation, a foreign limited liability partnership, a foreign limited partnership (including a foreign limited liability limited partnership), a foreign limited liability company, or a foreign statutory trust. . . .

(e) Every registered agent shall:

(1) If an entity, maintain a business office in the State of Delaware which is generally open, or if an individual, be generally present at a designated location in the State of Delaware, at sufficiently frequent times to accept service of process and otherwise perform the functions of a registered agent;

(2) If a foreign entity, be authorized to transact business in the State of Delaware;

(3) Accept service of process and other communications directed to the limited liability companies (and any protected series or registered series thereof) and foreign limited liability companies for which it serves as registered agent and forward same to the limited liability company or foreign limited liability company to which the service or communication is directed; and

(4) Forward to the limited liability companies and foreign limited liability companies for which it serves as registered agent the statement for the annual tax for such limited liability company (and each registered series thereof) or such foreign limited liability company, as applicable, as described in §18-1107 of this title or an electronic notification of same in a form satisfactory to the Secretary of State; and

(5) Satisfy and adhere to regulations established by the Secretary regarding the verification of both the identity of the entity's contacts and individuals for which the registered agent maintains a record for the reduction of risk of unlawful business purposes. . . .

§18-105. Service of Process on Domestic Limited Liability Companies and Protected Series or Registered Series Therof

(a) Service of legal process upon any domestic limited liability company or any protected series or registered series thereof shall be made by delivering a copy personally to any manager of the limited liability company in the State of Delaware, or the registered agent of the limited liability company in the State of Delaware, or by leaving it at the dwelling house or usual place of abode in the State of Delaware of any such manager or registered agent (if the registered agent be an individual), or at the registered office or other place of business of the limited liability company in the State of Delaware. If service of legal process is made upon the registered agent of the limited liability company in the State of Delaware on behalf of any such protected series or registered series, such process shall include the name of the limited liability company and the name of such protected series or registered series. If the registered agent be a corporation, service of process upon it as such may be made by serving, in the State of Delaware, a copy thereof on the president, vice-president, secretary, assistant secretary or any director of the corporate registered agent. Service by copy left at the dwelling house or usual place of abode of a manager or registered agent, or at the registered office or other place of business of the limited liability company in the State of Delaware, to be effective, must be delivered thereat at least 6 days before the return date of the process, and in the presence of an adult person, and the officer serving the process shall distinctly state the manner of service in the officer's return thereto. Process returnable forthwith must be delivered personally to the manager or registered agent.

(b) In case the officer whose duty it is to serve legal process cannot by due diligence serve the process in any manner provided for by subsection (a) of this section, it shall be lawful to serve the process against the limited liability company or any protected series or registered series thereof the Secretary of State, and such service shall be as effectual for all intents and purposes as if made in any of the ways provided for in subsection (a) of this section. If service of legal process is made upon the Secretary of State on behalf of any such protected series or registered series, such process shall include the name of the limited liability company and the name of such protected series or registered series. Process may be served upon the Secretary of State under this subsection by means of electronic transmission but only as prescribed by the Secretary of State. The Secretary of State is authorized to issue such rules and regulations with respect to such service as the Secretary of State deems necessary or appropriate. In the event that service is effected through the Secretary of State in accordance with this subsection, the Secretary of State shall forthwith notify the limited liability company by letter, directed to the limited liability company at its address as it appears on the records relating to such limited liability company on file with the Secretary of State or, if no such address appears, at its last registered office. Such letter shall be sent by a mail or courier service that includes a record of mailing or deposit with the courier and a record of delivery evidenced by the signature of the recipient. Such letter shall enclose a copy of the process and any other papers served on the Secretary of State pursuant to this subsection. It shall be the duty of the plaintiff in the event of such service to serve process and any other papers in duplicate, to notify the Secretary of State that service is being effected pursuant to this subsection, and to pay the Secretary of State the sum of $50 for the use of the State of Delaware, which sum shall be taxed as part of the costs in the proceeding if the plaintiff shall prevail therein. The Secretary of State shall maintain an alphabetical record of any such service setting forth the name of the plaintiff and defendant, the title, docket number and nature of the proceeding in which process has been served upon the Secretary, the fact that service has been effected pursuant to this subsection, the return date thereof, and the day and hour when the service was made. The Secretary of State shall not be required to retain such information for a period longer than 5 years from the Secretary's receipt of the service of process.

§18-106. Nature of Business Permitted; Powers

(a) A limited liability company may carry on any lawful business, purpose or activity, whether or not for profit, with the exception of the business of banking as defined in §126 of Title 8.

(b) A limited liability company shall possess and may exercise all the powers and privileges granted by this chapter or by any other law or by its limited liability company agreement, together with any powers incidental thereto, including such powers and privileges as are necessary or convenient to the conduct, promotion or attainment of the business, purposes or activities of the limited liability company.

(c) Notwithstanding any provision of this chapter to the contrary, without limiting the general powers enumerated in subsection (b) of this section, a limited liability company shall, subject to such standards and restrictions, if any, as are set forth in its limited liability company agreement, have the power and authority to make contracts of guaranty and suretyship and enter into interest rate, basis, currency, hedge or other swap agreements or cap, floor, put, call, option, exchange or collar agreements, derivative agreements, or other agreements similar to any of the foregoing.

(d) Unless otherwise provided in a limited liability company agreement, a limited liability company has the power and authority to grant, hold or exercise a power of attorney, including an irrevocable power of attorney.

(e) Any act or transaction that may be taken by or in respect of a limited liability company under this chapter or a limited liability company agreement, but that is void or voidable when taken, may be ratified (or the failure to comply with any requirements of the limited liability company agreement making such act or transaction void or voidable may be waived) by the members, managers or other persons whose approval would be required under the limited liability company agreement (i) for such act or transaction to be validly taken, or (ii) to amend the limited liability company agreement in a manner that would permit such act or transaction to be validly taken, in each case at the time of such ratification or waiver; provided, that if the void or voidable act or transaction was the issuance or assignment of any limited liability company interests, the limited liability company interests purportedly issued or assigned shall be deemed not to have been issued or assigned for purposes of determining whether the void or voidable act or transaction was ratified or waived pursuant to this subsection (e). Any act or transaction ratified, or with respect to which the failure to comply with any requirements of the limited liability company agreement is waived, pursuant to this subsection (e) shall be deemed validly taken at the time of such act or transaction. If an amendment to the limited liability company agreement to permit any such act or transaction to be validly taken would require notice to any members, managers or other persons under the limited liability company agreement and the ratification or waiver of such act or transaction is effectuated pursuant to this subsection (e) by the members, managers or other persons whose approval would be required to amend the limited liability company agreement, notice of such ratification or waiver shall be given following such ratification or waiver to the members, managers or other persons who would have been entitled to notice of such an amendment and who have not otherwise received notice of, or participated in, such ratification or waiver. The provisions of this subsection (e) shall not be construed to limit the accomplishment of a ratification or waiver of a void or voidable act by other means permitted by law. Upon application of the limited liability company, any member, any manager or any person claiming to be substantially and adversely affected by a ratification or waiver pursuant to this subsection (e) (excluding any harm that would have resulted if such act or transaction had been valid when taken), the Court of Chancery may hear and determine the validity and effectiveness of the ratification of, or waiver with respect to, any void or voidable act or transaction effectuated pursuant to this subsection (e), and in any such application, the limited liability company shall be named as a party and service of the application upon the registered agent of the limited liability company shall be deemed to be service upon the limited liability company, and no other party need be joined in order for the Court to adjudicate the validity and effectiveness of the ratification or waiver, and the Court may make such order respecting further or other notice of such application as it deems proper under these circumstances; provided, that nothing herein limits or affects the right to serve process in any other manner now or hereafter provided by law, and this sentence is an extension of and not a limitation upon the right otherwise existing of service of legal process upon nonresidents.

§18-107. Business Transactions of Member or Manager with the Limited Liability Company

Except as provided in a limited liability company agreement, a member or manager may lend money to, borrow money from, act as a surety, guarantor or endorser for, guarantee or assume 1 or more obligations of, provide collateral for, and transact other business with, a limited liability company and, subject to other applicable law, has the same rights and obligations with respect to any such matter as a person who is not a member or manager.

§18-108. Indemnification

Subject to such standards and restrictions, if any, as are set forth in its limited liability company agreement, a limited liability company may, and shall have the power to, indemnify and hold harmless any member or manager or other person from and against any and all claims and demands whatsoever.

§18-109. Service of Process on Managers and Liquidating Trustees

(a) A manager or a liquidating trustee of a limited liability company may be served with process in the manner prescribed in this section in all civil actions or proceedings brought in the State of Delaware involving or relating to the business of the limited liability company or a violation by the manager or the liquidating trustee of a duty to the limited liability company or any member of the limited liability company, whether or not the manager or the liquidating trustee is a manager or a liquidating trustee at the time suit is commenced. A manager's or a liquidating trustee's serving as such constitutes such person's consent to the appointment of the registered agent of the limited liability company (or, if there is none, the Secretary of State) as such person's agent upon whom service of process may be made as provided in this section. Such service as a manager or a liquidating trustee shall signify the consent of such manager or liquidating trustee that any process when so served shall be of the same legal force and validity as if served upon such manager or liquidating trustee within the State of Delaware and such appointment of the registered agent (or, if there is none, the Secretary of State) shall be irrevocable. As used in this subsection (a) and in subsections (b), (c) and (d) of this section, the term "manager" refers (i) to a person who is a manager as defined in §18-101 of this title and (ii) to a person, whether or not a member of a limited liability company, who, although not a manager as defined in §18-101 of this title, participates materially in the management of the limited liability company; provided however, that the power to elect or otherwise select or to participate in the election or selection of a person to be a manager as defined in §18-101 of this title shall not, by itself, constitute participation in the management of the limited liability company.

(b) Service of process shall be effected by serving the registered agent (or, if there is none, the Secretary of State) with 1 copy of such process in the manner provided by law for service of writs of summons. In the event service is made under this subsection upon the Secretary of State, the plaintiff shall pay to the Secretary of State the sum of $50 for the use of the State of Delaware, which sum shall be taxed as part of the costs of the proceeding if the plaintiff shall prevail therein. In addition, the Prothonotary or the Register in Chancery of the court in which the civil action or proceeding is pending shall, within 7 days of such service, deposit in the United States mails, by registered mail, postage prepaid, true and attested copies of the process, together with a statement that service is being made pursuant to this section, addressed to such manager or liquidating trustee at the principal place of business of the limited liability company (if such address is known) and at the manager's or liquidating trustee's address last known to the party desiring to make such service.

(c) In any action in which any such manager or liquidating trustee has been served with process as hereinabove provided, the time in which a defendant shall be required to appear and file a responsive pleading shall be computed from the date of mailing by the Prothonotary or the Register in Chancery as provided in subsection (b) of this section; however, the court in which such action has been commenced may order such continuance or continuances as may be necessary to afford such manager or liquidating trustee reasonable opportunity to defend the action.

(d) In a written limited liability company agreement or other writing, a manager or member may consent to be subject to the nonexclusive jurisdiction of the courts of, or arbitration in, a specified jurisdiction, or the exclusive jurisdiction of the courts of the State of Delaware, or the exclusivity of arbitration in a specified jurisdiction or the State of Delaware, and to be served with legal process in the manner prescribed in such limited liability company agreement or other writing. Except by agreeing to arbitrate any arbitrable matter in a specified jurisdiction or in the State of Delaware, a member who is not a manager may not waive its right to maintain a legal action or proceeding in the courts of the State of Delaware with respect to matters relating to the organization or internal affairs of a limited liability company.

(e) Nothing herein contained limits or affects the right to serve process in any other manner now or hereafter provided by law. This section is an extension of and not a limitation upon the right otherwise existing of service of legal process upon nonresidents.

(f) The Court of Chancery and the Superior Court may make all necessary rules respecting the form of process, the manner of issuance and return thereof and such other rules which may be necessary to implement this section and are not inconsistent with this section.

§18-110. Contested Matters Relating to Managers; Contested Votes

(a) Upon application of any member or manager, the Court of Chancery may hear and determine the validity of any admission, election, appointment, removal or resignation of a manager of a limited liability company, and the right of any person to become or continue to be a manager of a limited liability company, and, in case the right to serve as a manager is claimed by more than 1 person, may determine the person or persons entitled to serve as managers; and to that end make such order or decree in any such case as may be just and proper, with power to enforce the production of any books, papers and records of the limited liability company relating to the issue. In any such application, the limited liability company shall be named as a party and service of copies of the application upon the registered agent of the limited liability company shall be deemed to be service upon the limited liability company and upon the person or persons whose right to serve as a manager is contested and upon the person or persons, if any, claiming to be a manager or claiming the right to be a manager; and the registered agent shall forward immediately a copy of the application to the limited liability company and to the person or persons whose right to serve as a manager is contested and to the person or persons, if any, claiming to be a manager or the right to be a manager, in a postpaid, sealed, registered letter addressed to such limited liability company and such person or persons at their post-office addresses last known to the registered agent or furnished to the registered agent by the applicant member or manager. The Court may make such order respecting further or other notice of such application as it deems proper under these circumstances.

(b) Upon application of any member or manager, the Court of Chancery may hear and determine the result of any vote of members or managers upon matters as to which the members or managers of the limited liability company, or any class or group of members or managers, have the right to vote pursuant to the limited liability company agreement or other agreement or this chapter (other than the admission, election, appointment, removal or resignation of managers). In any such application, the limited liability company shall be named as a party and service of the application upon the registered agent of the limited liability company shall be deemed to be service upon the limited liability company, and no other party need be joined in order for the Court to adjudicate the result of the vote. The Court may make such order respecting further or other notice of such application as it deems proper under these circumstances.

(c) As used in this section, the term "manager" refers to a person:

a. Who is a manager as defined in §18-101 of this title; and

b. Whether or not a member of a limited liability company, who, although not a manager as defined in §18-101 of this title, participates materially in the management of the limited liability company;

provided however, that the power to elect or otherwise select or to participate in the election or selection of a person to be a manager as defined in §18-101 of this title shall not, by itself, constitute participation in the management of the limited liability company.

(d) Nothing herein contained limits or affects the right to serve process in any other manner now or hereafter provided by law. This section is an extension of and not a limitation upon the right otherwise existing of service of legal process upon nonresidents.

§18-111. Interpretation and Enforcement of Limited Liability Company Agreement

Any action to interpret, apply or enforce the provisions of a limited liability company agreement, or the duties, obligations or liabilities of a limited liability company to the members or managers of the limited liability company, or the duties, obligations or liabilities among members or managers and of members or managers to the limited liability company, or the rights or powers of, or restrictions on, the limited liability company, members or managers, or any provision of this chapter, or any other instrument, document, agreement or certificate contemplated by any provision of this chapter, may be brought in the Court of Chancery.

As used in this section, the term "manager" refers to a person:

(1) Who is a manager as defined in §18-101 of this title; and

(2) Whether or not a member of a limited liability company, who, although not a manager as defined in §18-101 of this title, participates materially in the management of the limited liability company;

provided however, that the power to elect or otherwise select or to participate in the election or selection of a person to be a manager as defined in §18-101 of this title shall not, by itself, constitute participation in the management of the limited liability company.

§18-112. Judicial Cancellation of Certificate of Formation; Proceedings

(a) Upon motion by the Attorney General, the Court of Chancery shall have jurisdiction to cancel the certificate of formation of any domestic limited liability company for abuse or misuse of its limited liability company powers, privileges or existence. The Attorney General shall proceed for this purpose in the Court of Chancery.

(b) The Court of Chancery shall have power, by appointment of trustees, receivers or otherwise, to administer and wind up the affairs of any domestic limited liability company whose certificate of formation shall be canceled by the Court of Chancery under this section, and to make such orders and decrees with respect thereto as shall be just and equitable respecting its affairs and assets and the rights of its members and creditors.

§18-113. Document form, Signature and Delivery

(a) Except as provided in subsection (b) of this section, without limiting the manner in which any act or transaction may be documented, or the manner in which a document may be signed or delivered:

(1) Any act or transaction contemplated or governed by this chapter or the limited liability company agreement may be provided for in a document, and an electronic transmission is the equivalent of a written document.

(2) Whenever this chapter or the limited liability company agreement requires or permits a signature, the signature may be a manual, facsimile, conformed or electronic signature. "Electronic signature" means an electronic symbol or process that is attached to, or logically associated with, a document and executed or adopted by a person with an intent to execute, authenticate or adopt the document. A person may execute a document with such person's signature.

(3) Unless otherwise provided in the limited liability company agreement or agreed between the sender and recipient, an electronic transmission is delivered to a person for purposes of this chapter and the limited liability company agreement when it enters an information processing system that the person has designated for the purpose of receiving electronic transmissions of the type delivered, so long as the electronic transmission is in a form capable of being processed by that system and such person is able to retrieve the electronic transmission. Whether a person has so designated an information processing system is determined by the limited liability company agreement or from the context and surrounding circumstances, including the parties' conduct. An electronic transmission is delivered under this section even if no person is aware of its receipt. Receipt of an electronic acknowledgement from an information processing system establishes that an electronic transmission was received but, by itself, does not establish that the content sent corresponds to the content received.

This chapter shall not prohibit 1 or more persons from conducting a transaction in accordance with Chapter 12A of this title so long as the part or parts of the transaction that are governed by this chapter are documented, signed and delivered in accordance with this subsection or otherwise in accordance with this chapter. This subsection shall apply solely for purposes of determining whether an act or transaction has been documented, and the document has been signed and delivered, in accordance with this chapter and the limited liability company agreement.

(b) Subsection (a) of this section shall not apply to:

(1) A document filed with or submitted to the Secretary of State, the Register in Chancery, or a court or other judicial or governmental body of this State;

(2) A certificate of limited liability company interest, except that a signature on a certificate of limited liability company interest may be a manual, facsimile, or electronic signature; and

(3) An act or transaction effected pursuant to §18-104, §18-105 or §18-109 or subchapter IX or X of this title.

The foregoing shall not create any presumption about the lawful means to document a matter addressed by this subsection, or the lawful means to sign or deliver a document addressed by this subsection. A provision of the limited liability company agreement shall not limit the application of subsection (a) of this section unless the provision expressly restricts one or more of the means of documenting an act or transaction, or of signing or delivering a document, permitted by subsection (a) of this section.

(c) In the event that any provision of this chapter is deemed to modify, limit or supersede the Electronic Signatures in Global and National Commerce Act, 15 U.S.C. §7001 et. seq., the provisions of this chapter shall control to the fullest extent permitted by §7002(a)(2) of such act.

Subchapter II. Formation; Certificate of Formation

§18-201. Certificate of Formation

(a) In order to form a limited liability company, 1 or more authorized persons must execute a certificate of formation. The certificate of formation shall be filed in the office of the Secretary of State and set forth:

(1) The name of the limited liability company;

(2) The address of the registered office and the name and address of the registered agent for service of process required to be maintained by §18-104 of this title; and

(3) Any other matters the members determine to include therein.

(b) A limited liability company is formed at the time of the filing of the initial certificate of formation in the office of the Secretary of State or at any later date or time specified in the certificate of formation if, in either case, there has been substantial compliance with the requirements of this section. A limited liability company formed under this chapter shall be a separate legal entity, the existence of which as a separate legal entity shall continue until cancellation of the limited liability company's certificate of formation.

(c) The filing of the certificate of formation in the office of the Secretary of State shall make it unnecessary to file any other documents under Chapter 31 of this title.

(d) A limited liability company agreement shall be entered into or otherwise existing either before, after or at the time of the filing of a certificate of formation and, whether entered into or otherwise existing before, after or at the time of such filing, may be made effective as of the effective time of such filing or at such other time or date as provided in or reflected by the limited liability company agreement.

(e) A certificate of formation substantially complies with §18-201(a)(2) of this title if it contains the name of the registered agent and the address of the registered office even if the certificate of formation does not expressly designate such person as the registered agent or such address as the registered office or the address of the registered agent.

§18-202. Amendment to Certificate of Formation

(a) A certificate of formation is amended by filing a certificate of amendment thereto in the office of the Secretary of State. The certificate of amendment shall set forth:

(1) The name of the limited liability company; and

(2) The amendment to the certificate of formation.

(b) A manager or, if there is no manager, then any member who becomes aware that any statement in a certificate of formation was false when made, or that any matter described has changed making the certificate of formation false in any material respect, shall promptly amend the certificate of formation.

(c) A certificate of formation may be amended at any time for any other proper purpose.

(d) Unless otherwise provided in this chapter or unless a later effective date or time (which shall be a date or time certain) is provided for in the certificate of amendment, a certificate of amendment shall be effective at the time of its filing with the Secretary of State.

§18-203. Cancellation of Certificate

(a) A certificate of formation shall be canceled upon the dissolution and the completion of winding up of a limited liability company, or as provided in §18-104(d), §18-104(i)(4), §18-112 or §18-1108 of this title, or upon the filing of a certificate of merger or consolidation or a certificate of ownership and merger if the limited liability company is not the surviving or resulting entity in a merger or consolidation or upon the future effective date or time of a certificate of merger or consolidation or a certificate of ownership and merger if the limited liability company is not the surviving or resulting entity in a merger or consolidation, or upon the filing of a certificate of transfer, or upon the future effective date or time of a certificate of transfer, or upon the filing of a certificate of conversion to non-Delaware entity or upon the future effective date or time of a certificate of conversion to non-Delaware entity or upon the filing of a certificate of division if the limited liability company is a dividing company that is not a surviving company or upon the future effective date or time of a certificate of division if the limited liability company is a dividing company that is not a surviving company. A certificate of cancellation shall be filed in the office of the Secretary of State to accomplish the cancellation of a certificate of formation upon the dissolution and the completion of winding up of a limited liability company and shall set forth:

(1) The name of the limited liability company;

(2) The date of filing of its certificate of formation;

(3) If the limited liability company has formed one or more registered series whose certificate of registered series has not been canceled prior to the filing of the certificate of cancellation, the name of each such registered series;

(4) The future effective date or time (which shall be a date or time certain) of cancellation if it is not to be effective upon the filing of the certificate; and

(5) Any other information the person filing the certificate of cancellation determines.

(b) A certificate of cancellation that is filed in the office of the Secretary of State prior to the dissolution or the completion of winding up of a limited liability company may be corrected as an erroneously executed certificate of cancellation by filing with the office of the Secretary of State a certificate of correction of such certificate of cancellation in accordance with §18-211 of this title.

(c) The Secretary of State shall not issue a certificate of good standing with respect to a limited liability company (or any registered series thereof) if its certificate of formation is canceled.

§18-204. Execution

(a) Each certificate required by this subchapter to be filed in the office of the Secretary of State shall be executed by 1 or more authorized persons or, in the case of a certificate of conversion to limited liability company or certificate of limited liability company domestication, by any person authorized to execute such certificate on behalf of the other entity or non United States entity, respectively, except that a certificate of merger or consolidation filed by a surviving or resulting other business entity shall be executed by any person authorized to execute such certificate on behalf of such other business entity.

(b) Unless otherwise provided in a limited liability company agreement, any person may sign any certificate or amendment thereof or enter into a limited liability company agreement or amendment thereof by an agent, including an attorney-in-fact. An authorization, including a power of attorney, to sign any certificate or amendment thereof or to enter into a limited liability company agreement or amendment thereof need not be in writing, need not be sworn to, verified or acknowledged, and need not be filed in the office of the Secretary of State, but if in writing, must be retained by the limited liability company.

(c) For all purposes of the laws of the State of Delaware, unless otherwise provided in a limited liability company agreement, a power of attorney or proxy with respect to a limited liability company granted to any person shall be irrevocable if it states that it is irrevocable and it is coupled with an interest sufficient in law to support an irrevocable power or proxy. Such irrevocable power of attorney or proxy, unless otherwise provided therein or in a limited liability company agreement, shall not be affected by subsequent death, disability, incapacity, dissolution, termination of existence or bankruptcy of, or any other event concerning, the principal. A power of attorney or proxy with respect to matters relating to the organization, internal affairs or termination of a limited liability company or granted by a person as a member or an assignee of a limited liability company interest or by a person seeking to become a member or an assignee of a limited liability company interest and, in either case, granted to the limited liability company, a manager or member thereof, or any of their respective officers, directors, managers, members, partners, trustees, employees or agents shall be deemed coupled with an interest sufficient in law to support an irrevocable power or proxy. The provisions of this subsection shall not be construed to limit the enforceability of a power of attorney or proxy that is part of a limited liability company agreement.

(d) The execution of a certificate by a person who is authorized by this chapter to execute such certificate constitutes an oath or affirmation, under the penalties of perjury in the third degree, that, to the best of such person's knowledge and belief, the facts stated therein are true at the time such certificate becomes effective as provided in this chapter.

§18-205. Execution, Amendment or Cancellation by Judicial Order

(a) If a person required to execute a certificate required by this subchapter fails or refuses to do so, any other person who is adversely affected by the failure or refusal may petition the Court of Chancery to direct the execution of the certificate. If the Court finds that the execution of the certificate is proper and that any person so designated has failed or refused to execute the certificate, it shall order the Secretary of State to record an appropriate certificate.

(b) If a person required to execute a limited liability company agreement or amendment thereof fails or refuses to do so, any other person who is adversely affected by the failure or refusal may petition the Court of Chancery to direct the execution of the limited liability company agreement or amendment thereof. If the Court finds that the limited liability company agreement or amendment thereof should be executed and that any person required to execute the limited liability company agreement or amendment thereof has failed or refused to do so, it shall enter an order granting appropriate relief.

§18-206. Filing

(a) The signed copy of any certificate authorized to be filed under this chapter shall be delivered to the Secretary of State. A person who executes a certificate as an agent or fiduciary need not exhibit evidence of that person's authority as a prerequisite to filing. Any signature on any certificate authorized to be filed with the Secretary of State under any provision of this chapter may be a facsimile, a conformed signature or an electronically transmitted signature. Upon delivery of any certificate, the Secretary of State shall record the date and time of its delivery. Unless the Secretary of State finds that any certificate does not conform to law, upon receipt of all filing fees required by law the Secretary of State shall:

(1) Certify that any certificate authorized to be filed under this chapter has been filed in the Secretary of State's office by endorsing upon the signed certificate the word "Filed," and the date and time of the filing. This endorsement is conclusive of the date and time of its filing in the absence of actual fraud. Except as provided in subdivision (a)(5) or (a)(6) of this section, such date and time of filing of a certificate shall be the date and time of delivery of the certificate. . . .

(b) Notwithstanding any other provision of this chapter, any certificate filed under this chapter shall be effective at the time of its filing with the Secretary of State or at any later date or time (not later than a time on the one hundred and eightieth day after the date of its filing if such date of filing is on or after January 1, 2012) specified in the certificate. . . .

§18-207. Notice

The fact that a certificate of formation is on file in the office of the Secretary of State is notice that the entity formed in connection with the filing of the certificate of formation is a limited liability company formed under the laws of the State of

Delaware and is notice of all other facts set forth therein which are required to be set forth in a certificate of formation by §18-201(a)(1) and (2) or §18-1202 of this title and which are permitted to be set forth in a certificate of formation by §18-215(b) or §18-218(b) of this title. The fact that a certificate of registered series is on file in the office of the Secretary of State is notice that the registered series named in such certificate of registered series has been formed pursuant to §18-218 of this title and is notice of all other facts set forth therein which are required to be set forth in a certificate of registered series by §18-218(d) of this title.

§18-209. Merger and Consolidation

(a) As used in this section and in §§18-204, 18-217, 18-219, 18-220 and 18-221 of this title, "other business entity" means a corporation, a statutory trust, a business trust, an association, a real estate investment trust, a common-law trust, or any other incorporated or unincorporated business or entity, including a partnership (whether general (including a limited liability partnership) or limited (including a limited liability limited partnership)), and a foreign limited liability company, but excluding a domestic limited liability company. As used in this section and in §§18-210 and 18-301 of this title, "plan of merger" means a writing approved by a domestic limited liability company, in the form of resolutions or otherwise, that states the terms and conditions of a merger under subsection (i) of this section.

(b) Pursuant to an agreement of merger or consolidation, 1 or more domestic limited liability companies may merge or consolidate with or into 1 or more domestic limited liability companies or 1 or more other business entities formed or organized under the laws of the State of Delaware or any other state or the United States or any foreign country or other foreign jurisdiction, or any combination thereof, with such domestic limited liability company or other business entity as the agreement shall provide being the surviving or resulting domestic limited liability company or other business entity. Unless otherwise provided in the limited liability company agreement, an agreement of merger or consolidation or a plan of merger shall be approved by each domestic limited liability company which is to merge or consolidate by members who own more than 50 percent of the then current percentage or other interest in the profits of the domestic limited liability company owned by all of the members. In connection with a merger or consolidation hereunder, rights or securities of, or interests in, a domestic limited liability company or other business entity which is a constituent party to the merger or consolidation may be exchanged for or converted into cash, property, rights or securities of, or interests in, the surviving or resulting domestic limited liability company or other business entity or, in addition to or in lieu thereof, may be exchanged for or converted into cash, property, rights or securities of, or interests in, a domestic limited liability company or other business entity which is not the surviving or resulting limited liability company or other business entity in the merger or consolidation, may remain outstanding or may be canceled. Notwithstanding prior approval, an agreement of merger or consolidation or a plan of merger may be terminated or amended pursuant to a provision for such termination or amendment contained in the agreement of merger or consolidation or plan of merger. Unless otherwise provided in a limited liability company agreement, a limited liability company whose original certificate of formation was filed with the Secretary of State and effective on or prior to July 31, 2015, shall continue to be governed by the second sentence of this subsection as in effect on July 31, 2015.

(c) Except in the case of a merger under subsection (i) of this section, if a domestic limited liability company is merging or consolidating under this section, the domestic limited liability company or other business entity surviving or resulting in or from the merger or consolidation shall file a certificate of merger or consolidation executed by 1 or more authorized persons on behalf of the domestic limited liability company when it is the surviving or resulting entity in the office of the Secretary of State. The certificate of merger or consolidation shall state:

(1) The name, jurisdiction of formation or organization and type of entity of each of the domestic limited liability companies and other business entities which is to merge or consolidate;

(2) That an agreement of merger or consolidation has been approved and executed by each of the domestic limited liability companies and other business entities which is to merge or consolidate;

(3) The name of the surviving or resulting domestic limited liability company or other business entity;

(4) In the case of a merger in which a domestic limited liability company is the surviving entity, such amendments, if any, to the certificate of formation of the surviving domestic limited liability company to change its name, registered office or registered agent as are desired to be effected by the merger;

(5) The future effective date or time (which shall be a date or time certain) of the merger or consolidation if it is not to be effective upon the filing of the certificate of merger or consolidation;

(6) That the agreement of merger or consolidation is on file at a place of business of the surviving or resulting domestic limited liability company or other business entity, and shall state the address thereof;

(7) That a copy of the agreement of merger or consolidation will be furnished by the surviving or resulting domestic limited liability company or other business entity, on request and without cost, to any member of any domestic limited liability company or any person holding an interest in any other business entity which is to merge or consolidate; and

(8) If the surviving or resulting entity is not a domestic limited liability company, or a corporation, partnership (whether general (including a limited liability partnership) or limited (including a limited liability limited partnership)) or statutory trust organized under the laws of the State of Delaware, a statement that such surviving or resulting other business entity agrees that it may be served with process in the State of Delaware in any action, suit or proceeding for the enforcement of any obligation of any domestic limited liability company which is to merge or consolidate, irrevocably appointing the Secretary of State as its agent to accept service of process in any such action, suit or proceeding and specifying the address to which a copy of such process shall be mailed to it by the Secretary of State. Process may be served upon the Secretary of State under this subsection by means of electronic transmission but only as prescribed by the Secretary of State. The Secretary of State is authorized to issue such rules and regulations with respect to such service as the Secretary of State deems necessary or appropriate.

In the event of service hereunder upon the Secretary of State, the procedures set forth in §18-911(c) of this title shall be applicable, except that the plaintiff in any such action, suit or proceeding shall furnish the Secretary of State with the address specified in the certificate of merger or consolidation provided for in this section and any other address which the plaintiff may elect to furnish, together with copies of such process as required by the Secretary of State, and the Secretary of State shall notify such surviving or resulting other business entity at all such addresses furnished by the plaintiff in accordance with the procedures set forth in §18-911(c) of this title.

(d) Unless a future effective date or time is provided in a certificate of merger or consolidation, or in the case of a merger under subsection (i) of this section in a certificate of ownership and merger, in which event a merger or consolidation shall be effective at any such future effective date or time, a merger or consolidation shall be effective upon the filing in the office of the Secretary of State of a certificate of merger or consolidation or a certificate of ownership and merger.

(e) A certificate of merger or consolidation or a certificate of ownership and merger shall act as a certificate of cancellation for a domestic limited liability company which is not the surviving or resulting entity in the merger or consolidation. A certificate of merger that sets forth any amendment in accordance with subsection (c)(4) of this section shall be deemed to be an amendment to the certificate of formation of the limited liability company, and the limited liability company shall not be required to take any further action to amend its certificate of formation under §18-202 of this title with respect to such amendments set forth in the certificate of merger. Whenever this section requires the filing of a certificate of merger or consolidation, such requirement shall be deemed satisfied by the filing of an agreement of merger or consolidation containing the information required by this section to be set forth in the certificate of merger or consolidation.

(f) An agreement of merger or consolidation or a plan of merger approved in accordance with subsection (b) of this section may:

(1) Effect any amendment to the limited liability company agreement; or

(2) Effect the adoption of a new limited liability company agreement, for a limited liability company if it is the surviving or resulting limited liability company in the merger or consolidation.

Any amendment to a limited liability company agreement or adoption of a new limited liability company agreement made pursuant to the foregoing sentence shall be effective at the effective time or date of the merger or consolidation and shall be effective notwithstanding any provision of the limited liability company agreement relating to amendment or adoption of a new limited liability company agreement, other than a provision that by its terms applies to an amendment to the limited liability company agreement or the adoption of a new limited liability company agreement, in either case, in connection with a merger or consolidation. The provisions of this subsection shall not be construed to limit the accomplishment of a merger or of any of the matters referred to herein by any other means provided for in a limited liability company agreement or other agreement or as otherwise permitted by law, including that the limited liability company agreement of any constituent limited liability company to the merger or consolidation (including a limited liability company formed for the purpose of consummating a merger or consolidation) shall be the limited liability company agreement of the surviving or resulting limited liability company.

(g) When any merger or consolidation shall have become effective under this section, for all purposes of the laws of the State of Delaware, all of the rights, privileges and powers of each of the domestic limited liability companies and other business entities that have merged or consolidated, and all property, real, personal and mixed, and all debts due to any of said domestic limited liability companies and other business entities, as well as all other things and causes of action belonging to each of such domestic limited liability companies and other business entities, shall be vested in the surviving or resulting domestic limited liability company or other business entity, and shall thereafter be the property of the surviving or resulting domestic limited liability company or other business entity as they were of each of the domestic limited liability companies and other business entities that have merged or consolidated, and the title to any real property vested by deed or otherwise, under the laws of the State of Delaware, in any of such domestic limited liability companies and other business entities, shall not revert or be in any way impaired by reason of this chapter; but all rights of creditors and all liens upon any property of any of said domestic limited liability companies and other business entities shall be preserved unimpaired, and all debts, liabilities and duties of each of the said domestic limited liability companies and other business entities that have merged or consolidated shall thenceforth attach to the surviving or resulting domestic limited liability company or other business entity, and may be enforced against it to the same extent as if said debts, liabilities and duties had been incurred or contracted by it. Unless otherwise agreed, a merger or consolidation of a domestic limited liability company, including a domestic limited liability company which is not the surviving or resulting entity in the merger or consolidation, shall not require such domestic limited liability company to wind up its affairs under §18-803 of this title or pay its liabilities and distribute its assets under §18-804 of this title, and the merger or consolidation shall not constitute a dissolution of such limited liability company.

(h) A limited liability company agreement may provide that a domestic limited liability company shall not have the power to merge or consolidate as set forth in this section.

(i) In any case in which (x) at least 90% of the outstanding shares of each class of the stock of a corporation or corporations (other than a corporation which has in its certificate of incorporation the provision required by §251(g)(7)(A) and (B) of Title 8), of which class there are outstanding shares that, absent §267(a) of Title 8, would be entitled to vote on such merger, is owned by a domestic limited liability company, (y) 1 or more of such corporations is a corporation of the State of Delaware, and (z) any corporation that is not a corporation of the State of Delaware is a corporation of any other state or the District of Columbia or another jurisdiction, the laws of which do not forbid such merger, the domestic limited liability company having such stock ownership may either merge the corporation or corporations into itself and assume all of its or their obligations, or merge itself, or itself and 1 or more of such corporations, into 1 of the other corporations, pursuant to a plan of merger. If a domestic limited liability company is causing a merger under this subsection, the domestic limited liability company shall file a certificate of ownership and merger executed by 1 or more authorized persons on behalf of the domestic limited liability company in the office of the Secretary of State. The certificate of ownership and merger shall certify that such merger was authorized in accordance with the domestic limited liability company's limited liability company agreement and this chapter, and if the domestic limited liability company shall not own all the outstanding stock of all the corporations that are parties to the merger, shall state the terms and conditions of the merger, including the securities, cash, property, or rights to be issued, paid, delivered or granted by the surviving domestic limited liability company or corporation upon surrender of each share of the corporation or corporations not owned by the domestic limited liability company, or the cancellation of some or all of such shares. If a corporation surviving a merger under this subsection is not a corporation organized under the laws of the State of Delaware, then the terms and conditions of the merger shall obligate such corporation to agree that it may be served with process in the State of Delaware in any proceeding for enforcement of any obligation of the domestic limited liability company or any obligation of any constituent corporation of the State of Delaware, as well as for enforcement of any obligation of the surviving corporation, including any suit or other proceeding to enforce the right of any stockholders as determined in appraisal proceedings pursuant to §262 of Title 8, and to irrevocably appoint the Secretary of State as its agent to accept service of process in any such suit or other proceedings, and to specify the address to which a copy of such process shall be mailed by the Secretary of State. Process may be served upon the Secretary of State under this subsection by means of electronic transmission but only as prescribed by the Secretary of State. The Secretary of State is authorized to issue such rules and regulations with respect to such service as the Secretary of State deems necessary or appropriate. In the event of such service upon the Secretary of State in accordance with this subsection, the Secretary of State shall forthwith notify such surviving corporation thereof by letter, directed to such surviving corporation at its address so specified, unless such surviving corporation shall have designated in writing to the Secretary of State a different address for such purpose, in which case it shall be mailed to the last address so designated. Such letter shall be sent by a mail or courier service that includes a record of mailing or deposit with the courier and a record of delivery evidenced by the signature of the recipient. Such letter shall enclose a copy of the process and any other papers served on the Secretary of State pursuant to this subsection. It shall be the duty of the plaintiff in the event of such service to serve process and any other papers in duplicate, to notify the Secretary of State that service is being effected pursuant to this subsection and to pay the Secretary of State the sum of $50 for the use of the State of Delaware, which sum shall be taxed as part of the costs in the proceeding, if the plaintiff shall prevail therein. The Secretary of State shall maintain an alphabetical record of any such service setting forth the name of the plaintiff and the defendant, the title, docket number and nature of the proceeding in which process has been served, the fact that service has been effected pursuant to this subsection, the return date thereof, and the day and hour service was made. The Secretary of State shall not be required to retain such information longer than 5 years from receipt of the service of process.

§18-210. No Statutory Appraisal Rights

Unless otherwise provided in a limited liability company agreement or an agreement of merger or consolidation or a plan of merger or a plan of division, no appraisal rights shall be available with respect to a limited liability company interest or another interest in a limited liability company, including in connection with any amendment of a limited liability company agreement, any merger or consolidation in which the limited liability company or a registered series of the limited liability company is a constituent party to the merger or consolidation, any division of the limited liability company, any conversion of the limited liability company to another business form, any conversion of a protected series of the limited liability company to a registered series of such limited liability company, any conversion of a registered series of the limited liability company to a protected series of such limited liability company, any transfer to or domestication or continuance in any jurisdiction by the limited liability company, or the sale of all or substantially all of the limited liability company's assets. The Court of Chancery shall have jurisdiction to hear and determine any matter relating to any appraisal rights provided in a limited liability company agreement or an agreement of merger or consolidation or a plan of merger or a plan of division.

§18-213. Transfer or Continuance of Domestic Limited Liability Companies

(a) Upon compliance with this section, any limited liability company may transfer to or domesticate or continue in any jurisdiction, other than any state, and, in connection therewith, may elect to continue its existence as a limited liability company in the State of Delaware. . . .

(h) A limited liability company agreement may provide that a domestic limited liability company shall not have the power to transfer, domesticate or continue as set forth in this section.

§18-214. Conversion of Certain Entities to a Limited Liability Company

(a) As used in this section and in §18-204 of this title, the term "other entity" means a corporation, a statutory trust, a business trust, an association, a real estate investment trust, a common-law trust or any other incorporated or unincorporated business or entity, including a partnership (whether general (including a limited liability partnership) or limited (including a limited liability limited partnership)) or a foreign limited liability company.

(b) Any other entity may convert to a domestic limited liability company by complying with subsection (h) of this section and filing in the office of the Secretary of State in accordance with §18-206 of this title:

(1) A certificate of conversion to limited liability company that has been executed in accordance with §18-204 of this title; and

(2) A certificate of formation that complies with §18-201 of this title and has been executed by 1 or more authorized persons in accordance with §18-204 of this title. . . .

§18-215. Series of Members, Managers, Limited Liability Company Interests or Assets

(a) A limited liability company agreement may establish or provide for the establishment of 1 or more designated series of members, managers, limited liability company interests or assets. Any such series may have separate rights, powers or duties with respect to specified property or obligations of the limited liability company or profits and losses associated with specified property or obligations, and any such series may have a separate business purpose or investment objective. No provision of subsection (b) of this section or §18-218 of this title shall be construed to limit the application of the principle of freedom of contract to a series that is not a protected series or a registered series. Other than pursuant to §§18-219, 18-220 and 18-221, a series may not merge, convert or consolidate pursuant to any section of this title or any other statute of this State.

(b) A series established in accordance with the following sentence is a protected series. Notwithstanding anything to the contrary set forth in this chapter or under other applicable law, in the event that a limited liability company agreement establishes or provides for the establishment of 1 or more series, and to the extent the records maintained for any such series account for the assets associated with such series separately from the other assets of the limited liability company, or any other series thereof, and if the limited liability company agreement so provides, and if notice of the limitation on liabilities of a series as referenced in this subsection is set forth in the certificate of formation of the limited liability company, then the debts, liabilities, obligations and expenses incurred, contracted for or otherwise existing with respect to such series shall be enforceable against the assets of such series only, and not against the assets of the limited liability company generally or any other series thereof, and, unless otherwise provided in the limited liability company agreement, none of the debts, liabilities, obligations and expenses incurred, contracted for or otherwise existing with respect to the limited liability company generally or any other series thereof shall be enforceable against the assets of such series. Neither the preceding sentence nor any provision pursuant thereto in a limited liability company agreement or certificate of formation shall (i) restrict a protected series or limited liability company on behalf of a protected series from agreeing in the limited liability company agreement or otherwise that any or all of the debts, liabilities, obligations and expenses incurred, contracted for or otherwise existing with respect to the limited liability company generally or any other series thereof shall be enforceable against the assets of such protected series or (ii) restrict a limited liability company from agreeing in the limited liability company agreement or otherwise that any or all of the debts, liabilities, obligations and expenses incurred, contracted for or otherwise existing with respect to a protected series shall be enforceable against the assets of the limited liability company generally. A limited liability company agreement does not need to use the term protected when referencing series or refer to this §18-215. Assets associated with a protected series may be held directly or indirectly, including in the name of such series, in the name of the limited liability company, through a nominee or otherwise. Records maintained for a protected series that reasonably identify its assets, including by specific listing, category, type, quantity, computational or allocational formula or procedure (including a percentage or share of any asset or assets) or by any other method where the identity of such assets is objectively determinable, will be deemed to account for the assets associated with such series separately from the other assets of the limited liability company, or any other series thereof. Notice in a certificate of formation of the limitation on liabilities of a protected series as referenced in this subsection shall be sufficient for all purposes of this subsection whether or not the limited liability company has established any protected series when such notice is included in the certificate of formation, and there shall be no requirement that (i) any specific protected series of the limited liability company be referenced in such notice, or (ii) such notice use the term protected when referencing series or include a reference to this §18-215. The fact that a certificate of formation that contains the foregoing notice of the limitation on liabilities of a protected series is on file in the office of the Secretary of State shall constitute notice of such limitation on liabilities of a protected series. As used in this chapter, a reference to assets of a protected series includes assets associated with such series, a reference to assets associated with a protected series includes assets of such series, a reference to members or managers of a protected series includes members or managers associated with such series, and a reference to members or managers associated with a protected series includes members or managers of such series. The following shall apply to a protected series:

(1) A protected series may carry on any lawful business, purpose or activity, whether or not for profit, with the exception of the business of banking as defined in §126 of Title 8. Unless otherwise provided in a limited liability company agreement, a protected series shall have the power and capacity to, in its own name, contract, hold title to assets (including real, personal and intangible property), grant liens and security interests, and sue and be sued.

(2) Except as otherwise provided by this chapter, no member or manager of a protected series shall be obligated personally for any debt, obligation or liability of such series, whether arising in contract, tort or otherwise, solely by reason of being a member or acting as manager of such series. Notwithstanding the preceding sentence, under a limited liability company agreement or under another agreement, a member or manager may agree to be obligated personally for any or all of the debts, obligations and liabilities of 1 or more protected series.

(3) A limited liability company agreement may provide for classes or groups of members or managers associated with a protected series having such relative rights, powers and duties as the limited liability company agreement may provide, and may make provision for the future creation in the manner provided in the limited liability company agreement of additional classes or groups of members or managers associated with such series having such relative rights, powers and duties as may from time to time be established, including rights, powers and duties senior to existing classes and groups of members or managers associated with such series. A limited liability company agreement may provide for the taking of an action, including the amendment of the limited liability company agreement, without the vote or approval of any member or manager or class or group of members or managers, including an action to create under the provisions of the limited liability company agreement a class or group of a protected series of limited liability company interests that was not previously outstanding. A limited liability company agreement may provide that any member or class or group of members associated with a protected series shall have no voting rights.

(4) A limited liability company agreement may grant to all or certain identified members or managers or a specified class or group of the members or managers associated with a protected series the right to vote separately or with

all or any class or group of the members or managers associated with such series, on any matter. Voting by members or managers associated with a protected series may be on a per capita, number, financial interest, class, group or any other basis.

(5) Unless otherwise provided in a limited liability company agreement, the management of a protected series shall be vested in the members associated with such series in proportion to the then current percentage or other interest of members in the profits of such series owned by all of the members associated with such series, the decision of members owning more than 50 percent of the said percentage or other interest in the profits controlling; provided, however, that if a limited liability company agreement provides for the management of a protected series, in whole or in part, by a manager, the management of such series, to the extent so provided, shall be vested in the manager who shall be chosen in the manner provided in the limited liability company agreement. The manager of a protected series shall also hold the offices and have the responsibilities accorded to the manager as set forth in a limited liability company agreement. A protected series may have more than 1 manager. Subject to §18-602 of this title, a manager shall cease to be a manager with respect to a protected series as provided in a limited liability company agreement. Except as otherwise provided in a limited liability company agreement, any event under this chapter or in a limited liability company agreement that causes a manager to cease to be a manager with respect to a protected series shall not, in itself, cause such manager to cease to be a manager of the limited liability company or with respect to any other series thereof.

(6) Notwithstanding §18-606 of this title, but subject to paragraphs (b)(7) and (b)(10) of this section, and unless otherwise provided in a limited liability company agreement, at the time a member of a protected series becomes entitled to receive a distribution with respect to such series, the member has the status of, and is entitled to all remedies available to, a creditor of such series, with respect to the distribution. A limited liability company agreement may provide for the establishment of a record date with respect to allocations and distributions with respect to a protected series.

(7) Notwithstanding §18-607(a) of this title, a limited liability company may make a distribution with respect to a protected series. A limited liability company shall not make a distribution with respect to a protected series to a member to the extent that at the time of the distribution, after giving effect to the distribution, all liabilities of such series, other than liabilities to members on account of their limited liability company interests with respect to such series and liabilities for which the recourse of creditors is limited to specified property of such series, exceed the fair value of the assets associated with such series, except that the fair value of property of such series that is subject to a liability for which the recourse of creditors is limited shall be included in the assets associated with such series only to the extent that the fair value of that property exceeds that liability. For purposes of the immediately preceding sentence, the term "distribution" shall not include amounts constituting reasonable compensation for present or past services or reasonable payments made in the ordinary course of business pursuant to a bona fide retirement plan or other benefits program. A member who

receives a distribution in violation of this paragraph (b)(7), and who knew at the time of the distribution that the distribution violated this paragraph (b)(7), shall be liable to the protected series for the amount of the distribution. A member who receives a distribution in violation of this paragraph (b)(7), and who did not know at the time of the distribution that the distribution violated this paragraph (b)(7), shall not be liable for the amount of the distribution. Subject to §18-607(c) of this title, which shall apply to any distribution made with respect to a protected series under this paragraph (b)(7), this paragraph (b)(7) shall not affect any obligation or liability of a member under an agreement or other applicable law for the amount of a distribution.

(8) Unless otherwise provided in the limited liability company agreement, a member shall cease to be associated with a protected series and to have the power to exercise any rights or powers of a member with respect to such series upon the assignment of all of the member's limited liability company interest with respect to such series. Except as otherwise provided in a limited liability company agreement, any event under this chapter or a limited liability company agreement that causes a member to cease to be associated with a protected series shall not, in itself, cause such member to cease to be associated with any other series or terminate the continued membership of a member in the limited liability company or cause the termination of the protected series, regardless of whether such member was the last remaining member associated with such series.

(9) Subject to §18-801 of this title, except to the extent otherwise provided in the limited liability company agreement, a protected series may be terminated and its affairs wound up without causing the dissolution of the limited liability company. The termination of a protected series shall not affect the limitation on liabilities of such series provided by this subsection (b). A protected series is terminated and its affairs shall be wound up upon the dissolution of the limited liability company under §18-801 of this title or otherwise upon the first to occur of the following:

a. At the time specified in the limited liability company agreement;

b. Upon the happening of events specified in the limited liability company agreement;

c. Unless otherwise provided in the limited liability company agreement, upon the vote or consent of members associated with such series who own more than 2/3 of the then-current percentage or other interest in the profits of such series of the limited liability company owned by all of the members associated with such series; or

d. The termination of such series under paragraph (b)(11) of this section.

Unless otherwise provided in a limited liability company agreement, a limited liability company whose original certificate of formation was filed with the Secretary of State and effective on or prior to July 31, 2015, shall continue to be governed by paragraph (k)(3) of this section as in effect on July 31, 2015 (except that "affirmative" and "written" shall be deleted from such paragraph (k)(3) of this section).

(10) Notwithstanding §18-803(a) of this title, unless otherwise provided in the limited liability company agreement, a manager associated with a protected

series who has not wrongfully terminated such series or, if none, the members associated with such series or a person approved by the members associated with such series, in either case, by members who own more than 50 percent of the then current percentage or other interest in the profits of such series owned by all of the members associated with such series, may wind up the affairs of such series; but the Court of Chancery, upon cause shown, may wind up the affairs of a protected series upon application of any member or manager associated with such series, or the member's personal representative or assignee, and in connection therewith, may appoint a liquidating trustee. The persons winding up the affairs of a protected series may, in the name of the limited liability company and for and on behalf of the limited liability company and such series, take all actions with respect to such series as are permitted under §18-803(b) of this title. The persons winding up the affairs of a protected series shall provide for the claims and obligations of such series and distribute the assets of such series as provided in §18-804 of this title, which section shall apply to the winding up and distribution of assets of a protected series. Actions taken in accordance with this paragraph (b)(10) shall not affect the liability of members and shall not impose liability on a liquidating trustee. Unless otherwise provided in a limited liability company agreement, a limited liability company whose original certificate of formation was filed with the Secretary of State and effective on or prior to July 31, 2015, shall continue to be governed by the first sentence of this paragraph (b)(10) as in effect on July 31, 2015.

(11) On application by or for a member or manager associated with a protected series, the Court of Chancery may decree termination of such series whenever it is not reasonably practicable to carry on the business of such series in conformity with a limited liability company agreement.

(12) For all purposes of the laws of the State of Delaware, a protected series is an association, regardless of the number of members or managers, if any, of such series.

(c) If a foreign limited liability company that is registering to do business in the State of Delaware in accordance with §18-902 of this title is governed by a limited liability company agreement that establishes or provides for the establishment of designated series of members, managers, limited liability company interests or assets having separate rights, powers or duties with respect to specified property or obligations of the foreign limited liability company or profits and losses associated with specified property or obligations, that fact shall be so stated on the application for registration as a foreign limited liability company. In addition, the foreign limited liability company shall state on such application whether the debts, liabilities and obligations incurred, contracted for or otherwise existing with respect to a particular series, if any, shall be enforceable against the assets of such series only, and not against the assets of the foreign limited liability company generally or any other series thereof, and whether any of the debts, liabilities, obligations and expenses incurred, contracted for or otherwise existing with respect to the foreign limited liability company generally or any other series thereof shall be enforceable against the assets of such series.

§18-216. Approval of Conversion of a Limited Liability Company

(a) Upon compliance with this section, a domestic limited liability company may convert to a corporation, a statutory trust, a business trust, an association, a real estate investment trust, a common-law trust or any other incorporated or unincorporated business or entity, including a partnership (whether general (including a limited liability partnership) or limited (including a limited liability limited partnership)) or a foreign limited liability company.

(b) If the limited liability company agreement specifies the manner of authorizing a conversion of the limited liability company, the conversion shall be authorized as specified in the limited liability company agreement. If the limited liability company agreement does not specify the manner of authorizing a conversion of the limited liability company and does not prohibit a conversion of the limited liability company, the conversion shall be authorized in the same manner as is specified in the limited liability company agreement for authorizing a merger or consolidation that involves the limited liability company as a constituent party to the merger or consolidation. If the limited liability company agreement does not specify the manner of authorizing a conversion of the limited liability company or a merger or consolidation that involves the limited liability company as a constituent party and does not prohibit a conversion of the limited liability company, the conversion shall be authorized by the approval by members who own more than 50 percent of the then current percentage or other interest in the profits of the domestic limited liability company owned by all of the members. Unless otherwise provided in a limited liability company agreement, a limited liability company whose original certificate of formation was filed with the Secretary of State and effective on or prior to July 31, 2015, shall continue to be governed by the third sentence of this subsection as in effect on July 31, 2015.

(c) Unless otherwise agreed, the conversion of a domestic limited liability company to another entity or business form pursuant to this section shall not require such limited liability company to wind up its affairs under §18-803 of this title or pay its liabilities and distribute its assets under §18-804 of this title, and the conversion shall not constitute a dissolution of such limited liability company. When a limited liability company has converted to another entity or business form pursuant to this section, for all purposes of the laws of the State of Delaware, the other entity or business form shall be deemed to be the same entity as the converting limited liability company and the conversion shall constitute a continuation of the existence of the limited liability company in the form of such other entity or business form.

(d) In connection with a conversion of a domestic limited liability company to another entity or business form pursuant to this section, rights or securities of or interests in the domestic limited liability company which is to be converted may be exchanged for or converted into cash, property, rights or securities of or interests in the entity or business form into which the domestic limited liability company is being converted or, in addition to or in lieu thereof, may be exchanged for or converted into cash, property, rights or securities of or interests in another entity or business form, may remain outstanding or may be canceled.

(e) If a limited liability company shall convert in accordance with this section to another entity or business form organized, formed or created under the laws of a jurisdiction other than the State of Delaware, a certificate of conversion to non-Delaware entity executed in accordance with §18-204 of this title, shall be filed in the office of the Secretary of State in accordance with §18-206 of this title. The certificate of conversion to non-Delaware entity shall state:

(1) The name of the limited liability company and, if it has been changed, the name under which its certificate of formation was originally filed;

(2) The date of filing of its original certificate of formation with the Secretary of State;

(3) The jurisdiction in which the entity or business form, to which the limited liability company shall be converted, is organized, formed or created, and the name of such entity or business form;

(4) The future effective date or time (which shall be a date or time certain) of the conversion if it is not to be effective upon the filing of the certificate of conversion to non-Delaware entity;

(5) That the conversion has been approved in accordance with this section;

(6) The agreement of the limited liability company that it may be served with process in the State of Delaware in any action, suit or proceeding for enforcement of any obligation of the limited liability company arising while it was a limited liability company of the State of Delaware, and that it irrevocably appoints the Secretary of State as its agent to accept service of process in any such action, suit or proceeding;

(7) The address to which a copy of the process referred to in paragraph (e)(6) of this section shall be mailed to it by the Secretary of State. Process may be served upon the Secretary of State under paragraph (e)(6) of this section by means of electronic transmission but only as prescribed by the Secretary of State. The Secretary of State is authorized to issue such rules and regulations with respect to such service as the Secretary of State deems necessary or appropriate. In the event of service hereunder upon the Secretary of State, the procedures set forth in §18-911(c) of this title shall be applicable, except that the plaintiff in any such action, suit or proceeding shall furnish the Secretary of State with the address specified in this subdivision and any other address that the plaintiff may elect to furnish, together with copies of such process as required by the Secretary of State, and the Secretary of State shall notify the limited liability company that has converted out of the State of Delaware at all such addresses furnished by the plaintiff in accordance with the procedures set forth in §18-911(c) of this title.

(f) Upon the filing in the office of the Secretary of State of the certificate of conversion to non-Delaware entity or upon the future effective date or time of the certificate of conversion to non-Delaware entity and payment to the Secretary of State of all fees prescribed in this chapter, the limited liability company shall cease to exist as a limited liability company of the State of Delaware. A copy of the certificate of conversion to non-Delaware entity certified by the Secretary of State shall be prima facie evidence of the conversion by such limited liability company out of the State of Delaware.

(g) The conversion of a limited liability company out of the State of Delaware in accordance with this section and the resulting cessation of its existence as a limited liability company of the State of Delaware pursuant to a certificate of conversion to non-Delaware entity shall not be deemed to affect any obligations or liabilities of the limited liability company incurred prior to such conversion or the personal liability of any person incurred prior to such conversion, nor shall it be deemed to affect the choice of law applicable to the limited liability company with respect to matters arising prior to such conversion.

(h) When any conversion shall have become effective under this section, for all purposes of the laws of the State of Delaware, all of the rights, privileges and powers of the limited liability company that has converted, and all property, real, personal and mixed, and all debts due to such limited liability company, as well as all other things and causes of action belonging to such limited liability company, shall remain vested in the other entity or business form to which such limited liability company has converted and shall be the property of such other entity or business form, and the title to any real property vested by deed or otherwise in such limited liability company shall not revert or be in any way impaired by reason of this chapter; but all rights of creditors and all liens upon any property of such limited liability company shall be preserved unimpaired, and all debts, liabilities and duties of the limited liability company that has converted shall remain attached to the other entity or business form to which such limited liability company has converted, and may be enforced against it to the same extent as if said debts, liabilities and duties had originally been incurred or contracted by it in its capacity as such other entity or business form. The rights, privileges, powers and interests in property of the limited liability company that has converted, as well as the debts, liabilities and duties of such limited liability company, shall not be deemed, as a consequence of the conversion, to have been transferred to the other entity or business form to which such limited liability company has converted for any purpose of the laws of the State of Delaware.

(i) A limited liability company agreement may provide that a domestic limited liability company shall not have the power to convert as set forth in this section.

§18-217. Division of a limited liability company.

(a) As used in this section and §§18-203 and 18-301:

(1) "Dividing company" means the domestic limited liability company that is effecting a division in the manner provided in this section.

(2) "Division" means the division of a dividing company into two or more domestic limited liability companies in accordance with this section.

(3) "Division company" means a surviving company, if any, and each resulting company.

(4) "Division contact" means, in connection with any division, a natural person who is a Delaware resident, any division company in such division or any other domestic limited liability company or other business entity as defined in §18-209 of this title formed or organized under the laws of the State of Delaware, which division contact shall maintain a copy of the plan of division for a period of six (6) years from the effective date of the division and shall comply with subsection (g)(3) of this section.

(5) "Organizational documents" means the certificate of formation and limited liability company agreement of a domestic limited liability company.

(6) "Resulting company" means a domestic limited liability company formed as a consequence of a division.

(7) "Surviving company" means a dividing company that survives the division.

(b) Pursuant to a plan of division, any domestic limited liability company may, in the manner provided in this section, be divided into two or more domestic limited liability companies. The division of a domestic limited liability company in accordance with this section and, if applicable, the resulting cessation of the existence of the dividing company pursuant to a certificate of division shall not be deemed to affect the personal liability of any person incurred prior to such division with respect to matters arising prior to such division, nor shall it be deemed to affect the validity or enforceability of any obligations or liabilities of the dividing company incurred prior to such division; provided, that the obligations and liabilities of the dividing company shall be allocated to and vested in, and valid and enforceable obligations of, such division company or companies to which such obligations and liabilities have been allocated pursuant to the plan of division, as provided in subsection (l) of this section. Each resulting company in a division shall be formed in compliance with the requirements of this chapter and subsection (i) of this section.

(c) If the limited liability company agreement of the dividing company specifies the manner of adopting a plan of division, the plan of division shall be adopted as specified in the limited liability company agreement. If the limited liability company agreement of the dividing company does not specify the manner of adopting a plan of division and does not prohibit a division of the limited liability company, the plan of division shall be adopted in the same manner as is specified in the limited liability company agreement for authorizing a merger or consolidation that involves the limited liability company as a constituent party to the merger or consolidation. If the limited liability company agreement of the dividing company does not specify the manner of adopting a plan of division or authorizing a merger or consolidation that involves the limited liability company as a constituent party and does not prohibit a division of the limited liability company, the adoption of a plan of division shall be authorized by the approval by members who own more than 50 percent of the then current percentage or other interest in the profits of the dividing company owned by all of the members. Notwithstanding prior approval, a plan of division may be terminated or amended pursuant to a provision for such termination or amendment contained in the plan of division.

(d) Unless otherwise provided in a plan of division, the division of a domestic limited liability company pursuant to this section shall not require such limited liability company to wind up its affairs under §18-803 of this title or pay its liabilities and distribute its assets under §18-804 of this title, and the division shall not constitute a dissolution of such limited liability company.

(e) In connection with a division under this section, rights or securities of, or interests in, the dividing company may be exchanged for or converted into cash, property, rights or securities of, or interests in, the surviving company or any resulting company or, in addition to or in lieu thereof, may be exchanged for or converted into cash, property, rights or securities of, or interests in, a domestic limited liability company or any other business entity which is not a division company or may be canceled or remain outstanding (if the dividing company is a surviving company).

(f) A plan of division adopted in accordance with subsection (c) of this section:

(1) May effect any amendment to the limited liability company agreement of the dividing company if it is a surviving company in the division; or

(2) May effect the adoption of a new limited liability company agreement for the dividing company if it is a surviving company in the division; and

(3) Shall effect the adoption of a limited liability company agreement for each resulting company.

Any amendment to a limited liability company agreement or adoption of a new limited liability company agreement for the dividing company, if it is a surviving company in the division, or adoption of a limited liability company agreement for each resulting company made pursuant to the foregoing sentence shall be effective at the effective time or date of the division. Any amendment to a limited liability company agreement or adoption of a limited liability company agreement for the dividing company, if it is a surviving company in the division, shall be effective notwithstanding any provision in the limited liability company agreement of the dividing company relating to amendment or adoption of a new limited liability company agreement, other than a provision that by its terms applies to an amendment to the limited liability company agreement or the adoption of a new limited liability company agreement, in either case, in connection with a division, merger or consolidation.

(g) If a domestic limited liability company is dividing under this section, the dividing company shall adopt a plan of division which shall set forth:

(1) The terms and conditions of the division, including:

(i) Any conversion or exchange of the limited liability company interests of the dividing company into or for limited liability company interests or other securities or obligations of any division company or cash, property or rights or securities or obligations of or interests in any other business entity or domestic limited liability company which is not a division company, or that the limited liability company interests of the dividing company shall remain outstanding or be canceled, or any combination of the foregoing; and

(ii) The allocation of assets, property, rights, series, debts, liabilities and duties of the dividing company among the division companies;

(2) The name of each resulting company and, if the dividing company will survive the division, the name of the surviving company;

(3) The name and business address of a division contact which shall have custody of a copy of the plan of division. The division contact, or any successor division contact, shall serve for a period of six (6) years following the effective date of the division. During such six (6) year period the division contact shall provide, without cost, to any creditor of the dividing company, within thirty (30) days following the division contact's receipt of a written request from any creditor of the dividing company, the name and business address of the division company to which the claim of such creditor was allocated pursuant to the plan of division; and

(4) Any other matters that the dividing company determines to include therein.

(h) If a domestic limited liability company divides under this section, the dividing company shall file a certificate of division executed by 1 or more authorized persons on behalf of such division company in the office of the Secretary of State in accordance with §18-204 of this title and a certificate of formation that complies with §18-201 of this title for each resulting company executed by one or more authorized persons in accordance with §18-204 of this title. The certificate of division shall state:

(1) The name of the dividing company and, if it has been changed, the name under which its certificate of formation was originally filed and whether the dividing company is a surviving company;

(2) The date of filing of the dividing company's original certificate of formation with the Secretary of State;

(3) The name of each division company;

(4) The name and business address of the division contact required by subsection (g)(3) of this section;

(5) The future effective date or time (which shall be a date or time certain) of the division if it is not to be effective upon the filing of the certificate of division;

(6) That the division has been approved in accordance with this section;

(7) That the plan of division is on file at a place of business of such division company as is specified therein, and shall state the address thereof;

(8) That a copy of the plan of division will be furnished by such division company as is specified therein, on request and without cost, to any member of the dividing company; and

(9) Any other information the dividing company determines to include therein.

(i) The certificate of division and each certificate of formation for each resulting company required by subsection (h) of this section shall be filed simultaneously in the office of the Secretary of State and, if such certificates are not to become effective upon their filing as permitted by §18-206(b) of this title, then each such certificate shall provide for the same effective date or time in accordance with §18-206(b) of this title. Concurrently with the effective date or time of a division, the limited liability company agreement of each resulting company shall become effective.

(j) A certificate of division shall act as a certificate of cancellation for a dividing company which is not a surviving company.

(k) A limited liability company agreement may provide that a domestic limited liability company shall not have the power to divide as set forth in this section.

(l) Upon the division of a domestic limited liability company becoming effective:

(1) The dividing company shall be divided into the distinct and independent resulting companies named in the plan of division, and, if the dividing company is not a surviving company, the existence of the dividing company shall cease.

(2) For all purposes of the laws of the State of Delaware, all of the rights, privileges and powers, and all the property, real, personal and mixed, of the dividing company and all debts due on whatever account to it, as well as all other things and other causes of action belonging to it, shall without further action be allocated to and vested in the applicable division company in such a manner and

basis and with such effect as is specified in the plan of division, and the title to any real property or interest therein allocated to and vested in any division company shall not revert or be in any way impaired by reason of the division.

(3) Each division company shall, from and after effectiveness of the certificate of division, be liable as a separate and distinct domestic limited liability company for such debts, liabilities and duties of the dividing company as are allocated to such division company pursuant to the plan of division in the manner and on the basis provided in subsection (g)(1)(ii) of this section.

(4) Each of the debts, liabilities and duties of the dividing company shall without further action be allocated to and be the debts, liabilities and duties of such division company as is specified in the plan of division as having such debts, liabilities and duties allocated to it, in such a manner and basis and with such effect as is specified in the plan of division, and no other division company shall be liable therefor, so long as the plan of division does not constitute a fraudulent transfer under applicable law, and all liens upon any property of the dividing company shall be preserved unimpaired, and all debts, liabilities and duties of the dividing company shall remain attached to the division company to which such debts, liabilities and duties have been allocated in the plan of division, and may be enforced against such division company to the same extent as if said debts, liabilities and duties had originally been incurred or contracted by it in its capacity as a domestic limited liability company.

(5) In the event that any allocation of assets, debts, liabilities and duties to division companies in accordance with a plan of division is determined by a court of competent jurisdiction to constitute a fraudulent transfer, each division company shall be jointly and severally liable on account of such fraudulent transfer notwithstanding the allocations made in the plan of division; provided, however, the validity and effectiveness of the division are not otherwise affected thereby.

(6) Debts and liabilities of the dividing company that are not allocated by the plan of division shall be the joint and several debts and liabilities of all of the division companies.

(7) It shall not be necessary for a plan of division to list each individual asset, property, right, series, debt, liability or duty of the dividing company to be allocated to a division company so long as the assets, property, rights, series, debts, liabilities or duties so allocated are reasonably identified by any method where the identity of such assets, property, rights, series, debts, liabilities or duties is objectively determinable.

(8) The rights, privileges, powers and interests in property of the dividing company that have been allocated to a division company, as well as the debts, liabilities and duties of the dividing company that have been allocated to such division company pursuant to a plan of division, shall remain vested in each such division company and shall not be deemed, as a result of the division, to have been assigned or transferred to such division company for any purpose of the laws of the State of Delaware.

(9) Any action or proceeding pending against a dividing company may be continued against the surviving company as if the division did not occur, but subject to subsection (l)(4) of this section, and against any resulting company to

which the asset, property, right, series, debt, liability or duty associated with such action or proceeding was allocated pursuant to the plan of division by adding or substituting such resulting company as a party in the action or proceeding.

(m) In applying the provisions of this chapter on distributions, a direct or indirect allocation of property or liabilities in a division is not deemed a distribution for purposes of this chapter.

(n) The provisions of this section shall not be construed to limit the means of accomplishing a division by any other means provided for in a limited liability company agreement or other agreement or as otherwise permitted by this chapter or as otherwise permitted by law.

(o) All limited liability companies formed on or after August 1, 2018 shall be governed by this section. All limited liability companies formed prior to August 1, 2018 shall be governed by this section; provided, that if the dividing company is a party to any written contract, indenture or other agreement entered into prior to August 1, 2018 that, by its terms, restricts, conditions or prohibits the consummation of a merger or consolidation by the dividing company with or into another party, or the transfer of assets by the dividing company to another party, then such restriction, condition or prohibition shall be deemed to apply to a division as if it were a merger, consolidation or transfer of assets, as applicable.

§18-218. Registered Series of Members, Managers, Limited Liability Company Interests or Assets

(a) If a limited liability company agreement provides for the establishment or formation of 1 or more series, then a registered series may be formed by complying with this §18-218. A limited liability company agreement does not need to use the term registered when referencing series or refer to this §18-852, and a reference in a limited liability company agreement for a registered series, including a registered series resulting from the conversion of a protected series to a registered series, may continue to refer to §18-215 of this title, which reference shall be deemed a reference to this §18-852 with respect to such registered series. A registered series is formed by the filing of a certificate of registered series in the office of the Secretary of State.

(b) Notice of the limitation on liabilities of a registered series as referenced in §18-218(c) shall be set forth in the certificate of formation of the limited liability company. Notice in a certificate of formation of the limitation on liabilities of a registered series as referenced in §18-218(c) shall be sufficient for all purposes of this subsection whether or not the limited liability company has formed any registered series when such notice is included in the certificate of formation, and there shall be no requirement that (i) any specific registered series of the limited liability company be referenced in such notice, (ii) such notice use the term registered when referencing series or include a reference to this §18-218, or (iii) the certificate of formation be amended if it includes a reference to §18-215 of this title. Any reference to §18-215 of this title in a certificate of formation of a limited liability company that has one or more registered series shall be deemed a reference to this §18-218 with respect to such registered series. The fact that a certificate of formation that contains the foregoing notice of the limitation on liabilities of a series is on file in the office of the Secretary of State shall constitute notice of such limitation on liabilities of a registered series.

(c) Notwithstanding anything to the contrary set forth in this chapter or under other applicable law, to the extent the records maintained for a registered series account for the assets associated with such series separately from the other assets of the limited liability company, or any other series thereof, then the debts, liabilities, obligations and expenses incurred, contracted for or otherwise existing with respect to such series shall be enforceable against the assets of such series only, and not against the assets of the limited liability company generally or any other series thereof, and, unless otherwise provided in the limited liability company agreement, none of the debts, liabilities, obligations and expenses incurred, contracted for or otherwise existing with respect to the limited liability company generally or any other series thereof shall be enforceable against the assets of such series. Neither the preceding sentences nor any provision pursuant thereto in a limited liability company agreement, certificate of formation or certificate of registered series shall (i) restrict a registered series or limited liability company on behalf of a registered series from agreeing in the limited liability company agreement or otherwise that any or all of the debts, liabilities, obligations and expenses incurred, contracted for or otherwise existing with respect to the limited liability company generally or any other series thereof shall be enforceable against the assets of such registered series or (ii) restrict a limited liability company from agreeing in the limited liability company agreement or otherwise that any or all of the debts, liabilities, obligations and expenses incurred, contracted for or otherwise existing with respect to a registered series shall be enforceable against the assets of the limited liability company generally. Assets associated with a registered series may be held directly or indirectly, including in the name of such series, in the name of the limited liability company, through a nominee or otherwise. Records maintained for a registered series that reasonably identify its assets, including by specific listing, category, type, quantity, computational or allocational formula or procedure (including a percentage or share of any asset or assets) or by any other method where the identity of such assets is objectively determinable, will be deemed to account for the assets associated with such series separately from the other assets of the limited liability company, or any other series thereof. As used in this chapter, a reference to assets of a registered series includes assets associated with such series, a reference to assets associated with a registered series includes assets of such series, a reference to members or managers of a registered series includes members or managers associated with such series, and a reference to members or managers associated with a registered series includes members or managers of such series. The following shall apply to a registered series:

(1) A registered series may carry on any lawful business, purpose or activity, whether or not for profit, with the exception of the business of banking as defined in §126 of Title 8. Unless otherwise provided in a limited liability company agreement, a registered series shall have the power and capacity to, in its own name, contract, hold title to assets (including real, personal and intangible property), grant liens and security interests, and sue and be sued.

(2) Except as otherwise provided by this chapter, no member or manager of a registered series shall be obligated personally for any debt, obligation or

liability of such series, whether arising in contract, tort or otherwise, solely by reason of being a member or acting as manager of such series. Notwithstanding the preceding sentence, under a limited liability company agreement or under another agreement, a member or manager may agree to be obligated personally for any or all of the debts, obligations and liabilities of one or more registered series.

(3) A limited liability company agreement may provide for classes or groups of members or managers associated with a registered series having such relative rights, powers and duties as the limited liability company agreement may provide, and may make provision for the future creation in the manner provided in the limited liability company agreement of additional classes or groups of members or managers associated with such series having such relative rights, powers and duties as may from time to time be established, including rights, powers and duties senior to existing classes and groups of members or managers associated with such series. A limited liability company agreement may provide for the taking of an action, including the amendment of the limited liability company agreement, without the vote or approval of any member or manager or class or group of members or managers, including an action to create under the provisions of the limited liability company agreement a class or group of a registered series of limited liability company interests that was not previously outstanding. A limited liability company agreement may provide that any member or class or group of members associated with a registered series shall have no voting rights.

(4) A limited liability company agreement may grant to all or certain identified members or managers or a specified class or group of the members or managers associated with a registered series the right to vote separately or with all or any class or group of the members or managers associated with such series, on any matter. Voting by members or managers associated with a registered series may be on a per capita, number, financial interest, class, group or any other basis.

(5) Unless otherwise provided in a limited liability company agreement, the management of a registered series shall be vested in the members associated with such series in proportion to the then current percentage or other interest of members in the profits of such series owned by all of the members associated with such series, the decision of members owning more than 50 percent of the said percentage or other interest in the profits controlling; provided, however, that if a limited liability company agreement provides for the management of a registered series, in whole or in part, by a manager, the management of such series, to the extent so provided, shall be vested in the manager who shall be chosen in the manner provided in the limited liability company agreement. The manager of a registered series shall also hold the offices and have the responsibilities accorded to the manager as set forth in a limited liability company agreement. A registered series may have more than 1 manager. Subject to §18-602 of this title, a manager shall cease to be a manager with respect to a registered series as provided in a limited liability company agreement. Except as otherwise provided in a limited liability company agreement, any event under this chapter or in a limited liability company agreement that causes a manager to cease to be a manager with respect to a registered series shall not, in itself, cause such manager

to cease to be a manager of the limited liability company or with respect to any other series thereof.

(6) Notwithstanding §18-606 of this title, but subject to subsections (c)(7) and (c)(10) of this section, and unless otherwise provided in a limited liability company agreement, at the time a member of a registered series becomes entitled to receive a distribution with respect to such series, the member has the status of, and is entitled to all remedies available to, a creditor of such series, with respect to the distribution. A limited liability company agreement may provide for the establishment of a record date with respect to allocations and distributions with respect to a registered series.

(7) Notwithstanding §18-607(a) of this title, a limited liability company may make a distribution with respect to a registered series. A limited liability company shall not make a distribution with respect to a registered series to a member to the extent that at the time of the distribution, after giving effect to the distribution, all liabilities of such series, other than liabilities to members on account of their limited liability company interests with respect to such series and liabilities for which the recourse of creditors is limited to specified property of such series, exceed the fair value of the assets associated with such series, except that the fair value of property of such series that is subject to a liability for which the recourse of creditors is limited shall be included in the assets associated with such series only to the extent that the fair value of that property exceeds that liability. For purposes of the immediately preceding sentence, the term "distribution" shall not include amounts constituting reasonable compensation for present or past services or reasonable payments made in the ordinary course of business pursuant to a bona fide retirement plan or other benefits program. A member who receives a distribution in violation of this subsection, and who knew at the time of the distribution that the distribution violated this subsection, shall be liable to the registered series for the amount of the distribution. A member who receives a distribution in violation of this subsection, and who did not know at the time of the distribution that the distribution violated this subsection, shall not be liable for the amount of the distribution. Subject to §18-607(c) of this title, which shall apply to any distribution made with respect to a registered series under this subsection, this subsection shall not affect any obligation or liability of a member under an agreement or other applicable law for the amount of a distribution.

(8) Unless otherwise provided in the limited liability company agreement, a member shall cease to be associated with a registered series and to have the power to exercise any rights or powers of a member with respect to such series upon the assignment of all of the member's limited liability company interest with respect to such series. Except as otherwise provided in a limited liability company agreement, any event under this chapter or a limited liability company agreement that causes a member to cease to be associated with a registered series shall not, in itself, cause such member to cease to be associated with any other series or terminate the continued membership of a member in the limited liability company or cause the dissolution of the registered series, regardless of whether such member was the last remaining member associated with such series.

(9) Subject to §18-801 of this title, except to the extent otherwise provided in the limited liability company agreement, a registered series may be dissolved and its affairs wound up without causing the dissolution of the limited liability company. The dissolution of a registered series shall not affect the limitation on liabilities of such series provided by this subsection (c). A registered series is dissolved and its affairs shall be wound up upon the dissolution of the limited liability company under §18-801 of this title or otherwise upon the first to occur of the following:

a. At the time specified in the limited liability company agreement;

b. Upon the happening of events specified in the limited liability company agreement;

c. Unless otherwise provided in the limited liability company agreement, upon the vote or consent of members associated with such series who own more than 2/3 of the then-current percentage or other interest in the profits of such series of the limited liability company owned by all of the members associated with such series; or

d. The dissolution of such series under subsection (b)(11) of this section.

(10) Notwithstanding §18-803(a) of this title, unless otherwise provided in the limited liability company agreement, a manager associated with a registered series who has not wrongfully dissolved such series or, if none, the members associated with such series or a person approved by the members associated with such series, in either case, by members who own more than 50 percent of the then current percentage or other interest in the profits of such series owned by all of the members associated with such series, may wind up the affairs of such series; but the Court of Chancery, upon cause shown, may wind up the affairs of a registered series upon application of any member or manager associated with such series, or the member's personal representative or assignee, and in connection therewith, may appoint a liquidating trustee. The persons winding up the affairs of a registered series may, in the name of the limited liability company and for and on behalf of the limited liability company and such series, take all actions with respect to such series as are permitted under §18-803(b) of this title. The persons winding up the affairs of a registered series shall provide for the claims and obligations of such series and distribute the assets of such series as provided in §18-804 of this title, which section shall apply to the winding up and distribution of assets of a registered series. Actions taken in accordance with this subsection shall not affect the liability of members and shall not impose liability on a liquidating trustee.

(11) On application by or for a member or manager associated with a registered series, the Court of Chancery may decree dissolution of such series whenever it is not reasonably practicable to carry on the business of such series in conformity with a limited liability company agreement.

(12) For all purposes of the laws of the State of Delaware, a registered series is an association, regardless of the number of members or managers, if any, of such series.

(d) In order to form a registered series of a limited liability company, a certificate of registered series must be filed in accordance with this §18-218(d).

(1) A certificate of registered series:

a. Shall set forth:

(i) The name of the limited liability company; and

(ii) The name of the registered series.

b. May include any other matter that the members of such registered series determine to include therein.

(2) A certificate of registered series shall be executed in accordance with §18-204 of this title and shall be filed in the office of the Secretary of State in accordance with §18-206 of this title. A certificate of registered series shall be effective as of the effective time of such filing unless a later effective date or time (which shall be a date or time certain) is provided for in the certificate of registered series. A certificate of registered series is not an amendment to the certificate of formation of the limited liability company. The filing of a certificate of registered series in the office of the Secretary of State shall make it unnecessary to file any other documents under Chapter 31 of this title.

(3) A certificate of registered series is amended by filing a certificate of amendment thereto in the office of the Secretary of State. The certificate of amendment of certificate of registered series shall set forth:

a. The name of the limited liability company;

b. The name of the registered series; and

c. The amendment to the certificate of registered series.

(4) A manager of a registered series or, if there is no manager, then any member of a registered series who becomes aware that any statement in a certificate of registered series filed with respect to such registered series was false when made, or that any matter described therein has changed making the certificate of registered series false in any material respect or non-compliant with §18-218(e)(1), shall promptly amend the certificate of registered series.

(5) A certificate of registered series may be amended at any time for any other proper purpose.

(6) Unless otherwise provided in this chapter or unless a later effective date or time (which shall be a date or time certain) is provided for in the certificate of amendment of certificate of registered series, a certificate of amendment of certificate of registered series shall be effective at the time of its filing with the Secretary of State.

(7) A certificate of registered series shall be canceled upon the cancellation of the certificate of formation of the limited liability company named in the certificate of registered series, or upon the filing of a certificate of cancellation of the certificate of registered series or upon the future effective date or time of a certificate of cancellation of the certificate of registered series, or as provided in §18-1108(b), or upon the filing of a certificate of merger or consolidation of registered series if the registered series is not the surviving or resulting registered series in a merger or consolidation or upon the future effective date or time of a certificate of merger or consolidation of registered series if the registered series is not the surviving or resulting registered series in a merger or consolidation, or upon the filing of a certificate of conversion of registered series to protected series or upon the future effective date or time of a certificate of conversion to

a protected series. A certificate of cancellation of the certificate of registered series may be filed at any time, and shall be filed, in the office of the Secretary of State to accomplish the cancellation of a certificate of registered series upon the dissolution of a registered series for which a certificate of registered series was filed and completion of the winding up of such registered series. A certificate of cancellation of the certificate of registered series shall set forth:

a. The name of the limited liability company;

b. The name of the registered series;

c. The date of filing of the certificate of registered series;

d. The future effective date or time (which shall be a date or time certain) of cancellation if it is not to be effective upon the filing of the certificate of cancellation; and

e. Any other information the person filing the certificate of cancellation of the certificate of registered series determines.

(8) A certificate of cancellation of the certificate of registered series that is filed in the office of the Secretary of State prior to the dissolution or the completion of winding up of a registered series may be corrected as an erroneously executed certificate of cancellation of the certificate of registered series by filing with the office of the Secretary of State a certificate of correction of such certificate of cancellation of the certificate of registered series in accordance with §18-211.

(9) The Secretary of State shall not issue a certificate of good standing with respect to a registered series if its certificate of registered series is canceled or the limited liability company has ceased to be in good standing.

(e) The name of each registered series as set forth in its certificate of registered series:

(1) Shall begin with the name of the limited liability company, including any word, abbreviation or designation required by §18-102;

(2) May contain the name of a member or manager;

(3) Must be such as to distinguish it upon the records in the office of the Secretary of State from the name on such records of any corporation, partnership, limited partnership, statutory trust, limited liability company, registered series of a limited liability company, or registered series of a limited partnership reserved, registered, formed or organized under the laws of the State of Delaware or qualified to do business or registered as a foreign corporation, foreign limited partnership, foreign statutory trust, foreign partnership or foreign limited liability company in the State of Delaware; provided, however, that a registered series may register under any name which is not such as to distinguish it upon the records in the office of the Secretary of State from the name on such records of any domestic or foreign corporation, partnership, limited partnership, statutory trust, registered series of a limited liability company, registered series of a limited partnership, or foreign limited liability company reserved, registered, formed or organized under the laws of the State of Delaware with the written consent of the other corporation, partnership, limited partnership, statutory trust, registered series of a limited liability company, registered series of a limited partnership, or foreign limited liability company, which written consent shall be filed with the Secretary of State;

(4) May contain the following words: "Company," "Association," "Club," "Foundation," "Fund," "Institute," "Society," "Union," "Syndicate," "Limited," "Public Benefit" or "Trust" (or abbreviations of like import); and

(5) Shall not contain the word "bank," or any variation thereof, except for the name of a bank reporting to and under the supervision of the State Bank Commissioner of this State or a subsidiary of a bank or savings association (as those terms are defined in the Federal Deposit Insurance Act, as amended, at 12 U.S.C. §1813), or a limited liability company regulated under the Bank Holding Company Act of 1956, as amended, 12 U.S.C. §1841 et seq., or the Home Owners' Loan Act, as amended, 12 U.S.C. §1461 et seq.; provided, however, that this section shall not be construed to prevent the use of the word "bank," or any variation thereof, in a context clearly not purporting to refer to a banking business or otherwise likely to mislead the public about the nature of the business of the limited liability company or the registered series, or to lead to a pattern and practice of abuse that might cause harm to the interests of the public or this State as determined by the Division of Corporations in the Department of State.

Subchapter III. Members

§18-301. Admission of Members

(a) In connection with the formation of a limited liability company, a person is admitted as a member of the limited liability company upon the later to occur of:

(1) The formation of the limited liability company; or

(2) The time provided in and upon compliance with the limited liability company agreement or, if the limited liability company agreement does not so provide, when the person's admission is reflected in the records of the limited liability company or as otherwise provided in the limited liability company agreement.

(b) After the formation of a limited liability company, a person is admitted as a member of the limited liability company:

(1) In the case of a person who is not an assignee of a limited liability company interest, including a person acquiring a limited liability company interest directly from the limited liability company and a person to be admitted as a member of the limited liability company without acquiring a limited liability company interest in the limited liability company at the time provided in and upon compliance with the limited liability company agreement or, if the limited liability company agreement does not so provide, upon the consent of all members or as otherwise provided in the limited liability company agreement;

(2) In the case of an assignee of a limited liability company interest, as provided in §18-704(a) of this title;

(3) In the case of a person being admitted as a member of a surviving or resulting limited liability company pursuant to a merger or consolidation approved in accordance with §18-209(b) of this title, as provided in the limited liability company agreement of the surviving or resulting limited liability company or in the agreement of merger or consolidation or plan of merger, and in

the event of any inconsistency, the terms of the agreement of merger or consolidation or plan of merger shall control; and in the case of a person being admitted as a member of a limited liability company pursuant to a merger or consolidation in which such limited liability company is not the surviving or resulting limited liability company in the merger or consolidation, as provided in the limited liability company agreement of such limited liability company; or

(4) In the case of a person being admitted as a member of a division company pursuant to a division approved in accordance with §18-217(c) of this title, as provided in the limited liability company agreement of such division company or in the plan of division, and in the event of any inconsistency, the terms of the plan of division shall control; and in the case of a person being admitted as a member of a limited liability company pursuant to a division in which such limited liability company is not a division company in the division, as provided in the limited liability company agreement of such limited liability company.

(c) In connection with the domestication of a non-United States entity (as defined in §18-212 of this title) as a limited liability company in the State of Delaware in accordance with §18-212 of this title or the conversion of an other entity (as defined in §18-214 of this title) to a domestic limited liability company in accordance with §18-214 of this title, a person is admitted as a member of the limited liability company as provided in the limited liability company agreement.

(d) A person may be admitted to a limited liability company as a member of the limited liability company and may receive a limited liability company interest in the limited liability company without making a contribution or being obligated to make a contribution to the limited liability company. Unless otherwise provided in a limited liability company agreement, a person may be admitted to a limited liability company as a member of the limited liability company without acquiring a limited liability company interest in the limited liability company. Unless otherwise provided in a limited liability company agreement, a person may be admitted as the sole member of a limited liability company without making a contribution or being obligated to make a contribution to the limited liability company or without acquiring a limited liability company interest in the limited liability company.

(e) Unless otherwise provided in a limited liability company agreement or another agreement, a member shall have no preemptive right to subscribe to any additional issue of limited liability company interests or another interest in a limited liability company.

§18-302. Classes and Voting

(a) A limited liability company agreement may provide for classes or groups of members having such relative rights, powers and duties as the limited liability company agreement may provide, and may make provision for the future creation in the manner provided in the limited liability company agreement of additional classes or groups of members having such relative rights, powers and duties as may from time to time be established, including rights, powers and duties senior to existing classes and groups of members. A limited liability company agreement may provide for the taking of an action, including the amendment of the limited liability company agreement, without the vote or approval of any member or class or group of members, including an action to create under the provisions of the limited liability company agreement a class or group of limited liability company interests that was not previously outstanding. A limited liability company agreement may provide that any member or class or group of members shall have no voting rights.

(b) A limited liability company agreement may grant to all or certain identified members or a specified class or group of the members the right to vote separately or with all or any class or group of the members or managers, on any matter. Voting by members may be on a per capita, number, financial interest, class, group or any other basis.

(c) A limited liability company agreement may set forth provisions relating to notice of the time, place or purpose of any meeting at which any matter is to be voted on by any members, waiver of any such notice, action by consent without a meeting, the establishment of a record date, quorum requirements, voting in person or by proxy, or any other matter with respect to the exercise of any such right to vote.

(d) Unless otherwise provided in a limited liability company agreement, meetings of members may be held by means of conference telephone or other communications equipment by means of which all persons participating in the meeting can hear each other, and participation in a meeting pursuant to this subsection shall constitute presence in person at the meeting. Unless otherwise provided in a limited liability company agreement, on any matter that is to be voted on, consented to or approved by members, the members may take such action without a meeting, without prior notice and without a vote if consented to or approved, in writing, by electronic transmission or by any other means permitted by law, by members having not less than the minimum number of votes that would be necessary to authorize or take such action at a meeting at which all members entitled to vote thereon were present and voted. Unless otherwise provided in a limited liability company agreement, if a person (whether or not then a member) consenting as a member to any matter provides that such consent will be effective at a future time (including a time determined upon the happening of an event), then such person shall be deemed to have consented as a member at such future time so long as such person is then a member. Unless otherwise provided in a limited liability company agreement, on any matter that is to be voted on by members, the members may vote in person or by proxy, and such proxy may be granted in writing, by means of electronic transmission or as otherwise permitted by applicable law. Unless otherwise provided in a limited liability company agreement, a consent transmitted by electronic transmission by a member or by a person or persons authorized to act for a member shall be deemed to be written and signed for purposes of this subsection.

(e) If a limited liability company agreement provides for the manner in which it may be amended, including by requiring the approval of a person who is not a party to the limited liability company agreement or the satisfaction of conditions, it may be amended only in that manner or as otherwise permitted by law, including as permitted by §18-209(f) of this title (provided that the approval of any person may be waived by such person and that any such conditions may be waived by all persons for whose benefit such conditions were intended). Unless otherwise provided in a limited liability company agreement, a supermajority amendment provision shall only apply to provisions of the limited liability company agreement that are expressly included in the limited liability company agreement. As used in this section, "supermajority amendment provision" means any amendment provision set forth in a limited liability company agreement requiring that an amendment to a provision of the limited liability company agreement be adopted by no less than the vote or consent required to take action under such latter provision.

(f) If a limited liability company agreement does not provide for the manner in which it may be amended, the limited liability company agreement may be amended with the approval of all of the members or as otherwise permitted by law, including as permitted by §18-209(f) of this title. This subsection shall only apply to a limited liability company whose original certificate of formation was filed with the Secretary of State on or after January 1, 2012.

§18-303. Liability to 3rd Parties

(a) Except as otherwise provided by this chapter, the debts, obligations and liabilities of a limited liability company, whether arising in contract, tort or otherwise, shall be solely the debts, obligations and liabilities of the limited liability company, and no member or manager of a limited liability company shall be obligated personally for any such debt, obligation or liability of the limited liability company solely by reason of being a member or acting as a manager of the limited liability company.

(b) Notwithstanding the provisions of subsection (a) of this section, under a limited liability company agreement or under another agreement, a member or manager may agree to be obligated personally for any or all of the debts, obligations and liabilities of the limited liability company.

§18-304. Events of Bankruptcy

A person ceases to be a member of a limited liability company upon the happening of any of the following events:

(1) Unless otherwise provided in a limited liability company agreement, or with the consent of all members, a member:

a. Makes an assignment for the benefit of creditors;

b. Files a voluntary petition in bankruptcy;

c. Is adjudged a bankrupt or insolvent, or has entered against the member an order for relief, in any bankruptcy or insolvency proceeding;

d. Files a petition or answer seeking for the member any reorganization, arrangement, composition, readjustment, liquidation, dissolution or similar relief under any statute, law or regulation;

e. Files an answer or other pleading admitting or failing to contest the material allegations of a petition filed against the member in any proceeding of this nature;

f. Seeks, consents to or acquiesces in the appointment of a trustee, receiver or liquidator of the member or of all or any substantial part of the member's properties; or

(2) Unless otherwise provided in a limited liability company agreement, or with the consent of all members, 120 days after the commencement of any proceeding against the member seeking reorganization, arrangement, composition, readjustment, liquidation, dissolution or similar relief under any statute, law or regulation, if the proceeding has not been dismissed, or if within 90 days after the appointment without the member's consent or acquiescence of a trustee, receiver or liquidator

of the member or of all or any substantial part of the member's properties, the appointment is not vacated or stayed, or within 90 days after the expiration of any such stay, the appointment is not vacated.

§18-305. Access to and Confidentiality of Information; Records

(a) Each member of a limited liability company, in person or by attorney or other agent, has the right, subject to such reasonable standards (including standards governing what information (including books, records and other documents) is to be furnished at what time and location and at whose expense) as may be set forth in a limited liability company agreement or otherwise established by the manager or, if there is no manager, then by the members, to obtain from the limited liability company from time to time upon reasonable demand for any purpose reasonably related to the member's interest as a member of the limited liability company:

(1) True and full information regarding the status of the business and financial condition of the limited liability company;

(2) Promptly after becoming available, a copy of the limited liability company's federal, state and local income tax returns for each year;

(3) A current list of the name and last known business, residence or mailing address of each member and manager;

(4) A copy of any written limited liability company agreement and certificate of formation and all amendments thereto, together with executed copies of any written powers of attorney pursuant to which the limited liability company agreement and any certificate and all amendments thereto have been executed;

(5) True and full information regarding the amount of cash and a description and statement of the agreed value of any other property or services contributed by each member and which each member has agreed to contribute in the future, and the date on which each became a member; and

(6) Other information regarding the affairs of the limited liability company as is just and reasonable.

(b) Each manager shall have the right to examine all of the information described in subsection (a) of this section for a purpose reasonably related to the position of manager.

(c) The manager of a limited liability company shall have the right to keep confidential from the members, for such period of time as the manager deems reasonable, any information which the manager reasonably believes to be in the nature of trade secrets or other information the disclosure of which the manager in good faith believes is not in the best interest of the limited liability company or could damage the limited liability company or its business or which the limited liability company is required by law or by agreement with a 3rd party to keep confidential.

(d) A limited liability company may maintain its books, records and other documents in other than paper form, including on, by means of, or in the form of any information storage device, method, or 1 or more electronic networks or databases (including 1 or more distributed electronic networks or databases), if such form is capable of conversion into paper form within a reasonable time.

(e) Any demand under this section shall be in writing and shall state the purpose of such demand. In every instance where an attorney or other agent shall be the person who seeks the right to obtain the information described in subsection (a) of this section, the demand shall be accompanied by a power of attorney or such other writing which authorizes the attorney or other agent to so act on behalf of the member.

(f) Any action to enforce any right arising under this section shall be brought in the Court of Chancery. If the limited liability company refuses to permit a member, or attorney or other agent acting for the member, to obtain or a manager to examine the information described in subsection (a) of this section or does not reply to the demand that has been made within 5 business days (or such shorter or longer period of time as is provided for in a limited liability company agreement but not longer than 30 business days) after the demand has been made, the demanding member or manager may apply to the Court of Chancery for an order to compel such disclosure. The Court of Chancery is hereby vested with exclusive jurisdiction to determine whether or not the person seeking such information is entitled to the information sought. The Court of Chancery may summarily order the limited liability company to permit the demanding member to obtain or manager to examine the information described in subsection (a) of this section and to make copies or abstracts therefrom, or the Court of Chancery may summarily order the limited liability company to furnish to the demanding member or manager the information described in subsection (a) of this section on the condition that the demanding member or manager first pay to the limited liability company the reasonable cost of obtaining and furnishing such information and on such other conditions as the Court of Chancery deems appropriate. When a demanding member seeks to obtain or a manager seeks to examine the information described in subsection (a) of this section, the demanding member or manager shall first establish:

(1) that the demanding member or manager has complied with the provisions of this section respecting the form and manner of making demand for obtaining or examining of such information, and

(2) that the information the demanding member or manager seeks is reasonably related to the member's interest as a member or the manager's position as a manager, as the case may be.

The Court of Chancery may, in its discretion, prescribe any limitations or conditions with reference to the obtaining or examining of information, or award such other or further relief as the Court of Chancery may deem just and proper. The Court of Chancery may order books, records and other documents, pertinent extracts therefrom, or duly authenticated copies thereof, to be brought within the State of Delaware and kept in the State of Delaware upon such terms and conditions as the order may prescribe.

(g) If a member is entitled to obtain information under this chapter or a limited liability company agreement for a purpose reasonably related to the member's interest as a member or other stated purpose, the member's right shall be to obtain such information as is necessary and essential to achieving that purpose. The rights of a member or manager to obtain or examine information as provided in this section may be expanded or restricted in an original limited liability company agreement or in any subsequent amendment approved or adopted by all of the members or in compliance with any applicable requirements of the limited liability company agreement. The provisions of this subsection shall not be construed to limit the ability to expand or restrict the rights of a member or manager to obtain or examine information by any other means permitted by law.

(h) A limited liability company shall maintain a current record that identifies the name and last known business, residence, or mailing address of each member and manager.

§18-306. Remedies for Breach of Limited Liability Company Agreement by Member

A limited liability company agreement may provide that:

(1) A member who fails to perform in accordance with, or to comply with the terms and conditions of, the limited liability company agreement shall be subject to specified penalties or specified consequences; and

(2) At the time or upon the happening of events specified in the limited liability company agreement, a member shall be subject to specified penalties or specified consequences.

Such specified penalties or specified consequences may include and take the form of any penalty or consequence set forth in §18-502(c) of this title.

Subchapter IV. Managers

§18-401. Admission of Managers

A person may be named or designated as a manager of the limited liability company as provided in §18-101(10) of this title.

§18-402. Management of Limited Liability Company

Unless otherwise provided in a limited liability company agreement, the management of a limited liability company shall be vested in its members in proportion to the then current percentage or other interest of members in the profits of the limited liability company owned by all of the members, the decision of members owning more than 50 percent of the said percentage or other interest in the profits controlling; provided however, that if a limited liability company agreement provides for the management, in whole or in part, of a limited liability company by a manager, the management of the limited liability company, to the extent so provided, shall be vested in the manager who shall be chosen in the manner provided in the limited liability company agreement. The manager shall also hold the offices and have the responsibilities accorded to the manager by or in the manner provided in a limited liability company agreement. Subject to §18-602 of this title, a manager shall cease to be a manager as provided in a limited liability company agreement. A limited liability company may have more than 1 manager. Unless otherwise provided in a limited liability company agreement, each member and manager has the authority to bind the limited liability company.

§18-403. Contributions by a Manager

A manager of a limited liability company may make contributions to the limited liability company and share in the profits and losses of, and in distributions from, the limited liability company as a member. A person who is both a manager and a member has the rights and powers, and is subject to the restrictions and liabilities, of a manager and, except as provided in a limited liability company agreement, also has the rights and powers, and is subject to the restrictions and liabilities, of a member to the extent of the manager's participation in the limited liability company as a member.

§18-404. Classes and Voting

(a) A limited liability company agreement may provide for classes or groups of managers having such relative rights, powers and duties as the limited liability company agreement may provide, and may make provision for the future creation in the manner provided in the limited liability company agreement of additional classes or groups of managers having such relative rights, powers and duties as may from time to time be established, including rights, powers and duties senior to existing classes and groups of managers. A limited liability company agreement may provide for the taking of an action, including the amendment of the limited liability company agreement, without the vote or approval of any manager or class or group of managers, including an action to create under the provisions of the limited liability company agreement a class or group of limited liability company interests that was not previously outstanding.

(b) A limited liability company agreement may grant to all or certain identified managers or a specified class or group of the managers the right to vote, separately or with all or any class or group of managers or members, on any matter. Voting by managers may be on a per capita, number, financial interest, class, group or any other basis.

(c) A limited liability company agreement may set forth provisions relating to notice of the time, place or purpose of any meeting at which any matter is to be voted on by any manager or class or group of managers, waiver of any such notice, action by consent without a meeting, the establishment of a record date, quorum requirements, voting in person or by proxy, or any other matter with respect to the exercise of any such right to vote.

(d) Unless otherwise provided in a limited liability company agreement, meetings of managers may be held by means of conference telephone or other communications equipment by means of which all persons participating in the meeting can hear each other, and participation in a meeting pursuant to this subsection shall constitute presence in person at the meeting. Unless otherwise provided in a limited liability company agreement, on any matter that is to be voted on, consented to or approved by managers, the managers may take such action without a meeting, without prior notice and without a vote if consented to or approved, in writing, by electronic transmission or by any other means permitted by law, by managers having not less than the minimum number of votes that would be necessary to authorize or take such action at a meeting at which all managers entitled to vote thereon were present and voted. Unless otherwise provided in a limited liability company agreement, if a person (whether or not then a manager) consenting as a manager to any matter provides that such consent will be effective at a future time (including a time determined upon the happening of an event), then such person shall be deemed to have consented as a manager at such future time so long as such person is then a manager. Unless otherwise provided in a limited liability company agreement, on any matter that is to be voted on by managers, the managers may vote in person or by proxy, and such proxy may be granted in writing, by means of electronic transmission or as otherwise permitted by applicable law. Unless otherwise provided in a limited liability company agreement, a consent transmitted by electronic transmission by a manager or by a person or persons authorized to act for a manager shall be deemed to be written and signed for purposes of this subsection.

§18-405. Remedies for Breach of Limited Liability Company Agreement by Manager

A limited liability company agreement may provide that:

(1) A manager who fails to perform in accordance with, or to comply with the terms and conditions of, the limited liability company agreement shall be subject to specified penalties or specified consequences; and

(2) At the time or upon the happening of events specified in the limited liability company agreement, a manager shall be subject to specified penalties or specified consequences.

§18-406. Reliance on Reports and Information by Member or Manager

A member, manager or liquidating trustee of a limited liability company shall be fully protected in relying in good faith upon the records of the limited liability company and upon information, opinions, reports or statements presented by another manager, member or liquidating trustee, an officer or employee of the limited liability company, or committees of the limited liability company, members or managers, or by any other person as to matters the member, manager or liquidating trustees reasonably believes are within such other person's professional or expert competence, including information, opinions, reports or statements as to the value and amount of the assets, liabilities, profits or losses of the limited liability company, or the value and amount of assets or reserves or contracts, agreements or other undertakings that would be sufficient to pay claims and obligations of the limited liability company or to make reasonable provision to pay such claims and obligations, or any other facts pertinent to the existence and amount of assets from which distributions to members or creditors might properly be paid.

§18-407. Delegation of Rights and Powers to Manage

Unless otherwise provided in the limited liability company agreement, a member or manager of a limited liability company has the power and authority to delegate to 1 or more other persons any or all of the member's or manager's, as the case may be, rights, powers and duties to manage and control the business and affairs of the limited liability company , which delegation may be made irrespective of whether the member or manager has a conflict of interest with respect to the matter as to which its rights, powers or duties are being delegated, and the person or persons to whom any such rights, powers or duties are being delegated shall not be deemed conflicted solely by reason of the conflict of interest of the member or manager. Any such delegation may be to agents, officers and employees of a member or manager or the limited liability company, and by a management agreement or another agreement with, or otherwise to,. other persons, including a committee of 1 or more persons. Unless otherwise provided in the limited liability company agreement, such delegation by a member or manager shall be irrevocable if it states that it is irrevocable. Unless otherwise provided in the limited liability company agreement, such delegation by a member or manager of a limited liability company shall not cause the member or manager to cease to be a member or manager, as the case may be, of the limited liability company or cause the person to whom any such rights, powers and duties have been delegated to be a member or manager, as the case may be, of the limited liability company. No other provision of this chapter or other law shall be construed to restrict a member's or manager's power and authority to delegate any or all of its rights, powers and duties to manage and control the business and affairs of the limited liability company.

SUBCHAPTER V. FINANCE

§18-501. Form of Contribution

The contribution of a member to a limited liability company may be in cash, property or services rendered, or a promissory note or other obligation to contribute cash or property or to perform services.

§18-502. Liability for Contribution

(a) Except as provided in a limited liability company agreement, a member is obligated to a limited liability company to perform any promise to contribute cash or property or to perform services, even if the member is unable to perform because of death, disability or any other reason. If a member does not make the required contribution of property or services, the member is obligated at the option of the limited liability company to contribute cash equal to that portion of the agreed value (as stated in the records of the limited liability company) of the contribution that has not been made. The foregoing option shall be in addition to, and not in lieu of, any other rights, including the right to specific performance, that the limited liability company may have against such member under the limited liability company agreement or applicable law.

(b) Unless otherwise provided in a limited liability company agreement, the obligation of a member to make a contribution or return money or other property paid or distributed in violation of this chapter may be compromised only by consent of all the members. Notwithstanding the compromise, a creditor of a limited liability company who extends credit, after the entering into of a limited liability company agreement or an amendment thereto which, in either case, reflects the obligation, and before the amendment thereof to reflect the compromise, may enforce the original obligation to the extent that, in extending credit, the creditor reasonably relied on the obligation of a member to make a contribution or return. A conditional obligation of a member to make a contribution or return money or other property to a limited liability company may not be enforced unless the conditions of the obligation have been satisfied or waived as to or by such member. Conditional obligations include contributions payable upon a discretionary call of a limited liability company prior to the time the call occurs.

(c) A limited liability company agreement may provide that the interest of any member who fails to make any contribution that the member is obligated to make shall be subject to specified penalties for, or specified consequences of, such failure. Such penalty or consequence may take the form of reducing or eliminating the defaulting member's proportionate interest in a limited liability company, subordinating the member's limited liability company interest to that of nondefaulting members, a forced sale of that limited liability company interest, forfeiture of the defaulting member's limited liability company interest, the lending by other members of the amount necessary to meet the defaulting member's commitment, a fixing of the value of the defaulting member's limited liability company interest by appraisal or by formula and redemption or sale of the limited liability company interest at such value, or other penalty or consequence.

§18-503. Allocation of Profits and Losses

The profits and losses of a limited liability company shall be allocated among the members, and among classes or groups of members, in the manner provided in a limited liability company agreement. If the limited liability company agreement does not so provide, profits and losses shall be allocated on the basis of the agreed value (as stated in the records of the limited liability company) of the contributions made by each member to the extent they have been received by the limited liability company and have not been returned.

§18-504. Allocation of Distributions

Distributions of cash or other assets of a limited liability company shall be allocated among the members, and among classes or groups of members, in the manner provided in a limited liability company agreement. If the limited liability company agreement does not so provide, distributions shall be made on the basis of the agreed value (as stated in the records of the limited liability company) of the contributions made by each member to the extent they have been received by the limited liability company and have not been returned.

§18-505. Defense of Usury not Available

No obligation of a member or manager of a limited liability company to the limited liability company, or to a member or manager of the limited liability company, arising under the limited liability company agreement or a separate agreement or writing, and no note, instrument or other writing evidencing any such obligation of a member or manager, shall be subject to the defense of usury, and no member or manager shall interpose the defense of usury with respect to any such obligation in any action.

Subchapter VI. Distributions and Resignation

§18-601. Interim Distributions

Except as provided in this subchapter, to the extent and at the times or upon the happening of the events specified in a limited liability company agreement, a member is entitled to receive from a limited liability company distributions before the member's resignation from the limited liability company and before the dissolution and winding up thereof.

§18-602. Resignation of Manager

A manager may resign as a manager of a limited liability company at the time or upon the happening of events specified in a limited liability company agreement and in accordance with the limited liability company agreement. A limited liability company agreement may provide that a manager shall not have the right to resign as a manager of a limited liability company. Notwithstanding that a limited liability company agreement provides that a manager does not have the right to resign as a manager of a limited liability company, a manager may resign as a manager of a limited liability company at any time by giving written notice to the members and other managers. If the resignation of a manager violates a limited liability company agreement, in addition to any remedies otherwise available under applicable law, a limited liability company may recover from the resigning manager damages for breach of the limited liability company agreement and offset the damages against the amount otherwise distributable to the resigning manager.

§18-603. Resignation of Member

A member may resign from a limited liability company only at the time or upon the happening of events specified in a limited liability company agreement and in accordance with the limited liability company agreement. Notwithstanding anything to the contrary under applicable law, unless a limited liability company agreement provides otherwise, a member may not resign from a limited liability company prior to the dissolution and winding up of the limited liability company. Notwithstanding anything to the contrary under applicable law, a limited liability company agreement may provide that a limited liability company interest may not be assigned prior to the dissolution and winding up of the limited liability company.

Unless otherwise provided in a limited liability company agreement, a limited liability company whose original certificate of formation was filed with the Secretary of State and effective on or prior to July 31, 1996, shall continue to be governed by this section as in effect on July 31, 1996.

§18-604. Distribution Upon Resignation

Except as provided in this subchapter, upon resignation any resigning member is entitled to receive any distribution to which such member is entitled under a limited liability company agreement and, if not otherwise provided in a limited liability company agreement, such member is entitled to receive, within a reasonable time after resignation, the fair value of such member's limited liability company interest as of the date of resignation based upon such member's right to share in distributions from the limited liability company.

§18-605. Distribution in Kind

Except as provided in a limited liability company agreement, a member, regardless of the nature of the member's contribution, has no right to demand and receive any distribution from a limited liability company in any form other than cash. Except as provided in a limited liability company agreement, a member may not be compelled to accept a distribution of any asset in kind from a limited liability company to the extent that the percentage of the asset distributed exceeds a percentage of that asset which is equal to the percentage in which the member shares in distributions from the limited liability company. Except as provided in the limited liability company agreement, a member may be compelled to accept a distribution of any asset in kind from a limited liability company to the extent that the percentage of the asset distributed is equal to a percentage of that asset which is equal to the percentage in which the member shares in distributions from the limited liability company.

§18-606. Right to Distribution

Subject to §§18-607 and 18-804 of this title, and unless otherwise provided in a limited liability company agreement, at the time a member becomes entitled to receive a distribution, the member has the status of, and is entitled to all remedies available to, a creditor of a limited liability company with respect to the distribution. A limited liability company agreement may provide for the establishment of a record date with respect to allocations and distributions by a limited liability company.

§18-607. Limitations on Distribution

(a) A limited liability company shall not make a distribution to a member to the extent that at the time of the distribution, after giving effect to the distribution, all liabilities of the limited liability company, other than liabilities to members on account of their limited liability company interests and liabilities for which the recourse of creditors is limited to specified property of the limited liability company, exceed the fair value of the assets of the limited liability company, except that the fair value of property that is subject to a liability for which the recourse of creditors is limited shall be included in the assets of the limited liability company only to the extent that the fair value of that property exceeds that liability. For purposes of this subsection (a), the term "distribution" shall not include amounts constituting reasonable compensation for present or past services or reasonable payments made in the ordinary course of business pursuant to a bona fide retirement plan or other benefits program.

(b) A member who receives a distribution in violation of subsection (a) of this section, and who knew at the time of the distribution that the distribution violated subsection (a) of this section, shall be liable to a limited liability company for the amount of the distribution. A member who receives a distribution in violation of subsection (a) of this section, and who did not know at the time of the distribution that the distribution violated subsection (a) of this section, shall not be liable for the amount of the distribution. Subject to subsection (c) of this section, this subsection shall not affect any obligation or liability of a member under an agreement or other applicable law for the amount of a distribution.

(c) Unless otherwise agreed, a member who receives a distribution from a limited liability company shall have no liability under this chapter or other applicable law for the amount of the distribution after the expiration of 3 years from the date of the distribution unless an action to recover the distribution from such member is commenced prior to the expiration of the said 3-year period and an adjudication of liability against such member is made in the said action.

Subchapter VII. Assignment of Limited Liability Company Interests

§18-701. Nature of Limited Liability Company Interest

A limited liability company interest is personal property. A member has no interest in specific limited liability company property.

§18-702. Assignment of Limited Liability Company Interest

(a) A limited liability company interest is assignable in whole or in part except as provided in a limited liability company agreement. The assignee of a member's limited liability company interest shall have no right to participate in the management of the business and affairs of a limited liability company except as provided in a limited liability company agreement or, unless otherwise provided in the limited liability company agreement, upon the vote or consent of all of the members of the limited liability company.

(b) Unless otherwise provided in a limited liability company agreement:

(1) An assignment of a limited liability company interest does not entitle the assignee to become or to exercise any rights or powers of a member;

(2) An assignment of a limited liability company interest entitles the assignee to share in such profits and losses, to receive such distribution or distributions, and to receive such allocation of income, gain, loss, deduction, or credit or similar item to which the assignor was entitled, to the extent assigned; and

(3) A member ceases to be a member and to have the power to exercise any rights or powers of a member upon assignment of all of the member's limited liability company interest. Unless otherwise provided in a limited liability company agreement, the pledge of, or granting of a security interest, lien or other encumbrance in or against, any or all of the limited liability company interest of a member shall not cause the member to cease to be a member or to have the power to exercise any rights or powers of a member.

(c) Unless otherwise provided in a limited liability company agreement, a member's interest in a limited liability company may be evidenced by a certificate of limited liability company interest issued by the limited liability company. A limited liability company agreement may provide for the assignment or transfer of any limited liability company interest represented by such a certificate and make other provisions with respect to such certificates. A limited liability company shall not have the power to issue a certificate of limited liability company interest in bearer form.

(d) Unless otherwise provided in a limited liability company agreement and except to the extent assumed by agreement, until an assignee of a limited liability company interest becomes a member, the assignee shall have no liability as a member solely as a result of the assignment.

(e) Unless otherwise provided in the limited liability company agreement, a limited liability company may acquire, by purchase, redemption or otherwise, any limited liability company interest or other interest of a member or manager in the limited liability company. Unless otherwise provided in the limited liability company agreement, any such interest so acquired by the limited liability company shall be deemed canceled.

§18-703. Member's Limited Liability Company Interest Subject to Charging Order

(a) On application by a judgment creditor of a member or of a member's assignee, a court having jurisdiction may charge the limited liability company interest of the judgment debtor to satisfy the judgment. To the extent so charged, the judgment creditor has only the right to receive any distribution or distributions to which the judgment debtor would otherwise have been entitled in respect of such limited liability company interest.

(b) A charging order constitutes a lien on the judgment debtor's limited liability company interest.

(c) This chapter does not deprive a member or member's assignee of a right under exemption laws with respect to the judgment debtor's limited liability company interest.

(d) The entry of a charging order is the exclusive remedy by which a judgment creditor of a member or a member's assignee may satisfy a judgment out of the judgment debtor's limited liability company interest and attachment, garnishment, foreclosure or other legal or equitable remedies are not available to the judgment creditor, whether the limited liability company has 1 member or more than 1 member.

(e) No creditor of a member or of a member's assignee shall have any right to obtain possession of, or otherwise exercise legal or equitable remedies with respect to, the property of the limited liability company.

(f) The Court of Chancery shall have jurisdiction to hear and determine any matter relating to any such charging order.

§18-704. Right of Assignee to Become Member

(a) An assignee of a limited liability company interest becomes a member:

(1) As provided in the limited liability company agreement;

(2) Unless otherwise provided in the limited liability company agreement, upon the vote or consent of all of the members of the limited liability company; or

(3) Unless otherwise provided in the limited liability company agreement by a specific reference to this subsection or otherwise provided in connection with the assignment, upon the voluntary assignment by the sole member of the

limited liability company of all of the limited liability company interests in the limited liability company to a single assignee. An assignment will be voluntary for purposes of this subsection if it is consented to by the member at the time of the assignment and is not effected by foreclosure or other similar legal process.

(b) An assignee who has become a member has, to the extent assigned, the rights and powers, and is subject to the restrictions and liabilities, of a member under a limited liability company agreement and this chapter. Notwithstanding the foregoing, unless otherwise provided in a limited liability company agreement, an assignee who becomes a member is liable for the obligations of the assignor to make contributions as provided in §18-502 of this title, but shall not be liable for the obligations of the assignor under subchapter VI of this chapter. However, the assignee is not obligated for liabilities, including the obligations of the assignor to make contributions as provided in §18-502 of this title, unknown to the assignee at the time the assignee became a member and which could not be ascertained from a limited liability company agreement.

(c) Whether or not an assignee of a limited liability company interest becomes a member, the assignor is not released from liability to a limited liability company under subchapters V and VI of this chapter.

§18-705. Powers of Estate of Deceased or Incompetent Member

If a member who is an individual dies or a court of competent jurisdiction adjudges the member to be incompetent to manage the member's person or property, the member's personal representative may exercise all of the member's rights for the purpose of settling the member's estate or administering the member's property, including any power under a limited liability company agreement of an assignee to become a member. If a member is a corporation, trust or other entity and is dissolved or terminated, the powers of that member may be exercised by its personal representative.

SUBCHAPTER VIII. DISSOLUTION

§18-801. Dissolution

(a) A limited liability company is dissolved and its affairs shall be wound up upon the first to occur of the following:

(1) At the time specified in a limited liability company agreement, but if no such time is set forth in the limited liability company agreement, then the limited liability company shall have a perpetual existence;

(2) Upon the happening of events specified in a limited liability company agreement;

(3) Unless otherwise provided in a limited liability company agreement, upon the vote or consent of members who own more than 2/3 of the then-current percentage or other interest in the profits of the limited liability company owned by all of the members;

(4) At any time there are no members; provided, that the limited liability company is not dissolved and is not required to be wound up if:

a. Unless otherwise provided in a limited liability company agreement, within 90 days or such other period as is provided for in the limited liability company agreement after the occurrence of the event that terminated the continued membership of the last remaining member, the personal representative of the last remaining member agrees to continue the limited liability company and to the admission of the personal representative of such member or its nominee or designee to the limited liability company as a member, effective as of the occurrence of the event that terminated the continued membership of the last remaining member; provided, that a limited liability company agreement may provide that the personal representative of the last remaining member shall be obligated to agree to continue the limited liability company and to the admission of the personal representative of such member or its nominee or designee to the limited liability company as a member, effective as of the occurrence of the event that terminated the continued membership of the last remaining member, or

b. A member is admitted to the limited liability company in the manner provided for in the limited liability company agreement, effective as of the occurrence of the event that terminated the continued membership of the last remaining member, within 90 days or such other period as is provided for in the limited liability company agreement after the occurrence of the event that terminated the continued membership of the last remaining member, pursuant to a provision of the limited liability company agreement that specifically provides for the admission of a member to the limited liability company after there is no longer a remaining member of the limited liability company.

(5) The entry of a decree of judicial dissolution under §18-802 of this title.

Unless otherwise provided in a limited liability company agreement, a limited liability company whose original certificate of formation was filed with the Secretary of State and effective on or prior to July 31, 2015, shall continue to be governed by paragraph (a)(3) of this section as in effect on July 31, 2015 (except that "affirmative" and "written" shall be deleted from such paragraph (a)(3) of this section).

(b) Unless otherwise provided in a limited liability company agreement, the death, retirement, resignation, expulsion, bankruptcy or dissolution of any member or the occurrence of an event that terminates the continued membership of any member shall not cause the limited liability company to be dissolved or its affairs to be wound up, and upon the occurrence of any such event, the limited liability company shall be continued without dissolution.

§18-802. Judicial Dissolution

On application by or for a member or manager the Court of Chancery may decree dissolution of a limited liability company whenever it is not reasonably practicable to carry on the business in conformity with a limited liability company agreement.

§18-803. Winding Up

(a) Unless otherwise provided in a limited liability company agreement, a manager who has not wrongfully dissolved a limited liability company or, if none, the members or a person approved by the members, in either case, by members who own more than 50 percent of the then current percentage or other interest in the profits of the limited liability company owned by all of the members, may wind up the limited liability company's affairs; but the Court of Chancery, upon cause shown, may wind up the limited liability company's affairs upon application of any member or manager, or the member's personal representative or assignee, and in connection therewith, may appoint a liquidating trustee. Unless otherwise provided in a limited liability company agreement, a limited liability company whose original certificate of formation was filed with the Secretary of State and effective on or prior to July 31, 2015, shall continue to be governed by this subsection as in effect on July 31, 2015.

(b) Upon dissolution of a limited liability company and until the filing of a certificate of cancellation as provided in §18-203 of this title, the persons winding up the limited liability company's affairs may, in the name of, and for and on behalf of, the limited liability company, prosecute and defend suits, whether civil, criminal or administrative, gradually settle and close the limited liability company's business, dispose of and convey the limited liability company's property, discharge or make reasonable provision for the limited liability company's liabilities, and distribute to the members any remaining assets of the limited liability company, all without affecting the liability of members and managers and without imposing liability on a liquidating trustee.

§18-804. Distribution of Assets

(a) Upon the winding up of a limited liability company, the assets shall be distributed as follows:

(1) To creditors, including members and managers who are creditors, to the extent otherwise permitted by law, in satisfaction of liabilities of the limited liability company (whether by payment or the making of reasonable provision for payment thereof) other than liabilities for which reasonable provision for payment has been made and liabilities for distributions to members and former members under §18-601 or §18-604 of this title;

(2) Unless otherwise provided in a limited liability company agreement, to members and former members in satisfaction of liabilities for distributions under §18-601 or §18-604 of this title; and

(3) Unless otherwise provided in a limited liability company agreement, to members first for the return of their contributions and second respecting their limited liability company interests, in the proportions in which the members share in distributions.

(b) A limited liability company which has dissolved:

(1) Shall pay or make reasonable provision to pay all claims and obligations, including all contingent, conditional or unmatured contractual claims, known to the limited liability company;

(2) Shall make such provision as will be reasonably likely to be sufficient to provide compensation for any claim against the limited liability company which is the subject of a pending action, suit or proceeding to which the limited liability company is a party; and

(3) Shall make such provision as will be reasonably likely to be sufficient to provide compensation for claims that have not been made known to the limited liability company or that have not arisen but that, based on facts known to the limited liability company, are likely to arise or to become known to the limited liability company within 10 years after the date of dissolution.

If there are sufficient assets, such claims and obligations shall be paid in full and any such provision for payment made shall be made in full. If there are insufficient assets, such claims and obligations shall be paid or provided for according to their priority and, among claims of equal priority, ratably to the extent of assets available therefor. Unless otherwise provided in the limited liability company agreement, any remaining assets shall be distributed as provided in this chapter. Any liquidating trustee winding up a limited liability company's affairs who has complied with this section shall not be personally liable to the claimants of the dissolved limited liability company by reason of such person's actions in winding up the limited liability company.

(c) A member who receives a distribution in violation of subsection (a) of this section, and who knew at the time of the distribution that the distribution violated subsection (a) of this section, shall be liable to the limited liability company for the amount of the distribution. For purposes of the immediately preceding sentence, the term "distribution" shall not include amounts constituting reasonable compensation for present or past services or reasonable payments made in the ordinary course of business pursuant to a bona fide retirement plan or other benefits program. A member who receives a distribution in violation of subsection (a) of this section, and who did not know at the time of the distribution that the distribution violated subsection (a) of this section, shall not be liable for the amount of the distribution. Subject to subsection (d) of this section, this subsection shall not affect any obligation or liability of a member under an agreement or other applicable law for the amount of a distribution.

(d) Unless otherwise agreed, a member who receives a distribution from a limited liability company to which this section applies shall have no liability under this chapter or other applicable law for the amount of the distribution after the expiration of 3 years from the date of the distribution unless an action to recover the distribution from such member is commenced prior to the expiration of the said 3-year period and an adjudication of liability against such member is made in the said action.

(e) Section 18-607 of this title shall not apply to a distribution to which this section applies.

§18-805. Trustees or Receivers for Limited Liability Companies; Appointment; Powers; Duties

When the certificate of formation of any limited liability company formed under this chapter shall be canceled by the filing of a certificate of cancellation pursuant to §18-203 of this title, the Court of Chancery, on application of any creditor, member or manager of the limited liability company, or any other person who shows good cause therefor, at any time, may either appoint 1 or more of the managers of the limited liability company to be trustees, or appoint 1 or more persons to be receivers, of and for the limited liability company, to take charge of the limited liability company's property, and to collect the debts and property due and belonging to the limited liability company, with the power to prosecute and defend, in the name of the limited liability company, or otherwise, all such suits as may be necessary or proper for the purposes aforesaid, and to appoint an agent or agents under them, and to do all other acts which might be done by the limited liability company, if in being, that may be necessary for the final settlement of the unfinished business of the limited liability company. The powers of the trustees or receivers may be continued as long as the Court of Chancery shall think necessary for the purposes aforesaid.

§18-806. Revocation of Dissolution

If a limited liability company agreement provides the manner in which a dissolution may be revoked, it may be revoked in that manner and, unless a limited liability company agreement prohibits revocation of dissolution, then notwithstanding the occurrence of an event set forth in §18-801(a)(1), (2), (3) or (4) of this title, the limited liability company shall not be dissolved and its affairs shall not be wound up if, prior to the filing of a certificate of cancellation in the office of the Secretary of State, the limited liability company is continued, effective as of the occurrence of such event:

(1) In the case of dissolution effected by the vote or consent of the members or other persons, pursuant to such vote or consent (and the approval of any members or other persons whose approval is required under the limited liability company agreement to revoke a dissolution contemplated by this paragraph);

(2) In the case of dissolution under §18-801(a)(1) or (2) of this title (other than a dissolution effected by the vote or consent of the members or other persons or the occurrence of an event that causes the last remaining member to cease to be a member), pursuant to such vote or consent that, pursuant to the terms of the limited liability company agreement, is required to amend the provision of the limited liability company agreement effecting such dissolution (and the approval of any members or other persons whose approval is required under the limited liability company agreement to revoke a dissolution contemplated by this paragraph); and

(3) In the case of dissolution effected by the occurrence of an event that causes the last remaining member to cease to be a member, pursuant to the vote or consent of the personal representative of the last remaining member of the limited liability company or the assignee of all of the limited liability company interests in the limited liability company (and the approval of any other persons whose approval is required under the limited liability company agreement to revoke a dissolution contemplated by this paragraph).

If there is no remaining member of the limited liability company and the personal representative of the last remaining member or the assignee of all of the limited liability company interests in the limited liability company votes in favor of or consents to the continuation of the limited liability company, such personal representative or such assignee, as applicable, shall be required to agree to the admission of a nominee or designee as a member, effective as of the occurrence of the event that terminated the continued membership of the last remaining member. The provisions of this section shall not be construed to limit the accomplishment of a revocation of dissolution by other means permitted by law.

Subchapter IX. Foreign Limited Liability Companies

§18-901. Law Governing

(a) Subject to the Constitution of the State of Delaware:

(1) The laws of the state, territory, possession, or other jurisdiction or country under which a foreign limited liability company is organized govern its organization and internal affairs and the liability of its members and managers; and

(2) A foreign limited liability company may not be denied registration by reason of any difference between those laws and the laws of the State of Delaware.

(b) A foreign limited liability company shall be subject to §18-106 of this title.

§18-902. Registration Required; Application

Before doing business in the State of Delaware, a foreign limited liability company shall register with the Secretary of State. . . .

Subchapter X. Derivative Actions

§18-1001. Right to Bring Action

A member or an assignee of a limited liability company interest may bring an action in the Court of Chancery in the right of a limited liability company to recover a judgment in its favor if managers or members with authority to do so have refused to bring the action or if an effort to cause those managers or members to bring the action is not likely to succeed.

§18-1002. Proper Plaintiff

In a derivative action, the plaintiff must be a member or an assignee of a limited liability company interest at the time of bringing the action and:

(1) At the time of the transaction of which the plaintiff complains; or

(2) The plaintiff's status as a member or an assignee of a limited liability company interest had devolved upon the plaintiff by operation of law or pursuant to the terms of a limited liability company agreement from a person who was a member or an assignee of a limited liability company interest at the time of the transaction.

§18-1003. Complaint

In a derivative action, the complaint shall set forth with particularity the effort, if any, of the plaintiff to secure initiation of the action by a manager or member or the reasons for not making the effort.

§18-1004. Expenses

If a derivative action is successful, in whole or in part, as a result of a judgment, compromise or settlement of any such action, the court may award the plaintiff reasonable expenses, including reasonable attorney's fees, from any recovery in any such action or from a limited liability company.

Subchapter XI. Miscellaneous

§18-1101. Construction and Application of Chapter and Limited Liability Company Agreement

(a) The rule that statutes in derogation of the common law are to be strictly construed shall have no application to this chapter.

(b) It is the policy of this chapter to give the maximum effect to the principle of freedom of contract and to the enforceability of limited liability company agreements.

(c) To the extent that, at law or in equity, a member or manager or other person has duties (including fiduciary duties) to a limited liability company or to another member or manager or to another person that is a party to or is otherwise bound by a limited liability company agreement, the member's or manager's or other person's duties may be expanded or restricted or eliminated by provisions in the limited liability company agreement; provided, that the limited liability company agreement may not eliminate the implied contractual covenant of good faith and fair dealing.

(d) Unless otherwise provided in a limited liability company agreement, a member or manager or other person shall not be liable to a limited liability company or to another member or manager or to another person that is a party to or is otherwise bound by a limited liability company agreement for breach of fiduciary duty for the member's or manager's or other person's good faith reliance on the provisions of the limited liability company agreement.

(e) A limited liability company agreement may provide for the limitation or elimination of any and all liabilities for breach of contract and breach of duties (including fiduciary duties) of a member, manager or other person to a limited liability company or to another member or manager or to another person that is a party to or is otherwise bound by a limited liability company agreement; provided, that a limited liability company agreement may not limit or eliminate liability for any act or omission that constitutes a bad faith violation of the implied contractual covenant of good faith and fair dealing.

(f) Unless the context otherwise requires, as used herein, the singular shall include the plural and the plural may refer to only the singular. The use of any gender shall be applicable to all genders. The captions contained herein are for purposes of convenience only and shall not control or affect the construction of this chapter.

(g) Sections 9-406 and 9-408 of this title do not apply to any interest in a limited liability company, including all rights, powers and interests arising under a limited liability company agreement or this chapter. This provision prevails over §§9-406 and 9-408 of this title.

(h) Action validly taken pursuant to 1 provision of this chapter shall not be deemed invalid solely because it is identical or similar in substance to an action that could have been taken pursuant to some other provision of this chapter but fails to satisfy 1 or more requirements prescribed by such other provision.

(i) A limited liability company agreement that provides for the application of Delaware law shall be governed by and construed under the laws of the State of Delaware in accordance with its terms.

(j) The provisions of this chapter shall apply whether a limited liability company has 1 member or more than 1 member.

§18-1102. Short Title

This chapter may be cited as the "Delaware Limited Liability Company Act."

§18-1103. Severability

If any provision of this chapter or its application to any person or circumstances is held invalid, the invalidity does not affect other provisions or applications of the chapter which can be given effect without the invalid provision or application, and to this end, the provisions of this chapter are severable.

§18-1104. Cases not Provided for in this Chapter

In any case not provided for in this chapter, the rules of law and equity, including the rules of law and equity relating to fiduciary duties and the law merchant, shall govern.

§18-1106. Reserved Power of State of Delaware to Alter or Repeal Chapter

All provisions of this chapter may be altered from time to time or repealed and all rights of members and managers are subject to this reservation. Unless expressly stated to the contrary in this chapter, all amendments of this chapter shall apply to limited liability companies and members and managers whether or not existing as such at the time of the enactment of any such amendment.

§18-1107. Taxation of Limited Liability Companies

(a) For purposes of any tax imposed by the State of Delaware or any instrumentality, agency or political subdivision of the State of Delaware, a domestic limited liability company or a foreign limited liability company qualified to do business in the State of Delaware shall be classified as a partnership unless classified otherwise for federal income tax purposes, in which case the domestic or foreign limited liability company shall be classified in the same manner as it is classified for federal income tax purposes. For purposes of any tax imposed by the State of Delaware or any instrumentality, agency or political subdivision of the State of Delaware, a member or an assignee of a member of a domestic limited liability company or a foreign limited liability company qualified to do business in the State of Delaware shall be treated as either a resident or nonresident partner unless classified otherwise for federal income tax purposes, in which case the member or assignee of a member shall have the same status as such member or assignee of a member has for federal income tax purposes.

(b) Every domestic limited liability company and every foreign limited liability company registered to do business in the State of Delaware shall pay an annual tax, for the use of the State of Delaware, in the amount of $300. There shall be paid by or on behalf of each registered series of a domestic limited liability company an annual tax, for use of the State of Delaware, in the amount of $75 per registered series. . . .

Subchapter XII. Statutory Public Benefit Limited Liability Companies

§18-1201. Law Applicable to Statutory Public Benefit Limited Liability Companies; How Formed

This subchapter applies to all statutory public benefit limited liability companies, as defined in §18-1202(a) of this title. If a limited liability company is formed as or elects to become a statutory public benefit limited liability company in the manner prescribed in this section, it shall be subject in all respects to the provisions of this chapter, except to the extent this subchapter imposes additional or different requirements, in which case such additional or different requirements shall apply, and notwithstanding §18-1101 of this title or any other provision of this title, such additional or different requirements imposed by this subchapter may not be altered in the limited liability company agreement. If a limited liability company is not formed as a statutory public benefit limited liability company, it may become a statutory public benefit limited liability company in the manner specified in its limited liability company agreement or by amending its limited liability company agreement and certificate of formation to comply with the requirements of this subchapter.

§18-1202. Statutory Public Benefit Limited Liability Company Defined; Contents of Certificate of Formation and Limited Liability Company Agreement

(a) A "statutory public benefit limited liability company" is a for-profit limited liability company formed under and subject to the requirements of this chapter that is intended to produce a public benefit or public benefits and to operate in a responsible and sustainable manner. To that end, a statutory public benefit limited liability company shall be managed in a manner that balances the members' pecuniary interests, the best interests of those materially affected by the limited liability company's conduct, and the public benefit or public benefits set forth in its limited liability company agreement and in its certificate of formation. A statutory public benefit limited liability company shall state in its limited liability company agreement and in the heading of its certificate of formation that it is a statutory public benefit limited liability company and shall set forth in its limited liability company agreement and in its certificate of formation 1 or more specific public benefits to be promoted by the limited liability company. In the event of any inconsistency between the public benefit or benefits to be promoted by the limited liability company as set forth in its limited liability company agreement and in its certificate of formation, the limited liability company agreement shall control as among the members, the managers and other persons who are party to or otherwise bound by the liability company agreement. A manager of a statutory public benefit limited liability company or, if there is no manager, then any member of a statutory public benefit limited liability company who becomes aware that the specific public benefit or benefits to be promoted by the limited liability company as set forth in its limited liability company agreement are inaccurately set forth in its certificate of formation, shall promptly amend the certificate of formation. Any provision in the limited liability company agreement or certificate of formation of a statutory public benefit limited liability company that is inconsistent with this subchapter shall not be effective to the extent of such inconsistency.

(b) "Public benefit" means a positive effect (or reduction of negative effects) on 1 or more categories of persons, entities, communities or interests (other than members in their capacities as members) including, but not limited to, effects of an artistic, charitable, cultural, economic, educational, environmental, literary, medical, religious, scientific or technological nature. "Public benefit provisions" means the provisions of a limited liability company agreement contemplated by this subchapter.

81 Del. Laws, c. 357, §34; 83 Del. Laws, c. 61, §6;

§18-1203. Certain Amendments and Mergers; Votes Required [Repealed]

81 Del. Laws, c. 357, §34; repealed by 83 Del. Laws, c. 61, §7, effective Aug. 1, 2021.;

§18-1204. Duties of Members or Managers

(a) The members or managers or other persons with authority to manage or direct the business and affairs of a statutory public benefit limited liability company shall manage or direct the business and affairs of the statutory public benefit limited liability company in a manner that balances the pecuniary interests of the members, the best interests of those materially affected by the limited liability company's conduct, and the specific public benefit or public benefits set forth in its limited liability company agreement and certificate of formation. Unless otherwise provided in a limited liability company agreement, no member, manager or other person with authority to manage or direct the business and affairs of the statutory public benefit limited liability company shall have any liability for monetary damages for the failure to manage or direct the business and affairs of the statutory public benefit limited liability company as provided in this subsection.

(b) A member or manager of a statutory public benefit limited liability company or any other person with authority to manage or direct the business and affairs of the statutory public benefit limited liability company shall not, by virtue of the public benefit provisions or §18-1202(a) of this title, have any duty to any person on account of any interest of such person in the public benefit or public benefits set forth in its limited liability company agreement and certificate of formation or on account of any interest materially affected by the limited liability company's conduct and, with respect to a decision implicating the balance requirement in subsection (a) of this section, will be deemed to satisfy such person's fiduciary duties to members and the limited liability company if such person's decision is both informed and disinterested and not such that no person of ordinary, sound judgment would approve.

81 Del. Laws, c. 357, §34; 83 Del. Laws, c. 61, §8;

§18-1205. Periodic Statements and Third-Party Certification

A statutory public benefit limited liability company shall no less than biennially provide its members with a statement as to the limited liability company's promotion of the public benefit or public benefits set forth in its limited liability company agreement and certificate of formation and as to the best interests of those materially affected by the limited liability company's conduct. The statement shall include:

(1) The objectives that have been established to promote such public benefit or public benefits and interests;

(2) The standards that have been adopted to measure the limited liability company's progress in promoting such public benefit or public benefits and interests;

(3) Objective factual information based on those standards regarding the limited liability company's success in meeting the objectives for promoting such public benefit or public benefits and interests; and

(4) An assessment of the limited liability company's success in meeting the objectives and promoting such public benefit or public benefits and interests.

81 Del. Laws, c. 357, §34; 83 Del. Laws, c. 61, §9;

§18-1206. Derivative Suits

Members of a statutory public benefit limited liability company or assignees of limited liability company interests in a statutory public benefit limited liability company owning individually or collectively, as of the date of instituting such derivative suit, at least 2% of the then-current percentage or other interest in the profits of the limited liability company or, in the case of a limited liability company with limited liability company interests listed on a national securities exchange, the lesser of such percentage or limited liability company interests of at least $2,000,000 in market value, may maintain a derivative lawsuit to enforce the requirements set forth in §18-1204(a) of this title.

81 Del. Laws, c. 357, §34;

§18-1207. No Effect on Other Limited Liability Companies

This subchapter shall not affect a statute or rule of law that is applicable to a limited liability company that is not a statutory public benefit limited liability company.

81 Del. Laws, c. 357, §34;

§18-1208. Accomplishment by Other Means

The provisions of this subchapter shall not be construed to limit the accomplishment by any other means permitted by law of the formation or operation of a limited liability company that is formed or operated for a public benefit (including a limited liability company that is designated as a public benefit limited liability company) that is not a statutory public benefit limited liability company.

Uniform Limited Liability Company Act (2006)

ARTICLE 1. GENERAL PROVISIONS

ARTICLE 2. FORMATION; CERTIFICATE OF ORGANIZATION AND OTHER FILINGS

ARTICLE 3. RELATIONS OF MEMBERS AND MANAGERS TO PERSONS DEALING WITH LIMITED LIABILITY COMPANY

ARTICLE 4. RELATIONS OF MEMBERS TO EACH OTHER AND TO LIMITED LIABILITY COMPANY

ARTICLE 5. TRANSFERABLE INTERESTS AND RIGHTS OF TRANSFEREES AND CREDITORS

ARTICLE 6. MEMBER'S DISSOCIATION

ARTICLE 7. DISSOLUTION AND WINDING UP

ARTICLE 8. FOREIGN LIMITED LIABILITY COMPANIES

Article 1. General Provisions

§101. Short Title

This [act] may be cited as the Revised Uniform Limited Liability Company Act.

§102. Definitions

In this [act]:

(1) "Certificate of organization" means the certificate required by Section 201. The term includes the certificate as amended or restated.

(2) "Contribution" means any benefit provided by a person to a limited liability company:

(A) in order to become a member upon formation of the company and in accordance with an agreement between or among the persons that have agreed to become the initial members of the company;

(B) in order to become a member after formation of the company and in accordance with an agreement between the person and the company; or

(C) in the person's capacity as a member and in accordance with the operating agreement or an agreement between the member and the company.

(3) "Debtor in bankruptcy" means a person that is the subject of:

(A) an order for relief under Title 11 of the United States Code or a successor statute of general application; or

(B) a comparable order under federal, state, or foreign law governing insolvency.

(4) "Designated office" means:

(A) the office that a limited liability company is required to designate and maintain under Section 113; or

(B) the principal office of a foreign limited liability company.

(5) "Distribution", except as otherwise provided in Section 405(g), means a transfer of money or other property from a limited liability company to another person on account of a transferable interest.

(6) "Effective", with respect to a record required or permitted to be delivered to the [Secretary of State] for filing under this [act], means effective under Section 205(c).

(7) "Foreign limited liability company" means an unincorporated entity formed under the law of a jurisdiction other than this state and denominated by that law as a limited liability company.

(8) "Limited liability company", except in the phrase "foreign limited liability company", means an entity formed under this [act].

(9) "Manager" means a person that under the operating agreement of a manager-managed limited liability company is responsible, alone or in concert with others, for performing the management functions stated in Section 407(c).

(10) "Manager-managed limited liability company" means a limited liability company that qualifies under Section 407(a).

(11) "Member" means a person that has become a member of a limited liability company under Section 401 and has not dissociated under Section 602.

(12) "Member-managed limited liability company" means a limited liability company that is not a manager-managed limited liability company.

(13) "Operating agreement" means the agreement, whether or not referred to as an operating agreement and whether oral, in a record, implied, or in any combination thereof, of all the members of a limited liability company, including a sole member, concerning the matters described in Section 110(a). The term includes the agreement as amended or restated.

(14) "Organizer" means a person that acts under Section 201 to form a limited liability company.

(15) "Person" means an individual, corporation, business trust, estate, trust, partnership, limited liability company, association, joint venture, public corporation, government or governmental subdivision, agency, or instrumentality, or any other legal or commercial entity.

(16) "Principal office" means the principal executive office of a limited liability company or foreign limited liability company, whether or not the office is located in this state.

(17) "Record" means information that is inscribed on a tangible medium or that is stored in an electronic or other medium and is retrievable in perceivable form.

(18) "Sign" means, with the present intent to authenticate or adopt a record:

(A) to execute or adopt a tangible symbol; or

(B) to attach to or logically associate with the record an electronic symbol, sound, or process.

(19) "State" means a state of the United States, the District of Columbia, Puerto Rico, the United States Virgin Islands, or any territory or insular possession subject to the jurisdiction of the United States.

(20) "Transfer" includes an assignment, conveyance, deed, bill of sale, lease, mortgage, security interest, encumbrance, gift, and transfer by operation of law.

(21) "Transferable interest" means the right, as originally associated with a person's capacity as a member, to receive distributions from a limited liability company in accordance with the operating agreement, whether or not the person remains a member or continues to own any part of the right.

(22) "Transferee" means a person to which all or part of a transferable interest has been transferred, whether or not the transferor is a member.

§103. Knowledge; Notice

(a) A person knows a fact when the person:

(1) has actual knowledge of it; or

(2) is deemed to know it under subsection (d)(1) or law other than this [act].

(b) A person has notice of a fact when the person:

(1) has reason to know the fact from all of the facts known to the person at the time in question; or

(2) is deemed to have notice of the fact under subsection (d)(2).

(c) A person notifies another of a fact by taking steps reasonably required to inform the other person in ordinary course, whether or not the other person knows the fact.

(d) A person that is not a member is deemed:

(1) to know of a limitation on authority to transfer real property as provided in Section 302(g); and

(2) to have notice of a limited liability company's:

(A) dissolution, 90 days after a statement of dissolution under Section 702(b)(2)(A) becomes effective;

(B) termination, 90 days after a statement of termination Section 702(b)(2)(F) becomes effective; and

(C) merger, conversion, or domestication, 90 days after articles of merger, conversion, or domestication under [Article] 10 become effective.

§104. *Nature, Purpose, and Duration of Limited Liability Company*

(a) A limited liability company is an entity distinct from its members.

(b) A limited liability company may have any lawful purpose, regardless of whether for profit.

(c) A limited liability company has perpetual duration.

§105. *Powers*

A limited liability company has the capacity to sue and be sued in its own name and the power to do all things necessary or convenient to carry on its activities.

§106. *Governing Law*

The law of this state governs:

(1) the internal affairs of a limited liability company; and

(2) the liability of a member as member and a manager as manager for the debts, obligations, or other liabilities of a limited liability company.

§107. *Supplemental Principles of Law*

Unless displaced by particular provisions of this [act], the principles of law and equity supplement this [act].

§108. *Name*

(a) The name of a limited liability company must contain the words "limited liability company" or "limited company" or the abbreviation "L.L.C.", "LLC", "L.C.", or "LC". "Limited" may be abbreviated as "Ltd.", and "company" may be abbreviated as "Co.". . . .

§110. *Operating Agreement; Scope, Function, and Limitations*

(a) Except as otherwise provided in subsections (b) and (c), the operating agreement governs:

(1) relations among the members as members and between the members and the limited liability company;

(2) the rights and duties under this [act] of a person in the capacity of manager;

(3) the activities of the company and the conduct of those activities; and

(4) the means and conditions for amending the operating agreement.

(b) To the extent the operating agreement does not otherwise provide for a matter described in subsection (a), this [act] governs the matter.

(c) An operating agreement may not:

(1) vary a limited liability company's capacity under Section 105 to sue and be sued in its own name;

(2) vary the law applicable under Section 106;

(3) vary the power of the court under Section 204;

(4) subject to subsections (d) through (g), eliminate the duty of loyalty, the duty of care, or any other fiduciary duty;

(5) subject to subsections (d) through (g), eliminate the contractual obligation of good faith and fair dealing under Section 409(d);

(6) unreasonably restrict the duties and rights stated in Section 410;

(7) vary the power of a court to decree dissolution in the circumstances specified in Section 701(a)(4) and (5);

(8) vary the requirement to wind up a limited liability company's business as specified in Section 702(a) and (b)(1);

(9) unreasonably restrict the right of a member to maintain an action under [Article] 9;

(10) restrict the right to approve a merger, conversion, or domestication under Section 1014 to a member that will have personal liability with respect to a surviving, converted, or domesticated organization; or

(11) except as otherwise provided in Section 112(b), restrict the rights under this [act] of a person other than a member or manager.

(d) If not manifestly unreasonable, the operating agreement may:

(1) restrict or eliminate the duty:

(A) as required in Section 409(b)(1) and (g), to account to the limited liability company and to hold as trustee for it any property, profit, or benefit derived by the member in the conduct or winding up of the company's business, from a use by the member of the company's property, or from the appropriation of a limited liability company opportunity;

(B) as required in Section 409(b)(2) and (g), to refrain from dealing with the company in the conduct or winding up of the company's business as or on behalf of a party having an interest adverse to the company; and

(C) as required by Section 409(b)(3) and (g), to refrain from competing with the company in the conduct of the company's business before the dissolution of the company;

(2) identify specific types or categories of activities that do not violate the duty of loyalty;

(3) alter the duty of care, except to authorize intentional misconduct or knowing violation of law;

(4) alter any other fiduciary duty, including eliminating particular aspects of that duty; and

(5) prescribe the standards by which to measure the performance of the contractual obligation of good faith and fair dealing under Section 409(d).

(e) The operating agreement may specify the method by which a specific act or transaction that would otherwise violate the duty of loyalty may be authorized or ratified by one or more disinterested and independent persons after full disclosure of all material facts.

(f) To the extent the operating agreement of a member-managed limited liability company expressly relieves a member of a responsibility that the member would otherwise have under this [act] and imposes the responsibility on one or more other members, the operating agreement may, to the benefit of the member that the operating agreement relieves of the responsibility, also eliminate or limit any fiduciary duty that would have pertained to the responsibility.

(g) The operating agreement may alter or eliminate the indemnification for a member or manager provided by Section 408(a) and may eliminate or limit a member or manager's liability to the limited liability company and members for money damages, except for:

(1) breach of the duty of loyalty;

(2) a financial benefit received by the member or manager to which the member or manager is not entitled;

(3) a breach of a duty under Section 406;

(4) intentional infliction of harm on the company or a member; or

(5) an intentional violation of criminal law.

(h) The court shall decide any claim under subsection (d) that a term of an operating agreement is manifestly unreasonable. The court:

(1) shall make its determination as of the time the challenged term became part of the operating agreement and by considering only circumstances existing at that time; and

(2) may invalidate the term only if, in light of the purposes and activities of the limited liability company, it is readily apparent that:

(A) the objective of the term is unreasonable; or

(B) the term is an unreasonable means to achieve the provision's objective.

§111. *Operating Agreement; Effect on Limited Liability Company and Persons Becoming Members; Preformation Agreement*

(a) A limited liability company is bound by and may enforce the operating agreement, whether or not the company has itself manifested assent to the operating agreement.

(b) A person that becomes a member of a limited liability company is deemed to assent to the operating agreement.

(c) Two or more persons intending to become the initial members of a limited liability company may make an agreement providing that upon the formation of the company the agreement will become the operating agreement. One person intending to become the initial member of a limited liability company may assent to terms providing that upon the formation of the company the terms will become the operating agreement.

§112. *Operating Agreement; Effect on Third Parties and Relationship to Records Effective on Behalf of Limited Liability Company*

(a) An operating agreement may specify that its amendment requires the approval of a person that is not a party to the operating agreement or the satisfaction of a condition. An amendment is ineffective if its adoption does not include the required approval or satisfy the specified condition.

(b) The obligations of a limited liability company and its members to a person in the person's capacity as a transferee or dissociated member are governed by the operating agreement. Subject only to any court order issued under Section 503(b)(2) to effectuate a charging order, an amendment to the operating agreement made after a person becomes a transferee or dissociated member is effective with regard to any debt, obligation, or other liability of the limited liability company or its members to the person in the person's capacity as a transferee or dissociated member.

(c) If a record that has been delivered by a limited liability company to the [Secretary of State] for filing and has become effective under this [act] contains a provision that would be ineffective under Section 110(c) if contained in the operating agreement, the provision is likewise ineffective in the record.

(d) Subject to subsection (c), if a record that has been delivered by a limited liability company to the [Secretary of State] for filing and has become effective under this [act] conflicts with a provision of the operating agreement:

(1) the operating agreement prevails as to members, dissociated members, transferees, and managers; and

(2) the record prevails as to other persons to the extent they reasonably rely on the record.

§113. Office and Agent for Service of Process

(a) A limited liability company shall designate and continuously maintain in this state:

(1) an office, which need not be a place of its activity in this state; and

(2) an agent for service of process.

(b) A foreign limited liability company that has a certificate of authority under Section 802 shall designate and continuously maintain in this state an agent for service of process.

(c) An agent for service of process of a limited liability company or foreign limited liability company must be an individual who is a resident of this state or other person with authority to transact business in this state.

Article 2. Formation; Certificate of Organization and Other Filings

§201. Formation of Limited Liability Company; Certificate of Organization

(a) One or more persons may act as organizers to form a limited liability company by signing and delivering to the [Secretary of State] for filing a certificate of organization.

(b) A certificate of organization must state:

(1) the name of the limited liability company, which must comply with Section 108;

(2) the street and mailing addresses of the initial designated office and the name and street and mailing addresses of the initial agent for service of process of the company; and

(3) if the company will have no members when the [Secretary of State] files the certificate, a statement to that effect.

(c) Subject to Section 112(c), a certificate of organization may also contain statements as to matters other than those required by subsection (b). However, a statement in a certificate of organization is not effective as a statement of authority.

(d) Unless the filed certificate of organization contains the statement as provided in subsection (b)(3), the following rules apply:

(1) A limited liability company is formed when the [Secretary of State] has filed the certificate of organization and the company has at least one member, unless the certificate states a delayed effective date pursuant to Section 205(c).

(2) If the certificate states a delayed effective date, a limited liability company is not formed if, before the certificate takes effect, a statement of cancellation is signed and delivered to the [Secretary of State] for filing and the [Secretary of State] files the certificate.

(3) Subject to any delayed effective date and except in a proceeding by this state to dissolve a limited liability company, the filing of the certificate of organization by the [Secretary of State] is conclusive proof that the organizer satisfied all conditions to the formation of a limited liability company.

(e) If a filed certificate of organization contains a statement as provided in subsection (b)(3), the following rules apply:

(1) The certificate lapses and is void unless, within [90] days from the date the [Secretary of State] files the certificate, an organizer signs and delivers to the [Secretary of State] for filing a notice stating:

(A) that the limited liability company has at least one member; and

(B) the date on which a person or persons became the company's initial member or members.

(2) If an organizer complies with paragraph (1), a limited liability company is deemed formed as of the date of initial membership stated in the notice delivered pursuant to paragraph (1).

(3) Except in a proceeding by this state to dissolve a limited liability company, the filing of the notice described in paragraph (1) by the [Secretary of State] is conclusive proof that the organizer satisfied all conditions to the formation of a limited liability company.

§209. Annual Report for [Secretary of State]

(a) Each year, a limited liability company or a foreign limited liability company authorized to transact business in this state shall deliver to the [Secretary of State] for filing a report that states:

(1) the name of the company;

(2) the street and mailing addresses of the company's designated office and the name and street and mailing addresses of its agent for service of process in this state;

(3) the street and mailing addresses of its principal office; and

(4) in the case of a foreign limited liability company, the state or other jurisdiction under whose law the company is formed and any alternate name adopted under Section 805(a). . . .

Article 3. Relations of Members and Managers to Persons Dealing with Limited Liability Company

§301. No Agency Power of Member as Member

(a) A member is not an agent of a limited liability company solely by reason of being a member.

(b) A person's status as a member does not prevent or restrict law other than this [act] from imposing liability on a limited liability company because of the person's conduct.

§302. Statement of Authority

(a) A limited liability company may deliver to the [Secretary of State] for filing a statement of authority. The statement:

(1) must include the name of the company and the street and mailing addresses of its designated office;

(2) with respect to any position that exists in or with respect to the company, may state the authority, or limitations on the authority, of all persons holding the position to:

(A) execute an instrument transferring real property held in the name of the company; or

(B) enter into other transactions on behalf of, or otherwise act for or bind, the company; and

(3) may state the authority, or limitations on the authority, of a specific person to:

(A) execute an instrument transferring real property held in the name of the company; or

(B) enter into other transactions on behalf of, or otherwise act for or bind, the company.

(b) To amend or cancel a statement of authority filed by the [Secretary of State] under Section 205(a), a limited liability company must deliver to the [Secretary of State] for filing an amendment or cancellation stating:

(1) the name of the company;

(2) the street and mailing addresses of the company's designated office;

(3) the caption of the statement being amended or canceled and the date the statement being affected became effective; and

(4) the contents of the amendment or a declaration that the statement being affected is canceled.

(c) A statement of authority affects only the power of a person to bind a limited liability company to persons that are not members.

(d) Subject to subsection (c) and Section 103(d) and except as otherwise provided in subsections (f), (g), and (h), a limitation on the authority of a person or a position contained in an effective statement of authority is not by itself evidence of knowledge or notice of the limitation by any person.

(e) Subject to subsection (c), a grant of authority not pertaining to transfers of real property and contained in an effective statement of authority is conclusive in favor of a person that gives value in reliance on the grant, except to the extent that when the person gives value:

(1) the person has knowledge to the contrary;

(2) the statement has been canceled or restrictively amended under subsection (b); or

(3) a limitation on the grant is contained in another statement of authority that became effective after the statement containing the grant became effective.

(f) Subject to subsection (c), an effective statement of authority that grants authority to transfer real property held in the name of the limited liability company and that is recorded by certified copy in the office for recording transfers of the real property is conclusive in favor of a person that gives value in reliance on the grant without knowledge to the contrary, except to the extent that when the person gives value:

(1) the statement has been canceled or restrictively amended under subsection (b) and a certified copy of the cancellation or restrictive amendment has been recorded in the office for recording transfers of the real property; or

(2) a limitation on the grant is contained in another statement of authority that became effective after the statement containing the grant became effective and a certified copy of the later-effective statement is recorded in the office for recording transfers of the real property.

(g) Subject to subsection (c), if a certified copy of an effective statement containing a limitation on the authority to transfer real property held in the name of a limited liability company is recorded in the office for recording transfers of that real property, all persons are deemed to know of the limitation.

(h) Subject to subsection (i), an effective statement of dissolution or termination is a cancellation of any filed statement of authority for the purposes of subsection (f) and is a limitation on authority for the purposes of subsection (g).

(i) After a statement of dissolution becomes effective, a limited liability company may deliver to the [Secretary of State] for filing and, if appropriate, may record a statement of authority that is designated as a post-dissolution statement of authority. The statement operates as provided in subsections (f) and (g).

(j) Unless earlier canceled, an effective statement of authority is canceled by operation of law five years after the date on which the statement, or its most recent amendment, becomes effective. This cancellation operates without need for any recording under subsection (f) or (g).

(k) An effective statement of denial operates as a restrictive amendment under this section and may be recorded by certified copy for the purposes of subsection (f)(1).

§303. Statement of Denial

A person named in a filed statement of authority granting that person authority may deliver to the [Secretary of State] for filing a statement of denial that:

(1) provides the name of the limited liability company and the caption of the statement of authority to which the statement of denial pertains; and

(2) denies the grant of authority.

§304. Liability of Members and Managers

(a) The debts, obligations, or other liabilities of a limited liability company, whether arising in contract, tort, or otherwise:

(1) are solely the debts, obligations, or other liabilities of the company; and

(2) do not become the debts, obligations, or other liabilities of a member or manager solely by reason of the member acting as a member or manager acting as a manager.

(b) The failure of a limited liability company to observe any particular formalities relating to the exercise of its powers or management of its activities is not a ground for imposing liability on the members or managers for the debts, obligations, or other liabilities of the company.

Article 4. Relations of Members to Each Other and to Limited Liability Company

§401. Becoming Member

(a) If a limited liability company is to have only one member upon formation, the person becomes a member as agreed by that person and the organizer of the company. That person and the organizer may be, but need not be, different persons. If different, the organizer acts on behalf of the initial member.

(b) If a limited liability company is to have more than one member upon formation, those persons become members as agreed by the persons before the formation of the company. The organizer acts on behalf of the persons in forming the company and may be, but need not be, one of the persons.

(c) If a filed certificate of organization contains the statement required by Section 201(b)(3), a person becomes an initial member of the limited liability company with the consent of a majority of the organizers. The organizers may consent to more than one person simultaneously becoming the company's initial members.

(d) After formation of a limited liability company, a person becomes a member:

(1) as provided in the operating agreement;

(2) as the result of a transaction effective under [Article] 10;

(3) with the consent of all the members; or

(4) if, within 90 consecutive days after the company ceases to have any members:

(A) the last person to have been a member, or the legal representative of that person, designates a person to become a member; and

(B) the designated person consents to become a member.

(e) A person may become a member without acquiring a transferable interest and without making or being obligated to make a contribution to the limited liability company.

§402. Form of Contribution

A contribution may consist of tangible or intangible property or other benefit to a limited liability company, including money, services performed, promissory notes, other agreements to contribute money or property, and contracts for services to be performed.

§403. Liability for Contributions

(a) A person's obligation to make a contribution to a limited liability company is not excused by the person's death, disability, or other inability to perform personally. If a person does not make a required contribution, the person or the person's estate is obligated to contribute money equal to the value of the part of the contribution which has not been made, at the option of the company.

(b) A creditor of a limited liability company which extends credit or otherwise acts in reliance on an obligation described in subsection (a) may enforce the obligation.

§404. Sharing of and Right to Distributions Before Dissolution

(a) Any distributions made by a limited liability company before its dissolution and winding up must be in equal shares among members and dissociated members, except to the extent necessary to comply with any transfer effective under Section 502 and any charging order in effect under Section 503.

(b) A person has a right to a distribution before the dissolution and winding up of a limited liability company only if the company decides to make an interim distribution. A person's dissociation does not entitle the person to a distribution.

(c) A person does not have a right to demand or receive a distribution from a limited liability company in any form other than money. Except as otherwise provided in Section 708(c), a limited liability company may distribute an asset in kind if each part of the asset is fungible with each other part and each person receives a percentage of the asset equal in value to the person's share of distributions.

(d) If a member or transferee becomes entitled to receive a distribution, the member or transferee has the status of, and is entitled to all remedies available to, a creditor of the limited liability company with respect to the distribution.

§405. Limitations on Distribution

(a) A limited liability company may not make a distribution if after the distribution:

(1) the company would not be able to pay its debts as they become due in the ordinary course of the company's activities; or

(2) the company's total assets would be less than the sum of its total liabilities plus the amount that would be needed, if the company were to be dissolved, wound up, and terminated at the time of the distribution, to satisfy the preferential rights upon dissolution, winding up, and termination of members whose preferential rights are superior to those of persons receiving the distribution.

(b) A limited liability company may base a determination that a distribution is not prohibited under subsection (a) on financial statements prepared on the basis of accounting practices and principles that are reasonable in the circumstances or on a fair valuation or other method that is reasonable under the circumstances.

(c) Except as otherwise provided in subsection (f), the effect of a distribution under subsection (a) is measured:

(1) in the case of a distribution by purchase, redemption, or other acquisition of a transferable interest in the company, as of the date money or other property is transferred or debt incurred by the company; and

(2) in all other cases, as of the date:

(A) the distribution is authorized, if the payment occurs within 120 days after that date; or

(B) the payment is made, if the payment occurs more than 120 days after the distribution is authorized.

(d) A limited liability company's indebtedness to a member incurred by reason of a distribution made in accordance with this section is at parity with the company's indebtedness to its general, unsecured creditors.

(e) A limited liability company's indebtedness, including indebtedness issued in connection with or as part of a distribution, is not a liability for purposes of subsection (a) if the terms of the indebtedness provide that payment of principal and interest are made only to the extent that a distribution could be made to members under this section.

(f) If indebtedness is issued as a distribution, each payment of principal or interest on the indebtedness is treated as a distribution, the effect of which is measured on the date the payment is made.

(g) In subsection (a), "distribution" does not include amounts constituting reasonable compensation for present or past services or reasonable payments made in the ordinary course of business under a bona fide retirement plan or other benefits program.

§406. Liability for Improper Distributions

(a) Except as otherwise provided in subsection (b), if a member of a member-managed limited liability company or manager of a manager-managed limited liability company consents to a distribution made in violation of Section 405 and in consenting to the distribution fails to comply with Section 409, the member or manager is personally liable to the company for the amount of the distribution that exceeds the amount that could have been distributed without the violation of Section 405.

(b) To the extent the operating agreement of a member-managed limited liability company expressly relieves a member of the authority and responsibility to consent to distributions and imposes that authority and responsibility on one or more other members, the liability stated in subsection (a) applies to the other members and not the member that the operating agreement relieves of authority and responsibility.

(c) A person that receives a distribution knowing that the distribution to that person was made in violation of Section 405 is personally liable to the limited liability company but only to the extent that the distribution received by the person exceeded the amount that could have been properly paid under Section 405.

(d) A person against which an action is commenced because the person is liable under subsection (a) may:

(1) implead any other person that is subject to liability under subsection (a) and seek to compel contribution from the person; and

(2) implead any person that received a distribution in violation of subsection (c) and seek to compel contribution from the person in the amount the person received in violation of subsection (c).

(e) An action under this section is barred if not commenced within two years after the distribution.

§407. *Management of Limited Liability Company*

(a) A limited liability company is a member-managed limited liability company unless the operating agreement:

(1) expressly provides that:

(A) the company is or will be "manager-managed";

(B) the company is or will be "managed by managers"; or

(C) management of the company is or will be "vested in managers"; or

(2) includes words of similar import.

(b) In a member-managed limited liability company, the following rules apply:

(1) The management and conduct of the company are vested in the members.

(2) Each member has equal rights in the management and conduct of the company's activities.

(3) A difference arising among members as to a matter in the ordinary course of the activities of the company may be decided by a majority of the members.

(4) An act outside the ordinary course of the activities of the company may be undertaken only with the consent of all members.

(5) The operating agreement may be amended only with the consent of all members.

(c) In a manager-managed limited liability company, the following rules apply:

(1) Except as otherwise expressly provided in this [act], any matter relating to the activities of the company is decided exclusively by the managers.

(2) Each manager has equal rights in the management and conduct of the activities of the company.

(3) A difference arising among managers as to a matter in the ordinary course of the activities of the company may be decided by a majority of the managers.

(4) The consent of all members is required to:

(A) sell, lease, exchange, or otherwise dispose of all, or substantially all, of the company's property, with or without the good will, outside the ordinary course of the company's activities;

(B) approve a merger, conversion, or domestication under [Article] 10;

(C) undertake any other act outside the ordinary course of the company's activities; and

(D) amend the operating agreement.

(5) A manager may be chosen at any time by the consent of a majority of the members and remains a manager until a successor has been chosen, unless the

manager at an earlier time resigns, is removed, or dies, or, in the case of a manager that is not an individual, terminates. A manager may be removed at any time by the consent of a majority of the members without notice or cause.

(6) A person need not be a member to be a manager, but the dissociation of a member that is also a manager removes the person as a manager. If a person that is both a manager and a member ceases to be a manager, that cessation does not by itself dissociate the person as a member.

(7) A person's ceasing to be a manager does not discharge any debt, obligation, or other liability to the limited liability company or members which the person incurred while a manager.

(d) An action requiring the consent of members under this [act] may be taken without a meeting, and a member may appoint a proxy or other agent to consent or otherwise act for the member by signing an appointing record, personally or by the member's agent.

(e) The dissolution of a limited liability company does not affect the applicability of this section. However, a person that wrongfully causes dissolution of the company loses the right to participate in management as a member and a manager.

(f) This [act] does not entitle a member to remuneration for services performed for a member-managed limited liability company, except for reasonable compensation for services rendered in winding up the activities of the company.

§408. *Indemnification and Insurance*

(a) A limited liability company shall reimburse for any payment made and indemnify for any debt, obligation, or other liability incurred by a member of a member-managed company or the manager of a manager-managed company in the course of the member's or manager's activities on behalf of the company, if, in making the payment or incurring the debt, obligation, or other liability, the member or manager complied with the duties stated in Sections 405 and 409.

(b) A limited liability company may purchase and maintain insurance on behalf of a member or manager of the company against liability asserted against or incurred by the member or manager in that capacity or arising from that status even if, under Section 110(g), the operating agreement could not eliminate or limit the person's liability to the company for the conduct giving rise to the liability.

§409. *Standards of Conduct for Members and Managers*

(a) A member of a member-managed limited liability company owes to the company and, subject to Section 901(b), the other members the fiduciary duties of loyalty and care stated in subsections (b) and (c).

(b) The duty of loyalty of a member in a member-managed limited liability company includes the duties:

(1) to account to the company and to hold as trustee for it any property, profit, or benefit derived by the member:

(A) in the conduct or winding up of the company's activities;

(B) from a use by the member of the company's property; or

(C) from the appropriation of a limited liability company opportunity;

(2) to refrain from dealing with the company in the conduct or winding up of the company's activities as or on behalf of a person having an interest adverse to the company; and

(3) to refrain from competing with the company in the conduct of the company's activities before the dissolution of the company.

(c) Subject to the business judgment rule, the duty of care of a member of a member-managed limited liability company in the conduct and winding up of the company's activities is to act with the care that a person in a like position would reasonably exercise under similar circumstances and in a manner the member reasonably believes to be in the best interests of the company. In discharging this duty, a member may rely in good faith upon opinions, reports, statements, or other information provided by another person that the member reasonably believes is a competent and reliable source for the information.

(d) A member in a member-managed limited liability company or a manager-managed limited liability company shall discharge the duties under this [act] or under the operating agreement and exercise any rights consistently with the contractual obligation of good faith and fair dealing.

(e) It is a defense to a claim under subsection (b)(2) and any comparable claim in equity or at common law that the transaction was fair to the limited liability company.

(f) All of the members of a member-managed limited liability company or a manager-managed limited liability company may authorize or ratify, after full disclosure of all material facts, a specific act or transaction that otherwise would violate the duty of loyalty.

(g) In a manager-managed limited liability company, the following rules apply:

(1) Subsections (a), (b), (c), and (e) apply to the manager or managers and not the members.

(2) The duty stated under subsection (b)(3) continues until winding up is completed.

(3) Subsection (d) applies to the members and managers.

(4) Subsection (f) applies only to the members.

(5) A member does not have any fiduciary duty to the company or to any other member solely by reason of being a member.

§410. Right of Members, Managers, and Dissociated Members to Information

(a) In a member-managed limited liability company, the following rules apply:

(1) On reasonable notice, a member may inspect and copy during regular business hours, at a reasonable location specified by the company, any record maintained by the company regarding the company's activities, financial condition, and other circumstances, to the extent the information is material to the member's rights and duties under the operating agreement or this [act].

(2) The company shall furnish to each member:

(A) without demand, any information concerning the company's activities, financial condition, and other circumstances which the company knows and is material to the proper exercise of the member's rights and duties under the operating agreement or this [act], except to the extent the company can establish that it reasonably believes the member already knows the information; and

(B) on demand, any other information concerning the company's activities, financial condition, and other circumstances, except to the extent the demand or information demanded is unreasonable or otherwise improper under the circumstances.

(3) The duty to furnish information under paragraph (2) also applies to each member to the extent the member knows any of the information described in paragraph (2).

(b) In a manager-managed limited liability company, the following rules apply:

(1) The informational rights stated in subsection (a) and the duty stated in subsection (a)(3) apply to the managers and not the members.

(2) During regular business hours and at a reasonable location specified by the company, a member may obtain from the company and inspect and copy full information regarding the activities, financial condition, and other circumstances of the company as is just and reasonable if:

(A) the member seeks the information for a purpose material to the member's interest as a member;

(B) the member makes a demand in a record received by the company, describing with reasonable particularity the information sought and the purpose for seeking the information; and

(C) the information sought is directly connected to the member's purpose.

(3) Within 10 days after receiving a demand pursuant to paragraph (2)(B), the company shall in a record inform the member that made the demand:

(A) of the information that the company will provide in response to the demand and when and where the company will provide the information; and

(B) if the company declines to provide any demanded information, the company's reasons for declining.

(4) Whenever this [act] or an operating agreement provides for a member to give or withhold consent to a matter, before the consent is given or withheld, the company shall, without demand, provide the member with all information that is known to the company and is material to the member's decision.

(c) On 10 days' demand made in a record received by a limited liability company, a dissociated member may have access to information to which the person was entitled while a member if the information pertains to the period during which the person was a member, the person seeks the information in good faith, and the person satisfies the requirements imposed on a member by subsection (b)(2). The company shall respond to a demand made pursuant to this subsection in the manner provided in subsection (b)(3).

(d) A limited liability company may charge a person that makes a demand under this section the reasonable costs of copying, limited to the costs of labor and material.

(e) A member or dissociated member may exercise rights under this section through an agent or, in the case of an individual under legal disability, a legal representative. Any restriction or condition imposed by the operating agreement or under subsection (g) applies both to the agent or legal representative and the member or dissociated member.

(f) The rights under this section do not extend to a person as transferee.

(g) In addition to any restriction or condition stated in its operating agreement, a limited liability company, as a matter within the ordinary course of its activities, may impose reasonable restrictions and conditions on access to and use of information to be furnished under this section, including designating information confidential and imposing nondisclosure and safeguarding obligations on the recipient. In a dispute concerning the reasonableness of a restriction under this subsection, the company has the burden of proving reasonableness.

ARTICLE 5. TRANSFERABLE INTERESTS AND RIGHTS OF TRANSFEREES AND CREDITORS

§501. *Nature of Transferable Interest*

A transferable interest is personal property.

§502. *Transfer of Transferable Interest*

(a) A transfer, in whole or in part, of a transferable interest:

(1) is permissible;

(2) does not by itself cause a member's dissociation or a dissolution and winding up of the limited liability company's activities; and

(3) subject to Section 504, does not entitle the transferee to:

(A) participate in the management or conduct of the company's activities; or

(B) except as otherwise provided in subsection (c), have access to records or other information concerning the company's activities.

(b) A transferee has the right to receive, in accordance with the transfer, distributions to which the transferor would otherwise be entitled.

(c) In a dissolution and winding up of a limited liability company, a transferee is entitled to an account of the company's transactions only from the date of dissolution.

(d) A transferable interest may be evidenced by a certificate of the interest issued by the limited liability company in a record, and, subject to this section, the interest represented by the certificate may be transferred by a transfer of the certificate.

(e) A limited liability company need not give effect to a transferee's rights under this section until the company has notice of the transfer.

(f) A transfer of a transferable interest in violation of a restriction on transfer contained in the operating agreement is ineffective as to a person having notice of the restriction at the time of transfer.

(g) Except as otherwise provided in Section 602(4)(B), when a member transfers a transferable interest, the transferor retains the rights of a member other than the interest in distributions transferred and retains all duties and obligations of a member.

(h) When a member transfers a transferable interest to a person that becomes a member with respect to the transferred interest, the transferee is liable for the member's obligations under Sections 403 and 406(c) known to the transferee when the transferee becomes a member.

§504. Power of Personal Representative of Deceased Member

If a member dies, the deceased member's personal representative or other legal representative may exercise the rights of a transferee provided in Section 502(c) and, for the purposes of settling the estate, the rights of a current member under Section 410.

ARTICLE 6. MEMBER'S DISSOCIATION

§601. Member's Power to Dissociate; Wrongful Dissociation

(a) A person has the power to dissociate as a member at any time, rightfully or wrongfully, by withdrawing as a member by express will under Section 602(1).

(b) A person's dissociation from a limited liability company is wrongful only if the dissociation:

(1) is in breach of an express provision of the operating agreement; or

(2) occurs before the termination of the company and:

(A) the person withdraws as a member by express will;

(B) the person is expelled as a member by judicial order under Section 602(5);

(C) the person is dissociated under Section 602(7)(A) by becoming a debtor in bankruptcy; or

(D) in the case of a person that is not a trust other than a business trust, an estate, or an individual, the person is expelled or otherwise dissociated as a member because it willfully dissolved or terminated.

(c) A person that wrongfully dissociates as a member is liable to the limited liability company and, subject to Section 901, to the other members for damages caused by the dissociation. The liability is in addition to any other debt, obligation, or other liability of the member to the company or the other members.

§602. Events Causing Dissociation

A person is dissociated as a member from a limited liability company when:

(1) the company has notice of the person's express will to withdraw as a member, but, if the person specified a withdrawal date later than the date the company had notice, on that later date;

(2) an event stated in the operating agreement as causing the person's dissociation occurs;

(3) the person is expelled as a member pursuant to the operating agreement;

(4) the person is expelled as a member by the unanimous consent of the other members if:

(A) it is unlawful to carry on the company's activities with the person as a member;

(B) there has been a transfer of all of the person's transferable interest in the company, other than:

(i) a transfer for security purposes; or

(ii) a charging order in effect under Section 503 which has not been foreclosed;

(C) the person is a corporation and, within 90 days after the company notifies the person that it will be expelled as a member because the person has filed a certificate of dissolution or the equivalent, its charter has been revoked, or its right to conduct business has been suspended by the jurisdiction of its incorporation, the certificate of dissolution has not been revoked or its charter or right to conduct business has not been reinstated; or

(D) the person is a limited liability company or partnership that has been dissolved and whose business is being wound up;

(5) on application by the company, the person is expelled as a member by judicial order because the person:

(A) has engaged, or is engaging, in wrongful conduct that has adversely and materially affected, or will adversely and materially affect, the company's activities;

(B) has willfully or persistently committed, or is willfully and persistently committing, a material breach of the operating agreement or the person's duties or obligations under Section 409; or

(C) has engaged in, or is engaging, in conduct relating to the company's activities which makes it not reasonably practicable to carry on the activities with the person as a member;

(6) in the case of a person who is an individual:

(A) the person dies; or

(B) in a member-managed limited liability company:

(i) a guardian or general conservator for the person is appointed; or

(ii) there is a judicial order that the person has otherwise become incapable of performing the person's duties as a member under [this act] or the operating agreement;

(7) in a member-managed limited liability company, the person:

(A) becomes a debtor in bankruptcy;

(B) executes an assignment for the benefit of creditors; or

(C) seeks, consents to, or acquiesces in the appointment of a trustee, receiver, or liquidator of the person or of all or substantially all of the person's property;

(8) in the case of a person that is a trust or is acting as a member by virtue of being a trustee of a trust, the trust's entire transferable interest in the company is distributed;

(9) in the case of a person that is an estate or is acting as a member by virtue of being a personal representative of an estate, the estate's entire transferable interest in the company is distributed;

(10) in the case of a member that is not an individual, partnership, limited liability company, corporation, trust, or estate, the termination of the member;

(11) the company participates in a merger under [Article] 10, if:

(A) the company is not the surviving entity; or

(B) otherwise as a result of the merger, the person ceases to be a member;

(12) the company participates in a conversion under [Article] 10;

(13) the company participates in a domestication under [Article] 10, if, as a result of the domestication, the person ceases to be a member; or

(14) the company terminates.

§603. Effect of Person's Dissociation as Member

(a) When a person is dissociated as a member of a limited liability company:

(1) the person's right to participate as a member in the management and conduct of the company's activities terminates;

(2) if the company is member-managed, the person's fiduciary duties as a member end with regard to matters arising and events occurring after the person's dissociation; and

(3) subject to Section 504 and [Article] 10, any transferable interest owned by the person immediately before dissociation in the person's capacity as a member is owned by the person solely as a transferee.

(b) A person's dissociation as a member of a limited liability company does not of itself discharge the person from any debt, obligation, or other liability to the company or the other members which the person incurred while a member.

Article 7. Dissolution and Winding Up

§701. Events Causing Dissolution

(a) A limited liability company is dissolved, and its activities must be wound up, upon the occurrence of any of the following:

(1) an event or circumstance that the operating agreement states causes dissolution;

(2) the consent of all the members;

(3) the passage of 90 consecutive days during which the company has no members;

(4) on application by a member, the entry by [appropriate court] of an order dissolving the company on the grounds that:

(A) the conduct of all or substantially all of the company's activities is unlawful; or

(B) it is not reasonably practicable to carry on the company's activities in conformity with the certificate of organization and the operating agreement; or

(5) on application by a member, the entry by [appropriate court] of an order dissolving the company on the grounds that the managers or those members in control of the company:

(A) have acted, are acting, or will act in a manner that is illegal or fraudulent; or

(B) have acted or are acting in a manner that is oppressive and was, is, or will be directly harmful to the applicant.

(b) In a proceeding brought under subsection (a)(5), the court may order a remedy other than dissolution.

§702. *Winding Up*

(a) A dissolved limited liability company shall wind up its activities, and the company continues after dissolution only for the purpose of winding up.

(b) In winding up its activities, a limited liability company:

(1) shall discharge the company's debts, obligations, or other liabilities, settle and close the company's activities, and marshal and distribute the assets of the company; and

(2) may:

(A) deliver to the [Secretary of State] for filing a statement of dissolution stating the name of the company and that the company is dissolved;

(B) preserve the company activities and property as a going concern for a reasonable time;

(C) prosecute and defend actions and proceedings, whether civil, criminal, or administrative;

(D) transfer the company's property;

(E) settle disputes by mediation or arbitration;

(F) deliver to the [Secretary of State] for filing a statement of termination stating the name of the company and that the company is terminated; and

(G) perform other acts necessary or appropriate to the winding up.

(c) If a dissolved limited liability company has no members, the legal representative of the last person to have been a member may wind up the activities of the company. If the person does so, the person has the powers of a sole manager under Section 407(c) and is deemed to be a manager for the purposes of Section 304(a)(2).

(d) If the legal representative under subsection (c) declines or fails to wind up the company's activities, a person may be appointed to do so by the consent of transferees owning a majority of the rights to receive distributions as transferees at the time the consent is to be effective. A person appointed under this subsection:

(1) has the powers of a sole manager under Section 407(c) and is deemed to be a manager for the purposes of Section 304(a)(2); and

(2) shall promptly deliver to the [Secretary of State] for filing an amendment to the company's certificate of organization to:

(A) state that the company has no members;

(B) state that the person has been appointed pursuant to this subsection to wind up the company; and

(C) provide the street and mailing addresses of the person.

(e) The [appropriate court] may order judicial supervision of the winding up of a dissolved limited liability company, including the appointment of a person to wind up the company's activities:

(1) on application of a member, if the applicant establishes good cause;

(2) on the application of a transferee, if:

(A) the company does not have any members;

(B) the legal representative of the last person to have been a member declines or fails to wind up the company's activities; and

(C) within a reasonable time following the dissolution a person has not been appointed pursuant to subsection (d); or

(3) in connection with a proceeding under Section 701(a)(4) or (5).

Article 8. Foreign Limited Liability Companies

§801. *Governing Law*

(a) The law of the state or other jurisdiction under which a foreign limited liability company is formed governs:

(1) the internal affairs of the company; and

(2) the liability of a member as member and a manager as manager for the debts, obligations, or other liabilities of the company.

(b) A foreign limited liability company may not be denied a certificate of authority by reason of any difference between the law of the jurisdiction under which the company is formed and the law of this state.

(c) A certificate of authority does not authorize a foreign limited liability company to engage in any business or exercise any power that a limited liability company may not engage in or exercise in this state.

Article 9. Actions by Members

§901. *Direct Action by Member*

(a) Subject to subsection (b), a member may maintain a direct action against another member, a manager, or the limited liability company to enforce the member's rights and otherwise protect the member's interests, including rights and interests under the operating agreement or this [act] or arising independently of the membership relationship.

(b) A member maintaining a direct action under this section must plead and prove an actual or threatened injury that is not solely the result of an injury suffered or threatened to be suffered by the limited liability company.

§902. *Derivative Action*

A member may maintain a derivative action to enforce a right of a limited liability company if:

(1) the member first makes a demand on the other members in a member-managed limited liability company, or the managers of a manager-managed limited liability company, requesting that they cause the company to bring an action

to enforce the right, and the managers or other members do not bring the action within a reasonable time; or

(2) a demand under paragraph (1) would be futile.

§903. Proper Plaintiff

(a) Except as otherwise provided in subsection (b), a derivative action under Section 902 may be maintained only by a person that is a member at the time the action is commenced and remains a member while the action continues.

(b) If the sole plaintiff in a derivative action dies while the action is pending, the court may permit another member of the limited liability company to be substituted as plaintiff.

§904. Pleading

In a derivative action under Section 902, the complaint must state with particularity:

(1) the date and content of the plaintiff's demand and the response to the demand by the managers or other members; or

(2) if a demand has not been made, the reasons a demand under Section 902(1) would be futile.

§905. Special Litigation Committee

(a) If a limited liability company is named as or made a party in a derivative proceeding, the company may appoint a special litigation committee to investigate the claims asserted in the proceeding and determine whether pursuing the action is in the best interests of the company. If the company appoints a special litigation committee, on motion by the committee made in the name of the company, except for good cause shown, the court shall stay discovery for the time reasonably necessary to permit the committee to make its investigation. This subsection does not prevent the court from enforcing a person's right to information under Section 410 or, for good cause shown, granting extraordinary relief in the form of a temporary restraining order or preliminary injunction.

(b) A special litigation committee may be composed of one or more disinterested and independent individuals, who may be members.

(c) A special litigation committee may be appointed:

(1) in a member-managed limited liability company:

(A) by the consent of a majority of the members not named as defendants or plaintiffs in the proceeding; and

(B) if all members are named as defendants or plaintiffs in the proceeding, by a majority of the members named as defendants; or

(2) in a manager-managed limited liability company:

(A) by a majority of the managers not named as defendants or plaintiffs in the proceeding; and

(B) if all managers are named as defendants or plaintiffs in the proceeding, by a majority of the managers named as defendants.

(d) After appropriate investigation, a special litigation committee may determine that it is in the best interests of the limited liability company that the proceeding:

(1) continue under the control of the plaintiff;

(2) continue under the control of the committee;

(3) be settled on terms approved by the committee; or

(4) be dismissed.

(e) After making a determination under subsection (d), a special litigation committee shall file with the court a statement of its determination and its report supporting its determination, giving notice to the plaintiff. The court shall determine whether the members of the committee were disinterested and independent and whether the committee conducted its investigation and made its recommendation in good faith, independently, and with reasonable care, with the committee having the burden of proof. If the court finds that the members of the committee were disinterested and independent and that the committee acted in good faith, independently, and with reasonable care, the court shall enforce the determination of the committee. Otherwise, the court shall dissolve the stay of discovery entered under subsection (a) and allow the action to proceed under the direction of the plaintiff.

§906. Proceeds and Expenses

(a) Except as otherwise provided in subsection (b):

(1) any proceeds or other benefits of a derivative action under Section 902, whether by judgment, compromise, or settlement, belong to the limited liability company and not to the plaintiff; and

(2) if the plaintiff receives any proceeds, the plaintiff shall remit them immediately to the company.

(b) If a derivative action under Section 902 is successful in whole or in part, the court may award the plaintiff reasonable expenses, including reasonable attorney's fees and costs, from the recovery of the limited liability company.

Delaware Revised Uniform Limited Partnership Act

SUBCHAPTER I. GENERAL PROVISIONS

SUBCHAPTER II. FORMATION; CERTIFICATE OF LIMITED PARTNERSHIP

SUBCHAPTER VII. ASSIGNMENT OF PARTNERSHIP INTERESTS

SUBCHAPTER VIII. DISSOLUTION

SUBCHAPTER X. DERIVATIVE ACTIONS

SUBCHAPTER XI. MISCELLANEOUS

Delaware Revised Uniform Limited Partnership Act

Subchapter I. General Provisions

§17-101. Definitions.

As used in this chapter unless the context otherwise requires:

(1) "Certificate of limited partnership" means the certificate referred to in §17-201 of this title, and the certificate as amended.

(2) "Contribution" means any cash, property, services rendered or a promissory note or other obligation to contribute cash or property or to perform services, which a partner contributes to a limited partnership in the capacity as a partner.

(3) "Document" means:

a. Any tangible medium on which information is inscribed, and includes handwritten, typed, printed or similar instruments, and copies of such instruments; and

b. An electronic transmission.

(4) "Electronic transmission" means any form of communication not directly involving the physical transmission of paper, including the use of, or participation in, 1 or more electronic networks or databases (including 1 or more distributed electronic networks or databases), that creates a record that may be retained, retrieved and reviewed by a recipient thereof and that may be directly reproduced in paper form by such a recipient through an automated process.

(5) "Event of withdrawal of a general partner" means an event that causes a person to cease to be a general partner as provided in §17-402 of this title.

(6) "Foreign limited partnership" includes a partnership formed under the laws of any state or under the laws of any foreign country or other foreign jurisdiction consisting of 2 or more persons and having 1 or more general partners and 1 or more limited partners. When used in this title in reference to a foreign limited partnership, the terms "partnership agreement," "partnership interest," "general partner" or "limited partner" shall mean a partnership agreement, partnership interest, general partner or limited partner, respectively, under the laws of the state or foreign country or other foreign jurisdiction under which the foreign limited partnership is formed.

(7) "General partner" means a person who is named as a general partner in the certificate of limited partnership or similar instrument under which a limited partnership is formed if so required and who is admitted to the limited partnership as a general partner in accordance with the partnership agreement or this chapter, and includes a general partner of the limited partnership generally and a general partner associated with a series of the limited partnership. Unless the context otherwise requires, references in this chapter to a general partner (including references in this chapter to a general partner of a limited partnership) shall be deemed to be references to a general partner of the limited partnership generally and to a general partner associated with a series with respect to such series.

(8) "Knowledge" means a person's actual knowledge of a fact, rather than the person's constructive knowledge of the fact.

(9) "Limited liability limited partnership" means a limited partnership complying with §17-214 of this title.

(10) "Limited partner" means a person who is admitted to a limited partnership as a limited partner as provided in §17-301 of this title, and includes a limited partner of the limited partnership generally and a limited partner associated with a series of the limited partnership. Unless the context otherwise requires, references in this chapter to a limited partner (including references in this chapter to a limited partner of a limited partnership) shall be deemed to be references to a limited partner of the limited partnership generally and to a limited partner associated with a series with respect to such series.

(11) "Limited partnership" and "domestic limited partnership" mean a partnership formed under the laws of the State of Delaware consisting of 2 or more persons and having 1 or more general partners and 1 or more limited partners, and includes, for all purposes of the laws of the State of Delaware, a limited liability limited partnership.

(12) "Liquidating trustee" means a person, other than a general partner, but including a limited partner, carrying out the winding up of a limited partnership.

(13) "Partner" means a limited or general partner.

(14) "Partnership agreement" means any agreement, written, oral or implied, of the partners as to the affairs of a limited partnership and the conduct of its business. A partner of a limited partnership or an assignee of a partnership interest is bound by the partnership agreement whether or not the partner or assignee executes the partnership agreement. A limited partnership (including any protected series or registered series thereof) is not required to execute its partnership agreement. A limited partnership (including any protected series or registered series thereof) is bound by its partnership agreement whether or not the limited partnership (or any protected series or registered series thereof) executes the partnership agreement. A partnership agreement is not subject to any statute of frauds (including §2714 of this title). A partnership agreement may provide rights to any person, including a person who is not a party to the partnership agreement, to the extent set forth therein. A written partnership agreement or another written agreement or writing;

a. May provide that a person shall be admitted as a limited partner of a limited partnership, or shall become an assignee of a partnership interest or other rights or powers of a limited partner to the extent assigned (i) if such person (or a representative authorized by such person orally, in writing or by other action such as payment for a partnership interest) executes the partnership agreement or any other writing evidencing the intent of such person to become a limited partner or assignee, or (ii) without such execution, if such person (or a representative authorized by such person orally, in writing or by other action such as payment for a partnership interest) complies with the conditions for becoming a limited partner or assignee as set forth in the partnership agreement or any other writing;

b. Shall not be unenforceable by reason of its not having been signed by a person being admitted as a limited partner or becoming an assignee as provided in paragraph (14)a. of this section, or by reason of its having been signed by a representative as provided in this title; and

c. May consist of 1 or more agreements, instruments or other writings and may include or incorporate 1 or more schedules, supplements or other writings containing provisions as to the conduct of the business and affairs of the limited partnership or any series thereof.

(15) "Partnership interest" means a partner's share of the profits and losses of a limited partnership and the right to receive distributions of partnership assets.

(16) "Person" means a natural person, partnership (whether general or limited), limited liability company, trust (including a common law trust, business trust, statutory trust, voting trust or any other form of trust), estate, association (including any group, organization, co-tenancy, plan, board, council or committee), corporation, government (including a country, state, county or any other governmental subdivision, agency or instrumentality), custodian, nominee or any other individual or entity (or series thereof) in its own or any representative capacity, in each case, whether domestic or foreign.

(17) "Personal representative" means, as to a natural person, the executor, administrator, guardian, conservator or other legal representative thereof and, as to a person other than a natural person, the legal representative or successor thereof.

(18) "Protected series" means a designated series of limited partners, general partners, partnership interests or assets that is established in accordance with §17-218(b) of this title.

(19) "Registered series" means a designated series of limited partners, general partners, partnership interests or assets that is formed in accordance with §17-221 of this title.

(20) "Series" means a designated series of limited partners, general partners, partnership interests or assets that is a protected series or a registered series, or that is neither a protected series nor a registered series.

(21) "State" means the District of Columbia or the Commonwealth of Puerto Rico or any state, territory, possession, or other jurisdiction of the United States other than the State of Delaware.

§17-102. Name set forth in certificate.

The name of each limited partnership as set forth in its certificate of limited partnership:

(1) Shall contain the words "Limited Partnership" or the abbreviation "L.P." or the designation "LP" or, in the case of a limited partnership that is formed as or becomes a limited liability limited partnership, shall contain the words, abbreviation or designation required by §17-214(a) of this title;

(2) May contain the name of a partner;

(3) Must be such as to distinguish it upon the records in the office of the Secretary of State from the name on such records of any corporation, partnership, limited partnership, statutory trust, limited liability company, registered series of a limited liability company or registered series of a limited partnership reserved, registered, formed or organized under the laws of the State of Delaware or qualified to do business or registered as a foreign corporation, foreign limited partnership, foreign statutory trust, foreign partnership or foreign limited liability company in the State of Delaware; provided, however, that a limited partnership may register under any name which is not such as to distinguish it upon the records in the office of the Secretary of State from the name on such records of any domestic or foreign corporation, partnership, statutory trust, limited liability company, registered series

of a limited liability company, registered series of a limited partnership, or foreign limited partnership reserved, registered, formed or organized under the laws of the State of Delaware with the written consent of the other corporation, partnership, statutory trust, limited liability company, registered series of a limited liability company, registered series of a limited partnership, or foreign limited partnership, which written consent shall be filed with the Secretary of State; provided further, that, if on July 31, 2011, a limited partnership is registered (with the consent of another limited partnership) under a name which is not such as to distinguish it upon the records in the office of the Secretary of State from the name on such records of such other domestic limited partnership, it shall not be necessary for any such limited partnership to amend its certificate of limited partnership to comply with this subsection;

(4) May contain the following words: "Company," "Association," "Club," "Foundation," "Fund," "Institute," "Society," "Union," "Syndicate," "Limited," "Public Benefit" or "Trust" (or abbreviations of like import); and

(5) Shall not contain the word "bank," or any variation thereof, except for the name of a bank reporting to and under the supervision of the State Bank Commissioner of this State or a subsidiary of a bank or savings association (as those terms are defined in the Federal Deposit Insurance Act, as amended, at 12 U.S.C. §1813), or a limited partnership regulated under the Bank Holding Company Act of 1956, as amended, 12 U.S.C. §1841 et seq., or the Home Owners' Loan Act, as amended, 12 U.S.C. §1461 et seq.; provided, however, that this section shall not be construed to prevent the use of the word "bank," or any variation thereof, in a context clearly not purporting to refer to a banking business or otherwise likely to mislead the public about the nature of the business of the limited partnership or to lead to a pattern and practice of abuse that might cause harm to the interests of the public or this State as determined by the Division of Corporations in the Department of State.

§17-104. Registered office; registered agent.

(a) Each limited partnership shall have and maintain in the State of Delaware:

(1) A registered office, which may but need not be a place of its business in the State of Delaware; and

(2) A registered agent for service of process on the limited partnership, having a business office identical with such registered office, which agent may be any of

a. The limited partnership itself,

b. An individual resident in the State of Delaware,

c. A domestic limited liability company, a domestic corporation, a domestic partnership (whether general (including a limited liability partnership) or limited (other than the limited partnership itself, including a limited liability limited partnership)), or a domestic statutory trust, or

d. A foreign corporation, a foreign limited liability partnership, a foreign limited partnership (including a foreign limited liability limited partnership), a foreign limited liability company, or a foreign statutory trust. . . .

§17-106. Nature of business permitted; powers.

(a) A limited partnership may carry on any lawful business, purpose or activity, whether or not for profit, with the exception of the business of banking as defined in §126 of Title 8.

(b) A limited partnership shall possess and may exercise all the powers and privileges granted by this chapter or by any other law or by its partnership agreement, together with any powers incidental thereto, including such powers and privileges as are necessary or convenient to the conduct, promotion or attainment of the business, purposes or activities of the limited partnership.

(c) Notwithstanding any provision of this chapter to the contrary, without limiting the general powers enumerated in subsection (b) of this section above, a limited partnership shall, subject to such standards and restrictions, if any, as are set forth in its partnership agreement, have the power and authority to make contracts of guaranty and suretyship and enter into interest rate, basis, currency, hedge or other swap agreements or cap, floor, put, call, option, exchange or collar agreements, derivative agreements or other agreements similar to any of the foregoing.

(d) Unless otherwise provided in a partnership agreement, a limited partnership has the power and authority to grant, hold or exercise a power of attorney, including an irrevocable power of attorney.

§17-107. Business transactions of partner with the partnership.

Except as provided in the partnership agreement, a partner may lend money to, borrow money from, act as a surety, guarantor or endorser for, guarantee or assume 1 or more specific obligations of, provide collateral for and transact other business with, the limited partnership and, subject to other applicable law, has the same rights and obligations with respect thereto as a person who is not a partner.

§17-108. Indemnification.

Subject to such standards and restrictions, if any, as are set forth in its partnership agreement, a limited partnership may, and shall have the power to, indemnify and hold harmless any partner or other person from and against any and all claims and demands whatsoever.

§17-109. Service of process on partners and liquidating trustees.

(a) A general partner or a liquidating trustee of a limited partnership may be served with process in the manner prescribed in this section in all civil actions or proceedings brought in the State of Delaware involving or relating to the business of the limited partnership or a violation by the general partner or the liquidating trustee of a duty to the limited partnership, or any partner of the limited partnership, whether or not the general partner or the liquidating trustee is a general partner or a liquidating trustee at the time suit is commenced. The filing in the Office of the Secretary of State of a certificate of limited partnership executed, and the execution thereof, by a resident or nonresident of the State of Delaware which names such person as a general partner or a liquidating trustee of a limited partnership, or the acceptance by a general partner or a liquidating trustee after August 1, 1999, of election or appointment as a general partner or a liquidating trustee of a limited partnership, or a general partner or a liquidating trustee of a limited partnership serving in such capacity after August 1, 1999, constitute such person's consent to the appointment of the registered agent of the limited partnership (or, if there is none, the Secretary of State) as such person's agent upon whom service of process may be made as provided in this section. Such execution and filing, or such acceptance or service, shall signify the consent of such general partner or liquidating trustee that any process when so served shall be of the same legal force and validity as if served upon such general partner or liquidating trustee within the State of Delaware and such appointment of the registered agent (or, if there is none, the Secretary of State) shall be irrevocable. . . .

(d) In a written partnership agreement or other writing, a partner may consent to be subject to the nonexclusive jurisdiction of the courts of, or arbitration in, a specified jurisdiction, or the exclusive jurisdiction of the courts of the State of Delaware, or the exclusivity of arbitration in a specified jurisdiction or the State of Delaware, and to be served with legal process in the manner prescribed in such partnership agreement or other writing. Except by agreeing to arbitrate any arbitrable matter in a specified jurisdiction or in the State of Delaware, a limited partner may not waive its right to maintain a legal action or proceeding in the courts of the State of Delaware with respect to matters relating to the organization or internal affairs of a limited partnership.

(e) Nothing herein contained limits or affects the right to serve process in any other manner now or hereafter provided by law. This section is an extension of and not a limitation upon the right otherwise existing of service of legal process upon nonresidents.

(f) The Court of Chancery and the Superior Court may make all necessary rules respecting the form of process, the manner of issuance and return thereof and such other rules which may be necessary to implement this section and are not inconsistent with this section.

§17-110. Contested matters relating to general partners; contested votes.

(a) Upon application of any partner, the Court of Chancery may hear and determine the validity of any admission, election, appointment or removal or other withdrawal of a general partner of a limited partnership, and the right of any person to become or continue to be a general partner of a limited partnership, and, in case the right to serve as a general partner is claimed by more than 1 person, may determine the person or persons entitled to serve as general partners; and to that end make such order or decree in any such case as may be just and proper, with power to enforce the production of any books, papers and records of the limited partnership relating to the issue. In any such application, the limited partnership shall be named as a party and service of copies of the application upon the registered agent of the limited partnership shall be deemed to be service upon the limited partnership and upon the person or persons whose right to serve as a general partner is contested and upon the person or persons, if any, claiming to be a general partner or claiming the right to be a general partner; and the registered agent shall forward immediately a copy of the application to the limited partnership and to the person or persons whose right to serve as a general partner is contested and to the person or persons, if any, claiming to be a general partner or the right to be a general partner, in a postpaid, sealed, registered letter addressed to such limited partnership and such person or persons at their post-office addresses last known to the registered agent or furnished to the registered agent by the applicant partner. The Court may make such order respecting further or other notice of such application as it deems proper under the circumstances.

(b) Upon application of any partner, the Court of Chancery may hear and determine the result of any vote of partners upon matters as to which the partners of the limited partnership, or any class or group of partners, have the right to vote pursuant to the partnership agreement or other agreement or this chapter (other than the admission, election, appointment or removal or other withdrawal of general partners). In any such application, the limited partnership shall be named as a party and service of the application upon the registered agent of the limited partnership shall be deemed to be service upon the limited partnership, and no other party need be joined in order for the Court to adjudicate the result of the vote. The Court may make such order respecting further or other notice of such application as it deems proper under the circumstances.

(c) Nothing herein contained limits or affects the right to serve process in any other manner now or hereafter provided by law. This section is an extension of and not a limitation upon the right otherwise existing of service of legal process upon nonresidents.

§17-111. Interpretation and enforcement of partnership agreement.

Any action to interpret, apply or enforce the provisions of a partnership agreement, or the duties, obligations or liabilities of a limited partnership to the partners of the limited partnership, or the duties, obligations or liabilities among partners or of partners to the limited partnership, or the rights or powers of, or restrictions on, the limited partnership or partners, or any provision of this chapter, or any other instrument, document, agreement or certificate contemplated by any provision of this chapter, may be brought in the Court of Chancery.

§17-112. Judicial cancellation of certificate of limited partnership; proceedings.

(a) Upon motion by the Attorney General, the Court of Chancery shall have jurisdiction to cancel the certificate of limited partnership of any domestic limited partnership for abuse or misuse of its limited partnership powers, privileges or existence. The Attorney General shall proceed for this purpose in the Court of Chancery.

(b) The Court of Chancery shall have power, by appointment of trustees, receivers or otherwise, to administer and wind up the affairs of any domestic limited partnership whose certificate of limited partnership shall be canceled by the Court of Chancery under this section, and to make such orders and decrees with respect thereto as shall be just and equitable respecting its affairs and assets and the rights of its partners and creditors.

SUBCHAPTER II. FORMATION; CERTIFICATE OF LIMITED PARTNERSHIP

§17-201. Certificate of limited partnership.

(a) In order to form a limited partnership, 1 or more persons (but not less than all of the general partners) must execute a certificate of limited partnership.

The certificate of limited partnership shall be filed in the Office of the Secretary of State and set forth:

(1) The name of the limited partnership;

(2) The address of the registered office and the name and address of the registered agent for service of process required to be maintained by §17-104 of this title;

(3) The name and the business, residence or mailing address of each general partner; and

(4) Any other matters the partners determine to include therein.

(b) A limited partnership is formed at the time of the filing of the initial certificate of limited partnership in the Office of the Secretary of State or at any later date or time specified in the certificate of limited partnership if, in either case, there has been substantial compliance with the requirements of this section. A limited partnership formed under this chapter shall be a separate legal entity, the existence of which as a separate legal entity shall continue until cancellation of the limited partnership's certificate of limited partnership.

(c) The filing of the certificate of limited partnership in the Office of the Secretary of State shall make it unnecessary to file any other documents under Chapter 31 of this title.

(d) A partnership agreement shall be entered into or otherwise existing either before, after or at the time of the filing of a certificate of limited partnership and, whether entered into or otherwise existing before, after or at the time of such filing, may be made effective as of the effective time of such filing or at such other time or date as provided in or reflected by the partnership agreement.

(e) A certificate of limited partnership substantially complies with §17-201(a)(2) of this title if it contains the name of the registered agent and the address of the registered office even if the certificate of limited partnership does not expressly designate such person as the registered agent or such address as the registered office or the address of the registered agent.

§17-202. Amendment to certificate.

(a) A certificate of limited partnership is amended by filing a certificate of amendment thereto in the Office of the Secretary of State. The certificate of amendment shall set forth:

(1) The name of the limited partnership; and

(2) The amendment to the certificate.

(b) A general partner who becomes aware that any statement in a certificate of limited partnership was false when made, or that any matter described has changed making the certificate false in any material respect, shall promptly amend the certificate.

(c) Notwithstanding the requirements of subsection (b) of this section, no later than 90 days after the happening of any of the following events an amendment to a certificate of limited partnership reflecting the occurrence of the event or events shall be filed by a general partner:

(1) The admission of a new general partner;

(2) The withdrawal of a general partner; or

(3) A change in the name of the limited partnership, or, except as provided in §17-104(b) and (c) of this title, a change in the address of the registered office or a change in the name or address of the registered agent of the limited partnership.

(d) A certificate of limited partnership may be amended at any time for any other proper purpose the general partners may determine.

(e) Unless otherwise provided in this chapter or in the certificate of amendment, a certificate of amendment shall be effective at the time of its filing with the Secretary of State.

(f) If after the dissolution of a limited partnership but prior to the filing of a certificate of cancellation as provided in §17-203 of this title:

(1) A certificate of limited partnership has been amended to reflect the withdrawal of all general partners of a limited partnership, the certificate of limited partnership shall be amended to set forth the name and the business, residence or mailing address of each person winding up the limited partnership's affairs, each of whom shall execute and file such certificate of amendment, and each of whom shall not be subject to liability as a general partner by reason of such amendment; or

(2) A person shown on a certificate of limited partnership as a general partner is not winding up the limited partnership's affairs, the certificate of limited partnership shall be amended to add the name and the business, residence or mailing address of each person winding up the limited partnership's affairs, each of whom shall execute and file such certificate of amendment, and each of whom shall not be subject to liability as a general partner by reason of such amendment. A person shown on a certificate of limited partnership as a general partner who is not winding up a limited partnership's affairs need not execute a certificate of amendment which is being executed and filed as required under this subsection.

§17-206. Filing.

(a) The signed copy of any certificate authorized to be filed under this chapter shall be delivered to the Secretary of State. . . .

(b) Notwithstanding any other provision of this chapter, any certificate filed under this chapter shall be effective at the time of its filing with the Secretary of State or at any later date or time (not later than a time on the one hundred and eightieth day after the date of its filing if such date of filing is on or after January 1, 2012) specified in the certificate. . . .

§17-207. Liability for false statement.

(a) If any certificate authorized to be filed under this chapter contains a materially false statement, one who suffers loss by reasonable reliance on the statement may recover damages for the loss from:

(1) Any general partner who executes the certificate and knew or should have known the statement to be false in any material respect at the time the certificate was executed; and

(2) Any general partner that filed the certificate, who thereafter knows that any arrangement or other fact described in the certificate is false in any material respect or has changed, making the statement false in any material respect, if that general partner had sufficient time to amend, correct or cancel the certificate, or to file a petition for its amendment, correction or cancellation, before the statement was reasonably relied upon.

(b) No general partner shall have any liability for failing to cause the amendment, correction or cancellation of a certificate to be filed or failing to file a petition for its amendment, correction or cancellation pursuant to subsection (a) of this section if the certificate of amendment, certificate of correction, certificate of cancellation or petition is filed within 90 days of when that general partner knew or should have known to the extent provided in subsection (a) of this section that the statement in the certificate was false in any material respect.

§17-208. Notice.

The fact that a certificate of limited partnership is on file in the Office of the Secretary of State is notice that the partnership is a limited partnership and is notice of all other facts set forth therein which are required to be set forth in a certificate of limited partnership by §17-201(a)(1)-(3) or §17-1202 of this title and by §17-202(f) of this title and which are permitted to be set forth in a certificate of limited partnership by §17-218(b) or §17-221(b) of this title. The fact that a certificate of registered series is on file in the office of the Secretary of State is notice that the registered series named in such certificate of registered series has been formed pursuant to §17-221 of this title and is notice of all other facts set forth therein which are required to be set forth in a certificate of registered series by §17-221(d) of this title.

§17-209. Delivery of certificates to limited partners.

Upon the return by the Secretary of State pursuant to §17-206 of this title of a certificate marked "Filed," the general partners shall promptly deliver or mail a copy of the certificate to each limited partner if the partnership agreement so requires.

§17-210. Restated certificate.

(a) *Restated certificate of limited partnership.* — (1) A limited partnership may, whenever desired, integrate into a single instrument all of the provisions of its certificate of limited partnership which are then in effect and operative as a result of there having theretofore been filed with the Secretary of State 1 or more certificates or other instruments pursuant to any of the sections referred to in this subchapter and it may at the same time also further amend its certificate of limited partnership by adopting a restated certificate of limited partnership. . . .

§17-211. Merger and consolidation.

(a) As used in this section and in §§17-220, 17-222, 17-223 and 17-224 of this title, "other business entity" means a corporation, a statutory trust, a business trust, an association, a real estate investment trust, a common-law trust, a limited liability company, or any other incorporated or unincorporated business or entity, including a partnership (whether general (including a limited liability partnership) or limited (including a foreign limited liability limited partnership), but excluding a domestic limited partnership). As used in this section and in §§17-212 and 17-301 of this title, "plan of merger" means a writing approved by a domestic limited partnership, in the form of resolutions or otherwise, that states the terms and conditions of a merger under subsection (*l*) of this section.

(b) Pursuant to an agreement of merger or consolidation, 1 or more domestic limited partnerships may merge or consolidate with or into 1 or more domestic limited partnerships or 1 or more other business entities formed or organized under the laws of the State of Delaware or any other state or the United States or any foreign country or other foreign jurisdiction, or any combination thereof, with such domestic limited partnership or other business entity as the agreement shall provide being the surviving or resulting domestic limited partnership or other business entity. Unless otherwise provided in the partnership agreement, an agreement of merger or consolidation or a plan of merger shall be approved by each domestic limited partnership which is to merge or consolidate: (1) by all general partners; and (2) by limited partners who own more than 50 percent of the then current percentage or other interest in the profits of the domestic limited partnership owned by all of the limited partners. In connection with a merger or consolidation hereunder, rights or securities of, or interests in, a limited partnership or other business entity which is a constituent party to the merger or consolidation may be exchanged for or converted into cash, property, rights or securities of, or interests in, the surviving or resulting limited partnership or other business entity or, in addition to or in lieu thereof, may be exchanged for or converted into cash, property, rights or securities of, or interests in, a limited partnership or other business entity which is not the surviving or resulting limited partnership or other business entity in the merger or consolidation, may remain outstanding or may be canceled. Notwithstanding prior approval, an agreement of merger or consolidation or a plan of merger may be terminated or amended pursuant to a provision for such termination or amendment contained in the agreement of merger or consolidation or plan of merger. Unless otherwise provided in a partnership agreement, a limited partnership whose original certificate of limited partnership was filed with the Secretary of State and effective on or prior to July 31, 2015, shall continue to be governed by clause (2) of this subsection as in effect on July 31, 2015.

(c) Except in the case of a merger under subsection (*l*) of this section, if a domestic limited partnership is merging or consolidating under this section, the domestic limited partnership or other business entity surviving or resulting in or from the merger or consolidation shall file a certificate of merger or consolidation executed by at least 1 general partner on behalf of the domestic limited partnership when it is the surviving or resulting entity in the office of the Secretary of State. The certificate of merger or consolidation shall state:

(1) The name, jurisdiction of formation or organization and type of entity of each of the domestic limited partnerships and other business entities which is to merge or consolidate;

(2) That an agreement of merger or consolidation has been approved and executed by each of the domestic limited partnerships and other business entities which is to merge or consolidate;

(3) The name of the surviving or resulting domestic limited partnership or other business entity;

(4) In the case of a merger in which a domestic limited partnership is the surviving entity, such amendments, if any, to the certificate of limited partnership of the surviving domestic limited partnership (and in the case of a surviving domestic limited partnership that is a limited liability limited partnership, to the statement of qualification of such surviving domestic limited partnership filed under §15-1001 of this title) to change its name, registered office or registered agent as are desired to be effected by the merger;

(5) The future effective date or time (which shall be a date or time certain) of the merger or consolidation if it is not to be effective upon the filing of the certificate of merger or consolidation;

(6) That the agreement of merger or consolidation is on file at a place of business of the surviving or resulting domestic limited partnership or other business entity, and shall state the address thereof;

(7) That a copy of the agreement of merger or consolidation will be furnished by the surviving or resulting domestic limited partnership or other business entity, on request and without cost, to any partner of any domestic limited partnership or any person holding an interest in any other business entity which is to merge or consolidate; and

(8) If the surviving or resulting entity is not a domestic limited partnership (including a limited liability limited partnership), or a corporation, limited liability company, partnership (including a limited liability partnership) or statutory trust organized under the laws of the State of Delaware, a statement that such surviving or resulting other business entity agrees that it may be served with process in the State of Delaware in any action, suit or proceeding for the enforcement of any obligation of any domestic limited partnership which is to merge or consolidate, irrevocably appointing the Secretary of State as its agent to accept service of process in any such action, suit or proceeding and specifying the address to which a copy of such process shall be mailed to it by the Secretary of State. Process may be served upon the Secretary of State under this subsection by means of electronic transmission but only as prescribed by the Secretary of State. The Secretary of State is authorized to issue such rules and regulations with respect to such service as the Secretary of State deems necessary or appropriate. In the event of service hereunder upon the Secretary of State, the procedures set forth in §17-911(c) of this title shall be applicable, except that the plaintiff in any such action, suit or proceeding shall furnish the Secretary of State with the address specified in the certificate of merger or consolidation provided for in this section and any other address which the plaintiff may elect to furnish, together with copies of such process as required by the Secretary of State, and the Secretary of State shall notify such surviving or resulting other business entity at

all such addresses furnished by the plaintiff in accordance with the procedures set forth in §17-911(c) of this title.

(d) Any failure to file a certificate of merger or consolidation in connection with a merger or consolidation pursuant to this section which was effective prior to September 1, 1988, shall not affect the validity or effectiveness of any such merger or consolidation.

(e) Unless a future effective date or time is provided in a certificate of merger or consolidation, or in the case of a merger under subsection (*l*) of this section in a certificate of ownership and merger, in which event a merger or consolidation shall be effective at any such future effective date or time, a merger or consolidation shall be effective upon the filing in the Office of the Secretary of State of a certificate of merger or consolidation or a certificate of ownership and merger.

(f) A certificate of merger or consolidation or a certificate of ownership and merger shall act as a certificate of cancellation for a domestic limited partnership which is not the surviving or resulting entity in the merger or consolidation. A certificate of merger that sets forth any amendment in accordance with paragraph (c)(4) of this section shall be deemed to be an amendment to the certificate of limited partnership (and if applicable to the statement of qualification) of the limited partnership, and the limited partnership shall not be required to take any further action to amend its certificate of limited partnership under §17-202 of this title (or if applicable its statement of qualification under §15-105 of this title) with respect to such amendments set forth in the certificate of merger. Whenever this section requires the filing of a certificate of merger or consolidation, such requirement shall be deemed satisfied by the filing of an agreement of merger or consolidation containing the information required by this section to be set forth in the certificate of merger or consolidation.

(g) An agreement of merger or consolidation or a plan of merger approved in accordance with subsection (b) of this section may (1) effect any amendment to the partnership agreement or (2) effect the adoption of a new partnership agreement for a limited partnership if it is the surviving or resulting limited partnership in the merger or consolidation. Any amendment to a partnership agreement or adoption of a new partnership agreement made pursuant to the foregoing sentence shall be effective at the effective time or date of the merger or consolidation and shall be effective notwithstanding any provision of the partnership agreement relating to amendment or adoption of a new partnership agreement, other than a provision that by its terms applies to an amendment to the partnership agreement or the adoption of a new partnership agreement, in either case, in connection with a merger or consolidation. The provisions of this subsection shall not be construed to limit the accomplishment of a merger or of any of the matters referred to herein by any other means provided for in a partnership agreement or other agreement or as otherwise permitted by law, including that the partnership agreement of any constituent limited partnership to the merger or consolidation (including a limited partnership formed for the purpose of consummating a merger or consolidation) shall be the partnership agreement of the surviving or resulting limited partnership. Unless otherwise provided in a partnership agreement, a limited partnership whose original certificate of limited partnership was filed with the Secretary of State and effective on or prior to July 31, 2005, shall continue to be governed by this subsection as in effect on July 31, 2005.

(h) When any merger or consolidation shall have become effective under this section, for all purposes of the laws of the State of Delaware, all of the rights, privileges and powers of each of the domestic limited partnerships and other business entities that have merged or consolidated, and all property, real, personal and mixed, and all debts due to any of said domestic limited partnerships and other business entities, as well as all other things and causes of action belonging to each of such domestic limited partnerships and other business entities, shall be vested in the surviving or resulting domestic limited partnership or other business entity, and shall thereafter be the property of the surviving or resulting domestic limited partnership or other business entity as they were of each of the domestic limited partnerships and other business entities that have merged or consolidated, and the title to any real property vested by deed or otherwise, under the laws of the State of Delaware, in any of such domestic limited partnerships and other business entities, shall not revert or be in any way impaired by reason of this chapter; but all rights of creditors and all liens upon any property of any of said domestic limited partnerships and other business entities shall be preserved unimpaired, and all debts, liabilities and duties of each of the said domestic limited partnerships and other business entities that have merged or consolidated shall thenceforth attach to the surviving or resulting domestic limited partnership or other business entity, and may be enforced against it to the same extent as if said debts, liabilities and duties had been incurred or contracted by it. Unless otherwise agreed, a merger or consolidation of a domestic limited partnership, including a domestic limited partnership which is not the surviving or resulting entity in the merger or consolidation, shall not require such domestic limited partnership to wind up its affairs under §17-803 of this title or pay its liabilities and distribute its assets under §17-804 of this title, and the merger or consolidation shall not constitute a dissolution of such limited partnership.

(i) Except as provided by agreement with a person to whom a general partner of a limited partnership is obligated, a merger or consolidation of a limited partnership that has become effective shall not affect any obligation or liability existing at the time of such merger or consolidation of a general partner of a limited partnership which is merging or consolidating.

(j) If a limited partnership is a constituent party to a merger or consolidation that shall have become effective, but the limited partnership is not the surviving or resulting entity of the merger or consolidation, then a judgment creditor of a general partner of such limited partnership may not levy execution against the assets of the general partner to satisfy a judgment based on a claim against the surviving or resulting entity of the merger or consolidation unless:

(1) A judgment based on the same claim has been obtained against the surviving or resulting entity of the merger or consolidation and a writ of execution on the judgment has been returned unsatisfied in whole or in part;

(2) The surviving or resulting entity of the merger or consolidation is a debtor in bankruptcy;

(3) The general partner has agreed that the creditor need not exhaust the assets of the limited partnership that was not the surviving or resulting entity of the merger or consolidation;

(4) The general partner has agreed that the creditor need not exhaust the assets of the surviving or resulting entity of the merger or consolidation;

(5) A court grants permission to the judgment creditor to levy execution against the assets of the general partner based on a finding that the assets of the surviving or resulting entity of the merger or consolidation that are subject to execution are clearly insufficient to satisfy the judgment, that exhaustion of the assets of the surviving or resulting entity of the merger or consolidation is excessively burdensome, or that the grant of permission is an appropriate exercise of the court's equitable powers; or

(6) Liability is imposed on the general partner by law or contract independent of the existence of the surviving or resulting entity of the merger or consolidation.

(k) A partnership agreement may provide that a domestic limited partnership shall not have the power to merge or consolidate as set forth in this section.

(l) In any case in which (i) at least 90% of the outstanding shares of each class of the stock of a corporation or corporations (other than a corporation which has in its certificate of incorporation the provision required by §251(g)(7)(A) and (B) of Title 8), of which class there are outstanding shares that, absent §267(a) of Title 8, would be entitled to vote on such merger, is owned by a domestic limited partnership, (ii) 1 or more of such corporations is a corporation of the State of Delaware, and (iii) any corporation that is not a corporation of the State of Delaware is a corporation of any other state or the District of Columbia or another jurisdiction, the laws of which do not forbid such merger, the domestic limited partnership having such stock ownership may either merge the corporation or corporations into itself and assume all of its or their obligations, or merge itself, or itself and 1 or more of such corporations, into 1 of the other corporations, pursuant to a plan of merger. If a domestic limited partnership is causing a merger under this subsection, the domestic limited partnership shall file a certificate of ownership and merger executed by at least 1 general partner on behalf of the domestic limited partnership in the office of the Secretary of State. The certificate of ownership and merger shall certify that such merger was authorized in accordance with the domestic limited partnership's partnership agreement and this chapter, and if the domestic limited partnership shall not own all the outstanding stock of all the corporations that are parties to the merger, shall state the terms and conditions of the merger, including the securities, cash, property, or rights to be issued, paid, delivered or granted by the surviving domestic limited partnership or corporation upon surrender of each share of the corporation or corporations not owned by the domestic limited partnership, or the cancellation of some or all of such shares. The terms and conditions of the merger may not result in a holder of stock in a corporation becoming a general partner in a surviving domestic limited partnership (other than a limited liability limited partnership). If a corporation surviving a merger under this subsection is not a corporation organized under the laws of the State of Delaware, then the terms and conditions of the merger shall obligate such corporation to agree that it may be served with process in the State of Delaware in any proceeding for enforcement of any obligation of the domestic limited partnership or any obligation of any constituent corporation of the State of Delaware, as well as for enforcement of any obligation of the surviving corporation, including any suit or other proceeding to enforce the right of any stockholders as determined in appraisal proceedings pursuant to §262 of Title 8, and to irrevocably appoint the Secretary of State as its agent to accept service of process in any such suit or other proceedings, and to specify the address to which a copy of such process shall be mailed by the Secretary of State. Process may be served upon the Secretary of State under this subsection by means of electronic transmission but only as prescribed by the Secretary of State. The Secretary of State is authorized to issue such rules and regulations with respect to such service as the Secretary of State deems necessary or appropriate. In the event of such service upon the Secretary of State in accordance with this subsection, the Secretary of State shall forthwith notify such surviving corporation thereof by letter, directed to such surviving corporation at its address so specified, unless such surviving corporation shall have designated in writing to the Secretary of State a different address for such purpose, in which case it shall be mailed to the last address so designated. Such letter shall be sent by a mail or courier service that includes a record of mailing or deposit with the courier and a record of delivery evidenced by the signature of the recipient. Such letter shall enclose a copy of the process and any other papers served on the Secretary of State pursuant to this subsection. It shall be the duty of the plaintiff in the event of such service to serve process and any other papers in duplicate, to notify the Secretary of State that service is being effected pursuant to this subsection and to pay the Secretary of State the sum of $50 for the use of the State of Delaware, which sum shall be taxed as part of the costs in the proceeding, if the plaintiff shall prevail therein. The Secretary of State shall maintain an alphabetical record of any such service setting forth the name of the plaintiff and the defendant, the title, docket number and nature of the proceeding in which process has been served, the fact that service has been effected pursuant to this subsection, the return date thereof, and the day and hour service was made. The Secretary of State shall not be required to retain such information longer than 5 years from receipt of the service of process.

§17-212. No statutory appraisal rights.

Unless otherwise provided in a partnership agreement or an agreement of merger or consolidation or a plan of merger or a plan of division, no appraisal rights shall be available with respect to a partnership interest or another interest in a limited partnership, including in connection with any amendment of a partnership agreement, any merger or consolidation in which the limited partnership or a registered series of the limited partnership is a constituent party to the merger or consolidation, any division of the limited partnership, any conversion of the limited partnership to another business form, any conversion of a protected series of the limited partnership to a registered series of such limited partnership, any conversion of a registered series of the limited partnership to a protected series of such limited partnership, any transfer to or domestication or continuance in any jurisdiction by the limited partnership, or the sale of all or substantially all of the limited partnership's assets. The Court of Chancery shall have jurisdiction to hear and determine any matter relating to any appraisal rights provided in a partnership agreement or an agreement of merger or consolidation or a plan of merger or a plan of division.

§17-214. Limited partnerships as limited liability limited partnerships.

(a) A limited partnership may be formed as, or may become, a limited liability limited partnership pursuant to this section. A limited partnership may become a limited liability limited partnership as permitted by the limited partnership's partnership agreement or, if the limited partnership's partnership agreement does not provide for the limited partnership's becoming a limited liability limited partnership, with the approval (i) by all general partners, and (ii) by limited partners who own more than 50 percent of the then current percentage or other interest in the profits of the limited partnership owned by all of the limited partners. To be formed or to become, and to continue as, a limited liability limited partnership, a limited partnership shall, in addition to complying with the requirements of this chapter:

(1) File a statement of qualification as provided in §15-1001 of this title and thereafter an annual report as provided in §15-1003 of this title; and

(2) Have as the last words or letters of its name the words "Limited Liability Limited Partnership," or the abbreviation "L.L.L.P.," or the designation "LLLP." . . .

§17-217. Conversion of certain entities to a limited partnership.

(a) As used in this section and in §17-204 of this title, the term "other entity" means a corporation, a statutory trust, a business trust, an association, a real estate investment trust, a common-law trust, or any other incorporated or unincorporated business or entity, including a general partnership (including a limited liability partnership) or a foreign limited partnership (including a foreign limited liability limited partnership) or a limited liability company.

(b) Any other entity may convert to a domestic limited partnership (including a limited liability limited partnership) by complying with subsection (h) of this section and filing in the office of the Secretary of State in accordance with §17-206 of this title:

(1) A certificate of conversion to limited partnership that has been executed in accordance with §17-204 of this title;

(2) A certificate of limited partnership that complies with §17-201 of this title and has been executed in accordance with §17-204 of this title; and

(3) In the case of a conversion to a limited liability limited partnership, a statement of qualification in accordance with of §15-1001(c) of this title.

Each of the certificates (and, as applicable, the statement) required by this subsection (b) shall be filed simultaneously in the office of the Secretary of State and, if such certificates (and, as applicable, such statement) are not to become effective upon their filing as permitted by §17-206(b) of this title, then each such certificate (and, as applicable, such statement) shall provide for the same effective date or time in accordance with §17-206(b) of this title.

(c) The certificate of conversion to limited partnership shall state:

(1) The date on which and jurisdiction where the other entity was first created, incorporated, formed or otherwise came into being and, if it has changed, its jurisdiction immediately prior to its conversion to a domestic limited partnership;

(2) The name and type of entity of the other entity immediately prior to the filing of the certificate of conversion to limited partnership;

(3) The name of the limited partnership as set forth in its certificate of limited partnership filed in accordance with subsection (b) of this section; and

(4) The future effective date or time (which shall be a date or time certain) of the conversion to a limited partnership if it is not to be effective upon the

filing of the certificate of conversion to limited partnership and the certificate of limited partnership.

(d) Upon the filing in the office of the Secretary of State of the certificate of conversion to limited partnership, the certificate of limited partnership and the statement of qualification (if applicable), or upon the future effective date or time of the certificate of conversion to limited partnership, the certificate of limited partnership and the statement of qualification (if applicable), the other entity shall be converted into a domestic limited partnership (including a limited liability limited partnership, if applicable) and the limited partnership shall thereafter be subject to all of the provisions of this chapter, except that notwithstanding §17-201 of this title, the existence of the limited partnership shall be deemed to have commenced on the date the other entity commenced its existence in the jurisdiction in which the other entity was first created, formed, incorporated or otherwise came into being.

(e) The conversion of any other entity into a domestic limited partnership (including a limited liability limited partnership) shall not be deemed to affect any obligations or liabilities of the other entity incurred prior to its conversion to a domestic limited partnership, or the personal liability of any person incurred prior to such conversion.

(f) When any conversion shall have become effective under this section, for all purposes of the laws of the State of Delaware, all of the rights, privileges and powers of the other entity that has converted, and all property, real, personal and mixed, and all debts due to such other entity, as well as all other things and causes of action belonging to such other entity, shall remain vested in the domestic limited partnership to which such other entity has converted and shall be the property of such domestic limited partnership, and the title to any real property vested by deed or otherwise in such other entity shall not revert or be in any way impaired by reason of this chapter; but all rights of creditors and all liens upon any property of such other entity shall be preserved unimpaired, and all debts, liabilities and duties of the other entity that has converted shall remain attached to the domestic limited partnership to which such other entity has converted, and may be enforced against it to the same extent as if said debts, liabilities and duties had originally been incurred or contracted by it in its capacity as a domestic limited partnership. The rights, privileges, powers and interests in property of the other entity, as well as the debts, liabilities and duties of the other entity, shall not be deemed, as a consequence of the conversion, to have been transferred to the domestic limited partnership to which such other entity has converted for any purpose of the laws of the State of Delaware.

(g) Unless otherwise agreed, for all purposes of the laws of the State of Delaware, the converting other entity shall not be required to wind up its affairs or pay its liabilities and distribute its assets, and the conversion shall not be deemed to constitute a dissolution of such other entity. When an other entity has been converted to a limited partnership pursuant to this section, for all purposes of the laws of the State of Delaware, the limited partnership shall be deemed to be the same entity as the converting other entity and the conversion shall constitute a continuation of the existence of the converting other entity in the form of a domestic limited partnership.

(h) Prior to filing a certificate of conversion to limited partnership with the office of the Secretary of State, the conversion shall be approved in the manner provided for by the document, instrument, agreement or other writing, as the case may be, governing the internal affairs of the other entity and the conduct of its business or by applicable law, as appropriate, and a partnership agreement shall be approved by the same authorization required to approve the conversion; provided, that in any event, such approval shall include the approval of any person who, at the effective date or time of the conversion, shall be a general partner of the limited partnership.

(i) In connection with a conversion hereunder, rights or securities of, or interests in, the other entity which is to be converted to a domestic limited partnership may be exchanged for or converted into cash, property, rights or securities of, or interests in, such domestic limited partnership or, in addition to or in lieu thereof, may be exchanged for or converted into cash, property, rights or securities of, or interests in, another domestic limited partnership or other entity, may remain outstanding or may be canceled.

(j) The provisions of this section shall not be construed to limit the accomplishment of a change in the law governing, or the domicile of, an other entity to the State of Delaware by any other means provided for in a partnership agreement or other agreement or as otherwise permitted by law, including by the amendment of a partnership agreement or other agreement.

§17-218. Series of limited partners, general partners, partnership interests or assets.

(a) A partnership agreement may establish or provide for the establishment of 1 or more designated series of limited partners, general partners, partnership interests or assets. Any such series may have separate rights, powers or duties with respect to specified property or obligations of the limited partnership or profits and losses associated with specified property or obligations, and any such series may have a separate business purpose or investment objective. No provision of subsection (b) of this section or §17-221 of this title shall be construed to limit the application of the principle of freedom of contract to a series that is not a protected series or a registered series. Other than pursuant to §§17-222, 17-223 and 17-224 of this title a series may not merge, convert or consolidate pursuant to any section of this title or any other statute of this State.

(b) A series established in accordance with the following sentence is a protected series. Notwithstanding anything to the contrary set forth in this chapter or under other applicable law, in the event that a partnership agreement establishes or provides for the establishment of 1 or more series, and to the extent the records maintained for any such series account for the assets associated with such series separately from the other assets of the limited partnership, or any other series thereof, and if the partnership agreement so provides, and if notice of the limitation on liabilities of a series as referenced in this subsection is set forth in the certificate of limited partnership, then the debts, liabilities, obligations and expenses incurred, contracted for or otherwise existing with respect to such series shall be enforceable only against the assets of such series or the general partners associated with such series and not against the assets of the limited partnership generally, any other series thereof, or any general partner not associated with such series, and, unless otherwise provided in the partnership agreement, none of the debts, liabilities, obligations and expenses incurred, contracted for or otherwise existing with respect to the limited partnership generally or any other series thereof shall be enforceable against the assets of such series or the general partners associated with such series who are not also general partners of the limited partnership generally or general partners associated with the other series, as the case may be. . . .

§17-219. Approval of conversion of a limited partnership.

(a) Upon compliance with this section, a domestic limited partnership may convert to a corporation, a statutory trust, a business trust, an association, a real estate investment trust, a common-law trust or any other incorporated or unincorporated business or entity, including a general partnership (including a limited liability partnership) or a foreign limited partnership (including a foreign limited liability limited partnership) or a limited liability company.

(b) If the partnership agreement specifies the manner of authorizing a conversion of the limited partnership, the conversion shall be authorized as specified in the partnership agreement. If the partnership agreement does not specify the manner of authorizing a conversion of the limited partnership and does not prohibit a conversion of the limited partnership, the conversion shall be authorized in the same manner as is specified in the partnership agreement for authorizing a merger or consolidation that involves the limited partnership as a constituent party to the merger or consolidation. If the partnership agreement does not specify the manner of authorizing a conversion of the limited partnership or a merger or consolidation that involves the limited partnership as a constituent party and does not prohibit a conversion of the limited partnership, the conversion shall be authorized by the approval (1) by all general partners, and (2) by limited partners who own more than 50 percent of the then current percentage or other interest in the profits of the domestic limited partnership owned by all of the limited partners. Unless otherwise provided in a partnership agreement, a limited partnership whose original certificate of limited partnership was filed with the Secretary of State and effective on or prior to July 31, 2015, shall continue to be governed by clause (2) of this subsection as in effect on July 31, 2015.

(c) Unless otherwise agreed, the conversion of a domestic limited partnership to another entity or business form pursuant to this section shall not require such limited partnership to wind up its affairs under §17-803 of this title or pay its liabilities and distribute its assets under §17-804 of this title, and the conversion shall not constitute a dissolution of such limited partnership. When a limited partnership has converted to another entity or business form pursuant to this section, for all purposes of the laws of the State of Delaware, the other entity or business form shall be deemed to be the same entity as the converting limited partnership and the conversion shall constitute a continuation of the existence of the limited partnership in the form of such other entity or business form.

(d) In connection with a conversion of a domestic limited partnership to another entity or business form pursuant to this section, rights or securities of or interests in the domestic limited partnership which is to be converted may be exchanged for or converted into cash, property, rights or securities of or interests in the entity or business form into which the domestic limited partnership is being converted or, in addition to or in lieu thereof, may be exchanged for or converted into cash, property, rights or securities of or interests in another entity or business form, may remain outstanding or may be canceled.

(e) If a limited partnership shall convert in accordance with this section to another entity or business form organized, formed or created under the laws of a jurisdiction other than the State of Delaware, a certificate of conversion to non-Delaware entity executed in accordance with §17-204 of this title shall be filed in the office of the Secretary of State in accordance with §17-206 of this title. The certificate of conversion to non-Delaware entity shall state:

(1) The name of the limited partnership and, if it has been changed, the name under which its certificate of limited partnership was originally filed;

(2) The date of filing of its original certificate of limited partnership with the Secretary of State;

(3) The jurisdiction in which the entity or business form, to which the limited partnership shall be converted, is organized, formed or created, and the name of such entity or business form;

(4) The future effective date or time (which shall be a date or time certain) of the conversion if it is not to be effective upon the filing of the certificate of conversion to non-Delaware entity;

(5) That the conversion has been approved in accordance with this section;

(6) The agreement of the limited partnership that it may be served with process in the State of Delaware in any action, suit or proceeding for enforcement of any obligation of the limited partnership arising while it was a limited partnership of the State of Delaware, and that it irrevocably appoints the Secretary of State as its agent to accept service of process in any such action, suit or proceeding;

(7) The address to which a copy of the process referred to in paragraph (e)(6) of this section shall be mailed to it by the Secretary of State. Process may be served upon the Secretary of State under paragraph (e)(6) of this section by means of electronic transmission but only as prescribed by the Secretary of State. The Secretary of State is authorized to issue such rules and regulations with respect to such service as the Secretary of State deems necessary or appropriate. In the event of service hereunder upon the Secretary of State, the procedures set forth in §17-911(c) of this title shall be applicable, except that the plaintiff in any such action, suit or proceeding shall furnish the Secretary of State with the address specified in this paragraph and any other address that the plaintiff may elect to furnish, together with copies of such process as required by the Secretary of State, and the Secretary of State shall notify the limited partnership that has converted out of the State of Delaware at all such addresses furnished by the plaintiff in accordance with the procedures set forth in §17-911(c) of this title.

(f) Upon the filing in the office of the Secretary of State of the certificate of conversion to non-Delaware entity or upon the future effective date or time of the certificate of conversion to non-Delaware entity and payment to the Secretary of State of all fees prescribed in this chapter, the limited partnership shall cease to exist as a limited partnership of the State of Delaware. A copy of the certificate of conversion to non-Delaware entity certified by the Secretary of State shall be prima facie evidence of the conversion by such limited partnership out of the State of Delaware.

(g) The conversion of a limited partnership out of the State of Delaware in accordance with this section and the resulting cessation of its existence as a limited partnership of the State of Delaware pursuant to a certificate of conversion to non-Delaware entity shall not be deemed to affect any obligations or liabilities of the limited partnership incurred prior to such conversion or the personal liability of any person incurred prior to such conversion, nor shall it be deemed to affect the choice of law applicable to the limited partnership with respect to matters arising prior to such conversion.

(h) When any conversion shall have become effective under this section, for all purposes of the laws of the State of Delaware, all of the rights, privileges and powers of the limited partnership that has converted, and all property, real, personal and mixed, and all debts due to such limited partnership, as well as all other things and causes of action belonging to such limited partnership, shall remain vested in the other entity or business form to which such limited partnership has converted and shall be the property of such other entity or business form, and the title to any real property vested by deed or otherwise in such limited partnership shall not revert or be in any way impaired by reason of this chapter; but all rights of creditors and all liens upon any property of such limited partnership shall be preserved unimpaired, and all debts, liabilities and duties of the limited partnership that has converted shall remain attached to the other entity or business form to which such limited partnership has converted, and may be enforced against it to the same extent as if said debts, liabilities and duties had originally been incurred or contracted by it in its capacity as such other entity or business form. The rights, privileges, powers and interests in property of the limited partnership that has converted, as well as the debts, liabilities and duties of such limited partnership, shall not be deemed, as a consequence of the conversion, to have been transferred to the other entity or business form to which such limited partnership has converted for any purpose of the laws of the State of Delaware.

(i) A partnership agreement may provide that a domestic limited partnership shall not have the power to convert as set forth in this section.

§17-220. Division of a limited partnership.

(a) As used in this section and §§17-203, 17-301 and 17-1203:

(1) "Dividing partnership" means the domestic limited partnership that is effecting a division in the manner provided in this section.

(2) "Division" means the division of a dividing partnership into two or more domestic limited partnerships in accordance with this section.

(3) "Division contact" means, in connection with any division, a natural person who is a Delaware resident, any division partnership in such division or any other domestic limited partnership or other business entity as defined in §17-211 of this title formed or organized under the laws of the State of Delaware, which division contact shall maintain a copy of the plan of division for a period of 6 years from the effective date of the division and shall comply with paragraph (g)(3) of this section.

(4) "Division partnership" means a surviving partnership, if any, and each resulting partnership.

(5) "Organizational documents" means the certificate of limited partnership and partnership agreement of a domestic limited partnership.

(6) "Resulting partnership" means a domestic limited partnership formed as a consequence of a division.

(7) "Surviving partnership" means a dividing partnership that survives the division.

(b) Pursuant to a plan of division, any domestic limited partnership may, in the manner provided in this section, be divided into 2 or more domestic limited partnerships. The division of a domestic limited partnership in accordance with this section and, if applicable, the resulting cessation of the existence of the dividing partnership pursuant to a certificate of division shall not be deemed to affect the personal liability of any person (including any general partner of the dividing partnership) incurred prior to such division with respect to matters arising prior to such division, nor shall it be deemed to affect the validity or enforceability of any obligations or liabilities of the dividing partnership incurred prior to such division; provided, that the obligations and liabilities of the dividing partnership shall be allocated to and vested in, and valid and enforceable obligations of, such division partnership or partnerships to which such obligations and liabilities have been allocated pursuant to the plan of division, as provided in subsection (*l*) of this section. Each resulting partnership in a division shall be formed in compliance with the requirements of this chapter and subsection (i) of this section. . . .

§17-221. Registered series of limited partners, general partners, partnership interests or assets.

(a) If a partnership agreement provides for the establishment or formation of 1 or more series, then a registered series may be formed by complying with this section. A partnership agreement does not need to use the term registered when referencing series or refer to this section, and a reference in a partnership agreement for a registered series, including a registered series resulting from the conversion of a protected series to a registered series, may continue to refer to §17-218 of this title, which reference shall be deemed a reference to this section with respect to such registered series. A registered series is formed by the filing of a certificate of registered series in the office of the Secretary of State.

(b) Notice of the limitation on liabilities of a registered series as referenced in subsection (c) of this section shall be set forth in the certificate of limited partnership of the limited partnership. Notice in a certificate of limited partnership of the limitation on liabilities of a registered series as referenced in subsection (c) of this section shall be sufficient for all purposes of this subsection whether or not the limited partnership has formed any registered series when such notice is included in the certificate of limited partnership, and there shall be no requirement that (i) any specific registered series of the limited partnership be referenced in such notice, (ii) such notice use the term registered when referencing series or include a reference to this section, or (iii) the certificate of limited partnership be amended if it includes a reference to §17-218 of this title. Any reference to §17-218 of this title in a certificate of limited partnership of a limited partnership that has 1 or more registered series shall be deemed a reference to this section with respect to such registered series. The fact that a certificate of limited partnership that contains the foregoing notice of the limitation on liabilities of a series is on file in the office of the Secretary of State shall constitute notice of such limitation on liabilities of a registered series.

(c) Notwithstanding anything to the contrary set forth in this chapter or under other applicable law, to the extent the records maintained for a registered series account for the assets associated with such series separately from the other assets of the limited partnership, or any other series thereof, then the debts, liabilities, obligations and expenses incurred, contracted for or otherwise existing with respect to such series shall be enforceable against the assets of such series or the general partners associated with such series only, and not against the assets of the limited partnership generally, any other series thereof, or any general partner not associated with such series, and, unless otherwise provided in the partnership agreement, none of the debts, liabilities, obligations and expenses incurred, contracted for or otherwise existing with respect to the limited partnership generally or any other series thereof shall be enforceable against the assets of such series or the general partners associated with such series who are not also general partners of the limited partnership generally or general partners associated with the other series, as the case may be. . . . The following shall apply to a registered series: . . .

(13) For all purposes of the laws of the State of Delaware, a registered series is an association, regardless of the number of partners of such series. . . .

Subchapter III. Limited Partners

§17-301. Admission of limited partners.

(a) In connection with the formation of a limited partnership, a person is admitted as a limited partner of the limited partnership upon the later to occur of:

(1) The formation of the limited partnership; or

(2) The time provided in and upon compliance with the partnership agreement or, if the partnership agreement does not so provide, when the person's admission is reflected in the records of the limited partnership or as otherwise provided in the partnership agreement.

(b) After the formation of a limited partnership, a person is admitted as a limited partner of the limited partnership:

(1) In the case of a person who is not an assignee of a partnership interest, including a person acquiring a partnership interest directly from the limited partnership and a person to be admitted as a limited partner of the limited partnership without acquiring a partnership interest in the limited partnership, at the time provided in and upon compliance with the partnership agreement or, if the partnership agreement does not so provide, upon the consent of all partners or as otherwise provided in the partnership agreement;

(2) In the case of an assignee of a partnership interest, as provided in §17-704(a) of this title;

(3) In the case of a person being admitted as a partner of a surviving or resulting limited partnership pursuant to a merger or consolidation approved

in accordance with §17-211(b) of this title, as provided in the partnership agreement of the surviving or resulting limited partnership or in the agreement of merger or consolidation or plan of merger, and in the event of any inconsistency, the terms of the agreement of merger or consolidation or plan of merger shall control; and in the case of a person being admitted as a partner of a limited partnership pursuant to a merger or consolidation in which such limited partnership is not the surviving or resulting limited partnership in the merger or consolidation, as provided in the partnership agreement of such limited partnership; or

(4) In the case of a person being admitted as a partner of a division partnership pursuant to a division approved in accordance with §17-220 of this title, as provided in the partnership agreement of such division partnership or in the plan of division, and in the event of any inconsistency, the terms of the plan of division shall control; and in the case of a person being admitted as a partner of a limited partnership pursuant to a division in which such limited partnership is not a division partnership in the division, as provided in the partnership agreement of such limited partnership.

(c) In connection with the domestication of a non-United States entity (as defined in §17-215 of this title) as a limited partnership in the State of Delaware in accordance with §17-215 of this title or the conversion of an other entity (as defined in §17-217 of this title) to a domestic limited partnership in accordance with §17-217 of this title, a person is admitted as a limited partner of the limited partnership as provided in the partnership agreement.

(d) A person may be admitted to a limited partnership as a limited partner of the limited partnership and may receive a partnership interest in the limited partnership without making a contribution or being obligated to make a contribution to the limited partnership. Unless otherwise provided in a partnership agreement, a person may be admitted to a limited partnership as a limited partner of the limited partnership without acquiring a partnership interest in the limited partnership. Unless otherwise provided in a partnership agreement, a person may be admitted as the sole limited partner of a limited partnership without making a contribution or being obligated to make a contribution to the limited partnership or without acquiring a partnership interest in the limited partnership.

(e) Unless otherwise provided in a partnership agreement or another agreement, a limited partner shall have no preemptive right to subscribe to any additional issue of partnership interests or another interest in a limited partnership.

§17-302. Classes and voting.

(a) A partnership agreement may provide for classes or groups of limited partners having such relative rights, powers and duties as the partnership agreement may provide, and may make provision for the future creation in the manner provided in the partnership agreement of additional classes or groups of limited partners having such relative rights, powers and duties as may from time to time be established, including rights, powers and duties senior to existing classes and groups of limited partners.

A partnership agreement may provide for the taking of an action, including the amendment of the partnership agreement, without the vote or approval of any limited partner or class or group of limited partners, including an action to create under the provisions of the partnership agreement a class or group of partnership interests that was not previously outstanding.

(b) Subject to §17-303 of this title, the partnership agreement may grant to all or certain identified limited partners or a specified class or group of the limited partners the right to vote separately or with all or any class or group of the limited partners or the general partners, on any matter. Voting by limited partners may be on a per capita, number, financial interest, class, group or any other basis.

(c) A partnership agreement may set forth provisions relating to notice of the time, place or purpose of any meeting at which any matter is to be voted on by any limited partners, waiver of any such notice, action by consent without a meeting, the establishment of a record date, quorum requirements, voting in person or by proxy, or any other matter with respect to the exercise of any such right to vote.

(d) Any right or power, including voting rights, granted to limited partners as permitted under §17-303 of this title shall be deemed to be permitted by this section.

(e) Unless otherwise provided in a partnership agreement, meetings of limited partners may be held by means of conference telephone or other communications equipment by means of which all persons participating in the meeting can hear each other, and participation in a meeting pursuant to this subsection shall constitute presence in person at the meeting. Unless otherwise provided in a partnership agreement, on any matter that is to be voted on, consented to or approved by limited partners, the limited partners may take such action without a meeting, without prior notice and without a vote if consented to or approved, in writing, by electronic transmission or by any other means permitted by law, by limited partners having not less than the minimum number of votes that would be necessary to authorize or take such action at a meeting at which all limited partners entitled to vote thereon were present and voted. Unless otherwise provided in a partnership agreement, if a person (whether or not then a limited partner) consenting as a limited partner to any matter provides that such consent will be effective at a future time (including a time determined upon the happening of an event), then such person shall be deemed to have consented as a limited partner at such future time so long as such person is then a limited partner. Unless otherwise provided in a partnership agreement, on any matter that is to be voted on by limited partners, the limited partners may vote in person or by proxy, and such proxy may be granted in writing, by means of electronic transmission or as otherwise permitted by applicable law. Unless otherwise provided in a partnership agreement, a consent transmitted by electronic transmission by a limited partner or by a person or persons authorized to act for a limited partner shall be deemed to be written and signed for purposes of this subsection.

(f) If a partnership agreement provides for the manner in which it may be amended, including by requiring the approval of a person who is not a party to the partnership agreement or the satisfaction of conditions, it may be amended only in that manner or as otherwise permitted by law, including as permitted by §17-211(g) of this title (provided that the approval of any person may be waived by such person and that any such conditions may be waived by all persons for whose benefit such conditions were intended). If a partnership agreement does not provide for the manner in which it may be amended, the partnership agreement may be amended with the approval of all the partners or as otherwise permitted by law, including as permitted by §17-211(g) of this title. A limited partner and any class or group of limited partners have the right to vote only on matters as specifically set forth in this chapter, on matters specifically provided by agreement, including a partnership agreement, and on any matter with respect to which a general partner may determine in its discretion to seek a vote of a limited partner or a class or group of limited partners if a vote on such matter is not contrary to a partnership agreement or another agreement to which a general partner or the limited partnership is a party. A limited partner and any class or group of limited partners have no other voting rights. A partnership agreement may provide that any limited partner or class or group of limited partners shall have no voting rights. Unless otherwise provided in a partnership agreement, a supermajority amendment provision shall only apply to provisions of the partnership agreement that are expressly included in the partnership agreement. As used in this section, "supermajority amendment provision" means any amendment provision set forth in a partnership agreement requiring that an amendment to a provision of the partnership agreement be adopted by no less than the vote or consent required to take action under such latter provision.

§17-303. Liability to third parties.

(a) A limited partner is not liable for the obligations of a limited partnership unless he or she is also a general partner or, in addition to the exercise of the rights and powers of a limited partner, he or she participates in the control of the business. However, if the limited partner does participate in the control of the business, he or she is liable only to persons who transact business with the limited partnership reasonably believing, based upon the limited partner's conduct, that the limited partner is a general partner.

(b) A limited partner does not participate in the control of the business within the meaning of subsection (a) of this section by virtue of possessing or, regardless of whether or not the limited partner has the rights or powers, exercising or attempting to exercise 1 or more of the following rights or powers or having or, regardless of whether or not the limited partner has the rights or powers, acting or attempting to act in 1 or more of the following capacities:

(1) To be an independent contractor for or to transact business with, including being a contractor for, or to be an agent or employee of, the limited partnership or a general partner, or to be an officer, director, stockholder, or interest holder of a corporate general partner, or to be a partner or interest holder of a partnership that is a general partner of the limited partnership, or to be a trustee, administrator, executor, custodian, fiduciary, beneficiary, or interest holder of an estate or trust which is a general partner, or to be a trustee, officer, advisor, stockholder, beneficiary, beneficial owner, or interest holder of a business trust or a statutory trust which is a general partner or to be a member, manager, agent, employee, or interest holder of a limited liability company which is a general partner;

(2) To consult with or advise a general partner or any other person with respect to any matter, including the business of the limited partnership, or to act or cause a general partner or any other person to take or refrain from taking any action, including by proposing, approving, consenting or disapproving, by voting or otherwise, with respect to any matter, including the business of the limited partnership;

(3) To act as surety, guarantor or endorser for the limited partnership or a general partner, to guaranty or assume 1 or more obligations of the limited partnership or a general partner, to borrow money from the limited partnership or a general partner, to lend money to the limited partnership or a general partner, or to provide collateral for the limited partnership or a general partner;

(4) To call, request, or attend or participate at a meeting of the partners or the limited partners;

(5) To wind up a limited partnership pursuant to §17-803 of this title;

(6) To take any action required or permitted by law to bring, pursue or settle or otherwise terminate a derivative action in the right of the limited partnership;

(7) To serve on a committee of the limited partnership or the limited partners or partners or to appoint, elect or otherwise participate in the choice of a representative or another person to serve on any such committee, and to act as a member of any such committee directly or by or through any such representative or other person;

(8) To act or cause the taking or refraining from the taking of any action, including by proposing, approving, consenting or disapproving, by voting or otherwise, with respect to 1 or more of the following matters:

a. The dissolution and winding up of the limited partnership or an election to continue the limited partnership or an election to continue the business of the limited partnership;

b. The sale, exchange, lease, mortgage, assignment, pledge or other transfer of, or granting of a security interest in, any asset or assets of the limited partnership;

c. The incurrence, renewal, refinancing or payment or other discharge of indebtedness by the limited partnership;

d. A change in the nature of the business;

e. The admission, removal or retention of a general partner;

f. The admission, removal or retention of a limited partner;

g. A transaction or other matter involving an actual or potential conflict of interest;

h. An amendment to the partnership agreement or certificate of limited partnership;

i. The merger or consolidation of a limited partnership;

j. In respect of a limited partnership which is registered as an investment company under the Investment Company Act of 1940, as amended [15 U.S.C. §80a-1 et seq.], any matter required by the Investment Company Act of 1940, as amended, or the rules and regulations of the Securities and Exchange Commission thereunder, to be approved by the holders of beneficial interests in an investment company, including the electing of directors or trustees of the investment company, the approving or terminating of investment advisory or underwriting contracts and the approving of auditors;

k. The indemnification of any partner or other person;

l. The making of, or calling for, or the making of other determinations in connection with, contributions;

m. The making of, or the making of other determinations in connection with or concerning, investments, including investments in property, whether real, personal or mixed, either directly or indirectly, by the limited partnership;

n. The nomination, appointment, election or other manner of selection or removal of an independent contractor for, or an agent or employee of, the limited partnership or a general partner, or an officer, director or stockholder of a corporate general partner, or a partner of a partnership which is a general partner, or a trustee, administrator, executor, custodian or other fiduciary or beneficiary of an estate or trust which is a general partner, or a trustee, officer, advisor, stockholder or beneficiary of a business trust or a statutory trust which is a general partner, or a member or manager of a limited liability company which is a general partner, or a member of a governing body of, or a fiduciary for, any person, whether domestic or foreign, which is a general partner; or

o. Such other matters as are stated in the partnership agreement or in any other agreement or in writing;

(9) To serve on the board of directors or a committee of, to consult with or advise, to be an officer, director, stockholder, partner, member, manager, trustee, agent or employee of, or to be a fiduciary or contractor for, any person in which the limited partnership has an interest or any person providing management, consulting, advisory, custody or other services or products for, to or on behalf of, or otherwise having a business or other relationship with, the limited partnership or a general partner of the limited partnership; or

(10) Any right or power granted or permitted to limited partners under this chapter and not specifically enumerated in this subsection.

(c) The enumeration in subsection (b) of this section does not mean that the possession or exercise of any other powers or having or acting in other capacities by a limited partner constitutes participation by him or her in the control of the business of the limited partnership.

(d) A limited partner does not participate in the control of the business within the meaning of subsection (a) of this section by virtue of the fact that all or any part of the name of such limited partner is included in the name of the limited partnership.

(e) This section does not create rights or powers of limited partners. Such rights and powers may be created only by a certificate of limited partnership, a partnership agreement or any other agreement or in writing, or other sections of this chapter.

(f) A limited partner does not participate in the control of the business within the meaning of subsection (a) of this section regardless of the nature, extent, scope, number or frequency of the limited partner's possessing or, regardless of whether or not the limited partner has the rights or powers, exercising or attempting to exercise 1 or more of the rights or powers or having or, regardless of whether or not the limited partner has the rights or powers, acting or attempting to act in 1 or more of the capacities which are permitted under this section.

§17-304. Person erroneously believing himself or herself limited partner.

(a) Except as provided in subsection (b) of this section, a person who makes a contribution to a partnership and erroneously but in good faith believes that he or she has become a limited partner in the partnership is not a general partner in the partnership and is not bound by its obligations by reason of making the contribution, receiving distributions from the partnership or exercising any rights of a limited partner, if, within a reasonable time after ascertaining the mistake:

(1) In the case of a person who wishes to be a limited partner, he or she causes an appropriate certificate to be executed and filed; or

(2) In the case of a person who wishes to withdraw from the partnership, that person takes such action as may be necessary to withdraw.

(b) A person who makes a contribution under the circumstances described in subsection (a) of this section is liable as a general partner to any third party who transacts business with the partnership prior to the occurrence of either of the events referred to in subsection (a) of this section:

(1) If such person knew or should have known either that no certificate has been filed or that the certificate inaccurately refers to the person as a general partner; and

(2) If the third party actually believed in good faith that such person was a general partner at the time of the transaction, acted in reasonable reliance on such belief and extended credit to the partnership in reasonable reliance on the credit of such person.

§17-305. Access to and confidentiality of information; records.

(a) Each limited partner, in person or by attorney or other agent, has the right, subject to such reasonable standards (including standards governing what information and documents are to be furnished, at what time and location and at whose expense) as may be set forth in the partnership agreement or otherwise established by the general partners, to obtain from the general partners from time to time upon reasonable demand for any purpose reasonably related to the limited partner's interest as a limited partner:

(1) True and full information regarding the status of the business and financial condition of the limited partnership;

(2) Promptly after becoming available, a copy of the limited partnership's federal, state and local income tax returns for each year;

(3) A current list of the name and last known business, residence or mailing address of each partner;

(4) A copy of any written partnership agreement and certificate of limited partnership and all amendments thereto, together with executed copies of any written powers of attorney pursuant to which the partnership agreement and any certificate and all amendments thereto have been executed;

(5) True and full information regarding the amount of cash and a description and statement of the agreed value of any other property or services contributed by each partner and which each partner has agreed to contribute in the future, and the date on which each became a partner; and

(6) Other information regarding the affairs of the limited partnership as is just and reasonable.

(b) A general partner shall have the right to keep confidential from limited partners for such period of time as the general partner deems reasonable, any information which the general partner reasonably believes to be in the nature of trade secrets or other information the disclosure of which the general partner in good faith believes is not in the best interest of the limited partnership or could damage the limited partnership or its business or which the limited partnership is required by law or by agreement with a third party to keep confidential.

(c) A limited partnership may maintain its records in other than paper form, including on, by means of, or in the form of any information storage device, method, or 1 or more electronic networks or databases (including 1 or more distributed electronic networks or databases), if such form is capable of conversion into paper form within a reasonable time.

(d) Any demand under this section shall be in writing and shall state the purpose of such demand. In every instance where an attorney or other agent shall be the person who seeks the right to obtain the information described in subsection (a) of this section, the demand shall be accompanied by a power of attorney or such other writing which authorizes the attorney or other agent to so act on behalf of the limited partner.

(e) Any action to enforce any right arising under this section shall be brought in the Court of Chancery. If a general partner refuses to permit a limited partner, or attorney or other agent acting for the limited partner, to obtain from the general partner the information described in subsection (a) of this section or does not reply to the demand that has been made within 5 business days (or such shorter or longer period of time as is provided for in a partnership agreement but not longer than 30 business days) after the demand has been made, the limited partner may apply to the Court of Chancery for an order to compel such disclosure. The Court of Chancery is hereby vested with exclusive jurisdiction to determine whether or not the person seeking such information is entitled to the information sought. The Court of Chancery may summarily order the general partner to permit the limited partner to obtain the information described in subsection (a) of this section and to make copies or abstracts therefrom, or the Court of Chancery may summarily order the general partner to furnish to the limited partner the information described in subsection (a) of this section on the condition that the limited partner first pay to the limited partnership the reasonable cost of obtaining and furnishing such information and on such other conditions as the Court of Chancery deems appropriate. When a limited partner seeks to obtain the information described in subsection (a) of this section, the limited partner shall first establish: (1) that the limited partner has complied with the provisions of this section respecting the form and manner of making demand for obtaining such information, and (2) that the information the limited partner seeks is reasonably related to the limited partner's interest as a limited partner. The Court of Chancery may, in its discretion, prescribe any limitations or conditions with reference to the obtaining of information, or award such other or further relief as the Court of Chancery may deem just and proper. The Court of Chancery may order books, documents and records, pertinent extracts therefrom, or duly authenticated copies thereof, to be brought within the State of Delaware and kept in the State of Delaware upon such terms and conditions as the order may prescribe.

(f) The rights of a limited partner to obtain information as provided in this section may be restricted in an original partnership agreement or in any subsequent amendment approved or adopted by all of the partners or in compliance with any applicable requirements of the partnership agreement. The provisions of this subsection shall not be construed to limit the ability to impose restrictions on the rights of a limited partner to obtain information by any other means permitted under this chapter.

(g) A limited partnership shall maintain a current record that identifies the name and last known business, residence, or mailing address of each partner.

§17-306. Remedies for breach of partnership agreement by limited partner.

A partnership agreement may provide that:

(1) A limited partner who fails to perform in accordance with, or to comply with the terms and conditions of, the partnership agreement shall be subject to specified penalties or specified consequences; and

(2) At the time or upon the happening of events specified in the partnership agreement, a limited partner shall be subject to specified penalties or specified consequences.

Such specified penalties or specified consequences may include and take the form of any penalty or consequence set forth in §17-502(c) of this title.

Subchapter IV. General Partners

§17-401. Admission of general partners.

(a) A person may be admitted to a limited partnership as a general partner of the limited partnership and may receive a partnership interest in the limited partnership without making a contribution or being obligated to make a contribution to the limited partnership. Unless otherwise provided in a partnership agreement, a person may be admitted to a limited partnership as a general partner of the limited partnership without acquiring a partnership interest in the limited partnership. Unless otherwise provided in a partnership agreement, a person may be admitted as the sole general partner of a limited partnership without making a contribution or being obligated to make a contribution to the limited partnership or without acquiring a partnership interest in the limited partnership. Nothing contained in this subsection shall affect the first sentence of §17-403(b) of this title.

(b) After the filing of a limited partnership's initial certificate of limited partnership, unless otherwise provided in the partnership agreement, additional general partners may be admitted only with the consent of each partner.

(c) Unless otherwise provided in a partnership agreement or another agreement, a general partner shall have no preemptive right to subscribe to any additional issue of partnership interests or another interest in a limited partnership.

§17-402. Events of withdrawal.

(a) A person ceases to be a general partner of a limited partnership upon the happening of any of the following events:

(1) The general partner withdraws from the limited partnership as provided in §17-602 of this title;

(2) The general partner ceases to be a general partner of the limited partnership as provided in §17-702 of this title;

(3) The general partner is removed as a general partner in accordance with the partnership agreement;

(4) Unless otherwise provided in the partnership agreement, or with the consent of all partners, the general partner:

a. Makes an assignment for the benefit of creditors;

b. Files a voluntary petition in bankruptcy;

c. Is adjudged a bankrupt or insolvent, or has entered against him or her an order for relief in any bankruptcy or insolvency proceeding;

d. Files a petition or answer seeking for himself or herself any reorganization, arrangement, composition, readjustment, liquidation, dissolution or similar relief under any statute, law or regulation;

e. Files an answer or other pleading admitting or failing to contest the material allegations of a petition filed against him or her in any proceeding of this nature; or

f. Seeks, consents to or acquiesces in the appointment of a trustee, receiver or liquidator of the general partner or of all or any substantial part of his or her properties;

(5) Unless otherwise provided in the partnership agreement, or with the consent of all partners, 120 days after the commencement of any proceeding against the general partner seeking reorganization, arrangement, composition, readjustment, liquidation, dissolution or similar relief under any statute, law or regulation, the proceeding has not been dismissed, or if within 90 days after the appointment without the general partner's consent or acquiescence of a trustee, receiver or liquidator of the general partner or of all or any substantial part of his or her properties, the appointment is not vacated or stayed, or within 90 days after the expiration of any such stay, the appointment is not vacated;

(6) In the case of a general partner who is a natural person:

a. The general partner's death; or

b. The entry by a court of competent jurisdiction adjudicating the general partner incompetent to manage his or her person or property;

(7) In the case of a general partner who is acting as a general partner by virtue of being a trustee of a trust, the termination of the trust (but not merely the substitution of a new trustee);

(8) In the case of a general partner that is a separate partnership, the dissolution and commencement of winding up of the separate partnership;

(9) In the case of a general partner that is a corporation, the filing of a certificate of dissolution, or its equivalent, for the corporation or the revocation of its charter and the expiration of 90 days after the date of notice to the corporation of revocation without a reinstatement of its charter;

(10) Unless otherwise provided in the partnership agreement, or with the consent of all partners, in the case of a general partner that is an estate, the distribution by the fiduciary of the estate's entire interest in the limited partnership;

(11) In the case of a general partner that is a limited liability company, the dissolution and commencement of winding up of the limited liability company; or

(12) In the case of a general partner who is not an individual, partnership, limited liability company, corporation, trust or estate, the termination of the general partner.

(b) A general partner who suffers an event that with the passage of the specified period becomes an event of withdrawal under paragraph (a)(4) or (5) of this section shall notify each other general partner, or in the event that there is no other general partner, each limited partner, of the occurrence of the event within 30 days after the date of occurrence of the event of withdrawal.

§17-403. General powers and liabilities.

(a) Except as provided in this chapter or in the partnership agreement, a general partner of a limited partnership has the rights and powers and is subject to the restrictions of a partner in a partnership that is governed by the Delaware Uniform Partnership Law in effect on July 11, 1999 (6 Del. C. §1501 et seq.).

(b) Except as provided in this chapter, a general partner of a limited partnership has the liabilities of a partner in a partnership that is governed by the Delaware Uniform Partnership Law in effect on July 11, 1999 (6 Del. C. §1501 et seq.) to persons other than the partnership and the other partners. Except as provided in this chapter or in the partnership agreement, a general partner of a limited partnership has the liabilities of a partner in a partnership that is governed by the Delaware Uniform Partnership Law in effect on July 11, 1999 (6 Del. C. §1501 et seq.) to the partnership and to the other partners.

(c) Unless otherwise provided in the partnership agreement, a general partner of a limited partnership has the power and authority to delegate to 1 or more other persons any or all of the general partner's rights, powers and duties to manage and control the business and affairs of the limited partnership. Any such delegation may be to agents, officers, and employees of the general partner or the limited partnership and by a management agreement or another agreement with, or otherwise to, other persons. Unless otherwise provided in the partnership agreement, such delegation by a general partner of a limited partnership shall be irrevocable if it states that it is irrevocable. Unless otherwise provided in the partnership agreement, such delegation by a general partner of a limited partnership shall not cause the general partner to cease to be a general partner of the limited partnership or cause the person to whom any such rights, powers and duties have been delegated to be a general partner of the limited partnership. No other provision of this chapter shall be construed to restrict a general partner's power and authority to delegate any or all of its rights, powers, and duties to manage and control the business and affairs of the limited partnership.

(d) A judgment creditor of a general partner of a limited partnership may not levy execution against the assets of the general partner to satisfy a judgment based on a claim against the limited partnership unless:

(1) A judgment based on the same claim has been obtained against the limited partnership and a writ of execution on the judgment has been returned unsatisfied in whole or in part;

(2) The limited partnership is a debtor in bankruptcy;

(3) The general partner has agreed that the creditor need not exhaust the assets of the limited partnership;

(4) A court grants permission to the judgment creditor to levy execution against the assets of the general partner based on a finding that the assets of the limited partnership that are subject to execution are clearly insufficient to satisfy the judgment, that exhaustion of the assets of the limited partnership is excessively burdensome, or that the grant of permission is an appropriate exercise of the court's equitable powers; or

(5) Liability is imposed on the general partner by law or contract independent of the existence of the limited partnership.

§17-404. Contributions by a general partner.

A general partner of a limited partnership may make contributions to the limited partnership and share in the profits and losses of, and in distributions from, the limited partnership as a general partner. A general partner also may make contributions to and share in profits, losses and distributions as a limited partner. A person who is both a general partner and a limited partner has the rights and powers, and is subject to the restrictions and liabilities, of a general partner and, except as provided in the partnership agreement, also has the rights and powers, and is subject to the restrictions, of a limited partner to the extent of his or her participation in the partnership as a limited partner.

§17-405. Classes and voting.

(a) A partnership agreement may provide for classes or groups of general partners having such relative rights, powers and duties as the partnership agreement may provide, and may make provision for the future creation in the manner provided in the partnership agreement of additional classes or groups of general partners having such relative rights, powers and duties as may from time to time be established, including rights, powers and duties senior to existing classes and groups of general partners. A partnership agreement may provide for the taking of an action, including the amendment of the partnership agreement, without the vote or approval of any general partner or class or group of general partners, including an action to create under the provisions of the partnership agreement a class or group of partnership interests that was not previously outstanding.

(b) The partnership agreement may grant to all or certain identified general partners or a specified class or group of the general partners the right to vote, separately or with all or any class or group of the limited partners or the general partners, on any matter. Voting by general partners may be on a per capita, number, financial interest, class, group or any other basis.

(c) A partnership agreement may set forth provisions relating to notice of the time, place or purpose of any meeting at which any matter is to be voted on by any general partner, waiver of any such notice, action by consent without a meeting, the establishment of a record date, quorum requirements, voting in person or by proxy, or any other matter with respect to the exercise of any such right to vote.

(d) Unless otherwise provided in a partnership agreement, meetings of general partners may be held by means of conference telephone or other communications equipment by means of which all persons participating in the meeting can hear each other, and participation in a meeting pursuant to this subsection shall constitute presence in person at the meeting. Unless otherwise provided in a partnership agreement, on any matter that is to be voted on, consented to or approved by general partners, the general partners may take such action without a meeting, without prior notice and without a vote if consented to or approved, in writing, by electronic transmission or by any other means permitted by law, by general partners having not less than the minimum number of votes that would be necessary to authorize or take such action at a meeting at which all general partners entitled to vote thereon were present and voted. Unless otherwise provided in a partnership agreement, if a person (whether or not then a general partner) consenting as a general partner to any matter provides that such consent will be effective at a future time (including a time determined upon the happening of an event), then such person shall be deemed to have consented as a general partner at such future time so long as such person is then a general partner. Unless otherwise provided in a partnership agreement, on any matter that is to be voted on by general partners, the general partners may vote in person or by proxy, and such proxy may be granted in writing, by means of electronic transmission or as otherwise permitted by applicable law. Unless otherwise provided in a partnership agreement, a consent transmitted by electronic transmission by a general partner or by a person or persons authorized to act for a general partner shall be deemed to be written and signed for purposes of this subsection (d).

§17-406. Remedies for breach of partnership agreement by general partner.

A partnership agreement may provide that (1) a general partner who fails to perform in accordance with, or to comply with the terms and conditions of, the partnership agreement shall be subject to specified penalties or specified consequences, and (2) at the time or upon the happening of events specified in the partnership agreement, a general partner shall be subject to specified penalties or specified consequences. Such specified penalties or specified consequences may include and take the form of any penalty or consequence set forth in §17-502(c) of this title.

§17-407. Reliance on reports and information by limited partners, liquidating trustees, and general partners.

(a) A limited partner or liquidating trustee of a limited partnership shall be fully protected in relying in good faith upon the records of the limited partnership and upon information, opinions, reports or statements presented by a general partner of the limited partnership, an officer or employee of a general partner of the limited partnership, another liquidating trustee, or committees of the limited partnership, limited partners or partners, or by any other person as to matters the limited partner or liquidating trustee reasonably believes are within such other person's professional or expert competence, including information, opinions, reports or statements as to the value and amount of the assets, liabilities, profits or losses of the limited partnership, or the value and amount of assets or reserves or contracts, agreements or other undertakings that would be sufficient to pay claims and obligations of the limited partnership or to make reasonable provision to pay such claims and obligations, or any other facts pertinent to the existence and amount of assets from which distributions to partners or creditors might properly be paid.

(b) A general partner of a limited liability limited partnership shall be fully protected in relying in good faith upon the records of the limited partnership and upon information, opinions, reports or statements presented by another general partner of the limited partnership, an officer or employee of the limited partnership, a liquidating trustee, or committees of the limited partnership, limited partners or partners, or by any other person as to matters the general partner reasonably believes are within such other person's professional or expert competence, including information, opinions, reports or statements as to the value and amount of the assets, liabilities, profits or losses of the limited partnership, or the value and amount of assets or reserves or contracts, agreements or other undertakings that would be sufficient to pay claims and obligations of the limited partnership or to make reasonable provision to pay such claims and obligations, or any other facts pertinent to the existence and amount of assets from which distributions to partners or creditors might properly be paid.

(c) A general partner of a limited partnership that is not a limited liability limited partnership shall be fully protected from liability to the limited partnership, its partners or other persons party to or otherwise bound by the partnership agreement in relying in good faith upon the records of the limited partnership and upon information, opinions, reports or statements presented by another general partner of the limited partnership, an officer or employee of the limited partnership, a liquidating trustee, or committees of the limited partnership, limited partners or partners, or by any other person as to matters the general partner reasonably believes are within such other person's professional or expert competence, including information, opinions, reports or statements as to the value and amount of the assets, liabilities, profits or losses of the limited partnership, or the value and amount of assets or reserves or contracts, agreements or other undertakings that would be sufficient to pay claims and obligations of the limited partnership or to make reasonable provision to pay such claims and obligations, or any other facts pertinent to the existence and amount of assets from which distributions to partners or creditors might properly be paid.

SUBCHAPTER V. FINANCE

§17-501. Form of contribution.

The contribution of a partner may be in cash, property or services rendered, or a promissory note or other obligation to contribute cash or property or to perform services.

§17-502. Liability for contribution.

(a) (1) Except as provided in the partnership agreement, a partner is obligated to the limited partnership to perform any promise to contribute cash or property or to perform services, even if that partner is unable to perform because of death, disability or any other reason. If a partner does not make the required contribution of property or services, he or she is obligated at the option of the limited partnership to contribute cash equal to that portion of the agreed value (as stated in the records of the limited partnership) of the contribution that has not been made.

(2) The foregoing option shall be in addition to, and not in lieu of, any other rights, including the right to specific performance, that the limited partnership may have against such partner under the partnership agreement or applicable law.

(b) (1) Unless otherwise provided in the partnership agreement, the obligation of a partner to make a contribution or return money or other property paid or distributed in violation of this chapter may be compromised only by consent of all the partners. Notwithstanding the compromise, a creditor of a limited partnership who extends credit, after the entering into of a partnership agreement or an amendment thereto which, in either case, reflects the obligation, and before the amendment thereof to reflect the compromise, may enforce the original obligation to the extent that, in extending credit, the creditor reasonably relied on the obligation of a partner to make a contribution or return.

(2) A conditional obligation of a partner to make a contribution or return money or other property to a limited partnership may not be enforced unless the conditions to the obligation have been satisfied or waived as to or by such partner. Conditional obligations include contributions payable upon a discretionary call of a limited partnership or a general partner prior to the time the call occurs.

(c) A partnership agreement may provide that the interest of any partner who fails to make any contribution that he or she is obligated to make shall be subject to specified penalties for, or specified consequences of, such failure. Such penalty or consequence may take the form of reducing or eliminating the defaulting partner's proportionate interest in the limited partnership, subordinating the partnership interest to that of nondefaulting partners, a forced sale of his or her partnership interest, forfeiture of that partnership interest, the lending by other partners of the amount necessary to meet his or her commitment, a fixing of the value of that partnership interest by appraisal or by formula and redemption or sale of the partnership interest at such value, or other penalty or consequence.

§17-503. Allocation of profits and losses.

The profits and losses of a limited partnership shall be allocated among the partners, and among classes or groups of partners, in the manner provided in the partnership agreement. If the partnership agreement does not so provide, profits and losses shall be allocated on the basis of the agreed value (as stated in the records of the limited partnership) of the contributions made by each partner to the extent they have been received by the limited partnership and have not been returned.

§17-504. Allocation of distributions.

Distributions of cash or other assets of a limited partnership shall be allocated among the partners, and among classes or groups of partners, in the manner provided in the partnership agreement. If the partnership agreement does not so provide, distributions shall be made on the basis of the agreed value (as stated in the records of the limited partnership) of the contributions made by each partner to the extent they have been received by the limited partnership and have not been returned.

§17-505. Defense of usury not available.

No obligation of a partner of a limited partnership to the limited partnership, or to a partner of the limited partnership, arising under the partnership agreement or a separate agreement or writing, and no note, instrument or other writing evidencing any such obligation of a partner, shall be subject to the defense of usury, and no partner shall interpose the defense of usury with respect to any such obligation in any action.

Subchapter VI. Distributions and Withdrawal

§17-601. Interim distributions.

Except as provided in this subchapter, to the extent and at the times or upon the happening of the events specified in the partnership agreement, a partner is entitled to receive from a limited partnership distributions before withdrawing from the limited partnership and before the dissolution and winding up thereof.

§17-602. Withdrawal of general partner and assignment of general partner's partnership interest.

(a) A general partner may withdraw from a limited partnership at the time or upon the happening of events specified in the partnership agreement and in accordance with the partnership agreement. A partnership agreement may provide that a general partner shall not have the right to withdraw as a general partner of a limited partnership. Notwithstanding that a partnership agreement provides that a general partner does not have the right to withdraw as a general partner of a limited partnership, a general partner may withdraw from a limited partnership at any time by giving written notice to the other partners. If the withdrawal of a general partner violates a partnership agreement, in addition to any remedies otherwise available under applicable law, the limited partnership may recover from the withdrawing general partner damages for breach of the partnership agreement and offset the damages against the amount otherwise distributable to the withdrawing general partner.

(b) Notwithstanding anything to the contrary set forth in this chapter, a partnership agreement may provide that a general partner may not assign a partnership interest in a limited partnership prior to the dissolution and winding up of the limited partnership.

§17-603. Withdrawal of limited partner.

A limited partner may withdraw from a limited partnership only at the time or upon the happening of events specified in the partnership agreement and in accordance with the partnership agreement. Notwithstanding anything to the contrary under applicable law, unless a partnership agreement provides otherwise, a limited partner may not withdraw from a limited partnership prior to the dissolution and winding up of the limited partnership. Notwithstanding anything to the contrary under applicable law, a partnership agreement may provide that a partnership interest may not be assigned prior to the dissolution and winding up of the limited partnership.

Unless otherwise provided in a partnership agreement, a limited partnership whose original certificate of limited partnership was filed with the Secretary of State and effective on or prior to July 31, 1996, shall continue to be governed by this section as in effect on July 31, 1996.

§17-604. Distribution upon withdrawal.

Except as provided in this subchapter, upon withdrawal any withdrawing partner is entitled to receive any distribution to which such partner is entitled under a partnership agreement and, if not otherwise provided in a partnership agreement, such partner is entitled to receive, within a reasonable time after withdrawal, the fair value of such partner's partnership interest in the limited partnership as of the date of withdrawal based upon such partner's right to share in distributions from the limited partnership.

§17-605. Distribution in kind.

Except as provided in the partnership agreement, a partner, regardless of the nature of the partner's contribution, has no right to demand and receive any distribution from a limited partnership in any form other than cash. Except as provided in the partnership agreement, a partner may not be compelled to accept a distribution of any asset in kind from a limited partnership to the extent that the percentage of the asset distributed exceeds a percentage of that asset which is equal to the percentage in which the partner shares in distributions from the limited partnership. Except as provided in the partnership agreement, a partner may be compelled to accept a distribution of any asset in kind from a limited partnership to the extent that the percentage of the asset distributed is equal to a percentage of that asset which is equal to the percentage in which the partner shares in distributions from the limited partnership.

§17-606. Right to distribution.

(a) Subject to §§17-607 and 17-804 of this title, and unless otherwise provided in the partnership agreement, at the time a partner becomes entitled to receive a distribution, he or she has the status of, and is entitled to all remedies available to, a creditor of the limited partnership with respect to the distribution.

(b) A partnership agreement may provide for the establishment of a record date with respect to allocations and distributions by a limited partnership.

§17-607. Limitations on distribution.

(a) A limited partnership shall not make a distribution to a partner to the extent that at the time of the distribution, after giving effect to the distribution, all liabilities of the limited partnership, other than liabilities to partners on account of their partnership interests and liabilities for which the recourse of creditors is limited to specified property of the limited partnership, exceed the fair value of the assets of the limited partnership, except that the fair value of property that is subject to a liability for which the recourse of creditors is limited shall be included in the assets of the limited partnership only to the extent that the fair value of that property exceeds that liability. For purposes of this subsection (a), the term "distribution" shall not include amounts constituting reasonable compensation for present or past services or reasonable payments made in the ordinary course of business pursuant to a bona fide retirement plan or other benefits program.

(b) A limited partner who receives a distribution in violation of subsection (a) of this section, and who knew at the time of the distribution that the distribution violated subsection (a) of this section, shall be liable to the limited partnership for the amount of the distribution. A limited partner who receives a distribution in violation of subsection (a) of this section, and who did not know at the time of the distribution that the distribution violated subsection (a) of this section, shall not be liable for the amount of the distribution. Subject to subsection (c) of this section, this subsection shall not affect any obligation or liability of a limited partner under an agreement or other applicable law for the amount of a distribution.

(c) Unless otherwise agreed, a limited partner who receives a distribution from a limited partnership shall have no liability under this chapter or other applicable law for the amount of the distribution after the expiration of 3 years from the date of the distribution.

Subchapter VII. Assignment of Partnership Interests

§17-701. Nature of partnership interest.

A partnership interest is personal property. A partner has no interest in specific limited partnership property.

§17-702. Assignment of partnership interest.

(a) Unless otherwise provided in the partnership agreement:

(1) A partnership interest is assignable in whole or in part;

(2) An assignment of a partnership interest does not dissolve a limited partnership or entitle the assignee to become or to exercise any rights or powers of a partner;

(3) An assignment of a partnership interest entitles the assignee to share in such profits and losses, to receive such distribution or distributions, and to receive such allocation of income, gain, loss, deduction, or credit or similar item to which the assignor was entitled, to the extent assigned; and

(4) A partner ceases to be a partner and to have the power to exercise any rights or powers of a partner upon assignment of all of its partnership interests. Unless otherwise provided in a partnership agreement, the pledge of, or granting of a security interest, lien or other encumbrance in or against, any or all of the partnership interest of a partner shall not cause the partner to cease to be a partner or to have the power to exercise any rights or powers of a partner.

(b) Unless otherwise provided in a partnership agreement, a partner's interest in a limited partnership may be evidenced by a certificate of partnership interest issued by the limited partnership. A partnership agreement may provide for the assignment or transfer of any partnership interest represented by such a certificate and make other provisions with respect to such certificates. A limited partnership shall not have the power to issue a certificate of partnership interest in bearer form.

(c) Unless otherwise provided in a partnership agreement and except to the extent assumed by agreement, until an assignee of a partnership interest becomes a partner, the assignee shall have no liability as a partner solely as a result of the assignment.

(d) Unless otherwise provided in the partnership agreement, a limited partnership may acquire, by purchase, redemption or otherwise, any partnership interest or other interest of a partner in the limited partnership. Unless otherwise provided in the partnership agreement, any such interest so acquired by the limited partnership shall be deemed canceled.

§17-703. *Partner's partnership interest subject to charging order.*

(a) On application by a judgment creditor of a partner or of a partner's assignee, a court having jurisdiction may charge the partnership interest of the judgment debtor to satisfy the judgment. To the extent so charged, the judgment creditor has only the right to receive any distribution or distributions to which the judgment debtor would otherwise have been entitled in respect of such partnership interest.

(b) A charging order constitutes a lien on the judgment debtor's partnership interest.

(c) This chapter does not deprive a partner or partner's assignee of a right under exemption laws with respect to the judgment debtor's partnership interest.

(d) The entry of a charging order is the exclusive remedy by which a judgment creditor of a partner or of a partner's assignee may satisfy a judgment out of the judgment debtor's partnership interest and attachment, garnishment, foreclosure or other legal or equitable remedies are not available to the judgment creditor.

(e) No creditor of a partner or of a partner's assignee shall have any right to obtain possession of, or otherwise exercise legal or equitable remedies with respect to, the property of the limited partnership.

(f) The Court of Chancery shall have jurisdiction to hear and determine any matter relating to any such charging order.

§17-704. *Right of assignee to become limited partner.*

(a) An assignee of a partnership interest, including an assignee of a general partner, becomes a limited partner:

(1) As provided in the partnership agreement; or

(2) Unless otherwise provided in the partnership agreement, upon the vote or consent of all partners.

(b) An assignee who has become a limited partner has, to the extent assigned, the rights and powers, and is subject to the restrictions and liabilities, of a limited partner under the partnership agreement and this chapter. Notwithstanding the foregoing, unless otherwise provided in the partnership agreement, an assignee who becomes a limited partner is liable for the obligations of his or her assignor to make contributions as provided in §17-502 of this title, but shall not be liable for the obligations of the assignor under subchapter VI of this chapter. However, the assignee is not obligated for liabilities, including the obligations of the assignor to make contributions as provided in §17-502 of this title, unknown to the assignee at the time the assignee became a limited partner and which could not be ascertained from the partnership agreement.

(c) Whether or not an assignee of a partnership interest becomes a limited partner, the assignor is not released from liability to the limited partnership under subchapters V and VI of this chapter.

§17-705. Powers of estate of deceased or incompetent partner.

If a partner who is an individual dies or a court of competent jurisdiction adjudges the partner to be incompetent to manage the partner's person or property, the partner's personal representative may exercise all of the partner's rights for the purpose of settling the partner's estate or administering the partner's property, including any power under the partnership agreement of an assignee to become a limited partner. If a partner is a corporation, trust or other entity and is dissolved or terminated, the powers of that partner may be exercised by its personal representative.

SUBCHAPTER VIII. DISSOLUTION

§17-801. Nonjudicial dissolution.

A limited partnership is dissolved and its affairs shall be wound up upon the first to occur of the following:

(1) At the time specified in a partnership agreement, but if no such time is set forth in the partnership agreement, then the limited partnership shall have a perpetual existence;

(2) Unless otherwise provided in a partnership agreement, upon the vote or consent of (i) all general partners and (ii) limited partners who own more than 2/3 of the then-current percentage or other interest in the profits of the limited partnership owned by all of the limited partners;

(3) An event of withdrawal of a general partner unless at the time there is at least 1 other general partner and the partnership agreement permits the business of the limited partnership to be carried on by the remaining general partner and that partner does so, but the limited partnership is not dissolved and is not required to be wound up by reason of any event of withdrawal if (i) within 90 days or such other period as is provided for in a partnership agreement after the withdrawal either (A) if provided for in the partnership agreement, the then-current percentage or other interest in the profits of the limited partnership specified in the partnership agreement owned by the remaining partners agree or vote to continue the business of the limited partnership and to appoint, effective as of the date of withdrawal, 1 or more additional general partners if necessary or desired, or (B) if no such right to agree or vote to continue the business of the limited partnership and to appoint 1 or more additional general partners

is provided for in the partnership agreement, then more than 50 percent of the then-current percentage or other interest in the profits of the limited partnership owned by the remaining partners agree or vote to continue the business of the limited partnership and to appoint, effective as of the date of withdrawal, 1 or more additional general partners if necessary or desired, or (ii) the business of the limited partnership is continued pursuant to a right to continue stated in the partnership agreement and the appointment, effective as of the date of withdrawal, of 1 or more additional general partners if necessary or desired;

(4) At the time there are no limited partners; provided, that the limited partnership is not dissolved and is not required to be wound up if:

a. Unless otherwise provided in a partnership agreement, within 90 days or such other period as is provided for in the partnership agreement after the occurrence of the event that caused the last remaining limited partner to cease to be a limited partner, the personal representative of the last remaining limited partner and all of the general partners agree or vote to continue the business of the limited partnership and to the admission of the personal representative of such limited partner or its nominee or designee to the limited partnership as a limited partner, effective as of the occurrence of the event that caused the last remaining limited partner to cease to be a limited partner; provided, that a partnership agreement may provide that the general partners or the personal representative of the last remaining limited partner shall be obligated to agree to continue the business of the limited partnership and to the admission of the personal representative of such limited partner or its nominee or designee to the limited partnership as a limited partner, effective as of the occurrence of the event that caused the last limited partner to cease to be a limited partner; or

b. A limited partner is admitted to the limited partnership in the manner provided for in the partnership agreement, effective as of the occurrence of the event that caused the last remaining limited partner to cease to be a limited partner, within 90 days or such other period as is provided for in the partnership agreement after the occurrence of the event that caused the last remaining limited partner to cease to be a limited partner, pursuant to a provision of the partnership agreement that specifically provides for the admission of a limited partner to the limited partnership after there is no longer a remaining limited partner of the limited partnership.

(5) Upon the happening of events specified in a partnership agreement; or

(6) Entry of a decree of judicial dissolution under §17-802 of this title.

Unless otherwise provided in a partnership agreement, a limited partnership whose original certificate of limited partnership was filed with the Secretary of State and effective on or prior to July 31, 2015, shall continue to be governed by clause (ii) of paragraph (2) of this section and clause (i)(B) of paragraph (3) of this section as in effect on July 31, 2015 (except that "in writing" shall be deleted from such clause (i)(B) of paragraph (3) of this section).

§17-802. Judicial dissolution.

On application by or for a partner the Court of Chancery may decree dissolution of a limited partnership whenever it is not reasonably practicable to carry on the business in conformity with the partnership agreement.

§17-803. Winding up.

(a) Unless otherwise provided in the partnership agreement, the general partners who have not wrongfully dissolved a limited partnership or, if none, the limited partners, or a person approved by the limited partners, in either case, by limited partners who own more than 50 percent of the then current percentage or other interest in the profits of the limited partnership owned by all of the limited partners may wind up the limited partnership's affairs; but the Court of Chancery, upon cause shown, may wind up the limited partnership's affairs upon application of any partner, the partner's personal representative or assignee, and in connection therewith, may appoint a liquidating trustee. Unless otherwise provided in a partnership agreement, a limited partnership whose original certificate of limited partnership was filed with the Secretary of State and effective on or prior to July 31, 2015, shall continue to be governed by this subsection as in effect on July 31, 2015.

(b) Upon dissolution of a limited partnership and until the filing of a certificate of cancellation as provided in §17-203 of this title, the persons winding up the limited partnership's affairs may, in the name of, and for and on behalf of, the limited partnership, prosecute and defend suits, whether civil, criminal or administrative, gradually settle and close the limited partnership's business, dispose of and convey the limited partnership's property, discharge or make reasonable provision for the limited partnership's liabilities, and distribute to the partners any remaining assets of the limited partnership, all without affecting the liability of limited partners and without imposing the liability of a general partner on a liquidating trustee.

§17-804. Distribution of assets.

(a) Upon the winding up of a limited partnership, the assets shall be distributed as follows:

(1) To creditors, including partners who are creditors, to the extent otherwise permitted by law, in satisfaction of liabilities of the limited partnership (whether by payment or the making of reasonable provision for payment thereof) other than liabilities for which reasonable provision for payment has been made and liabilities for distributions to partners and former partners under §17-601 or §17-604 of this title;

(2) Unless otherwise provided in the partnership agreement, to partners and former partners in satisfaction of liabilities for distributions under §17-601 or §17-604 of this title; and

(3) Unless otherwise provided in the partnership agreement, to partners first for the return of their contributions and second respecting their partnership interests, in the proportions in which the partners share in distributions.

(b) A limited partnership which has dissolved:

(1) Shall pay or make reasonable provision to pay all claims and obligations, including all contingent, conditional or unmatured contractual claims, known to the limited partnership;

(2) Shall make such provision as will be reasonably likely to be sufficient to provide compensation for any claim against the limited partnership which is the

subject of a pending action, suit or proceeding to which the limited partnership is a party and

(3) Shall make such provision as will be reasonably likely to be sufficient to provide compensation for claims that have not been made known to the limited partnership or that have not arisen but that, based on facts known to the limited partnership, are likely to arise or to become known to the limited partnership within 10 years after the date of dissolution.

If there are sufficient assets, such claims and obligations shall be paid in full and any such provision for payment made shall be made in full. If there are insufficient assets, such claims and obligations shall be paid or provided for according to their priority and, among claims of equal priority, ratably to the extent of assets available therefor. Unless otherwise provided in the partnership agreement, any remaining assets shall be distributed as provided in this chapter. Any liquidating trustee winding up a limited partnership's affairs who has complied with this section shall not be personally liable to the claimants of the dissolved limited partnership by reason of such person's actions in winding up the limited partnership.

(c) A limited partner who receives a distribution in violation of subsection (a) of this section, and who knew at the time of the distribution that the distribution violated subsection (a) of this section, shall be liable to the limited partnership for the amount of the distribution. For purposes of the immediately preceding sentence, the term "distribution" shall not include amounts constituting reasonable compensation for present or past services or reasonable payments made in the ordinary course of business pursuant to a bona fide retirement plan or other benefits program. A limited partner who receives a distribution in violation of subsection (a) of this section, and who did not know at the time of the distribution that the distribution violated subsection (a) of this section, shall not be liable for the amount of the distribution. Subject to subsection (d) of this section, this subsection shall not affect any obligation or liability of a limited partner under an agreement or other applicable law for the amount of a distribution.

(d) Unless otherwise agreed, a limited partner who receives a distribution from a limited partnership to which this section applies shall have no liability under this chapter or other applicable law for the amount of the distribution after the expiration of 3 years from the date of the distribution.

(e) Section 17-607 of this title shall not apply to a distribution to which this section applies.

§17-805. Trustees or receivers for limited partnerships; appointment; powers; duties.

When the certificate of limited partnership of any limited partnership formed under this chapter shall be canceled by the filing of a certificate of cancellation pursuant to §17-203 of this title, the Court of Chancery, on application of any creditor or partner of the limited partnership, or any other person who shows good cause therefor, at any time, may either appoint 1 or more of the general partners of the limited partnership to be trustees, or appoint 1 or more persons to be receivers, of and for the limited partnership, to take charge of the limited partnership's property, and to collect the debts and property due and belonging to the limited partnership, with the power to prosecute and defend, in the name of the limited partnership, or otherwise, all such suits as may be necessary or proper for the purposes aforesaid, and to appoint an agent or agents under them, and to do all other acts which might be done by the limited partnership, if in being, that may be necessary for the final settlement of the unfinished business of the limited partnership. The powers of the trustees or receivers may be continued as long as the Court of Chancery shall think necessary for the purposes aforesaid.

§17-806. Revocation of dissolution.

If a partnership agreement provides the manner in which a dissolution may be revoked, it may be revoked in that manner and, unless a partnership agreement prohibits revocation of dissolution, then notwithstanding the occurrence of an event set forth in §17-801(1), (2), (3), (4) or (5) of this title, the limited partnership shall not be dissolved and its affairs shall not be wound up if, prior to the filing of a certificate of cancellation in the office of the Secretary of State, the business of the limited partnership is continued, effective as of the occurrence of such event:

(1) In the case of dissolution effected by the vote or consent of the partners or other persons, pursuant to such vote or consent (and the approval of any partners or other persons whose approval is required under the partnership agreement to revoke a dissolution contemplated by this paragraph);

(2) In the case of dissolution under §17-801(1) or (5) of this title (other than a dissolution effected by the vote or consent of the partners or other persons, an event of withdrawal of a general partner or the occurrence of an event that causes the last remaining limited partner to cease to be a limited partner), pursuant to such vote or consent that, pursuant to the terms of the partnership agreement, is required to amend the provision of the partnership agreement effecting such dissolution (and the approval of any partners or other persons whose approval is required under the partnership agreement to revoke a dissolution contemplated by this paragraph); and

(3) In the case of dissolution effected by an event of withdrawal of a general partner or the occurrence of an event that causes the last remaining limited partner to cease to be a limited partner, pursuant to the vote or consent of:

a. All remaining general partners; and

b. Limited partners who own more than ⅔ of the then-current percentage or other interest in the profits of the limited partnership owned by all of the limited partners, or if there is no remaining limited partner the personal representative of the last remaining limited partner of the limited partnership or the assignee of all of the limited partners' partnership interests in the limited partnership (and the approval of any partners or other persons whose approval is required under the partnership agreement to revoke a dissolution contemplated by this paragraph).

If dissolution is revoked pursuant to paragraph (3) of this section above and there is no remaining general partner of the limited partnership, 1 or more general partners shall be appointed, effective as of the date of withdrawal of the last remaining general partner, by the vote or consent of the limited partners of the limited partnership who own more than 2/3 of the then-current percentage or other interest in the profits of the limited partnership owned by all of the limited partners. If dissolution is revoked pursuant to paragraph (3) of this section above and there is no remaining limited partner of the limited partnership, a nominee or designee of such personal representative or such assignee, as applicable, shall be appointed as a limited partner, effective as of the occurrence of the event that caused the last remaining limited partner to cease to be a limited partner, by the vote or consent of the remaining general partners and such personal representative or such assignee, as applicable. If dissolution is revoked pursuant to paragraph (3) of this section above and there is no remaining general partner of the limited partnership and no remaining limited partner of the limited partnership, 1 or more general partners shall be appointed, effective as of the date of withdrawal of the last remaining general partner, and a nominee or designee of such personal representative or such assignee, as applicable, shall be appointed as a limited partner, effective as of the occurrence of the event that caused the last remaining limited partner to cease to be a limited partner, in each case, by the vote or consent of such personal representative or such assignee, as applicable. The provisions of this section shall not be construed to limit the accomplishment of a revocation of dissolution by other means permitted by law.

Subchapter X. Derivative Actions

§17-1001. Right to bring action.

A limited partner or an assignee of a partnership interest may bring an action in the Court of Chancery in the right of a limited partnership to recover a judgment in its favor if general partners with authority to do so have refused to bring the action or if an effort to cause those general partners to bring the action is not likely to succeed.

§17-1002. Proper plaintiff.

In a derivative action, the plaintiff must be a partner or an assignee of a partnership interest at the time of bringing the action and:

(1) At the time of the transaction of which the plaintiff complains; or

(2) The plaintiff's status as a partner or an assignee of a partnership interest had devolved upon the plaintiff by operation of law or pursuant to the terms of the partnership agreement from a person who was a partner or an assignee of a partnership interest at the time of the transaction.

§17-1003. Complaint.

In a derivative action, the complaint shall set forth with particularity the effort, if any, of the plaintiff to secure initiation of the action by a general partner or the reasons for not making the effort.

§17-1004. Expenses.

If a derivative action is successful, in whole or in part, as a result of a judgment, compromise or settlement of any such action, the court may award the plaintiff reasonable expenses, including reasonable attorney's fees, from any recovery in any such action or from a limited partnership.

Subchapter XI. Miscellaneous

§17-1101. Construction and application of chapter and partnership agreement.

(a) This chapter shall be so applied and construed to effectuate its general purpose to make uniform the law with respect to the subject of this chapter among states enacting it.

(b) The rule that statutes in derogation of the common law are to be strictly construed shall have no application to this chapter.

(c) It is the policy of this chapter to give maximum effect to the principle of freedom of contract and to the enforceability of partnership agreements.

(d) To the extent that, at law or in equity, a partner or other person has duties (including fiduciary duties) to a limited partnership or to another partner or to another person that is a party to or is otherwise bound by a partnership agreement, the partner's or other person's duties may be expanded or restricted or eliminated by provisions in the partnership agreement; provided that the partnership agreement may not eliminate the implied contractual covenant of good faith and fair dealing.

(e) Unless otherwise provided in a partnership agreement, a partner or other person shall not be liable to a limited partnership or to another partner or to another person that is a party to or is otherwise bound by a partnership agreement for breach of fiduciary duty for the partner's or other person's good faith reliance on the provisions of the partnership agreement.

(f) A partnership agreement may provide for the limitation or elimination of any and all liabilities for breach of contract and breach of duties (including fiduciary duties) of a partner or other person to a limited partnership or to another partner or to an other person that is a party to or is otherwise bound by a partnership agreement; provided, that a partnership agreement may not limit or eliminate liability for any act or omission that constitutes a bad faith violation of the implied contractual covenant of good faith and fair dealing.

(g) Sections 9-406 and 9-408 of this title do not apply to any interest in a limited partnership, including all rights, powers and interests arising under a partnership agreement or this chapter. This provision prevails over §§9-406 and 9-408 of this title.

(h) Action validly taken pursuant to 1 provision of this chapter shall not be deemed invalid solely because it is identical or similar in substance to an action that could have been taken pursuant to some other provision of this chapter but fails to satisfy 1 or more requirements prescribed by such other provision.

(i) A partnership agreement that provides for the application of Delaware law shall be governed by and construed under the laws of the State of Delaware in accordance with its terms.

§17-1102. Short title.

This chapter may be cited as the "Delaware Revised Uniform Limited Partnership Act."

§17-1103. Severability.

If any provision of this chapter or its application to any person or circumstances is held invalid, the invalidity does not affect other provisions or applications of the chapter which can be given effect without the invalid provision or application, and to this end the provisions of this chapter are severable.

§17-1105. Cases not provided for in this chapter.

In any case not provided for in this chapter, the Delaware Uniform Partnership Law in effect on July 11, 1999 [6 Del. C. §1501, et seq.] and the rules of law and equity, including the law merchant, shall govern.

§17-1106. Prior law.

Except as set forth in §17-1104 of this title, [former] Chapter 17 of this title is hereby repealed.

§17-1108. Reserved power of State of Delaware to alter or repeal chapter.

All provisions of this chapter may be altered from time to time or repealed and all rights of partners are subject to this reservation. Unless expressly stated to the contrary in this chapter, all amendments of this chapter shall apply to limited partnerships and partners whether or not existing as such at the time of the enactment of any such amendment.

§17-1109. Annual tax of domestic limited partnership and foreign limited partnership and registered series.

(a) Every domestic limited partnership and every foreign limited partnership registered to do business in the State of Delaware shall pay an annual tax, for the use of the State of Delaware, in the amount of $300. There shall be paid by or on behalf of each registered series of a domestic limited partnership an annual tax, for use of the State of Delaware, in the amount of $75 per registered series. . . .

Federal Securities Laws, Regulations, and Forms

Securities Act of 1933

15 U.S.C. §§77a et seq.

Act	15 U.S.C.	Section
1	77a	Short Title
2	77b	Definitions
2A	77b-1	Swap agreements
3	77c	Classes of Securities under this Subchapter
4	77d	Exempted Transactions
4A	77d-1	Requirements with Respect to Certain Small Transactions
5	77e	Prohibitions Relating to Interstate Commerce and the Mails
6	77f	Registration of Securities
7	77g	Information Required in Registration Statement
8	77h	Taking Effect of Registration Statements and Amendments Thereto
8A	77h-l	Cease-and-Desist Proceedings [omitted]
9	77i	Court Review of Orders [omitted]
10	77j	Information Required in Prospectus
11	77k	Civil Liabilities on Account of False Registration Statement
12	77l	Civil Liabilities Arising in Connection with Prospectuses and Communications
13	77m	Limitation of Actions
14	77n	Contrary Stipulations Void
15	77o	Liability of Controlling Persons
16	77p	Additional Remedies; Limitation on Remedies
17	77q	Fraudulent Interstate Transactions
18	77r	Exemption from State Regulation of Securities Offerings
18A	77r-1	Preemption of State law
19	77s	Special Powers of Commission
20	77t	Injunctions and Prosecution of Offenses [omitted]
21	77u	Hearings by Commission
22	77v	Jurisdiction of Offenses and Suits
23	77w	Unlawful Representations [omitted]
24	77x	Penalties
25	77y	Jurisdiction of Other Government Agencies Over Securities [omitted]

§1. Short Title

This subchapter may be cited as the "Securities Act of 1933."

§2. Definitions

(a) Definitions

When used in this subchapter, unless the context otherwise requires—

(1) The term "security" means any note, stock, treasury stock, security future, security based swap, bond, debenture, evidence of indebtedness, certificate of interest or participation in any profit-sharing agreement, collateral-trust certificate, preorganization certificate or subscription, transferable share, investment contract, voting-trust certificate, certificate of deposit for a security, fractional undivided interest in oil, gas, or other mineral rights, any put, call, straddle, option, or privilege on any security, certificate of deposit, or group or index of securities (including any interest therein or based on the value thereof), or any put, call, straddle, option, or privilege entered into on a national securities exchange relating to foreign currency, or, in general, any interest or instrument commonly known as a "security," or any certificate of interest or participation in, temporary or interim certificate for, receipt for, guarantee of, or warrant or right to subscribe to or purchase, any of the foregoing. . . .

(3) The term "sale" or "sell" shall include every contract of sale or disposition of a security or interest in a security, for value. The term "offer to sell," "offer for sale," or "offer" shall include every attempt or offer to dispose of, or solicitation of an offer to buy, a security or interest in a security, for value. The terms defined in this paragraph and the term "offer to buy" as used in subsection (c) of section 5 of this title shall not include preliminary negotiations or agreements between an issuer (or any person directly or indirectly controlling or controlled by an issuer, or under direct or indirect common control with an issuer) and any underwriter or among underwriters who are or are to be in privity of contract with an issuer (or any person directly or indirectly controlling or controlled by an issuer, or under direct or indirect common control with an issuer). Any security given or delivered with, or as a bonus on account of, any purchase of securities or any other thing, shall be conclusively presumed to constitute a part of the subject of such purchase and to have been offered and sold for value. The issue or transfer of a right or privilege, when originally issued or transferred with a security, giving the holder of such security the right to convert such security into another security of the same issuer or of another person, or giving a right to subscribe to another security of the same issuer or

of another person, which right cannot be exercised until some future date, shall not be deemed to be an offer or sale of such other security; but the issue or transfer of such other security upon the exercise of such right of conversion or subscription shall be deemed a sale of such other security. Any offer or sale of a security-based swap by or on behalf of the issuer of the securities upon which such security-based swap is based or is referenced, an affiliate of the issuer, or an underwriter, shall constitute a contract for sale of, sale of, offer for sale, or offer to sell such securities. The publication or distribution by a broker or dealer of a research report about an emerging growth company that is the subject of a proposed public offering of the common equity securities of such emerging growth company pursuant to a registration statement that the issuer proposes to file, or has filed, or that is effective shall be deemed for purposes of paragraph (10) of this subsection and section 5(c) not to constitute an offer for sale or offer to sell a security, even if the broker or dealer is participating or will participate in the registered offering of the securities of the issuer. As used in this paragraph, the term "research report" means a written, electronic, or oral communication that includes information, opinions, or recommendations with respect to securities of an issuer or an analysis of a security or an issuer, whether or not it provides information reasonably sufficient upon which to base an investment decision.

(4) The term "issuer" means every person who issues or proposes to issue any security; except that with respect to certificates of deposit, voting-trusts certificates, or collateral-trust certificates, or with respect to certificates of interest or shares in an unincorporated investment trust not having a board of directors (or persons performing similar functions) or of the fixed, restricted management, or unit type, the term "issuer" means the person or persons performing the acts and assuming the duties of depositor or manager pursuant to the provisions of the trust or other agreement or instrument under which such securities are issued; except that in the case of an unincorporated association which provides by its articles for limited liability of any or all of its members, or in the case of a trust, committee, or other legal entity, the trustees or members thereof shall not be individually liable as issuers of any security issued by the association, trust, committee, or other legal entity; except that with respect to equipment-trust certificates or like securities, the term "issuer" means the person by whom the equipment or property is or is to be used; and except that with respect to fractional undivided interests in oil, gas, or other mineral rights, the term "issuer" means the owner of any such right or of any interest in such right (whether whole or fractional) who creates fractional interests therein for the purpose of public offering.

(5) The term "Commission" means the Securities and Exchange Commission. . . .

(7) The term "interstate commerce" means trade or commerce in securities or any transportation or communication relating thereto among the several States or between the District of Columbia or any Territory of the United States and any State or other Territory, or between any foreign country and any State, Territory, or the District of Columbia, or within the District of Columbia.

(8) The term "registration statement" means the statement provided for in section 6 of this title, and includes any amendment thereto and any report, document, or memorandum filed as part of such statement or incorporated therein by reference.

(9) The term "write" or "written" shall include printed, lithographed, or any means of graphic communication.

(10) The term "prospectus" means any prospectus, notice, circular, advertisement, letter, or communication, written or by radio or television, which offers any security for sale or confirms the sale of any security; except that (a) a communication sent or given after the effective date of the registration statement (other than a prospectus permitted under subsection (b) of section 10 of this title) shall not be deemed a prospectus if it is proved that prior to or at the same time with such communication a written prospectus meeting the requirements of subsection (a) of section 10 of this title at the time of such communication was sent or given to the person to whom the communication was made, and (b) a notice, circular, advertisement, letter, or communication in respect of a security shall not be deemed to be a prospectus if it states from whom a written prospectus meeting the requirements of section 10 of this title may be obtained and, in addition, does no more than identify the security, state the price thereof, state by whom orders will be executed, and contain such other information as the Commission, by rules or regulations deemed necessary or appropriate in the public interest and for the protection of investors, and subject to such terms and conditions as may be prescribed therein, may permit.

(11) The term "underwriter" means any person who has purchased from an issuer with a view to, or offers or sells for an issuer in connection with, the distribution of any security, or participates or has a direct or indirect participation in any such undertaking, or participates or has a participation in the direct or indirect underwriting of any such undertaking; but such term shall not include a person whose interest is limited to a commission from an underwriter or dealer not in excess of the usual and customary distributors' or sellers' commission. As used in this paragraph the term "issuer" shall include, in addition to an issuer, any person directly or indirectly controlling or controlled by the issuer, or any person under direct or indirect common control with the issuer.

(12) The term "dealer" means any person who engages either for all or part of his time, directly or indirectly, as agent, broker, or principal, in the business of offering, buying, selling, or otherwise dealing or trading in securities issued by another person. . . .

(15) The term "accredited investor" shall mean—

(i) a bank as defined in section 3(a)(2) whether acting in its individual or fiduciary capacity; an insurance company as defined in paragraph (13); an investment company registered under the Investment Company Act of 1940 or a business development company as defined in section 2(a)(48) of that Act; a Small Business Investment Company licensed by the Small Business Administration; or an employee benefit plan, including an individual retirement account, which is subject to the provisions of the Employee Retirement Income Security Act of 1974 if the investment decision is made by a plan fiduciary, as defined in section 3(21) of such Act, which is either a bank, insurance company, or registered investment adviser; or

(ii) any person who, on the basis of such factors as financial sophistication, net worth, knowledge, and experience in financial matters, or amount of assets under management qualifies as an accredited investor under rules and regulations which the Commission shall prescribe. . . .

(19) The term "emerging growth company" means an issuer that had total annual gross revenues of less than $1,000,000,000 (as such amount is indexed for inflation every 5 years by the Commission to reflect the change in the Consumer Price Index for All Urban Consumers published by the Bureau of Labor Statistics, setting the threshold to the nearest 1,000,000) during its most recently completed fiscal year. An issuer that is an emerging growth company as of the first day of that fiscal year shall continue to be deemed an emerging growth company until the earliest of—

(A) the last day of the fiscal year of the issuer during which it had total annual gross revenues of $1,000,000,000 (as such amount is indexed for inflation every 5 years by the Commission to reflect the change in the Consumer Price Index for All Urban Consumers published by the Bureau of Labor Statistics, setting the threshold to the nearest 1,000,000) or more;

(B) the last day of the fiscal year of the issuer following the fifth anniversary of the date of the first sale of common equity securities of the issuer pursuant to an effective registration statement under this title;

(C) the date on which such issuer has, during the previous 3-year period, issued more than $1,000,000,000 in non-convertible debt; or

(D) the date on which such issuer is deemed to be a "large accelerated filer", as defined in [Rule]12b-2, or any successor thereto.

(b) Consideration of Promotion of Efficiency, Competition, and Capital Formation

Whenever pursuant to this title the Commission is engaged in rulemaking and is required to consider or determine whether an action is necessary or appropriate in the public interest, the Commission shall also consider, in addition to the protection of investors, whether the action will promote efficiency, competition, and capital formation.

§3. Classes of Securities under this Subchapter

(a) Exempted Securities

Except as hereinafter expressly provided, the provisions of this subchapter shall not apply to any of the following classes of securities:

(1) Reserved.

(2) Any security issued or guaranteed by the United States or any territory thereof, or by the District of Columbia, or by any State of the United States, or by any political subdivision of a State or territory, or by any public instrumentality

of one or more States or territories, or by any person controlled or supervised by and acting as an instrumentality of the Government of the United States pursuant to authority granted by the Congress of the United States; or any certificate of deposit for any of the foregoing; or any security issued or guaranteed by any bank; or any security issued by or representing an interest in or a direct obligation of a Federal Reserve bank; or any interest or participation in any common trust fund or similar fund maintained by a bank exclusively for the collective investment and reinvestment of assets contributed thereto by such bank in its capacity as trustee, executor, administrator, or guardian; . . . [and various other similar securities].

(3) Any note, draft, bill of exchange, or banker's acceptance which arises out of a current transaction or the proceeds of which have been or are to be used for current transactions, and which has a maturity at the time of issuance of not exceeding nine months, exclusive of days of grace, or any renewal thereof the maturity of which is likewise limited;

(4) Any security issued by a person organized and operated exclusively for religious, educational, benevolent, fraternal, charitable, or reformatory purposes and not for pecuniary profit, and no part of the net earnings of which inures to the benefit of any person, private stockholder, or individual, or any security of a fund that is excluded from the definition of an investment company under section 3(c)(10)(B) of the Investment Company Act of 1940; . . .

(11) Any security which is a part of an issue offered and sold only to persons resident within a single State or Territory, where the issuer of such security is a person resident and doing business within or, if a corporation, incorporated by and doing business within, such State or Territory. . . .

(b) Additional Exemptions

(1) Small Issues Exemptive Authority. The Commission may from time to time by its rules and regulations, and subject to such terms and conditions as may be prescribed therein, add any class of securities to the securities exempted as provided in this section, if it finds that the enforcement of this subchapter with respect to such securities is not necessary in the public interest and for the protection of investors by reason of the small amount involved or the limited character of the public offering; but no issue of securities shall be exempted under this subsection where the aggregate amount at which such issue is offered to the public exceeds $5,000,000.

(2) Additional Issues.—The Commission shall by rule or regulation add a class of securities to the securities exempted pursuant to this section in accordance with the following terms and conditions:

(A) The aggregate offering amount of all securities offered and sold within the prior 12-month period in reliance on the exemption added in accordance with this paragraph shall not exceed $50,000,000.

(B) The securities may be offered and sold publicly.

(C) The securities shall not be restricted securities within the meaning of the Federal securities laws and the regulations promulgated thereunder.

(D) The civil liability provision in section 12(a)(2) shall apply to any person offering or selling such securities.

(E) The issuer may solicit interest in the offering prior to filing any offering statement, on such terms and conditions as the Commission may prescribe in the public interest or for the protection of investors.

(F) The Commission shall require the issuer to file audited financial statements with the Commission annually.

(G) Such other terms, conditions, or requirements as the Commission may determine necessary in the public interest and for the protection of investors, which may include—

(i) a requirement that the issuer prepare and electronically file with the Commission and distribute to prospective investors an offering statement, and any related documents, in such form and with such content as prescribed by the Commission, including audited financial statements, a description of the issuer's business operations, its financial condition, its corporate governance principles, its use of investor funds, and other appropriate matters; and

(ii) disqualification provisions under which the exemption shall not be available to the issuer or its predecessors, affiliates, officers, directors, underwriters, or other related persons, which shall be substantially similar to the disqualification provisions contained in the regulations adopted in accordance with section 926 of the Dodd-Frank Wall Street Reform and Consumer Protection Act (15 U.S.C. 77d note).

(3) Limitation.—Only the following types of securities may be exempted under a rule or regulation adopted pursuant to paragraph (2): equity securities, debt securities, and debt securities convertible or exchangeable to equity interests, including any guarantees of such securities.

(4) Periodic Disclosures.—Upon such terms and conditions as the Commission determines necessary in the public interest and for the protection of investors, the Commission by rule or regulation may require an issuer of a class of securities exempted under paragraph (2) to make available to investors and file with the Commission periodic disclosures regarding the issuer, its business operations, its financial condition, its corporate governance principles, its use of investor funds, and other appropriate matters, and also may provide for the suspension and termination of such a requirement with respect to that issuer.

(5) Adjustment.—Not later than 2 years after the date of enactment of the Small Company Capital Formation Act of 2011 and every 2 years thereafter, the Commission shall review the offering amount limitation described in paragraph (2)(A) and shall increase such amount as the Commission determines appropriate. If the Commission determines not to increase such amount, it shall report to the Committee on Financial Services of the House of Representatives and the Committee on Banking, Housing, and Urban Affairs of the Senate on its reasons for not increasing the amount.

(c) Securities Issued by Small Investment Company

The Commission may from time to time by its rules and regulations and subject to such terms and conditions as may be prescribed therein, add to the securities exempted as provided in this section any class of securities issued by a small business investment company under the Small Business Investment Act of 1958 if it finds, having regard to the purposes of that Act, that the enforcement of this subchapter with respect to such securities is not necessary in the public interest and for the protection of investors. . . .

§4. *Exempted Transactions*

(a) The provisions of section 5 of this title shall not apply to—

(1) transactions by any person other than an issuer, underwriter, or dealer.

(2) transactions by an issuer not involving any public offering.

(3) transactions by a dealer (including an underwriter no longer acting as an underwriter in respect of the security involved in such transaction), except—

(A) transactions taking place prior to the expiration of forty days after the first date upon which the security was bona fide offered to the public by the issuer or by or through an underwriter.

(B) transactions in a security as to which a registration statement has been filed taking place prior to the expiration of forty days after the effective date of such registration statement or prior to the expiration of forty days after the first date upon which the security was bona fide offered to the public by the issuer or by or through an underwriter after such effective date, whichever is later (excluding in the computation of such forty days any time during which a stop order issued under section 8 of this title is in effect as to the security), or such shorter period as the Commission may specify by rules and regulations or order, and

(C) transactions as to securities constituting the whole or a part of an unsold allotment to or subscription by such dealer as a participant in the distribution of such securities by the issuer or by or through an underwriter.

With respect to transactions referred to in clause (B), if securities of the issuer have not previously been sold pursuant to an earlier effective registration statement the applicable period, instead of forty days, shall be ninety days, or such shorter period as the Commission may specify by rules and regulations or order.

(4) brokers' transactions executed upon customers' orders on any exchange or in the over-the-counter market but not the solicitation of such orders.

(5) transactions involving offers or sales by an issuer solely to one or more accredited investors, if the aggregate offering price of an issue of securities offered in reliance on this paragraph does not exceed the amount allowed under section 3(b)(1) of this title, if there is no advertising or public solicitation in connection with the transaction by the issuer or anyone acting on the issuer's behalf, and if the issuer files such notice with the Commission as the Commission shall prescribe.

(6) transactions involving the offer or sale of securities by an issuer (including all entities controlled by or under common control with the issuer), provided that—

(A) the aggregate amount sold to all investors by the issuer, including any amount sold in reliance on the exemption provided under this paragraph during the 12-month period preceding the date of such transaction, is not more than $1,000,000;

(B) the aggregate amount sold to any investor by an issuer, including any amount sold in reliance on the exemption provided under this paragraph during the 12-month period preceding the date of such transaction, does not exceed—

(i) the greater of $2,000 or 5 percent of the annual income or net worth of such investor, as applicable, if either the annual income or the net worth of the investor is less than $100,000; and

(ii) 10 percent of the annual income or net worth of such investor, as applicable, not to exceed a maximum aggregate amount sold of $100,000, if either the annual income or net worth of the investor is equal to or more than $100,000;

(C) the transaction is conducted through a broker or funding portal that complies with the requirements of section 4A(a); and

(D) the issuer complies with the requirements of section 4A(b).

(7) transactions meeting the requirements of subsection (d).

(b) Offers and sales exempt under [Rule] 506 (as revised pursuant to section 201 of the Jumpstart Our Business Startups Act) shall not be deemed public offerings under the Federal securities laws as a result of general advertising or general solicitation.

(1) With respect to securities offered and sold in compliance with Rule 506 of Regulation D under this Act, no person who meets the conditions set forth in paragraph (2) shall be subject to registration as a broker or dealer pursuant to section 15(a)(1) of this title, solely because—

(A) that person maintains a platform or mechanism that permits the offer, sale, purchase, or negotiation of or with respect to securities, or permits general solicitations, general advertisements, or similar or related activities by issuers of such securities, whether online, in person, or through any other means;

(B) that person or any person associated with that person co-invests in such securities; or

(C) that person or any person associated with that person provides ancillary services with respect to such securities.

(2) The exemption provided in paragraph (1) shall apply to any person described in such paragraph if—

(A) such person and each person associated with that person receives no compensation in connection with the purchase or sale of such security;

(B) such person and each person associated with that person does not have possession of customer funds or securities in connection with the purchase or sale of such security; and

(C) such person is not subject to a statutory disqualification as defined in section 3(a)(39) of this title and does not have any person associated with that person subject to such a statutory disqualification.

(3) For the purposes of this subsection, the term "ancillary services" means—

(A) the provision of due diligence services, in connection with the offer, sale, purchase, or negotiation of such security, so long as such services do not include, for separate compensation, investment advice or recommendations to issuers or investors; and

(B) the provision of standardized documents to the issuers and investors, so long as such person or entity does not negotiate the terms of the issuance for and on behalf of third parties and issuers are not required to use the standardized documents as a condition of using the service. . . .

(d) Certain accredited investor transactions—The transactions referred to in subsection (a)(7) are transactions meeting the following requirements:

(1) Accredited investor requirement.—Each purchaser is an accredited investor, as that term is defined in section 230.501(a) of title 17, Code of Federal Regulations (or any successor regulation).

(2) Prohibition on general solicitation or advertising.—Neither the seller, nor any person acting on the seller's behalf, offers or sells securities by any form of general solicitation or general advertising.

(3) Information requirement.—In the case of a transaction involving the securities of an issuer that is neither subject to section 13 or 15d of this title, nor exempt from reporting pursuant to section 240.12g3–2(b) of title 17, Code of Federal Regulations, nor a foreign government (as defined in section 230.405 of title 17, Code of Federal Regulations) eligible to register securities under Schedule B, the seller and a prospective purchaser designated by the seller obtain from the issuer, upon request of the seller, and the seller in all cases makes available to a prospective purchaser, the following information (which shall be reasonably current in relation to the date of resale under this section):

(A) The exact name of the issuer and the issuer's predecessor (if any).

(B) The address of the issuer's principal executive offices.

(C) The exact title and class of the security.

(D) The par or stated value of the security.

(E) The number of shares or total amount of the securities outstanding as of the end of the issuer's most recent fiscal year.

(F) The name and address of the transfer agent, corporate secretary, or other person responsible for transferring shares and stock certificates.

(G) A statement of the nature of the business of the issuer and the products and services it offers, which shall be presumed reasonably current if the statement is as of 12 months before the transaction date.

(H) The names of the officers and directors of the issuer.

(I) The names of any persons registered as a broker, dealer, or agent that shall be paid or given, directly or indirectly, any commission or remuneration for such person's participation in the offer or sale of the securities.

(J) The issuer's most recent balance sheet and profit and loss statement and similar financial statements, which shall—

(i) be for such part of the 2 preceding fiscal years as the issuer has been in operation;

(ii) be prepared in accordance with generally accepted accounting principles or, in the case of a foreign private issuer, be prepared in accordance with generally accepted accounting principles or the International Financial Reporting Standards issued by the International Accounting Standards Board;

(iii) be presumed reasonably current if—

(I) with respect to the balance sheet, the balance sheet is as of a date less than 16 months before the transaction date; and

(II) with respect to the profit and loss statement, such statement is for the 12 months preceding the date of the issuer's balance sheet; and

(iv) if the balance sheet is not as of a date less than 6 months before the transaction date, be accompanied by additional statements of profit and loss for the period from the date of such balance sheet to a date less than 6 months before the transaction date.

(K) To the extent that the seller is a control person with respect to the issuer, a brief statement regarding the nature of the affiliation, and a statement certified by such seller that they have no reasonable grounds to believe that the issuer is in violation of the securities laws or regulations.

(4) Issuers disqualified.—The transaction is not for the sale of a security where the seller is an issuer or a subsidiary, either directly or indirectly, of the issuer.

(5) Bad actor prohibition.—Neither the seller, nor any person that has been or will be paid (directly or indirectly) remuneration or a commission for their participation in the offer or sale of the securities, including solicitation of purchasers for the seller is subject to an event that would disqualify an issuer or other covered person under Rule 506(d)(1) of Regulation D (17 CFR 230.506(d)(1)) or is subject to a statutory disqualification described under section 78c(a)(39) of this title.

(6) Business requirement.—The issuer is engaged in business, is not in the organizational stage or in bankruptcy or receivership, and is not a blank check, blind pool, or shell company that has no specific business plan or purpose or has indicated that the issuer's primary business plan is to engage in a merger or combination of the business with, or an acquisition of, an unidentified person.

(7) Underwriter prohibition.—The transaction is not with respect to a security that constitutes the whole or part of an unsold allotment to, or a subscription or participation by, a broker or dealer as an underwriter of the security or a redistribution.

(8) Outstanding class requirement.—The transaction is with respect to a security of a class that has been authorized and outstanding for at least 90 days prior to the date of the transaction.

(e) Additional requirements

(1) In general.—With respect to an exempted transaction described under subsection (a)(7):

(A) Securities acquired in such transaction shall be deemed to have been acquired in a transaction not involving any public offering.

(B) Such transaction shall be deemed not to be a distribution for purposes of section 2(a)(11).

(C) Securities involved in such transaction shall be deemed to be restricted securities within the meaning of Rule 144.

(2) Rule of construction.—The exemption provided by subsection (a)(7) shall not be the exclusive means for establishing an exemption from the registration requirements of section 5.

§4A. *Requirements with Respect to Certain Small Transactions*

(a) Requirements on Intermediaries.—A person acting as an intermediary in a transaction involving the offer or sale of securities for the account of others pursuant to section 4(6) shall—

(1) register with the Commission as—

(A) a broker; or

(B) a funding portal (as defined in section 3(a)(80) of the Securities Exchange Act of 1934);

(2) register with any applicable self-regulatory organization (as defined in section 3(a)(26) of the Securities Exchange Act of 1934);

(3) provide such disclosures, including disclosures related to risks and other investor education materials, as the Commission shall, by rule, determine appropriate;

(4) ensure that each investor—

(A) reviews investor-education information, in accordance with standards established by the Commission, by rule;

(B) positively affirms that the investor understands that the investor is risking the loss of the entire investment, and that the investor could bear such a loss; and

(C) answers questions demonstrating—

(i) an understanding of the level of risk generally applicable to investments in startups, emerging businesses, and small issuers;

(ii) an understanding of the risk of illiquidity; and

(iii) an understanding of such other matters as the Commission determines appropriate, by rule;

(5) take such measures to reduce the risk of fraud with respect to such transactions, as established by the Commission, by rule, including obtaining a background and securities enforcement regulatory history check on each officer, director, and person holding more than 20 percent of the outstanding equity of every issuer whose securities are offered by such person;

(6) not later than 21 days prior to the first day on which securities are sold to any investor (or such other period as the Commission may establish), make available to the Commission and to potential investors any information provided by the issuer pursuant to subsection (b);

(7) ensure that all offering proceeds are only provided to the issuer when the aggregate capital raised from all investors is equal to or greater than a target offering amount, and allow all investors to cancel their commitments to invest, as the Commission shall, by rule, determine appropriate;

(8) make such efforts as the Commission determines appropriate, by rule, to ensure that no investor in a 12-month period has purchased securities offered pursuant to section 4(6) that, in the aggregate, from all issuers, exceed the investment limits set forth in section 4(6)(B);

(9) take such steps to protect the privacy of information collected from investors as the Commission shall, by rule, determine appropriate;

(10) not compensate promoters, finders, or lead generators for providing the broker or funding portal with the personal identifying information of any potential investor;

(11) prohibit its directors, officers, or partners (or any person occupying a similar status or performing a similar function) from having any financial interest in an issuer using its services; and

(12) meet such other requirements as the Commission may, by rule, prescribe, for the protection of investors and in the public interest.

(b) Requirements for Issuers.—For purposes of section 4(6), an issuer who offers or sells securities shall—

(1) file with the Commission and provide to investors and the relevant broker or funding portal, and make available to potential investors—

(A) the name, legal status, physical address, and website address of the issuer;

(B) the names of the directors and officers (and any persons occupying a similar status or performing a similar function), and each person holding more than 20 percent of the shares of the issuer;

(C) a description of the business of the issuer and the anticipated business plan of the issuer;

(D) a description of the financial condition of the issuer, including, for offerings that, together with all other offerings of the issuer under section 4(6) within the preceding 12-month period, have, in the aggregate, target offering amounts of—

(i) $100,000 or less—

(I) the income tax returns filed by the issuer for the most recently completed year (if any); and

(II) financial statements of the issuer, which shall be certified by the principal executive officer of the issuer to be true and complete in all material respects;

(ii) more than $100,000, but not more than $500,000, financial statements reviewed by a public accountant who is independent of the issuer, using professional standards and procedures for such review or standards and procedures established by the Commission, by rule, for such purpose; and

(iii) more than $500,000 (or such other amount as the Commission may establish, by rule), audited financial statements;

(E) a description of the stated purpose and intended use of the proceeds of the offering sought by the issuer with respect to the target offering amount;

(F) the target offering amount, the deadline to reach the target offering amount, and regular updates regarding the progress of the issuer in meeting the target offering amount;

(G) the price to the public of the securities or the method for determining the price, provided that, prior to sale, each investor shall be provided in writing the final price and all required disclosures, with a reasonable opportunity to rescind the commitment to purchase the securities;

(H) a description of the ownership and capital structure of the issuer, including—

(i) terms of the securities of the issuer being offered and each other class of security of the issuer, including how such terms may be modified, and a summary of the differences between such securities, including how the rights of the securities being offered may be materially limited, diluted, or qualified by the rights of any other class of security of the issuer;

(ii) a description of how the exercise of the rights held by the principal shareholders of the issuer could negatively impact the purchasers of the securities being offered;

(iii) the name and ownership level of each existing shareholder who owns more than 20 percent of any class of the securities of the issuer;

(iv) how the securities being offered are being valued, and examples of methods for how such securities may be valued by the issuer in the future, including during subsequent corporate actions; and

(v) the risks to purchasers of the securities relating to minority ownership in the issuer, the risks associated with corporate actions, including additional issuances of shares, a sale of the issuer or of assets of the issuer, or transactions with related parties; and

(I) such other information as the Commission may, by rule, prescribe, for the protection of investors and in the public interest;

(2) not advertise the terms of the offering, except for notices which direct investors to the funding portal or broker;

(3) not compensate or commit to compensate, directly or indirectly, any person to promote its offerings through communication channels provided by a broker or funding portal, without taking such steps as the Commission shall, by rule, require to ensure that such person clearly discloses the receipt, past or prospective, of such compensation, upon each instance of such promotional communication;

(4) not less than annually, file with the Commission and provide to investors reports of the results of operations and financial statements of the issuer, as the Commission shall, by rule, determine appropriate, subject to such exceptions and termination dates as the Commission may establish, by rule; and

(5) comply with such other requirements as the Commission may, by rule, prescribe, for the protection of investors and in the public interest.

(c) Liability for Material Misstatements and Omissions.—

(1) Actions authorized.—

(A) In general.—Subject to paragraph (2), a person who purchases a security in a transaction exempted by the provisions of section 4(6) may bring an action against an issuer described in paragraph (2), either at law or in equity in any court of competent jurisdiction, to recover the consideration paid for such security with interest thereon, less the amount of any income received thereon, upon the tender of such security, or for damages if such person no longer owns the security.

(B) Liability.—An action brought under this paragraph shall be subject to the provisions of section 12(b) and section 13, as if the liability were created under section 12(a)(2).

(2) Applicability.—An issuer shall be liable in an action under paragraph (1), if the issuer—

(A) by the use of any means or instruments of transportation or communication in interstate commerce or of the mails, by any means of any written or oral communication, in the offering or sale of a security in a transaction exempted by the provisions of section 4(6), makes an untrue statement of a material fact or omits to state a material fact required to be stated or necessary in order to make the statements, in the light of the circumstances under which they were made, not misleading, provided that the purchaser did not know of such untruth or omission; and

(B) does not sustain the burden of proof that such issuer did not know, and in the exercise of reasonable care could not have known, of such untruth or omission.

(3) Definition.—As used in this subsection, the term 'issuer' includes any person who is a director or partner of the issuer, and the principal executive officer or officers, principal financial officer, and controller or principal accounting officer of the issuer (and any person occupying a similar status or performing a similar function) that offers or sells a security in a transaction exempted by the provisions of section 4(6), and any person who offers or sells the security in such offering.

(d) Information Available to States.—The Commission shall make, or shall cause to be made by the relevant broker or funding portal, the information described in subsection (b) and such other information as the Commission, by rule, determines appropriate, available to the securities commission (or any agency or office performing like functions) of each State and territory of the United States and the District of Columbia.

(e) Restrictions on Sales.—Securities issued pursuant to a transaction described in section 4(6)—

(1) may not be transferred by the purchaser of such securities during the 1-year period beginning on the date of purchase, unless such securities are transferred—

(A) to the issuer of the securities;

(B) to an accredited investor;

(C) as part of an offering registered with the Commission; or

(D) to a member of the family of the purchaser or the equivalent, or in connection with the death or divorce of the purchaser or other similar circumstance, in the discretion of the Commission; and

(2) shall be subject to such other limitations as the Commission shall, by rule, establish.

(f) Applicability.—Section 4(6) shall not apply to transactions involving the offer or sale of securities by any issuer that—

(1) is not organized under and subject to the laws of a State or territory of the United States or the District of Columbia;

(2) is subject to the requirement to file reports pursuant to section 13 or section 15(d) of the Securities Exchange Act of 1934;

(3) is an investment company, as defined in section 3 of the Investment Company Act of 1940, or is excluded from the definition of investment company by section 3(b) or section 3(c) of that Act; or

(4) the Commission, by rule or regulation, determines appropriate.

(g) Rule of Construction.—Nothing in this section or section 4(6) shall be construed as preventing an issuer from raising capital through methods not described under section 4(6).

(h) Certain Calculations.—

(1) Dollar amounts.—Dollar amounts in section 4(6) and subsection (b) of this section shall be adjusted by the Commission not less frequently than once

every 5 years, by notice published in the Federal Register to reflect any change in the Consumer Price Index for All Urban Consumers published by the Bureau of Labor Statistics.

(2) Income and net worth.—The income and net worth of a natural person under section 4(6)(B) shall be calculated in accordance with any rules of the Commission under this title regarding the calculation of the income and net worth, respectively, of an accredited investor.

§5. Prohibitions Relating to Interstate Commerce and the Mails

(a) Sale or Delivery after Sale of Unregistered Securities

Unless a registration statement is in effect as to a security, it shall be unlawful for any person, directly or indirectly—

(1) to make use of any means or instruments of transportation or communication in interstate commerce or of the mails to sell such security through the use or medium of any prospectus or otherwise; or

(2) to carry or cause to be carried through the mails or in interstate commerce, by any means or instruments of transportation, any such security for the purpose of sale or for delivery after sale.

(b) Necessity of Prospectus Meeting Requirements of Section 10 of this Title

It shall be unlawful for any person, directly or indirectly—

(1) to make use of any means or instruments of transportation or communication in interstate commerce or of the mails to carry or transmit any prospectus relating to any security with respect to which a registration statement has been filed under this subchapter, unless such prospectus meets the requirements of section 10 of this title; or

(2) to carry or cause to be carried through the mails or in interstate commerce any such security for the purpose of sale or for delivery after sale, unless accompanied or preceded by a prospectus that meets the requirements of subsection (a) of section 10 of this title.

(c) Necessity of Filing Registration Statement

It shall be unlawful for any person, directly or indirectly, to make use of any means or instruments of transportation or communication in interstate commerce or of the mails to offer to sell or offer to buy through the use or medium of any prospectus or otherwise any security, unless a registration statement has been filed as to such security, or while the registration statement is the subject of a refusal order or stop order or (prior to the effective date of the registration statement) any public proceeding or examination under section 8 of this title.

(d) Limitation

Notwithstanding any other provision of this section, an emerging growth company or any person authorized to act on behalf of an emerging growth company may engage in oral or written communications with potential investors that are qualified institutional buyers or institutions that are accredited investors, as such terms are respectively defined in section 230.144A and section 230.501(a) of title 17, Code of

Federal Regulations, or any successor thereto, to determine whether such investors might have an interest in a contemplated securities offering, either prior to or following the date of filing of a registration statement with respect to such securities with the Commission, subject to the requirement of subsection (b)(2).

(e) Notwithstanding the provisions of section 3 or 4, unless a registration statement meeting the requirements of section 10(a) is in effect as to a security-based swap, it shall be unlawful for any person, directly or indirectly, to make use of any means or instruments of transportation or communication in interstate commerce or of the mails to offer to sell, offer to buy or purchase or sell a security-based swap to any person who is not an eligible contract participant as defined in section 1a(18) of the Commodity Exchange Act (7 U.S.C. 1a(18)).

§6. *Registration of Securities*

(a) Method of Registration

Any security may be registered with the Commission under the terms and conditions hereinafter provided, by filing a registration statement in triplicate, at least one of which shall be signed by each issuer, its principal executive officer or officers, its principal financial officer, its comptroller or principal accounting officer, and the majority of its board of directors or persons performing similar functions (or, if there is no board of directors or persons performing similar functions, by the majority of the persons or board having the power of management of the issuer), and in case the issuer is a foreign or Territorial person by its duly authorized representative in the United States; except that when such registration statement relates to a security issued by a foreign government, or political subdivision thereof, it need be signed only by the underwriter of such security. Signatures of all such persons when written on the said registration statements shall be presumed to have been so written by authority of the person whose signature is so affixed and the burden of proof, in the event such authority shall be denied, shall be upon the party denying the same. The affixing of any signature without the authority of the purported signer shall constitute a violation of this subchapter. A registration statement shall be deemed effective only as to the securities specified therein as proposed to be offered. . . .

(e) Emerging Growth Companies

(1) In general.—Any emerging growth company, prior to its initial public offering date, may confidentially submit to the Commission a draft registration statement, for confidential nonpublic review by the staff of the Commission prior to public filing, provided that the initial confidential submission and all amendments thereto shall be publicly filed with the Commission not later than 15 days before the date on which the issuer conducts a road show, as such term is defined in section 230.433(h)(4) of title 17, Code of Federal Regulations, or any successor thereto.

(2) Confidentiality.—Notwithstanding any other provision of this title, the Commission shall not be compelled to disclose any information provided to or obtained by the Commission pursuant to this subsection. For purposes of section 552 of title 5, United States Code, this subsection shall be considered a statute described in subsection (b)(3)(B) of such section 552. Information described in or obtained

pursuant to this subsection shall be deemed to constitute confidential information for purposes of section 24(b)(2) of the Securities Exchange Act of 1934.

§7. *Information Required in Registration Statement*

(a) Information Required in Registration Statement

(1) In general. The registration statement, when relating to a security other than a security issued by a foreign government, or political subdivision thereof, shall contain the information, and be accompanied by the documents, specified in Schedule A, and when relating to a security issued by a foreign government, or political subdivision thereof, shall contain the information, and be accompanied by the documents, specified in Schedule B; except that the Commission may by rules or regulations provide that any such information or document need not be included in respect of any class of issuers or securities if it finds that the requirement of such information or document is inapplicable to such class and that disclosure fully adequate for the protection of investors is otherwise required to be included within the registration statement. If any accountant, engineer, or appraiser, or any person whose profession gives authority to a statement made by him, is named as having prepared or certified any part of the registration statement, or is named as having prepared or certified a report or valuation for use in connection with the registration statement, the written consent of such person shall be filed with the registration statement. If any such person is named as having prepared or certified a report or valuation (other than a public official document or statement) which is used in connection with the registration statement, but is not named as having prepared or certified such report or valuation for use in connection with the registration statement, the written consent of such person shall be filed with the registration statement unless the Commission dispenses with such filing as impracticable or as involving undue hardship on the person filing the registration statement. Any such registration statement shall contain such other information, and be accompanied by such other documents, as the Commission may by rules or regulations require as being necessary or appropriate in the public interest or for the protection of investors.

(2) Treatment of emerging growth companies.—An emerging growth company—

(A) need not present more than 2 years of audited financial statements in order for the registration statement of such emerging growth company with respect to an initial public offering of its common equity securities to be effective, and in any other registration statement to be filed with the Commission, an emerging growth company need not present selected financial data in accordance with section 229.301 of title 17, Code of Federal Regulations, for any period prior to the earliest audited period presented in connection with its initial public offering; and

(B) may not be required to comply with any new or revised financial accounting standard until such date that a company that is not an issuer (as defined under section 2(a) of the Sarbanes-Oxley Act of 2002 (15 U.S.C. 7201(a))) is required to comply with such new or revised accounting standard, if such standard applies to companies that are not issuers.

[Editors' Note: A portion of the JOBS Act not codified as part of the Securities Act permits emerging growth companies to choose to forgo the various exemptions provided to them, but as to choosing compliance with new or revised financial accounting standards provided under this section, the emerging company (1) must make such choice at the time the company is first required to file a registration statement, periodic report, or other report with the Commission under section 13 of the Securities Exchange Act of 1934 and notify the Securities and Exchange Commission of such choice; (2) may not select some standards to comply with in such manner and not others, but must comply with all such standards to the same extent that a non-emerging growth company is required to comply with such standards; and (3) must continue to comply with such standards to the same extent that a non-emerging growth company is required to comply with such standards for as long as the company remains an emerging growth company.]

. . .

(c) Disclosure Requirements.—

(1) In general.—

The Commission shall adopt regulations under this subsection requiring each issuer of an asset-backed security to disclose, for each tranche or class of security, information regarding the assets backing that security.

(2) Content of regulations.—

In adopting regulations under this subsection, the Commission shall—

(A) set standards for the format of the data provided by issuers of an asset-backed security, which shall, to the extent feasible, facilitate comparison of such data across securities in similar types of asset classes; and

(B) require issuers of asset-backed securities, at a minimum, to disclose asset-level or loan-level data, if such data are necessary for investors to independently perform due diligence, including—

(i) data having unique identifiers relating to loan brokers or originators;

(ii) the nature and extent of the compensation of the broker or originator of the assets backing the security; and

(iii) the amount of risk retention by the originator and the securitizer of such assets.

§8. *Taking Effect of Registration Statements and Amendments Thereto*

(a) Effective Date of Registration Statement

Except as hereinafter provided, the effective date of a registration statement shall be the twentieth day after the filing thereof or such earlier date as the Commission may determine, having due regard to the adequacy of the information respecting the issuer theretofore available to the public, to the facility with which the nature of the securities to be registered, their relationship to the capital structure of the issuer and the rights of holders thereof can be understood, and to the public interest and the protection of investors. If any amendment to any such statement is filed prior to the effective date of such statement, the registration statement shall be deemed to have been filed when such amendment was filed; except that an amendment filed with the consent of the Commission, prior to the effective date of the registration statement, or filed pursuant to an order of the Commission, shall be treated as a part of the registration statement.

(b) Incomplete or Inaccurate Registration Statement

If it appears to the Commission that a registration statement is on its face incomplete or inaccurate in any material respect, the Commission may, after notice by personal service or the sending of confirmed telegraphic notice not later than ten days after the filing of the registration statement, and opportunity for hearing (at a time fixed by the Commission) within ten days after such notice by personal service or the sending of such telegraphic notice, issue an order prior to the effective date of registration refusing to permit such statement to become effective until it has been amended in accordance with such order. When such statement has been amended in accordance with such order the Commission shall so declare and the registration shall become effective at the time provided in subsection (a) of this section or upon the date of such declaration, whichever date is the later.

(c) Effective Date of Amendment to Registration Statement

An amendment filed after the effective date of the registration statement, if such amendment, upon its face, appears to the Commission not to be incomplete or inaccurate in any material respect, shall become effective on such date as the Commission may determine, having due regard to the public interest and the protection of investors.

(d) Untrue Statements or Omissions in Registration Statement

If it appears to the Commission at any time that the registration statement includes any untrue statement of a material fact or omits to state any material fact required to be stated therein or necessary to make the statements therein not misleading, the Commission may, after notice by personal service or the sending of confirmed telegraphic notice, and after opportunity for hearing (at a time fixed by the Commission) within fifteen days after such notice by personal service or the sending of such telegraphic notice, issue a stop order suspending the effectiveness of the registration statement. When such statement has been amended in accordance with such stop order, the Commission shall so declare and thereupon the stop order shall cease to be effective.

(e) Examination for Issuance of Stop Order

The Commission is empowered to make an examination in any case in order to determine whether a stop order should issue under subsection (d) of this section. In making such examination the Commission or any officer or officers designated by it shall have access to and may demand the production of any books and papers of, and may administer oaths and affirmations to and examine, the issuer, underwriter, or any other person, in respect of any matter relevant to the examination, and may, in its discretion, require the production of a balance sheet exhibiting the assets and liabilities of the issuer, or its income statement, or both, to be certified to by a public or certified accountant approved by the Commission. If the issuer or underwriter shall fail to cooperate, or shall obstruct or refuse to permit the making of an examination, such conduct shall be proper ground for the issuance of a stop order.

(f) Notice Requirements . . .

§10. Information Required in Prospectus

(a) Information in Registration Statement; Documents Not Required

Except to the extent otherwise permitted or required pursuant to this subsection or subsections (c), (d), or (e) of this section—

(1) a prospectus relating to a security other than a security issued by a foreign government or political subdivision thereof, shall contain the information contained in the registration statement, but it need not include the documents referred to in paragraphs (28) to (32), inclusive, of schedule A;

(2) a prospectus relating to a security issued by a foreign government or political subdivision thereof shall contain the information contained in the registration statement, but it need not include the documents referred to in paragraphs (13) and (14) of schedule B;

(3) notwithstanding the provisions of paragraphs (1) and (2) of this subsection when a prospectus is used more than nine months after the effective date of the registration statement, the information contained therein shall be as of a date not more than sixteen months prior to such use, so far as such information is known to the user of such prospectus or can be furnished by such user without unreasonable effort or expense;

(4) there may be omitted from any prospectus any of the information required under this subsection which the Commission may by rules or regulations designate as not being necessary or appropriate in the public interest or for the protection of investors.

(b) Summarizations and Omissions Allowed by Rules and Regulations

In addition to the prospectus permitted or required in subsection (a) of this section, the Commission shall by rules or regulations deemed necessary or appropriate in the public interest or for the protection of investors permit the use of a prospectus for the purposes of subsection (b)(1) of section 5 of this title which omits in part or summarizes information in the prospectus specified in subsection (a) of this section. A prospectus permitted under this subsection shall, except to the extent the Commission by rules or regulations deemed necessary or appropriate in the public interest or for the protection of investors otherwise provides, be filed as part of the registration statement but shall not be deemed a part of such registration statement for the purposes of section 11 of this title. . . .

(c) Additional Information Required by Rules and Regulations

Any prospectus shall contain such other information as the Commission may by rules or regulations require as being necessary or appropriate in the public interest or for the protection of investors. . . .

§11. *Civil Liabilities on Account of False Registration Statement*

(a) Persons Possessing Cause of Action; Persons Liable

In case any part of the registration statement, when such part became effective, contained an untrue statement of a material fact or omitted to state a material fact required to be stated therein or necessary to make the statements therein not misleading, any person acquiring such security (unless it is proved that at the time of such acquisition he knew of such untruth or omission) may, either at law or in equity, in any court of competent jurisdiction, sue—

(1) every person who signed the registration statement;

(2) every person who was a director of (or person performing similar functions) or partner in the issuer at the time of the filing of the part of the registration statement with respect to which his liability is asserted;

(3) every person who, with his consent, is named in the registration statement as being or about to become a director, person performing similar functions, or partner;

(4) every accountant, engineer, or appraiser, or any person whose profession gives authority to a statement made by him, who has with his consent been named as having prepared or certified any part of the registration statement, or as having prepared or certified any report or valuation which is used in connection with the registration statement, with respect to the statement in such registration statement, report, or valuation, which purports to have been prepared or certified by him;

(5) every underwriter with respect to such security.

If such person acquired the security after the issuer has made generally available to its security holders an earning statement covering a period of at least twelve months beginning after the effective date of the registration statement, then the right of recovery under this subsection shall be conditioned on proof that such person acquired the security relying upon such untrue statement in the registration statement or relying upon the registration statement and not knowing of such omission, but such reliance may be established without proof of the reading of the registration statement by such person.

(b) Persons Exempt from Liability upon Proof of Issues

Notwithstanding the provisions of subsection (a) of this section no person, other than the issuer, shall be liable as provided therein who shall sustain the burden of proof—

(1) that before the effective date of the part of the registration statement with respect to which his liability is asserted (A) he had resigned from or had taken such steps as are permitted by law to resign from, or ceased or refused to act in, every office, capacity, or relationship in which he was described in the registration statement as acting or agreeing to act, and (B) he had advised the Commission and the issuer in writing that he had taken such action and that he would not be responsible for such part of the registration statement; or

(2) that if such part of the registration statement became effective without his knowledge, upon becoming aware of such fact he forthwith acted and advised

the Commission, in accordance with paragraph (1) of this subsection, and, in addition, gave reasonable public notice that such part of the registration statement had become effective without his knowledge; or

(3) that (A) as regards any part of the registration statement not purporting to be made on the authority of an expert, and not purporting to be a copy of or extract from a report or valuation of an expert, and not purporting to be made on the authority of a public official document or statement, he had, after reasonable investigation, reasonable ground to believe and did believe, at the time such part of the registration statement became effective, that the statements therein were true and that there was no omission to state a material fact required to be stated therein or necessary to make the statements therein not misleading; and (B) as regards any part of the registration statement purporting to be made upon his authority as an expert or purporting to be a copy of or extract from a report or valuation of himself as an expert, (i) he had, after reasonable investigation, reasonable ground to believe and did believe, at the time such part of the registration statement became effective, that the statements therein were true and that there was no omission to state a material fact required to be stated therein or necessary to make the statements therein not misleading, or (ii) such part of the registration statement did not fairly represent his statement as an expert or was not a fair copy of or extract from his report or valuation as an expert; and (C) as regards any part of the registration statement purporting to be made on the authority of an expert (other than himself) or purporting to be a copy of or extract from a report or valuation of an expert (other than himself), he had no reasonable ground to believe and did not believe, at the time such part of the registration statement became effective, that the statements therein were untrue or that there was an omission to state a material fact required to be stated therein or necessary to make the statements therein not misleading, or that such part of the registration statement did not fairly represent the statement of the expert or was not a fair copy of or extract from the report or valuation of the expert; and (D) as regards any part of the registration statement purporting to be a statement made by an official person or purporting to be a copy of or extract from a public official document, he had no reasonable ground to believe and did not believe, at the time such part of the registration statement became effective, that the statements therein were untrue, or that there was an omission to state a material fact required to be stated therein or necessary to make the statements therein not misleading, or that such part of the registration statement did not fairly represent the statement made by the official person or was not a fair copy of or extract from the public official document.

(c) Standard of Reasonableness

In determining, for the purpose of paragraph (3) of subsection (b) of this section, what constitutes reasonable investigation and reasonable ground for belief, the standard of reasonableness shall be that required of a prudent man in the management of his own property. . . .

(e) Measure of Damages; Undertaking for Payment of Costs

The suit authorized under subsection (a) of this section may be to recover such damages as shall represent the difference between the amount paid for the security (not exceeding the price at which the security was offered to the public) and (1) the value thereof as of the time such suit was brought, or (2) the price at which such security shall have been disposed of in the market before suit, or (3) the price at which such security shall have been disposed of after suit but before judgment if such damages shall be less than the damages representing the difference between the amount paid for the security (not exceeding the price at which the security was offered to the public) and the value thereof as of the time such suit was brought: *Provided,* That if the defendant proves that any portion or all of such damages represents other than the depreciation in value of such security resulting from such part of the registration statement, with respect to which his liability is asserted, not being true or omitting to state a material fact required to be stated therein or necessary to make the statements therein not misleading, such portion of or all such damages shall not be recoverable. In no event shall any underwriter (unless such underwriter shall have knowingly received from the issuer for acting as an underwriter some benefit, directly or indirectly, in which all other underwriters similarly situated did not share in proportion to their respective interests in the underwriting) be liable in any suit or as a consequence of suits authorized under subsection (a) of this section for damages in excess of the total price at which the securities underwritten by him and distributed to the public were offered to the public. In any suit under this or any other section of this subchapter the court may, in its discretion, require an undertaking for the payment of the costs of such suit, including reasonable attorney's fees, and if judgment shall be rendered against a party litigant, upon the motion of the other party litigant, such costs may be assessed in favor of such party litigant (whether or not such undertaking has been required) if the court believes the suit or the defense to have been without merit, in an amount sufficient to reimburse him for the reasonable expenses incurred by him, in connection with such suit, such costs to be taxed in the manner usually provided for taxing of costs in the court in which the suit was heard.

(f) Joint and Several Liability

(1) Except as provided in paragraph (2) all or any one or more of the persons specified in subsection (a) of this section shall be jointly and severally liable, and every person who becomes liable to make any payment under this section may recover contribution as in cases of contract from any person who, if sued separately, would have been liable to make the same payment, unless the person who has become liable was, and the other was not, guilty of fraudulent misrepresentation.

(2) (A) The liability of an outside director under subsection (e) shall be determined in accordance with section 21D(f) of the Securities Exchange Act of 1934.

(B) For purposes of this paragraph, the term "outside director" shall have the meaning given such term by rule or regulation of the Commission.

(g) Offering Price to Public as Maximum Amount Recoverable

In no case shall the amount recoverable under this section exceed the price at which the security was offered to the public.

§12. *Civil Liabilities Arising in Connection with Prospectuses and Communications*

(a) In General

Any person who—

(1) offers or sells a security in violation of section 5 of this title, or

(2) offers or sells a security (whether or not exempted by the provisions of section 3 of this title, other than paragraph (2) of subsection (a) of said section), by the use of any means or instruments of transportation or communication in interstate commerce or of the mails, by means of a prospectus or oral communication, which includes an untrue statement of a material fact or omits to state a material fact necessary in order to make the statements, in the light of the circumstances under which they were made, not misleading (the purchaser not knowing of such untruth or omission), and who shall not sustain the burden of proof that he did not know, and in the exercise of reasonable care could not have known, of such untruth or omission,

shall be liable, subject to subsection (b), to the person purchasing such security from him, who may sue either at law or in equity in any court of competent jurisdiction, to recover the consideration paid for such security with interest thereon, less the amount of any income received thereon, upon the tender of such security, or for damages if he no longer owns the security.

(b) Loss Causation

In an action described in subsection (a)(2), if the person who offered or sold such security proves that any portion or all of the amount recoverable under subsection (a)(2) represents other than the depreciation in value of the subject security resulting from such part of the prospectus or oral communication, with respect to which the liability of that person is asserted, not being true or omitting to state a material fact required to be stated therein or necessary to make the statement not misleading, then such portion or amount, as the case may be, shall not be recoverable.

§13. *Limitation of Actions*

No action shall be maintained to enforce any liability created under section 11 or 12(a)(2) of this title unless brought within one year after the discovery of the untrue statement or the omission, or after such discovery should have been made by the exercise of reasonable diligence, or, if the action is to enforce a liability created under section 12(a)(1) of this title, unless brought within one year after the violation upon which it is based. In no event shall any such action be brought to enforce a liability created under section 11 or 12(a)(1) of this title more than three years after the security was bona fide offered to the public, or under section 12(a)(2) of this title more than three years after the sale.

§14. *Contrary Stipulations Void*

Any condition, stipulation, or provision binding any person acquiring any security to waive compliance with any provision of this subchapter or of the rules and regulations of the Commission shall be void.

§15. Liability of Controlling Persons

(a) Control Person

Every person who, by or through stock ownership, agency, or otherwise, or who, pursuant to or in connection with an agreement or understanding with one or more other persons by or through stock ownership, agency, or otherwise, controls any person liable under sections 11 or 12 of this title, shall also be liable jointly and severally with and to the same extent as such controlled person to any person to whom such controlled person is liable, unless the controlling person had no knowledge of or reasonable ground to believe in the existence of the facts by reason of which the liability of the controlled person is alleged to exist. . . .

(b) Prosecution of Persons Who Aid and Abet Violations.—

For purposes of any action brought by the Commission under subparagraph (b) or (d) of section 20, any person that knowingly or recklessly provides substantial assistance to another person in violation of a provision of this Act, or of any rule or regulation issued under this Act, shall be deemed to be in violation of such provision to the same extent as the person to whom such assistance is provided.

§16. Additional Remedies; Limitation on Remedies

(a) Remedies Additional

Except as provided in subsection (b), the rights and remedies provided by this title shall be in addition to any and all other rights and remedies that may exist at law or in equity.

(b) Class Action Limitations

No covered class action based upon the statutory or common law of any State or subdivision thereof may be maintained in any State or Federal court by any private party alleging—

(1) An untrue statement or omission of a material fact in connection with the purchase or sale of a covered security; or

(2) that the defendant used or employed any manipulative or deceptive device or contrivance in connection with the purchase or sale of a covered security.

(c) Removal of Covered Class Actions

Any covered class action brought in any State court involving a covered security, as set forth in subsection (b), shall be removable to the Federal district court for the district in which the action is pending, and shall be subject to subsection (b).

(d) Preservation of Certain Actions

(1) Actions under State Law of State of Incorporation

(A) Actions Preserved.—Notwithstanding subsection (b) or (c), a covered class action described in subparagraph (B) of this paragraph that is based upon the statutory or common law of the State in which the issuer is incorporated (in the case of a corporation) or organized (in the case of any other entity) may be maintained in a State or Federal court by a private party.

(B) Permissible Actions.—A covered class action is described in this subparagraph if it involves—

(i) the purchase or sale of securities by the issuer or an affiliate of the issuer exclusively from or to holders of equity securities of the issuer; or

(ii) any recommendation, position, or other communication with respect to the sale of securities of the issuer that—

(I) is made by or on behalf of the issuer or an affiliate of the issuer to holders of equity securities of the issuer; and

(II) concerns decisions of those equity holders with respect to voting their securities, acting in response to a tender or exchange offer, or exercising dissenters' or appraisal rights.

(2) State Actions

(A) In General.—Notwithstanding any other provision of this section, nothing in this section may be construed to preclude a State or political subdivision thereof or a State pension plan from bringing an action involving a covered security on its own behalf, or as a member of a class comprised solely of other States, political subdivisions, or State pension plans that are named plaintiffs, and that have authorized participation, in such action.

(B) State Pension Plan Defined.—For purposes of this paragraph, the term 'State pension plan' means a pension plan established and maintained for its employees by the government of the State or political subdivision thereof, or by any agency or instrumentality thereof.

(3) Actions under Contractual Agreements Between Issuers and Indenture Trustees.—Notwithstanding subsection (b) or (c), a covered class action that seeks to enforce a contractual agreement between an issuer and an indenture trustee may be maintained in a State or Federal court by a party to the agreement or a successor to such party.

(4) Remand of Removed Actions.—In an action that has been removed from a State court pursuant to subsection (c), if the Federal court determines that the action may be maintained in State court pursuant to this subsection, the Federal court shall remand such action to such State court.

(e) Preservation of State Jurisdiction

The securities commission (or any agency or office performing like functions) of any State shall retain jurisdiction under the laws of such State to investigate and bring enforcement actions.

(f) Definitions

For purposes of this section, the following definitions shall apply:

(1) Affiliate of the Issuer.—The term "affiliate of the issuer" means a person that directly or indirectly, through one or more intermediaries, controls or is controlled by or is under common control with, the issuer.

(2) Covered Class Action

(A) In General.—The term "covered class action" means—

(i) any single lawsuit in which—

(I) damages are sought on behalf of more than 50 persons or prospective class members, and questions of law or fact common to those persons or members of the prospective class, without reference to issues of individualized reliance on an alleged misstatement or omission, predominate over any questions affecting only individual persons or members; or

(II) one or more named parties seek to recover damages on a representative basis on behalf of themselves and other unnamed parties similarly situated, and questions of law or fact common to those persons or members of the prospective class predominate over any questions affecting only individual persons or members; or

(ii) any group of lawsuits filed in or pending in the same court and involving common questions of law or fact, in which—

(I) damages are sought on behalf of more than 50 persons; and

(II) the lawsuits are joined, consolidated, or otherwise proceed as a single action for any purpose.

(B) Exception for Derivative Actions.—Notwithstanding subparagraph (A), the term "covered class action" does not include an exclusively derivative action brought by one or more shareholders on behalf of a corporation.

(C) Counting of Certain Class Members.—For purposes of this paragraph, a corporation, investment company, pension plan, partnership, or other entity, shall be treated as one person or prospective class member, but only if the entity is not established for the purpose of participating in the action.

(D) Rule of Construction.—Nothing in this paragraph shall be construed to affect the discretion of a State court in determining whether actions filed in such court should be joined, consolidated, or otherwise allowed to proceed as a single action.

(3) Covered Security.—The term "covered security" means a security that satisfies the standards for a covered security specified in paragraph (1) or (2) of section 18(b) at the time during which it is alleged that the misrepresentation, omission, or manipulative or deceptive conduct occurred, except that such term shall not include any debt security that is exempt from registration under this title pursuant to rules issued by the Commission under section 4(2).

§17. Fraudulent Interstate Transactions

(a) Use of Interstate Commerce for Purpose of Fraud or Deceit

It shall be unlawful for any person in the offer or sale of any securities (including security-based swaps) . . . by the use of any means or instruments of transportation or communication in interstate commerce or by the use of the mails, directly or indirectly—

(1) to employ any device, scheme, or artifice to defraud, or

(2) to obtain money or property by means of any untrue statement of a material fact or any omission to state a material fact necessary in order to make the statements made, in the light of the circumstances under which they were made, not misleading, or

(3) to engage in any transaction, practice, or course of business which operates or would operate as a fraud or deceit upon the purchaser.

(b) Use of Interstate Commerce for Purpose of Offering for Sale

It shall be unlawful for any person, by the use of any means or instruments of transportation or communication in interstate commerce or by the use of the mails, to publish, give publicity to, or circulate any notice, circular, advertisement, newspaper, article, letter, investment service, or communication which, though not purporting to offer a security for sale, describes such security for a consideration received or to be received, directly or indirectly, from an issuer, underwriter, or dealer, without fully disclosing the receipt, whether past or prospective, of such consideration and the amount thereof.

(c) Exemptions of Section 3 Not Applicable to This Section

The exemptions provided in section 3 of this title shall not apply to the provisions of this section. . . .

§18. Exemption from State Regulation of Securities Offerings

(a) Scope of Exemption

Except as otherwise provided in this section, no law, rule, regulation, or order, or other administrative action of any State or any political subdivision thereof—

(1) requiring, or with respect to, registration or qualification of securities, or registration or qualification of securities transactions, shall directly or indirectly apply to a security that—

(A) is a covered security; or

(B) will be a covered security upon completion of the transaction;

(2) shall directly or indirectly prohibit, limit, or impose any conditions upon the use of—

(A) with respect to a covered security described in subsection (b), any offering document that is prepared by or on behalf of the issuer; or

(B) any proxy statement, report to shareholders, or other disclosure document relating to a covered security or the issuer thereof that is required to be and is filed with the Commission or any national securities organization registered under section 15A or the Securities Exchange Act of 1934, except that this subparagraph does not apply to the laws, rules, regulations, or orders, or other administrative actions of the State of incorporation of the issuer; or

(3) shall directly or indirectly prohibit, limit, or impose conditions, based on the merits of such offering or issuer, upon the offer or sale of any security described in paragraph (1).

(b) Covered Securities

For purposes of this section, the following are covered securities:

(1) Exclusive federal registration of nationally traded securities.—A security is a covered security if such security is—

(A) listed, or authorized for listing, on the New York Stock Exchange or the American Stock Exchange, or listed, or authorized for listing on the National Market System of the Nasdaq Stock Market (or any successor to such entities);

(B) listed, or authorized for listing, on a national securities exchange (or tier or segment thereof) that has listing standards that the Commission determines by rule (on its own initiative or on the basis of a petition) are substantially similar to the listing standards applicable to securities described in subparagraph (A); or

(C) a security of the same issuer that is equal in seniority or that is a senior security to a security described in subparagraph (A) or (B).

(2) Exclusive federal registration of investment companies.—A security is a covered security if such security is a security issued by an investment company that is registered, or that has filed a registration statement, under the Investment Company Act of 1940.

(3) Sales to qualified purchasers.—A security is a covered security with respect to the offer or sale of the security to qualified purchasers, as defined by the Commission by rule. In prescribing such rule, the Commission may define the term "qualified purchaser" differently with respect to different categories of securities, consistent with the public interest and the protection of investors.

(4) Exemption in connection with certain exempt offerings.—A security is a covered security with respect to a transaction that is exempt from registration under this title pursuant to—

(A) paragraph (1) or (3) of section 4, and the issuer of such security files reports with the Commission pursuant to section 13 or 15(d) of the Securities Exchange Act of 1934;

(B) section 4(4);

(C) section 4(6);

(D) a rule or regulation adopted pursuant to section 3(b)(2) and such security is—

(i) offered or sold on a national securities exchange; or

(ii) offered or sold to a qualified purchaser, as defined by the Commission pursuant to paragraph (3) with respect to that purchase or sale;

(D) section 3(a), other than the offer or sale of a security that is exempt from such registration pursuant to paragraph (4), (10), or (11) of such section, except that a municipal security that is exempt from such registration pursuant to paragraph (2) of such section is not a covered security with respect to the offer or sale of such security in the State in which the issuer of such security is located; or

(E) Commission rules or regulations issued under section 4(2), except that this subparagraph does not prohibit a State from imposing notice filing requirements that are substantially similar to those required by rule or regulation under section 4(2) that are in effect on September 1, 1996.

(c) Preservation of Authority

(1) Fraud authority.—Consistent with this section, the securities commission (or any agency or office performing like functions) of any State shall retain jurisdiction under the laws of such State to investigate and bring enforcement actions in connection with securities or securities transactions

(A) with respect to—

(i) fraud or deceit; or

(ii) unlawful conduct by a broker dealer or funding portal; and

(B) in connection to a transaction described under section 4(6), with respect to—

(i) fraud or deceit; or

(ii) unlawful conduct by a broker, dealer, funding portal, or issuer.

(2) Preservation of filing requirements.—

(A) Notice filings permitted—Nothing in this section prohibits the securities commission (or any agency or office performing like functions) of any State from requiring the filing of any document filed with the Commission pursuant to this title, together with annual or periodic reports of the value of securities sold or offered to be sold to persons located in the State (if such sales data is not included in documents filed with the Commission), solely for notice purposes and the assessment of any fee, together with a consent to service of process and any required fee. . . .

(F) Fees not permitted on crowdfunded securities.—Notwithstanding subparagraphs (A), (B), and (C), no filing or fee may be required with respect to any security that is a covered security pursuant to subsection (b)(4)(B), or will be such a covered security upon completion of the transaction, except for the securities commission (or any agency or office performing like functions) of the State of the principal place of business of the issuer, or any State in which purchasers of 50 percent or greater of the aggregate amount of the issue are residents, provided that for purposes of this subparagraph, the term "State" includes the District of Columbia and the territories of the United States.

§19. Special Powers of Commission

(a) The Commission shall have authority from time to time to make, amend, and rescind such rules and regulations as may be necessary to carry out the provisions of this subchapter, including rules and regulations governing registration statements and prospectuses for various classes of securities and issuers, and defining accounting, technical, and trade terms used in this subchapter. Among other things, the Commission shall have authority, for the purposes of this subchapter, to prescribe the form or forms in which required information shall be set forth, the items or details to be shown in the balance sheet and earning statement, and the methods to be followed in the preparation of accounts, in the appraisal or valuation of assets and liabilities, in the determination of depreciation and depletion, in the differentiation of recurring and nonrecurring income, in the differentiation of investment and operating income, and in the preparation, where the Commission deems it necessary or desirable, of consolidated balance sheets or income accounts of any person directly or indirectly controlling or controlled by the issuer, or any person under direct or indirect common control with the issuer. The rules and regulations of the Commission shall be effective upon publication in the manner which the Commission shall prescribe. No provision of this subchapter imposing any liability shall apply to any act done or omitted in good faith in conformity with any rule or regulation of the Commission, notwithstanding that such rule or regulation may, after such act or omission, be amended or rescinded or be determined by judicial or other authority to be invalid for any reason. . . .

(b) Recognition of Accounting Standards

(1) In general.—In carrying out its authority under subsection (a) and under section 13(b) of the Securities Exchange Act of 1934, the Commission may recognize, as 'generally accepted' purposes of the securities laws, any accounting principles established by a standard body—

(A) that—

(i) is organized as a private entity;

(ii) has, for administrative and operational purposes, a board of trustees (or equivalent body) serving in the public interest, the majority of whom are not, concurrent with their service on such board, and have not been during the 2-year period preceding such service, associated persons of any registered public accounting firm;

(iii) is funded as provided in section 109 of the Sarbanes-Oxley Act of 2002;

(iv) has adopted procedures to ensure prompt consideration, by majority vote of its members, of changed to accounting principles necessary to reflect emerging accounting issues and changing business practices; and

(v) considers, in adopting accounting principles, the need to keep standards current in order to reflect changed in the business environment, the extent to which international convergence on high quality accounting standards is necessary or appropriate in the public interest and for the protection of investors; and

(B) that the Commission determines has the capacity to assist the Commission in fulfilling the requirements of subsection (a) and section 13(b) of the Securities Exchange Act of 1934, because, at a minimum, the standard setting body is capable of improving the accuracy and effectiveness of financial reporting and the protection of investors under the securities laws. . . .

§21. Hearings by Commission

All hearings shall be public and may be held before the Commission or an officer or officers of the Commission designated by it, and appropriate records thereof shall be kept.

§22. Jurisdiction of Offenses and Suits

(a) Federal and State Courts; Venue; Service of Process; Review; Removal; Costs

The district courts of the United States and the United States courts of any Territory shall have jurisdiction of offenses and violations under this subchapter and under the rules and regulations promulgated by the Commission in respect thereto, and, concurrent with State and Territorial courts, except as provided in Section 16 with respect to covered class actions, of all suits in equity and actions at law brought to enforce any liability or duty created by this subchapter. Any such suit or action may be brought in the district wherein the defendant is found or is an inhabitant or transacts business, or in the district where the offer or sale took place, if the defendant participated therein, and process in such cases may be served in any other district of which the defendant is an inhabitant or wherever the defendant may be found. Judgments and decrees so rendered shall be subject to review as provided in sections 1254, 1291, 1292, and 1294 of title 28. Except as provided in Section 16(c), no case arising under this subchapter and brought in any State court of competent jurisdiction shall be removed to any court of the United States. No costs shall be assessed for or against the Commission in any proceeding under this subchapter brought by or against it in the Supreme Court or such other courts.

(b) Contumacy or Refusal to Obey Subpoena; Contempt

In case of contumacy or refusal to obey a subpoena issued to any person, any of the said United States courts, within the jurisdiction of which said person guilty of contumacy or refusal to obey is found or resides, upon application by the Commission may issue to such person an order requiring such person to appear before the Commission, or one of its examiners designated by it, there to produce documentary evidence if so ordered, or there to give evidence touching the matter in question; and any failure to obey such order of the court may be punished by said court as a contempt thereof.

(c) Extraterritorial Jurisdiction.—

The district courts of the United States and the United States courts of any Territory shall have jurisdiction of an action or proceeding brought or instituted by the Commission or the United States alleging a violation of section 17(a) involving—

(1) conduct within the United States that constitutes significant steps in furtherance of the violation, even if the securities transaction occurs outside the United States and involves only foreign investors; or

(2) conduct occurring outside the United States that has a foreseeable substantial effect within the United States.

§24. Penalties

Any person who willfully violates any of the provisions of this subchapter, or the rules and regulations promulgated by the Commission under authority thereof, or any person who willfully, in a registration statement filed under this subchapter, makes any untrue statement of a material fact or omits to state any material fact required to be stated therein or necessary to make the statements therein not misleading, shall upon conviction be fined not more than $10,000 or imprisoned not more than five years, or both.

§27. Private Securities Litigation

[This section replicates §21D of the 1934 Act printed later in this book, except there is no 1933 Act counterpart for §21D(a)(8), (b)(1), (b)(2), (b)(3)(A), (b)(4), (e), and (f), so that (a)(9) of the 1934 Act corresponds to (a)(8) of the 1933 Act and §21D(b)(3), (B), (C), and (D) of the 1934 Act correspond to §27(b)(1), (2), and (3) of the 1933 Act.]

§27A. *Application of Safe Harbor for Forward-Looking Statements*

[The section replicates §21E of the 1934 Act printed later in this book.]

§27B. *Conflicts of interest relating to certain securitizations*

(a) In general.—

An underwriter, placement agent, initial purchaser, or sponsor, or any affiliate or subsidiary of any such entity, of an asset-backed security (as such term is defined in section 3 of the Securities . . . Exchange Act of 1934, which for the purposes of this section shall include a synthetic asset-backed security), shall not, at any time for a period ending on the date that is one year after the date of the first closing of the sale of the asset-backed security, engage in any transaction that would involve or result in any material conflict of interest with respect to any investor in a transaction arising out of such activity. . . .

(c) Exception.—

The prohibitions of subsection (a) shall not apply to—

(1) risk-mitigating hedging activities in connection with positions or holdings arising out of the underwriting, placement, initial purchase, or sponsorship of an asset-backed security, provided that such activities are designed to reduce the specific risks to the underwriter, placement agent, initial purchaser, or sponsor associated with positions or holdings arising out of such underwriting, placement, initial purchase, or sponsorship; or

(2) purchases or sales of asset-backed securities made pursuant to and consistent with—

(A) commitments of the underwriter, placement agent, initial purchaser, or sponsor, or any affiliate or subsidiary of any such entity, to provide liquidity for the asset-backed security, or

(B) bona fide market-making in the asset backed security. . . .

§28. *General Exemptive Authority*

The Commission, by rule or regulation, may conditionally or unconditionally exempt any person, security, or transaction, or any class or classes of persons, securities, or transactions, from any provision or provisions of this title or of any rule or regulation issued under this title, to the extent that such exemption is necessary or appropriate in the public interest, and is consistent with the protection of investors.

Selected Rules and Regulations Under the Securities Act of 1933

17 C.F.R. §§230.147-230.508

GENERAL

REGULATION D—RULES GOVERNING THE LIMITED OFFER AND SALE OF SECURITIES WITHOUT REGISTRATION UNDER THE SECURITIES ACT OF 1933

REGULATION CE—COORDINATED EXEMPTIONS FOR CERTAIN ISSUES OF SECURITIES EXEMPT UNDER STATE LAW

Rule 147. Intrastate Offers and Sales

(a) This section shall not raise any presumption that the exemption provided by section 3(a)(11) of the Act (15 U.S.C. 77c(a)(11)) is not available for transactions by an issuer which do not satisfy all of the provisions of this section.

(b) *Manner of offers and sales.* An issuer, or any person acting on behalf of the issuer, shall be deemed to conduct an offering in compliance with section 3(a)(11) of the Act (15 U.S.C. 77c(a)(11)), where offers and sales are made only to persons resident within the same state or territory in which the issuer is resident and doing business, within the meaning of section 3(a)(11) of the Act, so long as the issuer complies with the provisions of paragraphs (c), (d), and (f) through (h) of this section.

(c) *Nature of the issuer.* The issuer of the securities shall at the time of any offers and sales be a person resident and doing business within the state or territory in which all of the offers and sales are made.

(1) The issuer shall be deemed to be a resident of the state or territory in which:

(i) It is incorporated or organized, and it has its principal place of business, if a corporation, limited partnership, trust or other form of business organization that is organized under state or territorial law. The issuer shall be deemed to have its principal place of business in a state or territory in which the officers, partners or managers of the issuer primarily direct, control and coordinate the activities of the issuer;

(ii) It has its principal place of business, as defined in paragraph (c)(1)(i) of this section, if a general partnership or other form of business organization that is not organized under any state or territorial law;

(iii) Such person's principal residence is located, if an individual.

INSTRUCTION TO PARAGRAPH (c)(1)

An issuer that has previously conducted an intrastate offering pursuant to this section (§230.147) or Rule 147A (§230.147A) may not conduct another intrastate offering pursuant to this section (§230.147) in a different state or territory, until the expiration of the time period specified in paragraph (e) of this section (§230.147(e)) or paragraph (e) of Rule 147A (§230.147A(e)), calculated on the basis of the date of the last sale in such offering.

(2) The issuer shall be deemed to be doing business within a state or territory if the issuer satisfies at least one of the following requirements:

(i) The issuer derived at least 80% of its consolidated gross revenues from the operation of a business or of real property located in or from the rendering of services within such state or territory;

INSTRUCTION TO PARAGRAPH (c)(2)(I)

Revenues must be calculated based on the issuer's most recent fiscal year, if the first offer of securities pursuant to this section is made during the first six months of the issuer's current fiscal year, and based on the first six months of the issuer's current fiscal year or during the twelve-month fiscal period ending with such six-month period, if the first offer of securities pursuant to this section is made during the last six months of the issuer's current fiscal year.

(ii) The issuer had at the end of its most recent semi-annual fiscal period prior to an initial offer of securities in any offering or subsequent offering pursuant to this section, at least 80% of its assets and those of its subsidiaries on a consolidated basis located within such state or territory;

(iii) The issuer intends to use and uses at least 80% of the net proceeds to the issuer from sales made pursuant to this section (§230.147) in connection with the operation of a business or of real property, the purchase of real property located in, or the rendering of services within such state or territory; or

(iv) A majority of the issuer's employees are based in such state or territory.

(d) *Residence of offerees and purchasers.* Offers and sales of securities pursuant to this section (§230.147) shall be made only to residents of the state or territory in which the issuer is resident, as determined pursuant to paragraph (c) of this section, or who the issuer reasonably believes, at the time of the offer and sale, are residents of the state or territory in which the issuer is resident. For purposes of determining the residence of offerees and purchasers:

(1) A corporation, partnership, limited liability company, trust or other form of business organization shall be deemed to be a resident of a state or territory

if, at the time of the offer and sale to it, it has its principal place of business, as defined in paragraph (c)(1)(i) of this section, within such state or territory.

INSTRUCTION TO PARAGRAPH (d)(1)

A trust that is not deemed by the law of the state or territory of its creation to be a separate legal entity is deemed to be a resident of each state or territory in which its trustee is, or trustees are, resident.

(2) Individuals shall be deemed to be residents of a state or territory if such individuals have, at the time of the offer and sale to them, their principal residence in the state or territory.

(3) A corporation, partnership, trust or other form of business organization, which is organized for the specific purpose of acquiring securities offered pursuant to this section (§230.147), shall not be a resident of a state or territory unless all of the beneficial owners of such organization are residents of such state or territory.

INSTRUCTION TO PARAGRAPH (d)

Obtaining a written representation from purchasers of in-state residency status will not, without more, be sufficient to establish a reasonable belief that such purchasers are in-state residents.

(e) *Limitation on resales.* For a period of six months from the date of the sale by the issuer of a security pursuant to this section (§230.147), any resale of such security shall be made only to persons resident within the state or territory in which the issuer was resident, as determined pursuant to paragraph (c) of this section, at the time of the sale of the security by the issuer.

INSTRUCTION TO PARAGRAPH (e)

In the case of convertible securities, resales of either the convertible security, or if it is converted, the underlying security, could be made during the period described in paragraph (e) only to persons resident within such state or territory. For purposes of this paragraph (e), a conversion in reliance on section 3(a)(9) of the Act (15 U.S.C. 77c(a)(9)) does not begin a new period.

(f) *Precautions against interstate sales.* (1) The issuer shall, in connection with any securities sold by it pursuant to this section:

(i) Place a prominent legend on the certificate or other document evidencing the security stating that: "Offers and sales of these securities were made under an exemption from registration and have not been registered under the Securities Act of 1933. For a period of six months from the date of the sale by the issuer of these securities, any resale of these securities (or the underlying securities in the case of convertible securities) shall be made only to persons resident within the state or territory of [identify the name of the state or territory in which the issuer was resident at the time of the sale of the securities by the issuer].";

(ii) Issue stop transfer instructions to the issuer's transfer agent, if any, with respect to the securities, or, if the issuer transfers its own securities, make a notation in the appropriate records of the issuer; and

(iii) Obtain a written representation from each purchaser as to his or her residence.

(2) The issuer shall, in connection with the issuance of new certificates for any of the securities that are sold pursuant to this section (§230.147) that are presented for transfer during the time period specified in paragraph (e), take the steps required by paragraphs (f)(1)(i) and (ii) of this section.

(3) The issuer shall, at the time of any offer or sale by it of a security pursuant to this section (§230.147), prominently disclose to each offeree in the manner in which any such offer is communicated and to each purchaser of such security in writing a reasonable period of time before the date of sale, the following: "Sales will be made only to residents of [identify the name of the state or territory in which the issuer was resident at the time of the sale of the securities by the issuer]. Offers and sales of these securities are made under an exemption from registration and have not been registered under the Securities Act of 1933. For a period of six months from the date of the sale by the issuer of the securities, any resale of the securities (or the underlying securities in the case of convertible securities) shall be made only to persons resident within the state or territory of [identify the name of the state or territory in which the issuer was resident at the time of the sale of the securities by the issuer]."

(g) *Integration with other offerings.* To determine whether offers and sales should be integrated, refer to §230.152.

Rule 147A. Intrastate Sales Exemption

(a) *Scope of the exemption.* Offers and sales by or on behalf of an issuer of its securities made in accordance with this section (§230.147A) are exempt from section 5 of the Act (15 U.S.C. 77e). This exemption is not available to an issuer that is an investment company registered or required to be registered under the Investment Company Act of 1940 (15 U.S.C. 80a-1 et seq.).

(b) *Manner of offers and sales.* An issuer, or any person acting on behalf of the issuer, may rely on this exemption to make offers and sales using any form of general solicitation and general advertising, so long as the issuer complies with the provisions of paragraphs (c), (d), and (f) through (h) of this section.

(c) *Nature of the issuer.* The issuer of the securities shall at the time of any offers and sales be a person resident and doing business within the state or territory in which all of the sales are made.

(1) The issuer shall be deemed to be a resident of the state or territory in which it has its principal place of business. The issuer shall be deemed to have its principal place of business in a state or territory in which the officers, partners or managers of the issuer primarily direct, control and coordinate the activities of the issuer.

(2) The issuer shall be deemed to be doing business within a state or territory if the issuer satisfies at least one of the following requirements:

(i) The issuer derived at least 80% of its consolidated gross revenues from the operation of a business or of real property located in or from the rendering of services within such state or territory.

INSTRUCTION TO PARAGRAPH (c)(2)(i)

Revenues must be calculated based on the issuer's most recent fiscal year, if the first offer of securities pursuant to this section is made during the first six months of the issuer's current fiscal year, and based on the first six months of the issuer's current fiscal year or during the twelve-month fiscal period ending with such six-month period, if the first offer of securities pursuant to this section is made during the last six months of the issuer's current fiscal year.

(ii) The issuer had at the end of its most recent semi-annual fiscal period prior to an initial offer of securities in any offering or subsequent offering pursuant to this section, at least 80% of its assets and those of its subsidiaries on a consolidated basis located within such state or territory;

(iii) The issuer intends to use and uses at least 80% of the net proceeds to the issuer from sales made pursuant to this section (§230.147A) in connection with the operation of a business or of real property, the purchase of real property located in, or the rendering of services within such state or territory; or

(iv) A majority of the issuer's employees are based in such state or territory.

INSTRUCTION TO PARAGRAPH (c)

An issuer that has previously conducted an intrastate offering pursuant to this section (§230.147A) or Rule 147 (§230.147) may not conduct another intrastate offering pursuant to this section (§230.147A) in a different state or territory, until the expiration of the time period specified in paragraph (e) of this section (§230.147A(e)) or paragraph (e) of Rule 147 (§230.147(e)), calculated on the basis of the date of the last sale in such offering.

(d) *Residence of purchasers.* Sales of securities pursuant to this section (§230.147A) shall be made only to residents of the state or territory in which the issuer is resident, as determined pursuant to paragraph (c) of this section, or who the issuer reasonably believes, at the time of sale, are residents of the state or territory in which the issuer is resident. For purposes of determining the residence of purchasers:

(1) A corporation, partnership, limited liability company, trust or other form of business organization shall be deemed to be a resident of a state or territory if, at the time of sale to it, it has its principal place of business, as defined in paragraph (c)(1) of this section, within such state or territory.

INSTRUCTION TO PARAGRAPH (d)(1)

A trust that is not deemed by the law of the state or territory of its creation to be a separate legal entity is deemed to be a resident of each state or territory in which its trustee is, or trustees are, resident.

(2) Individuals shall be deemed to be residents of a state or territory if such individuals have, at the time of sale to them, their principal residence in the state or territory.

(3) A corporation, partnership, trust or other form of business organization, which is organized for the specific purpose of acquiring securities offered pursuant to this section (§230.147A), shall not be a resident of a state or territory unless all of the beneficial owners of such organization are residents of such state or territory.

INSTRUCTION TO PARAGRAPH (d)

Obtaining a written representation from purchasers of in-state residency status will not, without more, be sufficient to establish a reasonable belief that such purchasers are in-state residents.

(e) *Limitation on resales.* For a period of six months from the date of the sale by the issuer of a security pursuant to this section (§230.147A), any resale of such security shall be made only to persons resident within the state or territory in which the issuer was resident, as determined pursuant to paragraph (c) of this section, at the time of the sale of the security by the issuer.

INSTRUCTION TO PARAGRAPH (e)

In the case of convertible securities, resales of either the convertible security, or if it is converted, the underlying security, could be made during the period described in paragraph (e) only to persons resident within such state or territory. For purposes of this paragraph (e), a conversion in reliance on section 3(a)(9) of the Act (15 U.S.C. 77c(a)(9)) does not begin a new period.

(f) *Precautions against interstate sales.* (1) The issuer shall, in connection with any securities sold by it pursuant to this section:

(i) Place a prominent legend on the certificate or other document evidencing the security stating that: "Offers and sales of these securities were made under an exemption from registration and have not been registered under the Securities Act of 1933. For a period of six months from the date of the sale by the issuer of these securities, any resale of these securities (or the underlying securities in the case of convertible securities) shall be made only to persons resident within the state or territory of [identify the name of the state or territory in which the issuer was resident at the time of the sale of the securities by the issuer].";

(ii) Issue stop transfer instructions to the issuer's transfer agent, if any, with respect to the securities, or, if the issuer transfers its own securities, make a notation in the appropriate records of the issuer; and

(iii) Obtain a written representation from each purchaser as to his or her residence.

(2) The issuer shall, in connection with the issuance of new certificates for any of the securities that are sold pursuant to this section (§230.147A) that are

presented for transfer during the time period specified in paragraph (e), take the steps required by paragraphs (f)(1)(i) and (ii) of this section.

(3) The issuer shall, at the time of any offer or sale by it of a security pursuant to this section (§230.147A), prominently disclose to each offeree in the manner in which any such offer is communicated and to each purchaser of such security in writing a reasonable period of time before the date of sale, the following: "Sales will be made only to residents of the state or territory of [identify the name of the state or territory in which the issuer was resident at the time of the sale of the securities by the issuer]. Offers and sales of these securities are made under an exemption from registration and have not been registered under the Securities Act of 1933. For a period of six months from the date of the sale by the issuer of the securities, any resale of the securities (or the underlying securities in the case of convertible securities) shall be made only to persons resident within the state or territory of [identify the name of the state or territory in which the issuer was resident at the time of the sale of the securities by the issuer]."

(g) *Integration with other offerings.* To determine whether offers and sales should be integrated, refer to §230.152. (omitted)

Rule 163. Exemption from Section 5(c) of the Act for Certain Communications by or on Behalf of Well-known Seasoned Issuers

PRELIMINARY NOTE

Attempted compliance with this section does not act as an exclusive election and the issuer also may claim the availability of any other applicable exemption or exclusion. Reliance on this section does not affect the availability of any other exemption or exclusion from the requirements of section 5 of the Act.

(a) In an offering by or on behalf of a well-known seasoned issuer, as defined in Rule 405, that will be or is at the time intended to be registered under the Act, an offer by or on behalf of such issuer is exempt from the prohibitions in section 5(c) of the Act on offers to sell, offers for sale, or offers to buy its securities before a registration statement has been filed, provided that:

(1) Any written communication that is an offer made in reliance on this exemption will be a free writing prospectus as defined in Rule 405 and a prospectus under section 2(a)(10) of the Act relating to a public offering of securities to be covered by the registration statement to be filed; and

(2) The exemption from section 5(c) of the Act provided in this section for such written communication that is an offer shall be conditioned on satisfying the conditions in paragraph (b) of this section.

(b) *Conditions*

(1) *Legend*

(i) Every written communication that is an offer made in reliance on this exemption shall contain substantially the following legend:

The issuer may file a registration statement (including a prospectus) with the SEC for the offering to which this communication relates. Before you invest, you should read the prospectus in that registration statement and other documents the issuer has filed with the SEC for more complete information about the issuer and this offering. You may get these documents for free by visiting EDGAR on the SEC Web site at www.sec.gov. Alternatively, the company will arrange to send you the prospectus after filing if you request it by calling toll-free 1-8[xx-xxx-xxxx].

(ii) The legend also may provide an e-mail address at which the documents can be requested and may indicate that the documents also are available by accessing the issuer's Web site, and provide the Internet address and the particular location of the documents on the Web site.

(iii) An immaterial or unintentional failure to include the specified legend in a free writing prospectus required by this section will not result in a violation of section 5(c) of the Act or the loss of the ability to rely on this section so long as:

(A) A good faith and reasonable effort was made to comply with the specified legend condition;

(B) The free writing prospectus is amended to include the specified legend as soon as practicable after discovery of the omitted or incorrect legend; and

(C) If the free writing prospectus has been transmitted without the specified legend, the free writing prospectus is retransmitted with the legend by substantially the same means as, and directed to substantially the same prospective purchasers to whom, the free writing prospectus was originally transmitted.

(2) *Filing condition*

(i) Subject to paragraph (b)(2)(ii) of this section, every written communication that is an offer made in reliance on this exemption shall be filed by the issuer with the Commission promptly upon the filing of the registration statement, if one is filed, or an amendment, if one is filed, covering the securities that have been offered in reliance on this exemption.

(ii) The condition that an issuer shall file a free writing prospectus with the Commission under this section shall not apply in respect of any communication that has previously been filed with, or furnished to, the Commission or that the issuer would not be required to file with the Commission pursuant to the conditions of Rule 433 if the communication was a free writing prospectus used after the filing of the registration statement. The condition that the issuer shall file a free writing prospectus with the Commission under this section shall be satisfied if the issuer satisfies the filing conditions (other than timing of filing which is provided in this section) that would apply under Rule 433 if the communication was a free writing prospectus used after the filing of the registration statement.

(iii) An immaterial or unintentional failure to file or delay in filing a free writing prospectus to the extent provided in this section will not result in a violation of section 5(c) of the Act or the loss of the ability to rely on this section so long as:

(A) A good faith and reasonable effort was made to comply with the filing condition; and

(B) The free writing prospectus is filed as soon as practicable after discovery of the failure to file.

(3) *Ineligible offerings.* The exemption in paragraph (a) of this section shall not be available to:

(i) Communications relating to business combination transactions that are subject to Rule 165 or Rule 166;

(ii) Communications by an issuer that is an investment company registered under the Investment Company Act of 1940; or

(iii) Communications by an issuer that is a business development company as defined in section 2(a)(48) of the Investment Company Act of 1940.

(c) For purposes of this section, a communication is made by or on behalf of an issuer if the issuer or an agent or representative of the issuer, other than an offering participant who is an underwriter or dealer, authorizes or approves the communication before it is made.

(d) For purposes of this section, a communication for which disclosure would be required under section 17(b) of the Act as a result of consideration given or to be given, directly or indirectly, by or on behalf of an issuer is deemed to be an offer by the issuer and, if a written communication, is deemed to be a free writing prospectus of the issuer.

(e) A communication exempt from section 5(c) of the Act pursuant to this section will not be considered to be in connection with a securities offering registered under the Securities Act for purposes of Rule 100(b)(2)(iv) of Regulation FD under the Securities Exchange Act of 1934.

Rule 175. Liability for Certain Statements by Issuers

(a) A statement within the coverage of paragraph (b) of this section which is made by or on behalf of an issuer or by an outside reviewer retained by the issuer shall be deemed not to be a fraudulent statement (as defined in paragraph (d) of this section), unless it is shown that such statement was made or reaffirmed without a reasonable basis or was disclosed other than in good faith.

(b) This rule applies to the following statements:

(1) A forward-looking statement (as defined in paragraph (c) of this section) made in a document filed with the Commission, in Part I of a quarterly report on Form 10-Q, or in an annual report to security holders meeting the requirements of Rules 14a-3(b) and (c) or 14c-3(a) and (b) under the Securities Exchange Act of 1934, a statement reaffirming such forward-looking statement after the date the document was filed or the annual report was made publicly available, or a forward-looking statement made before the date the document was filed or the date the annual report was publicly available if such statement is reaffirmed in a filed document, in Part I of a quarterly report on Form 10-Q, or in an annual report made publicly available within a reasonable time after the making of such forward-looking statement; *Provided,* That

(i) At the time such statements are made or reaffirmed, either the issuer is subject to the reporting requirements of section 13(a) or 15(d) of the Securities

Exchange Act of 1934 and has complied with the requirements of Rule 13a-1 or 15d-1 thereunder, if applicable, to file its most recent annual report on Form 10-K, Form 20-F, or Form 40-F or if the issuer is not subject to the reporting requirements of section 13(a) or 15(d) of the Securities Exchange Act of 1934, the statements are made in a registration statement filed under the Act, offering statement or solicitation of interest written document or broadcast script under Regulation A or pursuant to section 12(b) or (g) of the Securities Exchange Act of 1934, and

(ii) The statements are not made by or on behalf of an issuer that is an investment company registered under the Investment Company Act of 1940; and

(2) Information which is disclosed in a document filed with the Commission, in Part I of a quarterly report on Form 10-Q or in an annual report to shareholders meeting the requirements of Rules 14a-3(b) and (c) or 14c-3(a) and (b) under the Securities Exchange Act of 1934 and which relates to (i) the effects of changing prices on the business enterprise, presented voluntarily or pursuant to Item 303 of Regulation S-K or Regulation S-B "Management's Discussion and Analysis of Financial Condition and Results of Operations," Item 5 of Form 20-F, Operating and Financial Review and Prospects, Item 302 of Regulation S-K, "Supplementary financial information," or Rule 3-20(c) of Regulation S-X, or (ii) the value of proved oil and gas reserves (such as a standardized measure of discounted future net cash flows relating to proved oil and gas reserves as set forth in FASB ASC paragraphs 932-235-50-29 through 932-235-50-36 (Extractive Activities—Oil and Gas Topic) presented voluntarily or pursuant to Item 302 of Regulation S-K.

(c) For the purpose of this rule, the term *forward-looking statement* shall mean and shall be limited to:

(1) A statement containing a projection of revenues, income (loss), earnings (loss) per share, capital expenditures, dividends, capital structure or other financial items;

(2) A statement of management's plans and objectives for future operations;

(3) A statement of future economic performance contained in management's discussion and analysis of financial condition and results of operations included pursuant to Item 303 of Regulation S-K or Item 5 of Form 20-F; or

(4) Disclosed statements of the assumptions underlying or relating to any of the statements described in paragraphs (c)(1), (2), or (3) of this section.

(d) For the purpose of this rule the term *fraudulent statement* shall mean a statement which is an untrue statement of a material fact, a statement false or misleading with respect to any material fact, an omission to state a material fact necessary to make a statement not misleading, or which constitutes the employment of a manipulative, deceptive, or fraudulent device, contrivance, scheme, transaction, act, practice, course of business, or an artifice to defraud, as those terms are used in the Securities Act of 1933 or the rules or regulations promulgated thereunder.

Rule 215. Accredited investor

. . .

(e) Any natural person whose individual net worth, or joint net worth with that person's spouse, exceeds $1,000,000.

(1) Except as provided in paragraph (e)(2) of this section, for purposes of calculating net worth under this paragraph (e):

(i) The person's primary residence shall not be included as an asset;

(ii) Indebtedness that is secured by the person's primary residence, up to the estimated fair market value of the primary residence at the time of the sale of securities, shall not be included as a liability (except that if the amount of such indebtedness outstanding at the time of the sale of securities exceeds the amount outstanding 60 days before such time, other than as a result of the acquisition of the primary residence, the amount of such excess shall be included as a liability); and

(iii) Indebtedness that is secured by the person's primary residence in excess of the estimated fair market value of the primary residence shall be included as a liability.

(2) Paragraph (1) of this section will not apply to any calculation of a person's net worth made in connection with a purchase of securities in accordance with a right to purchase such securities, provided that:

(i) Such right was held by the person on July 20, 2010;

(ii) The person qualified as an accredited investor on the basis of net worth at the time the person acquired such right; and

(iii) The person held securities of the same issuer, other than such right, on July 20, 2010.

Regulation A — Conditional Small Issues Exemption

Rule 251. Scope of Exemption

(a) *Tier 1 and Tier 2.* A public offer or sale of eligible securities, as defined in Rule 261, pursuant to Regulation A shall be exempt under section 3(b) from the registration requirements of the Securities Act of 1933 (the "Securities Act").

(1) *Tier 1.* Offerings pursuant to Regulation A in which the sum of all cash and other consideration to be received for the securities being offered ("aggregate offering price") plus the gross proceeds for all securities sold pursuant to other offering statements within the 12 months before the start of and during the current offering of securities ("aggregate sales") does not exceed $20,000,000, including not more than $6,000,000 offered by all selling securityholders that are affiliates of the issuer ("Tier 1 offerings").

(2) *Tier 2.* Offerings pursuant to Regulation A in which the sum of the aggregate offering price and aggregate sales does not exceed $75,000,000, including not more than $22,500,000 offered by all selling securityholders that are affiliates of the issuer ("Tier 2 offerings").

(3) *Additional limitation on secondary sales in first year.* The portion of the aggregate offering price attributable to the securities of selling securityholders shall not exceed 30% of the aggregate offering price of a particular offering in:

(i) The issuer's first offering pursuant to Regulation A; or

(ii) Any subsequent Regulation A offering that is qualified within one year of the qualification date of the issuer's first offering.

NOTE TO PARAGRAPH (a)

Where a mixture of cash and non-cash consideration is to be received, the aggregate offering price must be based on the price at which the securities are offered for cash. Any portion of the aggregate offering price or aggregate sales attributable to cash received in a foreign currency must be translated into United States currency at a currency exchange rate in effect on, or at a reasonable time before, the date of the sale of the securities. If securities are not offered for cash, the aggregate offering price or aggregate sales must be based on the value of the consideration as established by bona fide sales of that consideration made within a reasonable time, or, in the absence of sales, on the fair value as determined by an accepted standard. Valuations of non-cash consideration must be reasonable at the time made. If convertible securities or warrants are being offered and such securities are convertible, exercisable, or exchangeable within one year of the offering statement's qualification or at the discretion of the issuer, the underlying securities must also be qualified and the aggregate offering price must include the actual or maximum estimated conversion, exercise, or exchange price of such securities.

(b) *Issuer.* The issuer of the securities:

(1) Is an entity organized under the laws of the United States or Canada, or any State, Province, Territory or possession thereof, or the District of Columbia, with its principal place of business in the United States or Canada;

(2) (Reserved)

(3) Is not a development stage company that either has no specific business plan or purpose, or has indicated that its business plan is to merge with or acquire an unidentified company or companies;

(4) Is not an investment company registered or required to be registered under the Investment Company Act of 1940 or a business development company as defined in section 2(a)(48) of the Investment Company Act of 1940;

(5) Is not issuing fractional undivided interests in oil or gas rights, or a similar interest in other mineral rights;

(6) Is not, and has not been, subject to any order of the Commission entered pursuant to Section 12(j) of the Exchange Act within five years before the filing of the offering statement;

(7) Has filed with the Commission all reports required to be filed, if any, pursuant to Rule 257 or pursuant to section 13 or 15(d) of the Exchange Act (15 U.S.C. 78m or 15 U.S.C. 78o) during the two years before the filing of the offering statement (or for such shorter period that the issuer was required to file such reports); and

(8) Is not disqualified under Rule 262.

(c) *Integration with other offerings.* To determine whether offers and sales should be integrated, see §230.152.

(d) *Offering conditions*—(1) *Offers.* (i) Except as allowed by Rule 255, no offer of securities may be made unless an offering statement has been filed with the Commission.

(ii) After the offering statement has been filed, but before it is qualified:

(A) Oral offers may be made;

(B) Written offers pursuant to Rule 254 may be made; and

(C) Solicitations of interest and other communications pursuant to Rule 255 may be made.

(iii) Offers may be made after the offering statement has been qualified, but any written offers must be accompanied with or preceded by the most recent offering circular filed with the Commission for such offering.

(2) *Sales.* (i) No sale of securities may be made:

(A) Until the offering statement has been qualified;

(B) By issuers that are not currently required to file reports pursuant to Rule 257(b), until a Preliminary Offering Circular is delivered at least 48 hours before the sale to any person that before qualification of the offering statement had indicated an interest in purchasing securities in the offering, including those persons that responded to an issuer's solicitation of interest materials; and

(C) In a Tier 2 offering of securities that are not listed on a registered national securities exchange upon qualification, unless the purchaser is either an accredited investor (as defined in Rule 501) or the aggregate purchase price to be paid by the purchaser for the securities (including the actual or maximum estimated conversion, exercise, or exchange price for any underlying securities that have been qualified) is no more than ten percent (10%) of the greater of such purchaser's:

(1) Annual income or net worth if a natural person (with annual income and net worth for such natural person purchasers determined as provided in Rule 501; or

(2) Revenue or net assets for such purchaser's most recently completed fiscal year end if a non-natural person.

NOTE TO PARAGRAPH (d)(2)(i)(c)

When securities underlying warrants or convertible securities are being qualified pursuant to Tier 2 of Regulation A one year or more after the qualification of an offering for which investment limitations previously applied, purchasers of the underlying securities for which investment limitations would apply at that later date may determine compliance with the ten percent (10%) investment limitation using the conversion, exercise, or exchange price to acquire the underlying securities at that later time without aggregating such price with the price of the overlying warrants or convertible securities.

(D) The issuer may rely on a representation of the purchaser when determining compliance with the ten percent (10%) investment limitation in this paragraph (d)(2)(i)(C), provided that the issuer does not know at the time of sale that any such representation is untrue.

(ii) In a transaction that represents a sale by the issuer or an underwriter, or a sale by a dealer within 90 calendar days after qualification of the offering statement, each underwriter or dealer selling in such transaction must deliver to each purchaser from it, not later than two business days following the completion of such sale, a copy of the Final Offering Circular, subject to the following provisions: (A) If the sale was by the issuer and was not effected by or through an underwriter or dealer, the issuer is responsible for delivering the Final Offering Circular as if the issuer were an underwriter;

(B) For continuous or delayed offerings pursuant to paragraph (d)(3) of this section, the 90 calendar day period for dealers shall commence on the day of the first bona fide offering of securities under such offering statement;

(C) If the security is listed on a registered national securities exchange, no offering circular need be delivered by a dealer more than 25 calendar days after the later of the qualification date of the offering statement or the first date on which the security was bona fide offered to the public;

(D) No offering circular need be delivered by a dealer if the issuer is subject, immediately prior to the time of the filing of the offering statement, to the reporting requirements of Rule 257(b); and

(E) The Final Offering Circular delivery requirements set forth in paragraph (d)(2)(ii) of this section may be satisfied by delivering a notice to the effect that the sale was made pursuant to a qualified offering statement that includes the uniform resource locator ("URL"), which, in the case of an electronic-only offering, must be an active hyperlink, where the Final Offering Circular, or the offering statement of which such Final Offering Circular is part, may be obtained on the Commission's Electronic Data Gathering, Analysis and Retrieval System ("EDGAR") and contact information sufficient to notify a purchaser where a request for a Final Offering Circular can be sent and received in response.

(3) *Continuous or delayed offerings.* (i) Continuous or delayed offerings may be made under this Regulation A, so long as the offering statement pertains only to:

(A) Securities that are to be offered or sold solely by or on behalf of a person or persons other than the issuer, a subsidiary of the issuer, or a person of which the issuer is a subsidiary;

(B) Securities that are to be offered and sold pursuant to a dividend or interest reinvestment plan or an employee benefit plan of the issuer;

(C) Securities that are to be issued upon the exercise of outstanding options, warrants, or rights;

(D) Securities that are to be issued upon conversion of other outstanding securities;

(E) Securities that are pledged as collateral; or

(F) Securities the offering of which will be commenced within two calendar days after the qualification date, will be made on a continuous basis, may continue for a period in excess of 30 calendar days from the date of initial qualification, and will be offered in an amount that, at the time the offering statement is qualified, is reasonably expected to be offered and sold within two years from the initial qualification date. These securities may be offered and sold only if not more than three years have elapsed since the initial qualification date of the offering statement under which they are being offered and sold; provided, however, that if a new offering statement has been filed pursuant to this paragraph (d)(3)(i)(F), securities covered by the prior offering statement may continue to be offered and sold until the earlier of the qualification date of the new offering statement or 180 calendar days after the third anniversary of the initial qualification date of the prior offering statement. Before the end of such three-year period, an issuer may file a new offering statement covering the securities. The new offering statement must include all the information that would be required at that time in an offering statement relating to all offerings that it covers. Before the qualification date of the new offering statement, the issuer may include as part of such new offering statement any unsold securities covered by the earlier offering statement by identifying on the cover page of the new offering circular, or the latest amendment, the amount of such unsold securities being included. The offering of securities on the earlier offering statement will be deemed terminated as of the date of qualification of the new offering statement. Securities may be sold pursuant to this paragraph (d)(3)(i)(F) only if the issuer is current in its annual and semiannual filings pursuant to Rule 257(b), at the time of such sale.

(ii) At the market offerings, by or on behalf of the issuer or otherwise, are not permitted under this Regulation A. As used in this paragraph (d)(3)(ii), the term *at the market offering* means an offering of equity securities into an existing trading market for outstanding shares of the same class at other than a fixed price.

(e) *Confidential treatment.* A request for confidential treatment may be made under Rule 406 for information required to be filed, and Rule 83 for information not required to be filed.

(f) *Electronic filing.* Documents filed or otherwise provided to the Commission pursuant to this Regulation A must be submitted in electronic format by means of EDGAR in accordance with the EDGAR rules set forth in Regulation S-T.

Rule 252. Offering Statement

(a) *Documents to be included.* The offering statement consists of the contents required by Form 1-A (§239.90 of this chapter) and any other material information necessary to make the required statements, in light of the circumstances under which they are made, not misleading.

(b) *Paper, printing, language and pagination.* Except as otherwise specified in this rule, the requirements for offering statements are the same as those specified in Rule 403 for registration statements under the Act. No fee is payable to the Commission upon either the submission or filing of an offering statement on Form 1-A, or any amendment to an offering statement.

(c) *Signatures.* The issuer, its principal executive officer, principal financial officer, principal accounting officer, and a majority of the members of its board of directors or other governing body, must sign the offering statement in the manner prescribed by Form 1-A. If a signature is by a person on behalf of any other person, evidence of authority to sign must be filed, except where an executive officer signs for the issuer.

(d) *Non-public submission.* An issuer whose securities have not been previously sold pursuant to a qualified offering statement under this Regulation A or an effective registration statement under the Securities Act may submit a draft offering statement to the Commission for non-public review by the staff of the Commission before public filing, provided that the offering statement shall not be qualified less than 21 calendar days after the public filing with the Commission of:

(1) The initial non-public submission;

(2) All non-public amendments; and

(3) All non-public correspondence submitted by or on behalf of the issuer to the Commission staff regarding such submissions (subject to any separately approved confidential treatment request under Rule 251(e).

(e) *Qualification.* An offering statement and any amendment thereto can be qualified only at such date and time as the Commission may determine.

(f) *Amendments.* (1) (i) Amendments to an offering statement must be signed and filed with the Commission in the same manner as the initial filing. Amendments to an offering statement must be filed under cover of Form 1-A and must be numbered consecutively in the order in which filed.

(ii) Every amendment that includes amended audited financial statements must include the consent of the certifying accountant to the use of such accountant's certification in connection with the amended financial statements in the offering statement or offering circular and to being named as having audited such financial statements.

(iii) Amendments solely relating to Part III of Form 1-A must comply with the requirements of paragraph (f)(1)(i) of this section, except that such amendments may be limited to Part I of Form 1-A, an explanatory note, and all of the information required by Part III of Form 1-A.

(2) Post-qualification amendments must be filed in the following circumstances for ongoing offerings:

(i) At least every 12 months after the qualification date to include the financial statements that would be required by Form 1-A as of such date; or

(ii) To reflect any facts or events arising after the qualification date of the offering statement (or the most recent post-qualification amendment thereof) which, individually or in the aggregate, represent a fundamental change in the information set forth in the offering statement.

Rule 253. Offering Circular

(a) *Contents.* An offering circular must include the information required by Form 1-A for offering circulars.

(b) *Information that may be omitted.* Notwithstanding paragraph (a) of this section, a qualified offering circular may omit information with respect to the public offering price, underwriting syndicate (including any material relationships between the issuer or selling securityholders and the unnamed underwriters, brokers or dealers), underwriting discounts or commissions, discounts or commissions to dealers, amount of proceeds, conversion rates, call prices and other items dependent upon the offering price, delivery dates, and terms of the securities dependent upon the offering date; provided, that the following conditions are met:

(1) The securities to be qualified are offered for cash.

(2) The outside front cover page of the offering circular includes a bona fide estimate of the range of the maximum offering price and the maximum number of shares or other units of securities to be offered or a bona fide estimate of the principal amount of debt securities offered, subject to the following conditions:

(i) The range must not exceed $2 for offerings where the upper end of the range is $10 or less or 20% if the upper end of the price range is over $10; and

(ii) The upper end of the range must be used in determining the aggregate offering price under Rule 251(a).

(3) The offering statement does not relate to securities to be offered by competitive bidding.

(4) The volume of securities (the number of equity securities or aggregate principal amount of debt securities) to be offered may not be omitted in reliance on this paragraph (b).

NOTE TO PARAGRAPH (b)

A decrease in the volume of securities offered or a change in the bona fide estimate of the offering price range from that indicated in the offering circular filed as part of a qualified offering statement may be disclosed in the offering circular filed with the Commission pursuant to Rule 253(g), so long as the decrease in the volume of securities offered or change in the price range would not materially change the disclosure contained in the offering statement at qualification. Notwithstanding the foregoing, any decrease in the volume of securities offered and any deviation from the low or high end of the price range may be reflected in the offering circular supplement filed with the Commission pursuant to Rule 253(g)(1) or (3) if, in the aggregate, the decrease in volume and/or change in price represent no more than a 20% change from the maximum aggregate offering price calculable using the information in the qualified offering statement. In no circumstances may this paragraph be used to offer securities where the maximum aggregate offering price would result in the offering exceeding the limit set forth in Rule 251(a) or if the change would result in a Tier 1 offering becoming a Tier 2 offering. An offering circular supplement may not be used to increase the volume of securities being offered. Additional securities may only be offered pursuant to a new offering statement or post-qualification amendment qualified by the Commission.

(c) *Filing of omitted information.* The information omitted from the offering circular in reliance upon paragraph (b) of this section must be contained in an offering circular filed with the Commission pursuant to paragraph (g) of this section; except that if such offering circular is not so filed by the later of 15 business days after the qualification date of the offering statement or 15 business days after the qualification of a post-qualification amendment thereto that contains an offering circular, the information omitted in reliance upon paragraph (b) of this section must be contained in a qualified post-qualification amendment to the offering statement.

(d) *Presentation of information.* (1) Information in the offering circular must be presented in a clear, concise and understandable manner and in a type size that is easily readable. Repetition of information should be avoided; cross-referencing of information within the document is permitted.

(2) Where an offering circular is distributed through an electronic medium, issuers may satisfy legibility requirements applicable to printed documents by presenting all required information in a format readily communicated to investors.

(e) *Date.* An offering circular must be dated approximately as of the date it was filed with the Commission.

(f) *Cover page legend.* The cover page of every offering circular must display the following statement highlighted by prominent type or in another manner:

The United States Securities and Exchange Commission does not pass upon the merits of or give its approval to any securities offered or the terms of the offering, nor does it pass upon the accuracy or completeness of any offering circular or other solicitation materials. These securities are offered pursuant to an exemption from registration with the Commission; however, the Commission has not made an independent determination that the securities offered are exempt from registration.

(g) *Offering circular supplements.* (1) An offering circular that discloses information previously omitted from the offering circular in reliance upon Rule 253(b) must be filed with the Commission no later than two business days following the earlier of the date of determination of the offering price or the date such offering circular is first used after qualification in connection with a public offering or sale.

(2) An offering circular that reflects information other than that covered in paragraph (g)(1) of this section that constitutes a substantive change from or addition to the information set forth in the last offering circular filed with the Commission must be filed with the Commission no later than five business days after the date it is first used after qualification in connection with a public offering or sale. If an offering circular filed pursuant to this paragraph (g)(2) consists of an offering circular supplement attached to an offering circular that previously had been filed or was not required to be filed pursuant to paragraph (g) of this section because it did not contain substantive changes from an offering circular that previously was filed, only the offering circular supplement need be filed under paragraph (g) of this section, provided that the cover page of the offering circular supplement identifies the date(s) of the related offering circular and any offering circular supplements thereto that together constitute the offering circular with respect to the securities currently being offered or sold.

(3) An offering circular that discloses information, facts or events covered in both paragraphs (g)(1) and (2) of this section must be filed with the Commission no later than two business days following the earlier of the date of the determination of the offering price or the date it is first used after qualification in connection with a public offering or sale.

(4) An offering circular required to be filed pursuant to paragraph (g) of this section that is not filed within the time frames specified in paragraphs (g)(1) through (3) of this section, as applicable, must be filed pursuant to this paragraph (g)(4) as soon as practicable after the discovery of such failure to file.

(5) Each offering circular filed under this section must contain in the upper right corner of the cover page the paragraphs of paragraphs (g)(1) through (4) of this section under which the filing is made, and the file number of the offering statement to which the offering circular relates.

Rule 254. Preliminary Offering Circular

After the filing of an offering statement, but before its qualification, written offers of securities may be made if they meet the following requirements:

(a) *Outside front cover page.* The outside front cover page of the material bears the caption *Preliminary Offering Circular,* the date of issuance, and the following legend, which must be highlighted by prominent type or in another manner:

An offering statement pursuant to Regulation A relating to these securities has been filed with the Securities and Exchange Commission. Information contained in this Preliminary Offering Circular is subject to completion or amendment. These securities may not be sold nor may offers to buy be accepted before the offering statement filed with the Commission is qualified. This Preliminary Offering Circular shall not constitute an offer to sell or the solicitation of an offer to buy nor may there be any sales of these securities in any state in which such offer, solicitation or sale would be unlawful before registration or qualification under the laws of any such state. We may elect to satisfy our obligation to deliver a Final Offering Circular by sending you a notice within two business days after the completion of our sale to you that contains the URL where the Final Offering Circular or the offering statement in which such Final Offering Circular was filed may be obtained.

(b) *Other contents.* The Preliminary Offering Circular contains substantially the information required to be in an offering circular by Form 1-A (§239.90 of this chapter), except that certain information may be omitted under Rule 253(b) subject to the conditions set forth in such rule.

(c) *Filing.* The Preliminary Offering Circular is filed as a part of the offering statement.

Rule 255. Solicitations of Interest and Other Communications

(a) *Solicitation of interest.* At any time before the qualification of an offering statement, including before the non-public submission or public filing of such offering statement, an issuer or any person authorized to act on behalf of an issuer may communicate orally or in writing to determine whether there is any interest in a contemplated securities offering. Such communications are deemed to be an offer of a security for sale for purposes of the antifraud provisions of the federal securities laws. No solicitation or acceptance of money or other consideration, nor of any commitment, binding or otherwise, from any person is permitted until qualification of the offering statement.

(b) *Conditions.* The communications must:

(1) State that no money or other consideration is being solicited, and if sent in response, will not be accepted;

(2) State that no offer to buy the securities can be accepted and no part of the purchase price can be received until the offering statement is qualified, and any such offer may be withdrawn or revoked, without obligation or commitment of any kind, at any time before notice of its acceptance given after the qualification date;

(3) State that a person's indication of interest involves no obligation or commitment of any kind; and

(4) After the public filing of the offering statement:

(i) State from whom a copy of the most recent version of the Preliminary Offering Circular may be obtained, including a phone number and address of such person;

(ii) Provide the URL where such Preliminary Offering Circular, or the offering statement in which such Preliminary Offering Circular was filed, may be obtained; or

(iii) Include a complete copy of the Preliminary Offering Circular.

(c) *Indications of interest.* Any written communication under this rule may include a means by which a person may indicate to the issuer that such person is interested in a potential offering. This issuer may require the name, address, telephone number, and/or e-mail address in any response form included pursuant to this paragraph (c).

(d) *Revised solicitations of interest.* If solicitation of interest materials are used after the public filing of the offering statement and such solicitation of interest materials contain information that is inaccurate or inadequate in any material respect, revised solicitation of interest materials must be redistributed in a substantially similar manner as such materials were originally distributed. Notwithstanding the foregoing in this paragraph (d), if the only information that is inaccurate or inadequate is contained in a Preliminary Offering Circular provided with the solicitation of interest materials pursuant to paragraphs (b)(4)(i) or (ii) of this section, no such redistribution is required in the following circumstances:

(1) in the case of paragraph (b)(4)(i) of this section, the revised Preliminary Offering Circular will be provided to any persons making new inquiries and will be recirculated to any persons making any previous inquiries; or

(2) in the case of paragraph (b)(4)(ii) of this section, the URL continues to link directly to the most recent Preliminary Offering Circular or to the offering statement in which such revised Preliminary Offering Circular was filed.

Rule 256. Definition of "Qualified Purchaser"

For purposes of Section 18(b)(3) of the Securities Act, a "qualified purchaser" means any person to whom securities are offered or sold pursuant to a Tier 2 offering of this Regulation A.

Rule 257. Periodic and Current Reporting; Exit Report

(a) *Tier 1: Exit report.* Each issuer that has filed an offering statement for a Tier 1 offering that has been qualified pursuant to this Regulation A must file an exit report on Form 1-Z (§239.94 of this chapter) not later than 30 calendar days after the termination or completion of the offering.

(b) *Tier 2: Periodic and current reporting.* Each issuer that has filed an offering statement for a Tier 2 offering that has been qualified pursuant to this Regulation A must file with the Commission the following periodic and current reports:

(1) *Annual reports.* An annual report on Form 1-K (§239.91 of this chapter) for the fiscal year in which the offering statement became qualified and for any fiscal year thereafter, unless the issuer's obligation to file such annual report is suspended under paragraph (d) of this section. Annual reports must be filed within the period specified in Form 1-K.

(2) *Special financial report.* (i) A special financial report on Form 1-K or Form 1-SA if the offering statement did not contain the following:

(A) audited financial statements for the issuer's most recent fiscal year (or for the life of the issuer if less than a full fiscal year) preceding the fiscal year in which the issuer's offering statement became qualified; or

(B) unaudited financial statements covering the first six months of the issuer's current fiscal year if the offering statement was qualified during the last six months of that fiscal year.

(ii) The special financial report described in paragraph (b)(2)(i)(A) of this section must be filed under cover of Form 1-K within 120 calendar days after the qualification date of the offering statement and must include audited financial statements for such fiscal year or other period specified in that paragraph, as the case may be. The special financial report described in paragraph (b)(2)(i)(B) of this section must be filed under cover of Form 1-SA within 90 calendar days after the qualification date of the offering statement and must include the semiannual financial statements for the first six months of the issuer's fiscal year, which may be unaudited.

(iii) A special financial report must be signed in accordance with the requirements of the form on which it is filed.

(3) *Semiannual report.* A semiannual report on Form 1-SA (§239.92 of this chapter) within the period specified in Form 1-SA. Semiannual reports must cover the first six months of each fiscal year of the issuer, commencing with the first six months of the fiscal year immediately following the most recent fiscal year for which full financial statements were included in the offering statement, or, if the offering statement included financial statements for the first six months of the fiscal year following the most recent full fiscal year, for the first six months of the following fiscal year.

(4) *Current reports.* Current reports on Form 1-U (§239.93 of this chapter) with respect to the matters and within the period specified in that form, unless substantially the same information has been previously reported to the Commission by the issuer under cover of Form 1-K or Form 1-SA.

(5) *Reporting by successor issuers.* Where in connection with a succession by merger, consolidation, exchange of securities, acquisition of assets or otherwise, securities of any issuer that is not required to file reports pursuant to paragraph (b) of this section are issued to the holders of any class of securities of another issuer that is required to file such reports, the duty to file reports pursuant to paragraph (b) of this section shall be deemed to have been assumed by the issuer of the class of securities so issued. The successor issuer must, after the consummation of the succession, file reports in accordance with paragraph (b) of this section, unless that issuer is exempt from filing such reports or the duty to file such reports is terminated or suspended under paragraph (d) of this section.

(6) *Exchange Act reporting requirements.* The duty to file reports under this rule shall be deemed to have been met if the issuer is subject to the reporting requirements of Section 13 or 15(d) of the Exchange Act and, as of each Form 1-K and Form 1-SA due date, has filed all reports required to be filed by Section 13 or 15(d) of the Exchange Act during the 12 months (or such shorter period that the registrant was required to file such reports) preceding such due date.

(c) *Amendments.* All amendments to the reports described in paragraphs (a) and (b) of this section must be filed under cover of the form amended, marked with the letter *A* to designate the document as an amendment, *e.g.*, "1-K/A," and in compliance with pertinent requirements applicable to such reports. Amendments filed pursuant to this paragraph (c) must set forth the complete text of each item as amended, but need not include any items that were not amended. Amendments must be numbered sequentially and be filed separately for each report amended. Amendments must be signed on behalf of the issuer by a duly authorized representative of the issuer. An amendment to any report required to include certifications as specified in the applicable form must include new certifications by the appropriate persons.

(d) *Suspension of duty to file reports.*

(1) (Reserved)

(2) The duty to file reports under paragraph (b) of this section with respect to a class of securities held of record (as defined in Rule 12g5-1 by less than 300 persons, or less than 1,200 persons for a bank (as defined in Section 3(a)(6) of the Exchange Act, or a bank holding company (as defined in section 2 of the Bank Holding Company Act of 1956 (12 U.S.C. 1841)))), shall be suspended for such class of securities immediately upon filing with the Commission an exit report on

Form 1-Z (§239.94 of this chapter) if the issuer of such class has filed all reports due pursuant to this rule before the date of such Form 1-Z filing for the shorter of:

(i) The period since the issuer became subject to such reporting obligation; or

(ii) Its most recent three fiscal years and the portion of the current year preceding the date of filing Form 1-Z.

(3) For the purposes of paragraph (d)(2) of this section, the term *class* shall be construed to include all securities of an issuer that are of substantially similar character and the holders of which enjoy substantially similar rights and privileges. If the Form 1-Z is subsequently withdrawn or if it is denied because the issuer was ineligible to use the form, the issuer must, within 60 calendar days, file with the Commission all reports which would have been required if such exit report had not been filed. If the suspension resulted from the issuer's merger into, or consolidation with, another issuer or issuers, the notice must be filed by the successor issuer.

(4) The ability to suspend reporting, as described in paragraph (d)(2) of this section, is not available for any class of securities if:

(i) During that fiscal year a Tier 2 offering statement was qualified;

(ii) The issuer has not filed an annual report under this rule or the Ex-change Act for the fiscal year in which a Tier 2 offering statement was qualified; or

(iii) Offers or sales of securities of that class are being made pursuant to a Tier 2 Regulation A offering.

(e) *Termination of duty to file reports.* If the duty to file reports is deemed to have been met pursuant to paragraph (b)(6) of this section and such status ends because the issuer terminates or suspends its duty to file reports under the Exchange Act, the issuer's obligation to file reports under paragraph (b) of this section shall:

(1) Automatically terminate if the issuer is eligible to suspend its duty to file reports under paragraphs (d)(2) and (3) of this section; or

(2) Recommence with the report covering the most recent financial period after that included in any effective registration statement or filed Exchange Act report.

Rule 260. Insignificant Deviations from a Term, Condition or Requirement of Regulation A

(a) *Failure to comply.* A failure to comply with a term, condition or requirement of Regulation A will not result in the loss of the exemption from the requirements of section 5 of the Securities Act for any offer or sale to a particular individual or entity, if the person relying on the exemption establishes that:

(1) The failure to comply did not pertain to a term, condition or requirement directly intended to protect that particular individual or entity;

(2) The failure to comply was insignificant with respect to the offering as a whole, provided that any failure to comply with Rule 251(a), (b), and (d)(1) and (3) shall be deemed to be significant to the offering as a whole; and

(3) A good faith and reasonable attempt was made to comply with all applicable terms, conditions and requirements of Regulation A.

(b) *Action by Commission.* A transaction made in reliance upon Regulation A must comply with all applicable terms, conditions and requirements of the regulation. Where an exemption is established only through reliance upon paragraph (a) of this section, the failure to comply shall nonetheless be actionable by the Commission under section 20 of the Securities Act.

(c) *Suspension.* This provision provides no relief or protection from a proceeding under Rule 258.

Rule 262. Disqualification Provisions

(a) *Disqualification events.* No exemption under this Regulation A shall be available for a sale of securities if the issuer; any predecessor of the issuer; any affiliated issuer; any director, executive officer, other officer participating in the offering, general partner or managing member of the issuer; any beneficial owner of 20% or more of the issuer's outstanding voting equity securities, calculated on the basis of voting power; any promoter connected with the issuer in any capacity at the time of filing, any offer after qualification, or such sale; any person that has been or will be paid (directly or indirectly) remuneration for solicitation of purchasers in connection with such sale of securities; any general partner or managing member of any such solicitor; or any director, executive officer or other officer participating in the offering of any such solicitor or general partner or managing member of such solicitor:

[The list of various disqualifying events is omitted].

(b) *Transition, waivers, reasonable care exception.* Paragraph (a) of this section shall not apply:

. . .

(2) Upon a showing of good cause and without prejudice to any other action by the Commission, if the Commission determines that it is not necessary under the circumstances that an exemption be denied;

(3) If, before the filing of the offering statement or the relevant sale, the court or regulatory authority that entered the relevant order, judgment or decree advises in writing (whether contained in the relevant judgment, order or decree or separately to the Commission or its staff) that disqualification under paragraph (a) of this section should not arise as a consequence of such order, judgment or decree; or

(4) If the issuer establishes that it did not know and, in the exercise of reasonable care, could not have known that a disqualification existed under paragraph (a) of this section.

NOTE TO PARAGRAPH (b)(4)

An issuer will not be able to establish that it has exercised reasonable care unless it has made, in light of the circumstances, factual inquiry into whether any disqualifications exist. The nature and scope of the factual inquiry will vary based on the facts and circumstances concerning, among other things, the issuer and the other offering participants.

(c) *Affiliated issuers.* For purposes of paragraph (a) of this section, events relating to any affiliated issuer that occurred before the affiliation arose will be not considered disqualifying if the affiliated entity is not:

(1) In control of the issuer; or

(2) Under common control with the issuer by a third party that was in control of the affiliated entity at the time of such events.

(d) *Disclosure of prior "bad actor" events.* The issuer must include in the offering circular a description of any matters that would have triggered disqualification under paragraphs (a)(3) and (5) of this section but occurred before xx/xx/xxxx. The failure to provide such information shall not prevent an issuer from relying on Regulation A if the issuer establishes that it did not know and, in the exercise of reasonable care, could not have known of the existence of the undisclosed matter or matters.

Regulation C — Registration

Rule 405. Definitions of Terms

Unless the context otherwise requires, all terms used in Rules 400 to 494, inclusive, or in the forms for registration have the same meanings as in the Act and in the general rules and regulations. In addition, the following definitions apply, unless the context otherwise requires:

Affiliate. An *affiliate* of, or person *affiliated* with, a specified person, is a person that directly, or indirectly through one or more intermediaries, controls or is controlled by, or is under common control with, the person specified. . . .

Associate. The term *associate,* when used to indicate a relationship with any person, means (1) a corporation or organization (other than the registrant or a majority-owned subsidiary of the registrant) of which such person is an officer or partner or is, directly or indirectly, the beneficial owner of 10 percent or more of any class of equity securities, (2) any trust or other estate in which such person has a substantial beneficial interest or as to which such person serves as trustee or in a similar capacity, and (3) any relative or spouse of such person, or any relative of such spouse, who has the same home as such person or who is a director or officer of the registrant or any of its parents or subsidiaries. . . .

Charter. The term *charter* includes articles of incorporation, declarations of trust, articles of association or partnership, or any similar instrument, as amended, affecting (either with or without filing with any governmental agency) the organization or creation of an incorporated or unincorporated person.

Common equity. The term *common equity* means any class of common stock or an equivalent interest, including but not limited to a unit of beneficial interest in a trust or a limited partnership interest.

Commission. The term *Commission* means the Securities and Exchange Commission.

Control. The term *control* (including the terms *controlling, controlled by* and *under common control with*) means the possession, direct or indirect, of the power to direct or cause the direction of the management and policies of a person, whether through the ownership of voting securities, by contract, or otherwise.

Depositary share. The term *depositary share* means a security, evidenced by an American Depositary Receipt, that represents a foreign security or a multiple of or fraction thereof deposited with a depositary.

Director. The term *director* means any director of a corporation or any person performing similar functions with respect to any organization whether incorporated or unincorporated. . . .

Employee. The term *employee* does not include a director, trustee, or officer. . . .

Employee benefit plan. . . .

Emerging Growth Company.

(1) The term *emerging growth company* means an issuer that had total annual gross revenues of less than $1,235,000,000 during its most recently completed fiscal year.

(2) An issuer that is an emerging growth company as of the first day of that fiscal year shall continue to be deemed an emerging growth company until the earliest of:

(i) the last day of the fiscal year of the issuer during which it had total annual gross revenues of $1,235,000,000 or more;

(ii) the last day of the fiscal year of the issuer following the fifth anniversary of the date of the first sale of common equity securities of the issuer pursuant to an effective registration statement under the Securities Act of 1933;

(iii) the date on which such issuer has, during the previous three-year period, issued more than $1,000,000,000 in non-convertible debt; or

(iv) the date on which such issuer is deemed to be a large accelerated filer, as defined in Rule 12b-2 of the Exchange Act, or any successor thereto.

Equity security. The term *equity security* means any stock or similar security, certificate of interest or participation in any profit sharing agreement, preorganization certificate or subscription, transferable share, voting trust certificate or certificate of deposit for an equity security, limited partnership interest, interest in a joint venture, or certificate of interest in a business trust; any security future on any such security; or any security convertible, with or without consideration into such a security, or carrying any warrant or right to subscribe to or purchase such a security; or any such warrant or right; or any put, call, straddle, or other option or privilege of buying such a security from or selling such a security to another without being bound to do so.

Executive officer. The term *executive officer,* when used with reference to a registrant, means its president, any vice president of the registrant in charge of a principal business unit, division or function (such as sales, administration or finance), any other officer who performs a policy making function or any other person who performs similar policy making functions for the registrant. Executive officers of subsidiaries may be deemed executive officers of the registrant if they perform such policy making functions for the registrant. . . .

Material. The term *material,* when used to qualify a requirement for the furnishing of information as to any subject, limits the information required to those matters to which there is a substantial likelihood that a reasonable investor would attach importance in determining whether to purchase the security registered.

Officer. The term *officer* means a president, vice president, secretary, treasurer or principal financial officer, comptroller or principal accounting officer, and any person routinely performing corresponding functions with respect to any organization whether incorporated or unincorporated.

Parent. A *parent* of a specified person is an affiliate controlling such person directly, or indirectly through one or more intermediaries. . . .

Promoter. (1) The term *promoter* includes:

(i) Any person who, acting alone or in conjunction with one or more other persons, directly or indirectly takes initiative in founding and organizing the business or enterprise of an issuer; or

(ii) Any person who, in connection with the founding and organizing of the business or enterprise of an issuer, directly or indirectly receives in consideration of services or property, or both services and property, 10 percent or more of any class of securities of the issuer or 10 percent or more of the proceeds from the sale of any class of such securities. However, a person who receives such securities or proceeds either solely as underwriting commissions or solely in consideration of property shall not be deemed a promoter within the meaning of this paragraph if such person does not otherwise take part in founding and organizing the enterprise.

(2) All persons coming within the definition of *promoter* in paragraph (1) of this definition may be referred to as *founders* or *organizers* or by another term provided that such term is reasonably descriptive of those persons' activities with respect to the issuer.

Prospectus. Unless otherwise specified or the context otherwise requires, the term *prospectus* means a prospectus meeting the requirements of section 10(a) of the Act.

Registrant. The term *registrant* means the issuer of the securities for which the registration statement is filed.

Share. The term *share* means a share of stock in a corporation or unit of interest in an unincorporated person. . . .

Smaller reporting company. As used in this part, the term *smaller reporting company* means an issuer that is not an investment company, an asset-backed issuer, or a majority-owned subsidiary of a parent that is not a smaller reporting company and that:

(1) Had a public float of less than $250 million; or

(2) Had annual revenues of less than $100 million and either:

(i) No public float; or

(ii) A public float of less than $700 million.

(3) Whether an issuer is a smaller reporting company is determined on an annual basis . . .

Regulation D — Rules Governing the Limited Offer and Sale of Securities Without Registration Under the Securities Act of 1933

Rule 500. Use of Regulation D

Users of Regulation D (§§230.500 *et seq.*) should note the following:

(a) Regulation D relates to transactions exempted from the registration requirements of section 5 of the Securities Act of 1933 (the Act) (15 U.S.C.77a *et seq.*, as amended). Such transactions are not exempt from the antifraud, civil liability, or other provisions of the federal securities laws. Issuers are reminded of their obligation to provide such further material information, if any, as may be necessary to make the information required under Regulation D, in light of the circumstances under which it is furnished, not misleading.

(b) Nothing in Regulation D obviates the need to comply with any applicable state law relating to the offer and sale of securities. Regulation D is intended to be a basic element in a uniform system of federal-state limited offering exemptions consistent with the provisions of sections 18 and 19(c) of the Act (15 U.S.C. 77r and 77(s)(c)). In those states that have adopted Regulation D, or any version of

Regulation D, special attention should be directed to the applicable state laws and regulations, including those relating to registration of persons who receive remuneration in connection with the offer and sale of securities, to disqualification of issuers and other persons associated with offerings based on state administrative orders or judgments, and to requirements for filings of notices of sales.

(c) Attempted compliance with any rule in Regulation D does not act as an exclusive election; the issuer can also claim the availability of any other applicable exemption. For instance, an issuer's failure to satisfy all the terms and conditions of rule 506 (§230.506) shall not raise any presumption that the exemption provided by section 4(a)(2) of the Act (15 U.S.C. 77d(a)(2)) is not available.

(d) Regulation D is available only to the issuer of the securities and not to any affiliate of that issuer or to any other person for resales of the issuer's securities. Regulation D provides an exemption only for the transactions in which the securities are offered or sold by the issuer, not for the securities themselves.

(e) Regulation D may be used for business combinations that involve sales by virtue of rule 145(a) (§230.145(a)) or otherwise.

(f) In view of the objectives of Regulation D and the policies underlying the Act, Regulation D is not available to any issuer for any transaction or chain of transactions that, although in technical compliance with Regulation D, is part of a plan or scheme to evade the registration provisions of the Act. In such cases, registration under the Act is required.

(g) Securities offered and sold outside the United States in accordance with Regulation S (§230.901 through 905) need not be registered under the Act. See Release No. 33-6863. Regulation S may be relied upon for such offers and sales even if coincident offers and sales are made in accordance with Regulation D inside the United States. See §230.152(b)(2). Thus, for example, persons who are offered and sold securities in accordance with Regulation S would not be counted in the calculation of the number of purchasers under Regulation D. Similarly, proceeds from such sales would not be included in the aggregate offering price. The provisions of this paragraph (g), however, do not apply if the issuer elects to rely solely on Regulation D for offers or sales to persons made outside the United States. See §§230.502(a) and 230.152.

Rule 501. Definitions and Terms Used in Regulation D

As used in Regulation D (Rules 500 *et seq.*), the following terms shall have the meaning indicated:

(a) *Accredited investor. Accredited investor* shall mean any person who comes within any of the following categories, or who the issuer reasonably believes comes within any of the following categories, at the time of the sale of the securities to that person:

(1) Any bank as defined in section 3(a)(2) of the Act, or any savings and loan association or other institution as defined in section 3(a)(5)(A) of the Act whether acting in its individual or fiduciary capacity; any broker or dealer registered pursuant to section 15 of the Securities Exchange Act of 1934; any insurance company as defined in section 2(a)(13) of the Act, any investment company registered under the Investment Company Act of 1940 or a business development company as defined in Section 2(a)(48) of that Act; any Small Business Investment Company licensed by the U.S. Small Business Administration under section 301(c) or (d) of the Small Business Investment Act of 1958; any plan established and maintained by a state, its political

subdivisions, or any agency or instrumentality of a state or its political subdivisions, for the benefit of its employees, if such plan has total assets in excess of $5,000,000; any employee benefit plan within the meaning of the Employee Retirement Income Security Act of 1974 if the investment decision is made by a plan fiduciary, as defined in section 3(21) of such act, which is either a bank, savings and loan association, insurance company, or registered investment adviser, or if the employee benefit plan has total assets in excess of $5,000,000 or, if a self-directed plan, with investment decisions made solely by persons that are accredited investors;

(2) Any private business development company as defined in section 202(a)(22) of the Investment Advisers Act of 1940;

(3) Any organization described in section 501(c)(3) of the Internal Revenue Code, corporation, Massachusetts or similar business trust, or partnership, not formed for the specific purpose of acquiring the securities offered, with total assets in excess of $5,000,000;

(4) Any director, executive officer, or general partner of the issuer of the securities being offered or sold, or any director, executive officer, or general partner of a general partner of that issuer;

(5) Any natural person whose individual net worth, or joint net worth with that person's spouse, exceeds $1,000,000.

(i) Except as provided in paragraph (a)(5)(ii) of this section, for purposes of calculating net worth under this paragraph (a)(5):

(A) The person's primary residence shall not be included as an asset;

(B) Indebtedness that is secured by the person's primary residence, up to the estimated fair market value of the primary residence at the time of the sale of securities, shall not be included as a liability (except that if the amount of such indebtedness outstanding at the time of sale of securities exceeds the amount outstanding 60 days before such time, other than as a result of the acquisition of the primary residence, the amount of such excess shall be included as a liability); and

(C) Indebtedness that is secured by the person's primary residence in excess of the estimated fair market value of the primary residence at the time of the sale of securities shall be included as a liability;

(ii) Paragraph (a)(5)(i) of this section will not apply to any calculation of a person's net worth made in connection with a purchase of securities in accordance with a right to purchase such securities, provided that:

(A) Such right was held by the person on July 20, 2010;

(B) The person qualified as an accredited investor on the basis of net worth at the time the person acquired such right; and

(C) The person held securities of the same issuer, other than such right, on July 20, 2010.

(6) Any natural person who had an individual income in excess of $200,000 in each of the two most recent years or joint income with that person's spouse in excess of $300,000 in each of those years and has a reasonable expectation of reaching the same income level in the current year;

(7) Any trust, with total assets in excess of $5,000,000, not formed for the specific purpose of acquiring the securities offered, whose purchase is directed by a sophisticated person as described in Rule 506(b)(2)(ii); and

(8) Any entity in which all of the equity owners are accredited investors.

(b) *Affiliate.* An *affiliate* of, or person *affiliated* with, a specified person shall mean a person that directly, or indirectly through one or more intermediaries, controls or is controlled by, or is under common control with, the person specified.

(c) *Aggregate offering price. Aggregate offering price* shall mean the sum of all cash, services, property, notes, cancellation of debt, or other consideration to be received by an issuer for issuance of its securities. Where securities are being offered for both cash and non-cash consideration, the aggregate offering price shall be based on the price at which the securities are offered for cash. Any portion of the aggregate offering price attributable to cash received in a foreign currency shall be translated into United States currency at the currency exchange rate in effect at a reasonable time prior to or on the date of the sale of the securities. If securities are not offered for cash, the aggregate offering price shall be based on the value of the consideration as established by bona fide sales of that consideration made within a reasonable time, or, in the absence of sales, on the fair value as determined by an accepted standard. Such valuations of non-cash consideration must be reasonable at the time made.

(d) *Business combination. Business combination* shall mean any transaction of the type specified in paragraph (a) of Rule 145 under the Act and any transaction involving the acquisition by one issuer, in exchange for all or a part of its own or its parent's stock, of stock of another issuer if, immediately after the acquisition, the acquiring issuer has control of the other issuer (whether or not it had control before the acquisition).

(e) *Calculation of number of purchasers.* For purposes of calculating the number of purchasers under Rules 506(b) only, the following shall apply:

(1) The following purchasers shall be excluded:

(i) Any relative, spouse or relative of the spouse of a purchaser who has the same primary residence as the purchaser;

(ii) Any trust or estate in which a purchaser and any of the persons related to him as specified in paragraph (e)(1)(i) or (e)(1)(iii) of this section collectively have more than 50 percent of the beneficial interest (excluding contingent interests);

(iii) Any corporation or other organization of which a purchaser and any of the persons related to him as specified in paragraph (e)(1)(i) or (e)(1)(ii) of this section collectively are beneficial owners of more than 50 percent of the equity securities (excluding directors' qualifying shares) or equity interests; and

(iv) Any accredited investor.

(2) A corporation, partnership or other entity shall be counted as one purchaser. If, however, that entity is organized for the specific purpose of acquiring the securities offered and is not an accredited investor under paragraph (a)(8) of this section, then each beneficial owner of equity securities or equity interests in the entity shall count as a separate purchaser for all provisions of Regulation D (Rules 501-508), except to the extent provided in paragraph (e)(1) of this section.

(3) A non-contributory employee benefit plan within the meaning of Title I of the Employee Retirement Income Security Act of 1974 shall be counted as one purchaser where the trustee makes all investment decisions for the plan.

(f) *Executive officer. Executive officer* shall mean the president, any vice president in charge of a principal business unit, division or function (such as sales, administration or finance), any other officer who performs a policy making function, or any other person who performs similar policy making functions for the issuer. Executive officers of subsidiaries may be deemed executive officers of the issuer if they perform such policy making functions for the issuer.

(g) *Final order. Final order* shall mean a written directive or declaratory statement issued by a federal or state agency described in §230.506(d)(1)(iii) under applicable statutory authority that provides for notice and an opportunity for hearing, which constitutes a final disposition or action by that federal or state agency.

(h) *Issuer.* The definition of the term *issuer* in section 2(a)(4) of the Act shall apply, except that in the case of a proceeding under the Federal Bankruptcy Code, the trustee or debtor in possession shall be considered the issuer in an offering under a plan or reorganization, if the securities are to be issued under the plan.

(i) *Purchaser representative. Purchaser representative* shall mean any person who satisfies all of the following conditions or who the issuer reasonably believes satisfies all of the following conditions:

(1) Is not an affiliate, director, officer or other employee of the issuer, or beneficial owner of 10 percent or more of any class of the equity securities or 10 percent or more of the equity interest in the issuer, except where the purchaser is:

(i) A relative of the purchaser representative by blood, marriage or adoption and not more remote than a first cousin;

(ii) A trust or estate in which the purchaser representative and any persons related to him as specified in paragraph (h)(1)(i) or (h)(1)(iii) of this section collectively have more than 50 percent of the beneficial interest (excluding contingent interest) or of which the purchaser representative serves as trustee, executor, or in any similar capacity; or

(iii) A corporation or other organization of which the purchaser representative and any persons related to him as specified in paragraph (h)(1)(i) or (h)(1)(ii) of this section collectively are the beneficial owners of more than 50 percent of the equity securities (excluding directors' qualifying shares) or equity interests;

(2) Has such knowledge and experience in financial and business matters that he is capable of evaluating, alone, or together with other purchaser representatives of the purchaser, or together with the purchaser, the merits and risks of the prospective investment;

(3) Is acknowledged by the purchaser in writing, during the course of the transaction, to be his purchaser representative in connection with evaluating the merits and risks of the prospective investment; and

(4) Discloses to the purchaser in writing a reasonable time prior to the sale of securities to that purchaser any material relationship between himself or his affiliates and the issuer or its affiliates that then exists, that is mutually understood to be contemplated, or that has existed at any time during the previous two years, and any compensation received or to be received as a result of such relationship.

Rule 502. General Conditions to Be Met

The following conditions shall be applicable to offers and sales made under Regulation D.

(a) *Integration.* To determine whether offers and sales should be integrated, see §230.152.

(b) *Information requirements*— (1) *When information must be furnished.* If the issuer sells securities under Rule 506(b) to any purchaser that is not an accredited investor, the issuer shall furnish the information specified in paragraph (b)(2) of this section to such purchaser a reasonable time prior to sale. The issuer is not required to furnish the specified information to purchasers when it sells securities under Rule 504, or to any accredited investor.

NOTE

When an issuer provides information to investors pursuant to paragraph (b)(1), it should consider providing such information to accredited investors as well, in view of the anti-fraud provisions of the federal securities laws.

(2) *Type of information to be furnished.* (i) If the issuer is not subject to the reporting requirements of section 13 or 15(d) of the Exchange Act, at a reasonable time prior to the sale of securities the issuer shall furnish to the purchaser, to the extent material to an understanding of the issuer, its business, and the securities being offered:

(A) *Non-financial statement information.* If the issuer is eligible to use Regulation A, the same kind of information as would be required in Part II of Form 1-A. If the issuer is not eligible to use Regulation A, the same kind of information as required in Part I of a registration filed under the Securities Act on the form that issuer would be entitled to use.

(B) *Financial statement information.*

(1) *Offerings up to $20,000,000.* The financial statement information required by paragraph (b) of Part F/S of Form 1-A. Such financial statement information must be prepared in accordance with generally accepted accounting principles in the United States (US GAAP). If the issuer is a foreign private issuer, such financial statements must be prepared in accordance with either US GAAP or International Financial Reporting Standards (IFRS) as issued by the International Accounting Standards Board (IASB). If the financial statements comply with IFRS, such compliance must be explicitly and unreservedly stated in the notes to the financial statements and if the financial statements are audited, the auditor's report must include an opinion on whether the financial statements comply with IFRS as issued by the IASB.

(2) *Offerings over $20,000,000.* The financial statement information required by paragraph (c) of Part F/S of Form 1-A (referenced in §239.90 of this chapter). If the issuer is a foreign private issuer, such financial statements must be prepared in accordance with either US

GAAP or IFRS as issued by the IASB. If the financial statements comply with IFRS, such compliance must be explicitly and unreservedly stated in the notes to the financial statements and the auditor's report must include an opinion on whether the financial statements comply with IFRS as issued by the IASB.

(C) If the issuer is a foreign private issuer eligible to use Form 20-F, the issuer shall disclose the same kind of information required to be included in a registration statement filed under the Act on the form that the issuer would be entitled to use. The financial statements need be certified only to the extent required by paragraph (b)(2)(i)(B)(1)(2) or (3) of this section, as appropriate.

(ii) If the issuer is subject to the reporting requirements of section 13 or 15(d) of the Exchange Act, at a reasonable time prior to the sale of securities the issuer shall furnish to the purchaser the information specified in paragraph (b)(2)(ii)(A) or (B) of this section, and in either event the information specified in paragraph (b)(2)(ii)(C) of this section:

(A) The issuer's annual report to shareholders for the most recent fiscal year, if such annual report meets the requirements of Rules 14a-3 or 14c-3 under the Exchange Act, the definitive proxy statement filed in connection with that annual report, and, if requested by the purchaser in writing, a copy of the issuer's most recent Form 10-K under the Exchange Act.

(B) The information contained in an annual report on Form 10-K under the Exchange Act or in a registration statement on Form S-1 or Form S-11 under the Act or on Form 10 under the Exchange Act, whichever filing is the most recent required to be filed.

(C) The information contained in any reports or documents required to be filed by the issuer under sections 13(a), 14(a), 14(c), and 15(d) of the Exchange Act since the distribution or filing of the report or registration statement specified in paragraphs (A) or (B), and a brief description of the securities being offered, the use of the proceeds from the offering, and any material changes in the issuer's affairs that are not disclosed in the documents furnished.

(D) If the issuer is foreign private issuer, the issuer may provide in lieu of the information specified in paragraphs (b)(2)(ii)(A) or (B) of this section, the information contained in its most recent filing on Form 20-F or Form F-1.

(iii) Exhibits required to be filed with the Commission as part of a registration statement or report, other than an annual report to shareholders or parts of that report incorporated by reference in a Form 10-K report, need not be furnished to each purchaser that is not an accredited investor if the contents of material exhibits are identified and such exhibits are made available to a purchaser, upon his or her written request, a reasonable time prior to his or her purchase.

(iv) At a reasonable time prior to the sale of securities to any purchaser that is not an accredited investor in a transaction under Rule 506(b), the issuer shall furnish to the purchaser a brief description in writing of any material written information concerning the offering that has been provided by the issuer to any accredited investor but not previously delivered to such unaccredited purchaser. The issuer shall furnish any portion or all of this information to the purchaser, upon his written request a reasonable time prior to his purchase.

(v) The issuer shall also make available to each purchaser at a reasonable time prior to his purchase of securities in a transaction under Rule 506(b) the opportunity to ask questions and receive answers concerning the terms and conditions of the offering and to obtain any additional information which the issuer possesses or can acquire without unreasonable effort or expense that is necessary to verify the accuracy of information furnished under paragraph (b)(2)(i) or (ii) of this section.

(vi) For business combinations or exchange offers, in addition to information required by Form S-4, the issuer shall provide to each purchaser at the time the plan is submitted to security holders, or, with an exchange, during the course of the transaction and prior to sale, written information about any terms or arrangements of the proposed transactions that are materially different from those for all other security holders. For purposes of this subsection, an issuer which is not subject to the reporting requirements of section 13 or 15(d) of the Exchange Act may satisfy the requirements of Part I.B. or C. of Form S-4 by compliance with paragraph (b)(2)(i) of this Rule 502.

(vii) At a reasonable time prior to the sale of securities to any purchaser that is not an accredited investor in a transaction under Rule 506(b), the issuer shall advise the purchaser of the limitations on resale in the manner contained in paragraph (d)(2) of this section. Such discloser may be contained in other materials required to be provided by this paragraph.

(viii) At a reasonable time prior to the sale of securities to any purchaser that is not an accredited investor in a transaction under §230.506(b), the issuer shall provide the purchaser with any written communication or broadcast script used under the authorization of §230.241 within 30 days prior to such sale.

(c) *Limitation on manner of offering.* Except as provided in Rule 504(b)(1) or Rule 506(c), neither the issuer nor any person acting on its behalf shall offer or sell the securities by any form of general solicitation or general advertising, including, but not limited to, the following:

(1) Any advertisement, article, notice or other communication published in any newspaper, magazine, or similar media or broadcast over television or radio; and

(2) Any seminar or meeting whose attendees have been invited by any general solicitation or general advertising.

Provided, however, that publication by an issuer of a notice in accordance with Rule 135c or filing with the Commission by an issuer of a notice of sales on Form D in which the issuer has made of good faith and reasonable attempt to comply with the requirements of such form shall not be deemed to constitute general solicitation or general advertising for purposes of this section; *Provided further,* that, if the requirements of Rule 135e are satisfied, providing any journalist with access to press conferences held outside of the United States, to meetings with issuer or selling security holder representatives conducted outside the United States, or to written press-related materials released outside the United States, at or in which a present or proposed offering of securities is discussed, will not be deemed to constitute general solicitation or general advertising for purposes of this section.

(d) *Limitations on resale.* Except as provided in Rule 504(b)(1), securities acquired in a transaction under Regulation D shall have the status of securities acquired in a transaction under section 4(a)(2) of the Act and cannot be resold without registration under the Act or an exemption therefrom. The issuer shall exercise reasonable care to assure that the purchasers of the securities are not underwriters within the meaning of section 2(a)(11) of the Act, which reasonable care may be demonstrated by the following:

(1) Reasonable inquiry to determine if the purchaser is acquiring the securities for himself or for other persons;

(2) Written disclosure to each purchaser prior to sale that the securities have not been registered under the Act and, therefore, cannot be resold unless they are registered under the Act or unless an exemption from registration is available; and

(3) Placement of a legend on the certificate or other document that evidences the securities stating that the securities have not been registered under the Act and setting forth or referring to the restrictions on transferability and sale of the securities.

While taking these actions will establish the requisite reasonable care, it is not the exclusive method to demonstrate such care. Other actions by the issuer may satisfy this provision. In addition, Rules 502(b)(2)(vii) and 504(b)(2)(ii) require the delivery of written disclosure of the limitations on resale to investors in certain instances.

Rule 503. Filing of Notice of Sales

(a) *When notice of sales on Form D is required and permitted to be filed.*

(1) An issuer offering or selling securities in reliance on Rule 504 or Rule 506 must file with the Commission a notice of sales containing the information required by Form D for each new offering of securities no later than 15 calendar days after the first sale of securities in the offering, unless the end of that period falls on a Saturday, Sunday or holiday, in which case the due date would be the first business day following.

(2) An issuer may file an amendment to a previously filed notice of sales on Form D at any time.

(3) An issuer must file an amendment to a previously filed notice of sales on Form D for an offering:

(i) To correct a material mistake of fact or error in the previously filed notice of sales on Form D, as soon as practicable after discovery of the mistake or error;

(ii) To reflect a change in the information provided in the previously filed notice of sales on Form D, as soon as practicable after the change, except that no amendment is required to reflect a change that occurs after the offering terminates or a change that occurs solely in the following information:

(A) The address or relationship to the issuer of a related person identified in response to Item 3 of the notice of sales on Form D;

(B) An issuer's revenues or aggregate net asset value;

(C) The minimum investment amount, if the change is an increase, or if the change, together with all other changes in that amount since the previously filed notice of sales on Form D, does not result in a decrease of more than 10%;

(D) Any address or state(s) of solicitation shown in response to Item 12 of the notice of sales on Form D;

(E) The total offering amount, if the change is a decrease, or if the change, together with all other changes in that amount since the previously filed notice of sales on Form D, does not result in an increase of more than 10%;

(F) The amount of securities sold in the offering or the amount remaining to be sold;

(G) The number of non-accredited investors who have invested in the offering, as long as the change does not increase the number to more than 35;

(H) The total number of investors who have invested in the offering; or

(I) The amount of sales commissions, finders' fees or use of proceeds for payments to executive officers, directors or promoters, if the change is a decrease, or if the change, together with all other changes in that amount since the previously filed notice of sales on Form D, does not result in an increase of more than 10%; and

(iii) Annually, on or before the first anniversary of the filing of the notice of sales on Form D or the filing of the most recent amendment to the notice of sales on Form D, if the offering is continuing at that time.

(4) An issuer that files an amendment to a previously filed notice of sales on Form D must provide current information in response to all requirements of the notice of sales on Form D regardless of why the amendment is filed.

(b) *How notice of sales on Form D must be filed and signed.*

(1) A notice of sales on Form D must be filed with the Commission in electronic format by means of the Commission's Electronic Data Gathering, Analysis, and Retrieval System (EDGAR) in accordance with EDGAR rules set forth in Regulation S-T.

(2) Every notice of sales on Form D must be signed by a person duly authorized by the issuer.

Rule 504. Exemption for Limited Offerings and Sales of Securities Not Exceeding $10,000,000

(a) *Exemption.* Offers and sales of securities that satisfy the conditions in paragraph (b) of this Rule 504 by an issuer that is not:

(1) subject to the reporting requirements of section 13 or 15(d) of the Exchange Act;

(2) an investment company; or

(3) a development stage company that either has no specific business plan or purpose or has indicated that its business plan is to engage in a merger or acquisition with an unidentified company or companies, or other entity or person,

shall be exempt from the provision of section 5 of the Act under section 3(b) of the Act.

(b) *Conditions to be met.*

(1) General conditions. To qualify for exemption under this Rule 504, offers and sales must satisfy the terms and conditions of Rules 501 and 502(a), (c) and (d), except that the provisions of Rule 502(c) and (d) will not apply to offers and sales of securities under this Rule 504 that are made:

(i) Exclusively in one or more states that provide for the registration of the securities, and require the public filing and delivery to investors of a substantive disclosure document before sale, and are made in accordance with those state provisions;

(ii) In one or more states that have no provision for the registration of the securities or the public filing or delivery of a disclosure document before sale, if the securities have been registered in at least one state that provides for such registration, public filing and delivery before sale, offers and sales are made in that state in accordance with such provisions, and the disclosure document is delivered before sale to all purchasers (including those in the states that have no such procedure); or

(iii) Exclusively according to state law exemptions from registration that permit general solicitation and general advertising so long as sales are made only to "accredited investors" as defined in Rule 501(a).

(2) The aggregate offering price for an offering of securities under this Rule 504, as defined in Rule 501(c), shall not exceed $10,000,000, less the aggregate offering price for all securities sold within the twelve months before the start of and during the offering of securities under this Rule 504 or violation of section 5(a) of the Act.

INSTRUCTION TO PARAGRAPH (b)(2)

If a transaction under §230.504 fails to meet the limitation on the aggregate offering price, it does not affect the availability of this Rule 504 for the other transactions considered in applying such limitation. For example, if an issuer sold $10,000,000 of its securities on June 1, 2021 under this §230.504 and an additional $500,000 of its securities on December 1, 2021, this Rule 504 would not be available for the later sale, but would still be applicable to the June 1, 2021 sale.

(3) *Disqualifications.* No exemption under this section shall be available for the securities of any issuer if such issuer would be subject to disqualification under Rule 506(d) on or after January 20, 2017; provided that disclosure of prior "bad actor" events shall be required in accordance with Rule 506(e).

INSTRUCTION TO PARAGRAPH (b)(3)

For purposes of disclosure of prior "bad actor" events pursuant to §230.506(e), an issuer shall furnish to each purchaser, a reasonable time prior to sale, a description in writing of any matters that would have triggered disqualification under this paragraph (b)(3) but occurred before January 20, 2017.

Rule 506. Exemption for Limited Offers and Sales Without Regard to Dollar Amount of Offering

(a) *Exemption.* Offers and sales of securities by an issuer that satisfy the conditions in paragraph (b) or (c) of this section shall be deemed to be transactions not involving any public offering within the meaning of section 4(a)(2) of the Act.

(b) *Conditions to be met in offerings subject to limitation on manner of offering*—(1) *General conditions.* To qualify for an exemption under this section, offers and sales must satisfy all the terms and conditions of Rules 501 and 502.

(2) *Specific Conditions*— (i) *Limitation on number of purchasers.* There are no more than or the issuer reasonably believes that there are no more than 35 purchasers of securities from the issuer in offerings under this section in any 90-calendar-day period.

NOTE TO PARAGRAPH (b)(2)(i)

See Rule 501(c) for the calculation of the number of purchasers and Rule 502(a) for what may or may not constitute an offering under paragraph (b) of this section.

(ii) *Nature of purchasers.* Each purchaser who is not an accredited investor either alone or with his purchaser representative(s) has such knowledge and experience in financial and business matters that he is capable of evaluating the merits and risks of the prospective investment, or the issuer reasonably believes immediately prior to making any sale that such purchaser comes within this description.

(c) *Conditions to be met in offerings not subject to limitation on manner of offering.*

(1) *General conditions.* To qualify for exemption under this section, sales must satisfy all the terms and conditions of Rule 501 and Rule 502(a) and (d).

(2) *Specific conditions.*

(i) *Nature of purchasers.* All purchasers of securities sold in any offering under this Rule 506(c) are accredited investors.

(ii) *Verification of accredited investor status.* The issuer shall take reasonable steps to verify that purchasers of securities sold in any offering under Rule 506(c) are accredited investors. The issuer shall be deemed to take reasonable steps to verify if the issuer uses, at its option, one of the following non-exclusive and non-mandatory methods of verifying that a natural person who purchases securities in such offering is an accredited investor; provided, however, that the issuer does not have knowledge that such person is not an accredited investor:

(A) In regard to whether the purchaser is an accredited investor on the basis of income, reviewing any Internal Revenue Service form that reports the purchaser's income for the two most recent years (including, but not limited to, Form W-2, Form 1099, Schedule K-1 to Form 1065, and Form 1040) and obtaining a written representation from the purchaser that he or she has a reasonable expectation of reaching the income level necessary to qualify as an accredited investor during the current year;

(B) In regard to whether the purchaser is an accredited investor on the basis of net worth, reviewing one or more of the following types of documentation dated within the prior three months and obtaining a written representation from the purchaser that all liabilities necessary to make a determination of net worth have been disclosed:

(*1*) With respect to assets: bank statements, brokerage statements and other statements of securities holdings, certificates of deposit, tax assessments, and appraisal reports issued by independent third parties; and

(*2*) With respect to liabilities: a consumer report from at least one of the nationwide consumer reporting agencies;

(C) Obtaining a written confirmation from one of the following persons or entities that such person or entity has taken reasonable steps to verify that the purchaser is an accredited investor within the prior three months and has determined that such purchaser is an accredited investor:

(*1*) A registered broker-dealer;

(*2*) An investment adviser registered with the Securities and Exchange Commission;

(*3*) A licensed attorney who is in good standing under the laws of the jurisdictions in which he or she is admitted to practice law; or

(*4*) A certified public accountant who is duly registered and in good standing under the laws of the place of his or her residence or principal office;

(D) In regard to any person who purchased securities in an issuer's Rule 506(b) offering as an accredited investor prior to September 23, 2013 and continues to hold such securities, for the same issuer's Rule 506(c) offering, obtaining a certification by such person at the time of sale that he or she qualifies as an accredited investor; or

(E) In regard to any person that the issuer previously took reasonable steps to verify as an accredited investor in accordance with this paragraph (c)(2)(ii), so long as the issuer is not aware of information to the contrary, obtaining a written representation from such person at the time of sale that he or she qualifies as an accredited investor. A written representation under this method of verification will satisfy the issuer's obligation to verify the person's accredited investor status for a period of five years from the date the person was previously verified as an accredited investor.

INSTRUCTIONS TO PARAGRAPH (c)(2)(ii)

1. The issuer is not required to use any of these methods in verifying the accredited investor status of natural persons who are purchasers. These methods are examples of the types of non-exclusive and non-mandatory methods that satisfy the verification requirement in §230.506(c)(2)(ii).

2. In the case of a person who qualifies as an accredited investor based on joint income with that person's spouse, the issuer would be deemed to satisfy the verification requirement in §230.506(c)(2)(ii)(A) by reviewing copies of Internal Revenue Service forms that report income for the two most recent years in regard to, and obtaining written representations from, both the person and the spouse.

3. In the case of a person who qualifies as an accredited investor based on joint net worth with that person's spouse, the issuer would be deemed to satisfy the verification requirement in §230.506(c)(2)(ii)(B) by reviewing such documentation in regard to, and obtaining written representations from, both the person and the spouse.

(d) "*Bad Actor*" *disqualification*. (1) No exemption under this section shall be available for a sale of securities if the issuer; any predecessor of the issuer; any affiliated issuer; any director, executive officer, other officer participating in the offering, general partner or managing member of the issuer; any beneficial owner of 20% or more of the issuer's outstanding voting equity securities, calculated on the basis of voting power; any promoter connected with the issuer in any capacity at the time of such sale; any investment manager of an issuer that is a pooled investment fund; any person that has been or will be paid (directly or indirectly) remuneration for solicitation of purchasers in connection with such sale of securities; any general partner or managing member of any such investment manager or solicitor; or any director, executive officer or other officer participating in the offering of any such investment manager or solicitor or general partner or managing member of such investment manager or solicitor:

(i) Has been convicted, within ten years before such sale (or five years, in the case of issuers, their predecessors and affiliated issuers), of any felony or misdemeanor:

(A) In connection with the purchase or sale of any security;

(B) Involving the making of any false filing with the Commission; or

(C) Arising out of the conduct of the business of an underwriter, broker, dealer, municipal securities dealer, investment adviser or paid solicitor of purchasers of securities;

(ii) Is subject to any order, judgment or decree of any court of competent jurisdiction, entered within five years before such sale, that, at the time of such sale, restrains or enjoins such person from engaging or continuing to engage in any conduct or practice:

(A) In connection with the purchase or sale of any security;

(B) Involving the making of any false filing with the Commission; or

(C) Arising out of the conduct of the business of an underwriter, broker, dealer, municipal securities dealer, investment adviser or paid solicitor of purchasers of securities;

(iii) Is subject to a final order of a state securities commission (or an agency or officer of a state performing like functions); a state authority that supervises or examines banks, savings associations, or credit unions; a state insurance commission (or an agency or officer of a state performing like functions); an appropriate federal banking agency; the U.S. Commodity Futures Trading Commission; or the National Credit Union Administration that:

(A) At the time of such sale, bars the person from:

(*1*) Association with an entity regulated by such commission, authority, agency, or officer;

(*2*) Engaging in the business of securities, insurance or banking; or

(*3*) Engaging in savings association or credit union activities; or

(B) Constitutes a final order based on a violation of any law or regulation that prohibits fraudulent, manipulative, or deceptive conduct entered within ten years before such sale;

(iv) Is subject to an order of the Commission entered pursuant to section 15(b) or 15B(c) of the Securities Exchange Act of 1934 (15 U.S.C. 78*o*(b) or 78o-4(c)) or section 203(e) or (f) of the Investment Advisers Act of 1940 (15 U.S.C. 80b-3(e) or (f)) that, at the time of such sale:

(A) Suspends or revokes such person's registration as a broker, dealer, municipal securities dealer or investment adviser;

(B) Places limitations on the activities, functions or operations of such person; or

(C) Bars such person from being associated with any entity or from participating in the offering of any penny stock;

(v) Is subject to any order of the Commission entered within five years before such sale that, at the time of such sale, orders the person to cease and desist from committing or causing a violation or future violation of:

(A) Any scienter-based anti-fraud provision of the federal securities laws, including without limitation section 17(a)(1) of the Securities Act of 1933 (15 U.S.C. 77q(a)(1)), section 10(b) of the Securities Exchange Act of 1934 (15 U.S.C. 78j(b)) and 17 CFR 240.10b-5, section 15(c)(1) of the Securities Exchange Act of 1934 (15 U.S.C. 78*o*(c)(1)) and section 206(1) of the Investment Advisers Act of 1940 (15 U.S.C. 80b-6(1)), or any other rule or regulation thereunder; or

(B) Section 5 of the Securities Act of 1933 (15 U.S.C. 77e).

(vi) Is suspended or expelled from membership in, or suspended or barred from association with a member of, a registered national securities exchange or a registered national or affiliated securities association for any act or omission to act constituting conduct inconsistent with just and equitable principles of trade;

(vii) Has filed (as a registrant or issuer), or was named as an underwriter in, any registration statement or Regulation A offering statement filed with the Commission that, within five years before such sale, was the subject of a refusal order, stop order, or order suspending the Regulation A exemption, or is, at the time of such sale, the subject of an investigation or proceeding to determine whether a stop order or suspension order should be issued; or

(viii) Is subject to a United States Postal Service false representation order entered within five years before such sale, or is, at the time of such sale, subject to a temporary restraining order or preliminary injunction with respect to conduct alleged by the United States Postal Service to constitute a scheme or device for obtaining money or property through the mail by means of false representations.

(2) Paragraph (d)(1) of this section shall not apply:

(i) With respect to any conviction, order, judgment, decree, suspension, expulsion or bar that occurred or was issued before September 23, 2013;

(ii) Upon a showing of good cause and without prejudice to any other action by the Commission, if the Commission determines that it is not necessary under the circumstances that an exemption be denied;

(iii) If, before the relevant sale, the court or regulatory authority that entered the relevant order, judgment or decree advises in writing (whether contained in the relevant judgment, order or decree or separately to the Commission or its staff) that disqualification under paragraph (d)(1) of this section should not arise as a consequence of such order, judgment or decree; or

(iv) If the issuer establishes that it did not know and, in the exercise of reasonable care, could not have known that a disqualification existed under paragraph (d)(1) of this section.

INSTRUCTION TO PARAGRAPH (d)(2)(iv)

An issuer will not be able to establish that it has exercised reasonable care unless it has made, in light of the circumstances, factual inquiry into whether any disqualifications exist. The nature and scope of the factual inquiry will vary based on the facts and circumstances concerning, among other things, the issuer and the other offering participants.

(3) For purposes of paragraph (d)(1) of this section, events relating to any affiliated issuer that occurred before the affiliation arose will be not considered disqualifying if the affiliated entity is not:

(i) In control of the issuer; or

(ii) Under common control with the issuer by a third party that was in control of the affiliated entity at the time of such events.

(e) *Disclosure of prior "bad actor" events.* The issuer shall furnish to each purchaser, a reasonable time prior to sale, a description in writing of any matters that would have triggered disqualification under paragraph (d)(1) of this section but occurred before September 23, 2013. The failure to furnish such information timely shall not prevent an issuer from relying on this section if the issuer establishes that it did not know and, in the exercise of reasonable care, could not have known of the existence of the undisclosed matter or matters.

INSTRUCTION TO PARAGRAPH (E)

An issuer will not be able to establish that it has exercised reasonable care unless it has made, in light of the circumstances, factual inquiry into whether any disqualifications exist. The nature and scope of the factual inquiry will vary based on the facts and circumstances concerning, among other things, the issuer and the other offering participants.

Rule 507. Disqualifying Provision Relating to Exemptions Under Rules 504 and 506

(a) No exemption under Rule 504 or 506 shall be available for an issuer if such issuer, any of its predecessors or affiliates have been subject to any order, judgment, or decree of any court of competent jurisdiction temporarily, preliminary or permanently enjoining such person for failure to comply with Rule 503.

(b) Paragraph (a) of this section shall not apply if the Commission determines, upon a showing of good cause, that it is not necessary under the circumstances that the exemption be denied.

Rule 508. Insignificant Deviations from a Term, Condition or Requirement of Regulation D

(a) A failure to comply with a term, condition or requirement of Rule 504 or 506 will not result in the loss of the exemption from the requirements of section 5 of the Act for any offer or sale to a particular individual or entity, if the person relying on the exemption shows:

(1) The failure to comply did not pertain to a term, condition or requirement directly intended to protect that particular individual or entity; and

(2) The failure to comply was insignificant with respect to the offering as a whole, provided that any failure to comply with paragraph (c) of Rule 502, paragraph (b)(2) of Rule 504 and paragraph (b)(2)(i) of Rule 506 shall be deemed to be significant to the offering as a whole; and

(3) A good faith and reasonable attempt was made to comply with all applicable terms, conditions and requirements of Rule 504 or Rule 506.

(b) A transaction made in reliance on Rule 504 or Rule 506 shall comply with all applicable terms, conditions and requirements of Regulation D. Where an exemption is established only through reliance upon paragraph (a) of this section, the failure to comply shall nonetheless be actionable by the Commission under section 20 of the Act.

REGULATION CE — COORDINATED EXEMPTIONS FOR CERTAIN ISSUES OF SECURITIES EXEMPT UNDER STATE LAW

Rule 1001. Exemption for Transactions Exempt from Qualification under §25102(n) of the California Corporations Code

PRELIMINARY NOTES

1. Nothing in this rule is intended to be or should be construed as in any way relieving issuers or persons acting on behalf of issuers from providing disclosure to prospective investors necessary to satisfy the antifraud provisions of the federal securities laws. This rule only provides an exemption from the registration requirements of the Securities Act of 1933.
2. Nothing in this rule obviates the need to comply with any applicable state law relating to the offer and sales of securities.
3. Attempted compliance with this rule does not act as an exclusive election; the issuer also can claim the availability of any other applicable exemption.
4. This exemption is not available to any issuer for any transaction which, while in technical compliance with the provision of this rule, is part of a plan or scheme to evade the registration provisions of the Act. In such cases, registration under the Act is required.

(a) *Exemption.* Offers and sales of securities that satisfy the conditions of paragraph (n) of §25102 of the California Corporations Code, and paragraph (b) of this section, shall be exempt from the provisions of Section 5 of the Securities Act of 1933 by virtue of Section 3(b) of that Act.

(b) *Limitation on and computation of offering price.* The sum of all cash and other consideration to be received for the securities shall not exceed $5,000,000, less the aggregate offering price for all other securities sold in the same offering of securities, whether pursuant to this or another exemption.

(c) *Resale limitations.* Securities issued pursuant to this rule are deemed to be "restricted securities" as defined in Securities Act Rule 144. Resales of such securities must be made in compliance with the registration requirements of the Act or an exemption therefrom.

Forms Under the Securities Act of 1933

Form S-1, Registration Statement under the Securities Act of 1933

This Form shall be used for registration under the Securities Act of 1933 of securities of all issuers for which no other form is authorized or prescribed, except that this Form shall not be used for securities of foreign governments or political subdivisions thereof or asset-backed securities as defined in 17 CFR 229.1100.

General Instructions

* * *

VII. Eligibility to Use Incorporation by Reference

If a registrant meets the following requirements in paragraphs A-F immediately prior to the time of filing a registration statement on this Form, it may elect to provide information required by Items 3 through 11 of this Form in accordance with Item 11A and Item 12 of this Form. Notwithstanding the foregoing, in the financial statements, incorporating by reference or cross-referencing to information outside of the financial statements is not permitted unless otherwise specifically permitted or required by the Commission's rules or by U.S. Generally Accepted Accounting Principles or International Financial Reporting Standards as issued by the International Accounting Standards Board, whichever is applicable:

A. The registrant is subject to the requirement to file reports pursuant to Section 13 or Section 15(d) of the Securities Exchange Act of 1934 ("Exchange Act").

B. The registrant has filed all reports and other materials required to be filed by Sections 13(a), 14, or 15(d) of the Exchange Act during the preceding 12 months (or for such shorter period that the registrant was required to file such reports and materials).

C. The registrant has filed an annual report required under Section 13(a) or Section 15(d) of the Exchange Act for its most recently completed fiscal year.

D. The registrant is not:

1. And during the past three years neither the registrant nor any of its predecessors was:

(a) A blank check company as defined in Rule 491(a)(2);

(b) A shell company, other than a business combination related shell company, each as defined in Rule 405; or

(c) A registrant for an offering of penny stock as defined in Rule 3a51-1 of the Exchange Act.

2. Registering an offering that effectuates a business combination transaction as defined in Rule 165(f)(1).

E. If a registrant is a successor registrant it shall be deemed to have satisfied conditions A., B., C., and D.2 above if:

1. Its predecessor and it, taken together, do so, provided that the succession was primarily for the purpose of changing the state of incorporation of the predecessor or forming a holding company and that the assets and liabilities of the successor at the time of succession were substantially the same as those of the predecessor; or

2. All predecessors met the conditions at the time of succession and the registrant has continued to do so since the succession.

F. The registrant makes its periodic and current reports filed pursuant to Section 13 or Section 15(d) of the Exchange Act that are incorporated by reference pursuant to Item 11A or Item 12 of this Form readily available and accessible on a Web site maintained by or for the registrant and containing information about the registrant.

PART I — INFORMATION REQUIRED IN PROSPECTUS

Item 1. Forepart of the Registration Statement and Outside Front Cover Page of Prospectus

Set forth in the forepart of the registration statement and on the outside front cover page of the prospectus the information required by Item 501 of Regulation S-K.

Item 2. Inside Front and Outside Back Cover Pages of Prospectus

Set forth on the inside front cover page of the prospectus or, where permitted, on the outside back cover page, the information required by Item 502 of Regulation S-K.

Item 3. Summary Information, Risk Factors and Ratio of Earnings to Fixed Charges

Furnish the information required by Items 105 and 503 of Regulation S-K.

Item 4. Use of Proceeds

Furnish the information required by Item 504 of Regulation S-K.

Item 5. Determination of Offering Price

Furnish the information required by Item 505 of Regulation S-K.

Item 6. Dilution

Furnish the information required by Item 506 of Regulation S-K.

Item 7. Selling Security Holders

Furnish the information required by Item 507 of Regulation S-K.

Item 8. Plan of Distribution

Furnish the information required by Item 508 of Regulation S-K.

Item 9. Description of Securities to Be Registered

Furnish the information required by Item 202 of Regulation S-K.

Item 10. Interests of Named Experts and Counsel

Furnish the information required by Item 509 of Regulation S-K.

Item 11. Information with Respect to the Registrant

Furnish the following information with respect to the registrant:

(a) Information required by Item 101 of Regulation S-K, description of business;

(b) Information required by Item 102 of Regulation S-K, description of property;

(c) Information required by Item 103 of Regulation S-K, legal proceedings;

(d) Where common equity securities are being offered, information required by Item 201 of Regulation S-K, market price of and dividends on the registrant's common equity and related stockholder matters;

(e) Financial statements meeting the requirements of Regulation S-X (Schedules required under Regulation S-X shall be filed as "Financial Statement Schedules" pursuant to Item 15, Exhibits and Financial Statement Schedules, of this Form), as well as any Financial information required by Rule 3-05 and Article 11 of Regulation S-X. A smaller reporting company may provide the information in Rule 8-04 and 8-05 of Regulation S-X in lieu of the financial information required by Rule 3-05 and Article 11 of Regulation S-X.

(f) (reserved)

(g) Information required by Item 302 of Regulation S-K, supplementary financial information;

(h) Information required by Item 303 of Regulation S-K, management's discussion and analysis of financial condition and results of operations;

(i) Information required by Item 304 of Regulation S-K, changes in and disagreements with accountants on accounting and financial disclosure;

(j) Information required by Item 305 of Regulation S-K, quantitative and qualitative disclosures about market risk.

(k) Information required by Item 401 of Regulation S-K, directors and executive officers;

(l) Information required by Item 402 of Regulation S-K, executive compensation and information required by paragraph (e)(4) of Item 407 of Regulation S-K, corporate governance;

(m) Information required by Item 403 of Regulation S-K, security ownership of certain beneficial owners and management; and

(n) Information required by Item 404 of Regulation S-K, transactions with related persons, promoters and certain control persons, and Item 407 or Regulation S-K, corporate governance.

Item 11A. Material Changes

If the registrant elects to incorporate information by reference pursuant to General Instruction VII., describe any and all material changes in the registrant's affairs that have occurred since the end of the latest fiscal year for which audited financial statements were included in the latest Form 10-K and which have not been described in a Form 10-Q or Form 8-K filed under the Exchange Act.

Item 12. Incorporation of Certain Information by Reference

If the registrant elects to incorporate information by reference pursuant to General Instruction VII.:

(a) It must specifically incorporate by reference into the prospectus contained in the registration statement the following documents by means of a statement to that effect in the prospectus listing all such documents:

(1) The registrant's latest annual report on Form 10-K filed pursuant to Section 13(a) or Section 15(d) of the Exchange Act which contains financial statements for the registrant's latest fiscal year for which a Form 10-K was required to have been filed; and

(2) All other reports filed pursuant to Section 13(a) or 15(d) of the Exchange Act or proxy or information statements filed pursuant to Section 14 of the Exchange Act since the end of the fiscal year covered by the annual report referred to in paragraph (a)(1) above.

Note to Item 12(a). Attention is directed to Rule 439 regarding consent to use of material incorporated by reference.

(b)(1) The registrant must state:

(i) That it will provide to each person, including any beneficial owner, to whom a prospectus is delivered, a copy of any or all of the reports or documents that have been incorporated by reference in the prospectus contained in the registration statement but not delivered with the prospectus;

(ii) That it will provide these reports or documents upon written or oral request;

(iii) That it will provide these reports or documents at no cost to the requester;

(iv) The name, address, telephone number, and e-mail address, if any, to which the request for these reports or documents must be made; and

(v) The registrant's Web site address, including the uniform resource locator (URL) where the incorporated reports and other documents may be accessed.

(2) The registrant must:

(i) Identify the reports and other information that it files with the SEC; and

(ii) State that the public may read and copy any materials it files with the SEC at the SEC's Public Reference Room at 100 F Street, N.E., Washington, DC 20549. State that the public may obtain information on the operation of the Public Reference Room by calling the SEC at 1-800-SEC-0330. If the registrant is an electronic filer, state that the SEC maintains an Internet site that contains reports, proxy and information statements, and other information regarding issuers that file electronically with the SEC and state the address of that site (http://www.sec.gov). . . .

Item 12A. Disclosure of Commission Position on Indemnification for Securities Act Liabilities

Furnish the information required by Item 510 of Regulation S-K.

PART II — INFORMATION NOT REQUIRED IN PROSPECTUS

Item 13. Other Expenses of Issuance and Distribution

Furnish the information required by Item 511 of Regulation S-K.

Item 14. Indemnification of Directors and Officers

Furnish the information required by Item 702 of Regulation S-K.

Item 15. Recent Sales of Unregistered Securities

Furnish the information required by Item 701 of Regulation S-K.

Item 16. Exhibits and Financial Statement Schedules

(a) Subject to the rules regarding incorporation by reference, furnish the exhibits as required by Item 601 of Regulation S-K.

(b) Furnish the financial statement schedules required by Regulation S-X and Item 11(e) of this Form. These schedules shall be lettered or numbered in the manner described for exhibits in paragraph (a).

Item 17. Undertakings

Furnish the undertakings required by Item 512 of Regulation S-K. . . .

Form S-3, for Registration under the Securities Act of 1933 of Securities of Certain Issuers Offered Pursuant to Certain Types of Transactions

General Instructions

. . . Any registrant which meets the requirements of I.A below (*Registrant Requirements*), may use this Form for the registration of securities under the Securities Act of 1933 (*Securities Act*) which are offered in any transaction specified in I.B below (*Transaction Requirements*), provided that the requirements applicable to the specified transaction are met. With respect to majority-owned subsidiaries, see I.C below. With respect to well-known seasoned issuers and majority-owned subsidiaries of well-known seasoned issuers see Instruction I.D below.

A. *Registrant requirements.* Registrants must meet the following conditions in order to use this Form for registration under the Securities Act of securities offered in the transactions specified in B below:

1. The registrant is organized under the laws of the United States or any State or Territory or the District of Columbia and has its principal business operations in the United States or its territories.

2. The registrant has a class of securities registered pursuant to section 12(b) of the Securities Exchange Act of 1934 (*Exchange Act*) or a class of equity securities registered pursuant to section 12(g) of the Exchange Act or is required to file reports pursuant to section 15(d) of the Exchange Act;

3. The registrant: (a) Has been subject to the requirements of section 12 or 15(d) of the Exchange Act and has filed all the material required to be filed pursuant to sections 13, 14 or 15(d) for a period of at least twelve calendar months immediately preceding the filing of the registration statement on this Form; and (b) has filed in a timely manner all reports required to be filed during the twelve calendar months and any portion of a month immediately preceding the filing of the registration statement other than a report that is required solely pursuant to Item 1.01, 1.02, 1.04, 2.03, 2.04, 2.05, 2.06, 4.02(a), or 5.02 (e) of Form 8-K. If the registrant has used (during the twelve calendar months and any portion of a month immediately preceding the filing of the registration statement) Rule 12b-25(b) under the Exchange Act with respect to a report or a portion of a report, that report or portion thereof has actually been filed within the time period prescribed by the Rule; and . . .

4. Neither the registrant nor any of its consolidated or unconsolidated subsidiaries have, since the end of the last fiscal year for which certified financial statements of the registrant and its consolidated subsidiaries were included in a report filed pursuant to section 13(a) or 15(d) of the Exchange Act: (a) Failed to

pay any dividend or sinking fund installment on preferred stock; or (b) defaulted (i) on any installment or installments on indebtedness for borrowed money, or (ii) on any rental on one or more long term leases, which defaults in the aggregate are material to the financial position of the registrant and its consolidated and unconsolidated subsidiaries, taken as a whole.

5. A foreign private issuer which satisfies all of the above provisions of these registrant eligibility requirements except the provisions in A.1 relating to organization and principal business shall be deemed to have met these registrant eligibility requirements provided that such foreign issuer files the same reports with the Commission under section 13(a) or 15(d) of the Exchange Act as a domestic registrant pursuant to A.3 of this section.

6. If the registrant is a successor registrant, it shall be deemed to have met conditions in paragraphs A.1, 2, 3, and 4 of this section if: (i) its predecessor and it, taken together, do so, provided that the succession was primarily for the purpose of changing the state of incorporation of the predecessor or forming a holding company and that the assets and liabilities of the successor at the time of succession were substantially the same as those of the predecessor; or (ii) if all predecessors met the conditions at the time of succession and the registrant has continued to do so since the succession.

7. *Electronic filings.* In addition to satisfying the foregoing conditions, a registrant subject to the electronic filing requirements of Rule 101 of Regulation S-T shall have:

(a) Filed with the Commission all required electronic filings, including electronic copies of documents submitted in paper pursuant to a hardship exemption as provided by Rule 201 or Rule 202(d) of Regulation S-T (of this chapter); and

(b) Submitted electronically to the Commission and posted on its corporate Web site, if any, all Interactive Data Files required to be submitted and posted pursuant to Rule 405 of Regulation S-T during the twelve calendar months and any portion of a month immediately preceding the filing of the registration statement on this Form (or for such shorter period of time that the registrant was required to submit and post such files).

B. *Transaction requirements.* Security offerings meeting and of the following conditions and made by registrants meeting the Registrant Requirements above may be registered on this Form:

1. *Primary offerings by certain registrants.* Securities to be offered for cash by or on behalf of a registrant, or outstanding securities to be offered for cash for the account of any person other than the registrant, including securities acquired by stand-by underwriters in connection with the call or redemption by the registrant of warrants or a class of convertible securities; *provided* that the aggregate market value of the voting stock held by non-affiliates of the registrant is $75 million or more.

2. *Primary offerings of non-convertible securities other than common equity . . .*

3. *Transactions involving secondary offerings.* Outstanding securities to be offered for the account of any person other than the issuer, including securities

acquired by standby underwriters in connection with the call or redemption by the issuer of warrants or a class of convertible securities, if securities of the same class are listed and registered on a national securities exchange or are quoted on the automated quotation system of a national securities association. . . .

4. *Rights offerings, dividend or interest reinvestment plans, and conversions or warrants.* . . .

5. *This Form shall not be used to register offerings of asset-backed securities as defined in 17 CFR 229.1101(c)* . . .

C. *Majority-owned subsidiaries* . . .

D. *Automatic shelf offerings by well-known seasoned issuers* . . .

6. *Limited primary offerings by certain other registrants* . . .

INFORMATION REQUIRED IN PROSPECTUS . . .

Item 11. Material Changes

(a) Describe any and all material changes in the registrant's affairs which have occurred since the end of the latest fiscal year for which certified financial statements were included in the latest annual report to security holders and which have not been described in a report on Form 10-Q or Form 8-K filed under the Exchange Act.

(b) Include in the prospectus, if not incorporated by reference therein from the reports filed under the Exchange Act specified in Item 12(a), a proxy or information statement filed pursuant to Section 14 of the Exchange Act, a prospectus previously filed pursuant to Rule 424(b) or (c) under the Securities Act or, where no prospectus was required to be filed pursuant to Rule 424(b), the prospectus included in the registration statement at effectiveness, or a Form 8-K filed during either of the two preceding years:

(i) information required by Rule 3-05 and Article 11 of Regulation S-X;

(ii) restated financial statements prepared in accordance with Regulation S-X if there has been a change in accounting principles or a correction in an error where such change or correction requires a material retroactive restatement of financial statements;

(iii) restated financial statements prepared in accordance with Regulation S-X where a combination of entities under common control has been consummated subsequent to the most recent fiscal year and the transferred businesses, considered in the aggregate, are significant pursuant to Rule 11-01(b), or

(iv) any financial information required because of a material disposition of assets outside the normal course of business.

Item 12. Incorporation of Certain Information by Reference

(a) The documents listed in (1) and (2) below shall be specifically incorporated by reference into the prospectus, by means of a statement to that effect in the prospectus listing all such documents.

(1) the registrant's latest annual report on Form 10-K filed pursuant to Section 13(a) or 15(d) of the Exchange Act which contains financial statements

for the registrant's latest fiscal year for which a Form 10-K was required to have been filed; and

(2) all other reports filed pursuant to Section 13(a) or 15(d) of the Exchange Act since the end of the fiscal year covered by the annual report referred to in (1) above; and

(3) if capital stock is to be registered and securities of the same class are registered under Section 12 of the Exchange Act, the description of such class of securities which is contained in a registration statement filed under the Exchange Act, including any amendment or reports filed for the purpose of updating such description.

(b) The prospectus shall also state that all documents subsequently filed by the registrant pursuant to Sections 13(a), 13(c), 14 or 15(d) of the Exchange Act, prior to the termination of the offering shall be deemed to be incorporated by reference into the prospectus.

(c)(1) You must state (i) that you will provide to each person, including any beneficial owner, to whom a prospectus is delivered, a copy of any or all of the information that has been incorporated by reference in the prospectus but not delivered with the prospectus;

(ii) that you will provide this information upon written or oral request;

(iii) that you will provide this information at no cost to the requester; and

(iv) the name, address, and telephone number to which the request for this information must be made . . .

Securities Exchange Act of 1934

15 U.S.C. §§78a et seq.

Act	15 U.S.C. Section	
1	78a	Short Title
2	78b	Necessity for Regulation
3	78c	Definitions and Application
3A	78c-1	Swap Agreements [omitted]
3B	78c-2	Securities-Related Derivatives [omitted]
3C	78c-3	Clearing for Security-Based Swaps [omitted]
3D	78c-4	Security-Based Swap Execution Facilities [omitted]
3E	78c-5	Segregation of Assets Held as Collateral in Security-Based Swap Transactions [omitted]
4	78d	Securities and Exchange Commission [Sections 4A-4I omitted]
5	78e	Transactions on Unregistered Exchanges
6	78f	National Securities Exchanges
7	78g	Margin Requirements [omitted]
8	78h	Restrictions on Borrowing and Lending by Members, Brokers, and Dealers [omitted]
9	78i	Manipulation of Security Prices
10	78j	Manipulative and Deceptive Devices
10A	A 78j-1	Audit Requirements
10B	78j-2	Position Limits and Position Accountability for Security-Based Swaps and Large Trader Reporting [omitted]
10C	78j-3	Compensation Committees
10D	78j-4	Recovery of Erroneously Awarded Compensation Policy
11	78k	Trading by Members of Exchanges, Brokers, and Dealers [omitted]
11A	78k-1	National Market System for Securities; Securities Information Processors
12	78l	Registration Requirements for Securities
13	78m	Periodical and Other Reports
13A	78m-1	Reporting and Recordkeeping for Certain Security-Based Swaps [omitted]
13B	78m-2	Reporting Requirements Regarding Coal or other Mine Safety
14	78n	Proxies

14A	78n-1	Shareholder Approval of Executive Compensation
14B	78n-2	Corporate Governance
15	78o	Registration and Regulation of Brokers and Dealers
15A	78o-3	Registered Securities Associations [omitted]
15B	78o-4	Municipal Securities [omitted]
15C	78o-5	Government Securities Brokers and Dealers [omitted]
15D	78o-6	Securities Analysts and Research Reports
15E	78o-7	Registration of Nationally Recognized Statistical Rating Organizations [omitted]
15F	78o-8	Registration and Regulation of Security-Based Swap Dealers and Major Security-Based Swap Participants [omitted]
15G	78o-9	Credit Risk Retention [omitted]
16	78p	Directors, Officers, and Principal Stockholders
17	78q	Records and Reports [omitted]
17A	78q-1	National System for Clearance and Settlement of Securities Transactions
17B	78q-2	Automated Quotation Systems for Penny Stocks [omitted]
18	78r	Liability for Misleading Statements
19	78s	Registration, Responsibilities, and Oversight of Self-Regulatory Organizations
20	78t	Liabilities of Controlling Persons and Persons Who Aid and Abet Violations
20A	78t-1	Liability to Contemporaneous Traders for Insider Trading
21	78u	Investigations and Actions
21A	78u-1	Civil Penalties for Insider Trading
21B	78u-2	Civil Remedies in Administrative Proceedings
21C	78u-3	Cease-and-Desist Proceedings
21D	78u-4	Private Securities Litigation
21E	78u-5	Application of Safe Harbor for Forward-Looking Statements
21E	78u-6	Securities Whistleblower Incentives and Protection [omitted]
22	78v	Hearings by Commission [omitted]
23	78w	Rules, Regulations, and Orders; Annual Reports
24	78x	Public Availability of Information [omitted]
25	78y	Court Review of Orders and Rules
26	78z	Unlawful Representations
27	78aa	Jurisdiction of Offenses and Suits
27A	78aa-1	Special Provision Relating to Statute of Limitations on Private Causes of Action [omitted]
28	78bb	Effect on Existing Law
29	78cc	Validity of Contracts
30	78dd	Foreign Securities Exchanges
30A	78dd-1	Prohibited Foreign Trade Practices by Issuers
30B	77dd-2	Prohibited Foreign Trade Practices by Domestic Concerns [omitted]
31	78ee	Transaction Fees [omitted]
32	78ff	Penalties

§1. Short Title

This chapter may be cited as the "Securities Exchange Act of 1934."

§2. Necessity for Regulation

For the reasons hereinafter enumerated, transactions in securities as commonly conducted upon securities exchanges and over-the-counter markets are effected with a national public interest which makes it necessary to provide for regulation and control of such transactions and of practices and matters related thereto, including transactions by officers, directors, and principal security holders, to require appropriate reports to remove impediments to and perfect the mechanisms of a national market system for securities and a national system for the clearance and settlement of securities transactions and the safeguarding of securities and funds related thereto, and to impose requirements necessary to make such regulation and control reasonably complete and effective, in order to protect interstate commerce, the national credit, the Federal taxing power, to protect and make more effective the national banking system and Federal Reserve System, and to insure the maintenance of fair and honest markets in such transactions:

(1) Such transactions (a) are carried on in large volume by the public generally and in large part originate outside the States in which the exchanges and over-the-counter markets are located and/or are effected by means of the mails and instrumentalities of interstate commerce; (b) constitute an important part of the current of interstate commerce; (c) involve in large part the securities of issuers engaged in interstate commerce; (d) involve the use of credit, directly affect the financing of trade, industry, and transportation in interstate commerce, and directly affect and influence the volume of interstate commerce; and affect the national credit.

(2) The prices established and offered in such transactions are generally disseminated and quoted throughout the United States and foreign countries and constitute a basis for determining and establishing the prices at which securities are bought and sold, the amount of certain taxes owing to the United States and to the several States by owners, buyers, and sellers of securities, and the value of collateral for bank loans.

(3) Frequently the prices of securities on such exchanges and markets are susceptible to manipulation and control, and the dissemination of such prices gives rise to excessive speculation, resulting in sudden and unreasonable fluctuations in the prices of securities which (a) cause alternately unreasonable expansion and unreasonable contraction of the volume of credit available for trade, transportation, and

industry in interstate commerce, (b) hinder the proper appraisal of the value of securities and thus prevent a fair calculation of taxes owing to the United States and to the several States by owners, buyers, and sellers of securities, and (c) prevent the fair valuation of collateral for bank loans and/or obstruct the effective operation of the national banking system and Federal Reserve System.

(4) National emergencies, which produce widespread unemployment and the dislocation of trade, transportation, and industry, and which burden interstate commerce and adversely affect the general welfare, are precipitated, intensified, and prolonged by manipulation and sudden and unreasonable fluctuations of security prices and by excessive speculation on such exchanges and markets, and to meet such emergencies the Federal Government is put to such great expense as to burden the national credit.

§3. *Definitions and Application*

(a) Definitions

When used in this chapter, unless the context otherwise requires—

(1) The term "exchange" means any organization, association, or group of persons, whether incorporated or unincorporated, which constitutes, maintains, or provides a market place or facilities for bringing together purchasers and sellers of securities or for otherwise performing with respect to securities the functions commonly performed by a stock exchange as that term is generally understood, and includes the market place and the market facilities maintained by such exchange.

(4)(A) In general.—The term "broker" means any person engaged in the business of effecting transactions in securities for the account of others. . .

(B) Exception for certain bank activities. . .

(5)(A) In general.—The term "dealer" means any person engaged in the business of buying and selling securities (not including security-based swaps, other than security-based swaps with or for persons that are not eligible contract participants) for his own account, through a broker or otherwise,

(B) Exception for person not engaged in the business of dealing

The term "dealer" does not include a person that buys or sells securities (not including security-based swaps, other than security-based swaps with or for persons that are not eligible contract participants) for such person's own account, either individually or in a fiduciary capacity, but not as a part of a regular business.

(C) Exception for certain bank activities. . .

(7) The term "director" means any director of a corporation or any person performing similar functions with respect to any organization, whether incorporated or unincorporated.

(8) The term "issuer" means any person who issues or proposes to issue any security; except that with respect to certificates of deposit for securities, voting-trust certificates, or collateral-trust certificates, or with respect to certificates of interest or shares in an unincorporated investment trust not having a board of directors or of the fixed, restricted management, or unit type, the term "issuer" means the

person or persons performing the acts and assuming the duties of depositor or manager pursuant to the provisions of the trust or other agreement or instrument under which such securities are issued; and except that with respect to equipment-trust certificates or like securities, the term "issuer" means the person by whom the equipment or property is, or is to be, used.

(9) The term "person" means a natural person, company, government, or political subdivision, agency, or instrumentality of a government.

(10) The term "security" means any note, stock, treasury stock, security future, security-based swap, bond, debenture, certificate of interest or participation in any profit-sharing agreement or in any oil, gas, or other mineral royalty or lease, any collateral-trust certificate, preorganization certificate or subscription, transferable share, investment contract, voting-trust certificate, certificate of deposit for a security, any put, call, straddle, option, or privilege on any security, certificate of deposit, or group or index of securities (including any interest therein or based on the value thereof), or any put, call, straddle, option, or privilege entered into on a national securities exchange relating to foreign currency, or in general, any instrument commonly known as a "security"; or any certificate of interest or participation in, temporary or interim certificate for, receipt for, or warrant or right to subscribe to or purchase, any of the foregoing; but shall not include currency or any note, draft, bill of exchange, or banker's acceptance which has a maturity at the time of issuance of not exceeding nine months, exclusive of days of grace, or any renewal thereof the maturity of which is likewise limited.

(11) The term "equity security" means any stock or similar security; or any security future on any such security; security convertible, with or without consideration, into such a security, or carrying any warrant or right to subscribe to or purchase such a security; or any such warrant or right; or any other security which the Commission shall deem to be of similar nature and consider necessary or appropriate, by such rules and regulations as it may prescribe in the public interest or for the protection of investors, to treat as an equity security.

(12) (A) The term "exempted security" or "exempted securities" includes—

(i) government securities, as defined in paragraph (42) of this subsection;

(ii) municipal securities, as defined in paragraph (29) of this subsection;

(iii) any interest or participation in any common trust fund or similar fund that is excluded from the definition of the term "Investment Company" under §3(c)(3) of the Investment Company Act of 1940;

(iv) any interest or participation in a single trust fund, or a collective trust fund maintained by a bank, or any security arising out of a contract issued by an insurance company, which interest, participation, or security is issued in connection with a qualified plan as defined in subparagraph (C) of this paragraph;

(v) any security issued by or any interest or participation in any pooled income fund, collective trust fund, collective investment fund, or similar fund that is excluded from the definition of an investment company under section 3(c)(3) of the Investment Company Act of 1940;

(vi) solely for purposes of sections 12, 13, 14, and 16 of this title, any security issued by or any interest or participation in any church plan, company, or account that is excluded from the definition of an investment company under section 3(c)(3) of the Investment Company Act of 1940; and

(vii) such other securities (which may include, among others, unregistered securities, the market in which is predominantly intrastate) as the Commission may, by such rules and regulations as it deems consistent with the public interest and the protection of investors, either unconditionally or upon specified terms and conditions or for stated periods, exempt from the operation of any one or more provisions of this chapter which by their terms do not apply to an "exempted security" or to "exempted securities."

(B)(i) Notwithstanding subparagraph (A)(i) of this paragraph, government securities shall not be deemed to be "exempted securities" for the purposes of section 17A of this title.

(ii) Notwithstanding subparagraph (A)(ii) of this paragraph, municipal securities shall not be deemed to be "exempted securities" for the purposes of sections 15 and 17A of this title. . . .

(13) The terms "buy" and "purchase" each include any contract to buy, purchase, or otherwise acquire. For security futures product, such term includes any contract, agreement, or transaction for future delivery.

(14) The terms "sale" and "sell" each include any contract to sell or otherwise dispose of. For security futures product, such term includes any contract, agreement or transaction for future delivery.

(15) The term "Commission" means the Securities and Exchange Commission established by section 4 of this title.

(17) The term "interstate commerce" means trade, commerce, transportation, or communication among the several States, or between any foreign country and any State, or between any State and any place or ship outside thereof. The term also includes intrastate use of (A) any facility of a national securities exchange or of a telephone or other interstate means of communication, or (B) any other interstate instrumentality. . . .

(19) The terms "investment company," "affiliated person," "insurance company," "separate account," and "company" have the same meanings as in the Investment Company Act of 1940.

(20) The terms "investment adviser" and "underwriter" have the same meanings as in the Investment Advisers Act of 1940. . . .

(26) The term "self-regulatory organization" means any national securities exchange, registered securities association, or registered clearing agency, or (solely for purposes of sections 19(b), 19(c), and 23(b) of this title) the Municipal Securities Rulemaking Board established by section 15B of this title.

(38) The term "market maker" means any specialist permitted to act as a dealer, any dealer acting in the capacity of block positioner, and any dealer who, with respect to a security, holds himself out (by entering quotations in an inter-dealer communications system or otherwise) as being willing to buy and sell such security for his own account on a regular or continuous basis. . . .

(58) Audit Committee.—The term 'audit committee' means—

(A) a committee (or equivalent body) established by and amongst the board of directors of an issuer for the purpose of overseeing the accounting and financial reporting processes of the issuer and audits of the financial statements of the issuer; and

(B) if no such committee exists with respect to an issuer, the entire board of directors of the issuer. . . .

(79) Asset-backed security.—

The term 'asset-backed security'—

(A) means a fixed-income or other security collateralized by any type of self-liquidating financial asset (including a loan, a lease, a mortgage, or a secured or unsecured receivable) that allows the holder of the security to receive payments that depend primarily on cash flow from the asset, including—

(i) a collateralized mortgage obligation;

(ii) a collateralized debt obligation;

(iii) a collateralized bond obligation;

(iv) a collateralized debt obligation of asset-backed securities;

(v) a collateralized debt obligation of collateralized debt obligations; and

(vi) a security that the Commission, by rule, determines to be an asset-backed security for purposes of this section; and

(B) does not include a security issued by a finance subsidiary held by the parent company or a company controlled by the parent company, if none of the securities issued by the finance subsidiary are held by an entity that is not controlled by the parent company.

(80) Emerging growth company.—The term "emerging growth company" means an issuer that had total annual gross revenues of less than $1,000,000,000 (as such amount is indexed for inflation every 5 years by the Commission to reflect the change in the Consumer Price Index for All Urban Consumers published by the Bureau of Labor Statistics, setting the threshold to the nearest 1,000,000) during its most recently completed fiscal year. An issuer that is an emerging growth company as of the first day of that fiscal year shall continue to be deemed an emerging growth company until the earliest of—

(A) the last day of the fiscal year of the issuer during which it had total annual gross revenues of $1,000,000,000 (as such amount is indexed for inflation every 5 years by the Commission to reflect the change in the Consumer Price Index for All Urban Consumers published by the Bureau of Labor Statistics, setting the threshold to the nearest 1,000,000) or more;

(B) the last day of the fiscal year of the issuer following the fifth anniversary of the date of the first sale of common equity securities of the issuer pursuant to an effective registration statement under the Securities Act of 1933;

(C) the date on which such issuer has, during the previous 3-year period, issued more than $1,000,000,000 in non-convertible debt; or

(D) the date on which such issuer is deemed to be a "large accelerated filer", as defined in section 240.12b–2 of title 17, Code of Federal Regulations, or any successor thereto.

(80) Funding portal.—The term "funding portal" means any person acting as an intermediary in a transaction involving the offer or sale of securities for the

account of others, solely pursuant to section 4(6) of the Securities Act of 1933, that does not—

(A) offer investment advice or recommendations;

(B) solicit purchases, sales, or offers to buy the securities offered or displayed on its website or portal;

(C) compensate employees, agents, or other persons for such solicitation or based on the sale of securities displayed or referenced on its website or portal;

(D) hold, manage, possess, or otherwise handle investor funds or securities; or

(E) engage in such other activities as the Commission, by rule, determines appropriate.

(f) Consideration of Promotion of Efficiency, Competition, and Capital Formation

Whenever pursuant to this title the Commission is engaged in rulemaking, or in the review of a rule of a self-regulatory organization, and is required to consider or determine whether an action is necessary or appropriate in the public interest, the Commission shall also consider, in addition to the protection of investors, whether the action will promote efficiency, competition, and capital formation. . . .

(h) Limited Exemption for Funding Portals.—

(1) In general.—The Commission shall, by rule, exempt, conditionally or unconditionally, a registered funding portal from the requirement to register as a broker or dealer under section 15(a)(1), provided that such funding portal—

(A) remains subject to the examination, enforcement, and other rulemaking authority of the Commission;

(B) is a member of a national securities association registered under section 15A; and

(C) is subject to such other requirements under this title as the Commission determines appropriate under such rule.

(2) National securities association membership.—For purposes of sections 15(b)(8) and 15A, the term "broker or dealer" includes a funding portal and the term "registered broker or dealer" includes a registered funding portal, except to the extent that the Commission, by rule, determines otherwise, provided that a national securities association shall only examine for and enforce against a registered funding portal rules of such national securities association written specifically for registered funding portals.

§3B. Securities-Related Derivatives

(a) Any agreement, contract, or transaction (or class thereof) that is exempted by the Commodity Futures Trading Commission pursuant to section 4(c)(1) of the Commodity Exchange Act (7 U.S.C. 6(c)(1)) with the condition that the Commission exercise concurrent jurisdiction over such agreement, contract, or transaction (or class thereof) shall be deemed a security for purposes of the securities laws.

(b) With respect to any agreement, contract, or transaction (or class thereof) that is exempted by the Commodity Futures Trading Commission pursuant to section 4(c)(1) of the Commodity Exchange Act (7 U.S.C. 6(c)(1)) with the condition that the Commission exercise concurrent jurisdiction over such agreement, contract, or transaction (or class thereof), references in the securities laws to the 'purchase' or 'sale' of a security shall be deemed to include the execution, termination (prior to its scheduled maturity date), assignment, exchange, or similar transfer or conveyance of, or extinguishing of rights or obligations under such agreement, contract, or transaction, as the context may require

§4. *Securities and Exchange Commission*

(a) Establishment; Composition; Limitations on Commissioners; Terms of Office

There is hereby established a Securities and Exchange Commission (hereinafter referred to as the "Commission") to be composed of five commissioners to be appointed by the President by and with the advice and consent of the Senate. Not more than three of such commissioners shall be members of the same political party, and in making appointments members of different political parties shall be appointed alternately as nearly as may be practicable. No commissioner shall engage in any other business, vocation, or employment than that of serving as commissioner, nor shall any commissioner participate, directly or indirectly, in any stock-market operations or transactions of a character subject to regulation by the Commission pursuant to this chapter. Each commissioner shall hold office for a term of five years and until his successor is appointed and has qualified, except that he shall not so continue to serve beyond the expiration of the next session of Congress subsequent to the expiration of said fixed term of office, and except (1) any commissioner appointed to fill a vacancy occurring prior to the expiration of the term for which his predecessor was appointed shall be appointed for the remainder of such term. . . .

§5. *Transactions on Unregistered Exchanges*

It shall be unlawful for any broker, dealer, or exchange, directly or indirectly, to make use of the mails or any means or instrumentality of interstate commerce for the purpose of using any facility of an exchange within or subject to the jurisdiction of the United States to effect any transaction in a security, or to report any such transaction, unless such exchange (1) is registered as national securities exchange under section 6 of this title, or (2) is exempted from such registration upon application by the exchange because, in the opinion of the Commission, by reason of the limited volume of transactions effected on such exchange, it is not practicable and not necessary or appropriate in the public interest or for the protection of investors to require such registration.

§6. National Securities Exchanges

(a) Registration; Application

An exchange may be registered as a national securities exchange under the terms and conditions hereinafter provided in this section and in accordance with the provisions of section 19(a) of this title, by filing with the Commission an application for registration in such form as the Commission, by rule, may prescribe containing the rules of the exchange and such other information and documents as the Commission, by rule, may prescribe as necessary or appropriate in the public interest or for the protection of investors. . . .

(b) Determination by Commission requisite to registration of applicant as a national securities exchange

An exchange shall not be registered as a national securities exchange unless the Commission determines that . . . —

(10) (A) The rules of the exchange prohibit any member that is not the beneficial owner of a security registered under section 12 from granting a proxy to vote the security in connection with a shareholder vote described in subparagraph (B), unless the beneficial owner of the security has instructed the member to vote the proxy in accordance with the voting instructions of the beneficial owner.

(B) A shareholder vote described in this subparagraph is a shareholder vote with respect to the election of a member of the board of directors of an issuer, executive compensation, or any other significant matter, as determined by the Commission, by rule, and does not include a vote with respect to the uncontested election of a member of the board of directors of any investment company registered under the Investment Company Act of 1940 (15 U.S.C. 80b-1 et seq.).

(C) Nothing in this paragraph shall be construed to prohibit a national securities exchange from prohibiting a member that is not the beneficial owner of a security registered under section 12 from granting a proxy to vote the security in connection with a shareholder vote not described in subparagraph (A).

§9. Manipulation of Security Prices

(a) Transactions Relating to Purchase or Sale of Security

It shall be unlawful for any person, directly or indirectly, by the use of the mails or any means or instrumentality of interstate commerce, or of any facility of any national securities exchange, or for any member of a national securities exchange—

(1) For the purpose of creating a false or misleading appearance of active trading in any security other than a government security, or a false or misleading appearance with respect to the market for any such security, (A) to effect any transaction in such security which involves no change in the beneficial ownership

thereof, or (B) to enter an order or orders for the purchase of such security with the knowledge that an order or orders of substantially the same size, at substantially the same time, and at substantially the same price, for the sale of any such security, has been or will be entered by or for the same or different parties, or (C) to enter any order or orders for the sale of any such security with the knowledge that an order or orders of substantially the same size, at substantially the same time, and at substantially the same price, for the purchase of such security, has been or will be entered by or for the same or different parties. . . .

(2) To effect, alone or with one or more other persons, a series of transactions in any security other than a government security creating actual or apparent active trading in such security or raising or depressing the price of such security, for the purpose of inducing the purchase or sale of such security by others.

(3) If a dealer or broker, or other person selling or offering for sale or purchasing or offering to purchase the security, to induce the purchase or sale of any security other than a government security by the circulation or dissemination in the ordinary course of business of information to the effect that the price of any such security will or is likely to rise or fall because of market operations of any one or more persons conducted for the purpose of raising or depressing the prices of such security.

(4) If a dealer or broker, or other person selling or offering for sale or purchasing or offering to purchase the security, to make, regarding any security other than a government security for the purpose of inducing the purchase or sale of such security, any statement which was at the time and in the light of the circumstances under which it was made, false or misleading with respect to any material fact, and which he knew or had reasonable ground to believe was so false or misleading.

(5) For a consideration, received directly or indirectly from a dealer or broker, or other person selling or offering for sale or purchasing or offering to purchase the security, to induce the purchase or sale of any security other than a government security by the circulation or dissemination of information to the effect that the price of any such security will or is likely to rise or fall because of the market operations of any one or more persons conducted for the purpose of raising or depressing the price of such security.

(6) To effect either alone or with one or more other persons any series of transactions for the purchase and/or sale of any security other than a government security for the purpose of pegging, fixing, or stabilizing the price of such security in contravention of such rules and regulations as the Commission may prescribe as necessary or appropriate in the public interest or for the protection of investors.

(b) Transactions Relating to Puts, Calls, Straddles, or Options

It shall be unlawful for any person to effect, in contravention of such rules and regulations as the Commission may prescribe as necessary or appropriate in the public interest or for the protection of investors—

(1) any transaction in connection with any security whereby any party to such transaction acquires any put, call, straddle, or other option or privilege of buying the security from or selling the security to another without being bound to do so; or

(2) any transaction in connection with any security with relation to which he has, directly or indirectly, any interest in any such put, call, straddle, option, or privilege; or

(3) any transaction in any security for the account of any person who he has reason to believe has, and who actually has, directly or indirectly, any interest in any such put, call, straddle, option, or privilege with relation to such security.

(c) Endorsement or Guarantee of Puts, Calls, Straddles, or Options

It shall be unlawful for any broker, dealer, or member of a national securities exchange directly or indirectly to endorse or guarantee the performance of any put, call, straddle, option, or privilege in relation to any security other than a government security, in contravention of such rules and regulations as the Commission may prescribe as necessary or appropriate in the public interest or for the protection of investors.

(d) Transactions Relating to Short Sales of Securities

It shall be unlawful for any person, directly or indirectly, by the use of the mails or any means or instrumentality of interstate commerce, or of any facility of any national securities exchange, or for any member of a national securities exchange to effect, alone or with one or more other persons, a manipulative short sale of any security. The Commission shall issue such other rules as are necessary or appropriate to ensure that the appropriate enforcement options and remedies are available for violations of this subsection in the public interest or for the protection of investors.

(e) Registered Warrant, Right, or Convertible Security Not Included in "Put," "Call," "Straddle," or "Option"

The terms "put," "call," "straddle," "option," or "privilege" as used in this section shall not include any registered warrant, right, or convertible security.

(f) Persons Liable; Suits at Law or in Equity

Any person who willfully participates in any act or transaction in violation of subsections (a), (b), or (c) of this section, shall be liable to any person who shall purchase or sell any security at a price which was affected by such act or transaction, and the person so injured may sue in law or in equity in any court of competent jurisdiction to recover the damages sustained as a result of any such act or transaction. In any such suit the court may, in its discretion, require an undertaking for the payment of the costs of such suit, and assess reasonable costs, including reasonable attorneys' fees, against either party litigant. Every person who becomes liable to make any payment under this subsection may recover contribution as in cases of contract from any person who, if joined in the original suit, would have been liable to make the same payment. No action shall be maintained to enforce any liability created under this section, unless brought within one year after the discovery of the facts constituting the violation and within three years after such violation.

(g) Subsection (a) Not Applicable to Exempted Securities

The provisions of subsection (a) of this section shall not apply to an exempted security.

(h) Foreign Currencies

Notwithstanding any other provision of law, the Commission shall have the authority to regulate the trading of any put, call, straddle, option, or privilege on any security, certificate of deposit, or group or index of securities (including any interest therein or based on the value thereof), or any put, call, straddle, option, or privilege entered into on a national securities exchange relating to foreign currency (but not, with respect to any of the foregoing, an option on a contract for future delivery).

(i) Limitations on Practices That Affect Market Volatility

It shall be unlawful for any person, by the use of the mails or any means or instrumentality of interstate commerce or of any facility of any national securities exchange, to use or employ any act or practice in connection with the purchase or sale of any equity security in contravention of such rules or regulations as the Commission may adopt, consistent with the public interest, the protection of investors, and the maintenance of fair and orderly markets—

(1) to prescribe means reasonably designed to prevent manipulation of price levels of the equity securities market or a substantial segment thereof; and

(2) to prohibit or constrain, during periods of extraordinary market volatility, and trading practice in connection with the purchase or sale of equity securities that the Commission determines (A) has previously contributed significantly to extraordinary levels of volatility that have threatened the maintenance of fair and orderly markets; and (B) is reasonably certain to engender such levels of volatility if not prohibited or constrained.

In adopting rules under paragraph (2), the Commission shall, consistent with the purposes of this subsection, minimize the impact on the normal operations of the market and a natural person's freedom to buy or sell any equity security.

(j) It shall be unlawful for any person, directly or indirectly, by the use of any means or instrumentality of interstate commerce or of the mails, or of any facility of any national securities exchange, to effect any transaction in, or to induce or attempt to induce the purchase or sale of, any security-based swap, in connection with which such person engages in any fraudulent, deceptive, or manipulative act or practice, makes any fictitious quotation, or engages in any transaction, practice, or course of business which operates as a fraud or deceit upon any person. The Commission shall, for the purposes of this subsection, by rules and regulations define, and prescribe means reasonably designed to prevent, such transactions, acts, practices, and courses of business as are fraudulent, deceptive, or manipulative, and such quotations as are fictitious.

§10. Manipulative and Deceptive Devices

It shall be unlawful for any person, directly or indirectly, by the use of any means or instrumentality of interstate commerce or of the mails, or of any facility of any national securities exchange—

(a)(1) To effect a short sale, or to use or employ any stop-loss order in connection with the purchase or sale, of any security other than a government security, in contravention of such rules and regulations as the Commission may prescribe as necessary or appropriate in the public interest or for the protection of investors.

(2) Paragraph (1) of this subsection shall not apply to security futures products.

(b) To use or employ, in connection with the purchase or sale of any security registered on a national securities exchange or any security not so registered or any securities-based swap agreement, any manipulative or deceptive device or contrivance in contravention of such rules and regulations as the Commission may prescribe as necessary or appropriate in the public interest or for the protection of investors.

(c)(1) To effect, accept, or facilitate a transaction involving the loan or borrowing of securities in contravention of such rules and regulations as the Commission may prescribe as necessary or appropriate in the public interest or for the protection of investors. . . .

§10A. Audit Requirements

(a) In General

Each audit required pursuant to this title of the financial statements of an issuer by a registered public accounting firm shall include, in accordance with generally accepted auditing standards, as may be modified or supplemented from time to time by the Commission—

(1) procedures designed to provide reasonable assurance of detecting illegal acts that would have a direct and material effect on the determination of financial statement amounts;

(2) procedures designed to identify related party transactions that are material to the financial statements or otherwise require disclosure therein; and

(3) an evaluation of whether there is substantial doubt about the ability of the issuer to continue as a going concern during the ensuing fiscal year.

(b) Required Response to Audit Discoveries

(1) Investigation and Report to Management

If, in the course of conducting an audit pursuant to this title to which subsection (a) applies, the registered public accounting firm detects or otherwise becomes aware of information indicating that an illegal act (whether or not perceived to have a material effect on the financial statements of the issuer) has or may have occurred, the firm shall, in accordance with generally accepted auditing standards, as may be modified or supplemented from time to time by the Commission—

(A)(i) determine whether it is likely that an illegal act has occurred; and

(ii) if so, determine and consider the possible effect of the illegal act on the financial statements of the issuer, including any contingent monetary effects, such as fines, penalties, and damages; and

(B) as soon as practicable, inform the appropriate level of the management of the issuer and assure that the audit committee of the issuer, or the board of directors of the issuer in the absence of such a committee, is adequately informed with respect to illegal acts that have been detected or have otherwise come to the attention of such firm in the course of the audit, unless the illegal act is clearly inconsequential.

(2) Response to Failure to Take Remedial Action

If, after determining that the audit committee of the board of directors of the issuer, or the board of directors of the issuer in the absence of an audit committee, is adequately informed with respect to illegal acts that have been detected or have otherwise come to the attention of the accountant in the course of the audit of such firm, the registered public accounting firm concludes that—

(A) the illegal act has a material effect on the financial statements of the issuer;

(B) the senior management has not taken, and the board of directors has not caused senior management to take, timely and appropriate remedial actions with respect to the illegal act; and

(C) the failure to take remedial action is reasonably expected to warrant departure from a standard report of the auditor, when made, or warrant resignation from the audit engagement;

the registered public accounting firm shall, as soon as practicable, directly report its conclusions to the board of directors.

(3) Notice to Commission; Response to Failure to Notify

An issuer whose board of directors receives a report under paragraph (2) shall inform the Commission by notice not later than 1 business day after the receipt of such report and shall furnish the registered public accounting firm making such report with a copy of the notice furnished to the Commission. If the registered public accounting firm fails to receive a copy of the notice before the expiration of the required 1-business-day period, the registered public accounting firm shall—

(A) resign from the engagement; or

(B) furnish to the Commission a copy of its report (or the documentation of any oral report given) not later than 1 business day following such failure to receive notice.

(4) Report After Resignation

If a registered public accounting firm resigns from an engagement under paragraph (3)(A), the firm shall, not later than 1 business day following the failure by the issuer to notify the Commission under paragraph (3), furnish to the Commission a copy of the report of the firm (or the documentation of any oral report given).

(c) Auditor Liability Limitation

No registered public accounting firm shall be liable in a private action for any finding, conclusion, or statement expressed in a report made pursuant to paragraph (3) or (4) of subsection (b), including any rule promulgated pursuant thereto.

(d) Civil Penalties in Cease-and-Desist Proceedings

If the Commission finds, after notice and opportunity for hearing in a proceeding instituted pursuant to section 21C, that a registered public accounting firm has willfully violated paragraph (3) or (4) of subsection (b), the Commission may, in addition to entering an order under section 21C, impose a civil penalty against the registered public accounting firm and any other person that the Commission finds was a cause of such violation. The determination to impose a civil penalty and the amount of the penalty shall be governed by the standards set forth in section 21B.

(e) Preservation of Existing Authority

Except as provided in subsection (d), nothing in this section shall be held to limit or otherwise affect the authority of the Commission under this title.

(f) Definitions

As used in this section, the term "illegal act" means an act or omission that violates any law, or any rule or regulation having the force of law. . . .

(g) Prohibited Activities

Except as provided in subsection (h), it shall be unlawful for a registered public accounting firm (and any associated person of that firm, to the extent determined appropriate by the Commission) that performs for any issuer any audit required by this title or the rules of the Commission under this title or, beginning 180 days after the date of commencement of the operations of the Public Company Accounting Oversight Board established under section 101 of the Sarbanes-Oxley Act of 2002 (in this section referred to as the "Board"), the rules of the Board, to provide to that issuer, contemporaneously with the audit, and non-audit service, including—

(1) bookkeeping or other services related to the accounting records or financial statements of the audit client;

(2) financial information systems design and implementation;

(3) appraisal or valuation services, fairness opinions, or contribution-in-kind reports;

(4) actuarial services;

(5) internal audit outsourcing services;

(6) management functions or human resources;

(7) broker or dealer, investment adviser, or investment banking services;

(8) legal services and expert services unrelated to the audit; and

(9) any other service that the Board determines, by regulation, is impermissible.

(h) Preapproval Required for Non-Audit Services

A registered public accounting firm may engage in any non-audit service, including tax services, that is not described in any of paragraphs (1) through (9) of subsection (g) for an audit client, only if the activity is approved in advance by the audit committee of the issuer, in accordance with subsection (i).

(i) Preapproval Requirements

(1) In general.—

(A) Audit committee action.—All auditing services (which may entail providing comfort letters in connection with securities underwritings or statutory audits required for insurance companies for purposes of State law) and non-audit services, other than as provided in subparagraph (B), provided to an issuer by the auditor or the issuer shall be preapproved by the audit committee of the issuer.

(B) De Minimis Exception.—The preapproval requirement under subparagraph (A) is waived with respect to the provision of non-audit services for an issuer, if

(i) the aggregate amount of all such non-audit services provided to the issuer constitutes not more than 5 percent of the total amount of revenues paid by the issuer to its auditor during the fiscal year in which the nonaudit services are provided;

(ii) such services were not recognized by the issuer at the time of the engagement to be non-audit services; and

(iii) such services are promptly brought to the attention of the audit committee of the issuer and approved prior to the completion of the audit by the audit committee or by 1 or more members of the audit committee who are members of the board of directors to whom authority to grant such approvals has been delegated by the audit committee.

(2) Disclosure to investors.—Approval by an audit committee of an issuer under this subsection of a non-audit service to be performed by the auditor of the issuer shall be disclosed to investors in periodic reports required by section 13(a).

(3) Delegation authority.—The audit committee of an issuer may delegate to 1 or more designated members of the audit committee who are independent directors of the board of directors, the authority to grant preapprovals required by this subsection. The decisions of any member to whom authority is delegated under this paragraph to preapprove an activity under this subsection shall be presented to the full audit committee at each of its scheduled meetings.

(4) Approval of audit services for other purposes.—In carrying out its duties under subsection (m)(2), if the audit committee of an issuer approves an audit service within the scope of the engagement of the auditor, such audit service shall be deemed to have been preapproved for purposes of this subsection.

(j) Audit Partner Rotation

It shall be unlawful for a registered public accounting firm to provide audit services to an issuer if the lead (or coordinating) audit partner (having primary responsibility for the audit), or the audit partner responsible for reviewing the audit, has performed audit services for that issuer in each of the 5 previous fiscal years of that issuer.

(k) Reports to Audit Committees

Each registered public accounting firm that performs for any issuer any audit required by this title shall timely report to the audit committee of the issuer

(1) all critical accounting policies and practices to be used.

(2) all alternative treatments of financial information within generally accepted accounting principles that have been discussed with management officials of the issuer, ramifications of the use of such alternative disclosures and treatments, and the treatment preferred by the registered public accounting firm; and

(3) other material written communications between the registered public accounting firm and the management of the issuer, such as any management letter or schedule of unadjusted differences.

(l) Conflicts of Interest

It shall be unlawful for a registered public accounting firm to perform for an issuer any audit service required by this title, if a chief executive officer, controller, chief financial officer, chief accounting officer, or any person serving in an equivalent position for the issuer, was employed by that registered independent public accounting firm and participated in any capacity in the audit of that issuer during the 1 year period preceding the date of the initiation of the audit.

(m) Standards Relating to Audit Committees.

(1) Commission rules.

(A) In general.—Effective not later that 270 days after the date of enactment of this subsection, the Commission shall, by rule, direct the national securities exchanges and national securities associations to prohibit the listing of any security of an issuer that is not in compliance with the requirements of any portion of paragraphs (2) through (6).

(B) Opportunity to cure defects.—The rules of the Commission under subparagraph (A) shall provide for appropriate procedures for an issuer to have an opportunity to cure any defects that would be the basis for a prohibition under subparagraph (A), before the imposition of such prohibition.

(2) Responsibilities relating to registered public accounting firms.—The audit committee of each issuer, in its capacity as a committee of the board of directors, shall be directly responsible for the appointment, compensation, and oversight of the work of any registered public accounting firm employed by that issuer (including resolution of disagreements between management and the auditor regarding financial reporting) for the purpose of preparing or issuing an audit report or related work, and each such registered public accounting firm shall report directly to the audit committee.

(3) Independence.

(A) In general.—Each member of the audit committee of the issuer shall be a member of the board of directors of the issuer, and shall otherwise be independent.

(B) Criteria.—In order to be considered to be independent for purposes of this paragraph, a member of an audit committee of an issuer may not, other than in his or her capacity as a member of the audit committee, the board of directors, or any other board committee

(i) accept any consulting, advisory, or other compensatory fee from the issuer; or

(ii) be an affiliated person of the issuer or any subsidiary thereof.

(C) Exemption authority—The Commission may exempt from the requirements of subparagraph (B) a particular relationship with respect to audit committee members, as the Commission determines appropriate in light of the circumstances.

(4) Complaints.—Each audit committee shall establish procedures for

(A) the receipt, retention, and treatment of complaints received by the issuer regarding accounting, internal accounting controls, or auditing matters; and

(B) the confidential, anonymous submission by employees of the issuer of concerns regarding questionable accounting or auditing matters.

(5) Authority to engage advisers.—Each audit committee shall have the authority to engage independent counsel and other advisers, as it deems necessary to carry out its duties.

(6) Funding.—Each issuer shall provide for appropriate funding, as determined by the audit committee, in its capacity as a committee of the board of directors, for payment of compensation.

(A) to the registered public accounting firm employed by the issuer for the purpose of rendering or issuing an audit report; and

(B) to any advisers employed by the audit committee under paragraph (5).

§10C. Compensation Committees

(a) Independence of Compensation Committees

(1) Listing standards.—

The Commission shall, by rule, direct the national securities exchanges and national securities associations to prohibit the listing of any equity security of an issuer, other than an issuer that is a controlled company, limited partnership, company in bankruptcy proceedings, openended management investment company that is registered under the Investment Company Act of 1940, or a foreign private issuer that provides annual disclosures to shareholders of the reasons that the foreign private issuer does not have an independent compensation committee, that does not comply with the requirements of this subsection.

(2) Independence of compensation committees

The rules of the Commission under paragraph (1) shall require that each member of the compensation committee of the board of directors of an issuer be—

(A) a member of the board of directors of the issuer; and

(B) independent.

(3) Independence

The rules of the Commission under paragraph (1) shall require that, in determining the definition of the term 'independence' for purposes of paragraph (2), the national securities exchanges and the national securities associations shall consider relevant factors, including—

(A) the source of compensation of a member of the board of directors of an issuer, including any consulting, advisory, or other compensatory fee paid by the issuer to such member of the board of directors; and

(B) whether a member of the board of directors of an issuer is affiliated with the issuer, a subsidiary of the issuer, or an affiliate of a subsidiary of the issuer.

(4) Exemption authority

The rules of the Commission under paragraph (1) shall permit a national securities exchange or a national securities association to exempt a particular relationship from the requirements of paragraph (2), with respect to the members of a compensation committee, as the national securities exchange or national securities association determines is appropriate, taking into consideration the size of an issuer and any other relevant factors.

(b) Independence of Compensation Consultants and Other Compensation Committee Advisers

(1) In general

The compensation committee of an issuer may only select a compensation consultant, legal counsel, or other adviser to the compensation committee after taking into consideration the factors identified by the Commission under paragraph (2).

(2) Rules

The Commission shall identify factors that affect the independence of a compensation consultant, legal counsel, or other adviser to a compensation committee of an issuer. Such factors shall be competitively neutral among categories of consultants, legal counsel, or other advisers and preserve the ability of compensation committees to retain the services of members of any such category, and shall include—

(A) the provision of other services to the issuer by the person that employs the compensation consultant, legal counsel, or other adviser;

(B) the amount of fees received from the issuer by the person that employs the compensation consultant, legal counsel, or other adviser, as a percentage of the total revenue of the person that employs the compensation consultant, legal counsel, or other adviser;

(C) the policies and procedures of the person that employs the compensation consultant, legal counsel, or other adviser that are designed to prevent conflicts of interest;

(D) any business or personal relationship of the compensation consultant, legal counsel, or other adviser with a member of the compensation committee; and

(E) any stock of the issuer owned by the compensation consultant, legal counsel, or other adviser.

(c) Compensation Committee Authority Relating to Compensation Consultants

(1) Authority to retain compensation consultant

(A) In general.—

The compensation committee of an issuer, in its capacity as a committee of the board of directors, may, in its sole discretion, retain or obtain the advice of a compensation consultant.

(B) Direct responsibility of compensation committee.—

The compensation committee of an issuer shall be directly responsible for the appointment, compensation, and oversight of the work of a compensation consultant.

(C) Rule of construction.—

This paragraph may not be construed—

(i) to require the compensation committee to implement or act consistently with the advice or recommendations of the compensation consultant; or

(ii) to affect the ability or obligation of a compensation committee to exercise its own judgment in fulfillment of the duties of the compensation committee.

(2) Disclosure

In any proxy or consent solicitation material for an annual meeting of the shareholders (or a special meeting in lieu of the annual meeting) occurring on or after the date that is 1 year after the date of enactment of this section, each issuer shall disclose in the proxy or consent material, in accordance with regulations of the Commission, whether—

(A) the compensation committee of the issuer retained or obtained the advice of a compensation consultant; and

(B) the work of the compensation consultant has raised any conflict of interest and, if so, the nature of the conflict and how the conflict is being addressed.

(d) Authority to Engage Independent Legal Counsel and Other Advisers

(1) In general

The compensation committee of an issuer, in its capacity as a committee of the board of directors, may, in its sole discretion, retain and obtain the advice of independent legal counsel and other advisers.

(2) Direct responsibility of compensation committee

The compensation committee of an issuer shall be directly responsible for the appointment, compensation, and oversight of the work of independent legal counsel and other advisers.

(3) Rule of construction

This subsection may not be construed—

(A) to require a compensation committee to implement or act consistently with the advice or recommendations of independent legal counsel or other advisers under this subsection; or

(B) to affect the ability or obligation of a compensation committee to exercise its own judgment in fulfillment of the duties of the compensation committee.

(e) Compensation of Compensation Consultants, Independent Legal Counsel, and Other Advisers

Each issuer shall provide for appropriate funding, as determined by the compensation committee in its capacity as a committee of the board of directors, for payment of reasonable compensation—

(1) to a compensation consultant; and

(2) to independent legal counsel or any other adviser to the compensation committee.

(f) Commission Rules

(1) In general

Not later than 360 days after the date of enactment of this section, the Commission shall, by rule, direct the national securities exchanges and national securities associations to prohibit the listing of any security of an issuer that is not in compliance with the requirements of this section.

(2) Opportunity to cure defects.—

The rules of the Commission under paragraph (1) shall provide for appropriate procedures for an issuer to have a reasonable opportunity to cure any defects that would be the basis for the prohibition under paragraph (1), before the imposition of such prohibition.

(3) Exemption authority

(A) In general.—

The rules of the Commission under paragraph (1) shall permit a national securities exchange or a national securities association to exempt a category of issuers from the requirements under this section, as the national securities exchange or the national securities association determines is appropriate.

(B) Considerations.—

In determining appropriate exemptions under subparagraph (A), the national securities exchange or the national securities association shall take into account the potential impact of the requirements of this section on smaller reporting issuers.

(g) Controlled Company Exemption

(1) In general

This section shall not apply to any controlled company.

(2) Definition

For purposes of this section, the term 'controlled company' means an issuer—

(A) that is listed on a national securities exchange or by a national securities association; and

(B) that holds an election for the board of directors of the issuer in which more than 50 percent of the voting power is held by an individual, a group, or another issuer.

§10D. Recovery of Erroneously Awarded Compensation Policy

(a) Listing Standards

The Commission shall, by rule, direct the national securities exchanges and national securities associations to prohibit the listing of any security of an issuer that does not comply with the requirements of this section.

(b) Recovery of Funds

The rules of the Commission under subsection (a) shall require each issuer to develop and implement a policy providing—

(1) for disclosure of the policy of the issuer on incentive based compensation that is based on financial information required to be reported under the securities laws; and

(2) that, in the event that the issuer is required to prepare an accounting restatement due to the material noncompliance of the issuer with any financial reporting requirement under the securities laws, the issuer will recover from any current or former executive officer of the issuer who received incentive-based compensation (including stock options awarded as compensation) during the 3-year period preceding the date on which the issuer is required to prepare an accounting restatement, based on the erroneous data, in excess of what would have been paid to the executive officer under the accounting restatement.

§11A. National Market System for Securities; Securities Information Processors

(a) Congressional Findings; Facilitating Establishment of National Market System for Securities; Designation of Qualified Securities

(1) The Congress finds that—

(A) The securities markets are an important national asset which must be preserved and strengthened.

(B) New data processing and communications techniques create the opportunity for more efficient and effective market operations.

(C) It is in the public interest and appropriate for the protection of investors and the maintenance of fair and orderly markets to assure—

(i) economically efficient execution of securities transactions;

(ii) fair competition among brokers and dealers, among exchange markets, and between exchange markets and markets other than exchange markets;

(iii) the availability to brokers, dealers, and investors of information with respect to quotations for and transactions in securities;

(iv) the practicability of brokers executing investors' orders in the best market; and

(v) an opportunity, consistent with the provisions of clauses (i) and (iv) of this subparagraph, for investors' orders to be executed without the participation of a dealer.

(D) The linking of all markets for qualified securities through communication and data processing facilities will foster efficiency, enhance competition, increase the information available to brokers, dealers, and investors, facilitate the offsetting of investors' orders, and contribute to best execution of such orders.

(2) The Commission is directed, therefore, having due regard for the public interest, the protection of investors, and the maintenance of fair and orderly markets, to use its authority under this chapter to facilitate the establishment of a national market system for securities (which may include subsystems for particular types of securities with unique trading characteristics) in accordance with the findings and to carry out the objectives set forth in paragraph (1) of this subsection. The Commission, by rule, shall designate the securities or classes of securities qualified for trading in the national market system from among securities other than exempted securities. (Securities or classes of securities so designated hereinafter in this section referred to as "qualified securities.") . . .

§12. Registration Requirements for Securities

(a) General Requirement of Registration

It shall be unlawful for any member, broker, or dealer to effect any transaction in any security (other than an exempted security) on a national securities exchange unless a registration is effective as to such security for such exchange in accordance with the provisions of this chapter and the rules and regulations thereunder.

(b) Procedure for Registration; Information

A security may be registered on a national securities exchange by the issuer filing an application with the exchange (and filing with the Commission such duplicate originals thereof as the Commission may require), which application shall contain—

(1) Such information, in such detail, as to the issuer and any person directly or indirectly controlling or controlled by, or under direct or indirect common control with, the issuer, and any guarantor of the security as to principal or interest or both, as the Commission may by rules and regulations require, as necessary or appropriate in the public interest or for the protection of investors . . .

(g) Registration of Securities by Issuer; Exemptions

(1) Every issuer which is engaged in interstate commerce, or in a business affecting interstate commerce, or whose securities are traded by use of the mails or any means or instrumentality of interstate commerce shall—. . .

(A) within 120 days after the last day of its first fiscal year ended on which the issuer has total assets exceeding $10,000,000 and a class of equity security (other than an exempted security) held of record by either—

(i) 2,000 persons, or

(ii) 500 persons who are not accredited investors (as such term is defined by the Commission), and

(B) in the case of an issuer that is a bank, a savings and loan holding company (as defined in section 10 of 24 the Home Owners' Loan Act), or a bank holding company, as such term is defined in section 2 of the Bank Holding Company Act of 1956 (12 U.S.C. 1841), not later than 120 days after the last day of its first fiscal year ended after the effective date of this subsection, on which the issuer has total assets exceeding $10,000,000 and a class of equity security (other than an exempted security) held of record by 2,000 or more persons,

register such security by filing with the Commission a registration statement (and such copies thereof as the Commission may require) with respect to such security containing such information and documents as the Commission may specify comparable to that which is required in an application to register a security pursuant to subsection (b) of this section . . .

(2) The provisions of this subsection shall not apply in respect of—

(A) any security listed and registered on a national securities exchange. . . .

(4) Registration of any class of security pursuant to this subsection shall be terminated ninety days, or such shorter period as the Commission may determine, after the issuer files a certification with the Commission that the number of holders of record of such class of security is reduced to less than 300 persons, or, in the case of a bank, a savings and loan holding company (as defined in section 10 of 24 the Home Owners' Loan Act), or a bank holding company, as such term is defined in section 2 of the Bank Holding Company Act of 1956 (12 U.S.C. 1841), 1,200 persons. The Commission shall after notice and opportunity for hearing deny termination of registration if it finds that the certification is untrue. Termination of registration shall be deferred pending final determination on the question of denial.

(5) For the purposes of this subsection the term "class" shall include all securities of an issuer which are of substantially similar character and the holders of which enjoy substantially similar rights and privileges. The Commission may

for the purpose of this subsection define by rules and regulations the terms "total assets" and "held of record" as it deems necessary or appropriate in the public interest or for the protection of investors in order to prevent circumvention of the provisions of this subsection. For purposes of determining whether an issuer is required to register a security with the Commission pursuant to paragraph (1), the definition of "held of record" shall not include securities held by persons who received the securities pursuant to an employee compensation plan in transactions exempted from the registration requirements of section 5 of the Securities Act of 1933.

(6) Exclusion for persons holding certain securities.—The Commission shall, by rule, exempt, conditionally or unconditionally, securities acquired pursuant to an offering made under section 4(6) of the Securities Act of 1933 from the provisions of this subsection.

(h) Exemption by Rules and Regulations from Certain Provisions of Section

The Commission may by rules and regulations, or upon application of an interested person, by order, after notice and opportunity for hearing, exempt in whole or in part any issuer or class of issuers from the provisions of subsection (g) of this section or from section 13, 14, or 15(d) of this title or may exempt from section 16 of this title any officer, director, or beneficial owner of securities of any issuer, any security of which is required to be registered pursuant to subsection (g) hereof, upon such terms and conditions and for such period as it deems necessary or appropriate, if the Commission finds, by reason of the number of public investors, amount of trading interest in the securities, the nature and extent of the activities of the issuer, income or assets of the issuer, or otherwise, that such action is not inconsistent with the public interest or the protection of investors. The Commission may, for the purposes of any of the above-mentioned sections or subsections of this chapter, classify issuers and prescribe requirements appropriate for each such class.

(i) Securities Issued by Banks

In respect of any securities issued by banks and savings associations the deposits of which are insured in accordance with the Federal Deposit Insurance Act, the powers, functions, and duties vested in the Commission to administer and enforce this section and sections 13, 14(a), 14(c), 14(d), 14(f), and 16 of this title, (1) with respect to national banks and Federal savings associations, the accounts of which are insured by the Federal Deposit Insurance Corporation and banks operating under the Code of Law for the District of Columbia are vested in the Comptroller of the Currency, (2) with respect to all other member banks of the Federal Reserve System are vested in the Board of Governors of the Federal Reserve System and (3) with respect to all other insured banks and State savings associations, the accounts of which are insured by the Federal Deposit Insurance Corporation, are vested in the Federal Deposit Insurance Corporation. The Comptroller of the Currency, the Board of Governors of the Federal Reserve System, and the Federal Deposit Insurance Corporation shall have the power to make such rules and regulations as may be necessary for the execution of the functions vested in them as provided in this subsection. In carrying out their responsibilities under this subsection, the agencies named in the first sentence of this subsection shall issue substantially similar regulations to regulations and rules issued by the Commission under this section and sections 13, 14(a), 14(c), 14(d), 14(f), and 16 of this title unless they find that implementation of substantially similar regulations with respect to insured banks and insured institutions are not necessary or appropriate in the public interest or for protection of investors, and publish such findings, and the detailed reasons therefor, in the Federal Register. . . .

(j) Denial, Suspension, or Revocation of Registration;
Notice and Hearing

The Commission is authorized, by order, as it deems necessary or appropriate for the protection of investors to deny, to suspend the effective date of, to suspend for a period not exceeding twelve months, or to revoke the registration of a security, if the Commission finds, on the record after notice and opportunity for hearing, that the issuer, of such security has failed to comply with any provision of this chapter or the rules and regulations thereunder. No member of a national securities exchange, broker, or dealer shall make use of the mails or any means or instrumentality of interstate commerce to effect any transaction in, or to induce the purchase or sale of, any security the registration of which has been and is suspended or revoked pursuant to the preceding sentence.

(k) Trading Suspensions; Emergency Authority

(1) Trading Suspensions

If in its opinion the public interest and the protection of investors so require, the Commission is authorized by order—

(A) summarily to suspend trading in any security (other than an exempted security) for a period not exceeding 10 business days, and

(B) summarily to suspend all trading on any national securities exchange or otherwise, in securities other than exempted securities, for a period not exceeding 90 calendar days.

The action described in subparagraph (B) shall not take effect unless the Commission notifies the President of its decision and the President notifies the Commission that the President does not disapprove of such decision.

(2) Emergency Orders

(A) The Commission, in an emergency, may by order summarily take such action to alter, supplement, suspend, or impose requirements or restrictions with respect to any matter or action subject to regulation by the Commission or a self-regulatory organization under this chapter, as the Commission determines is necessary in the public interest and for the protection of investors—

(i) to maintain or restore fair and orderly securities markets (other than markets in exempted securities); or

(ii) to ensure prompt, accurate, and safe clearance and settlement of transactions in securities (other than exempted securities).

(B) An order of the Commission under this paragraph (2) shall continue in effect for the period specified by the Commission, and may be extended, except that in no event shall the Commission's action continue in effect for more than 10 business days, including extensions. In exercising its authority under this paragraph, the Commission shall not be required to comply with the provisions of section 553 of Title 5, or with the provisions of section 19(c) of this title.

(3) Termination of Emergency Actions by President

The President may direct that action taken by the Commission under paragraph (1)(B) or paragraph (2) of this subsection shall not continue in effect.

(4) Compliance with Orders

No member of a national securities exchange, broker, or dealer shall make use of the mails or any means or instrumentality of interstate commerce to effect any transaction in, or to induce the purchase or sale of, any security in contravention of an order of the Commission under this subsection unless such order has been stayed, modified, or set aside as provided in paragraph (5) of this subsection or has ceased to be effective upon direction of the President as provided in paragraph (3).

(5) Limitations on Review of Orders

An order of the Commission pursuant to this subsection shall be subject to review only as provided in section 25(a) of this title. Review shall be based on an examination of all the information before the Commission at the time such order was issued. The reviewing court shall not enter a stay, write of mandamus, or similar relief unless the court finds, after notice and hearing before a panel of the court, that the Commission's action is arbitrary, capricious, an abuse of discretion, or otherwise not in accordance with law.

(6) Definition of Emergency

For purposes of this subsection, the term "emergency" means a major market disturbance characterized by or constituting—

(A) sudden and excessive fluctuations of securities prices generally, or a substantial threat thereof, that threaten fair and orderly markets, or

(B) a substantial disruption of the safe or efficient operation of the national system for clearance and settlement of securities, or a substantial threat thereof. . . .

§13. Periodical and Other Reports

(a) Reports by Issuer of Security; Contents

Every issuer of a security registered pursuant to section 12 of this title shall file with the Commission, in accordance with such rules and regulations as the

Commission may prescribe as necessary or appropriate for the proper protection of investors and to insure fair dealing in the security—

(1) such information and documents (and such copies thereof) as the Commission shall require to keep reasonably current the information and documents required to be included in or filed with an application or registration statement filed pursuant to section 12 of this title. . .

(2) such annual reports (and such copies thereof), certified if required by the rules and regulations of the Commission by independent public accountants, and such quarterly reports (and such copies thereof), as the Commission may prescribe.

Every issuer of a security registered on a national securities exchange shall also file a duplicate original of such information, documents, and reports with the exchange. In any registration statement, periodic report, or other reports to be filed with the Commission, an emerging growth company need not present selected financial data in accordance with section 229.301 of title 17, Code of Federal Regulations, for any period prior to the earliest audited period presented in connection with its first registration statement that became effective under this Act or the Securities Act of 1933 and, with respect to any such statement or reports, an emerging growth company may not be required to comply with any new or revised financial accounting standard until such date that a company that is not an issuer as defined under section 2(a) of the Sarbanes-Oxley Act of 2002 (15 U.S.C. 7201(a)) is required to comply with such new or revised accounting standard, if such standard applies to companies that are not issuers.

[Editors' Note: A portion of the JOBS Act not codified as part of the Securities Exchange Act permits emerging growth companies to choose to forgo the various exemptions provided to them, but as to choosing compliance with new or revised financial accounting standards provided under this section, the emerging company (1) must make such choice at the time the company is first required to file a registration statement, periodic report, or other report with the Commission under section 13 of the Securities Exchange Act of 1934 and notify the Securities and Exchange Commission of such choice; (2) may not select some standards to comply with in such manner and not others, but must comply with all such standards to the same extent that a non-emerging growth company is required to comply with such standards; and (3) must continue to comply with such standards to the same extent that a non-emerging growth company is required to comply with such standards for as long as the company remains an emerging growth company.]

(b) Form of Report; Books, Records, and Internal Accounting; Directives

(1) The Commission may prescribe, in regard to reports made pursuant to this chapter, the form or forms in which the required information shall be set forth, the items or details to be shown in the balance sheet and the earnings statement, and the methods to be followed in the preparation of reports, in the appraisal or valuation of assets and liabilities, in the determination of depreciation and depletion, in the differentiation of recurring and nonrecurring

income, in the differentiation of investment and operating incomes, and in the preparation, where the Commission deems it necessary or desirable, of separate and/or consolidated balance sheets or income accounts of any person directly or indirectly controlling or controlled by the issuer, or any person under direct or indirect common control with the issuer; but in the case of the reports of any person whose methods of accounting are prescribed under the provisions of any law of the United States, or any rule or regulation thereunder, the rules and regulations of the Commission with respect to reports shall not be inconsistent with the requirements imposed by such law or rule or regulation in respect of the same subject matter (except that such rules and regulations of the Commission may be inconsistent with such requirements to the extent that the Commission determines that the public interest or the protection of investors so requires).

(2) Every issuer which has a class of securities registered pursuant to section 12 of this title and every issuer which is required to file reports pursuant to section 15(d) of this title shall—

(A) make and keep books, records, and accounts, which, in reasonable detail, accurately and fairly reflect the transactions and dispositions of the assets of the issuer;

(B) devise and maintain a system of internal accounting controls sufficient to provide reasonable assurances that—

(i) transactions are executed in accordance with management's general or specific authorization;

(ii) transactions are recorded as necessary (I) to permit preparation of financial statements in conformity with generally accepted accounting principles or any other criteria applicable to such statements, and (II) to maintain accountability for assets;

(iii) access to assets is permitted only in accordance with management's general or specific authorization; and

(iv) the recorded accountability for assets is compared with the existing assets at reasonable intervals and appropriate action is taken with respect to any differences. . . .; and

(C) notwithstanding any other provision of law, pay the allocable share of such issuer of a reasonable annual accounting support fee or fees, determined in accordance with section 109 of the Sarbanes-Oxley Act of 2002.

(d) Reports by Persons Acquiring More Than Five Per Centum of Certain Classes of Securities

(1) Any person who, after acquiring directly or indirectly the beneficial ownership of any equity security of a class which is registered pursuant to section 12 of this title, or any equity security of an insurance company which would have been required to be so registered except for the exemption contained in section 12(g)(2)(G) of this title, or any equity security issued by a closed-end investment company registered under the Investment Company Act of 1940 or any equity security issued by a Native Corporation pursuant to section 1629c(d)(6) of title 43 or otherwise

becomes or is deemed to become a beneficial owner of any of the foregoing upon the purchase or sale of a security-based swap that the Commission may define by rule, and is directly or indirectly the beneficial owner of more than 5 per centum of such class shall, within ten days after such acquisition or within such shorter time as the Commission may establish by rule, file with the Commission, a statement containing such of the following information, and such additional information, as the Commission may by rules and regulations, prescribe as necessary or appropriate in the public interest or for the protection of investors—

(A) the background, and identity, residence, and citizenship of, and the nature of such beneficial ownership by, such person and all other persons by whom or on whose behalf the purchases have been or are to be effected;

(B) the source and amount of the funds or other consideration used or to be used in making the purchases, and if any part of the purchase price is represented or is to be represented by funds or other consideration borrowed or otherwise obtained for the purpose of acquiring, holding, or trading such security, a description of the transaction and the names of the parties thereto, except that where a source of funds is a loan made in the ordinary course of business by a bank, as defined in section 3(a)(6) of this title, if the person filing such statement so requests, the name of the bank shall not be made available to the public.

(C) if the purpose of the purchases or prospective purchases is to acquire control of the business of the issuer of the securities, any plans or proposals which such persons may have to liquidate such issuer, to sell its assets to or merge it with any other persons, or to make any other major change in its business or corporate structure;

(D) the number of shares of such security which are beneficially owned, and the number of shares concerning which there is a right to acquire, directly or indirectly, by (i) such person, and (ii) by each associate of such person, giving the background, identity, residence, and citizenship of each such associate; and

(E) information as to any contracts, arrangements, or understandings with any person with respect to any securities of the issuer, including but not limited to transfer of any of the securities, joint ventures, loan or option arrangements, puts or calls, guaranties of loans, guaranties against loss or guaranties of profits, division of losses or profits, or the giving or withholding of proxies, naming the persons with whom such contracts, arrangements, or understandings have been entered into, and giving the details thereof.

(2) If any material change occurs in the facts set forth in the statement filed with the Commission, an amendment shall be filed with the Commission, in accordance with such rules and regulations as the Commission may prescribe as necessary or appropriate in the public interest or for the protection of investors.

(3) When two or more persons act as a partnership, limited partnership, syndicate, or other group for the purpose of acquiring, holding, or disposing of securities of an issuer, such syndicate or group shall be deemed a "person" for the purposes of this subsection.

(4) In determining, for purposes of this subsection, any percentage of a class of any security, such class shall be deemed to consist of the amount of the outstanding securities of such class, exclusive of any securities of such class held by or for the account of the issuer or a subsidiary of the issuer.

(5) The Commission, by rule or regulation or by order, may permit any person to file in lieu of the statement required by paragraph (1) of this subsection or the rules and regulations thereunder, a notice stating the name of such person, the number of shares of any equity securities subject to paragraph (1) which are owned by him, the date of their acquisition and such other information as the Commission may specify, if it appears to the Commission that such securities were acquired by such person in the ordinary course of his business and were not acquired for the purpose of and do not have the effect of changing or influencing the control of the issuer nor in connection with or as a participant in any transaction having such purpose or effect.

(6) The provisions of this subsection shall not apply to—

(A) any acquisition or offer to acquire securities made or proposed to be made by means of a registration statement under the Securities Act of 1933;

(B) any acquisition of the beneficial ownership of a security which, together with all other acquisitions by the same person of securities of the same class during the preceding twelve months, does not exceed 2 per centum of that class;

(C) any acquisition of an equity security by the issuer of such security;

(D) any acquisition or proposed acquisition of a security which the Commission, by rules or regulations or by order, shall exempt from the provisions of this subsection as not entered into for the purpose of, and not having the effect of, changing or influencing the control of the issuer or otherwise as not comprehended within the purposes of this subsection.

(e) Purchase of Securities by Issuer

(1) It shall be unlawful for an issuer which has a class of equity securities registered pursuant to section 12 of this title, or which is a closed-end investment company registered under the Investment Company Act of 1940, to purchase any equity security issued by it if such purchase is in contravention of such rules and regulations as the Commission, in the public interest or for the protection of investors, may adopt (A) to define acts and practices which are fraudulent, deceptive, or manipulative, and (B) to prescribe means reasonably designed to prevent such acts and practices. Such rules and regulations may require such issuer to provide holders of equity securities of such class with such information relating to the reasons for such purchase, the source of funds, the number of shares to be purchased, the price to be paid for such securities, the method of purchase, and such additional information, as the Commission deems necessary or appropriate in the public interest or for the protection of investors, or which the Commission deems to be material to a determination whether such security should be sold.

(2) For the purpose of this subsection, a purchase by or for the issuer or any person controlling, controlled by, or under common control with the issuer, or a purchase subject to control of the issuer or any such person, shall be deemed to

be a purchase by the issuer. The Commission shall have power to make rules and regulations implementing this paragraph in the public interest and for the protection of investors, including exemptive rules and regulations covering situations in which the Commission deems it unnecessary or inappropriate that a purchase of the type described in this paragraph shall be deemed to be a purchase by the issuer for purposes of some or all of the provisions of paragraph (1) of this subsection.

(3) At the time of filing such statement as the Commission may require by rule pursuant to paragraph (1) of this subsection, the person making the filing shall pay to the Commission a fee at a rate that subject to paragraph 4, is equal to $92 per $1,000,000 of the value of securities proposed to be purchased. The fee shall be reduced with respect to securities in an amount equal to any fee paid with respect to any securities issued in connection with the proposed transaction under section 6(b) of the Securities Act of 1933, or the fee paid under that section shall be reduced in an amount equal to the fee paid to the Commission in connection with such transaction under this paragraph. . . .

(f) Reports by Institutional Investment Managers

(1) Every institutional investment manager which uses the mails, or any means or instrumentality of interstate commerce in the course of its business as an institutional investment manager and which exercises investment discretion with respect to accounts holding equity securities of a class described in subsection (d)(1) of this section or otherwise becomes or is deemed to become a beneficial owner of any security of a class described in subsection (d)(1) upon the purchase or sale of a security-based swap that the Commission may define by rule, having an aggregate fair market value on the last trading day in any of the preceding twelve months of at least $100,000,000 or such lesser amount (but in no case less than $10,000,000) as the Commission, by rule, may determine, shall file reports with the Commission in such form, for such periods, and at such times after the end of such periods as the Commission, by rule, may prescribe, but in no event shall such reports be filed for periods longer than one year or shorter than one quarter. Such reports shall include for each such equity security held on the last day of the reporting period by accounts (in aggregate or by type as the Commission, by rule, may prescribe) with respect to which the institutional investment manager exercises investment discretion (other than securities held in amounts which the Commission, by rule, determines to be insignificant for purposes of this subsection), the name of the issuer and the title, class, CUSIP number, number of shares or principal amount, and aggregate fair market value of each such security. Such reports may also include for accounts (in aggregate or by type) with respect to which the institutional investment manager exercises investment discretion such of the following information as the Commission, by rule, prescribes—

(A) the name of the issuer and the title, class, CUSIP number, number of shares or principal amount, and aggregate fair market value or cost or amortized cost of each other security (other than an exempted security) held on the last day of the reporting period by such accounts;

(B) the aggregate fair market value or cost or amortized cost of exempted securities (in aggregate or by class) held on the last day of the reporting period by such accounts;

(C) the number of shares of each equity security of a class described in subsection (d)(1) of this section held on the last day of the reporting period by such accounts with respect to which the institutional investment manager possesses sole or shared authority to exercise the voting rights evidenced by such securities;

(D) the aggregate purchases and aggregate sales during the reporting period of each security (other than an exempted security) effected by or for such accounts; and

(E) with respect to any transaction or series of transactions having a market value of at least $500,000 or such other amount as the Commission, by rule, may determine, effected during the reporting period by or for such accounts in any equity security of a class described in subsection (d)(1) of this section—

(i) the name of the issuer and the title, class, and CUSIP number of the security;

(ii) the number of shares or principal amount of the security involved in the transaction;

(iii) whether the transaction was a purchase or sale;

(iv) the per share price or prices at which the transaction was effected;

(v) the date or dates of the transaction;

(vi) the date or dates of the settlement of the transaction;

(vii) the broker or dealer through whom the transaction was effected;

(viii) the market or markets in which the transaction was effected; and

(ix) such other related information as the Commission, by rule, may prescribe.

(2) The Commission shall prescribe rules providing for the public disclosure of the name of the issuer and the title, class, CUSIP number, aggregate amount of the number of short sales of each security, and any additional information determined by the Commission following the end of the reporting period. At a minimum, such public disclosure shall occur every month.

(3) The Commission, by rule, or order, may exempt, conditionally or unconditionally, any institutional investment manager or security or any class of institutional investment managers or securities from any or all of the provisions of this subsection or the rules thereunder.

(4) The Commission shall make available to the public for a reasonable fee a list of all equity securities of a class described in subsection (d)(1) of this section, updated no less frequently than reports are required to be filed pursuant to paragraph (1) of this subsection. The Commission shall tabulate the information contained in any report filed pursuant to this subsection in a manner which will, in the view of the Commission, maximize the usefulness of the information to other Federal and State authorities and the public. Promptly after the filing of any such report, the Commission shall make the information contained therein conveniently available to the public for a reasonable fee in such form as the Commission, by

rule, may prescribe, except that the Commission, as it determines to be necessary or appropriate in the public interest or for the protection of investors, may delay or prevent public disclosure of any such information in accordance with section 552 of title 5. Notwithstanding the preceding sentence, any such information identifying the securities held by the account of a natural person or an estate or trust (other than a business trust or investment company) shall not be disclosed to the public. . . .

(g) Statement of Equity Security Ownership

(1) Any person who is directly or indirectly the beneficial owner of more than 5 per centum of any security of a class described in subsection (d)(1) of this section or otherwise becomes or is deemed to become a beneficial owner of any security of a class described in subsection (d)(1) upon the purchase or sale of a security-based swap that the Commission may define by rule shall file with the Commission a statement setting forth, in such form and at such time as the Commission may, by rule, prescribe—

(A) such person's identity, residence, and citizenship; and

(B) the number and description of the shares in which such person has an interest and the nature of such interest.

(2) If any material change occurs in the facts set forth in the statement filed with the Commission, an amendment shall be filed with the Commission, in accordance with such rules and regulations as the Commission may prescribe as necessary or appropriate in the public interest or for the protection of investors.

(3) When two or more persons act as a partnership, limited partnership, syndicate, or other group for the purpose of acquiring, holding, or disposing of securities of an issuer, such syndicate or group shall be deemed a "person" for the purposes of this subsection.

(4) In determining, for purposes of this subsection, any percentage of a class of any security, such class shall be deemed to consist of the amount of the outstanding securities of such class, exclusive of any securities of such class held by or for the account of the issuer or a subsidiary of the issuer.

(5) In exercising its authority under this subsection, the Commission shall take such steps as it deems necessary or appropriate in the public interest or for the protection of investors (A) to achieve centralized reporting of information regarding ownership, (B) to avoid unnecessarily duplicative reporting by and minimize the compliance burden on persons required to report, and (C) to tabulate and promptly make available the information contained in any report filed pursuant to this subsection in a manner which will, in the view of the Commission, maximize the usefulness of the information to other Federal and State agencies and the public.

(6) The Commission may, by rule or order, exempt, in whole or in part, any person or class of persons from any or all of the reporting requirements of this subsection as it deems necessary or appropriate in the public interest or for the protection of investors.

(h) Large Trader Reporting

(1) Identification Requirements for Large Traders

For the purpose of monitoring the impact on the securities markets of securities transactions involving a substantial volume or a large fair market value or exercise value and for the purpose of otherwise assisting the Commission in the enforcement of this chapter, each large trader shall—

(A) provide such information to the Commission as the Commission may by rule or regulation prescribe as necessary or appropriate, identifying such large trader and all accounts in or through which such large trader effects such transactions; and

(B) identify, in accordance with such rules or regulations as the Commission may prescribe as necessary or appropriate, to any registered broker or dealer by or through whom such large trader directly or indirectly effects securities transactions, such large trader and all accounts directly or indirectly maintained with such broker or dealer by such large trader in or through which such transactions are effected.

(2) Recordkeeping and Reporting Requirements for Brokers and Dealers

Every registered broker or dealer shall make and keep for prescribed periods such records as the Commission by rule or regulation prescribes as necessary or appropriate in the public interest, for the protection of investors, or otherwise in furtherance of the purposes of this chapter, with respect to securities transactions that equal or exceed the reporting activity level effected directly or indirectly by or through such registered broker or dealer of or for any person that such broker or dealer knows is a large trader, or any person that such broker or dealer has reason to know is a large trader on the basis of transactions in securities effected by or through such broker or dealer. . . .

(i) Accuracy of Financial Reports

Each financial report that contains financial statements, and that is required to be prepared in accordance with (or reconciled to) generally accepted accounting principles under this title and filed with the Commission shall reflect all material correcting adjustments that have been identified by a registered public accounting firm in accordance with generally accepted accounting principles and the rules and regulations of the Commission.

(j) Off-Balance Sheet Transactions

Not later that 180 days after the date of enactment of the Sarbanes-Oxley Act of 2002, the Commission shall issue final rules providing that each annual and quarterly financial report required to be filed with the Commission shall disclose all material off-balance sheet transactions, arrangements, obligations (including contingent obligations), and other relationships of the issuer with unconsolidated entities or other persons, that may have a material current or future effect on financial condition, changes in financial condition, results of operations, liquidity, capital expenditures, capital resources, or significant components of revenues or expenses.

(k) Prohibition on Personal Loans to Executives

(1) In general.—It shall be unlawful for any issuer (as defined in section 2 of the Sarbanes-Oxley Act of 2002), directly or indirectly, including through any subsidiary, to extend or maintain credit, to arrange for the extension of credit, or to renew an extension of credit, in the form of a personal loan to or for any director or executive director (or equivalent thereof) of that issuer. An extension of credit maintained by the issuer on the date of enactment of this subsection shall not be subject to the provisions of this subsection, provided that there is no material modification to any term of any such extension of credit or any renewal of any such extension of credit on or after that date of enactment.

(2) Limitation. Paragraph (1) does not preclude any home improvement and manufactured home loans (as that term is defined in section 5 of the Home Owners' Loan Act (12 U.S.C. 1464), consumer credit (as defined in section 103 of the Truth in Lending Act (15 U.S.C. 1602)), or any extension of credit under an open end credit plan (as defined in section 103 of the Truth in Lending Act (15 U.S.C. 1602)), or a charge card (as defined in section 127(c)(4)(e) of the Truth in Lending Act (15 U.S.C. 1637 (c)(4)(e), or any extension of credit by a broker or dealer registered under section 15 of this title to an employee of that broker or dealer to buy, trade, or carry securities, that is permitted under rules or regulations of the Board of Governors of the Federal Reserve System pursuant to section 7 of this title (other than an extension of credit that would be used to purchase stock of that issuer), that is

(A) made or provided in the ordinary course of the consumer credit business of such issuer;

(B) of a type that is generally made available by such issuer to the public; and

(C) made by such an issuer on market terms, or terms that are no more favorable than those offered by the issuer to the general public for such extensions of credit.

(3) Rule of construction for certain loans.—Paragraph (1) does not apply to any loan made or maintained by an insured depository institution (as defined in section 3 of the Federal Deposit Insurance Act (12 U.S.C. 1813)), if the loan is subject to the insider lending restrictions of section 22(h) of the Federal Reserve Act (12 U.S.C. 375b).

(l) Real Time Issuer Disclosures

Each issuer reporting under section 13(a) or 15(d) shall disclose to the public on a rapid and current basis such additional information concerning material changes in the financial condition or operations of the issuer, in plain English, which may include trend and qualitative information and graphic presentations, as the Commission determines, by rule, is necessary or useful for the protection of investors and in the public interest.

(m) Public Availability of Security-Based Swap Transaction Data (omitted)

(n) Security-Based Swap Data Repositories (omitted)

(o) Beneficial Ownership.—

For purposes of this section and section 16, a person shall be deemed to acquire beneficial ownership of an equity security based on the purchase or sale of a security-based swap, only to the extent that the Commission, by rule, determines after consultation with the prudential regulators and the Secretary of the Treasury, that the purchase or sale of the security-based swap, or class of security-based swap, provides incidents of ownership comparable to direct ownership of the equity security, and that it is necessary to achieve the purposes of this section that the purchase or sale of the security-based swaps, or class of security-based swap, be deemed the acquisition of beneficial ownership of the equity security.

(p) Disclosures Relating to Conflict Minerals Originating in the Democratic Republic of the Congo.—

(1) Regulations.—

(A) In general.—

Not later than 270 days after the date of the enactment of this subsection, the Commission shall promulgate regulations requiring any person described in paragraph (2) to disclose annually, beginning with the person's first full fiscal year that begins after the date of promulgation of such regulations, whether conflict minerals that are necessary as described in paragraph (2)(B), in the year for which such reporting is required, did originate in the Democratic Republic of the Congo or an adjoining country and, in cases in which such conflict minerals did originate in any such country, submit to the Commission a report that includes, with respect to the period covered by the report—

(i) a description of the measures taken by the person to exercise due diligence on the source and chain of custody of such minerals, which measures shall include an independent private sector audit of such report submitted through the Commission that is conducted in accordance with standards established by the Comptroller General of the United States, in accordance with rules promulgated by the Commission, in consultation with the Secretary of State; and

(ii) a description of the products manufactured or contracted to be manufactured that are not DRC conflict free ('DRC conflict free' is defined to mean the products that do not contain minerals that directly or indirectly finance or benefit armed groups in the Democratic Republic of the Congo or an adjoining country), the entity that conducted the independent private sector audit in accordance with clause (i), the facilities used to process the conflict minerals, the country of origin of the conflict minerals, and the efforts to determine the mine or location of origin with the greatest possible specificity.

(B) Certification.—

The person submitting a report under subparagraph (A) shall certify the audit described in clause (i) of such subparagraph that is included in such report. Such a certified audit shall constitute a critical component of due diligence in establishing the source and chain of custody of such minerals.

(C) Unreliable determination.—

If a report required to be submitted by a person under subparagraph (A) relies on a determination of an independent private sector audit, as described under subparagraph (A)(i), or other due diligence processes previously determined by the Commission to be unreliable, the report shall not satisfy the requirements of the regulations promulgated under subparagraph (A)(i).

(D) DRC conflict free.—

For purposes of this paragraph, a product may be labeled as 'DRC conflict free' if the product does not contain conflict minerals that directly or indirectly finance or benefit armed groups in the Democratic Republic of the Congo or an adjoining country.

(E) Information available to the public.—

Each person described under paragraph (2) shall make available to the public on the Internet website of such person the information disclosed by such person under subparagraph (A).

(2) Person described.—

A person is described in this paragraph if—

(A) the person is required to file reports with the Commission pursuant to paragraph (1)(A); and

(B) conflict minerals are necessary to the functionality or production of a product manufactured by such person.

(3) Revisions and waivers.—

The Commission shall revise or temporarily waive the requirements described in paragraph (1) if the President transmits to the Commission a determination that—

(A) such revision or waiver is in the national security interest of the United States and the President includes the reasons therefor; and

(B) establishes a date, not later than 2 years after the initial publication of such exemption, on which such exemption shall expire.

(4) Termination of disclosure requirements.—

The requirements of paragraph (1) shall terminate on the date on which the President determines and certifies to the appropriate congressional committees, but in no case earlier than the date that is one day after the end of the 5-year period beginning on the date of the enactment of this subsection, that no armed groups continue to be directly involved and benefitting from commercial activity involving conflict minerals.

(5) Definitions.—

For purposes of this subsection, the terms 'adjoining country', 'appropriate congressional committees', 'armed group', and 'conflict mineral' have the meaning given those terms under section 1502 of the Dodd-Frank Wall Street Reform and Consumer Protection Act.

(q) Disclosure of payments by resource extraction issuers.—

(1) Definitions.—

In this subsection—

(A) the term 'commercial development of oil, natural gas, or minerals' includes exploration, extraction, processing, export, and other significant actions relating to oil, natural gas, or minerals, or the acquisition of a license for any such activity, as determined by the Commission;

(B) the term 'foreign government' means a foreign government, a department, agency, or instrumentality of a foreign government, or a company owned by a foreign government, as determined by the Commission;

(C) the term 'payment'—

(i) means a payment that is—

(I) made to further the commercial development of oil, natural gas, or minerals; and

(II) not de minimis; and

(ii) includes taxes, royalties, fees (including license fees), production entitlements, bonuses, and other material benefits, that the Commission, consistent with the guidelines of the Extractive Industries Transparency Initiative (to the extent practicable), determines are part of the commonly recognized revenue stream for the commercial development of oil, natural gas, or minerals;

(D) the term 'resource extraction issuer' means an issuer that—

(i) is required to file an annual report with the Commission; and

(ii) engages in the commercial development of oil, natural gas, or minerals;

(E) the term 'interactive data format' means an electronic data format in which pieces of information are identified using an interactive data standard; and

(F) the term 'interactive data standard' means standardized list of electronic tags that mark information included in the annual report of a resource extraction issuer.

(2) Disclosure.—

(A) Information required.—

Not later than 270 days after the date of enactment of the Dodd-Frank Wall Street Reform and Consumer Protection Act, the Commission shall issue final rules that require each resource extraction issuer to include in an annual report of the resource extraction issuer information relating to any payment made by the resource extraction issuer, a subsidiary of the resource extraction issuer, or an entity under the control of the resource extraction issuer to a foreign government or the Federal Government for the purpose of the commercial development of oil, natural gas, or minerals, including—

(i) the type and total amount of such payments made for each project of the resource extraction issuer relating to the commercial development of oil, natural gas, or minerals; and

(ii) the type and total amount of such payments made to each government.

(B) Consultation in rulemaking.—

In issuing rules under subparagraph (A), the Commission may consult with any agency or entity that the Commission determines is relevant.

(C) Interactive data format.—

The rules issued under subparagraph (A) shall require that the information included in the annual report of a resource extraction issuer be submitted in an interactive data format.

(D) Interactive data standard.—

(i) In general.—

The rules issued under subparagraph (A) shall establish an interactive data standard for the information included in the annual report of a resource extraction issuer.

(ii) Electronic tags.—

The interactive data standard shall include electronic tags that identify, for any payments made by a resource extraction issuer to a foreign government or the Federal Government—

(I) the total amounts of the payments, by category;

(II) the currency used to make the payments;

(III) the financial period in which the payments were made;

(IV) the business segment of the resource extraction issuer that made the payments;

(V) the government that received the payments, and the country in which the government is located;

(VI) the project of the resource extraction issuer to which the payments relate; and

(VII) such other information as the Commission may determine is necessary or appropriate in the public interest or for the protection of investors.

(E) International transparency efforts.—

To the extent practicable, the rules issued under subparagraph (A) shall support the commitment of the Federal Government to international transparency promotion efforts relating to the commercial development of oil, natural gas, or minerals.

(F) Effective date.—

With respect to each resource extraction issuer, the final rules issued under subparagraph (A) shall take effect on the date on which the resource extraction issuer is required to submit an annual report relating to the fiscal year of the resource extraction issuer that ends not earlier than 1 year after the date on which the Commission issues final rules under subparagraph (A).

(3) Public availability of information.—

(A) In general.—

To the extent practicable, the Commission shall make available online, to the public, a compilation of the information required to be submitted under the rules issued under paragraph (2)(A).

(B) Other information.—

Nothing in this paragraph shall require the Commission to make available online information other than the information required to be submitted under the rules issued under paragraph (2)(A).

(r) Disclosure of Certain Activities Relating to Iran.—

(1) In General.—

Each issuer required to file an annual or quarterly report under subsection (a) shall disclose in that report the information required by paragraph

(2) if, during the period covered by the report, the issuer or any affiliate of the issuer—

(A) knowingly engaged in an activity described in subsection (a) or (b) of section 5 of the Iran Sanctions Act of 1996 (Public Law 104–172; 50 U.S.C. 1701 note);

(B) knowingly engaged in an activity described in subsection (c)(2) of section 104 of the Comprehensive Iran Sanctions, Accountability, and Divestment Act of 2010 (22 U.S.C. 8513) or a transaction described in subsection (d)(1) of that section;

(C) knowingly engaged in an activity described in section 105A(b)(2) of that Act; or

(D) knowingly conducted any transaction or dealing with—

(i) any person the property and interests in property of which are blocked pursuant to Executive Order No. 13224 (66 Fed. Reg. 49079; relating to blocking property and prohibiting transactions with persons who commit, threaten to commit, or support terrorism);

(ii) any person the property and interests in property of which are blocked pursuant to Executive Order No. 13382 (70 Fed. Reg. 38567; relating to blocking of property of weapons of mass destruction proliferators and their supporters); or

(iii) any person or entity identified under section 560.304 of title 31, Code of Federal Regulations (relating to the definition of the Government of Iran) without the specific authorization of a Federal department or agency.

(2) Information Required.—

If an issuer or an affiliate of the issuer has engaged in any activity described in paragraph (1), the issuer shall disclose a detailed description of each such activity, including—

(A) the nature and extent of the activity;

(B) the gross revenues and net profits, if any, attributable to the activity; and

(C) whether the issuer or the affiliate of the issuer (as the case may be) intends to continue the activity.

(3) Notice of Disclosure.—

If an issuer reports under paragraph (1) that the issuer or an affiliate of the issuer has knowingly engaged in any activity described in that paragraph, the issuer shall separately file with the Commission, concurrently with the annual or quarterly report under subsection (a), a notice that the disclosure of that activity has been included in that annual or quarterly report that identifies the issuer and contains the information required by paragraph (2).

(4) Public Disclosure of Information.—

Upon receiving a notice under paragraph (3) that an annual or quarterly report includes a disclosure of an activity described in paragraph (1), the Commission shall promptly—

(A) transmit the report to—

(i) the President;

(ii) the Committee on Foreign Affairs and the Committee on Financial Services of the House of Representatives; and

(iii) the Committee on Foreign Relations and the Committee on Banking, Housing, and Urban Affairs of the Senate; and

(B) make the information provided in the disclosure and the notice available to the public by posting the information on the Internet website of the Commission.

(5) Investigations.—

Upon receiving a report under paragraph (4) that includes a disclosure of an activity described in paragraph (1) (other than an activity described in subparagraph (D)(iii) of that paragraph), the President shall—

(A) initiate an investigation into the possible imposition of sanctions under the Iran Sanctions Act of 1996 (Public Law 104–172; 50 U.S.C. 1701 note), section 104 or 105A of the Comprehensive Iran Sanctions, Accountability, and Divestment Act of 2010, an Executive order specified in clause (i) or (ii) of paragraph (1)(D), or any other provision of law relating to the imposition of sanctions with respect to Iran, as applicable; and

(B) not later than 180 days after initiating such an investigation, make a determination with respect to whether sanctions should be imposed with respect to the issuer or the affiliate of the issuer (as the case may be).

(6) Sunset.—

The provisions of this subsection shall terminate on the date that is 30 days after the date on which the President makes the certification described in section 401(a) of the Comprehensive Iran Sanctions, Accountability, and Divestment Act of 2010 (22 U.S.C. 8551(a)).

§14. Proxies

(a) Solicitation of Proxies in Violation of Rules and Regulations

(1) It shall be unlawful for any person, by the use of the mails or by any means or instrumentality of interstate commerce or of any facility of a national securities exchange or otherwise, in contravention of such rules and regulations as the Commission may prescribe as necessary or appropriate in the public interest or for the protection of investors, to solicit or to permit the use of his name to solicit any proxy or consent or authorization in respect of any security (other than an exempted security) registered pursuant to section 12 of this title.

(2) The rules and regulations prescribed by the Commission under paragraph (1) may include—

(A) a requirement that a solicitation of proxy, consent, or authorization by (or on behalf of) an issuer include a nominee submitted by a shareholder to serve on the board of directors of the issuer; and

(B) a requirement that an issuer follow a certain procedure in relation to a solicitation described in subparagraph (A).

(b) Giving or Refraining from Giving Proxy in Respect of any Security Carried for Account of Customer

(1) It shall be unlawful for any member of a national securities exchange, or any broker or dealer registered under this chapter, or any bank, association, or other entity that exercises fiduciary powers, in contravention of such rules and

regulations as the Commission may prescribe as necessary or appropriate in the public interest or for the protection of investors, to give, or to refrain from giving a proxy, consent, or authorization or information statement in respect of any security registered pursuant to section 12 of this title or any security issued by an investment company registered under the Investment Company Act of 1940 and carried for the account of a customer.

(2) With respect to banks, the rules and regulations prescribed by the Commission under paragraph (1) shall not require the disclosure of the names of beneficial owners of securities in an account held by the bank on December 28, 1985, unless the beneficial owner consents to the disclosure. The provisions of this paragraph shall not apply in the case of a bank which the Commission finds has not made a good faith effort to obtain such consent from such beneficial owners.

(c) Information to Holders of Record Prior to Annual or Other Meeting

Unless proxies, consents, or authorizations in respect of a security registered pursuant to section 12 of this title or security issued by an investment company registered under the Investment Company Act of 1940, are solicited by or on behalf of the management of the issuer from the holders of record of such security in accordance with the rules and regulations prescribed under subsection (a) of this section, prior to any annual or other meeting of the holders of such security, such issuer shall, in accordance with rules and regulations prescribed by the Commission, file with the Commission and transmit to all holders of record of such security information substantially equivalent to the information which would be required to be transmitted if a solicitation were made, but no information shall be required to be filed or transmitted pursuant to this subsection before July 1, 1964.

(d) Tender Offer by Owner of More Than Five Per Centum of Class of Securities; Exceptions

(1) It shall be unlawful for any person, directly or indirectly, by use of the mails or by any means or instrumentality of interstate commerce or of any facility of a national securities exchange or otherwise, to make a tender offer for, or a request or invitation for tenders of, any class of any equity security which is registered pursuant to section 12 of this title, or any equity security of an insurance company which would have been required to be so registered except for the exemption contained in section 12(g)(2)(G) of this title, or any equity security issued by a closed-end investment company registered under the Investment Company Act of 1940, if, after consummation thereof, such person would, directly or indirectly, be the beneficial owner of more than 5 per centum of such class, unless at the time copies of the offer or request or invitation are first published or sent or given to security holders such person has filed with the Commission a statement containing such of the information specified in section 13(d) of this title, and such additional information as the Commission may by rules and regulations

prescribe as necessary or appropriate in the public interest or for the protection of investors. All requests or invitations for tenders or advertisements making a tender offer or requesting or inviting tenders of such a security shall be filed as a part of such statement and shall contain such of the information contained in such statement as the Commission may by rules and regulations prescribe. Copies of any additional material soliciting or requesting such tender offers subsequent to the initial solicitation or request shall contain such information as the Commission may by rules and regulations prescribe as necessary or appropriate in the public interest or for the protection of investors, and shall be filed with the Commission not later than the time copies of such material are first published or sent or given to security holders. Copies of all statements, in the form in which such material is furnished to security holders and the Commission, shall be sent to the issuer not later than the date such material is first published or sent or given to any security holders.

(2) When two or more persons act as a partnership, limited partnership, syndicate, or other group for the purpose of acquiring, holding, or disposing of securities of an issuer, such syndicate or group shall be deemed a "person" for purposes of this subsection.

(3) In determining, for purposes of this subsection, any percentage of a class of any security, such class shall be deemed to consist of the amount of the outstanding securities of such class, exclusive of any securities of such class held by or for the account of the issuer or a subsidiary of the issuer.

(4) Any solicitation or recommendation to the holders of such a security to accept or reject a tender offer or request or invitation for tenders shall be made in accordance with such rules and regulations as the Commission may prescribe as necessary or appropriate in the public interest or for the protection of investors.

(5) Securities deposited pursuant to a tender offer or request or invitation for tenders may be withdrawn by or on behalf of the depositor at any time until the expiration of seven days after the time definitive copies of the offer or request or invitation are first published or sent or given to security holders, and at any time after sixty days from the date of the original tender offer or request or invitation, except as the Commission may otherwise prescribe by rules, regulations, or order as necessary or appropriate in the public interest or for the protection of investors.

(6) Where any person makes a tender offer, or request or invitation for tenders, for less than all the outstanding equity securities of a class, and where a greater number of securities is deposited pursuant thereto within ten days after copies of the offer or request or invitation are first published or sent or given to security holders than such person is bound or willing to take up and pay for, the securities taken up shall be taken up as nearly as may be pro rata, disregarding fractions, according to the number of securities deposited by each depositor. The provisions of this subsection shall also apply to securities deposited within ten days after notice of an increase in the consideration offered to security holders, as described in paragraph (7), is first published or sent or given to security holders.

(7) Where any person varies the terms of a tender offer or request or invitation for tenders before the expiration thereof by increasing the consideration

offered to holders of such securities, such person shall pay the increased consideration to each security holder whose securities are taken up and paid for pursuant to the tender offer or request or invitation for tenders whether or not such securities have been taken up by such person before the variation of the tender offer or request or invitation.

(8) The provisions of this subsection shall not apply to any offer for, or request or invitation for tenders of, any security—

(A) if the acquisition of such security, together with all other acquisitions by the same person of securities of the same class during the preceding twelve months, would not exceed 2 per centum of that class;

(B) by the issuer of such security; or

(C) which the Commission, by rules or regulations or by order, shall exempt from the provisions of this subsection as not entered into for the purpose of, and not having the effect of, changing or influencing the control of the issuer or otherwise as not comprehended within the purposes of this subsection.

(e) Untrue Statement of Material Fact or Omission of Fact with Respect to Tender Offer

It shall be unlawful for any person to make any untrue statement of a material fact or omit to state any material fact necessary in order to make the statements made, in the light of the circumstances under which they are made, not misleading, or to engage in any fraudulent, deceptive, or manipulative acts or practices, in connection with any tender offer or request or invitation for tenders, or any solicitation of security holders in opposition to or in favor of any such offer, request, or invitation. The Commission shall, for the purposes of this subsection, by rules and regulations define, and prescribe means reasonably designed to prevent, such acts and practices as are fraudulent, deceptive, or manipulative.

(f) Election or Designation of Majority of Directors of Issuer by Owner of More Than Five Per Centum of Class of Securities at Other Than Meeting of Security Holders

If, pursuant to any arrangement or understanding with the person or persons acquiring securities in a transaction subject to subsection (d) of this section or subsection (d) of section 13 of this title, any persons are to be elected or designated as directors of the issuer, otherwise than at a meeting of security holders, and the persons so elected or designated will constitute a majority of the directors of the issuer, then, prior to the time any such person takes office as a director, and in accordance with rules and regulations prescribed by the Commission, the issuer shall file with the Commission, and transmit to all holders of record of securities of the issuer who would be entitled to vote at a meeting for election of directors, information substantially equivalent to the information which would be required by subsection (a) or (c) of this section to be transmitted if such person or persons were nominees for election as directors at a meeting of such security holders. . . .

(h) Proxy Solicitations and Tender Offers in Connection with Limited Partnership Roll-Up Transactions [omitted]

(i) Disclosure of Pay Versus Performance.—

The Commission shall, by rule, require each issuer to disclose in any proxy or consent solicitation material for an annual meeting of the shareholders of the issuer a clear description of any compensation required to be disclosed by the issuer under section 229.402 of title 17, Code of Federal Regulations (or any successor thereto), including for any issuer other than an emerging growth company, information that shows the relationship between executive compensation actually paid and the financial performance of the issuer, taking into account any change in the value of the shares of stock and dividends of the issuer and any distributions. The disclosure under this subsection may include a graphic representation of the information required to be disclosed.

[Editors' note: In an uncodified section of Dodd-Frank, passed in 2010, Congress also required that the SEC amend Item 402 of Regulation S-K to require each issuer to disclose—

(a) the median of the annual total compensation of all employees of the issuer, except the chief executive officer (or any equivalent position) of the issuer;

(b) the annual total compensation of the chief executive officer (or any equivalent position) of the issuer; and

(c) the ratio of the amount described in subparagraph (A) to the amount described in subparagraph (B).]

(j) Disclosure of Hedging by Employees and Directors.—

The Commission shall, by rule, require each issuer to disclose in any proxy or consent solicitation material for an annual meeting of the shareholders of the issuer whether any employee or member of the board of directors of the issuer, or any designee of such employee or member, is permitted to purchase financial instruments (including prepaid variable forward contracts, equity swaps, collars, and exchange funds) that are designed to hedge or offset any decrease in the market value of equity securities—

(1) granted to the employee or member of the board of directors by the issuer as part of the compensation of the employee or member of the board of directors; or

(2) held, directly or indirectly, by the employee or member of the board of directors.

§14A. Shareholder Approval of Executive Compensation

(a) Separate Resolution Required.—

(1) In general.—

Not less frequently than once every 3 years, a proxy or consent or authorization for an annual or other meeting of the shareholders for which the proxy solicitation rules of the Commission require compensation disclosure shall include a separate resolution subject to shareholder vote to approve the compensation of executives, as disclosed pursuant to section 229.402 of title 17, Code of Federal Regulations, or any successor thereto.

(2) Frequency of vote.—

Not less frequently than once every 6 years, a proxy or consent or authorization for an annual or other meeting of the shareholders for which the proxy solicitation rules of the Commission require compensation disclosure shall include a separate resolution subject to shareholder vote to determine whether votes on the resolutions required under paragraph (1) will occur every 1, 2, or 3 years.

(3) Effective date.—

The proxy or consent or authorization for the first annual or other meeting of the shareholders occurring after the end of the 6-month period beginning on the date of enactment of this section shall include—

(A) the resolution described in paragraph (1); and

(B) a separate resolution subject to shareholder vote to determine whether votes on the resolutions required under paragraph (1) will occur every 1, 2, or 3 years.

(b) Shareholder Approval of Golden Parachute Compensation.—

(1) Disclosure.—

In any proxy or consent solicitation material (the solicitation of which is subject to the rules of the Commission pursuant to subsection (a)) for a meeting of the shareholders occurring after the end of the 6-month period beginning on the date of enactment of this section, at which shareholders are asked to approve an acquisition, merger, consolidation, or proposed sale or other disposition of all or substantially all the assets of an issuer, the person making such solicitation shall disclose in the proxy or consent solicitation material, in a clear and simple form in accordance with regulations to be promulgated by the Commission, any agreements or understandings that such person has with any named executive officers of such issuer (or of the acquiring issuer, if such issuer is not the acquiring issuer) concerning any type of compensation (whether present, deferred, or contingent) that is based on or otherwise relates to the acquisition, merger, consolidation, sale, or other disposition of all or substantially all of the assets of the issuer and the aggregate total of all such compensation that may (and the conditions upon which it may) be paid or become payable to or on behalf of such executive officer.

(2) Shareholder approval.—

Any proxy or consent or authorization relating to the proxy or consent solicitation material containing the disclosure required by paragraph (1) shall include a separate resolution subject to shareholder vote to approve such agreements or understandings and compensation as disclosed, unless such agreements or understandings have been subject to a shareholder vote under subsection (a).

(c) Rule of Construction.—

The shareholder vote referred to in subsections (a) and (b) shall not be binding on the issuer or the board of directors of an issuer, and may not be construed—

(1) as overruling a decision by such issuer or board of directors;

(2) to create or imply any change to the fiduciary duties of such issuer or board of directors;

(3) to create or imply any additional fiduciary duties for such issuer or board of directors; or

(4) to restrict or limit the ability of shareholders to make proposals for inclusion in proxy materials related to executive compensation.

(d) Disclosure of Votes.—

Every institutional investment manager subject to section 13(f) shall report at least annually how it voted on any shareholder vote pursuant to subsections (a) and (b), unless such vote is otherwise required to be reported publicly by rule or regulation of the Commission.

(e) Exemption.—

(1) In General

The Commission may, by rule or order, exempt any other issuer or class of issuers from the requirement under subsection (a) or (b). In determining whether to make an exemption under this subsection, the Commission shall take into account, among other considerations, whether the requirements under subsections (a) and (b) disproportionately burdens small issuers.

(2) Treatment of emerging growth companies.—

(A) In general.—An emerging growth company shall be exempt from the requirements of subsections (a) and (b).

(B) Compliance after termination of emerging growth company treatment.—An issuer that was an emerging growth company but is no longer an emerging growth company shall include the first separate resolution described under subsection (a)(1) not later than the end of—

(i) in the case of an issuer that was an emerging growth company for less than 2 years after the date of first sale of common equity securities of the issuer pursuant to an effective registration statement under the Securities Act of 1933, the 3-year period beginning on such date; and

(ii) in the case of any other issuer, the 1-year period beginning on the date the issuer is no longer an emerging growth company.

§14B. Corporate Governance

Not later than 180 days after the date of enactment of this subsection, the Commission shall issue rules that require an issuer to disclose in the annual proxy sent to investors the reasons why the issuer has chosen—

(1) the same person to serve as chairman of the board of directors and chief executive officer (or in equivalent positions); or

(2) different individuals to serve as chairman of the board of directors and chief executive officer (or in equivalent positions of the issuer).

§15. Registration and Regulation of Brokers and Dealers

(a) Registration of all Persons Utilizing Exchange Facilities to Effect Transactions; Exemptions

(1) It shall be unlawful for any broker or dealer which is either a person other than a natural person or a natural person not associated with a broker or dealer which is a person other than a natural person (other than such a broker or dealer whose business is exclusively intrastate and who does not make use of any facility of a national securities exchange) to make use of the mails or any means or instrumentality of interstate commerce to effect any transactions in, or to induce or attempt to induce the purchase or sale of, any security (other than an exempted security or commercial paper, bankers' acceptances, or commercial bills) unless such broker or dealer is registered in accordance with subsection (b) of this section.

(2) The Commission, by rule or order, as it deems consistent with the public interest and the protection of investors, may conditionally or unconditionally exempt from paragraph (1) of this subsection any broker or dealer or class of brokers or dealers specified in such rule or order.

(b) Manner of Registration of Brokers and Dealers

(1) A broker or dealer may be registered by filing with the Commission an application for registration in such form and containing such information and documents concerning such broker or dealer and any person associated with such broker or dealer as the Commission by rule, may prescribe as necessary or appropriate in the public interest or for the protection of investors. . . .

(d) Filing of Supplementary and Periodic Information

(1) In general.— Each issuer which has filed a registration statement containing an undertaking which is or becomes operative under this subsection as in effect prior to the date of enactment of the Securities Acts Amendments of 1964, and each issuer which shall after such date file a registration statement which has become effective pursuant to the Securities Act of 1933, as amended, shall file with the Commission, in accordance with such rules and regulations as the Commission may prescribe as necessary or appropriate in the public interest or for the protection of investors, such supplementary and periodic information, documents, and reports as may be required pursuant to section 13 of this title in respect of a security registered pursuant to section 12 of this title. The duty to file under this subsection shall be automatically suspended if and so long as any issue of securities of such issuer is registered pursuant to section 12 of this title. The duty to file under this subsection shall also be automatically suspended as to any fiscal year, other than the fiscal year within which

such registration statement became effective, if, at the beginning of such fiscal year, the securities of each class, other than any class of asset-backed securities, to which the registration statement relates are held of record by less than 300 persons, or, in the case of a bank, a savings and loan holding company (as defined in section 10 of 24 the Home Owners' Loan Act), or a bank holding company, as such term is defined in section 2 of the Bank Holding Company Act of 1956 (12 U.S.C. 1841), 1,200 persons. For the purposes of this subsection, the term "class" shall be construed to include all securities of an issuer which are of substantially similar character and the holders of which enjoy substantially similar rights and privileges. The Commission may, for the purpose of this subsection, define by rules and regulations the term "held of record" as it deems necessary or appropriate in the public interest or for the protection of investors in order to prevent circumvention of the provisions of this subsection. Nothing in this subsection shall apply to securities issued by a foreign government or political subdivision thereof. . . .

(e) Notices to Customers Regarding Securities Lending.—

Every registered broker or dealer shall provide notice to its customers that they may elect not to allow their fully paid securities to be used in connection with short sales. If a broker or dealer uses a customer's securities in connection with short sales, the broker or dealer shall provide notice to its customer that the broker or dealer may receive compensation in connection with lending the customer's securities. The Commission, by rule, as it deems necessary or appropriate in the public interest and for the protection of investors, may prescribe the form, content, time, and manner of delivery of any notice required under this paragraph. . . .

(g) Prevention of Misuse of Material, Nonpublic Information

Every registered broker or dealer shall establish, maintain, and enforce written policies and procedures reasonably designed, taking into consideration the nature of such broker's or dealer's business, to prevent the misuse in violation of this chapter, or the rules or regulations thereunder, of material, nonpublic information by such broker or dealer or any person associated with such broker or dealer. The Commission, as it deems necessary or appropriate in the public interest or for the protection of investors, shall adopt rules or regulations to require specific policies or procedures reasonably designed to prevent misuse in violation of this chapter (or the rules or regulations thereunder) of material, nonpublic information. . . .

(i) Limitations on State Law . . .

(2) Funding portals.—

(A) Limitation on state laws.—Except as provided in subparagraph (B), no State or political subdivision thereof may enforce any law, rule, regulation, or other administrative action against a registered funding portal with respect to its business as such.

(B) Examination and enforcement authority.— Subparagraph (A) does not apply with respect to the examination and enforcement of any law, rule, regulation, or administrative action of a State or political subdivision thereof in which the principal place of business of a registered funding portal is located, provided that such law, rule, regulation, or administrative action is not in addition to or different from the requirements for registered funding portals established by the Commission.

(C) Definition.—For purposes of this paragraph, the term "State" includes the District of Columbia and the territories of the United States.

(k) Standard of Conduct.—

(1) In general.—

Notwithstanding any other provision of this Act or the Investment Advisers Act of 1940, the Commission may promulgate rules to provide that, with respect to a broker or dealer, when providing personalized investment advice about securities to a retail customer (and such other customers as the Commission may by rule provide), the standard of conduct for such broker or dealer with respect to such customer shall be the same as the standard of conduct applicable to an investment adviser under section 211 of the Investment Advisers Act of 1940. The receipt of compensation based on commission or other standard compensation for the sale of securities shall not, in and of itself, be considered a violation of such standard applied to a broker or dealer. Nothing in this section shall require a broker or dealer or registered representative to have a continuing duty of care or loyalty to the customer after providing personalized investment advice about securities.

(2) Disclosure of range of products offered.—

Where a broker or dealer sells only proprietary or other limited range of products, as determined by the Commission, the Commission may by rule require that such broker or dealer provide notice to each retail customer and obtain the consent or acknowledgment of the customer. The sale of only proprietary or other limited range of products by a broker or dealer shall not, in and of itself, be considered a violation of the standard set forth in paragraph (1).

(*l*) Other Matters.—

The Commission shall—

(1) facilitate the provision of simple and clear disclosures to investors regarding the terms of their relationships with brokers, dealers, and investment advisers, including any material conflicts of interest; and

(2) examine and, where appropriate, promulgate rules prohibiting or restricting certain sales practices, conflicts of interest, and compensation schemes for brokers, dealers, and investment advisers that the Commission deems contrary to the public interest and the protection of investors. . . .

(n) Disclosures to Retail Investors.—

(1) In general.—

Notwithstanding any other provision of the securities laws, the Commission may issue rules designating documents or information that shall be provided by a broker or dealer to a retail investor before the purchase of an investment product or service by the retail investor

(o) Authority to Restrict Mandatory Pre-dispute Arbitration.—

The Commission, by rule, may prohibit, or impose conditions or limitations on the use of, agreements that require customers or clients of any broker, dealer, or municipal securities dealer to arbitrate any future dispute between them arising under the Federal securities laws, the rules and regulations thereunder, or the rules of a self-regulatory organization if it finds that such prohibition, imposition of conditions, or limitations are in the public interest and for the protection of investors.

§15D. Securities Analysts and Research Reports

(a) Analyst Protections.—The Commission, or upon the authorization and direction of the Commission, a registered securities association or national securities exchange, shall have adopted, not later than 1 year after the date of enactment of this section, rules reasonably designed to address conflicts of interest that can arise when securities analysts recommend equity securities in research reports and public appearances, in order to improve the objectivity of research and provide investors with more useful and reliable information, including rules designed

(1) to foster greater public confidences in securities research, and to protect the objectivity and independence of securities analysts by

(A) restricting the prepublication clearance or approval of research reports by persons employed by the broker or dealer who are engaged in investment banking activities, or persons not directly responsible for investment research, other than legal or compliance staff;

(B) limiting the supervision and compensatory evaluation of securities analysts to officials employed by the broker or dealer who are not engaged in investment banking activities; and

(C) requiring that a broker or dealer and persons employed by a broker or dealer who are involved with investment banking activities may not, directly or indirectly, retaliate against or threaten to retaliate against any securities analyst employed by that broker or dealer or its affiliates as a result of an adverse, negative, or otherwise unfavorable research report that may adversely affect the present or prospective investment banking relationship of the broker or dealer with the issuer that is the subject of the research report, except that such rules may not limit the authority of a broker or dealer to discipline a securities analyst for causes other than such research report in accordance with the policies and procedures of the firm;

(2) to define periods during which brokers or dealers who have participated, or are to participate, in a public offering of securities as underwriters or dealers should not publish or otherwise distribute research reports relating to such securities or to the issuer of such securities;

(3) to establish structural and institutional safeguards within registered brokers or dealers to assure that securities analysts are separated by appropriate

informational partitions within the firm from the review, pressure, or oversight of those whose involvement in investment banking activities might potentially bias their judgment or supervision; and

(4) to address such other issues as the Commission, or such association or exchange, determines appropriate.

(b) Disclosure.—The Commission, or upon the authorization and direction of the Commission, a registered securities association or national securities exchange, shall have adopted, not later than 1 year after the date of enactment of this section, rules reasonably designed to require each securities analyst to disclose in public appearances, and each registered broker or dealer to disclose in each research report, as applicable, conflicts of interest that are known or should have been known by the securities analyst or the broker or dealer, to exist at the time of the appearance or the date of distribution of the report, including

(1) the extent to which the securities analyst has debt or equity investments in the issuer that is the subject of the appearance or research report;

(2) whether any compensation has been received by the registered broker or dealer, or any affiliate thereof, including the securities analyst, from the issuer that is the subject of the appearance or research report, subject to such exemptions as the Commission may determine appropriate and necessary to prevent disclosure by virtue of this paragraph of material non-public information regarding specific potential future investment banking transactions of such issuer, as is appropriate in the public interest and consistent with the protection of investors;

(3) whether an issuer, the securities of which are recommended in the appearance or research report, currently is, or during the 1-year period preceding the date of the appearance or date of distribution of the report has been, a client of the registered broker or dealer, and if so, stating the types of services provided to the issuer;

(4) whether the securities analyst received compensation with respect to a research report, based upon (among any other factors) the investment banking revenues (either generally or specifically earned from the issuer being analyzed) of the registered broker or dealer; and

(5) such other disclosures of conflicts of interest that are material to investors, research analysts, or the broker or dealer as the Commission, or such association or exchange, determines appropriate.

(c) Limiation.—Notwithstanding subsection (a) or any other provision of law, neither the Commission nor any national securities association registered under section 15A may adopt or maintain any rule or regulation in connection with an initial public offering of the common equity of an emerging growth company—

(1) restricting, based on functional role, which associated persons of a broker, dealer, or member of a national securities association, may arrange for communications between a securities analyst and a potential investor; or

(2) restricting a securities analyst from participating in any communications with the management of an emerging growth company that is also attended by any other associated person of a broker, dealer, or member of a national securities association whose functional role is other than as a securities analyst.

(d) Definitions.—In this section—

(1) the term "securities analyst" means any associated person of a registered broker or dealer that is principally responsible for, and any associated person who reports directly or indirectly to a securities analyst in connection with, the preparation of the substance of a research report, whether or not any such person has the job title of "securities analyst", and

(2) the term "research report" means a written or electronic communication that includes an analysis of equity securities of individual companies or industries, and that provides information reasonable sufficient upon which to base an investment decision.

§16. *Directors, Officers, and Principal Stockholders*

(a) Disclosures Required

(1) Directors, officers, and principal stockholders required to file.—Every person who is directly or indirectly the beneficial owner of more than 10 percent of any class of any equity security (other than an exempted security) which is registered pursuant to section 12, or who is a director or an officer of the issuer of such security, shall file the statements required by this subsection with the Commission.

(2) Time of filing.—The statements required by this subsection shall be filed.—

(A) at the time of the registration of such security on a national securities exchange or by the effective date of a registration statement filed pursuant to section 12(g);

(B) within 10 days after he or she becomes such beneficial owner, director, or officer or within such shortor time as the Commission may establish by rule;

(C) if there has been a change in such ownership, or if such person shall have purchased or sold a security-based swap agreement involving such equity security, before the end of the second business day following the day on which the subject transaction has been executed, or at such other time as the Commission shall establish, by rule, in any case in which the Commission determines that such 2-day period is not feasible.

(3) Contents of statements.—A statement filed.—

(A) under subparagraph (A) or (B) of paragraph (2) shall contain a statement of the amount of all equity securities of such issuer of which the filing person is the beneficial owner; and

(B) under subparagraph (C) of such paragraph shall indicate ownership by the filing person at the date of filing, any such changes in such ownership, and such purchases and sales of the security-based swap agreements or security-based swaps as have occurred since the most recent such filing under such subparagraph.

(4) Electronic filing and availability.—

Beginning not later than 1 year after July 30, 2002.

(A) a statement filed under subparagraph (C) of paragraph (2) shall be filed electronically;

(B) the Commission shall provide each such statement on a publicly accessible Internet site not later than the end of the business day following that filing; and

(C) the issuer (if the issuer maintains a corporate website) shall provide that statement on that corporate website, not later than the end of the business day following that filing.

(b) Profits from Purchase and Sale of Security Within Six Months

For the purpose of preventing the unfair use of information which may have been obtained by such beneficial owner, director, or officer by reason of his relationship to the issuer, any profit realized by him from any purchase and sale, or any sale and purchase, of any equity security of such issuer (other than an exempted security) or a security-based swap agreement involving any such equity security within any period of less than six months, unless such security or security-based swap agreement was acquired in good faith in connection with a debt previously contracted, shall inure to and be recoverable by the issuer, irrespective of any intention on the part of such beneficial owner, director, or officer in entering into such transaction of holding the security or security-based swap agreement purchased or of not repurchasing the security or security-based swap agreement sold for a period exceeding six months. Suit to recover such profit may be instituted at law or in equity in any court of competent jurisdiction by the issuer, or by the owner of any security of the issuer in the name and in behalf of the issuer if the issuer shall fail or refuse to bring such suit within sixty days after request or shall fail diligently to prosecute the same thereafter; but no such suit shall be brought more than two years after the date such profit was realized. This subsection shall not be construed to cover any transaction where such beneficial owner was not such both at the time of the purchase and sale, or the sale and purchase, of the security or security-based swap agreement involved, or any transaction or transactions which the Commission by rules and regulations may exempt as not comprehended within the purpose of this subsection.

(c) Conditions for Sale of Security by Beneficial Owner, Director, or Officer

It shall be unlawful for any such beneficial owner, director, or officer, directly or indirectly, to sell any equity security of such issuer (other than an exempted security), if the person selling the security or his principal (1) does not own the security sold, or (2) if owning the security, does not deliver it against such sale within twenty days thereafter, or does not within five days after such sale deposit it in the mails or other usual channels of transportation; but no person shall be deemed to have violated this subsection if he proves that notwithstanding the exercise of good faith he was unable to make such delivery or deposit within such time, or that to do so would cause undue inconvenience or expense.

(d) Securities Held in Investment Account, Transactions in Ordinary Course of Business, and Establishment of Primary or Secondary Market

The provisions of subsection (b) of this section shall not apply to any purchase and sale, or sale and purchase, and the provisions of subsection (c) of this section shall not apply to any sale, of an equity security not then or theretofore held by him in an investment account, by a dealer in the ordinary course of his business and incident to the establishment or maintenance by him of a primary or secondary market (otherwise than on a national securities exchange or an exchange exempted from registration under section 5 of this title) for such security. The Commission may, by such rules and regulations as it deems necessary or appropriate in the public interest, define and prescribe terms and conditions with respect to securities held in an investment account and transactions made in the ordinary course of business and incident to the establishment or maintenance of a primary or secondary market.

(e) Application of Section to Foreign or Domestic Arbitrage Transactions

The provisions of this section shall not apply to foreign or domestic arbitrage transactions unless made in contravention of such rules and regulations as the Commission may adopt in order to carry out the purposes of this section.

(f) Treatment of Transactions in Security Futures Products

The provisions of this section shall apply to ownership of and transactions in security futures products. . .

§17A. National System for Clearance and Settlement of Securities Transactions

(a) Congressional Findings; Facilitating Establishment of System

(1) The Congress finds that—

(A) The prompt and accurate clearance and settlement of securities transactions, including the transfer of record ownership and the safeguarding of securities and funds related thereto, are necessary for the protection of investors and persons facilitating transactions by and acting on behalf of investors.

(B) Inefficient procedures for clearance and settlement impose unnecessary costs on investors and persons facilitating transactions by and acting on behalf of investors.

(C) New data processing and communications techniques create the opportunity for more efficient, effective, and safe procedures for clearance and settlement.

(D) The linking of all clearance and settlement facilities and the development of uniform standards and procedures for clearance and settlement will reduce unnecessary costs and increase the protection of investors and persons facilitating transactions by and acting on behalf of investors.

(2)(A) The Commission is directed, therefore, having due regard for the public interest, the protection of investors, the safeguarding of securities and funds, and maintenance of fair competition among brokers and dealers, clearing agencies, and transfer agents, to use its authority under this chapter—

(i) to facilitate the establishment of a national system for the prompt and accurate clearance and settlement of transactions in securities (other than exempt securities); and

(ii) to facilitate the establishment of linked or coordinated facilities for clearance and settlement of transactions in securities, securities options, contracts of sale for future delivery and options thereon, and commodity options;

in accordance with the findings and to carry out the objectives set forth in paragraph (1) of this subsection.

(B) The Commission shall use its authority under this chapter to assure equal regulation under this chapter of registered clearing agencies and registered transfer agents. In carrying out its responsibilities set forth in subparagraph (A)(ii) of this paragraph, the Commission shall coordinate with the Commodity Futures Trading Commission and consult with the Board of Governors of the Federal Reserve System. . . .

(e) Physical Movement of Securities Certificates

The Commission shall use its authority under this chapter to end the physical movement of securities certificates in connection with the settlement among brokers and dealers of transactions in securities consummated by means of the mails or any means or instrumentalities of interstate commerce. . . .

(g) Registration Requirement

It shall be unlawful for a clearing agency, unless registered with the Commission, directly or indirectly to make use of the mails or any means or instrumentality of interstate commerce to perform the functions of a clearing agency with respect to a security-based swap.

(h) Voluntary Registration [omitted]

§18. Liability for Misleading Statements

(a) Persons Liable; Persons Entitled to Recover; Defense of Good Faith; Suit at Law or in Equity; Costs, Etc.

Any person who shall make or cause to be made any statement in any application, report, or document filed pursuant to this chapter or any rule or regulation thereunder or any undertaking contained in a registration statement as provided in subsection (d) of section 15 of this title, which statement was at the time and in the light of the circumstances under which it was made false or misleading with respect to any material fact, shall be liable to any person (not knowing that such statement was false or misleading) who, in reliance upon such statement, shall have purchased or sold a security at a price which was affected by such statement, for damages caused by such reliance, unless the person sued shall prove that he acted in good faith and had no knowledge that such statement was false or misleading. A person seeking to enforce such liability may sue at law or in equity in any court of competent jurisdiction. In any such suit the court may, in its discretion, require an undertaking for the payment of the costs of such suit, and assess reasonable costs, including reasonable attorneys' fees, against either party litigant.

(b) Contribution

Every person who becomes liable to make payment under this section may recover contribution as in cases of contract from any person who, if joined in the original suit, would have been liable to make the same payment.

(c) Period of Limitations

No action shall be maintained to enforce any liability created under this section unless brought within one year after the discovery of the facts constituting the cause of action and within three years after such cause of action accrued.

§19. Registration, Responsibilities, and Oversight of Self-Regulatory Organizations . . .

(b) Proposed Rule Changes; Notice; Proceedings

(1) Each self-regulatory organization shall file with the Commission, in accordance with such rules as the Commission may prescribe, copies of any proposed rule or any proposed change in, addition to, or deletion from the rules of such self-regulatory organization (hereinafter in this subsection collectively referred to as a "proposed rule change") accompanied by a concise general statement of the basis and purpose of such proposed rule change. The Commission shall, as soon as practicable after the date of the filing of any proposed rule change, publish notice thereof together with the terms of substance of the proposed rule change or a description of the subjects and issues involved. The Commission shall give interested persons an opportunity to submit written data, views, and arguments concerning such proposed rule change. No proposed rule change shall take effect unless approved by the Commission or otherwise permitted in accordance with the provisions of this subsection.

(2) Approval process.—

(A) Approval process established.—

(i) In general.—Except as provided in clause (ii), not later than 45 days after the date of publication of a proposed rule change under paragraph (1), the Commission shall—

(I) by order, approve or disapprove the proposed rule change; or

(II) institute proceedings under subparagraph (B) to determine whether the proposed rule change should be disapproved.

(ii) Extension of time period.—The Commission may extend the period established under clause (i) by not more than an additional 45 days, if—

(I) the Commission determines that a longer period is appropriate and publishes the reasons for such determination; or

(II) the self-regulatory organization that filed the proposed rule change consents to the longer period.

(B) Proceedings.—

(i) Notice and hearing.—If the Commission does not approve or disapprove a proposed rule change under subparagraph (A), the Commission shall provide to the self-regulatory organization that filed the proposed rule change—

(I) notice of the grounds for disapproval under consideration; and

(II) opportunity for hearing, to be concluded not later than 180 days after the date of publication of notice of the filing of the proposed rule change.

(ii) Order of approval or disapproval.—

(I) In general.—Except as provided in subclause (II), not later than 180 days after the date of publication under paragraph (1), the Commission shall issue an order approving or disapproving the proposed rule change.

(3)(A) Notwithstanding the provisions of paragraph (2) of this subsection, a proposed rule change shall take effect upon filing with the Commission if designated by the self-regulatory organization as (i) constituting a stated policy, practice, or interpretation with respect to the meaning, administration, or enforcement of an existing rule of the self-regulatory organization, (ii) establishing or changing a due, fee, or other charge imposed by the self-regulatory organization on any person, whether or not the person is a member of the self-regulatory organization, or (iii) concerned solely with the administration of the self-regulatory organization or other matters which the Commission, by rule, consistent with the public interest and the purposes of this subsection, may specify as without the provisions of such paragraph (2).

(B) Notwithstanding any other provision of this subsection, a proposed rule change may be put into effect summarily if it appears to the Commission that such action is necessary for the protection of investors, the maintenance of fair and orderly markets, or the safeguarding of securities or funds. Any proposed rule change so put into effect shall be filed promptly thereafter in accordance with the provisions of paragraph (1) of this subsection.

(C) Any proposed rule change of a self-regulatory organization which has taken effect pursuant to subparagraph (A) or (B) of this paragraph may be enforced by such organization to the extent it is not inconsistent with the provisions of this chapter, the rules and regulations thereunder, and applicable Federal and State law. At any time within the sixty days beginning on of the date of filing of such a proposed rule change in accordance with the provisions of paragraph (1), the Commission summarily may temporarily suspend the change in the rules of the self-regulatory organization made thereby, if it appears to the

Commission that such action is necessary or appropriate in the public interest, for the protection of investors, or otherwise in furtherance of the purposes of this title. If the Commission takes such action, the Commission shall institute proceedings under paragraph (2)(B) to determine whether the proposed rule should be approved or disapproved. Commission action pursuant to this paragraph shall not affect the validity or force of the rule change during the period it was in effect and shall not be reviewable under section 25 of this title nor deemed to be "final agency action" for purposes of section 704 of title 5. . . .

(c) Amendment by Commission of Rules of Self-Regulatory Organizations

The Commission, by rule, may abrogate, add to, and delete from (hereinafter in this subsection collectively referred to as "amend") the rules of a self-regulatory organization (other than a registered clearing agency) as the Commission deems necessary or appropriate to insure the fair administration of the self-regulatory organization, to conform its rules to requirements of this chapter and the rules and regulations thereunder applicable to such organization, or otherwise in furtherance of the purposes of this chapter, in the following manner:

(1) The Commission shall notify the self-regulatory organization and publish notice of the proposed rulemaking in the Federal Register. The notice shall include the text of the proposed amendment to the rules of the self-regulatory organization and a statement of the Commission's reasons, including any pertinent facts, for commencing such proposed rulemaking.

(2) The Commission shall give interested persons an opportunity for the oral presentation of data, views, and arguments, in addition to an opportunity to make written submissions. A transcript shall be kept of any oral presentation.

(3) A rule adopted pursuant to this subsection shall incorporate the text of the amendment to the rules of the self-regulatory organization and a statement of the Commission's basis for and purpose in so amending such rules. This statement shall include an identification of any facts on which the Commission considers its determination so to amend the rules of the self-regulatory agency to be based, including the reasons for the Commission's conclusions as to any of such facts which were disputed in the rulemaking.

(4) (A) Except as provided in paragraphs (1) through (3) of this subsection, rulemaking under this subsection shall be in accordance with the procedures specified in section 553 of title 5 for rulemaking not on the record.

(B) Nothing in this subsection shall be construed to impair or limit the Commission's power to make, or to modify or alter the procedures the Commission may follow in making, rules and regulations pursuant to any other authority under this chapter.

(C) Any amendment to the rules of a self-regulatory organization made by the Commission pursuant to this subsection shall be considered for all purposes of this chapter to be part of the rules of such self-regulatory organization and shall not be considered to be a rule of the Commission. . . .

§20. Liabilities of Controlling Persons and Persons Who Aid and Abet Violations

(a) Joint and Several Liability; Good Faith Defense

Every person who, directly or indirectly, controls any person liable under any provision of this chapter or of any rule or regulation thereunder shall also be liable jointly and severally with and to the same extent as such controlled person to any person to whom such controlled person is liable (including to the Commission in any action brought under paragraph (1) or (3) of section 21(d)), unless the controlling person acted in good faith and did not directly or indirectly induce the act or acts constituting the violation or cause of action.

(b) Unlawful Activity Through or by Means of any Other Person

It shall be unlawful for any person, directly or indirectly, to do any act or thing which it would be unlawful for such person to do under the provisions of this chapter or any rule or regulation thereunder through or by means of any other person.

(c) Hindering, Delaying, or Obstructing the Making or Filing of any Document, Report, or Information

It shall be unlawful for any director or officer of, or any owner of any securities issued by, any issuer required to file any document, report, or information under this chapter or any rule or regulation thereunder without just cause to hinder, delay, or obstruct the making or filing of any such document, report, or information.

(d) Liability for Trading in Securities While in Possession of Material Nonpublic Information

Wherever communicating, or purchasing or selling a security while in possession of, material nonpublic information would violate, or result in liability to any purchaser or seller of the security under any provision of this chapter, or any rule or regulation thereunder, such conduct in connection with a purchase or sale of a put, call, straddle, option, or privilege or security-based swap agreement with respect to such security or with respect to a group or index of securities including such security, shall also violate and result in comparable liability to any purchaser or seller of that security under such provision, rule, or regulation.

(e) Prosecution of Persons Who Aid and Abet Violations

For purposes of any action brought by the Commission under paragraph (1) or (3) of section 21(d), any person that knowingly or recklessly provides substantial assistance to another person in violation of a provision of this title, or of any rule or regulation issued under this title, shall be deemed to be in violation of such provision to the same extent as the person to whom such assistance is provided. . . .

§20A. Liability to Contemporaneous Traders for Insider Trading

(a) Private Rights of Action Based on Contemporaneous Trading

Any person who violates any provision of this chapter or the rules or regulations thereunder by purchasing or selling a security while in possession of material, nonpublic information shall be liable in an action in any court of competent jurisdiction to any person who, contemporaneously with the purchase or sale of securities that is the subject of such violation, has purchased (where such violation is based on a sale of securities) or sold (where such violation is based on a purchase of securities) securities of the same class.

(b) Limitations on Liability

(1) Contemporaneous Trading Actions Limited to Profit Gained or Loss Avoided

The total amount of damages imposed under subsection (a) of this section shall not exceed the profit gained or loss avoided in the transaction or transactions that are the subject of the violation.

(2) Offsetting Disgorgements Against Liability

The total amount of damages imposed against any person under subsection (a) of this section shall be diminished by the amounts, if any, that such person may be required to disgorge, pursuant to a court order obtained at the instance of the Commission, in a proceeding brought under section 21(d) of this title relating to the same transaction or transactions.

(3) Controlling Person Liability

No person shall be liable under this section solely by reason of employing another person who is liable under this section, but the liability of a controlling person under this section shall be subject to section 20(a) of this title.

(4) Statute of Limitations

No action may be brought under this section more than 5 years after the date of the last transaction that is the subject of the violation.

(c) Joint and Several Liability for Communicating

Any person who violates any provision of this chapter or the rules or regulations thereunder by communicating material, nonpublic information shall be jointly and severally liable under subsection (a) of this section with, and to the same extent as, any person or persons liable under subsection (a) of this section to whom the communication was directed.

(d) Authority Not to Restrict Other Express or Implied Rights of Action

Nothing in this section shall be construed to limit or condition the right of any person to bring an action to enforce a requirement of this chapter or the availability of any cause of action implied from a provision of this chapter.

(e) Provisions Not to Affect Public Prosecutions

This section shall not be construed to bar or limit in any manner any action by the Commission or the Attorney General under any other provision of this chapter, nor shall it bar or limit in any manner any action to recover penalties, or to seek any other order regarding penalties.

§21. *Investigations and Actions*

(a) Authority and Discretion of Commission to Investigate Violations

(1) The Commission may, in its discretion, make such investigations as it deems necessary to determine whether any person has violated, is violating, or is about to violate any provision of this chapter, the rules or regulations thereunder, the rules of a national securities exchange or registered securities association of which such person is a member or a person associated, or, as to any act or practice, or omission to act, while associated with a member, formerly associated with a member, the rules of a registered clearing agency in which such person is a participant, or, as to any act or practice, or omission to act, while a participant, was a participant," the rules of the Public Company Accounting Oversight Board, of which such person is a registered public accounting firm, a person associated with such a firm, or, as to any act, practice, or omission to act, while associated with such firm, a person formerly associated with such a firm, or the rules of the Municipal Securities Rulemaking Board, and may require or permit any person to file with it a statement in writing, under oath or otherwise as the Commission shall determine, as to all the facts and circumstances concerning the matter to be investigated. The Commission is authorized in its discretion, to publish information concerning any such violations, and to investigate any facts, conditions, practices, or matters which it may deem necessary or proper to aid in the enforcement of such provisions, in the prescribing of rules and regulations under this chapter, or in securing information to serve as a basis for recommending further legislation concerning the matters to which this chapter relates. . . .

(d) Injunction Proceedings

(1) Whenever it shall appear to the Commission that any person is engaged or is about to engage in acts or practices constituting a violation of any provision of this chapter, the rules or regulations thereunder, the rules of a national securities exchange or registered securities association of which such person is a member or a person associated with a member, the rules of a registered clearing agency in which

such person is a participant, the rules of the Public Company Accounting Oversight Board, of which such person is a registered public accounting firm or a person associated with such a firm, or the rules of the Municipal Securities Rulemaking Board, it may in its discretion bring an action in the proper district court of the United States, the United States District Court for the District of Columbia, or the United States courts of any territory or other place subject to the jurisdiction of the United States, to enjoin such acts or practices, and upon a proper showing a permanent or temporary injunction or restraining order shall be granted without bond. The Commission may transmit such evidence as may be available concerning such acts or practices as may constitute a violation of any provision of this chapter of the rules or regulations thereunder to the Attorney General, who may, in his discretion, institute the necessary criminal proceedings under this chapter.

(2) Authority of a Court to Prohibit Persons from Serving as Officers and Directors

In any proceeding under paragraph (1) of this subsection, the court may prohibit, conditionally or unconditionally, and permanently or for such period of time as it shall determine, any person who violated section 10(b) of this title or the rules or regulations thereunder from acting as an officer or director of any issuer that has a class of securities registered pursuant to section 12 of this title or that is required to file reports pursuant to section 15(d) of this title if the person's conduct demonstrates unfitness to serve as an officer or director of any such issuer.

(3) Money Penalties in Civil Actions

(A) Authority of Commission

Whenever it shall appear to the Commission that any person has violated any provision of this chapter, the rules or regulations thereunder, or a cease-and-desist order entered by the Commission pursuant to section 21C of this title, other than by committing a violation subject to a penalty pursuant to section 21A of this title, the Commission may bring an action in a United States district court to seek, and the court shall have jurisdiction to impose, upon a proper showing, a civil penalty to be paid by the person who committed such violation.

(B) Amount of Penalty [omitted]

(4) Prohibition of Attorneys' Fees Paid from Commission Disgorgement Funds

Except as otherwise ordered by the court upon motion by the Commission, or, in the case of an administrative action, as otherwise ordered by the Commission, funds disgorged as the result of an action brought by the Commission in Federal court, or as a result of any Commission administrative action, shall not be distributed as payment for attorneys' fees or expenses incurred by private parties seeking distribution of the disgorged funds.

(5) Equitable Relief

In any action or proceeding brought or instituted by the Commission under any provision of the securities laws, the Commission may seek, and any Federal court may grant, any equitable relief that may be appropriate or necessary for the benefit of investors. . . .

§21A. *Civil Penalties for Insider Trading*

(a) Authority to Impose Civil Penalties

(1) Judicial Actions by Commission Authorized

Whenever it shall appear to the Commission that any person has violated any provision of this chapter or the rules or regulations thereunder by purchasing or selling a security or security-based swap agreement while in possession of material, nonpublic information in, or has violated any such provision by communicating such information in connection with, a transaction on or through the facilities of a national securities exchange or from or through a broker or dealer, and which is not part of a public offering by an issuer of securities other than standardized options, the Commission—

(A) may bring an action in a United States district court to seek, and the court shall have jurisdiction to impose, a civil penalty to be paid by the person who committed such violation; and

(B) may, subject to subsection (b)(1) of this section, bring an action in a United States district court to seek, and the court shall have jurisdiction to impose, a civil penalty to be paid by a person who, at the time of the violation, directly or indirectly controlled the person who committed such violation.

(2) Amount of Penalty for Person Who Committed Violation

The amount of the penalty which may be imposed on the person who committed such violation shall be determined by the court in light of the facts and circumstances, but shall not exceed three times the profit gained or loss avoided as a result of such unlawful purchase, sale, or communication.

(3) Amount of Penalty for Controlling Person

The amount of the penalty which may be imposed on any person who, at the time of the violation, directly or indirectly controlled the person who committed such violation, shall be determined by the court in light of the facts and circumstances, but shall not exceed the greater of $1,000,000, [as adjusted for inflation by 17 C.F.R. § 201.1001] or three times the amount of the profit gained or loss avoided as a result of such controlled person's violation. If such controlled person's violation was a violation by communication, the profit gained or loss avoided as a result of the violation shall, for purposes of this paragraph only, be deemed to be limited to the profit gained or loss avoided by the person or persons to whom the controlled person directed such communication.

(b) Limitations on Liability

(1) Liability of Controlling Persons

No controlling person shall be subject to a penalty under subsection (a) (1) (B) of this section unless the Commission establishes that—

(A) such controlling person knew or recklessly disregarded the fact that such controlled person was likely to engage in the act or acts constituting the violation and failed to take appropriate steps to prevent such act or acts before they occurred; or

(B) such controlling person knowingly or recklessly failed to establish, maintain, or enforce any policy or procedure required under section 15(f) of this title or section 80b-4a of this title and such failure substantially contributed to or permitted the occurrence of the act or acts constituting the violation.

(2) Additional Restrictions on Liability

No person shall be subject to a penalty under subsection (a) of this section solely by reason of employing another person who is subject to a penalty under such subsection, unless such employing person is liable as a controlling person under paragraph (1) of this subsection. Section 20(a) of this title shall not apply to actions under subsection (a) of this section.

(c) Authority of Commission

The Commission, by such rules, regulations, and orders as it considers necessary or appropriate in the public interest or for the protection of investors, may exempt, in whole or in part, either unconditionally or upon specific terms and conditions, any person or transaction or class of persons or transactions from this section.

(d) Procedures for Collection

(1) Payment of Penalty to Treasury

A penalty imposed under this section shall be payable into the Treasury of the United States, except as otherwise provided in section 308 of the Sarbanes-Oxley Act of 2002 and section 21F of this title.

(2) Collection of Penalties

If a person upon whom such a penalty is imposed shall fail to pay such penalty within the time prescribed in the court's order, the Commission may refer the matter to the Attorney General who shall recover such penalty by action in the appropriate United States district court.

(3) Remedy Not Exclusive

The actions authorized by this section may be brought in addition to any other actions that the Commission or the Attorney General are entitled to bring.

(4) Jurisdiction and Venue

For purposes of section 27 of this title, actions under this section shall be actions to enforce a liability or a duty created by this chapter.

(5) Statute of Limitations

No action may be brought under this section more than 5 years after the date of the purchase or sale. This section shall not be construed to bar or limit in any manner any action by the Commission or the Attorney General under any other provision of this chapter, nor shall it bar or limit in any manner any action to recover penalties, or to seek any other order regarding penalties, imposed in an action commenced within 5 years of such transaction.

(e) Definition

For purposes of this section, "profit gained" or "loss avoided" is the difference between the purchase or sale price of the security and the value of that security as measured by the trading price of the security a reasonable period after public dissemination of the nonpublic information. . . .

§21B. Civil Remedies in Administrative Proceedings

(a) Commission Authority to Assess Money Penalties

(1) In general.—

In any proceeding instituted pursuant to sections 15(b)(4), 15(b)(6), 15B, 15C, 15D, or 17A of this title against any person, the Commission or the appropriate regulatory agency may impose a civil penalty if it finds, on the record after notice and opportunity for hearing, that such penalty is in the public interest that such person—

(A) has willfully violated any provision of the Securities Act of 1933, the Investment Company Act of 1940, the Investment Advisers Act of 1940, or this chapter, or the rules or regulations thereunder, or the rules of the Municipal Securities Rulemaking Board;

(B) has willfully aided, abetted, counseled, commanded, induced, or procured such a violation by any other person;

(C) has willfully made or caused to be made in any application for registration or report required to be filed with the Commission or with any other appropriate regulatory agency under this chapter, or in any proceeding before the Commission with respect to registration, any statement which was, at the time and in the light of the circumstances under which it was made, false or misleading with respect to any material fact, or has omitted to state in any such application or report any material fact which is required to be stated therein; or

(D) has failed reasonably to supervise, within the meaning of section 15(b)(4)(E) of this title, with a view to preventing violations of the provisions of such statutes, rules and regulations, another person who commits such a violation, if such other person is subject to his supervision;

(2) Cease-and-desist proceedings.—

In any proceeding instituted under section 21C against any person, the Commission may impose a civil penalty, if the Commission finds, on the record after notice and opportunity for hearing, that such person—

(A) is violating or has violated any provision of this title, or any rule or regulation issued under this title; or

(B) is or was a cause of the violation of any provision of this title, or any rule or regulation issued under this title.

§21C. Cease-and-Desist Proceedings

(a) Authority of the Commission

If the Commission finds, after notice and opportunity for hearing, that any person is violating, has violated, or is about to violate any provision of this chapter, or any rule or regulation thereunder, the Commission may publish its findings and enter an order requiring such person, and any other person that is, was, or would be a cause of the violation, due to an act or omission the person knew or should have known would contribute to such violation, to cease and desist from committing or causing such violation and any future violation of the same provision, rule, or regulation. Such order may, in addition to requiring a person to cease and desist from committing or causing a violation, require such person to comply, or to take steps to effect compliance, with such provision, rule, or regulation, upon such terms and conditions and within such time as the Commission may specify in such order. Any such order may, as the Commission deems appropriate, require future compliance or steps to effect future compliance, either permanently or for such period of time as the Commission may specify, with such provision, rule, or regulation with respect to any security, any issuer, or any other person. . . .

(e) Authority to Enter an Order Requiring an Accounting and Disgorgement

In any cease-and-desist proceeding under subsection (a) of this section, the Commission may enter an order requiring accounting and disgorgement, including reasonable interest. The Commission is authorized to adopt rules, regulations, and orders concerning payments to investors, rates of interest, periods of accrual, and such other matters as it deems appropriate to implement this subsection.

(f) Authority of the Commission to Prohibit Persons from Serving as Officers or Directors.

In any cease-and-desist proceeding under subsection (a), the Commission may issue an order to prohibit, conditionally or unconditionally, and permanently or for such period of time as it shall determine, any person who has violated section 10(b) or the rules or regulations thereunder, from acting as an officer or director of any issuer that has a class of securities registered pursuant to section 12, or that is required to file reports pursuant to section 15(d), if the conduct of that person demonstrates unfitness to serve as an officer or director of any such issuer.

§21D. Private Securities Litigation

(a) Private Class Actions

(1) In General

The provisions of this subsection shall apply in each private action arising under this title that is brought as a plaintiff class action pursuant to the Federal Rules of Civil Procedure.

(2) Certification Filed with Complaint

(A) In General

Each plaintiff seeking to serve as a representative party on behalf of a class shall provide a sworn certification, which shall be personally signed by such plaintiff and filed with the complaint, that—

(i) states that the plaintiff has reviewed the complaint and authorized its filing;

(ii) states that the plaintiff did not purchase the security that is the subject of the complaint at the direction of plaintiff's counsel or in order to participate in any private action arising under this title;

(iii) states that the plaintiff is willing to serve as a representative party on behalf of a class, including providing testimony at deposition and trial, if necessary;

(iv) sets forth all of the transactions of the plaintiff in the security that is the subject of the complaint during the class period specified in the complaint;

(v) identifies any other action under this title, filed during the 3-year period preceding the date on which the certification is signed by the plaintiff, in which the plaintiff has sought to serve as a representative party on behalf of a class; and

(vi) states that the plaintiff will not accept any payment for serving as a representative party on behalf of a class beyond the plaintiff's pro rata share of any recovery, except as ordered or approved by the court in accordance with paragraph (4).

(B) Nonwaiver of Attorney-Client Privilege

The certification filed pursuant to subparagraph (A) shall not be construed to be a waiver of the attorney-client privilege.

(3) Appointment of Lead Plaintiff

(A) Early Notice to Class Members

(i) In General

Not later than 20 days after the date on which the complaint is filed, the plaintiff or plaintiffs shall cause to be published, in a widely circulated national business-oriented publication or wire service, a notice advising members of the purported plaintiff class—

(I) of the pendency of the action, the claims asserted therein, and the purported class period; and

(II) that, not later than 60 days after the date on which the notice is published, any member of the purported class may move the court to serve as lead plaintiff of the purported class.

(ii) Multiple Actions

If more than one action on behalf of a class asserting substantially the same claim or claims arising under this title is filed, only the plaintiff or plaintiffs in the first filed action shall be required to cause notice to be published in accordance with clause (i).

(iii) Additional Notices May Be Required Under Federal Rules

Notice required under clause (i) shall be in addition to any notice required pursuant to the Federal Rules of Civil Procedure.

(B) Appointment of Lead Plaintiff

(i) In General

Not later than 90 days after the date on which a notice is published under subparagraph (A)(i), the court shall consider any motion made by a purported class member in response to the notice, including any motion by a class member who is not individually named as a plaintiff in the complaint or complaints, and shall appoint as lead plaintiff the member or members of the purported plaintiff class that the court determines to be most capable of adequately representing the interests of class members (hereafter in this paragraph referred to as the "most adequate plaintiff") in accordance with this subparagraph.

(ii) Consolidated Actions

If more than one action on behalf of a class asserting substantially the same claim or claims arising under this title has been filed, and any party has sought to consolidate those actions for pretrial purposes or for trial, the court shall not make the determination required by clause (i) until after the decision on the motion to consolidate is rendered. As soon as practicable after such decision is rendered, the court shall appoint the most adequate plaintiff as lead plaintiff for the consolidated actions in accordance with this paragraph.

(iii) Rebuttable Presumption

(I) In General

Subject to subclause (II), for purposes of clause (i), the court shall adopt a presumption that the most adequate plaintiff in any private action arising under this title is the person or group of persons that—

(aa) has either filed the complaint or made a motion in response to a notice under subparagraph (A)(i);

(bb) in the determination of the court, has the largest financial interest in the relief sought by the class; and

(cc) otherwise satisfies the requirements of Rule 23 of the Federal Rules of Civil Procedure.

(II) Rebuttal Evidence

The presumption described in subclause (I) may be rebutted only upon proof by a member of the purported plaintiff class that the presumptively most adequate plaintiff—

(aa) will not fairly and adequately protect the interests of the class; or

(bb) is subject to unique defenses that render such plaintiff incapable of adequately representing the class.

(iv) Discovery

For purposes of this subparagraph, discovery relating to whether a member or members of the purported plaintiff class is the most adequate plaintiff may be conducted by a plaintiff only if the plaintiff first demonstrates a reasonable basis for a finding that the presumptively most adequate plaintiff is incapable of adequately representing the class.

(v) Selection of Lead Counsel

The most adequate plaintiff shall, subject to the approval of the court, select and retain counsel to represent the class.

(vi) Restrictions on Professional Plaintiffs

Except as the court may otherwise permit, consistent with the purposes of this section, a person may be a lead plaintiff, or an officer, director, or fiduciary of a lead plaintiff, in no more than 5 securities class actions brought as plaintiff class actions pursuant to the Federal Rules of Civil Procedure during any 3-year period.

(4) Recovery by Plaintiffs

The share of any final judgment or of any settlement that is awarded to a representative party serving on behalf of a class shall be equal, on a per share basis, to the portion of the final judgment or settlement awarded to all other members of the class. Nothing in this paragraph shall be construed to limit the award of reasonable costs and expenses (including lost wages) directly relating to the representation of the class to any representative party serving on behalf of a class.

(5) Restrictions on Settlements under Seal

The terms and provisions of any settlement agreement of a class action shall not be filed under seal, except that on motion of any party to the settlement, the court may order filing under seal for those portions of a settlement agreement as to which good cause is shown for such filing under seal. For purposes of this paragraph, good cause shall exist only if publication of a term or provision of a settlement agreement would cause direct and substantial harm to any party.

(6) Restrictions on Payment of Attorneys' Fees and Expenses

Total attorneys' fees and expenses awarded by the court to counsel for the plaintiff class shall not exceed a reasonable percentage of the amount of any damages and prejudgment interest actually paid to the class.

(7) Disclosure of Settlement Terms to Class Members

Any proposed or final settlement agreement that is published or otherwise disseminated to the class shall include each of the following statements, along with a cover page summarizing the information contained in such statements:

(A) Statement of Plaintiff Recovery

The amount of the settlement proposed to be distributed to the parties to the action, determined in the aggregate and on an average per share basis.

(B) Statement of Potential Outcome of Case

(i) Agreement on Amount of Damages

If the settling parties agree on the average amount of damages per share that would be recoverable if the plaintiff prevailed on each claim alleged under this title, a statement concerning the average amount of such potential damages per share.

(ii) Disagreement on Amount of Damages

If the parties do not agree on the average amount of damages per share that would be recoverable if the plaintiff prevailed on each claim alleged under this title, a statement from each settling party concerning the issue or issues on which the parties disagree.

(iii) Inadmissibility for Certain Purposes

A statement made in accordance with clause (i) or (ii) concerning the amount of damages shall not be admissible in any Federal or State judicial action or administrative proceeding, other than an action or proceeding arising out of such statement.

(C) Statement of Attorneys' Fees or Costs Sought

If any of the settling parties or their counsel intend to apply to the court for an award of attorneys' fees or costs from any fund established as part of the settlement, a statement indicating which parties or counsel intend to make such an application, the amount of fees and costs that will be sought (including the amount of such fees and costs determined on an average per share basis), and a brief explanation supporting the fees and costs sought. Such information shall be clearly summarized on the cover page of any notice to a party of any proposed or final settlement agreement.

(D) Identification of Lawyers' Representatives

The name, telephone number, and address of one or more representatives of counsel for the plaintiff class who will be reasonably available to answer questions from class members concerning any matter contained in any notice of settlement published or otherwise disseminated to the class.

(E) Reasons for Settlement

A brief statement explaining the reasons why the parties are proposing the settlement.

(F) Other Information

Such other information as may be required by the court.

(8) Security for Payment of Costs in Class Actions

In any private action arising under this title that is certified as a class action pursuant to the Federal Rules of Civil Procedure, the court may require an undertaking from the attorneys for the plaintiff class, the plaintiff class, or both, or from the attorneys for the defendant, the defendant, or both, in such proportions and at such times as the court determines are just and equitable, for the payment of fees and expenses that may be awarded under this subsection.

(9) Attorney Conflict of Interest

If a plaintiff class is represented by an attorney who directly owns or otherwise has a beneficial interest in the securities that are the subject of the litigation, the court shall make a determination of whether such ownership or other interest constitutes a conflict of interest sufficient to disqualify the attorney from representing the plaintiff class.

(b) Requirements for Securities Fraud Actions

(1) Misleading Statements and Omissions

In any private action arising under this title in which the plaintiff alleges that the defendant—

(A) made an untrue statement of a material fact; or

(B) omitted to state a material fact necessary in order to make the statements made, in the light of the circumstances in which they were made, not misleading;

the complaint shall specify each statement alleged to have been misleading, the reason or reasons why the statement is misleading, and, if an allegation regarding the statement or omission is made on information and belief, the complaint shall state with particularity all facts on which that belief is formed.

(2) Required State of Mind

(A) In general.—Except as provided in paragraph (B), in any private action arising under this title in which the plaintiff may recover money damages only on proof that the defendant acted with a particular state of mind, the complaint shall, with respect to each act or omission alleged to violate this title, state with particularity facts giving rise to a strong inference that the defendant acted with the required state of mind.

(B) Exception

In the case of an action for money damages brought against a credit rating agency or a controlling person under this title, it shall be sufficient, for purposes of pleading any required state of mind in relation to such action, that the complaint state with particularity facts giving rise to a strong inference that the credit rating agency knowingly or recklessly failed—

(i) to conduct a reasonable investigation of the rated security with respect to the factual elements relied upon by its own methodology for evaluating credit risk; or

(ii) to obtain reasonable verification of such factual elements (which verification may be based on a sampling technique that does not amount to an audit) from other sources that the credit rating agency considered to be competent and that were independent of the issuer and underwriter.

(3) Motion to Dismiss; Stay of Discovery

(A) Dismissal for Failure to Meet Pleading Requirements

In any private action arising under this title, the court shall, on the motion of any defendant, dismiss the complaint if the requirements of paragraphs (1) and (2) are not met.

(B) Stay of Discovery

In any private action arising under this title, all discovery and other proceedings shall be stayed during the pendency of any motion to dismiss, unless the court finds upon the motion of any party that particularized discovery is necessary to preserve evidence or to prevent undue prejudice to that party.

(C) Preservation of Evidence

(i) In General

During the pendency of any stay of discovery pursuant to this paragraph, unless otherwise ordered by the court, any party to the action with actual notice of the allegations contained in the complaint shall treat all documents, data compilations (including electronically recorded or stored data), and tangible objects that are in the custody or control of such person and that are relevant to the allegations, as if they were the subject of a continuing request for production of documents from an opposing party under the Federal Rules of Civil Procedure.

(ii) Sanction for Willful Violation

A party aggrieved by the willful failure of an opposing party to comply with clause (i) may apply to the court for an order awarding appropriate sanctions.

(D) Circumvention of Stay of Discovery

Upon a proper showing, a court may stay discovery proceedings in any private action in a State court, as necessary in aid of its jurisdiction, or to protect or effectuate its judgments, in an action subject to a stay of discovery pursuant to this paragraph.

(4) Loss Causation

In any private action arising under this title, the plaintiff shall have the burden of proving that the act or omission of the defendant alleged to violate this title caused the loss for which the plaintiff seeks to recover damages.

(c) Sanctions for Abusive Litigation

(1) Mandatory Review by Court

In any private action arising under this title, upon final adjudication of the action, the court shall include in the record specific findings regarding compliance by each party and each attorney representing any party with each requirement of Rule 11(b) of the Federal Rules of Civil Procedure as to any complaint, responsive pleading, or dispositive motion.

(2) Mandatory Sanctions

If the court makes a finding under paragraph (1) that a party or attorney violated any requirement of Rule 11(b) of the Federal Rules of Civil Procedure as to any complaint, responsive pleading, or dispositive motion, the court shall impose sanctions on such party or attorney in accordance with Rule 11 of the Federal Rules of Civil Procedure. Prior to making a finding that any party or attorney has violated Rule 11 of the Federal Rules of Civil Procedure, the court shall give such party or attorney notice and an opportunity to respond.

(3) Presumption in Favor of Attorneys' Fees and Costs

(A) In General

Subject to subparagraphs (B) and (C), for purposes of paragraph (2), the court shall adopt a presumption that the appropriate sanction—

(i) for failure of any responsive pleading or dispositive motion to comply with any requirement of Rule 11(b) of the Federal Rules of Civil Procedure is an award to the opposing party of the reasonable attorneys' fees and other expenses incurred as a direct result of the violation; and

(ii) for substantial failure of any complaint to comply with any requirement of Rule 11(b) of the Federal Rules of Civil Procedure is an award to the opposing party of the reasonable attorneys' fees and other expenses incurred in the action.

(B) Rebuttal Evidence

The presumption described in subparagraph (A) may be rebutted only upon proof by the party or attorney against whom sanctions are to be imposed that—

(i) the award of attorneys' fees and other expenses will impose an unreasonable burden on that party or attorney and would be unjust, and the failure to make such an award would not impose a greater burden on the party in whose favor sanctions are to be imposed; or

(ii) the violation of Rule 11(b) of the Federal Rules of Civil Procedure was de minimis.

(C) Sanctions

If the party or attorney against whom sanctions are to be imposed meets its burden under subparagraph (B), the court shall award the sanctions that the court deems appropriate pursuant to Rule 11 of the Federal Rules of Civil Procedure.

(d) Defendant's Right to Written Interrogatories

In any private action arising under this title in which the plaintiff may recover money damages, the court shall, when requested by a defendant, submit to the jury a written interrogatory on the issue of each such defendant's state of mind at the time the alleged violation occurred.

(e) Limitation on Damages

(1) In General

Except as provided in paragraph (2), in any private action arising under this title in which the plaintiff seeks to establish damages by reference to the market price of a security, the award of damages to the plaintiff shall not exceed the difference between the purchase or sale price paid or received, as appropriate, by the plaintiff for the subject security and the mean trading price of that security during the 90-day period beginning on the date on which the information correcting the misstatement or omission that is the basis for the action is disseminated to the market.

(2) Exception

In any private action arising under this title in which the plaintiff seeks to establish damages by reference to the market price of a security, if the plaintiff sells or repurchases the subject security prior to the expiration of the 90-day period described in paragraph (1), the plaintiff's damages shall not exceed the difference between the purchase or sale price paid or received, as appropriate, by the plaintiff for the security and the mean trading price of the security during the period beginning immediately after dissemination of information correcting the misstatement or omission and ending on the date on which the plaintiff sells or repurchases the security.

(3) Definition

For purposes of this subsection, the "mean trading price" of a security shall be an average of the daily trading price of that security, determined as of the close of the market each day during the 90-day period referred to in paragraph (1).

(f) Proportionate Liability

(1) Applicability

Nothing in this subsection shall be construed to create, affect, or in any manner modify, the standard for liability associated with any action arising under the securities laws.

(2) Liability for Damages

(A) Joint and Several Liability

Any covered person against whom a final judgment is entered in a private action shall be liable for damages jointly and severally only if the trier of fact specifically determines that such covered person knowingly committed a violation of the securities laws.

(B) Proportionate Liability

(i) In General

Except as provided in subparagraph (A), a covered person against whom a final judgment is entered in a private action shall be liable solely for the portion of the judgment that corresponds to the percentage of responsibility of that covered person, as determined under paragraph (3).

(ii) Recovery by and Costs of Covered Person

In any case in which a contractual relationship permits, a covered person that prevails in any private action may recover the attorney's fees and costs of that covered person in connection with the action.

(3) Determination of Responsibility

(A) In General

In any private action, the court shall instruct the jury to answer special interrogatories, or if there is no jury, shall make findings, with respect to each covered person and each of the other persons claimed by any of the parties to have caused or contributed to the loss incurred by the plaintiff, including persons who have entered into settlements with the plaintiff or plaintiffs, concerning—

(i) whether such person violated the securities laws;

(ii) the percentage of responsibility of such person, measured as a percentage of the total fault of all persons who caused or contributed to the loss incurred by the plaintiff; and

(iii) whether such person knowingly committed a violation of the securities laws.

(B) Contents of Special Interrogatories or Findings

The responses to interrogatories, or findings, as appropriate, under subparagraph (A) shall specify the total amount of damages that the plaintiff is entitled to recover and the percentage of responsibility of each covered person found to have caused or contributed to the loss incurred by the plaintiff or plaintiffs.

(C) Factors for Consideration

In determining the percentage of responsibility under this paragraph, the trier of fact shall consider—

(i) the nature of the conduct of each covered person found to have caused or contributed to the loss incurred by the plaintiff or plaintiffs; and

(ii) the nature and extent of the causal relationship between the conduct of each such person and the damages incurred by the plaintiff or plaintiffs.

(4) Uncollectible Share

(A) In General

Notwithstanding paragraph (2)(B), upon motion made not later than 6 months after a final judgment is entered in any private action, the court determines that all or part of the share of the judgment of the covered person is not collectible against that covered person, and is also not collectible against a covered person described in paragraph (2)(A), each covered person described in paragraph (2)(B) shall be liable for the uncollectible share as follows:

(i) Percentage of Net Worth

Each covered person shall be jointly and severally liable for the uncollectible share if the plaintiff establishes that—

(I) the plaintiff is an individual whose recoverable damages under the final judgment are equal to more than 10 percent of the net worth of the plaintiff; and

(II) the net worth of the plaintiff is equal to less than $200,000.

(ii) Other Plaintiffs

With respect to any plaintiff not described in subclauses (I) and (II) of clause (i), each covered person shall be liable for the uncollectible share in proportion to the percentage of responsibility of that covered person, except that the total liability of a covered person under this clause may not exceed 50 percent of the proportionate share of that covered person, as determined under paragraph (3)(B).

(iii) Net Worth

For purposes of this subparagraph, net worth shall be determined as of the date immediately preceding the date of the purchase or sale (as applicable) by the plaintiff of the security that is the subject of the action, and shall be equal to the fair market value of assets, minus liabilities, including the net value of the investments of the plaintiff in real and personal property (including personal residences).

(B) Overall Limit

In no case shall the total payments required pursuant to subparagraph (A) exceed the amount of the uncollectible share.

(C) Covered Persons Subject to Contribution

A covered person against whom judgment is not collectible shall be subject to contribution and to any continuing liability to the plaintiff on the judgment.

(5) Right of Contribution

To the extent that a covered person is required to make an additional payment pursuant to paragraph (4), that covered person may recover contribution—

(A) from the covered person originally liable to make the payment;

(B) from any covered person liable jointly and severally pursuant to paragraph (2)(A);

(C) from any covered person held proportionately liable pursuant to this paragraph who is liable to make the same payment and has paid less than his or her proportionate share of that payment; or

(D) from any other person responsible for the conduct giving rise to the payment that would have been liable to make the same payment.

(6) Nondisclosure to Jury

The standard for allocation of damages under paragraphs (2) and (3) and the procedure for reallocation of uncollectible shares under paragraph (4) shall not be disclosed to members of the jury.

(7) Settlement Discharge

(A) In General

A covered person who settles any private action at any time before final verdict or judgment shall be discharged from all claims for contribution brought by other persons. Upon entry of the settlement by the court, the court shall enter a bar order constituting the final discharge of all obligations to the plaintiff of the settling covered person arising out of the action. The order shall bar all future claims for contribution arising out of the action—

(i) by any person against the settling covered person; and

(ii) by the settling covered person against any person, other than a person whose liability has been extinguished by the settlement of the settling covered person.

(B) Reduction

If a covered person enters into a settlement with the plaintiff prior to final verdict or judgment, the verdict or judgment shall be reduced by the greater of—

(i) an amount that corresponds to the percentage of responsibility of that covered person; or

(ii) the amount paid to the plaintiff by that covered person.

(8) Contribution

A covered person who becomes jointly and severally liable for damages in any private action may recover contribution from any other person who, if joined in the original action, would have been liable for the same damages. A claim for contribution shall be determined based on the percentage of responsibility of the claimant and of each person against whom a claim for contribution is made.

(9) Statute of Limitations for Contribution

In any private action determining liability, an action for contribution shall be brought not later than 6 months after the entry of a final, nonappealable judgment in the action, except that an action for contribution brought by a covered person who was required to make an additional payment pursuant to paragraph (4) may be brought not later than 6 months after the date on which such payment was made.

(10) Definitions

For purposes of this subsection—

(A) a covered person "knowingly commits a violation of the securities laws"—

(i) with respect to an action that is based on an untrue statement of material fact or omission of a material fact necessary to make the statement not misleading, if—

(I) that covered person makes an untrue statement of a material fact, with actual knowledge that the representation is false, or omits to state a fact necessary in order to make the statement made not misleading, with actual knowledge that, as a result of the omission, one of the material representations of the covered person is false; and

(II) persons are likely to reasonably rely on that misrepresentation or omission; and

(ii) with respect to an action that is based on any conduct that is not described in clause (i), if that covered person engages in that conduct with actual knowledge of the facts and circumstances that make the conduct of that covered person a violation of the securities laws;

(B) reckless conduct by a covered person shall not be construed to constitute a knowing commission of a violation of the securities laws by that covered person;

(C) the term "covered person" means—

(i) a defendant in any private action arising under this title; or

(ii) a defendant in any private action arising under section 11 of the Securities Act of 1933, who is an outside director of the issuer of the securities that are the subject of the action; and

(D) the term "outside director" shall have the meaning given such term by rule or regulation of the Commission.

§21E. *Application of Safe Harbor for Forward-Looking Statements*

(a) Applicability

This section shall apply only to a forward-looking statement made by—

(1) an issuer that, at the time that the statement is made, is subject to the reporting requirements of section 13(a) or section 15(d);

(2) a person acting on behalf of such issuer;

(3) an outside reviewer retained by such issuer making a statement on behalf of such issuer; or

(4) an underwriter, with respect to information provided by such issuer or information derived from information provided by such issuer.

(b) Exclusions

Except to the extent otherwise specifically provided by rule, regulation, or order of the Commission, this section shall not apply to a forward-looking statement—

(1) that is made with respect to the business or operations of the issuer, if the issuer—

(A) during the 3-year period preceding the date on which the statement was first made—

(i) was convicted of any felony or misdemeanor described in clauses (i) through (iv) of section 15(b)(4)(B); or

(ii) has been made the subject of a judicial or administrative decree or order arising out of a governmental action that—

(I) prohibits future violations of the antifraud provisions of the securities laws;

(II) requires that the issuer cease and desist from violating the antifraud provisions of the securities laws; or

(III) determines that the issuer violated the antifraud provisions of the securities laws;

(B) makes the forward-looking statement in connection with an offering of securities by a blank check company;

(C) issues penny stock;

(D) makes the forward-looking statement in connection with a rollup transaction; or

(E) makes the forward-looking statement in connection with a going private transaction; or

(2) that is—

(A) included in a financial statement prepared in accordance with generally accepted accounting principles;

(B) contained in a registration statement of, or otherwise issued by, an investment company;

(C) made in connection with a tender offer;

(D) made in connection with an initial public offering;

(E) made in connection with an offering by, or relating to the operations of, a partnership, limited liability company, or a direct participation investment program; or

(F) made in a disclosure of beneficial ownership in a report required to be filed with the Commission pursuant to section 13(d).

(c) Safe Harbor

(1) In General

Except as provided in subsection (b), in any private action arising under this title that is based on an untrue statement of a material fact or omission of a material fact necessary to make the statement not misleading, a person referred to in subsection (a) shall not be liable with respect to any forward-looking statement, whether written or oral, if and to the extent that—

(A) the forward-looking statement is—

(i) identified as a forward-looking statement, and is accompanied by meaningful cautionary statements identifying important factors that could cause actual results to differ materially from those in the forward-looking statement; or

(ii) immaterial; or

(B) the plaintiff fails to prove that the forward-looking statement—

(i) if made by a natural person, was made with actual knowledge by that person that the statement was false or misleading; or

(ii) if made by a business entity; was—

(I) made by or with the approval of an executive officer of that entity; and

(II) made or approved by such officer with actual knowledge by that officer that the statement was false or misleading.

(2) Oral Forward-Looking Statements

In the case of an oral forward-looking statement made by an issuer that is subject to the reporting requirements of section 13(a) or section 15(d), or by a person acting on behalf of such issuer, the requirement set forth in paragraph (1)(A) shall be deemed to be satisfied—

(A) if the oral forward-looking statement is accompanied by a cautionary statement—

(i) that the particular oral statement is a forward-looking statement; and

(ii) that the actual results might differ materially from those projected in the forward-looking statement; and

(B) if—

(i) the oral forward-looking statement is accompanied by an oral statement that additional information concerning factors that could cause actual results to materially differ from those in the forward-looking statement is contained in a readily available written document, or portion thereof;

(ii) the accompanying oral statement referred to in clause (i) identifies the document, or portion thereof, that contains the additional information about those factors relating to the forward-looking statement; and

(iii) the information contained in that written document is a cautionary statement that satisfies the standard established in paragraph (1)(A).

(3) Availability

Any document filed with the Commission or generally disseminated shall be deemed to be readily available for purposes of paragraph (2).

(4) Effect on Other Safe Harbors

The exemption provided for in paragraph (1) shall be in addition to any exemption that the Commission may establish by rule or regulation under subsection (g).

(d) Duty to Update

Nothing in this section shall impose upon any person a duty to update a forward-looking statement.

(e) Dispositive Motion

On any motion to dismiss based upon subsection (c)(1), the court shall consider any statement cited in the complaint and any cautionary statement accompanying the forward-looking statement, which are not subject to material dispute, cited by the defendant.

(f) Stay Pending Decision on Motion

In any private action arising under this title, the court shall stay discovery (other than discovery that is specifically directed to the applicability of the exemption provided for in this section) during the pendency of any motion by a defendant for summary judgment that is based on the grounds that—

(1) the statement or omission upon which the complaint is based is a forward-looking statement within the meaning of this section; and

(2) the exemption provided for in this section precludes a claim for relief.

(g) Exemption Authority

In addition to the exemptions provided for in this section, the Commission may, by rule or regulation, provide exemptions from or under any provision of this title, including with respect to liability that is based on a statement or that is based on projections or other forward-looking information, if and to the extent that any such exemption is consistent with the public interest and the protection of investors, as determined by the Commission.

(h) Effect on Other Authority of Commission

Nothing in this section limits, either expressly or by implication, the authority of the Commission to exercise similar authority or to adopt similar rules and regulations with respect to forward-looking statements under any other statute under which the Commission exercises rule-making authority.

(i) Definitions

For purposes of this section, the following definitions shall apply:

(1) Forward-Looking Statement

The term "forward-looking statement" means—

(A) a statement containing a projection of revenues, income (including income loss), earnings (including earnings loss) per share, capital expenditures, dividends, capital structure, or other financial items;

(B) a statement of the plans and objectives of management for future operations, including plans or objectives relating to the products or services of the issuer;

(C) a statement of future economic performance, including any such statement contained in a discussion and analysis of financial condition by the management or in the results of operations included pursuant to the rules and regulations of the Commission;

(D) any statement of the assumptions underlying or relating to any statement described in subparagraph (A), (B), or (C);

(E) any report issued by an outside reviewer retained by an issuer, to the extent that the report assesses a forward-looking statement made by the issuer; or

(F) a statement containing a projection or estimate of such other items as may be specified by rule or regulation of the Commission. . . .

(3) Going Private Transaction

The term "going private transaction" has the meaning given that term under the rules or regulations of the Commission issued pursuant to section 13(e).

(4) Person Acting on Behalf of an Issuer

The term "person acting on behalf of an issuer" means any officer, director, or employee of such issuer.

(5) Other Terms

The terms "blank check company", "rollup transaction", "partnership", "limited liability company", "executive officer of an entity" and "direct participation investment program", have the meanings given those terms by rule or regulation of the Commission. . . .

§23. Rules, Regulations, and Orders; Annual Reports

(a) Power to Make Rules and Regulations; Considerations; Public Disclosure

(1) The Commission, the Board of Governors of the Federal Reserve System, and the other agencies enumerated in section 3(a)(34) of this title shall each have power to make such rules and regulations as may be necessary or appropriate to implement the provisions of this chapter for which they are responsible or for the execution of the functions vested in them by this chapter, and may for such purposes classify persons, securities, transactions, statements, applications, reports, and other matters within their respective jurisdictions, and prescribe greater, lesser, or different requirements for different classes thereof. No provision of this chapter imposing any liability shall apply to any act done or omitted in good faith in conformity with a rule, regulation, or order of the Commission, the Board of Governors of the Federal Reserve System, other agency enumerated in section 3(a)(34) of this title, or any self-regulatory organization, notwithstanding that such rule, regulation, or order may thereafter be amended or rescinded or determined by judicial or other authority to be invalid for any reason.

(2) The Commission and the Secretary of the Treasury, in making rules and regulations pursuant to any provisions of this chapter, shall consider among other matters the impact any such rule or regulation would have on competition. The Commission and the Secretary of the Treasury shall not adopt any such rule or regulation which would impose a burden on competition not necessary or appropriate in furtherance of the purposes of this chapter. The Commission and the Secretary of the Treasury shall include in the statement of basis and purpose incorporated in any rule or regulation adopted under this chapter, the reasons for the Commission's or the Secretary's determination that any burden on competition imposed by such rule or regulation is necessary or appropriate in furtherance of the purposes of this chapter. . . .

§25. Court Review of Orders and Rules

(a) Final Commission Orders; Persons Aggrieved; Petition; Record; Findings; Affirmance, Modification, Enforcement, or Setting Aside of Orders; Remand to Adduce Additional Evidence

(1) A person aggrieved by a final order of the Commission entered pursuant to this chapter may obtain review of the order in the United States Court of Appeals for the circuit in which he resides or has his principal place of business, or for the District of Columbia Circuit, by filing in such court, within sixty days after the entry of the order, a written petition requesting that the order be modified or set aside in whole or in part. . . .

§26. *Unlawful Representations*

No action or failure to act by the Commission or the Board of Governors of the Federal Reserve System, in the administration of this chapter shall be construed to mean that the particular authority has in any way passed upon the merits of, or given approval to, any security or any transaction or transactions therein, nor shall such action or failure to act with regard to any statement or report filed with or examined by such authority pursuant to this chapter or rules and regulations thereunder, be deemed a finding by such authority that such statement or report is true and accurate on its face or that it is not false or misleading. It shall be unlawful to make, or cause to be made, to any prospective purchaser or seller of a security any representation that any such action or failure to act by any such authority is to be so construed or has such effect.

§27. *Jurisdiction of Offenses and Suits*

(a) In general.—The district courts of the United States and the United States courts of any Territory or other place subject to the jurisdiction of the United States shall have exclusive jurisdiction of violations of this chapter or the rules and regulations thereunder, and of all suits in equity and actions at law brought to enforce any liability or duty created by this chapter or the rules and regulations thereunder. Any criminal proceeding may be brought in the district wherein any act or transaction constituting the violation occurred. Any suit or action to enforce any liability or duty created by this chapter or rules and regulations thereunder, or to enjoin any violation of such chapter or rules and regulations, may be brought in any such district or in the district wherein the defendant is found or is an inhabitant or transacts business, and process in such cases may be served in any other district of which the defendant is an inhabitant or wherever the defendant may be found. Judgments and decrees so rendered shall be subject to review as provided in sections 1254, 1291, 1292, and 1294 of title 28. No costs shall be assessed for or against the Commission in any proceeding under this chapter brought by or against it in the Supreme Court or such other courts.

(b) Extraterritorial Jurisdiction

The district courts of the United States and the United States courts of any Territory shall have jurisdiction of an action or proceeding brought or instituted by the Commission or the United States alleging a violation of the antifraud provisions of this title involving—

(1) conduct within the United States that constitutes significant steps in furtherance of the violation, even if the securities transaction occurs outside the United States and involves only foreign investors; or

(2) conduct occurring outside the United States that has a foreseeable substantial effect within the United States.

§28. Effect on Existing Law

(a) Limitation on judgments

(1) In general

No person permitted to maintain a suit for damages under the provisions of this title shall recover, through satisfaction of judgment in 1 or more actions, a total amount in excess of the actual damages to that person on account of the act complained of. Except as otherwise specifically provided in this title, nothing in this title shall affect the jurisdiction of the securities commission (or any agency or officer performing like functions) of any State over any security or any person insofar as it does not conflict with the provisions of this title or the rules and regulations under this title.

(2) Rule of construction

Except as provided in subsection (f), the rights and remedies provided by this title shall be in addition to any and all other rights and remedies that may exist at law or in equity.

(3) State bucket shop laws

No State law which prohibits or regulates the making or promoting of wagering or gaming contracts, or the operation of 'bucket shops' or other similar or related activities, shall invalidate—

(A) any put, call, straddle, option, privilege, or other security subject to this title (except any security that has a pari-mutuel payout or otherwise is determined by the Commission, acting by rule, regulation, or order, to be appropriately subject to such laws), or apply to any activity which is incidental or related to the offer, purchase, sale, exercise, settlement, or closeout of any such security;

(B) any security-based swap between eligible contract participants; or

(C) any security-based swap effected on a national securities exchange registered pursuant to section 6(b).

(4) Other state provisions

No provision of State law regarding the offer, sale, or distribution of securities shall apply to any transaction in a security-based swap or a security futures product, except that this paragraph may not be construed as limiting any State antifraud law of general applicability. A security-based swap may not be regulated as an insurance contract under any provision of State law.

(f) Limitations on Remedies

(1) Class Action Limitations.—No covered class action based upon the statutory or common law of any State or subdivision thereof may be maintained in any State or Federal court by any private party alleging—

(A) a misrepresentation or omission of a material fact in connection with the purchase or sale of a covered security; or

(B) that the defendant used or employed any manipulative or deceptive device or contrivance in connection with the purchase or sale of a covered security.

(2) Removal of Covered Class Actions.—Any covered class action brought in any State court involving a covered security, as set forth in paragraph (1), shall be removable to the Federal district court for the district in which the action is pending, and shall be subject to paragraph (1).

(3) Preservation of Certain Actions.—

(A) Actions under State Law of State of Incorporation.—

(i) Actions Preserved.—Notwithstanding paragraph (1) or (2), a covered class action described in clause (ii) of this subparagraph that is based upon the statutory or common law of the State in which the issuer is incorporated (in the case of a corporation) or organized (in the case of any other entity) may be maintained in a State or Federal court by a private party.

(ii) Permissible Actions.—A covered class action is described in this clause if it involves—

(I) the purchase or sale of securities by the issuer or an affiliate of the issuer exclusively from or to holders of equity securities of the issuer; or

(II) any recommendation, position, or other communication with respect to the sale of securities of an issuer that—

(aa) is made by or on behalf of the issuer or an affiliate of the issuer to holders of equity securities of the issuer; and

(bb) concerns decisions of such equity holders with respect to voting their securities, acting in response to a tender or exchange offer, or exercising dissenters' or appraisal rights.

(B) State Actions.—

(i) In General.—Notwithstanding any other provision of this subsection, nothing in this subsection may be construed to preclude a State or political subdivision thereof or a State pension plan from bringing an action involving a covered security on its own behalf, or as a member of a class comprised solely of other States, political subdivisions, or State pension plans that are named plaintiffs, and that have authorized participation, in such action.

(ii) State Pension Plan Defined.—For purposes of this subparagraph, the term 'State pension plan' means a pension plan established and maintained for its employees by the government of a State or political subdivision thereof, or by any agency or instrumentality thereof.

(C) Actions under Contractual Agreements Between Issuers and Indenture Trustees.—Notwithstanding paragraph (1) or (2), a covered class action that seeks to enforce a contractual agreement between an issuer and an indenture trustee may be maintained in a State or Federal court by a party to the agreement or a successor to such party.

(D) Remand of Removed Actions.—In an action that has been removed from a State court pursuant to paragraph (2), if the Federal court determines that the action may be maintained in State court pursuant to this subsection, the Federal court shall remand such action to such State court.

(4) Preservation of State Jurisdiction.—The securities commission (or any agency or office performing like functions) of any State shall retain jurisdiction under the laws of such State to investigate and bring enforcement actions.

(5) Definitions.—For purposes of this subsection, the following definitions shall apply:

(A) Affiliate of the Issuer.—The term 'affiliate of the issuer' means a person that directly or indirectly, through one or more intermediaries, controls or is controlled by or is under common control with, the issuer.

(B) Covered Class Action.—The term 'covered class action' means—

(i) any single lawsuit in which—

(I) damages are sought on behalf of more than 50 persons or prospective class members, and questions of law or fact common to those persons or members of the prospective class, without reference to issues of individualized reliance on an alleged misstatement or omission, predominate over any questions affecting only individual persons or members; or

(II) one or more named parties seek to recover damages on a representative basis on behalf of themselves and other unnamed parties similarly situated, and questions of law or fact common to those persons or members of the prospective class predominate over any questions affecting only individual persons or members; or

(ii) any group of lawsuits filed in or pending in the same court and involving common questions of law or fact, in which—

(I) damages are sought on behalf of more than 50 persons; and

(II) the lawsuits are joined, consolidated, or otherwise proceed as a single action for any purpose.

(C) Exception for Derivative Actions.—Notwithstanding subpara- graph (B), the term 'covered class action' does not include an exclusively derivative action brought by one or more shareholders on behalf of a corporation.

(D) Counting of Certain Class Members.—For purposes of this paragraph, a corporation, investment company, pension plan, partnership, or other entity, shall be treated as one person or prospective class member, but only if the entity is not established for the purpose of participating in the action.

(E) Covered Security.—The term 'covered security' means a security that satisfies the standards for a covered security specified in paragraph (1) or (2) of section 18(b) of the Securities Act of 1933, at the time during which it is alleged that the misrepresentation, omission, or manipulative or deceptive conduct occurred, except that such term shall not include any debt security that is exempt from registration under the Securities Act of 1933 pursuant to rules issued by the Commission under section 4(2) of that Act.

(F) Rule of Construction.—Nothing in this paragraph shall be construed to affect the discretion of a State court in determining whether actions filed in such court should be joined, consolidated, or otherwise allowed to proceed as a single action.

§29. Validity of Contracts

(a) Waiver Provisions

Any condition, stipulation, or provision binding any person to waive compliance with any provision of this chapter or of any rule or regulation thereunder, or of any rule of, self-regulatory organization shall be void.

(b) Contract Provisions in Violation of Chapter

Every contract made in violation of any provision of this chapter or of any rule or regulation thereunder, and every contract (including any contract for listing a security on an exchange) heretofore or hereafter made, the performance of which involves the violation of, or the continuance of any relationship or practice in violation of, any provision of this chapter or any rule or regulation thereunder, shall be void (1) as regards the rights of any person who, in violation of any such provision, rule, or regulation, shall have made or engaged in the performance of any such contract, and (2) as regards the rights of any person who, not being a party to such contract, shall have acquired any right thereunder with actual knowledge of the facts by reason of which the making or performance of such contract was in violation of any such provision, rule, or regulation: *Provided,* (A) That no contract shall be void by reason of this subsection because of any violation of any rule or regulation prescribed pursuant to paragraph (3) of subsection (c) of section 15 of this title, and (B) that no contract shall be deemed to be void by reason of this subsection in any action maintained in reliance upon this subsection, by any person to or for whom any broker or dealer sells, or from or for whom any broker or dealer purchases, a security in violation of any rule or regulation prescribed pursuant to paragraph (1) or (2) of subsection (c) of section 15 of this title, unless such action is brought within one year after the discovery that such sale or purchase involves such violation and within three years after such violation. The Commission may, in a rule or regulation prescribed pursuant to such paragraph (2) of such section 15(c) of this title, designate such rule or regulation, or portion thereof, as a rule or regulation, or portion thereof, a contract in violation of which shall not be void by reason of this subsection. . . .

§30. Foreign Securities Exchanges

(a) It shall be unlawful for any broker or dealer, directly or indirectly, to make use of the mails or of any means or instrumentality of interstate commerce for the purpose of effecting on an exchange not within or subject to the jurisdiction of the United States, any transaction in any security the issuer of which is a resident of, or is organized under the laws of, or has its principal place of business in, a place within or subject to the jurisdiction of the United States, in contravention of such rules and regulations as the Commission may prescribe as necessary or appropriate in the public interest or for the protection of investors or to prevent the evasion of this title.

(b) The provisions of this title or of any rule or regulation thereunder shall not apply to any person insofar as he transacts a business in securities without the jurisdiction of the United States, unless he transacts such business in contravention of such rules and regulations as the Commission may prescribe as necessary or appropriate to prevent the evasion of this title.

(c) Rule of construction. . .

§30A. Prohibited Foreign Trade Practices by Issuers

(a) Prohibition

It shall be unlawful for any issuer which has a class of securities registered pursuant to section 12 of this title or which is required to file reports under section 15(d) of this title, or for any officer, director, employee, or agent of such issuer or any stockholder thereof acting on behalf of such issuer, to make use of the mails or any means or instrumentality of interstate commerce corruptly in furtherance of an offer, payment, promise to pay, or authorization of the payment of any money, or offer, gift, promise to give, or authorization of the giving of anything of value to—

(1) any foreign official for purposes of—

(A)(i) influencing any act or decision of such foreign official in his official capacity, or (ii) inducing such foreign official to do or omit to do any act in violation of the lawful duty of such official, or

(B) inducing such foreign official to use his influence with a foreign government or instrumentality thereof to affect or influence any act or decision of such government or instrumentality,

in order to assist such issuer in obtaining or retaining business for or with, or directing business to, any person;

(2) any foreign political party or official thereof or any candidate for foreign political office for purposes of—

(A) (i) influencing any act or decision of such party, official, or candidate in its or his official capacity, or (ii) inducing such party, official, or candidate to do or omit to do an act in violation of the lawful duty of such party, official, or candidate,

(B) inducing such party, official, or candidate to use its or his influence with a foreign government or instrumentality thereof to affect or influence any act or decision of such government or instrumentality,

in order to assist such issuer in obtaining or retaining business for or with, or directing business to, any person; or

(3) any person, while knowing that all or a portion of such money or thing of value will be offered, given, or promised, directly or indirectly, to any foreign official, to any foreign political party or official thereof, or to any candidate for foreign political office, for purposes of—

(A)(i) influencing any act or decision of such foreign official, political party, party official, or candidate in his or its official capacity, or (ii) inducing such foreign official, political party, party official, or candidate to do or omit to do any act in violation of the lawful duty of such foreign official, political party, party official, or candidate, or

(B) inducing such foreign official, political party, party official, or candidate to use his or its influence with a foreign government or instrumentality thereof to affect or influence any act or decision of such government or instrumentality,

in order to assist such issuer in obtaining or retaining business for or with, or directing business to, any person.

(b) Exception for Routine Governmental Action

Subsection (a) of this section shall not apply to any facilitating or expediting payment to a foreign official, political party, or party official the purpose of which is to expedite or to secure the performance of a routine governmental action by a foreign official, political party, or party official.

(c) Affirmative Defenses

It shall be an affirmative defense to actions under subsection (a) of this section that—

(1) the payment, gift, offer, or promise of anything of value that was made, was lawful under the written laws and regulations of the foreign official's, political party's, party official's, or candidate's country; or

(2) the payment, gift, offer, or promise of anything of value that was made, was a reasonable and bona fide expenditure, such as travel and lodging expenses, incurred by or on behalf of a foreign official, party, party official, or candidate and was directly related to—

(A) the promotion, demonstration, or explanation of products or services; or

(B) the execution or performance of a contract with a foreign government or agency thereof. . . .

(e) Opinions of Attorney General

(1) The Attorney General, after consultation with appropriate departments and agencies of the United States and after obtaining the views of all interested persons through public notice and comment procedures, shall establish a procedure to provide responses to specific inquiries by issuers concerning conformance of their conduct with the Department of Justice's present enforcement policy regarding the preceding provisions of this section. . . .

(f) Definitions

For purposes of this section:

(1) The term "foreign official" means any officer or employee of a foreign government or any department, agency, or instrumentality thereof, or any person acting in an official capacity for or on behalf of any such government or department, agency, or instrumentality.

(2) (A) A person's state of mind is "knowing" with respect to conduct, a circumstance, or a result if—

(i) such person is aware that such person is engaging in such conduct, that such circumstance exists, or that such result is substantially certain to occur; or

(ii) such person has a firm belief that such circumstance exists or that such result is substantially certain to occur.

(B) When knowledge of the existence of a particular circumstance is required for an offense, such knowledge is established if a person is aware of a high probability of the existence of such circumstance, unless the person actually believes that such circumstance does not exist.

(3) (A) The term "routine governmental action" means only an action which is ordinarily and commonly performed by a foreign official in—

(i) obtaining permits, licenses, or other official documents to qualify a person to do business in a foreign country;

(ii) processing governmental papers, such as visas and work orders;

(iii) providing police protection, mail pick-up and delivery, or scheduling inspections associated with contract performance or inspections related to transit of goods across country;

(iv) providing phone service, power and water supply, loading and unloading cargo, or protecting perishable products or commodities from deterioration; or

(v) actions of a similar nature.

(B) The term "routine governmental action" does not include any decision by a foreign official whether, or on what terms, to award new business to or to continue business with a particular party, or any action taken by a foreign official involved in the decision-making process to encourage a decision to award new business to or continue business with a particular party. . . .

§32. Penalties

(a) Willful Violations; False and Misleading Statements

Any person who willfully violates any provision of this chapter (other than section 30A of this title), or any rule or regulation thereunder the violation of which is made unlawful or the observance of which is required under the terms of this chapter, or any person who willfully and knowingly makes, or causes to be made, any statement in any application, report, or document required to be filed under this chapter or any rule or regulation thereunder or any undertaking contained in a registration statement as provided in subsection (d) of section 15 of this title, or by any self-regulatory organization in connection with an application for membership or participation therein or to become associated with a member thereof which statement was false or misleading with respect to any material fact, shall upon conviction be fined not more than $5,000,000, or imprisoned not more than 20 years, or both, except that when such person is a person other than a natural person, a fine not exceeding $25,000,000 may be imposed; but no person shall be subject to imprisonment under this section for the violation of any rule or regulation if he proves that he had no knowledge of such rule or regulation.

(b) Failure to File Information, Documents, or Reports

Any issuer which fails to file information, documents, or reports required to be filed under subsection (d) of section 15 of this title or any rule of regulation thereunder shall forfeit to the United States the sum of $100 [as adjusted for inflation by 17 C.F.R. § 201.1001] for each and every day such failure to file shall continue. Such forfeiture, which shall be in lieu of any criminal penalty for such failure to file which might be deemed to arise under subsection (a) of this section, shall be payable into the Treasury of the United States and shall be recoverable in a civil suit in the name of the United States.

(c) Violations by Issuers, Officers, Directors, Stockholders, Employees, or Agents of Issuers

(1) (A) Any issuer that violates section 30A-(a) of this title shall be fined not more than $2,000,000.

(B) Any issuer that violates section 30A-(a) of this title shall be subject to a civil penalty of not more than $10,000 [as adjusted for inflation by 17 C.F.R. § 201.1001] imposed in an action brought by the Commission.

(2) (A) Any officer or director of an issuer, or stockholder acting on behalf of such issuer, who willfully violates section 30A-(a) of this title shall be fined not more than $100,000, or imprisoned not more than 5 years, or both.

(B) Any employee or agent of an issuer who is a United States citizen, national, or resident or is otherwise subject to the jurisdiction of the United States (other than an officer, director, or stockholder acting on behalf of such issuer), and who willfully violates section 30A-(a) of this title, shall be fined not more than $100,000, or imprisoned not more than 5 years, or both.

(C) Any officer, director, employee, or agent of an issuer, or stockholder acting on behalf of such issuer, who violates section 30A-(a) of this title shall be subject to a civil penalty of not more than $10,000 [as adjusted for inflation by 17 C.F.R. § 201.1001] imposed in an action brought by the Commission.

(3) Whenever a fine is imposed under paragraph (2) upon any officer, director, employee, agent, or stockholder of an issuer, such fine may not be paid, directly or indirectly, by such issuer.

§33. Separability of Provisions

If any provision of this chapter, or the application of such provision to any person or circumstances, shall be held invalid, the remainder of the chapter and the application of such provision to persons or circumstances other than those as to which it is held invalid, shall not be affected thereby.

§36. *General Exemptive Authority*

(a) Authority

(1) In general

Except as provided in subsection (b), but notwithstanding any other provision of this title, the Commission, by rule, regulation, or order, may conditionally or unconditionally exempt any person, security, or transaction, or any class or classes of persons, securities, or transactions, from any provision or provisions of this title or of any rule or regulation thereunder, to the extent that such exemption is necessary or appropriate in the public interest, and is consistent with the protection of investors.

(2) Procedures

The Commission shall, by rule or regulation, determine the procedures under which an exemptive order under this section shall be granted and may, in its sole discretion, decline to entertain any application for an order of exemption under this section.

(b) Limitation

The Commission may not, under this section, exempt any person, security, or transaction, or any class or classes of persons, securities, or transactions from section 15C or the rules or regulations issued thereunder or (for purposes of section 15C and the rules and regulations issued thereunder) from any definition in paragraph (42), (43), (44), or (45) of section 3(a).

(c) Derivatives [omitted].

The Sarbanes-Oxley Act of 2002

TITLE II — AUDITOR INDEPENDENCE

Sec. 208 ...

(b) Auditor Independence.—It shall be unlawful for any registered public accounting firm (or an associated person thereof, as applicable) to prepare or issue and audit report with respect to any issuer, if the firm or associated person engages in any activity with respect to that issuer prohibited by any of subsections (g) through (l) of section 10A of the Securities Exchange Act of 1934, as added by this title, or any rule or regulation of the Commission or of the Board issued thereunder.

Title III — Corporate Responsibility

Sec. 302. Corporate Responsibility for Financial Reports

(a) Regulations Required.—The Commission shall, by rule, require, for each company filing periodic reports under section 13(a) or 15(d) of the Securities Exchange Act of 1934, that the principal executive officer or officers and the principal financial officer or officers, or persons performing similar functions, certify in each annual or quarterly report filed or submitted under either such section of such Act that —

(1) the signing officer has reviewed the report;

(2) based on the officer's knowledge, the report does not contain any untrue statement of a material fact or omit to state a material fact necessary in order to make the statements made, in light of the circumstances under which such statements were made, not misleading;

(3) based on such officer's knowledge, the financial statements, and other financial information included in the report, fairly present in all material respects the financial condition and results of operations of the issuer as of, and for, the periods presented in the report;

(4) the signing officers

(A) are responsible for establishing and maintaining internal controls;

(B) have designed such internal controls to ensure that material information relating to the issuer and its consolidated subsidiaries is made known to such officers by others within those entities, particularly during the period in which the periodic reports are being prepared;

(C) have evaluated the effectiveness of the issuer's internal controls as of a date within 90 days prior to the report; and

(D) have presented in the report their conclusions about the effectiveness of their internal controls based on their evaluation as of that date;

(5) the signing officers have disclosed to the issuer's auditors and the audit committee of the board of directors (or persons fulfilling the equivalent function) —

(A) all significant deficiencies in the design or operation of internal controls which could adversely affect the issuer's ability to record, process, summarize, and report financial data and have identified for the issuer's auditors any material weaknesses in internal controls; and

(B) any fraud, whether or not material, that involves management or other employees who have a significant role in the issuer's internal controls; and

(6) the signing officers have indicated in the report whether or not there were significant changes in internal controls or in other factors that could significantly affect internal controls subsequent to the date of their evaluation, including any corrective actions with regard to significant deficiencies and material weaknesses.

(b) Foreign Reincorporations Have No Effect.—Nothing in this section 302 shall be interpreted or applied in any way to allow any issuer to lessen the legal force of the statement required under this section 302, by an issuer having reincorporated or having engaged in any other transaction that resulted in the transfer of the corporate domicile or offices of the issuer from inside the United States to outside the United States. . . .

Sec. 303. Improper Influence on Conduct of Audits

(a) Rules to Prohibit.—It shall be unlawful, in contravention of such rules or regulations as the Commission shall prescribe as necessary and appropriate in the public interest or for the protection of investors, for any officer or director of an issuer, or any other person acting under the direction thereof, to take any action to fraudulently influence, coerce, manipulate, or mislead any independent public or certified accountant engaged in the performance of an audit of the financial statements of that issuer for the purpose of rendering such financial statements materially misleading.

(b) Enforcement.—In any civil proceeding, the Commission shall have exclusive authority to enforce this section and any rule or regulation issued under this section.

(c) No Preemption of Other Law.—The provisions of subsection (a) shall be in addition to, and shall not supersede or preempt, any other provision of law or any rule or regulation issued thereunder. . . .

Sec. 304. Forfeiture of Certain Bonuses and Profits

(a) Additional Compensation Prior to Noncompliance with Commission Financial Reporting Requirements.—If an issuer is required to prepare an accounting restatement due to the material noncompliance of the issuer, as a result of misconduct, with any financial reporting requirement under the securities law, the chief executive officer and chief financial officer of the issuer shall reimburse the issuer for—

(1) any bonus or other incentive-based or equity-based compensation received by that person from the issuer during the 12-month period following the first public issuance or filing with the Commission (whichever first occurs) of the financial document embodying such financial reporting requirement; and

(2) any profits realized from the sale of securities of the issuer during that 12-month period.

(b) Commission Exemption Authority. The Commission may exempt any person from the application of subsection (a), as it deems necessary and appropriate.

Sec. 306. Insider Trades During Pension Fund Blackout Periods

(a) Prohibition of Insider Trading During Pension Fund Blackout Periods.—

(1) In general.—Except to the extent otherwise provided by rule of the Commission pursuant to paragraph (3), it shall be unlawful for any director or executive officer of an issuer of any equity security (other than an exempted security), directly or indirectly, to purchase, sell, or otherwise acquire or transfer any equity security of the issuer (other than an exempted security) during any

blackout period with respect to such equity security if such director or officer acquires such equity security in connection with his or her service or employment as a director or executive officer.

(2) Remedy. —

(A) In general.—Any profit realized by a director or executive officer referred to in paragraph (1) from any purchase, sale, or other acquisitions or transfer in violation of this subsection shall inure to and be recoverable by the issuer, irrespective of any intention on the part of such director or executive officer in entering into the transaction.

(B) Actions to recover profits.—An action to recover profits in accordance with this subsection may be instituted at law or in equity in any court of competent jurisdiction by the issuer, or by the owner of any security of the issuer in the name and in behalf of the issuer if the issuer fails or refuses to bring such action within 60 days after the date of request, or fails diligently to prosecute the action thereafter, except that no such suit shall be brought more than 2 years after the date on which such profit was realized.

(3) Rulemaking Authorized.—The Commission shall, in consultation with the Secretary of Labor, issue rules to clarify the application of this subsection and to prevent evasion thereof. Such rules shall provide for the application of the requirements of paragraph (1) with respect to entities treated as a single employer with respect to an issuer under section 414(b), (c), (m), or (o) of the Internal Revenue Code of 1986 to the extent necessary to clarify the application of such requirements and to prevent evasion thereof. Such rules may also provide for appropriate exceptions from the requirements of this subsection, including exceptions for purchases pursuant to an automatic dividend reinvestment program or purchases or sales made pursuant to an advance election.

(4) Blackout period.—For purposes of this subsection, the term "blackout period," with respect to the equity securities of any issuer—

(A) means any period of more than 3 consecutive business days during which the ability of not fewer than 50 percent of the participants or beneficiaries under all individual account plans maintained by the issuer to purchase, sell, or otherwise acquire or transfer an interest in any equity of such issuer held in such an individual account plan is temporarily suspended by the issuer or by a fiduciary of the plan; and

(B) does not include, under regulations which shall be prescribed by the Commission —

(i) a regularly scheduled period in which the participants and beneficiaries may not purchase, sell, or otherwise acquire or transfer an interest in any equity of such issuer; if such period is —

(I) incorporated into the individual account plan; and

(II) timely disclosed to employees before becoming participants under the individual account plan or as a subsequent amendment to the plan; or

(ii) any suspension described in subparagraph (A) that is imposed solely in connection with persons becoming participants or beneficiaries, or ceasing to be participants or beneficiaries, in an individual account plan by reason of a corporate merger, acquisition, divestiture, or similar transaction involving the plan or plan sponsor.

(5) Individual account plan.—For purposes of this subsection, the term "individual account plan" has the meaning provided in section 3(34) of the Employee Retirement Income Security Act of 1974 (29 U.S.C. 1002(34), except that such term shall not include a one-participant retirement plan (within the meaning of section 101(i)(8)(B) of such Act (29 U.S.C. 102(i)(8)(B))).

(6) Notice to directors, executive officers, and the commission.—In any case in which a director or executive officer is subject to the requirements of this subsection in connection with a blackout period (as defined in paragraph (4) with respect to any equity securities, the issuer of such equity securities shall timely notify such director or officer and the Securities and Exchange Commission of such blackout period.

Sec. 307. Rules of Professional Responsibility for Attorneys

Not later than 180 days after the date of enactment of this Act, the Commission shall issue rules, in the public interest and for the protection of investors, setting forth minimum standards of professional conduct for attorneys appearing and practicing before the Commission in any way in the representation of issuers, including a rule —

(1) requiring an attorney to report evidence of a material violation of securities law or breach of fiduciary duty or similar violation by the company or any agent thereof, to the chief legal counsel or the chief executive officer of the company (or the equivalent thereof); and

(2) if the counsel or officer does not appropriately respond to the evidence (adopting, as necessary, appropriate remedial measures or sanctions with respect to the violation), requiring the attorney to report the evidence to the audit committee of the board of directors of the issuer or to another committee of the board of directors comprised solely of directors not employed directly or indirectly by the issuer, or to the board of directors.

Sec. 308. Fair Funds for Investors

(a) Civil Penalties Added to Disgorgement Funds for the Relief of Victims.—If in any judicial or administrative action brought by the Commission under the securities laws (as such term is defined in section 3(a)(47) of the Securities Exchange Act of 1934) the Commission obtains an order requiring disgorgement against any person for a violation of such laws or the rules or regulations thereunder, or such person agrees in settlement of any such action to such disgorgement, and the Commission also obtains pursuant to such laws a civil penalty against such person, the amount of such civil penalty shall, on the motion or at the direction of the Commission, be added to and become part of the disgorgement fund to the benefit of the victims of such violation.

(b) Acceptance of Additional Donations.—The Commission is authorized to accept, hold, administer, and utilize gifts, bequests and devises of property, both real and personal, to the United States for a disgorgement fund described in subsection (a). . . .

Title IV — Enhanced Financial Disclosures

Sec. 401. Disclosure in Periodic Reports

(b) Commission Rules on Pro Forma Figures.—

Not later than 180-days after the date of enactment of the Sarbanes-Oxley Act for 2002, the Commission shall issue final rules providing that pro forma financial information included in any periodic or other report filed with the Commission pursuant to the securities laws, or in any public disclosure or press or other release, shall be presented in a matter that —

(1) does not contain an untrue statement of a material fact or omit to state a material fact necessary in order to make the pro forma financial information, in light of the circumstances under which it is presented, not misleading; and

(2) reconciles it with the financial condition and results of operations of the issuer under generally accepted accounting principles.

Sec. 404. Management Assessment of Internal Controls

(a) Rules Required.—The Commission shall prescribe rules requiring each annual report required by section 13(a) or 15(d) of the Securities Exchange Act of 1934 to contain an internal control report, which shall —

(1) state the responsibility of management for establishing and maintaining an adequate internal control structure and procedures for financial reporting; and

(2) contain an assessment, as of the end of the most recent fiscal year of the issuer, of the effectiveness of the internal control structure and procedures of the issuer for financial reporting.

(b) Internal Control Evaluation and Reporting.—With respect to the internal control assessment required by subsection (a), each registered public accounting firm that prepares or issues the audit report for the issuer other than an issuer that is an emerging growth company (as defined by section 3 of the Securities Exchange Act of 1934) shall attest to, and report on, the assessment made by the management of the issuer. An attestation made under this subsection shall be made in accordance with standards for attestation engagements issued or adopted by the Board. Any such attestation shall not be subject of a separate engagement.

(c) Exemption for Smaller Issuers.—Subsection (b) shall not apply with respect to any audit report prepared for an issuer that is neither a 'large accelerated filer' nor an 'accelerated filer' as those terms are defined in Rule 12b-2 of the Commission.

Sec. 406. Code of Ethics for Senior Financial Officers

(a) Code of Ethics Disclosure.—The Commission shall issue rules to require each issuer, together with periodic reports required pursuant to section 13(a) or

15(d) of the Securities Exchange Act of 1934, to disclose whether or not, and if not, the reason therefore, such issuer has adopted a code of ethics for senior financial officers, applicable to its principal financial officer and comptroller or principal accounting officer, or persons performing similar functions.

(b) Changes in Codes of Ethics.—The Commission shall revise its regulations concerning matters requiring prompt disclosure on Form 8-K (or any successor thereto) to require the immediate disclosure, by means of the filing of such form, dissemination by the Internet or by other electronic means, by any issuer of any change in or waiver of the code of ethics for senior financial officers.

(c) Definition.—In this section, the term "code of ethics" means such standards as are reasonably necessary to promote

(1) honest and ethical conduct, including the ethical handling of actual or apparent conflicts of interest between personal and professional relationships;

(2) full, fair, accurate, timely, and understandable disclosure in the periodic reports required to be filed by the issuer; and

(3) compliance with applicable governmental rules and regulations. . . .

Sec. 407. Disclosure of Audit Committee Financial Expert

(a) Rules defining "Financial Expert."—The Commission shall issue rules, as necessary or appropriate in the public interest and consistent with the protection of investors, to require each issuer, together with periodic reports required pursuant to sections 13(a) and 15(d) of the Securities Exchange Act of 1934, to disclose whether or not, and if not, the reasons therefor, the audit committee of that issuer is comprised of at least 1 member who is a financial expert, as such term is defined by the Commission.

(b) Considerations.—In defining the term "financial expert", for purposes of subsection (a), the Commission shall consider whether a person has, through education and experience as a public accountant or auditor or a principal financial officer, comptroller, or principal accounting officer of an issuer, or from a position involving the performance of similar functions

(1) an understanding of generally accepted accounting principles and financial statements;

(2) experience in

(A) the preparation of auditing of financial statements of generally comparable issuers; and

(B) the application of such principles in connection with the accounting for estimates, accruals, and reserves;

(3) experience with internal accounting controls; and

(4) an understanding of audit committee functions.

Sec. 408. Enhanced Review of Periodic Disclosures by Issuers . . .

(a) Regular and Systematic Review.—The Commission shall review disclosures made by issuers reporting under section 13(a) of the Securities Exchange Act of 1934 (including reports filed on Form 10-K), and which have a class of securities listed on a national securities exchange or traded on an automated quotation facility of a national securities association, on a regular and systematic basis for the protection of investors. Such review shall include a review of an issuer's financial statement.

Title VIII — Corporate and Criminal Fraud Accountability

Sec. 804. Statue of Limitations for Securities Fraud

(a) In general. Section 1658 of title 28, United States Code, is amended . . .

(2) by adding at the end the following:

(b) Notwithstanding subsection (a), a private right of action that involves a claim of fraud, deceit, manipulation, or contrivance in contravention of a regulatory requirement concerning the securities law, as defined in section 3(a)(47) of the Securities Exchange Act of 1934, may be brought not later than the earlier of—

(1) 2 years after the discovery of the facts constituting the violation; or

(2) 5 years after such violation.

Rules, Regulations, and Forms Under the Securities Exchange Act of 1934

17 C.F.R. §§240.10b-5 to 240.16b-7

REGULATION 13A: REPORTS OF ISSUERS OF SECURITIES REGISTERED PURSUANT TO SECTION 12

REGULATION 13D

REGULATION 14A: SOLICITATION OF PROXIES

REGULATION 14D

REGULATION 14E

REGULATION 15D: REPORTS OF REGISTRANTS UNDER THE SECURITIES ACT OF 1933

REPORTS OF DIRECTORS, OFFICERS, AND PRINCIPAL SHAREHOLDERS

16a-1.	Definition of Terms
16a-2.	Persons and Transactions Subject to Section 16
16a-3.	Reporting Transactions and Holdings
16a-4.	Derivative Securities
16a-8.	Trusts
16a-9.	Stock Splits, Stock Dividends, and Pro Rata Rights

EXEMPTION FROM CERTAIN TRANSACTIONS FROM SECTION 16(B)

16b-5.	Bona Fide Gifts and Inheritance
16b-6.	Derivative Securities
16b-7.	Mergers, Reclassifications, and Consolidations

Manipulative and Deceptive Devices and Contrivances

Rule 10b-5. Employment of Manipulative and Deceptive Devices

It shall be unlawful for any person, directly or indirectly, by the use of any means or instrumentality of interstate commerce, or of the mails or of any facility of any national securities exchange,

(a) To employ any device, scheme, or artifice to defraud,

(b) To make any untrue statement of a material fact or to omit to state a material fact necessary in order to make the statements made, in the light of the circumstances under which they were made, not misleading, or

(c) To engage in any act, practice, or course of business which operates or would operate as a fraud or deceit upon any person,

in connection with the purchase or sale of any security.

Rule 10b5-1. Trading "On the Basis Of" Material Nonpublic Information in Insider Trading Cases

Preliminary Note to Rule 10b5-1

(a) The "manipulative and deceptive device[s] or contrivance[s]" prohibited by Section 10(b) of the Act and Rule 10b-5 thereunder include, among other things, the purchase or sale of a security of any issuer, on the basis of material nonpublic information about that security or issuer, in breach of a duty of trust or confidence that is owed directly, indirectly, or derivatively to the issuer of that security or the shareholders of that issuer, or to any other person who is the source of the material nonpublic information.

(b) *Awareness of material nonpublic information.* Subject to the affirmative defenses in paragraph (c) of this section, a purchase or sale of a security of an issuer is on the basis of material nonpublic information when the person made the purchase or sale. The law of insider trading is otherwise defined by judicial opinions construing Rule 10b-5, and Rule 10b5-1 does not modify the scope of insider trading law in any other respect.

(c) *Affirmative defenses.*

(1)(i) Subject to paragraph (c)(l)(ii) of this section, a person's purchase or sale is not on the basis of material nonpublic information if the person making the purchase or sale demonstrates that:

(A) Before becoming aware of the information, the person had:

(1) entered into a binding contract to purchase or sell the security,

(2) instructed another person to purchase or sell the security for the instructing person's account, or

(3) adopted a written plan for trading securities;

(B) The contract, instruction, or plan described in paragraph (c)(1)(i)(A) of this section:

(1) Specified the amount of securities to be purchased or sold and the price at which and the date on which the securities were to be purchased or sold;

(2) Included a written formula or algorithm, or computer program, for determining the amount of securities to be purchased or sold and the price at which and the date on which the securities were to be purchased or sold; or

(3) Did not permit the person to exercise any subsequent influence over how, when, or whether to effect purchases or sales; provided, in addition, that any other person who, pursuant to the contract, instruction, or plan, did exercise such influence must not have been aware of the material nonpublic information when doing so; and

(C) The purchase or sale that occurred was pursuant to the contract, instruction, or plan. A purchase or sale is not "pursuant to a contract, instruction, or plan" if, among other things, the person who entered into the contract, instruction, or plan altered or deviated from the contract, instruction, or plan to purchase or sell securities (whether by changing the amount, price, or timing of the purchase or sale), or entered into or altered a corresponding or hedging transaction or position with respect to those securities.

(ii) Paragraph (c)(1)(i) of this section is applicable only when:

(A) The contract, instruction, or plan to purchase or sell securities was given or entered into in good faith and not as part of a plan or scheme to evade the prohibitions of this section and the person who entered into the contract, instruction, or plan has acted in good faith with respect to the contract, instruction or plan;.

(B) If the person who entered into the contract, instruction, or plan is:

(1) A director or officer (as defined in § 240.16a-1(f) (Rule 16a-1(f)) of the issuer, no purchases or sales occur until expiration of a cooling-off period consisting of the later of:

(i) Ninety days after the adoption of the contract, instruction, or plan or

(ii) Two business days following the disclosure of the issuer's financial results in a Form 10-Q (§ 249.308a of this chapter) or Form 10-K (§ 249.310 of this chapter) for the completed fiscal quarter in which the plan was adopted or, for foreign private issuers, in a Form 20-F (§ 249.220f of this chapter) or Form 6-K (§249.306 of this chapter) that discloses the issuer's financial results (but, in any event, this required cooling-off period is subject to a maximum of 120 days after adoption of the contract, instruction, or plan); or

(2) Not the issuer and not a director or officer (as defined in § 240.16a-1(f) (Rule 16a- 1(f)) of the issuer, no purchases or sales occur until the expiration of a cooling-off period that is 30 days after the adoption of the contract, instruction or plan;

(C) If the person who entered into a plan as described in paragraph (c)(1)(i)(A)(3) of this section is a director or officer (as defined in Rule 16a-1(f) (§240.16a-1(f)) of the issuer of the securities, such director or officer included a representation in the plan certifying that, on the date of adoption of the plan:

(1) The individual director or officer is not aware of any material nonpublic information about the security or issuer; and

(2) The individual director or officer is adopting the plan in good faith and not as part of a plan or scheme to evade the prohibitions of this section;

(D) The person (other than the issuer) who entered into the contract, instruction, or plan has no outstanding (and does not subsequently enter into any additional) contract, instruction, or plan that would qualify for the affirmative defense under paragraph (c)(1) of this section for purchases or sales of the issuer's securities on the open market; except that:

(1) For purposes of this paragraph (c)(1)(ii)(D), a series of separate contracts with different broker-dealers or other agents acting on behalf of the person (other than the issuer) to execute trades thereunder may be treated as a single "plan," provided that the individual constituent contracts with each broker-dealer or other agent, when taken together as a whole, meet all of the applicable conditions of and remain collectively subject to the provisions of this rule, including that a modification of any individual contract acts as modification of the whole contract, instruction of plan, as defined in paragraph (c)(1)(iv) of this section. The substitution of a broker-dealer or other agent acting on behalf of the person (other than the issuer) for another broker-dealer that is executing trades pursuant to a contract, instruction or plan shall not be a modification of the contract, instruction, or plan (as defined in paragraph (c)(1)(iv) of this section) as long as the purchase or sales instructions applicable to the substitute and substituted broker are identical with respect to the prices of securities to be purchased or sold, dates of the purchases or sales to be executed, and amount of securities to be purchased or sold; and

(2) The person (other than the issuer) may have one later-commencing contract, instruction, or plan for purchases or sales of any securities of the issuer on the open market under which trading is not authorized to begin until after all trades under the earlier-commencing contract, instruction, or plan are completed or expired without execution; provided, however, that if the first trade under the later-commencing contract, instruction, or plan is scheduled during the Effective Cooling-Off Period, the later-commencing contract, instruction, or plan may not

rely on this paragraph (c)(1)(ii)(D)(2). For purposes of this paragraph (c)(1)(ii)(D)(2), "Effective Cooling-Off Period" means the cooling-off period that would be applicable under paragraph (c)(1)(ii)(B) of this section with respect to the later-commencing contract, instruction, or plan if the date of adoption of the later-commencing contract, instruction, or plan were deemed to be the date of termination of the earlier-commencing contract, instruction, or plan; and

(3) A contract, instruction, or plan providing for an eligible sell-to-cover transaction shall not be considered an outstanding or additional contract, instruction, or plan under paragraph (c)(1)(ii)(D) of this section, and such eligible sell-to-cover transaction shall not be subject to the limitation under paragraph (c)(1)(ii)(D) of this section. A contract, instruction, or plan provides for an eligible sell-to-cover transaction where the contract, instruction, or plan authorizes an agent to sell only such securities as are necessary to satisfy tax withholding obligations arising exclusively from the vesting of a compensatory award, such as restricted stock or stock appreciation rights, and the insider does not otherwise exercise control over the timing of such sales; and

(E) With respect to persons (other than the issuer), if the contract, instruction, or plan does not provide for an eligible sell-to-cover transaction as described in paragraph (c)(1)(ii)(D)(3) of this section and is designed to effect the open-market purchase or sale of the total amount of securities as a single transaction, the person who entered into the contract, instruction, or plan has not during the prior 12-month period adopted a contract, instruction, or plan that:

(1) was designed to effect the open-market purchase or sale of all of the securities covered by such prior contract, instruction or plan, in a single transaction; and

(2) Would otherwise qualify for the affirmative defense under paragraph (c)(1) of this section. . . .

(iv) Any modification or change to the amount, price, or timing of the purchase or sale of the securities underlying a contract, instruction, or written plan as described in paragraph (c)(1)(i)(A) of this section is a termination of such contract, instruction, or written plan, and the adoption of a new contract, instruction, or written plan. A plan modification, such as the substitution or removal of a broker that is executing trades pursuant to a Rule 10b5-1 arrangement on behalf of the person, that changes the price or date on which purchases or sales are to be executed, is a termination of such plan and the adoption of a new plan.

Rule 10b5-2. Duties of Trust or Confidence in Misappropriation Insider Trading Cases

Preliminary Note to Rule 10b5-2

This section provides a non-exclusive definition of circumstances in which a person has a duty of trust or confidence for purposes of the "misappropriation" theory of insider trading under Section 10(b) of the Act and Rule 10b-5. The law of insider trading is otherwise defined by judicial opinions construing Rule 10b-5, and Rule 10b5-2 does not modify the scope of insider trading law in any other respect.

(a) *Scope of Rule.* This rule shall apply to any violation of Section 10(b) of the Act and Rule 10b-5 thereunder that is based on the purchase or sale of securities on the basis of, or the communication of, material nonpublic information misappropriated in breach of a duty of trust or confidence.

(b) *Enumerated "duties of trust or confidence."* For purposes of this rule, a "duty of trust or confidence" exists in the following circumstances, among others:

(1) Whenever a person agrees to maintain information in confidence;

(2) Whenever the person communicating the material nonpublic information and the person to whom it is communicated have a history, pattern, or practice of sharing confidences, such that the recipient of the information knows or reasonably should know that the person communicating the material nonpublic information expects that the recipient will maintain its confidentiality; or

(3) Whenever a person receives or obtains material nonpublic information from his or her spouse, parent, child, or sibling; *provided, however,* That the person receiving or obtaining the information may demonstrate that no duty of trust or confidence existed with respect to the information, by establishing that he or she neither knew nor reasonably should have known that the person who was the source of the information expected that the person would keep the information confidential, because of the parties' history, pattern, or practice of sharing and maintaining confidences, and because there was no agreement or understanding to maintain the confidentiality of the information.

Rule 10b-18. Purchases of Certain Equity Securities by the Issuer and Others

Preliminary Notes to Rule 10b-18

1. Rule 10b-18 provides an issuer (and its affiliated purchasers) with a "safe harbor" from liability for manipulation under section 9(a)(2) of the Act and Rule 10b-5 under the Act *solely* by reason of the manner, timing, price, and volume of their repurchases when they repurchase the issuer's common stock in the market in accordance with the section's manner, timing, price, and volume conditions. As a safe harbor, compliance with Rule 10b-18 is voluntary. To come within the safe harbor, however, an issuer's repurchases must satisfy (on a daily basis) each of the section's four conditions. Failure to meet any one of the four conditions will remove all of the issuer's repurchases from the safe harbor for that day. The safe harbor, moreover, is not available for repurchases that, although made in technical compliance with the section, are part of a plan or scheme to evade the federal securities laws.

2. Regardless of whether the repurchases are effected in accordance with Rule 10b-18, reporting issuers must report their repurchasing activity as required by Item 703 of Regulations S-K and S-B and Item 15(e) of Form 20-F (regarding foreign private issuers), and closed-end management investment companies that are registered under the Investment Company Act of 1940 must report their repurchasing activity as required by Item 8 of Form N-CSR.

(a) *Definitions.* Unless otherwise provided, all terms used in this section shall have the same meaning as in the Act. In addition, the following definitions shall apply:

(1) *ADTV* means the average daily trading volume reported for the security during the four calendar weeks preceding the week in which the Rule 10b-18 purchase is to be effected.

(2) *Affiliate* means any person that directly or indirectly controls, is controlled by, or is under common control with, the issuer.

(3) *Affiliated purchaser* means:

(i) A person acting, directly or indirectly, in concert with the issuer for the purpose of acquiring the issuer's securities; or

(ii) An affiliate who, directly or indirectly, controls the issuer's purchases of such securities, whose purchases are controlled by the issuer, or whose purchases are under common control with those of the issuer; *Provided, however,* that "affiliated purchaser" shall not include a broker, dealer, or other person solely by reason of such broker, dealer, or other person effecting Rule 10b-18 purchases on behalf of the issuer or for its account, and shall not include an officer or director of the issuer solely by reason of that officer or director's participation in the decision to authorize Rule 10b-18 purchases by or on behalf of the issuer.

(4) *Agent independent of the issuer* has the meaning contained in §242.100 of this chapter.

(5) *Block* means a quantity of stock that either:

(i) Has a purchase price of $200,000 or more; or

(ii) Is at least 5,000 shares and has a purchase price of at least $50,000; or

(iii) Is at least 20 round lots of the security and totals 150 percent or more of the trading volume for that security or, in the event that trading volume data are unavailable, is at least 20 round lots of the security and totals at least one-tenth of one percent (.001) of the outstanding shares of the security, exclusive of any shares owned by any affiliate; *Provided, however,* That a block under paragraph (a)(5)(i), (ii), and (iii) shall not include any amount a broker or dealer, acting as principal, has accumulated for the purpose of sale or resale to the issuer or to any affiliated purchaser of the issuer if the issuer or such affiliated purchaser knows or has reason to know that such amount was accumulated for such purpose, nor shall it include any amount that a broker or dealer has sold short to the issuer or to any affiliated purchaser of the issuer if the issuer or such affiliated purchaser knows or has reason to know that the sale was a short sale.

(6) *Consolidated system* means a consolidated transaction or quotation reporting system that collects and publicly disseminates on a current and continuous basis transaction or quotation information in common equity securities pursuant to an effective transaction reporting plan (as defined in Rule 11Aa3-1) or a national market system plan (as defined in Rule 11Aa3-2).

(7) *Market-wide trading suspension* means a market-wide trading halt of 30 minutes or more that is:

(i) Imposed pursuant to the rules of a national securities exchange or a national securities association in response to a market-wide decline during a single trading session; or

(ii) Declared by the Commission pursuant to its authority under section 12(k) of the Act.

(8) *Plan* has the meaning contained in §242.100 of this chapter.

(9) *Principal market* for a security means the single securities market with the largest reported trading volume for the security during the six full calendar months preceding the week in which the Rule 10b-18 purchase is to be effected.

(10) *Public float value* has the meaning contained in §242.100 of this chapter.

(11) *Purchase price* means the price paid per share as reported, exclusive of any commission paid to a broker acting as agent, or commission equivalent, mark-up, or differential paid to a dealer.

(12) *Riskless principal transaction* means a transaction in which a broker or dealer after having received an order from an issuer to buy its security, buys the security as principal in the market at the same price to satisfy the issuer's buy order. The issuer's buy order must be effected at the same price per-share at which the broker or dealer bought the shares to satisfy the issuer's buy order, exclusive of any explicitly disclosed markup or markdown, commission equivalent, or other fee. In addition, only the first leg of the transaction, when the broker or dealer buys the security in the market as principal, is reported under the rules of a self-regulatory organization or under the Act. For purposes of this section, the broker or dealer must have written policies and procedures in place to assure that, at a minimum, the issuer's buy order was received prior to the offsetting transaction; the offsetting transaction is allocated to a riskless principal account or the issuer's account within 60 seconds of the execution; and the broker or dealer has supervisory systems in place to produce records that enable the broker or dealer to accurately and readily reconstruct, in a time-sequenced manner, all orders effected on a riskless principal basis.

(13) *Rule 10b-18 purchase* means a purchase (or any bid or limit order that would effect such purchase) of an issuer's common stock (or an equivalent interest, including a unit of beneficial interest in a trust or limited partnership or a depository share) by or for the issuer or any affiliated purchaser (including riskless principal transactions). However, it does *not* include any purchase of such security:

(i) Effected during the applicable restricted period of a distribution that is subject to §242.102 of this chapter;

(ii) Effected by or for an issuer plan by an agent independent of the issuer;

(iii) Effected as a fractional share purchase (a fractional interest in a security) evidenced by a script certificate, order form, or similar document;

(iv) Effected during the period from the time of public announcement (as defined in Rule 165(f)) of a merger, acquisition, or similar transaction involving a recapitalization, until the earlier of the completion of such transaction or the completion of the vote by target shareholders. This exclusion does *not* apply to Rule 10b-18 purchases:

(A) Effected during such transaction in which the consideration is solely cash and there is no valuation period; or

(B) Where:

(*1*) The total volume of Rule 10b-18 purchases effected on any single day does not exceed the lesser of 25% of the security's four-week ADTV or the issuer's average daily Rule 10b-18 purchases during the three full calendar months preceding the date of the announcement of such transaction;

(*2*) The issuer's block purchases effected pursuant to paragraph (b)(4) of this section do not exceed the average size and frequency of the issuer's block purchases effected pursuant to paragraph (b)(4) of this section during the three full calendar months preceding the date of the announcement of such transaction; and

(*3*) Such purchases are not otherwise restricted or prohibited;

(v) Effected pursuant to Rule 13e-1;

(vi) Effected pursuant to a tender offer that is subject to Rule 13e-4 or specifically excepted from Rule 13e-4; or

(vii) Effected pursuant to a tender offer that is subject to section 14(d) of the Act and the rules and regulations thereunder.

(b) *Conditions to be met.* Rule 10b-18 purchases shall not be deemed to have violated the anti-manipulation provisions of sections 9(a)(2) or 10(b) of the Act, or Rule 10b-5 under the Act, solely by reason of the time, price, or amount of the Rule 10b-18 purchases, or the number of brokers or dealers used in connection with such purchases, if the issuer or affiliated purchaser of the issuer effects the Rule 10b-18 purchases according to each of the following conditions:

(1) *One broker or dealer.* Rule 10b-18 purchases must be effected from or through only one broker or dealer on any single day; *Provided, however,* that:

(i) The "one broker or dealer" condition shall not apply to Rule 10b-18 purchases that are not solicited by or on behalf of the issuer or its affiliated purchaser(s);

(ii) Where Rule 10b-18 purchases are effected by or on behalf of more than one affiliated purchaser of the issuer (or the issuer and one or more of its affiliated purchasers) on a single day, the issuer and all affiliated purchasers must use the same broker or dealer; and

(iii) Where Rule 10b-18 purchases are effected on behalf of the issuer by a broker-dealer that is not an electronic communication network (ECN) or other alternative trading system (ATS), that broker-dealer can access ECN or other ATS liquidity in order to execute repurchases on behalf of the issuer (or any affiliated purchaser of the issuer) on that day.

(2) *Time of purchases.* Rule 10b-18 purchases must not be:

(i) The opening (regular way) purchase reported in the consolidated system;

(ii) Effected during the 10 minutes before the scheduled close of the primary trading session in the principal market for the security, and the 10 minutes before the scheduled close of the primary trading session in the market where the purchase is effected, for a security that has an ADTV value of $1 million or more and a public float value of $150 million or more; and

(iii) Effected during the 30 minutes before the scheduled close of the primary trading session in the principal market for the security, and the

30 minutes before the scheduled close of the primary trading session in the market where the purchase is effected, for all other securities;

(iv) However, for purposes of this section, Rule 10b-18 purchases may be effected following the close of the primary trading session until the termination of the period in which last sale prices are reported in the consolidated system so long as such purchases are effected at prices that do not exceed the lower of the closing price of the primary trading session in the principal market for the security and any lower bids or sale prices subsequently reported in the consolidated system, and all of this section's conditions are met. However, for purposes of this section, the issuer may use one broker or dealer to effect Rule 10b-18 purchases during this period that may be different from the broker or dealer that it used during the primary trading session. However, the issuer's Rule 10b-18 purchase may not be the opening transaction of the session following the close of the primary trading session.

(3) *Price of purchases.* Rule 10b-18 purchases must be effected at a purchase price that:

(i) Does not exceed the highest independent bid or the last independent transaction price, whichever is higher, quoted or reported in the consolidated system at the time the Rule 10b-18 purchase is effected;

(ii) For securities for which bids and transaction prices are not quoted or reported in the consolidated system, Rule 10b-18 purchases must be effected at a purchase price that does not exceed the highest independent bid or the last independent transaction price, whichever is higher, displayed and disseminated on any national securities exchange or on any inter-dealer quotation system (as defined in §240.15c2-11) that displays at least two priced quotations for the security, at the time the Rule 10b-18 purchase is effected; and

(iii) For all other securities, Rule 10b-18 purchases must be effected at a price no higher than the highest independent bid obtained from three independent dealers.

(4) *Volume of purchases.* The total volume of Rule 10b-18 purchases effected by or for the issuer and any affiliated purchasers effected on any single day must not exceed 25 percent of the ADTV for that security; *However*, once each week, in lieu of purchasing under the 25 percent of ADTV limit for that day, the issuer or an affiliated purchaser of the issuer may effect one block purchase if:

(i) No other Rule 10b-18 purchases are effected that day, and

(ii) The block purchase is *not* included when calculating a security's four week ADTV under this section.

(c) *Alternative conditions.* The conditions of paragraph (b) of this section shall apply in connection with Rule 10b-18 purchases effected during a trading session following the imposition of a market-wide trading suspension, except:

(1) That the time of purchases condition in paragraph (b)(2) of this section shall not apply, either:

(i) From the reopening of trading until the scheduled close of trading on the day that the market-wide trading suspension is imposed; or

(ii) At the opening of trading on the next trading day until the scheduled close of trading that day, if a market-wide trading suspension was in effect at the close of trading on the preceding day; and

(2) The volume of purchases condition in paragraph (b)(4) of this section is modified so that the amount of Rule 10b-18 purchases must not exceed 100 percent of the ADTV for that security.

(d) *Other purchases.* No presumption shall arise that an issuer or an affiliated purchaser has violated the anti-manipulation provisions of sections 9(a)(2) or 10(b) of the Act, or Rule 10b-5 under the Act, if the Rule 10b-18 purchases of such issuer or affiliated purchaser do not meet the conditions specified in paragraph (b) or (c) of this section.

Audit Requirements

Rule 10A-3. Listing Standards Relating to Audit Committees

(a) Pursuant to section 10A(m) of the Act and section 3 of the Sarbanes-Oxley Act of 2002:

(1) *National securities exchanges.* The rules of each national securities exchange registered pursuant to section 6 of the Act must, in accordance with the provisions of this section, prohibit the initial or continued listing of any security of an issuer that is not in compliance with the requirements of any portion of paragraph (b) or (c) of this section.

(2) *National securities associations.* The rules of each national securities association registered pursuant to section 15A of the Act must, in accordance with the provisions of this section, prohibit the initial or continued listing in an automated inter-dealer quotation system of any security of an issuer that is not in compliance with the requirements of any portion of paragraph (b) or (c) of this section.

(3) *Opportunity to cure defects.* The rules required by paragraphs (a)(1) and (a)(2) of this section must provide for appropriate procedures for a listed issuer to have an opportunity to cure any defects that would be the basis for a prohibition under paragraph (a) of this section, before the imposition of such prohibition. Such rules also may provide that if a member of an audit committee ceases to be independent in accordance with the requirements of this section for reasons outside the member's reasonable control, that person, with notice by the issuer to the applicable national securities exchange or national securities association, may remain an audit committee member of the listed issuer until the earlier of the next annual shareholders meeting of the listed issuer or one year from the occurrence of the event that caused the member to be no longer independent.

(4) *Notification of noncompliance.* The rules required by paragraphs (a)(1) and (a)(2) of this section must include a requirement that a listed issuer must notify the applicable national securities exchange or national securities association promptly after an executive officer of the listed issuer becomes aware of any material noncompliance by the listed issuer with the requirements of this section. . . .

(b) *Required standards.*

(1) *Independence.*

(i) Each member of the audit committee must be a member of the board of directors of the listed issuer, and must otherwise be independent; provided that, where a listed issuer is one of two dual holding companies, those companies may designate one audit committee for both companies so long as each member of the audit committee is a member of the board of directors of at least one of such dual holding companies.

(ii) *Independence requirements for non-investment company issuers.* In order to be considered to be independent for purposes of this paragraph (b)(1), a member of an audit committee of a listed issuer that is not an investment company may not, other than in his or her capacity as a member of the audit committee, the board of directors, or any other board committee:

(A) Accept directly or indirectly any consulting, advisory, or other compensatory fee from the issuer or any subsidiary thereof, provided that, unless the rules of the national securities exchange or national securities association provide otherwise, compensatory fees do not include the receipt of fixed amounts of compensation under a retirement plan (including deferred compensation) for prior service with the listed issuer (provided that such compensation is not contingent in any way on continued service); or

(B) Be an affiliated person of the issuer or any subsidiary thereof.

(iii) *Independence requirements for investment company issuers.* . . .

(iv) *Exemptions from the independence requirements.*

(A) For an issuer listing securities pursuant to a registration statement under section 12 of the Act, or for an issuer that has a registration statement under the Securities Act of 1933 covering an initial public offering of securities to be listed by the issuer, where in each case the listed issuer was not, immediately prior to the effective date of such registration statement, required to file reports with the Commission pursuant to section 13(a) or 15(d) of the Act:

(*1*) All but one of the members of the listed issuer's audit committee may be exempt from the independence requirements of paragraph (b)(1)(ii) of this section for 90 days from the date of effectiveness of such registration statement; and

(*2*) A minority of the members of the listed issuer's audit committee may be exempt from the independence requirements of paragraph (b)(1)(ii) of this section for one year from the date of effectiveness of such registration statement.

(B) An audit committee member that sits on the board of directors of a listed issuer and an affiliate of the listed issuer is exempt from the requirements of paragraph (b)(1)(ii)(B) of this section if the member, except for being a director on each such board of directors, otherwise meets the independence requirements of paragraph (b)(1)(ii) of this section for each such entity, including the receipt of only ordinary-course compensation for serving as a member of the board of directors, audit committee or any other board committee of each such entity. . . .

(2) *Responsibilities relating to registered public accounting firms.* The audit committee of each listed issuer, in its capacity as a committee of the board of directors, must be directly responsible for the appointment, compensation, retention and oversight of the work of any registered public accounting firm engaged

(including resolution of disagreements between management and the auditor regarding financial reporting) for the purpose of preparing or issuing an audit report or performing other audit, review or attest services for the listed issuer, and each such registered public accounting firm must report directly to the audit committee.

(3) *Complaints.* Each audit committee must establish procedures for:

(i) The receipt, retention, and treatment of complaints received by the listed issuer regarding accounting, internal accounting controls, or auditing matters; and

(ii) The confidential, anonymous submission by employees of the listed issuer of concerns regarding questionable accounting or auditing matters.

(4) *Authority to engage advisers.* Each audit committee must have the authority to engage independent counsel and other advisers, as it determines necessary to carry out its duties.

(5) *Funding.* Each listed issuer must provide for appropriate funding, as determined by the audit committee, in its capacity as a committee of the board of directors, for payment of:

(i) Compensation to any registered public accounting firm engaged for the purpose of preparing or issuing an audit report or performing other audit, review or attest services for the listed issuer;

(ii) Compensation to any advisers employed by the audit committee under paragraph (b)(4) of this section; and

(iii) Ordinary administrative expenses of the audit committee that are necessary or appropriate in carrying out its duties.

(c) *General exemptions.*

(1) At any time when an issuer has a class of securities that is listed on a national securities exchange or national securities association subject to the requirements of this section, the listing of other classes of securities of the listed issuer on a national securities exchange or national securities association is not subject to the requirements of this section.

(2) At any time when an issuer has a class of common equity securities (or similar securities) that is listed on a national securities exchange or national securities association subject to the requirements of this section, the listing of classes of securities of a direct or indirect consolidated subsidiary or an at least 50% beneficially owned subsidiary of the issuer (except classes of equity securities, other than non-convertible, non-participating preferred securities, of such subsidiary) is not subject to the requirements of this section. . . .

(d) *Disclosure.* Any listed issuer availing itself of an exemption from the independence standards contained in paragraph (b)(1)(iv) of this section (except paragraph (b)(1)(iv)(B) of this section), the general exemption contained in paragraph (c)(3) of this section or the last sentence of paragraph (a)(3) of this section, must:

(1) Disclose its reliance on the exemption and its assessment of whether, and if so, how, such reliance would materially adversely affect the ability of the audit committee to act independently and to satisfy the other requirements of this section in any proxy or information statement for a meeting of shareholders

at which directors are elected that is filed with the Commission pursuant to the requirements of section 14 of the Act; and

(2) Disclose the information specified in paragraph (d)(1) of this section in, or incorporate such information by reference from such proxy or information statement filed with the Commission into, its annual report filed with the Commission pursuant to the requirements of section 13(a) or 15(d) of the Act.

(e) *Definitions.* Unless the context otherwise requires, all terms used in this section have the same meaning as in the Act. In addition, unless the context otherwise requires, the following definitions apply for purposes of this section:

(1)(i) The term *affiliate* of, or a person *affiliated* with, a specified person, means a person that directly, or indirectly through one or more intermediaries, controls, or is controlled by, or is under common control with, the person specified.

(ii) (A) A person will be deemed not to be in control of a specified person for purposes of this section if the person:

(*1*) Is not the beneficial owner, directly or indirectly, of more than 10% of any class of voting equity securities of the specified person; and

(*2*) Is not an executive officer of the specified person.

(B) Paragraph (e)(1)(ii)(A) of this section only creates a safe harbor position that a person does not control a specified person. The existence of the safe harbor does not create a presumption in any way that a person exceeding the ownership requirement in paragraph (e)(1)(ii)(A)(1) of this section controls or is otherwise an affiliate of a specified person.

(iii) The following will be deemed to be affiliates:

(A) An executive officer of an affiliate;

(B) A director who also is an employee of an affiliate;

(C) A general partner of an affiliate; and

(D) A managing member of an affiliate.

(iv) For purposes of paragraph (e)(1)(i) of this section, dual holding companies will not be deemed to be affiliates of or persons affiliated with each other by virtue of their dual holding company arrangements with each other, including where directors of one dual holding company are also directors of the other dual holding company, or where directors of one or both dual holding companies are also directors of the businesses jointly controlled, directly or indirectly, by the dual holding companies (and, in each case, receive only ordinary-course compensation for serving as a member of the board of directors, audit committee or any other board committee of the dual holding companies or any entity that is jointly controlled, directly or indirectly, by the dual holding companies).

(2) In the case of foreign private issuers with a two-tier board system, the term *board of directors* means the supervisory or non-management board.

(3) In the case of a listed issuer that is a limited partnership or limited liability company where such entity does not have a board of directors or equivalent body, the term *board of directors* means the board of directors of the managing general partner, managing member or equivalent body.

(4) The term *control* (including the terms *controlling, controlled by* and under *common control with*) means the possession, direct or indirect, of the power to

direct or cause the direction of the management and policies of a person, whether through the ownership of voting securities, by contract, or otherwise.

(5) The term *dual holding companies* means two foreign private issuers that:

(i) Are organized in different national jurisdictions;

(ii) Collectively own and supervise the management of one or more businesses which are conducted as a single economic enterprise; and

(iii) Do not conduct any business other than collectively owning and supervising such businesses and activities reasonably incidental thereto.

(6) The term *executive officer* has the meaning set forth in Rule 3b-7.

(7) The term *foreign private issuer* has the meaning set forth in Rule 3b-4(c).

(8) The term *indirect* acceptance by a member of an audit committee of any consulting, advisory or other compensatory fee includes acceptance of such a fee by a spouse, a minor child or stepchild or a child or stepchild sharing a home with the member or by an entity in which such member is a partner, member, an officer such as a managing director occupying a comparable position or executive officer, or occupies a similar position (except limited partners, non-managing members and those occupying similar positions who, in each case, have no active role in providing services to the entity) and which provides accounting, consulting, legal, investment banking or financial advisory services to the issuer or any subsidiary of the issuer.

(9) The terms *listed* and *listing* refer to securities listed on a national securities exchange or listed in an automated inter-dealer quotation system of a national securities association or to issuers of such securities.

Instructions Rule 10a-3

1. The requirements in paragraphs (b)(2) through (b)(5), (c)(3)(v) and (c)(3)(vi) of this section do not conflict with, and do not affect the application of, any requirement or ability under a listed issuer's governing law or documents or other home country legal or listing provisions that requires or permits shareholders to ultimately vote on, approve or ratify such requirements. The requirements instead relate to the assignment of responsibility as between the audit committee and management. In such an instance, however, if the listed issuer provides a recommendation or nomination regarding such responsibilities to shareholders, the audit committee of the listed issuer, or body performing similar functions, must be responsible for making the recommendation or nomination.
2. The requirements in paragraphs (b)(2) through (b)(5), (c)(3)(v), (c)(3)(vi) and Instruction 1 of this section do not conflict with any legal or listing requirement in a listed issuer's home jurisdiction that prohibits the full board of directors from delegating such responsibilities to the listed issuer's audit committee or limits the degree of such delegation. In that case, the audit committee, or body performing similar functions, must be granted such responsibilities, which can include advisory powers, with respect to such matters to the extent permitted by law, including submitting nominations or recommendations to the full board.
3. The requirements in paragraphs (b)(2) through (b)(5), (c)(3)(v) and (c)(3)(vi) of this section do not conflict with any legal or listing requirement in a listed issuer's home jurisdiction that vests such responsibilities with a government entity or tribunal. In that case, the audit committee, or body performing similar functions, must be granted such responsibilities, which can include advisory powers, with respect to such matters to the extent permitted by law.

4. For purposes of this section, the determination of a person's beneficial ownership must be made in accordance with Rule 13d-3.

Requirements Under Section 10C

Rule 10C-1. Listing Standards Relating to Compensation Committees

(a) Pursuant to section 10C(a) of the Act and section 952 of the Dodd-Frank Wall Street Reform and Consumer Protection Act of 2010 (Pub. L. 111-203, 124 Stat. 1900):

(1) *National securities exchanges.* The rules of each national securities exchange registered pursuant to section 6 of the Act, to the extent such national securities exchange lists equity securities, must, in accordance with the provisions of this section, prohibit the initial or continued listing of any equity security of an issuer that is not in compliance with the requirements of any portion of paragraph (b) or (c) of this section.

(2) *National securities associations.* The rules of each national securities association registered pursuant to section 15A of the Act, to the extent such national securities association lists equity securities in an automated inter-dealer quotation system, must, in accordance with the provisions of this section, prohibit the initial or continued listing in an automated inter-dealer quotation system of any equity security of an issuer that is not in compliance with the requirements of any portion of paragraph (b) or (c) of this section.

(3) *Opportunity to cure defects.* The rules required by paragraphs (a)(1) and (a)(2) of this section must provide for appropriate procedures for a listed issuer to have a reasonable opportunity to cure any defects that would be the basis for a prohibition under paragraph (a) of this section, before the imposition of such prohibition. Such rules may provide that if a member of a compensation committee ceases to be independent in accordance with the requirements of this section for reasons outside the member's reasonable control, that person, with notice by the issuer to the applicable national securities exchange or national securities association, may remain a compensation committee member of the listed issuer until the earlier of the next annual shareholders meeting of the listed issuer or one year from the occurrence of the event that caused the member to be no longer independent in accordance with the requirements of this section for reasons outside the member's reasonable control, that person, with notice by the issuer to the applicable national securities exchange or national securities association, may retain a compensation committee member of the listed issuer until the earlier of the next annual shareholders meeting of the listed issuer for one year from the occurrence of the event that caused the member to be no longer independent.

(4) *Implementation.* (i) Each national securities exchange and national securities association that lists equity securities must provide to the Commission, no later than 90 days after publication of this section in the Federal Register, proposed rules or rule amendments that comply with this section. Each submission must include, in addition to any other information required under section 19(b) of the Act and the rules thereunder, a review of whether and how existing or

proposed listing standards satisfy the requirements of this rule, a discussion of the consideration of factors relevant to compensation committee independence conducted by the national securities exchange or national securities association, and the definition of independence applicable to compensation committee members that the national securities exchange or national securities association proposes to adopt or retain in light of such review.

(ii) Each national securities exchange and national securities association that lists equity securities must have rules or rule amendments that comply with this section approved by the Commission no later than one year after publication of this section in the Federal Register.

(b) *Required standards.* The requirements of this section apply to the compensation committees of listed issuers.

(1) *Independence.*

(i) Each member of the compensation committee must be a member of the board of directors of the listed issuer, and must otherwise be independent.

(ii) *Independence requirements.* In determining independence requirements for members of compensation committees, the national securities exchanges and national securities associations shall consider relevant factors, including, but not limited to:

(A) The source of compensation of a member of the board of directors of an issuer, including any consulting, advisory or other compensatory fee paid by the issuer to such member of the board of directors; and

(B) Whether a member of the board of directors of an issuer is affiliated with the issuer, a subsidiary of the issuer or an affiliate of a subsidiary of the issuer.

(iii) *Exemptions from the independence requirements.*

(A) The listing of equity securities of the following categories of listed issuers is not subject to the requirements of paragraph (b)(1) of this section:

(1) Limited partnerships;

(2) Companies in bankruptcy proceedings;

(3) Open-end management investment companies registered under the Investment Company Act of 1940; and

(4) Any foreign private issuer that discloses in its annual report the reasons that the foreign private issuer does not have an independent compensation committee.

(B) In addition to the issuer exemptions set forth in paragraph (b)(1)(iii)(A) of this section, a national securities exchange or a national securities association, pursuant to section 19(b) of the Act and the rules thereunder, may exempt from the requirements of paragraph (b)(1) of this section a particular relationship with respect to members of the compensation committee, as each national securities exchange or national securities association determines is appropriate, taking into consideration the size of an issuer and any other relevant factors.

(2) *Authority to retain compensation consultants, independent legal counsel and other compensation advisers.*

(i) The compensation committee of a listed issuer, in its capacity as a committee of the board of directors, may, in its sole discretion, retain or obtain the advice of a compensation consultant, independent legal counsel or other adviser.

(ii) The compensation committee shall be directly responsible for the appointment, compensation and oversight of the work of any compensation consultant, independent legal counsel and other adviser retained by the compensation committee.

(iii) Nothing in this paragraph (b)(2) shall be construed:

(A) To require the compensation committee to implement or act consistently with the advice or recommendations of the compensation consultant, independent legal counsel or other adviser to the compensation committee; or

(B) To affect the ability or obligation of a compensation committee to exercise its own judgment in fulfillment of the duties of the compensation committee.

(3) *Funding.* Each listed issuer must provide for appropriate funding, as determined by the compensation committee, in its capacity as a committee of the board of directors, for payment of reasonable compensation to a compensation consultant, independent legal counsel or any other adviser retained by the compensation committee.

(4) *Independence of compensation consultants and other advisers.* The compensation committee of a listed issuer may select a compensation consultant, legal counsel or other adviser to the compensation committee only after taking into consideration the following factors, as well as any other factors identified by the relevant national securities exchange or national securities association in its listing standards:

(i) The provision of other services to the issuer by the person that employs the compensation consultant, legal counsel or other adviser;

(ii) The amount of fees received from the issuer by the person that employs the compensation consultant, legal counsel or other adviser, as a percentage of the total revenue of the person that employs the compensation consultant, legal counsel or other adviser;

(iii) The policies and procedures of the person that employs the compensation consultant, legal counsel or other adviser that are designed to prevent conflicts of interest;

(iv) Any business or personal relationship of the compensation consultant, legal counsel or other adviser with a member of the compensation committee;

(v) Any stock of the issuer owned by the compensation consultant, legal counsel or other adviser; and

(vi) Any business or personal relationship of the compensation consultant, legal counsel, other adviser or the person employing the adviser with an executive officer of the issuer.

Instruction to paragraph (b)(4) of this section: A listed issuer's compensation committee is required to conduct the independence assessment outlined in paragraph (b)(4) of this section with respect to any compensation consultant, legal counsel or other adviser that provides advice to the compensation committee, other than in-house legal counsel.

(5) *General exemptions.* (i) The national securities exchanges and national securities associations, pursuant to section 19(b) of the Act (15 U.S.C. 78s(b)) and the rules thereunder, may exempt from the requirements of this section certain categories of issuers, as the national securities exchange or national securities association determines is appropriate, taking into consideration, among other relevant factors, the potential impact of such requirements on smaller reporting issuers.

(ii) The requirements of this section shall not apply to any controlled company or to any smaller reporting company.

(iii) The listing of a security futures product cleared by a clearing agency that is registered pursuant to section 17A of the Act or that is exempt from the registration requirements of section 17A(b)(7)(A) is not subject to the requirements of this section.

(iv) The listing of a standardized option, as defined in Rule 9b-1(a)(4), issued by a clearing agency that is registered pursuant to section 17A of the Act is not subject to the requirements of this section.

(c) *Definitions.* Unless the context otherwise requires, all terms used in this section have the same meaning as in the Act and the rules and regulations thereunder. In addition, unless the context otherwise requires, the following definitions apply for purposes of this section:

(1) In the case of foreign private issuers with a two-tier board system, the term *board of directors* means the supervisory or non-management board.

(2) The term *compensation committee* means:

(i) A committee of the board of directors that is designated as the compensation committee; or

(ii) In the absence of a committee of the board of directors that is designated as the compensation committee, a committee of the board of directors performing functions typically performed by a compensation committee, including oversight of executive compensation, even if it is not designated as the compensation committee or also performs other functions; or

(iii) For purposes of this section other than paragraphs (b)(2)(i) and (b)(3), in the absence of a committee as described in paragraphs (c)(2)(i) or (ii) of this section, the members of the board of directors who oversee executive compensation matters on behalf of the board of directors.

(3) The term *controlled company* means an issuer:

(i) That is listed on a national securities exchange or by a national securities association; and

(ii) Of which more than 50 percent of the voting power for the election of directors is held by an individual, a group or another company.

(4) The terms *listed* and *listing* refer to equity securities listed on a national securities exchange or listed in an automated inter-dealer quotation system of a national securities association or to issuers of such securities.

(5) The term *open-end management investment company* means an open-end company, as defined by Section 5(a)(1) of the Investment Company Act of 1940 that is registered under that Act.

REQUIREMENTS UNDER SECTION 10D

Rule 10D-1. Listing Standards Relating to Recovery of Erroneously Awarded Compensation

(a) Each national securities exchange registered pursuant to section 6 of the Act (15 U.S.C. 78f) and each national securities association registered pursuant to section 15A of the Act (15 U.S.C. 78o-3), to the extent such national securities exchange or association lists securities, must:

(1) In accordance with the provisions of this section, prohibit the initial or continued listing of any security of an issuer that is not in compliance with the requirements of any portion of this section;

(2) . . . [P]ropose rules or rule amendments that comply with this section. Such rules or rule amendments that comply with this section must be effective no later than one year . . .

(3) Require that each listed issuer:

(i) Adopt the recovery policy required by this section no later than 60 days following the effective date of the listing standard referenced in paragraph (a)(2) of this section to which the issuer is subject;

(ii) Comply with that recovery policy for all incentive-based compensation received (as defined in paragraph (d) of this section) by executive officers on or after the effective date of the applicable listing standard;

(iii) Provide the disclosures required by this section and in the applicable Commission filings required on or after the effective date of the listing standard referenced in paragraph (a)(2) of this section to which the issuer is subject.

(b) *Recovery of Erroneously Awarded Compensation.* The issuer must:

(1) Adopt and comply with a written policy providing that the issuer will recover reasonably promptly the amount of erroneously awarded incentive-based compensation in the event that the issuer is required to prepare an accounting restatement due to the material noncompliance of the issuer with any financial reporting requirement under the securities laws, including any required accounting restatement to correct an error in previously issued financial statements that is material to the previously issued financial statements, or that would result in a material misstatement if the error were corrected in the current period or left uncorrected in the current period. . . .

(iv) The issuer must recover erroneously awarded compensation in compliance with its recovery policy except to the extent that the conditions of paragraphs (b)(1)(iv)(A), (B), or (C) of this section are met, and the issuer's committee of independent directors responsible for executive compensation decisions, or in the absence of such a committee, a majority of the independent directors serving on the board, has made a determination that recovery would be impracticable. . . .

(c) *General Exemptions.* [omitted]

(d) *Definitions.* [Omitted]

REGULATION 12B: REGISTRATION AND REPORTING

Rule 12b-2. Definitions . . .

* * *

Accelerated filer and large accelerated filer. (1) *Accelerated filer.* The term *accelerated filer* means an issuer after it first meets the following conditions as of the end of its fiscal year:

(i) The issuer had an aggregate worldwide market value of the voting and non-voting common equity held by its non-affiliates of $75 million or more, but less than $700 million, as of the last business day of the issuer's most recently completed second fiscal quarter;

(ii) The issuer has been subject to the requirements of section 13(a) or 15(d) of the Act for a period of at least twelve calendar months;

(iii) The issuer has filed at least one annual report pursuant to section 13(a) or 15(d) of the Act; and

(iv) The issuer is not eligible to use the requirements for smaller reporting companies under the revenue test in paragraph (2) or (3)(iii)(B) of the "smaller reporting company" definition in this section, as applicable.

(2) *Large accelerated filer.* The term *large accelerated filer* means an issuer after it first meets the following conditions as of the end of its fiscal year:

(i) The issuer had an aggregate worldwide market value of the voting and non-voting common equity held by its non-affiliates of $700 million or more, as of the last business day of the issuer's most recently completed second fiscal quarter;

(ii) The issuer has been subject to the requirements of section 13(a) or 15(d) of the Act for a period of at least twelve calendar months;

(iii) The issuer has filed at least one annual report pursuant to section 13(a) or 15(d) of the Act; and

(iv) The issuer is not eligible to use the requirements for smaller reporting companies under the revenue test in paragraph (2) or (3)(iii)(B) of the "smaller reporting company" definition in this section, as applicable.

(3) *Entering and exiting accelerated filer and large accelerated filer status.*

(i) The determination at the end of the issuer's fiscal year for whether a non-accelerated filer becomes an accelerated filer, or whether a non-accelerated filer or accelerated filer becomes a large accelerated filer, governs the deadlines for the annual report to be filed for that fiscal year, the quarterly and annual reports to be filed for the subsequent fiscal year and all annual and quarterly reports to be filed thereafter while the issuer remains an accelerated filer or large accelerated filer.

(ii) Once an issuer becomes an accelerated filer, it will remain an accelerated filer unless: the issuer determines, at the end of a fiscal year, that the aggregate worldwide market value of the voting and non-voting common equity held by its non-affiliates was less than $60 million, as of the last business day of the issuer's most recently completed second fiscal quarter; or it determines that it is eligible to use the requirements for smaller reporting companies under the revenue test in paragraph (2) or (3)(iii)(B) of the "smaller reporting company" definition in this section, as applicable. An issuer that makes either of these determinations becomes a non-accelerated filer. The issuer will not become an accelerated filer again unless it subsequently meets the conditions in paragraph (1) of this definition.

(iii) Once an issuer becomes a large accelerated filer, it will remain a large accelerated filer unless: it determines, at the end of a fiscal year, that the aggregate worldwide market value of the voting and non-voting common equity held by its non-affiliates ("aggregate worldwide market value") was less than $560 million, as of the last business day of the issuer's most recently completed second fiscal quarter or it determines that it is eligible to use the requirements for smaller reporting companies under the revenue test in paragraph (2) or (3)(iii)(B) of the "smaller reporting company" definition in this section, as applicable. If the issuer's aggregate worldwide market value was $60 million or more, but less than $560 million, as of the last business day of the issuer's most recently completed second fiscal quarter, and it is not eligible to use the requirements for smaller reporting companies under the revenue test in paragraph (2) or (3)(iii)(B) of the "smaller reporting company" definition in this section, as applicable, it becomes an accelerated filer. If the issuer's aggregate worldwide market value was less than $60 million, as of the last business day of the issuer's most recently completed second fiscal quarter, or it is eligible to use the requirements for smaller reporting companies under the revenue test in paragraph (2) or (3)(iii)(B) of the "smaller reporting company" definition in this section, it becomes a non-accelerated filer. An issuer will not become a large accelerated filer again unless it subsequently meets the conditions in paragraph (2) of this definition.

(iv) The determination at the end of the issuer's fiscal year for whether an accelerated filer becomes a non-accelerated filer, or a large accelerated filer becomes an accelerated filer or a non-accelerated filer, governs the deadlines for the annual report to be filed for that fiscal year, the quarterly and annual reports to be filed for the subsequent fiscal year and all annual and quarterly reports to be filed thereafter while the issuer remains an accelerated filer or non-accelerated filer.

(4) For purposes of paragraphs (1), (2), and (3) of this definition only, a business development company is considered to be eligible to use the requirements for smaller reporting companies under the revenue test in paragraph (2) or (3)(iii)(B) of the "smaller reporting company" definition in this section, provided that the business development company meets the requirements of the test using annual investment income under Rule 6-07.1 of Regulation S-X (17 CFR 210.6-07.1) as the measure of its "annual revenues" for purposes of the test.

NOTE TO PARAGRAPHS (1), (2) AND (3)

The aggregate worldwide market value of the issuer's outstanding voting and non-voting common equity shall be computed by use of the price at which the common equity was last sold, or the average of the bid and asked prices of such common equity, in the principal market for such common equity.

* * *

Emerging Growth Company.

(1) The term *emerging growth company* means an issuer that had total annual gross revenues of less than $1,235,000,000 during its most recently completed fiscal year.

(2) An issuer that is an emerging growth company as of the first day of that fiscal year shall continue to be deemed an emerging growth company until the earliest of:

(i) the last day of the fiscal year of the issuer during which it had total annual gross revenues of $1,235,000,000 or more;

(ii) the last day of the fiscal year of the issuer following the fifth anniversary of the date of the first sale of common equity securities of the issuer pursuant to an effective registration statement under the Securities Act of 1933;

(iii) the date on which such issuer has, during the previous three year period, issued more than $1,000,000,000 in non-convertible debt; or

(iv) the date on which such issuer is deemed to be a large accelerated filer, as defined in Rule 12b-2 or any successor thereto.

. . . .

Smaller reporting company: As used in this part, the term *smaller reporting company* means an issuer that is not an investment company, an asset-backed issuer (as defined in Item 1101 of Regulation S-K), or a majority-owned subsidiary of a parent that is not a smaller reporting company and that:

(1) Had a public float of less than $250 million; or

(2) Had annual revenues of less than $100 million and either:

(i) No public float; or

(ii) A public float of less than $700 million.

(3) Whether an issuer is a smaller reporting company is determined on an annual basis.

EXTENSIONS AND TEMPORARY EXEMPTIONS; DEFINITIONS

Rule 12g-1. Registration of Securities; Exemption from Section 12(g)

An issuer is not required to register a class of equity securities pursuant to section 12(g)(1) of the Act if on the last day of its most recent fiscal year:

(a) The issuer had total assets not exceeding $10 million; or

(b) (1) The class of equity securities was held of record by fewer than 2,000 persons and fewer than 500 of those persons were not accredited investors (as such term is defined in Rule 501 (§230.501(a) of this chapter), determined as of such day rather than at the time of the sale of the securities); or

(2) The class of equity securities was held of record by fewer than 2,000 persons in the case of a bank; a savings and loan holding company, as such term is defined in section 10 of the Home Owners' Loan Act (12 U.S.C. 1461); or a bank holding company, as such term is defined in section 2 of the Bank Holding Company Act of 1956 (12 U.S.C. 1841).

Rule 12g-4. Certifications of Termination of Registration under Section 12(g)

(a) Termination of registration of a class of securities under section 12(g) of the Act shall take effect 90 days, or such shorter period as the Commission may determine, after the issuer certifies to the Commission on Form 15 that the class of securities is held of record by:

(1) Fewer than 300 persons, or in the case of a bank; a savings and loan holding company, as such term is defined in section 10 of the Home Owners' Loan Act (12 U.S.C. 1461); or a bank holding company, as such term is defined in section 2 of the Bank Holding Company Act of 1956 (12 U.S.C. 1841), 1,200 persons; or

(2) Fewer than 500 persons, where the total assets of the issuer have not exceeded $10 million on the last day of each of the issuer's most recent three fiscal years.

(b) The issuer's duty to file any reports required under section 13(a) shall be suspended immediately upon filing a certification on Form 15; *Provided, however,* That if the certification on Form 15 is subsequently withdrawn or denied, the issuer shall within 60 days after the date of such withdrawal or denial, file with the Commission all reports which would have been required had the certification on Form 15 not been filed. If the suspension resulted from the issuer's merger into, or consolidation with, another issuer or issuers, the certification shall be filed by the successor issuer.

Rule 12g5-1. Definition of Securities "Held of Record"

(a) For the purpose of determining whether an issuer is subject to the provisions of sections 12(g) and 15(d) of the Act, securities shall be deemed to be "held of record" by each person who is identified as the owner of such securities on records of security holders maintained by or on behalf of the issuer, subject to the following:

(1) In any case where the records of security holders have not been maintained in accordance with accepted practice, any additional person who would be identified as such an owner on such records if they had been maintained in accordance with accepted practice shall be included as a holder of record.

(2) Except as specified in paragraph (a)(9) of this section, securities identified as held of record by a corporation, a partnership, a trust whether or not the

trustees are named, or other organization shall be included as so held by one person.

(3) Securities identified as held of record by one or more persons as trustees, executors, guardians, custodians or in other fiduciary capacities with respect to a single trust, estate or account shall be included as held of record by one person.

(4) Securities held by two or more persons as coowners shall be included as held by one person.

(5) Each outstanding unregistered or bearer certificate shall be included as held of record by a separate person, except to the extent that the issuer can establish that, if such securities were registered, they would be held of record, under the provisions of this rule, by a lesser number of persons.

(6) Securities registered in substantially similar names where the issuer has reason to believe because of the address or other indications that such names represent the same person, may be included as held of record by one person.

(7) Other than when determining compliance with Rule 257(d)(2) of Regulation A the definition of "held of record" shall not include securities issued in a Tier 2 offering pursuant to Regulation A by an issuer that:

(i) Is required to file reports pursuant to Rule 257(b) of Regulation A;

(ii) Is current in filing annual, semiannual and special financial reports pursuant to such rule as of its most recently completed fiscal year end;

(iii) Has engaged a transfer agent registered pursuant to Section 17A(c) of the Act to perform the function of a transfer agent with respect to such securities; and

(iv) Had a public float of less than $75 million as of the last business day of its most recently completed semiannual period, computed by multiplying the aggregate worldwide number of shares of its common equity securities held by non-affiliates by the price at which such securities were last sold (or the average bid and asked prices of such securities) in the principal market for such securities or, in the event the result of such public float calculation was zero, had annual revenues of less than $50 million as of its most recently completed fiscal year. An issuer that would be required to register a class of securities under Section 12(g) of the Act as a result of exceeding the applicable threshold in this paragraph (a)(7)(iv), may continue to exclude the relevant securities from the definition of "held of record" for a transition period ending on the penultimate day of the fiscal year two years after the date it became ineligible. The transition period terminates immediately upon the failure of an issuer to timely file any periodic report due pursuant to Rule 257 at which time the issuer must file a registration statement that registers that class of securities under the Act within 120 days.

(8) (i) For purposes of determining whether an issuer is required to register a class of equity securities with the Commission pursuant to section 12(g)(1) of the Act (15 U.S.C. 78*l*(g)(1)), an issuer may exclude securities:

(A) Held by persons who received the securities pursuant to an employee compensation plan in transactions exempt from, or not subject to, the registration requirements of section 5 of the Securities Act of 1933 (15 U.S.C. 77e); and

(B) Held by persons who received the securities in a transaction exempt from, or not subject to, the registration requirements of section 5 of the Securities Act (15 U.S.C. 77e) from the issuer, a predecessor of the issuer or an acquired company in substitution or exchange for excludable securities under paragraph (a)(8)(i)(A) of this section, as long as the persons were eligible to receive securities pursuant to §230.701(c) of this chapter at the time the excludable securities were originally issued to them.

(ii) As a non-exclusive safe harbor under this paragraph (a)(8):

(A) An issuer may deem a person to have received the securities pursuant to an employee compensation plan if such plan and the person who received the securities pursuant to the plan met the plan and participant conditions of §230.701(c) of this chapter; and

(B) An issuer may, solely for the purposes of Section 12(g) of the Act (15 U.S.C. 78*l*(g)(1)), deem the securities to have been issued in a transaction exempt from, or not subject to, the registration requirements of Section 5 of the Securities Act (15 U.S.C. 77e) if the issuer had a reasonable belief at the time of the issuance that the securities were issued in such a transaction.

(9) For purposes of determining whether a crowdfunding issuer, as defined in §270.3a-9(b)(1) of this chapter, or a crowdfunding vehicle, as defined in §270.3a-9(b)(2) of this chapter, is required to register a class of equity securities with the Commission pursuant to section 12(g)(1) of the Act, both the crowdfunding issuer and the crowdfunding vehicle:

(i) May exclude securities issued by a crowdfunding vehicle, as defined in §270.3a-9(b)(2) of this chapter, in an offering under §§227.100 through 227.504 (Regulation Crowdfunding) in which the crowdfunding vehicle and the crowdfunding issuer are deemed to be co-issuers under the Securities Act (15 U.S.C. 77a *et seq.*) and that are held by natural persons; and

(ii) Shall include securities issued by a crowdfunding vehicle, as defined in §270.3a-9(b)(2) of this chapter, in an offering under Regulation Crowdfunding in which the crowdfunding vehicle and the crowdfunding issuer are deemed to be co-issuers under the Securities Act and that are held by investors that are not natu-ral persons.

(b) Notwithstanding paragraph (a) of this section:

(1) Securities held, to the knowledge of the issuer, subject to a voting trust, deposit agreement or similar arrangement shall be included as held of record by the record holders of the voting trust certificates, certificates of deposit, receipts or similar evidences of interest in such securities: *Provided, however,* That the issuer may rely in good faith on such information as is received in response to its request from a non-affiliated issuer of the certificates or evidences of interest.

(2) Whole or fractional securities issued by a savings and loan association, building and loan association, cooperative bank, homestead association, or similar institution for the sole purpose of qualifying a borrower for membership in the issuer, and which are to be redeemed or repurchased by the issuer when the borrower's loan is terminated, shall not be included as held of record by any person.

(3) If the issuer knows or has reason to know that the form of holding securities of record is used primarily to circumvent the provisions of section 12(g) or

15(d) of the Act, the beneficial owners of such securities shall be deemed to be the record owners thereof.

Rule 12g-6. Exemption for Securities Issued Pursuant to Section 4(a)(6) of the Securities Act of 1933 or Regulation Crowdfunding.

(a) For purposes of determining whether an issuer is required to register a security with the Commission pursuant to Section 12(g)(1) of the Act, the definition of held of record shall not include securities issued pursuant to the offering exemption under section 4(a)(6) of the Securities Act or §§227.100 through 227.504 (Regulation Crowdfunding) by an issuer that:

(1) Is current in filing its ongoing annual reports required pursuant to §227.202 of this chapter;

(2) Has total assets not in excess of $25 million as of the end of its most recently completed fiscal year; and

(3) Has engaged a transfer agent registered pursuant to Section 17A(c) of the Act to perform the function of a transfer agent with respect to such securities.

(b) An issuer that would be required to register a class of securities under Section 12(g) of the Act as a result of exceeding the asset threshold in paragraph (2) may continue to exclude the relevant securities from the definition of "held of record" for a transition period ending on the penultimate day of the fiscal year two years after the date it became ineligible. The transition period terminates immediately upon the failure of an issuer to timely file any periodic report due pursuant to §227.202 at which time the issuer must file a registration statement that registers that class of securities under the Act within 120 days.

REGULATION 13A: REPORTS OF ISSUERS OF SECURITIES REGISTERED PURSUANT TO SECTION 12

Rule 13a-1. Requirements of Annual Reports

Every issuer having securities registered pursuant to section 12 of the Act shall file an annual report on the appropriate form authorized or prescribed therefor for each fiscal year after the last full fiscal year for which financial statements were filed in its registration statement. Registrants on Form 8-B shall file an annual report for each fiscal year beginning on or after the date as of which the succession occurred. Annual reports shall be filed within the period specified in the appropriate form.

Rule 13a-11. Current Reports on Form 8-K

(a) Except as provided in paragraph (b) of this section, every registrant subject to Rule 13a-1 shall file a current report on Form 8-K within the period specified in that form unless substantially the same information as that required by Form 8-K has been previously reported by the registrant. . . .

(c) No failure to file a report on Form 8-K that is required solely pursuant to Item 1.01, 1.02, 2.03, 2.04, 2.05, 2.06, 4.02(a), 5.02(e), or 6.03 of Form 8-K shall be deemed to be a violation of 15 U.S.C. 78j(b) and Rule 10b-5.

Rule 13a-13. Quarterly Reports on Form 10-Q

(a) Except as provided in paragraphs (b) and (c) of this section, every issuer that has securities registered pursuant to section 12 of the Act and is required to file annual reports pursuant to section 13 of the Act and has filed or intends to file such reports on Form 10-K, shall file a quarterly report on Form 10-Q within the period specified in General Instruction A.1. to that form for each of the first three quarters of each fiscal year of the issuer, commencing with the first fiscal quarter following the most recent fiscal year for which full financial statements were included in the registration statement, or, if the registration statement included financial statements for an interim period subsequent to the most recent fiscal year end meeting the requirements of Article 10 of Regulation S-X and Rule 8-03 of Regulation S-X for smaller reporting companies, for the first fiscal quarter subsequent to the quarter reported upon in the registration statement. . . .

Rule 13a-14. Certification of Disclosure in Annual and Quarterly Reports

(a) Each report, including transition reports, filed on Form 10-Q, Form 10-K, Form 20-F or Form 40-F under section 13(a) of the Act, other than a report filed by an Asset-Backed Issuer (as defined in Item 1101 of Regulation S-K)or a report or Form 20-F filed under Rule 13a-19, must include certifications in the form specified in the applicable exhibit filing requirement of such report and such certification must be filed as an exhibit to such report. Each principal executive and principal financial officer of the issuer, or persons performing similar functions, at the time of filing of the report must sign a certification. The principal executive and principal financial officer of an issuer may omit the portion of the introductory language in paragraph 4 as well as language in paragraph 4(b) of the certification that refers to the certifying officer's responsibility for designing, establishing, and maintaining internal controls over financial reporting for the issuer until the issuer becomes subject to the internal control over financial reporting requirements in Rules 13a-15 or 15d-15.

(b) Each periodic report containing financial statements filed by an issuer pursuant to section 13(a) of the Act must be accompanied by the certifications required by Section 1350 of Chapter 63 of Title 18 of the United States Code and such certifications must be furnished as an exhibit to such report as specified in the applicable exhibit requirements for such report. Each principal executive and principal financial officer of the issuer (or equivalent thereof) must sign a certification. This requirement may be satisfied by a single certification signed by an issuer's principal executive and principal financial officers.

(c) A person required to provide a certification specified in paragraph (a), (b) or (d) of this section may not have the certification signed on his or her behalf pursuant to a power of attorney or other form of confirming authority.

(d) Each annual report and transaction report filed by an Asset-Backed Issuer under section 13(a) of the Act must include a certification in the form specified in the applicable exhibit filing requirement of such report. . . .

Rule 13a-15. Controls and Procedures

(a) Every issuer that has a class of securities registered pursuant to section 12 of the Act, other than an Asset-Backed Issuer (as defined in Item 1101 of Regulation

S-K), a small business investment company registered on Form N-5, or a unit investment trust as defined by Section 4(2) of the Investment Company Act of 1940 (15 U.S.C. 80(2)), must maintain disclosure controls and procedures (as defined in paragraph(e) of this section) and, if the issuer either had been required to file an annual report pursuant to sections 13(a) or 15(d) of the Act for the prior fiscal year or had filed an annual report with the Commission for the prior fiscal year, internal control over financial reporting (as defined in paragraph(f) of this section).

(b) Each such issuer's management must evaluate, with the participation of the issuer's principal executive and principal financial officers, or persons performing similar functions, the effectiveness of the issuer's disclosure controls and procedures, as of the end of each fiscal quarter, except that management must perform this evaluation:

(1) In the case of a foreign private issuer (as defined in Rule 3b-4) as of the end of each fiscal year; and

(2) In the case of an investment company registered under section 8 of the Investment Company Act of 1940, within the 90-day period prior to the filing date of each report requiring certification under Rule 30a-2 of this chapter.

(c) The management of each such issuer that either had been required to file an annual report pursuant to section 13(a) or 15(d) of the Act for the prior fiscal year or previously had filed an annual report with the Commission for the prior fiscal year, other than an investment company registered under section 8 of the Investment Company Act of 1940, must evaluate, with the participation of the issuer's principal executive and principal financial officers, or persons performing similar functions, the effectiveness, as of the end of each fiscal year, of the issuer's internal control over financial reporting. The framework on which management's evaluation of the issuer's internal control over financial reporting is based must be a suitable, recognized control framework that is established by a body or group that has followed due-process procedures, including the broad distribution of the framework for public comment.

(d) The management of each such issuer that either had been required to file an annual report pursuant to section 13(a) or 15(d) of the Act for the prior fiscal year or previously had filed an annual report with the Commission for the prior fiscal year, other than an investment company registered under section 8 of the Investment Company Act of 1940, must evaluate, with the participation of the issuer's principal executive and principal financial officers, or persons performing similar functions, any change in the issuer's internal control over financial reporting, that occurred during each of the issuer's fiscal quarters, or fiscal year in the case of a foreign private issuer, that has materially affected, or is reasonably likely to materially affect, the issuer's internal control over financial reporting.

(e) For purposes of this section, the term *disclosure controls and procedures* means controls and other procedures of an issuer that are designed to ensure that information required to be disclosed by the issuer in the reports that it files or submits under the Act is recorded, processed, summarized and reported, within the time periods specified in the Commission's rules and forms. Disclosure controls and procedures include, without limitation, controls and procedures designed to ensure that information required to be disclosed by an issuer in the reports that it files or submits under the Act is accumulated and communicated to the issuer's management, including its principal executive and principal financial officers, or persons performing similar functions, as appropriate to allow timely decisions regarding required disclosure.

Rule 13a-20. Plain English Presentation of Specified Information

(a) Any information included or incorporated by reference in a report filed under section 13(a) of the Act that is required to be disclosed pursuant to Item 402, 403, 404, or 407 or Regulation S-K must be presented in a clear, concise and understandable manner. You must prepare the disclosure using the following standards:

(1) Present information in clear, concise sections, paragraphs and sentences;

(2) Use short sentences;

(3) Use definite, concrete, everyday words;

(4) Use the active voice;

(5) Avoid multiple negatives;

(6) Use descriptive headings and subheadings;

(7) Use a tabular presentation or bullet lists for complex material, wherever possible;

(8) Avoid legal jargon and highly technical business and other terminology;

(9) Avoid frequent reliance on glossaries or defined terms as the primary means of explaining information. Define terms in a glossary or other section of the document only if the meaning is unclear from the context. Use a glossary only if it facilitates understanding of the disclosure; and

(10) In designing the presentation of the information you may include pictures, logos, charts, graphs and other design elements so long as the design is not misleading and the required information is clear. You are encouraged to use schedules, charts, and graphic illustrations that present relevant data in an understandable manner, so long as such presentations are consistent with applicable disclosure requirements and consistent with other information in the document. You must draw graphs and charts to scale. Any information you provide must not be misleading.

(b) Reserved.

NOTE TO RULE 13A-20

In drafting the disclosure to comply with this section, you should avoid the following:

1. Legalistic or overly complex presentations that make the substance of the disclosure difficult to understand;

2. Vague "boilerplate" explanations that are imprecise and readily subject to different interpretations;

3. Complex information copied directly from legal documents without any clear and concise explanation of the provision(s); and

4. Disclosure repeated in different sections of the document that increases the size of the document but does not enhance the quality of the information.

Form 8-K: Current Report Pursuant to Section 13 or 15(d) of the Securities Exchange Act of 1934

GENERAL INSTRUCTIONS

A. Rule as to Use of Form 8-K

1. Form 8-K shall be used for current reports under Section 13 or 15(d) of the Securities Exchange Act of 1934, filed pursuant to Rule 13a-11 or Rule 15d-11.

2. Form 8-K may be used by a registrant to satisfy its filing obligations pursuant to Rule 425 under the Securities Act, regarding written communications related to business combination transactions, or Rules 14a-12(b) or Rule 14d-2(b) under the Exchange Act, relating to soliciting materials and pre-commencement communications pursuant to tender offers, respectively, provided that the Form 8-K filing satisfies all the substantive requirements of those rules (other than the Rule 425(c) requirement to include certain specified information in any prospectus filed pursuant to such rule). Such filing is also deemed to be filed pursuant to any rule for which the box is checked. A registrant is not required to check the box in connection with Rule 14a-12(b) or Rule 14d-2(b) if the communication is filed pursuant to Rule 425. Communications filed pursuant to Rule 425 are deemed filed under the other applicable sections. See Note 2 to Rule 425, Rule 14a-12(b) and Instruction 2 to Rule 14d-2(b)(2).

B. Events to Be Reported and Time for Filing of Reports

1. A report on this form is required to be filed or furnished, as applicable, upon the occurrence of any one or more of the events specified in the items in Sections 1–6 and 9 of this form. Unless otherwise specified, a report is to be filed or furnished within four business days after occurrence of the event. If the event occurs on a Saturday, Sunday or holiday on which the Commission is not open for business, then the four business day period shall begin to run on, and include, the first business day thereafter. A registrant either furnishing a report on this form under Item 7.01 (Regulation FD Disclosure) or electing to file a report on this form under Item 8.01 (Other Events) solely to satisfy its obligations under Regulation FD must furnish such report or make such filing, as applicable, in accordance with the requirements of Rule 100(a) of Regulation FD, including the deadline for furnishing or filing such report.

2. The information in a report furnished pursuant to Item 2.02 (Results of Operations and Financial Condition) or Item 7.01 (Regulation FD Disclosure) shall not be deemed to be "filed" for purposes of Section 18 of the Exchange Act or otherwise subject to the liabilities of that section, unless the registrant specifically states that the information is to be considered "filed" under the Exchange Act or incorporates it by reference into a filing under the Securities Act or the Exchange Act. If a report on Form 8-K contains disclosures under Item 2.02 or Item 7.01, whether or not the report contains disclosures regarding other items, all exhibits to such

report relating to Item 2.02 or Item 7.01 will be deemed furnished, and not filed, unless the registrant specifies, under Item 9.01 (Financial Statements and Exhibits), which exhibits, or portions of exhibits, are intended to be deemed filed rather than furnished pursuant to this instruction.

3. If the registrant previously has reported substantially the same information as required by this form, the registrant need not make an additional report of the information on this form. To the extent that an item calls for disclosure of developments concerning a previously reported event or transaction, any information required in the new report or amendment about the previously reported event or transaction may be provided by incorporation by reference to the previously filed report. The term *previously reported* is defined in Rule 12b-2.

4. Copies of agreements, amendments or other documents or instruments required to be filed pursuant to Form 8-K are not required to be filed or furnished as exhibits to the Form 8-K unless specifically required to be filed or furnished by the applicable Item. This instruction does not affect the requirement to otherwise file such agreements, amendments or other documents or instruments, including as exhibits to registration statements and periodic reports pursuant to the requirements of Item 601 of Regulation S-K.

5. When considering current reporting on this form, particularly of other events of material importance pursuant to Item 7.01 (Regulation FD Disclosure) and Item 8.01 (Other Events), registrants should have due regard for the accuracy, completeness and currency of the information in registration statements filed under the Securities Act which incorporate by reference information in reports filed pursuant to the Exchange Act, including reports on this form.

6. A registrant's report under Item 7.01 (Regulation FD Disclosure) or Item 8.01 (Other Events) will not be deemed an admission as to the materiality of any information in the report that is required to be disclosed solely by Regulation FD. . . .

INFORMATION TO BE INCLUDED IN THE REPORT

Section 1 - Registrant's Business and Operations

Item 1.01 Entry into a Material Definitive Agreement

(a) If the registrant has entered into a material definitive agreement not made in the ordinary course of business of the registrant, or into any amendment of such agreement that is material to the registrant, disclose the following information:

(1) the date on which the agreement was entered into or amended, the identity of the parties to the agreement or amendment and a brief description of any material relationship between the registrant or its affiliates and any of the parties, other than in respect of the material definitive agreement or amendment; and

(2) a brief description of the terms and conditions of the agreement or amendment that are material to the registrant.

(b) For purposes of this Item 1.01, a *material definitive agreement* means an agreement that provides for obligations that are material to and enforceable against the registrant, or rights that are material to the registrant and enforceable by the registrant against one or more other parties to the agreement, in each case whether or not subject to conditions.

Instructions. 1. Any material definitive agreement of the registrant not made in the ordinary course of the registrant's business must be disclosed under this Item 1.01. An agreement is deemed to be not made in the ordinary course of a registrant's business even if the agreement is such as ordinarily accompanies the kind of business conducted by the registrant if it involves the subject matter identified in Item 601(b)(10)(ii)(A)-(D) of Regulation S-K. An agreement involving the subject matter identified in Item 601(b)(10)(iii)(A) or (B) need not be disclosed under this item.

2. A registrant must provide disclosure under this Item 1.01 if the registrant succeeds as a party to the agreement or amendment to the agreement by assumption or assignment (other than in connection with a merger or acquisition or similar transaction). . . .

Item 1.02 Termination of a Material Definitive Agreement

(a) If a material definitive agreement which was not made in the ordinary course of business of the registrant and to which the registrant is a party is terminated otherwise than by expiration of the agreement on its stated termination date, or as a result of all parties completing their obligations under such agreement, and such termination of the agreement is material to the registrant, disclose the following information:

(1) the date of the termination of the material definitive agreement, the identity of the parties to the agreement and a brief description of any material relationship between the registrant or its affiliates and any of the parties other than in respect of the material definitive agreement;

(2) a brief description of the terms and conditions of the agreement that are material to the registrant;

(3) a brief description of the material circumstances surrounding the termination; and

(4) any material early termination penalties incurred by the registrant.

(b) For purposes of this Item 1.02, the term *material definitive agreement* shall have the same meaning as set forth in Item 1.01(b).

Instructions. 1. No disclosure is required solely by reason of this Item 1.02 during negotiations or discussions regarding termination of a material definitive agreement unless and until the agreement has been terminated.

2. No disclosure is required solely by reason of this Item 1.02 if the registrant believes in good faith that the material definitive agreement has not been terminated, unless the registrant has received a notice of termination pursuant to the terms of agreement. . . .

Item 1.03 Bankruptcy or Receivership

(a) If a receiver, fiscal agent or similar officer has been appointed for a registrant or its parent, in a proceeding under the Bankruptcy Act or in any other proceeding under state or federal law in which a court or governmental authority has assumed jurisdiction over substantially all of the assets or business of the registrant or its parent, or if such jurisdiction has been assumed by leaving the existing directors and officers in possession but subject to the supervision and orders of a court or governmental authority, disclose the following information:

(1) the name or other identification of the proceeding;

(2) the identity of the court or governmental authority;

(3) the date that jurisdiction was assumed; and

(4) the identity of the receiver, fiscal agent or similar officer and the date of his or her appointment.

(b) If an order confirming a plan of reorganization, arrangement or liquidation has been entered by a court or governmental authority having supervision or jurisdiction over substantially all of the assets or business of the registrant or its parent, disclose the following;

(1) the identity of the court or governmental authority;

(2) the date that the order confirming the plan was entered by the court or governmental authority;

(3) a summary of the material features of the plan and, pursuant to Item 9.01 (Financial Statements and Exhibits), a copy of the plan as confirmed;

(4) the number of shares or other units of the registrant or its parent issued and outstanding, the number reserved for future issuance in respect of claims and interests filed and allowed under the plan, and the aggregate total of such numbers; and

(5) information as to the assets and liabilities of the registrant or its parent as of the date that the order confirming the plan was entered, or a date as close thereto as practicable.

Item 1.04 Mine Safety – Reporting of Shutdowns and Patterns of Violations

(a) If the registrant or a subsidiary of the registrant has received, with respect to a coal or other mine of which the registrant or a subsidiary of the registrant is an operator

- an imminent danger order issued under section 107(a) of the Federal Mine Safety and Health Act of 1977 (30 U.S.C. 817(a));
- a written notice from the Mine Safety and Health Administration that the coal or other mine has a pattern of violations of mandatory health or safety standards that are of such nature as could have significantly and substantially contributed to the cause and effect of coal or other mine health or safety hazards under section 104(e) of such Act (30 U.S.C. 814(e)); or
- a written notice from the Mine Safety and Health Administration that the coal or other mine has the potential to have such a pattern,

disclose the following information:

(1) The date of receipt by the issuer or a subsidiary of such order or notice.

(2) The category of the order or notice.

(3) The name and location of the mine involved.

Section 2 - Financial Information

Item 2.01 Completion of Acquisition or Disposition of Assets

If the registrant or any of its subsidiaries consolidated has completed the acquisition or disposition of a significant amount of assets, otherwise than in the ordinary course of business, disclose the following information. . .:

Item 2.02 Results of Operations and Financial Condition

(a) If a registrant, or any person acting on its behalf, makes any public announcement or release (including any update of an earlier announcement or release) disclosing material non-public information regarding the registrant's results of operations or financial condition for a completed quarterly or annual fiscal period, the registrant shall disclose the date of the announcement or release, briefly identify the announcement or release and include the text of that announcement or release as an exhibit.

(b) A Form 8-K is not required to be furnished to the Commission under this Item 2.02 in the case of disclosure of material non-public information that is disclosed orally, telephonically, by webcast, by broadcast, or by similar means if:

(1) the information is provided as part of a presentation that is complementary to, and initially occurs within 48 hours after, a related, written announcement or release that has been furnished on Form 8-K pursuant to this Item 2.02 prior to the presentation;

(2) the presentation is broadly accessible to the public by dial-in conference call, by webcast, by broadcast or by similar means;

(3) the financial and other statistical information contained in the presentation is provided on the registrant's website, together with any information that would be required under 17 CFR 244.100; and

(4) the presentation was announced by a widely disseminated press release, that included instructions as to when and how to access the presentation and the location on the registrant's website where the information would be available.

Item 2.03 Creation of a Direct Financial Obligation or an Obligation Under an Off-Balance Sheet Arrangement of a Registrant

(a) If the registrant becomes obligated on a direct financial obligation that is material to the registrant, disclose the following information:

(1) the date on which the registrant becomes obligated on the direct financial obligation and a brief description of the transaction or agreement creating the obligation;

(2) the amount of the obligation, including the terms of its payment and, if applicable, a brief description of the material terms under which it may be accelerated or increased and the nature of any recourse provisions that would enable the registrant to recover from third parties; and

(3) a brief description of the other terms and conditions of the transaction or agreement that are material to the registrant.

(b) If the registrant becomes directly or contingently liable for an obligation that is material to the registrant arising out of an off-balance sheet arrangement, disclose the following information:

(1) the date on which the registrant becomes directly or contingently liable on the obligation and a brief description of the transaction or agreement creating the arrangement and obligation;

(2) a brief description of the nature and amount of the obligation of the registrant under the arrangement, including the material terms whereby it may become a direct obligation, if applicable, or may be accelerated or increased and the nature of any recourse provisions that would enable the registrant to recover from third parties;

(3) the maximum potential amount of future payments (undiscounted) that the registrant may be required to make, if different; and

(4) a brief description of the other terms and conditions of the obligation or arrangement that are material to the registrant.

(c) For purposes of this Item 2.03, *direct financial obligation* means any of the following:

(1) a long-term debt obligation, as defined in Item 303(a)(5)(ii)(A) of Regulation S-K;

(2) a capital lease obligation, as defined in Item 303(a)(5)(ii)(B) of Regulation S-K;

(3) an operating lease obligation, as defined in Item 303(a)(5)(ii)(C) of Regulation S-K; or

(4) a short-term debt obligation that arises other than in the ordinary course of business.

(d) For purposes of this Item 2.03, *off-balance sheet arrangement* means any transaction, agreement or other contractual arrangement to which an entity unconsolidated with the registrant is a party, under which the registrant has:

(1) Any obligation under a guarantee contract that has any of the characteristics identified in FASB ASC paragraph 460-10-15-4 (Guarantees Topic), as may be modified or supplemented, and that is not excluded from the initial recognition and measurement provisions of FASB ASC paragraphs 460-10-15-7, 460-10-25-1, and 460-10-30-1.

(2) A retained or contingent interest in assets transferred to an unconsolidated entity or similar arrangement that serves as credit, liquidity or market risk support to such entity for such assets;

(3) Any obligation, including a contingent obligation, under a contract that would be accounted for as a derivative instrument, except that it is both indexed to the registrant's own stock and classified in stockholders' equity in the registrant's statement of financial position, and therefore excluded from the scope of FASB ASC Topic 815, Derivatives and Hedging, pursuant to FASB ASC subparagraph 815-10-15-74(a), as may be modified or supplemented; or

(4) Any obligation, including a contingent obligation, arising out of a variable interest (as defined in the FASB ASC Master Glossary), as may be modified or supplemented) in an unconsolidated entity that is held by, and material to, the registrant, where such entity provides financing, liquidity, market risk or credit risk support to, or engages in leasing, hedging or research and development services with, the registrant.

(e) For purposes of this Item 2.03, *short-term debt obligation* means a payment obligation under a borrowing arrangement that is scheduled to mature within one year, or, for those registrants that use the operating cycle concept of working capital, within a registrant's operating cycle that is longer than one year, as discussed in FASB ASC paragraph 210-10-45-3 (Balance Sheet Topic).

Item 2.04 Triggering Events That Accelerate or Increase a Direct Financial Obligation or an Obligation Under an Off-Balance Sheet Arrangement

(a) If a triggering event causing the increase or acceleration of a direct financial obligation of the registrant occurs and the consequences of the event, taking into account those described in paragraph (a)(4) of this Item 2.04, are material to the registrant, disclose the following information:

(1) the date of the triggering event and a brief description of the agreement or transaction under which the direct financial obligation was created and is increased or accelerated;

(2) a brief description of the triggering event;

(3) the amount of the direct financial obligation, as increased if applicable, and the terms of payment or acceleration that apply; and

(4) any other material obligations of the registrant that may arise, increase, be accelerated or become direct financial obligations as a result of the triggering event or the increase or acceleration of the direct financial obligation.

(b) If a triggering event occurs causing an obligation of the registrant under an off-balance sheet arrangement to increase or be accelerated, or causing a contingent obligation of the registrant under an off-balance sheet arrangement to become a direct financial obligation of the registrant, and the consequences of the event, taking into account those described in paragraph (b)(4) of this Item 2.04, are material to the registrant, disclose the following information:

(1) the date of the triggering event and a brief description of the off-balance sheet arrangement;

(2) a brief description of the triggering event;

(3) the nature and amount of the obligation, as increased if applicable, and the terms of payment or acceleration that apply; and

(4) any other material obligations of the registrant that may arise, increase, be accelerated or become direct financial obligations as a result of the triggering event or the increase or acceleration of the obligation under the off-balance sheet arrangement or its becoming a direct financial obligation of the registrant.

(c) For purposes of this Item 2.04, the term *direct financial obligation* has the meaning provided in Item 2.03 of this form, but shall also include an obligation arising out of an off-balance sheet arrangement that is accrued under FASB ASC section 450-20-25 (Contingencies—Loss Contingencies—Recognition) as a probable loss contingency.

(d) For purposes of this Item 2.04, the term *off-balance sheet arrangement* has the meaning provided in Item 2.03 of this form.

(e) For purposes of this Item 2.04, a *triggering event* is an event, including an event of default, event of acceleration or similar event, as a result of which a direct financial obligation of the registrant or an obligation of the registrant arising under an off-balance sheet arrangement is increased or becomes accelerated or as a result of which a contingent obligation of the registrant arising out of an off-balance sheet arrangement becomes a direct financial obligation of the registrant.

Instructions. 1. Disclosure is required if a triggering event occurs in respect of an obligation of the registrant under an off-balance sheet arrangement and the consequences are material to the registrant, whether or not the registrant is also a party to the transaction or agreement under which the triggering event occurs.

2. No disclosure is required under this Item 2.04 unless and until a triggering event has occurred in accordance with the terms of the relevant agreement, transaction or arrangement, including, if required, the sending to the registrant of notice of the occurrence of a triggering event pursuant to the terms of the agreement, transaction or arrangement and the satisfaction of all conditions to such occurrence, except the passage of time.

3. No disclosure is required solely by reason of this Item 2.04 if the registrant believes in good faith that no triggering event has occurred, unless the registrant has received a notice described in Instruction 2 to this Item 2.04.

4. Where a registrant is subject to an obligation arising out of an off-balance sheet arrangement, whether or not disclosed pursuant to Item 2.03 of this form, if a triggering event occurs as a result of which under that obligation an accrual for a probable loss is required under FASB ASC section 450-20-25 the obligation arising out of the off-balance sheet arrangement becomes a direct financial obligation as defined in this Item 2.04. In that situation, if the consequences as determined under Item 2.04(b) are material to the registrant, disclosure is required under this Item 2.04. . . .

Item 2.05 Costs Associated with Exit or Disposal Activities

If the registrant's board of directors, a committee of the board of directors or the officer or officers of the registrant authorized to take such action if board action is not required, commits the registrant to an exit or disposal plan, or otherwise disposes of a long-lived asset or terminates employees under a plan of termination described in FASB ASC paragraph 420-10-25-4 (Exit or Disposal Cost Obligations Topic), under which material charges will be incurred under generally accepted accounting principles applicable to the registrant, disclose the following information:

(a) the date of the commitment to the course of action and a description of the course of action, including the facts and circumstances leading to the expected action and the expected completion date;

(b) for each major type of cost associated with the course of action (for example, one-time termination benefits, contract termination costs and other associated costs), an estimate of the total amount or range of amounts expected to be incurred in connection with the action;

(c) an estimate of the total amount or range of amounts expected to be incurred in connection with the action; and

(d) the registrant's estimate of the amount or range of amounts of the charge that will result in future cash expenditures,

provided, however, that if the registrant determines that at the time of filing it is unable in good faith to make a determination of an estimate required by paragraphs (b), (c) or (d) of this Item 2.05, no disclosure of such estimate shall be required; *provided further, however,* that in any such event, the registrant shall file an amended report on Form 8-K under this Item 2.05 within four business days after it makes a determination of such an estimate or range of estimates.

Item 2.06 Material Impairments

If the registrant's board of directors, a committee of the board of directors or the officer or officers of the registrant authorized to take such action if board action is not required, concludes that a material charge for impairment to one or more of its assets, including, without limitation, impairments of securities or goodwill, is required under generally accepted accounting principles applicable to the registrant, disclose the following information:

(a) the date of the conclusion that a material charge is required and a description of the impaired asset or assets and the facts and circumstances leading to the conclusion that the charge for impairment is required;

(b) the registrant's estimate of the amount or range of amounts of the impairment charge; and

(c) the registrant's estimate of the amount or range of amounts of the impairment charge that will result in future cash expenditures,

provided, however, that if the registrant determines that at the time of filing it is unable in good faith to make a determination of an estimate required by paragraphs (b) or (c) of this Item 2.06, no disclosure of such estimate shall be required; *provided further, however,* that in any such event, the registrant shall file an amended report on Form 8-K under this Item 2.06 within four business days after it makes a determination of such an estimate or range of estimates.

Section 3 - Securities and Trading Markets

Item 3.01 Notice of Delisting or Failure to Satisfy a Continued Listing Rule or Standard; Transfer of Listing

(a) If the registrant has received notice from the national securities exchange or national securities association (or a facility thereof) that maintains the principal listing for any class of the registrant's common equity (as defined in Exchange Act Rule 12b-2) that:

- the registrant or such class of the registrant's securities does not satisfy a rule or standard for continued listing on the exchange or association;
- the exchange has submitted an application under Exchange Act Rule 12d2-2 to the Commission to delist such class of the registrant's securities; or
- the association has taken all necessary steps under its rules to delist the security from its automated inter-dealer quotation system,

the registrant must disclose:

(i) the date that the registrant received the notice;

(ii) the rule or standard for continued listing on the national securities exchange or national securities association that the registrant fails, or has failed to, satisfy; and

(iii) any action or response that, at the time of filing, the registrant has determined to take in response to the notice.

(b) If the registrant has notified the national securities exchange or national securities association (or a facility thereof) that maintains the principal listing for any class of the registrant's common equity (as defined in Exchange Act Rule 12b-2) that the registrant is aware of any material noncompliance with a rule or standard for continued listing on the exchange or association, the registrant must disclose:

(i) the date that the registrant provided such notice to the exchange or association;

(ii) the rule or standard for continued listing on the exchange or association that the registrant fails, or has failed, to satisfy; and

(iii) any action or response that, at the time of filing, the registrant has determined to take regarding its noncompliance.

(c) If the national securities exchange or national securities association (or a facility thereof) that maintains the principal listing for any class of the registrant's common equity (as defined in Exchange Act Rule 12b-2), in lieu of suspending trading in or delisting such class of the registrant's securities, issues a public reprimand letter or similar communication indicating that the registrant has violated a rule or standard for continued listing on the exchange or association, the registrant must state the date, and summarize the contents of the letter or communication.

(d) If the registrant's board of directors, a committee of the board of directors or the officer or officers of the registrant authorized to take such action if board action is not required, has taken definitive action to cause the listing of a class of its common equity to be withdrawn from the national securities exchange, or terminated from the automated inter-dealer quotation system of a registered national securities association, where such exchange or association maintains the principal listing for such class of securities, including by reason of a transfer of the listing or quotation to another securities exchange or quotation system, describe the action taken and state the date of the action.

Item 3.02 Unregistered Sales of Equity Securities

(a) If the registrant sells equity securities in a transaction that is not registered under the Securities Act, furnish the information set forth in paragraphs (a) and (c) through (e) of Item 701 of Regulation S-K or for purposes of determining the required filing date for the Form 8-K under this Item 3.02(a), the registrant has no obligation to disclose information under this Item 3.02 until the registrant enters into an agreement enforceable against the registrant, whether or not subject to conditions, under which the equity securities are to be sold. If there is no such agreement, the registrant must provide the disclosure within four business days after the occurrence of the closing or settlement of the transaction or arrangement under which the equity securities are to be sold.

(b) No report need be filed under this Item 3.02 if the equity securities sold, in the aggregate since its last report filed under this Item 3.02 or its last periodic report, whichever is more recent, constitute less than 1% of the number of shares outstanding of the class of equity securities sold. In the case of smaller reporting company no report need be filed if the equity securities sold, in the aggregate since its last report filed under this Item 3.02 or its last periodic report, whichever is more recent, constitute less than 5% of the number of shares outstanding of the class of equity securities sold.

Item 3.03 Material Modification to Rights of Security Holders

(a) If the constituent instruments defining the rights of the holders of any class of registered securities of the registrant have been materially modified, disclose the date of the modification, the title of the class of securities involved and briefly describe the general effect of such modification upon the rights of holders of such securities.

(b) If the rights evidenced by any class of registered securities have been materially limited or qualified by the issuance or modification of any other class of securities by the registrant, briefly disclose the date of the issuance or modification, the general effect of the issuance or modification of such other class of securities upon the rights of the holders of the registered securities.

Section 4 - Matters Related to Accountants and Financial Statements

Item 4.01 Changes in Registrant's Certifying Accountant

(a) If an independent accountant who was previously engaged as the principal accountant to audit the registrant's financial statements, or an independent accountant upon whom the principal accountant expressed reliance in its report regarding a significant subsidiary, resigns (or indicates that it declines to stand for re-appointment after completion of the current audit) or is dismissed, disclose the information required by Item 304(a)(1) of Regulation S-K, including compliance with Item 304(a)(3) of Regulation S-K.

(b) If a new independent accountant has been engaged as either the principal accountant to audit the registrant's financial statements or as an independent accountant on whom the principal accountant is expected to express reliance in its report regarding a significant subsidiary, the registrant must disclose the information required by Item 304(a)(2) of Regulation S-K.

Instruction. The resignation or dismissal of an independent accountant, or its refusal to stand for re-appointment, is a reportable event separate from the engagement of a new independent accountant. On some occasions, two reports on Form 8-K are required for a single change in accountants, the first on the resignation (or refusal to stand for re-appointment) or dismissal of the former accountant and the second when the new accountant is engaged. Information required in the second Form 8-K in such situations need not be provided to the extent that it has been reported previously in the first Form 8-K.

Item 4.02 Non-Reliance on Previously Issued Financial Statements or a Related Audit Report or Completed Interim Review

(a) If the registrant's board of directors, a committee of the board of directors or the officer or officers of the registrant authorized to take such action if board action is not required, concludes that any previously issued financial statements, covering one or more years or interim periods for which the registrant is required to provide financial statements under Regulation S-X, should no longer be relied upon because of an error in such financial statements as addressed in FASB ASC Topic 250 Accounting Changes and Error Corrections, as may be modified, supplemented or succeeded, disclose the following information:

(1) the date of the conclusion regarding the non-reliance and an identification of the financial statements and years or periods covered that should no longer be relied upon;

(2) a brief description of the facts underlying the conclusion to the extent known to the registrant at the time of filing; and

(3) a statement of whether the audit committee, or the board of directors in the absence of an audit committee, or authorized officer or officers, discussed with the registrant's independent accountant the matters disclosed in the filing pursuant to this Item 4.02(a).

(b) If the registrant is advised by, or receives notice from, its independent accountant that disclosure should be made or action should be taken to prevent future reliance on a previously issued audit report or completed interim review related to previously issued financial statements, disclose the following information:

(1) the date on which the registrant was so advised or notified;

(2) identification of the financial statements that should no longer be relied upon;

(3) a brief description of the information provided by the accountant; and

(4) a statement of whether the audit committee, or the board of directors in the absence of an audit committee, or authorized officer or officers, discussed with the independent accountant the matters disclosed in the filing pursuant to this Item 4.02(b).

(c) If the registrant receives advisement or notice from its independent accountant requiring disclosure under paragraph (b) of this Item 4.02, the registrant must:

(1) provide the independent accountant with a copy of the disclosures it is making in response to this Item 4.02 that the independent accountant shall receive no later than the day that the disclosures are filed with the Commission;

(2) request the independent accountant to furnish to the registrant as promptly as possible a letter addressed to the Commission stating whether the independent accountant agrees with the statements made by the registrant in response to this Item 4.02 and, if not, stating the respects in which it does not agree; and

(3) amend the registrant's previously filed Form 8-K by filing the independent accountant's letter as an exhibit to the filed Form 8-K no later than two business days after the registrant's receipt of the letter.

Section 5 - Corporate Governance and Management

Item 5.01 Changes in Control of Registrant

(a) If, to the knowledge of the registrant's board of directors, a committee of the board of directors or authorized officer or officers of the registrant, a change in control of the registrant has occurred, furnish the following information:

(1) the identity of the person(s) who acquired such control;

(2) the date and a description of the transaction(s) which resulted in the change in control;

(3) the basis of the control, including the percentage of voting securities of the registrant now beneficially owned directly or indirectly by the person(s) who acquired control;

(4) the amount of the consideration used by such person(s);

(5) the source(s) of funds used by the person(s), *unless* all or any part of the consideration used is a loan made in the ordinary course of business by a bank as defined by section 3(a)(6) of the Act, in which case the identity of such bank may be omitted provided the person who acquired control:

(1) has made a request for confidentiality pursuant to section 13(d)(1)(B) of the Act; and

(2) states in the report that the identity of the bank has been so omitted and filed separately with the Commission.

(6) the identity of the person(s) from whom control was assumed

(7) any arrangements or understandings among members of both the former and new control groups and their associates with respect to election of directors or other matters and

(8) if the registrant was a shell company, other than a business combination related shell company, as those terms are defined in Rule 12b-2 under the Exchange Act, immediately before the change in control, the information that would be required if the registrant were filing a general form for registration of securities on Form 10, under the Exchange Act reflecting all classes of the registrant's securities subject to the reporting requirements of Section 13 or Section 15(d) of such Act upon consummation of the change of control, with such information reflecting the registrant and its securities upon consummation of the transaction. Notwithstanding General Instruction B.3. to Form 8-K, if any disclosure required by this Item 5.01(a)(8) is previously reported, as that term is defined in Rule 12b-2 under the Exchange Act, the registrant may identify the filing in which that disclosure is included instead of including that disclosure in this report.

(b) Furnish the information required by Item 403(c) of Regulation S-K, as applicable.

Item 5.02 Departure of Directors or Certain Officers; Election of Directors; Appointment of Certain Officers; Compensatory Arrangements of Certain Officers

(a)(1) If a director has resigned or refuses to stand for re-election to the board of directors since the date of the last annual meeting of shareholders because of a disagreement with the registrant, known to an executive officer of the registrant, as defined in 17 CFR 240.3b-7, on any matter relating to the registrant's operations, policies or practices, or if a director has been removed for cause from the board of directors, disclose the following information:

(i) the date of such resignation, refusal to stand for re-election or removal;

(ii) any positions held by the director on any committee of the board of directors at the time of the director's resignation, refusal to stand for re-election or removal; and

(iii) a brief description of the circumstances representing the disagreement that the registrant believes caused, in whole or in part, the director's resignation, refusal to stand for re-election or removal.

(2) If the director has furnished the registrant with any written correspondence concerning the circumstances surrounding his or her resignation, refusal or removal, the registrant shall file a copy of the document as an exhibit to the report on Form 8-K.

(3) The registrant also must:

(i) provide the director with a copy of the disclosures it is making in response to this Item 5.02 no later than the day the registrant file the disclosures with the Commission;

(ii) provide the director with the opportunity to furnish the registrant as promptly as possible with a letter addressed to the registrant stating whether he or she agrees with the statements made by the registrant in response to this Item 5.02 and, if not, stating the respects in which he or she does not agree; and

(iii) file any letter received by the registrant from the director with the Commission as an exhibit by an amendment to the previously filed Form 8-K within two business days after receipt by the registrant.

(b) If the registrant's principal executive officer, president, principal financial officer, principal accounting officer, principal operating officer or any person performing similar functions, or any named executive officer, retires, resigns or is terminated from that position, or if a director retires, resigns, is removed, or refuses to stand for re-election (except in circumstances described in paragraph (a) of this Item 5.02), disclose the fact that the event has occurred and the date of the event.

(c) If the registrant appoints a new principal executive officer, president, principal financial officer, principal accounting officer, principal operating officer, or person performing similar functions, disclose the following information with respect to the newly appointed officer:

(1) the name and position of the newly appointed officer and the date of the appointment;

(2) the information required by Items 401(b), (d), (e) and Item 404(a) of Regulation S-K, and

(3) a brief description of any material plan, contract or arrangement (whether or not written) to which a covered officer is a party or in which he or she participates that is entered into or material amendment in connection with the triggering event or any grant or award to any covered person or modification thereto under any such plan, contract or arrangement in connection with any such event.

Instruction to paragraph (c). If the registrant intends to make a public announcement of the appointment other than by means of a report on Form 8-K, the registrant may delay filing the Form 8-K containing the disclosures required by this Item 5.02(c) until the day on which the registrant otherwise makes public announcement of the appointment of such officer.

(d) If the registrant elects a new director, except by a vote of security holders at an annual meeting or special meeting convened for such purpose, disclose the following information:

(1) the name of the newly elected director and the date of election;

(2) a brief description of any arrangement or understanding between the new director and any other persons, naming such persons, pursuant to which such director was selected as a director;

(3) the committees of the board of directors to which the new director has been, or at the time of this disclosure is expected to be, named; and

(4) the information required by Item 404(a) of Regulation S-K.

(5) a brief description of any material plan, contract or arrangement (whether or not written) to which the director is a party or in which he or she participates that is entered into or material amendment in connection with the triggering event or any grant or award to any such covered person or modification thereto, under any such plan, contract or arrangement in connection with any such event.

(e) If the registrant enters into, adopts, or otherwise commences a material compensatory plan, contract or arrangement (whether or not written), as to which the registrant's principal executive officer, principal financial officer, or a named executive officer participates or is a party, or such compensatory plan, contract or arrangement is materially amended or modified, or a material grant or award under any such plan, contract or arrangement to any such person is made or materially modified, then the registrant shall provide a brief description of the terms and conditions of the plan, contract or arrangement and the amounts payable to the officer thereunder.

INSTRUCTIONS TO PARAGRAPH (e)

1. Disclosure under this Item 5.02(e) shall be required whether or not the specified event is in connection with events otherwise triggering disclosure pursuant to this Item 5.02.

2. Grants or awards (or modifications thereto) made pursuant to a plan, contract or arrangement (whether involving cash to equity), that are materially consistent with the previously disclosed terms of such plan, contract or arrangement, need not be disclosed under this Item 5.02(e), provided the registrant has previously disclosed such terms and the grant, award or modification is disclosed when Item 402 of Regulation S-K requires such disclosure.

(f)(1) If the salary or bonus of a named executive officer cannot be calculated as of the most recent practicable date and is omitted from the Summary Compensation Table as specified in Instruction 1 to Item 402(c)(2)(iii) and (iv) of Regulation S-K, disclose the appropriate information under this Item 5.02(f) when there is a payment, grant, award, decision or other occurrence as a result of which such amounts become calculable in whole or part. Disclosure under this Item 5.02(f) shall include a new total compensation figure for the named executive officer, using the new salary or bonus information to recalculate the information that was previously provided with respect to the named executive officer in the registrant's Summary Compensation Table for which the salary and bonus information was omitted in reliance on Instruction 1 to Item 402(c)(2)(iii) and (iv) or Regulation S-K.

(2) As specified in Instruction 6 to Item 402(u) of Regulation S-K, disclosure under this Item 5.02(f) with respect to the salary or bonus of a principal executive officer shall include pay ratio disclosure pursuant to Item 402(u) of Regulation S-K calculated using the new total compensation figure for the principal executive officer. Pay ratio disclosure is not required under this Item 5.02(f) until the omitted salary or bonus amounts for such principal executive officer become calculable in whole.

*****

INSTRUCTIONS TO ITEM 5.02. . . .

3. The registrant need not provide information with respect to plans, contracts, and arrangements to the extent they do not discriminate in scope, terms or operation, in favor of executive officers or directors of the registrant and that are available generally to all salaried employees.

4. For purposes of this Item, the term "named executive officer" shall refer to those executive officers for whom disclosure was required in the registrant's most recent filling with the Commission under the Securities Act or Exchange Act that required disclosure pursuant to Item 402(c) of Regulation S-K.

Item 5.03 Amendments to Articles of Incorporation or Bylaws; Change in Fiscal Year

(a) If a registrant with a class of equity securities registered under Section 12 of the Exchange Act amends its articles of incorporation or bylaws and a proposal for the amendment was not disclosed in a proxy statement or information statement filed by the registrant, disclose the following information:

(1) the effective date of the amendment; and

(2) a description of the provision adopted or changed by amendment and, if applicable, the previous provision.

(b) If the registrant determines to change the fiscal year from that used in its most recent filing with the Commission other than by means of:

(1) a submission to a vote of security holders through the solicitation of proxies or otherwise; or

(2) an amendment to its articles of incorporation or bylaws,

disclose the date of such determination, the date of the new fiscal year end and the form (for example, Form 10-K, Form 10-KSB, Form 10-Q or Form 10-QSB) on which the report covering the transition period will be filed.

Item 5.04 Temporary Suspension of Trading Under Registrant's Employee Benefit Plans

(a) No later than the fourth business day after which the registrant receives the notice required by section 101(i)(2)(E) of the Employment Retirement Income Security Act of 1974, or, if such notice is not received by the registrant, on the same date by which the registrant transmits a timely notice to an affected officer or director within the time period prescribed by Rule 104(b)(2)(i)(B) or 104(b)(2)(ii) of Regulation BTR, provide the information specified in Rule 104(b) and the date the registrant received the notice required by section 101(i)(2)(E) of the Employment Retirement Income Security Act of 1974, if applicable.

(b) On the same date by which the registrant transmits a timely updated notice to an affected officer or director, as required by the time period under Rule 104(b)(2)(iii) of Regulation BTR, provide the information specified in Rule 104(b)(3)(iii).

Item 5.05 Amendments to the Registrant's Code of Ethics, or Waiver of a Provision of the Code of Ethics

(a) Briefly describe the date and nature of any amendment to a provision of the registrant's code of ethics that applies to the registrant's principal executive officer, principal financial officer, principal accounting officer or controller or persons performing similar functions and that relates to any element of the code of ethics definition enumerated in Item 406(b) of Regulations S-K.

(b) If the registrant has granted a waiver, including an implicit waiver, from a provision of the code of ethics to an officer or person described in paragraph (a) of this Item 5.05, and the waiver relates to one or more of the elements of the code of ethics definition referred to in paragraph (a) of this Item 5.05, briefly describe the nature of the waiver, the name of the person to whom the waiver was granted, and the date of the waiver.

(c) The registrant does not need to provide any information pursuant to this Item 5.05 if it discloses the required information on its Internet website within four business days following the date of the amendment or waiver and the registrant has disclosed in its most recently filed annual report its Internet address and intention to provide disclosure in this manner. If the registrant elects to disclose the information required by this Item 5.05 through its website, such information must remain available on the website for at least a 12-month period. Following the 12-month period, the registrant must retain the information for a period of not less than five years. Upon request, the registrant must furnish to the Commission or its staff a copy of any or all information retained pursuant to this requirement.

INSTRUCTIONS

1. The registrant does not need to disclose technical, administrative or other non-substantive amendments to its code of ethics.

2. For purposes of this Item 5.05:

(i) The term *waiver* means the approval by the registrant of a material departure from a provision of the code of ethics; and

(ii) The term *implicit waiver* means the registrant's failure to take action within a reasonable period of time regarding a material departure from a provision of the code of ethics that has been made known to an executive officer, as defined in Rule 3b-7 of the registrant.

Item 5.06 Change in Shell Company Status

If a registrant that was a shell company, other than a business combination related shell company, as those terms are defined in Rule 12b-2 under the Exchange Act, has completed a transaction that has the effect of causing it to cease being a shell company, as defined in Rule 12b-2, disclose the material terms of the transaction. Notwithstanding General Instruction B.3. to Form 8-K, if any disclosure required by this Item 5.06 is previously reported, as that term is defined in Rule 12b-2 under the Exchange Act, the registrant may identify the filing in which that disclosure is included instead of including that disclosure in this report.

Item 5.07 Submission of Matters to a Vote of Security Holders

If any matter was submitted to a vote of security holders, through the solicitation of proxies or otherwise, provide the following information:

(a) The date of the meeting and whether it was an annual or special meeting. This information must be provided only if a meeting of security holders was held.

(b) If the meeting involved the election of directors, the name of each director elected at the meeting, as well as a brief description of each other matter voted upon at the meeting; and state the number of votes cast for, against or withheld, as well as the number of abstentions and broker non-votes as to each such matter, including a separate tabulation with respect to each nominee for office. For the vote on the frequency of shareholder advisory votes on executive compensation required by section 14A(a)(2) of the Securities Exchange Act of 1934 and Rule 14a-21(b), state the number of votes cast for each of 1 year, 2 years, and 3 years, as well as the number of abstentions.

(c) A description of the terms of any settlement between the registrant and any other participant (as defined in Instruction 3 to Item 4 of Schedule 14A) terminating any solicitation subject to Rule 14a-12(c), including the cost or anticipated cost to the registrant.

Instruction 1 to Item 5.07. The four business day period for reporting the event under this Item 5.07 shall begin to run on the day on which the meeting ended. The registrant shall disclose on Form 8-K under this Item 5.07 the preliminary voting results. The registrant shall file an amended report on Form 8-K under this Item 5.07 to disclose the final voting results within four business days after the final voting results are known. However, no preliminary voting results need be disclosed under this Item 5.07 if the registrant has disclosed final voting results on Form 8-K under this Item.

Instruction 2 to Item 5.07. If any matter has been submitted to a vote of security holders otherwise than at a meeting of such security holders, corresponding information with respect to such submission shall be provided. The solicitation of any authorization or consent (other than a proxy to vote at a stockholders' meeting) with respect to any matter shall be deemed a submission of such matter to a vote of security holders within the meaning of this item.

Instruction 3 to Item 5.07. If the registrant did not solicit proxies and the board of directors as previously reported to the Commission was re-elected in its entirety, a statement to that effect in answer to paragraph (b) will suffice as an answer there to regarding the election of directors.

Instruction 4 to Item 5.07. If the registrant has furnished to its security holders proxy soliciting material containing the information called for by paragraph (c), the paragraph may be answered by reference to the information contained in such material.

Instruction 5 to Item 5.07. A registrant may omit the information called for by this Item 5.07 if, on the date of the filing of its report on Form 8-K, the registrant meets the following conditions:

1. All of the registrant's equity securities are owned, either directly or indirectly, by a single person which is a reporting company under the Exchange Act and which has filed all the material required to be filed pursuant to Section 13, 14 or 15(d) thereof, as applicable; and

2. During the preceding thirty-six calendar months and any subsequent period of days, there has not been any material default in the payment of principal, interest, a sinking or purchase fund installment, or any other material default not cured within thirty days, with respect to any indebtedness of the registrant or its subsidiaries, and there has not been any material default in the payment of rentals under material long-term leases.

Section 6 - Asset-Backed Securities [omitted]

Section 7 - Regulation FD

Item 7.01 Regulation FD Disclosure

Unless filed under Item 8.01, disclose under this item only information that the registrant elects to disclose through Form 8-K pursuant to Regulation FD.

Section 8 - Other Events

Item 8.01 Other Events

The registrant may, at its option, disclose under this Item 8.01 any events, with respect to which information is not otherwise called for by this form, that the registrant deems of importance to security holders. The registrant may, at its option, file a report under this Item 8.01 disclosing the nonpublic information required to be disclosed by Regulation FD.

Section 9 - Financial Statements and Exhibits

Item 9.01 Financial Statements and Exhibits

List below the financial statements, pro forma financial information and exhibits, if any, filed as a part of this report.

(a) *Financial statements of businesses acquired. . . .*

(b) *Pro forma financial information. . . .*

Form 10-Q: Quarterly Report Pursuant to Section 13 or 15(d) of the Securities Exchange Act of 1934

GENERAL INSTRUCTIONS

A. *Rule as to Use of Form 10-Q*

1. Form 10-Q shall be used for quarterly reports under Section 13 or 15(d) of the Securities Exchange Act of 1934, filed pursuant to Rule 13a-13 or Rule 15d-13. A quarterly report on this form pursuant to Rule 13a-13 or Rule 15d-13 shall be filed within the following period after the end of each of the first three fiscal quarters of each fiscal year, but no report need be filed for the fourth quarter of any fiscal year:

a. 40 days after the end of the fiscal quarter for large accelerated filers and accelerated filers (as defined in Rule 12b-2);

b. 45 days after the end of the fiscal quarter for all other registrants. . . .

D. *Incorporation by Reference*

1. If the registrant makes available to its stockholders or otherwise publishes, within the period prescribed for filing the report, a document or statement containing information meeting some or all of the requirements of Part I of this form, the information called for may be incorporated by reference from such published document or statement, in answer or partial answer to any item or items of Part I of this form, provided copies thereof are filed as an exhibit to Part I of the report on this form.

2. Other information may be incorporated by reference in answer or partial answer to any item or items of Part II of this form in accordance with the provisions of Rule 12b-23.

3. If any information required by Part I or Part II is incorporated by reference into an electronic format document from the quarterly report to security holders as provided in General Instruction D, any portion of the quarterly report to security holders incorporated by reference shall be filed as an exhibit in electronic format, as required by Item 601(b)(13) of Regulation S-K.

E. *Integrated Reports to Security Holders*

Quarterly reports to security holders may be combined with the required information of Form 10-Q and will be suitable for filing with the Commission if the following conditions are satisfied:

1. The combined report contains full and complete answers to all items required by Part I of this form. When responses to a certain item of required disclosure are separated within the combined report, an appropriate cross-reference should be made.
2. If not included in the combined report, the cover page, appropriate responses to Part II, and the required signatures shall be included in the

Form 10-Q. Additionally, as appropriate, a cross-reference sheet should be filed indicating the location of information required by the items of the form.

3. If an electronic filer files any portion of a quarterly report to security holders in combination with the required information of Form 10-Q, as provided in this instruction, only such portions filed in satisfaction of the Form 10-Q requirements shall be filed in electronic format.

F. Filed Status of Information Presented

1. Pursuant to Rule 13a-13(d) and Rule 15d-13(d), the information presented in satisfaction of the requirements of Items 1 and 2 of Part I of this form, whether included directly in a report on this form, incorporated therein by reference from a report, document or statement filed as an exhibit to Part I of this form pursuant to Instruction D(1) above, included in an integrated report pursuant to Instruction E above, or contained in a statement regarding computation of per share earnings or a letter regarding a change in accounting principles filed as an exhibit to Part I pursuant to Item 601 of Regulation S-K, except as provided by Instruction F(2) below, shall not be deemed filed for the purpose of Section 18 of the Act or otherwise subject to the liabilities of that section of the Act but shall be subject to the other provisions of the Act.

2. Information presented in satisfaction of the requirements of this form other than those of Items 1 and 2 of Part I shall be deemed filed for the purpose of Section 18 of the Act; except that, where information presented in response to Item 1 or 2 of Part I (or as an exhibit thereto) is also used to satisfy Part II requirements through incorporation by reference, only that portion of Part I (or exhibit thereto) consisting of the information required by Part II shall be deemed so filed. . . .

Part I—Financial Information

Item 1. Financial Statements

Provide the information required by Rule 10-01 of Regulation S-X. A smaller reporting company defined in Rule 12b-2 may provide the information required by Article 8-03 of Regulation S-X.

Item 2. Management's Discussion and Analysis of Financial Condition and Results of Operations

Furnish the information required by Item 303 of Regulation S-K. . . .

Item 4. Controls and Procedures

Furnish the information required by Item 307 of Regulation S-K and Item 308(c) of Regulation S-K.

Part II—Other Information

Item 1. Legal Proceedings

Furnish the information required by Item 103 of Regulation S-K. As to such proceedings which have been terminated during the period covered by the report, provide similar information, including the date of termination and a description of the disposition thereof with respect to the registrant and its subsidiaries.

Instruction. A legal proceeding need only be reported in the 10-Q filed for the quarter in which it first became a reportable event and in subsequent quarters in which there have been material developments. Subsequent Form 10-Q filings in the same fiscal year in which a legal proceeding or a material development is reported should reference any previous reports in that year.

Item 1A. Risk Factors

Set forth any material changes from risk factors as previously disclosed in the registrant's Form 10-K in reponse to Item 1A to Part I of Form 10-K. Smaller reporting companies are not required to provide the information required by this item.

Item 2. Unregistered Sales of Equity Securities and Use of Proceeds

(a) Furnish the information required by Item 701 of Regulation S-K as to all equity securities of the registrant sold by the registrant during the period covered by the report that were not registered under the Securities Act. If the Item 701 information previously has been included in a current report on Form 8-K, however it need not be furnished. . . .

(c) Furnish the information required by Item 703 of Regulation S-K for any repurchases made in the quarter covered by the report. Provide disclosure covering repurchases made on a monthly basis. . . .

Instruction. Working capital restrictions and other limitations upon the payment of dividends are to be reported hereunder.

Item 3. Defaults Upon Senior Securities

(a) If there has been any material default in the payment of principal, interest, a sinking or purchase fund installment, or any other material default not cured within 30 days, with respect to any indebtedness of the registrant or any of its significant subsidiaries exceeding 5 percent of the total assets of the registrant and its consolidated subsidiaries, identify the indebtedness and state the nature of the default. In the case of such a default in the payment of principal, interest, or a sinking or purchase fund installment, state the amount of the default and the total arrearage on the date of filing this report.

Instructions to Item 3. 1. Item 3 need not be answered as to any default or arrearage with respect to any class of securities all of which is held by or for the account of the registrant or its totally held subsidiaries.

2. The information required by Item 3 need not be made if previously disclosed on a report on Form 8-K.

(b) If any material arrearage in the payment of dividends has occurred or if there has been any other material delinquency not cured within 30 days, with respect to any class of preferred stock of the registrant which is registered or which ranks prior to any class of registered securities, or with respect to any class of preferred stock of any significant subsidiary of the registrant, give the title of the class and state the nature of the arrearage or delinquency. In the case of an arrearage in the payment of dividends, state the amount and the total arrearage on the date of filing this report.

Instruction. Item 3 need not be answered as to any default or arrearage with respect to any class of securities all of which is held by, or for the account of, the registrant or its totally held subsidiaries.

Item 4. Mine Safety Disclosures

If applicable, provide a statement that the information concerning mine safety violations or other regulatory matters required by Section 1503(a) of the Dodd-Frank Wall Street Reform and Consumer Protection Act and Item 104 of Regulation S-K (17 CFR 229.104) is included in exhibit 95 to the quarterly report.

Item 5. Other Information

(a) The registrant must disclose under this item any information required to be disclosed in a report on Form 8-K during the period covered by this Form 10-Q, but not reported, whether or not otherwise required by this Form 10-Q. If disclosure of such information is made under this item, it need not be repeated in a report on Form 8-K which would otherwise be required to be filed with respect to such information or in a subsequent report on Form 10-Q.

(b) Furnish the information required by Item 407(c)(3) of Regulation S-K. . . .

FORM 10-K: ANNUAL REPORT PURSUANT TO SECTION 13 OR 15(D) OF THE SECURITIES EXCHANGE ACT OF 1934

GENERAL INSTRUCTIONS

A. Rule as to Use of Form 10-K

(1) This Form shall be used for annual reports pursuant to Section 13 or 15(d) of the Securities Exchange Act of 1934 (the "Act") for which no other form is prescribed. This Form also shall be used for transition reports filed pursuant to Section 13 or 15(d) of the Act.

(2) Annual reports on this Form shall be filed within the following period:

(a) 60 days after the end of the fiscal year covered by the report (75 days for fiscal years ending before December 15, 2006) for large accelerated filers (as defined in Rule 12b-2);

(b) 75 days after the end of the fiscal year covered by the report for accelerated filers (as defined in Rule 12b-2); and

(c) 90 days after the end of the fiscal year covered by the report for all other registrants.

G. *Information to Be Incorporated by Reference*

(1) Attention is directed to Rule 12b-23 which provides for the incorporation by reference of information contained in certain documents in answer or partial answer to any item of a report.

(2) The information called for by Parts I and II of this Form (Items 1 through 9A or any portion thereof) may, at the registrant's option, be incorporated by reference from the registrant's annual report to security holders furnished to the Commission pursuant to Rule 14a-3(b) or Rule 14c-3(a) or from the registrant's annual report to security holders, even if not furnished to the Commission pursuant to Rule 14a-3(b) or Rule 14c-3(a), provided such annual report contains the information required by Rule 14a-3.

Notes

1. In order to fulfill the requirements of Part I of Form 10-K, the incorporated portion of the annual report to security holders must contain the information required by Items 1-3 of Form 10-K, to the extent applicable.
2. If any information required by Part I or Part II is incorporated by reference into an electronic format document from the annual report to security holders as provided in General Instruction G, any portion of the annual report to security holders incorporated by reference shall be filed as an exhibit in electronic format, as required by Item 601(b)(13) of Regulation S-K.

(3) The information required by Part III (Items 10, 11, 12, 13 and 14) shall be incorporated by reference from the registrant's definitive proxy statement (filed or required to be filed pursuant to Regulation 14A) or definitive information statement (filed or to be filed pursuant to Regulation 14C) which involves the election of directors, if such definitive proxy statement or information statement is filed with the Commission not later than 120 days after the end of the fiscal year covered by the Form 10-K. However, if such definitive proxy or information statement is not filed with the Commission in the 120-day period or is not required to be filed with the Commission by virtue of Rule 3a12-3(b) under the Exchange Act, the Items comprising the Part III information must be filed as part of the Form 10-K, or as an amendment to the Form 10-K, not later than the end of the 120-day period. It should be noted that the information regarding executive officers required by Item 401 of Regulation S-K may be included in part I of Form 10-K under an appropriate caption. See Instruction 3 to Item 401 of Regulation S-K.

(4) No item numbers of captions of items need be contained in the material incorporated by reference into the report. When the registrant combines all of

the information in Parts I and II of this Form (Items 1 through 9A) by incorporation by reference from the registrant's annual report to security holders and all of the information in Part III of this Form (Items 10 through 14) by incorporating by reference from a definitive proxy statement or information statement involving the election of directors, then, notwithstanding General Instruction C(1), this Form shall consist of the facing or cover page, those sections incorporated from the annual report to security holders, the proxy or information statement, and the information, if any, required by Part IV of this Form, signatures, and a cross reference sheet setting forth the item numbers and captions in Parts I, II and III of this Form and the page and/or pages in the referenced materials where the corresponding information appears.

H. Integrated Reports to Security Holders

Annual reports to security holders may be combined with the required information of Form 10-K and will be suitable for filing with the Commission if the following conditions are satisfied:

(1) The combined report contains full and complete answers to all items required by Form 10-K. When responses to a certain item of required disclosure are separated within the combined report, an appropriate cross-reference should be made. If the information required by Part III of Form 10-K is omitted by virtue of General Instruction G, a definitive proxy or information statement shall be filed.

(2) The cover page and the required signatures are included. As appropriate, a cross-reference sheet should be filed indicating the location of information required by the items of the Form.

(3) If an electronic filer files any portion of an annual report to security holders in combination with the required information of Form 10-K, as provided in this instruction, only such portions filed in satisfaction of the Form 10-K requirements shall be filed in electronic format. . . .

[INFORMATION TO BE INCLUDED IN THE REPORT]

FORM 10-K . . .

Indicate by check mark whether the registrant is a large accelerated filer, an accelerated filer, a non-accelerated filer, a smaller reporting company, or an emerging growth company. See the definitions of "large accelerated filer," "accelerated filer," "smaller reporting company," and "emerging growth company" in Rule 12b-2 of the Exchange Act.

Large accelerated filer _____ Accelerated filer _____ Non-accelerated filer _____ Smaller reporting company _____ Emerging growth company _____

Indicate by check mark whether the registrant (1) has filed all reports required to be filed by Section 13 or 15(d) of the Securities Exchange Act of 1934 during the preceding 12 months (or for such shorter period that the registrant was required to file such reports), and (2) has been subject to such filing requirements for the past 90 days.

Yes _____ No _____

If securities are registered pursuant to Section 12(b) of the Act, indicate by check mark whether the financial statements of the registrant included in the filing reflect the correction of an error to previously issued financial statements Indicate by check mark whether any of those error corrections are restatements that required a recovery analysis of incentive-based compensation received by any of the registrant' executive officers during the relevant recovery period pursuant to §240.10D-1(b).
Yes _____ No _____

Indicate by check mark whether the registrant is a shell company (as defined by Rule 12b-2 of the Act).
Yes ____ No ____

If an emerging growth company, indicate by check mark if the registrant has elected not to use the extended transition period for complying with any new or revised financial accounting standards provided pursuant to Section 13(a) of the Exchange Act.

Indicate by check mark whether the registrant has filed a report on and attestation to its management's assessment of the effectiveness of its internal control over financial reporting under Section 404(b) of the Sarbanes-Oxley Act (15 U.S.C. 7262(b)) by the registered public accounting firm that prepared or issued its audit report.

State the aggregate market value of the voting and non-voting common equity held by non-affiliates of the registrant. The aggregate market value shall be computed by reference to the price at which the common equity was sold, or the average bid and asked prices of such common equity, as of a specified date within 60 days prior to the date of filing. (See definition of affiliate in Rule 405.)

NOTE

If a determination as to whether a particular person or entity is an affiliate cannot be made without involving unreasonable effort and expense, the aggregate market value of the common stock held by non-affiliates may be calculated on the basis of assumptions reasonable under the circumstances, provided that the assumptions are set forth in this Form. . . .

Documents Incorporated by Reference

List hereunder the following documents if incorporated by reference and the Part of the Form 10-K (e.g., Part I, Part II, etc.) into which the document is incorporated: (1) Any annual report to security holders; (2) Any proxy or information statement; and (3) Any prospectus filed pursuant to Rule 424(b) or (c) under the Securities Act of 1933. The listed documents should be clearly described for identification purposes (e.g., annual report to security holders for fiscal year ended December 24, 1980).

Part I [See General Instruction G(2)]

Item 1. Business

Furnish the information required by Item 101 of Regulation S-K except that the discussion of the development of the registrant's business need only include developments since the beginning of the fiscal year for which this report is filed.

Item 1A. Risk Factors

Set forth, under the caption "Risk Factors," where appropriate, the risk factors described in Item 105 of Regulation S-K applicable to the registrant. Provide any discussion of risk factors in plain English in accordance with Rule 421(d) of the Securities Act of 1933. Smaller reporting companies are not required to provide the information required by this Item.

Item 1B. Unresolved Staff Comments

If the registrant is an accelerated filer or a large accelerated filer, as defined in Rule 12b-2 of the Exchange Act, or is a well-known seasoned issuer as defined in Rule 405 of the Securities Act and has received written comments from the Commission staff regarding its periodic or current reports under the Act not less than 180 days before the end of its fiscal year to which the annual report relates, and such comments remain unresolved, disclose the substance of any such unresolved comments that the registrant believes are material. Such disclosure may provide other information including the position of the registrant with respect to any such comment.

Item 2. Properties

Furnish the information required by Item 102 of Regulation S-K.

Item 3. Legal Proceedings

(a) Furnish the information required by Item 103 of Regulation S-K.

(b) As to any proceeding that was terminated during the fourth quarter of the fiscal year covered by this report, furnish information similar to that required by Item 103 of Regulation S-K, including the date of termination and a description of the disposition thereof with respect to the registrant and its subsidiaries.

Item 4. Mine Safety Disclosures

If applicable, provide a statement that the information concerning mine safety violation or other regulatory matters required by Section 1503(a) of the Dodd-Frank Wall Street Reform and Consumer Protection Act and Item 104 of Regulation S-K (17 CFR 229.104) is included in exhibit 95 to the annual report.

Part II [See General Instruction G(2)]

Item 5. Market for Registrant's Common Equity and Related Stockholder Matters

(a) Furnish the information required by Item 201 of Regulation S-K and Item 701 of Regulation S-K as to all equity securities of the registrant sold by the registrant during the period covered by the report that were not registered under the Securities Act. If the Item 701 information previously has been included in a Quarterly Report on Form 10-Q or in a Current Report on Form 8-K, it need not be furnished.

(c) Furnish the information required by Item 703 of Regulation S-K for any repurchase made in a month within the fourth quarter of the fiscal year covered by the report. Provide disclosures covering repurchases made on a monthly basis. For example, if the fourth quarter began on January 16 and ended on April 15, the chart would show repurchases for the months from January 16 through February 15, February 16 through March 15, and March 16 through April 15.

Item 6. Selected Financial Data

Furnish the information required by Item 301 of Regulation S-K.

Item 7. Management's Discussion and Analysis of Financial Condition and Results of Operation

Furnish the information required by Item 303 of Regulation S-K.

Item 8. Financial Statements and Supplementary Data

(a) Furnish financial statements meeting the requirements of Regulation S-X, except §210.3-05 and Article 11 thereof, and the supplementary financial information required by Item 302 of Regulation S-K. . . .

(b) A smaller reporting company may provide the information required by Article 8 of Regulation S-X in lieu of the financial statements required by Item 8 of this Form.

Item 9. Changes in and Disagreements with Accountants on Accounting and Financial Disclosure

Furnish the information required by Item 304(b) of Regulation S-K.

Item 9A. Controls and Procedures

Furnish the information required by Items 307 and 308 of Regulation S-K.

Item 9B. Other Information

The registrant must disclose under this item any information required to be disclosed in a report on Form 8-K during the fourth quarter of the year covered by this Form 10-K, but not reported, whether or not otherwise required by this Form 10-K. If disclosure of such information is made under this item, it need not be repeated in a report on Form 8-K which would otherwise be required to be filed with respect to such information or in a subsequent report on Form 10-K.

Part III [See General Instruction G(3)]

Item 10. Directors, Executive Officers, and Corporate Governance

Furnish the information required by Items 401, 405, 406, and 407(c)(3), d(4), and d(5) of Regulation S-K.

Instruction. Checking the box provided on the cover page of this Form to indicate that Item 405 disclosure of delinquent Form 3, 4, or 5 filers is not contained herein is intended to facilitate Form processing and review. Failure to provide such indication will not create liability for violation of the federal securities laws. The space should be checked only if there is no disclosure in this Form of reporting person delinquencies in response to Item 405 and the registrant, at the time of filing the Form 10-K, has reviewed the information necessary to ascertain, and has determined that, Item 405 disclosure is not expected to be contained in Part III of the Form 10-K or incorporated by reference.

Item 11. Executive Compensation

Furnish the information required by Item 402 Regulation S-K and paragraphs (e)(4) and (e)(5) of Item 407 of Regulation S-K.

Item 12. Security Ownership of Certain Beneficial Owners and Management

Furnish the information required by Item 201(d) of Regulation S-K and by Item 403 of Regulation S-K.

Item 13. Certain Relationships and Related Transactions, and Director Independence

Furnish the information required by Item 404 of Regulation S-K and Item 407(a) of Regulation S-K.

Part IV

Item 14. Principal Accountant Fees and Services

Furnish the information required by Item 9(e) of Schedule 14A.

(1) Disclose, under the caption *Audit Fees,* the aggregate fees billed for each of the last two fiscal years for professional services rendered by the principal accountant for the audit of the registrant's annual financial statements and review of financial statements include in the registrant's Form 10-Q or services that are normally provided by the accountant in connection with statutory and regulatory fillings or engagements for those fiscal years.

(2) Disclose, under the caption *Audit-Related Fees,* the aggregate fees billed in each of the last two fiscal years for assurance and related services by the principal

accountant that are reasonably related to the performance of the audit or review of the registrant's financial statements and are not reported under Item 9(e)(1) of Schedule 14A. Registrants shall describe the nature of the services comprising the fees disclosed under this category.

(3) Disclose, under the caption *Tax Fees,* the aggregate fees billed in each of the last two fiscal years for professional services rendered by the principal accountant for tax compliance, tax advice, and tax planning. Registrants shall describe the nature of the services comprising the fees disclosed under this category.

(4) Disclose, under the caption *All Other Fees,* the aggregate fees billed in each of the last two fiscal years for products and services provided by the principal accountant, other than the services reported in Items 9(e)(1) through 9(e)(3) of Schedule 14A. Registrants shall describe the nature of the services comprising the fees disclosed under this category.

(5)(i) Disclose the audit committee's pre-approval policies and procedures described in paragraph (c)(7)(i) of Rule 2-01 of Regulation S-X.

(ii) Disclose the percentage of services described in each of Items 9(e)(2) through 9(e)(4) of Schedule 14A that were approved by the audit committee pursuant to paragraph (c)(7)(ii)(C) of Rule 2-01 of Regulation S-X.

(6) If greater than 50 percent, disclose the percentage of hours expended on the principal accountant's engagement to audit the registrant's financial statements for the most recent fiscal year that were attributed to work performed by persons other than the principal accountant's full-time, permanent employees.

Item 15. Exhibits, Financial Statement Schedules, and Reports on Form 8-K

(a) List the following Documents filed as a part of the report:

1. All financial statements;

2. Those financial statement schedules required to be filed by Item 8 of this Form, and by paragraph (d) below.

3. Those exhibits required by Item 601 of Regulation S-K and by paragraph (c) below. Identify in the list each management contract or compensatory plan or arrangement required to be filed as an exhibit to this form pursuant to Item 14(c) of this report.

(b) Reports on Form 8-K. State whether any reports on Form 8-K have been filed during the last quarter of the period covered by this report, listing the items reported, any financial statements filed and the dates of any such reports.

(c) Registrants shall file, as exhibits to this Form, the exhibits required by Item 601 of Regulation S-K.

(d) Registrants shall file, as financial statement schedules to this Form, the financial statements required by Regulation S-X which are excluded from the annual report to shareholders by Rule 14a-3(b), including (1) separate financial statements of subsidiaries not consolidated and fifty percent or less owned persons; (2) separate financial statements of affiliates whose securities are pledged as collateral and (3) schedules. . . .

Regulation 13D-G

Rule 13d-1. Filing of Schedules 13D and 13G

(a) Any person who, after acquiring directly or indirectly the beneficial ownership of any equity security of a class which is specified in paragraph (i) of this section, is directly or indirectly the beneficial owner of more than 5 percent of the class shall, within 10 days after such acquisition, file with the Commission, a statement containing the information required by Schedule 13D. . . .

Rule 13d-2. Filing of Amendments to Schedules 13D or 13G

(a) Schedule 13D—If any material change occurs in the facts set forth in the statement required by Rule 13d-1(a), including, but not limited to, any material increase or decrease in the percentage of the class beneficially owned, the person or persons who were required to file such statement shall promptly file or cause to be filed with the Commission an amendment disclosing such change. An acquisition or disposition of beneficial ownership of securities in an amount equal to one percent or more of the class of securities shall be deemed "material" for purposes of this rule; acquisitions or dispositions of less than such amounts may be material, depending upon the facts and circumstances. . . .

Rule 13d-3. Determination of Beneficial Owner

(a) For the purposes of sections 13(d) and 13(g) of the Act a beneficial owner of a security includes any person who, directly or indirectly, through any contract, arrangement, understanding, relationship, or otherwise has or shares:

(1) Voting power which includes the power to vote, or to direct the voting of, such security; and/or,

(2) Investment power which includes the power to dispose, or to direct the disposition of, such security.

(b) Any person who, directly or indirectly, creates or uses a trust, proxy, power of attorney, pooling arrangement or any other contract, arrangement, or device with the purpose or effect of divesting such person of beneficial ownership of a security or preventing the vesting of such beneficial ownership as part of a plan or scheme to evade the reporting requirements of section 13(d) or (g) of the Act shall be deemed for purposes of such sections to be the beneficial owner of such security.

(c) All securities of the same class beneficially owned by a person, regardless of the form which such beneficial ownership takes, shall be aggregated in calculating the number of shares beneficially owned by such person.

(d) Notwithstanding the provisions of paragraphs (a) and (c) of this rule:

(1)(i) A person shall be deemed to be the beneficial owner of a security, subject to the provisions of paragraph (b) of this rule, if that person has the right to acquire beneficial ownership of such security, as defined in Rule 13d-3(a) within sixty days, including but not limited to any right to acquire: (A) Through the exercise of any option, warrant or right; (B) through the conversion of a security; (C) pursuant to the power to revoke a trust, discretionary account, or similar arrangement; or (D) pursuant to the automatic termination of a trust, discretionary account or similar arrangement; provided, however, any person who acquires a security or power specified in paragraphs (d)(1)(i)(A), (B) or (C), of this section, with the purpose or effect of changing or influencing the control of the issuer, or in connection with or as a participant in any transaction having such purpose or effect, immediately upon such acquisition shall be deemed to be the beneficial owner of the securities which may be acquired through the exercise or conversion of such security or power. Any securities not outstanding which are subject to such options, warrants, rights or conversion privileges shall be deemed to be outstanding for the purpose of computing the percentage of outstanding securities of the class owned by such person but shall not be deemed to be outstanding for the purpose of computing the percentage of the class by any other person.

(ii) Paragraph (i) remains applicable for the purpose of determining the obligation to file with respect to the underlying security even though the option, warrant, right or convertible security is of a class of equity security, as defined in Rule 13d-1(i), and may therefore give rise to a separate obligation to file.

(2) A member of a national securities exchange shall not be deemed to be a beneficial owner of securities held directly or indirectly by it on behalf of another person solely because such member is the record holder of such securities and, pursuant to the rules of such exchange, may direct the vote of such securities, without instruction, on other than contested matters or matters that may affect substantially the rights or privileges of the holders of the securities to be voted, but is otherwise precluded by the rules of such exchange from voting without instruction.

(3) A person who in the ordinary course of his business is a pledgee of securities under a written pledge agreement shall not be deemed to be the beneficial owner of such pledged securities until the pledgee has taken all formal steps necessary which are required to declare a default and determines that the power to vote or to direct the vote or to dispose or to direct the disposition of such pledged securities will be exercised, provided, that:

(i) The pledgee agreement is bona fide and was not entered into with the purpose nor with the effect of changing or influencing the control of the issuer, not in connection with any transaction having such purpose or effect, including any transaction subject to Rule 13d-3(b);

(ii) The pledgee is a person specified in Rule 13d-1(b)(ii), including persons meeting the conditions set forth in paragraph (G) thereof; and

(iii) The pledgee agreement, prior to default, does not grant to the pledgee:

(A) The power to vote or to direct the vote of the pledged securities; or

(B) The power to dispose or direct the disposition of the pledged securities, other than the grant of such power(s) pursuant to a pledge agreement under which credit is extended subject to regulation T and in which the pledgee is a broker or dealer registered under section 15 of the act.

(4) A person engaged in business as an underwriter of securities who acquires securities through his participation in good faith in a firm commitment underwriting registered under the Securities Act of 1933 shall not be deemed to be the beneficial owner of such securities until the expiration of forty days after the date of such acquisition.

Rule 13d-5. Acquisition of Securities

(a) A person who becomes a beneficial owner of securities shall be deemed to have acquired such securities for purposes of section 13(d)(1) of the Act, whether such acquisition was through purchase or otherwise. However, executors or administrators of a decedent's estate generally will be presumed not to have acquired beneficial ownership of the securities in the decedent's estate until such time as such executors or administrators are qualified under local law to perform their duties.

(b)(1) When two or more persons agree to act together for the purpose of acquiring, holding, voting or disposing, of equity securities of an issuer, the group formed thereby shall be deemed to have acquired beneficial ownership, for purposes of sections 13(d) and (g) of the Act, as of the date of such agreement, of all equity securities of that issuer beneficially owned by any such persons.

(2) Notwithstanding the previous paragraph, a group shall be deemed not to have acquired any equity securities beneficially owned by the other members of the group solely by virtue of their concerted actions relating to the purchase of equity securities directly from an issuer in a transaction not involving a public offering: *Provided,* That:

(i) All the members of the group are persons specified in Rule 13d-1(b)(1)(ii);

(ii) The purchase is in the ordinary course of each member's business and not with the purpose nor with the effect of changing or influencing control of the issuer, nor in connection with or as a participant in any transaction having such purpose or effect, including any transaction subject to Rule 13d-3(b);

(iii) There is no agreement among, or between any members of the group to act together with respect to the issuer or its securities except for the purpose of facilitating the specific purchase involved; and

(iv) The only actions among or between any members of the group with respect to the issuer or its securities subsequent to the closing date of the non-public offering are those which are necessary to conclude ministerial matters directly related to the completion of the offer or sale of the securities.

Schedule 13D. Information to Be Included in Statements Filed Pursuant to Rule 13d-1(a) and Amendments Thereto Filed Pursuant to Rule 13d-2(a)

SPECIAL INSTRUCTIONS FOR COMPLYING WITH SCHEDULE 13D . . .

Item 1. Security and Issuer.

State the title of the class of equity securities to which this statement relates and the name and address of the principal executive offices of the issuer of such securities.

Item 2. Identity and Background.

If the person filing this statement or any person enumerated in Instruction C of this statement is a corporation, general partnership, limited partnership, syndicate or other group of persons, state its name, the state or other place of its organization, its principal business, the address of its principal office and the information required by (d) and (e) of this Item. If the person filing this statement or any person enumerated in Instruction C is a natural person, provide the information specified in (a) through (f) of this Item with respect to such person(s).

(a) Name;

(b) Residence or business address;

(c) Present principal occupation or employment and the name, principal business and address of any corporation or other organization in which such employment is conducted;

(d) Whether or not, during the last five years, such person has been convicted in a criminal proceeding (excluding traffic violations or similar misdemeanors) and, if so, give the dates, nature of conviction, name and location of court, any penalty imposed, or other disposition of the case;

(e) Whether or not, during the last five years, such person was a party to a civil proceeding of a judicial or administrative body of competent jurisdiction and as a result of such proceeding was or is subject to a judgment, decree or final order enjoining future violations of, or prohibiting or mandating activities subject to, federal or state securities laws or finding any violation with respect to such laws; and, if so, identify and describe such proceedings and summarize the terms of such judgment, degree or final order; and

(f) Citizenship.

Item 3. Source and Amount of Funds or Other Consideration.

State the source and the amount of funds or other consideration used or to be used in making the purchases, and if any part of the purchase price is or will be represented by funds or other consideration borrowed or otherwise obtained for the purpose of acquiring, holding, trading or voting the securities, a description of the transaction and the names of the parties thereto. Where material, such information should also be provided with respect to prior acquisitions not previously reported pursuant to this regulation. If the source of all or any part of the funds is a loan made in the ordinary course of business by a bank, as defined in section 3(a)(6) of the Act, the name of the bank shall not be made available to the public if the person at the time of filing the statement so requests in writing and files such request, naming such bank, with the Secretary of the Commission. If the securities were acquired other than by purchase, describe the method of acquisition.

Item 4. Purpose of Transaction.

State the purpose or purposes of the acquisition of securities of the issuer. Describe any plans or proposals which the reporting persons may have which relate to or would result in:

(a) The acquisition by any person of additional securities of the issuer, or the disposition of securities of the issuer;

(b) An extraordinary corporate transaction, such as a merger, reorganization or liquidation, involving the issuer or any of its subsidiaries;

(c) A sale or transfer of a material amount of assets of the issuer or any of its subsidiaries;

(d) Any change in the present board of directors or management of the issuer, including any plans or proposals to change the number or term of directors or to fill any existing vacancies on the board;

(e) Any material change in the present capitalization or dividend policy of the issuer;

(f) Any other material change in the issuer's business or corporate structure, including but not limited to, if the issuer is a registered closed-end investment company, any plans or proposals to make any changes in its investment policy for which a vote is required by section 13 of the Investment Company Act of 1940;

(g) Changes in the issuer's charter, bylaws or instruments corresponding thereto or other actions which may impede the acquisition of control of the issuer by any person;

(h) Causing a class of securities of the issuer to be delisted from a national securities exchange or to cease to be authorized to be quoted in an inter-dealer quotation system of a registered national securities association;

(i) A class of equity securities of the issuer becoming eligible for termination of registration pursuant to section 12(g)(4) of the Act; or

(j) Any action similar to any of those enumerated above.

Item 5. Interest in Securities of the Issuer.

(a) State the aggregate number and percentage of the class of securities identified pursuant to Item 1 (which may be based on the number of securities outstanding as contained in the most recently available filing with the Commission by the issuer unless the filing person has reason to believe such information is not current) beneficially owned (identifying those shares which there is a right to acquire) by each person named in Item 2. The above mentioned information should also be furnished with respect to persons who, together with any of the persons named in Item 2, comprise a group within the meaning of section 13(d)(3) of the Act;

(b) For each person named in response to paragraph (a), indicate the number of shares as to which there is sole power to vote or to direct the vote, sole power to dispose or to direct the disposition, or shared power to dispose or to direct the disposition. Provide the applicable information required by Item 2 with respect to each person with whom the power to vote or to direct the vote or to dispose or direct the disposition is shared;

(c) Describe any transactions in the class of securities reported on that were effected during the past sixty days or since the most recent filing of Schedule 13D, whichever is less, by the persons named in response to paragraph (a).

Instruction. The description of a transaction required by Item 5(c) shall include, but not necessarily be limited to: (1) The identity of the person covered by Item 5(c) who effected the transaction; (2) the date of transaction; (3) the amount of securities involved; (4) the price per share or unit; and (5) where and how the transaction was effected.

(d) If any other person is known to have the right to receive or the power to direct the receipt of dividends from, or the proceeds from the sale of, such securities, a statement to that effect should be included in response to this item and, if such interest relates to more than five percent of the class, such person should be identified. A listing of the shareholders of an investment company registered under the Investment Company Act of 1940 or the beneficiaries of an employee benefit plan, pension fund or endowment fund is not required.

(e) If applicable, state the date on which the reporting person ceased to be the beneficial owner of more than five percent of the class of securities.

Instruction. For computations regarding securities which represent a right to acquire an underlying security, see Rule 13d-3(d)(1) and the note thereto.

Item 6. Contracts, Arrangements, Understandings or Relationships With Respect to Securities of the Issuer.

Describe any contracts, arrangements, understandings or relationships (legal or otherwise) among the persons named in Item 2 and between such persons and any person with respect to any securities of the issuer, including but not limited to transfer or voting of any of the securities, finder's fees, joint ventures, loan or option arrangements, puts or calls, guarantees of profits, division of profits or loss, or the giving or withholding of proxies, naming the persons with whom such contracts, arrangements, understanding or relationships have been entered into. Include such information for any of the securities that are pledged or otherwise subject to a contingency the occurrence of which would give another person voting power or investment power over such securities except that disclosure of standard default and similar provisions contained in loan agreements need not be included. . . .

Rule 13e-1. Purchase of Securities by the Issuer During a Third-Party Tender Offer

An issuer that has received notice that it is the subject of a tender offer made under Section 14(d)(1) of the Act that has commenced under Rule 14d-2 must not purchase any of its equity securities during the tender offer unless the issuer first:

(a) Files a statement with the Commission containing the following information:

(1) The title and number of securities to be purchased;

(2) The names of the persons or classes of persons from whom the issuer will purchase the securities;

(3) The name of any exchange, inter-dealer quotation system or any other market on or through which the securities will be purchased;

(4) The purpose of the purchase;

(5) Whether the issuer will retire the securities, hold the securities in its treasury, or dispose of the securities. If the issuer intends to dispose of the securities, describe how it intends to do so; and

(6) The source and amount of funds or other consideration to be used to make the purchase. If the issuer borrows any funds or other consideration to make the purchase or enters any agreement for the purpose of acquiring, holding, or trading the securities, describe the transaction and agreement and identify the parties; and

(b) Pays the fee required by Rule 0-11 when it files the initial statement.

(c) This section does not apply to periodic repurchases in connection with an employee benefit plan or other similar plan of the issuer so long as the purchases are made in the ordinary course and not in response to the tender offer.

Rule 13e-3. Going Private Transactions by Certain Issuers or Their Affiliates

(a) *Definitions.* Unless indicated otherwise or the context otherwise requires, all terms used in this section and in Schedule 13E-3 shall have the same meaning as in the Act or elsewhere in the General Rules and Regulations thereunder. In addition, the following definitions apply:

(1) An *affiliate* of an issuer is a person that directly or indirectly through one or more intermediaries controls, is controlled by, or is under common control with such issuer. For the purposes of this section only, a person who is not an affiliate of an issuer at the commencement of such person's tender offer for a class of equity securities of such issuer will not be deemed an affiliate of such issuer prior to the stated termination of such tender offer and any extensions thereof;

(2) The term *purchase* means any acquisition for value including, but not limited to, (i) any acquisition pursuant to the dissolution of an issuer subsequent to the sale or other disposition of substantially all the assets of such issuer to its affiliate, (ii) any acquisition pursuant to a merger, (iii) any acquisition of fractional interests in connection with a reverse stock split, and (iv) any acquisition subject to the control of an issuer or an affiliate of such issuer;

(3) A *Rule 13e-3 transaction* is any transaction or series of transactions involving one or more of the transactions described in paragraph (a)(3)(i) of this section which has either a reasonable likelihood or a purpose of producing, either directly or indirectly, any of the effects described in paragraph (a)(3)(ii) of this section;

(i) The transactions referred to in paragraph (a)(3) of this section are:

(A) A purchase of any equity security by the issuer of such security or by an affiliate of such issuer;

(B) A tender offer for or request or invitation for tenders of any equity security made by the issuer of such class of securities or by an affiliate of such issuer; or

(C) A solicitation subject to Regulation 14A of any proxy, consent or authorization of, or a distribution subject to Regulation 14C of information statements to, any equity security holder by the issuer of the class of securities or by an affiliate of such issuer, in connection with: a merger, consolidation, reclassification, recapitalization, reorganization or similar corporate transaction of an issuer or between an issuer (or its subsidiaries) and its affiliate; a sale of substantially all the assets of an issuer to its affiliate or group of affiliates; or a reverse stock split of any class of equity securities of the issuer involving the purchase of fractional interests.

(ii) The effects referred to in paragraph (a)(3) of this section are:

(A) Causing any class of equity securities of the issuer which is subject to section 12(g) or section 15(d) of the Act to become eligible for termination of registration under Rule 12g-4 or Rule 12h-6 or causing the reporting obligations with respect to such class to become eligible for termination under Rule 12h-6; or suspension under Rule 12h-3 or section 15(d); or

(B) Causing any class of equity securities of the issuer which is either listed on a national securities exchange or authorized to be quoted in an inter-dealer quotation system of a registered national securities association to be neither listed on any national securities exchange nor authorized to be quoted on an inter-dealer quotation system of any registered national securities association.

(4) An *unaffiliated security holder* is any security holder of an equity security subject to a Rule 13e-3 transaction who is not an affiliate of the issuer of such security.

(b) *Application of section to an issuer (or an affiliate of such issuer) subject to section 12 of the Act.* (1) It shall be a fraudulent, deceptive or manipulative act or practice, in connection with a Rule 13e-3 transaction, for an issuer which has a class of equity securities registered pursuant to section 12 of the Act or which is a closed-end investment company registered under the Investment Company Act of 1940, or an affiliate of such issuer, directly or indirectly

(i) To employ any device, scheme or artifice to defraud any person;

(ii) To make any untrue statement of a material fact or to omit to state a material fact necessary in order to make the statements made, in light of the circumstances under which they were made, not misleading; or

(iii) To engage in any act, practice or course of business which operates or would operate as a fraud or deceit upon any person.

(2) As a means reasonably designed to prevent fraudulent, deceptive or manipulative acts or practices in connection with any Rule 13e-3 transaction, it shall be unlawful for an issuer which has a class of equity securities registered pursuant to section 12 of the Act, or an affiliate of such issuer, to engage, directly or indirectly, in a Rule 13e-3 transaction unless:

(i) Such issuer or affiliate complies with the requirements of paragraphs (d), (e) and (f) of this section; and

(ii) The Rule 13e-3 transaction is not in violation of paragraph (b)(1) of this section.

(c) *Application of section to an issuer (or an affiliate of such issuer) subject to section 15(d) of the Act.* (1) It shall be unlawful as a fraudulent, deceptive or manipulative act or practice for an issuer which is required to file periodic reports pursuant to Section 15(d) of the Act, or an affiliate of such issuer, to engage, directly or indirectly, in a Rule 13e-3 transaction unless such issuer or affiliate complies with the requirements of paragraphs (d), (e) and (f) of this section.

(2) An issuer or affiliate which is subject to paragraph (c)(1) of this section and which is soliciting proxies or distributing information statements in connection with a transaction described in paragraph (a)(3)(i)(A) of this section may elect to use the timing procedures for conducting a solicitation subject to Regulation 14A or a distribution subject to Regulation 14C in complying with paragraphs (d), (e) and (f) of this section, provided that if an election is made, such solicitation or distribution is conducted in accordance with the requirements of the respective regulations, including the filing of preliminary copies of soliciting materials or an information statement at the time specified in Regulation 14A or 14C, respectively.

(d) *Material required to be filed.* The issuer or affiliate engaging in a Rule 13e-3 transaction must file with the Commission:

(1) A Schedule 13E-3 including all exhibits;

(2) An amendment to Schedule 13E-3 reporting promptly any material changes in the information set forth in the schedule previously filed; and

(3) A final amendment to Schedule 13E-3 reporting promptly the results of the Rule 13e-3 transaction.

(e) *Disclosure of information to security holders.*

(1) In addition to disclosing the information required by any other applicable rule or regulation under the federal securities laws, the issuer or affiliate engaging in a Rule 13e-3 transaction must disclose to security holders of the class that is the subject of the transaction, as specified in paragraph (f) of this section, the following:

(i) The information required by Item 1 of Schedule 13E-3 (Summary Term Sheet);

(ii) The information required by Items 7, 8 and 9 of Schedule 13E-3, which must be prominently disclosed in a "Special Factors" section in the front of the disclosure document;

(iii) A prominent legend on the outside front cover page that indicates that neither the Securities and Exchange Commission nor any state securities commission has: approved or disapproved of the transaction; passed upon the merits or fairness of the transaction; or passed upon the adequacy or accuracy of the disclosure in the document. The legend also must make it clear that any representation to the contrary is a criminal offense;

(iv) The information concerning appraisal rights required by Item 1016(f) of [Regulation M-A]; and

(v) The information required by the remaining items of Schedule 13E-3, except for (exhibits), or a fair and adequate summary of the information. . . .

Rule 13e-4. Tender Offers by Issuers

(a) *Definitions.* Unless the context otherwise requires, all terms used in this section and in Schedule TO shall have the same meaning as in the Act or elsewhere in the General Rules and Regulations thereunder. In addition, the following definitions shall apply:

(1) The term *issuer* means any issuer which has a class of equity security registered pursuant to section 12 of the Act, or which is required to file periodic reports pursuant to section 15(d) of the Act, or which is a closed-end investment company registered under the Investment Company Act of 1940.

(2) The term *issuer tender offer* refers to a tender offer for, or a request or invitation for tenders of, any class of equity security, made by the issuer of such class of equity security or by an affiliate of such issuer. . . .

(b) As soon as practicable on the date of commencement of the issuer tender offer, the issuer or affiliate making the issuer tender offer must comply with:

(1) The filing requirements of paragraph (c)(2) of this section;

(2) The disclosure requirements of paragraph (d)(1) of this section; and

(3) The dissemination requirements of paragraph (e) of this section.

(c) *Material required to be filed.* The issuer or affiliate making the issuer tender offer must file with the Commission:

(1) All written communications made by the issuer or affiliate relating to the issuer tender offer, from and including the first public announcement, as soon as practicable on the date of the communication;

(2) A Schedule TO including all exhibits;

(3) An amendment to Schedule TO reporting promptly any material changes in the information set forth in the schedule previously filed; and

(4) A final amendment to Schedule TO reporting promptly the results of the issuer tender offer.

(d) *Disclosure of tender offer information to security holders.*

(1) The issuer or affiliate making the issuer tender offer must disclose, in a manner prescribed by paragraph (e)(1) of this section, the following:

(i) The information required by Item 1 of Schedule TO (summary term sheet); and

(ii) The information required by the remaining items of Schedule TO for issuer tender offers, except for Item 12 (exhibits), or a fair and adequate summary of the information.

(2) If there are any material changes in the information previously disclosed to security holders, the issuer or affiliate must disclose the changes promptly to security holders in a manner specified in paragraph (e)(3) of this section.

(3) If the issuer or affiliate disseminates the issuer tender offer by means of summary publication as described in paragraph (e)(1)(iii) of this section, the summary advertisement must not include a transmittal letter that would permit security holders to tender securities sought in the offer and must disclose at least the following information:

(i) The identity of the issuer or affiliate making the issuer tender offer;

(ii) The information required by Regulation M-A, Items 1004(a)(1) and 1006(a) of this chapter;

(iii) Instructions on how security holders can obtain promptly a copy of the statement required by paragraph (d)(1) of this section, at the issuer or affiliate's expense; and

(iv) A statement that the information contained in the statement required by paragraph (d)(1) of this section is incorporated by reference.

(e) *Dissemination of tender offers to security holders.* An issuer tender offer will be deemed to be published, sent or given to security holders if the issuer or affiliate making the issuer tender offer complies fully with one or more of the methods described in this section.

(1) For issuer tender offers in which the consideration offered consists solely of cash and/or securities exempt from registration under Section 3 of the Securities Act of 1933:

(i) Dissemination of cash issuer tender offers by long-form publication: By making adequate publication of the information required by paragraph (d)(1) of this section in a newspaper or newspapers, on the date of commencement of the issuer tender offer.

(ii) Dissemination of any issuer tender offer by use of stockholder and other lists:

(A) By mailing or otherwise furnishing promptly a statement containing the information required by paragraph (d)(1) of this section to each security holder whose name appears on the most recent stockholder list of the issuer;

(B) By contacting each participant on the most recent security position listing of any clearing agency within the possession or access of the issuer or affiliate making the issuer tender offer, and making inquiry of each participant as to the approximate number of beneficial owners of the securities sought in the offer that are held by the participant;

(C) By furnishing to each participant a sufficient number of copies of the statement required by paragraph (d)(1) of this section for transmittal to the beneficial owners; and

(D) By agreeing to reimburse each participant promptly for its reasonable expenses incurred in forwarding the statement to beneficial owners.

(iii) Dissemination of certain cash issuer tender offers by summary publication:

(A) If the issuer tender offer is not subject to Rule 13e-3, by making adequate publication of a summary advertisement containing the information required by paragraph (d)(3) of this section in a newspaper or newspapers, on the date of commencement of the issuer tender offer; and

(B) By mailing or otherwise furnishing promptly the statement required by paragraph (d)(1) of this section and a transmittal letter to any security holder who requests a copy of the statement or transmittal letter.

(2) For tender offers in which the consideration consists solely or partially of securities registered under the Securities Act of 1933, a registration statement containing all of the required information, including pricing information, has been filed and a preliminary prospectus or a prospectus that meets the requirements of Section 10(a) of the Securities Act, including a letter of transmittal, is delivered to security holders. However, for going-private transactions (as defined by Rule 13e-3) and roll-up transactions (as described by Item 901 of Regulation S-K), a registration statement registering the securities to be offered must have become effective and only a prospectus that meets the requirements of Section 10(a) of the Securities Act may be delivered to security holders on the date of commencement.

(3) If a material change occurs in the information published, sent or given to security holders, the issuer or affiliate must disseminate promptly disclosure of the change in a manner reasonably calculated to inform security holders of the change. In a registered securities offer where the issuer or affiliate disseminates the preliminary prospectus as permitted by paragraph (e)(2) of this section, the offer must remain open from the date that material changes to the tender offer materials are disseminated to security holders, as follows:

(i) Five business days for a prospectus supplement containing a material change other than price or share levels;

(ii) Ten business days for a prospectus supplement containing a change in price, the amount of securities sought, the dealer's soliciting fee, or other similarly significant change;

(iii) Ten business days for a prospectus supplement included as part of a post-effective amendment; and

(iv) Twenty business days for a revised prospectus when the initial prospectus was materially deficient.

(f) *Manner of making tender offer.* (1) The issuer tender offer, unless withdrawn, shall remain open until the expiration of:

(i) At least twenty business days from its commencement; and

(ii) At least ten business days from the date that notice of an increase or decrease in the percentage of the class of securities being sought or the consideration offered or the dealer's soliciting fee to be given is first published, sent or given to security holders. *Provided, however,* That, for purposes of this paragraph, the acceptance for payment by the issuer or affiliate of an additional amount of securities not to exceed two percent of the class of securities that is the subject of the tender offer shall not be deemed to be an increase.

For purposes of this paragraph, the percentage of a class of securities shall be calculated in accordance with section 14(d)(3) of the Act.

(2) The issuer or affiliate making the issuer tender offer shall permit securities tendered pursuant to the issuer tender offer to be withdrawn:

(i) At any time during the period such issuer tender offer remains open; and

(ii) If not yet accepted for payment, after the expiration of forty business days from the commencement of the issuer tender offer.

(3) If the issuer or affiliate makes a tender offer for less than all of the outstanding equity securities of a class, and if a greater number of securities is tendered pursuant thereto than the issuer or affiliate is bound or willing to take up and pay for, the securities taken up and paid for shall be taken up and paid for as nearly as may be pro rata, disregarding fractions, according to the number of securities tendered by each security holder during the period such offer remains open; *Provided, however,* That this provision shall not prohibit the issuer or affiliate making the issuer tender offer from:

(i) Accepting all securities tendered by persons who own, beneficially or of record, an aggregate of not more than a specified number which is less than one hundred shares of such security and who tender all their securities, before prorating securities tendered by others; or

(ii) Accepting by lot securities tendered by security holders who tender all securities held by them and who, when tendering their securities, elect to have either all or none of at least a minimum amount or none accepted, if the issuer or affiliate first accepts all securities tendered by security holders who do not so elect;

(4) In the event the issuer or affiliate making the issuer tender increases the consideration offered after the issuer tender offer has commenced, such issuer or affiliate shall pay such increased consideration to all security holders whose tendered securities are accepted for payment by such issuer or affiliate.

(5) The issuer or affiliate making the tender offer shall either pay the consideration offered, or return the tendered securities, promptly after the termination or withdrawal of the tender offer.

(6) Until the expiration of at least ten business days after the date of termination of the issuer tender offer, neither the issuer nor any affiliate shall make any purchases, otherwise than pursuant to the tender offer, of:

(i) Any security which is the subject of the issuer tender offer, or any security of the same class and series, or any right to purchase any such securities; and

(ii) In the case of an issuer tender offer which is an exchange offer, any security being offered pursuant to such exchange offer, or any security of the same class and series, or any right to purchase any such security.

(7) The time periods for the minimum offering periods pursuant to this section shall be computed on a concurrent as opposed to a consecutive basis.

(8) No issuer or affiliate shall make a tender offer unless:

(i) The tender offer is open to all security holders of the class of securities subject to the tender offer; and

(ii) The consideration paid to any security holder for securities tendered in the tender offer is the highest consideration paid to any other security holder for securities tendered in the tender offer.

(9) Paragraph (f)(8)(i) of this section shall not:

(i) Affect dissemination under paragraph (e) of this section; or

(ii) Prohibit an issuer or affiliate from making a tender offer excluding all security holders in a state where the issuer or affiliate is prohibited from making the tender offer by administrative or judicial action pursuant to a state statute after a good faith effort by the issuer or affiliate to comply with such statute.

(10) Paragraph (f)(8)(ii) of this section shall not prohibit the offer of more than one type of consideration in a tender offer, provided that:

(i) Security holders are afforded equal right to elect among each of the types of consideration offered; and

(ii) The highest consideration of each type paid to any security holder is paid to any other security holder receiving that type of consideration.

(11) If the offer and sale of securities constituting consideration offered in an issuer tender offer is prohibited by the appropriate authority of a state after a good faith effort by the issuer or affiliate to register or qualify the offer and sale of such securities in such state:

(i) The issuer or affiliate may offer security holders in such state an alternative form of consideration; and

(ii) Paragraph (f)(10) of this section shall not operate to require the issuer or affiliate to offer or pay the alternative form of consideration to security holders in any other state.

(12) (i) Paragraph (f)(8)(ii) of this section shall not prohibit the negotiation, execution or amendment of an employment compensation, severance or other employee benefit arrangement, or payments made or to be made or benefits granted or to be granted according to such an arrangement, with respect to any security holder of the issuer, where the amount payable under the arrangement:

(A) Is being paid or granted as compensation for past services performed, future services to be performed, or future services to be refrained from performing, by the security holder (and matters incidental thereto); and

(B) Is not calculated based on the number of securities tendered or to be tendered in the tender offer by the security holder.

(ii) The provisions of paragraph (f)(12)(i) of this section shall be satisfied and, therefore, pursuant to this non-exclusive safe harbor, the negotiation, execution or amendment of an arrangement and any payments made or to be made or benefits granted or to be granted according to that arrangement shall not be prohibited by paragraph (f)(8)(ii) of this section, if the arrangement is approved as an employment compensation, severance or other employee benefit arrangement solely by independent directors as follows:

(A) The compensation committee of the board of directors that performs functions similar to a compensation committee of the issuer approves the arrangement, regardless of whether the issuer is a party to the arrangement, or, if an affiliate is a party to the arrangement, the compensation committee or a committee of the board of directors that performs functions similar to a compensation committee of the affiliate approves the arrangement; or

(B) If the issuer's or affiliate's board of directors, as applicable, does not have a compensation committee or a committee of the board of directors that performs functions similar to a compensation committee or if none of the members of the issuer's or affiliate's compensation committee or committee that performs functions similar to a compensation committee is independent, a special committee of the board of directors formed to consider and approve the arrangement approves the arrangement; or

(C) If the issuer or affiliate, as applicable, is a foreign private issuer, any or all members of the board of directors or any committee of the board of directors authorized to approve employment compensation, severance or other employee benefit arrangements under the laws or regulations of the home country approves the arrangement.

INSTRUCTIONS TO PARAGRAPH (f)(12)(ii)

For purposes of determining whether the members of the committee approving an arrangement in accordance with the provisions of paragraph (f)(12)(ii) of this section are independent, the following provisions shall apply:

1. If the issuer or affiliate, as applicable, is a listed issuer (as defined in Rule 10A-3) whose securities are listed either on a national securities exchange registered pursuant to section 6(a) of the Exchange Act or in an inter-dealer quotation system of a national securities association registered pursuant to section 15A(a) of the Exchange Act that has independence requirements for compensation committee members that have been approved by the Commission (as those requirements may be modified or supplemented), apply the issuer's or affiliate's definition that it uses for determining that the members of the compensation committee are independent in compliance with the listing standards to compensation committee members of the listed issuer.

2. If the issuer or affiliate, as applicable, is not a listed issuer (as defined in Rule 10A-3), apply the independence requirements for compensation committee members of a national securities exchange registered pursuant to section 6(a) of the Exchange Act or an inter-dealer quotation system of a national securities association registered pursuant to section 15A(a) of the Exchange Act that have been approved by the Commission (as those requirements may be modified or supplemented). Whatever definition the issuer or affiliate, as applicable, chooses, it must apply that definition consistently to all members of the committee approving the arrangement.

3. Notwithstanding Instructions 1 and 2 paragraph(f)(12)(ii), if the issuer or affiliate, as applicable, is a closed-end investment company registered under the Investment Company Act of 1940, a director is considered to be independent if the director is not, other than in his or her capacity as a member of the board of directors or any board committee, an "interested person" of the investment company, as defined in section 2(a)(19) of the Investment Company Act of 1940.

4. If the issuer or affiliate, as applicable, is a foreign private issuer, apply either the independence standards set forth in Instructions 1 and 2 paragraph (f)(12)(ii) or the independence

requirements of the laws, regulations, codes or standards of the home country of the issuer or affiliate, as applicable, for members of the board of directors or the committee of the board of directors approving the arrangement.

5. A determination by the issuer's or affiliate's board of directors, as applicable, that the members of the board of directors or the committee of the board of directors, as applicable, approving an arrangement in accordance with the provisions of paragraph (f)(12)(ii) are independent in accordance with the provisions of this instruction to paragraph (f)(12)(ii) shall satisfy the independence requirements of paragraph (f)(12)(ii).

Instruction to paragraph (f)(12): The fact that the provisions of paragraph (f)(12) of this section extend only to employment compensation, severance and other employee benefit arrangements and not to other arrangements, such as commercial arrangements, does not raise any inference that a payment under any such other arrangement constitutes consideration paid for securities in a tender offer.

(13) Electronic filings. If the issuer or affiliate is an electronic filer, the minimum offering periods set forth in paragraph (f)(1) of this section shall be tolled for any period during which it fails to file in electronic format, absent a hardship exemption, the Schedule TO, the tender offer material specified in Item 1016(a)(1) of Regulation M-A, and any amendments thereto. If such documents were filed in paper pursuant to a temporary hardship exemption, the minimum offering periods shall be tolled for any period during which a required confirming electronic copy of such Schedule and tender offer material is delinquent. . . .

(h) This section shall not apply to:

(1) Calls or redemptions of any security in accordance with the terms and conditions of its governing instruments;

(2) Offers to purchase securities evidenced by a scrip certificate, order form or similar document which represents a fractional interest in a share of stock or similar security;

(3) Offers to purchase securities pursuant to a statutory procedure for the purchase of dissenting security holders' securities;

(4) Any tender offer which is subject to section 14(d) of the Act;

(5) Offers to purchase from security holders who own an aggregate of not more than a specified number of shares that is less than one hundred: *Provided, however,* That:

(i) The offer complies with paragraph (f)(8)(i) of this section with respect to security holders who own a number of shares equal to or less than the specified number of shares, except that an issuer can elect to exclude participants in an issuer's plan as that term is defined in §242.100 of Regulation M, or to exclude security holders who do not own their shares as of a specified date determined by the issuer; and

(ii) The offer complies with paragraph (f)(8)(ii) of this section or the consideration paid pursuant to the offer is determined on the basis of a uniformly applied formula based on the market price of the subject security;

(6) An issuer tender offer made solely to effect a rescission offer: *Provided, however,* That the offer is registered under the Securities Act of 1933, and the

consideration is equal to the price paid by each security holder, plus legal interest if the issuer elects to or is required to pay legal interest;

(7) Offers by closed-end management investment companies, to repurchase equity securities pursuant to §270.23C-3 of this chapter;

(8) Cross-border tender offers. . . .

(9) Any other transaction or transactions, if the Commission, upon written request or upon its own motion, exempts such transaction or transactions, either unconditionally, or on specified terms and conditions, as not constituting a fraudulent, deceptive or manipulative act or practice comprehended within the purpose of this section.

(i) Cross-border tender offers (Tier II). . .

(j)(1) It shall be a fraudulent, deceptive or manipulative act or practice, in connection with an issuer tender offer, for an issuer or an affiliate of such issuer, in connection with an issuer tender offer:

(i) To employ any device, scheme or artifice to defraud any person;

(ii) To make any untrue statement of a material fact or to omit to state a material fact necessary in order to make the statements made, in the light of the circumstances under which they were made, not misleading; or

(iii) To engage in any act, practice or course of business which operates or would operate as a fraud or deceit upon any person.

(2) As a means reasonably designed to prevent fraudulent, deceptive or manipulative acts or practices in connection with any issuer tender offer, it shall be unlawful for an issuer or an affiliate of such issuer to make an issuer tender offer unless:

(i) Such issuer or affiliate complies with the requirements of paragraphs (b), (c), (d), (e) and (f) of this section; and

(ii) The issuer tender offer is not in violation of paragraph (j)(1) of this section.

Schedule 13e-3. Transaction Statement Pursuant to Section 13(e) of the Securities Exchange Act of 1934 and Rule 13e-3 Thereunder

Item 1. Summary Term Sheet.

Furnish the information required by Item 1001 of Regulation M-A unless information is disclosed to security holders in a prospectus that meets the requirements of Rule 421(d) of this chapter.

Item 2. Subject Company Information.

Furnish the information required by Item 1002 of Regulation M-A.

Item 3. Identity and Background of Filing Person.

Furnish the information required by Item 1003(a) through (c) of Regulation M-A.

Item 4. Terms of the Transaction.

Furnish the information required by Item 1004(a) and (c) through (f) of Regulation M-A.

Item 5. Past Contacts, Transactions, Negotiations and Agreements.

Furnish the information required by Item 1005(a) through (c) and (e) of Regulation M-A.

Item 6. Purposes of the Transaction and Plans or Proposals.

Furnish the information required by Item 1006(b) and (c)(1) through (8) of Regulation M-A.

Item 7. Purposes, Alternatives, Reasons and Effects.

Furnish the information required by Item 1013 of Regulation M-A.

Item 8. Fairness of the Transaction.

Furnish the information required by Item 1014 of Regulation M-A.

Item 9. Reports, Opinions, Appraisal and Negotiations.

Furnish the information required by Item 1015 of Regulation M-A.

Item 10. Source and Amounts of Funds or Other Consideration.

Furnish the information required by Item 1007 of Regulation M-A.

Item 11. Interest in Securities of the Subject Company.

Furnish the information required by Item 1008 of Regulation M-A.

Item 12. The Solicitation or Recommendation.

Furnish the information required by Item 1012(d) and (e) of Regulation M-A.

Item 13. Financial Statements.

Furnish the information required by Item 1010(a) through (b) of Regulation M-A for the issuer of the subject class of securities.

Item 14. Persons/Assets, Retained, Employed, Compensated or Used.

Furnish the information required by Item 1009 of Regulation M-A.

Item 15. Additional Information.

Furnish the information required by Item 1011(b) and (c) of Regulation M-A.

Item 16. Exhibits.

File as an exhibit to the Schedule all documents specified in Item 1016(a) through (d), (f) and (g) of Regulation M-A.

Signature. . . .

INSTRUCTION TO SIGNATURE

The statement must be signed by the filing person or that person's authorized representative. If the statement is signed on behalf of a person by an authorized representative (other than an executive officer of a corporation or general partner of a partnership), evidence of the representative's authority to sign on behalf of the person must be filed with the statement. The name and any title of each person who signs the statement must be typed or printed beneath the signature. See Rule 12b-11 with respect to signature requirements.

Rule 13f-1. Reporting by Institutional Investment Managers of Information with Respect to Accounts over Which They Exercise Investment Discretion

(a)(1) Every institutional investment manager which exercises investment discretion with respect to accounts holding section 13(f) securities, as defined in paragraph (c) of this section, having an aggregate fair market value on the last trading day of any month of any calendar year of at least $100,000,000 shall file a report on Form 13F with the Commission within 45 days after the last day of such calendar year and within 45 days after the last day of each of the first three calendar quarters of the subsequent calendar year. . . .

(b) For the purposes of this rule, "investment discretion" has the meaning set forth in section 3(a)(35) of the Act. An institutional investment manager shall also be deemed to exercise "investment discretion" with respect to all accounts over which any person under its control exercises investment discretion.

(c) For purposes of this rule "section 13(f) securities" shall mean equity securities of a class described in section 13(d)(1) of the Act that are admitted to trading on a national securities exchange or quoted on the automated quotation system of a registered securities association. In determining what classes of securities are section 13(f) securities, an institutional investment manager may rely on the most recent list of such securities published by the Commission pursuant to section 13(f)(4) of the Act. Only securities of a class on such list shall be counted in determining whether an institutional investment manager must file a report under this rule and only those securities shall be reported in such report. Where a person controls the issuer of a class of equity securities which are "section 13(f) securities" as defined in this rule, those securities shall not be deemed to be "section 13(f) securities" with respect to the controlling person, provided that such person does not otherwise exercise investment discretion with respect to accounts with fair market value of at least $100,000,000 within the meaning of paragraph (a) of this section.

Rule 13p-1 Requirement of Report Regarding Disclosure of Registrant's Supply Chain Information Regarding Conflict Minerals

Every registrant that files reports with the Commission under Sections 13(a) (15 U.S.C. 78m(a)) or 15(d) (15 U.S.C. 78o(d)) of the Exchange Act, having conflict minerals that are necessary to the functionality or production of a product manufactured or contracted by that registrant to be manufactured, shall file a report on Form SD within the period specified in that Form disclosing the information required by the applicable items of Form SD as specified in that Form (17 CFR 249b.400).

[Editors' Note: Form SD requires that if any conflict minerals necessary to the functionality or production of a product manufactured by the registrant or contracted by the registrant to be manufactured are required to be reported, the registrant must conduct in good faith a reasonable country of origin inquiry regarding those conflict minerals that is reasonably designed to determine whether any of the conflict minerals originated in the Democratic Republic of the Congo or an adjoining country or are from recycled or scrap sources. It must also disclose in its filings and on its internet site the determination and the inquiry it performed. In some instances, it must exercise due diligence as to the source and the chain of custody of conflict minerals that conforms to a nationally or internationally recognized due diligence framework, if available, and include a statement that the registrant has obtained an independent private sector audit of the Conflict Minerals Report. For products that have not been found to be "DRC conflict free", the registrant must provide additional information. Conflict minerals are defined to include four identified minerals or their derivatives or any other the Secretary of State determines to be financing conflict in the Democratic Republic of the Congo].

Rule 13q-1 Disclosure of Payments Made by Resource Extraction Issuers

(a) A resource extraction issuer, as defined by paragraph (b) of this section, shall file a report on Form SD (17 CFR 249b.400) within the period specified in that Form disclosing the information required by the applicable items of Form SD as specified in that Form.

(b) *Definitions.* For the purpose of this section:

(1) *Resource extraction issuer* means an issuer that:

(i) Is required to file an annual report with the Commission; and

(ii) Engages in the commercial development of oil, natural gas, or minerals.

(2) *Commercial development of oil, natural gas, or minerals* includes exploration, extraction, processing, and export of oil, natural gas, or minerals, or the acquisition of a license for any such activity.

[Editors' Note: For resource extraction issuers, Form SD requires disclosure relating to type and amount of payments (including currency of payment) made by the issuer or a subsidiary to foreign governments or the U.S. government for purposes of the commercial development of oil, natural gas, or minerals.]

Regulation 14A: Solicitation of Proxies

Rule 14a-1. Definitions

Unless the context otherwise requires, all terms used in this regulation have the same meanings as in the Act or elsewhere in the general rules and regulations thereunder. In addition, the following definitions apply unless the context otherwise requires:

(a) *Associate.* The term "associate," used to indicate a relationship with any person, means:

(1) Any corporation or organization (other than the registrant or a majority owned subsidiary of the registrant) of which such person is an officer or partner or is, directly or indirectly, the beneficial owner of 10 percent or more of any class of equity securities;

(2) Any trust or other estate in which such person has a substantial beneficial interest or as to which such person serves as trustee or in a similar fiduciary capacity; and

(3) Any relative or spouse of such person, or any relative of such spouse, who has the same home as such person or who is a director or officer of the registrant or any of its parents or subsidiaries.

(b) *Employee benefit plan.* For purposes of Rules 14a-13, 14b-1 and 14b-2, the term "employee benefit plan" means any purchase, savings, options, bonus, appreciation, profit sharing, thrift, incentive, pension or similar plan primarily for employees, directors, trustees or officers.

(c) *Entity that exercises fiduciary powers.* The term "entity that exercises fiduciary powers" means any entity that holds securities in nominee name or otherwise on behalf of a beneficial owner but does not include a clearing agency registered pursuant to section 17A of the Act or a broker or a dealer.

(d) *Exempt employee benefit plan securities.* For purposes of Rules 14a-13, 14b-1, and 14b-2, the term "exempt employee benefit plan securities" means:

(1) Securities of the registrant held by an employee benefit plan, as defined in paragraph (b) of this section, where such plan is established by the registrant; or

(2) If notice regarding the current solicitation has been given pursuant to 14a-13(a)(1)(ii)(C) or if notice regarding the current request for a list of names, addresses and securities positions of beneficial owners has been given pursuant to Rule 14a-13(b)(3), securities of the registrant held by an employee benefit plan, as defined in paragraph (b) of this section, where such plan is established by an affiliate of the registrant.

(e) *Last fiscal year.* The term "last fiscal year" of the registrant means the last fiscal year of the registrant ending prior to the date of the meeting for which proxies are to be solicited or if the solicitation involves written authorization or consents in lieu of a meeting, the earliest date they may be used to effect corporate action.

(f) *Proxy.* The term "proxy" includes every proxy, consent or authorization within the meaning of section 14(a) of the Act. The consent or authorization may take the form of failure to object or to dissent.

(g) *Proxy statement.* The term "proxy statement" means the statement required by Rule 14a-3(a) whether or not contained in a single document.

(h) *Record date.* The term "record date" means the date as of which the record holders of securities entitled to vote at a meeting or by written consent or authorization shall be determined.

(i) *Record holder.* For purposes of Rules 14a-13, 14b-1 and 14b-2, the term "record holder" means any broker, dealer, voting trustee, bank, association or other entity that exercises fiduciary powers which holds securities of record in nominee name or otherwise or as a participant in a clearing agency registered pursuant to section 17A of the Act.

(j) *Registrant.* The term "registrant" means the issuer of the securities in respect of which proxies are to be solicited.

(k) *Respondent bank.* For purposes of Rules 14a-13, 14b-1 and 14b-2, the term "respondent bank" means any bank, association or other entity that exercises fiduciary powers which holds securities on behalf of beneficial owners and deposits such securities for safekeeping with another bank, association or other entity that exercises fiduciary powers.

(l) *Solicitation.* (1) The terms "solicit" and "solicitation" include:

(i) Any request for a proxy whether or not accompanied by or included in a form of proxy:

(ii) Any request to execute or not to execute, or to revoke, a proxy; or

(iii) The furnishing of a form of proxy or other communication to security holders under circumstances reasonably calculated to result in the procurement, withholding or revocation of a proxy, including:

(A) Any proxy voting advice that makes a recommendation to a security holder as to its vote, consent, or authorization on a specific matter for which security holder approval is solicited, and that is furnished by a person that markets its expertise as a provider of such proxy voting advice, separately from other forms of investment advice, and sells such proxy voting advice for a fee.

(B) [Reserved]

(2) The terms do not apply, however, to:

(i) The furnishing of a form of proxy to a security holder upon the unsolicited request of such security holder;

(ii) The performance by the registrant of acts required by Rule 14a-7;

(iii) The performance by any person of ministerial acts on behalf of a person soliciting a proxy; or

(iv) A communication by a security holder who does not otherwise engage in a proxy solicitation (other than a solicitation exempt under Rule 14a-2) stating how the security holder intends to vote and the reasons therefor, provided that the communication:

(A) Is made by means of speeches in public forums, press releases, published or broadcast opinions, statements, or advertisements appearing in a broadcast media, or newspaper, magazine or other bona fide publication disseminated on a regular basis.

(B) Is directed to persons to whom the security holder owes a fiduciary duty in connection with the voting of securities of a registrant held by the security holder, or

(C) Is made in response to unsolicited requests for additional information with respect to a prior communication by the security holder made pursuant to this paragraph (*l*)(2)(iv).

(v) The furnishing of any proxy voting advice by a person who furnishes such advice only in response to an unprompted request.

Rule 14a-2. Solicitations to Which Rules 14a-3 to 14a-15 Apply

Rules 14a-3 to 14a-15, except as specified below, apply to every solicitation of a proxy with respect to securities registered pursuant to section 12 of the Act, whether or not trading in such securities has been suspended. To the extent specified below, certain of these sections also apply to roll-up transactions that do not involve an entity with securities registered pursuant to section 12 of the Act.

(a) Rules 14a-3 to 14a-15 do not apply to the following:

(1) Any solicitation by a person in respect to securities carried in his name or in the name of his nominee (otherwise than as voting trustee) or held in his custody, if such person—

(i) Receives no commission or remuneration for such solicitation, directly or indirectly, other than reimbursement of reasonable expenses,

(ii) Furnishes promptly to the person solicited (or person's household in accordance with Rule 14a-3(e)(1)) a copy of all soliciting material with respect to the same subject matter or meeting received from all persons who shall furnish copies thereof for such purpose and who shall, if requested, defray the reasonable expenses to be incurred in forwarding such material, and

(iii) In addition, does no more than impartially instruct the person solicited to forward a proxy to the person, if any, to whom the person solicited desires to give a proxy, or impartially request from the person solicited instructions as to the authority to be conferred by the proxy and state that a proxy will be given if no instructions are received by a certain date.

(2) Any solicitation by a person in respect of securities of which he is the beneficial owner;

(3) Any solicitation involved in the offer and sale of securities registered under the Securities Act of 1933; *Provided,* That this paragraph shall not apply to securities to be issued in any transaction of the character specified in paragraph (a) of Rule 145 under that Act;

(4) Any solicitation with respect to a plan of reorganization under Chapter 11 of the Bankruptcy Reform Act of 1978, as amended, if made after the entry of an order approving the written disclosure statement concerning a plan

of reorganization pursuant to section 1125 of said Act and after, or concurrently with, the transmittal of such disclosure statement as required by section 1125 of said Act;

(5) [Reserved]; and

(6) Any solicitation through the medium of a newspaper advertisement which informs security holders of a source from which they may obtain copies of a proxy statement, form of proxy and any other soliciting material and does not more than:

(i) Name the registrant,

(ii) State the reason for the advertisement, and

(iii) Identify the proposal or proposals to be acted upon by security holders.

(b) Rules 14a-3 to 14a-6 (other than 14a-6(g) and (p)), Rules 14a-8, 14a-10, 14a-12 through 14a-15, and Rule 14a-19 do not apply to the following:

(1) Any solicitation by or on behalf of any person who does not, at any time during such solicitation, seek directly or indirectly, either on its own or another's behalf, the power to act as proxy for a security holder and does not furnish or otherwise request, or act on behalf of a person who furnishes or requests, a form of revocation, abstention, consent or authorization. *Provided, however,* That the exemption set forth in this paragraph shall not apply to:

(i) The registrant or an affiliate or associate of the registrant (other than an officer or director or any person serving in a similar capacity);

(ii) An officer or director of the registrant or any person serving in a similar capacity engaging in a solicitation financed directly or indirectly by the registrant;

(iii) An officer, director, affiliate or associate of a person that is ineligible to rely on the exemption set forth in this paragraph (other than persons specified in paragraph (b)(1)(i) of this section), or any person serving in a similar capacity.

(iv) Any nominee for whose election as a director proxies are solicited;

(v) Any person soliciting in opposition to a merger, recapitalization, reorganization, sale of assets or other extraordinary transaction recommended or approved by the board of directors of the registrant who is proposing or intends to propose an alternative transaction to which such person or one of its affiliates is a party;

(vi) Any person who is required to report beneficial ownership of the registrant's equity securities on a Schedule 13D, unless such person has filed a Schedule 13D and has not disclosed pursuant to Item 4 thereto an intent, or reserved the right, to engage in a control transaction, or any contested solicitation for the election of directors;

(vii) Any person who receives compensation from an ineligible person directly related to the solicitation of proxies, other than pursuant to Rule 14a-13;

(viii) Where the registrant is an investment company registered under the Investment Company Act of 1940, an "interested person" of that investment company, as that term is defined in section 2(a)(19) of the Investment Company Act;

(ix) Any person who, because of a substantial interest in the subject matter of the solicitation, is likely to receive a benefit from a successful solicitation that would not be shared pro rata by all other holders of the same class of securities, other than a benefit arising from the person's employment with the registrant; and

(x) Any person acting on behalf of any of the foregoing.

(2) Any solicitation made otherwise than on behalf of the registrant where the total number of persons solicited is not more than ten; and

(3) The furnishing of proxy voting advice by any person (the "advisor") to any other person with whom the advisor has a business relationship, if:

(i) The advisor renders financial advice in the ordinary course of his business;

(ii) The advisor discloses to the recipient of the advice any significant relationship with the registrant or any of its affiliates, or a security holder proponent of the matter on which advice is given, as well as any material interests of the advisor in such matter;

(iii) The advisor receives no special commission or remuneration for furnishing the proxy voting advice from any person other than a recipient of the advice and other persons who receive similar advice under this subsection; and

(iv) The proxy voting advice is not furnished on behalf of any person soliciting proxies or on behalf of a participant in an election subject to the provisions of Rule 14a-12(c).

(4) Any solicitation in connection with a roll-up transaction as defined in Item 901(c) of Regulation S-K in which the holder of a security that is the subject of a proposed roll-up transaction engages in preliminary communications with other holders of securities that are the subject of the same limited partnership roll-up transaction for the purpose of determining whether to solicit proxies, consents, or authorizations in opposition to the proposed limited partnership roll-up transaction; *provided, however,* that:

(i) This exemption shall not apply to a security holder who is an affiliate of the registrant or general partner or sponsor; and

(ii) This exemption shall not apply to a holder of five percent (5%) or more of the outstanding securities of a class that is the subject of the proposed roll-up transaction who engages in the business of buying and selling limited partnership interests in the secondary market unless that holder discloses to the persons to whom the communications are made such ownership interest and any relations of the holder to the parties of the transaction or to the transaction itself, as required by Rule 14a-6(n)(1) and specified in the Notice of Exempt Preliminary Roll-up Communication (Schedule 14a-104). If the communication is oral, this disclosure may be provided to the security holder orally. Whether the communication is written or oral, the notice required by Rule 14a-6(n) and Schedule 14a-104 shall be furnished to the Commission.

(5) Publication or distribution by a broker or a dealer of a research report in accordance with Rule 138 or Rule 139 during a transaction in which the broker or dealer or its affiliate participates or acts in an advisory role.

(6) Any solicitation by or on behalf of any person who does not seek directly or indirectly, either on its own or another's behalf, the power to act as proxy for a shareholder and does not furnish or otherwise request, or act on behalf of a person who furnishes or requests, a form of revocation, abstention, consent, or authorization in an electronic shareholder forum that is established, maintained or operated pursuant to the provisions of Rule 14a-17, provided that the solicitation is made more than 60 days prior to the date announced by a registrant for its next annual or special meeting of shareholders. If the registrant announces the date of its next annual or special meeting of shareholders less than 60 days before the meeting date, then the solicitation may not be made more than two days following the date of the registrant's announcement of the meeting date. Participation in an electronic shareholder forum does not eliminate a person's eligibility to solicit proxies after the date that this exemption is no longer available, or is no longer being relied upon, provided that any such solicitation is conducted in accordance with this regulation.

. . .

(9) Paragraphs (b)(1) and (b)(3) of this section shall not be available to a person furnishing proxy voting advice covered by §240.14a-1(l)(1)(iii)(A) ("proxy voting advice business") unless the proxy voting advice business includes in its proxy voting advice or in an electronic medium used to deliver the proxy voting advice prominent disclosure of:

(i) Any information regarding an interest, transaction, or relationship of the proxy voting advice business (or its affiliates) that is material to assessing the objectivity of the proxy voting advice in light of the circumstances of the particular interest, transaction, or relationship; and

(ii) Any policies and procedures used to identify, as well as the steps taken to address, any such material conflicts of interest arising from such interest, transaction, or relationship.

Rule 14a-3. Information to be Furnished to Security Holders

(a) No solicitation subject to this regulation shall be made unless each person solicited is concurrently furnished or has previously been furnished with:

(1) A publicly-filed preliminary or definitive proxy statement, in the form and manner described in Rule 14a-16, containing the information specified in Schedule 14A; or

(2) A preliminary or definitive written proxy statement included in a registration filed under the Securities Act of 1933 on Form S-4 or F-4 or Form N-14 and containing the information specified in such Form; or

(3) A publicly filed preliminary or definitive proxy statement, not in the form and manner described in Rule 14a-16, containing the information specified in Schedule 14A, if:

(i) The solicitation relates to a business combination transaction as defined in Rule 165 of this chapter as well as transactions for cash consideration requiring disclosure under Item 14 of schedule 14A; or

(ii) The solicitation may not follow the form and manner described in Rule 14a-16 pursuant to the laws of the state of incorporation of the registrant.

(b) If the solicitation is made on behalf of the registrant and relates to an annual (or special meeting in lieu of the annual) meeting of security holders, or written consent in lieu of such meeting, at which directors are to be elected, each proxy statement furnished pursuant to paragraph (a) of this section shall be accompanied or preceded by an annual report to security holders as follows:

(1) The report shall include, for the registrant and its subsidiaries consolidated audited balance sheets as of the end of each of the two most recent fiscal years and audited statements of income and cash flow for each of the three most recent fiscal years prepared in accordance with Regulation S-X, except that the provisions of Article 3 (other than §§210.3-03(e), 210.3-04 and 210.3-20) and Article 11 shall not apply. Any financial statement schedules or exhibits or separate financial statements which may otherwise be required in filings with the Commission may be omitted. If the financial statements of the registrant and its subsidiaries consolidated in the annual report filed or to be filed with the Commission are not required to be audited, the financial statements required by this paragraph may be unaudited. A smaller reporting company may provide the information in Article 8 of Regulation S-X in lieu of the financial information required by this paragraph 9(b)(1).

NOTE 1 TO PARAGRAPH (b)(1)

If the financial statements for a period prior to the most recently completed fiscal year have been examined by a predecessor accountant, the separate report of the predecessor accountant may be omitted in the report to security holders, provided the registrant has obtained from the predecessor accountant a reissued report covering the prior period presented and the successor accountant clearly indicates in the scope paragraph of his or her report (a) that the financial statements of the prior period were examined by other accountants, (b) the date of their report, (c) the type of opinion expressed by the predecessor accountant and (d) the substantive reasons therefore, if it was other than unqualified. It should be noted, however, that the separate report of any predecessor accountant is required in filings with the Commission. If, for instance, the financial statements in the annual report to security holders are incorporated by reference in a Form 10-K, the separate report of a predecessor accountant shall be filed in Part II or in Part IV as a financial statement schedule.

(2)(i) Financial statements and notes thereto shall be presented in roman type at least as large and as legible as 10-point modern type. If necessary for convenient presentation, the financial statements may be in roman type as large and as legible as 8-point modern type. All type shall be leaded at least 2 points.

(ii) Where the annual report to security holders is delivered through an electronic medium, issuers may satisfy legibility requirements applicable to printed documents, such as type size and font, by presenting all required information in a format readily communicated to investors.

(3) The report shall contain the supplementary financial information required by item 302 of Regulation S-K.

(4) The report shall contain information concerning changes in and disagreements with accountants on accounting and financial disclosure required by Item 304 of Regulation S-K.

(5)(i) (reserved)

(ii) The report shall contain management's discussion and analysis of financial condition and results of operations required by Item 303 of Regulation S-K.

(6) The report shall contain a brief description of the business done by the registrant and its subsidiaries during the most recent fiscal year which will, in the opinion of management, indicate the general nature and scope of the business of the registrant and its subsidiaries.

(7) The report shall contain information relating to the registrant's industry segments, classes of similar products or services, foreign and domestic operations and exports sales required by paragraphs (b), (c)(1)(i) and (d) of Item 101 of Regulation S-K.

(8) The report shall identify each of the registrant's directors and executive officers, and shall indicate the principal occupation or employment of each such person and the name and principal business of any organization by which such person is employed.

(9) The report shall contain the market price of and dividends on the registrant's common equity and related security holder matters required by Item 201(a), (b) and (c) of Regulation S-K. If the report precedes or accompanies a proxy statement or information statement relating to an annual meeting of security holders at which directors are to be elected (or special meeting or written consent in lieu of such meeting), furnish the performance graphs required by Item 201 (e).

(10) The registrant's proxy statement, or the report, shall contain an undertaking in bold face or otherwise reasonably prominent type to provide without charge to each person solicited upon the written request of any such person, a copy of the registrant's annual report on Form 10-K, including the financial statements and the financial statement schedules, required to be filed with the Commission pursuant to Rule 13a-1 under the Act for the registrant's most recent fiscal year, and shall indicate the name and address (including title or department) of the person to whom such a written request is to be directed. In the discretion of management, a registrant need not undertake to furnish without charge copies of all exhibits to its Form 10-K provided that the copy of the annual report on Form 10-K furnished without charge to requesting security holders is accompanied by a list briefly describing all the exhibits not contained therein and indicating that the registrant will furnish any exhibit upon the payment of a specified reasonable fee, which fee shall be limited to the registrant's reasonable expenses in furnishing such exhibit. If the registrant's annual report to security holders complies with all of the disclosure requirements of Form 10-K and is filed with the Commission in satisfaction of its Form 10-K filing requirements, such

registrant need not furnish a separate Form 10-K to security holders who receive a copy of such annual report. . . .

(c) Seven copies of the report sent to security holders pursuant to this rule shall be mailed to the Commission, solely for its information, not later than the date on which such report is first sent or given to security holders or the date on which preliminary copies, or definitive copies, if preliminary filing was not required, of solicitation material are filed with the Commission pursuant to Rule 14a-6, whichever date is later. The report is not deemed to be "soliciting material" or to be "filed" with the Commission or subject to this regulation otherwise than as provided in this Rule, or to the liabilities of section 18 of the Act, except to the extent that the registrant specifically requests that it be treated as a part of the proxy soliciting material or incorporates it in the proxy statement or other filed report by reference. . . .

(f) The provisions of paragraph (a) of this section shall not apply to a communication made by means of speeches in public forums, press releases, published or broadcast opinions, statements, or advertisements appearing in a broadcast media, newspaper, magazine or other bona fide publication disseminated on a regular basis, provided that:

(1) No form of proxy, consent or authorization or means to execute the same is provided to a security holder in connection with the communication; and

(2) At the time the communication is made, a definitive proxy statement is on file with the Commission pursuant to Rule 14a-6(b).

Rule 14a-4. Requirements as to Proxy

(a) The form of proxy

(1) shall indicate in bold-face type whether or not the proxy is solicited on behalf of the registrant's board of directors or, if provided other than by a majority of the board of directors, shall indicate in bold-face type on whose behalf the solicitation is made;

(2) Shall provide a specifically designated blank space for dating the proxy card; and

(3) Shall identify clearly and impartially each separate matter intended to be acted upon, whether or not related to or conditioned on the approval of other matters, and whether proposed by the registrant or by security holders. No reference need be made, however, to proposals as to which discretionary authority is conferred pursuant to paragraph (c) of this section.

NOTE TO PARAGRAPH (a)(3) (ELECTRONIC FILERS)

Electronic filers shall satisfy the filing requirements of Rule 14a-6(a) or (b) with respect to the form of proxy by filing the form of proxy as an appendix at the end of the proxy statement. Forms of proxy shall not be filed as exhibits or separate documents within an electronic submission.

(b)(1) Means shall be provided in the form of proxy whereby the person solicited is afforded an opportunity to specify by boxes a choice between approval or disapproval of, or abstention with respect to, each separate matter referred to therein as intended to be acted upon, other than elections to office and votes to determine the frequency of shareholder votes on executive compensation pursuant to §240.14a-21(b) of this chapter. A proxy may confer discretionary authority with respect to matters as to which a choice is not specified by the security holder provided that the form of proxy states in bold-face type how it is intended to vote the shares represented by the proxy in each such case.

(2) A form of proxy which provides for the election of directors shall set forth the names of persons nominated for election as directors, including any person whose nomination by a shareholder or shareholder group satisfies the requirements of an applicable state or foreign law provision, or a registrant's governing documents as they relate to the inclusion of shareholder director nominees in the registrant's proxy materials.

(3) Except as otherwise provided in Rule.14a-19, a form of proxy that provides for the election of directors may provide a means for the security holder to grant authority to vote for the nominees set forth, as a group, provided that there is a similar means for the security holder to withhold authority to vote for such group of nominees (or, when applicable state law gives legal effect to votes cast against a nominee, a similar means for the security holder to vote against such group of nominees and a means for security holders to abstain from voting for such group of nominees). Any such form of proxy which is executed by the security holder in such manner as not to withhold authority to vote for the election of any nominee, or not to grant authority to vote against the election of any nominee, shall be deemed to grant authority to vote for the election of any nominee, provided that the form of proxy so states in bold-face type. Means to grant authority to vote for any nominees as a group or to withhold authority for any nominees as a group or to vote against any nominees as a group may not be provided if the form of proxy includes one or more shareholder nominees in accordance with an applicable state or foreign law provision, or a registrant's governing documents as they relate to the inclusion of shareholder director nominees in the registrant's proxy materials.

(4) When applicable state law gives legal effect to votes cast against a nominee, then in lieu of providing a means for security holders to withhold authority to vote, the form of proxy shall provide a means for security holders to vote against each nominee and a means for security holders to abstain from voting. When applicable state law does not give legal effect to votes cast against a nominee, such form of proxy shall not provide a means for security holders to vote against any nominee and such form of proxy shall clearly provide any of the following means for security holders to withhold authority to vote for each nominee:

(i) A box opposite the name of each nominee which may be marked to indicate that authority to vote for such nominee is withheld; or

(ii) An instruction in bold-face type which indicates that the security holder may withhold authority to vote for any nominee by lining through or otherwise striking out the name of any nominee; or

(iii) Designated blank spaces in which the security holder may enter the names of nominees with respect to whom the security holder chooses to withhold authority to vote; or

(iv) Any other similar means, provided that clear instructions are furnished indicating how the security holder may withhold authority to vote for any nominee.

Instruction 1 to paragraphs (b)(2), (3), and (4). Paragraphs (b)(2), (3), and (4) do not apply in the case of a merger, consolidation or other plan if the election of directors is an integral part of the plan.

(5) A form of proxy which provides for a shareholder vote on the frequency of shareholder votes to approve the compensation of executives required by section 14A(a)(2) of the Securities Exchange Act of 1934 shall provide means whereby the person solicited is afforded an opportunity to specify by boxes a choice among 1, 2 or 3 years, or abstain.

(c) A proxy may confer discretionary authority to vote on any of the following matters:

(1) For an annual meeting of shareholders, if the registrant did not have notice of the matter at least 45 days before the date on which the registrant first sent its proxy materials for the prior year's annual meeting of shareholders (or date specified by an advance notice provision), and a specific statement to that effect is made in the proxy statement or form of proxy. If during the prior year the registrant did not hold an annual meeting, or if the date of the meeting has changed more than 30 days from the prior year, then notice must not have been received a reasonable time before the registrant sends its proxy materials for the current year.

(2) In the case in which the registrant has received timely notice in connection with an annual meeting of shareholders (as determined under paragraph (c)(1) of this Rule), if the registrant includes, in the proxy statement, advice on the nature of the matter and how the registrant intends to exercise its discretion to vote on each matter. However, even if the registrant includes this information in its proxy statement, it may not exercise discretionary voting authority on a particular proposal if the proponent:

(i) Provides the registrant with a written statement, within the time-frame determined under paragraph (c)(1) of this Rule, that the proponent intends to deliver a proxy statement and form of proxy to holders of at least the percentage of the company's voting shares required under applicable law to carry the proposal;

(ii) Includes the same statement in its proxy materials filed under Rule 14a-6; and

(iii) Immediately after soliciting the percentage of shareholders required to carry the proposal, provides the registrant with a statement from any solicitor or other person with knowledge that the necessary steps have been taken to deliver a proxy statement and form of proxy to holders of at least the percentage of the company's voting shares required under applicable law to carry the proposal.

(3) For solicitations other than for annual meetings or for solicitations by persons other than the registrant, matters which the persons making the solicitation do not know, a reasonable time before the solicitation, are to be presented at

the meeting, if a specific statement to that effect is made in the proxy statement or form of proxy.

(4) Approval of the minutes of the prior meeting if such approval does not amount to ratification of the action taken at that meeting;

(5) The election of any person to any office for which a bona fide nominee is named in a proxy statement and such nominee is unable to serve or for good cause will not serve.

(6) Any proposal omitted from the proxy statement and form of proxy pursuant to Rule 14a-8 or 14a-9 of this chapter.

(7) Matters incident to the conduct of the meeting.

(d) No proxy shall confer authority:

(1) To vote for the election of any person to any office for which a bona fide nominee is not named in the proxy statement:

(i) A person shall not be deemed to be a bona fide nominee and shall not be named as such unless the person has consented to being named in a proxy statement relating to the registrant's next annual meeting of shareholders at which directors are to be elected (or a special meeting in lieu of such meeting) and to serve if elected.

(ii) Notwithstanding paragraph (d)(1)(i) of this section, if the registrant is an investment company registered under the Investment Company Act of 1940 (15 U.S.C. 80a-1 et seq.) or a business development company as defined by section 2(a)(48) of the Investment Company Act of 1940 (15 U.S.C. 80a-2(a)(48)), a person shall not be deemed to be a bona fide nominee and shall not be named as such unless the person has consented to being named in the proxy statement and to serve if elected. Provided, however, that nothing in this section shall prevent any person soliciting in support of nominees who, if elected, would constitute a minority of the board of directors of an investment company registered under the Investment Company Act of 1940 or a business development company as defined by section 2(a)(48) of the Investment Company Act of 1940, from seeking authority to vote for nominees named in the registrant's proxy statement, so long as the soliciting party:

(A) Seeks authority to vote in the aggregate for the number of director positions then subject to election;

(B) Represents that it will vote for all the registrant nominees, other than those registrant nominees specified by the soliciting party;

(C) Provides the security holder an opportunity to withhold authority with respect to any other registrant nominee by writing the name of that nominee on the form of proxy; and

(D) States on the form of proxy and in the proxy statement that there is no assurance that the registrant's nominees will serve if elected with any of the soliciting party's nominees; (2) To vote at any annual meeting other than the next annual meeting (or any adjournment thereof) to be held after the date on which the proxy statement and form of proxy are first sent or given to security holders;

(3) To vote with respect to more than one meeting (and any adjournment thereof) or more than one consent solicitation; or

(4) To consent to or authorize any action other than the action proposed to be taken in the proxy statement, or matters referred to in paragraph (c) of this rule.

(e) The proxy statement or form of proxy shall provide, subject to reasonable specified conditions, that the shares represented by the proxy will be voted and that where the person solicited specifies by means of a ballot provided pursuant to paragraph (b) of this section a choice with respect to any matter to be acted upon, the shares will be voted in accordance with the specifications so made.

(f) No person conducting a solicitation subject to this regulation shall deliver a form of proxy, consent or authorization to any security holder unless the security holder concurrently receives, or has previously received, a definitive proxy statement that has been filed with the Commission pursuant to Rule 14a-6(b).

Rule 14a-5. Presentation of Information in Proxy Statement

(a) The information included in the proxy statement shall be clearly presented and the statements made shall be divided into groups according to subject matter and the various groups of statements shall be preceded by appropriate headings. The order of items and sub-items in the schedule need not be followed. Where practicable and appropriate, the information shall be presented in tabular form. All amounts shall be stated in figures. Information required by more than one applicable item need not be repeated. No statement need be made in response to any item or sub-item which is inapplicable.

(b) Any information required to be included in the proxy statement as to terms of securities or other subject matter which from a standpoint of practical necessity must be determined in the future may be stated in terms of present knowledge and intention. To the extent practicable, the authority to be conferred concerning each such matter shall be confined within limits reasonably related to the need for discretionary authority. Subject to the foregoing, information which is not known to the persons on whose behalf the solicitation is to be made and which it is not reasonably within the power of such persons to ascertain or procure may be omitted, if a brief statement of the circumstances rendering such information unavailable is made.

(c) Any information contained in any other proxy soliciting material which has been or will be furnished to each person solicited in connection with the same meeting or subject matter may be omitted from the proxy statement, if a clear reference is made to the particular document containing such information.

(d)(1) All printed proxy statements shall be in roman type at least as large and as legible as 10-point modern type, except that to the extent necessary for convenient presentation financial statements and other tabular data, but not the notes thereto, may be in roman type at least as large and as legible as 8-point modern type. All such type shall be leaded at least 2 points.

(2) Where a proxy statement is delivered through an electronic medium, issuers may satisfy legibility requirements applicable to printed documents, such as type size and font, by presenting all required information in a format readily communicated to investors.

(e) All proxy statements shall disclose, under an appropriate caption, the following dates:

(1) The deadline for submitting shareholder proposals for inclusion in the registrant's proxy statement and form of proxy for the registrant's next annual meeting, calculated in the manner provided in Rule 14a-8(d) (Question 4); and

(2) The date after which notice of a shareholder proposal submitted outside the processes of Rule 14a-8 is considered untimely, either calculated in the manner provided by Rule 14a-4(c)(1) or as established by the registrant's advance notice provision, if any, authorized by applicable state law. . . . .

(4) The deadline for providing notice of a solicitation of proxies in support of director nominees other than the registrant's nominees pursuant to Rule.14a-19 for the registrant's next annual meeting unless the registrant is an investment company registered under the Investment Company Act of 1940 (15 U.S.C. 80a-1 et seq.) or a business development company as defined by section 2(a)(48) of the Investment Company Act of 1940 (15 U.S.C. 80a-2(a)(48)).

(f) If the date of the next annual meeting is subsequently advanced or delayed by more than 30 calendar days from the date of the annual meeting to which the proxy statement relates, the registrant shall, in a timely manner, inform shareholders of such change, and the new dates referred to in paragraphs (e)(1) and (e)(2) of this Rule, by including a notice, under Item 5, in its earliest possible quarterly report on Form 10-Q, or, in the case of investment companies, in a shareholder report under Rule 30d-1 under the Investment Company Act of 1940, or, if impracticable, any means reasonably calculated to inform shareholders.

Rule 14a-6. Filing Requirements

(a) *Preliminary proxy statement.* Five preliminary copies of the proxy statement and form of proxy shall be filed with the Commission at least 10 calendar days prior to the date definitive copies of such material are first sent or given to security holders, or such shorter period prior to that date as the Commission may authorize upon a showing of good cause thereunder. A registrant, however, shall not file with the Commission a preliminary proxy statement, form of proxy or other soliciting material to be furnished to security holders concurrently therewith if the solicitation relates to an annual (or special meeting in lieu of the annual) meeting or for an investment company registered under the Investment Company Act of 1940 or a business development company, if the solicitation relates to any meeting of security holders at which the only matters to be acted upon are:

(1) The election of directors;

(2) The election, approval or ratification of accountant(s);

(3) A security holder proposal included pursuant to Rule 14a-8;

(4) The approval or ratification of a plan as defined in paragraph (a)(6)(ii) of Item 402 of Regulation S-K or amendments to such a plan;

(5) With respect to an investment company registered under the Investment Company Act of 1940 or a business development company, a proposal to continue, without change, any advisory or other contract or agreement that previously has been the subject of a proxy solicitation for which proxy material was filed with the Commission pursuant to this rule;

(6) With respect to an open-end investment company registered under the Investment Company Act of 1940, a proposal to increase the number of shares authorized to be issued; and/or

(7) A vote to approve the compensation of executives as required pursuant to section 14A(a)(1) of the Securities Exchange Act of 1934 and Rule 14a-21(a) of this chapter, or pursuant to section 111(e)(1) of the Emergency Economic Stabilization Act of 2008 (12 U.S.C. 5221(e)(1)) and Rule 14a-20 of this chapter, a vote to determine the frequency of shareholder votes to approve the compensation of executives as required pursuant to Section 14A(a)(2) of the Securities Exchange Act of 1934 and Rule 14a-21(b) of this chapter, or any other shareholder advisory vote on executive compensation.

This exclusion from filing preliminary proxy material does not apply if the registrant comments upon or refers to a solicitation in opposition in connection with the meeting in its proxy material.

Notes To Paragraph (a)

1. The filing of revised material does not recommence the ten day time period unless the revised material contains material revisions or material new proposal(s) that constitute a fundamental change in the proxy material.

2. The official responsible for the preparation of the proxy material should make every effort to verify the accuracy and completeness of the information required by the applicable rules. The preliminary material should be filed with the Commission at the earliest practicable date.

3. Solicitation in Opposition. For purposes of the exclusion from filing preliminary proxy material, a "solicitation in opposition" includes: {a} Any solicitation opposing a proposal supported by the registrant; {b} any solicitation supporting a proposal that the registrant does not expressly support, other than a security holder proposal included in the registrant's proxy material pursuant to Rule 14a-8; and {c} any solicitation subject to Rule 14a-19. The inclusion of a security holder proposal in the registrant's proxy material pursuant to Rule14a-8 does not constitute a "solicitation in opposition," even if the registrant opposes the proposal and/or includes a statement in opposition to the proposal. The inclusion of a shareholder nominee in the registrant's proxy materials pursuant to an applicable state or foreign law provision, or a registrant's governing documents as they relate to the inclusion of shareholder director nominees in the registrant's proxy materials does not constitute a "solicitation in opposition" for purposes of paragraph (a) of this section, even if the registrant opposes the shareholder nominee and solicits against the shareholder nominee and in favor of a registrant nominee.4. A registrant that is filing proxy material in preliminary form only because the registrant has commented on or referred to a solicitation in opposition should indicate that fact in a transmittal letter when filing the preliminary material with the Commission.

(b) *Definitive proxy statement and other soliciting materials.* Eight definitive copies of the proxy statement, form of proxy and all other soliciting materials, in the same form as the material sent to security holders, must be filed with the Commission no later than the date they are first sent or given to security holders. Three copies of these materials also must be filed with, or mailed for filing to, each national securities exchange on which the registrant has a class of securities listed and registered. . . .

(d) *Release dates.* All preliminary proxy statements and forms of proxy filed pursuant to paragraph (a) of this section shall be accompanied by a statement of the date on which definitive copies thereof filed pursuant to paragraph (b) of this section are intended to be released to security holders. All definitive material filed pursuant to paragraph (b) of this section shall be accompanied by a statement of the date on which copies of such material were released to security holders, or, if not released, the date on which copies thereof are intended to be released. All material filed pursuant to paragraph (c) of this section shall be accompanied by a statement of the date on which copies thereof were released to the individual who will make the actual solicitation or if not released, the date on which copies thereof are intended to be released.

(e)(1) *Public availability of information.* All copies of preliminary proxy statements and forms of proxy filed pursuant to paragraph (a) of this section shall be clearly marked "Preliminary Copies," and shall be deemed immediately available for public inspection unless confidential treatment is obtained pursuant to paragraph (e)(2) of this section.

(2) *Confidential treatment.* If action will be taken on any matter specified in Item 14 of Schedule 14A, all copies of the preliminary proxy statement and form of proxy filed under paragraph (a) of this section will be for the information of the Commission only and will not be deemed available for public inspection until filed with the Commission in definitive form so long as:

(i) The proxy statement does not relate to a matter of proposal subject to Rule 13e-3 or a roll-up transaction as defined in Item 901(c) of Regulation S-K;

(ii) Neither the parties to the transaction nor any persons authorized to act on their behalf have made any public communications relating to the transaction except for statements where the content is limited to the information specified in Rule 135; and

(iii) The materials are filed in paper and marked "Confidential, For Use of the Commission Only." In all cases, the materials may be disclosed to any department or agency of the United States Government and to the Congress, and the Commission may make any inquiries or investigation into the materials as may be necessary to conduct an adequate review by the Commission.

(g) *Solicitations subject to Rule 14a-2(b)(1).* (1) Any person who:

(i) Engages in a solicitation pursuant to Rule 14a-2(b)(1), and

(ii) At the commencement of that solicitation owns beneficially securities of the class which is the subject of the solicitation with a market value of over $5 million,

shall furnish or mail to the Commission, not later than three days after the date the written solicitation is first sent or given to any security holder, five copies of a statement containing the information specified in the Notice of Exempt Solicitation which statement shall attach as an exhibit all written soliciting materials. Five copies of an amendment to such statement shall be furnished or mailed to the Commission, in connection with dissemination of any additional communications, not later than three days after the date the additional material is first sent or given to any security holder. Three copies of the Notice of Exempt Solicitation and amendments thereto shall, at the same time the materials are furnished or mailed to the Commission, be furnished or mailed to each national securities exchange upon which any class of securities of the registrant is listed and registered.

(2) Notwithstanding paragraph (g)(1) of this section, no such submission need be made with respect to oral solicitations (other than with respect to scripts used in connection with such oral solicitations), speeches delivered in a public forum, press releases, published or broadcast opinions, statements, and advertisements appearing in a broadcast media, or a newspaper, magazine or other bona fide publication disseminated on a regular basis. . . .

(j) *Merger proxy materials.* Any proxy statement, form of proxy or other soliciting material required to be filed by this section that also is either: (i) included in a registration statement filed under the Securities Act of 1933 on Forms S-4, F-4 or N-14; or (ii) filed under Rules 424, 425 or 497 of this chapter is required to be filed only under the Securities Act, and is deemed filed under this section. In that case, the fee required under paragraph (i) of this section need not be paid. . . .

(n) *Solicitations subject to Rule 14a-2(b)(4).* Any person who:

(1) Engages in a solicitation pursuant to Rule 14a-2(b)(4), and

(2) At the commencement of that solicitation both owns five percent (5%) or more of the outstanding securities of a class that is the subject of the proposed roll-up transaction, and engages in the business of buying and selling limited partnership interests in the secondary market, shall furnish or mail to the Commission, not later than three days after the date an oral or written solicitation by that person is first made, sent or provided to any security holder, five copies of a statement containing the information specified in the Notice of Exempt Preliminary Roll-up Communication (Schedule 14a-104). Five copies of any amendment to such statement shall be furnished or mailed to the Commission not later than three days after a communication containing revised material is first made, sent or provided to any security holder.

(o) *Solicitations before furnishing a definitive proxy statement.* Solicitations that are published, sent, or given to security holders before they have been furnished a definitive proxy statement must be made in accordance with Rule 14a-12 unless there is an exemption available under Rule 14a-2.

Rule 14a-7. Obligations of Registrants to Provide a List of, or Mail Soliciting Material to Security Holders

(a) If the registrant has made or intends to make a proxy solicitation in connection with a security holder meeting or action by consent or authorization, upon the written request by any record or beneficial holder of securities of the class entitled to vote at the meeting or to execute a consent or authorization to provide a list of security holders or to mail the requesting security holder's materials, regardless of whether the request references this section, the registrant shall:

(1) Deliver to the requesting security holder within five business days after receipt of the request:

(i) Notification as to whether the registrant has elected to mail the security holder's soliciting materials or provide a security holder list if the election under paragraph (b) of this section is to be made by the registrant;

(ii) A statement of the approximate number of record holders and beneficial holders, separated by type of holder and class, owning securities in the same class or classes as holders which have been or are to be solicited on management's behalf, or any more limited group of such holders designated by the security holder if available or retrievable under the registrant's or its transfer agent's security holder data systems; and

(iii) The estimated cost of mailing a proxy statement, form of proxy or other communication to such holders, including to the extent known or reasonably available, the estimated costs of any bank, broker, and similar person through whom the registrant has solicited or intends to solicit beneficial owners in connection with the security holder meeting or action;

(2) Perform the acts set forth in either paragraphs (a)(2)(i) or (a)(2)(ii) of this section, at the registrant's or requesting security holder's option, as specified in paragraph (b) of this section:

(i) Send copies of any proxy statement, form of proxy, or other soliciting material, including a Notice of Internet Availability of Proxy Materials (as described in Rule 14a-16), furnished by the security holder to the record holders, including banks, brokers, and similar entities, designated by the security holder. A sufficient number of copies must be sent to the banks, brokers, and similar entities for distribution to all beneficial owners designated by the security holder. The security holder may designate only record holders and/or beneficial owners who have not requested paper and/or e-mail copies of the proxy statement. If the registrant has received affirmative written or implied consent to deliver a single proxy statement to security holders at a shared address in accordance with the procedures in Rule 14a-3(e)(1), a single copy of the proxy statement or Notice of Internet Availability of Proxy Materials furnished by the security holder shall be sent to that address, provided that if multiple copies of the Notice of Internet Availability of Proxy Materials are furnished by the security holder for that address, the registrant shall deliver those copies in a single envelope to that address. The registrant shall send the security holder material with reasonable promptness after tender of the material to be sent, envelopes or other containers therefore, postage or payment for postage and other reasonable expenses of effecting such distribution. The registrant shall not be responsible for the content of the material; or

(ii) Deliver the following information to the requesting security holder within five business days of receipt of the request:

(A) A reasonably current list of the names, addresses and security positions of the record holders, including banks, and similar entities holding securities in the same class or classes as holders which have been or are to be solicited on management's behalf, or any more limited group of such holders designated by the security holder if available or retrievable under the registrant's or its transfer agent's security holder data systems;

(B) The most recent list of names, addresses and security positions of beneficial owners as specified in Rule 14a-13(b), in the possession, or which subsequently comes into the possession, of the registrant;

(C) The names of security holders at a shared address that have consented to delivery of a single copy of proxy materials to a shared address, if the registrant has received written or implied consent in accordance with Rule 14a-3(e)(1); and

(D) If the registrant has relied on Rule 14a-16, the names of security holders who have requested papers copies of the proxy materials for all meetings and the names of security holders who, as of the date that the registrant receives the request, have requested paper copies of the proxy materials only for the meeting to which the solicitation relates.

(iii) All security holder list information shall be in the form requested by the security holder to the extent that such from is available to the registrant without undue burden or expense. The registrant shall furnish the security holder with updated record holder information on a daily basis or, if not available on a daily basis, at the shortest reasonable intervals; provided, however, the registrant need not provide beneficial or record holder information more current than the record date for the meeting or action.

(b)(1) The requesting security holder shall have the options set forth in paragraph (a)(2) of this section, and the registrant shall have corresponding obligations, if the registrant or general partner or sponsor is soliciting or intends to solicit with respect to:

(i) A proposal that is subject to Rule 13e-3;

(ii) A roll-up transaction as defined in Item 901(c) of Regulation S-K that involves an entity with securities registered pursuant to Section 12 of the Act; or

(iii) A roll-up transaction as defined in Item 901(c) of Regulation S-K that involves a limited partnership, unless the transaction involves only:

(A) Partnership whose investors will receive new securities or securities in another entity that are not reported under a transaction reporting plan declared effective before December 17, 1993 by the Commission under Section 11A of the Act; or

(B) Partnerships whose investors' securities are reported under a transaction reporting plan declared effective before December 17, 1993 by the Commission under Section 11A of the Act.

(2) With respect to all other requests pursuant to this section, the registrant shall have the option to either mail the security holder's material or furnish the security holder list as set forth in this section.

(c) At the time of a list request, the security holder making the request shall:

(1) If holding the registrant's securities through a nominee, provide the registrant with a statement by the nominee or other independent third party, or a copy of a current filing made with the Commission and furnished to the registrant, confirming such holder's beneficial ownership; and

(2) Provide the registrant with an affidavit, declaration, affirmation or other similar document provided for under applicable state law identifying the proposal or other corporate action that will be the subject of the security holder's solicitation or communication and attesting that:

(i) The security holder will not use the list information for any purpose other than to solicit security holders with respect to the same meeting or action by consent or authorization for which the registrant is soliciting or intends to solicit or to communicate with security holders with respect to a solicitation commenced by the registrant; and

(ii) The security holder will not disclose such information to any person other than a beneficial owner for whom the request was made and an employee or agent to the extent necessary to effectuate the communication or solicitation.

(d) The security holder shall not use the information furnished by the registrant pursuant to paragraph (a)(2)(ii) of this section for any purpose other than to solicit security holders with respect to the same meeting or action by consent or authorization for which the registrant is soliciting or intends to solicit or to communicate with security holders with respect to a solicitation commenced by the registrant; or disclose such information to any person other than an employee, agent, or beneficial owner for whom a request was made to the extent necessary to effectuate the communication or solicitation. The security holder shall return the information provided pursuant to paragraph (a)(2)(ii) of this section and shall not retain any copies thereof or of any information derived from such information after the termination of the solicitation.

(e) The security holder shall reimburse the reasonable expenses incurred by the registrant in performing the acts requested pursuant to paragraph (a) of this section.

Notes to Rule 14a-7

1. Reasonably prompt methods of distribution to security holders may be used instead of mailing. If an alternative distribution method is chosen, the costs of that method should be considered where necessary rather than the costs of mailing. . . .

Rule 14a-8. Shareholder Proposals

This section addresses when a company must include a shareholder's proposal in its proxy statement and identify the proposal in its form of proxy when the company holds an annual or special meeting of shareholders. In summary, in order to have your shareholder proposal included on a company's proxy card, and included along with any supporting statement in its proxy statement, you must be eligible and follow certain procedures. Under a few specific circumstances, the company is permitted to exclude your proposal, but only after submitting its reasons to the Commission. We structured this section in a question-and-answer format so that it is easier to understand. The references to "you" are to a shareholder seeking to submit the proposal.

(a) *Question 1: What is a proposal?* A shareholder proposal is your recommendation or requirement that the company and/or its board of directors take action, which you intend to present at a meeting of the company's shareholders. Your proposal should state as clearly as possible the course of action that you believe the company should follow. If your proposal is placed on the company's proxy card, the company must also provide in the form of proxy means for shareholders to specify by boxes a choice between approval or disapproval, or abstention. Unless otherwise indicated, the word "proposal" as used in this section refers both to your proposal, and to your corresponding statement in support of your proposal (if any).

(b) *Question 2: Who is eligible to submit a proposal, and how do I demonstrate to the company that I am eligible?*

(1) To be eligible to submit a proposal, you must satisfy the following requirements:

(i) You must have continuously held:

(A) At least $2,000 in market value of the company's securities entitled to vote on the proposal for at least three years; or

(B) At least $15,000 in market value of the company's securities entitled to vote on the proposal for at least two years; or

(C) At least $25,000 in market value of the company's securities entitled to vote on the proposal for at least one year; or

(D) The amounts specified in paragraph (b)(3) of this section. This paragraph (b)(1)(i)(D) will expire on the same date that §240.14a-8(b)(3) expires; and

(ii) You must provide the company with a written statement that you intend to continue to hold the requisite amount of securities, determined in accordance with paragraph (b)(1)(i)(A) through (C) of this section, through the date of the shareholders' meeting for which the proposal is submitted; and

(iii) You must provide the company with a written statement that you are able to meet with the company in person or via teleconference no less than 10 calendar days, nor more than 30 calendar days, after submission of the shareholder proposal. You must include your contact information as well as business days and specific times that you are available to discuss the proposal with the company. You must identify times that are within the regular business hours of the company's principal executive offices. If these hours are not disclosed in the company's proxy statement for the prior year's annual meeting, you must identify times that are between 9 a.m. and 5:30 p.m. in the time zone of the company's principal executive offices. If you elect to co-file a proposal, all co-filers must either:

(A) Agree to the same dates and times of availability, or

(B) Identify a single lead filer who will provide dates and times of the lead filer's availability to engage on behalf of all co-filers; and

(iv) If you use a representative to submit a shareholder proposal on your behalf, you must provide the company with written documentation that:

(A) Identifies the company to which the proposal is directed;

(B) Identifies the annual or special meeting for which the proposal is submitted;

(C) Identifies you as the proponent and identifies the person acting on your behalf as your representative;

(D) Includes your statement authorizing the designated representative to submit the proposal and otherwise act on your behalf;

(E) Identifies the specific topic of the proposal to be submitted;

(F) Includes your statement supporting the proposal; and

(G) Is signed and dated by you.

(v) The requirements of paragraph (b)(1)(iv) of this section shall not apply to shareholders that are entities so long as the representative's authority to act on the shareholder's behalf is apparent and self-evident such that a reasonable person would understand that the agent has authority to submit the proposal and otherwise act on the shareholder's behalf.

(vi) For purposes of paragraph (b)(1)(i) of this section, you may not aggregate your holdings with those of another shareholder or group of shareholders to meet the requisite amount of securities necessary to be eligible to submit a proposal.

(2) One of the following methods must be used to demonstrate your eligibility to submit a proposal:

(i) If you are the registered holder of your securities, which means that your name appears in the company's records as a shareholder, the company can verify your eligibility on its own, although you will still have to provide the company with a written statement that you intend to continue to hold the requisite amount of securities, determined in accordance with paragraph (b)(1)(i)(A) through (C) of this section, through the date of the meeting of shareholders.

(ii) If, like many shareholders, you are not a registered holder, the company likely does not know that you are a shareholder, or how many shares you own. In this case, at the time you submit your proposal, you must prove your eligibility to the company in one of two ways:

(A) The first way is to submit to the company a written statement from the "record" holder of your securities (usually a broker or bank) verifying that, at the time you submitted your proposal, you continuously held at least $2,000, $15,000, or $25,000 in market value of the company's securities entitled to vote on the proposal for at least three years, two years, or one year, respectively. You must also include your own written statement that you intend to continue to hold the requisite amount of securities, determined in accordance with paragraph (b)(1)(i)(A) through (C) of this section, through the date of the shareholders' meeting for which the proposal is submitted; or

(B) The second way to prove ownership applies only if you were required to file, and filed, a Schedule 13D (§240.13d-101), Schedule 13G (§240.13d-102), Form 3 (§249.103 of this chapter), Form 4 (§249.104 of this chapter), and/or Form 5 (§249.105 of this chapter), or amendments to those documents or updated forms, demonstrating that you meet at least one of the share ownership requirements under paragraph (b)(1)(i)(A) through (C) of this section. If you have filed one or more of these documents with the SEC, you may demonstrate your eligibility to submit a proposal by submitting to the company:

(1) A copy of the schedule(s) and/or form(s), and any subsequent amendments reporting a change in your ownership level;

(2) Your written statement that you continuously held at least $2,000, $15,000, or $25,000 in market value of the company's securities entitled to vote on the proposal for at least three years, two years, or one year, respectively; and

(3) Your written statement that you intend to continue to hold the requisite amount of securities, determined in accordance with paragraph (b)(1)(i)(A)

through (C) of this section, through the date of the company's annual or special meeting.

(3) If you continuously held at least $2,000 of a company's securities entitled to vote on the proposal for at least one year as of January 4, 2021, and you have continuously maintained a minimum investment of at least $2,000 of such securities from January 4, 2021 through the date the proposal is submitted to the company, you will be eligible to submit a proposal to such company for an annual or special meeting to be held prior to January 1, 2023. If you rely on this provision, you must provide the company with your written statement that you intend to continue to hold at least $2,000 of such securities through the date of the shareholders' meeting for which the proposal is submitted. You must also follow the procedures set forth in paragraph (b)(2) of this section to demonstrate that:

(i) You continuously held at least $2,000 of the company's securities entitled to vote on the proposal for at least one year as of January 4, 2021; and

(ii) You have continuously maintained a minimum investment of at least $2,000 of such securities from January 4, 2021through the date the proposal is submitted to the company.

(iii) This paragraph (b)(3) will expire on January 1, 2023.

(c) *Question 3: How many proposals may I submit?* Each person may submit no more than one proposal, directly or indirectly, to a company for a particular shareholders' meeting. A person may not rely on the securities holdings of another person for the purpose of meeting the eligibility requirements and submitting multiple proposals for a particular shareholders' meeting.

(d) *Question 4: How long can my proposal be?* The proposal, including any accompanying supporting statement, may not exceed 500 words.

(e) *Question 5: What is the deadline for submitting a proposal?* (1) If you are submitting your proposal for the company's annual meeting, you can in most cases find the deadline in last year's proxy statement. However, if the company did not hold an annual meeting last year, or has changed the date of its meeting for this year more than 30 days from last year's meeting, you can usually find the deadline in one of the company's quarterly reports on Form 10-Q or 10-QSB, or in shareholder reports of investment companies under §30d-1 of the Investment Company Act of 1940. In order to avoid controversy, shareholders should submit their proposals by means, including electronic means, that permit them to prove the date of delivery.

(2) The deadline is calculated in the following manner if the proposal is submitted for a regularly scheduled annual meeting. The proposal must be received at the company's principal executive offices not less than 120 calendar days before the date of the company's proxy statement released to shareholders in connection with the previous year's annual meeting. However, if the company did not hold an annual meeting the previous year, or if the date of this year's annual meeting has been changed by more than 30 days from the date of the previous year's meeting, then the deadline is a reasonable time before the company begins to print and send its proxy materials.

(3) If you are submitting your proposal for a meeting of shareholders other than a regularly scheduled annual meeting, the deadline is a reasonable time before the company begins to print and send its proxy materials.

(f) *Question 6: What if I fail to follow one of the eligibility or procedural requirements explained in answers to Questions 1 through 4 of this section?* (1) The company may exclude your proposal, but only after it has notified you of the problem, and you have failed adequately to correct it. Within 14 calendar days of receiving your proposal, the company must notify you in writing of any procedural or eligibility deficiencies, as well as of the time frame for your response. Your response must be postmarked, or transmitted electronically, no later than 14 days from the date you received the company's notification. A company need not provide you such notice of a deficiency if the deficiency cannot be remedied, such as if you fail to submit a proposal by the company's properly determined deadline. If the company intends to exclude the proposal, it will later have to make a submission under Rule 14a-8 and provide you with a copy under Question 10 below, Rule 14a-8(j).

(2) If you fail in your promise to hold the required number of securities through the date of the meeting of shareholders, then the company will be permitted to exclude all of your proposals from its proxy materials for any meeting held in the following two calendar years.

(g) *Question 7: Who has the burden of persuading the Commission or its staff that my proposal can be excluded?* Except as otherwise noted, the burden is on the company to demonstrate that it is entitled to exclude a proposal.

(h) *Question 8: Must I appear personally at the shareholders' meeting to present the proposal?* (1) Either you, or your representative who is qualified under state law to present the proposal on your behalf, must attend the meeting to present the proposal. Whether you attend the meeting yourself or send a qualified representative to the meeting in your place, you should make sure that you, or your representative, follow the proper state law procedures for attending the meeting and/or presenting your proposal.

(2) If the company holds its shareholder meeting in whole or in part via electronic media, and the company permits you or your representative to present your proposal via such media, then you may appear through electronic media rather than traveling to the meeting to appear in person.

(3) If you or your qualified representative fail to appear and present the proposal, without good cause, the company will be permitted to exclude all of your proposals from its proxy materials for any meetings held in the following two calendar years.

(i) *Question 9: If I have complied with the procedural requirements, on what other basis may a company rely to exclude my proposal?* (1) *Improper under state law.* If the proposal is not a proper subject for action by shareholders under the laws of the jurisdiction of the company's organization;

NOTE TO PARAGRAPH (i)(1)

Depending on the subject matter, some proposals are not considered proper under state law if they would be binding on the company if approved by shareholders. In our experience, most proposals that are cast as recommendations or requests that the board of directors take specified action are proper under state law. Accordingly, we will assume that a proposal drafted as a recommendation or suggestion is proper unless the company demonstrates otherwise.

(2) *Violation of law.* If the proposal would, if implemented, cause the company to violate any state, federal, or foreign law to which it is subject;

NOTE TO PARAGRAPH (i)(2)

We will not apply this basis for exclusion to permit exclusion of a proposal on grounds that it would violate foreign law if compliance with the foreign law would result in a violation of any state or federal law.

(3) *Violation of proxy rules.* If the proposal or supporting statement is contrary to any of the Commission's proxy rules, including Rule 14a-9, which prohibits materially false or misleading statements in proxy soliciting materials;

(4) *Personal grievance; special interest.* If the proposal relates to the redress of a personal claim or grievance against the company or any other person, or if it is designed to result in a benefit to you, or to further a personal interest, which is not shared by the other shareholders at large;

(5) *Relevance.* If the proposal relates to operations which account for less than 5 percent of the company's total assets at the end of its most recent fiscal year, and for less than 5 percent of its net earnings and gross sales for its most recent fiscal year, and is not otherwise significantly related to the company's business;

(6) *Absence of power/authority.* If the company would lack the power or authority to implement the proposal;

(7) *Management functions.* If the proposal deals with a matter relating to the company's ordinary business operations;

(8) *Director elections*: If the proposal:

(i) Would disqualify a nominee who is standing for election;

(ii) Would remove a director from office before his or her term expired;

(iii) Questions the competence, business judgment, or character of one or more nominees or directors;

(iv) Seeks to include specific individual in the company's proxy materials for election to the board of directors; or

(v) Otherwise could affect the outcome of the upcoming election of directors.

(9) *Conflicts with company's proposal.* If the proposal directly conflicts with one of the company's own proposals to be submitted to shareholders at the same meeting;

NOTE TO PARAGRAPH (i)(9)

A company's submission to the Commission under this section should specify the points of conflict with the company's proposal.

(10) *Substantially implemented.* If the company has already substantially implemented the proposal;

NOTE TO PARAGRAPH (i)(10):

A company may exclude a shareholder proposal that would provide an advisory vote or seek future advisory votes to approve the compensation of executives as disclosed pursuant to Item 402 of Regulation S-K or any successor to Item 402 (a "say-on-pay vote") or that relates to the frequency of say-on-pay votes, provided that in the most recent shareholder vote required by Rule 14a-21(b) of this chapter a single year (i.e., one, two, or three years) received approval of a majority of votes cast on the matter and the company has adopted a policy on the frequency of say-on-pay votes that is consistent with the choice of the majority of votes cast in the most recent shareholder vote required by Rule 14a-21(b) of this chapter.

(11) *Duplication.* If the proposal substantially duplicates another proposal previously submitted to the company by another proponent that will be included in the company's proxy materials for the same meeting;

(12) *Resubmissions.* If the proposal addresses substantially the same subject matter as a proposal, or proposals, previously included in the company's proxy materials within the preceding five calendar years if the most recent vote occurred within the preceding three calendar years and the most recent vote was:

(i) Less than 5 percent of the votes cast if previously voted on once;

(ii) Less than 15 percent of the votes cast if previously voted on twice; or

(iii) Less than 25 percent of the votes cast if previously voted on three or more times.

(13) *Specific amount of dividends.* If the proposal relates to specific amounts of cash or stock dividends.

(j) *Question 10: What procedures must the company follow if it intends to exclude my proposal?* (1) If the company intends to exclude a proposal from its proxy materials, it must file its reasons with the Commission no later than 80 calendar days before it files its definitive proxy statement and form of proxy with the Commission. The company must simultaneously provide you with a copy of its submission. The Commission staff may permit the company to make its submission later than 80 days before the company files its definitive proxy statement and form of proxy, if the company demonstrates good cause for missing the deadline.

(2) The company must file six paper copies of the following:

(i) The proposal;

(ii) An explanation of why the company believes that it may exclude the proposal, which should, if possible, refer to the most recent applicable authority, such as prior Division letters issued under the rule; and

(iii) A supporting opinion of counsel when such reasons are based on matters of state or foreign law.

(k) *Question 11: May I submit my own statement to the Commission responding to the company's arguments?* Yes, you may submit a response, but it is not required. You should try to submit any response to us, with a copy to the company, as soon as possible after the company makes its submission. This way, the Commission staff will have time to consider fully your submission before it issues its response. You should submit six paper copies of your response.

(l) *Question 12: If the company includes my shareholder proposal in its proxy materials, what information about me must it include along with the proposal itself?* (1) The company's proxy statement must include your name and address, as well as the number of the company's voting securities that you hold. However, instead of providing that information, the company may instead include a statement that it will provide the information to shareholders promptly upon receiving an oral or written request.

(2) The company is not responsible for the contents of your proposal or supporting statement.

(m) *Question 13: What can I do if the company includes in its proxy statement reasons why it believes shareholders should not vote in favor of my proposal, and I disagree with some if its statements?* (1) The company may elect to include in its proxy statement reasons why it believes shareholders should vote against your proposal. The company is allowed to make arguments reflecting its own point of view, just as you may express your own point of view in your proposal's supporting statement.

(2) However, if you believe that the company's opposition to your proposal contains materially false or misleading statements that may violate our anti-fraud rule, Rule 14a-9, you should promptly send to the Commission staff and the company a letter explaining the reasons for your view, along with a copy of the company's statements opposing your proposal. To the extent possible, your letter should include specific factual information demonstrating the inaccuracy of the company's claims. Time permitting, you may wish to try to work out your differences with the company by yourself before contacting the Commission staff.

(3) We require the company to send you a copy of its statements opposing your proposal before sends its proxy materials, so that you may bring to our attention any materially false or misleading statements, under the following timeframes:

(i) If our no-action response requires that you make revisions to your proposal or supporting statement as a condition to requiring the company to include it in its proxy materials, then the company must provide you with a copy of its opposition statements no later than 5 calendar days after the company receives a copy of your revised proposal; or

(ii) In all other cases, the company must provide you with a copy of its opposition statements no later than 30 calendar days before it files definitive copies of its proxy statement and form of proxy under Rule 14a-6.

Rule 14a-9. False or Misleading Statements

(a) No solicitation subject to this regulation shall be made by means of any proxy statement, form of proxy, notice of meeting or other communication, written or oral, containing any statement which, at the time and in the light of the circumstances under which it is made, is false or misleading with respect to any material fact, or which omits to state any material fact necessary in order to make the statements therein not false or misleading or necessary to correct any statement in any earlier communication with respect to the solicitation of a proxy for the same meeting or subject matter which has become false or misleading.

(b) The fact that a proxy statement, form of proxy or other soliciting material has been filed with or examined by the Commission shall not be deemed a finding by the Commission that such material is accurate or complete or not false or misleading, or that the Commission has passed upon the merits of or approved any statement contained therein or any matter to be acted upon by security holders. No representation contrary to the foregoing shall be made.

NOTE

The following are some examples of what, depending upon particular facts and circumstances, may be misleading within the meaning of this section.

(a) Predictions as to specific future market values.

(b) Material which directly or indirectly impugns character, integrity or personal reputation, or directly or indirectly makes charges concerning improper, illegal or immoral conduct or associations, without factual foundation.

(c) Failure to so identify a proxy statement, form of proxy and other soliciting material as to clearly distinguish it from the soliciting material of any other person or persons soliciting for the same meeting or subject matter.

(d) Claims made prior to a meeting regarding the results of a solicitation.

Rule 14a-10. Prohibition of Certain Solicitations

No person making a solicitation which is subject to Rules 14a-1 to 14a-10 shall solicit:

(a) Any undated or postdated proxy; or

(b) Any proxy which provides that it shall be deemed to be dated as of any date subsequent to the date on which it is signed by the security holder.

Rule 14a-12. Solicitation Before Furnishing a Proxy Statement

(a) Notwithstanding the provisions of Rule 14a-3(a), a solicitation may be made before furnishing security holders with a proxy statement meeting the requirements of Rule 14a-3(a) if:

(1) Each written communication includes:

(i) The identity of the participants in the solicitation (as defined in Instruction 3 to Item 4 of Schedule 14A) and a description of their direct or indirect interests, by security holdings or otherwise, a prominent legend in clear, plain language advising security holders where they can obtain that information; and

(ii) A prominent legend in clear, plain language advising security holders to read the proxy statement when it is available because it contains important information. The legend also must explain to investors that they can get the proxy statement, and any other relevant documents, for free at the Commission's web site and describe which documents are available free from the participants; and

(2) A definitive proxy statement meeting the requirements of Rule 14a-3(a) is sent or given to security holders solicited in reliance on this section before or at the same time as the forms of proxy, consent or authorization are furnished to or requested from security holders.

(b) Any soliciting material published, sent or given to security holders in accordance with paragraph (a) of this section must be filed with the Commission no later than the date the material is first published, sent or given to security holders. Three copies of the material must at the same time be filed with, or mailed for filing to, each national securities exchange upon which any class of securities of the registrant is listed and registered. The soliciting material must include a cover page in the form set forth in Schedule 14A and the appropriate box on the cover page must be marked. Soliciting material in connection with a registered offering is required to be filed only under Rules 424 or 425 of this chapter, and will be deemed filed under this section.

(c) Solicitations by any person or group of persons for the purpose of opposing a solicitation subject to this regulation by any other person or group of persons with respect to the election or removal of directors at any annual or special meeting of security holders also are subject to the following provisions:

(1) *Application of this rule to annual report to security holders.* Notwithstanding the provisions of Rule 14a-3(b) and (c), any portion of the annual report to security holders referred to in Rule 14a-3(b) that comments upon or refers to any solicitation subject to this rule, or to any participant in the solicitation, other than the solicitation by the management, must be filed with the Commission as proxy material subject to this regulation. This must be filed in electronic format unless an exemption is available under Rules 201 or 202 of Regulation S-T. . . .

Rule 14a-13. Obligation of Registrants in Communicating with Beneficial Owners

(a) If the registrant knows that securities of any class entitled to vote at a meeting (or by written consents or authorizations if no meeting is held) with respect to which the registrant intends to solicit proxies, consents or authorizations are held of record by a broker, dealer, voting trustee, bank, association, or other entity that exercises fiduciary powers in nominee name or otherwise, the registrant shall:

(1) By first class mail or other equally prompt means:

(i) Inquire of each such record holder:

(A) Whether other persons are the beneficial owners of such securities and if so, the number of copies of the proxy and other soliciting material necessary to supply such material to such beneficial owners;

(B) In the case of an annual (or special meeting in lieu of the annual) meeting, or written consents in lieu of such meeting, at which directors are to be elected, the number of copies of the annual report to security holders necessary to supply such report to beneficial owners to whom such reports are to be distributed by such record holder or its nominee and not by the registrant;

(C) If the record holder has no obligation under Rule 14b-1(b)(3) or 14b-2(b)(4)(ii) and (iii), whether an agent has been designated to act on its behalf in fulfilling such obligation and, if so, the name and address of such agent; and

(D) Whether it holds the registrant's securities on behalf of any respondent bank and, if so, the name and address of each such respondent bank; and

(ii) Indicate to each such record holder:

(A) Whether the registrant, pursuant to paragraph (c) of this section, intends to distribute the annual report to security holders to beneficial owners of its securities whose names, addresses and securities positions are disclosed pursuant to Rules 14b-1(b)(3) and 14b-2(b)(4)(ii) and (iii);

(B) The record date; and

(C) At the option of the registrant, any employee benefit plan established by an affiliate of the registrant that holds securities of the registrant that the registrant elects to treat as exempt employee benefit plan securities;

(2) Upon receipt of a record holder's or respondent bank's response indicating, pursuant to Rule 14b-2(b)(1)(i), the names and addresses of its respondent banks, within one business day after the date such response is received, make an inquiry of and give notification to each such respondent bank in the same manner required by paragraph (a)(1) of this section; *Provided, however,* the inquiry required by paragraphs (a)(1) and (a)(2) of this section shall not cover beneficial owners of exempt employee benefit plan securities;

(3) Make the inquiry required by paragraph (a)(1) of this section at least 20 business days prior to the record date of the meeting of security holders, or

(i) If such inquiry is impracticable 20 business days prior to the record date of a special meeting, as many days before the record date of such meeting as is practicable, or

(ii) If consents or authorizations are solicited, and such inquiry is impracticable 20 business days before the earliest date on which they may be used to effect corporate action, as many days before that date as is practicable, or

(iii) At such later time as the rules of a national securities exchange on which the class of securities in question is listed may permit for good cause shown; *Provided, however,* That if a record holder or respondent bank has informed the registrant that a designated office(s) or department(s) is to receive such inquiries, the inquiry shall be made to such designated office(s) or department(s); and

(4) Supply, in a timely manner, each record holder and respondent bank of whom the inquiries required by paragraphs (a)(1) and (a)(2) of this section are made with copies of the proxy, other proxy soliciting material, and/or the annual report to security holders, in such quantities, assembled in such form and at such place(s), as the record holder or respondent bank may reasonably request in order to send such material to each beneficial owner of securities who is to be furnished with such material by the record holder or respondent bank; and

(5) Upon the request of any record holder or respondent bank that is supplied with proxy soliciting material and/or annual reports to security holders pursuant to paragraph (a)(4) of this section, pay its reasonable expenses for completing the sending of such material to beneficial owners.

NOTES

1. If the registrant's list of security holders indicates that some of its securities are registered in the name of a clearing agency registered pursuant to Section 17A of the Act (e.g., "Cede & Co.," nominee for the Depository Trust Company), the registrant shall make

appropriate inquiry of the clearing agency and thereafter of the participants in such clearing agency who may hold on behalf of a beneficial owner or respondent bank, and shall comply with the above paragraph with respect to any such participant (see Rule 14a-1(i)).

2. The attention of registrants is called to the fact that each broker, dealer, bank, association and other entity that exercises fiduciary powers has an obligation pursuant to Rules 14b-1 and 14b-2 (except as provided therein with respect to exempt employee benefit plan securities held in nominee name) and, with respect to brokers and dealers, applicable self-regulatory organization requirements to obtain and forward, within the time periods prescribed therein, (a) proxies (or in lieu thereof requests for voting instructions) and proxy soliciting materials to beneficial owners on whose behalf it holds securities, and (b) annual reports to security holders to beneficial owners on whose behalf it holds securities, unless the registrant has notified the record holder or respondent bank that it has assumed responsibility to send such material to beneficial owners whose names, addresses and securities positions are disclosed pursuant to Rules 14b-1(b)(3) and 14b-2(b)(4)(ii) and (iii).

3. The attention of registrants is called to the fact that registrants have an obligation, pursuant to paragraph (d) of this section, to cause proxies (or in lieu thereof requests for voting instructions), proxy soliciting material and annual reports to security holders to be furnished, in a timely manner, to beneficial owners of exempt employee benefit plan securities.

(b) Any registrant requesting pursuant to Rules 14b-1(b)(3) and 14b-2(b)(4)(ii) and (iii) a list of names, addresses and securities positions of beneficial owners of its securities who either have consented or have not objected to disclosure of such information shall:

(1) By first class mail or other equally prompt means, inquire of each record holder and each respondent bank identified to the registrant pursuant to Rule 14b-2(b)(4)(i) whether such record holder or respondent bank holds the registrant's securities on behalf of any respondent banks and, if so, the name and address of each such respondent bank;

(2) Request such list to be compiled as of a date no earlier than five business days after the date the registrant's request is received by the record holder or respondent bank; *Provided, however,* That if the record holder or respondent bank has informed the registrant that a designated office(s) or department(s) is to receive such requests, the request shall be made to such designated office(s) or department(s);

(3) Make such request to the following persons that hold the registrant's securities on behalf of beneficial owners; all brokers, dealers, banks, associations and other entities that exercises fiduciary powers; *Provided however,* such request shall not cover beneficial owners of exempt employee benefit plan securities as defined in Rule 14a-1(d)(1); and, at the option of the registrant, such request may give notice of any employee benefit plan established by an affiliate of the registrant that holds securities of the registrant that the registrant elects to treat as exempt employee benefit plan securities;

(4) Use the information furnished in response to such request exclusively for purposes of corporate communications; and

(5) Upon the request of any record holder or respondent bank to whom such request is made, pay the reasonable expenses, both direct and indirect, of providing beneficial owner information.

NOTES

A registrant will be deemed to have satisfied its obligations under paragraph (b) of this section by requesting consenting and non-objecting beneficial owner lists from a designated agent acting on behalf of the record holder or respondent bank and paying to that designated agent the reasonable expenses of providing the beneficial owner information.

(c) A registrant, at its option, may mail its annual report to security holders to the beneficial owners whose identifying information is provided by record holders and respondent banks, pursuant to Rules 14b-1(b)(3) and 14b-2(b)(4)(ii) and (iii), provided that such registrant notifies the record holders and respondent banks, at the time it makes the inquiry required by paragraph (a) of this section, that the registrant will send the annual report to security holders to, the beneficial owners so identified.

(d) If a registrant solicits proxies, consents or authorizations from record holders and respondent banks who hold securities on behalf of beneficial owners, the registrant shall cause proxies (or in lieu thereof requests or voting instructions), proxy soliciting material and annual reports to security holders to be furnished, in a timely manner, to beneficial owners of exempt employee benefit plan securities. . . .

Rule 14a-16. Internet Availability of Proxy Materials

(a)(1) A registrant shall furnish a proxy statement pursuant to Rule 14a-3(a), or an annual report to security holders pursuant to Rule 14a-3(b), to a security holder by sending the security holder a Notice of Internet Availability of Proxy Materials, as described in this rule, 40 calendar days or more prior to the security holder meeting date, or if no meeting is to be held, 40 calendar days or more prior to the date the votes, consents or authorizations may be used to effect the corporate action, and complying with all other requirements of this rule.

(2) Unless the registrant chooses to follow the full set delivery option set forth in paragraph (n) of the Rule, it must provide the record holder or respondent bank with all information listed in paragraph (d) of this section in sufficient time for the record holder or respondent bank to prepare, print and send a Notice of Internet Availability of Proxy Materials to beneficial owners at least 40 calendar days before the meeting date.

(b)(1) All materials identified in the Notice of Internet Availability of Proxy Materials must be publicly accessible, free of charge, at the Web site address specified in the notice on or before the time that the notice is sent to the security holder and such materials must remain available on that Web site through the conclusion of the meeting of security holders.

(2) All additional soliciting materials sent to security holders or made public after the Notice of Internet Availability of Proxy Materials has been sent must be made publicly accessible at the specified Web site address no later than the day on which such materials are first sent to security holders or made public.

(3) The Web site address relied upon for compliance under this section may not be the address of the Commission's electronic filing system.

(4) The registrant must provide security holders with a means to execute a proxy as of the time the Notice of Internet Availability of Proxy Materials is first sent to security holders.

(c) The materials must be presented on the Web site in a format, or formats, convenient for both reading online and printing on paper.

(d) The Notice of Internet Availability of Proxy Materials must contain the following:

(1) A prominent legend in bold-face type that states:

Important Notice Regarding the Availability of Proxy Materials for the Shareholder Meeting to Be Held on [insert meeting date].

(2) An indication that the communication is not a form for voting and presents only an overview of the more complete proxy materials, which contain important information and are available on the Internet or by mail, and encouraging a security holder to access and review the proxy materials before voting;

(3) The Internet Web site address where the proxy materials are available;

(4) Instructions regarding how a security holder may request a paper or email copy of the proxy materials at no charge, including the date by which they should make the request to facilitate timely delivery, and an indication that they will not otherwise receive a paper or email copy;

(5) The date, time, and location of the meeting, or if corporate action is to be taken by written consent, the earliest date on which the corporate action may be effected;

(6) A clear and impartial identification of each separate matter intended to be acted on and the soliciting person's recommendations, if any, regarding those matters, but no supporting statements;

(7) A list of the materials being made available at the specified Web site;

(8) A toll-free telephone number, an e-mail address, and an Internet Web site where the security holder can request a copy of the proxy statement, annual report to security holders, and from of proxy, relating to all of the registrant's future security holder meetings and for the particular meeting to which the proxy materials being furnished relate;

(9) Any control/identification numbers that the security holder needs to access his or her form of proxy;

(10) Instructions on how to access the from of proxy, provided that such instructions do not enable a security holder to execute a proxy without having access to the proxy statement and, if required by Rule 14a-3(b), the annual report to security holders; and

(11) Information on how to obtain directions to be able to attend the meeting and vote in person.

(e)(1) The Notice of Internet Availability of Proxy Materials may not be incorporated into, or combined with, another document, except that it may be incorporated into, or combined with, a notice of security holder meeting required under state law, unless state law prohibits such incorporation or combination.

(2) The Notice of Internet Availability of Proxy Materials may contain only the information required by paragraph (d) of this section and any additional

information required to be included in a notice of security holders meeting under state law; provided that:

(i) The registrant must revise the information on the Notice of Internet Availability of Proxy Materials, including any title to the document, to reflect the fact that:

(A) The registrant is conducting a consent solicitation rather than a proxy solicitation; or

(B) The registrant is not soliciting proxy or consent authority, but is furnishing an information statement pursuant to Rule 14c-2; and

(ii) The registrant may include a statement on the Notice to educate security holders that no personal information other than the identification or control number is necessary to execute a proxy.

(f)(1) Except as provided in paragraph (h) of this section, the Notice of Internet Availability of Proxy Materials must be sent separately from other types of security holder communications and may not accompany any other document or materials, including the form of proxy.

(2) Notwithstanding paragraph (f)(1) of this section, the registrant may accompany the Notice of Internet Availability of Proxy Materials with:

(i) A pre-addressed, postage-paid reply card for requesting a copy of the proxy materials;

(ii) A copy of any notice of security holder meeting required under state law if that notice is not combined with the Notice of Internet Availability of Proxy Materials. . . .

(iv) An explanation of the reasons for a registrants use of the rules detailed in this section and the process of receiving and reviewing the proxy materials and voting as detailed in this section.

(g) *Plain English.*

(1) To enhance the readability of the Notice of Internet Availability of Proxy Materials, the registrant must use plain English principles in the organization, language, and design of the notice.

(2) The registrant must draft the language in the Notice of Internet Availability of Proxy Materials so that, at a minimum, it substantially complies with each of the following plain English writing principles:

(i) Short sentences;

(ii) Definite, concrete, everyday words;

(iii) Active voice;

(iv) Tabular presentation or bullet lists for complex material, whenever possible;

(v) No legal jargon or highly technical business terms; and

(vi) No multiple negatives.

(3) In designing the Notice of Internet Availability of Proxy Materials, the registrant may include pictures, logos, or similar design elements so long as the design is not misleading and the required information is clear.

(h) The registrant may send a form of proxy to security holders if:

(1) At least 10 calendar days or more have passed since the date it first sent the Notice of Internet Availability of Proxy Materials to security holders and the

form of proxy is accompanied by a copy of the Notice of Internet Availability of Proxy Materials; or

(2) The form of proxy is accompanied or preceded by a copy, via the same medium, of the proxy statement and any annual report to security holders that is required by Rule 14a-3(b).

(i) The registrant must file a form of the Notice of Internet Availability of Proxy Materials with the Commission pursuant to §240.14a-6(b) no later than the date that the registrant first sends the notice to security holders.

(j) *Obligation to provide copies.*

(1) The registrant must send, at no cost to the record holder or respondent bank and by U.S. first class mail or other reasonably prompt means, a paper copy of the proxy statement, information statement, annual report to security holders, and form of proxy (to the extent each of those documents is applicable) to any record holder or respondent bank requesting such a copy within three business days after receiving a request for a paper copy.

(2) The registrant must send, at no cost to the record holder or respondent bank and via e-mail, an electronic copy of the proxy statement, information statement, annual report to security holders, and form of proxy (to the extent each of those documents is applicable) to any record holder or respondent bank requesting such a copy within three business days after receiving a request for an electronic copy via e-mail.

(3) The registrant must provide copies of the proxy materials for one year after the conclusion of the meeting or corporate action to which the proxy materials relate provided that if the registrant receives the request after the conclusion of the meeting or corporate action to which the proxy materials relate the registrant need not send copies via first class mail and need not respond to such request within three business days.

(4) The registrant must maintain records of security holder requests to receive materials in paper or via e-main for future solicitations and must continue to provide copies of the materials to a security holder who has made such a request until the security holder revokes such request.

(k) *Security holder information.*

(1) A registrant or its agent shall maintain the Internet Web site on which it posts its proxy materials in a manner that does not infringe on the anonymity of a person accessing such Web site.

(2) The registrant and its agents shall not use any e-mail address obtained from a security holder solely for the purpose of requesting a copy proxy materials pursuant to paragraph (j) for any purpose other than to send a copy of those materials to that security holder. The registrant shall not disclose such information to any person other than an employee or agent to the extent necessary to send a copy of the proxy materials pursuant to paragraph (j).

(l) A person other than the registrant may solicit proxies pursuant to the conditions imposed on registrants by this section, provided that:

(1) A soliciting person other than the registrant is required to provide copies of its proxy materials only to security holders to whom it has sent a Notice of Internet Availability of Proxy Materials; and

(2) A soliciting person other than the registrant must send its Notice of Internet Availability of Proxy Materials by the later of:

(i) 40 calendar days prior to the security holder meeting date or, if no meeting is to be held, 40 calendar days prior to the date the votes, consents, or authorizations may be used to effect the corporate action; or

(ii) The date on which it files its definitive proxy statement with the Commission, provided its preliminary proxy statement is filed no later than 10 calendar days after the date that the registrant files its definitive proxy statement.

(3) *Content of the soliciting person's Notice of Internet Availability of Proxy Materials.*

(i) If, at the time a soliciting person other than the registrant sends its Notice of Internet Availability of Proxy Materials, the soliciting person is not aware of all matters on the registrant's agenda for the meeting of security holders, the soliciting person's Notice on Internet Availability of Proxy Materials must provide a clear and impartial identification of each separate matter on the agenda to the extent known by the soliciting person at that time. The soliciting person's notice also must include a clear statement indicating that there may be additional agenda items of which the soliciting person is not aware and that the security holder cannot direct a vote for those items on the soliciting person's proxy card provided at that time.

(ii) If a soliciting person other than the registrant sends a form of proxy not containing all matters intended to be acted upon, the Notice of Internet Availability of Proxy Materials must clearly state whether execution of the form of proxy will invalidate a security holder's prior vote on matters not presented on the form of proxy.

(m) This section shall not apply to a proxy solicitation in connection with a business combination transaction, as defined in Rule 165 of this chapter as well as transactions for cash consideration requiring disclosure under item 14 of Schedule 14A.

(n) *Full Set Delivery Option.*

(1) For purposes of this paragraph (n), the term "full set of proxy materials" shall include all of the following documents:

(i) A copy of the proxy statement;

(ii) A copy of the annual report to security holders if required by Rule 14a-3(b); and

(iii) A form of proxy.

(2) Notwithstanding paragraphs (e) and (f)(2) of this section, a registrant or other soliciting person may:

(i) Accompany the Notice of Internet Availability of Proxy Materials with a full set of proxy materials; or

(ii) Send a full set of proxy materials without a Notice of Internet Availability of Proxy Materials if all of the information required in a Notice of Internet Availability of Proxy Materials pursuant to paragraphs (d) and (n)(4) is incorporated in the proxy statement and the form of proxy.

(3) A registrant or other soliciting person that sends a full set of proxy materials to a security holder pursuant to this paragraph (n) need not comply with

(i) The timing provisions of paragraphs (a) and (1)(2); and

(ii) The obligation to provide copies pursuant to paragraph (j).

(4) A registrant or other soliciting person that sends a full set of proxy materials to a security holder pursuant to this paragraph (n) need not include in its Notice of Internet Availability of Proxy Materials, proxy statement, or form of proxy the following disclosures:

(i) Instructions regarding the nature of the communications pursuant to paragraph (d)(2) of this Rule;

(ii) Instructions on how to request a copy of the proxy materials; and

(iii) Instructions on how to access the form of proxy pursuant to paragraph (d)(10).

Rule 14a-17. Electronic Shareholder Forums

(a) A shareholder, registrant, or third-party acting on behalf of a shareholder or registrant may establish, maintain, or operate an electronic shareholder forum to facilitate interaction among the registrant's shareholders and between the registrant and its shareholders as the shareholder or registrant deems appropriate. Subject to paragraphs (b) and (c) of this section, the forum must comply with the federal securities laws, including Section 14(a) of the Act and its associated regulations, other applicable federal laws, applicable state laws, and the registrant's governing documents.

(b) No shareholder, registrant, or third party acting on behalf of a shareholder or registrant, by reason of establishing, maintaining, or operating an electronic shareholder forum, will be liable under the federal securities laws for any statement or information provided by another person to the electronic shareholder forum. Nothing in this section prevents or alters the application of the federal securities laws, including the provisions for liability for fraud, deception, or manipulation, or other applicable federal and state laws to the person or persons that provide a statement or information to an electronic shareholder forum.

(c) Reliance on the exemption in Rule 14a-2(b)(6) to participate in an electronic shareholder forum does not eliminate a person's eligibility to solicit proxies after the date that the exemption in Rule 14a-2(b)(6) is no longer available, or is no longer being relied upon, provided that any such solicitation is conducted in accordance with this regulation.

Rule 14a-19 Solicitation of Proxies in Support of Director Nominees Other Than the Registrant's Nominees.

(a) No person may solicit proxies in support of director nominees other than the registrant's nominees unless such person:

(1) Provides notice to the registrant in accordance with paragraph (b) of this section unless the information required by paragraph (b) of this section has been provided in a preliminary or definitive proxy statement previously filed by such person;

(2) Files a definitive proxy statement with the Commission in accordance with § Rule.14a-6(b) by the later of:

(i) 25 calendar days prior to the security holder meeting date; or

(ii) Five (5) calendar days after the date that the registrant files its definitive proxy statement; and

(3) Solicits the holders of shares representing at least 67% of the voting power of shares entitled to vote on the election of directors and includes a statement to that effect in the proxy statement or form of proxy

(b) The notice shall:

(1) Be postmarked or transmitted electronically to the registrant at its principal executive office no later than 60 calendar days prior to the anniversary of the previous year's annual meeting date, except that, if the registrant did not hold an annual meeting during the previous year, or if the date of the meeting has changed by more than 30 calendar days from the previous year, then notice must be provided by the later of 60 calendar days prior to the date of the annual meeting or the 10th calendar day following the day on which public announcement of the date of the annual meeting is first made by the registrant;

(2) Include the names of all nominees for whom such person intends to solicit proxies; and

(3) Include a statement that such person intends to solicit the holders of shares representing at least 67% of the voting power of shares entitled to vote on the election of directors in support of director nominees other than the registrant's nominees.

(c) If any change occurs with respect to such person's intent to solicit the holders of shares representing at least 67% of the voting power of shares entitled to vote on the election of directors in support of director nominees other than the registrant's nominees or with respect to the names of such person's nominees, such person shall notify the registrant promptly.

(d) A registrant shall notify the person conducting a proxy solicitation subject to this section of the names of all nominees for whom the registrant intends to solicit proxies unless the names have been provided in a preliminary or definitive proxy statement previously filed by the registrant. The notice shall be postmarked or transmitted electronically no later than 50 calendar days prior to the anniversary of the previous year's annual meeting date, except that, if the registrant did not hold an annual meeting during the previous year, or if the date of the meeting has changed by more than 30 calendar days from the previous year, then notice must be provided no later than 50 calendar days prior to the date of the annual meeting. If any change occurs with respect to the names of the registrant's nominees, the registrant shall notify the person conducting a proxy solicitation subject to this section promptly.

(e) Notwithstanding the provisions of Rule.14a-4(b)(2), if any person is conducting a proxy solicitation subject to this section, the form of proxy of the registrant and the form of proxy of any person soliciting proxies pursuant to this section shall:

(1) Set forth the names of all persons nominated for election by the registrant and by any person or group of persons that has complied with this section and the name of any person whose nomination by a shareholder or shareholder group satisfies the requirements of an applicable state or foreign law provision or a registrant's governing documents as they relate to the inclusion of shareholder director nominees in the registrant's proxy materials;

(2) Provide a means for the security holder to grant authority to vote for the nominees set forth;

(3) Clearly distinguish between the nominees of the registrant, the nominees of the person or group of persons that has complied with this section and the nominees of any shareholder or shareholder group whose nominees are included in a registrant's proxy materials pursuant to the requirements of an applicable state or foreign law provision or a registrant's governing documents;

(4) Within each group of nominees referred to in paragraph (e)(3) of this section, list nominees in alphabetical order by last name;

(5) Use the same font type, style and size for all nominees;

(6) Prominently disclose the maximum number of nominees for which authority to vote can be granted; and

(7) Prominently disclose the treatment and effect of a proxy executed in a manner that grants authority to vote for the election of fewer or more nominees than the number of directors being elected and the treatment and effect of a proxy executed in a manner that does not grant authority to vote with respect to any nominees.

(f) If any person is conducting a proxy solicitation subject to this section, the form of proxy of the registrant and the form of proxy of any person soliciting proxies pursuant to this section may provide a means for the security holder to grant authority to vote for the nominees of the registrant set forth, as a group, and a means for the security holder to grant authority to vote for the nominees of any other soliciting person set forth, as a group, provided that there is a similar means for the security holder to withhold authority to vote for such groups of nominees unless the number of nominees of the registrant or of any other soliciting person is less than the number of directors being elected. Means to grant authority to vote for any nominees as a group or to withhold authority for any nominees as a group may not be provided if the form of proxy includes one or more shareholder nominees in accordance with an applicable state or foreign law provision or a registrant's governing documents as they relate to the inclusion of shareholder director nominees in the registrant's proxy materials.

(g) This section shall not apply to:

(1) A consent solicitation; or

(2) A solicitation in connection with an election of directors at an investment company registered under the Investment Company Act of 1940 (15 U.S.C. 80a-1 et seq.) or a business development company as defined by section 2(a)(48) of the Investment Company Act of 1940 (15 U.S.C. 80a-2(a)(48)).

Instruction 1 to paragraphs (b)(1) and (d). Where the deadline falls on a Saturday, Sunday, or holiday, the deadline will be treated as the first business day following the Saturday, Sunday, or holiday. Instruction 2 to paragraph (f). Where applicable state law gives legal effect to votes cast against a nominee, the form of proxy may provide a means for the security holder to grant authority to vote for the nominees of the registrant set forth, as a group, and a means for the security holder to grant authority to vote for the nominees of any other soliciting person set forth, as a group, provided that, in lieu of the ability to withhold authority to vote as a group, there is a similar means for the security holder to vote against such group of nominees (as well as a means for security holders to abstain from voting for such group of nominees).

Rule 14a-21. Shareholder Approval of Executive Compensation, Frequency of Votes for Approval of Executive Compensation and Shareholder Approval of Golden Parachute Compensation

(a) If a solicitation is made by a registrant, other than an emerging growth company as defined in Rule 12b-2, and the solicitation relates to an annual or other meeting of shareholders at which directors will be elected and for which the rules of the Commission require executive compensation disclosure pursuant to Item 402 of Regulation S-K, the registrant shall, for the first annual or other meeting of shareholders on or after January 21, 2011, or for the first annual or other meeting of shareholders on or after January 21, 2013 if the registrant is a smaller reporting company, and thereafter no later than the annual or other meeting of shareholders held in the third calendar year after the immediately preceding vote under this subsection, include a separate resolution subject to shareholder advisory vote to approve the compensation of its named executive officers, as disclosed pursuant to Item 402 of Regulation S-K.

Instruction to Rule 14a-21(a)

The registrant's resolution shall indicate that the shareholder advisory vote under this subsection is to approve the compensation of the registrant's named executive officers as disclosed pursuant to Item 402 of Regulation S-K. The following is a non-exclusive example of a resolution that would satisfy the requirements of this subsection: "RESOLVED, that the compensation paid to the company's named executive officers, as disclosed pursuant to Item 402 of Regulation S-K, including the Compensation Discussion and Analysis, compensation tables and narrative discussion is hereby APPROVED."

(b) If a solicitation is made by a registrant, other than an emerging growth company as defined in Rule 12b-2, and the solicitation relates to an annual or other meeting of shareholders at which directors will be elected and for which the rules of the Commission require executive compensation disclosure pursuant to Item 402 of Regulation S-K, the registrant shall, for the first annual or other meeting of shareholders on or after January 21, 2011, or for the first annual or other meeting of shareholders on or after January 21, 2013 if the registrant is a smaller reporting company, and thereafter no later than the annual or other meeting of shareholders held in the sixth calendar year after the immediately preceding vote under this subsection, include a separate resolution subject to shareholder advisory vote as to whether the shareholder vote required by paragraph (a) of this section should occur every 1, 2 or 3 years. Registrants required to provide a separate shareholder vote pursuant to Rule 14a-20 of this chapter shall include the separate resolution required by this section for the first annual or other meeting of shareholders after the registrant has repaid all obligations arising from financial assistance provided under the TARP, as defined in section 3(8) of the Emergency Economic Stabilization Act of 2008 (12 U.S.C. 5202(8)), and thereafter no later than the annual or other meeting of shareholders held in the sixth calendar year after the immediately preceding vote under this subsection.

(c) If a solicitation is made by a registrant, other than an emerging growth company as defined in Rule 12b-2, for a meeting of shareholders at which shareholders are asked to approve an acquisition, merger, consolidation or proposed sale or other disposition of all or substantially all the assets of the registrant, the registrant shall include a separate resolution subject to shareholder advisory vote to approve any agreements or understandings and compensation disclosed pursuant to Item 402(t) of Regulation S-K, unless such agreements or understandings have been subject to a shareholder advisory vote under paragraph (a) of this section. Consistent with section 14A(b) of the Exchange Act, any agreements or understandings between an acquiring company and the named executive officers of the registrant, where the registrant is not the acquiring company, are not required to be subject to the separate shareholder advisory vote under this paragraph.

Schedule 14A. Information Required in Proxy Statement . . .

Item 1. Date, time and place information.

(a) State the date, time and place of the meeting of security holders, and the complete mailing address, including ZIP Code, of the principal executive offices of the registrant, unless such information is otherwise disclosed in material furnished to security holders with or preceding the proxy statement. If action is to be taken by written consent, state the date by which consents are to be submitted if state law requires that such a date be specified or if the person soliciting intends to set a date.

(b) On the first page of the proxy statement, as delivered to security holders, state the approximate date on which the proxy statement and form of proxy are first sent or given to security holders.

(c) Furnish the information required to be in the proxy statement by Rule 14a-5(e).

Item 2. Revocability of proxy.

State whether or not the person giving the proxy has the power to revoke it. If the right of revocation before the proxy is exercised is limited or is subject to compliance with any formal procedure, briefly describe such limitation or procedure.

Item 3. Dissenters' right of appraisal.

Outline briefly the rights of appraisal or similar rights of dissenters with respect to any matter to be acted upon and indicate any statutory procedure required to be followed by dissenting security holders in order to perfect such rights. Where such rights may be exercised only within a limited time after the date of adoption of a proposal, the filing of a charter amendment or other similar act, state whether the persons solicited will be notified of such date.

INSTRUCTIONS

1. Indicate whether a security holder's failure to vote against a proposal will constitute a waiver of his appraisal or similar rights and whether a vote against a proposal will be deemed to satisfy any notice requirements under State law with respect to appraisal rights. If the State law is unclear, state what position will be taken in regard to these matters. . . .

Item 4. Persons making the solicitation.

(a) Solicitations not subject to Rule 14a-12(c). (1) If the solicitation is made by the registrant, so state. Give the name of any director of the registrant who has informed the registrant in writing that he intends to oppose any action intended to be taken by the registrant and indicate the action which he intends to oppose.

(2) If the solicitation is made otherwise than by the registrant, so state and give the names of the participants in the solicitation, as defined in paragraphs (a) (iii), (iv), (v) and (vi) of Instruction 3 to this Item.

(3) If the solicitation is to be made otherwise than by the use of the mails or pursuant to Rule 14a-16, describe the methods to be employed. If the solicitation is to be made by specially, engaged employees or paid solicitors, state (i) the material features of any contract or arrangement for such solicitation and identify the parties, and (ii) the cost or anticipated cost thereof.

(4) State the names of the persons by whom the cost of solicitation has been or will be borne, directly or indirectly.

(b) *Solicitations subject to Rule 14a-12(c).* (1) State by whom the solicitation is made and describe the methods employed and to be employed to solicit security holders.

(2) If regular employees of the registrant or any other participant in a solicitation have been or are to be employed to solicit security holders, describe the class or classes of employees to be so employed, and the manner and nature of their employment for such purpose.

(3) If specially engaged employees, representatives or other persons have been or are to be employed to solicit security holders, state (i) the material features of any contract or arrangement for such solicitation and the identity of the parties, (ii) the cost or anticipated cost thereof and (iii) the approximate number of such employees of employees or any other person (naming such other person) who will solicit security holders.

(4) State the total amount estimated to be spent and the total expenditures to date for, in furtherance of, or in connection with the solicitation of security holders.

(5) State by whom the cost of the solicitation will be borne. If such cost is to be borne initially by any person other than the registrant, state whether reimbursement will be sought from the registrant, and, if so, whether the question of such reimbursement will be submitted to a vote of security holders.

(6) If any such solicitation is terminated pursuant to a settlement between the registrant and any other participant in such solicitation, describe the terms of such settlement, including the cost or anticipated cost thereof to the registrant.

INSTRUCTIONS

1. With respect to solicitations subject to Rule 14a-12(c), costs and expenditures within the meaning of this Item 4 shall include fees for attorneys, accountants, public relations or financial advisers, solicitors, advertising, printing, transportation, litigation and other costs incidental to the solicitation, except that the registrant may exclude the amount of such costs represented by the amount normally expended for a solicitation for an election of directors in the absence of a contest, and costs represented by salaries and wages of regular employees and officers, provided a statement to that effect is included in the proxy statement.

2. The information required pursuant to paragraph (b)(6) of this Item should be included in any amended or revised proxy statement or other soliciting materials relating to the same meeting or subject matter furnished to security holders by the registrant subsequent to the date of settlement.

3. For purposes of this Item 4 and Item 5 of this Schedule 14A:

(a) The terms "participant" and "participant in a solicitation" include the following:

(i) In the case of a solicitation made on behalf of the registrant, the registrant, each director of the registrant and each of the registrant's nominees for election as a director;

(ii) In the case of a solicitation made otherwise than on behalf of the registrant, each of the soliciting person's nominees for election as a director;

(iii) Any committee or group which solicits proxies, any member of such committee or group, and any person whether or not named as a member who, acting alone or with one or more other persons, directly or indirectly takes the initiative, or engages, in organizing, directing, or arranging for the financing of any such committee or group;

(iv) Any person who finances or joins with another to finance the solicitation of proxies, except persons who contribute not more than $500 and who are not otherwise participants;

(v) Any person who lends money or furnishes credit or enters into any other arrangements, pursuant to any contract or understanding with a participant, for the purpose of financing or otherwise inducing the purchase, sale, holding or voting of securities of the registrant by any participant or other persons, in support of or in opposition to a participant; except that such terms do not include a bank, broker or dealer who, in the ordinary course of business, lends money or executes orders for the purchase or sale of securities and who is not otherwise a participant; and

(vi) Any person who solicits proxies,

(b) The terms "participant" and "participant in a solicitation" do not include:

(i) Any person or organization retained or employed by a participant to solicit security holders and whose activities are limited to the duties required to be performed in the course of such employment;

(ii) Any person who merely transmits proxy soliciting material or performs other ministerial or clerical duties;

(iii) Any person employed by a participant in the capacity of attorney, accounting, or advertising, public relations or financial adviser, and whose activities are limited to the duties required to be performed in the course of such employment;

(iv) Any person regularly employed as an officer or employee of the registrant or any of its subsidiaries who is not otherwise a participant; or

(v) Any officer or director of, or any person regularly employed by, any other participant, if such officer, director or employee is not otherwise a participant.

Item 5. Interest of certain persons in matters to be acted upon.

(a) Solicitations not subject to Rule 14a-12(c). Describe briefly any substantial interest, direct or indirect, by security holdings or otherwise, of each of the following persons in any matter to be acted upon, other than elections to office:

(1) If the solicitation is made on behalf of the registrant, each person who has been a director or executive officer of the registrant at any time since the beginning of the last fiscal year.

(2) If the solicitation is made otherwise than on behalf of the registrant, each participant in the solicitation, as defined in paragraphs (a)(iii), (iv), (v), and (vi) of Instruction 3 to Item 4 of this Schedule 14A.

(3) Each nominee for election as a director of the registrant.

(4) Each associate of any of the foregoing persons.

(5) If the solicitation is made on behalf of the registrant, furnish the information required by Item 402(t) of Regulation S-K.

INSTRUCTION TO PARAGRAPH (a)

Except in the case of a solicitation subject to this regulation made in opposition to another solicitation subject to this regulation, this sub-item (a) shall not apply to any interest arising from the ownership of securities of the registrant where the security holder receives no extra or special benefit not shared on a pro rata basis by all other holders of the same class.

(b) *Solicitation subject to Rule 14a-12(c).* With respect to any solicitation subject to Rule 14a-12(c):

(1) Describe briefly any substantial interest, direct or indirect, by security holdings or otherwise, of each participant as defined in paragraphs (a)(ii), (iii), (iv), (v) and (vi) of Instruction 3 to Item 4 of this Schedule 14A, in any matter to be acted upon at the meeting, and include with respect to each participant the following information, or a fair and accurate summary thereof:

(i) Name and business address of the participant.

(ii) The participant's present principal occupation or employment and the name, principal business and address of any corporation or other organization in which such employment is carried on.

(iii) State whether or not, during the past ten years, the participant has been convicted in a criminal proceeding (excluding traffic violations or similar misdemeanors) and, if so, give dates, nature of conviction, name and location of court, and penalty imposed or other disposition of the case.

A negative answer need not be included in the proxy statement or other soliciting material.

(iv) State the amount of each class of securities of the registrant which the participant owns beneficially, directly or indirectly.

(v) State the amount of each class of securities of the registrant which the participant owns of record but not beneficially.

(vi) State with respect to all securities of the registrant purchased or sold within the past two years, the dates on which they were purchased or sold and the amount purchased or sold on each such date.

(vii) If any part of the purchase price or market value of any of the shares specified in paragraph (b)(1)(vi) of this Item is represented by funds borrowed or otherwise obtained for the purpose of acquiring or holding such securities, so state and indicate the amount of the indebtedness as of the latest practicable date. If such funds were borrowed or obtained otherwise than pursuant to a margin account or bank loan in the regular course of business of a bank, broker or dealer, briefly describe the transaction, and state the names of the parties.

(viii) State whether or not the participant is, or was within the past year, a party to any contract, arrangements or understandings with any person with respect to any securities of the registrant, including, but not limited to joint ventures, loan or option arrangements, puts or calls, guarantees against loss or guarantees of profit, division of losses or profits, or the giving or withholding of proxies. If so, name the parties to such contracts, arrangements or understandings and give the details thereof.

(ix) State the amount of securities of the registrant owned beneficially, directly or indirectly, by each of the participant's associates and the name and address of each such associate.

(x) State the amount of each class of securities of any parent or subsidiary of the registrant which the participant owns beneficially, directly or indirectly.

(xi) Furnish for the participant and associates of the participant the information required by Item 404(a) of Regulation S-K.

(xii) State whether or not the participant or any associates of the participant have any arrangement or understanding with any person—

(A) with respect to any future employment by the registrant or its affiliates; or

(B) with respect to any future transactions to which the registrant or any of its affiliates will or may be a party.

If so, describe such arrangement or understanding and state the names of the parties thereto.

(2) With respect to any person, other than a director or executive officer of the registrant acting solely in that capacity, who is a party to an arrangement or understanding pursuant to which a nominee for election as director is proposed to be elected, describe any substantial interest, direct or indirect, by security holdings or otherwise, that such person has in any matter to be acted upon at the meeting, and furnish the information called for by paragraphs (b)(1)(xi) and (xii) of this Item.

(3) If the solicitation is made on behalf of the registrant, furnish the information required by Item 402(t) of Regulation S-K.

INSTRUCTION TO PARAGRAPH (b)

For purposes of this Item 5, beneficial ownership shall be determined in accordance with Rule 13d-3 under the Act.

Item 6. Voting securities and principal holders thereof.

(a) As to each class of voting securities of the registrant entitled to be voted at the meeting (or by written consents or authorizations if no meeting is held), state the number of shares outstanding and the number of votes to which each class is entitled.

(b) State the record date, if any, with respect to this solicitation. If the right to vote or give consent is not to be determined, in whole or in part, by reference to a record date, indicate the criteria for the determination of security holders entitled to vote or give consent.

(c) If action is to be taken with respect to the election of directors and if the persons solicited have cumulative voting rights: (1) Make a statement that they have such rights, (2) briefly describe such rights, (3) state briefly the conditions precedent to the exercise thereof, and (4) if discretionary authority to cumulate votes is solicited, so indicate.

(d) Furnish the information required by Item 403 of Regulation S-K to the extent known by the persons on whose behalf the solicitation is made.

(e) If, to the knowledge of the persons on whose behalf the solicitation is made, a change in control of the registrant has occurred since the beginning of its last fiscal year, state the name of the person(s) who acquired such control, the amount and the source of the consideration used by such person or persons; the basis of the control, the date and a description of the transaction(s) which resulted in the change of control and the percentage of voting securities of the registrant now beneficially owned directly or indirectly by the person(s) who acquired control; and the identity of the person(s) from whom control was assumed. If the source of all or any part of the consideration used is a loan made in the ordinary course of business by a bank as defined by section 3(a)(6) of the Act, the identity of such bank shall be omitted provided a request for confidentiality has been made pursuant to section 13(d)(1)(B) of the Act by the person(s) who acquired control. In lieu thereof, the material shall indicate that the identity of the bank has been so omitted and filed separately with the Commission.

INSTRUCTIONS

1. State the terms of any loans or pledges obtained by the new control group for the purpose of acquiring control, and the names of the lenders or pledgees.

2. Any arrangements or understandings among members of both the former and new control groups and their associates with respect to election of directors or other matters should be described.

Item 7. Directors and executive officers.

If action is to be taken with respect to the election of directors, furnish the following information in tabular form to the extent practicable. If, however, the solicitation is made on behalf of persons other than the registrant, the information required need be furnished only as to nominees of the persons making the solicitation.

(a) The information required by instruction 4 to Item 103(c)(2) of Regulation S-K with respect to directors and executive officers.

(b) The information required by Items 401, 404(a) and (b), 405, 407, and 408(b) of Regulation S-K other than the information required by:

(i) Paragraph (c)(3) of Item 407 of Regulation S-K; and

(ii) Paragraphs (e)(4) and (e)(5) of Item 407 of Regulation S-K (which are required by Item 8 of this Schedule 14A).

(c) In lieu of the Information required by this Item 7, investment companies registered under the Investment Company Act of 1940 must furnish the information required by Item 12 of Schedule 14A. . . .

(f) If a person is conducting a solicitation that is subject to Rule 14a-19, the registrant must include in its proxy statement a statement directing shareholders to refer to any other soliciting person's proxy statement for information required by Item 7 of this Schedule 14A with regard to such person's nominee or nominees and a soliciting person other than the registrant must include in its proxy statement a statement directing shareholders to refer to the registrant's or other soliciting person's proxy statement for information required by Item 7 of this Schedule 14A with regard to the registrant's or other soliciting person's nominee or nominees. The statement must explain to shareholders that they can access the other soliciting person's proxy statement, and any other relevant documents, without cost on the Commission's website.

Item 8. Compensation of directors and executive officers.

Furnish the information required by Item 402 of Regulation S-K and paragraphs(e)(4) and (e)(5) of Item 407 of Regulation S-K if action is to be taken with regard to (a) the election of directors, (b) any bonus, profit sharing or other compensation plan, contract, or arrangement in which any director, nominee for election as a director, or executive officer of the registrant will participate, (c) any pension or retirement plan in which any such person will participate or (d) the granting or extension to any such person of any options, warrants or rights to purchase any securities, other than warrants or rights issued to security holders as such, on a pro rata basis. However, if the solicitation is made on behalf of persons other than the registrant the information required need to be furnished only as to nominees of the persons making the solicitation and associates of such nominees. . . .

INSTRUCTION

If an otherwise reportable compensation plan became subject to such requirements because of an acquisition or merger and, within one year of the acquisition or merger, such plan was terminated for purposes of prospective eligibility, the registrant may furnish a description of its obligation to the designated individuals pursuant to the compensation plan. Such description may be furnished in lieu of a description of the compensation plan in the proxy statement.

Item 9. Independent public accountants.

If the solicitation is made on behalf of the registrant and relates to: (1) The annual (or special meeting in lieu of annual) meeting of security holders at which directors are to be elected, or a solicitation of consents or authorizations in lieu of such meeting or (2) the election, approval or ratification of the registrant's accountant, furnish the following information describing the registrant's relationship with its independent public accountant:

(a) The name of the principal accountant selected or being recommended to security holders for election, approval or ratification for the current year. If no accountant has been selected or recommended, so state and briefly describe the reasons therefor.

(b) The name of the principal accountant for the fiscal year most recently completed if different from the accountant selected or recommended for the current year or if no accountant has yet been selected or recommended for the current year.

(c) The proxy statement shall indicate: (1) Whether or not representatives of the principal accountant for the current year and for the most recently completed fiscal year are expected to be present at the security holders' meeting, (2) whether or not they will have the opportunity to make a statement if they desire to do so, and (3) whether or not such representatives are expected to be available to respond to appropriate questions.

(d) If during the registrant's two most recent fiscal years or any subsequent interim period, (1) an independent accountant who was previously engaged as the principal accountant to audit the registrant's financial statements, or an independent accountant on whom the principal accountant expressed reliance in its report regarding a significant subsidiary, has resigned (or indicated it has declined to stand for re-election after the completion of the current audit) or was dismissed, or (2) a new independent accountant has been engaged as either the principal accountant to audit the registrant's financial statements or as an independent accountant on whom the principal accountant has expressed or is expected to express reliance in its report regarding a significant subsidiary, then, notwithstanding any previous disclosure, provide the information required by Item 304(a) of Regulation S-K.

(e)(1) Disclose, under the caption *Audit Fees*, the aggregate fees billed for each of the last two fiscal years for professional services rendered by the principal accountant for the audit of the registrant's annual financial statements and review of financial statements included in the registrant's Form 10-Q or services that are normally provided by the accountant in connection with statutory and regulatory filings or engagements for those fiscal years.

(2) Disclose, under the caption *Audit-Related Fees*, the aggregate fees billed in each of the last two fiscal years for assurance and related services by the principal

accountant that are reasonably related to the performance of the audit or review of the registrant's financial statements and are not reported under paragraph (e)(1) of this section. Registrants shall describe the nature of the services comprising the fees disclosed under this category.

(3) Disclose, under the caption *Tax Fees*, the aggregate fees billed in each of the last two fiscal years for professional services rendered by the principal accountant for tax compliance, tax advice, and tax planning. Registrants shall describe the nature of the services comprising the fees disclosed under this category.

(4) Disclose, under the caption *All Other Fees*, the aggregate fees billed in each of the last two fiscal years for products and services provided by the principal accountant, other than the services reported in paragraphs (e)(1) through (e)(3) of this section. Registrants shall describe the nature of the services comprising the fees disclosed under this category.

(5) (i) Disclose the audit committee's pre-approval policies and procedures described in Rule 2-01(c)(7)(i) of Regulation S-X.

(ii) Disclose the percentage of services described in each of paragraphs (e)(2) through (e)(4) of this section that were approved by the audit committee pursuant to Rule 2-01(c)(7)(ii)(C) of Regulation S-X.

(6) If greater than 50 percent, disclose the percentage of hours expended on the principal accountant's engagement to audit the registrant's financial statements for the most recent fiscal year that were attributed to work performed by persons other than principal accountant's full-time, permanent employees.

(7) If the registrant is an investment company, disclose the aggregate non-audit fees billed by the registrant's accountant for services rendered to the registrant, and to the registrant's investment adviser (not including any subadviser whose role is primarily portfolio management and is subcontracted with or overseen by another investment adviser), and any entity controlling, controlled by, or under common control with the adviser that provides ongoing services to the registrant for each of the last two fiscal years of the registrant.

(8) If the registrant is an investment company, disclose whether the audit committee of the board of directors has considered whether the provision of non-audit services that were rendered to the registrant's investment adviser (not including any subadviser whose role is primarily portfolio management and is subcontracted with or overseen by another investment adviser), and any entity controlling, controlled by, or under common control with the investment adviser that provides ongoing services to the registrant that were not pre-approved pursuant to Rule 210.2-01(c)(7)(ii) of Regulation S-X is compatible with maintaining the principal accountant's independence.

Item 10. Compensation plans.

If action is to be taken with respect to any plan pursuant to which cash or non-cash compensation may be paid or distributed, furnish the following information:

(a) *Plans subject to security holder action.* (1) Describe briefly the material features of the plan being acted upon, identify each class of persons who will be eligible to participate therein, indicate the approximate number of persons in each such class, and state the basis of such participation.

Plan Name		
Name and Position	*Dollar Value ($)*	*Number of Units*
CEO		
A		
B		
C		
D		
Executive Group		
Non-Executive Director Group		
Non-Executive Officer Employee Group		

(2) (i) In the tabular format specified below, disclose the benefits or amounts that will be received by or allocated to each of the following under the plan being acted upon, if such benefits or amounts are determinable:

(ii) The table required by paragraph (a) (2) (i) of this Item shall provide information as to the following persons:

(A) Each person (stating name and position) specified in paragraph (a) (3) of Item 402 of Regulation S-K.

(B) All current executive officers as a group;

(C) All current directors who are not executive officers as a group; and

(D) All employees, including all current officers who are not executive officers, as a group.

INSTRUCTION TO NEW PLAN BENEFITS TABLE

Additional columns should be added for each plan with respect to which security holder action is to be taken.

(iii) If the benefits or amounts specified in paragraph (a) (2) (i) of this item are not determinable, state the benefits or amounts which would have been received by or allocated to each of the following for the last completed fiscal year if the plan had been in effect, if such benefits or amounts may be determined, in the table specified in paragraph (a) (2) (i) of this Item:

(A) Each person (stating name and position) specified in paragraph (a) (3) of Item 402 of Regulation S-K;

(B) All current executive officers as a group;

(C) All current directors who are not executive officers as a group; and

(D) All employees, including all current officers who are not executive officers, as a group.

(3) If the plan to be acted upon can be amended, otherwise than by a vote of security holders, to increase the cost thereof to the registrant or to alter the allocation of the benefits as between the persons and groups specified in paragraph (a) (2) of this item, state the nature of the amendments which can be so made.

(b)(1) *Additional information regarding specified plans subject to security holder actions.* With respect to any pension or retirement plan submitted for security holder action, state:

(i) The approximate total amount necessary to fund the plan with respect to past services, the period over which such amount is to be paid and the estimated annual payments necessary to pay the total amount over such period; and

(ii) The estimated annual payment to be made with respect to current services. In the case of a pension or retirement plan, information called for by paragraph (a)(2) of this Item may be furnished in the format specified by paragraph (h)(2) of Item 402 of Regulation S-K.

(2) (i) With respect to any specific grant of or any plan containing options, warrants or rights submitted for security holder action, state:

(A) The title and amount of securities underlying such options, warrants or rights;

(B) The prices, expiration dates and other material conditions upon which the options, warrants or rights may be exercised;

(C) The consideration received or to be received by the registrant or subsidiary for the granting or extension of the options, warrants or rights;

(D) The market value of the securities underlying the options, warrants, or rights as of the latest practicable date; and

(E) In the case of options, the federal income tax consequences of the issuance and exercise of such options to the recipient and the registrant; and

(ii) State separately the amount of such options received or to be received by the following persons if such benefits or amounts are determinable:

(A) Each person (stating name and position) specified in paragraph (a)(3) of Item 402 of Regulation S-K;

(B) All current executive officers as a group;

(C) All current directors who are not executive officers as a group;

(D) Each nominee for election as a director;

(E) Each associate of any of such directors, executive officers or nominees;

(F) Each other person who received or is to receive 5 percent of such options, warrants or rights; and

(G) All employees, including all current officers who are not executive officers, as a group.

. . . (c) *Information regarding plans and other arrangements not subject to security holder action.* Furnish the information required by Item 201(d) of Regulation S-K. . . .

Item 14. Mergers, consolidations, acquisitions and similar matters.

(See Notes A and D at the beginning of this Schedule.)

INSTRUCTIONS TO ITEM 14

1. In transactions in which the consideration offered to security holders consists wholly or in part of securities registered under the Securities Act of 1933, furnish the information required by Form S-4, Form F-4, or Form N-14, as applicable, instead of this Item. Only a Form S-4, Form F-4, or Form N-14 must be filed in accordance with Rule 14a-6(j).

2. (a) In transactions in which the consideration offered to security holders consists wholly of cash, the information required by paragraph (c)(1) of this Item for the acquiring company need not be provided unless the information is material to an informed voting decision (*e.g.*, the security holders of the target company are voting and financing is not assured).

(b) Additionally, if only the security holders of the target company are voting:

(i) The financial information in paragraphs (b)(8)-(11) of this Item for the acquiring company and the target need not be provided; and

(ii) The information in paragraph (c)(2) of this Item for the target company need not be provided.

If, however, the transaction is a going-private transaction (as defined by Rule 13e-3), then the information required by paragraph (c)(2) of this Item must be provided and to the extent that the going-private rules require the information specified in paragraph (b)(8)-(b)(11) of this Item, that information must be provided as well.

(a) *Applicability.* If action is to be taken with respect to any of the following transactions, provide the information required by this Item:

(1) A merger or consolidation;

(2) An acquisition of securities of another person;

(3) An acquisition of any other going business or the assets of a going business;

(4) A sale or other transfer of all or any substantial part of assets; or

(5) A liquidation or dissolution.

(b) *Transaction information.* Provide the following information for each of the parties to the transaction unless otherwise specified:

(1) *Summary term sheet.* The information required by Item 1001 of Regulation M-A.

(2) *Contact information.* The name, complete mailing address and telephone number of the principal executive offices.

(3) *Business conducted.* A brief description of the general nature of the business conducted.

(4) *Terms of the transaction.* The information required by Item 1004(a)(2) of Regulation M-A.

(5) *Regulatory approvals.* A statement as to whether any federal or state regulatory requirements must be complied with or approval must be obtained in connection with the transaction and, if so, the status of the compliance or approval.

(6) *Reports, opinions, appraisals.* If a report, opinion or appraisal materially relating to the transaction has been received from an outside party, and is

referred to in the proxy statement, furnish the information required by Item 1015(b) of Regulation M-A.

(7) *Past contacts, transactions or negotiations.* The information required by Items 1005(b) and 1011(a)(1) of Regulation M-A, for the parties to the transaction and their affiliates during the periods for which financial statements are presented or incorporated by reference under this Item.

(8) – (10) (*reserved*).

(11) *Financial information.* If material, financial information required by Article 11 of Regulation S-X with respect to this transaction.

(c) *Information about the parties to the transaction.*

(1) *Acquiring company.* Furnish the information required by Part B (Registrant Information) of Form S-4 or Form F-4, as applicable, for the acquiring company. However, financial statements need only be presented for the latest two fiscal years and interim periods.

(2) *Acquired company.* Furnish the information required by Part C (Information with Respect to the Company Being Acquired) of Form S-4 or Form F-4, as applicable.

(d) *Information about parties to the transaction: registered investment companies and business development companies.*

If the acquiring company or the acquired company is an investment company registered under the Investment Company Act of 1940 or a business development company as defined by Section 2(a)(48) of the Investment Company Act of 1940, provide the following information for that company instead of the information specified by paragraph (c) of this Item:

(1) Information required by Item 101 of Regulation S-K, description of business;

(2) Information required by Item 102 of Regulation S-K, description of property;

(3) Information required by Item 103 of Regulation S-K, legal proceedings;

(4) Information required by Item 201 of Regulation S-K, market price of and dividends on the registrant's common equity and related stockholder matters;

(5) Financial statements meeting the requirements of Regulation S-X, including financial information required by Rule 3-05 and Article 11 of Regulation S-X with respect to transactions other than that as to which action is to be taken as described in this proxy statement;

(6) (reserved)

(7) Information required by Item 302 of Regulation S-K, supplementary financial information;

(8) Information required by Item 303 of Regulation S-K, management's discussion and analysis of financial condition and results of operations; and

(9) Information required by Item 304 of Regulation S-K, changes in and disagreements with accountants on accounting and financial disclosure.

INSTRUCTION TO PARAGRAPH (D) OF ITEM 14

Unless registered on a national securities exchange or otherwise required to furnish such information, registered investment companies need not furnish the information required by paragraphs (d)(6), (d)(7) and (d)(8) of this Item.

(e) *Incorporation by reference.*

(1) The information required by paragraph (c) of this section may be incorporated by reference into the proxy statement to the same extent as would be permitted by Form S-4 or Form F-4, as applicable.

(2) Alternatively, the registrant may incorporate by reference into the proxy statement the information required by paragraph (c) of this Item if it is contained in an annual report sent to security holders in accordance with Rule 14a-3 of this chapter with respect to the same meeting or solicitation of consents or authorizations that the proxy statement relates to and the information substantially meets the disclosure requirements of Item 14 or Item 17 of Form S-4 or Form F-4, as applicable. . . .

Item 20. Other proposed action

Registrants required to provide a separate shareholder vote pursuant to section 111(e)(1) of the Emergency Economic Stabilization Act of 2008 (12 U.S.C. 5221(e)(1)) and Rule 240.14a-20 shall disclose that they are providing such a vote as required pursuant to the Emergency Economic Stabilization Act of 2008, and briefly explain the general effect of the vote, such as whether the vote is non-binding.

Item 21. Voting Procedures

As to each matter which is to be submitted to a vote of security holders, furnish the following information:

(a) State the vote required for approval or election, other than for the approval of auditors.

(b) Disclose the method by which votes will be counted, including the treatment and effect under applicable state law and registrant charter and bylaw provisions of abstentions, broker non-votes, and, to the extent applicable, a security holder's withholding of authority to vote for a nominee in an election of directors.

(c) When applicable, disclose how the soliciting person intends to treat proxy authority granted in favor of any other soliciting person's nominees if such other soliciting person abandons its solicitation or fails to comply with Rule 14a-19.

Item 24. Shareholder approval of executive compensation

Registrants required to provide any of the separate shareholder votes pursuant to §240.14a-21 of this chapter shall disclose that they are providing each such vote as required pursuant to section 14A of the Securities Exchange Act (15 U.S.C. 78n-1), briefly explain the general effect of each vote, such as whether each such vote is non-binding, and, when applicable, disclose the current frequency of shareholder advisory votes on executive compensation required by Rule 14a-21(a) and when the next such shareholder advisory vote will occur. . . .

Rule 14b-1. Obligation of Registered Brokers and Dealers in Connection with the Prompt Forwarding of Certain Communications to Beneficial Owners

(a) *Definitions.* Unless the context otherwise requires, all terms used in this section shall have the same meanings as in the Act and, with respect to proxy soliciting material, as in Rule 14a-1 thereunder and, with respect to information statements, as in §240.14c-1 thereunder. In addition, as used in this section, the term "registrant" means:

(1) The issuer of a class of securities registered pursuant to section 12 of the Act; or

(2) An investment company registered under the Investment Company Act of 1940.

(b) *Dissemination and beneficial owner information requirements.* A broker or dealer registered under Section 15 of the Act shall comply with the following requirements for disseminating certain communications to beneficial owners and providing beneficial owner information to registrants.

(1) The broker or dealer shall respond, by first class mail or other equally prompt means, directly to the registrant no later than seven business days after the date it receives an inquiry made in accordance with Rule 14a-13(a) or Rule 14c-7(a) by indicting, by means of a search card or otherwise:

(i) The approximate number of customers of the broker or dealer who are beneficial owners of the registrant's securities that are held of record by the broker, dealer, or its nominee;

(ii) The number of customers of the broker or dealer who are beneficial owners of the registrant's securities who have objected to disclosure of their names, addresses, and securities positions if the registrant has indicated, pursuant to Rule 14a-13(a)(1)(ii)(A) or Rule 14c-7(a)(1)(ii)(A), that it will distribute the annual report to security holders to beneficial owners of its securities whose names, addresses and securities positions are disclosed pursuant to paragraph (b)(3) of this section; and

(iii) The identity of the designated agent of the broker or dealer, if any, acting on its behalf in fulfilling its obligations under paragraph (b)(3) of this section; *Provided, however,* that if the broker or dealer has informed the registrant that a designated office(s) or department(s) is to receive such inquiries, receipt for purposes of paragraph (b)(1) of this section shall mean receipt by such designated office(s) or department(s).

(2) The broker or dealer shall, upon receipt of the proxy, other proxy soliciting material, information statement, and/or annual reports to security holders from the registrant or other soliciting person, forward such materials to its customers who are beneficial owners of the registrant's securities no later than

five business days after receipt of the proxy material, information statement or annual report to security holders.

(3) The broker or dealer shall, through its agent or directly:

(i) Provide the registrant, upon the registrant's request, with the names, addresses, and securities positions, compiled as of a date specified in the registrant's request which is no earlier than five business days after the date the registrant's request is received, of its customers who are beneficial owners of the registrant's securities and who have not objected to disclosure of such information; *Provided, however,* that if the broker or dealer has informed the registrant that a designated office(s) or department(s) is to receive such requests, receipt shall mean receipt by such designated office(s) or department(s); and

(ii) Transmit the data specified in paragraph (b)(3)(i) of this section to the registrant no later than five business days after the record date or other date specified by the registrant.

Notes

1. Where a broker or dealer employs a designated agent to act on its behalf in performing the obligations imposed on the broker or dealer by paragraph (b)(3) of this section, the five business day time period for determining the date as of which the beneficial owner information is to be compiled is calculated from the date the designated agent receives the registrant's request. In complying with the registrant's request for beneficial owner information under paragraph (b)(3) of this section, a broker or dealer need only supply the registrant with the names, addresses, and securities positions of non-objecting beneficial owners.

2. If a broker or dealer receives a registrant's request less than five business days before the requested compilation date, it must provide a list compiled as of a date that is no more than five business days after receipt and transmit the list within five business days after the compilation date.

(c) *Exceptions to dissemination and beneficial owner information requirements.* A broker or dealer registered under section 15 of the Act shall be subject to the following with respect to its dissemination and beneficial owner information requirements.

(1) With regard to beneficial owners of exempt employee benefit plan securities, the broker or dealer shall:

(i) Not include information in its response pursuant to paragraph (b)(1) of this section or forward proxies (or in lieu thereof requests for voting instructions), proxy soliciting material, information statements, or annual reports to security holders pursuant to paragraph (b)(2) of this section to such beneficial owners; and

(ii) Not include in its response, pursuant to paragraph (b)(3) of this section, data concerning such beneficial owners.

(2) A broker or dealer need not satisfy:

(i) Its obligations under paragraphs (b)(2), (b)(3), and (d) of this section if the registrant or other soliciting person as applicable, does not provide assurance of reimbursement of the broker's or dealer's reasonable expenses, both direct and indirect, incurred in connection with performing the obligations imposed by paragraphs (b)(2), (b)(3), and (d) of this section; or

(ii) Its obligation under paragraph (b)(2) of this section to forward annual reports to non-objecting beneficial owners identified by the broker or dealer, through its agent or directly, pursuant to paragraph (b)(3) of this section if the registrant notifies the broker or dealer pursuant to Rule 14a-13(c) or Rule 14c-7(c) that the registrant will mail the annual report to such non-objecting beneficial owners identified by the broker or dealer and delivered in a list to the registrant pursuant to paragraph (b)(3) of this section. . . .

(d) *Compliance with Rule 14a-16.* Upon receipt from the soliciting person of all of the information listed in Rule 14a-16(d), the broker or dealer shall:

(1) Prepare and send a Notice of Internet Availability of Proxy Materials containing the information required in paragraph (e) of this section to beneficial owners no later than:

(i) With respect to a registrant, 40 calendar days prior to the security holder meeting date or, if no meeting is to be held, 40 calendar days prior to the date the votes, consents, or authorizations may be used to effect the corporate action; and

(ii) With respect to a soliciting person other than the registrant, the later of:

(A) 40 calendar days prior to the security holder meeting date or, if no meeting is to be held, 40 calendar days prior to the date the votes, consents, or authorizations may be used to effect the corporate action; or

(B) 10 calendar days after the date that the registrant first sends its proxy statement or Notice of Internet Availability of Proxy Materials to security holders.

(2) Establish a Web site at which beneficial owners are able to access the broker or dealer's request for voting instructions and, at the broker or dealer's option, establish a Web site at which beneficial owners are able to access the proxy statement and other soliciting materials, provided that such Web sites are maintained in a manner consistent with paragraphs (b), (c), and (k) of Rule 14a-16;

(3) Upon receipt of a request from the registrant or other soliciting person, send to security holders specified by the registrant or other soliciting person a copy of the request for voting instructions accompanied by a copy of the intermediary's Notice of Internet Availability of Proxy Materials 10 calendar days or more after the broker or dealer sends its Notice of Internet Availability of Proxy Materials pursuant to paragraph (d)(1); and

(4) Upon receipt of a request for a copy of the materials from a beneficial owner:

(i) Request a copy of the soliciting materials from the registrant or other soliciting person, in the form requested by the beneficial owner, within three business days after receiving the beneficial owner's request;

(ii) Forward a copy of the soliciting materials to the beneficial owner, in the form requested by the beneficial owner, within three business days after receiving the materials from the registrant or other soliciting person; and

(iii) Maintain records of security holder requests to receive a paper or e-mail copy of the proxy materials in connection with future proxy solicitations and provide copies of the proxy materials to a security holder who has made such a request for all securities held in the account of that security holder until the security holder revokes such request.

(5) Notwithstanding any other provisions in this paragraph (d), if the broker or dealer receives copies of the proxy statement and annual report to security holders (if applicable) from the soliciting person with instructions to forward such materials to beneficial owners, the broker or dealer:

(i) Shall either:

(A) Prepare a Notice of Internet Availability of Proxy Materials and forward it with the proxy statement and annual report to security holders (if applicable); or

(B) Incorporate any information required in the Notice of Internet Availability of Proxy Materials that does not appear in the proxy statement into the broker or dealer's request for voting instructions to be sent with the proxy statement and annual report (if applicable);

(ii) Need not comply with the following provisions:

(A) The timing provisions of paragraph (d)(1)(ii); and

(B) Paragraph (d)(4); and

(iii) Need not include in its Notice of Internet Availability of Proxy Materials or request for voting instructions the following disclosures:

(A) Legends 1 and 3 in Rule 14a-16(d)(1); and

(B) Instructions on how to request a copy of the proxy materials.

(e) *Content of Notice of Internet Availability of Proxy Materials.* The broker or dealer's Notice of Internet Availability of Proxy Materials shall:

(1) Include all information, as it relates to beneficial owners, required in a registrant's Notice of Internet Availability of Proxy Materials under Rule 14a-16(d), provided that the broker or dealer shall provide its own, or its agent's, toll-free telephone number, an e-mail address, and an Internet Web site to service requests for copies from beneficial owners;

(2) Include a brief description, if applicable, of the rules that permit the broker or dealer to vote the securities if the beneficial owner does not return his or her voting instructions; and

(3) Otherwise be prepared and sent in a manner consistent with paragraphs (e), (f), and (g) of Rule 14a-16.

Rule 14b-2. Obligation of Banks, Associations and Other Entities That Exercise Fiduciary Powers in Connection with the Prompt Forwarding of Certain Communications to Beneficial Owners . . .

REGULATION 14D

Rule 14d-1. Scope of and Definitions Applicable to Regulations 14D and 14E

(a) *Scope.* Regulation 14D shall apply to any tender offer which is subject to section 14(d)(1) of the Act, including, but not limited to, any tender offer for securities of a class described in that section that is made by an affiliate of the issuer of such class. Regulation 14E shall apply to any tender offer for securities (other than exempted securities) unless otherwise noted therein. . . .

(c) *Tier I.* Any tender offer for the securities of a foreign private issuer as defined in Rule 3b-4 is exempt from the requirements of Sections 14(d)(1) through 14(d)(7) of the Act, Regulation 14D and Schedules TO and 14D-9 thereunder, and Rules 14e-1 and 14e-2 of Regulation 14E under the Act if the following conditions are satisfied:

(1) *U.S. ownership limitation.* Except in the case of a tender offer that is commenced during the pendency of a tender offer made by a prior bidder in reliance on this paragraph or Rule 13e-4(h)(8), U.S. holders do not hold more than 10 percent of the class of securities sought in the offer (as determined under Instructions 2 or 3 to paragraphs (c) and (d) of this section).

(2) *Equal treatment.* The bidder must permit U.S. holders to participate in the offer on terms at least as favorable as those offered any other holder of the same class of securities that is the subject of the tender offer; however:

(i) *Registered exchange offers.* If the bidder offers securities registered under the Securities Act of 1933, the bidder need not extend the offer to security holders in those states or jurisdictions that prohibit the offer or sale of the securities after the bidder has made a good faith effort to register or qualify the offer and sale of securities in that state or jurisdiction, except that the bidder must offer the same cash alternative to security holders in any such state or jurisdiction that it has offered to security holders in any other state or jurisdiction.

(ii) *Exempt exchange offers.* If the bidder offers securities exempt from registration under Rule 802 of this chapter, the bidder need not extend the offer to security holders in those states or jurisdictions that require registration or qualification, except that the bidder must offer the same cash alternative to security holders in any such state or jurisdiction that it has offered to security holders in any other state or jurisdiction.

(iii) *Cash only consideration* . . .

(iv) *Disparate tax treatment.* If the bidder offers loan notes solely to offer sellers tax advantages not available in the United States and these notes are neither listed on any organized securities market nor registered under the Securities Act of 1933, the loan notes need not be offered to U.S. holders.

(3) *Informational documents.* (i) The bidder must disseminate any informational document to U.S. holders, including any amendments thereto, in English, on a comparable basis to that provided to security holders in the home jurisdiction.

(ii) If the bidder disseminates by publication in its home jurisdiction, the bidder must publish the information in the United States in a manner reasonably calculated to inform U.S. holders of the offer.

(iii) In the case of tender offers for securities described in Section 14(d)(1) of the Act, if the bidder publishes or otherwise disseminates an informational document to the holders of the securities in connection with the tender offer, the bidder must furnish that informational document, including any amendments thereto, in English, to the Commission on Form CB by the first business day after publication or dissemination. If the bidder is a foreign company, it must also file a Form F-X with the Commission at the same time as the submission of Form CB to appoint an agent for service in the United States.

(4) *Investment companies.* The issuer of the securities that are the subject of the tender offer is not an investment company registered or required to be registered under the Investment Company Act of 1940, other than a registered closed-end investment company.

(d) *Tier II.* A person conducting a tender offer (including any exchange offer) that meets the conditions in paragraph (d)(1) of this section shall be entitled to the exemptive relief specified in paragraph (d)(2) of this section, provided that such tender offer complies with all the requirements of this section other than those for which an exemption has been specifically provided in paragraph (d)(2) of this section. In addition, a person conducting a tendor offer subject only to the requirements of section 14(e) of the Act (15 U.S.C. 78n(e)) and Regulation 14E thereunder that meets the conditions in paragraph (d)(1) of the section also shall be entitled to the exemptive relief specified in paragraph (d)(2) of this section, to the extent needed under the requirements of Regulation 14E, so long as the tender offer complies with all requirements of Regulation 14E other than those for which an exemption has been specifically provided in paragraph (d)(2) of this section:

(1) *Conditions.* (i) The subject company is a foreign private issuer as defined in Rule 3b-4 and is not an investment company registered or required to be registered under the Investment Company Act of 1940, other than a registered closed-end investment company;

(ii) Except in the case of a tender offer that is commenced during the pendency of a tender offer made by a prior bidder in reliance on this paragraph or Rule 13e-4(i), U.S. holders do not hold more than 40 percent of the class of securities sought in the offer (as determined under Instructions 2 or 3 to paragraphs (c) and (d) of this section); and

(iii) The bidder complies with all applicable U.S. tender offer laws and regulations, other than those for which an exemption has been provided for in paragraph (d)(2) of this section.

(2) *Exemptions.* (i) *Equal treatment— loan notes.* If the bidder offers loan notes solely to offer sellers tax advantages not available in the United States and these notes are neither listed on any organized securities market nor registered under the Securities Act of 1933, the loan notes need not be offered to U.S. holders, notwithstanding Rule 14d-10.

(ii) *Equal treatment—separate U.S. and foreign offers.* Notwithstanding the provisions of Rule 14d-10, a bidder conducting a tender offer meeting the conditions of paragraph (d)(1) of this section may separate the offer into multiple offers: one offer made to U.S. holders which may also include all holders of American Depository Shares representing interests in the subject securities, and one or more offers made to non-U.S. holders. The offer to U.S. holders must be made on terms at least as favorable as those offered any other holder of the same class of securities that is the subject of the tender offers. U.S. holders may be included in the foreign offer(s) only where the laws of the jurisdiction governing such foreign offer(s) expressly preclude the exclusion of the U.S. holders from the foreign offer(s) and where the offer materials distributed to U.S. holders fully and adequately disclose the risks of participating in the foreign offer(s).

(iii) *Notice of extensions.* Notice of extensions made in accordance with the requirements of the home jurisdiction law or practice will satisfy the requirements of Rule 14e-1(d).

(iv) *Prompt payment.* Payment made in accordance with the requirements of the home jurisdiction law or practice will satisfy the requirements of Rule 14e-1(c). Where payment may not be made on a more expedited basis under home jurisdiction law or practice, payment for securities tendered during any subsequent offering period within 20 business days of the date of tender will satisfy the prompt payment requirements of Rule 14d-11(e). For purposes of this paragraph, a business day is determined with reference to the target's home jurisdiction.

(v) *Subsequent offering period/Withdrawal rights.* A bidder will satisfy the announcement and prompt payment requirements of Rule 14d-11(d), if the bidder announces the results of the tender offer, including the approximate number of securities deposited to date, and pays for tendered securities in accordance with the requirements of the home jurisdiction law or practice and the subsequent offering period commences immediately following such announcement. Notwithstanding Section 14(d)(5) of the Act, the bidder need not extend withdrawal rights following the close of the offer and prior to the commencement of the subsequent offering period.

(vi) *Payment of interest on securities tendered during subsequent offering period . . .*

(vii) *Suspension of withdrawal right during counting of tendered securities . . .*

(viii) *Mix and match elections and the subsequent offering period . . .*

(ix) *Early termination of an initial offering period.*

(e) *Definitions.* Unless the context otherwise requires, all terms used in Regulation 14D and Regulation 14E have the same meaning as in the Act and in Rule 12b-2 promulgated thereunder. In addition, for purposes of sections 14(d) and 14(e) of the Act and Regulations 14D and 14E, the following definitions apply:

(1) The term *bidder* means any person who makes a tender offer or on whose behalf a tender offer is made: *Provided, however,* That the term does not include an issuer which makes a tender offer for securities of any class of which it is the issuer;

(2) The term *subject company* means any issuer of securities which are sought by a bidder pursuant to a tender offer;

(3) The term *security holder* means holders of record and beneficial owners of securities which are the subject of a tender offer;

(4) The term *beneficial owner* shall have the same meaning as that set forth in Rule 13d-3; *Provided, however,* That, except with respect to Rule 14d-3, Rule 14d-9(d) and Item 6 of Schedule 14D-1, the term shall not include a person who does not have or share investment power or who is deemed to be a beneficial owner by virtue of Rule 13d-3(d)(1);

(5) The term *tender offer material* means:

(i) The bidder's formal offer, including all the material terms and conditions of the tender offer and all amendments thereto;

(ii) The related transmittal letter (whereby securities of the subject company which are sought in the tender offer may be transmitted to the bidder or its depositary) and all amendments thereto; and

(iii) Press releases, advertisements, letters and other documents published by the bidder or sent or given by the bidder to security holders which, directly or indirectly, solicit, invite or request tenders of the securities being sought in the tender offer;

(6) The term *business day* means any day, other than Saturday, Sunday or a federal holiday, and shall consist of the time period from 12:01 a.m. through 12:00 midnight Eastern time. In computing any time period under section 14(d)(5) or section 14(d)(6) of the Act or under Regulation 14D or Regulation 14E, the date of the event which begins the running of such time period shall be included *except that* if such event occurs on other than a business day such period shall begin to run on and shall include the first business day thereafter. . . .

Rule 14d-2. Commencement of a Tender Offer

(a) *Date of commencement.* A bidder will have commenced its tender offer for purposes of section 14(d) of the Act and the rules under that section at 12:01 a.m. on the date when the bidder has first published, sent or given the means to tender to security holders. For purposes of this section, the means to tender includes the transmittal form or a statement regarding how the transmittal form may be obtained.

(b) *Pre-commencement communications.* A communication by the bidder will not be deemed to constitute commencement of a tender offer if:

(1) It does not include the means for security holders to tender their shares into the offer; and

(2) All written communications relating to the tender offer, from and including the first public announcement, are filed under cover of Schedule TO with the Commission no later than the date of the communication. The bidder also must deliver to the subject company and any other bidder for the same class of securities the first communication relating to the transaction that is filed, or required to be filed, with the Commission.

(c) *Filing and other obligations triggered by commencement.* As soon as practicable on the date of commencement, a bidder must comply with the filing requirements of Rule 14d-3(a), the dissemination requirements of Rule 14d-4(a) or (b), and the disclosure requirements of Rule 14d-6(a).

Rule 14d-3. Filing and Transmission of Tender Offer Statement

(a) Filing and transmittal. No bidder shall make a tender offer if, after consummation thereof, such bidder would be the beneficial owner of more than 5 percent of the class of the subject company's securities for which the tender offer is made, unless as soon as practicable on the date of the commencement of the tender offer such bidder:

(1) Files with the Commission a Tender Offer Statement on Schedule TO, including all exhibits thereto;

(2) Delivers a copy of such Schedule TO, including all exhibits thereto:

(i) To the subject company at its principal executive office; and

(ii) To any other bidder, which has filed a Schedule 14D-1 with the Commission relating to a tender offer which has not yet terminated for the same class of securities of the subject company, at such bidder's principal executive office or at the address of the person authorized to receive notices and communications (which is disclosed on the cover sheet of such other bidder's Schedule TO);

(3) Gives telephonic notice of the information required by Rule 14d-6(d)(2)(i) and (ii) and mails by means of first class mail a copy of such Schedule TO, including all exhibits thereto:

(i) To each national securities exchange where such class of the subject company's securities is registered and listed for trading (which may be based upon information contained in the subject company's most recent Annual Report on Form 10-K filed with the Commission unless the bidder has reason to believe that such information is not current) which telephonic notice shall be made when practicable prior to the opening of each such exchange; and

(ii) To the National Association of Securities Dealers, Inc. ("NASD") if such class of the subject company's securities is authorized for quotation in the NASDAQ interdealer quotation system. . . .

Rule 14d-6. Disclosure of Tender Offer Information to Security Holders . . .

(d) *Information to be included.*

(1) *Tender offer materials other than summary publication.* The following information is required by paragraphs (a)(1), (a)(2)(ii), (a)(3)(ii) and (a)(4) of this section:

(i) The information required by Item 1 of Schedule TO (Summary Term Sheet); and

(ii) The information required by the remaining items of Schedule TO for third-party tender offers, except for Item 12 (exhibits) of Schedule TO, or a fair and adequate summary of the information.

(2) *Summary Publication.* The following information is required in a summary advertisement under paragraphs (a)(2)(i) and (a)(3)(i) of this section:

(i) The identity of the bidder and the subject company;

(ii) The information required by Item 1004(a)(1) of Regulation M-A;

(iii) If the tender offer is for less than all of the outstanding securities of a class of equity securities, a statement as to whether the purpose or one of the purposes of the tender offer is to acquire or influence control of the business of the subject company;

(iv) A statement that the information required by paragraph (d)(1) of this section is incorporated by reference into the summary advertisement;

(v) Appropriate instructions as to how security holders may obtain promptly, at the bidder's expense, the bidder's tender offer materials; and

(vi) In a tender offer published or sent or given to security holders by use of stockholder lists and security position listings under Rule 14d-4(a)(3), statement that a request is being made for such lists and listings. The summary publication also must state that tender offer materials will be mailed to record holders and will be furnished to brokers, banks and similar persons whose name appears or whose nominee appears on the list of security holders or, if applicable, who are listed as participants in a clearing agency's security position listing for subsequent transmittal to beneficial owners of such securities. If the list furnished to the bidder also included beneficial owners pursuant to Rule 14d-5(c)(1) and tender offer materials will be mailed directly to beneficial holders, include a statement to that effect.

(3) *No transmittal letter.* Neither the initial summary advertisement nor any subsequent summary advertisement may include a transmittal letter (the letter furnished to security holders for transmission of securities sought in the tender offer) or any amendment to the transmittal letter.

Rule 14d-7. Additional Withdrawal Rights

(a)(1) *Rights.* In addition to the provisions of section 14(d)(5) of the Act, any person who has deposited securities pursuant to a tender offer has the right to withdraw any such securities during the period such offer request or invitation remains open.

(a)(2) *Exemption during subsequent offering period.* Notwithstanding the provisions of Section 14(d)(5) of the Act and paragraph (a) of this section, the bidder need not offer withdrawal rights during a subsequent offering period.

(b) *Notice of withdrawal.* Notice of withdrawal pursuant to this section shall be deemed to be timely upon the receipt by the bidder's depositary of a written notice of withdrawal specifying the name(s) of the tendering stockholder(s), the number or amount of the securities to be withdrawn and the name(s) in which the certificate(s) is (are) registered, if different from that of the tendering security holder(s). A bidder may impose other reasonable requirements, including certificate numbers and a signed request for withdrawal accompanied by a signature guarantee, as conditions precedent to the physical release of withdrawn securities.

Rule 14d-8. Exemption from Statutory Pro Rata Requirements

Notwithstanding the pro rata provisions of section 14(d)(6) of the Act, if any person makes a tender offer or request or invitation for tenders, for less than all of the outstanding equity securities of a class, and if a greater number of securities are deposited pursuant thereto than such person is bound or willing to take up and pay for, the securities taken up and paid for shall be taken up and paid for as nearly as may be pro rata, disregarding fractions, according to the number of securities deposited by each depositor during the period such offer, request or invitation remains open.

Rule 14d-9. Recommendation or Solicitation by the Subject Company and Others

(a) *Pre-commencement communications.* A communication by a person described in paragraph (e) of this section with respect to a tender offer will not be deemed to constitute a recommendation or solicitation under this section if:

(1) The tender offer has not commenced under Rule 14d-2; and

(2) The communication is filed under cover of Schedule 14D-9 with the Commission no later than the date of the communication.

(b) *Post-commencement communications.* After commencement by a bidder under Rule 14d-2, no solicitation or recommendation to security holders may be made by any person described in paragraph (e) of this section with respect to a tender offer for such securities unless as soon as practicable on the date such solicitation or recommendation is first published or sent or given to security holders such person complies with the following:

(1) Such person shall file with the Commission a Tender Offer Solicitation/Recommendation Statement on Schedule 14D-9, including all exhibits thereto; and

(2) If such person is either the subject company or an affiliate of the subject company,

(i) Such person shall hand deliver a copy of the Schedule 14D-9 to the bidder at its principal office or at the address of the person authorized to receive notices and communications (which is set forth on the cover sheet of the bidder's Schedule TO filed with the Commission); and

(ii) Such person shall give telephonic notice (which notice to the extent possible shall be given prior to the opening of the market) of the information required by Items 1003(d) and 1012(a) of Regulation M-A and shall mail a copy of the Schedule to each national securities exchange where the class of securities is registered and listed for trading and, if the class is authorized for quotation in the NASDAQ interdealer quotation system, to the National Association of Securities Dealers, Inc. ("NASD").

(3) If such person is neither the subject company nor an affiliate of the subject company,

(i) Such person shall mail a copy of the schedule to the bidder at its principal office or at the address of the person authorized to receive notices and communications (which is set forth on the cover sheet of the bidder's Schedule TO filed with the Commission); and

(ii) Such person shall mail a copy of the Schedule to the subject company at its principal office.

(c) *Amendments.* If any material change occurs in the information set forth in the Schedule 14D-9 required by this section, the person who filed such Schedule 14D-9 shall:

(1) File with the Commission an amendment on Schedule 14D-9 disclosing such change promptly, but not later than the date such material is first published, sent or given to security holders; and

(2) Promptly deliver copies and give notice of the amendment in the same manner as that specified in paragraph (b)(2) or (3) of this section, whichever is applicable; and

(3) Promptly disclose and disseminate such change in a manner reasonably designed to inform security holders of such change.

(d) *Information required in solicitation or recommendation.* Any solicitation or recommendation to holders of a class of securities referred to in section 14(d)(1) of the Act with respect to a tender offer for such securities shall include the name of the person making such solicitation or recommendation and the information required by Items 1 through 8 of Schedule 14D-9 or a fair and adequate summary thereof: *Provided, however,* That such solicitation or recommendation may omit any of such information previously furnished to security holders of such class of securities by such person with respect to such tender offer.

(e) *Applicability.* (1) Except as is provided in paragraphs (e)(2) and (f) of this section, this section shall only apply to the following persons:

(i) The subject company, any director, officer, employee, affiliate or subsidiary of the subject company;

(ii) Any record holder or beneficial owner of any security issued by the subject company, by the bidder, or by any affiliate of either the subject company or the bidder; and

(iii) Any person who makes a solicitation or recommendation to security holders on behalf of any of the foregoing or on behalf of the bidder other than by means of a solicitation or recommendation to security holders which has been filed with the Commission pursuant to this section or Rule 14d-3.

(2) Notwithstanding paragraph (e)(1) of this section, shall not apply to the following persons:

(i) A bidder who has filed a Schedule TO pursuant to Rule 14d-3;

(ii) Attorneys, banks, brokers, fiduciaries or investment advisers who are not participating in a tender offer in more than a ministerial capacity and who furnish information and/or advice regarding such tender offer to their customers or clients on the unsolicited request of such customers or clients or solely pursuant to a contract or a relationship providing for advice to the customer or client to whom the information and/or advice is given.

(iii) Any person specified in paragraph (d)(1) of this section if:

(A) The subject company is the subject of a tender offer conducted under Rule 14d-1(c).

(B) Any person specified in paragraph (d)(1) of this section furnishes to the Commission on Form CB the entire informational document it publishes or otherwise disseminates to holders of the class of securities in connection with the tender offer no later than the next business day after publication or dissemination;

(C) Any person specified in paragraph (d)(1) of this section disseminates any informational document to U.S. holders, including any amendments thereto, in English, on a comparable basis to that provided to security holders in the issuer's home jurisdiction; and

(D) Any person specified in paragraph (d)(1) of this section disseminates by publication in its home jurisdiction, such person must publish the information in the United States in a manner reasonably calculated to inform U.S. security holders of the offer.

(f) *Stop-look-and-listen communication.* This section shall not apply to the subject company with respect to a communication by the subject company to its security holders which only:

(1) Identifies the tender offer by the bidder;

(2) States that such tender offer is under consideration by the subject company's board of directors and/or management;

(3) States that on or before a specified date (which shall be no later than 10 business days from the date of commencement of such tender offer) the subject company will advise such security holders of (i) whether the subject company recommends acceptance or rejection of such tender offer; expresses no opinion and remains neutral toward such tender offer; or is unable to take a position with respect to such tender offer and (ii) the reason(s) for the position taken by the subject company with respect to the tender offer (including the inability to take a position); and

(4) Requests such security holders to defer making a determination whether to accept or reject such tender offer until they have been advised of the subject company's position with respect thereto pursuant to paragraph (f)(3) of this section.

(g) *Statement of management's position.* A statement by the subject company's of its position with respect to a tender offer which is required to be published or sent or given to security holders pursuant to Rule 14e-2 shall be deemed to constitute a solicitation or recommendation within the meaning of this section and section 14(d)(4) of the Act.

Rule 14d-10. Equal Treatment of Security Holders

(a) No bidder shall make a tender offer unless:

(1) The tender offer is open to all security holders of the class of securities subject to the tender offer; and

(2) The consideration paid to any security holder for securities tendered in the tender offer is the highest consideration paid to any other security holder for securities tendered during such tender offer. . . .

(d)(1) Paragraph (a)(2) of this section shall not prohibit the negotiation, execution or amendment of an employment compensation, severance or other employee benefit arrangement, or payment made or to be made or benefits granted or to be granted according to such an arrangement, with respect to any security holder of the subject company, where the amount payable under the arrangement:

(i) Is being paid or granted as compensation for past services performed, future services to be performed, or future services to be refrained from performing, by the security holder (and matters incidental thereto); and

(ii) Is not calculated based on the number of securities tendered or to be tendered in the tender offer by the security holder.

(2) The provisions of paragraph (d)(1) of this section shall be satisfied and, therefore, pursuant to this non-exclusive safe harbor, the negotiation, execution or amendment of an arrangement and any payments made or to be made or benefits granted or to be granted according to that arrangement shall not be prohibited by paragraph (a)(2) of this section, if the arrangement is approved as an employment compensation, severance or other employee benefit arrangement solely by independent directors as follows:

(i) The compensation committee or a committee of the board of directors that performs functions similar to a compensation committee of the subject company approves the arrangement, regardless of whether the subject company is a party to the arrangement, or, if the bidder is a party to the arrangement, the compensation committee or a committee of the board of directors that performs functions similar to a compensation committee of the bidder approves the arrangement; or

(ii) If the subject company's or bidder's board of directors, as applicable, does not have a compensation committee or a committee of the board of the directors that performs functions similar to a compensation committee or if none of the members of the subject company's or bidder's compensation committee or committee or committee that performs functions similar to a compensation committee is independent, a special committee of the board of directors formed to consider and approve the arrangement approves the arrangement; or (iii) If the subject company or bidder, as applicable, is a foreign private issuer, any or all members of the board of directors or any committee of the board of directors authorized to approve employment compensation, severance or other employee benefit arrangements under the laws or regulations of the home country approves the arrangement.

Instructions to Paragraph (d)(2)

For purposes of determining whether the members of the committee approving an arrangement in accordance with the provisions of paragraph (d)(2) of this section are independent, the following provisions shall apply:

1. If the bidder or subject company, as applicable, is a listed issuer (as defined in Rule 10A-3 of this chapter) whose securities are listed either on a national securities exchange registered pursuant to section 6(a) of the Exchange Act or in an inter-dealer quotation system of a national securities association registered pursuant to section 15A(a) of the Exchange Act that has independence requirements for compensation committee members that have been approved by the Commission (as those requirements may be modified or supplemented), apply the bidder's or subject company's definition of independence that it uses for determining that the members of the compensation committee are independent in compliance with the listing standards applicable to compensation committee members of the listed issuer.

2. If the bidder or subject company, as applicable, is not a listed issuer (as defined in Rule 10A-3 of this chapter), apply the independence requirements for compensation committee members of a national securities exchange registered pursuant to section 6(a) of the Exchange Act or an inter-dealer quotation system of a national securities association registered pursuant to section 15A(a) of the Exchange Act that have been approved by the

Commission (as those requirements may be modified or supplemented). Whatever definition the bidder or subject company, as applicable, chooses, it must apply that definition consistently to all members of the committee approving the arrangement.

3. Notwithstanding Instruction 1 and 2 to paragraph (d)(2), if the bidder or subject company, as applicable, is a closed-end investment company registered under the Investment Company Act of 1940, a director is considered to be independent if the director is not, other than in his or her capacity as a member of the board of directors or any board committee, an "interested person" of the investment company, as defined in section 2(a)(19) of the Investment Act of 1940.

4. If the bidder or the subject company, as applicable, is a foreign private issuer, apply either the independence standards set forth in Instructions 1 and 2 to paragraph (d)(2) or the independence requirements of the laws, regulations, codes or standards of the home country of the bidder or subject company, as applicable, for members of the board of directors or the committee of the board of directors approving the arrangement.

5. A determination by the bidder-s or the subject company's board of directors, as applicable, that the members of the board of directors or the committee of the board of directors, as applicable, approving an arrangement in accordance with the provisions of paragraph (d)(2) are independent in accordance with the provisions of this instruction to paragraph (d)(2) shall satisfy the independence requirements of paragraph (d)(2).

Instruction to Paragraph (d)

The fact that the provisions of paragraph (d) of this section extend only to employment compensation, severance and other employee benefit arrangements and not to other arrangements, such as commercial arrangements, does not raise any inference that a payment under any such other arrangement constitutes consideration paid for securities in a tender offer.

Schedule TO. Tender Offer Statement Under Section 14(d)(1) or 13(e)(1) of the Securities Exchange Act of 1934 . . .

Item 1. Summary Term Sheet.

Furnish the information required by Item 1001 of Regulation M-A unless information is disclosed to security holders in a prospectus that meets the requirements of Rule 421(d).

Item 2. Subject Company Information.

Furnish the information required by Item 1002(a) through (c) of Regulation M-A.

Item 3. Identity and Background of Filing Person. . . .

Item 1003(a) through (c) of Regulation M-A for a third-party tender offer and the information required by Item 1003(a) of Regulation M-A for an issuer tender offer. . . .

Item 4. Terms of the Transaction. . . .

Item 1004(a) of Regulation M-A for a third-party tender offer and the information required by Item 1004(a) through (b) of Regulation M-A for an issuer tender offer.

Item 5. Past Contacts, Transactions, Negotiations and Agreements. . . .

Item 1005(a) and (b) of Regulation M-A for a third-party tender offer and the information required by Item 1005(e) of Regulation M-A for an issuer tender offer.

Item 6. Purposes of the Transaction and Plans or Proposals. . . .

Item 1006(a) and (c)(1) through (7) of Regulation M-A for a third-party tender offer and the information required by Item 1006(a) through (c) of Regulation M-A for an issuer tender offer.

Item 7. Source and Amount of Funds or Other Consideration. . . .

Item 1007(a), (b) and (d) of Regulation M-A.

Item 8. Interest in Securities of the Subject Company. . . .

Item 1008 of Regulation M-A.

Item 9. Persons/Assets, Retained, Employed, Compensated or Used. . . .

Item 1009(a) of Regulation M-A.

Item 10. Financial Statements. . . .

Item 1010(a) and (b) of Regulation M-A for the issuer in an issuer tender offer and for the offeror in a third-party tender offer.

INSTRUCTIONS TO ITEM 10

1. Financial statements must be provided when the offeror's financial condition is material to security holder's decision whether to sell, tender or hold the securities sought. The facts and circumstances of a tender offer, particularly the terms of the tender offer, may influence a determination as to whether financial statements are material, and thus required to be disclosed.

2. Financial statements are *not* considered material when: (a) the consideration offered consists solely of cash; (b) the offer is not subject to any financing condition; *and* either: (c) the offeror is a public reporting company under Section 13(a) or 15(d) of the Act that files reports electronically on EDGAR, or (d) the offer is for all outstanding securities of the subject class. Financial information may be required, however, in a two-tier transaction. *See* Instruction 5 below. . . .

4. If the offeror in a third-party tender offer is a natural person, and such person's financial information is material, disclose the net worth of the offeror. If the offeror's net worth is

derived from material amounts of assets that are not readily marketable or there are material guarantees and contingencies, disclose the nature and approximate amount of the individual's net worth that consists of illiquid assets and the magnitude of any guarantees or contingencies that may negatively affect the natural person's net worth.

5. Pro forma financial information is required in a negotiated third-party cash tender offer when securities are intended to be offered in a subsequent merger or other transaction in which remaining target securities are acquired and the acquisition of the subject company is significant to the offeror under Rule 11-01(b)(1) of this chapter. The offeror must disclose the financial information specified in Item 3(f) and Item 5 of Form S-4 in the schedule filed with the Commission, but may furnish only the summary financial information specified in Item 3(d), (e) and (f) of Form S-4 in the disclosure document sent to security holders. If pro forma financial information is required by this instruction, the historical financial statements specified in Item 1010 of Regulation M-A are required for the bidder.

Item 11. Additional Information. . . .

Item 1011 of Regulation M-A.

Item 12. Exhibits. . . .

Item 1016(a), (b), (d), (g) and (h) of Regulation M-A.

Item 13. Information Required by Schedule 13E-3.

If the Schedule TO is combined with Schedule 13E-3, set forth the information required by Schedule 13E-3 that is not included or covered by the items in Schedule TO.

Signature. . . .

INSTRUCTION TO SIGNATURE

The statement must be signed by the filing person or that person's authorized representative. If the statement is signed on behalf of a person by an authorized representative (other than an executive officer of a corporation or general partner of a partnership), evidence of the representative's authority to sign on behalf of the person must be filed with the statement. The name and any title of each person who signs the statement must be typed or printed beneath the signature. See Rules 12b-11 and 14d-1(h) with respect to signature requirements.

REGULATION 14E

Rule 14e-1. Unlawful Tender Offer Practices

As a means reasonably designed to prevent fraudulent, deceptive or manipulative acts or practices within the meaning of section 14(e) of the Act, no person who makes a tender offer shall:

(a) Hold such tender offer open for less than twenty business days from the date such tender offer is first published or sent or given to security holders; provided, *however,* that if the tender offer involves a roll-up transaction as defined in Item 901(c) of Regulation S-K and the securities being offered are registered (or authorized to be registered) on Form S-4 or Form F-4, the offer shall not be open for less than sixty calendar days from the date the tender offer is first published or sent to security holders:

(b) Increase or decrease the percentage of the class of securities being sought or the consideration offered or the dealer's soliciting fee to be given in a tender offer unless such tender offer remains open for at least ten business days from the date that notice of such increase or decrease is first published or sent or given to security holders.

Provided, however, That, for purposes of this paragraph, the acceptance for payment of an additional amount of securities not to exceed two percent of the class of securities that is the subject of the tender offer shall not be deemed to be an increase. For purposes of this paragraph, the percentage of a class of securities shall be calculated in accordance with section 14(d)(3) of the Act.

(c) Fail to pay the consideration offered or return the securities deposited by or on behalf of security holders promptly after the termination or withdrawal of a tender offer. This paragraph does not prohibit a bidder electing to offer a subsequent offering period under Rule 14d-11 from paying for securities during the subsequent offering period in accordance with that section.

(d) Extend the length of a tender offer without issuing a notice of such extension by press release or other public announcement, which notice shall include disclosure of the approximate number of securities deposited to date and shall be issued no later than the earlier of: (i) 9:00 a.m. Eastern time, on the next business day after the scheduled expiration date of the offer or (ii), if the class of securities which is the subject of the tender offer is registered on one or more national securities exchanges, the first opening of any one of such exchanges on the next business day after the scheduled expiration date of the offer.

(e) The periods of time required by paragraphs (a) and (b) of this section shall be tolled for any period during which the bidder has failed to file in electronic format, absent a hardship exemption, the Schedule TO Tender Offer Statement, any tender offer material required to be filed by Item 12 of that Schedule pursuant to paragraph (a) of Item 1016 of Regulation M-A, and any amendments thereto. If such documents were filed in paper pursuant to a hardship exemption, the minimum offering periods shall be tolled for any period during which a required confirming electronic copy of such Schedule and tender offer material is delinquent.

Rule 14e-2. Position of Subject Company with Respect to a Tender Offer

(a) *Position of subject company.* As a means reasonably designed to prevent fraudulent, deceptive or manipulative acts or practices within the meaning of section 14(e) of the Act, the subject company, no later than 10 business days from the date the tender offer is first published or sent or given, shall publish, send or give to security holders a statement disclosing that the subject company:

(1) Recommends acceptance or rejection of the bidder's tender offer;

(2) Expresses no opinion and is remaining neutral toward the bidder's tender offer; or

(3) Is unable to take a position with respect to the bidder's tender offer. Such statement shall also include the reason(s) for the position (including the inability to take a position) disclosed therein.

(b) *Material change.* If any material change occurs in the disclosure required by paragraph (a) of this section, the subject company shall promptly publish or send or give a statement disclosing such material change to security holders. . . .

Rule 14e-3. Transactions in Securities on the Basis of Material, Nonpublic Information in the Context of Tender Offers

(a) If any person has taken a substantial step or steps to commence, or has commenced, a tender offer (the "offering person"), it shall constitute a fraudulent, deceptive or manipulative act or practice within the meaning of section 14(e) of the Act for any other person who is in possession of material information relating to such tender offer which information he knows or has reason to know is nonpublic and which he knows or has reason to know has been acquired directly or indirectly from:

(1) The offering person,

(2) The issuer of the securities sought or to be sought by such tender offer, or

(3) Any officer, director, partner or employee or any other person acting on behalf of the offering person or such issuer, to purchase or sell or cause to be purchased or sold any of such securities or any securities convertible into or exchangeable for any such securities or any option or right to obtain or to dispose of any of the foregoing securities, unless within a reasonable time prior to any purchase or sale such information and its source are publicly disclosed by press release or otherwise.

(b) A person other than a natural person shall not violate paragraph (a) of this section if such person shows that:

(1) The individual(s) making the investment decision on behalf of such person to purchase or sell any security described in paragraph (a) of this section or to cause any such security to be purchased or sold by or on behalf of others did not know the material, nonpublic information; and

(2) Such person had implemented one or a combination of policies and procedures, reasonable under the circumstances, taking into consideration the nature of the person's business, to ensure that individual(s) making investment decision(s) would not violate paragraph (a) of this section, which policies and procedures may include, but are not limited to, (i) those which restrict any purchase, sale and causing any purchase and sale of any such security or (ii) those which prevent such individual(s) from knowing such information.

(c) Notwithstanding anything in paragraph (a) of this section to contrary, the following transactions shall not be violations of paragraph (a) of this section:

(1) Purchase(s) of any security described in paragraph (a) of this section by a broker or by another agent on behalf of an offering person; or

(2) Sale(s) by any person of any security described in paragraph (a) of this section to the offering person.

(d)(1) As a means reasonably designed to prevent fraudulent, deceptive or manipulative acts or practices within the meaning of section 14(e) of the Act, it shall be unlawful for any person described in paragraph (d)(2) of this section to communicate material, nonpublic information relating to a tender offer to any other person under circumstances in which it is reasonably foreseeable that such communication is likely to result in a violation of this section *except* that this paragraph shall not apply to a communication made in good faith,

(i) To the officers, directors, partners or employees of the offering person, to its advisors or to other persons, involved in the planning, financing, preparation or execution of such tender offer.

(ii) To the issuer whose securities are sought or to be sought by such tender offer, to its officers, directors, partners, employees or advisors or to other persons, involved in the planning, financing, preparation or execution of the activities of the issuer with respect to such tender offer; or

(iii) To any person pursuant to a requirement of any statute or rule or regulation promulgated thereunder.

(2) The persons referred to in paragraph (d)(1) of this section are:

(i) The offering person or its officers, directors, partners, employees or advisors;

(ii) The issuer of the securities sought or to be sought by such tender offer or its officers, directors, partners, employees or advisors;

(iii) Anyone acting on behalf of the persons in paragraph (d)(2)(i) of this section or the issuer or persons in paragraph (d)(2)(ii) of this section; and

(iv) Any person in possession of material information relating to a tender offer which information he knows or has reason to know is nonpublic and which he knows or has reason to know has been acquired directly or indirectly from any of the above.

Rule 14e-5. Prohibiting Purchases Outside of a Tender Offer

(a) *Unlawful activity.* As a means reasonably designed to prevent fraudulent, deceptive or manipulative acts or practices in connection with a tender offer for equity securities, no covered person may directly or indirectly purchase or arrange to purchase any subject securities or any related securities except as part of the tender offer. This prohibition applies from the time of public announcement of the tender offer until the tender offer expires. This prohibition does not apply to any purchases or arrangements to purchase made during the time of any subsequent offering period as provided for in Rule 14d-11 if the consideration paid or to be paid for the purchases or arrangements to purchase is the same in form and amount as the consideration offered in the tender offer.

(b) *Excepted activity.* The following transactions in subject securities or related securities are not prohibited by paragraph (a) of this section:

(1) *Exercises of securities.* Transactions by covered persons to convert, exchange, or exercise related securities into subject securities, if the covered person owned the related securities before public announcement;

(2) *Purchases for plans.* Purchases or arrangements to purchase by or for a plan that are made by an agent independent of the issuer;

(3) *Purchases during odd-lot offers.* Purchases or arrangements to purchase if the tender offer is excepted under Rule 13e-4(h)(5);

(4) *Purchases as intermediary.* Purchases or through a dealer-manager or its affiliates that are made in the ordinary course of business and made either:

(i) On an agency basis not for a covered person; or

(ii) As principal for its own account if the dealer-manager or its affiliate is not a market maker, and the purchase is made to offset a contemporaneous sale after having received an unsolicited order to buy from a customer who is not a covered person;

(5) *Basket transactions.* . . .

(6) *Covering transactions.* . . .

(7) *Purchases pursuant to contractual obligations.* . . .

(8) *Purchases or arrangements to purchase by an affiliate of the dealer-manager.* . . .

(9) *Purchases by connected exempt market makers or connected exempt principal traders.* . . .

(10) *Purchases during cross-border tender offers.* Purchases or arrangements to purchase if the following conditions are satisfied:

(i) The tender offer is excepted under Rule 13e-4(h)(8) or Rule 14d-1(c);

(ii) The offering documents furnished to U.S. holders prominently disclose the possibility of any purchases, or arrangements to purchase, or the intent to make such purchases;

(iii) The offering documents disclose the manner in which any information about any such purchases or arrangements to purchase will be disclosed;

(iv) The offeror discloses information in the United States about any such purchases or arrangements to purchase in a manner comparable to the disclosure made in the home jurisdiction, as defined in Rule 13e-4(i)(3); and

(v) The purchases comply with the applicable tender offer laws and regulations of the home jurisdiction.

(11) *Purchases or arrangements to purchase a foreign tender offer(s).* . . .

(12) *Purchases or arrangements to purchase by an affiliate of the financial advisor and an offeror and its affiliates.* . . .

(c) *Definitions.* . . .

Rule 14e-8. Prohibited Conduct in Connection with Pre-commencement Communications

It is a fraudulent, deceptive or manipulative act or practice within the meaning of section 14(e) of the Act for any person to publicly announce that the person (or a party on whose behalf the person is acting) plans to make a tender offer that has not yet been commenced, if the person:

(a) Is making the announcement of a potential tender offer without the intention to commence the offer within a reasonable time and complete the offer;

(b) Intends, directly or indirectly, for the announcement to manipulate the market price of the stock of the bidder or subject company; or

(c) Does not have the reasonable belief that the person will have the means to purchase securities to complete the offer.

Rule 14f-1. Change in Majority of Directors

If, pursuant to any arrangement or understanding with the person or persons acquiring securities in a transaction subject to section 13(d) or 14(d) of the Act, any persons are to be elected or designated as directors of the issuer, otherwise than at a meeting of security holders, and the persons so elected or designated will constitute a majority of the directors of the issuer, then, not less than 10 days prior to the date any such person take office as a director, or such shorter period prior to that date as the Commission may authorize upon a showing of good cause therefor, the issuer shall file with the Commission and transmit to all holders of record of securities of the issuer who would be entitled to vote at a meeting for election of directors, information substantially equivalent to the information which would be required by Items 6(a), (d) and (e), 7 and 8 of Schedule 14A of Regulation 14A to be transmitted if such person or persons were nominees for election as directors at a meeting of such security holders. Eight copies of such information shall be filed with the Commission.

REGULATION 15D: REPORTS OF REGISTRANTS UNDER THE SECURITIES ACT OF 1933

Rule 15d-11. Current Reports on Form 8-K. . . .

(c) No failure to file a report on Form 8-K that is required solely pursuant to Item 1.01, 1.02, 2.03, 2.04, 2.05, 2.06, 4.02(a), 5.02(e) or 6.03 of Form 8-K shall be deemed to be a violation of §10(b) and Rule 10b-5.

Rule 15d-15. Controls and Procedures

(a) Every issuer that files reports under section 15(d) of the Act other than an Asset Backed Issuer (as defined in Rule 1101 of Regulation S-K), a small business investment company registered on Form N-5, or a unit investment trust as defined section 4(2) of the Investment Company Act of 1940, must maintain disclosure controls and procedures (as defined in paragraph (e) of this section) and, if the issuer either had been required to file an annual report pursuant to section 13(a) or 15(d) of the Act for the prior fiscal year or had filed an annual report with the Commission for the prior fiscal year, internal control over financial reporting (as defined in paragraph (f) of this section). . . .

(c) The management of each such issuer that either had been required to file an annual report pursuant to section 13(a) or 15(d) of the Act for the prior fiscal year or had filed an annual report with the Commission for the prior fiscal year, other than an investment company registered under section 8 of the Investment Company Act of 1940, must evaluate, with the participation of the issuer's principal executive and principal financial officers, or persons performing similar functions, the effectiveness, as of the end of each fiscal year, of the issuer's internal control over financial reporting. . . .

(d) The management of each such issuer that previously either had been required to file an annual report pursuant to section 13(a) or 15(d) of the Act for the prior fiscal year or previously had filed an annual report with the Commission for the prior fiscal year, other than an investment company registered under section 8 of the Investment Company Act of 1940, must evaluate, with the participation of the issuer's principal executive and principal financial officers, or persons performing similar functions, any change in the issuer's internal control over financial reporting, that occurred during each of the issuer's fiscal quarters, or fiscal year in case of a foreign private issuer, that has materially affected, or is reasonably likely to materially affect, the issuer's internal control over financial reporting. . . .

Reports of Directors, Officers, and Principal Shareholders

Rule 16a-1. Definition of Terms

Terms defined in this rule shall apply solely to section 16 of the Act and the rules thereunder. These terms shall not be limited to section 16(a) of the Act but also shall apply to all other subsections under section 16 of the Act.

(a) The term *beneficial owner* shall have the following applications:

(1) Solely for purposes of determining whether a person is a beneficial owner of more than ten percent of any class of equity securities registered pursuant to section 12 of the Act, the term "beneficial owner" shall mean any person who is deemed a beneficial owner pursuant to section 13(d) of the Act and the rules thereunder; *provided, however,* that the following institutions or persons shall not be deemed the beneficial owner of securities of such class held for the benefit of third parties or in customer or fiduciary accounts in the ordinary course of business (or in the case of an employee benefit plan specified in paragraph (a)(1)(vi) of this section, of securities of such class allocated to plan participants where participants have voting power) as long as such shares are acquired by such institutions or persons without the purpose or effect of changing or influencing control of the issuer or engaging in any arrangement subject to Rule 13d-3(b):

(i) A broker or dealer registered under Section 15 of the Act;

(ii) A bank as defined in section 3(a)(6) of the Act;

(iii) An insurance company as defined in section 3(a)(19) of the Act;

(iv) An investment company registered under section 8 of the Investment Company Act of 1940;

(v) Any person registered as an investment adviser registered under section 203 of the Investment Advisers Act of 1940 or under the laws of any state;

(vi) An employee benefit plan as defined in Section 3(s) of the Employee Retirement Income Security Act of 1974, as amended, 29 U.S.C. 1001 *et seq.* ("Employee Retirement Income Security Act") that is subject to the provisions of ERISA, or any such plan that is not subject to ERISA that is maintained primarily for the benefit of the employees of a state or local government or instrumentality, or an endowment fund;

(vii) A parent holding company or control person, provided the aggregate amount held directly by the parent or control person, and directly and indirectly by their subsidiaries or affiliates that are not persons specified in Rule 16a-1(a)(1)(i) through (x), does not exceed one percent of the securities of the subject class;

(viii) A savings association as detailed in Section 3(b) of the Federal Deposit Insurance Act (12 U.S.C. 1813);

(ix) A church plan that is excluded from the definition of an investment company under Section 3(c)(4) of the Investment Company Act of 1940 (15 U.S.C. 80a-3);

(x) A non-U.S. institution that is the functional equivalent of any of the institutions listed in paragraphs (a)(1)(i) through (x) of this section, so long as the non-U.S. institution is subject to a regulatory scheme that is substantially comparable to the regulatory scheme applicable to equivalent U.S. institution and the non-U.S. institution is eligible to file a Schedule 13G pursuant to Rule 13d-1(b)(1)(ii)(J); and

(xi) A group, provided that all the members are persons specified in Rule 16a-1(a)(1)(i) through (x).

Note

Pursuant to this section, a person deemed a beneficial owner of more than ten percent of any class of equity securities registered under section 12 of the Act would file a Form 3, but the securities holdings disclosed on Form 3, and changes in beneficial ownership reported on subsequent Forms 4 or 5, would be determined by the definition of "beneficial owner" in paragraph (a)(2) of this section.

(2) Other than for purposes of determining whether a person is a beneficial owner of more than ten percent of any class of equity securities registered under Section 12 of the Act, the term *beneficial owner* shall mean any person who, directly or indirectly, through any contract, agreement, understanding, relationship or otherwise, has or shares a direct or indirect pecuniary interest in the equity securities, subject to the following:

(i) The term *pecuniary interest* in any class of equity securities shall mean the opportunity, directly or indirectly, to profit or share in any profit derived from a transaction in the subject securities.

(ii) The term *indirect pecuniary interest* in any class of equity securities shall include, but not be limited to:

(A) Securities held by members of a person's immediate family sharing the same household; *provided, however,* that the presumption of such beneficial ownership may be rebutted; see also Rule 16a-1(a)(4);

(B) A general partner's proportionate interest in the portfolio securities held by a general or limited partnership. The general partner's proportionate interest, as evidenced by the partnership agreement in effect at the time of the transaction and the partnership's most recent financial statements, shall be the greater of:

(1) The general partner's share of the partnership's profits, including profits attributed to any limited partnership interests held by the general partner and any other interests in profits that arise from the purchase and sale of the partnership's portfolio securities; or

(2) The general partner's share of the partnership capital account, including the share attributable to any limited partnership interest held by the general partner.

(C) A performance-related fee, other than an asset-based fee, received by any broker, dealer, bank, insurance company, investment company, investment adviser, investment manager, trustee or person or entity performing a similar function; *provided, however,* that no pecuniary interest shall be present where:

(1) The performance-related fee, regardless of when payable, is calculated based upon net capital gains and/or net capital appreciation generated from the portfolio or from the fiduciary's overall performance over a period of one year or more; and

(2) Equity securities of the issuer do not account for more than ten percent of the market value of the portfolio. A right to a nonperformance-related fee alone shall not represent a pecuniary interest in the securities;

(D) A person's right to dividends that is separated or separable from the underlying securities. Otherwise, a right to dividends alone shall not represent a pecuniary interest in the securities;

(E) A person's interest in securities held by a trust, as specified in Rule 16a-8(b); and

(F) A person's right to acquire equity securities through the exercise or conversion of any derivative security, whether or not presently exercisable.

(iii) A shareholder shall not be deemed to have a pecuniary interest in the portfolio securities held by a corporation or similar entity in which the person owns securities if the shareholder is not a controlling shareholder of the entity and does not have or share investment control over the entity's portfolio.

(3) Where more than one person subject to section 16 of the Act is deemed to be a beneficial owner of the same equity securities, all such persons must report as beneficial owners of the securities, either separately or jointly, as provided in Rule 16a-3(j). In such cases, the amount of short-swing profit recoverable shall not be increased above the amount recoverable if there were only one beneficial owner.

(4) Any person filing a statement pursuant to section 16(a) of the Act may state that the filing shall not be deemed an admission that such person is, for purposes of section 16 of the Act or otherwise, the beneficial owner of any equity securities covered by the statement.

(5) The following interests are deemed not to confer beneficial ownership for purposes of section 16 of the Act:

(i) Interests in portfolio securities held by an investment company registered under the Investment Company Act of 1940; and

(ii) Interests in securities comprising part of a broad-based, publicly traded market basket or index of stocks, approved for trading by the appropriate federal governmental authority.

(b) the term *call equivalent position* shall mean a derivative security position that increases in value as the value of the underlying equity increases, including, but not limited to, a long convertible security, a long call option, and a short put option position.

(c) The term *derivative securities* shall mean any option, warrant, convertible security, stock appreciation right, or similar right with an exercise or conversion privilege at a price related to an equity security, or similar securities with a value derived from the value of an equity security, but shall not include:

(1) Rights of a pledgee of securities to sell the pledged securities;

(2) Rights of all holders of a class of securities of an issuer to receive securities pro rata, or obligations to dispose of securities, as a result of a merger, exchange offer, or consolidation involving the issuer of the securities;

(3) Rights or obligations to surrender a security, or have a security withheld, upon the receipt or exercise of a derivative security or the receipt or vesting of equity securities, in order to satisfy the exercise price or the tax withholding consequences of receipt, exercise or vesting;

(4) Interests in broad-based index options, broad-based index futures, and broad-based publicly traded market baskets of stocks approved for trading by the appropriate federal governmental authority;

(5) Interests or rights to participate in employee benefit plans of the issuer;

(6) Rights with an exercise or conversion privilege at a price that is not fixed; or

(7) Options granted to an underwriter in a registered public offering for the purpose of satisfying over-allotments in such offering.

(d) The term *equity security of such issuer* shall mean any equity security or derivative security relating to an issuer, whether or not issued by that issuer.

(e) The term *immediate family* shall mean any child, stepchild, grandchild, parent, stepparent, grandparent, spouse, sibling, mother-in-law, father-in-law, son-in-law, daughter-in-law, brother-in-law, or sister-in-law, and shall include adoptive relationships.

(f) The term *officer* shall mean an issuer's president, principal financial officer, principal accounting officer (or, if there is no such accounting officer, the controller), any vice-president of the issuer in charge of a principal business unit, division or function (such as sales, administration or finance), any other officer who performs a policy-making function, or any other person who performs similar policy-making functions for the issuer. Officers of the issuer's parent(s) or subsidiaries shall be deemed officers of the issuer if they perform such policy-making functions for the issuer. In addition, when the issuer is a limited partnership, officers or employees of the general partner(s) who perform policy-making functions for the limited partnership are deemed officers of the limited partnership. When the issuer is a trust, officers or employees of the trustee(s) who perform policy-making functions for the trust are deemed officers of the trust.

NOTE

"Policy-making function" is not intended to include policy-making functions that are not significant. If pursuant to Item 401(b) of Regulation S-K the issuer identifies a person as an "executive officer," it is presumed that the Board of Directors has made that judgment and that the persons so identified are the officers for purposes of Section 16 of the Act, as are such other persons enumerated in this paragraph (f) but not in Item 401(b).

(g) The term *portfolio securities* shall mean all securities owned by an entity, other than securities issued by the entity.

(h) The term *put equivalent position* shall mean a derivative security position that increases in value as the value of the underlying equity decreases, including, but not limited to, a long put option and a short call option position.

Rule 16a-2. Persons and Transactions Subject to Section 16

Any person who is the beneficial owner, directly or indirectly, of more than ten percent of any class of equity securities ("ten percent beneficial owner") registered pursuant to section 12 of the Act, any director or officer of the issuer of such securities, and any person specified in section 30(h) of the Investment Company Act of 1940, including any person specified in Rule 16a-8, shall be subject to the provisions of section 16 of the Act. The rules under section 16 of the Act apply to any class of equity securities of an issuer whether or not registered under section 12 of the Act. The rules under section 16 of the Act also apply to non-equity securities as provided by the Investment Company Act of 1940. With respect to transactions by persons subject to section 16 of the Act:

(a) A transaction(s) carried out by a director or officer in the six months prior to the director or officer becoming subject to section 16 of the Act shall be subject to section 16 of the Act and reported on the first required Form 4 only if the transaction(s) occurred within six months of the transaction giving rise to the Form 4 filing obligation and the director or officer became subject to section 16 of the Act solely as a result of the issuer registering a class of equity securities pursuant to section 12 of the Act.

(b) A transaction(s) following the cessation of director or officer status shall be subject to section 16 of the Act only if:

(1) Executed within a period of less than six months of an opposite transaction subject to section 16(b) of the Act that occurred while that person was a director or officer; and

(2) Not otherwise exempted from section 16(b) of the Act pursuant to the provisions of this chapter.

NOTE

For purposes of this paragraph, an acquisition and a disposition each shall be an opposite transaction with respect to the other.

(c) The transaction that results in a person becoming a ten percent beneficial owner is not subject to section 16 of the Act unless the person otherwise is subject to section 16 of the Act. A ten percent beneficial owner not otherwise subject to section 16 of the Act must report only those transactions conducted while the beneficial owner of more than 10 percent of a class of equity securities of the issuer registered pursuant to section 12 of the Act.

(d)(1) Transactions by a person or entity shall be exempt from the provisions of section 16 of the Act for the 12 months following appointment and qualification, to the extent such person or entity is acting as:

(i) Executor or administrator of the estate of a decedent;

(ii) Guardian or member of a committee for an incompetent;

(iii) Receiver, trustee in bankruptcy, assignee for the benefit of creditors, conservator, liquidating agent, or other similar person duly authorized by law to administer the estate or assets of another person; or

(iv) Fiduciary in a similar capacity.

(2) Transactions by such person or entity acting in a capacity specified in paragraph (d)(1) of this section after the period specified in that paragraph shall be subject to section 16 of the Act only where the estate, trust or other entity is a beneficial owner of more than ten percent of any class of equity security registered pursuant to section 12 of the Act.

Rule 16a-3. Reporting Transactions and Holdings

(a) Initial statements of beneficial ownership of equity securities required by section 16(a) of the Act shall be filed on Form 3. Statements of changes in beneficial ownership required by that section shall be filed on Form 4. Annual statements shall be filed on Form 5. At the election of the reporting person, any transaction required to be reported on Form 5 may be reported on an earlier filed Form 4. All such statements shall be prepared and filed in accordance with the requirements of the applicable form. . . .

(f)(1) A Form 5 shall be filed by every person who at any time during the issuer's fiscal year was subject to section 16 of the Act with respect to such issuer, except as provided in paragraph (f)(2) of this section. The Form shall be filed within 45 days after the issuer's fiscal year end, and shall disclose the following holdings and transactions not reported previously on Forms 3, 4 or 5:

(i) All transactions during the most recent fiscal year that were exempt from section 16(b) of the Act, except:

(A) Exercises and conversions of derivative securities exempt under either Rule 16b-3 or Rule 16b-6(b), dispositions by bona fide gifts exempt under Rule 16b-5, and any transaction exempt under Rule 16b-3(d), (e) or (f) (these are required to be reported on Form 4);

(B) Transactions exempt from section 16(b) of the Act pursuant to Rule 16b-3(c), which shall be exempt from section 16(a) of the Act; and

(C) Transactions exempt from section 16(a) of the Act pursuant to another rule;

(ii) Transactions that constituted small acquisitions pursuant to Rule 16a-6(a);

(iii) All holdings and transactions that should have been reported during the most recent fiscal year, but were not; and

(iv) With respect to the first Form 5 requirement for a reporting person, all holdings and transactions that should have been reported in each of the issuer's last two fiscal years but were not, based on the reporting person's reasonable belief in good faith in the completeness and accuracy of the information.

(2) Notwithstanding the above, no Form 5 shall be required where all transactions otherwise required to be reported on the Form 5 have been reported before the due date of the Form 5.

NOTE

Persons no longer subject to section 16 of the Act, but who were subject to the Section at any time during the issuer's fiscal year, must file a Form 5 unless paragraph (f)(2) is satisfied. *See also* Rule 16a-2(b) regarding the reporting obligations of persons ceasing to be officers or directors.

(g)(1) A Form 4 must be filed to report: all transactions not exempt from section 16(b) of the Act; all transactions exempt from section 16(b) of the Act pursuant to Rules 16b-3(d), 16b-3(e), or 16b-3(f); and dispositions by bona fide gifts and all exercises and conversions of derivative securities, regardless of whether exempt from section 16(b) of the Act. Form 4 must be filed before the end of the second business day following the day on which the subject transaction has been executed.

(2) Solely for purposes of section 16(a)(2)(C) of the Act and paragraph (g)(1) of this section, the date on which the executing broker, dealer or plan administrator notifies the reporting person of the execution for the transaction where the following conditions are satisfied:

(i) the transaction is pursuant to a contract, instruction or written plan for the purchase or sale of equity securities of the issuer (as defined in §16a-1(d)) that satisfies the affirmative defense conditions of Rule 10b5-1(c) of this chapter; and

(ii) the reporting person does not select the date of execution.

(3) Solely for purposes of section 16(a)(2)(C) of the Act and paragraph (g)(1) of this section, the date on which the plan administrator notifies the reporting person that the transaction has been executed is deemed the date of execution for a discretionary transaction (as defined in §16b-3(b)(1)) for which the reporting person does not select the date of execution.

(4) In the case of the transactions described in paragraphs (g)(2) and (g)(3) of this section, if the notification date is later than the third business day following the trade date of the transaction, the date of execution is deemed to be the third business day following the trade date of the transaction.

(5) At the option of the reporting person, transactions that are reportable on Form 5 may be reported on Form 4, so long as the Form 4 is filed no later

than the due date of the Form 5 on which the transaction is otherwise required to be reported.

(h) The date of filing with the Commission shall be the date of receipt by the Commission.

(i) . . . .

(j) Where more than one person subject to section 16 of the Act is deemed to be a beneficial owner of the same equity securities, all such persons must report as beneficial owners of the securities, either separately or jointly. Where persons in a group are deemed to be beneficial owners of equity securities pursuant to Rule 16a-1(a)(1) due to the aggregation of holdings, a single Form 3, 4 or 5 may be filed on behalf of all persons in the group. Joint and group filings must include all required information for each beneficial owner, and such filings must be signed by each beneficial owner, or on behalf of such owner by an authorized person.

Rule 16a-4. Derivative Securities

(a) For purposes of section 16 of the Act, both derivative securities and the underlying securities to which they relate shall be deemed to be the same class of equity securities, *except that* the acquisition or disposition of any derivative security shall be separately reported.

(b) The exercise or conversion of a call equivalent position shall be reported on Form 4 and treated for reporting purposes as:

(1) A purchase of the underlying security; and

(2) A closing of the derivative security position.

(c) The exercise or conversion of a put equivalent position shall be reported on Form 4 and treated for reporting purposes as:

(1) A sale of the underlying security; and

(2) A closing of the derivative security position.

(d) The disposition or closing of a long derivative security position, as a result of cancellation or expiration, shall be exempt from section 16(a) of the Act if exempt from section 16(b) of the Act pursuant to Rule 16b-6(d).

NOTE

A purchase or sale resulting from an exercise or conversion of a derivative security may be exempt from section 16(b) of the Act pursuant to Rule 16b-3 or Rule 16b-6(b).

Rule 16a-8. Trusts

(a) *Persons subject to section 16.—(1) Trusts.* A trust shall be subject to section 16 of the Act with respect to securities of the issuer if the trust is a beneficial owner, pursuant to Rule 16a-1(a)(1), of more than ten percent of any class of equity securities of the issuer registered pursuant to section 12 of the Act ("ten percent beneficial owner").

(2) *Trustees, beneficiaries, and settlors.* In determining whether a trustee, beneficiary, or settlor is a ten percent beneficial owner with respect to the issuer:

(i) Such persons shall be deemed the beneficial owner of the issuer's securities held by the trust, to the extent specified by Rule 16a-1(a)(1); and

(ii) Settlors shall be deemed the beneficial owner of the issuer's securities held by the trust where they have the power to revoke the trust without the consent of another person. . . .

Rule 16a-9. Stock Splits, Stock Dividends, and Pro Rata Rights

The following shall be exempt from section 16 of the Act:

(a) The increase or decrease in the number of securities held as a result of a stock split or stock dividend applying equally to all securities of that class, including a stock dividend in which equity securities of a different issuer are distributed; and

(b) The acquisition of rights, such as shareholder or pre-emptive rights, pursuant to a pro rata grant to all holders of the same class of equity securities registered under section 12 of the Act.

NOTE

The exercise or sale of a pro rata right shall be reported pursuant to Rule 16a-4 and the exercise shall be eligible for exemption from section 16(b) of the Act pursuant to Rule 16b-6(b).

EXEMPTION FROM CERTAIN TRANSACTIONS FROM SECTION 16(B)

Rule 16b-5. Bona Fide Gifts and Inheritance

Both the acquisition and the disposition of equity securities shall be exempt from the operation of section 16(b) of the Act if they are: (a) Bona fide gifts; or (b) transfers of securities by will or the laws of descent and distribution.

Rule 16b-6. Derivative Securities

(a) The establishment of or increase in a call equivalent position or liquidation of or decrease in a put equivalent position shall be deemed a purchase of the underlying security for purposes of section 16(b) of the Act, and the establishment of or increase in a put equivalent position or liquidation of or decrease in a call equivalent position shall be deemed a sale of the underlying securities for purposes of section 16(b) of the Act: *Provided, however,* That if the increase or decrease occurs as a result of the fixing of the exercise price of a right initially issued without a fixed price, where the date the price is fixed is not known in advance and is outside the control of the recipient, the increase or decrease shall be exempt from section 16(b) of the Act with respect to any offsetting transaction within the six months prior to the date the price is fixed.

(b) The closing of a derivative security position as a result of its exercise or conversion shall be exempt from the operation of section 16(b) of the Act, and the acquisition of underlying securities at a fixed exercise price due to the exercise or conversion of a call equivalent position or the disposition of underlying securities at a fixed exercise price due to the exercise of a put equivalent position shall be exempt from the operation of section 16(b) of the Act: *Provided, however,* That the acquisition of underlying securities from the exercise of an out-of-the-money option, warrant, or right shall not be exempt unless the exercise is necessary to comport with the sequential exercise provisions of the Internal Revenue Code.

NOTE

The exercise or conversion of a derivative security that does not satisfy the conditions of this section is eligible for exemption from section 16(b) of the Act to the extent that the conditions of Rule 16b-3 are satisfied.

(c) In determining the short-swing profit recoverable pursuant to section 16(b) of the Act from transactions involving the purchase and sale or sale and purchase of derivative and other securities, the following rules apply:

(1) Short-swing profits in transactions involving the purchase and sale or sale and purchase of derivative securities that have identical characteristics (*e.g.,* purchases and sales of call options of the same strike price and expiration date, or purchases and sales of the same series of convertible debentures) shall be measured by the actual prices paid or received in the short-swing transactions.

(2) Short-swing profits in transactions involving the purchase and sale or sale and purchase of derivative securities having different characteristics but related to the same underlying security (*e.g.,* the purchase of a call option and the sale of a convertible debenture) or derivative securities and underlying securities shall not exceed the difference in price of the underlying security on the date of purchase or sale and the date of sale or purchase. Such profits may be measured by calculating the short-swing profits that would have been realized had the subject transactions involved purchases and sales solely of the derivative security that was purchased or solely of the derivative security that was sold, valued as of the time of the matching purchase or sale, and calculated for the of the number of underlying securities actually purchased or sold.

(d) Upon cancellation or expiration of an option within six months of the writing of the option, any profit derived from writing the option shall be recoverable under section 16(b) of the Act. The profit shall not exceed the premium received for writing the option. The disposition or closing of a long derivative security position, as a result of cancellation or expiration, shall be exempt from section 16(b) of the Act where no value is received from the cancellation or expiration.

Rule 16b-7. Mergers, Reclassifications, and Consolidations

(a) The following transactions shall be exempt from the provisions of section 16(b) of the Act:

(1) The acquisition of a security of a company, pursuant to a merger or consolidation, in exchange for a security of a company which, prior to the merger or consolidation, owned 85 percent or more of either

(i) The equity securities of all other companies involved in the merger or consolidation, or in the case of a consolidation, the resulting company; or

(ii) The combined assets of all the companies involved in the merger or consolidation, computed according to their book values prior to the merger or consolidation as determined by reference to their most recent available financial statements for a 12 month period prior to the merger or consolidation, or such shorter time as the company has been in existence.

(2) The disposition of a security, pursuant to a merger or consolidation, of a company which, prior to the merger or consolidation, owned 85 percent or more of either

(i) The equity securities of all other companies involved in the merger or consolidation or, in the case of a consolidation, the resulting company; or

(ii) The combined assets of all the companies undergoing merger or consolidation, computed according to their book values prior to the merger or consolidation as determined by reference to their most recent available financial statements for a 12 month period prior to the merger or consolidation.

(b) A merger within the meaning of this section shall include the sale or purchase of substantially all the assets of one company by another in exchange for equity securities which are then distributed to the security holders of the company that sold its assets.

(c) Notwithstanding the foregoing, if a person subject to section 16 of the Act makes any non-exempt purchase of a security in any company involved in the merger or consolidation and any nonexempt sale of a security in any company involved in the merger or consolidation within any period of less than six months during which the merger or consolidation took place, the exemption provided by this Rule shall be unavailable to the extent of such purchase and sale.

Regulation S-K—Standard Instructions for Filing Forms Under Securities Act of 1933, Securities Exchange Act of 1934, and Energy Policy and Conservation Act of 1975

17 C.F.R. §§229.10-229.1016

SUBPART 400—MANAGEMENT AND CERTAIN SECURITY HOLDERS

401. Directors, Executive Officers, Promoters, and Control Persons
402. Executive Compensation
403. Security Ownership of Certain Beneficial Owners and Management
404. Transactions with Related Persons, Promoters, and Certain Control Persons
405. Compliance with Section 16(a) of the Exchange Act
406. Code of Ethics
407. Corporate Governance
408. Insider Trading Arrangements and Policies

SUBPART 500—REGISTRATION STATEMENT AND PROSPECTUS PROVISIONS [OMITTED]

501. Forepart of Registration Statement and Outside Front Cover Page of Prospectus
502. Inside Front and Outside Back Cover Pages of Prospectus
503. Summary Information, Risk Factors, and Ratio of Earnings to Fixed Charges
504. Use of Proceeds
505. Determination of Offering Price
506. Dilution
507. Selling Security Holders
508. Plan of Distribution
509. Interests of Named Experts and Counsel
510. Disclosure of Commission Position on Indemnification for Securities Act Liabilities
511. Other Expenses of Issuance and Distribution
512. Undertakings

SUBPART 600—EXHIBITS [OMITTED]

601. Exhibits

SUBPART 700—MISCELLANEOUS [OMITTED]

701. Recent Sales of Unregistered Securities
702. Indemnification of Directors and Officers

SUBPART 800—LIST OF INDUSTRY GUIDES [OMITTED]

801. Securities Act Industry Guides
802. Exchange Act Industry Guides

SUBPART 900—ROLL-UP TRANSACTIONS [OMITTED]

901. Definitions
902. Individual Partnership Supplements

903. Summary
904. Risk Factors and Other Considerations
905. Comparative Information
906. Allocation of Roll-Up Consideration
907. Background of the Roll-Up Transaction
908. Reasons for and Alternatives to the Roll-Up Transaction
909. Conflicts of Interest
910. Fairness of the Transaction
911. Reports, Opinions and Appraisals
912. Source and Amount of Funds and Transactional Expenses
913. Other Provisions of the Transaction
914. Pro Forma Financial Statements; Selected Financial Data
915. Federal Income Tax Consequences

SUBPART 1000—MERGERS AND ACQUISITIONS (REGULATION M-A)

1000. Definitions
1001. Summary Term Sheet
1002. Subject Company Information
1003. Identity and Background of Filing Person
1004. Terms of the Transaction
1005. Past Contacts, Transactions, Negotiations and Agreements
1006. Purposes of the Transaction and Plans or Proposals
1007. Source and Amount of Funds or Other Consideration
1008. Interest in Securities of the Subject Company
1009. Persons/Assets, Retained, Employed, Compensated or Used
1010. Financial Statements
1011. Additional Information
1012. The Solicitation or Recommendation
1013. Purposes, Alternatives, Reasons and Effects in a Going-private Transaction
1014. Fairness of the Going-private Transaction
1015. Reports, Opinions, Appraisal and Negotiations
1016. Exhibits

SUBPART 1100—ASSET-BACKED SECURITIES (REGULATION AB) OMITTED

SUBPART 1 — GENERAL

Item 10. General

(a) *Application of Regulation S-K.* This part (together with the General Rules and Regulations under the Securities Act of 1933 (*Securities Act*), and the Securities Exchange Act of 1934, as amended (*Exchange Act*), the Interpretative Releases under these Acts and the forms under these Acts states the requirements applicable to the content of the non-financial statement portions of:

(1) Registration statements under the Securities Act to the extent provided in the forms to be used for registration under such Act; and

(2) Registration statements under section 12, annual or other reports under sections 13 and 15(d), going-private transaction statements under section 13, tender offer statements under sections 13 and 14, annual reports to security holders and proxy and information statements under section 14, and any other documents required to be filed under the Exchange Act, to the extent provided in the forms and rules under that Act.

(b) *Commission policy on projections.* The Commission encourages the use in documents specified in Rule 175 under the Securities Act and Rule 3b-6 under the Exchange Act of management's projections of future economic performance that have a reasonable basis and are presented in an appropriate format. The guidelines set forth herein represent the Commission's views on important factors to be considered in formulating and disclosing such projections.

(1) *Basis for projections.* The Commission believes that management must have the option to present in Commission filings its good faith assessment of a registrant's future performance. Management, however, must have a reasonable basis for such an assessment. Although a history of operations or experience in projecting may be among the factors providing a basis for management's assessment, the Commission does not believe that a registrant always must have had such a history or experience in order to formulate projections with a reasonable basis. An outside review of management's projections may furnish additional support for having a reasonable basis for a projection. If management decides to include a report of such a review in a Commission filing, there also should be disclosure of the qualifications of the reviewer, the extent of the review, the relationship between the reviewer and the registrant, and other material factors concerning the process by which any outside review was sought or obtained. Moreover, in the case of a registration statement under the Securities Act, the reviewer would be deemed an expert and an appropriate consent must be filed with the registration statement.

(2) *Format for projections.* In determining the appropriate format for projections included in Commission filings, consideration must be given to, among other things, the financial items to be projected, the period to be covered, and the manner of presentation to be used. Although traditionally projections have been given for three financial items generally considered to be of primary importance to investors (revenues, net income (loss) and earnings (loss) per share), projection information need not necessarily be limited to these three items. However, management should take care to assure that the choice of items projected is not susceptible of misleading inferences through selective projection of only favorable items. Revenues, net income (loss) and earnings (loss) per share usually are presented together in order to avoid any misleading inferences that may arise when the individual items reflect contradictory trends. There may be instances, however, when it is appropriate to present earnings (loss) from continuing operations, or income (loss) before extraordinary items in addition to or in lieu of net income (loss). It generally would be misleading to present sales or revenue projections without one of the foregoing measures of income.

The period that appropriately may be covered by a projection depends to a large extent on the particular circumstances of the company involved. For certain companies in certain industries, a projection covering a two or three year period may be entirely reasonable. Other companies may not have a reasonable basis for projections beyond the current year. Accordingly, management should select the period most appropriate in the circumstances. In addition, management, in making a projection, should disclose what, in its opinion, is the most probable specific amount or the most reasonable range for each financial item projected based on the selected assumptions. Ranges, however, should not be so wide as to make the disclosures meaningless. Moreover, several projections based on varying assumptions may be judged by management to be more meaningful than a single number or range and would be permitted.

(3) *Investor understanding.* (i) When management chooses to include its projections in a Commission filing, the disclosures accompanying the projections should facilitate investor understanding of the basis for and limitations of projections. In this regard investors should be cautioned against attributing undue certainty to management's assessment, and the Commission believes that investors would be aided by a statement indicating management's intention regarding the furnishing of updated projections. The Commission also believes that investor understanding would be enhanced by disclosure of the assumptions which in management's opinion are most significant to the projections or are the key factors upon which the financial results of the enterprise depend and encourages disclosure of assumptions in a manner that will provide a framework for analysis of the projection.

(ii) Management also should consider whether disclosure of the accuracy or inaccuracy of previous projections would provide investors with important insights into the limitations of projections. In this regard, consideration should be given to presenting the projections in a format that will facilitate subsequent analysis of the reasons for differences between actual and forecast results. An important benefit may arise from the systematic analysis of variances between projected and actual results on a continuing basis, since such disclosure may highlight for investors the most significant risk and profit-sensitive areas in a business operation.

(iii) With respect to previously issued projections, registrants are reminded of their responsibility to make full and prompt disclosure of material facts, both favorable and unfavorable, regarding their financial condition. This responsibility may extend to situations where management knows or has reason to know that its previously disclosed projects no longer have a reasonable basis.

(iv) Since a registrant's ability to make projections with relative confidence may vary with all the facts and circumstances, the responsibility for determining whether to discontinue or to resume making projections is best left to management. However, the Commission encourages registrants not to discontinue or to resume projections in Commission filings without a reasonable basis. . . .

(f) *Smaller reporting companies.* The requirements of this part apply to smaller reporting companies. A smaller reporting company may comply with either the requirements applicable to smaller reporting companies or the requirements applicable to other companies for each item, unless the requirements for smaller reporting companies specify that smaller reporting companies must comply with the smaller reporting company requirements. The following items of this part set forth requirements for smaller reporting companies that are different from requirements applicable to other companies:

Index of Scaled Disclosure Available to Smaller Reporting Companies	
Item 101	Description of business
Item 201	Market price of and dividends on registrant's common equity and related stockholder matters
Item 302	Supplementary financial information
Item 305	Quantitative and qualitative disclosures about market risk
Item 402	Executive compensation
Item 404	Transactions with related persons, promoters, and certain control persons
Item 407	Corporate governance
Item 503	Prospectus summary
Item 504	Use of proceeds
Item 601	Exhibits

(1) *Definition of smaller reporting company.* As used in this part, the term *smaller reporting company* means an issuer that is not an investment company, an asset-backed issuer (as defined in Item 1101), or a majority-owned subsidiary of a parent that is not a smaller reporting company and that:

(i) Had a public float of less than $250 million; or

(ii) Had annual revenues of less than $100 million and either:

a. No public float; or

b. A public float of less than $700 million.

(2) Whether an issuer is a smaller reporting company is determined on an annual basis. . . .

Subpart 100 — Business

Item 101. Description of Business

(a) *General development of business.* Describe the general development of the business of the registrant, its subsidiaries, and any predecessor(s).

(1) In describing developments, only information material to an understanding of the general development of the business is required. Disclosure may include, but should not be limited to, the following topics:

(i) Any material changes to a previously disclosed business strategy;

(ii) The nature and effects of any material bankruptcy, receivership, or any similar proceeding with respect to the registrant or any of its significant subsidiaries;

(iii) The nature and effects of any material reclassification, merger or consolidation of the registrant or any of its significant subsidiaries; and

(iv) The acquisition or disposition of any material amount of assets otherwise than in the ordinary course of business.

(2) Notwithstanding the provisions of §230.411(b) or §240.12b-23(a) of this chapter, as applicable, a registrant may only forgo providing a full discussion of the general development of its business for a filing other than an initial registration statement if it provides an update to the general development of its business, disclosing all of the material developments that have occurred since the most recent registration statement or report that includes a full discussion of the general development of its business. In addition, the registrant must incorporate by reference, and include one active hyperlink to one registration statement or report that includes, the full discussion of the general development of the registrant's business.

(b) (Reserved).

(c) *Narrative description of business.* (1) Describe the business done and intended to be done by the registrant and its subsidiaries, focusing upon the registrant's dominant segment or each reportable segment about which financial information is presented in the financial statements. . . .

(d) (Reserved)

(e) *Available information.* Disclose the information in paragraphs (e)(1), (e)(2), and (e)(3) of this section in any registration statement you file under the Securities Act, and disclose the information in paragraph (e)(3) of this section in your annual report on Form 10-K. Further disclose the information in paragraph (e)(4) of this section if you are an accelerated filer or a large accelerated filer (as defined in Rule 12b-2 of this chapter) filing an annual report on Form 10-K:

(1) Whether you file reports with the Securities and Exchange Commission. If you are a reporting company, identify the reports and other information you file with the SEC.

(2) State that the SEC maintains an Internet site that contains reports, proxy and information statements, and other information regarding issuers that file electronically with the SEC and state the address of that site (http://www.sec.gov).

(3) Disclose your Internet address, if you have one.

(4) (i) Whether you make available free of charge on or through your Internet website, if you have one, your annual report on Form 10-K, quarterly reports on Form 10-Q, current reports on Form 8-K, and amendments to those reports filed or furnished pursuant to Section 13(a) or 15(d) of the Exchange Act as soon as reasonably practicable after you electronically file such material with, or furnish it to, the SEC;

(ii) If you do not make your filings available in this manner, the reasons you do not do so (including, where applicable, that you do not have an Internet website); and

(iii) If you do not make your filings available in this manner, whether you voluntarily will provide electronic or paper copies of your filings free of charge upon request.

(f) *Reports to Security Holders.* Disclose the following information in any registration statement you file under the Securities Act:

(1) If the SEC's proxy rules or regulations, or stock exchange requirements, do not require you to send an annual report to security holders or to holders of American depository receipts, describe briefly the nature and frequency of reports that you will give to security holders. Specify whether the reports that you give will contain financial information that has been examined and reported on, with an opinion expressed "by" an independent public or certified public accountant.

(2) For a foreign private issuer, if the report will not contain financial information prepared in accordance with U.S. generally accepted accounting principles, you must state whether the report will include a reconciliation of this information with U.S. generally accepted accounting principles.

(g) *Enforceability of Civil Liabilities Against Foreign Persons.* Disclose the following if you are a foreign private issuer filing a registration statement under the Securities Act:

(1) Whether or not investors may bring actions under the civil liability provisions of the U.S. federal securities laws against the foreign private issuer, any of its officers and directors who are residents of a foreign country, any underwriters or experts named in the registration statement that are residents of a foreign country, and whether investors may enforce these civil liability provisions when the assets of the issuer or these other persons are located outside of the United States. The disclosure must address the following matters:

(i) The investor's ability to effect service of process within the United States on the foreign private issuer or any person;

(ii) The investor's ability to enforce judgments obtained in U.S. courts against foreign persons based upon the civil liability provisions of the U.S. federal securities laws;

(iii) The investor's ability to enforce, in an appropriate foreign court, judgments of U.S. courts based upon the civil liability provisions of the U.S. federal securities laws; and

(iv) The investor's ability to bring an original action in an appropriate foreign court to enforce liabilities against the foreign private issuer or any person based upon the U.S. federal securities laws.

(2) If you provide this disclosure based on an opinion of counsel, name counsel in the prospectus and file as an exhibit to the registration statement a signed consent of counsel to the use of its name and opinion.

(h) *Smaller reporting companies.* A smaller reporting company, as defined by Item 10(f)(1), may satisfy its obligations under this Item by describing the development of its business during the last three years. If the smaller reporting company has not been in business for three years, give the same information for predecessor(s) of the smaller reporting company if there are any. This business development description should include:

(1) Form and year of organization;

(2) Any bankruptcy, receivership or similar proceeding; and

(3) Any material reclassification, merger, consolidation, or purchase or sale of a significant amount of assets not in the ordinary course of business.

(4) *Business of the smaller reporting company.* Briefly describe the business and include, to the extent material to an understanding of the smaller reporting company:

(i) Principal products or services and their markets;

(ii) Distribution methods of the products or services;

(iii) Status of any publicly announced new product or service;

(iv) Competitive business conditions and the smaller reporting company's competitive position in the industry and methods of competition;

(v) Sources and availability of raw materials and the names of principal suppliers;

(vi) Dependence on one or a few major customers;

(vii) Patents, trademarks, licenses, franchises, concessions, royalty agreements or labor contracts, including duration;

(viii) Need for any government approval of principal products or services. If government approval is necessary and the smaller reporting company has not yet received that approval, discuss the status of the approval within the government approval process;

(ix) Effect of existing or probable governmental regulations on the business;

(x) Estimate of the amount spent during each of the last two fiscal years on research and development activities, and if applicable, the extent to which the cost of such activities is borne directly by customers;

(xi) Costs and effects of compliance with environmental laws (federal, state and local); and

(xii) Number of total employees and number of full-time employees.

(5) *Reports to security holders.* Disclose the following in any registration statement you file under the Securities Act of 1933:

(i) If you are not required to deliver an annual report to security holders, whether you will voluntarily send an annual report and whether the report will include audited financial statements;

(ii) Whether you file reports with the Securities and Exchange Commission. If you are a reporting company, identify the reports and other information you file with the Commission; and

(iii) State that the Commission maintains an Internet site that contains reports, proxy and information statements, and other information regarding issuers that file electronically with the Commission and state the address of that site (http://www.sec.gov). Disclose your Internet address, if available.

(6) *Foreign issuers.* Provide the information required by Item 101(g) of Regulation S-K.

Item 102. Description of Property

To the extent material, disclose the location and general character of the registrant's principal physical properties. In addition, identify the segment(s), as reported in the financial statements, that use the properties described. If any such property is not held in fee or is held subject to an encumbrance that is material to the registrant, so state and describe briefly how held.

Item 103. Legal Proceedings

(a) Describe briefly any material pending legal proceedings, other than ordinary routine litigation incidental to the business, to which the registrant or any of its subsidiaries is a party or of which any of their property is the subject. Include the name of the court or agency in which the proceedings are pending, the date instituted, the principal parties thereto, a description of the factual basis alleged to underlie the proceeding and the relief sought. Include similar information as to any such proceedings known to be contemplated by governmental authorities. . . .

Instructions to Item 103

1. If the business ordinarily results in actions for negligence or other claims, no such action or claim need be described unless it departs from the normal kind of such actions.

2. No information need be given with respect to any proceeding that involves primarily a claim for damages if the amount involved, exclusive of interest and costs, does not exceed 10 percent of the current assets of the registrant and its subsidiaries on a consolidated basis. However, if any proceeding presents in large degree the same legal and factual issues as other proceedings pending or known to be contemplated, the amount involved in such other proceedings shall be included in computing such percentage.

3. Notwithstanding Instructions 1 and 2, any material bankruptcy, receivership, or similar proceeding with respect to the registrant or any of its significant subsidiaries shall be described.

4. Any material proceedings to which any director, officer or affiliate of the registrant, any owner of record or beneficially of more than five percent of any class of voting securities of the registrant, or any associate of any such director, officer, affiliate of the registrant, or security holder is a party adverse to the registrant or any of its subsidiaries or has a material interest adverse to the registrant or any of its subsidiaries also shall be described.

5. Notwithstanding the foregoing, an administrative or judicial proceeding (including, for purposes of A and B of this Instruction, proceedings which present in large degree the same issues) arising under any Federal, State or local provisions that have been enacted or adopted regulating the discharge of materials into the environment or primary [primarily] for the purpose of protecting the environment shall not be deemed "ordinary routine litigation incidental to the business" and shall be described if:

A. Such proceeding is material to the business or financial condition of the registrant;

B. Such proceeding involves primarily a claim for damages, or involves potential monetary sanctions, capital expenditures, deferred charges or charges to income and the amount involved, exclusive of interest and costs, exceeds 10 percent of the current assets of the registrant and its subsidiaries on a consolidated basis; or

C. A governmental authority is a party to such proceeding and such proceeding involves potential monetary sanctions, unless the registrant reasonably believes that such proceeding will result in no monetary sanctions, or in monetary sanctions, exclusive of interest and costs, of less than $100,000; provided, however, that such proceedings which are similar in nature may be grouped and described generically.

Item 104. Mine Safety Disclosure

(a) A registrant that is the operator, or that has a subsidiary that is an operator, of a coal or other mine shall provide the information specified below for the time period covered by the report:

(1) For each coal or other mine of which the registrant or a subsidiary of the registrant is an operator, identify the mine and disclose:

(i) The total number of violations of mandatory health or safety standards that could significantly and substantially contribute to the cause and effect of a coal or other mine safety or health hazard under section 104 of the Federal Mine Safety and Health Act of 1977 (30 U.S.C. 814) for which the operator received a citation from the Mine Safety and Health Administration.

(ii) The total number of orders issued under section 104(b) of such Act (30 U.S.C. 814(b)).

(iii) The total number of citations and orders for unwarrantable failure of the mine operator to comply with mandatory health or safety standards under section 104(d) of such Act (30 U.S.C. 814(d)).

(iv) The total number of flagrant violations under section 110(b)(2) of such Act (30 U.S.C. 820(b)(2).

(v) The total number of imminent danger orders issued under section 107(a) of such Act (30 U.S.C. 817(a)).

(vi) The total dollar value of proposed assessments from the Mine Safety and Health Administration under such Act (30 U.S.C. 801 et seq.).

(vii) The total number of mining-related fatalities.

(2) A list of coal or other mines, of which the registrant or a subsidiary of the registrant is an operator, that receive written notice from the Mine Safety and Health Administration of:

(i) A pattern of violations of mandatory health or safety standards that are of such nature as could have significantly and substantially contributed to the cause and effect of coal or other mine health or safety hazards under section 104(e) of such Act (30 U.S.C. 814(e)); or

(ii) The potential to have such a pattern.

(3) Any pending legal action before the Federal Mine Safety and Health Review Commission involving such coal or other mine.

(b) *Definitions.* For purposes of this Item:

(1) The term *coal or other mine* means a coal or other mine, as defined in section 3 of the Federal Mine Safety and Health Act of 1977 (30 U.S.C. 802), that is subject to the provisions of such Act (30 U.S.C. 801 et seq.).

(2) The term *operator* has the meaning given the term in section 3 of the Federal Mine Safety and Health Act of 1977 (30 U.S.C. 802).

(3) The term *subsidiary* has the meaning given the term in Exchange Act Rule 12b-2 (17 CFR 240.12b-2).

Item 105. Risk Factors

(a) Where appropriate, provide under the caption "Risk Factors" a discussion of the material factors that make an investment in the registrant or offering speculative or risky. This discussion must be organized logically with relevant headings and each risk factor should be set forth under a subcaption that adequately describes the risk. The presentation of risks that could apply generically to any registrant or any offering is discouraged, but to the extent generic risk factors are presented, disclose them at the end of the risk factor section under the caption "General Risk Factors."

(b) Concisely explain how each risk affects the registrant or the securities being offered. If the discussion is longer than 15 pages, include in the forepart of the prospectus or annual report, as applicable, a series of concise, bulleted or numbered statements that is no more than two pages summarizing the principal factors that make an investment in the registrant or offering speculative or risky. If the risk factor discussion is included in a registration statement, it must immediately follow the summary section required by §229.503 (Item 503 of Regulation S-K). If you do not include a summary section, the risk factor section must immediately follow the cover page of the prospectus or the pricing information section that immediately follows the cover page. Pricing information means price and price-related information that you may omit from the prospectus in an effective registration statement based on Rule 430A (§230.430A of this chapter). The registrant must furnish this information in plain English. See §230.421(d) of Regulation C of this chapter.

Subpart 200 — Securities of the Registrant

Item 201. Market Price and Dividends on the Registrant's Common Equity and Related Stockholder Matters

. . . (d) *Securities authorized for issuance under equity compensation plans.*

(1) In the following tabular format, provide the information specified in paragraph (d)(2) of this Item as of the end of the most recently completed fiscal year with respect to compensation plans (including individual compensation arrangements)

under which equity securities of the registrant are authorized for issuance, aggregated as follows:

(i) All compensation plans previously approved by security holders; and

(ii) All compensation plans not previously approved by security holders.

(2) The table shall include the following information as of the end of the most recently completed fiscal year for each category of equity compensation plan described in paragraph (d)(1) of this Item:

(i) The number of securities to be issued upon the exercise of outstanding options, warrants and rights (column (a));

(ii) The weighted-average exercise price of the outstanding options, warrants and rights disclosed pursuant to paragraph (d)(2)(i) of this Item (column (b)); and

(iii) Other than securities to be issued upon the exercise of the outstanding options, warrants and rights disclosed in paragraph (d)(2)(i) of this item, the number of securities remaining available for future issuance under the plan (column (c)).

(3) For each compensation plan under which equity securities of the registrant are authorized for issuance that was adopted without the approval of security holders, describe briefly, in narrative form, the material features of the plan.

EQUITY COMPENSATION PLAN INFORMATION

Plan category	*Number of securities to be issued upon exercise of outstanding options, warrants and rights (a)*	*Weighted-average exercise price of outstanding options, warrants and rights (b)*	*Number of securities remaining available for future issuance under equity compensation plans (excluding securities reflected in column (a)) (c)*
Equity compensation plans approved by security holders			
Equity compensation plans not approved by security holders			
Total			

(e) *Performance graph.* (1) Provide a line graph comparing the yearly percentage change in the registrant's cumulative total shareholder return on a class of common stock registered under section 12 of the Exchange Act (as measured by dividing the sum of the cumulative amount of dividends for the measurement period, assuming dividend reinvestment, and the difference between the registrant's share price at the end and the beginning of the measurement period; by the share price at the beginning of the measurement period) with:

(i) The cumulative total return of a broad equity market index assuming reinvestment of dividends, that includes companies whose equity securities are traded on the same exchange or are of comparable market capitalization; *provided, however,* that if the registrant is a company within the Standard & Poor's 500 Stock Index, the registrant must use that index; and

(ii) The cumulative total return, assuming reinvestment of dividends, of:

(A) A published industry or line-of-business index;

(B) Peer issuer(s) selected in good faith. If the registrant does not select its peer issuer(s) on an industry or line-of-business basis, the registrant shall disclose the basis for its selection; or

(C) Issuer(s) with similar market capitalization(s), but only if the registrant does not use a published industry or line-or-business index and does not believe it can reasonably identify a peer group. If the registrant uses this alternative, the graph shall be accompanied by a statement of the reasons for this selection.

(2) For purposes of paragraph (e)(1) of this Item, the term "measurement period" shall be the period beginning at the "measurement point" established by the market close on the last trading day before the beginning of the registrant's fifth preceding fiscal year, through and including the end of registrant's last completed fiscal year. If the class of securities has been registered under section 12 of the Exchange Act for a shorter period of time, the period covered by the comparison may correspond to that time period.

(3) For purposes of paragraph (e)(1)(ii)(A) of this Item, the term "published industry or line-of-business index" means any index that is prepared by a party other than the registrant or an affiliate and is accessible to the registrant's security holders; provided, however, that registrants may use an index prepared by the registrant or affiliate if such index is widely recognized and used.

(4) If the registrant selects a different index from an index used for the immediately preceding fiscal year, explain the reason(s) for this change and also compare the registrant's total return with that of both the newly selected index and the index used in the immediately preceding fiscal year. . . .

(6) *Smaller reporting companies.* A registrant that qualifies as a smaller reporting company, as defined by Item 10(f)(1), is not required to provide the information required by paragraph (e) of this Item.

Instructions to Item 201(e)

1. In preparing the required graphic comparisons, the registrant should:

a. Use, to the extent feasible, comparable methods of presentation and assumptions for the total return calculations required by paragraph (e)(1) of this Item; *provided, however,* that if the registrant constructs its own peer group index under paragraph (e)(1)(ii)(B), the same methodology must be used in calculating both the registrant's total return and that on the peer group index; and

b. Assume the reinvestment of dividends into additional shares of the same class of equity securities at the frequency with which dividends are paid on such securities during the applicable fiscal year.

2. In constructing the graph:

a. The closing price at the measurement point must be converted into a fixed investment, stated in dollars, in the registrant's stock (or in the stocks represented by a given index) with cumulative returns for each subsequent fiscal year measured as a change from that investment; and

b. Each fiscal year should be plotted with points showing the cumulative total return as of that point. The value of the investment as of each point plotted on a given return line is the number of shares held at that point multiplied by the then-prevailing share price.

3. The registrant is required to present information for the registrant's last five fiscal years and may choose to graph a longer period; but the measurement point, however, shall remain the same.

4. Registrants may include comparisons using performance measures in addition to total return, such as return on average common shareholders' equity.

5. If the registrant uses a peer issuer(s) comparison or comparison with issuer(s) with similar market capitalization, the identity of those issuers must be disclosed and the returns of each component issuer of the group must be weighted according to the respective issuer's stock market capitalization at the beginning of each period for which a return is indicated.

6. A registrant that qualifies as a "small business issuer," as defined by Item 10(a)(1) of Regulation S-B is not required to provide the information required by paragraph (e) of this Item.

7. The information required by paragraph (e) of this Item need not be provided in any filings other than an annual report to security holders required by Exchange Act Rule 14a-3 or Exchange Act Rule 14c-3 that precedes or accompanies a registrant's proxy or information statement relating to an annual meeting of security holders at which directors are to be elected (or special meeting or written consents in lieu of such meeting). Such information will not be deemed to be incorporated by reference into any filing under the Securities Act or the Exchange Act, except to the extent that the registrant specifically incorporates it by reference.

8. The information required by paragraph (e) of this Item shall not be deemed to be "soliciting material" or to be "filed" with the Commission or subject to Regulation 14A or 14C, other than as provided in this Item, or to the liabilities of section 18 of the Exchange Act except to the extent that the registrant specifically requests that such information be treated as soliciting material or specifically incorporates it by reference into a filing under the Securities Act or the Exchange Act.

Subpart 300 — Financial Information

Item 301. (Reserved)

Item 303. Management's Discussion and Analysis of Financial Condition and Results of Operations

(a) *Objective.* The objective of the discussion and analysis is to provide material information relevant to an assessment of the financial condition and results of operations of the registrant including an evaluation of the amounts and certainty of cash flows from operations and from outside sources. The discussion and analysis must focus specifically on material events and uncertainties known to management that are reasonably likely to cause reported financial information not to be necessarily indicative of future operating results or of future financial condition. This includes descriptions and amounts of matters that have had a material impact on reported operations, as well as matters that are reasonably likely based on management's assessment to have a material impact on future operations. The discussion and analysis must be of the financial statements and other statistical data that the registrant believes will enhance a reader's understanding of the registrant's financial condition, cash flows and other changes in financial condition and results of operations. A discussion and analysis that meets the requirements of this paragraph (a) is expected to better allow investors to view the registrant from management's perspective.

(b) *Full fiscal years. . . .*

(1) *Liquidity and capital resources. . . .*

(2) *Results of operations. . . .*

(3) *Critical accounting estimates*

(c) *Interim periods. . . .*

* * *

Item 307. Disclosure Controls and Procedures

Disclose the conclusions of the registrant's principal executive and principal financial officers, or persons performing similar functions, regarding the effectiveness of the registrant's disclosure controls and procedures (as defined in Rule 13a-15(e) or Rule 15d-15(e) of this chapter) as of the end of the period covered by the report, based on the evaluation of these controls and procedures required by paragraph (b) of Rule 13a-15 or 15d-15 of this chapter.

Item 308. Internal Control over Financial Reporting

(a) *Management's annual report on internal control over financial reporting.* Provide a report of management on the registrant's internal control over financial reporting (as defined in Rule 13a-15(f) or 15d-15(f) of this chapter) that contains:

(1) A statement of management's responsibility for establishing and maintaining adequate internal control over financial reporting for the registrant;

(2) A statement identifying the framework used by management to evaluate the effectiveness of the registrant's internal control over financial reporting as required by paragraph (c) of Rule 13a-15 or 15d-15 of this chapter;

(3) Management's assessment of the effectiveness of the registrant's internal control over financial reporting as of the end of the registrant's most recent fiscal year, including a statement as to whether or not internal control over financial reporting is effective. This discussion must include disclosure of any material weakness in the registrant's internal control over financial reporting identified by management. Management is not permitted to conclude that the registrant's

internal control over financial reporting is effective if there are one or more material weaknesses in the registrant's internal control over financial reporting; and

(4) If the registrant is an accelerated filer or large accelerated filer (as defined in Rule 12b-2), or otherwise includes in its annual report a registered public accounting firm's attestation report on internal control over financial reporting, a statement that the registered public accounting firm that audited the financial statements included in the annual report containing the disclosure required by this Item has issued an attestation report on the registrant's internal control over financial reporting.

(b) *Attestation report of the registered public accounting firm.* If the registrant, other than a registrant that is an emerging growth company as defined in Rule 405 of the Securities Act of 1933 or Rule 12b-2 of the Securities Exchange Act of 1934, is an accelerated filer or large accelerated filer (as defined in Rule 12b-2), provide the registered public accounting firm's attestation report on management's assessment of the registrant's internal control over financial reporting in the registrant's annual report containing the disclosure required by this Item.

(c) *Changes in internal control over financial reporting.* Disclose any change in the registrant's internal control over financial reporting identified in connection with the evaluation required by paragraph (d) of Rule 13a-15 or 15d-15 of this chapter that occurred during the registrant's last fiscal quarter (the registrant's fourth fiscal quarter in the case of an annual report) that has materially affected, or is reasonably likely to materially affect, the registrant's internal control over financial reporting.

Instructions

1. A registrant need not comply with paragraphs (a) and (b) of this Item until it either had been required to file and annual report pursuant to section 13(a) or 15(d) of the Exchange Act for the prior fiscal year or had filed an annual report with the Commission for the prior fiscal year. A registrant that does not comply shall include a statement in the first annual report that it files in substantially the following form: "This annual report does not include a report of management's assessment regarding internal control over financial reporting or an attestation report of the company's registered public accounting firm due to a transition period established by rules of the Securities and Exchange Commission for newly public companies." . . .

Subpart 400 — Management and Certain Security Holders

Item 401. Directors, Executive Officers, Promoters, and Control Persons

(a) *Identification of directors.* List the names and ages of all directors of the registrant and all persons nominated or chosen to become directors; indicate all positions and offices with the registrant held by each such person; state his term of office as director and any period(s) during which he has served as such; describe briefly any arrangement or understanding between him and any other person(s) (naming such person(s)) pursuant to which he was or is to be selected as a director of nominee.

(b) *Identification of executive officers.* List the names and ages of all executive officers of the registrant and all persons chosen to become executive officers; indicate all positions and offices with the registrant held by each such person; state his term of office as officer and the period during which he has served as such and describe briefly any arrangement or understanding between him and any other person(s) (naming such person) pursuant to which he was or is to be selected as an officer.

(c) *Identification of certain significant employees.* Where the registrant employs persons such as production managers, sales managers, or research scientists who are not executive officers but who make or are expected to make significant contributions to the business of the registrant, such persons shall be identified and their background disclosed to the same extent as in the case of executive officers. Such disclosure need not be made if the registrant was subject to section 13(a) or 15(d) of the Exchange Act or was exempt from section 13(a) by section 12(g)(2)(G) of such Act immediately prior to the filing of the registration statement, report, or statement to which this Item is applicable.

(d) *Family relationships.* State the nature of any family relationship between any director, executive officer, or person nominated or chosen by the registrant to become a director or executive officer.

(e) *Business experience*— (1) *Background.* Briefly describe the business experience during the past five years of each director, executive officer, person nominated or chosen to become a director or executive officer, and each person named in answer to paragraph (c) of Item 401, including: each person's principal occupations and employment during the past five years; the name and principal business of any corporation or other organization in which such occupations and employment were carried on; and whether such corporation or organization is a parent, subsidiary or other affiliate of the registrant. In addition, for each director or person nominated or chosen to become a director, briefly discuss the specific experience, qualifications, attributes or skills that led to the conclusion that the person should serve as a director for the registrant at the time that the disclosure is made, in light of the registrant's business and structure. If material, this disclosure should cover more than the past five years, including information about the person's particular areas of expertise or other relevant qualifications. When an executive officer or person named in response to paragraph (c) of Item 401 has been employed by the registrant or a subsidiary of the registrant for less than five years, a brief explanation shall be included as to the nature of the responsibility undertaken by the individual in prior positions to provide adequate disclosure of his or her prior business experience. What is required is information relating to the level of his or her professional competence, which may include, depending upon the circumstances, such specific information as the size of the operation supervised.

(2) *Directorships.* Indicate any other directorships held, including any other directorships held during the past five years, by each director or person nominated or chosen to become a director in any company with a class of securities registered pursuant to section 12 of the Exchange Act or subject to the requirements

of section 15(d) of such Act or any company registered as an investment company under the Investment Company Act of 1940, as amended, naming such company.

(f) *Involvement in certain legal proceedings.* Describe any of the following events that occurred during the past ten years and that are material to an evaluation of the ability or integrity of any director, person nominated to become a director or executive officer of the registrant:

(1) A petition under the Federal bankruptcy laws or any state insolvency law was filed by or against, or a receiver, fiscal agent or similar officer was appointed by a court for the business or property of such person, or any partnership in which he was a general partner at or within two years before the time of such filing, or any corporation or business association of which he was an executive officer at or within two years before the time of such filing;

(2) Such person was convicted in a criminal proceeding or is a named subject of a pending criminal proceeding (excluding traffic violations and other minor offenses);

(3) Such person was the subject of any order, judgment, or decree, not subsequently reversed, suspended or vacated, of any court of competent jurisdiction, permanently or temporarily enjoining him from, or otherwise limiting, the following activities:

(i) Acting as a futures commission merchant, introducing broker, commodity trading advisor, commodity pool operator, floor broker, leverage transaction merchant, any other person regulated by the Commodity Futures Trading Commission, or an associated person of any of the foregoing, or as an investment adviser, underwriter, broker or dealer in securities, or as an affiliated person, director or employee of any investment company, bank, savings and loan association or insurance company, or engaging in or continuing any conduct or practice in connection with such activity;

(ii) Engaging in any type of business practice; or

(iii) Engaging in any activity in connection with the purchase or sale of any security or commodity or in connection with any violation of Federal or State securities laws or Federal commodities laws;

(4) Such person was the subject of any order, judgment or decree, not subsequently reversed, suspended or vacated, of any Federal or State authority barring, suspending or otherwise limiting for more than 60 days the right of such person to engage in any activity described in paragraph (f)(3)(i) of this section, or to be associated with persons engaged in any such activity;

(5) Such person was found by a court of competent jurisdiction in a civil action or by the Commission to have violated any Federal or State securities law, and the judgment in such civil action or finding by the Commission has not been subsequently reversed, suspended, or vacated;

(6) Such person was found by a court of competent jurisdiction in a civil action or by the Commodity Futures Trading Commission to have violated any Federal commodities law, and the judgment in such civil action or finding by the Commodity Futures Trading Commission has not been subsequently reversed, suspended or vacated;

(7) Such person was the subject of, or a party to, any Federal or State judicial or administrative order, judgment, decree, or finding, not subsequently reversed, suspended or vacated, relating to an alleged violation of:

(i) Any Federal or State securities or commodities law or regulation; or

(ii) Any law or regulation respecting financial institutions or insurance companies including, but not limited to, a temporary or permanent injunction, order of disgorgement or restitution, civil money penalty or temporary or permanent cease-and-desist order, or removal or prohibition order; or

(iii) Any law or regulation prohibiting mail or wire fraud or fraud in connection with any business entity; or

(8) Such person was the subject of, or a party to, any sanction or order, not subsequently reversed, suspended or vacated, of any self-regulatory organization (as defined in Section 3(a)(26) of the Exchange Act (15 U.S.C. 78c(a)(26))), any registered entity (as defined in Section 1(a)(29) of the Commodity Exchange Act (7 U.S.C. 1(a)(29))), or any equivalent exchange, association, entity or organization that has disciplinary authority over its members or persons associated with a member.

(g) *Promoters and control persons.* (1) Registrants, which have not been subject to the reporting requirements of section 13(a) or 15(d) of the Exchange Act for the twelve months immediately prior to the filing of the registration statement, report, or statement to which this Item is applicable, and which had a promoter at any time during the past five fiscal years, shall describe with respect to any promoter, any of the events enumerated in paragraphs (f)(1) through (f)(6) of this section that occurred during the past five years and that are material to a voting or investment decision.

(2) Registrants, which have not been subject to the reporting requirements of section 13(a) or 15(d) of the Exchange Act for the twelve months immediately prior to the filing of the registration statement, report, or statement to which this Item is applicable, shall describe with respect to any control person, any of the events enumerated in paragraphs (f)(1) through (f)(6) of this section that occurred during the past five years and that are material to a voting or investment decision.

(h) *Audit committee financial expert.* (1)(i) Disclose that the registrant's board of directors has determined that the registrant either:

(A) Has at least one audit committee financial expert serving on its audit committee; or

(B) Does not have an audit committee financial expert serving on its audit committee.

(ii) If the registrant provides the disclosure required by paragraph (h)(1)(i)(A) of this Item, it must disclose the name of the audit committee financial expert and whether that person is *independent,* as that term is used in Item 7(d)(3)(iv) of Schedule 14A under the Exchange Act.

(iii) If the registrant provides the disclosure required by paragraph (h)(1)(i)(B) of this Item, it must explain why it does not have an audit committee financial expert.

Item 402. Executive Compensation

(a) *General*

(1) *Treatment of foreign private issuers.* [Omitted.]

(2) *All compensation covered.* This Item requires clear, concise and understandable disclosure of all plan and not-plan compensation awarded to, earned by, or paid to the named executive officers designated under paragraph (a)(3) of this Item, and directors covered by paragraph (k) of this Item, by any person for all services rendered in all capacities to the registrant and its subsidiaries, unless otherwise specifically excluded from disclosure in this Item. All such compensation shall be reported pursuant to this Item, even if also called for by another requirement, including transactions between the registrant and a third party where a purpose of the transaction is to furnish compensation to any such named executive officer or director. No amount reported as compensation for one fiscal year need by reported in the same manner as compensation for a subsequent fiscal year; amounts reported as compensation for one fiscal year may be required to be reported in a different manner pursuant to this Item.

(3) *Persons covered.* Disclosure shall be provided pursuant to this Item for each of the following (the "named executive officers"):

(i) All individuals serving as the registrant's principal executive officer or acting in a similar capacity during the last completed fiscal year ("PEO"), regardless of compensation level;

(ii) All individuals serving as the registrant's principal financial officer or acting in a similar capacity during the last completed fiscal year ("PFO"), regardless of compensation level;

(iii) The registrant's three most highly compensated executive officers other than the PEO and PFO who were serving as executive officers at the end of the last completed fiscal year; and

(iv) Up to two additional individuals for whom disclosure would have been provided pursuant to paragraph (a)(3)(iii) of this Item but for the fact that the individual was not serving as an executive officer of the registrant at the end of the completed fiscal year.

Instructions to Item 402(a)(3)

1. *Determination of most highly compensated executive officers.* The determination as to which executive officers are most highly compensated shall be made by reference to total compensation for the last completed fiscal year (as required to be disclosed pursuant to paragraph (c)(2)(x) of this Item) reduced by the amount required to be disclosed pursuant to paragraph (c)(2)(viii) of this Item, provided, however, that no disclosure need be provided for any executive officer, other than the PEO and PFO, whose total compensation, as so reduced, does not exceed $100,000.

2. *Inclusion of executive officer of subsidiary.* It may be appropriate for a registrant to include as named executive officers one or more executive officers or other employees of subsidiaries in the disclosure required by this Item. See Rule 3b-7 under the Exchange Act.

3. *Exclusion of executive officer due to overseas compensation.* It may be appropriate in limited circumstances for a registrant not to include in the disclosure required by this Item an individual, other than its PEO or PFO, who is one of the registrant's most highly compensated executive officers due to the payment of amounts of cash compensation relating to overseas assignments attributed predominantly to such assignments.

4. *Information for full fiscal year.* If the PEO or PFO served in that capacity during any part of a fiscal year with respect to which information is required, information should be provided as to all of his or her compensation for the full fiscal year. If a named executive officer (other than the PEO or PFO) served as an executive officer of the registrant (whether or not in the same position) during any part of the fiscal year with respect to which information is required, information shall be provided as to all compensation of that individual for the full fiscal year.

5. *Omission of table or column.* A table or column may be omitted if there has been no compensation awarded to, earned by, or paid to any of the named executive officers or directors required to be reported in that table or column in any fiscal year covered by that table.

6. *Definitions.* For purposes of this Item:

(i) The term *stock* means instruments such as common stock, restricted stock, restricted stock units, phantom stock, phantom stock units, common stock equivalent units or any similar instruments that do not have option-like features, and the term *option* means instruments such as stock options, stock appreciation rights and similar instruments with option-like features. The term *stock appreciation rights* ("SARs") refers to SARs payable in cash or stock, including SARs payable in cash or stock at the election of the registrant or a named executive officer. The term *equity* is used to refer generally to stock and/or options.

(ii) The term *plan* includes, but is not limited to, the following: Any plan, contract, authorization, or arrangement, whether or not set forth in any formal document, pursuant to which cash, securities, similar instruments, or any other property may be received. A plan may be applicable to one person. Except with respect to the disclosure required by paragraph (t) of this item, registrants may omit information regarding group life, health, hospitalization, or medical reimbursement plans that do not discriminate in scope, terms, or operation, in favor of executive officers or directors of the registrant and that are available generally to all salaried employees.

(iii) The term *incentive plan* means any plan providing compensation intended to serve as incentive for performance to occur over a specified period, whether such performance is measured by reference to financial performance of the registrant or an affiliate, the registrant's stock price, or any other performance measure. An *equity incentive plan* is an incentive plan or portion of an incentive plan under which awards are granted that fall within the scope of FASB ASC Topic 718 Compensation—Stock Compensation. A *non-equity incentive plan* is an incentive plan or portion of an incentive plan that is not an equity incentive plan. The term *incentive plan award* means an award provided under an incentive plan.

(iv) The terms *date of grant* or *grant date* refer to the grant date determined for financial statement reporting purposes pursuant FASB ASC Topic 718.

(v) *Closing market price* is defined as the price at which the registrant's security was last sold in the principal United States market for such security as of the date for which the closing market price is determined.

(b) *Compensation discussion and analysis.*

(1) Discuss the compensation awarded to, earned by, or paid to the named executive officers. The discussion shall explain all material elements of the registrant's compensation of the named executive officers. The discussion shall describe the following:

(i) The objectives of the registrant's compensation programs;

(ii) What the compensation program is designed to reward;

(iii) Each elements of compensation;

(iv) Why the registrant chooses to pay each element;

(v) How the registrant determines the amount (and, where applicable, the formula) for each element to pay;

(vi) How each compensation element and the registrant's decisions regarding that element fit into the registrant's overall compensation objectives and affect decisions regarding other elements and

(vii) Whether and, if so, how the registrant has considered the results of the most recent shareholder advisory vote on executive compensation required by section 14A of the Exchange Act (15 U.S.C. 78n-1) or §240.14a-20 of this chapter in determining compensation policies and decisions and, if so, how that consideration has affected the registrant's executive compensation decisions and policies.

(2) While the material information to be disclosed under Compensation Discussion and Analysis will vary depending upon the facts and circumstances, examples of such information may include, in a given case, among other things, the following:

(i) The policies for allocating between long-term and currently paid out compensation;

(ii) The policies for allocating between cash and non-cash compensation, and among different forms of non-cash compensation;

(iii) For long-term compensation, the basis for allocating compensation to each different form of award (such as relationship of the award to the achievement of the registrant's long-term goals, management's exposure to downside equity performance risk, correlation between cost to registrant and expected benefits to the registrant);

(iv) How the determination is made as to when awards are granted, including awards of equity-based compensation such as options;

(v) What specific items of corporate performance are taken into account in setting compensation policies and making compensation decisions;

(vi) How specific forms of compensation are structured and implemented to reflect these items of the registrant's performance, including whether discretion can be or has been exercised (either to award compensation absent attainment of the relevant performance goal(s) or to reduce or increase the size of any award or payout), identifying any particular exercise of discretion, and stating whether it applied to one or more specified named executive officers or to all compensation subject to the relevant performance goal(s);

(vii) How specific forms of compensation are structured and implemented to reflect the named executive officer's individual performance and/or individual contribution to these items of the registrant's performance, describing the elements of individual performance and/or contribution that are taken into account;

(viii) Registrant policies and decisions regarding the adjustment or recovery of awards or payments if the relevant registrant performance measures upon which they are based are restated or otherwise adjusted in a manner that would reduce the size of an award or payment;

(ix) The factors considered in decision to increase or decrease compensation materially;

(x) How compensation or amounts realizable from prior compensation are considered in setting other elements of compensation (e.g., how gains from prior option or stock awards are considered in setting retirement benefits);

(xi) With respect to any contract, agreement, plan, or arrangement, whether written or unwritten, that provides for payment(s) at, following, or in connection with any termination or change-in-control, the basis for selecting particular events as triggering payment (e.g., the rationale for providing a single trigger for payment in the event of a change-in-control);

(xii) The impact of the accounting and tax treatments of the particular form of compensation;

(xiii) The registrant's equity or other security ownership requirements or guidelines (specifying applicable amounts and forms of ownership), and any registrant policies regarding hedging the economic risk of such ownership;

(xiv) Whether the registrant engaged in any benchmarking of total compensation, or any material element of compensation, identifying the benchmark, and, if applicable, its components (including component companies); and

(xv) The role of executive officers in determining executive compensation.

Instructions to Item 402(b)

1. The purpose of the Compensation Discussion and Analysis is to provide to investors material information that is necessary to an understanding of the registrant's compensation policies and decisions regarding the named executive officers.

2. The Compensation Discussion and Analysis should be of the information contained in the tables and otherwise disclosed pursuant to this Item. The Compensation Discussion and Analysis should also cover actions regarding executive compensation that were taken after the registrant's last fiscal year's end. Action that should be addressed might include, as examples only, the adoption or implementation of new or modified programs and policies or specific decisions that were made or steps that were taken that could affect a fair understanding of the named executive officer's compensation for the last fiscal year. Moreover, in some situations it may be necessary to discuss prior years in order to give context to the disclosure provided.

3. The Compensation Discussion and Analysis should focus on the material principles underlying the registrant's executive compensation policies and decisions and the most important factors relevant to analysis of those policies and decisions. The Compensation Discussion and Analysis shall reflect the individual circumstances of the registrant and shall avoid boilerplate language and repetition of the more detailed information set forth in the tables and narrative disclosures that follow.

4. Registrants are not required to disclose target levels with respect to specific quantitative or qualitative performance-related factors considered by the compensation committee or the board of directors, or any other factors or criteria involving confidential trade secrets or confidential commercial or financial information, the disclosure of which would result in competitive harm for the registrant. The standard to use when determining whether disclosure would cause competitive harm for the registrant is the same standard that would apply when a registrant requests confidential treatment of confidential trade secrets or confidential commercial or financial information pursuant to Securities Act Rule 406 (17 CFR 230.406) and Exchange Act Rule 24b-2 (17 CFR 240.24b-2), each of which incorporates the criteria for non-disclosure when relying upon Exemption 4 of the Freedom of Information Act (5 U.S.C. 552(b)(4)). A registrant is not required to seek confidential treatment under the procedures in Securities Act Rule 406 and Exchange Act Rule 24b-2 if it determines that the disclosure would cause competitive harm in reliance on this instruction; however, in that case, the registrant must discuss how difficult it will be for the executive or how likely it will be for the registrant to achieve the undisclosed target levels or other factors.

5. Disclosure of target levels that are non-GAAP financial measures will not be subject to Regulation G and Item 10(e); however, disclosure must be provided as to how the number is calculated from the registrant's audited financial statements.

6. In proxy or information statements with respect to the election of directors, if the information disclosed pursuant to Item 407(i) would satisfy paragraph (b)(2)(xiii) of this Item, a registrant may refer to the information disclosed pursuant to Item 407(i).

(c) *Summary compensation table.*

(1) *General.* Provide the information specified in paragraph (c)(2) of this Item, concerning the compensation of the named executive officers for each of the registrant's last three completed fiscal years, in Summary Compensation Table in the tabular format specified below.

(2) The Table shall include:

(i) The name and principal position of the named executive officer (column (a));

(ii) The fiscal year covered (column (b));

(iii) The dollar value of base salary (cash and non-cash) earned by the named executive officer during the fiscal year covered (column (c));

(iv) The dollar value of bonus (cash and non-cash) earned by the named executive officer during the fiscal year covered (column (d));

(v) For awards of stock, the aggregate grant date fair value computed in accordance with FASB ASC Topic 718 (column (e));

(vi) For awards of options, with or without tandem SARs (including awards that subsequently have been transferred) the aggregate grant date fair value computed in accordance with FASB ASC Topic 718 (column (f));

(vii) The dollar value of all earnings for services performed during the fiscal year pursuant to awards under non-equity incentive plans as defined in paragraph (a)(6)(iii) of this item, and all earnings on any outstanding awards (column (g));

(viii) The sum of the amounts specified in paragraphs (c)(2)(viii)(A) and (B) of this Item (column (h)) as follows:

(A) The aggregate change in the actuarial present value of the named executive officer's accumulated benefit under all defined benefit and actuarial pension plans (including supplemental plans) from the pension plan measurement date used for financial statement reporting purposes with respect to the registrant's audited financial statements for the prior completed fiscal year to the pension plan measurement date used for financial statement reporting purposes with respect to the registrant's audited financial statements for the covered fiscal year; and

(B) Above-market or preferential earnings on compensation that is deferred on a basis that is not tax-qualified, including such earnings on nonqualified defined contribution plans;

(ix) All other compensation for the covered fiscal year that the registrant could not properly report in any column of the Summary Compensation Table (column (i)). Each compensation item that is not properly reportable in columns (c)-(h), regardless of the amount of the compensation item, must be included in column (i). Such compensation must include, but is not limited to:

(A) Perquisites and other personal benefits, or property, unless the aggregate amount of such compensation is less than $10,000;

(B) All "gross-ups" or other amounts reimbursed during the fiscal year for the payment of taxes;

(C) For any security of the registrant or its subsidiaries purchased from the registrant or its subsidiaries (through deferral of salary or bonus, or otherwise) at a discount from the market price of such security at the date of purchase, unless that discount is available generally, either to all security holders or to all salaried employees of the registrant, the compensation cost, if any, computed in accordance with FAS 123R;

(D) The amount paid or accrued to any named executive officer pursuant to a plan or arrangement in connection with:

(*1*) Any termination, including without limitation through retirement, resignation, severance or constructive termination (including a change in responsibilities) of such executive officer's employment with the registrant and its subsidiaries; or

(*2*) A change in control of the registrant;

(E) Registrant contributions or other allocations to vested and unvested defined contribution plans;

(F) The dollar value of any insurance premiums paid by, or on behalf of, the registrant during the covered fiscal year with respect to life insurance for the benefit of a named executive officer; and

(G) The dollar value of any dividends or other earnings paid on stock or option awards, when those amounts were not factored into the grant date fair value required to be reported for the stock or option award in column (e) or (f).

(x) The dollar value of total compensation for the covered fiscal year (column (j)). With respect to each named executive officer, disclose the sum of all amounts reported in columns (c) through (i).

SUMMARY COMPENSATION TABLE

Name and Principal Position	*Year*	*Salary ($)*	*Bonus ($)*	*Stock Awards ($)*	*Option Awards ($)*	*Non-Equity Incentive Plan Compensation ($)*	*Change in Pension Value and Nonqualified Deferred Compensation Earnings ($)*	*All Other Compensation ($)*	*Total ($)*
(a)	(b)	(c)	(d)	(e)	(f)	(g)	(h)	(i)	(j)
PEO	___ ___ ___								
PFO	___ ___ ___								
A	___ ___ ___								
B	___ ___ ___								
C	___ ___ ___								

INSTRUCTIONS TO ITEM 402(c)

[Omitted.]

(d) *Grants of plan-based awards table.* (1) Provide the information specified in paragraph (d)(2) of this Item, concerning each grant of an award made to a named executive officer in the last completed fiscal year under any plan, including awards that subsequently have been transferred, in the following tabular format:

(2) The Table shall include:

(i) The name of the named executive officer (column (a));

(ii) The grant date for equity-based awards reported in the table (column (b)). If such grant date is different than the date on which the compensation committee (or a committee of the board of directors performing a similar function or the full board of directors) takes action or is deemed to take action to grant such awards, a separate, adjoining column shall be added between columns (b) and (c) showing such date;

(iii) The dollar value of the estimated future payout upon satisfaction of the conditions in question under non-equity incentive plan awards granted in the fiscal year, or the applicable range of estimated payouts denominated in dollars (threshold, target and maximum amount) (columns (c) through (e));

(iv) The number of shares of stock, or the number of shares underlying options to be paid out or vested upon satisfaction of the conditions in question under equity incentive plan awards granted in the fiscal year, or the applicable range of estimated payouts denominated in the number of shares of stock, or the number of shares underlying options under the award (threshold, target and maximum amount) (columns (f) through (h));

(v) The number of shares of stock granted in the fiscal year that are not required to be disclosed in columns (f) through (h) (column (i));

GRANTS OF PLAN-BASED AWARDS

Name	Grant Date	*Estimated Future Payouts Under Non-Equity Incentive Plan Awards*			*Estimated Future Payouts Under Equity Incentive Plan Awards*			*All Other Stock Awards: Number of Shares of Stock or Units (#)*	*All Other Option Awards: Number of Securities Underlying Options (#)*	*Exercise or Base Price of Option Awards ($/Sh)*	*Grant Date Fair Value of Stock and Option Awards*
		Threshold ($)	*Target ($)*	*Maximum ($)*	*Threshold (#)*	*Target (#)*	*Maximum (#)*				
(a)	(b)	(c)	(d)	(e)	(f)	(g)	(h)	(i)	(j)	(k)	(l)
PEO											
PFO											
A											
B											
C											

(vi) The number of securities underlying options granted in the fiscal year that are not required to be disclosed in columns (f) through (h) column (j));

(vii) The per-share exercise or base price of the options granted in the fiscal year (column (k)). If such exercise or base price is less than the closing market price of the underlying security on the date of the grant, a separate, adjoining column showing the closing market price on the date of the grant shall be added after column (k) and

(viii) The grant date fair value of each equity award computed in accordance with FAS 123R (column (1)). If at any time during the last completed fiscal year, the registrant has adjusted or amended the exercise or base price of options, SARs or similar option-like instruments previously awarded to a named executive officer, whether through amendment, cancellation or replacement grants, or any other means ("repriced"), or otherwise has materially modified such awards, the incremental fair value, computed as of the repricing or modification date in accordance with FAS 123R, with respect to that repriced or modified award, shall be reported.

INSTRUCTION TO ITEM 402(d)

1. Disclosure on a separate line shall be provided in the Table for each grant of an award made to a named executive officer during the fiscal year. If grants of awards were made to a named executive officer during the fiscal year under more than one plan, identify the particular plan under which each such grant was made. . . .

(e) *Narrative disclosure to summary compensation table and grants of plan-based awards table.*

(1) Provide a narrative description of any material factors necessary to an understanding of the information disclosed in the tables required by paragraphs (c) and (d) of this Item. Examples of such factors may include, in given cases, among other things:

(i) The material terms of each named executive officer's employment agreement or arrangement, whether written or unwritten;

(ii) If at any time during the last fiscal year, any outstanding option or other equity-based award was repriced or otherwise materially modified (such as by extension of exercise periods, the change of vesting or forfeiture conditions, the change or elimination of applicable performance criteria, or the change of the bases upon which return are determined), a description of each repricing or other material modification;

(iii) The material terms of any award reported in response to paragraph (d) of this Item, including a general description of the formula or criteria to be applied in determining the amounts payable, and the vesting schedule. For example, state where applicable that dividends will be paid on stock, and if so, the applicable dividend rate and whether that rate is preferential. Describe any performance-based conditions, and any other material conditions, that are applicable to the award. For purposes of the Table required by paragraph (d) of this Item and the narrative disclosure required by paragraph (e) of this Item, performance-based conditions include both performance conditions and market conditions, as those terms are defined in FASB ASC Topic 718 and

(iv) An explanation of the amount of salary and bonus in proportion to total compensation.

INSTRUCTION TO ITEM 402(e)(1)

1. The disclosure required by paragraph (e)(1)(ii) of this Item would not apply to any repricing that occurs through a pre-existing formula or mechanism in the plan or award that results in the periodic adjustment of the option or SAR exercise or base price, an antidilution provision in a plan or award, or a recapitalization or similar transaction equally affecting all holders of the class of securities underlying the options or SARs.

2. Instructions 4 and 5 to Item 402(b) apply regarding disclosure pursuant to paragraph (e)(1) of target levels with respect to specific quantitative or qualitative performance-related factors considered by the compensation committee or the board of directors, or any other factors or criteria involving confidential trade secrets or confidential commercial or financial information, the disclosure of which would result in competitive harm for the registrant.

(2) Reserved.

(f) *Outstanding equity awards at fiscal year-end table.* (1) Provide the information specified in paragraph (f)(2) of this Item, concerning unexercised options; stock that has not vested; and equity incentive plan awards for each named executive officer outstanding as of the end of the registrant's last completed fiscal year in the following tabular format:

(2) The Table shall include:

(i) The name of the named executive officer (column (a));

(ii) On an award-by-award basis, the number of securities underlying unexercised options, including awards that have been transferred other than for value, that are exercisable and that are not reported in column (d) (column (b));

(iii) On an award-by-award basis, the number of securities underlying unexercised options, including awards that have been transferred other than for value, that are unexercisable and that are not reported in column (d) (column (c));

(iv) On an award-by-award basis, the total number of shares underlying unexercised options awarded under any equity incentive plan that have not been earned (column (d));

(v) For each instrument reported in columns (b)(c) and (d), as applicable, the exercise or base price (column (e));

(vi) For each instrument reported in columns (b), (c), and (d), as applicable, the expiration date (column (f));

(vii) The total number of shares of stock that have not vested and that are not reported in column (i) (column (g));

OUTSTANDING EQUITY AWARDS AT FISCAL YEAR-END

	Option Awards					*Stock Awards*			
Name	*Number of Securities Underlying Unexercised Options (#) Exercisable*	*Number of Securities Underlying Unexercised Options (#) Unexercisable*	*Equity Incentive Plan Awards: Number of Securities Underlying Unexercised Unearned Options (#)*	*Option Exercise Price ($)*	*Option Expiration Date*	*Number of Shares or Units of Stock That Have Not Vested ($)*	*Market Value of Shares or Units of Stock That Have Not Vested ($)*	*Equity Incentive Plan Awards: Number of Unearned Shares, Units or Other Rights That Have Not Vested (#)*	*Equity Incentive Plan Awards: Market or Payout Value of Unearned Shares, Units or Other Rights That Have Not Vested ($)*
(a)	(b)	(c)	(d)	(e)	(f)	(g)	(h)	(i)	(j)
PEO									
PFO									
A									
B									
C									

(viii) The aggregate market value of shares of stock that have not vested and that are not reported in column (j) (column (h));

(ix) The total number of shares of stock, units or other rights awarded under any equity incentive plan that have not vested and that have not been earned, and, if applicable the number of shares underlying any such unit or right (column (i)); and

(x) The aggregate market or payout value of shares of stock, units or other rights awarded under any equity incentive plan that have not vested and that have not been earned (column (j)).

Instructions to Item 402(f)(2)

1. Identifying by footnote any award that has been transferred other than for value, disclosing the nature of the transfer.

2. The vesting dates of options, shares and stock and equity incentive plan awards held at fiscal-year end must be disclosed by footnote to the applicable column where the outstanding award is reported.

3. Compute the market value of stock reported in column (h) and equity incentive plan awards of stock reported in column (j) by multiplying the closing market price of the registrant's stock at the end of the last completed fiscal year by the number of shares or units of stock or the amount of equity incentive plan awards, respectively. The number of shares or units reported in columns (d) or (i), and the payout value reported in column (j), shall be based on achieving threshold performance goals, except that if the previous fiscal year's performance has exceeded the threshold, the disclosure shall be based on the next higher performance measure (target or maximum) that exceeds the previous fiscal year's performance. If the award provides only for a single estimated payout, that amount should be reported. If the target amount is not determinable, registrants must provide a representative amount based on the previous fiscal year's performance.

4. Multiple awards may be aggregated where the expiration date and the exercise and/or base price of the instruments is identical. A single award consisting of a combination of options, SARs and/or similar option-like instruments shall be reported as separate awards with respect to each tranche with a different exercise and/or base price or expiration date.

5. Options or stock awarded under an equity incentive plan are reported in columns (d) or (i) and (j), respectively, until the relevant performance condition has been satisfied. Once the relevant performance condition has been satisfied, even if the option or stock award is subject to forfeiture conditions, options are reported in column (b) or (c), as appropriate, until they are exercised or expire, or stock is reported in columns (g) and (h) until it vests.

(g) *Option exercises and stock vested table.* (1) Provide the information specified in paragraph (g)(2) of this Item, concerning each exercise of stock options, SARs and similar instruments, and each vesting of stock, including restricted stock, restricted stock units and similar instruments, during the last completed fiscal year for each of the named executive officers on an aggregated basis in the following tabular format:

OPTION EXERCISES AND STOCK VESTED

	Option Awards		*Stock Awards*	
Name (a)	*Number of Shares Acquired on Exercise (#)* (b)	*Value Realized on Exercise ($)* (c)	*Number of Shares Acquired on Vesting (#)* (d)	*Value Realized on Vesting ($)* (e)
PEO				
PFO				
A				
B				
C				

(2) The Table shall include:

(i) The name of the executive officer (column (a));

(ii) The number of securities for which the options were exercised (column (b));

(iii) The aggregate dollar value realized upon exercise of options, or upon the transfer of an award for value (column (c));

(iv) The number of shares of stock that have vested (column (d)); and

(v) The aggregate dollar value realized upon vesting of stock, or upon the transfer of an award for value (column (e)).

Instruction to Item 402(g)(2)

Report in column (c) the aggregate dollar amount realized by the named executive officer upon exercise of the options or upon the transfer of such instruments for value. Compute the dollar amount realized upon exercise by determining the difference between the market price of the underlying securities at exercise and the exercise or base price of the options. Do not include the value of any related payment or other consideration provided (or to be provided) by the registrant to or on behalf of a named executive officer, whether in payment of the exercise price or related taxes. (Any such payment or other consideration provided by the registrant is required to be disclosed in accordance with paragraph (c)(2)(ix) of this Item.) Report in column (e) the aggregate dollar amount realized by the named executive officer upon the vesting of stock or the transfer of such instruments for value. Compute the aggregate dollar amount realized upon vesting by multiplying the number of shares of stock or units by the market value of the underlying shares on the vesting date. For any amount realized upon exercise or vesting for which receipt has been deferred, provide a footnote quantifying the amount and disclosing the terms of the deferral.

(h) *Pension benefits*

(1) Provide the information specified in paragraph (h)(2) of this item with respect to each plan that provides for payments or other benefits at, following, or in connection with retirement, in the following tabular format:

PENSION BENEFITS

Name (a)	*Plan Name* (b)	*Number of Years Credited Service* (#) (c)	*Present Value of Accumulated Benefit* ($) (d)	*Payments During Last Fiscal Year* ($) (e)
PEO				
PFO				
A				
B				
C				

(2) The Table shall include:

(i) The name of the executive officer (column (a));

(ii) The name of the plan (column (b));

(iii) The number of years of service credited to the named executive officer under the plan, computed as of the same pension plan measurement date used for financial statement reporting purposes with respect to the registrant's audited financial statements for the last completed fiscal year (column (c));

(iv) The actuarial present value of the named executive officer's accumulated benefit under the plan, computed as of the same pension plan measurement date used for financial statement reporting purposes with respect to the registrant's audited financial statements for the last completed fiscal year (column (d)); and

(v) The dollar amount of any payments and benefits paid to the named executive officer during the registrant's last completed fiscal year (column (e)).

INSTRUCTIONS TO ITEM 402(h)(2)

1. The disclosure required pursuant to this Table applies to each plan that provides for specified retirement payments and benefits, or payments and benefits that will be provided primarily following retirement, including but not limited to tax-qualified defined benefit plans and supplemental executive retirement plans, but excluding tax-qualified defined contribution plans and nonqualified defined contribution plans. Provide a separate row for each such plan in which the named executive officer participates.

2. For purposes of the amount(s) reported in column (d), the registrant must use the same assumptions used for financial reporting purposes under generally accepted accounting principles, except that retirement age shall be assumed to be the normal retirement age as defined in the plan, or if not so defined, the earliest time at which a participant may retire under the plan without any benefit reduction due to age. The registrant must disclose in the accompanying textual narrative the valuation method and all material assumptions applied in quantifying the present value of the current accrued benefit. A benefit specified

in the plan document or the executive's contract itself is not an assumption. Registrants may satisfy all or part of this disclosure by reference to a discussion of those assumptions in the registrant's financial statements, footnotes to the financial statements, or discussion in the Management's Discussion and Analysis. The sections so referenced are deemed part of the disclosure provided pursuant to this Item.

3. For purposes of allocating the current accrued benefit between tax qualified defined benefit plans and related supplemental plans, apply the limitations applicable to tax qualified defined benefit plans established by the Internal Revenue Code and the regulations thereunder that applied as of the pension plan measurement date.

4. If a named executive officer's number of years of credited service with respect to any plan is different from the named executive officer's number of actual years of service with the registrant, provide footnote disclosure quantifying the difference and any resulting benefit augmentation.

(3) Provide a succinct narrative description of any material factors necessary to an understanding of each plan covered by the tabular disclosure required by this paragraph. While material factors will vary depending upon the facts, examples of such factors may include, in given cases, among other things:

(i) The material terms and conditions of payments and benefits available under the plan, including the plan's normal retirement payment and benefit formula and eligibility standards, and the effect of the form of benefit elected on the amount of annual benefits. For this purposes, normal retirement means retirement at the normal retirement age as defined in the plan, or if not so defined, the earliest time at which a participant may retire under the plan without any benefit reduction due to age;

(ii) If any named executive officer is currently eligible for early retirement under any plan, identify that named executive officer and the plan, and describe the plan's early retirement payment and benefit formula and eligibility standards. For this purpose, early retirement means retirement at the early retirement age as defined in the plan, or otherwise available to the executive under the plan;

(iii) The specific elements of compensation (*e.g.*, salary, bonus, etc.) included in applying the payment and benefit formula, identifying each such elements;

(iv) With respect to named executive officers' participation in multiple plans, the different purposes for each plan; and

(v) Registrant policies with regard to such matters as granting extra years of credited service.

(i) *Nonqualified defined contribution and other nonqualified deferred compensation plans.*

(1) Provide the information specified in paragraph (i)(2) of this Item with respect to each defined contribution or other plan that provides for the deferral of compensation on a basis that is not tax-qualified in the following tabular format:

NONQUALIFIED DEFERRED COMPENSATION

Name (a)	*Executive Contributions in Last FY ($)* (b)	*Registrant Contributions in Last FY ($)* (c)	*Aggregate Earnings in Last FY ($)* (d)	*Aggregate Withdrawals/ Distributions ($)* (e)	*Aggregate Balance at Last FYE ($)* (f)
PEO					
PFO					
A					
B					
C					

(2) The Table shall include:

(i) The name of the executive officer (column (a));

(ii) The dollar amount of aggregate executive contributions during the registrant's last fiscal year (column (b));

(iii) The dollar amount of aggregate registrant contributions during the registrant's last fiscal year (column (c));

(iv) The dollar amount of aggregate interest or other earnings accrued during the registrant's last fiscal year (column (d));

(v) The aggregate dollar amount of all withdrawals by and distributions to the executive during the registrant's last fiscal year (column (e)); and

(vi) The dollar amount of total balance of the executive's account as of the end of the registrant's last fiscal year (column (f)).

INSTRUCTION TO ITEM 402(i)(2)

Provide a footnote quantifying the extent to which amounts reported in the contributions and earnings columns are reported as compensation in the last completed fiscal year in the registrant's Summary Compensation Table and amounts reported in the aggregate balance at last fiscal year end (column (f)) previously were reported as compensation to the named executive officer in the registrant's Summary Compensation Table for previous years.

(3) Provide a succinct narrative description of any material factors necessary to an understanding of each plan covered by tabular disclosure required by this paragraph. While material factors will vary depending upon the facts, examples of such factors may include, in given cases, among other things:

(i) The type(s) of compensation permitted to be deferred, and any limitations (by percentage of compensation or otherwise) on the extent to which deferral is permitted;

(ii) The measures for calculating interest or other plan earnings (including whether such measure(s) are selected by the executive or the registrant and the frequency and manner in which selections may be changed), quantifying interest rates and other earnings measures applicable during the registrant's last fiscal year; and

(iii) Material terms with respect to payouts, withdrawals and other distributions.

(j) *Potential payments upon termination or change-in-control.* Regarding each contract, agreement, plan or arrangement, whether written or unwritten, that provides for payments(s) to a named executive officer at, following, or in connection with any termination, including without limitation resignation, severance, retirement or a constructive termination of a named executive officer, or a change in control of the registrant or a change in the named executive officer's responsibilities, with respect to each named executive officer:

(1) Describe and explain the specific circumstances that would trigger payment(s) or the provision of other benefits, including perquisites and health care benefits;

(2) Describe and quantify the estimated payments and benefits that would be provided in each covered circumstance, whether they would or could be lump sum, or annual, disclosing the duration, and by whom they would be provided;

(3) Describe and explain how the appropriate payment and benefit levels are determined under the various circumstances that trigger payments or provision of benefits;

(4) Describe and explain any material conditions or obligations applicable to the receipt of payments or benefits, including but not limited to non-compete, non-solicitation, non-disparagement or confidentiality agreements, including the duration of such agreements and provisions regarding waiver of breach of such agreements; and

(5) Describe any other material factors regarding each such contract, agreement, plan or arrangement.

INSTRUCTIONS TO ITEM 402(j)

1. The registrant must provide quantitative disclosure under these requirements, applying the assumptions that the triggering event took place on the last business day of the registrant's last completed fiscal year, and the price per share of the registrant's securities is the closing market price as of that date. In the event that uncertainties exist as to the provision of payments and benefits or the amounts involved, the registrant is required to make a reasonable estimate (or a reasonable estimated range of amounts) applicable to the payment or benefit and disclose material assumptions underlying such estimates or estimated ranges in its disclosure. In such event, the disclosure would require forward-looking information as appropriate.

2. Perquisites and other personal benefits or property may be excluded only if the aggregate amount of such compensation will be less than $10,000. Individual perquisites and personal benefits shall be identified and quantified as required by Instruction 4 to paragraph (c)(2)(ix) of this Item. For purposes of quantifying health care benefits, the registrant must use the assumptions used for financial reporting purposes under generally accepted accounting principles.

3. To the extent that the form and amount of any payment or benefit that would be provided in connection with any triggering event is fully disclosed pursuant to paragraph (h) or (i) of this Item, reference may be made to that disclosure. However, to the extent that the form or amount of any such payment or benefit would be enhanced or its vesting or other provisions accelerated in connection with any triggering events, such enhancement or acceleration must be disclosed pursuant to this paragraph.

4. Where a triggering event has actually occurred for a named executive officer and that individual was not serving as a named executive officer of the registrant at the end of the last completed fiscal year, the disclosure required by this paragraph for that named executive officer shall apply only to that triggering event.

5. The registrant need not provide information with respect to contracts, agreements, plans or arrangements to the extent they do not discriminate in scope, terms or operation, in favor of executive officers of the registrant and that are available generally to all salaried employees.

(k) *Compensation of directors.*

(1) Provide the information specified in paragraph (k)(2) of this Item, concerning the compensation of the directors for the registrant's last completed fiscal year, in the following tabular format:

(2) The Table shall include.

(i) The name of each director unless such director is also a named executive officer under paragraph (a) of this Item and his or her compensation for service as a director is fully reflected in the Summary Compensation Table pursuant to paragraph (c) of this Item and otherwise as required pursuant to paragraphs (d) through (j) of this Item (column (a));

(ii) The aggregate dollar amount of all fees earned or paid in cash for services as a director, including annual retainer fees, committee and/or chairmanship fees, and meeting fees (column (b));

(iii) For awards of stock, the aggregate grant date fair value computed in accordance FASB ASC Topic 718 (column (c));

(iv) For awards of stock options, with or without tandem SARs (including awards that subsequently have been transferred) the aggregate grant date fair value computed in accordance with FASB ASC Topic 718 (column (d));

(v) The dollar value of all earnings for services performed during the fiscal year pursuant to non-equity incentive plans as defined in paragraph (a)(6)(iii) of this Item, and all earnings on any outstanding awards (column (e));

(vi) The sum of the amounts specified in paragraphs (k)(2)(vi)(A) and (B) of this Item (column (f)) as follows:

(A) The aggregate change in the actuarial present value of the director's accumulated benefit under all defined benefit and actuarial pension plans (including supplemental plans) from the pension plan measurement date used for financial statement reporting purposes with respect to the registrant's audited financial statements for the prior completed fiscal year to the pension plan measurement date used for financial statement reporting purposes with respect to the registrant's audited financial statements for the covered fiscal year; and

(B) Above-market or preferential earnings on compensation that is deferred on a basis that is not tax-qualified, including such earnings on nonqualified defined contribution plans;

(vii) All other compensation for the covered fiscal year that the registrant could not properly report in any other column of the Director Compensation Table (column (g)). Each compensation item that is not properly reportable in column (b)-(f), regardless of the amount of the compensation item, must be included in column (g). Such compensation must include, but is not limited to:

(A) Perquisites and other personal benefits, or property, unless the aggregate amount of such compensation is less than $10,000;

(B) All "gross-ups" or other amounts reimbursed during the fiscal year for the payment of taxes;

(C) For any security of the registrant or its subsidiaries purchased from the registrant or its subsidiaries (through deferral of salary or bonus, or otherwise) at a discount from the market price of such security at the date of purchase, unless that discount is available generally, either to all security holders or to all salaried employees of the registrant, the compensation cost, if any, computed in accordance with FAS 123R;

(D) The amount paid or accrued to any director pursuant to a plan or arrangement in connection with:

(1) The resignation, retirement or any other termination of such director; or

(2) A change in control of the registrant;

(E) Registrant contributions or other allocations to vested and unvested defined contribution plans;

(F) Consulting fees earned from, or paid or payable by the registrant and/or its subsidiaries (including joint ventures);

(G) The annual costs of payments and promises or payments pursuant to director legacy programs and similar charitable award programs;

(H) The dollar value of any insurance premiums paid by, or on behalf of, the registrant during the covered fiscal year with respect to life insurance for the benefit of a director; and

(I) The dollar value of any dividends or other earnings paid on stock or option awards, when those amounts were not factored into the grant date fair value for the stock or option award in column (c) or (d); and

(viii) The dollar value of total compensation for the covered fiscal year (column (h)). With respect to each director, disclose the sum of all amounts reported in columns (b) through (g).

Instruction to Item 402(k)(2)

Two or more directors may be grouped in a single row in the Table if all elements of their compensation are identical. The names of the directors for whom disclosure is presented on a group basis should be clear from the Table.

DIRECTOR COMPENSATION

Name	*Fees Earned or Paid in Cash ($)*	*Stock Awards ($)*	*Option Awards ($)*	*Non-Equity Incentive Plan Compensation ($)*	*Change in Pension Value and Nonqualified Deferred Compensation Earnings*	*All Other Compensation ($)*	*Total ($)*
(a)	(b)	(c)	(d)	(e)	(f)	(g)	(h)
A							
B							
C							
D							
E							

(3) *Narrative to director compensation table.*

Provide a narrative description of any material factors necessary to an understanding of the director compensation disclosed in this Table. While material factors will vary depending upon the facts, examples of such factors may include, in given cases, among other things:

(i) A description of standard compensation arrangements (such as fees for retainer, committee service, service as chairman of the board or a committee, and meeting attendance); and

(ii) Whether any director has a different compensation arrangement, identifying that director and describing the terms of that arrangement.

INSTRUCTION TO ITEM 402(k)

In addition to the Instruction to paragraph 402(k)(2)(iii) and (iv) and the Instructions to paragraph (k)(2)(vii) of this Item, the following apply equally to paragraph (k) of this Item: Instructions 2 and 4 to paragraph (c) of this Item: Instructions to paragraphs (c)(2)(iii) and (iv) of this Item; Instructions to paragraphs (c)(2)(v) and (vi) of this Item; Instructions to paragraph (c)(2)(vii) of this Item; and Instructions 1 and 5 to paragraph (c)(2)(ix) of this Items. These Instructions apply to the columns in the Director Compensation Table that are analogous to the columns in the Summary Compensation Table to which they refer and to disclosures under paragraph (k) of this Item that correspond to analogous disclosures provided for in paragraph (c) of this Item to which they refer.

(l) *Smaller reporting companies and emerging growth companies.* A registrant that qualifies as a "smaller reporting company," as defined by Item 10(f), or is an "emerging growth company," as defined in Rule 405 of the Securities Act or Rule 12b-2 of the Exchange Act, may provide the scaled disclosure in paragraphs (m) through (r) instead of paragraphs (a) through (k), (s), and (u) of this Item. . . .

(t) *Golden Parachute Compensation.* (1) In connection with any proxy or consent solicitation material providing the disclosure required by section 14A(b)(1) of the Exchange Act or any proxy or consent solicitation that includes disclosure under Item 14 of Schedule 14A pursuant to Note A of Schedule 14A (excluding any proxy or consent solicitation of an "emerging growth company," as defined in Rule 405 of the Securities Act (§230.405 of this chapter) or Rule 12b-2 of the Exchange Act (§240.12b-2 of this chapter)), with respect to each named executive officer of the acquiring company and the target company, provide the information specified in paragraphs (t)(2) and (3) of this section regarding any agreement or understanding, whether written or unwritten, between such named executive officer and the acquiring company or target company, concerning any type of compensation, whether present, deferred or contingent, that is based on or otherwise relates to an acquisition, merger, consolidation, sale or other disposition of all or substantially all assets of the issuer, as follows:

GOLDEN PARACHUTE COMPENSATION

Name (a)	*Cash ($)* (b)	*Equity ($)* (c)	*Pension/ NQDC ($)* (d)	*Perquisites Benefits ($)* (e)	*Tax Reimbursement ($)* (f)	*Other ($)* (g)	*Total ($)* (h)
PEO							
PFO							
A							
B							
C							

(2) The table shall include, for each named executive officer:

(i) The name of the named executive officer (column (a):

(ii) The aggregate dollar value of any cash severance payments, including but not limited to payments of base salary, bonus, and pro-rated non-equity incentive compensation payments (column (b);

(iii) The aggregate dollar value of:

(A) Stock awards for which vesting would be accelerated;

(B) In-the-money option awards for which vesting would be accelerated; and

(C) Payments in cancellation of stock and option awards (column (c));

(iv) The aggregate dollar value of pension and nonqualified deferred compensation benefit enhancements (column (d));

(v) The aggregate dollar value of perquisites and other personal benefits or property, and health care and welfare benefits (column (e));

(vi) The aggregate dollar value of any tax reimbursements (column (f));

(vii) The aggregate dollar value of any other compensation that is based on or otherwise relates to the transaction not properly reported in columns (b) through (f) (column (g)); and

(viii) The aggregate dollar value of the sum of all amounts reported in columns (b) through (g) (column (h)).

(3) Provide a succinct narrative description of any material factors necessary to an understanding of each such contract, agreement, plan or arrangement and the payments quantified in the tabular disclosure required by this paragraph. Such factors shall include, but not be limited to a description of:

(i) The specific circumstances that would trigger payment(s);

(ii) Whether the payments would or could be lump sum, or annual, disclosing the duration, and by whom they would be provided; and

(iii) Any material conditions or obligations applicable to the receipt of payment or benefits, including but not limited to non-compete, non-solicitation, non-disparagement or confidentiality agreements, including the duration of such agreements and provisions regarding waiver or breach of such agreements.

(u) *Pay ratio disclosure.*—

(1) Disclose:

(i) The median of the annual total compensation of all employees of the registrant, except the PEO of the registrant;

(ii) The annual total compensation of the PEO of the registrant; and

(iii) The ratio of the amount in paragraph (u)(1)(i) of this Item to the amount in paragraph (u)(1)(ii) of this Item. For purposes of the ratio required by this paragraph (u)(1)(iii), the amount in paragraph (u)(1)(i) of this Item shall equal one, or, alternatively, the ratio may be expressed narratively as the multiple that the amount in paragraph (u)(1)(ii) of this Item bears to the amount in paragraph (u)(1)(i) of this Item.

(2) For purposes of this paragraph (u),

(i) Total compensation for the median of annual total compensation of all employees of the registrant and the PEO of the registrant shall be determined in accordance with paragraph (c)(2)(x) of this Item 402. In determining the total compensation, all references to "named executive officer" in this Item 402 and the instructions thereto may be deemed to refer instead, as applicable, to "employee" and, for non-salaried employees, references to "base salary" and "salary" in this Item 402 and the instructions thereto may be deemed to refer instead, as applicable, to "wages plus overtime";

(ii) Annual total compensation means total compensation for the registrant's last completed fiscal year; and

(iii) Registrant means the registrant and its consolidated subsidiaries.

(3) For purposes of this paragraph (u), employee or employee of the registrant means an individual employed by the registrant or any of its consolidated subsidiaries, whether as a full-time, part-time, seasonal, or temporary worker, as of

a date chosen by the registrant within the last three months of the registrant's last completed fiscal year. The definition of employee or employee of the registrant does not include those workers who are employed, and whose compensation is determined, by an unaffiliated third party but who provide services to the registrant or its consolidated subsidiaries as independent contractors or "leased" workers;

(4) For purposes of this paragraph (u), an employee located in a jurisdiction outside the United States (a "non-U.S. employee") may be exempt from the definition of employee or employee of the registrant under either of the following conditions:

(i) The employee is employed in a foreign jurisdiction in which the laws or regulations governing data privacy are such that, despite its reasonable efforts to obtain or process the information necessary for compliance with this paragraph (u), the registrant is unable to do so without violating such data privacy laws or regulations. . .

(ii) The registrant's non-U.S. employees account for 5% or less of the registrant's total employees. In that circumstance, if the registrant chooses to exclude any non-U.S. employees under this exemption, it must exclude all non-U.S. employees. Additionally, if a registrant's non-U.S. employees exceed 5% of the registrant's total U.S. and non-U.S. employees, it may exclude up to 5% of its total employees who are non-U.S. employees; provided, however, if a registrant excludes any non-U.S. employees in a particular jurisdiction, it must exclude all non-U.S. employees in that jurisdiction. . . .

INSTRUCTION 2 TO ITEM 402(u). IDENTIFYING THE MEDIAN EMPLOYEE.

A registrant is required to identify its median employee only once every three years and calculate total compensation for that employee each year; provided that, during a registrant's last completed fiscal year there has been no change in its employee population or employee compensation arrangements that it reasonably believes would result in a significant change to its pay ratio disclosure. . . .

INSTRUCTION 8 TO ITEM 402(u). EMERGING GROWTH COMPANIES.

A registrant is not required to comply with paragraph (u) of this Item if it is an emerging growth company as defined in Section 2(a)(19) of the Securities Act or Section 3(a)(80) of the Exchange Act. A registrant shall comply with paragraph (u) of this Item with respect to compensation for the first fiscal year commencing on or after the date the registrant ceases to be an emerging growth company. . . .

(v) *Pay versus performance.* In connection with any proxy or information statement for which the rules of the Commission require executive compensation disclosure pursuant to this section (excluding any proxy or information statement of an "emerging growth company," . . . :

(1) Provide the information specified in paragraph (v)(2) of this section for each of the registrant's last five completed fiscal years in the following tabular format:

PAY VERSUS PERFORMANCE

Year	*Summary Compensation Table Total for PEO*	*Compensation Actually Paid to PEO*	*Average Summary Compensation Table Total for Non-PEO Named Executive Officers*	*Average Compensation Actually Paid to Non-PEO Named Executive Officers*	*Value of Initial Fixed $100 Investment Based On:*		*Net Income*	*[Company Selected Measure] (i)*
(a)	(b)	(c)	(d)	(e)			(h)	(i)
					Total Shareholder Return (f)	Peer Group Total Shareholder Return (g)		

(2) The table required by paragraph (v)(1) of this section must include:

(i) The fiscal year covered (column (a)).

(ii) The PEO's (as defined in paragraph (a)(3) of this section) total compensation for the covered fiscal year as reported in the Summary Compensation Table pursuant to paragraph (c)(2)(x) of this section . . . and the average total compensation reported for the remaining named executive officers collectively reported pursuant to such applicable paragraph (column (d)) . . .

(iii) The executive compensation actually paid to the PEO (column (c)) and the average executive compensation actually paid to the remaining named executive officers collectively (column (e)). . . .

(iv) For purposes of columns (f) and (g) of the table required by paragraph (v)(1) of this section, for each fiscal year disclose the cumulative total shareholder return of the registrant (column (f)) and peer group cumulative total shareholder return (column (g)). . .

(v) The registrant's net income for each fiscal year (column (h)).

(vi) An amount for each fiscal year attributable to an additional financial performance measure included in the Tabular List provided pursuant to paragraph (v)(6) of this section, designated as the Company-Selected Measure, which in the registrant's assessment represents the most important financial performance measure (that is not otherwise required to be disclosed in the table) used by the registrant to link compensation actually paid to the registrant's named executive officers, for the most recently completed fiscal year, to company performance (column (i)). . .

(5) In proxy or information statements in which disclosure is required pursuant to this Item, use the information provided in the table required by paragraph (v) (1) of this section to provide a clear description (graphically, narratively, or a combination of the two) of the relationships:

(i) Between:

(A) The executive compensation actually paid by the registrant to the PEO (column (c)) and the average of the executive compensation actually paid to the named executive officers other than the PEO (column (e)) included in the Summary Compensation Table; and

(B) The cumulative total shareholder return of the registrant (column (f)), across the registrant's last five completed fiscal years;

(ii) Between:

(A) The executive compensation actually paid by the registrant to the PEO (column (c)) and the average of the executive compensation actually paid to the named executive officers other than the PEO (column (e)) included in the Summary Compensation Table; and

(B) Net income of the registrant (column (h)), across the registrant's last five completed fiscal years; and

(iii) Between:

(A) The executive compensation actually paid by the registrant to the PEO (column (c)) and the average of the executive compensation actually paid to the named executive officers other than the PEO (column (e)) included in the Summary Compensation Table; and

(B) The Company-Selected Measure (column (i)), across the registrant's last five completed fiscal years. . . .

(w) Disclosure of a registrant's action to recover erroneously awarded compensation.

(1) If at any time during or after the last completed fiscal year the registrant was required to prepare an accounting restatement that required recovery of erroneously awarded compensation pursuant to the registrant's compensation recovery policy required by the listing standards adopted pursuant to 17 CFR 240.10D-1, or there was an outstanding balance as of the end of the last completed fiscal year of erroneously awarded compensation to be recovered from the application of the policy to a prior restatement, the registrant must provide the following information:

(i) For each restatement:

(A) The date on which the registrant was required to prepare an accounting restatement;

(B) The aggregate dollar amount of erroneously awarded compensation attributable to such accounting restatement, including an analysis of how the amount was calculated;

(C) If the financial reporting measure as defined in 17 CFR 240.10D-1(d) related to a stock price or total shareholder return metric, the estimates that were used in determining the erroneously awarded compensation attributable to such accounting restatement and an explanation of the methodology used for such estimates;

(D) The aggregate dollar amount of erroneously awarded compensation that remains outstanding at the end of the last completed fiscal year; and

(E) If the aggregate dollar amount of erroneously awarded compensation has not yet been determined, disclose this fact, explain the reason(s) and disclose the information required in paragraphs (w)(1)(i)(B) through (D) of this section in the next filing that is required to include disclosure pursuant to Item 402 of Regulation S-K;

(ii) If recovery would be impracticable pursuant to 17 CFR 240.10D-1 (b)(1)(iv), for each current and former named executive officer and for all other current and former executive officers as a group, disclose the amount of recovery forgone and a brief description of the reason the listed registrant decided in each case not to pursue recovery; and

(iii) For each current and former named executive officer from whom, as of the end of the last completed fiscal year, erroneously awarded compensation had been outstanding for 180 days or longer since the date the registrant determined the amount the individual owed, disclose the dollar amount of outstanding erroneously awarded compensation due from each such individual.

(2) If at any time during or after its last completed fiscal year the registrant was required to prepare an accounting restatement, and the registrant concluded that recovery of erroneously awarded compensation was not required pursuant to the registrant's compensation recovery policy required by the listing standards adopted pursuant to 17 CFR 240.10D-1, briefly explain why application of the recovery policy resulted in this conclusion.

(3) The information must appear with, and in the same format as, the rest of the disclosure required to be provided pursuant to this Item 402. The information is required only in proxy or information statements that call for Item 402 disclosure and the registrant's annual report on Form 10-K, and will not be deemed to be incorporated by reference into any filing under the Securities Act, except to the extent that the listed registrant specifically incorporates it by reference.

(x) Disclosure of the registrant's policies and practices related to the grant of certain equity awards close in time to the release of material nonpublic information.

(1) Discuss the registrant's policies and practices on the timing of awards of options in relation to the disclosure of material nonpublic information by the registrant, including how the board determines when to grant such awards (for example, whether such awards are granted on a predetermined schedule); whether the board or compensation committee takes material nonpublic information into account when determining the timing and terms of such an award, and, if so, how the board or compensation committee takes material nonpublic information into account when determining the timing and terms of such an award; and whether the registrant has timed the disclosure of material nonpublic information for the purpose of affecting the value of executive compensation.

(2)(i) If, during the last completed fiscal year, the registrant awarded options to a named executive officer in the period beginning four business days before the filing of a periodic report on Form 10-Q (§249.308a of this chapter) or Form 10-K (§249.310 of this chapter), or the filing or furnishing of a current report on

Form 8-K (§ 249.308 of this chapter) that discloses material nonpublic information (other than a current report on Form 8-K disclosing a material new option award grant under Item 5.02(e) of that form), and ending one business day after the filing or furnishing of such report provide the information specified in paragraph (x)(2)(ii) of this section, concerning each such award for each of the named executive officers in the following tabular format:

Table 13 to paragraph (x)(2)(i)

Name (a)	*Grant date* (b)	*Number of securities underlying the award* (c)	*Exercise price of the award ($/Sh)* (d)	*Grant date fair value of the award* (e)	*Percentage change in the closing market price of the securities underlying the award between the trading day ending immediately prior to the disclosure of material nonpublic information and the trading day beginning immediately following the disclosure of material nonpublic information* (f)
PEO					
PFO					
A					
B					
C					

(ii) The Table shall include:

(A) The name of the named executive officer (column (a));

(B) On an award-by-award basis, the grant date of the option award reported in the table (column (b));

(C) On an award-by-award basis, the number of securities underlying the options, (column (c));

(D) On an award-by-award basis, the per-share exercise price of the options (column (d));

(E) On an award-by-award basis, the grant date fair value of each award computed using the same methodology as used for the registrant's financial statements under generally accepted accounting principles (column (e)).

(F) For each instrument reported in column (b), disclose the percentage change in the market price of the underlying securities between the closing market price of the security one trading day prior to and the trading day beginning immediately following the disclosure of material nonpublic information (column (f)).

Item 403. Security Ownership of Certain Beneficial Owners and Management

(a) *Security ownership of certain beneficial owners.* Furnish the following information, as of the most recent practicable date, substantially in the tabular form indicated, with respect to any person (including any "group" as that term is used in section 13(d)(3) of the Exchange Act) who is known to the registrant to be the beneficial owner of more than five percent of any class of the registrant's voting securities. The address given in column (2) may be a business, mailing or residence address. Show in column (3) the total number of shares beneficially owned and in column (4) the percentage of class so owned. Of the number of shares shown in column (3), indicate by footnote or otherwise the amount known to be shares with respect to which such listed beneficial owner has the right to acquire beneficial ownership, as specified in Rule 13d-3(d)(1) under the Exchange Act.

(1) Title of class	(2) Name and address of beneficial owner	(3) Amount and nature of beneficial ownership	(4) Percent of class

(b) *Security ownership of management.* Furnish the following information, as of the most recent practicable date, in substantially the tabular form indicated, as to each class of equity securities of the registrant or any of its parents or subsidiaries including directors' qualifying shares, beneficially owned by all directors and nominees, naming them, each of the named executive officers as defined in Item 402(a)(3), and directors and executive officers of the registrant as a group, without naming them. Show in column (3) the total number of shares beneficially owned and in column (4) the percent of the class so owned. Of the number of shares shown in column (3), indicate, by footnote or otherwise, the amount of shares that are pledged as security and the amount of shares with respect to which such persons have the right to acquire beneficial ownership as specified in Rule 13d-3(d)(1).

(1) Title of class	(2) Name of beneficial owner	(3) Amount and nature of beneficial ownership	(4) Percent of class

(c) *Changes in control.* Describe any arrangements, known to the registrant, including any pledge by any person of securities of the registrant or any of its parents, the operation of which may at a subsequent date result in a change in control of the registrant.

Item 404. Transactions with Related Persons, Promoters, and Certain Control Persons

(a) *Transactions with related persons.* Describe any transaction, since the beginning of the registrant's last fiscal year, or any currently proposed transaction, in which the registrant was or is to be a participant and the amount involved exceeds $120,000, and in which any related person had or will have a direct or indirect material interest. Disclose the following information regarding the transaction:

(1) The name of the related person and the basis on which the person is a related person.

(2) The related person's interest in the transaction with the registrant, including the related person's position(s) or relationship(s) with, or ownership in, a firm, corporation, or other entity that is a party to, or has an interest in, the transaction.

(3) The approximate dollar value of the amount involved in the transaction.

(4) The approximate dollar value of the amount of the related person's interest in the transaction, which shall be computed without regard to the amount of profit or loss.

(5) In the case of indebtedness, disclosure of the amount involved in the transaction shall include the largest aggregate amount of principal outstanding during the period for which disclosure is provided, the amount thereof outstanding as of the latest practicable date, the amount of principal paid during the periods for which disclosure is provided, the amount of interest paid during the period for which disclosure is provided, and the rate or amount of interest payable on the indebtedness.

(6) Any other information regarding the transaction or the related person in the context of the transaction that is material to investors in light of the circumstances of the particular transaction.

INSTRUCTIONS TO ITEM 404(a)

1. For the purposes of paragraph (a) of this Item, the term *related person* means:

a. Any person who was in any of the following categories at any time during the specified period for which disclosure under paragraph (a) of this Item is required:

i. Any director or executive officer of the registrant;

ii. Any nominee for director, when the information called for by paragraph (a) of this Item is being presented in a proxy or information statement relating to the election of that nominee for director; or

iiii. Any immediate family member of a director or executive officer of the registrant, or of any nominee for director when the information called for by paragraph (a) of this Item is being presented in a proxy or information statement relating to the election of that nominee for director, which means any child, stepchild, parent, stepparent, spouse, sibling, mother-in-law, father-in-law, son-in-law, daughter-in-law, brother-in-law, or sister-in-law of such director, executive officer or nominee for director, and any person (other than a tenant or employee) sharing the household of such director, executive officer or nominee for director; and

b. Any person who was in any of the following categories when a transaction in which such person had a direct or indirect material interest occurred or existed:

i. A security holder covered by Item 403(a) or

ii. Any immediate family member of any such security holder, which means any child, stepchild, parent, stepparent, spouse, sibling, mother-in-law, father-in-law, son-in-law, daughter-in-law, brother-in-law, or sister-in-law of such security holder, and any person (other than a tenant or employee) sharing the household of such security holder.

2. For purposes of paragraph (a) of this Item, a *transaction* includes, but is not limited to, any financial transaction, arrangement or relationship (including any indebtedness or guarantee of indebtedness) or any series of similar transactions, arrangements or relationships.

3. The amount involved in the transaction shall be computed by determining the dollar value of the amount involved in the transaction in question, which shall include:

a. In the case of any lease or other transaction providing for periodic payments or installments, the aggregate amount of all periodic payments or installments due on or after the beginning of the registrant's last fiscal year, including any required or optional payments due during or at the conclusion of the lease or other transaction providing for periodic payments or installments; and

b. In the case of indebtedness, the largest aggregate amount of all indebtedness outstanding at any time since the beginning of the registrant's last fiscal year and all amounts of interest payable on it during the last fiscal year.

4. In the case of a transaction involving indebtedness:

a. The following items of indebtedness may be excluded from the calculation of the amount of indebtedness and need not be disclosed: amounts due from the related person for purchases of goods and services subject to usual trade terms, for ordinary business travel and expense payments and for other transactions in the ordinary course of business;

b. Disclosure need not be provided of any indebtedness transaction for the related persons specified in Instruction 1.b. to paragraph (a) of this Item; and

c. If the lender is a bank, savings and loan association, or broker-dealer extending credit under Federal Reserve Regulation T and the loans are not disclosed as nonaccrual, past due, restructured or potential problems (see Item III.C.1. and 2. of Industry Guide 3, Statistical Disclosure by Bank Holding Companies), disclosure under paragraph (a) of this Item may consist of a statement, if such is the case, that the loans to such persons:

i. Were made in the ordinary course of business;

ii. Were made on substantially the same terms, including interest rates and collateral, as those prevailing at the time for comparable loans with persons not related to the lender; and

iii. Did not involve more than the normal risk of collectability or present other unfavorable features.

5.a. Disclosure of an employment relationship or transaction involving an executive officer and any related compensation solely resulting from that employment relationship or transaction need not be provided pursuant to paragraph (a) of this Item if:

i. The compensation arising from the relationship or transaction is reported pursuant to Item 402;

ii. The executive officer is not an immediate family member (as specified in Instruction 1 to paragraph (a) of this Item) and such compensation would have been reported under Item 402 as compensation earned for services to the registrant if the executive officer was a named executive officer as that term is defined in Item 402(a)(3), and such compensation had been approved, or recommended to the board of directors of the registrant for approval, by the compensation committee of the board of directors (or group of independent directors performing a similar function) of the registrant; or

iii. The transaction involves the recovery of erroneously awarded compensation computed as provided in Rule 10D-1(b)(1)(iii) and the applicable listing standard for registrant's securities disclosed pursuant to Item 402(w).

b. Disclosure of compensation to a director need not be provided pursuant to paragraph (a) of this Item if the compensation is reported pursuant to Item 402(k).

6. A person who has a position or relationship with a firm, corporation, or other entity that engages in a transaction with the registrant shall not be deemed to have an indirect material interest within the meaning of paragraph (a) of this Item where:

a. The interest arises only:

i. From such person's position as a director of another corporation or organization that is a party to the transaction; or

ii. From the direct or indirect ownership by such person and all other persons specified in Instruction 1 to paragraph (a) of this Item, in the aggregate, of less than a ten percent equity interest in another person (other than a partnership) which is a party to the transaction; or

iii. Form both such position and ownership; or

b. The interest arises only from such person's position as a limited partner in a partnership in which the person and all other persons specified in Instruction 1 to paragraph (a) of this Item, have an interest of less than ten percent, and the person is not a general partner of and does not hold another position in the partnership.

7. Disclosure need not be provided pursuant to paragraph (a) of this Item if:

a. The transaction is one where the rates or charges involved in the transaction are determined by competitive bids, or the transaction involves the rendering of services as a common or contract carrier, or public utility, at rates or charges fixed in conformity with law or governmental authority;

b. The transaction involves services as a bank depositary of funds, transfer agent, registrar, trustee under a trust indenture, or similar services; or

c. The interest of the related person arises solely from the ownership of a class of equity securities of the registrant and all holders of that class of equity securities of the registrant received the same benefit on a pro rata basis.

(b) *Review, approval, or ratification of transactions with related persons.*

(1) Describe the registrant's policies and procedures for the review, approval, or ratification of any transaction required to be reported under paragraph (a) of this Item. While the material features of such policies and procedures will vary depending on the particular circumstances, examples of such features may include, in given cases, among other things:

(i) The types of transactions that are covered by such policies and procedures;

(ii) The standards to be applied pursuant to such policies and procedures;

(iii) The persons or groups of persons on the board of directors or otherwise who are responsible for applying such policies and procedures; and

(iv) A statement of whether such policies and procedures are in writing and, if not, how such policies and procedures are evidenced.

(2) Identify any transaction required to be reported under paragraph (a) of this Item since the beginning of the registrant's last fiscal year where such policies and procedures did not require review, approval or ratification or where such policies and procedures were not followed.

Instruction to Item 404(b)

Disclosure need not be provided pursuant to this paragraph regarding any transaction that occurred at a time before the related person became one of the enumerated persons in Instruction 1. a.i., ii., or iii. to Item 404(a) if such transaction did not continue after the related person became one of the enumerated persons in Instruction 1.a.i., ii., or iii. to Item 404(a).

(c) *Promoters and certain control persons.*

(1) Registrants that are filing a registration statement on Form S-1 under the Securities Act or on Form 10 under the Exchange Act and that had a promoter at any time during the past five fiscal years shall:

(i) State the names of the promoter(s), the nature and amount of anything of value (including money, property, contracts, options or rights of any kind) received or to be received by each promoter, directly or indirectly, from the registrant and the nature and amount of any assets, services or other consideration therefore received or to be received by the registrant; and

(ii) As to any assets acquired or to be acquired by the registrant from a promoter, state the amount at which the assets were acquired or are to be acquired and the principle followed or to be followed in determining such amount, and identify the persons making the determination and their relationship, if any, with the registrant or any promoter. If the assets were acquired by the promoter within two years prior to their transfer to the registrant, also state the cost thereof to the promoter.

(2) Registrants shall provide the disclosure required by paragraphs (c)(1)(i) and (c)(1)(ii) of this Item as to any person who acquired control of a registrant that is a shell company, or any person that is part of a group, consisting of two or more persons that agree to act together for the purpose of acquiring, holding, voting or disposing of equity securities of a registrant, that acquired control of a registrant that is a shell company. For purposes of this Item, *shell company* has the same meaning as in Rule 405 under the Securities Act and Rule 12b-2 under the Exchange Act.

(d) *Smaller reporting companies.* A registrant that qualifies as a "smaller reporting company," as defined by Item 10(f)(1), must provide the following information in order to comply with this Item:

(1) The information required by paragraph (a) of this Item for the period specified there for a transaction in which the amount involved exceeds the lesser of $120,000 or one percent of the average of the smaller reporting company's total assets at year end for the last two completed fiscal years;

(2) The information required by paragraph (c) of this Item; and

(3) A list of all parents of the smaller reporting company showing the basis of control and as to each parent, the percentage of voting securities owned or other basis of control by its immediate parent, if any.

INSTRUCTION TO ITEM 404(d)

1. Include information for any material underwriting discounts and commissions upon the sale of securities by the smaller reporting company where any of the persons specified in paragraph (a) of this Item was or is to be a principal underwriter or is a controlling person or member of a firm that was or is to be a principal underwriter.

2. For smaller reporting companies information shall be given for the period specified in paragraph (a) of this Item and, in addition, for the fiscal year preceding the small reporting company's last fiscal year.

Item 405. Compliance with Section 16(a) of the Exchange Act

(a) *Reporting obligation.* Every registrant having a class of equity securities registered pursuant to Section 12 of the Exchange Act (15 U.S.C. 78l) and every closed-end investment company registered under the Investment Company Act of 1940 (15 U.S.C. 80a-1 et seq.) must:

(1) Under the caption "Delinquent Section 16(a) Reports," identify each person who, at any time during the fiscal year, was a director, officer, beneficial owner of more than ten percent of any class of equity securities of the registrant registered pursuant to Section 12 of the Exchange Act, or any other person subject to Section 16 of the Exchange Act with respect to the registrant because of the requirements of Section 30 of the Investment Company Act ("reporting person") that failed to file on a timely basis reports required by Section 16(a) of the Exchange Act during the most recent fiscal year or prior fiscal years.

(2) For each such person, set forth the number of late reports, the number of transactions that were not reported on a timely basis, and any known failure to file a required form. A known failure to file would include, but not be limited to, a failure to file a Form 3, which is required of all reporting persons, and a failure to file a Form 5 in the absence of the written representation referred to in paragraph (b)(3) of this section, unless the registrant otherwise knows that no Form 5 is required.

(b) *Scope of the Inquiry.* In determining whether disclosure is required pursuant to paragraph (a) of this section, the registrant may rely only on the following:

(1) A review of Forms 3 and 4 (17 CFR 249.103 and 249.104) and amendments thereto filed electronically with the Commission during the registrant's most recent fiscal year;

(2) A review of Forms 5 (17 CFR 249.105) and amendments thereto filed electronically with the Commission with respect to the registrant's most recent fiscal year; and

(3) Any written representation from the reporting person that no Form 5 is required. The registrant must maintain the representation in its records for two years, making a copy available to the Commission or its staff upon request.

Item 406. Code of Ethics

(a) Disclose whether the registrant has adopted a code of ethics that applies to the registrant's principal executive officer, principal financial officer, principal accounting officer or controller, or persons performing similar functions. If the registrant has not adopted such a code of ethics, explain why it has not done so.

(b) For purposes of this Item 406, the term *code of ethics* means written standards that are reasonably designed to deter wrongdoing and to promote:

(1) Honest and ethical conduct, including the ethical handling of actual or apparent conflicts of interest between personal and professional relationships;

(2) Full, fair, accurate, timely, and understandable disclosure in reports and documents that a registrant files with, or submits to, the Commission and in other public communications made by the registrant;

(3) Compliance with applicable governmental laws, rules and regulations;

(4) The prompt internal reporting of violations of the code to an appropriate person or persons identified in the code; and

(5) Accountability for adherence to the code.

(c) The registrant must:

(1) File with the Commission a copy of its code of ethics that applies to the registrant's principal executive officer, principal financial officer, principal accounting officer or controller, or persons performing similar functions, as an exhibit to its annual report;

(2) Post the text of such code of ethics on its Internet website and disclose, in its annual report, its Internet address and the fact that it has posted code of ethics on its Internet website; or

(3) Undertake in its annual report filed with the Commission to provide to any person without charge, upon request, a copy of such code of ethics and explain the manner in which such request may be made.

(d) If the registrant intends to satisfy the disclosure requirement under Item 5.05 of Form 8-K regarding an amendment to, or a waiver from, a provision of its code of ethics that applies to the registrant's principal executive officer, principal financial officer, principal accounting officer or controller, or persons performing similar functions and that relates to any element of the code of ethics definition enumerated in paragraph (b) of this Item by posting such information on its Internet website, disclose the registrant's Internet address and such intention.

Instructions to Item 406

1. A registrant may have separate codes of ethics for different types of officers. Furthermore, a *code of ethics* within the meaning of paragraph (b) of this Item may be a portion of a broader document that addresses additional topics or that applies to more persons than those specified in paragraph (a). In satisfying the requirements of paragraph (c), a registrant need only file, post or provide the portions of a broader document that constitutes a *code of ethics* as defined in paragraph (b) and that apply to the persons specified in paragraph (a).

2. If a registrant elects to satisfy paragraph (c) of this Item by posting its code of ethics on its website pursuant to paragraph (c)(2), the code of ethics must remain accessible on its website for as long as the registrant remains subject to requirements of this Item and chooses to comply with this Item by posting its code on its website pursuant to paragraph (c)(2).

Item 407. Corporate Governance

(a) *Director independence.* Identify each director and, when the disclosure called for by this paragraph is being presented in a proxy or information statement relating to the election of directors, each nominee for director, that is independent under the independence standards applicable to the registrant under paragraph (a)(1) of this Item. In addition, if such independence standards contain independence requirements for committees of the board of directors, identify each director that is a member of the compensation, nominating or audit committee that is not independent under such committee independence standards. If the registrant does not have a separately designated audit, nominating or compensation committee or committee performing similar functions, the registrant must provide the disclosure of directors that are not independent with respect to all members of the board of directors applying such committee independence standards.

(1) In determining whether or not the director or nominee for director is independent for the purposes of paragraph (a) of this Item, the registrant shall use the applicable definition of independence, as follows:

(i) If the registrant is a listed issuer whose securities are listed on a national securities exchange or in an inter-dealer quotation system which has requirements that a majority of the board of directors be independent, the registrant's definition of independence that it uses for determining if a majority of the board of directors is independent in compliance with the listing standards applicable to the registrant. When determining whether the members of a committee of the board of directors are independent, the registrant's definition of independence that it uses for determining if the members of that specific committee are independent in compliance with the independence standards applicable for the members of the specific committee in the listing standards of the national securities exchange or inter-dealer quotation system that the registrant uses for determining if a majority of the board of directors are independent. If the registrant does not have independence standards for a committee, the independence standards for that specific committee in the listing standards of the national securities exchange of inter-dealer quotation system that the registrant uses for determining if a majority of the board of directors are independent.

(ii) If the registrant is not a listed issuer, a definition of independence of a national securities exchange or of an inter-dealer quotation system which has requirements that a majority of the board of directors be independent, and state which definition is used. Whatever such definition the registrant chooses, it must use the same definition with respect to all directors and nominees for director. When determining whether the members of a specific committee of the board of directors are independent, if the national securities exchange or national securities association whose standards are used has independence standards for the members of a specific committee, use those committee specific standards.

(iii) If the information called for by paragraph (a) of this Item is being presented in a registration statement of Form S-1 under the Securities Act or on a Form 10 under the Exchange Act where the registrant has applied for listing with a national securities exchange or in an inter-dealer quotation system which has requirements that a majority of the board of directors be independent, the definition of independence that the registrant uses for determining if a majority of the board of directors is independent, and the definition of independence that the registrant uses for determining if members of the specific committee of the board of directors are independent, that is in compliance with the independence listing standards of the national securities exchange or inter-dealer quotation system on which it has applied for listing, or if the registrant has not adopted such definitions, the independence standards for determining if the majority of the board of directors is independent and if members of the committee of the board of directors are independent of that national securities exchange or inter-dealer quotation system.

(2) If the registrant uses its own definitions for determining whether its directors and nominees for director, and members of specific committees of the board of directors, are independent, disclose whether these definitions are available to security holders on the registrant's Web site. If so, provide the registrant's Web site address. If not, include a copy of these policies in an appendix to the registrant's proxy statement or information statement that is provided to security holders at least once every three fiscal years or if the policies have been materially amended since the beginning of the registrant's last fiscal year. If a current copy of the policies is not available to security holders on the registrant's Web site, and is not included as an appendix to the registrant's proxy statement or information statement, identify the most recent fiscal year in which the policies were so included in satisfaction of this requirement.

(3) For each director and nominee for director that is identified as independent, describe, by specific or type, any transactions, relationships or arrangements not disclosed pursuant to Item 404(a), or for investment companies, Item 22(b) of Schedule 14A, that were considered by the board of directors under the applicable independence definitions in determining that the director is independent.

INSTRUCTIONS TO ITEM 407(a)

1. If the registrant is a listed issuer whose securities are listed on a national securities exchange or in an inter-dealer quotation system which has requirement that a majority of the board of directors be independent, and also has exemptions to those requirements (for independence of majority of the board of directors or committee member independence) upon which the registrant relied, disclose the exemption relied upon and explain the basis for the registrant's conclusion that such exemption is applicable. The same disclosure should be provided if the registrant is not a listed issuer and the national securities exchange or inter-dealer quotation system selected by the registrant has exemptions that are applicable to the registrant. Any national securities exchange or inter-dealer quotation system which has requirements that at least 50 percent of the members of a small business issuer's board of directors must be independent shall be considered a national securities exchange or inter-dealer quotation system which has requirements that a majority of the board of directors be independent for the purposes of the disclosure required by paragraph (a) of this Item.

2. Registrants shall provide the disclosure required by paragraph (a) of this Item for any person who served as a director during any part of the last completed fiscal year, except that no information called for by paragraph (a) of this Item need be given in a registration statement filed at a time when the registrant is not subject to the reporting requirements of section 13(a) or 15(d) of the Exchange Act respecting any director who is no longer a director at the time of effectiveness of the registration statement.

3. The description of the specific categories or types of transactions, relationships or arrangements required by paragraph (a)(3) of this Item must be provided in such detail as is necessary to fully describe the nature of the transactions, relationships or arrangements.

(b) *Board meetings and committees; annual meeting attendance.*

(1) State the total number of meetings of the board of directors (including regularly scheduled and special meetings) which were held during the last full fiscal year. Name each incumbent director who during the last full fiscal year attended fewer than 75 percent of the aggregate of:

(i) The total number of meetings of the board of directors (held during the period for which he has been a director); and

(ii) The total number of meetings held by all committees of the board on which he served (during the periods that he served).

(2) Describe the registrant's policy, if any, with regard to board members' attendance at annual meetings of security holders and state the number of board members who attended the prior year's annual meeting.

INSTRUCTION TO ITEM 407(b)(2)

In lieu of providing the information required by paragraph (b)(2) of this Item in the proxy statement, the registrant may instead provide the registrant's Web site address where such information appears.

(3) State whether or not the registrant has standing audit, nominating and compensation committees of the board of directors, or committees performing similar functions. If the registrant has such committees, however designated, identify each committee member, state the number of committee meetings held by each such committee during the last fiscal year and describe briefly the functions performed by each such committee. Such disclosure need not be provided to the extent it is duplicative of disclosure provided in accordance with paragraph (c), (d), or (e) of this Item.

(c) *Nominating committee.* (1) If the registrant does not have a standing nominating committee or committee performing similar functions, state the basis for the view of the board of directors that it is appropriate for the registrant not to have such a committee and identify each director who participates in the consideration of director nominees.

(2) Provide the following information regarding the registrant's director nomination process:

(i) State whether or not the nominating committee has a charter. If the nominating committee has a charter, provide the disclosure required by Instruction 2 to this Item regarding the nominating committee charter;

(ii) If the nominating committee has a policy with regard to the consideration of any director candidates recommended by security holders, provide a description of the material elements of that policy, which shall include, but need not be limited to, a statement as to whether the committee will consider director candidates recommended by security holders;

(iii) If the nominating committee does not have a policy with regard to the consideration of any director candidates recommended by security holders, state that fact and state the basis for the view of the board of directors that it is appropriate for the registrant not to have such a policy;

(iv) If the nominating committee will consider candidates recommended by security holders, describe the procedures to be followed by security holders in submitting such recommendations;

(v) Describe any specific minimum qualifications that the nominating committee believes must be met by a nominating committee-recommended nominee for a position on the registrant's board of directors, and describe any specific qualities or skills that the nominating committee believes are necessary for one or more of the registrant's directors to possess;

(vi) Describe the nominating committee's process for identifying and evaluating nominees for director, including nominees recommended by security holders, and any differences in the manner in which the nominating committee evaluates nominees for director based on whether the nominee is recommended by a security holder, and whether, and if so how, the nominating committee (or the board) considers diversity in identifying nominees for director. If the nominating committee (or the board) has a policy with regard to the consideration of diversity in identifying director nominees, describe how this policy is implemented, as well as how the nominating committee (or the board) assessed the effectiveness of its policy;

(vii) With regard to each nominee approved by the nominating committee for inclusion on the registrant's proxy card (other than nominees who are executive officers or who are directors standing for re-election), state which one or more of the following categories of persons or entities recommended that nominee: security holder, non-management director, chief executive officer, other executive officer, third-party search firm, or other specified source. With regard to each such nominee approved by a nominating committee of an investment company, state which one or more of the following additional categories of persons or entities recommended that nominee: security holder, director, chief executive officer, other executive officer, or employee of the investment company's investment adviser, principal underwriter, or any affiliated person of the investment adviser or principal underwriter;

(viii) If the registrant pays a fee to any third party or parties to identify or evaluate or assist in identifying or evaluating potential nominees, disclose the function performed by each such third party; and

(ix) If the registrant's nominating committee received, by a date not later than the 120th calendar day before the date of the registrant's proxy statement released to security holders in connection with the previous year's annual meeting, a recommended nominee from a security holder that beneficially owned more than 5% of the registrant's voting common stock for at least one year as of the date the recommendation was made, or from a group of security holders that beneficially owned, in the aggregate, more than 5% of the registrant's voting common stock, with each of the securities used to calculate that ownership held for at least one year as of the date the recommendation was made, identify the candidate and the security holder or security holder group that recommended the candidate and disclose whether the nominating committee chose to nominate the candidate, *provided however*, that no such identification or disclosure is required without the written consent of both the security holder or security holder group and the candidate to be so identified.

Instructions to Item 407(c)(2)(ix)

1. For purposes of paragraph (c)(2)(ix) of this Item, the percentage of securities held by a nominating security holder may be determined using information set forth in the registrant's most recent quarterly or annual report, and any current report subsequent thereto, filed with the Commission pursuant to the Exchange Act (or, in the case of a registrant that is an investment company registered under the Investment Company Act of 1940, the registrant's most recent report on Form N-CSR, unless the party relying on such report knows or has reason to believe that the information contained therein is inaccurate.

2. For purposes of the registrant's obligation to provide the disclosure specified in paragraph (c)(2)(ix) of this Item, where the date of the annual meeting has been changed by more than 30 days form the date of the previous year's meeting, the obligation under that Item will arise where the registrant receives the security holder recommendation a reasonable time before the registrant begins to print and mail its proxy materials.

3. For purposes of paragraph (c)(2)(ix) of this Item, the percentage of securities held by a recommending security holder, as well as the holding period of those securities, may be determined by the registrant if the security holder is the registered holder of the securities. If the security holder is not the registered owner of the securities, he or she can submit one of the following to the registrant to evidence the required ownership percentage and holding period:

a. A written statement from the "record" holder of the securities (usually a broker or bank) verifying that, at the time the security holder made the recommendation, he or she had held the required securities for at least one year; or

b. If the security holder has filed a Schedule 13D, Schedule 13G, Form 3, Form 4, and/or Form 5, or amendments to those documents or updated forms, reflecting ownership of the securities as of or before the date of the recommendation, a copy of the schedule and/or form, and any subsequent amendments reporting a change in ownership level, as well as a written statement that the security holder continuously held the securities for the one-year period as of the date of the recommendation.

4. For purposes of the registrant's obligation to provide the disclosure specified in paragraph (c)(2)(ix) of this Item, the security holder or group must have provided to the registrant, at the time of the recommendation, the written consent of all parties to be identified and, where the security holder or group members are not registered holders, proof that the security holder or group satisfied the required ownership percentage and holding period as of the date of the recommendation.

Instruction to Item 407(c)(2)

For purposes of paragraph (c)(2) of this Item, the term *nominating committee* refers not only to nominating committees and committees performing similar functions, but also to groups of directors fulfilling the role of a nominating committee, including the entire board of directors.

(3) Describe any material changes to the procedures by which security holders may recommend nominees to the registrant's board of directors, where those changes were implemented after the registrant last provided disclosure in

response to the requirements of paragraph (c)(2)(iv) of this Item, or paragraph (c)(3) of this Item.

Instructions to Item 407(c)(3)

1. The disclosure required in paragraph (c)(3) of this Item need only be provided in a registrant's quarterly to annual reports.

2. For purposes of paragraph (c)(3) of this Item, adoption of procedures by which security holders may recommend nominees to the registrant's board of directors, where the registrant's most recent disclosure in response to the requirements of paragraph (c)(2)(iv) of this Item, or paragraph (c)(3) of this Item, indicated that the registrant did not have in place such procedures, will constitute a material change.

(d) *Audit committee*

(1) State whether or not audit committee has a charter. If the audit committee has a charter, provide the disclosure required by Instruction 2 to this Item regarding the audit committee charter.

(2) If a listed issuer's board of directors determines, in accordance with the listing standards applicable to the issuer, to appoint a director to the audit committee who is not independent (apart from the requirements in Rule 10A-3), including as a result of exceptional or limited or similar circumstances, disclose the nature of the relationship that makes that individual not independent and the reasons for the board of directors' determination.

(3)(i) The audit committee must state whether:

(A) The audit committee has reviewed and discussed the audited financial statements with management;

(B) The audit committee has discussed with the independent auditors the matters required to be discussed by the applicable requirements of the Public Company Accounting Oversight Board ("PCAOB") and the Commission;

(C) The audit committee has received the written disclosures and the letter from the independent accountant required by applicable requirements of the Public Company Accounting Oversight Board regarding the independent accountant's communications with the audit committee concerning independence, and has discussed with the independent accountant the independent accountant's independence; and

(D) Based on the review and discussions referred to in paragraphs (d)(3)(i)(A) through (d)(3)(i)(C) of this Item, the audit committee recommended to the board of directors that the audited financial statements be included in the company's annual report on Form 10-K (or, for closed end investment companies registered under the Investment Company Act of 1940, the annual report to shareholders required by section 30(e) of the Investment Company Act of 1940 and Rule 30d-1 thereunder) for the last fiscal year for filing with the Commission.

(ii) The name of each member of the company's audit committee (or, in the absence of an audit committee, the board committee performing equivalent functions or the entire board of directors) must appear below the disclosure required by paragraph (d)(3)(i) of this Item.

(4) (i) if the registrant meets the following requirements, provided the disclosure in paragraph (d) (4) (ii) of this Item:

(A) The registrant is a listed issuer, as defined in Rule 10A-3;

(B) The registrant is filing an annual report on Form 10-K or a proxy statement or information statement pursuant to the Exchange Act if action is to be taken with respect to the election of directors; and

(C) The registrant is neither:

(1) A subsidiary of another listed issuer that is relying on the exemption in Rule 10A-3(c) (2); nor

(2) Relying on any of the exemptions in Rule 10A-3(c) (4) through (c) (7) of this chapter.

(ii) (A) State whether or not the registrant has a separately-designated standing audit committee established in accordance with section 3(a) (58) (A) of the Exchange Act, or a committee performing similar functions. If the registrant has such a committee, however designated, identify each committee member. If the entire board of directors is acting as the registrant's audit committee as specified in section 3(a) (58) (B) of the Exchange Act, so state.

(B) If applicable, provide the disclosure required by Rule 10A-3(d) of this chapter regarding an exemption from the listing standards for audit committees.

(5) *Audit Committee financial expert.*

(i) (A) Disclose that the registrant's board of directors has determined that the registrant either:

(1) Has at least one audit committee financial expert serving on its audit committee; or

(2) Does not have an audit committee financial expert serving on its audit committee.

(B) If the registrant provides the disclosure required by paragraph (d) (5) (i) (A) (*1*) of this Item, it must disclose the name of the audit committee financial expert and whether that person is *independent*, as independence for audit committee members is defined in the listing standards applicable to the listed issuer.

(C) If the registrant provides the disclosure required by paragraph (d) (5) (i) (A) (*2*) of this Item, it must explain why it does not have an audit committee financial expert.

Instruction to Item 407(d) (5) (i)

If the registrant's board of directors has determined that the registrant has more than one audit committee financial expert serving on its audit committee, the registrant may, but is not required to, disclose the names of those additional persons. A registrant choosing to identify such persons must indicate whether they are independent pursuant to paragraph (d) (5) (i) (B) of this Item.

(ii) For purposes of this Item, an *audit committee financial expert* means a person who has the following attributes:

(A) An understanding of generally accepted accounting principles and financial statements;

(B) The ability to assess the general application of such principles in connection with the accounting for estimates, accruals, and reserves;

(C) Experience preparing, auditing, analyzing or evaluating financial statements that present a breadth and level of complexity of accounting issues that are generally comparable to the breadth and complexity of issues that can reasonably be expected to be raised by the registrant's financial statements, or experience actively supervising one or more persons engaged in such activities;

(D) An understanding of internal control over financial reporting; and

(E) An understanding of audit committee functions.

(iii) A person shall have acquired such attributes through:

(A) Education and experience as a principal financial officer, principal accounting officer, controller, public accountant or auditor or experience in one or more positions that involve the performance of similar functions;

(B) Experience actively supervising a principal financial officer, principal accounting officer, controller, public accountant, auditor or person performing similar functions;

(C) Experience overseeing or assessing the performance of companies or public accountants with respect to the preparation, auditing or evaluation of financial statements; or

(D) Other relevant experience.

(iv) *Safe harbor.*

(A) A person who is determined to be an audit committee financial expert will not be deemed an *expert* for any purpose, including without limitation for purposes of section 11 of the Securities Act, as a result of being designated or identified as an audit committee financial expert pursuant to this Item 407.

(B) The designation or identification of a person as an audit committee financial expert pursuant to this Item 407 does not impose on such person any duties, obligations or liability that are greater than the duties, obligations and liability imposed on such person as a member of the audit committee and board of directors is the absence of such designation or identification.

(C) The designation or identification of a person as an audit committee financial expert pursuant to this Item does not affect the duties, obligations or liability of any other member of the audit committee or board of directors.

Instructions to Item 407(d)(5)

1. The disclosure under paragraph (d)(5) of this Item is required only in a registrant's annual report. The registrant need not provide the disclosure required by paragraph (d)(5) of this Item in a proxy or information statement unless that registrant is electing to incorporate this information by reference from the proxy or information statement into its annual report pursuant to General Instruction G(3) to Form 10-K.

2. If a person qualifies as an audit committee financial expert by means of having held a position described in paragraph (d)(5)(iii)(D) of this Item, the registrant shall provide a brief listing of that person's relevant experience. Such disclosure may be made by reference to disclosures required under Item 401(e).

3. In the case of a foreign private issuer with a two-tier board of directors, for purposes of paragraph (d)(5) of this Item, the term *board of directors* means the supervisory or non-management board. In the case of a foreign private issuer meeting the requirements of Rule 10A-3(c)(3), for purposes of paragraph (d)(5) of this Item, the term *board of directors* means the issuer's board of auditors (or similar body) or statutory auditors, as applicable. Also, in the case of a foreign private issuer, the term *generally accepted accounting principles* in paragraph (d)(5)(ii)(A) of this Item means the body of generally accepted accounting principles used by that issuer in its primary financial statements filed with the Commission.

4. A registrant that is an Asset-Backed Issuer (as defined in Item 1101 of Regulation S-K) is not required to disclose the information required by paragraph (d)(5) of this Item.

Instruction to Item 407(d)

1. The information required by paragraph (d)(1)-(3) of this Item shall not be deemed to be "soliciting material," or to be "filed" with the Commission or subject to Regulation 14A or 14C, other than as provided in this Item, or to the liabilities of section 18 of the Exchange Act, except to the extent that the registrant specifically requests that the information be treated as soliciting material or specifically incorporates it by reference into a document filed under the Securities Act or the Exchange Act. Such information will not be deemed to be incorporated by reference into any filing under the Securities Act or the Exchange Act, except to the extent that the registrant specifically incorporates it by reference.

2. The disclosure required by paragraphs (d)(1)-(3) of this Item need only be provided one time during any fiscal year.

3. The disclosure required by paragraph (d)(3) of this Item need not be provided in any filings other than a registrant's proxy or information statement relating to an annual meeting of security holders at which directors are to be elected (or special meeting or written consents in lieu of such meeting).

(e) *Compensation committee.*

(1) If the registrant does not have a standing compensation committee or committee performing similar functions, state the basis for the view of the board of directors that it is appropriate for the registrant not to have such a committee and identify each director who participates in the consideration of executive officer and director compensation.

(2) State whether or not the compensation committee has a charter. If the compensation committee has a charter, provide the disclosure required by Instruction 2 to this Item regarding the compensation committee charter.

(3) Provide a narrative description of the registrant's processes and procedures for the consideration and determination of executive and director compensation, including:

(i)(A) The scope of authority of the compensation committee (or persons performing the equivalent functions); and

(B) The extent to which the compensation committee (or persons performing the equivalent functions) may delegate any authority described in paragraph (e)(3)(i)(A) of this Item to other persons, specifying what authority may be so delegated and to whom;

(ii) Any role of executive officers in determining or recommending the amount or form of executive and director compensation; and

(iii) Any role of compensation consultants in determining or recommending the amount or form of executive and director compensation (other than any role *limited* to consulting on any broad-based plan that does not discriminate in scope, terms, or operation, in favor of executive officers or directors of the registrant, and that is available generally to all salaried employees; or providing information that either is not customized for a particular registrant or that is customized based on parameters that are not developed by the compensation consultant, and about which the compensation consultant does not provide advice) during the registrant's last completed fiscal year, identifying such consultants, stating whether such consultants were engaged directly by the compensation committee (or persons performing the equivalent functions) or any other person, describing the nature and scope of their assignment, and the material elements of the instructions or directions given to the consultants with respect to the performance of their duties under the engagement:

(A) If such compensation consultant was engaged by the compensation committee (or persons performing the equivalent functions) to provide advice or recommendations on the amount or form of executive and director compensation (other than any role *limited* to consulting on any broad-based plan that does not discriminate in scope, terms, or operation, in favor of executive officers or directors of the registrant, and that is available generally to all salaried employees; or providing information that either is not customized for a particular registrant or that is customized based on parameters that are not developed by the compensation consultant, and about which the compensation consultant does not provide advice) and the compensation consultant or its affiliates also provided additional services to the registrant or its affiliates in an amount in excess of $120,000 during the registrant's last completed fiscal year, then disclose the aggregate fees for determining or recommending the amount or form of executive and director compensation and the aggregate fees for such additional services. Disclose whether the decision to engage the compensation consultant or its affiliates for these other services was made, or recommended, by management, and whether the compensation committee or the board approved such other services of the compensation consultant or its affiliates.

(B) If the compensation committee (or persons performing the equivalent functions) has not engaged a compensation consultant, but management has engaged a compensation consultant to provide advice or recommendations on the amount or form of executive and director compensation (other than any role *limited* to consulting on any broad-based plan that does not discriminate in scope, terms, or operation, in favor of executive officers or directors of the registrant, and that is available generally to all salaried employees; or providing information that either is not customized for a particular registrant or that is customized based on parameters that are not developed by the compensation consultant, and about which the compensation consultant does not provide advice) and such compensation consultant or its affiliates has provided additional services to the registrant in an amount in excess of $120,000 during the registrant's last completed fiscal year, then disclose the aggregate fees for determining or recommending the amount or form of executive and director compensation and the aggregate fees for any additional services provided by the compensation consultant or its affiliates.

(iv) With regard to any compensation consultant identified in response to Item 407(e)(3)(iii) whose work has raised a conflict of interest, disclose the nature of the conflict and how the conflict is being addressed.

(4) Under the caption "Compensation Committee Interlocks and Insider Participation":

(i) Identify each person who served as a member of the compensation committee of the registrant's board of directors (or board committee performing equivalent functions) during the last completed fiscal year, indicating each committee member who:

(A) Was, during the fiscal year, an officer or employee of the registrant;

(B) Was formerly an officer of the registrant; or

(C) Had any relationship requiring disclosure by the registrant under any paragraph of Item 404. In this event, the disclosure required by Item 404 shall accompany such identification.

(ii) If the registrant has no compensation committee (or other board committee performing equivalent functions), the registrant shall identify each officer and employee of the registrant, and any former officer of the registrant, who, during the last completed fiscal year, participated in deliberations of the registrant's board of directors concerning executive officer compensation.

(iii) Describe any of the following relationship that existed during the last completed fiscal year:

(A) An executive officer of the registrant served as a member of the compensation committee (or other board committee performing equivalent functions or,

in the absence of any committee, the entire board of directors) of another entity, one of whose executive officers served on the compensation committee (or other board committee performing equivalent functions or, in the absence of any such committee, the entire board of directors) of the registrant;

(B) An executive officer of the registrant served as a director of another entity, one of whose executive officers served on the compensation committee (or other board committee performing equivalent functions or, in the absence of any such committee, the entire board of directors) of the registrant; and

(C) An executive officer of the registrant served as a member of the compensation committee (or other board committee performing equivalent functions or, in the absence of any such committee, the entire board of directors) of another entity, one of whose executive officers served as a director of the registrant.

(iv) Disclosure required under paragraph (e)(4)(iii) of this Item regarding a compensation committee member or other director of the registrant who also served as an executive officer of another entity shall be accompanied by the disclosure called for by Item 404 with respect to that person.

Instruction to Item 407(e)(4)

For purposes of paragraph (e)(4) of this Item, the term *entity* shall not include an entity exempt from tax under section 501(c)(3) of the Internal Revenue Code.

(5) Under the caption "Compensation Committee Report:"

(i) The compensation committee (or other board committee performing equivalent functions or, in the absence of any such committee, the entire board of directors) must state whether:

(A) The compensation committee has reviewed and discussed the Compensation Discussion and Analysis required by Item 402(b) with management; and

(B) Based on the review and discussions referred to in paragraph (e)(5)(i)(A) of this Item, the compensation committee recommended to the board of directors that the Compensation Discussion and Analysis be included in the registrant's annual report on Form 10-K, proxy statement on Schedule 14A or information statement on Schedule 14C.

(ii) The name of each member of the registrant's compensation committee (or other board committee performing equivalent functions or, in the absence of any such committee, the entire board of directors) must appear below the disclosure required by paragraph (e)(5)(i) of this Item.

Instructions to Item 407(e)(5)

1. The information required by paragraph (e)(5) of this Item shall not be deemed to be "soliciting material," or to be "filed" with the Commission or subject to Regulation 14A or 14C, other than as provided in this Item, or to the liabilities of section 18 of the Exchange Act, except to the extent that the registrant specifically requests that the information be treated as soliciting material or specifically incorporates it by reference into a document filed under the Securities Act or the Exchange Act.

2. The disclosure required by paragraph (e)(5) of this Item need not be provided in any filings other than an annual report of Form 10-K, a proxy statement on Schedule 14A or an information statement on Schedule 14C, Such information will not be deemed to be incorporated by reference into any filing under the Securities Act or the Exchange Act, except to the extent that the registrant specifically incorporates it by reference. If the registrant elects to incorporate this information by reference from the proxy or information statement into its annual report on Form 10-K pursuant to General Instruction G(3) to Form 10-K, the disclosure required by paragraph (e)(5) of this Item will be deemed furnished in the annual report on Form 10-K and will not be deemed incorporated by reference into any filing under the Securities Act or the Exchange Act as a result of furnishing the disclosure in this manner.

3. The disclosure required by paragraph (e)(5) of this Item need only be provided one time during any fiscal year.

(f) *Shareholder communications.*

(1) State whether or not the registrant's board of directors provides a process for security holders to send communications to the board of directors and, if the registrant does not have such a process for security holders to send communications to the board of directors, state the basis for the view of the board of directors that it is appropriate for the registrant not to have such a process.

(2) If the registrant has a process for security holders to send communications to the board of directors:

(i) Describe the manner in which security holders can send communications to the board and, if applicable, to specified individual directors; and

(ii) If all security holder communications are not sent directly to board members, describe the registrant's process for determining which communications will be relayed to board members.

Instructions to Item 407(f)

1. In lieu of providing the information required by paragraph (f)(2) of this Item in the proxy statement, the registrant may instead provide the registrant's Web site address where such information appears.

2. For purposes of the disclosure required by paragraph (f)(2)(ii) of this Item, a registrant's process for collecting and organizing security holder communications, as well as similar or related activities, need not be disclosed provided that the registrant's process is approved by a majority of the independent directors or, in the case of a registrant that is an investment company, a majority of the directors who are not "interested persons" of the investment company as defined in section 2(a)(19) of the Investment Company Act of 1940.

3. For purposes of this paragraph, communications from an officer or director of the registrant will not be viewed as "security holder communications." Communications from an employee or agent of the registrant will be viewed as "security holder communications" for purposes of this paragraph only if those communications are made solely in such employee's or agent's capacity as a security holder.

4. For purposes of this paragraph, security holder proposals submitted pursuant to Rule 14a-8 of this chapter, and communications made in connection with such proposals, will not be viewed as "security holder communications."

(g) *Smaller reporting companies and emerging growth companies.* (1) A registrant that qualifies as a "smaller reporting company," as defined by Item 10(f)(1), is not required to provide:

(i) The disclosure required in paragraph (d)(5) of this Item in its first annual report filed pursuant to Section 13(a) or 15(d) of the Exchange Act; and

(ii) The disclosure required by paragraphs (e)(4) and (e)(5) of this Item.

(2) A registrant that qualifies as an "emerging growth company," as defined in Rule 405 of the Securities Act or Rule 12b-2 of the Exchange Act, is not required to provide the disclosure required by paragraph (e)(5) of this Item.

(h) *Board leadership structure and role in risk oversight.* Briefly describe the leadership structure of the registrant's board, such as whether the same person serves as both principal executive officer and chairman of the board, or whether two individuals serve in those positions, and, in the case of a registrant that is an investment company, whether the chairman of the board is an "interested person" of the registrant as defined in section 2(a)(19) of the Investment Company Act (15 U.S.C. 80a-2(a)(19)). If one person serves as both principal executive officer and chairman of the board, or if the chairman of the board of a registrant that is an investment company is an "interested person" of the registrant, disclose whether the registrant has a lead independent director and what specific role the lead independent director plays in the leadership of the board. This disclosure should indicate why the registrant has determined that its leadership structure is appropriate given the specific characteristics or circumstances of the registrant. In addition, disclose the extent of the board's role in the risk oversight of the registrant, such as how the board administers its oversight function, and the effect that this has on the board's leadership structure.

(i) *Employee, officer and director hedging.* In proxy or information statements with respect to the election of directors:

(1) Describe any practices or policies that the registrant has adopted regarding the ability of employees (including officers) or directors of the registrant, or any of their designees, to purchase financial instruments (including prepaid variable forward contracts, equity swaps, collars, and exchange funds), or otherwise engage in transactions, that hedge or offset, or are designed to hedge or offset, any decrease in the market value of registrant equity securities—

(i) Granted to the employee or director by the registrant as part of the compensation of the employee or director; or

(ii) Held, directly or indirectly, by the employee or director.

(2) A description provided pursuant to paragraph (1) shall provide a fair and accurate summary of the practices or policies that apply, including the categories of persons covered, or disclose the practices or policies in full.

(3) A description provided pursuant to paragraph (1) shall also describe any categories of hedging transactions that are specifically permitted and any categories of such transactions specifically disallowed.

(4) If the registrant does not have any such practices or policies regarding hedging, the registrant shall disclose that fact or state that the transactions described in paragraph (1) above are generally permitted.

Instructions to Item 407

1. For purposes of this Item:

a. *Listed issuer* means a listed issuer as defined in Rule 10A-3 of this chapter;

b. *National securities exchange* means a national securities exchange registered pursuant to section 6(a) of the Exchange Act;

c. *Inter-dealer quotation system* means an automated inter-dealer quotation system of a national securities association registered pursuant to section 15A(a) of the Exchange Act; and

d. *National securities association* means a national securities association registered pursuant to section 15A(a) of the Exchange Act that has been approved by the Commission (as that definition may be modified or supplemented).

2. With respect to paragraphs (c)(2)(i), (d)(1) and (e)(2) of this Item, disclose whether a current copy of the applicable committee charter is available to security holders on the

registrant's Web site, and if so, provide the registrant's Web site address. If a current copy of the charter is not available to security holders on the registrant's Web site, include a copy of the charter in an appendix to the registrant's proxy or information statement that is provided to security holders at least once every three fiscal years, or if the charter has been materially amended since the beginning of the registrant's last fiscal year. If a current copy of the charter is not available to security holders on the registrant's Web site, and is not included as an appendix to the registrant' proxy or information statement, identify in which of the prior fiscal years the charter was so included in satisfaction of this requirement.

Item 408. Insider Trading Arrangements and Policies

(a)(1) Disclose whether, during the registrant's last fiscal quarter (the registrant's fourth fiscal quarter in the case of an annual report), any director or officer (as defined in §240.16a-1(f) of this chapter) adopted or terminated:

(i) Any contract, instruction or written plan for the purchase or sale of securities of the registrant intended to satisfy the affirmative defense conditions of Rule 10b5-1(c) (§240.10b5-1(c) of this chapter) (a "Rule 10b5-1 trading arrangement"); and/or

(ii) Any "non-Rule 10b5-1 trading arrangement" as defined in paragraph (c) of this section.

(2) Identify whether the trading arrangement is intended to satisfy the affirmative defense of Rule 10b5-1(c), and provide a description of the material terms, other than terms with respect to the price at which the individual executing the Rule 10b5-1 trading arrangement or non-Rule 10b5-1 trading arrangement is authorized to trade, such as:

(A) The name and title of the director or officer;

(B) The date on which the director or officer adopted or terminated the trading arrangement;

(C) The duration of the trading arrangement; and

(D) The aggregate number of securities to be purchased or sold pursuant to the trading arrangement.

(3) The disclosure provided pursuant to paragraphs (a)(1) and (2) of this section must be provided in an Interactive Data File as required by 17 CFR 232.405 (Rule 405 of Regulation S-T) in accordance with the EDGAR Filer Manual.

(b)(1) Disclose whether the registrant has adopted insider trading policies and procedures governing the purchase, sale, and/or other dispositions of the registrant's securities by directors, officers and employees, or the registrant itself, that are reasonably designed to promote compliance with insider trading laws, rules and regulations, and any listing standards applicable to the registrant. If the registrant has not adopted such policies and procedures, explain why it has not done so.

(2) If the registrant has adopted insider trading policies and procedures, the registrant must file such policies and procedures as an exhibit. If all of the registrant's insider trading policies and procedures are included in its code of ethics (as defined in 17 CFR 229.406(b)) and the code of ethics is filed as an exhibit pursuant to 17 CFR 229.406(c)(1), that would satisfy the exhibit requirement of this paragraph.

(3) The disclosure provided pursuant to paragraph (b)(1) of this section must be provided in an Interactive Data File as required by 17 CFR 232.405 in accordance with the EDGAR Filer Manual.

(c) For purposes of this Item 408, a director or officer (as defined in §240.16a-1(f) of this chapter) (each a "covered person") has entered into a non-Rule 10b5-1 trading arrangement where:

(1) The covered person asserts that at a time when they were not aware of material nonpublic information about the security or the issuer of the security they had adopted a written arrangement for trading the securities; and

(2) The trading arrangement:

(i) Specified the amount of securities to be purchased or sold and the price at which and the date on which the securities were to be purchased or sold;

(ii) Included a written formula or algorithm, or computer program, for determining the amount of securities to be purchased or sold and the price at which and the date on which the securities were to be purchased or sold; or

(iii) Did not permit the covered person to exercise any subsequent influence over how, when, or whether to effect purchases or sales; provided, in addition, that any other person who, pursuant to the trading arrangement, did exercise such influence must not have been aware of material nonpublic information when doing so.

SUBPART 1000 — MERGERS AND ACQUISITIONS (REGULATION M-A)

Item 1000. Definitions

The following definitions apply to the terms used in Regulation M-A, unless specified otherwise:

(a) *Associate* has the same meaning as in Rule 12b-2 of this chapter;

(b) *Instruction C* means General Instruction C to Schedule 13E-3 and General Instruction C to Schedule TO;

(c) *Issuer tender offer* has the same meaning as in Rule 13e-4(a)(2) of this chapter;

(d) *Offeror* means any person who makes a tender offer or on whose behalf a tender offer is made;

(e) *Rule 13e-3 transaction* has the same meaning as in Rule 13e-3(a)(3) of this chapter;

(f) *Subject company* means the company or entity whose securities are sought to be acquired in the transaction (*e.g.*, the target), or that is otherwise the subject of the transaction;

(g) *Subject securities* means the securities or class of securities that are sought to be acquired in the transaction or that are otherwise the subject of the transaction; and

(h) *Third-party tender offer* means a tender offer that is not an issuer tender offer.

Item 1001. Summary Term Sheet

Summary term sheet. Provide security holders with a summary term sheet that is written in plain English. The summary term sheet must briefly describe in bullet point format the most material terms of the proposed transaction. The summary term sheet must provide security holders with sufficient information to understand the essential features and significance of the proposed transaction. The bullet points must cross-reference a more detailed discussion contained in the disclosure document that is disseminated to security holders.

Item 1002. Subject Company Information

(a) *Name and address.* State the name of the subject company (or the issuer in the case of an issuer tender offer), and the address and telephone number of its principal executive offices.

(b) *Securities.* State the exact title and number of shares outstanding of the subject class of equity securities as of the most recent practicable date. This may be based upon information in the most recently available filing with the Commission by the subject company unless the filing person has more current information.

(c) *Trading market and price.* Identify the principal market in which the subject securities are traded and state the high and low sales prices for the subject securities in the principal market (or, if there is no principal market, the range of high and low bid quotations and the source of the quotations) for each quarter during the past two years. If there is no established trading market for the securities (except for limited or sporadic quotations), so state.

(d) *Dividends.* State the frequency and amount of any dividends paid during the past two years with respect to the subject securities. Briefly describe any restriction on the subject company's current or future ability to pay dividends. If the filing person is not the subject company, furnish this information to the extent known after making reasonable inquiry.

(e) *Prior public offerings.* If the filing person has made an underwritten public offering of the subject securities for cash during the past three years that was registered under the Securities Act of 1933 or exempt from registration under Regulation A, state the date of the offering, the amount of securities offered, the offering price per share (adjusted for stock splits, stock dividends, etc. as appropriate) and the aggregate proceeds received by the filing person.

(f) *Prior stock purchases.* If the filing person purchased any subject securities during the past two years, state the amount of the securities purchased, the range of prices paid and the average purchase price for each quarter during that period. Affiliates need not give information for purchases made before becoming an affiliate.

Item 1003. Identity and Background of Filing Person

(a) *Name and address.* State the name, business address and business telephone number of each filing person. Also state the name and address of each person specified in Instruction C to the schedule (except for Schedule 14D-9). If the filing person is an affiliate of the subject company, state the nature of the affiliation. If the filing person is the subject company, so state.

(b) *Business and background of entities.* If any filing person (other than the subject company) or any person specified in Instruction C to the schedule is not a natural person, state the person's principal business, state or other place of organization, and the information required by paragraphs (c)(3) and (c)(4) of this section for each person.

(c) *Business and background of natural persons.* If any filing person or any person specified in Instruction C to the schedule is a natural person, provide the following information for each person:

(1) Current principal occupation or employment and the name, principal business and address of any corporation or other organization in which the employment or occupation is conducted;

(2) Material occupations, positions, offices or employment during the past five years, giving the starting and ending dates of each and the name, principal business and address of any corporation or other organization in which the occupation, position, office or employment was carried on;

(3) A statement whether or not the person was convicted in a criminal proceeding during the past five years (excluding traffic violations or similar misdemeanors). If the person was convicted, describe the criminal proceeding, including the dates, nature of conviction, name and location of court, and penalty imposed or other disposition of the case;

(4) A statement whether or not the person was a party to any judicial or administrative proceeding during the past five years (except for matters that were dismissed without sanction or settlement) that resulted in a judgment, decree or final order enjoining the person from future violations of, or prohibiting activities subject to, federal or state securities laws, or a finding of any violation of federal or state securities laws. Describe the proceeding, including a summary of the terms of the judgment, decree or final order; and

(5) Country of citizenship.

(d) *Tender offer.* Identify the tender offer and the class of securities to which the offer relates, the name of the offeror and its address (which may be based on the offeror's Schedule TO filed with the Commission).

Item 1004. Terms of the Transaction

(a) *Material terms.* State the material terms of the transaction.

(1) *Tender offers.* In the case of a tender offer, the information must include:

(i) The total number and class of securities sought in the offer;

(ii) The type and amount of consideration offered to security holders;

(iii) The scheduled expiration date;

(iv) Whether a subsequent offering period will be available, if the transaction is a third-party tender offer;

(v) Whether the offer may be extended, and if so, how it could be extended;

(vi) The dates before and after which security holders may withdraw securities tendered in the offer;

(vii) The procedures for tendering and withdrawing securities;

(viii) The manner in which securities will be accepted for payment;

(ix) If the offer is for less than all securities of a class, the periods for accepting securities on a pro rata basis and the offeror's present intentions in the event that the offer is oversubscribed;

(x) An explanation of any material differences in the rights of security holders as a result of the transaction, if material;

(xi) A brief statement as to the accounting treatment of the transaction, if material; and

(xii) The federal income tax consequences of the transaction, if material.

(2) *Mergers or similar transactions.* In the case of a merger or similar transaction, the information must include:

(i) A brief description of the transaction;

(ii) The consideration offered to security holders;

(iii) The reasons for engaging in the transaction;

(iv) The vote required for approval of the transaction;

(v) An explanation of any material differences in the rights of security holders as a result of the transaction, if material;

(vi) A brief statement as to the accounting treatment of the transaction, if material; and

(vii) The federal income tax consequences of the transaction, if material.

(b) *Purchases.* State whether any securities are to be purchased from any officer, director or affiliate of the subject company and provide the details of each transaction.

(c) *Different terms.* Describe any term or arrangement in the Rule 13e-3 transaction that treats any subject security holders differently from other subject security holders.

(d) *Appraisal rights.* State whether or not dissenting security holders are entitled to any appraisal rights. If so, summarize the appraisal rights. If there are no appraisal rights available under state law for security holders who object to the transaction, briefly outline any other rights that may be available to security holders under the law.

(e) *Provisions for unaffiliated security holders.* Describe any provision made by the filing person in connection with the transaction to grant unaffiliated security holders access to the corporate files of the filing person or to obtain counsel or appraisal services at the expense of the filing person. If none, so state.

(f) *Eligibility for listing or trading.* If the transaction involves the offer of securities of the filing person in exchange for equity securities held by unaffiliated security holders of the subject company, describe whether or not the filing person will take steps to assure that the securities offered are or will be eligible for trading on an automated quotations system operated by a national securities association.

Item 1005. Past Contacts, Transactions, Negotiations and Agreements

(a) *Transactions.* Briefly state the nature and approximate dollar amount of any transaction, other than those described in paragraphs (b) or (c) of this section, that occurred during the past two years, between the filing person (including any person specified in Instruction C of the schedule) and;

(1) The subject company or any of its affiliates that are not natural persons if the aggregate value of the transactions is more than one percent of the subject company's consolidated revenues for:

(i) The fiscal year when the transaction occurred; or

(ii) The past portion of the current fiscal year, if the transaction occurred in the current year; and

INSTRUCTION TO ITEM 1005(a)(1):

The information required by this Item may be based on information in the subject company's most recent filing with the Commission, unless the filing person has reason to believe the information is not accurate.

(2) Any executive officer, director or affiliate of the subject company that is a natural person if the aggregate value of the transaction or series of similar transactions with that person exceeds $60,000.

(b) *Significant corporate events.* Describe any negotiations, transactions or material contacts during the past two years between the filing person (including subsidiaries of the filing person and any person specified in Instruction C of the schedule) and the subject company or its affiliates concerning any:

(1) Merger;

(2) Consolidation;

(3) Acquisition;

(4) Tender offer for or other acquisition of any class of the subject company's securities;

(5) Election of the subject company's directors; or

(6) Sale or other transfer of a material amount of assets of the subject company.

(c) *Negotiations or contacts.* Describe any negotiations or material contacts concerning the matters referred to in paragraph (b) of this section during the past two years between:

(1) Any affiliates of the subject company; or

(2) The subject company or any of its affiliates and any person not affiliated with the subject company who would have a direct interest in such matters.

INSTRUCTION TO PARAGRAPHS (B) AND (C) OF ITEM 1005

Identify the person who initiated the contacts or negotiations.

(d) *Conflicts of interest.* If material, describe any agreement, arrangement or understanding and any actual or potential conflict of interest between the filing person or its affiliates and:

(1) The subject company, its executive officers, directors or affiliates; or

(2) The offeror, its executive officers, directors or affiliates.

INSTRUCTION TO ITEM 1005(d)

If the filing person is the subject company, no disclosure called for by this paragraph is required in the document disseminated to security holders, so long as substantially the same information was filed with the Commission previously and disclosed in a proxy statement, report or other communication sent to security holders by the subject company in the past year. The document disseminated to security holders, however, must refer specifically to the discussion in the proxy statement, report or other communication that was sent to security holders previously. The information also must be filed as an exhibit to the schedule.

(e) *Agreements involving the subject company's securities.* Describe any agreement, arrangement, or understanding, whether or not legally enforceable, between the filing person (including any person specified in Instruction C of the schedule) and any other person with respect to any securities of the subject company. Name all persons that are a party to the agreements, arrangements, or understandings and describe all material provisions.

INSTRUCTIONS TO ITEM 1005(e)

1. The information required by this Item includes: the transfer or voting of securities, joint ventures, loan or option arrangements, puts or calls, guarantees of loans, guarantees against loss, or the giving or withholding of proxies, consents or authorizations.

2. Include information for any securities that are pledged or otherwise subject to a contingency, the occurrence of which would give another person the power to direct the voting or disposition of the subject securities. No disclosure, however, is required about standard default and similar provisions contained in loan agreements.

Item 1006. Purposes of the Transaction and Plans or Proposals

(a) *Purposes.* State the purposes of the transaction.

(b) *Use of securities acquired.* Indicate whether the securities acquired in the transaction will be retained, retired, held in treasury, or otherwise disposed of.

(c) *Plans.* Describe any plans, proposals or negotiations that relate to or would result in:

(1) Any extraordinary transaction, such as a merger, reorganization or liquidation, involving the subject company or any of its subsidiaries;

(2) Any purchase, sale or transfer of a material amount of assets of the subject company or any of its subsidiaries;

(3) Any material change in the present dividend rate or policy, or indebtedness or capitalization of the subject company;

(4) Any change in the present board of directors or management of the subject company, including, but not limited to, any plans or proposals to change the number or the term of directors or to fill any existing vacancies on the board or to change any material term of the employment contract of any executive officer;

(5) Any other material change in the subject company's corporate structure or business, including, if the subject company is a registered closed-end investment company, any plans or proposals to make any changes in its investment policy for which a vote would be required by Section 13 of the Investment Company Act of 1940;

(6) Any class of equity securities of the subject company to be delisted from a national securities exchange or cease to be authorized to be quoted in an automated quotations system operated by a national securities association;

(7) Any class of equity securities of the subject company becoming eligible for termination of registration under Section 12(g)(4) of the Act;

(8) The suspension of the subject company's obligation to file reports under Section 15(d) of the Act;

(9) The acquisition by any person of additional securities of the subject company, or the disposition of securities of the subject company; or

(10) Any changes in the subject company's charter, bylaws or other governing instruments or other actions that could impede the acquisition of control of the subject company.

(d) *Subject company negotiations.* If the filing person is the subject company:

(1) State whether or not that person is undertaking or engaged in any negotiations in response to the tender offer that relate to:

(i) A tender offer or other acquisition of the subject company's securities by the filing person, any of its subsidiaries, or any other person; or

(ii) Any of the matters referred to in paragraphs (c)(1) through (c)(3) of this section; and

(2) Describe any transaction, board resolution, agreement in principle, or signed contract that is entered into in response to the tender offer that relates to one or more of the matters referred to in paragraph (d)(1) of this section.

Instruction to Item 1006(d)(1)

If an agreement in principle has not been reached at the time of filing, no disclosure under paragraph (d)(1) of this section is required of the possible terms of or the parties to the transaction if in the opinion of the board of directors of the subject company disclosure would jeopardize continuation of the negotiations. In that case, disclosure indicating that negotiations are being undertaken or are underway and are in the preliminary stages is sufficient.

Item 1007. Source and Amount of Funds or Other Consideration

(a) *Source of funds.* State the specific sources and total amount of funds or other consideration to be used in the transaction. If the transaction involves a tender offer, disclose the amount of funds or other consideration required to purchase the maximum amount of securities sought in the offer.

(b) *Conditions.* State any material conditions to the financing discussed in response to paragraph (a) of this section. Disclose any alternative financing arrangements or alternative financing plans in the event the primary financing plans fall through. If none, so state.

(c) *Expenses.* Furnish a reasonably itemized statement of all expenses incurred or estimated to be incurred in connection with the transaction including, but not limited to, filing, legal, accounting and appraisal fees, solicitation expenses and printing costs and state whether or not the subject company has paid or will be responsible for paying any or all expenses.

(d) *Borrowed funds.* If all or any part of the funds or other consideration required is, or is expected, to be borrowed, directly or indirectly, for the purpose of the transaction:

(1) Provide a summary of each loan agreement or arrangement containing the identity of the parties, the term, the collateral, the stated and effective interest rates, and any other material terms or conditions of the loan; and

(2) Briefly describe any plans or arrangements to finance or repay the loan, or, if no plans or arrangements have been made, so state.

Instruction to Item 1007(d)

If the transaction is a third-party tender offer and the source of all or any part of the funds used in the transaction is to come from a loan made in the ordinary course of business by a bank as defined by Section 3(a)(6) of the Act, the name of the bank will not be made available to the public if the filing person so requests in writing and files the request, naming the bank, with the Secretary of the Commission.

Item 1008. Interest in Securities of the Subject Company

(a) *Securities ownership.* State the aggregate number and percentage of subject securities that are beneficially owned by each person named in response to Item 1003 of Regulation M-A and by each associate and majority-owned subsidiary of those persons. Give the name and address of any associate or subsidiary.

(b) *Securities transactions.* Describe any transaction in the subject securities during the past 60 days. The description of transactions required must include, but not necessarily be limited to:

(1) The identity of the persons specified in the Instruction to this section who effected the transaction;

(2) The date of the transaction;

(3) The amount of securities involved;

(4) The price per share; and

(5) Where and how the transaction was effected.

Instructions to Item 1008(b)

1. Provide the required transaction information for the following persons:

(a) The filing person (for all schedules);

(b) Any person named in Instruction C of the schedule and any associate or majority-owned subsidiary of the issuer or filing person (for all schedules except Schedule 14D-9);

(c) Any executive officer, director, affiliate or subsidiary of the filing person (for Schedule 14D-9);

(d) The issuer and any executive officer or director of any subsidiary of the issuer or filing person (for an issuer tender offer on Schedule TO); and

(e) The issuer and any pension, profit-sharing or similar plan of the issuer or affiliate filing the schedule (for a going-private transaction on Schedule 13E-3).

2. Provide the information required by this Item if it is available to the filing person at the time the statement is initially filed with the Commission. If the information is not initially available, it must be obtained and filed with the Commission promptly, but in no event later than three business days after the date of the initial filing, and if material, disclosed in a manner reasonably designed to inform security holders. The procedure specified by this instruction

is provided to maintain the confidentiality of information in order to avoid possible misuse of inside information.

Item 1009. Persons/Assets, Retained, Employed, Compensated or Used

(a) *Solicitations or recommendations.* Identify all persons and classes of persons that are directly or indirectly employed, retained, or to be compensated to make solicitations or recommendations in connection with the transaction. Provide a summary of all material terms of employment, retainer or other arrangement for compensation.

(b) *Employees and corporate assets.* Identify any officer, class of employees or corporate assets of the subject company that has been or will be employed or used by the filing person in connection with the transaction. Describe the purpose for their employment or use.

Item 1010. Financial Statements

(a) *Financial information.* Furnish the following financial information:

(1) Audited financial statements for the two fiscal years required to be filed with the company's most recent annual report under Sections 13 and 15(d) of the Exchange Act;

(2) Unaudited balance sheets, comparative year-to-date income statements of comprehensive income (as defined in §210.1-02 of Regulation S-X of this chapter) and related earnings per share data and statements of cash flows required to be included in the company's most recent quarterly report filed under the Exchange Act;

(3) Ratio of earnings to fixed charges, computed in a manner consistent with Item 503(d) of Regulation S-K, for the two most recent fiscal years and the interim periods provided under paragraph (a)(2) of this section; and

(4) Book value per share as of the date of the most recent balance sheet presented.

(b) *Pro forma information.* If material, furnish pro forma information disclosing the effect of the transaction on:

(1) The company's balance sheet as of the date of the most recent balance sheet presented under paragraph (a) of this section;

(2) The company's statement of income, earnings per share, and ratio of earnings to fixed charges for the most recent fiscal year and the latest interim period provided under paragraph (a)(2) of this section; and

(3) The company's book value per share as of the date of the most recent balance sheet presented under paragraph (a) of this section.

(c) *Summary Information.* Furnish a fair and adequate summary of the information specified in paragraphs (a) and (b) of this section for the same periods specified. A fair and adequate summary includes:

(1) The summarized financial information specified in Item 1-02(bb)(1) of Regulation S-K;

(2) Income per common share from continuing operations (basic and diluted, if applicable);

(3) Net income per common share (basic and diluted, if applicable);

(4) Ratio of earnings to fixed charges, computed in a manner consistent with Item 503(d) of Regulation S-K;

(5) Book value per share as of the date of the most recent balance sheet; and

(6) If material, pro forma data for the summarized financial information specified in paragraph (c)(1) through (c)(5) of this section disclosing the effect of the transaction.

Item 1011. Additional Information

(a) *Agreements, regulatory requirements and legal proceedings.* If material to a security holder's decision whether to sell, tender or hold the securities sought in the tender offer, furnish the following information:

(1) Any present or proposed material agreement, arrangement, understanding or relationship between the offeror or any of its executive officers, directors, controlling persons or subsidiaries and the subject company or any of its executive officers, directors, controlling persons or subsidiaries (other than any agreement, arrangement or understanding disclosed under any other sections of Regulation M-A);

(2) To the extent known by the offeror after reasonable investigation, the applicable regulatory requirements which must be complied with or approvals which must be obtained in connection with the tender offer;

(3) The applicability of any anti-trust laws;

(4) The applicability of margin requirements under Section 7 of the Act and the applicable regulations; and

(5) Any material pending legal proceedings relating to the tender offer, including the name and location of the court or agency in which the proceedings are pending, the date instituted, the principal parties, and a brief summary of the proceedings and the relief sought.

(b) Furnish the information required by Item 402(t)(2) and (3) of this part and in the tabular format set forth in Item 402(t)(1) of this part with respect to each named executive officer

(1) Of the subject company in a Rule 13e-3 transaction; or

(2) Of the issuer whose securities are the subject of a third-party tender offer, regarding any agreement or understanding, whether written or unwritten, between such named executive officer and the subject company, issuer, bidder, or the acquiring company, as applicable, concerning any type of compensation, whether present, deferred or contingent, that is based upon or otherwise relates to the Rule 13e-3 transaction or third-party tender offer.

(c) *Other material information.* Furnish such additional material information, if any, as may be necessary to make the required statements, in light of the circumstances under which they are made, not materially misleading.

Item 1012. The Solicitation or Recommendation

(a) *Solicitation or recommendation.* State the nature of the solicitation or the recommendation. If this statement relates to a recommendation, state whether the filing person is advising holders of the subject securities to accept or reject the tender offer or to take other action with respect to the tender offer and, if so, describe the other action recommended. If the filing person is the subject company and is not making a recommendation, state whether the subject company is expressing no opinion and is remaining neutral toward the tender offer or is unable to take a position with respect to the tender offer.

(b) *Reasons.* State the reasons for the position (including the inability to take a position) stated in paragraph (a) of this section. Conclusory statements such as "The tender offer is in the best interests of shareholders" are not considered sufficient disclosure.

(c) *Intent to tender.* To the extent known by the filing person after making reasonable inquiry, state whether the filing person or any executive officer, director, affiliate or subsidiary of the filing person currently intends to tender, sell or hold the subject securities that are held of record or beneficially owned by that person.

(d) *Intent to tender or vote in a going-private transaction.* To the extent known by the filing person after making reasonable inquiry, state whether or not any executive officer, director or affiliate of the issuer (or any person specified in Instruction C to the schedule) currently intends to tender or sell subject securities owned or held by that person and/or how each person currently intends to vote subject securities, including any securities the person has proxy authority for. State the reasons for the intended action.

(e) *Recommendations of others.* To the extent known by the filing person after making reasonable inquiry, state whether or not any person specified in paragraph (d) of this section has made a recommendation either in support of or opposed to the transaction and the reasons for the recommendation.

Item 1013. Purposes, Alternatives, Reasons and Effects in a Going-private Transaction

(a) *Purposes.* State the purposes for the Rule 13e-3 transaction.

(b) *Alternatives.* If the subject company or affiliate considered alternative means to accomplish the stated purposes, briefly describe the alternatives and state the reasons for their rejection.

(c) *Reasons.* State the reasons for the structure of the Rule 13e-3 transaction and for undertaking the transaction at this time.

(d) *Effects.* Describe the effects of the Rule 13e-3 transaction on the subject company, its affiliates and unaffiliated security holders, including the federal tax consequences of the transaction.

Item 1014. Fairness of the Going-private Transaction

(a) *Fairness.* State whether the subject company or affiliate filing the statement reasonably believes that the Rule 13e-3 transaction is fair or unfair to unaffiliated security holders. If any director dissented to or abstained from voting on the Rule 13e-3 transaction, identify the director, and indicate, if known, after making reasonable inquiry, the reasons for the dissent or abstention.

(b) *Factors considered in determining fairness.* Discuss in reasonable detail the material factors upon which the belief stated in paragraph (a) of this section is based and, to the extent practicable, the weight assigned to each factor. The discussion must include an analysis of the extent, if any, to which the filing person's beliefs are based on the factors described in Instruction 2 of this section, paragraphs (c), (d) and (e) of this section and Item 1015 of Regulation M-A.

(c) *Approval of security holders.* State whether or not the transaction is structured so that approval of at least a majority of unaffiliated security holders is required.

(d) *Unaffiliated representative.* State whether or not a majority of directors who are not employees of the subject company has retained an unaffiliated representative to act solely on behalf of unaffiliated security holders for purposes of negotiating the terms of the Rule 13e-3 transaction and/or preparing a report concerning the fairness of the transaction.

(e) *Approval of directors.* State whether or not the Rule 13e-3 transaction was approved by a majority of the directors of the subject company who are not employees of the subject company.

(f) *Other offers.* If any offer of the type described in paragraph (viii) of Instruction 2 to this section has been received, describe the offer and state the reasons for its rejection.

Instructions to Item 1014

1. A statement that the issuer or affiliate has no reasonable belief as to the fairness of the Rule 13e-3 transaction to unaffiliated security holders will not be considered sufficient disclosure in response to paragraph (a) of this section.

2. The factors that are important in determining the fairness of a transaction to unaffiliated security holders and the weight, if any, that should be given to them in a particular context will vary. Normally such factors will include, among others, those referred to in paragraphs (c), (d) and (e) of this section and whether the consideration offered to unaffiliated security holders constitutes fair value in relation to:

(i) Current market prices;

(ii) Historical market prices;

(iii) Net book value;

(iv) Going concern value;

(v) Liquidation value;

(vi) Purchase prices paid in previous purchases disclosed in response to Item 1002(f) of Regulation M-A;

(vii) Any report, opinion, or appraisal described in Item 1015 of Regulation M-A; and

(viii) Firm offers of which the subject company or affiliate is aware made by any unaffiliated person, other than the filing persons, during the past two years for:

(A) The merger or consolidation of the subject company with or into another company, or *vice versa*;

(B) The sale or other transfer of all or any substantial part of the assets of the subject company; or

(C) A purchase of the subject company's securities that would enable the holder to exercise control of the subject company.

3. Conclusory statements, such as "The Rule 13e-3 transaction is fair to unaffiliated security holders in relation to net book value, going concern value and future prospects

of the issuer" will not be considered sufficient disclosure in response to paragraph (b) of this section.

Item 1015. Reports, Opinions, Appraisals and Negotiations

(a) *Report, opinion or appraisal.* State whether or not the subject company or affiliate has received any report, opinion (other than an opinion of counsel) or appraisal from an outside party that is materially related to the Rule 13e-3 transaction, including, but not limited to: any report, opinion or appraisal relating to the consideration or the fairness of the consideration to be offered to security holders or the fairness of the transaction to the issuer or affiliate or to security holders who are not affiliates.

(b) *Preparer and summary of the report, opinion or appraisal.* For each report, opinion or appraisal described in response to paragraph (a) of this section or any negotiation or report described in response to Item 1014(d) of Regulation M-A or Item 14(b)(6) of Schedule 14A concerning the terms of the transaction:

(1) Identify the outside party and/or unaffiliated representative;

(2) Briefly describe the qualifications of the outside party and/or unaffiliated representative;

(3) Describe the method of selection of the outside party and/or unaffiliated representative;

(4) Describe any material relationship that existed during the past two years or is mutually understood to be contemplated and any compensation received or to be received as a result of the relationship between:

(i) The outside party, its affiliates, and/or unaffiliated representative; and

(ii) The subject company or its affiliates;

(5) If the report, opinion or appraisal relates to the fairness of the consideration, state whether the subject company or affiliate determined the amount of consideration to be paid; and

(6) Furnish a summary concerning the negotiation, report, opinion or appraisal. The summary must include, but need not be limited to, the procedures followed; the findings and recommendations; the bases for and methods of arriving at such findings and recommendations; instructions received from the subject company or affiliate; and any limitation imposed by the subject company or affiliate on the scope of the investigation.

Instruction to Item 1015(b)

The information called for by paragraphs (b)(1), (2) and (3) of this section must be given with respect to the firm that provides the report, opinion or appraisal rather than the employees of the firm that prepared the report.

(c) *Availability of documents.* Furnish a statement to the effect that the report, opinion or appraisal will be made available for inspection and copying at the principal executive offices of the subject company or affiliate during its regular business hours by any interested equity security holder of the subject company or representative who has been so designated in writing. This statement also may provide that a copy of the report, opinion or appraisal will be transmitted by the subject company or affiliate to any interested equity security holder of the subject company or representative who has been so designated in writing upon written request and at the expense of the requesting security holder.

Item 1016. Exhibits . . .

Other Federal Regulations

Standards of Professional Conduct for Attorneys Appearing and Practicing Before the Commission in the Representation of an Issuer

17 C.F.R. §§205.1-205.7

Rule 205.1. Purpose and Scope

This part sets forth minimum standards of professional conduct for attorneys appearing and practicing before the Commission in the representation of an issuer. These standards supplement applicable standards of any jurisdiction where an attorney is admitted or practices and are not intended to limit the ability of any jurisdiction to impose additional obligations on an attorney not inconsistent with the application of this part. Where the standards of a state or other United States jurisdiction where an attorney is admitted or practices conflict with this part, this part shall govern.

Rule 205.2. Definitions

For purposes of this part, the following definitions apply:

(a) *Appearing and practicing* before the Commission:

(1) Means:

(i) Transacting any business with the Commission, including communications in any form;

(ii) Representing an issuer in a Commission administrative proceeding or in connection with any Commission investigation, inquiry, information request, or subpoena;

(iii) Providing advice in respect of the United States securities laws or the Commission's rules or regulations thereunder regarding any document that the attorney has notice will be filed with or submitted to, or incorporated into any document that will be filed with or submitted to, the Commission, including the provision of such advice in the context of preparing, or participating in the preparation of, any such document; or

(iv) Advising an issuer as to whether information or a statement, opinion, or other writing is required under the United States securities laws or the Commission's rules or regulations thereunder to be filed with or submitted to, or incorporated into any document that will be filed with or submitted to, the Commission; but

(2) Does not include an attorney who:

(i) Conducts the activities in paragraphs (a)(1)(i) through (a)(1)(iv) of this section other than in the context of providing legal services to an issuer with whom the attorney has an attorney-client relationship; or

(ii) Is a non-appearing foreign attorney.

(b) *Appropriate response* means a response to an attorney regarding reported evidence of a material violation as a result of which the attorney reasonably believes:

(1) That no material violation, as defined in paragraph (i) of this section, has occurred, is ongoing, or is about to occur;

(2) That the issuer has, as necessary, adopted appropriate remedial measures, including appropriate steps or sanctions to stop any material violations that are ongoing, to prevent any material violation that has yet to occur, and to remedy or otherwise appropriately address any material violation that has already occurred and to minimize the likelihood of its recurrence; or

(3) That the issuer, with the consent of the issuer's board of directors, a committee thereof to whom a report could be made pursuant to Rule 205.3(b)(3), or a qualified legal compliance committee, has retained or directed an attorney to review the reported evidence of a material violation and either:

(i) Has substantially implemented any remedial recommendations made by such attorney after a reasonable investigation and evaluation of the reported evidence; or

(ii) Has been advised that such attorney may, consistent with his or her professional obligations, assert a colorable defense on behalf of the issuer (or the issuer's officer, director, employee, or agent, as the case may be) in any investigation or judicial or administrative proceedings relating to the reported evidence of a material violation.

(c) *Attorney* means any person who is admitted, licensed, or otherwise qualified to practice law in any jurisdiction, domestic or foreign, or who holds himself or herself out as admitted, licensed, or otherwise qualified to practice law.

(d) *Breach of fiduciary duty* refers to any breach of fiduciary or similar duty to the issuer recognized under an applicable federal or state statute or at common law, including but not limited to misfeasance, nonfeasance, abdication of duty, abuse or trust, and approval of unlawful transactions.

(e) *Evidence of a material violation* means credible evidence, based upon which it would be unreasonable, under the circumstances, for a prudent and competent attorney not to conclude that it is reasonably likely that a material violation has occurred, is ongoing, or is about to occur.

(f) *Foreign government issuer* means a foreign issuer as defined in Rule 405 eligible to register securities on Schedule B of the Securities Act of 1933.

(g) *In the representation of an issuer* means providing legal services as an attorney for an issuer, regardless of whether the attorney is employed or retained by the issuer.

(h) *Issuer* means an issuer (as defined in section 3 of the Securities Exchange Act of 1934, the securities of which are registered under section 12 of that Act, or that is required to file reports under sections 15(d) of that Act, or that files or has filed a registration statement that has not yet become effective under the Securities Act of 1933, and that it has withdrawn, but does not include a foreign government issuer. For purposes of paragraphs (a) and (g) of this section, the term "issuer" includes any person controlled by an issuer, where an attorney provides legal services to such person on behalf of, or at the behest of, or for the benefit of the issuer, regardless of whether the attorney is employed or retained by the issuer.

(i) *Material violation* means a material violation of an applicable United States federal or state securities law, a material breach of fiduciary duty arising under United States federal or state law, or a similar material violation of any United States federal or state law.

(j) *Non-appearing foreign attorney* means an attorney:

(1) Who is admitted to practice law in a jurisdiction outside the United States;

(2) Who does not hold himself or herself out as practicing, and does not give legal advice regarding, United States federal or state securities or other laws (except as provided in paragraph (j)(3)(ii) of this section); and

(3) Who:

(i) Conducts activities that would constitute appearing and practicing before the Commission only incidentally to, and in the ordinary course of, the practice of law in a jurisdiction outside the United States; or

(ii) Is appearing and practicing before the Commission only in consultation with counsel, other than a non-appearing foreign attorney, admitted or licensed to practice in a state or other United States jurisdiction.

(k) *Qualified legal compliance committee* means a committee of an issuer (which also may be an audit or other committee of the issuer) that:

(1) Consists of at least one member of the issuer's audit committee (or, if the issuer has no audit committee, one member from an equivalent committee of independent directors) and two or more members of the issuer's board of directors who are not employed, directly or indirectly, by the issuer and who are not, in the case of a registered investment company, "interested persons" as defined in section 2(a)(19) of the Investment Company Act of 1940 (15 U.S.C. 80a-2(a)(19));

(2) Has adopted written procedures for the confidential receipt, retention, and consideration of any report of evidence of a material violation under Rule 205.3;

(3) Has been duly established by the issuer's board of directors, with the authority and responsibility:

(i) To inform the issuer's chief legal officer and chief executive officer (or the equivalents thereof) of any report of evidence of a material violation (except in the circumstances described in Rule 3(b)(4));

(ii) To determine whether an investigation is necessary regarding any report of evidence of a material violation by the issuer, its officers, directors, employees or agents and, if it determines an investigation is necessary or appropriate, to:

(A) Notify the audit committee or the full board of directors;

(B) Initiate an investigation, which may be conducted either by the chief legal officer (or the equivalent thereof) or by outside attorneys; and

(C) Retain such additional expert personnel as the committee deems necessary; and

(iii) At the conclusion of any such investigation, to:

(A) Recommend, by majority vote, that the issuer implement an appropriate response to evidence of a material violation; and

(B) Inform the chief legal officer and the chief executive officer (or the equivalents thereof) and the board of directors of the results of any such investigation under this section and the appropriate remedial measures to be adopted; and

(4) Has the authority and responsibility, acting by majority vote, to take all other appropriate action, including the authority to notify the Commission in the event that the issuer fails in any material respect to implement an appropriate response that the qualified legal compliance committee has recommended the issuer to take.

(l) *Reasonable* or *reasonably* denotes, with respect to the actions of an attorney, conduct that would not be unreasonable for a prudent and competent attorney.

(m) *Reasonably believes* means that an attorney believes the matter in question and that the circumstances are such that the belief is not unreasonable.

(n) *Report* means to make known to directly, either in person, by telephone, by e-mail, electronically, or in writing.

Rule 205.3. Issuer as Client

(a) *Representing an issuer.* An attorney appearing and practicing before the Commission in the representation of an issuer owes his or her professional and ethical duties to the issuer as an organization. That the attorney may work with and advise the issuer's officers, directors, or employees in the course of representing the issuer does not make such individuals the attorney's clients.

(b) *Duty to report evidence of a material violation.* (1) If an attorney, appearing and practicing before the Commission in the representation of an issuer, becomes aware of evidence of a material violation by the issuer or by any officer, director, employee, or agent of the issuer, the attorney shall report such evidence to the issuer's chief legal officer (or the equivalent thereof) or to both the issuer's chief legal officer and its chief executive officer (or the equivalent thereof) forthwith. By communicating such information to the issuer's officers or directors, an attorney does not reveal client confidences or secrets or privileged or otherwise protected information related to the attorney's representation of an issuer.

(2) The chief legal officer (or the equivalent thereof) shall cause such inquiry into the evidence of a material violation as he or she reasonably believes is appropriate to determine whether the material violation described in the report has occurred, is ongoing, or is about to occur. If the chief legal officer (or the equivalent thereof) determines no material violation has occurred, or is about to occur, he or she shall notify the reporting attorney and advise the reporting attorney of the basis for such determination. Unless the chief legal officer (or the equivalent thereof) reasonably believes that no material violation has occurred, is ongoing, or is about to occur, he or she shall take all reasonable steps to cause the issuer to adopt an appropriate response and shall advise the reporting attorney thereof. In lieu of causing an inquiry under this paragraph (b), a chief legal officer (or the equivalent thereof) may refer a report of evidence of a material violation to a qualified legal compliance committee under paragraph (c)(2) of this section if the issuer has duly established a qualified legal compliance committee prior to the report of evidence of a material violation.

(3) Unless an attorney who has made a report under paragraph (b)(1) of this section reasonably believes that the chief legal officer or the chief executive officer of the issuer (or the equivalent thereof) has provided an appropriate response within a reasonable time, the attorney shall report the evidence of a material violation to:

(i) The audit committee of the issuer's board of directors;

(ii) Another committee of the issuer's board of directors consisting solely of directors who are not employed, directly or indirectly, by the issuer and are not, in the case of a registered investment company, "interested persons" as defined in section 2(a)(19) of the Investment Company Act of 1940 (15 U.S.C. 80a-2(a)(19)) (if the issuer's board of directors has no audit committee); or

(iii) The issuer's board of directors (if the issuer's board of directors has no committee consisting solely of directors who are not employed, directly or indirectly, by the issuer are not, in the case of a registered investment company, "interested persons" as defined in section 2(a)(19) of the Investment Company Act of 1940 (15 U.S.C. 80a-2(a)(19))).

(4) If an attorney reasonably believes that it would be futile to report evidence of a material violation to the issuer's chief legal officer and chief executive officer (or the equivalents thereof) under paragraph (b)(1) of this section, the attorney may report such evidence as provided under paragraph (b)(3) of this section.

(5) An attorney retained or directed by an issuer to investigate evidence of a material violation reported under paragraph (b)(1), (b)(3), or (b)(4) or this section shall be deemed to be appearing and practicing before the Commission. Directing or retaining an attorney to investigate reported evidence of a material violation does not relieve an officer or director of the issuer to whom such evidence has been reported under paragraph (b)(1), (b)(3), or (b)(4) of this section from a duty to respond to the reporting attorney.

(6) An attorney shall not have any obligation to report evidence of a material violation under this paragraph (b) if:

(i) The attorney was retained or directed by the issuer's chief legal officer (or the equivalent thereof) to investigate such evidence of a material violation and:

(A) The attorney reports the results of such investigation to the chief legal officer (or the equivalent thereof); and

(B) Except where the attorney and the chief legal officer (or the equivalent thereof) each reasonably believes that no material violation has occurred, is ongoing, or is about to occur, the chief legal officer (or the equivalent thereof) reports the results of the investigation to the issuer's board of directors, a committee thereof to whom a report could be made pursuant to paragraph (b)(3) of this section, or a qualified legal compliance committee; or

(ii) The attorney was retained or directed by the chief legal officer (or the equivalent thereof) to assert, consistent with her or her professional obligations, a colorable defense on behalf of the issuer (or the issuer's officer, director, employee, or agent, as the case may be) in any investigation or judicial or administrative proceeding relating to such evidence of a material violation, and the chief legal officer (or the equivalent of) provides reasonable and timely reports on the progress and outcome of such proceeding to the issuer's board of directors, a committee thereof to whom a report could be made pursuant to paragraph (b)(3) of this section, or a qualified legal compliance committee.

(7) An attorney shall not have any obligation to report evidence of a material violation under this paragraph (b) if such attorney was retained or directed by a qualified legal compliance committee:

(i) To investigate such evidence of a material violation; or

(ii) To assert, consistent with his or her professional obligations, a colorable defense on behalf of the issuer (or the issuer's officer, director, employee, or agent, as the case may be) in any investigation or judicial or administrative proceeding relating to such evidence of a material violation.

(8) An attorney who receives what he or she reasonably believes is an appropriate and timely response to a report he or she made pursuant to paragraph (b)(1), or (b)(4) of this section need do nothing more under this section with respect to his or her report.

(9) An attorney who does not reasonably believe that the issuer has made an appropriate response within a reasonably time to the report or reports made pursuant to paragraph (b)(1), (b)(3), or (b)(4) of this section shall explain his or her reasons therefore to the chief legal officer (or the equivalent thereof), the chief executive officer (or the equivalent thereof), and directors to whom the attorney reported the evidence of a material violation pursuant to paragraph (b)(1), (b)(3), or (b)(4) of this section.

(10) An attorney formerly employed or retained by an issuer who has reported evidence of a material violation under this part and reasonably believes that he or she has been discharged for doing may notify the issuer's board of directors or any committee thereof that he or she believes that he or

she has been discharged for reporting evidence of a material violation under this section.

(c) *Alternative reporting procedures for attorneys retained or employed by an issuer that has established a qualified legal compliance committee.* (1) If an attorney, appearing and practicing before the Commission in the representation of an issuer, becomes aware of evidence of a material violation by the issuer or by any officer, director, employee, or agent of the issuer, the attorney may, as an alternative to the reporting requirements of paragraph (b) of this section, report such evidence to a qualified legal compliance committee, if the issuer has previously formed such a committee. An attorney who reports evidence of a material violation to such a qualified legal compliance committed has satisfied his or her obligation to report such evidence and is not required to assess the issuer's repose to the reported evidence of a material violation.

(2) A chief legal officer (or the equivalent thereof) may refer a report of evidence of a material violation to a previously establish qualified legal compliance committee in lieu of causing an inquiry to be conducted under paragraph (b)(2) of this section. The chief legal officer (or the equivalent thereof) shall inform the reporting attorney that the report has been referred to a qualified legal compliance committee. Thereafter, pursuant to the requirements under Rule 205.2(k), the qualified legal compliance violation reported to it under this paragraph (c).

(d) *Issuer confidence.* (1) Any report under this section (or the contemporaneous record thereof) or any response thereto (or the contemporaneous record thereof) may be used by an attorney in connection with any investigation, proceeding, or litigation in which the attorney's compliance with this part is in issue.

(2) An attorney appearing and practicing before the Commission in the representation of an issuer may reveal to the Commission, without the issuer's consent, confidential information related to the representation to the extent the attorney reasonably believes necessary:

(i) To prevent the issuer from committing a material violation that is likely to cause substantial injury to the financial interest or property of the issuer or investors;

(ii) To prevent the issuer, in a Commission investigation or administrative proceeding from committing perjury, proscribed in 18 U.S.C. 1621; suborning perjury, prescribed in 18 U.S.C. 1622; or committing any act proscribed in 18 U.S.C. 1001 that is likely to perpetuate a fraud upon the Commission; or

(iii) To rectify the consequences of a material violation by the issuer that caused, or may cause, substantial injury to the financial interest or of the issuer or investors in the furtherance of which the attorney's services were used.

Rule 205.4. Responsibilities of Supervisory Attorneys

(a) An attorney supervising or directing another attorney who is appearing and practicing before the Commission in the representation of an issuer is a supervisory attorney. An issuer's chief legal officer (or the equivalent thereof) is a supervisory attorney under this section.

(b) A supervisory attorney shall make reasonable efforts to ensure that a subordinate attorney, as defined in Rule 205.5(a), that he or she supervises or directs conforms to this part. To the extent a subordinate attorney appears and practices before the Commission in the representation of an issuer, that subordinate attorney's supervisory attorneys also appear and practice before the Commission.

(c) A supervisory attorney is responsible for complying with the reporting requirements in Rule 205.3 when a subordinate attorney has reported to the supervisory attorney evidence of a material violation.

(d) A supervisory attorney who has received a report of evidence of a material violation from a subordinate attorney under Rule 205.3 may report such evidence to the issuer's qualified legal compliance committee if the issuer has duly formed such a committee.

Rule 205.5. Responsibilities of a Subordinate Attorney

(a) An attorney who appears and practices before the Commission in the representation of an issuer on a matter under supervision or direction or another attorney (other than under the direct supervision or direction of the issuer's chief legal officer (or the equivalent thereof)) is a subordinate attorney.

(b) A subordinate attorney shall comply with this part notwithstanding that the subordinate attorney acted at the direction of or under the supervision of another person.

(c) A subordinate attorney complies with Rule 205.3 if the subordinate attorney reports to his or her supervising attorney under Rule 205.3(b) evidence of a material violation of which the subordinate attorney has become aware in appearing and practicing before the Commission.

(d) A subordinate attorney may take the steps permitted or required by Rule 205.3(b) or (c) if the subordinate attorney reasonably believes that a supervisory attorney to whom he or she has reported evidence of a supervisory attorney to whom he or she has reported evidence of a material violation under Rule 205.3(b) has failed to comply with Rule 205.3.

Rule 205.6. Sanctions and Discipline

(a) A violation of this part by any attorney appearing and practicing before the Commission in the representation of an issuer shall subject such attorney to the civil penalties and remedies for a violation of the federal securities laws available to the Commission in an action brought by the Commission thereunder.

(b) An attorney appearing and practicing before the Commission who violates any provision of this part is subject to the disciplinary authority of the Commission, regardless of whether the attorney may also be subject to discipline for the same conduct in a jurisdiction where the attorney is admitted or practices. An administrative disciplinary proceeding initiated by the Commission for violation of this part may result in an attorney being censured, or being temporarily or permanently denied the privilege of appearing, or practicing before the Commission.

(c) An attorney who complies in good faith with the provisions of this part shall not be subject to discipline or otherwise liable under inconsistent standards imposed by any state or other United States jurisdiction where the attorney is admitted or practices.

(d) An attorney practicing outside the United States shall not be required to comply with the requirements of this part to the extent that such compliance is prohibited by applicable foreign law.

Rule 205.7. No Private Right or Action

(a) Nothing is this part is intended to, or does, create a private right of action against any attorney, law firm, or issuer based upon compliance or noncompliance with its provisions.

(b) Authority to enforce compliance with this part is vested exclusively in the Commission.

Regulation Crowdfunding General Rules and Regulations

17 C.F.R. §§227.100-503

SUPART A — GENERAL

§227.100. Crowdfunding Exemption and Requirements

(a) Exemption. An issuer may offer or sell securities in reliance on section 4(a)(6) of the Securities Act of 1933 (the "Securities Act") provided that:

(1) The aggregate amount of securities sold to all investors by the issuer in reliance on section 4(a)(6) of the Securities Act during the 12-month period preceding the date of such offer or sale, including the securities offered in such transaction, shall not exceed $5,000,000;

(2) The aggregate amount of securities sold to any investor across all issuers in reliance on section 4(a)(6) of the Securities Act during the 12-month period preceding the date of such transaction, including the securities sold to such investor in such transaction, shall not exceed:

(i) The greater of $2,500 or 5 percent of the greater of the investor's annual income or net worth if either the investor's annual income or net worth is less than $124,000; or

(ii) 10 percent of the greater of the investor's annual income or net worth, not to exceed an amount sold of $124,000, if both the investor's annual income and net worth are equal to or more than $124,000;

Instruction 1 to paragraph (a)(2). To determine the investment limit for a natural person, the person's annual income and net worth shall be calculated as those values are calculated for purposes of determining accredited investor status in accordance with §230.501 of this chapter.

Instruction 2 to paragraph (a)(2). A person's annual income and net worth may be calculated jointly with that person's spouse; however, when such a joint calculation is used, the aggregate investment of the investor spouses may not exceed the limit that would apply to an individual investor at that income or net worth level.

Instruction 3 to paragraph (a)(2). An issuer offering and selling securities in reliance on section 4(a)(6) of the Securities Act may rely on the efforts of an intermediary required by §227.303(b) to ensure that the aggregate amount of securities purchased by an investor in offerings pursuant to section 4(a)(6) of the Securities Act will not cause the investor to exceed the limit set forth in section 4(a)(6) of the Securities Act and §227.100(a)(2), provided that the issuer does not know that the investor has exceeded the investor limits or would exceed the investor limits as a result of purchasing securities in the issuer's offering.

(3) The transaction is conducted through an intermediary that complies with the requirements in section 4A(a) of the Securities Act and the related requirements in this part, and the transaction is conducted exclusively through the intermediary's platform; and

Instruction to paragraph (a)(3). An issuer shall not conduct an offering or concurrent offerings in reliance on section 4(a)(6) of the Securities Act of 1933 using more than one intermediary.

(4) The issuer complies with the requirements in section 4A(b) of the Securities Act and the related requirements in this part; provided, however, that

the failure to comply with §§227.202, 227.203(a)(3) and 227.203(b) shall not prevent an issuer from relying on the exemption provided by section 4(a)(6) of the Securities Act)).

(b) *Applicability.* The crowdfunding exemption shall not apply to transactions involving the offer or sale of securities by any issuer that:

(1) Is not organized under, and subject to, the laws of a State or territory of the United States or the District of Columbia;

(2) Is subject to the requirement to file reports pursuant to section 13 or section 15(d) of the Securities Exchange Act of 1934 (the "Exchange Act");

(3) Is an investment company, as defined in section 3 of the Investment Company Act of 1940, or is excluded from the definition of investment company by section 3(b) or section 3(c) of that Act;

(4) Is not eligible to offer or sell securities in reliance on section 4(a)(6) of the Securities Act) as a result of a disqualification as specified in §227.503(a);

(5) Has sold securities in reliance on section 4(a)(6) of the Securities Act and has not filed with the Commission and provided to investors, to the extent required, the ongoing annual reports required by this part during the two years immediately preceding the filing of the required offering statement; or

(6) Has no specific business plan or has indicated that its business plan is to engage in a merger or acquisition with an unidentified company or companies.

(7) Seeks to rely on §227.201(aa) to conduct an offering on an expedited basis due to circumstances relating to coronavirus disease 2019 (COVID-19), where such offering is initiated between May 4, 2020, and February 28, 2021, or seeks to rely on §227.201(bb), where such offering is initiated between March 1, 2021, and August 28, 2022, and:

(i) Was organized and had operations less than six months prior to the commencement of the offering; or

(ii) Sold securities in reliance on section 4(a)(6) of the Securities Act and has not complied with the requirements in section 4A(b) of the Securities Act (15 U.S.C. 77d-1(b)) and the related requirements in this part.

(c) *Issuer.* For purposes of §227.201(r), calculating aggregate amounts offered and sold in §227.100(a) and §227.201(t), and determining whether an issuer has previously sold securities in §227.201(t)(3), issuer includes all entities controlled by or under common control with the issuer and any predecessors of the issuer.

(d) *Investor.* For purposes of this part, investor means any investor or any potential investor, as the context requires. A crowdfunding vehicle (as defined in §270.3a-9 of this chapter) is not considered an investor for the purposes of this part.

(e) *Integration with other offerings.* To determine whether offers and sales should be integrated, see §230.152 of this chapter.

Subpart B–Requirements for Issuers

§227.201. Disclosure Requirements

An issuer offering or selling securities in reliance on section 4(a)(6) of the Securities Act and in accordance with section 4A of the Securities Act and this part and any co-issuer jointly offering or selling securities with such an issuer in reliance on the same must file with the Commission and provide to investors and the relevant intermediary the following information:

(a) The name, legal status (including its form of organization, jurisdiction in which it is organized and date of organization), physical address and website of the issuer;

(b) The names of the directors and officers (and any persons occupying a similar status or performing a similar function) of the issuer, all positions and offices with the issuer held by such persons, the period of time in which such persons served in the position or office and their business experience during the past three years, including:

(1) Each person's principal occupation and employment, including whether any officer is employed by another employer; and

(2) The name and principal business of any corporation or other organization in which such occupation and employment took place.

(c) The name of each person, as of the most recent practicable date but no earlier than 120 days prior to the date the offering statement or report is filed, who is a beneficial owner of 20 percent or more of the issuer's outstanding voting equity securities, calculated on the basis of voting power;

(d) A description of the business of the issuer and the anticipated business plan of the issuer;

(e) The current number of employees of the issuer;

(f) A discussion of the material factors that make an investment in the issuer speculative or risky;

(g) The target offering amount and the deadline to reach the target offering amount, including a statement that if the sum of the investment commitments does not equal or exceed the target offering amount at the offering deadline, no securities will be sold in the offering, investment commitments will be cancelled and committed funds will be returned;

(h) Whether the issuer will accept investments in excess of the target offering amount and, if so, the maximum amount that the issuer will accept and how oversubscriptions will be allocated, such as on a prorata, first come first served, or other basis;

(i) A description of the purpose and intended use of the offering proceeds;

(j) A description of the process to complete the transaction or cancel an investment commitment, including a statement that:

(1) Investors may cancel an investment commitment until 48 hours prior to the deadline identified in the issuer's offering materials;

(2) The intermediary will notify investors when the target offering amount has been met;

(3) If an issuer reaches the target offering amount prior to the deadline identified in its offering materials, it may close the offering early if it provides notice about the new offering deadline at least five business days prior to such new offering deadline (absent a material change that would require an extension of the offering and reconfirmation of the investment commitment); and

(4) If an investor does not cancel an investment commitment before the 48-hour period prior to the offering deadline, the funds will be released to the issuer upon closing of the offering and the investor will receive securities in exchange for his or her investment;

(k) A statement that if an investor does not reconfirm his or her investment commitment after a material change is made to the offering, the investor's investment commitment will be cancelled and the committed funds will be returned;

(l) The price to the public of the securities or the method for determining the price, provided that, prior to any sale of securities, each investor shall be provided in writing the final price and all required disclosures;

(m) A description of the ownership and capital structure of the issuer, including:

(1) The terms of the securities being offered and each other class of security of the issuer, including the number of securities being offered and/or outstanding, whether or not such securities have voting rights, any limitations on such voting rights, how the terms of the securities being offered may be modified and a summary of the differences between such securities and each other class of security of the issuer, and how the rights of the securities being offered may be materially limited, diluted or qualified by the rights of any other class of security of the issuer;

(2) A description of how the exercise of rights held by the principal shareholders of the issuer could affect the purchasers of the securities being offered;

(3) The name and ownership level of each person, as of the most recent practicable date but no earlier than 120 days prior to the date the offering statement or report is filed, who is the beneficial owner of 20 percent or more of the issuer's outstanding voting equity securities, calculated on the basis of voting power;

(4) How the securities being offered are being valued, and examples of methods for how such securities may be valued by the issuer in the future, including during subsequent corporate actions;

(5) The risks to purchasers of the securities relating to minority ownership in the issuer and the risks associated with corporate actions including additional issuances of securities, issuer repurchases of securities, a sale of the issuer or of assets of the issuer or transactions with related parties; and

(6) A description of the restrictions on transfer of the securities, as set forth in §227.501;

(n) The name, SEC file number and Central Registration Depository (CRD) number (as applicable) of the intermediary through which the offering is being conducted;

(o) A description of the intermediary's financial interests in the issuer's transaction and in the issuer, including:

(1) The amount of compensation to be paid to the intermediary, whether as a dollar amount or a percentage of the offering amount, or a good faith estimate if the exact amount is not available at the time of the filing, for conducting the offering, including the amount of referral and any other fees associated with the offering, and

(2) Any other direct or indirect interest in the issuer held by the intermediary, or any arrangement for the intermediary to acquire such an interest;

(p) A description of the material terms of any indebtedness of the issuer, including the amount, interest rate, maturity date and any other material terms;

(q) A description of exempt offerings conducted within the past three years;

(r) A description of any transaction since the beginning of the issuer's last fiscal year, or any currently proposed transaction, to which the issuer was or is to be a party and the amount involved exceeds five percent of the aggregate amount of capital raised by the issuer in reliance on section 4(a)(6) of the Securities Act during the preceding 12-month period, inclusive of the amount the issuer seeks to raise in the current offering under section 4(a)(6) of the Securities Act, in which any of the following persons had or is to have a direct or indirect material interest:

(1) Any director or officer of the issuer;

(2) Any person who is, as of the most recent practicable date but no earlier than 120 days prior to the date the offering statement or report is filed, the beneficial owner of 20 percent or more of the issuer's outstanding voting equity securities, calculated on the basis of voting power;

(3) If the issuer was incorporated or organized within the past three years, any promoter of the issuer; or

(4) Any member of the family of any of the foregoing persons, which includes a child, stepchild, grandchild, parent, stepparent, grandparent, spouse or spousal equivalent, sibling, mother-in-law, father-in-law, son-in-law, daughter-in-law, brother-in-law, or sister-in-law, and shall include adoptive relationships. The term spousal equivalent means a cohabitant occupying a relationship generally equivalent to that of a spouse.

(s) A discussion of the issuer's financial condition, including, to the extent material, liquidity, capital resources and historical results of operations;

(t) For offerings that, together with all other amounts sold under section 4(a)(6) of the Securities Act within the preceding 12-month period, have, in the aggregate, the following target offering amounts:

(1) $124,000 or less, the amount of total income, taxable income and total tax, or the equivalent line items, as reported on the federal income tax returns filed by the issuer for the most recently completed year (if any), which shall be certified by the principal executive officer of the issuer to reflect accurately the information reported on the issuer's federal income tax returns, and financial statements of the issuer, which shall be certified by the principal executive officer of the issuer to be true and complete in all material respects. If financial statements of the issuer are available that have either been reviewed or audited by a public accountant that is independent of the issuer, the issuer must provide those financial statements instead and need not include the information reported on the federal income tax returns or the certifications of the principal executive officer;

(2) More than $124,000, but not more than $618,000, financial statements of the issuer reviewed by a public accountant that is independent of the issuer. If financial statements of the issuer are available that have been audited by a public accountant that is independent of the issuer, the issuer must provide those financial statements instead and need not include the reviewed financial statements; and

(3) More than $618,000, financial statements of the issuer audited by a public accountant that is independent of the issuer; provided, however, that for issuers that have not previously sold securities in reliance on section 4(a)(6) of the Securities Act, offerings that have a target offering amount of more than $618,000, but not more than $1,235,000, financial statements of the issuer reviewed by a public accountant that is independent of the issuer. If financial statements of the issuer are available that have been audited by a public accountant that is independent of the issuer, the issuer must provide those financial statements instead and need not include the reviewed financial completed fiscal

year when it is filed with the U.S. Internal Revenue Service (if the tax return is filed during the offering period). . .

(v) Updates regarding the progress of the issuer in meeting the target offering amount, to be provided in accordance with §227.203;

(w) Where on the issuer's website investors will be able to find the issuer's annual report, and the date by which such report will be available on the issuer's website;

(x) Whether the issuer or any of its predecessors previously failed to comply with the ongoing reporting requirements of §227.202;

(y) Any material information necessary in order to make the statements made, in light of the circumstances under which they were made, not misleading; and

(z) Any written communication or broadcast script provided in accordance with §227.206 or, if within 30 days of the initial filing of the offering statement, §230.241 of this chapter. . . .

§227.202. Ongoing Reporting Requirements

(a) An issuer that has offered and sold securities in reliance on section 4(a)(6) of the Securities Act and in accordance with section 4A of the Securities Act and this part must file with the Commission and post on the issuer's website an annual report along with the financial statements of the issuer certified by the principal executive officer of the issuer to be true and complete in all material respects and a description of the financial condition of the issuer as described in §227.201(s). If, however, an issuer has available financial statements that have either been reviewed or audited by a public accountant that is independent of the issuer, those financial statements must be provided and the certification by the principal executive officer will not be required. The annual report also must include the disclosure required by paragraphs (a), (b), (c), (d), (e), (f), (m), (p), (q), (r), and (x) of §227.201. The report must be filed in accordance with the requirements of §227.203 and Form C (§239.900 of this chapter) and no later than 120 days after the end of the fiscal year covered by the report.

§227.203. Filing Requirements and Form

(a) Form C: Offering statement and amendments (§239.900 of this chapter).

(1) *Offering statement.* Except as allowed by §227.206, an issuer offering or selling securities in reliance on section 4(a)(6) of the Securities Act (15 U.S.C. 77d(a)(6)) and in accordance with section 4A of the Securities Act (15 U.S.C. 77d-1) and this part, and any co-issuer jointly offering or selling securities with such an issuer in reliance on the same, must file with the Commission and provide to investors and the relevant intermediary a Form C: Offering Statement (Form C) (§239.900 of this chapter) prior to the commencement of the offering of securities. An issuer that is both offering or selling securities with a co-issuer and separately offering or selling securities on its own must file with the Commission and provide to investors and the relevant intermediary a separate Form C for such offering. Every Form C must include the information required by §227.201.

(2) *Amendments to offering statement.* An issuer must file with the Commission and provide to investors and the relevant intermediary an amendment to the offering statement filed on Form C (§239.900 of this chapter) to disclose any material changes, additions or updates to information that it provides to investors through the intermediary's platform, for any offering that has not yet been completed or terminated. The amendment must be filed on Form C: Amendment (Form C/A) (§239.900 of this chapter), and if the amendment reflects material changes, additions or updates, the issuer shall check the box indicating that investors must reconfirm an investment commitment within five business days or the investor's commitment will be considered cancelled.

(3) *Progress updates.* (i) An issuer must file with the Commission and provide to investors and the relevant intermediary a Form C: Progress Update (Form C-U) (§239.900 of this chapter) to disclose its progress in meeting the target offering amount no later than five business days after each of the dates when the issuer reaches 50 percent and 100 percent of the target offering amount. . . .

§227.204. Advertising

(a)(1) An issuer may not, directly or indirectly, advertise the terms of an offering made in reliance on section 4(a)(6) of the Securities Act except for oral or written communications that meet the requirements of paragraph (b) of this section.

(2) *Instruction to paragraph (a).* For purposes of this paragraph (a), issuer includes persons acting on behalf of the issuer.

(b) A notice may advertise any of the terms of an issuer's offering made in reliance on section 4(a)(6) of the Securities Act if it directs investors to the intermediary's platform and includes no more than the following information:

(1) A statement that the issuer is conducting an offering pursuant to section 4(a)(6) of the Securities Act (15 U.S.C. 77d(a)(6)), the name of the intermediary through which the offering is being conducted and information (including a link in any written communications) directing the potential investor to the intermediary's platform;

(2) The terms of the offering; and

(3) Factual information about the legal identity and business location of the issuer, limited to the name of the issuer of the security, the address, phone number and website of the issuer, the email address of a representative of the issuer and a brief description of the business of the issuer.

(c) Notwithstanding the prohibition on advertising any of the terms of the offering, an issuer, and persons acting on behalf of the issuer, may communicate with investors and potential investors about the terms of the offering through communication channels provided by the intermediary on the intermediary's platform, provided that an issuer identifies itself as the issuer in all communications. Persons acting on behalf of the issuer must identify their affiliation with the issuer in all communications on the intermediary's platform.

(d) Notwithstanding the requirement that a notice advertising any of the terms of an issuer's offering made in reliance on section 4(a)(6) of the Securities Act (15 U.S.C. 77d(a)(6)) include no more than the information specified in paragraph (b) of this section, an issuer conducting an offering in reliance on Regulation Crowdfunding concurrently with another offering that discloses the terms of the Regulation Crowdfunding offering in the disclosure document for the other offering will not be deemed to have exceeded these disclosure limitations if the disclosure document for the other offering satisfies all the other requirements of this section. If the disclosure document for the other offering is filed on the Commission's Electronic Data Gathering and Retrieval System (EDGAR), the link required by paragraph (b)(1) may not be a live hyperlink.

. . .

§227.205. Promoter Compensation

(a) An issuer, or person acting on behalf of the issuer, shall be permitted to compensate or commit to compensate, directly or indirectly, any person to promote the issuer's offerings made in reliance on section 4(a)(6) of the Securities Act through communication channels provided by an intermediary on the intermediary's platform, but only if the issuer or person acting on behalf of the issuer, takes reasonable steps to ensure that the person promoting the offering clearly discloses the receipt, past or prospective, of such compensation with any such communication.

(b) Other than as set forth in paragraph (a) of this section, an issuer or person acting on behalf of the issuer shall not compensate or commit to compensate, directly or indirectly, any person to promote the issuer's offerings made in reliance on section 4(a)(6) of the Securities Act, unless such promotion is limited to notices permitted by, and in compliance with, §227.204.

§227.206 Solicitations of interest and other communications. (omitted)

Subpart C — Requirements for Intermediaries

§227.300. Intermediaries

(a) Requirements. A person acting as an intermediary in a transaction involving the offer or sale of securities in reliance on section 4(a)(6) of the Securities Act must:

(1) Be registered with the Commission as a broker under section 15(b) of the Exchange Act or as a funding portal in accordance with the requirements of §227.400; and

(2) Be a member a national securities association registered under section 15A of the Exchange Act.

(b) Financial interests. Any director, officer or partner of an intermediary, or any person occupying a similar status or performing a similar function, may not have a financial interest in an issuer that is offering or selling securities in reliance on section 4(a)(6) of the Securities Act through the intermediary's platform, or receive a financial interest in an issuer as compensation for the services provided to or for the benefit of the issuer in connection with the offer or sale of such securities. An intermediary may not have a financial interest in an issuer that is offering or selling securities in reliance on section 4(a)(6) of the Securities Act through the intermediary's platform unless:

(1) the intermediary receives the financial interest from the issuer as compensation for the services provided to, or for the benefit of, the issuer in connection with the offer or sale of the securities being offered or sold in reliance on section 4(a)(6) of the Securities Act through the intermediary's platform; and

(2) the financial interest consists of securities of the same class and having the same terms, conditions and rights as the securities being offered or sold in reliance on section 4(a)(6) of the Securities Act through the intermediary's platform. For purposes of this paragraph, a financial interest in an issuer means a direct or indirect ownership of, or economic interest in, any class of the issuer's securities. . . .

§227.301. Measures to Reduce Risk of Fraud

An intermediary in a transaction involving the offer or sale of securities in reliance on section 4(a)(6) of the Securities Act must:

(a) Have a reasonable basis for believing that an issuer seeking to offer and sell securities in reliance on section 4(a)(6) of the Securities Act through the intermediary's platform complies with the requirements in section 4A(b) of the Act and the related requirements in this part. In satisfying this requirement, an intermediary may rely on the representations of the issuer concerning compliance with these requirements unless the intermediary has reason to question the reliability of those representations;

(b) Have a reasonable basis for believing that the issuer has established means to keep accurate records of the holders of the securities it would offer and sell through the intermediary's platform, provided that an intermediary may rely on the representations of the issuer concerning its means of record-keeping unless the intermediary has reason to question the reliability of those representations. An intermediary will be deemed to have satisfied this requirement if the issuer has engaged the services of a transfer agent that is registered under Section 17A of the Exchange Act.

(c) Deny access to its platform to an issuer if the intermediary:

(1) Has a reasonable basis for believing that the issuer or any of its officers, directors (or any person occupying a similar status or performing a similar function) or beneficial owners of 20 percent or more of the issuer's outstanding voting equity securities, calculated on the basis of voting power, is subject to a disqualification under §227.503. In satisfying this requirement, an intermediary must, at a minimum, conduct a background and securities enforcement regulatory history check on each issuer whose securities are to be offered by the intermediary and on each officer, director or beneficial owner of 20 percent or more of the issuer's outstanding voting equity securities, calculated on the basis of voting power.

(2) Has a reasonable basis for believing that the issuer or the offering presents the potential for fraud or otherwise raises concerns about investor protection. In satisfying this requirement, an intermediary must deny access if it reasonably believes that it is unable to adequately or effectively assess the risk of fraud of the issuer or its potential offering. In addition, if an intermediary becomes aware of

information after it has granted access that causes it to reasonably believe that the issuer or the offering presents the potential for fraud or otherwise raises concerns about investor protection, the intermediary must promptly remove the offering from its platform, cancel the offering, and return (or, for funding portals, direct the return of) any funds that have been committed by investors in the offering.

(d) . . .

(e) Have a reasonable basis for believing that an issuer seeking to initiate an offering of securities between March 1, 2021, and August 28, 2022, in reliance on section 4(a)(6) of the Securities Act through the intermediary's platform that is relying on §227.201(bb) and that has previously sold securities in reliance on section 4(a)(6) of the Securities Act has complied with the requirements in section 4A(b) of the Act (15 U.S.C. 77d1(b)) and the related requirements in this part. In satisfying the requirement in this paragraph (e), an intermediary may rely on the representations of the issuer concerning compliance with the requirements in this paragraph (e) unless the intermediary has reason to question the reliability of those representations.

§227.302. Account Opening [omitted]

§227.303. Requirements with Respect to Transactions

(a) *Issuer information.* An intermediary in a transaction involving the offer or sale of securities in reliance on section 4(a)(6) of the Securities Act must make available to the Commission and to investors any information required to be provided by the issuer of the securities under §§227.201 and 227.203(a).

(1) This information must be made publicly available on the intermediary's platform, in a manner that reasonably permits a person accessing the platform to save, download, or otherwise store the information;

(2) This information must be made publicly available on the intermediary's platform for a minimum of 21 days before any securities are sold in the offering, during which time the intermediary may accept investment commitments;

(3) This information, including any additional information provided by the issuer, must remain publicly available on the intermediary's platform until the offer and sale of securities in reliance on section 4(a)(6) of the Securities Act is completed or cancelled; and

(4) An intermediary may not require any person to establish an account with the intermediary to access this information.

(b) *Investor qualification.* Each time before accepting any investment commitment (including any additional investment commitment from the same person), an intermediary must:

(1) Have a reasonable basis for believing that the investor satisfies the investment limitations established by section 4(a)(6)(B) of the Act and this part. An intermediary may rely on an investor's representations concerning compliance with the investment limitation requirements concerning the investor's annual income, net worth, and the amount of the investor's other investments made pursuant to section 4(a)(6) of the Securities Act) unless the intermediary has reason to question the reliability of the representation.

(2) Obtain from the investor:

(i) A representation that the investor has reviewed the intermediary's educational materials delivered pursuant to §227.302(b), understands that the entire amount of his or her investment may be lost, and is in a financial condition to bear the loss of the investment; and

(ii) A questionnaire completed by the investor demonstrating the investor's understanding that:

(A) There are restrictions on the investor's ability to cancel an investment commitment and obtain a return of his or her investment;

(B) It may be difficult for the investor to resell securities acquired in reliance on section 4(a)(6) of the Securities Act and

(C) Investing in securities offered and sold in reliance on section 4(a)(6) of the Securities Act involves risk, and the investor should not invest any funds in an offering made in reliance on section 4(a)(6) of the Securities Act unless he or she can afford to lose the entire amount of his or her investment.

[(c) – (f) omitted here require the issuer to provide a communication channel, notice of commitment to proceed. Confirmation and certain rules regarding maintenance of funds]

§227.304. Completion of Offerings, Cancellations and Reconfirmations [omitted]

§227.305. Payments to Third Parties

(a) *Prohibition on payments for personally identifiable information.* An intermediary may not compensate any person for providing the intermediary with the personally identifiable information of any investor or potential investor in securities offered and sold in reliance on section 4(a)(6) of the Securities Act

(b) For purposes of this rule, personally identifiable information means information that can be used to distinguish or trace an individual's identity, either alone or when combined with other personal or identifying information that is linked or linkable to a specific individual.

Subpart D — Funding Portal Regulation

§227.400. Registration of Funding Portals

(a) *Registration.* A funding portal must register with the Commission, by filing a complete Form Funding Portal (§249.2000 of this chapter) in accordance with the instructions on the form, and become a member of a national securities association registered under section 15A of the Exchange Act. . . .

§227.401. Exemption

A funding portal that is registered with the Commission pursuant to §227.400 is exempt from the broker registration requirements of section 15(a)(1) of the Exchange Act in connection with its activities as a funding portal.

§227.402. Conditional Safe Harbor

(a) *General.* Under section 3(a)(80) of the Exchange Act a funding portal acting as an intermediary in a transaction involving the offer or sale of securities in reliance on section 4(a)(6) of the Securities Act)) may not: offer investment advice or recommendations; solicit purchases, sales, or offers to buy the securities offered or displayed on its platform or portal; compensate employees, agents, or other persons for such solicitation or based on the sale of securities displayed or referenced on its platform or portal; hold, manage, possess, or otherwise handle investor funds or securities; or engage in such other activities as the Commission, by rule, determines appropriate. This section is intended to provide clarity with respect to the ability of a funding portal to engage in certain activities, consistent with the prohibitions under section 3(a)(80) of the Exchange Act. No presumption shall arise that a funding portal has violated the prohibitions under section 3(a)(80) of the Exchange Act or this part by reason of the funding portal or its associated persons engaging in activities in connection with the offer or sale of securities in reliance on section 4(a)(6) of the Securities Act that do not meet the conditions specified in paragraph (b) of this section. The antifraud provisions and all other applicable provisions of the federal securities laws continue to apply to the activities described in paragraph (b) of this section.

(b) *Permitted activities.* A funding portal may, consistent with the prohibitions under section 3(a)(80) of the Exchange Act and this part:

(1) Determine whether and under what terms to allow an issuer to offer and sell securities in reliance on section 4(a)(6) of the Securities Act through its platform; provided that a funding portal otherwise complies with this part;

(2) Apply objective criteria to highlight offerings on the funding portal's platform [if certain conditions are met];

(3) Provide search functions or other tools that investors can use to search, sort, or categorize the offerings available through the funding portal's platform according to objective criteria [if certain conditions ae met].

(4) Provide communication channels by which investors can communicate with one another and with representatives of the issuer through the funding portal's platform about offerings through the platform, so long as the funding portal (and its associated persons) [with certain restrictions];

(5) Advise an issuer about the structure or content of the issuer's offering, including assisting the issuer in preparing offering documentation;

(6) Compensate a third party for referring a person to the funding portal, so long as the third party does not provide the funding portal with personally identifiable information of any potential investor, and the compensation, other than that paid to a registered broker or dealer, is not based, directly or indirectly, on the purchase or sale of a security in reliance on section 4(a)(6) of the Securities Act offered on or through the funding portal's platform;

(7) Pay or offer to pay any compensation to a registered broker or dealer for services, including referrals pursuant to paragraph (b)(6) of this section, in connection with the offer or sale of securities by the funding portal in reliance on section 4(a)(6) of the Act [with certain restrictions];

(8) Receive any compensation from a registered broker or dealer for services provided by the funding portal in connection with the offer or sale of securities

by the funding portal in reliance on section 4(a)(6) of the Securities Act)), [subject to certain restrictions];

(9) Advertise the existence of the funding portal and identify one or more issuers or offerings available on the portal on the basis of objective criteria, [subject to certain restrictions];

(10) Deny access to its platform to, or cancel an offering of an issuer, pursuant to §227.301(c)(2), if the funding portal has a reasonable basis for believing that the issuer or the offering presents the potential for fraud or otherwise raises concerns about investor protection;

(11) Accept, on behalf of an issuer, an investment commitment for securities offered in reliance on section 4(a)(6) of the Securities Act by that issuer on the funding portal's platform;

(12) Direct investors where to transmit funds or remit payment in connection with the purchase of securities offered and sold in reliance on section 4(a)(6) of the Securities Act; and

(13) Direct a qualified third party, as required by §227.303(e), to release proceeds to an issuer upon completion of a crowdfunding offering or to return proceeds to investors in the event an investment commitment or an offering is cancelled.

§227.403. Compliance [omitted]

§227.404. Records to Be Made and Kept by Funding Portals [omitted]

Subpart E — Miscellaneous Provisions

§227.501. Restrictions on Resales

(a) Securities issued in a transaction exempt from registration pursuant to section 4(a)(6) of the Securities Act and in accordance with section 4A of the Securities Act and this part may not be transferred by any purchaser of such securities during the one-year period beginning when the securities were issued in a transaction exempt from registration pursuant to section 4(a)(6) of the Securities Act unless such securities are transferred:

(1) To the issuer of the securities;

(2) To an accredited investor;

(3) As part of an offering registered with the Commission; or

(4) To a member of the family of the purchaser or the equivalent, to a trust controlled by the purchaser, to a trust created for the benefit of a member of the family of the purchaser or the equivalent, or in connection with the death or divorce of the purchaser or other similar circumstance.

(b) For purposes of this §227.501, the term accredited investor shall mean any person who comes within any of the categories set forth in §230.501(a) of this chapter, or who the seller reasonably believes comes within any of such categories, at the time of the sale of the securities to that person.

(c) For purposes of this section, the term member of the family of the purchaser or the equivalent includes a child, stepchild, grandchild, parent, stepparent, grandparent, spouse or spousal equivalent, sibling, mother-in-law, father-in-law, son-in-law, daughter-in-law, brother-in-law, or sister-in-law of the purchaser, and shall include adoptive relationships. For purposes of this paragraph (c), the term spousal equivalent means a cohabitant occupying a relationship generally equivalent to that of a spouse.

§227.502. Insignificant Deviations From a Term, Condition or Requirement of This Part (Regulation Crowdfunding) [omitted]

§227.503. Disqualification Provisions

(a) *Disqualification events.* No exemption under section 4(a)(6) of the Securities Act shall be available for a sale of securities if the issuer; any predecessor of the issuer; any affiliated issuer; any director, officer, general partner or managing member of the issuer; any beneficial owner of 20 percent or more of the issuer's outstanding voting equity securities, calculated on the basis of voting power; any promoter connected with the issuer in any capacity at the time of such sale; any person that has been or will be paid (directly or indirectly) remuneration for solicitation of purchasers in connection with such sale of securities; or any general partner, director, officer or managing member of any such solicitor:

[(1)–(8) lists various convictions, judgments, orders of the SEC, state securities commissioners and other agencies.]

Regulation FD

17 C.F.R. §§243.100-243.103

Rule 100. General Rule Regarding Selective Disclosure

(a) Whenever an issuer, or any person acting on its behalf, discloses any material non-public information regarding that issuer or its securities to any person described in paragraph (b)(1) of this section, the issuer shall make public disclosure of that information as provided in Rule 101(e):

(1) Simultaneously, in the case of an intentional disclosure; and

(2) Promptly, in the case of a non-intentional disclosure.

(b)(1) Except as provided in paragraph (b)(2) of this section, paragraph (a) of this section shall apply to a disclosure made to any person outside the issuer:

(i) Who is a broker or dealer, or a person associated with a broker or dealer, as those terms are defined in Section 3(a) of the Securities Exchange Act of 1934;

(ii) Who is an investment adviser, as that term is defined in Section 202(a)(11) of the Investment Advisers Act of 1940; an institutional investment manager, as that term is defined in Section 13(f)(6) of the Securities Exchange Act of 1934, that filed a report on Form 13F with the Commission for the most recent quarter ended prior to the date of the disclosure; or a person associated with either of the foregoing. For purposes of this paragraph, a "person associated with an investment adviser or institutional investment manager" has the meaning set forth in Section 202(a)(17) of the Investment Advisers Act of 1940, assuming for these purposes that an institutional investment manager is an investment adviser;

(iii) Who is a holder of the issuer's securities, under circumstances in which it is reasonably foreseeable that the person will purchase or sell the issuer's securities on the basis of the information.

(2) Paragraph (a) of this section shall not apply to a disclosure made:

(i) To a person who owes a duty of trust or confidence to the issuer (such as an attorney, investment banker, or accountant);

(ii) To a person who expressly agrees to maintain the disclosed information in confidence;

(iii) To the following entities solely for the purpose of determining or monitoring a credit rating:

(A) any nationally recognized statistical rating organization, as that term is defined in Section 3(a)(62) of the Securities Exchange Act of 1934, pursuant to Rule 17g-5(a)(3); or

(B) any credit rating agency, as that term is defined in Section 3(a)(61) of the Securities Exchange Act of 1934, that makes its credit ratings publicly available; or

(iv) In connection with a securities offering registered under the Securities Act, other than an offering of the type described in any of Rule 415(a)(1)(i) through (vi) under the Securities Act (§230.415(a)(1)(i) through (vi) of this chapter) (except an offering of the type described in Rule 415 (a)(1)(i) under the Securities Act (§230.415(a)(1)(i) of this chapter) also involving a registered offering, whether or not underwritten, for capital formation purposes for the account of the issuer (unless the issuer's offering is being registered for the purpose of evading the requirements of this section)), if the disclosure is by any of the following means:

(A) A registration statement filed under the Securities Act, including a prospectus contained therein;

(B) A free writing prospectus used after filing of the registration statement for the offering or a communication falling within the exception to the definition of prospectus contained in clause (a) of section 2(a)(10) of the Securities Act;

(C) Any other Section 10(b) prospectus;

(D) A notice permitted by Rule 135 under the Securities Act (§230.135 of this chapter);

(E) A communication permitted by Rule 134 under the Securities Act (§230.134 of this chapter); or

(F) An oral communication made in connection with the registered securities offering after filing of the registration statement for the offering under the Securities Act.

Rule 101. Definitions

This section defines certain terms as used in Regulation FD.

(a) *Intentional.* A selective disclosure of material nonpublic information is "intentional" when the person making the disclosure either knows, or is reckless in not knowing, that the information he or she is communicating is both material and nonpublic.

(b) *Issuer:* An "issuer" subject to this regulation is one that has a class of securities registered under Section 12 of the Securities Exchange Act of 1934, or is required to file reports under Section 15(d) of the Securities Exchange Act of 1934, including any closed-end investment company (as defined in Section 5(a)(2) of the Investment Company Act of 1940), but not including any other investment company or any foreign government or foreign private issuer, as those terms are defined in Rule 405 under the Securities Act.

(c) *Person acting on behalf of an issuer:* "Person acting on behalf of an issuer" means any senior official of the issuer (or, in the case of a closed-end investment company, a senior official of the issuer's investment adviser), or any other officer, employee, or agent of an issuer who regularly communicates with any person described in Rule 100(b)(1)(i), (ii), or (iii), or with holders of the issuer's securities. An officer, director, employee, or agent of an issuer who discloses material nonpublic information in breach of a duty of trust or confidence to the issuer shall not be considered to be acting on behalf of the issuer.

(d) *Promptly.* "Promptly" means as soon as reasonably practicable (but in no event after the later of 24 hours or the commencement of the next day's trading on the New York Stock Exchange) after a senior official of the issuer (or, in the case of a closed-end investment company, a senior official of the issuer's investment adviser) learns that there has been a non-intentional disclosure by the issuer or person acting on behalf of the issuer of information that the senior official knows, or is reckless in not knowing, is both material and nonpublic.

(e) *Public disclosure.*

(1) Except as provided in paragraph (e)(2) of this section, an issuer shall make the "public disclosure" of information required by Rule 100(a) by furnishing to or filing with the Commission a Form 8-K disclosing that information.

(2) An issuer shall be exempt from the requirement to furnish or file a Form 8-K if it instead disseminates the information through another method (or combination of methods) of disclosure that is reasonably designed to provide broad, non-exclusionary distribution of the information to the public.

(f) *Senior official.* "Senior official" means any director, executive officer (as defined in Rule 3b-7), investor relations or public relations officer, or other person with similar functions.

(g) *Securities offering.* For purposes of Rule 100(b)(2)(iv):

(1) *Underwritten offerings.* A securities offering that is underwritten commences when the issuer reaches an understanding with the broker-dealer that is to act as managing underwriter and continues until the later of the end of the period during which a dealer must deliver a prospectus or the sale of the securities (unless the offering is sooner terminated);

(2) *Non-underwritten offerings.* A securities offering that is not underwritten:

(i) If covered by Rule 415(a)(1)(x), commences when the issuer makes its first bona fide offer in a takedown of securities and continues until the later of the end of the period during which each dealer must deliver a prospectus or the sale of the securities in that takedown (unless the takedown is sooner terminated);

(ii) If a business combination as defined in Rule 165(f)(1), commences when the first public announcement of the transaction is made and continues until the completion of the vote or the expiration of the tender offer, as applicable (unless the transaction is sooner terminated);

(iii) If an offering other than those specified in paragraphs (a) and (b) of this section commences when the issuer files a registration statement and continues until the later of the end of the period during which each dealer must deliver a prospectus or the sale of the securities (unless the offering is sooner terminated).

Rule 102. No Effect on Antifraud Liability

No failure to make a public disclosure required solely by Rule 100 shall be deemed to be a violation of Rule 10b-5 under the Securities Exchange Act.

Rule 103. No Effect on Exchange Act Reporting Status

A failure to make a public disclosure required solely by Rule 100 shall not affect whether:

(a) For purposes of Forms S-3, S-8 and SF-3 under the Securities Act, . . . an issuer is deemed to have filed all the material required to be filed pursuant to Section 13 or 15(d) of the Securities Exchange Act of 1934 or, where applicable, has made those filings in a timely manner; or

(b) There is adequate current public information about the issuer for purposes of Rule 144(c).